CompTIA® Network+® 2009 In Depth

Tamara Dean

COURSE TECHNOLOGY
CENGAGE Learning™

Australia • Brazil • Japan • Korea • Mexico • Singapore • Spain • United Kingdom • United States

COURSE TECHNOLOGY
CENGAGE Learning

CompTIA® Network+® 2009
In Depth
Tamara Dean

Vice President, Career and Professional Editorial: Dave Garza
Publisher and General Manager, Course Technology PTR: Stacy L. Hiquet
Executive Editor: Stephen Helba
Associate Director of Marketing: Sarah Panella
Managing Editor: Marah Bellegarde
Manager of Editorial Services: Heather Talbot
Content Project Manager: Jessica McNavich
Senior Product Manager: Michelle Ruelos Cannistraci
Senior Marketing Manager: Erin Coffin
Marketing Manager: Jordan Casey
Acquisitions Editors: Nick Lombardi, Megan Belanger
Development Editor: Ann Shaffer
Copy Editor: Mark Goodin
Project Editor: Karen A. Gill
Proofreaders: Debra Kreiser, Karen A. Gill
Technical Reviewers: Serge Palladino, Danielle Shaw, and Marianne Snow
Interior Layout Tech: Cadmus Communications
Design Assistant: Hannah Wellman
Cover Designer: Mike Tanamachi
Cover Photo or Illustration: Veer.com
Indexer: Broccoli Information Management

Network+ is a registered trademark of the Computing Technology Industry Association, Inc.

All other trademarks are the property of their respective owners.

Library of Congress Control Number: 2008939962

ISBN-13: 978-1-59863-878-3

ISBN-10: 1-59863-878-5

Course Technology, a part of Cengage Learning
20 Channel Center Street
Boston, MA 02210
USA

Cengage Learning is a leading provider of customized learning solutions with office locations around the globe, including Singapore, the United Kingdom, Australia, Mexico, Brazil, and Japan. Locate your local office at **international.cengage.com/region**.

Cengage Learning products are represented in Canada by Nelson Education, Ltd.

For your lifelong learning solutions, visit **courseptr.com**.
Visit our corporate Web site at **cengage.com**.

Printed in Canada
2 3 4 5 6 7 11 10 09

Table of Contents

CHAPTER 3

Transmission Basics and Networking Media **57**

CHAPTER 4

Introduction to TCP/IP Protocols **113**

CHAPTER 8
Wireless Networking **299**

CHAPTER 9
Network Operating Systems **349**

CHAPTER 10
In-Depth TCP/IP Networking. **403**

CHAPTER 13
Troubleshooting Network Problems **529**

CHAPTER 14
Ensuring Integrity and Availability **571**

Preface

Knowing how to install, configure, and troubleshoot a computer network is a highly marketable and exciting skill. This book first introduces the fundamental building blocks that form a modern network, such as protocols, topologies, hardware, and network operating systems. It then provides in-depth coverage of the most important concepts in contemporary networking, such as TCP/IP, Ethernet, wireless transmission, and security. After reading the book and completing the end-of-chapter review questions, you will be prepared to select the best network design, hardware, and software for your environment. You will also have the skills to build a network from scratch and maintain, upgrade, and troubleshoot an existing network. Finally, you will be well prepared to pass CompTIA's (the Computing Technology Industry Association's) Network+ certification exam.

Because some technical topics can be difficult to grasp, this book explains concepts logically and in a clear, approachable style. In addition, concepts are reinforced by real-world examples of networking issues from a professional's standpoint. Each chapter opens with an On the Job story from a network engineer. (Though all the stories are true, some of the names and company affiliations have been changed at the request of the story's author.) These real-world examples make this book a practical learning tool. The numerous tables and illustrations, along with the glossary, appendixes, and review questions, make this book a valuable reference for any networking professional.

Intended Audience

This book is intended to serve the needs of professionals and would-be professionals who are interested in mastering fundamental, vendor-independent networking concepts. No previous networking experience is necessary to begin learning from this book, although knowledge of basic computer principles is helpful. Those seeking to pass CompTIA's Network+ certification exam will find the text's content, approach, and numerous review questions especially helpful. For more information on Network+ certification, visit CompTIA's Web site at *www.comptia.org*.

Chapter Descriptions

The following list summarizes the topics covered in each chapter of this book:

Chapter 1, "An Introduction to Networking," begins by answering the question, "What is a network?" Next, it presents the fundamental types of networks and describes the elements that constitute the most popular type: the client/server network. This chapter also introduces career options for those interested in mastering networking skills.

Chapter 2, "Networking Standards and the OSI Model," describes the organizations that set standards in the networking industry, including those that oversee wiring codes, network access methods, and Internet addressing. It also discusses, in depth, the OSI model, which is the industry standard for conceptualizing communication between computers on a network.

Chapter 3, "Transmission Basics and Networking Media," describes signaling techniques used on modern networks, including those used over coaxial cable, twisted pair cable, and fiber-optic cable. It also covers the characteristics—including cost, materials, and connector types—for physical media that can be used to carry signals. Finally, it describes structured cabling standards and best practices for installing network cables.

Chapter 4, "Introduction to TCP/IP Protocols," familiarizes you with the most popular set of protocols used by networks today: TCP/IP. Functions and interactions between each TCP/IP core protocol and subprotocol are described in the context of the OSI model. This chapter also explains IPv4 and IPv6 addressing and naming conventions.

Chapter 5, "Topologies and Ethernet Standards," discusses the variety of physical and logical topologies found on LANs (local area networks), with an emphasis on the most popular and fault-tolerant types. Next, it describes many Ethernet standards, from the older 10Mbps to the very latest 10Gbps transmission rates.

Chapters 6, "Network Hardware," examines the hardware associated with a network, including NICs (network interface cards), hubs, routers, bridges, gateways, and switches. In Chapter 6, you will find several photos portraying typical networking equipment. You'll also learn how to install network hardware.

Chapter 7, "WANs and Remote Connectivity," expands on your knowledge of networks by examining WAN (wide area network) topologies and transmission methods, such as T-carriers, ISDN, DSL, and broadband cable. This chapter also covers options for accessing networks from remote locations, including dial-up networking and VPNs (virtual private networks).

Chapter 8, "Wireless Networking," covers every popular wireless LAN and WAN networking standard, including its frequency range, maximum transmission distance, and maximum throughput. Here you'll also learn how data is converted to electromagnetic waves and how obstacles can impair wireless communication. Finally, this chapter teaches you how to perform a wireless site survey, install and configure a wireless access point, and troubleshoot wireless connectivity problems.

Chapter 9, "Network Operating Systems," covers the purpose and design of NOS (network operating system) software. It then provides an overview of the Microsoft Windows Server 2008 network operating system, including Active Directory, the NOS's method of organizing network elements. Next, this chapter introduces you to UNIX and Linux. It enumerates basic commands that can be used on UNIX-type systems and explains how these operating systems can share resources and communicate over networks.

Chapter 10, "In-Depth TCP/IP Networking," explores advanced concepts relating to TCP/IP-based networking, such as subnetting and NAT (Network Address Translation). It also details commands useful for evaluating devices and connections that run the TCP/IP protocol suite.

Chapter 11, "Voice and Video over IP," describes the very latest uses of packet-switched networks: delivering voice and video signals. These signals used to be carried over telephony or television networks only, but improvements in data networks' scale and speed have resulted in a convergence of data, voice, and video over the same transmission paths. You'll learn about the infrastructure, protocols, and equipment necessary to carry and receive such services over converged networks.

Chapter 12, "Network Security," discusses critical network security techniques, including the use of firewalls, encryption, intrusion detection, and enterprise-wide security policies. Network security is a major concern when designing and maintaining modern networks, which typically use open protocols and connect to public networks such as the Internet.

Chapter 13, "Troubleshooting Network Problems," approaches the tasks of troubleshooting and maintaining networks in a logical, practical manner. Further, this chapter teaches you how to use several software and hardware troubleshooting tools. A mastery of troubleshooting is not only critical for qualifying for Network+ certification, but it is also a highly valued skill in the workplace.

Chapter 14, "Ensuring Integrity and Availability," explains how to keep network resources available and connections reliable despite threats such as power outages or hardware and software failures. In this chapter, you will find information about backup power supplies, redundant disk arrays, data backups, and disaster recovery planning.

Chapter 15, "Network Managements," concludes the book by describing several aspects of network management, including documentation, policies and regulations, asset management, and change management. This chapter builds on all the knowledge you've gained about network fundamentals, design, maintenance, and troubleshooting.

The six appendixes at the end of this book serve as references for the networking professional:

Appendix A, "Network+ Examination Objectives," provides a complete list of the 2009 Network+ certification exam objectives, including the percentage of the exam's content they represent and which chapters in the book cover material associated with each objective.

Appendix B, "Network+ Practice Exam," offers a practice exam containing 100 questions similar in content and presentation to those you will find on CompTIA's Network+ examination.

Appendix C, "Visual Guide to Connectors," provides a visual connector reference chart for quick identification of connectors and receptacles used in contemporary networking.

Appendix D, "Answers to Chapter Review Questions," provides the answers to the questions found at the end of each chapter so you can check your understanding.

Appendix E, "Glossary," is a comprehensive listing of all the key terms defined throughout the book.

Appendix F, "Answers to Network+ Practice Exam Questions," presents the answers to the 100 questions found in Appendix B.

Features

To aid you in fully understanding networking concepts, this book includes many features designed to enhance your learning experience.

Chapter Objectives—Each chapter begins with a list of the concepts to be mastered within that chapter. This list provides you with both a quick reference to the chapter's contents and a useful study aid.

Illustrations and Tables—Numerous full-color illustrations of network media, methods of signaling, protocol behavior, hardware, topology, software screens, peripherals, and components help you visualize common network elements, theories, and concepts. In addition, the many tables included provide details and comparisons of both practical and theoretical information.

Chapter Summaries—Each chapter's text is followed by a summary of the concepts introduced in that chapter. These summaries provide a helpful way to recap and revisit the ideas covered in each chapter.

Key Terms—Here you'll find the essential terms introduced in the chapter. These are compiled into a Glossary in Appendix E that you can reference as a refresher before taking the exam.

Review Questions—These review questions reinforce the ideas introduced in each chapter. Many questions are situational. Rather than simply asking you to repeat what you've learned, these questions help you evaluate and apply the material you have learned. Answering these questions will ensure that you have mastered the important concepts and provide valuable practice for taking CompTIA's Network+ exam. Again, the answers to these questions are in Appendix D.

Text and Graphic Conventions

Wherever appropriate, additional information has been added to this book to help you better understand the topic at hand. The following icons are used throughout the text to alert you to additional materials:

The Note icon draws your attention to helpful material related to the subject being described.

All of the content that relates to CompTIA's Network+ certification exam, whether it is a page or a sentence, is highlighted with a Net+ icon and the relevant objective number. This unique feature highlights the important information at a glance, so you can pay extra attention to the certification material.

Acknowledgments

As with any large undertaking, this book is the result of many contributions and collaborative efforts. It would not exist without the help of friends, family, fellow networking professionals, and Course Technology/Cengage Learning staff. I'm again indebted to Nick Lombardi, Acquisitions Editor, and Stephen Helba, Executive Editor, for championing this book. Thanks to Michelle Ruelos Cannistraci, Senior Product Manager, and Jessica McNavich, Content Project Manager, for helping the project to advance smoothly. Many thanks to Ann Shaffer, Developmental Editor and friend, for handling extreme deadlines with grace and for insisting on coherence, clarity, and precision throughout each draft. With this edition, I am indebted to Andrea Clemente and Suresh Elumalai, of Cadmus Communications, who guided the book from final edits to finished product. Thanks also to John Bosco, Quality Assurance expert, for scrutinizing every page and alerting me to errors and inconsistencies. Thanks to Copy Editor Mark Goodin for watching the details. And thanks to Mary Pat Shaffer and Dean Robbins, who researched and obtained photos and permissions.

I'm also grateful to instructors who have used this text and offered suggestions for improvement. Thanks to reviewers Jeff McDowell, United Tribes Technical College; Dee Skinner, Highline Community College; Byron Todd, Tallahassee Community College; Dr. G. Jan Wilms, Union University; and especially, Mike Qaissaunee, Brookdale Community College, for letting me know how to make this edition more precise and engaging.

For sharing their expertise, thanks to networking professionals Marcin Antkiewicz, Steve Barnet, Martin Brown, David Butcher, Peyton Engel, Thom Jones, Brooke Noelke, Patrick Pejack, Mike Qaissaunee, Jeff Shuckra, Tracy Syslo, and Ron Young. Special thanks to David Klann, who generously contributed content, helped with research, and remained ever ready to discuss the implications of noncontiguous subnetting on a Saturday night. Finally, thanks again to Paul and Janet Dean, scientists and teachers both, for their encouragement, support, and continued interest in technology.

Photo Credits
Figure 1-5 © Gary Herrington Photography
Figure 2-6 Courtesy of 3Com Corporation
Figure 3-15 iConverter 10/100M2 image courtesy of Omnitron Systems
Figure 3-17 Courtesy of Stellar Labs (www.stellarlabs.com)
Figure 3-18 Image copyright, 2008. Used under license from Shutterstock.com
Figure 3-21 Courtesy of Belden, Inc.
Figure 3-23 © Gary Herrington Photography
Figure 3-27 Courtesy of BlackBox Corporation
Figure 3-28 Courtesy of Belkin Corporation
Figure 3-29 Courtesy of Belkin Corporation
Figure 3-30 Courtesy of Optical Cable Corporation
Figure 3-33 Courtesy of SENKO Advanced Components, Inc.
Figure 3-34 Courtesy of SENKO Advanced Components, Inc.
Figure 3-35 Courtesy of SENKO Advanced Components, Inc.
Figure 3-36 Courtesy of SENKO Advanced Components, Inc.
Figure 3-41 Courtesy of Siemon
Figure 3-42 Courtesy of Siemon
Figure 5-16 Photo courtesy of D-Link Systems
Figure 5-17 Photo courtesy of D-Link Systems
Figure 6-4 Courtesy of 3Com Corporation
Figure 6-5 Courtesy of PCMCIA
Figure 6-6 Courtesy of Linksys
Figure 6-7 Courtesy of TRT Business Network Solutions
Figure 6-8 Courtesy of Socket Communications
Figure 6-9 Courtesy of NETGEAR; Courtesy of SMC Networks, Inc.; Courtesy of Belkin Corporation
Figure 6-10 © Gary Herrington Photography
Figure 6-11 © Gary Herrington Photography
Figure 6-14 Courtesy of 3Com Corporation
Figure 6-16a Photo courtesy of Juniper Networks, Inc.

State of the Information Technology (IT) Field

Most organizations today depend on computers and information technology to improve business processes, productivity, and efficiency. Opportunities to become global organizations and reach customers, businesses, and suppliers are a direct result of the widespread use of the Internet. Changing technology further affects how companies do business. This fundamental shift in business practices has increased the need for skilled and certified IT workers across industries. This transformation moves many IT workers out of traditional IT businesses and into many IT-dependent industries such as banking, government, insurance, and health care.

In the latest *Occupational Outlook Handbook* from the Bureau of Labor Statistics (part of the United States Department of Labor), employment of computer support specialists is expected to increase faster than the average increase for all occupations through 2012. Job growth will continue to be driven by the continued expansion of computer system design and related services, which is projected to remain one of the fastest growing industries in the U.S. economy, despite recent job losses.

In any industry, the workforce is important to continually drive business. Having skilled workers in IT is always a struggle with ever-changing technologies. It has been estimated that technologies change approximately every two years. With such a quick product life cycle, IT workers must strive to keep up with these changes to continually bring value to their employers.

Certifications

Different levels of education are required for the many jobs in the IT industry. Additionally, the level of education and type of training required varies from employer to employer, but the need for qualified technicians remains a constant. As technology changes and advances in the industry continue to evolve rapidly, many employers look for employees who possess the skills necessary to implement these new technologies. Traditional degrees and diplomas do not identify the skills that a job applicant possesses. With the growth of the IT industry, companies are relying increasingly on technical certifications to adequately identify a job applicant's skills. Technical certifications are a way for employers to ensure the quality and skill qualifications of their computer professionals, and they can offer job seekers a competitive edge over their competition.

There are two types of certifications: vendor-neutral and vendor-specific. Vendor-neutral certifications are those that test for the skills and knowledge required in specific industry job roles and do not subscribe to a vendor's specific technology solutions. Some examples of vendor-neutral certifications include all of the CompTIA (Computing Technology Industry Association's) certifications, Project Management Institute's certifications, and Security Certified Program certifications. Vendor-specific certifications validate the skills and knowledge necessary to be successful while utilizing a specific vendor's technology solution. Some examples of vendor-specific certifications include those offered by Microsoft, IBM, Novell, and Cisco.

As employers struggle to fill open IT positions with qualified candidates, certifications are a means of validating the skill sets necessary to be successful within organizations. In most careers, salary and compensation are determined by experience and education, but in the IT field, the number and type of certifications an employee earns also determine salary and wage increases.

Certification provides job applicants with more than just a competitive edge over their noncertified counterparts applying for the same IT positions. Some institutions of higher education grant college credit to students who successfully pass certification exams, moving them further along in their degree programs. Certification also gives individuals who are interested in careers in the military the ability to move into higher positions more quickly. And many advanced certification programs accept, and sometimes require, entry-level certifications as part of their exams. For example, Cisco and Microsoft accept some CompTIA certifications as prerequisites for their certification programs.

Career Planning

Finding a career that fits your personality, skill set, and lifestyle is challenging and fulfilling but can often be difficult. What are the steps you should take to find that dream career? Is IT interesting to you? Chances are, if you are reading this book, this question has already been answered. What is it about IT that you like? The world of work in the IT industry is vast. Some questions to ask yourself: Are you a person who likes to work alone, or do you like to work in a group? Do you like speaking directly with customers, or do you prefer to stay behind the scenes? Does your lifestyle encourage a lot of travel, or do you need to stay in one location? All of these factors influence your job decision. Inventory assessments are a good first step to learning more about you, your interests, your work values, and your abilities. A variety of Web sites offer assistance with career planning and assessments.

CompTIA Authorized Curriculum Program

The logo of the CompTIA Authorized Curriculum Program and the status of this or other training material as "Authorized" under the CompTIA Authorized Curriculum Program signify that, in

CompTIA's opinion, such training material covers the content of the CompTIA-related certification exam. CompTIA has not reviewed or approved the accuracy of the contents of this training material and specifically disclaims any warranties of merchantability or fitness for a particular purpose. CompTIA makes no guarantee concerning the success of persons using any such "Authorized" or other training material to prepare for any CompTIA certification exam.

The contents of this training material were created for the CompTIA Network+ certification exam objectives that were current as of March 2009.

What's New with CompTIA Network+ Certification?

CompTIA has made the 2009 Network+ exam more technical and more in tune with the latest network technologies. Objectives that used to require only identifying protocols, devices, and standards now require demonstrating an ability to install and configure connectivity devices or to apply protocols and standards. Some objectives, such as knowledge of protocols related to VoIP and the use of IPS/IDS devices, are new. Older technologies (including IPX/SPX, NetBEUI, and Appletalk protocols; Bluetooth and Infrared wireless transmission; and the distinction between extranets and intranets) have been dropped from the objectives. However, bear in mind that some legacy protocols and standards appear in the objectives' list of acronyms, and the Network+ exam could refer to them.

As with the previous Network+ exam, the 2009 version includes many scenario-based questions. Mastering, rather than simply memorizing, the material in this book will help you succeed on the exam and on the job.

How to Become CompTIA Certified

This training material can help you prepare for and pass a related CompTIA certification exam or exams. To achieve CompTIA certification, you must register for and pass a CompTIA certification exam or exams.

To become CompTIA certified, you must:

1. Select a certification exam provider. For more information, please visit the following Web site: *certification.comptia.org/resources/registration.aspx.*
2. Register for and schedule a time to take the CompTIA certification exam(s) at a convenient location.
3. Take and pass the CompTIA certification exam(s).

For more information about CompTIA's certifications, such as their industry acceptance, benefits, or program news, please visit *certification.comptia.org/allcerts.aspx.*

CompTIA is dedicated to advancing industry growth through its educational programs, market research, networking events, professional certifications, and public policy advocacy.

CompTIA is a not-for-profit information technology trade association. CompTIA's certifications are designed by subject matter experts from across the IT industry. Each CompTIA certification is vendor neutral, covers multiple technologies, and requires demonstration of skills and knowledge widely sought after by the IT industry.

To contact CompTIA with any questions or comments, please call us at 1-630-678-8300, or submit your question via the Web form at *certification.comptia.org/customer_service/contact.aspx.*

An Introduction to Networking

After reading this chapter and completing the exercises, you will be able to:

- List the advantages of networked computing relative to stand-alone computing

- Distinguish between client/server and peer-to-peer networks

- List elements common to all client/server networks

- Describe several specific uses for a network

- Identify some of the certifications available to networking professionals

- Identify the kinds of skills and specializations that will help you excel as a networking professional

On the Job

My job as a recruiter is to match a candidate with a position that matches his or her skills and career goals. One time a new graduate came to me looking for work in the networking field. Although he had no previous networking experience, I was able to find him a position by emphasizing the hands-on experience he had gained in college networking courses. To help him look more appealing to employers, I reworded his resume and specified the software and hardware he used in his hands-on projects. I also asked him to tell me about technical obstacles he had overcome and what he had learned from the projects. Soon, my client found an assignment as a technical support specialist at a large pharmaceutical firm. Now, five years later, he is a network administrator for one of the country's largest banks. Although my client had little experience in the beginning, his always-positive attitude and a willingness to learn helped him advance quickly.

Tracy Syslo, Recruiter
Infostaff Services Corporation

Loosely defined, a **network** is a group of computers and other devices (such as printers) that are connected by some type of transmission media. Variations on the elements of a network and the way it is designed, however, are nearly infinite. Networks can be as small as two computers connected by a cable in a home office or as large as several thousand computers connected across the world via a combination of cable, phone lines, and satellite links. In addition to connecting personal computers, networks might link mainframe computers, printers, plotters, fax machines, and phone systems. They might communicate through copper wires, fiber-optic cable, radio waves, infrared, or satellite links. This chapter introduces you to the fundamental characteristics of networks.

Why Use Networks?

Using networks offers advantages relative to using a **stand-alone computer**—that is, a computer that is not connected to other computers and that uses software applications and data stored on its local disks. Most importantly, networks enable multiple users to share devices (for example, printers) and data (such as spreadsheet files), which are collectively known as the network's **resources**. Sharing devices saves money. For example, rather than buying 20 printers for 20 staff members, a company can buy one printer and have those 20 staff members share it over a network. Sharing devices also saves time. For example, it's faster for coworkers to share data over a network than to copy data to a removable storage device and physically transport the storage device from one computer to another—an outdated file-sharing method commonly referred to as **sneakernet** (presumably because people wore sneakers when walking from computer to computer). Before networks, transferring data via floppy disks was the only possible way to share data.

Networks also allow you to manage, or administer, resources on multiple computers from a central location. Imagine you work in the Information Technology (IT) department of a multinational bank and must verify that each of 5000 employees around the globe uses the same version of a database program. Without a network, you would have to visit every employee's machine to check and install the proper software. With a network, however, you could check the software installed on computers around the world from the computer on your desk. Because they allow you to share devices and administer computers centrally, networks increase productivity. It's not surprising, then, that virtually all organizations depend on their networks to stay competitive.

Types of Networks

Computers can be positioned on a network in different ways relative to each other. They can have different levels of control over shared resources. They can also be made to communicate and share resources according to different schemes. The following sections describe two fundamental network models: peer-to-peer and client/server.

Net+ Peer-to-Peer Networks

2.7   The simplest form of a network is a **peer-to-peer network**. In a peer-to-peer network, every computer can communicate directly with every other computer. By default, no computer on a peer-to-peer network has more authority than another. However, each computer can be configured to share only some of its resources and prevent access to other resources. Traditional peer-to-peer networks typically consist of two or more general-purpose personal computers, with modest processing capabilities. Every computer is capable of sending and receiving information to and from every other computer, as shown in Figure 1-1.

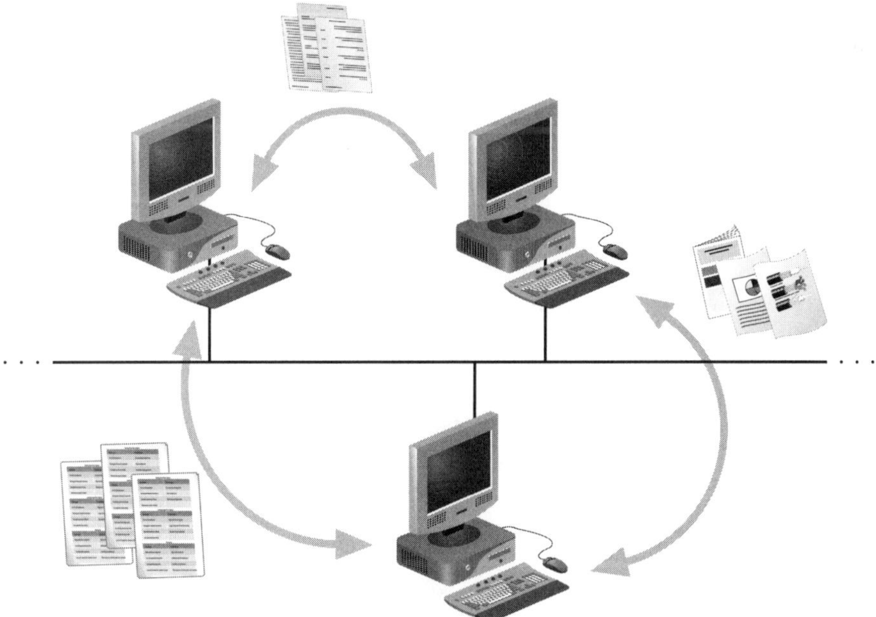

Figure 1-1 Resource sharing on a simple peer-to-peer network

Net+

2.7

The following are advantages of using traditional peer-to-peer networks:

- They are simple to configure. For this reason, they may be used in environments in which time or technical expertise is scarce.

- They are often less expensive to set up and maintain than other types of networks. This fact makes them suitable for environments in which saving money is critical.

The following are disadvantages of using traditional peer-to-peer networks:

- They are not very flexible. As a peer-to-peer network grows larger, adding or changing significant elements of the network may be difficult.

- They are not necessarily secure. In simple installations, data and other resources shared by network users can be easily discovered and used by unauthorized people.

- They are not practical for connecting more than a handful of computers. This is because traditional peer-to-peer networks do not always centralize resources.

For example, if your computer is part of a peer-to-peer network that includes five other computers, and each computer user stores her spreadsheets and word-processing files on her own hard disk, whenever your colleagues want to edit your files, they must access your machine on the network. If one colleague saves a changed version of one of your spreadsheets on her hard disk, you'll find it difficult to keep track of which version is the most current. As you can imagine, the more computers you add to a peer-to-peer network, the more difficult it becomes to find and manage resources.

A common way to share resources on a peer-to-peer network is by modifying the file-sharing controls via the computer's operating system. For example, you could choose to create a directory on your computer's hard disk called "SharedDocs" and then configure the directory to allow all networked computers to read its files. On a peer-to-peer network, each user is responsible for configuring her computer to allow access to certain resources and prevent access to others. In other words, resource sharing is not controlled by a central computer or authority. Because access depends on many different users, it might not be uniform or secure.

Although traditional peer-to-peer networks are typically small and contained within a home or office, examples of very large peer-to-peer networks have emerged to take advantage of the Internet. These newer types of peer-to-peer networks (commonly abbreviated **P2P networks**) link computers from around the world to share files between each others' hard disks. Unlike the older style of peer-to-peer network, they require specialized software (besides the computer's operating system) to allow resource sharing. Examples of these networks include Gnutella, Freenet, and the original Napster. In 2001, Napster, which allowed users around the globe to share music files, was forced to cease operation due to charges of copyright infringement from musicians and music producers. Later, the service was redesigned to provide legitimate music file-sharing services. More recently, a company called BitTorrent has made a unique high-speed data transfer technology (also called BitTorrent) the foundation of its business. The company specializes in allowing companies and individuals to share video, audio, software, and games over the Internet.

Client/Server Networks

Another way of designing a network is to use a central computer, known as a **server**, to facilitate communication and resource sharing between other computers on the network, which are known as **clients**. Clients usually take the form of personal computers, also known as

2.7

workstations. A network that uses a server to enable clients to share data, data storage space, and devices is known as a **client/server network**. (The term **client/server architecture** is sometimes used to refer to the design of a network in which clients rely on servers for resource sharing and processing.) In terms of resource sharing and control, you can compare the client/server network to a public library. Just as a librarian manages the use of books and other media by patrons, a server manages the use of shared resources by clients. For example, if a patron does not have the credentials to check out books, the librarian prevents the patron from doing so. Similarly, a server allows only authorized clients to access its resources.

Every computer on a client/server network acts as a client or a server. (It is possible, but uncommon, for some computers to act as both.) Clients on a network can still run applications from and save data to their local hard disk. But by connecting to a server, they also have the option of using shared applications, data, and devices. Clients on a client/server network do not share their resources directly with each other, but rather use the server as an intermediary. Clients and servers communicate through connectivity devices such as switches or routers. (These devices are covered in detail in Chapter 6.)

Figure 1-2 illustrates how resources are shared on a client/server network.

To function as a server, a computer must be running an **NOS** (**network operating system**). An NOS is a special type of software designed to do the following:

- Manage data and other resources for a number of clients.
- Ensure that only authorized users access the network.
- Control which type of files a user can open and read.

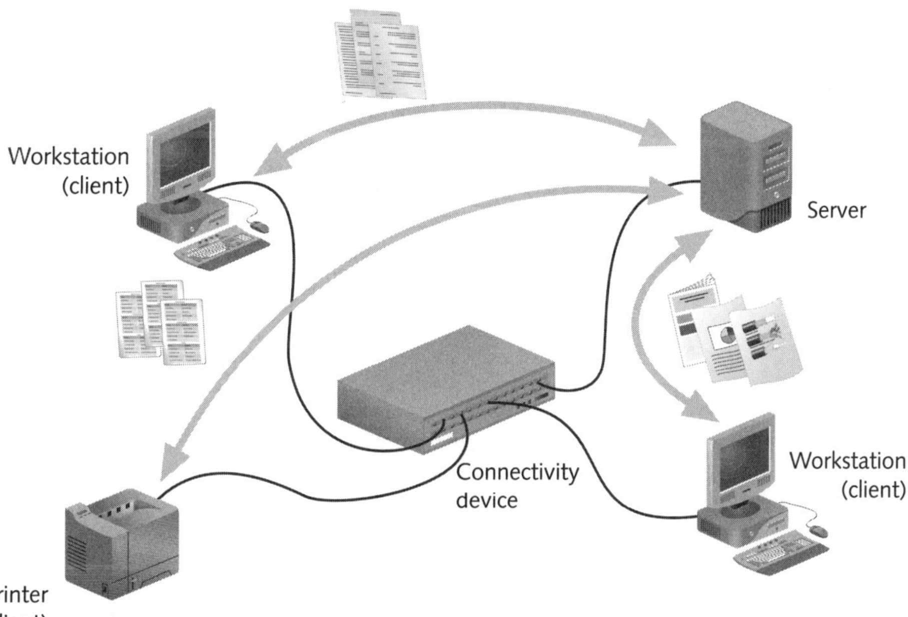

Figure 1-2 Resource sharing on a client/server network

2.7

- Restrict when and from where users can access the network.
- Dictate which rules computers will use to communicate.
- Supply applications to clients.

Examples of popular network operating systems include various forms of UNIX and Linux, Microsoft Windows Server 2003 or Server 2008, and Mac OS X Server. (By contrast, a stand-alone computer, or a client computer, uses an operating system, such as Windows XP or Windows Vista, which has more limited resource management capabilities.)

Usually, servers have more memory, processing, and storage capacity than clients. They may even be equipped with special hardware designed to provide network management functions beyond that provided by the network operating system. For example, a server might contain an extra hard disk and specialized software so that if the primary hard disk fails, the secondary hard disk automatically takes its place.

Although client/server networks are typically more complex in their design and maintenance than peer-to-peer networks, they offer many advantages over peer-to-peer networks, such as:

- User logon accounts and passwords for anyone on a server-based network can be assigned in one place.
- Access to multiple shared resources (such as data files or printers) can be centrally granted to a single user or groups of users.
- Problems on the network can be monitored, diagnosed, and often fixed from one location.
- Servers are optimized to handle heavy processing loads and dedicated to handling requests from clients, enabling faster response time.
- Because of their efficient processing and larger disk storage, servers can connect more than a handful of computers on a network.

Together, these advantages make client/server networks easier to manage, more secure, and more powerful than peer-to-peer networks. They are also more **scalable**—that is, they can be more easily added onto and extended—than peer-to-peer networks.

Because client/server networks are the most popular type of network for medium- and large-scale organizations, most of the concepts covered in this book and on the Network+ exam pertain to client/server networks. Next, you will learn how networks are classified according to size.

LANs, MANs, and WANs

As its name suggests, a **LAN** (**local area network**) is a network of computers and other devices that is confined to a relatively small space, such as one building or even one office. Small LANs first became popular in the early 1980s. At that time, LANs might have consisted of a handful of computers connected in a peer-to-peer fashion. Today's LANs are typically much larger and more complex client/server networks.

Often, separate LANs are interconnected and rely on several servers running many different applications and managing resources other than data. For example, imagine an office

building in which each of a company's departments runs its own LAN and all the LANs are connected. This network may contain dozens of servers, hundreds of workstations, and several shared storage devices, printers, plotters, fax machines, and even telephone interfaces. Figure 1-3 roughly depicts this type of network. (In reality, the network would probably contain many more clients.) As you progress through this book, you will learn about the devices on this network and how they communicate. After completing this book, you'll understand how to integrate clients, servers, and connectivity devices to create networks that are reliable, secure, and manageable.

Networks may extend beyond the boundaries of a building. A network that is larger than a LAN and connects clients and servers from multiple buildings—for example, a handful of government offices surrounding a state capitol—is known as a **MAN** (**metropolitan area network**). Because of the distance it covers, a MAN may use different transmission technology and media than a LAN.

A network that connects two or more geographically distinct LANs or MANs is called a **WAN** (**wide area network**). Because such networks carry data over longer distances than LANs, WANs require slightly different transmission methods and media and often use a greater variety of technologies than LANs. Most MANs can also be described as WANs; in fact, network engineers are more likely to refer to all networks that cover a broad geographical range as WANs.

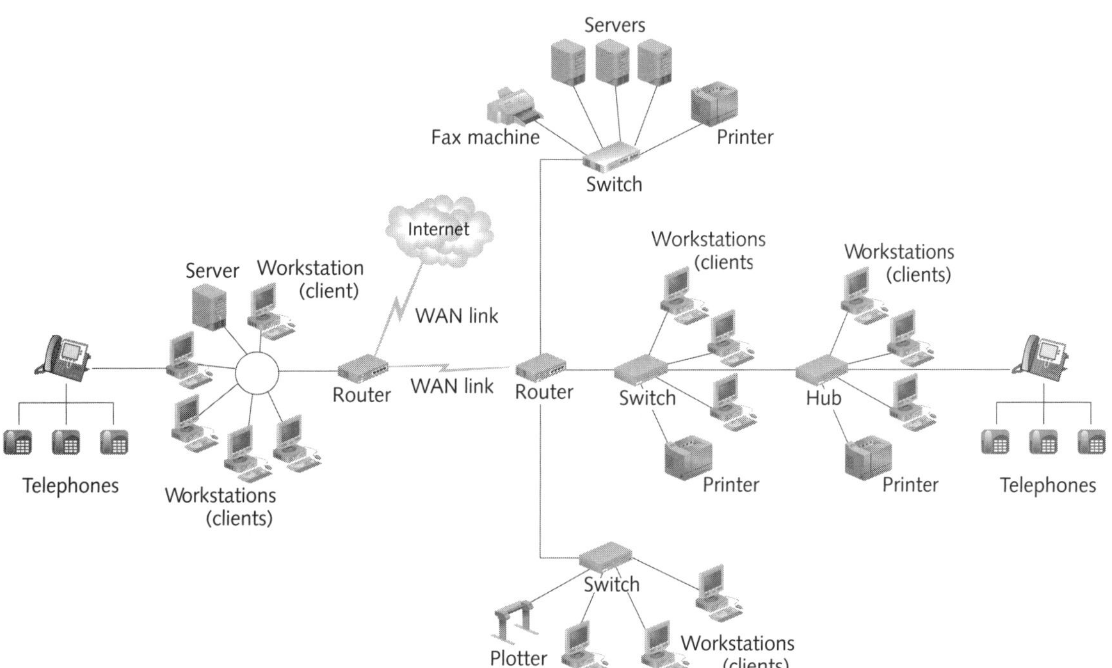

Figure 1-3 A more complex client/server network

WANs commonly connect separate offices in the same organization, whether they are across town or across the world from each other. For example, imagine you work for a nationwide plumbing supply company that keeps its inventory in warehouses in Topeka, Kansas, and Panama City, Florida. Suppose also that the company's headquarters is located in New York. When a customer calls and asks whether you have five faucets of a certain type available to ship overnight, you need to check the inventory databases for both the Topeka and Panama City warehouses. Thanks to your WAN, the data is accessible from your New York desktop. Twice a day the warehouses' inventory software automatically updates a database located on a central server in New York via WAN links that connect the locations.

WANs are also used to connect LANs that belong to different organizations. For example, all the public universities within a state might combine and share their resources via a WAN. The largest and most varied WAN in the world is the **Internet**. Figure 1-4 depicts a simple WAN.

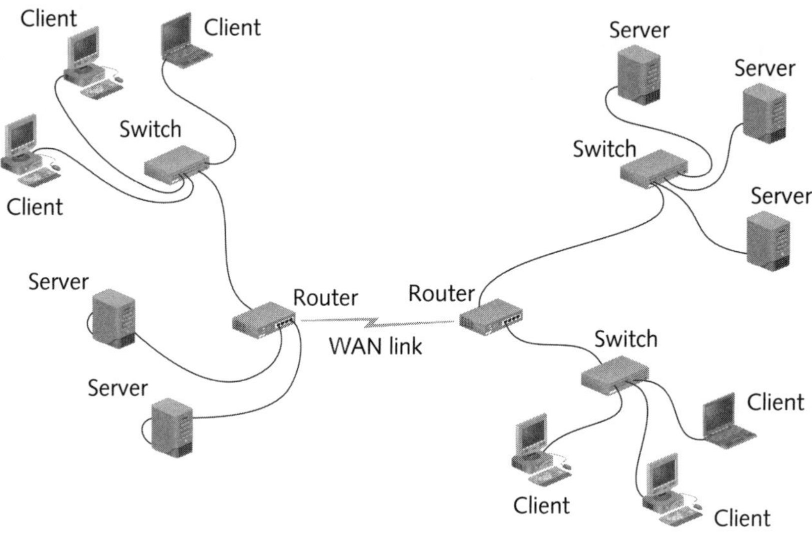

Figure 1-4 A simple WAN

Elements Common to Client/Server Networks

Net+

2.7

You have learned that networks—no matter how simple or how complex—provide some benefits over stand-alone computers. They also share terminology and common building blocks, some of which you have already encountered. The following list provides a more complete rundown of basic elements common to all client/server networks. You will learn more about these topics throughout this book:

- *Client*—A computer on the network that requests resources or services from another computer on a network; in some cases, a client could also act as a server. The term client may also refer to the human **user** of a client workstation or to client software installed on the workstation.

Net+

2.7

- *Server*—A computer on the network that manages shared resources; servers usually have more processing power, memory, and hard disk space than clients. They run network operating software that can manage not only data, but also users, groups, security, and applications on the network.

- *Workstation*—A personal computer (such as a desktop or laptop) that may or may not be connected to a network; most clients are workstation computers.

- **NIC** *(network interface card)*—The device (pronounced *nick*) inside a computer that connects a computer to the network media, thus allowing it to communicate with other computers; many companies (such as 3Com, IBM, Intel, SMC, and Xircom) manufacture NICs, which come with a variety of specifications that are tailored to the requirements of the workstation and the network. Some connect to the **motherboard,** which is the main circuit that controls the computer, some are integrated as part of the motherboard, and others connect via an external port. NICs are also known as **network adapters.** Figure 1-5 depicts a NIC connected to a computer's motherboard.

Because different PCs and network types require different kinds of NICs, you cannot assume that a NIC that works in one workstation will work in another.

- *NOS* *(network operating system)*—The software that runs on a server and enables the server to manage data, users, groups, security, applications, and other networking functions. Examples include various types of UNIX and Linux operating systems, Microsoft Windows Server 2003 or Windows Server 2008, and Mac OS X Server.

- *Host*—A computer that enables resource sharing by other computers on the same network.

- *Node*—A client, server, or other device that can communicate over a network and that is identified by a unique number, known as its network address.

- *Connectivity device*—A specialized device that allows multiple networks or multiple parts of one network to connect and exchange data. A client/server network can

Figure 1-5 A NIC (network interface card)

Net+

2.7

operate without connectivity devices. However, medium- and large-sized LANs use them to extend the network and to connect with WANs.

- *Segment*—A part of a network. Usually, a segment is composed of a group of nodes that use the same communications channel for all their traffic.

- *Backbone*—The part of a network to which segments and significant shared devices (such as routers, switches, and servers) connect. A backbone is sometimes referred to as "a network of networks," because of its role in interconnecting smaller parts of a LAN or WAN. Figure 1-6 shows a LAN with its backbone highlighted.

Net+

2.3

2.7

- *Topology*—The physical layout of a computer network. Topologies vary according to the needs of the organization and available hardware and expertise. Networks can be arranged in a ring, bus, or star formation, and the star formation is the most common. Hybrid combinations of these patterns are also possible. Figure 1-7 illustrates these network topologies, which you must understand to design and troubleshoot networks.

Net+

2.7

- *Protocol*—A standard method or format for communication between networked devices. Protocols ensure that data is transferred whole, in sequence, and without error from one node on the network to another.

- *Data packets*—The distinct units of data that are exchanged between nodes on a network. Breaking a large stream of data into many packets allows a network to deliver that data more efficiently and reliably.

- *Addressing*—The scheme for assigning a unique identifying number to every node on the network. The type of addressing used depends on the network's protocols and network operating system. Each network device must have a unique **address** so that data can be transmitted reliably to and from that device.

- *Transmission media*—The means through which data is transmitted and received. Transmission media may be physical, such as wire or cable, or atmospheric (wireless), such as radio waves. Figure 1-8 shows several examples of transmission media.

Now that you are familiar with basic network terminology, you are ready to appreciate the many uses of computer networks.

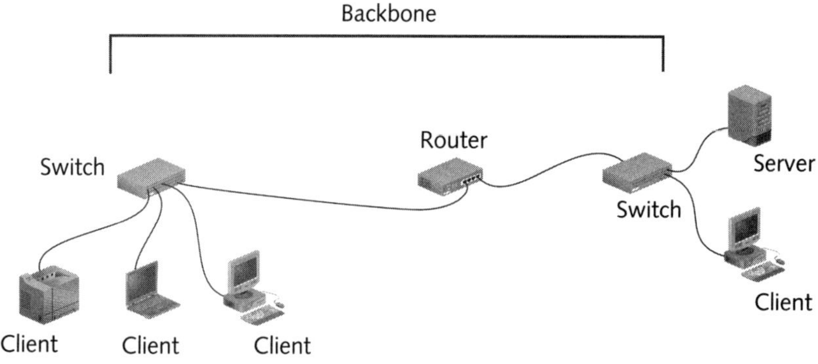

Figure 1-6 A LAN backbone

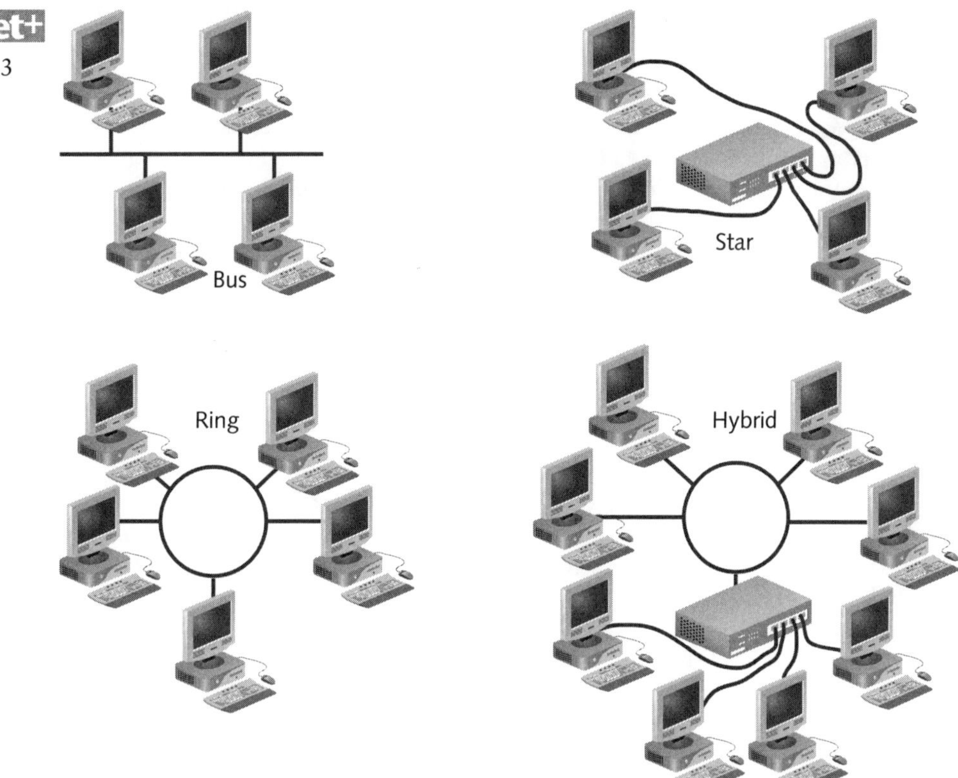

Figure 1-7 Common network topologies

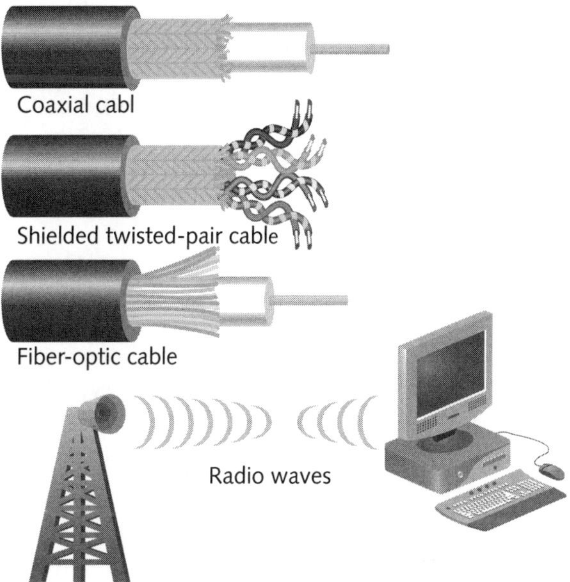

Figure 1-8 Examples of network transmission media

How Networks Are Used

The functions provided by a network are usually referred to as **network services**. Any network manager will tell you that the network service with the highest visibility is e-mail. If your company's e-mail system fails, users will notice within minutes—and they will not be shy about informing you of the failure. Although e-mail may be the most visible network service, other services can be just as vital. Printer sharing, file sharing, Internet access and Web site delivery, remote access capabilities, the provision of voice (telephone) and video services, and network management are all critical business functions provided through networks. In large organizations, separate servers may be dedicated to performing each of these functions. In offices with only a few users and little network traffic, one server may perform all functions.

File and Print Services

File services refer to the capability of a server to share data files, applications (such as word-processing or spreadsheet programs), and disk storage space. A server that provides file services is called a **file server**. File services accounted for the first use of networks and remain the foundation of networking today, for a number of reasons. As mentioned earlier, it is easier and faster to store shared data at a central location than to copy files to disks and then pass the disks around. Data stored at a central location is typically more secure because a network administrator can take charge of backing up this data, rather than relying on individual users to make their own copies. In addition, using a file server to run applications for multiple users requires the purchase of fewer copies of the application and less maintenance work for the network administrator.

Using **print services** to share printers across a network also saves time and money. A high-capacity printer can cost thousands of dollars, but it can handle the printing tasks of an entire department, thereby eliminating the need to buy a desktop printer for each worker. With one printer, less time is spent on maintenance and management. If a shared printer fails, the network administrator can diagnose the problem from a workstation anywhere on the network using the network operating system's printer control functions. Often, the administrator can solve the problem without even visiting the printer.

Access Services

A network's access services allow remote users to connect to the network. (The term **remote user** refers to a person working on a computer on a different network or in a different geographical location from the LAN's server.) Less frequently, access services allow network users to connect to machines outside the network. Most network operating systems include built-in access services that enable users to dial in to a **remote access server**, log on to the network, and take advantage of the network just as if they were logged on to a workstation on the office LAN. A remote access server may also be known as simply an **access server**.

Organizations commonly use access services to provide LAN connectivity for workers at home, workers on the road, and workers at small satellite offices where dedicated WAN connections are not cost effective. In addition, they may use access services to allow staff from other organizations (such as a software or hardware vendor) to help diagnose a network

problem. For example, suppose you work for a clothing manufacturer that uses embroidery software to control the machines that sew insignias on shirts and hats. You are an expert on networking, but you are less adept with the automated embroidery software. When the software causes problems, you turn to the software vendor for help. But suppose the vendor's technician can't solve the problem except by logging on to your network. In that case, it is much more efficient and less expensive to allow the technician to dial in to your network through a remote access server than to fly the technician to your office.

It is important to remember that remote access servers—no matter which platform (hardware or operating system software) they run on—allow external users to use network resources and devices just as if they were logged on to a workstation in the office. From a remote location, users can print files to shared printers, log on to hosts, retrieve mail from an internal messaging system, or run queries on internal databases. Because they can be accessed by the world outside the local network, remote access servers necessitate strict security measures.

Communications Services

Today's networks can help users communicate in many ways: e-mail, telephone, video, fax, cell phone, and personal digital assistant (for example, a BlackBerry). The phenomenon of offering multiple types of communications services on the same network is known as **convergence**. A similar term is **unified communications**, which refers to the centralized management of multiple network-based communications. For example, your company might use one software program to manage intraoffice phone calls, long-distance phone calls, cell phone calls, voice mail, faxes, and text messaging for all the users on your network.

The oldest and still most frequently used network communications services are **mail services**, which coordinate the storage and transfer of e-mail between users on a network. The computer responsible for mail services is called a **mail server**. Mail servers are usually connected to the Internet, but when clients only need to exchange e-mail within their organization, their mail server may be isolated on their LAN.

In addition to simply sending, receiving, and storing mail, mail servers can do the following:

- Intercept or filter unsolicited e-mail, known as **spam**.
- Find objectionable content in e-mails and perform functions (such as user notification) on that content.
- Route messages according to particular rules—for example, if a technical support representative has not opened a customer's message within 15 minutes of delivery, a mail server could automatically forward the message to a supervisor.
- Provide a Web-based client for checking e-mail.
- Notify administrators or users if certain events occur (for example, if a user's mailbox is close to exceeding its maximum amount of space on a server).
- Schedule e-mail transmission, retrieval, storage, and maintenance functions.
- Communicate with mail servers on other networks so that mail can be exchanged between users who do not connect to the same LAN.

To supply these services, a mail server runs specialized mail server software, examples of which include Sendmail and Microsoft Exchange Server. Because of their critical nature and heavy use, maintaining a mail server in any sizable organization requires a significant commitment of technical support and administration resources.

Internet Services

You have probably connected to the Internet without knowing or caring about all of the services running behind the scenes. But in fact, many servers are working together to bring Web pages to your desktop. For example, a **Web server** is a computer installed with the appropriate software to supply Web pages to many different clients upon demand. Supplying Web pages is only one type of Internet service. Other **Internet services** include file transfer capabilities, Internet addressing schemes, security filters, and a means for directly logging on to other computers on the Internet.

Management Services

When networks were small, they could be managed easily by a single network administrator and the network operating system's internal functions. For instance, suppose a user called to report a problem logging on to the network and the administrator diagnosed the problem as an addressing conflict (that is, two workstations having the same network address). In a very small network, the conflicting workstations might be located right around the corner from each other, and one address could be changed quickly. In another example, if a manager needed to report the number of copies of Adobe Photoshop in use in a certain department, the network administrator could probably get the desired information by just walking through the department and checking the various workstations.

As networks grow larger and more complex, however, they become more difficult to manage. Using network management services can help you keep track of a large network. Network **management services** centrally administer management tasks on the network, such as ensuring that no more than 20 workstations are using Adobe Photoshop at one time in an organization that purchased a 20-user license for the software. Some organizations dedicate a number of servers to network management functions, with each server performing only one or two unique services.

Numerous services fall under the category of network management. Some of the most important ones include the following:

- *Traffic monitoring and control*—Determining how much **traffic** (that is, data transmission activity) is taking place on a network and notifying administrators when the network becomes overloaded. In general, the larger the network, the more critical it is to monitor traffic.

- *Load balancing*—Distributing data transfer activity evenly across a network so that no single device becomes overwhelmed. Load balancing is especially important for networks in which it's difficult to predict the number of requests that will be issued to a server, as is the case with Web servers.

- *Hardware diagnosis and failure alert*—Determining when a network component fails and automatically notifying the network administrator through e-mail or paging

- *Asset management*—Collecting and storing data on the number and types of software and hardware assets in an organization's network. With asset management software, a server can electronically examine each client's software and hardware and automatically

save the data in a database. Other types of assets might be identified and tracked using RFID (radio frequency identification) tags, which emit a wireless signal at all times. Wireless detection devices connected to a network can track the locations of RFID-tagged devices. For example, a hospital might use RFID tags to keep track of the wheelchairs, beds, and IV pumps that circulate throughout its campus. Before asset management services, inventory data had to be gathered manually and typed into spreadsheets.

- *License tracking*—Determining how many copies of a single application are currently in use on the network and ensuring that number does not exceed the number of licenses purchased. This information is important for legal reasons, as software companies are vigilant about illegally copying software or using more than the authorized number of copies.

- *Security auditing*—Evaluating what security measures are currently in force and notifying the network administrator if a security breach occurs.

- *Software distribution*—Automatically transferring a file or installing an application from the server to a client on the network. The installation process can be started from either the server or the client. Several options are available when distributing software, such as warning users about updates, writing changes to a workstation's system files, and restarting the workstation after the update.

- *Address management*—Centrally managing a finite number of network addresses for an entire network. Usually this task can be accomplished without manually modifying the client workstation configurations.

- *Backup and restoration of data*—Copying (or **backing up**) critical data files to a secure storage area and then **restoring** (or retrieving) data if the original files are lost or deleted. Often backups are performed according to a formulaic schedule. Backup and data restoration services provide centralized management of data backup on multiple servers and on-demand restoration of files and directories.

Network management services will be covered in depth later in the book. For now, it is enough to be aware of the variety of services and the importance of this growing area of networking.

Becoming a Networking Professional

If you search online employment services, you'll probably find hundreds of postings for computer professionals. Of course, the level of expertise required for each of these jobs differs. Some companies simply need "warm bodies" to ensure that a higher-level engineer is notified if a critical network segment fails; other companies are looking for people to plan their global information technology strategies. Needless to say, the more extensive your skills, the better your chances for landing a lucrative and interesting job in networking. To prepare yourself to enter this job market, master a number of general networking technologies. Only then should you pick a few areas that interest you and study those specialties. Hone your communication and teamwork skills, and stay abreast of emerging technologies. Consider the tremendous advantages of attaining professional certification and getting to know others in your field. The following sections offer suggestions on how to approach a career in networking.

Mastering the Technical Challenges

Although computer networking is a varied field, some general technical skills will serve you well no matter which specialty you choose. Because you are already interested in computers, you probably enjoy an aptitude for logical and analytical thinking. You probably also want to acquire these skills:

- Installing, configuring, and troubleshooting network server software and hardware
- Installing, configuring, and troubleshooting network client software and hardware
- Understanding the characteristics of different transmission media
- Understanding network design
- Understanding network protocols
- Understanding how users interact with the network
- Constructing a network with clients, servers, media, and connectivity devices

Because you can expand your networking knowledge in almost any direction, you should pay attention to the general skills that interest you most, and then pick one or two of those areas and concentrate on them. The following specialties are currently in high demand:

- Network security
- Convergence (the delivery of voice, video, and data over a single network)
- In-depth knowledge about one or more NOSs: UNIX, Linux, Mac OS X Server, Microsoft Windows Server 2003, or Windows Server 2008
- Network management
- Internet and intranet design
- Configuration and optimization of routers and switches
- Centralized data storage and management for large-scale environments

Determine which method of learning works best for you. A small classroom with an experienced instructor and a hands-on projects lab is an excellent learning environment, because there you can ask questions and learn by doing. Many colleges offer courses or continuing education on networking topics. You may also want to enroll at a computer training center. These training centers can be found in every metropolitan area and in many small towns. If you are pursuing certification, be certain the training center you choose is authorized to provide training for that certification. Most computer training centers also operate a Web site that provides information on their course schedule, fees, and qualifications. Some of these sites even offer online class registration.

There is no substitute for hands-on experience when it comes to improving your networking hardware and software skills. If you don't already work in an IT department, try to find a position that puts you in that environment, even if it isn't your dream job. Volunteer a few hours a week if necessary. After you are surrounded with other information technology professionals and encounter real-life situations, you will have the opportunity to expand your skills by practicing and asking questions of more experienced staff. On the Web, you can find a number of searchable online job boards and recruiter sites. The placement office at your local college or university can also connect you with job opportunities.

Developing Your "Soft Skills"

Knowing how to configure a router or install UNIX will serve you well, but advanced soft skills will help you stand out. The term **soft skills** refers to those skills that are not easily measurable, such as customer relations, oral and written communications, dependability, teamwork, and leadership abilities. Some of these soft skills might appear to be advantages in any profession, but they are especially important when you must work in teams, in challenging technical circumstances, and under tight deadlines—requirements that apply to most networking projects. For this reason, soft skills merit closer examination:

- *Customer relations*—Perhaps one of the most important soft skills, customer relations involve an ability to listen to customers' frustrations and desires and then empathize, respond, and guide customers to their goals without acting arrogant. Bear in mind that some of your customers will not appreciate or enjoy technology as much as you do, and they will value your patience as you help them. The better your customer relations, the more respected and in demand you will be as a network professional.

- *Oral and written communications*—You may understand the most complicated technical details about a network, but if you cannot communicate them to colleagues and clients, the significance of your knowledge is diminished. Imagine that you are a networking consultant who is competing with several other firms to overhaul a metropolitan hospital's network, a project that could generate millions of dollars for your company. You may have designed the best solution and have it clearly mapped out in your head, but your plan is useless if you can't describe it clearly. The hospital's planning committee will accept whichever proposal makes the most sense to them—that is, the proposal whose suggestions and justifications are plainly communicated.

- *Dependability*—This characteristic will help you in any career. However, in the field of networking, where breakdowns or glitches can occur at any time of day or night and only a limited number of individuals have the expertise to fix them, being dependable is critical. Your career will benefit when you are the one who is available to address a problem, even if you don't always know the answer immediately.

- *Teamwork*—Individual computer professionals often have strong preferences for a certain type of hardware or software. Some technical people like to think that they have all of the answers. For these and other reasons, teamwork in IT departments is sometimes lacking. To be the best networking professional in your department, you must be open to new ideas, encourage cooperation among your colleagues, and allow others to help you and make suggestions.

- *Leadership abilities*—As a networking professional, you will sometimes need to make difficult or unpopular decisions under pressure. You may need to persuade opinionated colleagues to try a new product, tell a group of angry users that what they want is not possible, or manage a project with nearly impossible budgetary and time restrictions. In all of these situations, you will benefit from having strong leadership skills.

After your career in networking begins, you will discover which soft skills you already possess and which ones you need to cultivate. The important thing is that you realize the importance of these attributes and are willing to devote the time necessary to develop them.

Pursuing Certification

Certification is the process of mastering material pertaining to a particular hardware system, operating system, programming language, or software application, and then proving your mastery by passing a series of exams. Certification programs are developed and administered either by a manufacturer or a professional organization such as **CompTIA (Computing Technology Industry Association)**. You can pursue a number of different certifications, depending on your specialty interest. For example, if you want to become a PC technician, you should attain **A+** certification. If you want to specialize in Microsoft product support and development, pursue **MCSE (Microsoft Certified Systems Engineer)** certification. To specialize in the configuration and management of Cisco Systems' switches and routers, work toward Cisco's **CCNA (Cisco Certified Network Associate)** or go for their most difficult and prestigious distinction, **CCIE (Cisco Certified Internetwork Engineer)** certification. To prove a mastery of many aspects of networking, you can choose to become Network+ certified. **Network+ (Net+)** is a professional certification established by CompTIA that verifies broad, vendor-independent networking technology skills, such as an understanding of protocols, topologies, networking hardware, and network troubleshooting. Network+ may also be a stepping stone to more advanced certifications. The material in this book addresses the knowledge objectives you must understand to qualify for Network+ certification.

Certification is a popular career development tool for job seekers and a measure of an employee's qualifications for employers. Following are a list of benefits to becoming certified:

- *Better salary*—Professionals with certification can usually ask for higher salaries than those who aren't certified. Employers will also want to retain certified employees, especially if they helped pay for their training, and will offer incentives to keep certified professionals at the company.

- *Greater opportunities*—Certification may qualify you for additional degrees or more advanced technical positions.

- *Professional respect*—After you have proven your skills with a product or system, your colleagues and clients will gain great respect for your ability to solve problems with that system or product. They will therefore feel confident asking you for help.

- *Access to better support*—Many manufacturers reward certified professionals with less expensive, more detailed, and more direct access to their technical support.

One potential drawback of some certifications is the number of people attaining them—so many that certifications now have less value. Currently, hundreds of thousands of networking professionals have acquired the MCSE certification. When only tens of thousands of people had MCSEs, employers were willing to pay substantially higher salaries to workers with that certification than they are now. Other kinds of certifications, such as Cisco's CCIE program, require candidates to pass lab exams. These kinds of certifications, because they require rigorous proof of knowledge, are highly respected.

Finding a Job in Networking

With the proper credentials and demonstrated technical knowledge, you will qualify for a multitude of positions in networking. For this reason, you can and must be selective when searching for a job. Following are some ways to research your possibilities:

- *Search the Web*—Because your job will deal directly with technology, it makes sense to use technology to find it. Companies in the computer industry recruit intensively on the Web, either through searchable job databases or through links on their company Web sites. Unlike firms in other industries, these companies typically do not mind (and might prefer) receiving résumés and letters through e-mail. Most job database Web sites do not charge for their services, but they may require you to register with them. Some popular general Web job databases include Yahoo! Hot Jobs at *hotjobs.yahoo.com* and Monster at *www.monster.com*. IT-specific job sites include Dice at *www.dice.com*, Slashdot Jobs at *jobs.slashdot.org*, and *computerjobs.com*. A simple Web search could yield dozens more.

- *Read the newspaper*—A traditional place to look for jobs is the classified ad section of your local newspaper. Papers with large distributions often devote a section of their classified ads to careers in computing. Highlight the ads that sound interesting to you, even if you don't have all of the qualifications cited by the employer. In some ads, employers will list every skill they could possibly want a new hire to have, but they don't truly expect one person to have all of them.

- *Visit a career center*—Regardless of whether you are a registered university or college student, you can use career center services to find a list of job openings in your area. Companies that are hiring pay much attention to the collegiate career centers because of the number of job seekers served by these centers. Visit the college or university campus nearest you and search through its career center listings.

- *Network*—Find like-minded professionals with whom you can discuss job possibilities. You may meet these individuals through training classes, conferences, professional organizations, or career fairs. Let them know that you are looking for a job, and specify exactly what kind of job you want. If they can't suggest any leads for you, ask these people if they have other colleagues who might.

- *Attend career fairs*—Most metropolitan areas host career fairs for job seekers in the information technology field, and some large companies host their own job fairs. Even if you aren't sure you want to work for any of the companies represented at a job fair, attend the job fair to research the market. You can find out which skills are in high demand in your area and which types of companies are hiring the most networking professionals. You can also meet other people in your field who may offer valuable advice based on their employment experience.

- *Enlist a recruiter*—Many recruiting agencies deal strictly with clients in the technical fields. By signing up with such a recruiting agency, you may have access to job opportunities that you didn't know existed. You might also take advantage of a temporary assignment, to see if the fit between you and an employer is mutually beneficial, before accepting a permanent job with that employer.

Joining Professional Associations

At some point in your life, you have probably belonged to a club or organization. You know, therefore, that the benefits of joining can vary, depending on many factors. In the best case, joining an organization can connect you with people who have similar interests, provide new opportunities for learning, allow you to access specialized information, and give you more tangible assets such as free goods. Specifically, a networking professional organization might offer its own publications, technical workshops and conferences, free software, prerelease software, and access to expensive hardware labs.

You can choose from several prominent professional organizations in the field of networking. Because the field has grown so quickly and because so many areas in which to specialize exist, no single professional organization stands out as the most advantageous or highly respected. You will have to decide whether an organization is appropriate for you. Among other things, you will want to consider the organization's number of members, membership benefits, membership dues, technical emphasis, and whether it hosts a local chapter. Many organizations host student chapters on university campuses. You may also want to find a professional association that caters to your demographic group (such as Women in Technology International, if you are female). Table 1-1 lists some professional organizations and their Web sites.

Table 1-1 Networking Organizations

Professional Organization	Web Site
Association for Computing Machinery (ACM)	*www.acm.org*
Association for Information Technology Professionals	*www.aitp.org*
IEEE Computer Society	*www.computer.org*
Network Professional Association	*www.npanet.org*
Women in Technology International (WITI)	*www.witi.org*

Chapter Summary

- A network is a group of computers and other devices (such as printers) that are connected by some type of transmission media, such as copper or fiber-optic cable or the atmosphere, in the case of wireless transmission.

- All networks offer advantages relative to using a stand-alone computer. Networks enable multiple users to share devices and data. Sharing resources saves time and money. Networks also allow you to manage, or administer, resources on multiple computers from a central location.

- In a peer-to-peer network, every computer can communicate directly with every other computer. By default, no computer on a peer-to-peer network has more authority than another. However, each computer can be configured to share only some of its resources and keep other resources inaccessible.

- Traditional peer-to-peer networks are usually simple and inexpensive to set up. However, they are not necessarily flexible or secure.

- Client/server networks rely on a centrally administered server (or servers) to manage shared resources for multiple clients. In this scheme, the server has greater authority than the clients, which are typically desktop or laptop workstations.

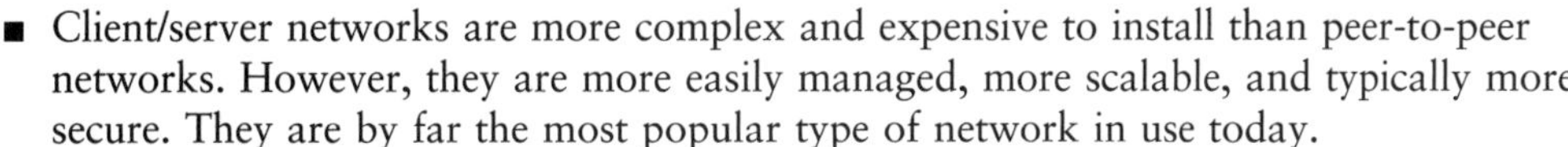

- Client/server networks are more complex and expensive to install than peer-to-peer networks. However, they are more easily managed, more scalable, and typically more secure. They are by far the most popular type of network in use today.

- Servers typically possess more processing power, hard disk space, and memory than client computers. To manage access to and use of shared resources, among other centralized functions, a server requires a network operating system.

- A LAN (local area network) is a network of computers and other devices that is confined to a relatively small space, such as one building or even one office.

- LANs can be interconnected to form WANs (wide area networks), which traverse longer distances and, therefore, require slightly different transmission methods and media than LANs. The Internet is the largest example of a WAN.

- Client/server networks share some common elements, including clients, servers, workstations, transmission media, connectivity devices, protocols, addressing, topology, NICs, data packets, network operating systems, hosts, backbones, segments, and nodes.

- Although e-mail is the most visible network service, networks also provide services for printing, file sharing, Internet access, remote access capabilities, communicating in multiple forms, and network management.

- File and print services provide the foundation for networking. They enable multiple users to share data, applications, storage areas, and printers.

- Networks use access services to allow remote users to connect to the network or network users to connect to machines outside the network.

- Communications services provided by networks include e-mail, telephone, video, fax, messaging, and voice mail.

- Mail services (running on mail servers) allow users on a network to exchange and store e-mail. Most mail packages also provide filtering, routing, scheduling, notification, and connectivity with other mail systems.

- Internet services such as World Wide Web servers and browsers, file transfer capabilities, addressing schemes, and security filters enable organizations to connect to and use the global Internet.

- Network management services centrally administer and simplify complicated management tasks on the network, such as asset management, security auditing, hardware problem diagnosis, backup and restore services, license tracking, load balancing, and data traffic control.

- To prepare yourself for a networking career, master a number of broad networking skills, such as installing and configuring client and server hardware and software. Then pick a few areas that interest you, such as network security or voice/data integration, and study those specialties.

- Certification is the process of mastering material pertaining to a particular hardware system, operating system, programming language, or other software program, and then proving your mastery by passing a series of exams. The benefits of certification can include a better salary, more job opportunities, greater professional respect, and better access to technical support.

- To excel in the field of networking, hone your soft skills, such as leadership abilities, written and oral communication, a professional attitude, dependability, and customer relations.

- Joining an association for networking professionals can connect you with like-minded people, give you access to workshops and technical publications, allow you to receive discounted or free software, and perhaps even help you find a job in the field.

Key Terms

A+   The professional certification established by CompTIA that verifies knowledge about PC operation, repair, and management.

access server   *See* remote access server.

address   A number that uniquely identifies each workstation and device on a network. Without unique addresses, computers on the network could not reliably communicate.

address management   The process of centrally administering a finite number of network addresses for an entire LAN. Usually this task can be accomplished without touching the client workstations.

addressing   The scheme for assigning a unique identifying number to every workstation and device on the network. The type of addressing used on a network depends on its protocols and network operating system.

asset management   The process of collecting and storing data on the number and types of software and hardware assets in an organization's network. The data collection is automated by electronically examining each network client from a server.

backbone   The part of a network to which segments and significant shared devices (such as routers, switches, and servers) connect. A backbone is sometimes referred to as "a network of networks" because of its role in interconnecting smaller parts of a LAN or WAN.

backing up   The process of copying critical data files to a secure storage area. Often, backups are performed according to a formulaic schedule.

CCIE (Cisco Certified Internetwork Expert)   An elite certification that recognizes expert-level installation, configuration, management, and troubleshooting skills on networks that use a range of Cisco Systems' devices.

CCNA (Cisco Certified Network Associate)   A professional certification that attests to one's skills in installing, configuring, maintaining, and troubleshooting medium-sized networks that use Cisco Systems' switches and routers.

certification   The process of mastering material pertaining to a particular hardware system, operating system, programming language, or other software program, and then proving your mastery by passing a series of exams.

Cisco Certified Internetwork Expert   *See* CCIE.

Cisco Certified Network Associate   *See* CCNA.

client   A computer on the network that requests resources or services from another computer on a network. In some cases, a client could also act as a server. The term *client*

may also refer to the user of a client workstation or a client software application installed on the workstation.

client/server architecture A network design in which clients (typically desktop or laptop computers) use a centrally administered server to share data, data storage space, and devices.

client/server network A network that uses centrally administered computers, known as servers, to enable resource sharing for and to facilitate communication between the other computers on the network.

CompTIA (Computing Technology Industry Association) An association of computer resellers, manufacturers, and training companies that sets industry-wide standards for computer professionals. CompTIA established and sponsors the A+ and Network+ (Net+) certifications.

Computing Technology Industry Association *See* CompTIA.

connectivity device One of several types of specialized devices that allows two or more networks or multiple parts of one network to connect and exchange data.

convergence The use of data networks to carry voice (or telephone), video, and other communications services in addition to data.

data packet A discrete unit of information sent from one node on a network to another.

file server A specialized server that enables clients to share applications and data across the network.

file services The functions of a file server that allow users to share data files, applications, and storage areas.

host A computer that enables resource sharing by other computers on the same network.

Internet A complex WAN that connects LANs and clients around the globe.

Internet services The services that enable a network to communicate with the Internet, including World Wide Web servers and browsers, file transfer capabilities, Internet addressing schemes, security filters, and a means for directly logging on to other computers.

LAN (local area network) A network of computers and other devices that is confined to a relatively small space, such as one building or even one office.

license tracking The process of determining the number of copies of a single application that are currently in use on the network and whether the number in use exceeds the authorized number of licenses.

load balancing The process of distributing data transfer activity evenly across a network so that no single device is overwhelmed.

local area network *See* LAN.

mail server A server that manages the storage and transfer of e-mail messages.

mail services The network services that manage the storage and transfer of e-mail between users on a network. In addition to sending, receiving, and storing mail, mail services can include filtering, routing, notification, scheduling, and data exchange with other mail servers.

MAN (metropolitan area network) A network that is larger than a LAN, typically connecting clients and servers from multiple buildings, but within a limited geographic area. For example, a MAN could connect multiple city government buildings around a city's center.

management services   The network services that centrally administer and simplify complicated management tasks on the network. Examples of management services include license tracking, security auditing, asset management, address management, software distribution, traffic monitoring, load balancing, and hardware diagnosis.

MCSE (Microsoft Certified Systems Engineer)   A professional certification established by Microsoft that demonstrates in-depth knowledge about Microsoft products.

metropolitan area network   *See* MAN.

Microsoft Certified Systems Engineer   *See* MCSE.

motherboard   The main circuit board that controls a computer.

network   A group of computers and other devices (such as printers) that are connected by and can exchange data via some type of transmission media, such as a cable, a wire, or the atmosphere.

network adapter   *See* NIC.

Network+ (Net+)   The professional certification established by CompTIA that verifies broad, vendor-independent networking technology skills, such as an understanding of protocols, topologies, networking hardware, and network troubleshooting.

network interface card   *See* NIC.

network operating system   *See* NOS.

network services   The functions provided by a network.

NIC (network interface card)   The device that enables a workstation to connect to the network and communicate with other computers. NICs are manufactured by several different companies and come with a variety of specifications that are tailored to the workstation's and the network's requirements. NICs are also called network adapters.

node   A computer or other device connected to a network that has a unique address and is capable of sending or receiving data.

NOS (network operating system)   The software that runs on a server and enables the server to manage data, users, groups, security, applications, and other networking functions. The most popular network operating systems are Microsoft Windows NT, Windows 2000 Server, Windows Server 2003, UNIX, Linux, and Novell NetWare.

P2P network   *See* peer-to-peer network.

peer-to-peer network   A network in which every computer can communicate directly with every other computer. By default, no computer on a peer-to-peer network has more authority than another. However, each computer can be configured to share only some of its resources and keep other resources inaccessible to other nodes on the network.

print services   The network service that allows printers to be shared by several users on a network.

protocol   A standard method or format for communication between network devices. Protocols ensure that data is transferred whole, in sequence, and without error from one node on the network to another.

remote access server   A server that runs communications services that enable remote users to log on to a network. Also known as an access server.

remote user A person working on a computer on a different network or in a different geographical location from the LAN's server.

resources The devices, data, and data storage space provided by a computer, whether stand-alone or shared.

restore The process of retrieving files from a backup. It is necessary to restore files if the original files are lost or deleted.

scalable The property of a network that allows you to add nodes or increase its size easily.

security auditing The process of evaluating security measures currently in place on a network and notifying the network administrator if a security breach occurs.

segment A part of a network. Usually, a segment is composed of a group of nodes that share the same communications channel for all their traffic.

server A computer on the network that manages shared resources. Servers usually have more processing power, memory, and hard disk space than clients. They run network operating software that can manage not only data, but also users, groups, security, and applications on the network.

sneakernet A way of exchanging data between computers that are not connected on a network. Sneakernet requires that data be copied from a computer to a removable storage device such as a floppy disk, carried (presumably by someone wearing sneakers) to another computer, and then copied from the storage device onto the second computer.

soft skills The skills such as customer relations, leadership ability, and dependability, which are not easily measured, but are nevertheless important in a networking career.

software distribution The process of automatically transferring a data file or installing a software application from the server to a client on the network.

spam An unsolicited, unwanted e-mail.

stand-alone computer A computer that uses applications and data only from its local disks and that is not connected to a network.

topology The physical layout of computers on a network.

traffic The data transmission and processing activity taking place on a computer network at any given time.

traffic monitoring The process of determining how much data transfer activity is taking place on a network or network segment and notifying administrators when a segment becomes overloaded.

transmission media The means through which data is transmitted and received. Transmission media may be physical, such as wire or cable, or atmospheric (wireless), such as radio waves.

unified communications The centralized management of multiple types of network-based communications, such as voice, video, fax, and messaging services.

user A person who uses a computer.

WAN (wide area network) A network that spans a long distance and connects two or more LANs.

Web server   A computer that manages Web site services, such as supplying a Web page to multiple users on demand.

wide area network   *See* WAN.

workstation   A computer that runs a desktop operating system and connects to a network.

Review Questions

1. Which of the following allows the sharing of resources and central location management for multiple computers?

   a. Workstations

   b. Clients

   c. Stand-alone computers

   d. Networks

2. What network design offers simplicity in configuration and low costs to set up and maintain?

   a. Client/server

   b. Peer-to-peer

   c. Bus topology

   d. Wide area network (WAN)

3. Which of the following is an advantage of a client/server network?

   a. It is simple to configure.

   b. It can connect more than a handful of computers on a network.

   c. It is often suitable for environments in which saving money is critical.

   d. It avoids scalability.

4. What term describes the phenomenon of offering multiple types of communications services on the same network?

   a. Unified communications

   b. Convergence

   c. Hybrid network topology

   d. Client/server architecture

5. Which network function is the oldest and still most frequently used?

   a. Internet services

   b. Print services

   c. Remote access services

   d. Mail services

6. True or false? The simplest form of a network is a client-server network.

7. True or false? A segment is part of a network usually composed of a group of nodes that use the same communications channel for all their traffic.

8. True or false? General technical skills are not useful in assisting networking professionals who choose to specialize in a particular area.

9. True or false? Soft skills refer to those skills that are easily measurable.

10. True or false? The Association for Computing Machinery (ACM) is the most advantageous and highly respected professional organization in the industry today.

11. A(n) ____ is a group of computers and other devices that are connected by some type of transmission media.

12. In a(n) ____ network, every computer can communicate directly with every other computer.

13. Client/server networks are more ____ than peer-to-peer networks, meaning client/server networks can be more easily added onto and extended than peer-to-peer networks.

14. The functions provided by a network are usually referred to as ____.

15. The process of proving your mastery in material pertaining to a particular hardware system, operating system, programming language, or software application by passing a series of exams is known as ____.

Networking Standards and the OSI Model

After reading this chapter and completing the exercises, you will be able to:

- Identify organizations that set standards for networking

- Describe the purpose of the OSI model and each of its layers

- Explain specific functions belonging to each OSI model layer

- Understand how two network nodes communicate through the OSI model

- Discuss the structure and purpose of data packets and frames

- Describe the two types of addressing covered by the OSI model

On the Job

When new technologies emerge, it's valuable to establish standards before the technology is widely deployed. Doing so requires getting many parties involved early—the technology developers, equipment suppliers, service providers, end users, marketers, and even organizations that set standards for different, but related, technologies.

For years I've worked on a technology called Metro Ethernet, which uses ubiquitous Ethernet to deliver high-speed data networking services directly to businesses over metropolitan area networks (MANs). This streamlined service bypasses the traditional voice-oriented telephone network often seen as a bottleneck for efficient data communications. My partners and I founded a company in July 1999 and first offered Metro Ethernet in February 2000. It rapidly became clear that this technology was hot. But at that time, no one in the industry agreed on exactly what Metro Ethernet included and how the services should be supplied. That's why I and others founded the Metro Ethernet Forum (MEF) in 2001. The MEF is a nonprofit organization with over 60 member companies working to create and accelerate the adoption of Metro Ethernet standards worldwide. Our members include traditional telephone companies, new types of network service providers, networking equipment manufacturers, electronic component suppliers, and other organizations.

Generating standards that are meaningful and lasting requires significant time and effort. The MEF relies on volunteers from its membership to participate in the work of our Technical or Marketing committees. In each, they review issues, draft recommendations, submit straw ballots, collaborate to achieve consensus, and craft and vote on subsequent ballots that gradually define our implementation agreements and standards. Finally, a letter ballot is submitted to the membership for review and a vote on acceptance at a quarterly meeting. Approximately 80 percent of proposed standards are accepted.

MEF is now working with other standards organizations, such as IEEE, IETF, and ITU, to foster national and international adoption of Metro Ethernet standards. The MEF has created liaisons with these organizations, sharing research and proposing specifications so that other standards bodies need not duplicate our efforts. Wishing to contribute to worldwide cooperation, in July 2003 the MEF hosted in San Francisco the ITU Forum Summit—the largest gathering to date of telecom forum leaders.

Ron Young, CEO, MetNet Communications, Inc. and Founding Chairman of the Board of the Metro Ethernet Forum

When trying to grasp a new theoretical concept, it often helps to form a picture of that concept in your mind. In the field of chemistry, for example, even though you can't see a water molecule, you can represent it with a simple drawing of two hydrogen atoms and one oxygen atom. Similarly, in the field of networking, even though you can't see the communication that occurs between two nodes on a network, you can use a model to depict how the communication takes place. The model commonly used to describe network communications is called the OSI (Open Systems Interconnection) model.

In this chapter, you will learn about the standards organizations that have helped create the various conventions (such as the OSI model) used in networking. Next, you'll be introduced to the seven layers of the OSI model and learn how they interact. You will then take a closer look at what goes on in each layer. Finally, you will learn to apply those details to a practical networking environment. Granted, learning the OSI model is not the most exciting part of becoming a networking expert. Thoroughly understanding it, however, is essential to proficient network design and troubleshooting.

Networking Standards Organizations

Standards are documented agreements containing technical specifications or other precise criteria that stipulate how a particular product or service should be designed or performed. Many different industries use standards to ensure that products, processes, and services suit their purposes. Because of the wide variety of hardware and software in use today, standards are especially important in the world of networking. Without standards, it would be very difficult to design a network because you could not be certain that software or hardware from different manufacturers would work together. For example, if one manufacturer designed a network cable with a 1-centimeter-wide plug and another company manufactured a wall plate with a 0.8-centimeter-wide opening, you would not be able to insert the plug into the wall plate.

When purchasing networking equipment, therefore, you want to verify that equipment meets the standards your network requires. However, bear in mind that standards define the *minimum* acceptable performance of a product or service—not the ideal. So, for example, you might purchase two different network cables that comply with the minimum standard for transmitting at a certain speed, but one cable might exceed that standard, allowing for better network performance. In the case of network cables, exceeding minimum standards often follows from the use of quality materials and careful production techniques.

Because the computer industry grew so quickly out of several technical disciplines, many different organizations evolved to oversee its standards. In some cases, a few organizations are responsible for a single aspect of networking. For example, both ANSI and IEEE are involved in setting standards for wireless networks. Whereas ANSI prescribes the kind of NIC (network interface card) that the consumer needs to accept a wireless connection, IEEE prescribes, among other things, how the network will ensure that different parts of a communication sent through the atmosphere arrive at their destination in the correct sequence.

A complete list of the standards that regulate computers and networking would fill an encyclopedia. Although you don't need to know the fine points of every standard, you should be familiar with the groups that set networking standards and the critical aspects of standards required by your network.

ANSI

ANSI (American National Standards Institute) is an organization composed of more than a thousand representatives from industry and government who together determine standards for the electronics industry and other fields, such as chemical and nuclear engineering, health and safety, and construction. ANSI also represents the United States in setting international standards. This organization does not dictate that manufacturers comply with its standards, but requests voluntarily compliance. Of course, manufacturers and developers benefit from compliance, because compliance assures potential customers that the systems are reliable and can be integrated with an existing infrastructure. New electronic equipment and methods must undergo rigorous testing to prove they are worthy of ANSI's approval.

You can purchase ANSI standards documents online from ANSI's Web site (*www.ansi.org*) or find them at a university or public library. You need not read complete ANSI standards to be a competent networking professional, but you should understand the breadth and significance of ANSI's influence.

EIA and TIA

Two related standards organizations are EIA and TIA. **EIA (Electronic Industries Alliance)** is a trade organization composed of representatives from electronics manufacturing firms across the United States. EIA not only sets standards for its members, but it helps write ANSI standards and lobbies for legislation favorable to the growth of the computer and electronics industries.

In 1988, one of the EIA's subgroups merged with the former United States Telecommunications Suppliers Association (USTSA) to form **TIA (Telecommunications Industry Association)**. TIA focuses on standards for information technology, wireless, satellite, fiber optics, and telephone equipment. Both TIA and EIA set standards, lobby governments and industry, and sponsor conferences, exhibitions, and forums in their areas of interest.

Probably the best-known standards to come from the TIA/EIA alliance are its guidelines for how network cable should be installed in commercial buildings, known as the "TIA/EIA 568-B Series." You can find out more about TIA from its Web site, *www.tiaonline.org*, and EIA from its Web site, *www.eia.org*.

IEEE

The **IEEE (Institute of Electrical and Electronics Engineers)**, or "I-triple-E," is an international society composed of engineering professionals. Its goals are to promote development and education in the electrical engineering and computer science fields. To this end, IEEE hosts numerous symposia, conferences, and local chapter meetings and publishes papers designed to educate members on technological advances. It also maintains a board that establishes its own standards for the electronics and computer industries and contributes to the work of other standards-setting bodies, such as ANSI.

IEEE technical papers and standards are highly respected in the networking profession. Among other places, you will find references to IEEE standards in the manuals that accompany NICs. You can purchase IEEE documents online from IEEE's Web site (*www.ieee.org*) or find them in a university or public library.

ISO

ISO (International Organization for Standardization), headquartered in Geneva, Switzerland, is a collection of standards organizations representing 157 countries. ISO's goal is to establish international technological standards to facilitate global exchange of information and barrier-free trade. Given the organization's full name, you might expect it to be called *IOS*, but ISO is not meant to be an acronym. In fact, *iso* is the Greek word for *equal*. Using this term conveys the organization's dedication to standards.

ISO's authority is not limited to the information-processing and communications industries. It also applies to the fields of textiles, packaging, distribution of goods, energy production and utilization, shipbuilding, and banking and financial services. The universal agreements on screw threads, bank cards, and even the names for currencies are all products of ISO's work. In fact, fewer than 3,000 of ISO's more than 17,000 standards apply to computer-related products and functions. You can find out more about ISO at its Web site: *www.iso.org*.

ITU

The **ITU (International Telecommunication Union)** is a specialized United Nations agency that regulates international telecommunications, including radio and TV frequencies, satellite and telephony specifications, networking infrastructure, and tariffs applied to global communications. It also provides developing countries with technical expertise and equipment to advance those nations' technological bases.

The ITU was founded in Paris in 1865. It became part of the United Nations in 1947 and relocated to Geneva, Switzerland. Its standards arm contains members from 191 countries and publishes detailed policy and standards documents that can be found on its Web site: *www.itu.int*. Typically, ITU documents pertain more to global telecommunications issues than to industry technical specifications. However, the ITU is deeply involved with the implementation of worldwide Internet services. As in other areas, the ITU cooperates with several different standards organizations, such as ISOC (discussed next), to develop these standards.

ISOC

ISOC (Internet Society), founded in 1992, is a professional membership society that helps to establish technical standards for the Internet. Some current ISOC concerns include the rapid growth of the Internet and keeping it accessible, information security, and the need for stable addressing services and open standards across the Internet. ISOC's membership consists of thousands of Internet professionals and companies from 90 chapters around the world.

ISOC oversees groups with specific missions, such as the **IAB (Internet Architecture Board)**. IAB is a technical advisory group of researchers and technical professionals interested in overseeing the Internet's design and management. As part of its charter, IAB is responsible for Internet growth and management strategy, resolution of technical disputes, and standards oversight.

Another ISOC group is the **IETF (Internet Engineering Task Force)**, the organization that sets standards for how systems communicate over the Internet—in particular, how protocols operate and interact. Anyone can submit a proposed standard for IETF approval. The standard then undergoes elaborate review, testing, and approval processes. On an international level, IETF works with the ITU to help give technical standards approved in the United States international acceptance.

You can learn more about ISOC and its member organizations, IAB and IETF, at their Web site: *www.isoc.org*.

IANA and ICANN

You have learned that every computer on a network must have a unique address. On the Internet, this is especially important because millions of different computers must be available to transmit and receive data at any time. Addresses used to identify computers on the Internet and other TCP/IP-based networks are known as **IP (Internet Protocol) addresses**. To ensure that every Internet-connected device has a unique IP address, organizations across the globe rely on centralized authorities.

In early Internet history, a nonprofit group called the **IANA (Internet Assigned Numbers Authority)** kept records of available and reserved IP addresses and determined how addresses were doled out. Starting in 1997, IANA coordinated its efforts with three **RIRs (Regional Internet Registries)**: ARIN (American Registry for Internet Numbers), APNIC (Asia Pacific Network Information Centre), and RIPE (Réseaux IP Européens). An RIR is a not-for-profit agency that manages the distribution of IP addresses to private and public entities. In the late 1990s, the United States Department of Commerce (DOC), which funded IANA, decided to overhaul IP addressing and domain name management. The DOC recommended the formation of **ICANN (Internet Corporation for Assigned Names and Numbers)**, a private, nonprofit corporation. ICANN is now ultimately responsible for IP addressing and domain name management. Technically speaking, however, IANA continues to perform the system administration.

Individuals and businesses do not typically obtain IP addresses directly from an RIR or IANA. Instead, they lease a group of addresses from their **ISP (Internet service provider)**, a business that provides organizations and individuals with access to the Internet and often, other services, such as e-mail and Web hosting. An ISP, in turn, arranges with its RIR for the right to use certain IP addresses on its network. The RIR obtains its right to dole out those addresses from ICANN. In addition, the RIR coordinates with IANA to ensure that the addresses are associated with devices connected to the ISP's network.

You can learn more about IANA and ICANN at their Web sites, *www.iana.org* and *www.icann.org*, respectively.

The OSI Model

4.1

In the early 1980s, ISO began work on a universal set of specifications that would enable computer platforms across the world to communicate openly. The result was a helpful model for understanding and developing computer-to-computer communications over a network. This model, called the **OSI (Open Systems Interconnection) model**, divides network communications into seven layers: physical, data link, network, transport, session, presentation, and application. At each layer, protocols perform services unique to that layer. While performing those services, the protocols also interact with protocols in the layers directly above and below. In addition, at the top of the OSI model, application layer protocols interact with the software you use (such an e-mail or spreadsheet program). At the bottom, physical layer services act on the networking cables and connectors to issue and receive signals.

You have already learned that protocols are the rules by which computers communicate. A protocol is simply a set of instructions written by a programmer to perform a function or

4.1

group of functions. Some protocols are included with a computer's operating system. Others are files installed with software programs. Chapter 4 covers protocols in depth; however, some protocols are briefly introduced in the following sections to better explain what happens at each layer of the OSI model.

The OSI model is a theoretical representation of what happens between two nodes communicating on a network. It does not prescribe the type of hardware or software that should support each layer. Nor does it describe how software programs interact with other software programs or how software programs interact with humans. Every process that occurs during network communications can be associated with a layer of the OSI model, so you should be familiar with the names of the layers and understand the key services and protocols that belong to each.

Networking professionals often devise a mnemonic way of remembering the seven layers of the OSI model. One strategy is to make a sentence using words that begin with the same first letter of each layer, starting with either the lowest (physical) or the highest (application) layer. For example, you might choose to remember the phrase "Programmers Dare Not Throw Salty Pretzels Away." Quirky phrases are often easiest to remember.

The path that data takes from one computer to another through the OSI model is illustrated in Figure 2-1. First, a user or device initiates a data exchange through the application layer. The application layer separates data into **PDUs (protocol data units)**, or discrete amounts of data. From there, application layer PDUs progress down through OSI model layers 6, 5, 4, 3,

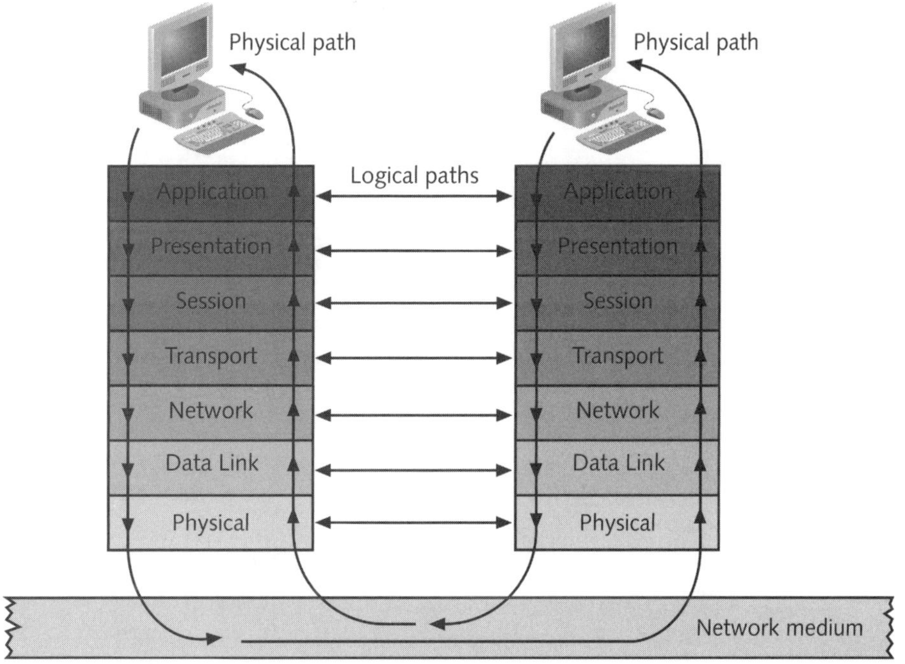

Figure 2-1 Flow of data through the OSI model

4.1

2, and 1 before being issued to the network medium—for example, the wire. The data traverses the network until it reaches the second computer's physical layer. Then at the receiving computer the data progresses up the OSI model until it reaches the second computer's application layer. This transfer of information happens in milliseconds.

Logically, however, each layer communicates with the same layer from one computer to another. In other words, the application layer protocols on one computer exchange information with the application layer protocols of the second computer. Protocols from other layers do not attempt to interpret application layer data. In the following sections, the OSI model layers are discussed from highest to lowest, beginning with the application layer, where the flow of information is initiated.

Bear in mind that the OSI model is a generalized and sometimes imperfect representation of network communication. In some cases, network functions can be associated with more than one layer of the model, and in other cases, network operations do not require services from every layer.

Application Layer

4.1

The top, or seventh, layer of the OSI model is the **application layer**. Contrary to what its name implies, the application layer does not include software applications, such as Microsoft Word or Firefox. Instead, application layer services facilitate communication between software applications and lower-layer network services so that the network can interpret an application's request and, in turn, the application can interpret data sent from the network. Through application layer protocols, software applications negotiate their formatting, procedural, security, synchronization, and other requirements with the network.

1.1

4.1

For example, when you choose to open a Web page in Firefox, an application layer protocol called **HTTP (Hypertext Transfer Protocol)** formats and sends your request from your client's browser (a software application) to the server. It also formats and sends the Web server's response back to your client's browser.

Suppose you choose to view the Exhibits page at the Library of Congress's Web site. You type "www.loc.gov/index.html" in Firefox and press Enter. At that point, Firefox's **API (application program interface)**, a set of routines that make up part of the software, transfers your request to the HTTP protocol. HTTP prompts lower-layer protocols to establish a connection between your computer and the Web server. Next, HTTP formats your request for the Web page and sends the request to the Web server. One part of the HTTP request includes a command that begins with "GET" and tells the server what page you want to retrieve. Other parts of the request indicate what version of HTTP you're using, what types of graphics and what language your browser can accept, and what browser version you're using, among other things.

After receiving your computer's HTTP request, the Web server responsible for *www.loc.gov* responds, also via HTTP. Its response includes the text and graphics that make up the Web page, plus specifications for the content contained in the page, the HTTP version used, the type of HTTP response, and the length of the page. However, if the Web page is unavailable, the host, *www.loc.gov*, sends an HTTP response containing an error message, such as "Error 404 – File Not Found."

After receiving the Web server's response, your workstation uses HTTP to interpret this response so that Firefox can present the *www.loc.gov/index.html* Web page in a format

Net+
1.1
4.1

you'll recognize, with neatly arranged text and images. Note that the information issued by one node's HTTP protocol is designed to be interpreted by the other node's HTTP protocol. However, as you will learn in later sections, HTTP requests cannot traverse the network without the assistance of lower-layer protocols.

Net+ Presentation Layer

4.1

Protocols at the **presentation layer** accept application layer data and format it so that one type of application and host can understand data from another type of application and host. In other words, the presentation layer serves as a translator. If you have spent any time working with computer graphics, you have probably heard of the GIF, JPG, and TIFF methods of compressing and encoding graphics. MPEG and QuickTime are two popular methods of compressing and encoding audio and video data. The popular audio format MP3, for example, uses MPEG compression. It can turn a music track that would require 30MB of space on a CD into a file no larger than 3MB—or even smaller, if lower quality were acceptable. Two well-known methods of encoding text are ASCII and EBCDIC. In each of these examples, it is the presentation layer protocols that perform the coding and compression. They also interpret coded and compressed formats in data received from other computers. In the previous example of requesting a Web page, the presentation layer protocols would interpret the JPG files transmitted within the Web server's HTTP response.

Presentation layer services also manage data encryption (such as the scrambling of passwords) and decryption. For example, if you look up your bank account status via the Internet, you are using a secure connection, and presentation layer protocols will encrypt your account data before it is transmitted. On your end of the network, the presentation layer will decrypt the data as it is received.

Net+ Session Layer

4.1

Protocols in the **session layer** coordinate and maintain communications between two nodes on the network. The term **session** refers to a connection for ongoing data exchange between two parties. Historically, it was used in the context of terminal and mainframe communications, in which the **terminal** is a device with little (if any) of its own processing or disk capacity that depends on a host to supply it with software and processing services. Today, the term *session* is often used in the context of a connection between a remote client and an access server or between a Web browser client and a Web server.

Among the session layer's functions are establishing and keeping alive the communications link for the duration of the session, keeping the communication secure, synchronizing the dialogue between the two nodes, determining whether communications have been cut off, and, if so, figuring out where to restart transmission, and terminating communications. Session layer services also set the terms of communication by deciding which node communicates first and how long a node can communicate. Finally, the session layer monitors the identification of session participants, ensuring that only the authorized nodes can access the session.

When you initiate a connection with your ISP, for example, the session layer services at your ISP's server and on your computer negotiate the connection. If your data cable accidentally falls out of the wall jack, session layer protocols on your end will detect the loss of a connection and initiate attempts to reconnect. If they cannot reconnect after a certain period of time, they will close the session and inform your client software that communication has ended.

Net+ Transport Layer

1.1

4.1

Protocols in the **transport layer** accept data from the session layer and manage end-to-end delivery of data. That means they can ensure that the data is transferred from point A to point B reliably, in the correct sequence, and without errors. Without transport layer services, data could not be verified or interpreted by its recipient. Transport layer protocols also handle **flow control**, which is the process of gauging the appropriate rate of transmission based on how fast the recipient can accept data. Dozens of different transport layer protocols exist, but most modern networks, such as the Internet, rely on only a few. In the example of retrieving a Web page, a transport layer protocol called TCP (Transmission Control Protocol) takes care of reliably transmitting the HTTP protocol's request from client to server and vice versa. You will learn more about this significant protocol later in this book.

Some transport layer protocols take steps to ensure that data arrives exactly as it was sent. Such protocols are **connection oriented**, because they establish a connection with another node before they begin transmitting data. TCP is one example of a connection-oriented protocol. In the case of requesting a Web page, the client's TCP protocol first sends a **SYN (synchronization)** packet request for a connection to the Web server. The Web server responds with a **SYN-ACK (synchronization-acknowledgment)** packet, or a confirmation, to indicate that it's willing to make a connection. Then the client responds with its own **ACK (acknowledgment)**. Through this three-step process, also known as a handshake, a connection is established. Only after TCP establishes this connection does it transmit the HTTP request for a Web page.

Acknowledgments are also used in subsequent communications to ensure that data was properly delivered. For every data unit a node sends, its connection-oriented protocol expects an acknowledgment from the recipient. For example, after a client's TCP protocol issued an HTTP request, it would expect to receive an acknowledgment from the Web server proving that the data arrived. If data isn't acknowledged within a given time period, the client's protocol assumes the data was lost and retransmits it.

To ensure further data integrity, connection-oriented protocols such as TCP use a checksum. A **checksum** is a unique character string that allows the receiving node to determine if an arriving data unit exactly matches the data unit sent by the source. Checksums are added to data at the source and verified at the destination. If at the destination a checksum doesn't match what the source predicted, the destination's transport layer protocols ask the source to retransmit the data. As you will learn, protocols at other layers of the OSI model also use checksums.

Not all transport layer protocols are concerned with reliability. Those that do not establish a connection before transmitting and make no effort to ensure that data is delivered free of errors are called **connectionless** protocols. A connectionless protocol's lack of sophistication makes it more efficient than a connection-oriented protocol and renders it useful when data must be transferred quickly, such as for live audio or video transmissions over the Internet. In these cases, connection-oriented protocols—with their acknowledgments, checksums, and flow control mechanisms—would add overhead to the transmission and potentially bog it down. In a video transmission, for example, this could result in pictures that are incomplete or aren't updated quickly enough to coincide with the audio.

In addition to ensuring reliable data delivery, transport layer protocols break large data units received from the session layer into multiple smaller units, called **segments**. This process is known as **segmentation**. On certain types of networks, segmentation increases data transmission efficiency. In some cases, segmentation is necessary for data units to match a

Net+

1.1

4.1

network's **MTU (maximum transmission unit)**, the largest data unit it will carry. Every network type specifies a default MTU (though its size can be modified to some extent by a network administrator). For example, by default, Ethernet networks cannot accept packets with data payloads larger than 1,500 bytes. Suppose an application wants to send a 6,000-byte unit of data. Before this data unit can be issued to an Ethernet network, it must be segmented into units no larger than 1,500 bytes. To learn a network's MTU size (and thereby determine whether it needs to segment packets), transport layer protocols perform a discovery routine upon establishing a connection with the network. Thereafter, the protocols will segment each data unit as necessary until closing the connection.

Segmentation is similar to the process of breaking down words into recognizable syllables that a child uses when learning to read. **Reassembly** is the process of reconstructing the segmented data units. To continue the reading analogy, when a child understands the separate syllables, he can combine them into a word—that is, he can reassemble the parts into a whole. To learn how reassembly works, suppose that you asked this question in history class: "Ms. Jones? How did poor farming techniques contribute to the Dust Bowl?" but that the words arrived at Ms. Jones's ear as "poor farming techniques Ms. Jones? how did to the Dust Bowl? contribute." On a network, the transport layer recognizes this kind of disorder and rearranges the data pieces so that they make sense.

Sequencing is a method of identifying segments that belong to the same group of subdivided data. Sequencing also indicates where a unit of data begins, as well as the order in which groups of data were issued and, therefore, should be interpreted. While establishing a connection, the transport layer protocols from two devices agree on certain parameters of their communication, including a sequencing scheme. For sequencing to work properly, the transport layer protocols of two nodes must synchronize their timing and agree on a starting point for the transmission.

Figure 2-2 illustrates the concept of segmentation and reassembly.

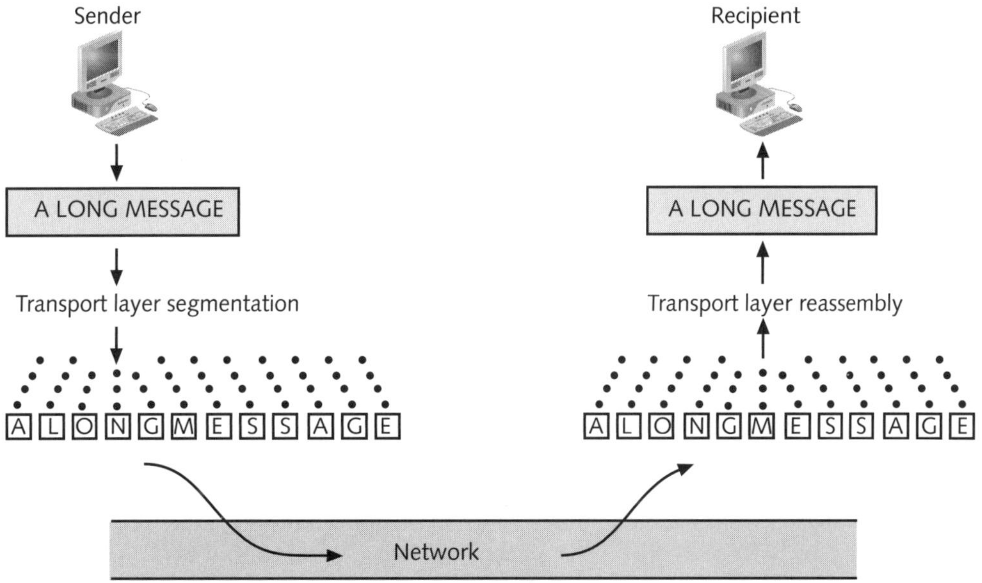

Figure 2-2 Segmentation and reassembly

 Figure 2-3 depicts the information contained in an actual TCP segment used to request the Web page *www.loc.gov/index.html*. After reading this section, you should recognize much of the segment's contents. After learning more about protocols later in this book, you will understand the meaning of everything contained in a TCP segment.

1.1

4.1

```
Transmission Control Protocol, Src Port: http (80), Dst Port: 1958 (1958), Seq: 3043958669, Ack:937013559, Len: 0
Source port: http (80)
   Destination port: 1958 (1958)
   Sequence number: 3043958669
   Acknowledgment number: 937013559
   Header length: 24 bytes
 Flags: 0x0012 (SYN, ACK)
      0... .... = Congestion Window Reduced (CWR): Not set
      .0.. .... = ECN-Echo: Not set
      ..0. .... = Urgent: Not set
      ...1 .... = Acknowledgment: Set
      .... 0... = Push: Not set
      .... .0.. = Reset: Not set
      .... ..1. = Syn: Set
      .... ...0 = Fin: Not set
   Window size: 5840
   Checksum: 0x206a (correct)
 Options: (4 bytes)
      Maximum segment size: 1460 bytes
```

Figure 2-3 A TCP segment

Network Layer

1.3

4.1

The primary function of protocols at the **Network layer,** the third layer in the OSI model, is to translate network addresses into their physical counterparts and decide how to route data from the sender to the receiver. Addressing is a system for assigning unique identification numbers to devices on a network. Each node has two types of addresses.

One type of address is called a network address. **Network addresses** follow a hierarchical addressing scheme and can be assigned through operating system software. They are hierarchical because they contain subsets of data that incrementally narrow the location of a node, just as your home address is hierarchical because it provides a country, state, ZIP code, city, street, house number, and person's name. Network layer address formats differ depending on which network layer protocol the network uses. Network addresses are also called **network layer addresses, logical addresses,** or **virtual addresses.** The second type of address assigned to each node is called a physical address, discussed in detail in the next section.

For example, a computer running on a TCP/IP network might have a network layer address of 10.34.99.12 and a physical address of 0060973E97F3. In the classroom example, this addressing scheme is like saying that "Ms. Jones" and "United States citizen with Social Security number 123-45-6789" are the same person. Even though there may be other people named "Ms. Jones" in the United States, only one person has the Social Security number 123-45-6789. Within the confines of your classroom, however, there is only one Ms. Jones, so you can be certain the correct person will respond when you say, "Ms. Jones?" There's no need to use her Social Security number.

4.1

Network layer protocols accept the transport layer segments and add logical addressing information in a network header. At this point, the data unit becomes a packet. Network layer protocols also determine the path from point A on one network to point B on another network by factoring in:

- Delivery priorities (for example, packets that make up a phone call connected through the Internet might be designated high priority, whereas a mass e-mail message is low priority)

- Network congestion

- Quality of service (for example, some packets may require faster, more reliable delivery)

- Cost of alternative routes

The process of determining the best path is known as routing. More formally, to **route** means to intelligently direct data based on addressing, patterns of usage, and availability. Because the network layer handles routing, **routers**—the devices that connect network segments and direct data—belong in the network layer.

1.1

4.1

Although there are numerous network layer protocols, one of the most common, and the one that underlies most Internet traffic, is the **IP**. In the example of requesting a Web page, IP is the protocol that instructs the network where the HTTP request is coming from and where it should go. Figure 2-4 depicts the data found in an IP packet used to contact the Web site *www.loc.gov/index.html*. Notice the Network layer addresses, or IP addresses, in the first line of the packet. The first, labeled "src Addr," reveals the unique IP address of the computer issuing the transmission. The next, labeled "Dst Add," indicates the unique IP address of the receiving computer.

On TCP/IP-based networks (such as the Internet), network layer protocols can perform an additional function called fragmentation. In **fragmentation**, a network layer protocol (such as IP) subdivides the segments it receives from the transport layer into smaller packets. If this process sounds familiar, it's because fragmentation accomplishes the same task at the network layer that segmentation performs at the transport layer. It ensures that packets issued to the network are no larger than the network's maximum transmission unit size.

```
⊟ Internet Protocol, src Addr: 140.147.249.7 (140.147.249.7), Dst Add: 10.11.11.51 (10.11.11.51)
      Version: 4
      Header length: 20 bytes
   ⊞ Differentiated Services Field: 0x00 (DSCP 0x00: Default; ECN: 0x00)
      Total Length: 44
      Identification: 0x0000 (0)
   ⊟ Flags: 0x04
         .1.. = Don't fragment: Set
         ..0. = More fragments: Not Set
      Fragment offset: 0
      Time to live: 64
      Protocol: TCP 0x06
      Header checksum: 0x9ff3 (correct)
      Source: 140.147.249.7 (140.147.249.7)
      Destination: 10.11.11.51 (10.11.11.51)
```

Figure 2-4 An IP packet

1.1

4.1

However, if a transport layer protocol performs segmentation, fragmentation may not be necessary. For greater network efficiency, segmentation is preferred. Not all transport layer protocols are designed to accomplish segmentation. If a transport layer protocol cannot perform segmentation, network layer protocols will perform fragmentation, if needed.

Data Link Layer

4.1

The primary function of protocols in the second layer of the OSI model, the **data link layer**, is to divide data they receive from the network layer into distinct frames that can then be transmitted by the physical layer. A **frame** is a structured package for moving data that includes not only the raw data, or "payload," but also the sender's and receiver's network addresses, and error checking and control information. The addresses tell the network where to deliver the frame, whereas the error checking and control information ensure that the frame arrives without problems.

To understand the function of the data link layer fully, pretend for a moment that computers communicate as humans do. Suppose you are in Ms. Jones's large classroom, which is full of noisy students, and you need to ask the teacher a question. To get your message through, you might say, "Ms. Jones? Can you explain more about the effects of railroads on commerce in the mid-nineteenth century?" In this example, you are the sender (in a busy network) and you have addressed your recipient, Ms. Jones, just as the data link layer addresses another computer on the network. In addition, you have formatted your thought as a question, just as the data link layer formats data into frames that can be interpreted by receiving computers.

What happens if the room is so noisy that Ms. Jones hears only part of your question? For example, she might receive "on commerce in the late-nineteenth century?" This kind of error can happen in network communications as well (because of wiring problems, for example). The data link layer protocols find out that information has been dropped and ask the first computer to retransmit its message—just as in a classroom setting Ms. Jones might say, "I didn't hear you. Can you repeat the question?" The data link layer accomplishes this task through a process called error checking.

Error checking is accomplished by a 4-byte **FCS (frame check sequence)** field, whose purpose is to ensure that the data at the destination exactly matches the data issued from the source. When the source node transmits the data, it performs an algorithm (or mathematical routine) called a **CRC (cyclic redundancy check)**. CRC takes the values of all of the preceding fields in the frame and generates a unique 4-byte number, the FCS. When the destination node receives the frame, its data link layer services unscramble the FCS via the same CRC algorithm and ensure that the frame's fields match their original form. If this comparison fails, the receiving node assumes that the frame has been damaged in transit and requests that the source node retransmit the data. Note that the receiving node, and not the sending node, is responsible for detecting errors.

In addition, the sender's data link layer waits for acknowledgment from the receiver's transport layer that data was received correctly. If the sender does not get this acknowledgment within a prescribed period of time, its data link layer gives instruction to retransmit the information. The data link layer never tries to figure out what went wrong. Similarly, as in a busy classroom, Ms. Jones will probably say, "Pardon me?" rather than, "It sounds as if you might have a question about railroads, and I heard only the last part of it, which dealt with commerce, so I assume you are asking about commerce and railroads; is that correct?" Obviously, the former method is more efficient.

Net+
4.1
Another communications mishap that might occur in a noisy classroom or on a busy network is a glut of communication requests. For example, at the end of class, 20 people might ask Ms. Jones 20 different questions at once. Of course, she can't pay attention to all of them simultaneously. She will probably say, "One person at a time, please," and then point to one student who asked a question. This situation is analogous to what the data link layer does for the physical layer. One node on a network (a Web server, for example) may receive multiple requests that include many frames of data each. The data link layer controls the flow of this information, allowing the NIC to process data without error.

In fact, the IEEE has divided the data link layer into two sublayers, as shown in Figure 2-5. The reason for this change was to allow higher layer protocols (for example, those operating in the network layer) to interact with data link layer protocols without regard for physical layer specifications.

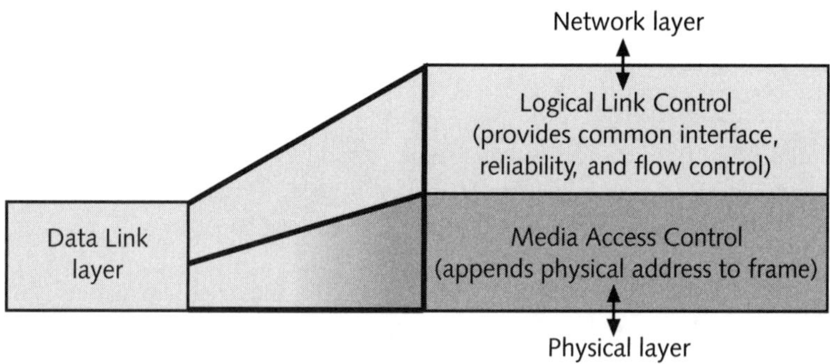

Figure 2-5 The data link layer and its sublayers

Net+
1.3
4.1
The upper sublayer of the data link layer, called the **LLC (logical link control)** sublayer, provides an interface to the network layer protocols, manages flow control, and issues requests for transmission for data that has suffered errors. The **MAC (media access control)** sublayer, the lower sublayer of the data link layer, manages access to the physical medium. It appends the **physical address** of the destination computer onto the data frame. The physical address is a fixed number associated with a device's NIC; it is initially assigned at the factory and stored in the NIC's on-board memory. Because this address is appended by the MAC sublayer of the data link layer, it is also known as a **MAC address** or a **data link layer address**. Sometimes, it's also called a **hardware address**.

You can find a NIC's MAC address through your computer's protocol configuration utility or by simply looking at the NIC. The MAC address will be stamped directly onto the NIC's circuit board or on a sticker attached to some part of the NIC, as shown in Figure 2-6.

MAC addresses contain two parts: a block ID and a device ID. The **block ID** is a six-character sequence unique to each vendor. IEEE manages which block IDs each manufacturer can use. For example, a series of Ethernet NICs manufactured by the 3Com Corporation begins with the six-character sequence "00608C," while a series of Ethernet NICs manufactured by Intel begins with "00AA00." Some manufacturers have several different block IDs. The remaining six characters in the MAC address are added at the factory, based on the NIC's model and manufacture date, and collectively form the **device ID**. An example of a device ID assigned by

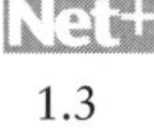

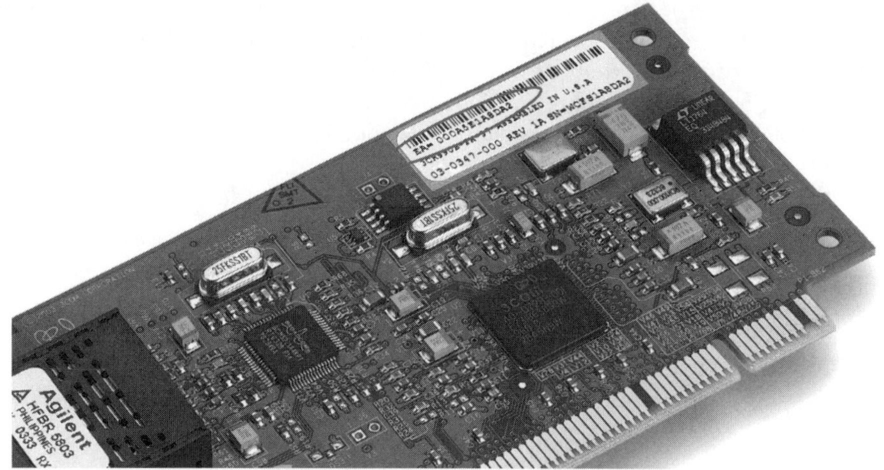

Figure 2-6 A NIC's MAC address

a manufacturer might be 005499. The combination of the block ID and device ID results in a unique, 12-character MAC address of 00608C005499. MAC addresses are also frequently depicted in their hexadecimal format—for example, 00:60:8C:00:54:99.

Hexadecimal, or base 16, is a numeral system that uses 0 through 9 to represent its first 10 numbers, and then uses the letters A through F to represent the next six numbers. (The system we use for everyday counting is base 10, or decimal, notation.) In hexadecimal notation, the decimal number 12 is represented by the letter C, for example. Starting with the decimal number 16, hexadecimal notation uses a 1 to represent the previous 15 digits and begins counting again at 0. In other words, a decimal number 16 is represented as 10 in hexadecimal, and a decimal number 32 is represented as 20 in hexadecimal. In computer science, hexadecimal notation (sometimes called, simply, "hex") is used as a shorter, readable version of the binary numbers that computers interpret. You won't often be asked to convert hexadecimal notation to decimal or binary notation, but you should understand the process. Chapter 4 describes binary notation in detail.

If you know a computer's MAC address, you can determine which company manufactured its NIC by looking up its block ID. IEEE maintains a database of block IDs and their manufacturers, which is accessible via the Web. At the time of this writing, the database search page could be found at *http://standards.ieee.org/regauth/oui/index.shtml*.

Because of their hardware addressing function, NICs can be said to perform in the data link layer of the OSI model. However, they also perform services in the physical layer, which is described next.

Net+ Physical Layer

4.1   The **physical layer** is the lowest, or first, layer of the OSI model. Protocols at the physical layer accept frames from the data link layer and generate signals as changes in voltage at the NIC. (Signals are made of electrical impulses that, when issued in a certain pattern, represent information.) When the network uses copper as its transmission medium, these

signals are also issued over the wire as voltage. In the case of fiber-optic cable, signals are issued as light pulses. When a network uses wireless transmission, the signals are sent from antennas as electromagnetic waves.

When receiving data, physical layer protocols detect and accept signals, which they pass on to the data link layer. Physical layer protocols also set the data transmission rate and monitor data error rates. However, even if they recognize an error, they cannot perform error correction. When you install a NIC in your desktop PC and connect it to a cable, you are establishing the foundation that allows the computer to be networked. In other words, you are providing a physical layer.

Simple connectivity devices such as hubs and repeaters operate at the physical layer. NICs operate at both the physical layer and the data link layer. As you would expect, physical network problems, such as a severed wire or a broken connectivity device, affect the physical layer. Similarly, if you insert a NIC but fail to seat it deeply enough in the computer's main circuit board, your computer will experience network problems at the physical layer.

Most of the functions that network administrators are most concerned with happen in the first four layers of the OSI model: physical, data link, network, and transport. Therefore, the bulk of material in this book and on the Network+ exam relates to these four layers. Software programmers, on the other hand, are more apt to be concerned with what happens at the application, presentation, and session layers.

Applying the OSI Model

Now that you have been introduced to the seven layers of the OSI model, you can take a closer look at exactly how the layers interact. For reference, Table 2-1 summarizes the functions of the seven OSI model layers.

Table 2-1 Functions of the OSI Layers

OSI Model Layer	Function
Application (layer 7)	Provides interface between software applications and network for interpreting applications' requests and requirements
Presentation (layer 6)	Allows hosts and applications to use a common language; performs data formatting, encryption, and compression
Session (layer 5)	Establishes, maintains, and terminates user connections
Transport (layer 4)	Ensures accurate delivery of data through flow control, segmentation and reassembly, error correction, and acknowledgment
Network (layer 3)	Establishes network connections; translates network addresses into their physical counterparts and determines routing
Data link (layer 2)	Packages data in frames appropriate to network transmission method
Physical (layer 1)	Manages signaling to and from physical network connections

Net+ Communication between Two Systems

4.1

Based on what you have learned about the OSI model, it should be clear to you that data issued from a software application is not in the same form as the data that your NIC sends to the network. At each layer of the OSI model, some information—for example, a format specification or a network address—is added to the original data. After it has followed the path from the application layer to the physical layer, data is significantly transformed, as shown in Figure 2-7. The following paragraphs describe this process in detail.

To understand how data changes, it is useful to trace the steps in a typical client/server exchange, such as retrieving a mail message from a mail server. Suppose that you connect to your company's network from your home computer via a broadband Internet connection, log on, start your e-mail application, and then click a button in the e-mail application to retrieve your mail from the server. At that point, application layer services on your computer accept data from your mail application and formulate a request meant for the mail server software. They add an application header to the data that the program wants to send. The application header contains information about the e-mail application's requirements, so that the mail server can fulfill its request properly. The application layer transfers the request to the presentation layer, in the form of a protocol data unit (PDU).

The presentation layer first determines whether and how it should format or encrypt the data request received from the application layer. For example, if your mail client requires

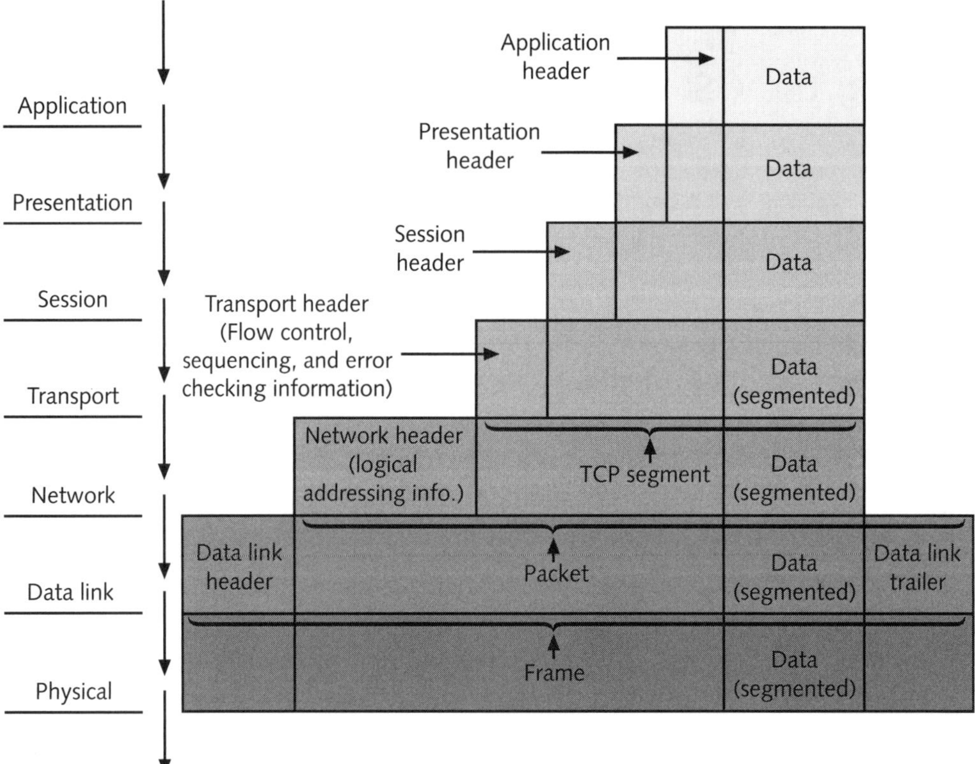

Figure 2-7 Data transformation through the OSI model

encryption, the presentation layer protocols will add that information to the PDU in a presentation header. If your e-mail message contains graphics or formatted text, that information will also be added.

Then the presentation layer sends its PDU to the session layer, which adds a session header that contains information about how your home computer communicates with the network. For example, the session header might indicate that your Internet connection can only transmit and receive data at 512Kbps. The session layer then passes the PDU to the transport layer.

At the transport layer, the PDU—your request for mail and the headers added by previous layers—is broken down into smaller pieces of data, or segments. The segments' maximum size is dictated by the type of network transmission method in use (for example, Ethernet). Suppose your mail request PDU is too large to be a single segment. In that case, transport layer protocols subdivide it into two or more smaller segments and assign sequence identifiers to all of the smaller segments. This information becomes part of the transport header. Protocols also add checksum, flow control, and acknowledgment data to the transport header. The transport layer then passes these segments, one at a time, to the network layer.

Next, network layer protocols add logical addressing information to the segments, so that your request will be properly routed to the mail server and the mail server will respond to your computer. This information is contained in the network header. With the addition of network address information, the pieces of data are called packets. The network layer then passes the packets to the data link layer.

At the data link layer, protocols add a header to the front of each packet and a trailer to the end of each packet to make frames. (The trailer indicates where a frame ends.) In other words, the data link layer protocols **encapsulate** the network layer packets. Encapsulation is frequently compared to placing a smaller envelope within a larger envelope. This analogy conveys the idea that the data link layer does not attempt to interpret any information added in the network layer, but simply surrounds it.

Using frames reduces the possibility of lost data or errors on the network, because built into each frame is a way of checking for errors. After verifying that the data has not been damaged, the data link layer then passes the frames to the physical layer.

Finally, your request for mail, in the form of many frames, hits the NIC at the physical layer. The physical layer does not interpret the frames or add information to the frames; it simply transmits them over the broadband connection to your LAN, across your office network, and to the mail server after the binary digits (bits), or ones and zeroes, have been converted to electrical pulses. As the frames arrive at the mail server, the server's physical layer accepts the frames and transfers them to the data link layer. The mail server begins to unravel your request, reversing the process just described, until it responds to your request with its own transmission, beginning from its application layer.

The terms *frame*, *packet*, *datagram*, and *PDU* are often used interchangeably to refer to a small piece of data formatted for network transmission. Technically, however, a *packet* is a piece of information that contains network addressing information, and a *frame* is a piece of data enclosed by a data link layer header and trailer. *Datagram* is synonymous with packet. *PDU* generically refers to a unit of data at any layer of the OSI model. However, networking professionals often use the term *packet* to refer to *frames*, *PDUs*, and transport layer segments alike.

Frame Specifications

You have learned that frames are composed of several smaller components, or fields. The characteristics of these components depend on the type of network on which the frames run and on the standards that they must follow. By far, the most popular type of networking technology in use today is Ethernet, which uses Ethernet frames. You'll learn much more about Ethernet in Chapter 5, but the following serves as an introduction, as well as a comparison between this favored network type and its historical rival, token ring.

Ethernet is a networking technology originally developed at Xerox in the early 1970s and improved by Digital Equipment Corporation, Intel, and Xerox. There are four types of Ethernet frames. The most popular form of Ethernet is characterized by the unique way in which devices share a common transmission channel, described in the IEEE **802.3** standard.

A much less common networking technology, **token ring**, was developed by IBM in the 1980s. It relies upon direct links between nodes and a ring topology. Nodes pass around **tokens**, special control frames that indicate to the network when a particular node is about to transmit data. Although this networking technology is nearly obsolete, there is a remote chance that you might work on a token ring network. The IEEE has defined token ring technology in its **802.5** standard.

Ethernet frames are different from token ring frames, and the two will not interact with each other on a network. In fact, most LANs do not support more than one frame type, because devices cannot support more than one frame type per physical interface, or NIC. (NICs can, however, support multiple protocols.) Although you can conceivably transmit both token ring and Ethernet frames on a network, Ethernet interfaces cannot interpret token ring frames, and vice versa. Normally, LANs use *either* Ethernet or token ring, and almost all contemporary LANs use Ethernet.

It is important to know what frame type (or types) your network environment requires. You will use this information when installing network operating systems, configuring servers and client workstations, installing NICs, troubleshooting network problems, and purchasing network equipment.

IEEE Networking Specifications

In addition to frame types and addressing, IEEE networking specifications apply to connectivity, networking media, error-checking algorithms, encryption, emerging technologies, and more. All of these specifications fall under the IEEE's Project 802, an effort to standardize physical and logical elements of a network. IEEE developed these standards before the OSI model was standardized by ISO, but IEEE's 802 standards can be applied to the layers of the OSI model. Table 2-2 describes just some of the IEEE 802 specifications. The Network+ certification exam includes questions about IEEE 802 specifications, with an emphasis on the technologies described by 802.3 and 802.11.

Table 2-2 IEEE 802 Standards

Standard	Name	Topic
802.1	Internetworking	Routing, bridging, and network-to-network communications
802.2	Logical link control	Error and flow control over data frames
802.3	Ethernet LAN	All forms of Ethernet media and interfaces
802.5	Token ring LAN	All forms of token ring media and interfaces
802.11	Wireless networks	Standards for wireless networking for many different broadcast frequencies and usage techniques
802.15	Wireless personal area networks	The coexistence of wireless personal area networks with other wireless devices in unlicensed frequency bands
802.16	Broadband wireless metropolitan area networks	The atmospheric interface and related functions associated with broadband wireless connectivity; also known as WiMAX
802.17	Resilient packet rings	Access method, physical layer specifications, and management of shared packet-based transmission on resilient rings (such as SONET)
802.20	Mobile broadband wireless network	Packet handling and other specifications for multivendor, mobile high-speed wireless transmission, nicknamed "mobile WiMAX"
802.22	Wireless regional area networks (WRAN)	Wireless, broadcast-style network to operate in the UHF/VHF frequency bands formerly used for TV channels

Chapter Summary

- Standards are documented agreements containing precise criteria that are used as guidelines to ensure that materials, products, processes, and services suit their purpose. Standards also help to ensure interoperability between software and hardware from different manufacturers.

- Some of the significant standards organizations are ANSI, EIA/TIA, IEEE, ISO, ITU, ISOC, IANA, and ICANN.

- ISO's OSI (Open Systems Interconnection) model represents communication between two computers on a network. It divides networking architecture into seven layers: physical, data link, network, transport, session, presentation, and application. Each layer has its own set of functions and interacts with the layers directly above and below it.

- Protocols in the application layer, the seventh layer of the OSI model, enable software programs to negotiate their formatting, procedural, security, synchronization, and other requirements with the network.

- Protocols in the presentation layer, the sixth OSI model layer, serve as translators between the application and the network, using a common language for different hosts and applications to exchange data.

- Protocols in the session layer, the fifth OSI model layer, coordinate and maintain links between two devices for the duration of their communication. They also synchronize dialogue, determine whether communications have been cut off, and, if so, figure out where to restart transmission.

- The primary function of protocols in the transport layer, the fourth OSI model layer, is to oversee end-to-end data delivery. In the case of connection-oriented protocols, this means data is delivered reliably. These protocols verify that data is received in the same sequence in which it was sent. They are also responsible for flow control, segmentation, and reassembly of packets. Connectionless transport layer protocols do not offer such guarantees.

- Protocols in the network layer, the third OSI model layer, manage logical addressing and determine routes based on addressing, patterns of usage, and availability. Routers belong to the network layer because they use this information to intelligently direct data from sender to receiver.

- Network layer addresses, also called logical or virtual addresses, are assigned to devices through operating system software. They are composed of hierarchical information, so they can be easily interpreted by routers and used to direct data to its destination.

- The primary function of protocols at the data link layer, the second layer of the OSI model, is to organize data they receive from the network layer into frames that contain error-checking routines and can then be transmitted by the physical layer.

- The data link layer is subdivided into the logical link control and MAC sublayers. The LLC sublayer ensures a common interface for the network layer protocols. The MAC sublayer is responsible for adding physical address data to frames. MAC addresses are hard-coded into a device's NIC.

- Protocols at the physical layer generate and detect signals to transmit and receive data over a network medium. These protocols also set the data transmission rate and monitor data error rates, but they do not provide error correction.

- A data request from a software program is received by the application layer protocols and is transferred down through the layers of the OSI model until it reaches the physical layer (the network cable, for example). At that point, data is sent to its destination over the network medium, and the physical layer protocols at the destination send it back up through the layers of the OSI model until it reaches the application layer.

- Data frames are small blocks of data with control, addressing, and handling information attached to them. Frames are composed of several fields. The characteristics of these fields depend on the type of network on which the frames run and the standards that they must follow. Ethernet and token ring networks use different frame types, and one type of network cannot interpret the others' frames.

- In addition to frame types and addressing schemes, the IEEE networking specifications apply to connectivity, networking media, error-checking algorithms, encryption, emerging technologies, and more. All of these specifications fall under the IEEE's Project 802, an effort to standardize the elements of networking.

- Significant IEEE 802 standards are 802.3, which describes Ethernet; 802.11, which describes wireless networking; and 802.16, which describes broadband wireless metropolitan area networks.

Key Terms

802.2 The IEEE standard for error and flow control in data frames.

802.3 The IEEE standard for Ethernet networking devices and data handling (using the CSMA/CD access method).

802.5 The IEEE standard for token ring networking devices and data handling.

802.11 The IEEE standard for wireless networking.

802.16 The IEEE standard for broadband wireless metropolitan area networking (also known as WiMAX).

ACK (acknowledgment) A response generated at the transport layer of the OSI model that confirms to a sender that its frame was received. The ACK packet is the third of three in the three-step process of establishing a connection.

acknowledgment *See* ACK.

American National Standards Institute *See* ANSI.

ANSI (American National Standards Institute) An organization composed of more than 1,000 representatives from industry and government who together determine standards for the electronics industry in addition to other fields, such as chemical and nuclear engineering, health and safety, and construction.

API (application program interface) A set of routines that make up part of a software application.

application layer The seventh layer of the OSI model. Application layer protocols enable software programs to negotiate formatting, procedural, security, synchronization, and other requirements with the network.

application program interface *See* API.

block ID The first set of six characters that make up the MAC address and that are unique to a particular manufacturer.

checksum A method of error checking that determines if the contents of an arriving data unit match the contents of the data unit sent by the source.

connection oriented A type of transport layer protocol that requires the establishment of a connection between communicating nodes before it will transmit data.

connectionless A type of transport layer protocol that services a request without requiring a verified session and without guaranteeing delivery of data.

CRC (cyclic redundancy check) An algorithm (or mathematical routine) used to verify the accuracy of data contained in a data frame.

cyclic redundancy check *See* CRC.

data link layer The second layer in the OSI model. The data link layer bridges the networking media with the network layer. Its primary function is to divide the data it receives from the network layer into frames that can then be transmitted by the physical layer.

data link layer address *See* MAC address.

device ID The second set of six characters that make up a network device's MAC address. The device ID, which is added at the factory, is based on the device's model and manufacture date.

EIA (Electronic Industries Alliance) A trade organization composed of representatives from electronics manufacturing firms across the United States that sets standards for electronic equipment and lobbies for legislation favorable to the growth of the computer and electronics industries.

Electronic Industries Alliance *See* EIA.

encapsulate   The process of wrapping one layer's PDU with protocol information so that it can be interpreted by a lower layer. For example, data link layer protocols encapsulate network layer packets in frames.

Ethernet   A networking technology originally developed at Xerox in the 1970s and improved by Digital Equipment Corporation, Intel, and Xerox. Ethernet, which is the most common form of network transmission technology, follows the IEEE 802.3 standard.

FCS (frame check sequence)   The field in a frame responsible for ensuring that data carried by the frame arrives intact. It uses an algorithm, such as CRC, to accomplish this verification.

flow control   A method of gauging the appropriate rate of data transmission based on how fast the recipient can accept data.

fragmentation   A network layer service that subdivides segments it receives from the transport layer into smaller packets.

frame   A package for data that includes not only the raw data, or "payload," but also the sender's and recipient's addressing and control information. Frames are generated at the data link layer of the OSI model and are issued to the network at the physical layer.

frame check sequence   *See* FCS.

hardware address   *See* MAC address.

HTTP (Hypertext Transfer Protocol)   An application layer protocol that formulates and interprets requests between Web clients and servers.

Hypertext Transfer Protocol   *See* HTTP.

IAB (Internet Architecture Board)   A technical advisory group of researchers and technical professionals responsible for Internet growth and management strategy, resolution of technical disputes, and standards oversight.

IANA (Internet Assigned Numbers Authority)   A nonprofit, United States government-funded group that was established at the University of Southern California and charged with managing IP address allocation and the domain name system. The oversight for many of IANA's functions was given to ICANN in 1998; however, IANA continues to perform Internet addressing and domain name system administration.

ICANN (Internet Corporation for Assigned Names and Numbers)   The nonprofit corporation currently designated by the United States government to maintain and assign IP addresses.

IEEE (Institute of Electrical and Electronics Engineers)   An international society composed of engineering professionals. Its goals are to promote development and education in the electrical engineering and computer science fields.

IETF (Internet Engineering Task Force)   An organization that sets standards for how systems communicate over the Internet (for example, how protocols operate and interact).

Institute of Electrical and Electronics Engineers   *See* IEEE.

International Organization for Standardization   *See* ISO.

International Telecommunication Union   *See* ITU.

Internet Architecture Board   *See* IAB.

Internet Assigned Numbers Authority   *See* IANA.

Internet Corporation for Assigned Names and Numbers   *See* ICANN.

Internet Engineering Task Force   *See* IETF.

Internet Protocol   *See* IP.

Internet Protocol address   *See* IP address.

Internet service provider   *See* ISP.

Internet Society   *See* ISOC.

IP (Internet Protocol)   A core protocol in the TCP/IP suite that operates in the network layer of the OSI model and provides information about how and where data should be delivered. IP is the subprotocol that enables TCP/IP to internetwork.

IP address (Internet Protocol address)   The network layer address assigned to nodes to uniquely identify them on a TCP/IP network. IP addresses consist of 32 bits divided into four octets, or bytes.

ISO (International Organization for Standardization)   A collection of standards organizations representing 157 countries with headquarters located in Geneva, Switzerland. Its goal is to establish international technological standards to facilitate the global exchange of information and barrier-free trade.

ISOC (Internet Society)   A professional organization with members from 90 chapters around the world that helps to establish technical standards for the Internet.

ISP (Internet service provider)   A business that provides organizations and individuals with Internet access and often, other services, such as e-mail and Web hosting.

ITU (International Telecommunication Union)   A United Nations agency that regulates international telecommunications and provides developing countries with technical expertise and equipment to advance their technological bases.

LLC (logical link control) sublayer   The upper sublayer in the data link layer. The LLC provides a common interface and supplies reliability and flow control services.

logical address   *See* network address.

logical link control sublayer   *See* LLC (logical link control) sublayer.

MAC address   A 12-character string that uniquely identifies a network node. The manufacturer hard-codes the MAC address into the NIC. This address is composed of the block ID and device ID.

MAC (media access control) sublayer   The lower sublayer of the data link layer. The MAC appends the physical address of the destination computer onto the frame.

maximum transmission unit   *See* MTU.

media access control sublayer   *See* MAC (media access control) sublayer.

MTU (maximum transmission unit)   The largest data unit that a network (for example, Ethernet or token ring) will accept for transmission.

network address   A unique identifying number for a network node that follows a hierarchical addressing scheme and can be assigned through operating system software. Network addresses are added to data packets and interpreted by protocols at the network layer of the OSI model.

network layer   The third layer in the OSI model. Protocols in the network layer translate network addresses into their physical counterparts and decide how to route data from the sender to the receiver.

network layer address   *See* network address.

Open Systems Interconnection model   *See* OSI (Open Systems Interconnection) model.

OSI (Open Systems Interconnection) model   A model for understanding and developing computer-to-computer communication developed in the 1980s by ISO. It divides networking functions among seven layers: physical, data link, network, transport, session, presentation, and application.

PDU (protocol data unit)   A unit of data at any layer of the OSI model.

physical address   *See* MAC address.

physical layer   The lowest, or first, layer of the OSI model. Protocols in the physical layer generate and detect signals so as to transmit and receive data over a network medium. These protocols also set the data transmission rate and monitor data error rates, but they do not provide error correction.

presentation layer   The sixth layer of the OSI model. Protocols in the presentation layer translate between the application and the network. Here, data is formatted in a schema that the network can understand, with the format varying according to the type of network used. The presentation layer also manages data encryption and decryption, such as the scrambling of system passwords.

protocol data unit   *See* PDU.

reassembly   The process of reconstructing data units that have been segmented.

Regional Internet Registry   *See* RIR.

RIR (Regional Internet Registry)   A not-for-profit agency that manages the distribution of IP addresses to private and public entities. ARIN is the RIR for North, Central, and South America and sub-Saharan Africa. APNIC is the RIR for Asia and the Pacific region. RIPE is the RIR for Europe and North Africa.

route   To intelligently direct data between networks based on addressing, patterns of usage, and availability of network segments.

router   A device that connects network segments and directs data based on information contained in the data packet.

segment   A unit of data that results from subdividing a larger protocol data unit.

segmentation   The process of decreasing the size of data units when moving data from a network that can handle larger data units to a network that can handle only smaller data units.

sequencing   The process of assigning a placeholder to each piece of a data block to allow the receiving node's transport layer to reassemble the data in the correct order.

session   A connection for data exchange between two parties. The term *session* may be used in the context of Web, remote access, or terminal and mainframe communications, for example.

session layer   The fifth layer in the OSI model. The session layer establishes and maintains communication between two nodes on the network. It can be considered the "traffic cop" for network communications.

standard   A documented agreement containing technical specifications or other precise criteria that are used as guidelines to ensure that materials, products, processes, and services suit their intended purpose.

SYN (synchronization)   The packet that one node sends to request a connection with another node on the network. The SYN packet is the first of three in the three-step process of establishing a connection.

SYN-ACK (synchronization-acknowledgment)   The packet a node sends to acknowledge to another node that it has received a SYN request for connection. The SYN-ACK packet is the second of three in the three-step process of establishing a connection.

synchronization   *See* SYN.

synchronization-acknowledgment   *See* SYN-ACK.

Telecommunications Industry Association   *See* TIA.

terminal   A device with little (if any) of its own processing or disk capacity that depends on a host to supply it with applications and data-processing services.

TIA (Telecommunications Industry Association)   A subgroup of the EIA that focuses on standards for information technology, wireless, satellite, fiber optics, and telephone equipment. Probably the best-known standards to come from the TIA/EIA alliance are its guidelines for how network cable should be installed in commercial buildings, known as the "TIA/EIA 568-B Series."

token   A special control frame that indicates to the rest of the network that a particular node has the right to transmit data.

token ring   A networking technology developed by IBM in the 1980s. It relies upon direct links between nodes and a ring topology, using tokens to allow nodes to transmit data.

transport layer   The fourth layer of the OSI model. In the transport layer, protocols ensure that data is transferred from point A to point B reliably and without errors. Transport layer services include flow control, acknowledgment, error correction, segmentation, reassembly, and sequencing.

virtual address   *See* network address.

Review Questions

1. Which of the following is the acceptable performance level of a product or service as defined by a standard?

    a. Maximum

    b. Minimum

    c. Standard

    d. Ideal

2. What international society is composed of engineering professionals with a goal of promoting the development and education in the electrical engineering and computer science fields?

    a. ANSI

    b. IEA

    c. IEEE

    d. ISO

3. Which OSI model layer accepts data from the session layer and manages end-to-end delivery of data?

    a. Network

    b. Physical

    c. Data link

    d. Transport

4. Which type of address contains subsets of data that incrementally narrow the location of a node?

    a. Network

    b. Physical

    c. Logical

    d. Segmented

5. Which OSI model layer divides data received from the network layer into distinct frames that can then be transmitted by the physical layer?

    a. Transport

    b. Application

    c. Session

    d. Data link

6. True or false? Standards help to assure network designers that hardware and software from different manufacturers will work together.

7. True or false? The OSI model is a physical representation of what happens between two nodes communicating on a network.

8. True or false? Software applications such Microsoft Word and Excel may be found in the OSI model's application layer.

9. True or false? The OSI model's presentation layer serves as a translator.

10. True or false? Most LANs will support both Ethernet and token ring frames.

11. The ANSI (American National Standards Institute) organization does not dictate that manufacturers comply with its standards, but it requests _____ compliance.

12. A(n) _____ is a not-for-profit agency that manages the distribution of IP addresses to private and public entities.

13. A helpful model for understanding and developing computer-to-computer communications over a network is known as the _____ model.

14. A user or device initiates a data exchange through the OSI _____ layer.

15. _____ occurs when OSI data link layer protocols add a header to the front of each packet and a trailer to the end of each packet to make frames.

Transmission Basics and Networking Media

After reading this chapter and completing the exercises, you will be able to:

- Explain basic data transmission concepts, including full duplexing, attenuation, latency, and noise

- Describe the physical characteristics of coaxial cable, STP, UTP, and fiber-optic media

- Compare the benefits and limitations of different networking media

- Explain the principles behind and uses for serial connector cables

- Identify wiring standards and the best practices for cabling buildings and work areas

On the Job

I was working for a company whose building was being gutted for renovations. The IT people told the architect about a problem with one of the planned data connections. One cabling run was going to be 105 meters—a problem, since the Institute of Electrical and Electronics Engineers (IEEE) recommends that cabling runs be limited to 100 meters to prevent problems with a network. The architect was concerned about the IT department's suggestion that he install an additional wiring closet to shorten the cabling run, given that it would cost another $2,000.

Our new network was going to be a switched Ethernet network, meaning that our connectivity devices would be switches rather than hubs. After some investigation and learning more details of the proposed network, a networking faculty member from a local college and I met with the architect and the director of IT. We explained that the 100-meter cabling limitation is only a problem for older networks that rely on hubs. With a newer switched environment, we might see some slight loss of speed for the end user with a 105-meter cabling run, but it would be fairly small.

We offered two options: We could put a repeater between the switch and the end user to shorten the cabling run, or we could allow the cabling run to go over 100 meters. Using free software available over the Internet, we ran simulations for each scenario to see what sort of loss we had. We determined that, at worst, the user would see about a 5-percent drop in the speed of the network in each case.

The institution decided to go with the longer cabling run. We've done some tests on the user's workstation subsequent to building the network and found that the reduction in throughput is even less than 5 percent. So with some free software and a little knowledge of modern network technology, we were able to save the institution the cost of a $2,000 wiring closet.

Michael Qaissaunee
Brookdale Community College

Just as highways and streets provide the foundation for automobile travel, networking media provide the physical foundation of data transmission. Media are the physical or atmospheric paths that signals follow. The first networks transmitted data over thick coaxial cables. Today, when not transmitted through the air, as in wireless networks, data is commonly transmitted over a type of cable that resembles telephone cords. It's sheathed in flexible plastic and contains twisted copper wire inside. For long-distance network connections, fiber-optic cable is preferred. And more and more, organizations are sending signals through the atmosphere to form wireless networks, which are covered in Chapter 8. Because networks are always evolving and demanding greater speed, versatility, and reliability, networking media change rapidly.

Network problems often occur at or below the physical layer. Therefore, understanding the characteristics of various networking media is critical to designing and troubleshooting networks. You also need to know how data is transmitted over the media. This chapter discusses physical networking media and the details of data transmission. You'll learn what it takes to make data transmission dependable and how to correct some common transmission problems.

Transmission Basics

In data networking, the term **transmit** means to issue signals along a network medium such as a cable. **Transmission** refers to either the process of transmitting or the progress of signals after they have been transmitted. In other words, you could say, "My NIC transmitted a message, but because the network is slow, the transmission took 10 seconds to reach the server." In fact, NICs both transmit and receive signals, which means they are a type of **transceiver**.

Long ago, people transmitted information across distances via smoke or fire signals. Needless to say, many different methods of data transmission have evolved since that time. The transmission techniques in use on today's networks are complex and varied. In the following sections, you will learn about some fundamental characteristics that define today's data transmission. In later chapters, you will learn about more subtle and specific differences between types of data transmission.

Analog and Digital Signaling

One important characteristic of data transmission is the type of signaling involved. On a data network, information can be transmitted via one of two signaling methods: analog or digital.

Computers generate and interpret digital signals as electrical current, the pressure of which is measured in **volts**. The strength of an electrical signal is directly proportional to its voltage. Thus, when network engineers talk about the strength of a signal, they often refer to the signal's **voltage**. After being generated, signals travel over copper cabling as electrical current. Over fiber-optic cable, they travel as light pulses. And through the atmosphere, they travel as electromagnetic waves.

Analog data signals are also generated as voltage. However, in **analog** signals, voltage varies continuously and appears as a wavy line when graphed over time, as shown in Figure 3-1.

An analog signal, like other waveforms, is characterized by four fundamental properties: amplitude, frequency, wavelength, and phase. A wave's **amplitude** is a measure of its strength at any given point in time. On a wave graph, the amplitude is the height of the wave at any point in time. In Figure 3-1, for example, the wave has an amplitude of 5 volts at .25 seconds, an amplitude of 0 volts at .5 seconds, and an amplitude of –5 volts at .75 seconds.

Whereas amplitude indicates an analog wave's strength, **frequency** is the number of times that a wave's amplitude cycles from its starting point, through its highest amplitude and its lowest amplitude, and back to its starting point over a fixed period of time. Frequency is expressed in cycles per second, or **hertz (Hz)**, named after German physicist Heinrich Hertz, who experimented with electromagnetic waves in the late nineteenth century. For example, in Figure 3-1 the wave cycles to its highest then lowest amplitude and returns to its starting point once in 1 second. Thus, the frequency of that wave would be 1 cycle per second, or 1Hz— which, as it turns out, is an extremely low frequency.

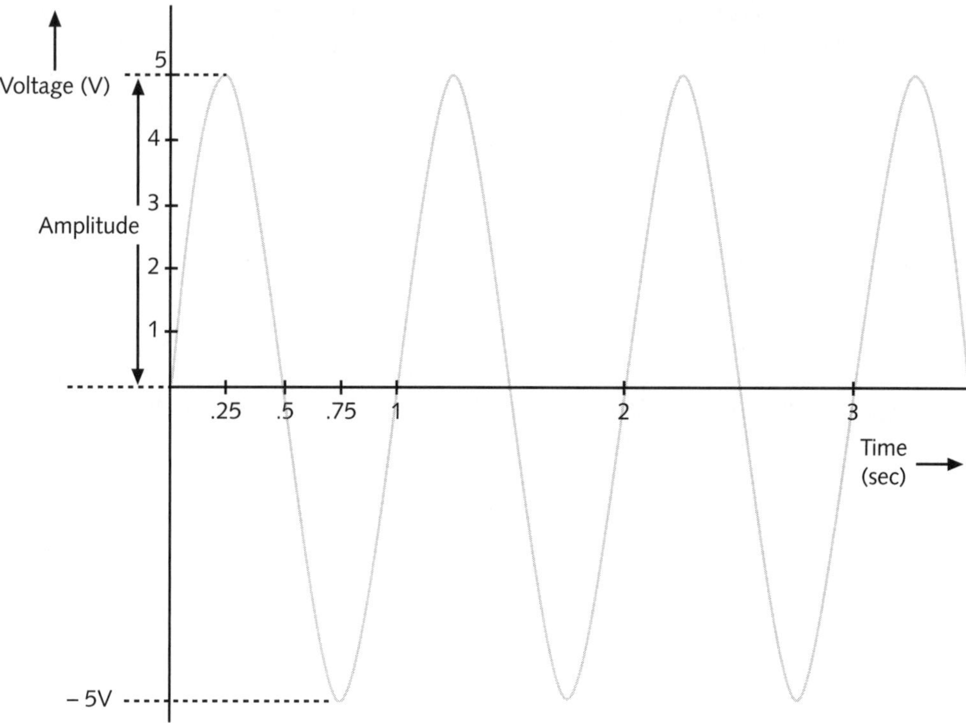

Figure 3-1 An example of an analog signal

Frequencies used to convey speech over telephone wires fall in the 300 to 3,300Hz range. Humans can hear frequencies between 20 and 20,000Hz. An FM radio station may use a frequency between 850,000Hz (or 850kHz) and 108,000,000Hz (or 108MHz) to transmit its signal through the air. You will learn more about radio frequencies used in networking later in this chapter.

The distance between corresponding points on a wave's cycle—for example, between one peak and the next—is called its **wavelength**. Wavelengths can be expressed in meters or feet. A wave's wavelength is inversely proportional to its frequency. In other words, the higher the frequency, the shorter the wavelength. For example, a radio wave with a frequency of 1,000,000 cycles per second (1MHz) has a wavelength of 300 meters, while a wave with a frequency of 2,000,000Hz (2MHz) has a wavelength of 150 meters.

The term **phase** refers to the progress of a wave over time in relationship to a fixed point. Suppose two separate waves have identical amplitudes and frequencies. If one wave starts at its lowest amplitude at the same time the second wave starts at its highest amplitude, these waves will have different phases. More precisely, they will be 180 degrees out of phase (using the standard assignment of 360 degrees to one complete wave). Had the second wave also started at its lowest amplitude, the two waves would be in phase. Figure 3-2 illustrates waves with identical amplitudes and frequencies whose phases are 90 degrees apart.

One benefit to analog signals is that, because they are more variable than digital signals, they can convey greater subtleties with less energy. For example, think of the difference between your voice and a digital voice, such as the automated service that some libraries use to notify

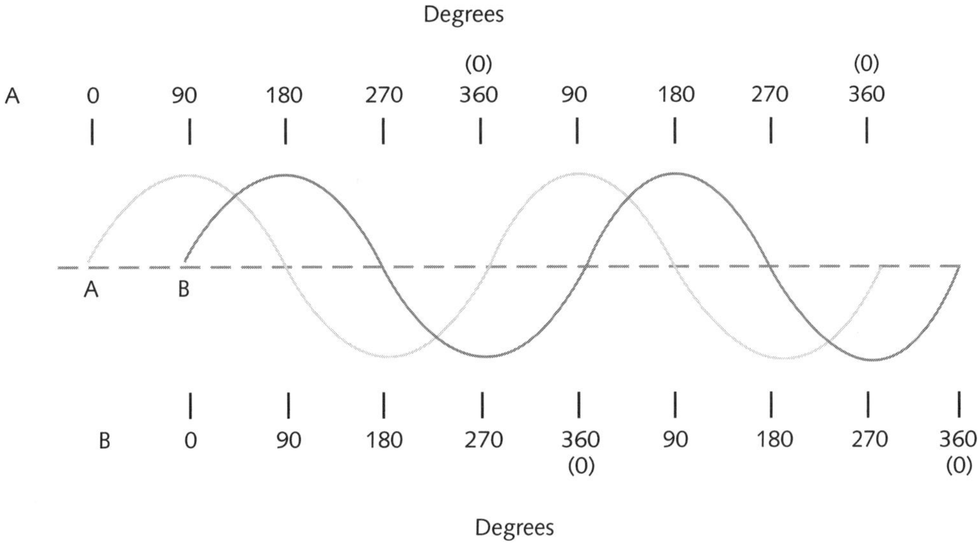

Figure 3-2 Waves with a 90-degree phase difference

you when a book you have requested is available. The digital voice has a poorer quality than your own voice—that is, it sounds like a machine. It can't convey the subtle changes in inflection that you expect in a human voice. Only very high-quality digital signals—for example, those used to record music on compact discs—can achieve such accuracy.

One drawback to analog signals is that their voltage is varied and imprecise. Thus, analog transmission is more susceptible to transmission flaws such as **noise,** or any type of interference that may degrade a signal, than digital signals. If you have tried to listen to AM radio on a stormy night, you have probably heard the crackle and static of noise affecting the signal.

Now contrast the analog signals pictured in Figures 3-1 and 3-2 to a digital signal, as shown in Figure 3-3. **Digital** signals are composed of pulses of precise, positive voltages and zero voltages. A pulse of positive voltage represents a 1. A pulse of zero voltage (in other words, the lack of any voltage) represents a 0. The use of 1s and 0s to represent information is characteristic of a **binary** system. Every pulse in the digital signal is called a binary digit, or **bit.**

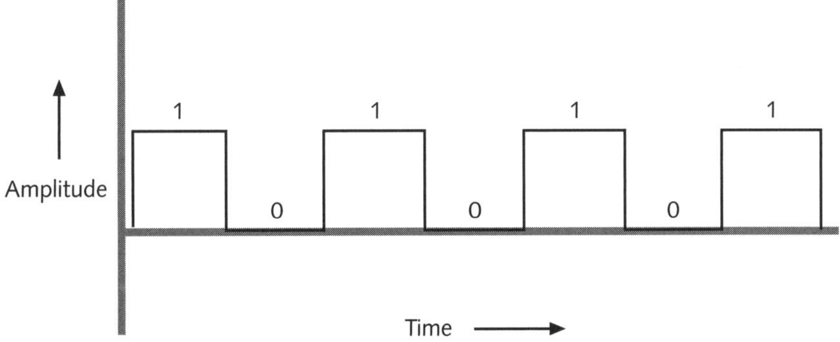

Figure 3-3 An example of a digital signal

A bit can have only one of two possible values: 1 or 0. Eight bits together form a **byte**. In broad terms, one byte carries one piece of information. For example, the byte 01111001 means 121 on a digital network.

Computers read and write information—for example, program instructions, routing information, and network addresses—in bits and bytes. When a number is represented in binary form (for example, 01111001), each bit position, or placeholder, in the number represents a specific multiple of 2. Because a byte contains eight bits, it has eight placeholders. When counting placeholders in a byte, you move from right to left. The placeholder farthest to the right is known as the zero position, the one to its left is in the first position, and so on. The placeholder farthest to the left is in the seventh position, as shown in Figure 3-4.

To find the decimal value of a bit, you multiply the 1 or 0 (whichever the bit is set to) by 2^x, where x equals the bit's position. For example, the 1 or 0 in the zero position must be multiplied by 2 to the 0 power, or 2^0, to determine its value. Any number (other than zero) raised to the power of 0 has a value of 1. Thus, if the zero-position bit is 1, it represents a value of 1×2^0, or 1×1, which equals 1. If a 0 is in the zero position, its value equals 0×2^0, or 0×1, which equals 0. In every position, if a bit is 0, that position represents a decimal number of 0.

To convert a byte to a decimal number, determine the value represented by each bit, and then add those values together. If a bit in the byte is 1 (in other words, if it's "on"), the bit's numerical equivalent in the coding scheme is added to the total. If a bit is 0, that position has no value and nothing is added to the total. For example, the byte 11111111 equals: $1 \times 2^7 + 1 \times 2^6 + 1 \times 2^5 + 1 \times 2^4 + 1 \times 2^3 + 1 \times 2^2 + 1 \times 2^1 + 1 \times 2^0$, or $128 + 64 + 32 + 16 + 8 + 4 + 2 + 1$. Its decimal equivalent, then, is 255. In another example, the byte 00100100 equals: $0 \times 2^7 + 0 \times 2^6 + 1 \times 2^5 + 0 \times 2^4 + 0 \times 2^3 + 1 \times 2^2 + 0 \times 2^1 + 0 \times 2^0$, or $0 + 0 + 32 + 0 + 0 + 4 + 0 + 0$. Its decimal equivalent, then, is 36.

Figure 3-4 illustrates placeholders in a byte, the exponential multiplier for each position, and the different decimal values that are represented by a 1 in each position.

To convert a decimal number to a byte, you reverse this process. For example, the decimal number 8 equals 2^3, which means a single "on" bit would be indicated in the fourth bit position as follows: 00001000. In another example, the decimal number 9 equals $8 + 1$, or $2^3 + 2^0$, and would be represented by the binary number 00001001.

The binary numbering scheme may be used with more than eight positions. However, in the digital world, bytes form the building blocks for messages, and bytes always include eight positions. In a data signal, multiple bytes are combined to form a message. If you were to peek at the 1s and 0s used to transmit an entire e-mail message, for example, you might see millions of 1s and 0s passing by. A computer can quickly translate these binary numbers into codes, such as ASCII or JPEG, that express letters, numbers, and pictures.

Bit position:	7	6	5	4	3	2	1	0
Binary exponential:	2^7	2^6	2^5	2^4	2^3	2^2	2^1	2^0
Value if bit = 1:	128	64	32	16	8	4	2	1

Figure 3-4 Components of a byte

Converting between decimal and binary numbers can be done by hand, as shown previously, or by using a scientific calculator, such as the one available with the Windows XP or Windows Vista operating systems. Take, for example, the number 131. To convert it to a binary number:

1. On a Windows XP or Windows Vista computer, click the **Start** button, select **All Programs**, select **Accessories**, and then select **Calculator**. The Calculator window opens.

2. Click **View**, and then click **Scientific**. Verify that the **Dec** option button is selected.

3. Type **131**, and then click the **Bin** option button. The binary equivalent of the number 131, 10000011, appears in the display window.

You can reverse this process to convert a binary number to a decimal number.

4. Close the Calculator window.

If you're connected to the Internet and using a Web browser, you can quickly convert binary and decimal numbers by using Google calculator. Simply point your browser to *www.google.com*, and then type in the number you want to convert, plus the format, in the search text box. For example, to convert the decimal number 131 into binary form, type "131 in binary" (without the quotation marks), and then press Enter. You see the following result: 131 = 0b10000011. The prefix "0b" indicates that the number is in binary format. To convert a binary number into decimal form, type "0b" (without the quotation marks) before the binary number. For example, entering "0b10000011 in decimal" (without the quotation marks) would return the number 131.

Because digital transmission involves sending and receiving only a pattern of 1s and 0s, represented by precise pulses, it is more reliable than analog transmission, which relies on variable waves. In addition, noise affects digital transmission less severely. On the other hand, digital transmission requires many pulses to transmit the same amount of information that an analog signal can transmit with a single wave. Nevertheless, the high reliability of digital transmission makes this extra signaling worthwhile. In the end, digital transmission is more efficient than analog transmission because it results in fewer errors and, therefore, requires less overhead to compensate for errors.

Overhead is a term used by networking professionals to describe the nondata information that must accompany data for a signal to be properly routed and interpreted by the network. For example, the data link layer header and trailer, the network layer addressing information, and the transport layer flow control information added to a piece of data to send it over the network are all part of the transmission's overhead.

It's important to understand that in both the analog and digital worlds, a variety of signaling techniques are used. For each technique, standards dictate what type of transmitter, communications channel, and receiver should be used. For example, the type of transmitter (NIC) used for computers on a LAN and the way in which this transmitter manipulates electric current to produce signals is different from the transmitter and signaling techniques used with a satellite link. While not all signaling methods are covered in this book, you will learn about the most common methods used for data networking.

Data Modulation

Data relies almost exclusively on digital transmission. However, in some cases the type of connection your network uses may be capable of handling only analog signals. For example, telephone lines are designed to carry analog signals. If you connect to your ISP's network via a telephone line, the data signals issued by your computer must be converted into analog form before they get to the phone line. Later, they must be converted back into digital form when they arrive at the ISP's access server. A modem accomplishes this translation. The word **modem** reflects this device's function as a *mo*dulator/*dem*odulator—that is, it modulates digital signals into analog signals at the transmitting end, and then it demodulates analog signals into digital signals at the receiving end.

Data modulation is a technology used to modify analog signals to make them suitable for carrying data over a communication path. In **modulation**, a simple wave, called a carrier wave, is combined with another analog signal to produce a unique signal that gets transmitted from one node to another. The carrier wave has preset properties (including frequency, amplitude, and phase). Its purpose is to help convey information; in other words, it's only a messenger. Another signal, known as the information or data wave, is added to the carrier wave. When the information wave is added, it modifies one property of the carrier wave (for example, the frequency, amplitude, or phase). The result is a new, blended signal that contains properties of both the carrier wave and added data. When the signal reaches its destination, the receiver separates the data from the carrier wave.

Modulation can be used to make a signal conform to a specific pathway, as in the case of **FM (frequency modulation)** radio, in which the data must travel along a particular frequency. In frequency modulation, the frequency of the carrier signal is modified by the application of the data signal. In **AM (amplitude modulation)**, the amplitude of the carrier signal is modified by the application of the data signal. Modulation may also be used to issue multiple signals to the same communications channel and prevent the signals from interfering with one another. Figure 3-5 depicts an unaltered carrier wave, a data wave, and the combined wave as modified through frequency modulation. Later in this book, you will learn about networking technologies, such as DSL, that make use of modulation.

Simplex, Half-Duplex, and Duplex

Data transmission, whether analog or digital, may also be characterized by the direction in which the signals travel over the media. In cases in which signals may travel in only one direction, the transmission is considered **simplex**. An example of simplex communication is a football coach calling out orders to his team through a megaphone. In this example, the coach's voice is the signal, and it travels in only one direction—away from the megaphone's mouthpiece and toward the team. Simplex is sometimes called one-way, or unidirectional, communication.

In **half-duplex** transmission, signals may travel in both directions over a medium but in only one direction at a time. Half-duplex systems contain only one channel for communication, and that channel must be shared for multiple nodes to exchange information. For example, a walkie-talkie or an apartment's intercom system that requires you to press a "talk" button to allow your voice to be transmitted uses half-duplex transmission. If you visit a friend's apartment building, you press the "talk" button to send your voice signals to his apartment. When

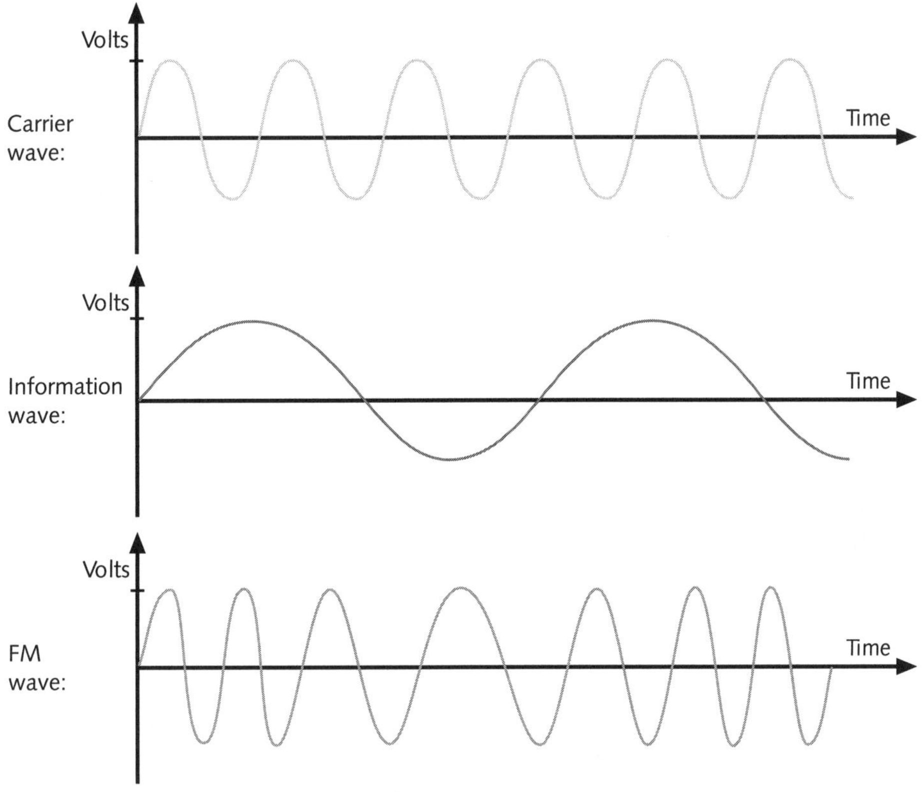

Figure 3-5 A carrier wave modified through frequency modulation

your friend responds, he presses the "talk" button in his apartment to send his voice signal in the opposite direction over the wire to the speaker in the lobby where you wait. If you press the "talk" button while he's talking, you will not be able to hear his voice transmission. In a similar manner, some networks operate with only half-duplex capability.

When signals are free to travel in both directions over a medium simultaneously, the transmission is considered **full-duplex**. Full-duplex may also be called bidirectional transmission or, sometimes, simply **duplex**. When you call a friend on the telephone, your connection is an example of a full-duplex transmission because your voice signals can be transmitted to your friend at the same time your friend's voice signals are transmitted in the opposite direction to you. In other words, both of you can talk and hear each other simultaneously.

Figure 3-6 compares simplex, half-duplex, and full-duplex transmissions.

Full-duplex transmission is also used on data networks. For example, modern Ethernet networks are capable of full-duplex. In this situation, full-duplex transmission uses multiple channels on the same medium. A **channel** is a distinct communication path between nodes, much as a lane is a distinct transportation path on a freeway. Channels may be separated either logically or physically. You will learn about logically separate channels in the next section. An example of physically separate channels occurs when one wire within a network cable is used for transmission while another wire is used for reception. In this example, each separate wire in the medium allows half-duplex transmission. When combined in a cable,

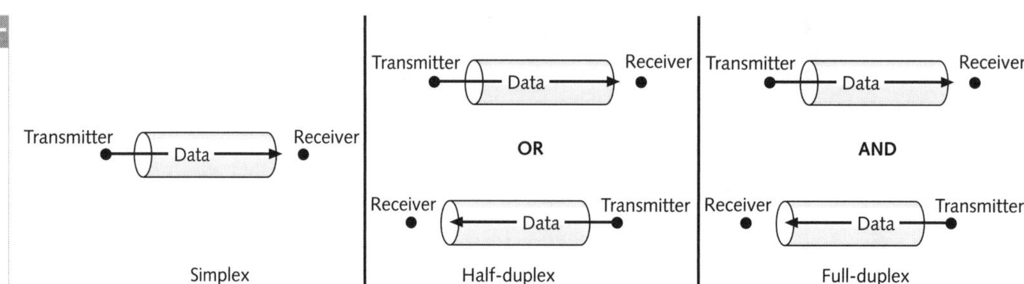

Figure 3-6 Simplex, half-duplex, and full-duplex transmission

they form a medium that provides full-duplex transmission. Full-duplex capability increases the speed with which data can travel over a network. In some cases—for example, when providing telephone service over the Internet—full-duplex data networks are a requirement.

Many network devices, such as modems and NICs, allow you to specify whether the device should use half- or full-duplex communication. It's important to know what type of transmission a network supports before installing network devices on that network. If you configure a computer's NIC to use full-duplex while the rest of the network is using half-duplex, for example, that computer will not be able to communicate on the network.

Multiplexing

A form of transmission that allows multiple signals to travel simultaneously over one medium is known as **multiplexing**. To carry multiple signals, the medium's channel is logically separated into multiple smaller channels, or **subchannels**. Many different types of multiplexing are available, and the type used in any given situation depends on what the media, transmission, and reception equipment can handle. For each type of multiplexing, a device that can combine many signals on a channel, a **multiplexer (mux)**, is required at the transmitting end of the channel. At the receiving end, a **demultiplexer (demux)** separates the combined signals and regenerates them in their original form. Networks rely on multiplexing to increase the amount of data that can be transmitted in a given time span over a given bandwidth.

One type of multiplexing, TDM (**time division multiplexing**), divides a channel into multiple intervals of time, or time slots. It then assigns a separate time slot to every node on the network and, in that time slot, carries data from that node. For example, if five stations are connected to a network over one wire, five different time slots are established in the communications channel. Workstation A may be assigned time slot 1, workstation B time slot 2, workstation C time slot 3, and so on. Time slots are reserved for their designated nodes regardless of whether the node has data to transmit. If a node does not have data to send, nothing is sent during its time slot. This arrangement can be inefficient if some nodes on the network rarely send data. Figure 3-7 shows a simple TDM model.

Statistical multiplexing is similar to time division multiplexing, but rather than assigning a separate slot to each node in succession, the transmitter assigns slots to nodes according to priority and need. This method is more efficient than TDM, because in statistical multiplexing time slots are unlikely to remain empty. To begin with, in statistical multiplexing, as in

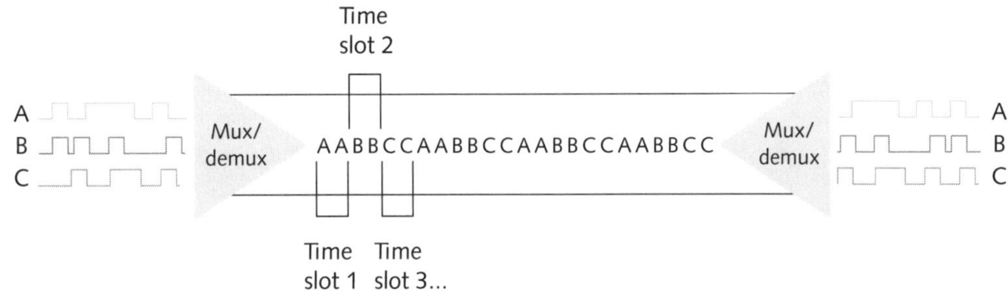

Figure 3-7 Time division multiplexing

TDM, each node is assigned one time slot. However, if a node doesn't use its time slot, statistical multiplexing devices recognize that and assign its slot to another node that needs to send data. The contention for slots may be arbitrated according to use or priority or even more sophisticated factors, depending on the network. Most importantly, statistical multiplexing maximizes available bandwidth on a network. Figure 3-8 depicts a simple statistical multiplexing system.

FDM (frequency division multiplexing) is a type of multiplexing that assigns a unique frequency band to each communications subchannel. Signals are modulated with different carrier frequencies, and then they are multiplexed to simultaneously travel over a single channel. The first use of FDM was in the early 20th century when telephone companies discovered they could send multiple voice signals over a single cable. That meant that rather than stringing separate lines for each residence (and adding to the urban tangle of wires), they could send as many as 24 multiplexed signals over a single neighborhood line. Each signal was then demultiplexed before being brought into the home.

Now, telephone companies also multiplex signals on the phone line that enters your residence. Voice communications use the frequency band of 300–3400Hz (because this matches approximately the range of human hearing), for a total bandwidth of 3100Hz. But the potential bandwidth of one phone line far exceeds this. Telephone companies implement FDM to subdivide and send signals in the bandwidth above 3400Hz. Because the frequencies can't be heard, you don't notice the data transmission occurring while you talk on the telephone. Figure 3-9 provides a simplified view of FDM, in which waves representing three different frequencies are carried simultaneously by one channel.

Different forms of FDM exist. One type is used in cellular telephone transmission and another by DSL Internet access. (You'll learn more about DSL in Chapter 7.)

WDM (wavelength division multiplexing) is a technology used with fiber-optic cable, which enables one fiber-optic connection to carry multiple light signals simultaneously. Using

Figure 3-8 Statistical multiplexing

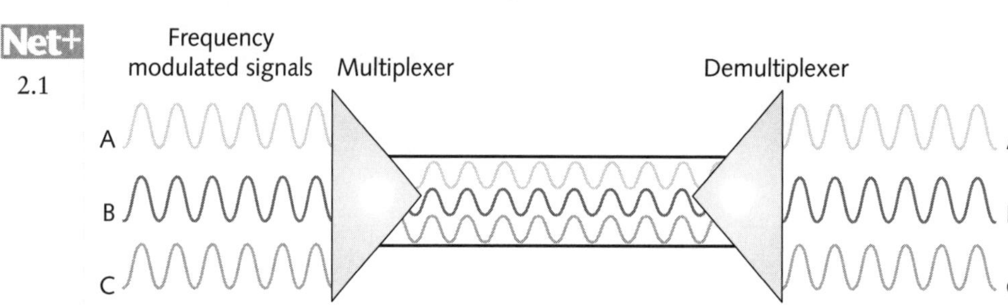

Figure 3-9 Frequency division multiplexing

WDM, a single fiber can transmit as many as 20 million telephone conversations at one time. WDM can work over any type of fiber-optic cable.

In the first step of WDM, a beam of light is divided into up to 40 different carrier waves, each with a different wavelength (and, therefore, a different color). Each wavelength represents a separate transmission channel capable of transmitting up to 10Gbps. Before transmission, each carrier wave is modulated with a different data signal. Then, through a very narrow beam of light, lasers issue the separate, modulated waves to a multiplexer. The multiplexer combines all of the waves, in the same way that a prism can accept light beams of different wavelengths and concentrate them into a single beam of white light. Next, another laser issues this multiplexed beam to a strand of fiber within a fiber-optic cable. The fiber carries the multiplexed signals to a receiver, which is connected to a demultiplexer. The demultiplexer acts as a prism to separate the combined signals according to their different wavelengths (or colors). Then, the separate waves are sent to their destinations on the network. If the signal risks losing strength between the multiplexer and demultiplexer, an amplifier might be used to boost it. Figure 3-10 illustrates WDM transmission.

The form of WDM used on most modern fiber-optic networks is **DWDM (dense wavelength division multiplexing)**. In DWDM, a single fiber in a fiber-optic cable can carry between 80 and 160 channels. It achieves this increased capacity because it uses more wavelengths for signaling. In other words, there is less separation between the usable carrier waves in DWDM than there is in the original form of WDM. Because of its extraordinary capacity,

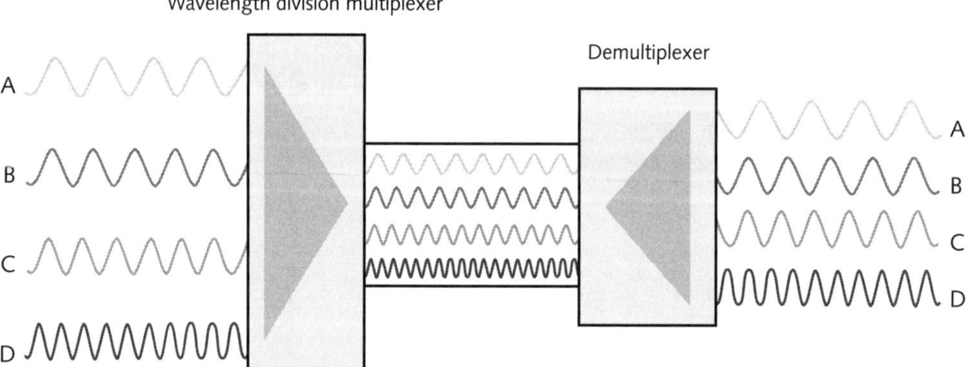

Figure 3-10 Wavelength division multiplexing

2.1 DWDM is typically used on high-bandwidth or long-distance WAN links, such as the connection between a large ISP and its (even larger) network service provider.

Relationships between Nodes

2.1 So far you have learned about two important characteristics of data transmission: the type of signaling (analog or digital) and the direction in which the signal travels (simplex, half-duplex, full-duplex, or multiplex). Another important characteristic is the number of senders and receivers, as well as the relationship between them. In general, data communications may involve a single transmitter with one or more receivers, or multiple transmitters with one or more receivers. The remainder of this section introduces the most common relationships between transmitters and receivers.

When a data transmission involves only one transmitter and one receiver, it is considered a **point-to-point** transmission. An office building in Dallas exchanging data with another office in St. Louis over a WAN connection is an example of point-to-point transmission. In this case, the sender only transmits data that is intended to be used by a specific receiver.

By contrast, **point-to-multipoint** transmission involves one transmitter and multiple receivers. Point-to-multipoint arrangements can be separated into two types: broadcast and nonbroadcast. **Broadcast** transmission involves one transmitter and multiple, *undefined* receivers. For example, a TV station indiscriminately transmitting a signal from its tower to thousands of homes with TV antennas uses broadcast transmission. A broadcast transmission sends data to any and all receivers, without regard for which receiver can use it. Broadcast transmissions are frequently used on both wired and wireless networks because they are simple and quick. They are used to identify certain nodes, to send data to certain nodes (even though every node is capable of picking up the transmitted data, only the destination node will actually do it), and to send announcements to all nodes.

When more tailored data transfer is desired, a network might use **nonbroadcast point-to-multipoint transmission**. In this scenario, a node issues signals to multiple, *defined* recipients. For example, a network administrator could schedule the LAN transmission of an instructional video that only she and all of her team's workstations could receive.

Figure 3-11 contrasts point-to-point and point-to-multipoint transmissions.

Throughput and Bandwidth

2.1 The data transmission characteristic most frequently discussed and analyzed by networking professionals is throughput. **Throughput** is the measure of how much data is transmitted during a given period of time. It may also be called **capacity** or bandwidth (though, as you will learn, bandwidth is technically different from throughput). Throughput is commonly expressed as a quantity of bits transmitted per second, with prefixes used to designate different throughput amounts. For example, the prefix *kilo* combined with the word *bit* (as in *kilobit*) indicates 1,000 bits per second. Rather than talking about a throughput of 1,000 bits per second, you typically say the throughput was 1 kilobit per second (1Kbps). Table 3-1 summarizes the terminology and abbreviations used when discussing different throughput amounts. As an example, a residential broadband Internet connection might be rated for a maximum throughput of 1.544Mbps. A fast LAN might transport up to 10Gbps of data. Contemporary networks commonly achieve throughputs of 10Mbps, 100Mbps, 1Gbps, or

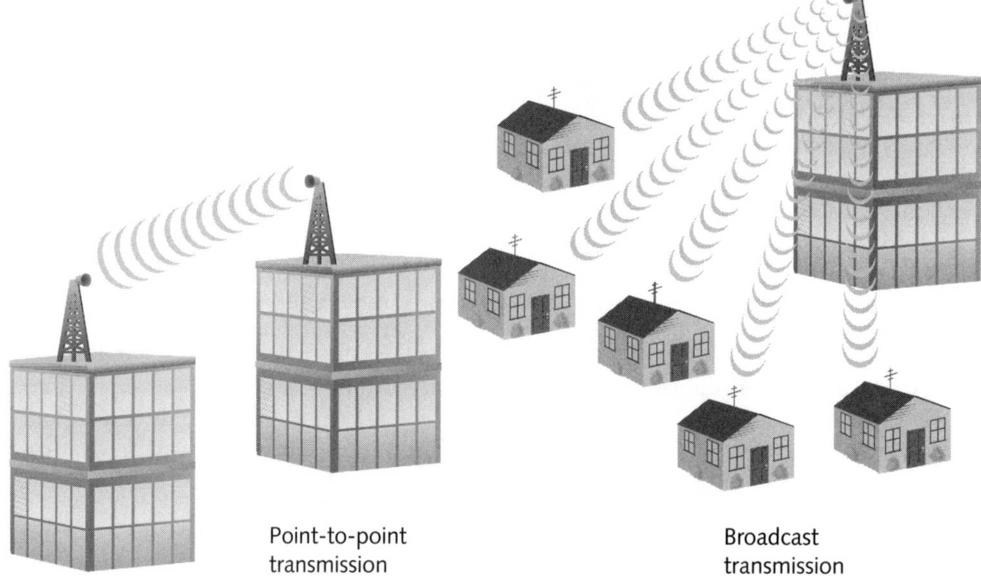

Figure 3-11 Point-to-point versus broadcast transmission

Table 3-1 Throughput Measures

Quantity	Prefix	Complete Example	Abbreviation
1 bit per second	n/a	1 bit per second	bps
1,000 bits per second	kilo	**1 kilobit per second**	Kbps
1,000,000 bits per second	mega	**1 megabit per second**	Mbps
1,000,000,000 bits per second	giga	**1 gigabit per second**	Gbps
1,000,000,000,000 bits per second	tera	**1 terabit per second**	Tbps

higher. Applications that require significant throughput include videoconferencing and telephone signaling. By contrast, instant messaging and e-mail, for example, require much less throughput.

Be careful not to confuse bits and bytes when discussing throughput. Although data storage quantities are typically expressed in multiples of bytes, data transmission quantities (in other words, throughput) are more commonly expressed in multiples of bits per second. When representing different data quantities, a small *b* represents bits, while a capital *B* represents bytes. To put this into context, a modem may transmit data at 56.6Kbps (kilobits per second); a data file may be 56KB (kilobytes) in size. Another difference between data storage and data throughput measures is that in data storage the prefix *kilo* means 2 to the 10th power, *or* 1,024, *not* 1,000.

Often, the term *bandwidth* is used interchangeably with throughput, and in fact, this may be the case on the Network+ certification exam. Bandwidth and throughput are similar

2.1

concepts, but strictly speaking, **bandwidth** is a measure of the difference between the highest and lowest frequencies that a medium can transmit. This range of frequencies, which is expressed in Hz, is directly related to throughput. For example, if the FCC told you that you could transmit a radio signal between 870 and 880MHz, your allotted bandwidth (literally, the width of your frequency band) would be 10MHz.

Baseband and Broadband

Baseband is a transmission form in which (typically) digital signals are sent through direct current (DC) pulses applied to the wire. This direct current requires exclusive use of the wire's capacity. As a result, baseband systems can transmit only one signal, or one channel, at a time. Every device on a baseband system shares the same channel. When one node is transmitting data on a baseband system, all other nodes on the network must wait for that transmission to end before they can send data. Baseband transmission supports half-duplexing, which means that computers can both send and receive information on the same length of wire. In some cases, baseband also supports full duplexing.

Ethernet is an example of a baseband system found on many LANs. In Ethernet, each device on a network can transmit over the wire—but only one device at a time. For example, if you want to save a file to the server, your NIC submits your request to use the wire; if no other device is using the wire to transmit data at that time, your workstation can go ahead. If the wire is in use, your workstation must wait and try again later. Of course, this retrying process happens so quickly that you don't even notice the wait.

Broadband is a form of transmission in which signals are modulated as radiofrequency (RF) analog waves that use different frequency ranges. Unlike baseband, broadband technology does not encode information as digital pulses.

As you may know, broadband transmission is used to bring cable TV to your home. Your cable TV connection can carry at least 25 times as much data as a typical baseband system (like Ethernet) carries, including many different broadcast frequencies on different channels. In traditional broadband systems, signals travel in only one direction—toward the user. To allow users to send data as well, cable systems allot a separate channel space for the user's transmission and use amplifiers that can separate data the user issues from data the network transmits. Broadband transmission is generally more expensive than baseband transmission because of the extra hardware involved. On the other hand, broadband systems can span longer distances than baseband.

In the field of networking, some terms have more than one meaning, depending on their context. *Broadband* is one of those terms. The *broadband* described in this chapter is the transmission system that carries RF signals across multiple channels on a coaxial cable, as used by cable TV. This definition was the original meaning of broadband. However, broadband has evolved to mean any of several different network types that use digital signaling to transmit data at very high transmission rates.

Transmission Flaws

2.1

Both analog and digital signals are susceptible to degradation between the time they are issued by a transmitter and the time they are received. One of the most common transmission flaws affecting data signals is noise.

Net+ **Noise** As you learned earlier, noise is any undesirable influence that may degrade or distort a signal. Many different types of noise may affect transmission. A common source of noise is **EMI (electromagnetic interference)**, or waves that emanate from electrical devices or cables carrying electricity. Motors, power lines, televisions, copiers, fluorescent lights, manufacturing machinery, and other sources of electrical activity (including a severe thunderstorm) can cause EMI. One type of EMI is **RFI (radiofrequency interference)**, or electromagnetic interference caused by radio waves. (Often, you'll see EMI referred to as EMI/RFI.) Strong broadcast signals from radio or TV towers can generate RFI. When EMI noise affects analog signals, this distortion can result in the incorrect transmission of data, just as if static prevented you from hearing a radio station broadcast. However, this type of noise affects digital signals much less. Because digital signals do not depend on subtle amplitude or frequency differences to communicate information, they are more apt to be readable despite distortions caused by EMI noise.

Another form of noise that hinders data transmission is cross talk. **Cross talk** occurs when a signal traveling on one wire or cable infringes on the signal traveling over an adjacent wire or cable. When cross talk occurs between two cables, it's called **alien cross talk**. When it occurs between wire pairs near the source of a signal, it's known as **NEXT (near end cross talk)**. One potential cause of NEXT is an improper termination—for example, one in which wire insulation has been damaged or wire pairs have been untwisted too far.

If you've ever been on the phone and heard the conversation on your second line in the background, you have heard the effects of cross talk. In this example, the current carrying a signal on the second line's wire imposes itself on the wire carrying your line's signal, as shown in Figure 3-12. The resulting noise, or cross talk, is equal to a portion of the second line's signal. Cross talk in the form of overlapping phone conversations is bothersome, but it does not usually prevent you from hearing your own line's conversation. In data networks, however, cross talk can be extreme enough to prevent the accurate delivery of data.

In addition to EMI and cross talk, less obvious environmental influences, including heat, can cause noise. In every signal, a certain amount of noise is unavoidable. However, engineers have designed a number of ways to limit the potential for noise to degrade a signal. One way is simply to ensure that the strength of the signal exceeds the strength of the noise. Proper cable design and installation are also critical for protecting against noise's effects. Note that all forms of noise are measured in decibels (dB).

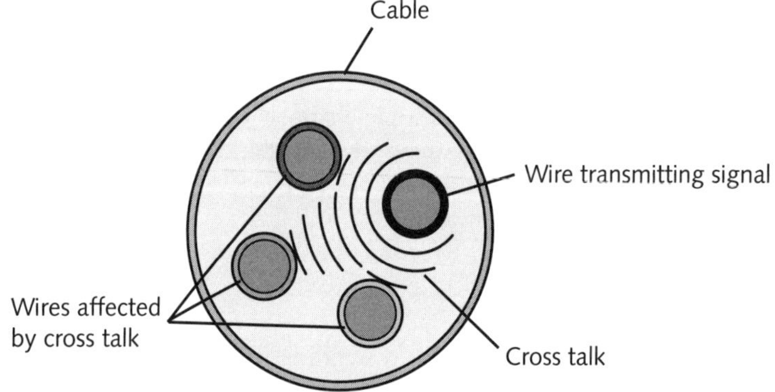

Figure 3-12 Cross talk between wires in a cable

Net+
4.7

Attenuation Another transmission flaw is **attenuation**, or the loss of a signal's strength as it travels away from its source. Just as your voice becomes fainter as it travels farther, so do signals fade with distance. To compensate for attenuation, both analog and digital signals are boosted en route. However, the technology used to boost an analog signal is different from that used to boost a digital signal. Analog signals pass through an **amplifier**, an electronic device that increases the voltage, or strength, of the signals. When an analog signal is amplified, the noise that it has accumulated is also amplified. This indiscriminate amplification causes the analog signal to worsen progressively. After multiple amplifications, an analog signal may become difficult to decipher. Figure 3-13 shows an analog signal distorted by noise and then amplified once.

When digital signals are repeated, they are actually retransmitted in their original form, without the noise they might have accumulated previously. This process is known as **regeneration**. A device that regenerates a digital signal is called a **repeater**. Figure 3-14 shows a digital signal distorted by noise and then regenerated by a repeater.

Amplifiers and repeaters belong to the physical layer of the OSI model. Both are used to extend the length of a network. Because most networks are digital, however, they typically use repeaters.

Net+
2.1
4.7

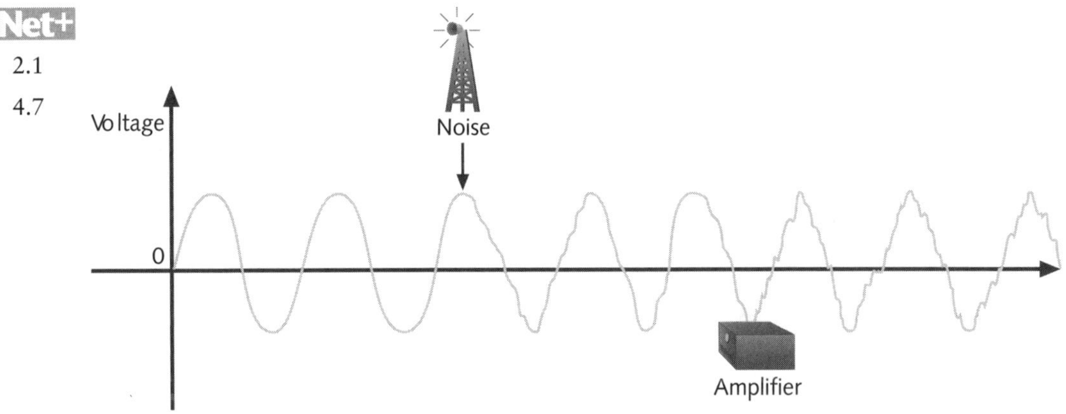

Figure 3-13 An analog signal distorted by noise and then amplified

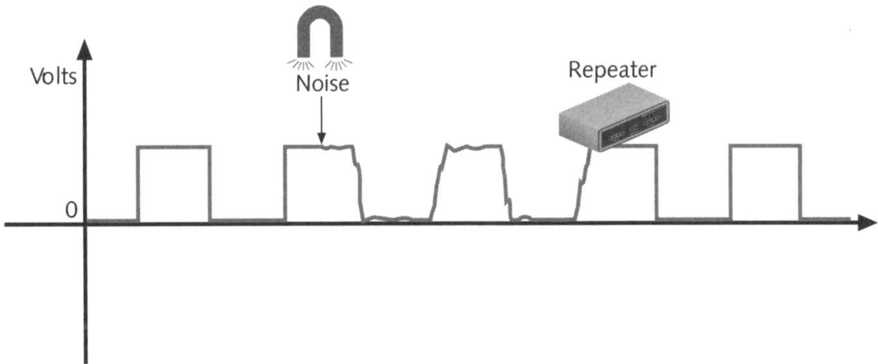

Figure 3-14 A digital signal distorted by noise and then repeated

Latency   In an ideal world, networks could transmit data instantaneously between sender and receiver, no matter how great the distance between the two. However, in the real world every network is subjected to a delay between the transmission of a signal and its eventual receipt. For example, when you press a key on your computer to save a file to a network server, the file's data must travel through your NIC, the network wire, one or more connectivity devices, more cabling, and the server's NIC before it lands on the server's hard disk. Although electrons travel rapidly, they still have to travel, and a brief delay takes place between the moment you press the key and the moment the server accepts the data. This delay is called **latency**.

The length of the cable involved affects latency, as does the existence of any intervening connectivity device, such as a router. Different devices affect latency to different degrees. For example, modems, which must modulate both incoming and outgoing signals, increase a connection's latency far more than hubs, which simply repeat a signal. The most common way to measure latency on data networks is by calculating a packet's **RTT (round trip time)**, or the length of time it takes for a packet to go from sender to receiver, and then back from receiver to sender. RTT is usually measured in milliseconds.

Latency causes problems only when a receiving node is expecting some type of communication, such as the rest of a data stream it has begun to accept. If that node does not receive the rest of the data stream within a given time period, it assumes that no more data is coming. This assumption may cause transmission errors on a network. When you connect multiple network segments and thereby increase the distance between sender and receiver, you increase the network's latency. To constrain the latency and avoid its associated errors, each type of cabling is rated for a maximum number of connected network segments, and each transmission method is assigned a maximum segment length.

Common Media Characteristics

Now that you are familiar with data-signaling characteristics, you are ready to learn more about the physical and atmospheric paths that these signals traverse. When deciding which kind of transmission media to use, you must match your networking needs with the characteristics of the media. This section describes the characteristics of several types of physical media, including throughput, cost, size and scalability, connectors, and noise immunity. The medium used for wireless transmission, the atmosphere, is discussed in detail in Chapter 8.

Throughput

Perhaps the most significant factor in choosing a transmission method is its throughput. All media are limited by the laws of physics that prevent signals from traveling faster than the speed of light. Beyond that, throughput is limited by the signaling and multiplexing techniques used in a given transmission method. Using fiber-optic cables allows faster throughput than copper or wireless connections. Noise and devices connected to the transmission medium can further limit throughput. A noisy circuit spends more time compensating for the noise and, therefore, has fewer resources available for transmitting data.

Cost

The precise costs of using a particular type of cable or wireless connection are often difficult to pinpoint. For example, although a vendor might quote you the cost-per-foot for new network cabling, you might also have to upgrade some hardware on your network to use that type of cabling. Thus, the cost of upgrading your media would actually include more than the cost of the cabling itself. Not only do media costs depend on the hardware that already exists in a network, but they also depend on the size of your network and the cost of labor in your area (unless you plan to install the cable yourself). The following variables can all influence the final cost of implementing a certain type of media:

- *Cost of installation*—Can you install the media yourself, or must you hire contractors to do it? Will you need to move walls or build new conduits or closets? Will you need to lease lines from a service provider?

- *Cost of new infrastructure versus reusing existing infrastructure*—Can you use existing wiring? In some cases, for example, installing all new Category 6 UTP wiring may not pay off if you can use existing Category 5 UTP wiring. If you replace only part of your infrastructure, will it be easily integrated with the existing media?

- *Cost of maintenance and support*—Reuse of an existing cabling infrastructure does not save any money if it is in constant need of repair or enhancement. Also, if you use an unfamiliar media type, it may cost more to hire a technician to service it. Will you be able to service the media yourself, or must you hire contractors to service it?

- *Cost of a lower transmission rate affecting productivity*—If you save money by reusing existing slower lines, are you incurring costs by reducing productivity? In other words, are you making staff wait longer to save and print reports or exchange e-mail?

- *Cost of obsolescence*—Are you choosing media that may become passing fads, requiring rapid replacement? Will you be able to find reasonably priced connectivity hardware that will be compatible with your chosen media for years to come?

Net+ Noise Immunity

2.1
As you learned earlier, noise can distort data signals. The extent to which noise affects a signal depends partly on the transmission media. Some types of media are more susceptible to noise than others. The type of media least susceptible to noise is fiber-optic cable, because it does not use electric current, but light waves, to conduct signals.

On most networks, noise is an ever-present threat, so you should take measures to limit its impact on your network. For example, install cabling well away from powerful electromagnetic forces. If your environment still leaves your network vulnerable, choose a type of transmission media that helps to protect the signal from noise. For example, wireless signals are more apt to be distorted by EMI/RFI than signals traveling over a cable. It is also possible to use antinoise algorithms to protect data from being corrupted by noise. If these measures don't ward off interference, in the case of wired media, you may need to use a metal **conduit**, or pipeline, to contain and further protect the cabling.

Now that you understand data transmission and the factors to consider when choosing a transmission medium, you are ready to learn about different types of transmission media. To qualify for Network+ certification, you must know the characteristics and limitations of each type of media, how to install and design a network with each type, how to troubleshoot networking media problems, and how to provide for future network growth with each option.

Size and Scalability

Three specifications determine the size and scalability of networking media: maximum nodes per segment, maximum segment length, and maximum network length. In cabling, each of these specifications is based on the physical characteristics of the wire and the electrical characteristics of data transmission. The maximum number of nodes per segment depends on attenuation and latency. Each device added to a network segment causes a slight increase in the signal's attenuation and latency. To ensure a clear, strong, and timely signal, you must limit the number of nodes on a segment.

The maximum segment length depends on attenuation and latency plus the segment type. A network can include two types of segments: populated and unpopulated. A **populated segment** is a part of a network that contains end nodes. For example, a switch connecting users in a classroom is part of a populated segment. An **unpopulated segment**, also known as a **link segment**, is a part of the network that does not contain end nodes, but simply connects two networking devices such as routers.

Segment lengths are limited because after a certain distance, a signal loses so much strength that it cannot be accurately interpreted. The maximum distance a signal can travel and still be interpreted accurately is equal to a segment's maximum length. Beyond this length, data loss is apt to occur. As with the maximum number of nodes per segment, maximum segment length varies between different cabling types. The same principle of data loss applies to maximum network length, which is the sum of the network's segment lengths.

Net+ Connectors and Media Converters

2.2

3.1

Connectors are the pieces of hardware that connect the wire to the network device, be it a file server, workstation, switch, or printer. Every networking medium requires a specific kind of connector. The type of connectors you use will affect the cost of installing and maintaining the network, the ease of adding new segments or nodes to the network, and the technical expertise required to maintain the network. The connectors you are most likely to encounter on modern networks are illustrated throughout this chapter and shown together in Appendix C.

Connectors are specific to a particular media type, but that doesn't prevent one network from using multiple media. Some connectivity devices are designed to accept more than one type of media. If you are working with a connectivity device that can't, you can integrate the two media types by using media converters. A **media converter** is a piece of hardware that enables networks or segments running on different media to interconnect and exchange signals. For example, suppose a segment leading from your company's data center to a group of workstations uses fiber-optic cable, but the workgroup hub can only accept twisted pair (copper) cable. In that case, you could use a media converter to interconnect the hub with the fiber-optic cable. The media converter completes the physical connection and also converts the electrical signals from the copper cable to light wave signals that can traverse the fiber-optic cable, and vice versa. Such a media converter is shown in Figure 3-15.

The terms *wire* and *cable* are used synonymously in some situations. Strictly speaking, however, *wire* is a subset of *cabling*, because the *cabling* category may also include fiber-optic cable, which is almost never called wire. The exact meaning of the term *wire* depends on context. For example, if you said, in a somewhat casual way, "We had 6 gigs of data go over the wire last night," you would be referring to whatever transmission media helped carry the data—whether fiber, radio waves, coax, or UTP.

Figure 3-15 Copper wire-to-fiber media converter

Coaxial Cable

Coaxial cable, called "coax" for short, was the foundation for Ethernet networks in the 1970s and remained a popular transmission medium for many years. Over time, however, twisted pair and fiber-optic cabling have replaced coax in modern LANs. If you work on long-established networks or cable systems, however, you might have to work with coaxial cable.

Coaxial cable consists of a central metal core (often copper) surrounded by an insulator, a braided metal shielding, called **braiding** or **shield**, and an outer cover, called the **sheath** or jacket. Figure 3-16 depicts a typical coaxial cable. The core may be constructed of one solid metal wire or several thin strands of metal wire. The core carries the electromagnetic signal, and the braided metal shielding acts as both a shield against noise and a ground for the signal. The insulator layer usually consists of a plastic material such as PVC (polyvinyl chloride) or Teflon. It protects the core from the metal shielding, because if the two made contact, the wire would short-circuit. The sheath, which protects the cable from physical damage, may be PVC or a more expensive, fire-resistant plastic.

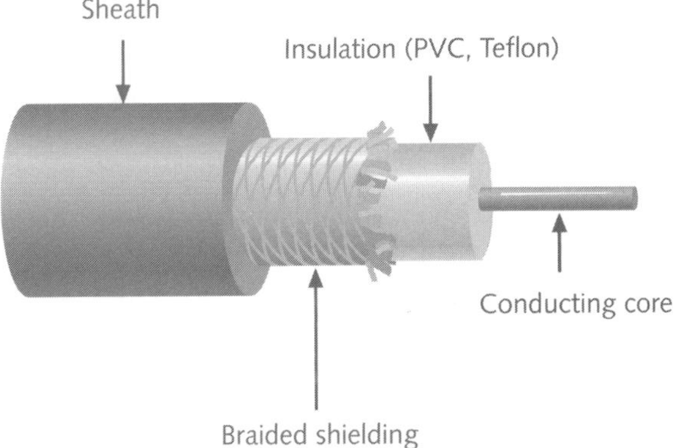

Figure 3-16 Coaxial cable

Because of its shielding, most coaxial cable has a high resistance to noise. It can also carry signals farther than twisted pair cabling before amplification of the signals becomes necessary (although not as far as fiber-optic cabling). On the other hand, coaxial cable is more expensive than twisted pair cable because it requires significantly more raw materials to manufacture.

Coaxial cabling comes in hundreds of specifications, although you are likely to see only two or three types of coax in use on data networks. All types have been assigned an RG specification number. (RG stands for *radio guide*, which is appropriate because coaxial cabling is used to guide radio frequencies in broadband transmission.) The significant differences between the cable types lie in the materials used for their shielding and conducting cores, which in turn influence their transmission characteristics, such as **impedance** (or the resistance that contributes to controlling the signal, as expressed in ohms), attenuation, and throughput. Each type of coax is suited to a different purpose. When discussing the size of the conducting core in a coaxial cable, we refer to its **American Wire Gauge (AWG)** size. The larger the AWG size, the smaller the diameter of a piece of wire. Following is a list of coaxial cable specifications used with data networks:

- *RG-6*—A type of coaxial cable that is characterized by an impedance of 75 ohms and contains an 18 AWG conducting core. The core is usually made of solid copper. RG-6 coaxial cables are used, for example, to deliver broadband cable Internet service and cable TV, particularly over long distances. If a service provider such as Comcast or Charter supplies you with Internet service, the cable entering your home is RG-6.

- *RG-8*—A type of coaxial cable characterized by a 50-ohm impedance and a 10 AWG core. RG-8 provided the medium for the first Ethernet networks, which followed the now-obsolete **10Base-5** standard. The *10* represents its maximum potential throughput of 10Mbps, the *Base* stands for *baseband transmission*, and the *5* represents its maximum segment length of 500 meters. As you'll learn, all Ethernet standards established by IEEE follow a similar naming convention. 10Base-5 is also known as **Thicknet**. You will never find Thicknet on new networks, but you might find it on older networks.

- *RG-58*—A type of coaxial cable characterized by a 50-ohm impedance and a 24 AWG core. RG-58 was a popular medium for Ethernet LANs in the 1980s. With a smaller diameter than RG-8, RG-58 is more flexible and easier to handle and install. Its core is typically made of several thin strands of copper. The Ethernet standard that relies on RG-58 coax is **10Base-2**, with the *10* representing its data transmission rate of 10Mbps, the *Base* representing the fact that it uses baseband transmission, and the *2* representing its maximum segment length of 185 meters (or roughly 200). Because it is thinner than Thicknet cables, it is also called **Thinnet**. Like Thicknet, Thinnet is almost never used on modern networks, although you might encounter it on networks installed in the 1980s.

- *RG-59*—A type of coaxial cable characterized by a 75-ohm impedance and a 20 or 22 AWG core, usually made of braided copper. Less expensive but suffering from greater attenuation than the more common RG-6 coax, RG-59 is still used for relatively short connections, for example, when distributing video signals from a central receiver to multiple monitors within a building.

The two coaxial cable types commonly used in networks today, RG-6 and RG-59, can terminate with one of two connector types: an F-type connector or a BNC connector. **F-type**

connectors attach to coaxial cable so that the pin in the center of the connector is the conducting core of the cable. Therefore, F-type connectors require that the cable contain a solid metal core. After being attached to the cable by crimping or compression, connectors are threaded and screw together like a nut and bolt assembly. A male F-type connector, or plug, attached to coax is shown in Figure 3-17. A corresponding female F-type connector, or jack, would be coupled with the male connector. F-type connectors are most often used with RG-6 cables.

BNC stands for Bayonet Neill-Concelman, a term that refers to both a style of connection and its two inventors. (Sometimes the term *British Naval Connector* is also used.) A **BNC connector** is crimped, compressed, or twisted onto a coaxial cable. It connects to another BNC connector via a turning and locking mechanism—this is the bayonet coupling referenced in its name. Unlike an F-type connector, male BNC connectors do not use the central conducting core of the coax as part of the connection, but provide their own conducting pin. BNC was once the standard for connecting coaxial-based Ethernet segments. Today, though, you're more likely to find BNC connectors used with RG-59 coaxial cable. Less commonly, they're also used with RG-6. Figure 3-18 shows a BNC connector that is not attached to a cable.

When sourcing connectors for coaxial cable, you need to specify the type of cable you are using. For instance, when working with RG-6 coax, choose an F-type connector made specifically for RG-6 cables. That way, you'll be certain that the connectors and cable share the same impedance rating. If impedance ratings don't match, data errors will result and network performance will suffer.

Next, you will learn about a medium you are more likely to find on modern LANs: twisted pair cable.

Figure 3-17 F-type connector

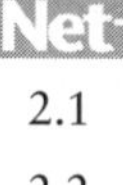

Figure 3-18 BNC connector

Twisted Pair Cable

Twisted pair cable consists of color-coded pairs of insulated copper wires, each with a diameter of 0.4 to 0.8mm (approximately the diameter of a straight pin). Every two wires are twisted around each other to form pairs, and all the pairs are encased in a plastic sheath, as shown in Figure 3-19. The number of pairs in a cable varies, depending on the cable type.

The more twists per foot in a pair of wires, the more resistant the pair will be to cross talk. Higher-quality, more expensive twisted pair cable contains more twists per foot. The number of twists per meter or foot is known as the **twist ratio**. Because twisting the wire pairs more tightly requires more cable, however, a high twist ratio can result in greater attenuation. For

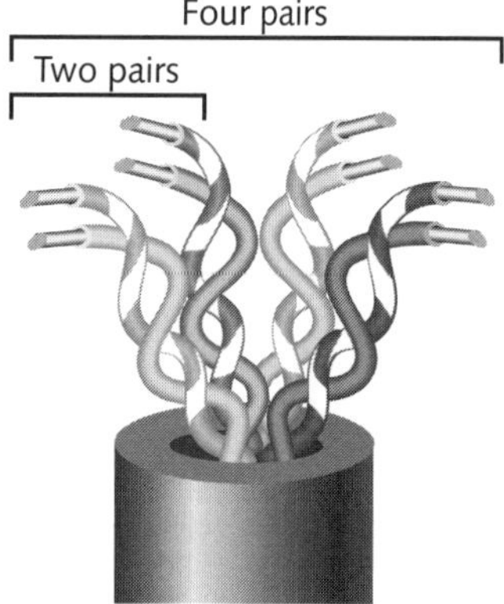

Figure 3-19 Twisted pair cable

optimal performance, cable manufacturers must strike a balance between minimizing cross talk and reducing attenuation.

Because twisted pair is used in such a wide variety of environments and for a variety of purposes, it comes in hundreds of different designs. These designs vary in their twist ratio, the number of wire pairs that they contain, the grade of copper used, the type of shielding (if any), and the materials used for shielding, among other things. A twisted pair cable may contain from 1 to 4,200 wire pairs. Modern networks typically use cables that contain four wire pairs, in which one pair is dedicated to sending data and another pair is dedicated to receiving data.

In 1991, two standards organizations, the TIA/EIA, finalized their specifications for twisted pair wiring in a standard called "TIA/EIA 568." Since then, this body has continually revised the international standards for new and modified transmission media. Its standards now cover cabling media, design, and installation specifications. The TIA/EIA 568 standard divides twisted pair wiring into several categories. The types of twisted pair wiring you will hear about most often are **Cat** (category) 3, 4, 5, 5e, 6, 6e, and 7. All of the category cables fall under the TIA/EIA 568 standard. Modern LANs use Cat 5 or higher wiring.

Twisted pair cable is relatively inexpensive, flexible, and easy to install, and it can span a significant distance before requiring a repeater (though not as far as coax). Twisted pair cable easily accommodates several different topologies, although it is most often implemented in star or star-hybrid topologies. Furthermore, twisted pair can handle the faster networking transmission rates currently being employed. Due to its wide acceptance, it will probably continue to be updated to handle the even faster rates that will emerge in the future. All twisted pair cable falls into one of two categories: STP (shielded twisted pair) or UTP (unshielded twisted pair).

STP (Shielded Twisted Pair)

STP (**shielded twisted pair**) cable consists of twisted wire pairs that are not only individually insulated, but also surrounded by a shielding made of a metallic substance such as foil. Some STP use a braided copper shielding. The shielding acts as a barrier to external electromagnetic forces, thus preventing them from affecting the signals traveling over the wire inside the shielding. It also contains the electrical energy of the signals inside. The shielding may be grounded to enhance its protective effects. The effectiveness of STP's shield depends on the level and type of environmental noise, the thickness and material used for the shield, the grounding mechanism, and the symmetry and consistency of the shielding. Figure 3-20 depicts an STP cable.

UTP (Unshielded Twisted Pair)

UTP (**unshielded twisted pair**) cabling consists of one or more insulated wire pairs encased in a plastic sheath. As its name implies, UTP does not contain additional shielding for the twisted pairs. As a result, UTP is both less expensive and less resistant to noise than STP. Figure 3-21 depicts a typical UTP cable.

Earlier, you learned that the TIA/EIA consortium designated standards for twisted pair wiring. To manage network cabling, you need to be familiar with the standards for use on modern networks, particularly Cat 3 and Cat 5 or higher:

- *Cat 3 (Category 3)*—A form of UTP that contains four wire pairs and can carry up to 10 Mbps of data with a possible bandwidth of 16MHz. Cat 3 has typically been used

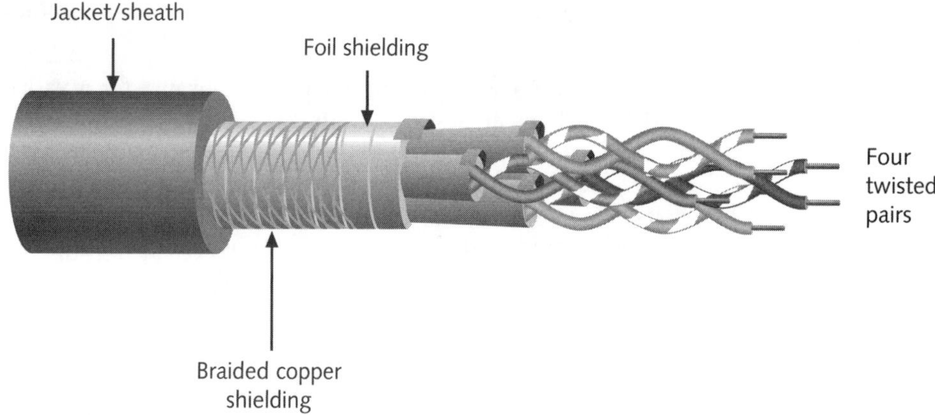

Figure 3-20 STP cable

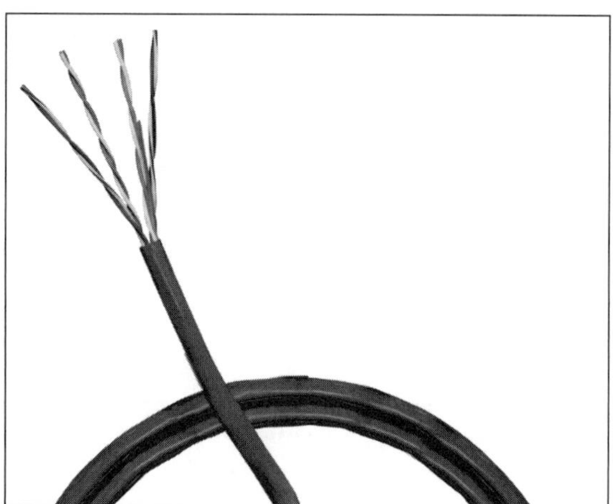

Figure 3-21 UTP cable

for 10Mbps Ethernet or 4Mbps token ring networks. Where it remains, network administrators are replacing their existing Cat 3 cabling with Cat 5 or better cabling to accommodate higher throughput.

- *Cat 4 (Category 4)*—A form of UTP that contains four wire pairs and can support up to 16Mbps throughput. Uncommon on new networks, Cat 4 may be found on older 16Mbps token ring or 10Mbps Ethernet networks. It is guaranteed for signals as high as 20MHz and provides more protection against cross talk and attenuation than Cat 3.

- *Cat 5 (Category 5)*—A form of UTP that contains four wire pairs and supports up to 1,000Mbps throughput and a 100MHz signal rate. Figure 3-22 depicts a typical Cat 5 UTP cable with its twisted pairs untwisted, allowing you to see their matched color coding. For example, the wire that is colored solid orange is twisted around the wire that is part orange and part white to form the pair responsible for transmitting data.

2.1

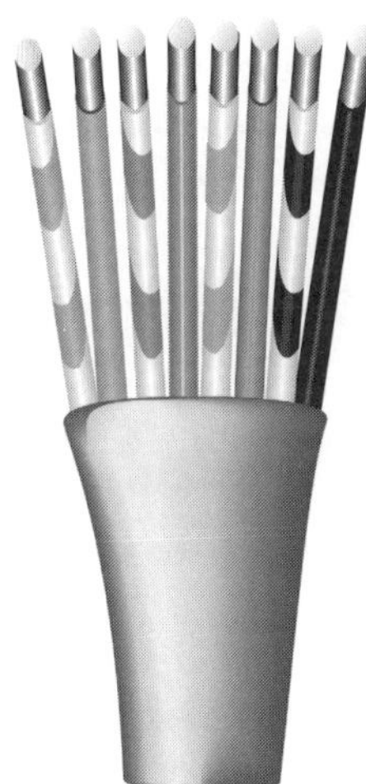

Figure 3-22 A Cat 5 UTP cable with pairs untwisted

It can be difficult to tell the difference between four-pair Cat 3 cables and four-pair Cat 5 or Cat 5e cables. However, some visual clues can help. On Cat 5 cable, the jacket is usually stamped with the manufacturer's name and cable type, including the Cat 5 specification. A cable whose jacket has no markings is more likely to be Cat 3. Also, pairs in Cat 5 cables have a significantly higher twist ratio than pairs in Cat 3 cables. Although Cat 3 pairs might be twisted as few as three times per foot, Cat 5 pairs are twisted at least 12 times per foot. Other clues, such as the date of installation (old cable is more likely to be Cat 3), the looseness of the jacket (Cat 3's jacket is typically looser than Cat 5's), and the extent to which pairs are untwisted before a termination (Cat 5 can tolerate only a small amount of untwisting) are also helpful, though less definitive.

- *Cat 5e (Enhanced Category 5)*—A higher-grade version of Cat 5 wiring that contains high-quality copper, offers a high twist ratio, and uses advanced methods for reducing cross talk. Cat 5e can support a signaling rate as high as 350MHz, more than triple the capability of regular Cat 5.

- *Cat 6 (Category 6)*—A twisted pair cable that contains four wire pairs, each wrapped in foil insulation. Additional foil insulation covers the bundle of wire pairs, and a fire-resistant plastic sheath covers the second foil layer. The foil insulation provides excellent resistance to cross talk and enables Cat 6 to support a 250MHz signaling rate and at least six times the throughput supported by regular Cat 5.

- *Cat 6e (Enhanced Category 6)*—A higher-grade version of Cat 6 wiring that reduces attenuation and cross talk and allows for potentially exceeding traditional network segment length limits. Cat 6e is capable of a 550MHz signaling rate and can reliably transmit data at multi-Gigabit per second rates.

- *Cat 7 (Category 7)*—A twisted pair cable that contains multiple wire pairs, each surrounded by its own shielding, and then packaged in additional shielding beneath the sheath. Although standards have not yet been finalized for Cat 7, cable supply companies are selling it, and some organizations are installing it. One advantage to Cat 7 cabling is that it can support signal rates up to 1GHz. However, it requires different connectors than other versions of UTP because its twisted pairs must be more isolated from each other to ward off cross talk. Because of its added shielding, Cat 7 cabling is also larger and less flexible than other versions of UTP cable. Cat 7 is uncommon on modern networks, but it will likely become popular as the final standard is released and network equipment is upgraded.

Technically, because Cat 6 and Cat 7 contain wires that are individually shielded, they are not unshielded twisted pair. Instead, they are more similar to shielded twisted pair.

UTP cabling may be used with any one of several IEEE physical layer networking standards that specify throughput maximums of 10, 100, 1,000, and even 10,000Mbps. These standards are described in detail in Chapter 5.

Comparing STP and UTP

STP and UTP share several characteristics. The following list highlights their similarities and differences:

- *Throughput*—STP and UTP can both transmit data at 10Mbps, 100Mbps, 1Gbps, and 10Gbps, depending on the grade of cabling and the transmission method in use.

- *Cost*—STP and UTP vary in cost, depending on the grade of copper used, the category rating, and any enhancements. Typically, STP is more expensive than UTP because it contains more materials and it has a lower demand. It also requires grounding, which can lead to more expensive installation. High-grade UTP can be expensive too, however. For example, Cat 6e costs more per foot than Cat 5 cabling.

- *Connector*—STP and UTP use **RJ-45 (Registered Jack 45)** modular connectors and data jacks, which look similar to analog telephone connectors and jacks. However, telephone connections follow the **RJ-11 (Registered Jack 11)** standard. Figure 3-23 shows a close-up of an RJ-45 connector for a cable containing four wire pairs. For comparison, this figure also shows a traditional RJ-11 phone line connector. All types of Ethernet that rely on twisted pair cabling use RJ-45 connectors.

Figure 3-23 RJ-45 and RJ-11 connectors

- *Noise immunity*—Because of its shielding, STP is more noise resistant than UTP. On the other hand, signals transmitted over UTP may be subject to filtering and balancing techniques to offset the effects of noise.

- *Size and scalability*—The maximum segment length for both STP and UTP is 100m, or 328 feet, on Ethernet networks that support data rates from 1Mbps to 10Gbps. These accommodate a maximum of 1024 nodes. (However, attaching so many nodes to a segment is very impractical, as it would slow traffic and make management nearly impossible.)

Terminating Twisted Pair Cable

Imagine you have been sent to one of your employer's remote offices and charged with upgrading all the old Cat 3 patch cables in a data closet with new, Cat 6 patch cables. A **patch cable** is a relatively short (usually between 3 and 25 feet) length of cabling with connectors at both ends. Based on the company's network documentation, you brought 50 premade cables with RJ-45 plugs on both ends, which you purchased from an online cable vendor. At the remote location, however, you discover that its data closet actually contains 60 patch cables that need replacing. No additional premade cables are available at that office, and you don't have time to order more. Luckily, you have brought your networking tool kit with spare RJ-45 plugs and a spool of Cat 6 cable. Knowing how to properly terminate Cat 6 cables allows you to make all the new patch cables you need and complete your work. Even if you are never faced with this situation, it's likely that at some point you will have to replace an RJ-45 connector on an existing cable. This section describes how to terminate twisted pair cable.

Proper cable termination is a basic requirement for two nodes on a network to communicate. Beyond that, however, poor terminations can lead to loss or noise—and consequently, errors—in a signal. Closely following termination standards, then, is critical. TIA/EIA has specified two different methods of inserting twisted pair wires into RJ-45 plugs: TIA/EIA 568A and TIA/EIA 568B. Functionally, there is no difference between the standards. You only have to be certain that you use the same standard on every RJ-45 plug and jack on your network, so that data is transmitted and received correctly. Figure 3-24 depicts pin numbers and assignments (or pinouts) for the TIA/EIA 568A standard when used on an Ethernet network. Figure 3-25 depicts pin numbers and assignments for the TIA/EIA 568B standard. (Although networking professionals commonly refer to wires in Figures 3-24 and 3-25 as *transmit* and *receive*, their original *T* and *R* designations stand for *Tip* and *Ring*, terms that come from early telephone technology but are irrelevant today.)

If you terminate the RJ-45 plugs at both ends of a patch cable identically, following one of the TIA/EIA 568 standards, you will create a **straight-through cable**. A straight-through cable is so named because it allows signals to pass "straight through" from one end to the other. This is the type used to connect a workstation to a hub or router, for example. However, in some cases you may want to reverse the pin locations of some wires—for example, when you want to connect two workstations without using a connectivity device or when you want to connect two hubs through their data ports. This can be accomplished through the use of a **crossover cable**, a patch cable in which the termination locations of the transmit and receive wires on one end of the cable are reversed, as shown in Figure 3-26. In this example, the TIA/EIA 568B standard is used on the left side, whereas the TIA/EIA 568A standard is used on the right side. Notice that only pairs 2 and 3 are switched, because those are the pairs sending and receiving data.

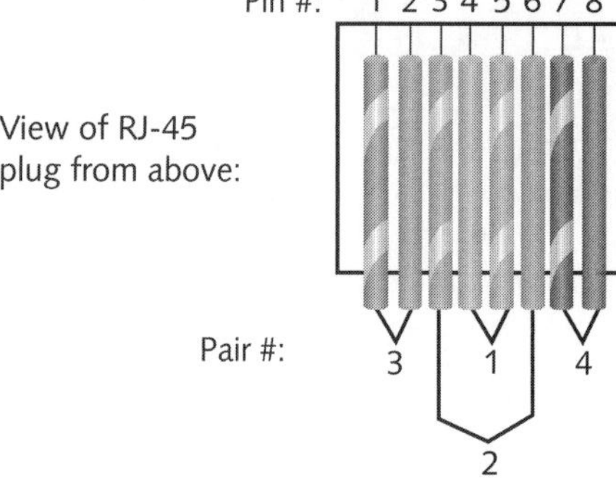

Pin #	Color	Pair #	Function
1	White with green stripe	3	Transmit +
2	Green	3	Transmit -
3	White with orange stripe	2	Receive +
4	Blue	1	Unused
5	White with blue stripe	1	Unused
6	Orange	2	Receive -
7	White with brown stripe	4	Unused
8	Brown	4	Unused

Figure 3-24 TIA/EIA 568A standard terminations

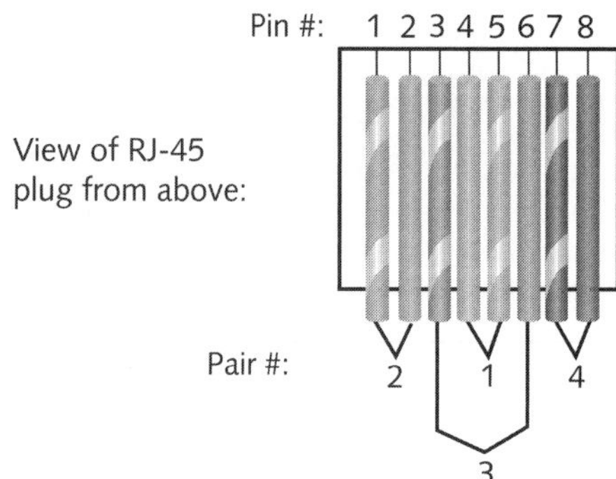

Pin #	Color	Pair #	Function
1	White with orange stripe	2	Transmit +
2	Orange	2	Transmit -
3	White with green stripe	3	Receive +
4	Blue	1	Unused
5	White with blue stripe	1	Unused
6	Green	3	Receive -
7	White with brown stripe	4	Unused
8	Brown	4	Unused

Figure 3-25 TIA/EIA 568B standard terminations

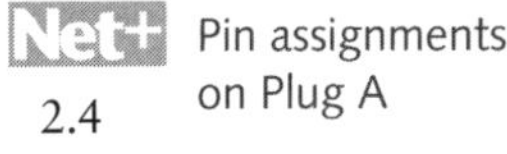

Pin assignments
on Plug A

Pin assignments
on Plug B (reversed)

Figure 3-26 RJ-45 terminations on a crossover cable

The tools you'll need to terminate a twisted-pair cable with an RJ-45 plug are a wire cutter, wire stripper, and crimping tool, which are pictured in Figures 3-27, 3-28, and 3-29, respectively. (In fact, you can find a single device that contains all three of these tools.)

Following are the steps to create a straight-through patch cable. To create a crossover cable, you would simply reorder the wires in step 4 to match Figure 3-26. The process of fixing wires inside the connector is called crimping, and it is a skill that requires practice—so don't be discouraged if the first cable you create doesn't reliably transmit and receive data.

1. Using the wire cutter, make a clean cut at both ends of the twisted-pair cable.

2. Using the wire stripper, remove the sheath off of one end of the twisted-pair cable, beginning at approximately one inch from the end. Be careful to neither damage nor remove the insulation that's on the twisted pairs inside.

3. Separate the four wire pairs slightly. Carefully unwind each pair no more than ½ inch.

4. To make a straight-through cable, align all eight wires on a flat surface, one next to the other, ordered according to their colors and positions listed in Figure 3-25. (It might be

Figure 3-27 Wire cutter

Figure 3-28 Wire stripper

Figure 3-29 Crimping tool

helpful first to "groom"—or pull steadily across the length of—the unwound section of each wire to straighten it out and help it stay in place.)

5. Keeping the wires in order and in line, gently slide them all the way into their positions in the RJ-45 plug.

6. After the wires are fully inserted, place the RJ-45 plug in the crimping tool and press firmly to crimp the wires into place. (Be careful not to rotate your hand or the wire as you do this; otherwise, only some of the wires will be properly terminated.) Crimping causes the internal RJ-45 pins to pierce the insulation of the wire, thus creating contact between the two conductors.

7. Now remove the RJ-45 connector from the crimping tool. Examine the end and see whether each wire appears to be in contact with the pin. It may be difficult to tell simply by looking at the connector. The real test is whether your cable will successfully transmit and receive signals.

8. Repeat steps 2 through 7 for the other end of the cable. After completing step 7 for the other end, you will have created a straight-through patch cable.

Even after you feel confident making your own cables, it's a good idea to verify that they can transmit and receive data at the necessary rates using a cable tester. Cable testing is discussed in Chapter 13.

In this section you've learned about twisted pair wiring, the most common network transmission medium in use today. The next section describes a transmission medium that, due to its many advantages, is enjoying ever-growing popularity.

Fiber-Optic Cable

Fiber-optic cable, or simply *fiber*, contains one or several glass or plastic fibers at its center, or **core**. Data is transmitted via pulsing light sent from a laser (in the case of 1- and 10-Gigabit technologies) or an LED (light-emitting diode) through the central fibers. Surrounding the fibers is a layer of glass or plastic called **cladding**. The cladding has a different density from the glass or plastic in the strands. It reflects light back to the core in patterns that vary depending on the transmission mode. This reflection allows the fiber to bend around corners without diminishing the integrity of the light-based signal. Outside the cladding, a plastic buffer protects the cladding and core. Because the buffer is opaque, it also absorbs any light that might escape. To prevent the cable from stretching, and to protect the inner core further, strands of Kevlar (a polymeric fiber) surround the plastic buffer. Finally, a plastic sheath covers the strands of Kevlar. Figure 3-30 shows a fiber-optic cable with multiple, insulated fibers.

Like twisted pair and coaxial cabling, fiber-optic cabling comes in a number of different varieties, depending on its intended use and the manufacturer. For example, fiber-optic cables used to connect the facilities of large telephone and data carriers may contain as many as 1,000 fibers and be heavily sheathed to prevent damage from extreme environmental conditions. At the other end of the spectrum, fiber-optic patch cables for use on LANs may contain only two strands of fiber and be pliable enough to wrap around your hand.

However, all fiber cable variations fall into two categories: single-mode and multimode.

SMF (Single-Mode Fiber)

SMF (single-mode fiber) uses a narrow core (less than 10 microns in diameter) through which light generated by a laser travels over one path, reflecting very little. Because it reflects little, the light does not disperse as the signal travels along the fiber. This continuity allows single-mode fiber to accommodate the highest bandwidths and longest distances (without requiring repeaters) of all network transmission media. Single-mode fiber may be used to connect a carrier's two facilities. However, it costs too much to be considered for use on

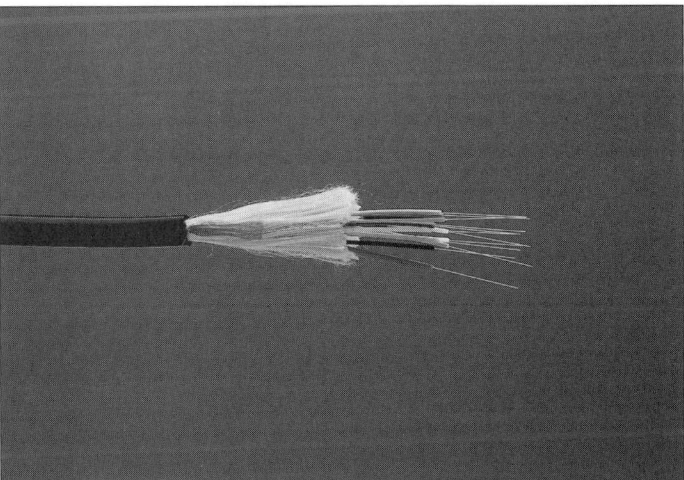

Figure 3-30 A fiber-optic cable

Net+
2.1

typical LANs and WANs. Figure 3-31 depicts a simplified version of how signals travel over single-mode fiber.

Net+ MMF (Multimode Fiber)

2.1

MMF (multimode fiber) contains a core with a larger diameter than single-mode fiber (between 50 and 115 microns in diameter; the most common size is 62.5 microns) over which many pulses of light generated by a laser or LED travel at different angles. It is commonly found on cables that connect a router to a switch or a server on the backbone of a network. Figure 3-32 depicts a simplified view of how signals travel over multimode fiber.

Because of its reliability, fiber is currently used primarily as a cable that connects the many segments of a network. Fiber-optic cable provides the following benefits over copper cabling:

- Extremely high throughput
- Very high resistance to noise
- Excellent security
- Ability to carry signals for much longer distances before requiring repeaters than copper cable
- Industry standard for high-speed networking

The most significant drawback to the use of fiber is that covering a certain distance with fiber-optic cable is much more expensive than using twisted pair cable. Also, fiber-optic cable requires special equipment to splice, which means that quickly repairing a fiber-optic

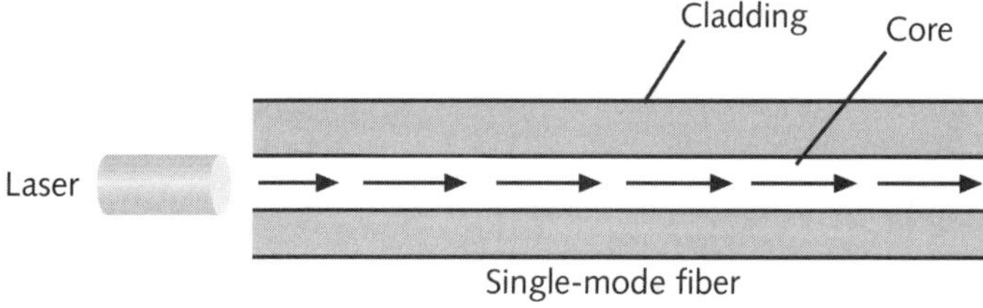

Figure 3-31 Transmission over single-mode fiber-optic cable

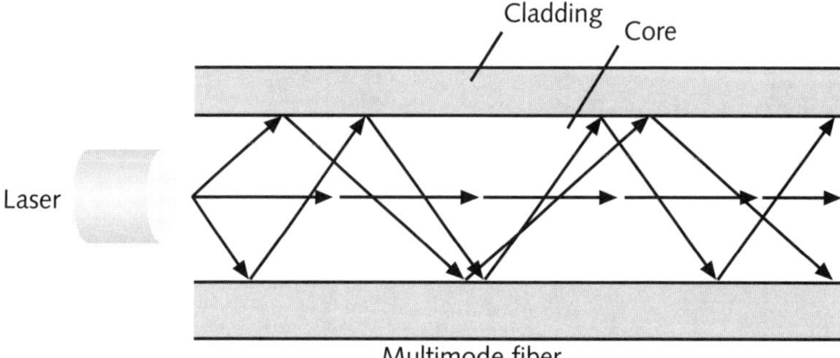

Figure 3-32 Transmission over multimode fiber-optic cable

2.1

cable in the field (given little time or resources) can be difficult. Fiber's characteristics are summarized in the following list:

- *Throughput*—Fiber has proved reliable in transmitting data at rates that can reach 100 gigabits (or 100,000 megabits) per second per channel. (Rates demanded by most networks are lower, however.) Fiber's amazing throughput is partly due to the physics of light traveling through glass. Unlike electrical pulses traveling over copper, the light experiences virtually no resistance. Therefore, light-based signals can be transmitted at faster rates and with fewer errors than electrical pulses. In fact, a pure glass strand can accept up to 1 billion laser light pulses per second. Its high throughput capability makes it suitable for network backbones and for serving applications that generate a great deal of traffic, such as video or audio conferencing.

- *Cost*—Fiber-optic cable is the most expensive transmission medium. Because of its cost, most organizations find it impractical to run fiber to every desktop. Not only is the cable itself more expensive than copper cabling, but fiber-optic NICs and hubs can cost as much as five times more than NICs and hubs designed for UTP networks. In addition, hiring skilled fiber cable installers costs more than hiring twisted pair cable installers.

2.1

2.2

- *Connector*—With fiber cabling, you can use any of 10 different types of connectors. Figures 3-33, 3-34, 3-35, and 3-36 show four of the most common connector types: the **ST (straight tip)**, **SC (subscriber connector or standard connector)**, **LC (local connector)**, and **MT-RJ (mechanical transfer registered jack)**. Each of these connectors can be obtained for single-mode or multimode fiber-optic cable. Existing fiber networks typically use ST or SC connectors. However, LC and MT-RJ connectors are used on the very latest fiber-optic technology. LC and MT-RJ connectors are preferable to ST and SC connectors because of their smaller size, which allows for a higher density of connections at each termination point. The MT-RJ connector is unique because it contains two strands of multimode fiber in a single **ferrule**, which is a short tube within a connector that encircles the fiber and keeps it properly aligned. With two strands in each ferrule, a single MT-RJ connector provides for a duplex signaling.

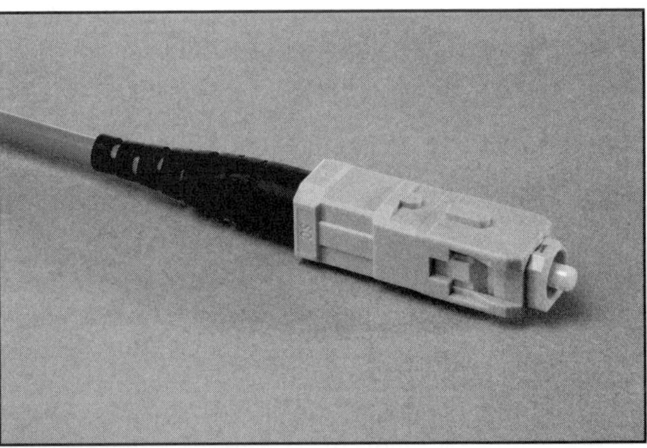

Figure 3-33 ST (straight tip) connector

Net+

2.1

2.2

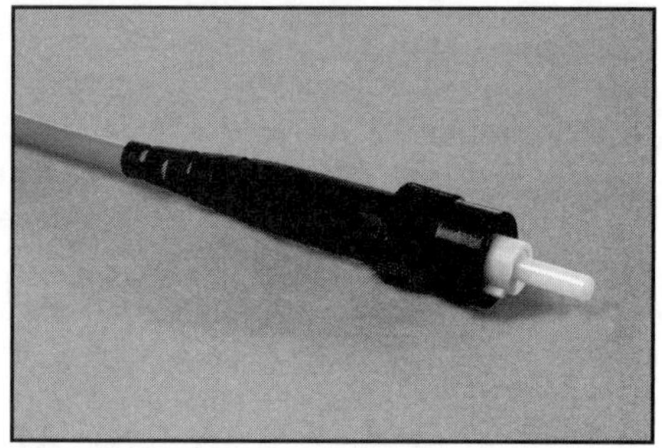

Figure 3-34 SC (subscriber connector or standard connector)

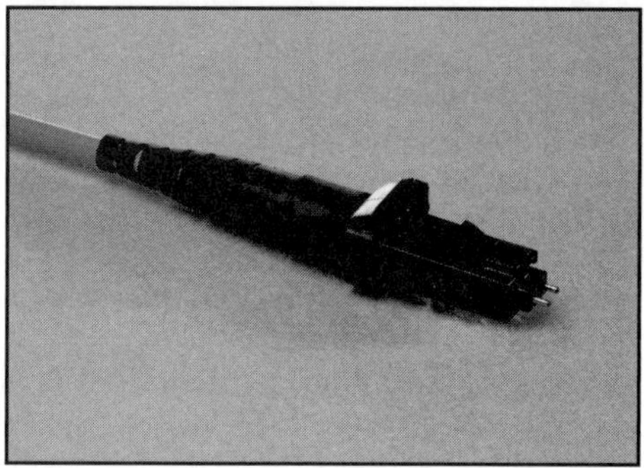

Figure 3-35 LC (local connector)

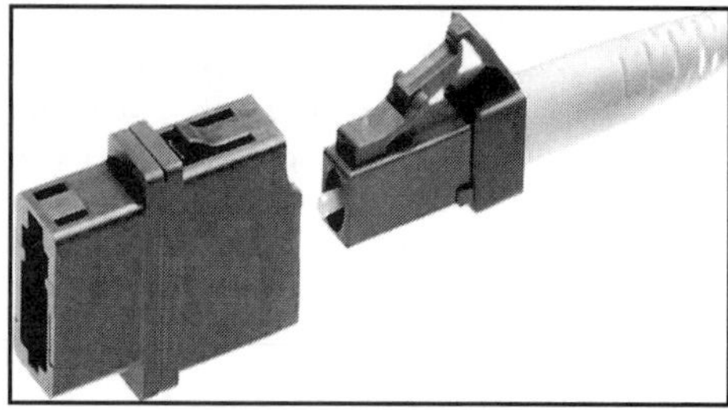

Figure 3-36 MT-RJ (mechanical transfer-register jack) connector

Net+

2.1

- *Noise immunity*—Because fiber does not conduct electrical current to transmit signals, it is unaffected by EMI. Its impressive noise resistance is one reason why fiber can span such long distances before it requires repeaters to regenerate its signal.

- *Size and scalability*—Depending on the type of fiber-optic cable used, segment lengths vary from 150 to 40,000 meters. This limit is due primarily to **optical loss**, or the degradation of the light signal after it travels a certain distance away from its source (just as the light of a flashlight dims after a certain number of feet). Optical loss accrues over long distances and grows with every connection point in the fiber network. Dust or oil in a connection (for example, from people handling the fiber while splicing it) can further exacerbate optical loss.

DTE (Data Terminal Equipment) and DCE (Data Circuit-Terminating Equipment) Connector Cables

Net+
2.1

So far you have learned about the kinds of physical media used between connectivity devices and with nodes on a LAN or WAN. This section describes some common cable types used to connect **DTE** (**data terminal equipment**) and **DCE** (**data circuit-terminating equipment**) found on a network. DTE refers to any end-user device, such as a workstation, a terminal (essentially a monitor with little or no independent data-processing capability), or a console (for example, the user interface for a router). DCE refers to a device, such as a multiplexer or modem, that processes signals. Importantly, DCE also supplies a clock signal to synchronize transmission between DTE and DCE. Most connectivity devices, such as routers and switches, can be configured to act as DTE or DCE, depending on the context in which they're used.

DTE and DCE are connected through special, typically short, cables that attach to the equipment's serial interface. **Serial** refers to a style of data transmission in which the pulses that represent bits follow one another along a single transmission line. In other words, they are issued sequentially, not simultaneously. A **serial cable** is one that carries serial transmissions. Several types of serial cables exist.

Net+
2.1
2.2

EIA/TIA has codified a popular serial data transmission method known as **RS-232 (Recommended Standard 232)**. This physical layer standard specifies, among other things, signal voltage and timing, plus the characteristics of compatible interfaces. Different connector types comply with this standard, including RJ-45 connectors, **DB-9 connectors**, and **DB-25 connectors**. You are already familiar with RJ-45 plugs. Figures 3-37 and 3-38 illustrate male DB-9 and DB-25 connectors, respectively. Notice that the arrangement of the pins on both connectors resembles a sideways letter D. Also notice that a DB-9 connector contains 9 contact points and a DB-25 connector contains 25.

You might connect a workstation (DTE) and an external modem (DCE) using RS-232. This was its primary use for many years. However, as an administrator on today's networks, you're more likely to use an RS-232 connection between a PC and a router to make your PC act as a console for configuring and managing that router. In fact, a higher-end router designed for use in your data center (not the kind of router you'd use at home) usually

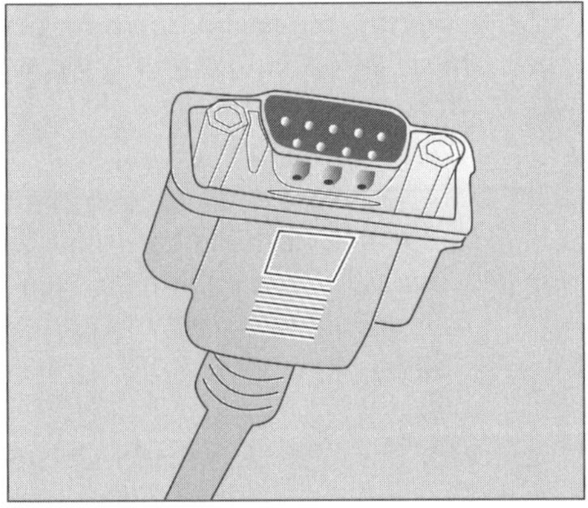

Figure 3-37 DB-9 connector

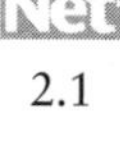

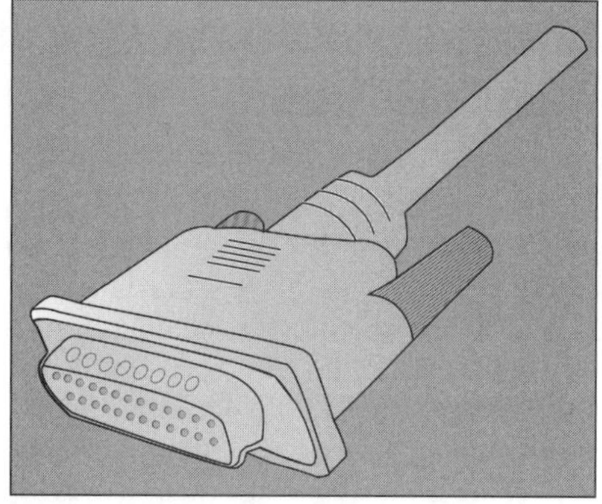

Figure 3-38 DB-25 connector

comes with an RS-232-compatible cable. The serial interface on the back of the connectivity device is often labeled "Console." (This is not to say that a serial cable is the only way of connecting to a router for configuring and managing it. However, if the router is brand new or for some other reason lacks an IP address, you need to access it directly, and not via a network connection.)

You can find RS-232 cables with different types of connectors at either end. For example, many Cisco routers come with a console port that's RJ-45 compliant. If you wanted to connect such a router to your laptop's DB-9 serial port, you could find an RS-232 cable with an RJ-45 plug on one end and a DB-9 plug on the other.

The fact that a serial cable terminates in an RJ-45 connector does not mean it will work if plugged into a device's RJ-45 Ethernet port! When using a serial cable with an RJ-45 connector, be certain to plug it into the appropriate serial interface.

In addition to using different connector types, the termination points on RS-232 cables can be arranged in various ways, depending on the cable's purpose. Earlier you learned about the difference between straight-through and crossover cables in the context of terminating twisted pair cables. An RS-232 cable, whether it uses DB-9, DB-25, or RJ-45 connectors, can also be straight-through. You also have the option of reversing the transmit and receive pins on one end, thereby making it into a crossover cable. Among other things, you could use such a crossover cable to directly connect two routers via their serial interfaces.

Yet another type of cable is a **rollover cable** (or rolled over cable). In a rollover cable, the usual wire positions are exactly reversed in one of the two RJ-45 terminations. (Imagine you were making a cable according to the steps described earlier in this chapter and flipped one end upside-down before inserting it into the RJ-45 jack.) Rollover cables are mainly used to connect a console to a connectivity device, such as a router. Do not confuse them with crossover cables, which reverse the transmit and receive pairs (pinouts 1, 2, 3 and 6) from one end of a cable to the other.

You'll learn more about the connectivity devices, such as routers and switches, that use DTE and DCE connector cables in Chapter 6. The following section describes how to arrange physical networking media between end users and connectivity devices on a LAN or WAN.

Structured Cabling

Net+
2.8

Organizations that pay attention to their **cable plant**—the hardware that makes up the enterprise-wide cabling system—are apt to experience fewer physical layer network problems, smoother network expansions, and simpler network troubleshooting. Following the cabling standards and best practices described in this chapter can help.

If you were to tour hundreds of data centers and equipment rooms at established enterprises, you would see similar cabling arrangements. That's because most organizations follow a cabling standard. One popular standard is TIA/EIA's joint 568 Commercial Building Wiring Standard, also known as **structured cabling**, for uniform, enterprise-wide, multivendor cabling systems. The standard suggests how networking media can best be installed to maximize performance and minimize upkeep. Structured cabling applies no matter what type of media or transmission technology a network uses. (It does, however, assume a network based on the star topology.) In other words, it's designed to work just as well for 10Mbps networks as it does for 10Gbps networks. Structured cabling is based on a hierarchical design that begins where a telecommunications company's service enters a building and ends at a user's workstation. Figure 3-39 illustrates the different components of structured cabling in an enterprise from a bird's eye view. Figure 3-40 gives a glimpse of how structured cabling appears within a building (in this case, one that is not part of a larger, enterprise-wide network). Detailed descriptions of the components referenced in these figures follow:

- *Entrance facilities*—The facilities necessary for a service provider (whether it is a local phone company, Internet service provider, or long-distance carrier) to connect with another organization's LAN or WAN. Entrance facilities may include fiber-optic cable and multiplexers, coaxial cable, UTP, satellite or wireless transceivers, and other devices or cabling. If the entrance facilities are supplied by a telecommunications carrier and rely on UTP, they may come in the form of 25-pair wire. As the name suggests, **25-pair wire** is a bundle of 25 wire pairs. As you might expect, **100-pair wire** contains 100 twisted wire pairs. More commonly, however, entrance facilities depend

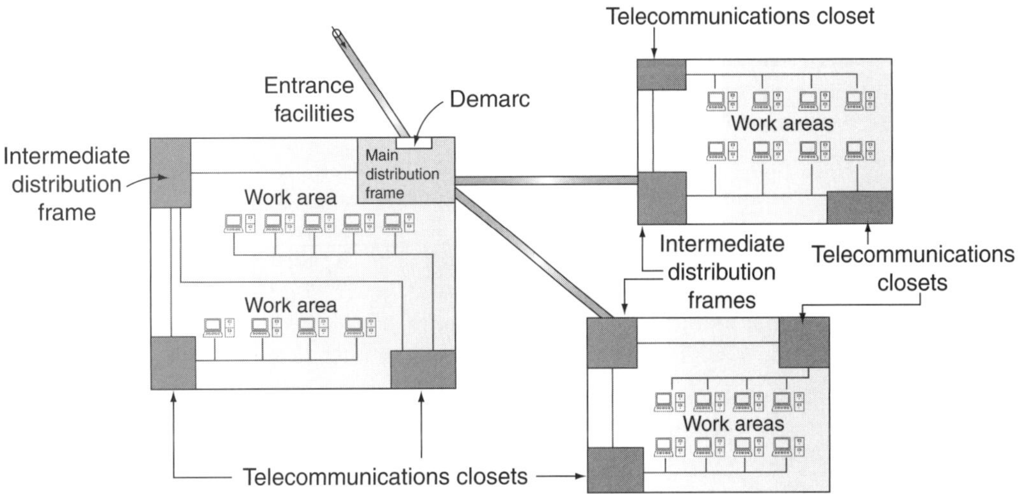

Figure 3-39 TIA/EIA structured cabling in an enterprise

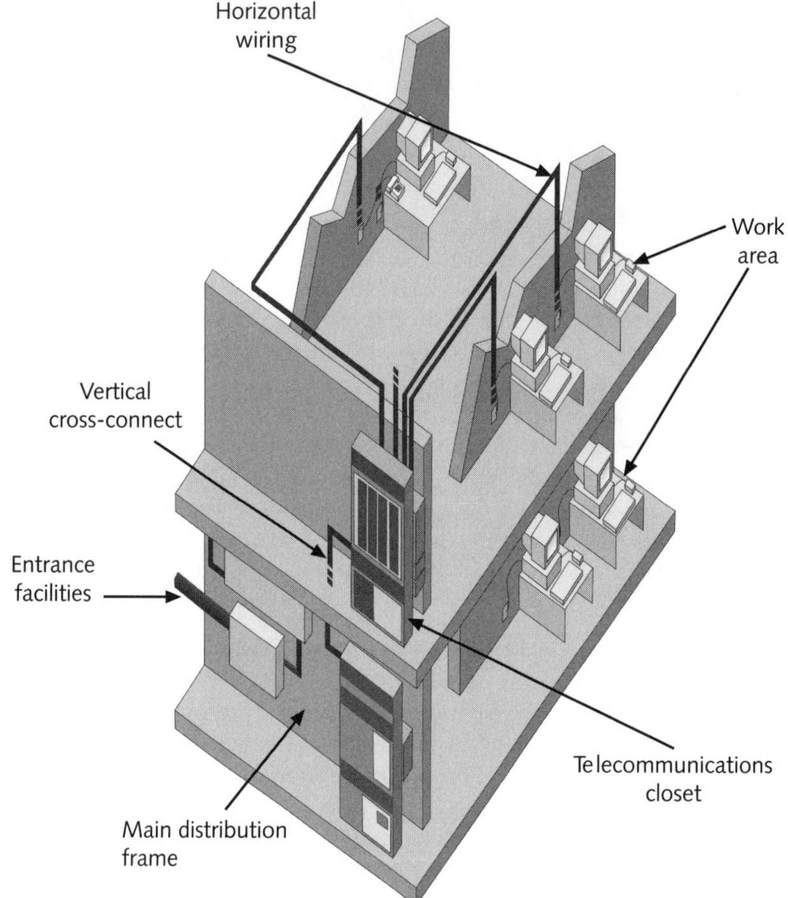

Figure 3-40 TIA/EIA structured cabling in a building

on fiber-optic cable. The entrance facility designates where the telecommunications service provider accepts responsibility for the (external) connection. The point of division between the service provider's network and the internal network is also known as the **demarcation point** (or **demarc**).

- *MDF (main distribution frame)*—Also known as the **main cross-connect**, the first point of interconnection between an organization's LAN or WAN and a service provider's facility. An MDF typically includes connectivity devices, such as switches and routers, and media, such as fiber-optic cable, capable of the greatest throughput. Often, it also houses an organization's main servers. In an enterprise-wide network, equipment in an MDF connects to equipment housed in another building's IDF. Sometimes the MDF is simply known as the computer room or equipment room.

- *Cross-connect facilities*—The points where circuits interconnect with other circuits. For example, when an MDF accepts UTP from a service provider, the wire pairs terminate at a punch-down block. A **punch-down block** is a panel of data receptors into which twisted pair wire is inserted, or punched down, to complete a circuit. Punch-down blocks were for many years the standard method of terminating telephone circuits,

Net+

2.8

the best known type being a **66 block**. Another, known as the **100 block**, meets standards for Cat 5 or better UTP terminations, and therefore, is used on data networks. Note that both 66 block and 100 block versions are available in several different capacities. That is, their numerical designation does not represent the number of wire pairs each can terminate. From a punch-down block, wires are distributed to a **patch panel**, a wall-mounted panel of data receptors. Figure 3-41 shows a patch panel and Figure 3-42 shows a punch-down block. A patch panel allows the insertion of patch cables. Note that cross-connect facilities are not limited to the MDF and may be used in other equipment rooms that are part of a building's cable infrastructure.

- *IDF (intermediate distribution frame)*—A junction point between the MDF and concentrations of fewer connections—for example, those that terminate in a telecommunications closet.

- *Backbone wiring*—The cables or wireless links that provide interconnection between entrance facilities and MDFs, MDFs and IDFs, and IDFs and telecommunications closets. One component of the backbone is given a special term: **vertical cross-connect**. A vertical cross-connect runs between a building's floors. For example, it might connect an MDF and IDF or IDFs and telecommunications closets (described next) within a

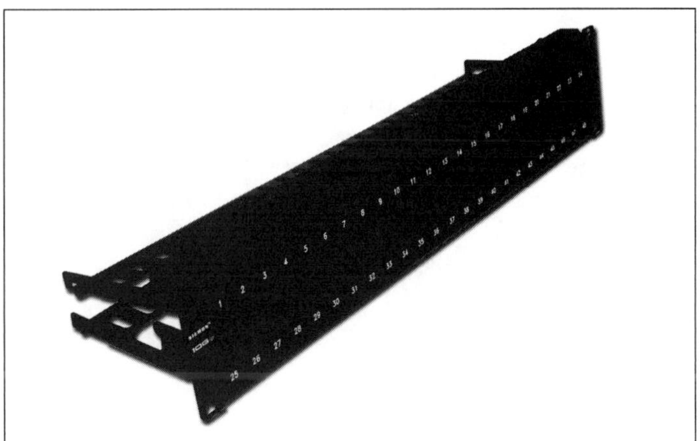

Figure 3-41 Patch panel

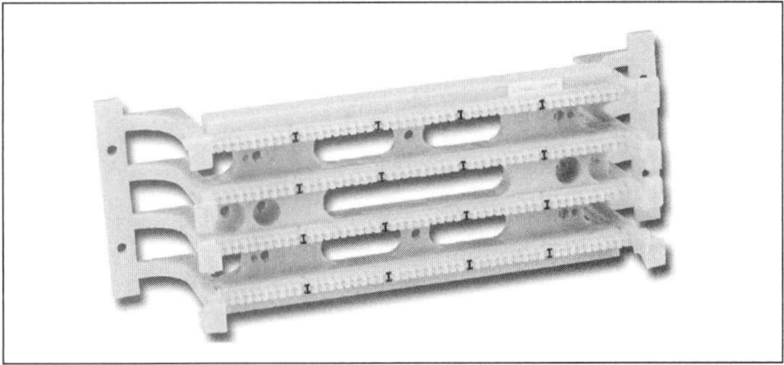

Figure 3-42 Punch-down block

building. The TIA/EIA standard designates distance limitations for backbones of varying cable types, as specified in Table 3-2. On modern networks, backbones are usually composed of fiber-optic or UTP cable.

- *Telecommunications closet*—Also known as a "telco room," it contains connectivity for groups of workstations in its area, plus cross-connections to IDFs or, in smaller organizations, an MDF. Large organizations may have several telco rooms per floor, but the TIA/EIA standard specifies at least one per floor. Telecommunications closets typically house patch panels, punch-down blocks, and connectivity devices for a work area. Because telecommunications closets are usually small, enclosed spaces, good cooling and ventilation systems are important to maintaining a constant temperature.

- *Horizontal wiring*—This is the wiring that connects workstations to the closest telecommunications closet. TIA/EIA recognizes three possible cabling types for horizontal wiring: STP, UTP or fiber-optic cable. The maximum allowable distance for horizontal wiring is 100m. This span includes 90m to connect a data jack on the wall to the telecommunications closet plus a maximum of 10m to connect a workstation to the data jack on the wall. Figure 3-43 depicts a horizontal wiring configuration.

- *Work area*—An area that encompasses all patch cables and horizontal wiring necessary to connect workstations, printers, and other network devices from their NICs to the telecommunications closet. The TIA/EIA standard calls for each wall jack to contain at least one voice and one data outlet, as pictured in Figure 3-44. Realistically,

Table 3-2 TIA/EIA Specifications for Backbone Cabling

Cable Type	Cross-Connects to Telecommunications Closet	MDF or IDF to Telecommunications Closet	Cross-Connects to IDF or MDF
UTP	800m (voice specification)	500m	300m
Single-mode fiber	3,000m	500m	1,500m
Multimode fiber	2,000m	500m	1,500m

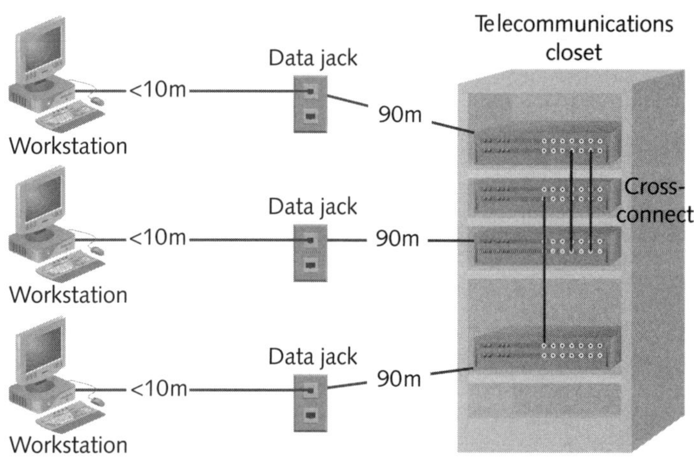

Figure 3-43 Horizontal wiring

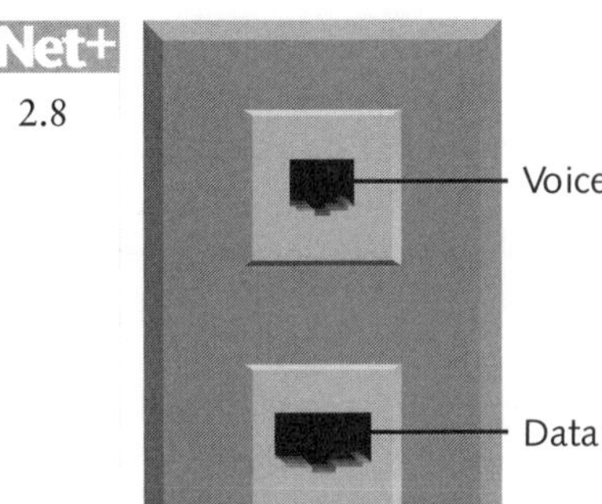

Figure 3-44 A standard TIA/EIA outlet

you will encounter a variety of wall jacks. For example, in a student computer lab lacking phones, a wall jack with a combination of voice and data outlets is unnecessary.

Figure 3-45 illustrates a cable installation using UTP from the telecommunications closet to the work area.

Knowing the standards for cabling a building or enterprise is key, but until you have practiced terminating, running, and testing cables, this knowledge is only theoretical. The following section provides some practical information that you can apply when working with physical networking media.

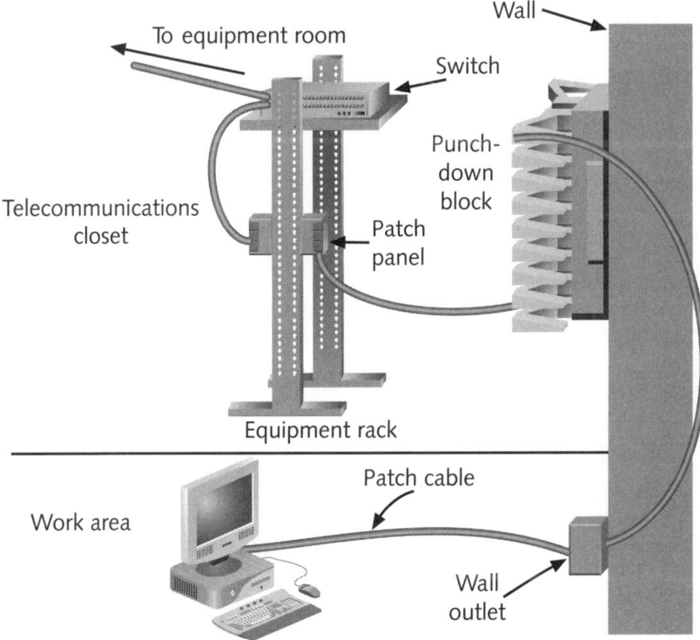

Figure 3-45 A typical UTP cabling installation

Best Practices for Cable Installation and Management

So far, you have read about the variety of cables used in networking and the limitations inherent in each. You may worry that with hundreds of varieties of cable, choosing the correct one and making it work with your network is next to impossible. The good news is that if you follow both the manufacturers' installation guidelines and the TIA/EIA standards, you are almost guaranteed success. Many network problems can be traced to poor cable installation techniques. For example, if you don't crimp twisted pair wires in the correct position in an RJ-45 connector, the cable will fail to transmit or receive data (or both—in which case, the cable will not function at all). Installing the wrong grade of cable can either cause your network to fail or render it more susceptible to damage.

The art of proper cabling could fill an entire book. If you plan to specialize in cable installation, design, or maintenance, you should invest in a reference dedicated to this topic. As a network professional, you will likely occasionally add new cables to a room or telecommunications closet, repair defective cable ends, or install a data outlet. Following are some cable installation tips that will help prevent physical layer failures:

- Do not untwist twisted pair cables more than one-half inch before inserting them into the punch-down block.

- Do not leave more than 1 inch of exposed (stripped) cable before a twisted pair termination. Doing so will increase the possibility for cross talk and data errors.

- Pay attention to the bend radius limitations for the type of cable you are installing. **Bend radius** is the radius of the maximum arc into which you can loop a cable before you will impair data transmission. Generally, a twisted pair cable's bend radius is equal to or greater than four times the diameter of the cable. Be careful not to exceed it.

- Use a cable tester to verify that each segment of cabling you install transmits data reliably. This practice will prevent you from later having to track down errors in multiple, long stretches of cable. Chapter 13, which covers troubleshooting network problems, explains the tools and methods needed to test cable continuity.

- Avoid cinching cables so tightly that you squeeze their outer covering, a practice that leads to difficult-to-diagnose data errors.

- Avoid laying cable across the floor where it might sustain damage from rolling chairs or foot traffic. If you must take this tack, cover the cable with a cable protector.

- Install cable at least 3 feet away from fluorescent lights or other sources of EMI. This will reduce the possibility for noise to affect your network's signals.

- Always leave some slack in cable runs. Stringing cable too tightly risks connectivity and data transmission problems.

- If you run cable in the **plenum**, the area above the ceiling tile or below the subflooring, make sure the cable sheath is plenum-rated, and consult with local electric installation codes to be certain you are installing it correctly. A plenum-rated cable is more fire resistant, and if burned, produces less smoke than other cables.

- Pay attention to grounding requirements and follow them religiously.

- Adhering to structured cabling hierarchies is only part of a smart cable management strategy. You or your network manager should also specify standards for the types of cable used by your organization and maintain a list of approved cabling vendors. Keep a supply room stocked with spare parts so that you can easily and quickly replace defective parts.

- Create documentation for your cabling plant, including the locations, installation dates, lengths, and grades of installed cable. Label every data jack, punch-down block, and connector. Use color-coded cables for different purposes. (Cables can be purchased in a variety of sheath colors.) For example, you might want to use pink for patch cables, green for horizontal wiring, and gray for vertical (backbone) wiring. Be certain to document your color schemes.

- Keep your cable plant documentation in a centrally accessible location and be certain to update it as you change the network. The more you document, the easier it will be to move or add cable segments.

- Finally, create a plan for expanding your cabling plant. For example, if your organization is rapidly enlarging, consider replacing your backbone with fiber, and leave plenty of space in your telecommunications closets for more racks.

Chapter Summary

- Information can be transmitted via two methods: analog or digital. Analog signals are continuous waves that result in variable and inexact transmission. Digital signals are based on electrical or light pulses that represent information encoded in binary form.

- In half-duplex transmission, signals can travel in both directions over a medium but in only one direction at a time. When signals can travel in both directions over a medium simultaneously, the transmission is considered full-duplex.

- A form of transmission that allows multiple signals to travel simultaneously over one medium is known as multiplexing. In multiplexing, the single medium is logically separated into multiple channels, or subchannels.

- Throughput is the amount of data that the medium can transmit during a given period of time. Throughput is usually measured in bits per second and depends on the physical nature of the medium.

- Baseband is a form of transmission in which digital signals are sent through direct current pulses applied to the wire. Baseband systems can transmit only one signal, or one channel, at a time. Broadband, on the other hand, uses modulated analog frequencies to transmit multiple signals over the same wire.

- Noise is interference that distorts an analog or digital signal. It may be caused by electrical sources, such as power lines, fluorescent lights, copiers, and microwave ovens, or by broadcast signals.

- Analog and digital signals both suffer attenuation, or loss of signal, as they travel farther from their sources. To compensate, analog signals are amplified, and digital signals are regenerated through repeaters.

- Every network is susceptible to a delay between the transmission of a signal and its receipt. This delay is called latency. The length of the cable contributes to latency, as does the presence of any intervening connectivity device.

- Coaxial cable consists of a central metal conducting core (often copper) surrounded by a plastic insulator, a braided metal shielding, and an outer plastic cover called the sheath. The conducting core carries the electromagnetic signal, and the shielding acts as both a protection against noise and a ground for the signal. The insulator layer protects the copper core from the metal shielding. The sheath protects the cable from physical damage.

- Most networks no longer rely on coaxial cable; however, if you obtain Internet service from a cable company, the cable that enters your home will be a type of coax known as RG-6.

- Twisted pair cable consists of color-coded pairs of insulated copper wires, each with a diameter of 0.4 to 0.8mm, twisted around each other and encased in plastic coating.

- STP (shielded twisted pair) cable consists of twisted wire pairs that are not only individually insulated, but also surrounded by a shielding made of a metallic substance such as foil, to reduce the effects of noise on the signal.

- UTP (unshielded twisted pair) cabling consists of one or more insulated wire pairs encased in a plastic sheath. As its name suggests, UTP does not contain additional shielding for the twisted pairs. As a result, UTP is both less expensive and less resistant to noise than STP.

- Fiber-optic cable contains one or several glass or plastic fibers in its core. Data is transmitted via pulsing light sent from a laser or light-emitting diode through the central fiber(s). Outside the fiber(s), cladding reflects light back to the core in different patterns that vary depending on the transmission mode.

- Fiber-optic cable provides the benefits of very high throughput, very high resistance to noise, and excellent security.

- Fiber cable variations fall into two categories: single-mode and multimode. Single-mode fiber uses a small-diameter core, over which light travels mostly down its center, reflecting very few times. This allows single-mode fiber to accommodate high bandwidths and long distances (without requiring repeaters).

- MMF (multimode fiber) uses a core with a larger diameter, over which many pulses of light travel at different angles. Multimode fiber is less expensive than SMF (single-mode fiber).

- Serial communication is often used on short links between DTE (data terminal equipment) and DCE (data circuit-terminating equipment). For example, you might use an RS-232 serial cable to connect your laptop to a router so that you can configure the router from your laptop.

- TIA/EIA's 568 Commercial Building Wiring Standard, also known as structured cabling, provides guidelines for uniform, enterprise-wide, multivendor cabling systems. Structured cabling is based on a hierarchical design that begins with a service provider's facilities and ends at users' workstations.

- The best practice for installing cable is to follow the TIA/EIA 568 specifications and the manufacturer's recommendations. Be careful not to exceed a cable's bend radius, untwist wire pairs more than one-half inch, or remove more than one inch of insulation from copper wire. Install plenum-rated cable in ceilings and floors, and run cabling away from where it might suffer physical damage. Maintain clear, comprehensive documentation on your cable plant.

Key Terms

1 gigabit per second (Gbps)   1,000,000,000 bits per second.

1 kilobit per second (Kbps)   1,000 bits per second.

1 megabit per second (Mbps)   1,000,000 bits per second.

1 terabit per second (Tbps)   1,000,000,000,000 bits per second.

10Base-2   *See* Thinnet.

10Base-5   *See* Thicknet.

25 pair wire   UTP supplied by a telecommunications carrier that contains 25 wire pairs.

66 block   Part of an organization's cross-connect facilities, a type of punch-down block used for many years to terminate telephone circuits. It does not meet Cat 5 or better standards, so it is infrequently used on data networks.

100 block   Part of an organization's cross-connect facilities, a type of punch-down block designed to terminate Cat 5 or better twisted pair wires.

100 pair wire   UTP supplied by a telecommunications carrier that contains 100 wire pairs.

alien cross talk   EMI interference induced on one cable by signals traveling over a nearby cable.

AM (amplitude modulation)   A modulation technique in which the amplitude of the carrier signal is modified by the application of a data signal.

American Wire Gauge   *See* AWG.

amplifier   A device that boosts, or strengthens, an analog signal.

amplitude   A measure of a signal's strength.

amplitude modulation   *See* AM.

analog   A signal that uses variable voltage to create continuous waves, resulting in an inexact transmission.

attenuation   The extent to which a signal has weakened after traveling a given distance.

AWG (American Wire Gauge)   A standard rating that indicates the diameter of a wire, such as the conducting core of a coaxial cable.

bandwidth   A measure of the difference between the highest and lowest frequencies that a medium can transmit.

baseband   A form of transmission in which digital signals are sent through direct current pulses applied to a wire. This direct current requires exclusive use of the wire's capacity, so baseband systems can transmit only one signal, or one channel, at a time. Every device on a baseband system shares a single channel.

bend radius   The radius of the maximum arc into which you can loop a cable before you will cause data transmission errors. Generally, a twisted pair cable's bend radius is equal to or greater than four times the diameter of the cable.

binary   A system founded on using 1s and 0s to encode information.

bit (binary digit)   A bit equals a single pulse in the digital encoding system. It may have only one of two values: 0 or 1.

BNC (Bayonet Neill-Concelman, or British Naval Connector)   A standard for coaxial cable connectors named after its coupling method and its inventors.

BNC connector   A coaxial cable connector type that uses a twist-and-lock (or bayonet) style of coupling. It may be used with several coaxial cable types, including RG-6 and RG-59.

braiding   A braided metal shielding used to insulate some types of coaxial cable.

broadband   A form of transmission in which signals are modulated as radiofrequency analog pulses with different frequency ranges. Unlike baseband, broadband technology does not involve binary encoding. The use of multiple frequencies enables a broadband system to operate over several channels and, therefore, carry much more data than a baseband system.

broadcast   A transmission that involves one transmitter and multiple, undefined receivers.

byte   Eight bits of information. In a digital signaling system, broadly speaking, one byte carries one piece of information.

cable plant   The hardware that constitutes the enterprise-wide cabling system.

capacity   *See* throughput.

Cat   Abbreviation for the word *category* when describing a type of twisted pair cable. For example, Category 3 unshielded twisted pair cable may also be called Cat 3.

Cat 3 (Category 3)   A form of UTP that contains four wire pairs and can carry up to 10Mbps, with a possible bandwidth of 16MHz. Cat 3 has typically been used for 10Mbps Ethernet or 4Mbps token ring networks. Network administrators are gradually replacing Cat 3 cabling with Cat 5 to accommodate higher throughput. Cat 3 is less expensive than Cat 5.

Cat 4 (Category 4)   A form of UTP that contains four wire pairs and can support up to 16Mbps throughput. Cat 4 may be used for 16Mbps token ring or 10Mbps Ethernet networks. It is guaranteed for data transmission up to 20MHz and provides more protection against cross talk and attenuation than Cat 1, Cat 2, or Cat 3.

Cat 5 (Category 5)   A form of UTP that contains four wire pairs and supports up to 100Mbps throughput and a 100MHz signal rate.

Cat 5e (Enhanced Category 5)   A higher-grade version of Cat 5 wiring that contains high-quality copper, offers a high twist ratio, and uses advanced methods for reducing cross talk. Enhanced Cat 5 can support a signaling rate of up to 350MHz, more than triple the capability of regular Cat 5.

Cat 6 (Category 6)   A twisted pair cable that contains four wire pairs, each wrapped in foil insulation. Additional foil insulation covers the bundle of wire pairs, and a fire-resistant plastic sheath covers the second foil layer. The foil insulation provides excellent resistance to cross talk and enables Cat 6 to support a signaling rate of 250MHz and at least six times the throughput supported by regular Cat 5.

Cat 6e (Enhanced Category 6)   A higher-grade version of Cat 6 wiring that further reduces attenuation and cross talk and allows for potentially exceeding traditional network segment length limits. Cat 6e is capable of a 550MHz signaling rate and can reliably transmit data at multi-gigabit per second rates.

Cat 7 (Category 7)   A twisted pair cable that contains multiple wire pairs, each separately shielded and then surrounded by another layer of shielding within the jacket. Cat 7 can support up to a 1GHz signal rate. But because of its extra layers, it is less flexible than other forms of twisted pair wiring.

Category 3   *See* Cat 3.

Category 4   *See* Cat 4.

Category 5   *See* Cat 5.

Category 6   *See* Cat 6.

Category 7   *See* Cat 7.

channel   A distinct communication path between two or more nodes, much like a lane is a distinct transportation path on a freeway. Channels may be separated either logically (as in multiplexing) or physically (as when they are carried by separate wires).

cladding   The glass or plastic shield around the core of a fiber-optic cable. Cladding reflects light back to the core in patterns that vary depending on the transmission mode. This reflection allows fiber to bend around corners without impairing the light-based signal.

coaxial cable   A type of cable that consists of a central metal conducting core, which might be solid or stranded and is often made of copper, surrounded by an insulator, a braided metal shielding, called braiding, and an outer cover, called the sheath or jacket. Coaxial cable, called "coax" for short, was the foundation for Ethernet networks in the 1980s. Today it's used to connect cable Internet and cable TV systems.

conduit   The pipeline used to contain and protect cabling. Conduit is usually made from metal.

connectors   The pieces of hardware that connect the wire to the network device, be it a file server, workstation, switch, or printer.

core   The central component of a cable designed to carry a signal. The core of a fiber-optic cable, for example, consists of one or several glass or plastic fibers. The core of a coaxial copper cable consists of one large or several small strands of copper.

cross talk   A type of interference caused by signals traveling on nearby wire pairs infringing on another pair's signal.

crossover cable   A twisted pair patch cable in which the termination locations of the transmit and receive wires on one end of the cable are reversed.

data circuit-terminating equipment   *See* DCE.

data terminal equipment   *See* DTE.

DB-9 connector   A type of connector with nine pins that's commonly used in serial communication that conforms to the RS-232 standard.

DB-25 connector   A type of connector with 25 pins that's commonly used in serial communication that conforms to the RS-232 standard.

DCE (data circuit-terminating equipment)   A device, such as a multiplexer or modem, that processes signals. DCE supplies a clock signal to synchronize transmission between DTE and DCE.

demarcation point (demarc)   The point of division between a telecommunications service carrier's network and a building's internal network.

demultiplexer (demux)   A device that separates multiplexed signals once they are received and regenerates them in their original form.

dense wavelength division multiplexing   *See* DWDM.

digital   As opposed to analog signals, digital signals are composed of pulses that can have a value of only 1 or 0.

DTE (data terminal equipment)   Any end-user device, such as a workstation, terminal (essentially a monitor with little or no independent data-processing capability), or a console (for example, the user interface for a router).

duplex   *See* full-duplex.

DWDM (dense wavelength division multiplexing)   A multiplexing technique used over single-mode or multimode fiber-optic cable in which each signal is assigned a different wavelength for its carrier wave. In DWDM, little space exists between carrier waves to achieve extraordinary high capacity.

electromagnetic interference   *See* EMI.

EMI (electromagnetic interference)   A type of interference that may be caused by motors, power lines, televisions, copiers, fluorescent lights, or other sources of electrical activity.

enhanced Category 5   *See* Cat 5e.

enhanced Category 6   *See* Cat 6e.

entrance facilities   The facilities necessary for a service provider (whether it is a local phone company, Internet service provider, or long-distance carrier) to connect with another organization's LAN or WAN.

F-type connector   A connector used to terminate coaxial cable used for transmitting television and broadband cable signals.

FDM (frequency division multiplexing)   A type of multiplexing that assigns a unique frequency band to each communications subchannel. Signals are modulated with different carrier frequencies, and then they are multiplexed to simultaneously travel over a single channel.

ferrule   A short tube within a fiber-optic cable connector that encircles the fiber strand and keeps it properly aligned.

fiber-optic cable   A form of cable that contains one or several glass or plastic fibers in its core. Data is transmitted via pulsing light sent from a laser or light-emitting diode (LED) through the central fiber (or fibers). Fiber-optic cables offer significantly higher throughput than copper-based cables. They may be single-mode or multimode and typically use wave-division multiplexing to carry multiple signals.

FM (frequency modulation)   A method of data modulation in which the frequency of the carrier signal is modified by the application of the data signal.

frequency   The number of times that a signal's amplitude changes over a fixed period of time, expressed in cycles per second, or hertz (Hz).

frequency division multiplexing   *See* FDM.

frequency modulation   *See* FM.

full-duplex   A type of transmission in which signals may travel in both directions over a medium simultaneously. May also be called, simply, "duplex."

half-duplex   A type of transmission in which signals may travel in both directions over a medium, but in only one direction at a time.

hertz (Hz)   A measure of frequency equivalent to the number of amplitude cycles per second.

IDF (intermediate distribution frame)   A junction point between the MDF and concentrations of fewer connections—for example, those that terminate in a telecommunications closet.

impedance   The resistance that contributes to controlling an electrical signal. Impedance is measured in ohms.

intermediate distribution frame   *See* IDF.

latency   The delay between the transmission of a signal and its receipt.

LC (local connector)   A connector used with single-mode or multimode fiber-optic cable.

link segment   *See* unpopulated segment.

local connector   *See* LC.

main cross-connect   *See* MDF.

main distribution frame   *See* MDF.

MDF (main distribution frame)   Also known as the main cross-connect, the first point of interconnection between an organization's LAN or WAN and a service provider's facility.

mechanical transfer-registered jack   *See* MT-RJ.

media converter   A device that enables networks or segments using different media to interconnect and exchange signals.

MMF (multimode fiber)   A type of fiber-optic cable that contains a core with a diameter between 50 and 100 microns, through which many pulses of light generated by a light-emitting diode (LED) travel at different angles.

modem   A device that modulates analog signals into digital signals at the transmitting end for transmission over telephone lines, and demodulates digital signals into analog signals at the receiving end.

modulation   A technique for formatting signals in which one property of a simple carrier wave is modified by the addition of a data signal during transmission.

MT-RJ (mechanical transfer-registered jack)   A connector used with single-mode or multimode fiber-optic cable.

multimode fiber   *See* MMF.

multiplexer (mux)   A device that separates a medium into multiple channels and issues signals to each of those subchannels.

multiplexing   A form of transmission that allows multiple signals to travel simultaneously over one medium.

near end cross talk   *See* NEXT.

NEXT (near end cross talk)   Cross talk, or the impingement of the signal carried by one wire onto a nearby wire, that occurs between wire pairs near the source of a signal.

noise   The unwanted signals, or interference, from sources near network cabling, such as electrical motors, power lines, and radar.

nonbroadcast point-to-multipoint transmission   A communications arrangement in which a single transmitter issues signals to multiple, defined recipients.

optical loss   The degradation of a light signal on a fiber-optic network.

overhead   The nondata information that must accompany data for a signal to be properly routed and interpreted by the network.

patch cable   A relatively short section (usually between 3 and 25 feet) of cabling with connectors on both ends.

patch panel   A wall-mounted panel of data receptors into which cross-connect patch cables from the punch-down block are inserted.

phase   A point or stage in a wave's progress over time.

plenum   The area above the ceiling tile or below the subfloor in a building.

point-to-multipoint   A communications arrangement in which one transmitter issues signals to multiple receivers. The receivers may be undefined, as in a broadcast transmission, or defined, as in a nonbroadcast transmission.

point-to-point   A data transmission that involves one transmitter and one receiver.

populated segment   A network segment that contains end nodes, such as workstations.

punch-down block   A panel of data receptors into which twisted pair wire is inserted, or punched down, to complete a circuit.

radiofrequency interference   *See* RFI.

Recommended Standard 232   *See* RS-232.

regeneration   The process of retransmitting a digital signal. Regeneration, unlike amplification, repeats the pure signal, with none of the noise it has accumulated.

registered jack 11   *See* RJ-11.

registered jack 45   *See* RJ-45.

repeater   A device used to regenerate a signal.

RFI (radiofrequency interference)   A kind of interference that may be generated by broadcast signals from radio or TV towers.

RG-6   A type of coaxial cable with an impedance of 75 ohms and that contains an 18 AWG core conductor. RG-6 is used for television, satellite, and broadband cable connections.

RG-8   A type of coaxial cable characterized by a 50-ohm impedance and a 10 AWG core. RG-8 provided the medium for the first Ethernet networks, which followed the now-obsolete 10Base-5 standard.

RG-58   A type of coaxial cable characterized by a 50-ohm impedance and a 24 AWG core. RG-58 was a popular medium for Ethernet LANs in the 1980s, used for the now-obsolete 10Base-2 standard.

RG-59   A type of coaxial cable characterized by a 75-ohm impedance and a 20 or 22 AWG core, usually made of braided copper. Less expensive but suffering greater attenuation than the more common RG-6 coax, RG-59 is used for relatively short connections.

RJ-11 (registered jack 11)   The standard connector used with unshielded twisted pair cabling (usually Cat 3 or Level 1) to connect analog telephones.

RJ-45 (registered jack 45)   The standard connector used with shielded twisted pair and unshielded twisted pair cabling.

rollover cable   A type of cable in which the terminations on one end are exactly the reverse of the terminations on the other end. It is used for serial connections between routers and consoles or other interfaces.

round trip time   *See* RTT.

RS-232 (Recommended Standard 232)   A physical layer standard for serial communications, as defined by EIA/TIA.

RTT (round trip time)   The length of time it takes for a packet to go from sender to receiver, and then back from receiver to sender. RTT is usually measured in milliseconds.

SC (subscriber connector or standard connector)   A connector used with single-mode or multimode fiber-optic cable.

serial   A style of data transmission in which the pulses that represent bits follow one another along a single transmission line. In other words, they are issued sequentially, not simultaneously.

serial cable   A cable, such as an RS-232 type, that permits serial data transmission.

sheath   The outer cover, or jacket, of a cable.

shield   *See* braiding.

shielded twisted pair   *See* STP.

simplex   A type of transmission in which signals may travel in only one direction over a medium.

single-mode fiber   *See* SMF.

SMF (single-mode fiber)   A type of fiber-optic cable with a narrow core that carries light pulses along a single path data from one end of the cable to the other end. Data can be transmitted faster and for longer distances on single-mode fiber than on multimode fiber. However, single-mode fiber is more expensive.

ST (straight tip)   A connector used with single-mode or multimode fiber-optic cable.

standard connector   *See* SC.

statistical multiplexing   A method of multiplexing in which each node on a network is assigned a separate time slot for transmission, based on the node's priority and need.

STP (shielded twisted pair)   A type of cable containing twisted-wire pairs that are not only individually insulated, but also surrounded by a shielding made of a metallic substance such as foil.

straight-through cable   A twisted pair patch cable in which the wire terminations in both connectors follow the same scheme.

straight tip   *See* ST.

structured cabling   A method for uniform, enterprise-wide, multivendor cabling systems specified by the TIA/EIA 568 Commercial Building Wiring Standard. Structured cabling is based on a hierarchical design using a high-speed backbone.

subchannel   One of many distinct communication paths established when a channel is multiplexed or modulated.

subscriber connector   *See* SC.

TDM (time division multiplexing)   A method of multiplexing that assigns a time slot in the flow of communications to every node on the network and, in that time slot, carries data from that node.

telecommunications closet   Also known as a "telco room," the space that contains connectivity for groups of workstations in a defined area, plus cross-connections to IDFs or, in smaller organizations, an MDF. Large organizations may have several telecommunications closets per floor, but the TIA/EIA standard specifies at least one per floor.

Thicknet   An IEEE physical layer standard for achieving a maximum of 10Mbps throughput over coaxial copper cable. Thicknet is also known as 10Base-5. Its maximum segment length is 500 meters, and it relies on a bus topology.

thickwire Ethernet   *See* Thicknet.

thin Ethernet   *See* Thinnet.

Thinnet   An IEEE physical layer standard for achieving 10Mbps throughput over coaxial copper cable. Thinnet is also known as 10Base-2. Its maximum segment length is 185 meters, and it relies on a bus topology.

throughput   The amount of data that a medium can transmit during a given period of time. Throughput is usually measured in megabits (1,000,000 bits) per second, or Mbps. The physical nature of every transmission media determines its potential throughput.

time division multiplexing   *See* TDM.

transceiver   A device that transmits and receives signals.

transmission   In networking, the application of data signals to a medium or the progress of data signals over a medium from one point to another.

transmit   To issue signals to the network medium.

twist ratio   The number of twists per meter or foot in a twisted pair cable.

twisted pair   A type of cable similar to telephone wiring that consists of color-coded pairs of insulated copper wires, each with a diameter of 0.4 to 0.8mm, twisted around each other and encased in plastic coating.

unpopulated segment   A network segment that does not contain end nodes, such as workstations. Unpopulated segments are also called link segments.

unshielded twisted pair   *See* UTP.

UTP (unshielded twisted pair)   A type of cabling that consists of one or more insulated wire pairs encased in a plastic sheath. As its name implies, UTP does not contain additional shielding for the twisted pairs. As a result, UTP is both less expensive and less resistant to noise than STP.

vertical cross-connect   Part of a network's backbone that supplies connectivity between a building's floors. For example, vertical cross-connects might connect an MDF and an IDF or IDFs and telecommunications closets within a building.

volt   The measurement used to describe the degree of pressure an electrical current exerts on a conductor.

voltage   The pressure (sometimes informally referred to as the strength) of an electrical current.

wavelength   The distance between corresponding points on a wave's cycle. Wavelength is inversely proportional to frequency.

wavelength division multiplexing   *See* WDM.

WDM (wavelength division multiplexing)   A multiplexing technique in which each signal on a fiber-optic cable is assigned a different wavelength, which equates to its own subchannel. Each wavelength is modulated with a data signal. In this manner, multiple signals can be simultaneously transmitted in the same direction over a length of fiber.

Review Questions

1. What terms characterize data transmission by the direction signals may travel over media?

    a. Noise, throughput, attenuation, and latency

    b. Amplitude, frequency, wavelength, and phase

    c. Simplex, half-duplex, full-duplex, and multiplex

    d. Multiplexing

2. Which of the following describes the loss of signal strength as it travels away from its source?

    a. Noise

    b. Crosstalk

    c. Attenuation

    d. Latency

3. What is the most significant factor in choosing a transmission method?

    a. Noise

    b. Throughput

    c. Cost

    d. Scalability

4. What cabling consists of one or more insulated wire pairs encased in a plastic sheath?

    a. Coaxial

    b. STP (shielded twisted pair)

    c. UTP (unshielded twisted pair)

    d. Fiber

5. What type of fiber uses a small-diameter core?

    a. Mini-mode

    b. Unimode

    c. Multimode

    d. Single-mode

6.   True or false? Digital signals are composed of pulses of precise, positive voltages and zero voltages.

7.   True or false? Throughput is the measure of how much data is transmitted during a given period of time.

8.   True or false? Broadband is a transmission form in which (typically) digital signals are sent through direct current (DC) pulses applied to the wire.

9.   True or false? Because of its shielding, most coaxial cable has a high resistance to noise.

10. True or false? A layer of glass or plastic surrounding the fibers in fiber-optic cable is called cladding.

11. ____ is a term used by networking professionals to describe the nonndata information that must accompany data for a signal to be properly routed and interpreted by the network.

12. In ____, a simple wave, called a carrier wave, is combined with another analog signal to produce a unique signal that gets transmitted from one node to another.

13. A form of transmission that allows multiple signals to travel simultaneously over one medium is known as ____.

14. If you terminate the RJ-45 plugs at both ends of a patch cable identically, following one of the TIA/EIA 568 standards, you will create a(n) ____ cable.

15. When connecting DTE (data terminal equipment) and DCE (data circuit-terminating equipment) using a serial cable, EIA/TIA has codified a popular serial data transmission method known as ____.

After reading this chapter and completing the exercises, you will be able to:

- Identify and explain the functions of the core TCP/IP protocols

- Explain how the TCP/IP protocols correlate to layers of the OSI model

- Discuss addressing schemes for TCP/IP in IPv4 and IPv6

- Describe the purpose and implementation of DNS (Domain Name System) and DHCP (Dynamic Host Configuration Protocol)

- Identify the well-known ports for key TCP/IP services

- Describe common application layer TCP/IP protocols

On the Job

I woke up to a message from an on-call engineer, Bill, saying, "Help, I am out of ideas for DNS troubleshooting!" Twenty minutes later, as I walked into the office, he recited a chaotic list of all the troubleshooting steps he took and every possible problem that could have caused the issue at hand. We took a walk to the vending machines so I could get caffeine and the story.

Dying server hardware forced Bill to move a number of services to new hardware. DNS was scheduled to be last, as the configuration was simple, and moving it was supposed to be a quick and easy task. Everything seemed to work fine, but queries for all of the Internet and a test internal domain were not being answered. The OS configuration, DNS server settings all seemed fine, but no matter what we tweaked, the service did not work right.

Since Bill knew more about DNS than I did, there was little reason for a detailed walk through the configurations. I took a quick look, in hope of finding something obvious that he had missed, but the configuration was sound. Since no trivial fix was available, I reverted to basic troubleshooting mode and started to work through a simple list of items to check: "ping localhost, ping the interface, ping the router, and a host beyond it...."

The last check returned "connect: Network is unreachable." A quick glance at the route table explained the issue: there was no default route. Without a way to forward traffic, no host outside of a few statically defined internal networks was reachable, including all of the root DNS servers.

The fix was simple and, once the service was restored, I helped a bit with moving other services. Another set of eyes is an invaluable asset during late-night work, and I had to work off all that caffeine.

Marcin Antkiewicz

A protocol is a rule that governs how networks communicate. Protocols define the standards for communication between network devices. Without protocols, devices could not interpret the signals sent by other devices, and data would go nowhere. In this chapter, you will learn about the most commonly used networking protocols, their components, and their functions. This chapter is not an exhaustive study of protocols, but rather a practical guide to applying them. At the end of the chapter, you will have the opportunity to read about some realistic networking scenarios pertaining to protocols and devise your own solutions. As protocols form the foundation of network communications, you must fully understand them to manage a network effectively.

In Chapter 2, you learned about the tasks associated with each layer of the OSI model, such as formatting, addressing, and error correction. You also learned that these tasks are performed by protocols, which are sets of instructions designed and coded by programmers. In the networking industry, the term *protocol* is often used to refer to a group, or suite, of individual protocols that work together.

In the sections that follow, you will learn about the networking protocol suite that is used on virtually all LANs and WANs today—TCP/IP. Other protocol suites, such as IPX/SPX, NetBIOS, and AppleTalk, do exist. However, these once-popular protocols have been replaced by TCP/IP on modern networks. As a network professional, you may occasionally encounter now-obsolete protocol suites, which are not detailed in this chapter. But you will definitely encounter TCP/IP both on the job and in the Network+ certification exam. To be successful, you need to understand TCP/IP in depth.

Characteristics of TCP/IP (Transmission Control Protocol/Internet Protocol)

Net+

1.1

TCP/IP (**Transmission Control Protocol/Internet Protocol**) is not simply one protocol, but rather a suite of specialized protocols—including TCP, IP, UDP, ARP, and many others—called **subprotocols**. Most network administrators refer to the entire group as "TCP/IP," or sometimes simply "IP." For example, a network administrator might say, "Our network only runs IP" when she means that all of the network's services rely on TCP/IP subprotocols.

TCP/IP's roots lie with the United States Department of Defense, which developed TCP/IP for its Advanced Research Projects Agency network (ARPANET, the precursor to today's Internet) in the late 1960s. TCP/IP has grown extremely popular thanks to its low cost, its ability to communicate between a multitude of dissimilar platforms, and its open nature. "Open" means that a software developer, for example, can use and modify TCP/IP's core protocols freely. TCP/IP is a de facto standard on the Internet and has become the protocol of choice on LANs and WANs. UNIX and Linux have always relied on TCP/IP. The most recent versions of NetWare and Windows network operating systems also use TCP/IP as their default protocol.

TCP/IP would not have become so popular if it weren't routable. Protocols that can span more than one LAN (or LAN segment) are **routable**, because they carry network layer addressing information that can be interpreted by a router. Not all protocols are routable, however. For example, the now-obsolete protocol NetBEUI is not routable. Protocol suites that are not routable do not enable data to traverse network segments. They are, therefore, unsuitable for most large networks.

TCP/IP also owes its popularity to its flexibility. It can run on virtually any combination of network operating systems or network media. Because of its flexibility, however, TCP/IP may require more configuration than other protocol suites.

TCP/IP is a broad topic with numerous technical, historical, and practical aspects. Advanced TCP/IP topics are covered in Chapter 10. If you want to become an expert on TCP/IP, consider investing in a book or study guide solely devoted to this suite of protocols.

The TCP/IP Core Protocols

Net+
1.1
Certain subprotocols of the TCP/IP suite, called **TCP/IP core protocols**, operate in the transport or network layers of the OSI model and provide basic services to protocols in other layers. As you might guess, TCP and IP are the most significant protocols in the TCP/IP suite. These and other core protocols are introduced in the following sections.

TCP (Transmission Control Protocol)

TCP (**Transmission Control Protocol**) operates in the transport layer of the OSI model and provides reliable data delivery services. TCP is a connection-oriented subprotocol, which means that a connection must be established between communicating nodes before this protocol will transmit data. TCP further ensures reliable data delivery through sequencing and checksums. Without such measures, data would be transmitted indiscriminately, without checking whether the destination node was offline, for example, or whether the data became corrupt during transmission. Finally, TCP provides flow control to ensure that a node is not flooded with data.

Figure 4-1 depicts the format of a TCP segment, the entity that becomes encapsulated by the IP datagram in the network layer (and, thus, becomes the IP datagram's "data"). Fields belonging to a TCP segment are described in the following list:

- *Source port*—Indicates the port number at the source node. A **port number** is the address on a host where an application makes itself available to incoming or outgoing data. One example is port 80, which is typically used to accept Web page requests from the HTTP protocol. The Source port field is 16 bits long.

- *Destination port*—Indicates the port number at the destination node. The Destination port field is 16 bits long.

- *Sequence number*—Identifies the data segment's position in the stream of data segments already sent. The Sequence number field is 32 bits long.

- *Acknowledgment number (ACK)*—Confirms receipt of the data via a return message to the sender. The Acknowledgment number field is 32 bits long.

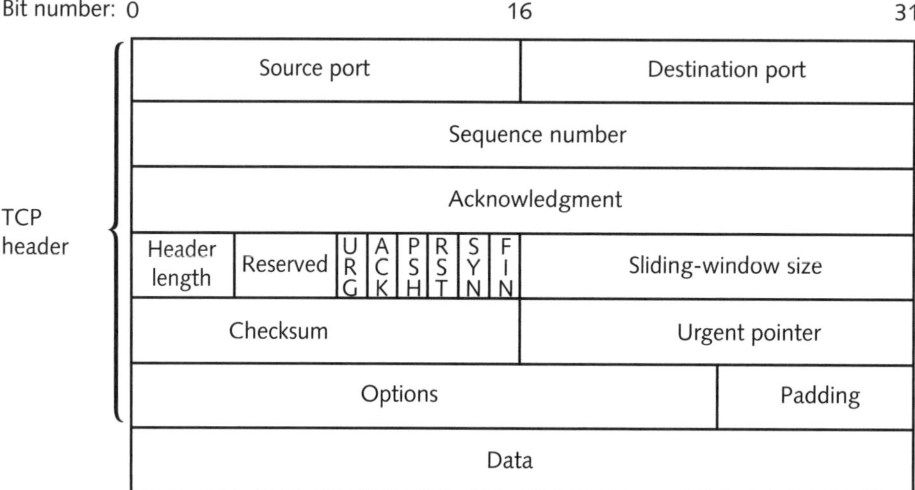

Figure 4-1 A TCP segment

1.1

- *TCP header length*—Indicates the length of the TCP header. This field is 4 bits long.
- *Reserved*—A 6-bit field reserved for later use.
- *Flags*—A collection of six 1-bit fields that signal special conditions through flags. The following flags are available for the sender's use:
    - URG—If set to *1*, the Urgent pointer field contains information for the receiver.
    - ACK—If set to *1*, the Acknowledgment field contains information for the receiver. (If set to *0*, the receiver will ignore the Acknowledgment field.)
    - PSH—If set to *1*, it indicates that data should be sent to an application without buffering.
    - RST—If set to *1*, the sender is requesting that the connection be reset.
    - SYN—If set to *1*, the sender is requesting a synchronization of the sequence numbers between the two nodes. This code is used when TCP requests a connection to set the initial sequence number.
    - FIN—If set to *1*, the segment is the last in a sequence and the connection should be closed.

- *Sliding-window size (or window)*—Indicates how many bytes the sender can issue to a receiver while acknowledgment for this segment is outstanding. This field performs flow control, preventing the receiver from being deluged with bytes. For example, suppose a server indicates a sliding window size of 4,000 bytes. Also suppose the client has already issued 1,000 bytes, 250 of which have been received and acknowledged by the server. That means that the server is still buffering 750 bytes. Therefore, the client can only issue 3,250 additional bytes before it receives acknowledgment from the server for the 750 bytes. This field is 16 bits long.
- *Checksum*—Allows the receiving node to determine whether the TCP segment became corrupted during transmission. The Checksum field is 16 bits long.
- *Urgent pointer*—Indicates a location in the data field where urgent data resides. This field is 16 bits long.
- *Options*—Specifies special options, such as the maximum segment size a network can handle. The size of this field can vary between 0 and 32 bits.
- *Padding*—Contains filler information to ensure that the size of the TCP header is a multiple of 32 bits. The size of this field varies; it is often 0.
- *Data*—Contains data originally sent by the source node. The size of the Data field depends on how much data needs to be transmitted, the constraints on the TCP segment size imposed by the network type, and the limitation that the segment must fit within an IP datagram.

In the Chapter 2 discussion of transport layer functions, you learned how TCP establishes connections for HTTP requests. You also saw an example of TCP segment data from an actual HTTP request. However, you might not have understood what all of the data meant. Now that you know the function of each TCP segment field, you can interpret its contents. Figure 4-2 offers another look at the TCP segment.

Suppose the segment in Figure 4-2 was sent from Computer B to Computer A. Begin interpreting the segment at the Source port line. Notice the segment was issued from Computer B's port 80, the port assigned to HTTP by default. It was addressed to port 1958 on

Transmission Control Protocol, Src Port: http (80), Dst Port: 1958 (1958), Seq: 3043958669, Ack: 937013559, Len: 0
        Source port : http (80)
        Destination port: 1958 (1958)
        Sequence number: 3043958669
        Acknowledgment number: 937013559
        Header length: 24 bytes
    ⊟ Flags:_ 0xx0012 (SYN, ACK)
            0... .... = Congestion Window Reduced (CWR): Not set
            .0.. .... = ECN-Echo: Not set
            ..0. .... = Urgent: Not set
            ...1 .... = Acknowledgment: Set
            .... 0... = Push: Not set
            .... .0.. = Reset: Not set
            .... ..1. = Syn: Set
            ....0 = Fin: not set
        window size; 5840
        Checksum: 0x206a (correct)
    ⊟ Options: (4bytes)
            Maximum segment size: 1460 bytes

Figure 4-2 TCP segment data

Computer A. The sequence number for this segment is 3043958669. The next segment that Computer B expects to receive from Computer A will have the sequence number of 937013559, because this is what Computer B has entered in the Acknowledgment field. By simply having a value, the Acknowledgment field performs its duty of letting a node know that its last communication was received. By indicating a sequence number, the Acknowledgment field does double-duty. Next, look at the Header length field. It indicates that the TCP header is 24 bytes long—4 bytes larger than its minimum size—which means that some of the available options were specified or the padding space was used.

In the flags category, notice that there are two unfamiliar flags: Congestion Window Reduced and ECN-Echo. These are optional flags that can be used to help TCP react to and reduce traffic congestion. They are only available when TCP is establishing a connection. However, in this segment, they are not set. Of all the possible flags in the Figure 4-2 segment, only the ACK and SYN flags are set. This means that Computer B is acknowledging the last segment it received from Computer A and also negotiating a synchronization scheme for sequencing. The window size is 5840, meaning that Computer B can accept 5840 more bytes of data from Computer A even while this segment remains unacknowledged. The Checksum field indicates the valid outcome of the error-checking algorithm used to verify the segment's header. In this case, the checksum is 0x206a. When Computer A receives this segment, it will perform the same algorithm, and if the result is 0x206a, it will know the TCP header arrived without damage. Finally, this segment uses its option field to specify a maximum TCP segment size of 1,460 bytes.

Note that a computer doesn't "see" the TCP segment as it's shown in Figure 4-2. This figure was obtained by using a data analyzer program that translates each packet into a user-friendly form. From the computer's standpoint, the TCP segment is encoded as hexadecimal characters. (The computer does not need labels to identify the fields, because as long as TCP/IP protocol standards are followed, it knows exactly where each byte of data is located.)

Net+

1.1

The TCP segment pictured in Figure 4-2 is part of the process of establishing a connection between Computer B and Computer A. In fact, it is the second segment of three used to establish a TCP connection. In the first step of establishing this connection, Computer A issues a message to Computer B with its SYN bit set, indicating the desire to communicate and synchronize sequence numbers. In its message, it sends a random number that will be used to synchronize the communication. In Figure 4-3, for example, this number is 937013558. (Its ACK bit is usually set to 0.) After Computer B receives this message, it responds with a segment whose ACK and SYN flags are both set. In Computer B's transmission, the ACK field contains a number that equals the sequence number Computer A originally sent plus 1. As Figure 4-3 illustrates, Computer B sends the number 937013559. In this manner, Computer B signals to Computer A that it has received the request for communication and further, it expects Computer A to respond with the sequence number 937013559. In its SYN field, Computer B sends its own random number (in Figure 4-3, this number is 3043958669), which Computer A will use to acknowledge that it received Computer B's transmission. Next, Computer A issues a segment whose sequence number is 937013559 (because this is what Computer B indicated it expects to receive). In the same segment, Computer A also communicates a sequence number via its Acknowledgment field. This number equals the sequence number that Computer B sent plus 1. In the example shown in Figure 4-3, Computer A expects 3043958670 to be the sequence number of the next segment it receives from Computer B. Thus, in its next communication (not shown in Figure 4-3), Computer B will respond with a segment whose sequence number is 937013560. The two nodes continue communicating this way until Computer A issues a segment whose FIN flag is set, indicating the end of the transmission.

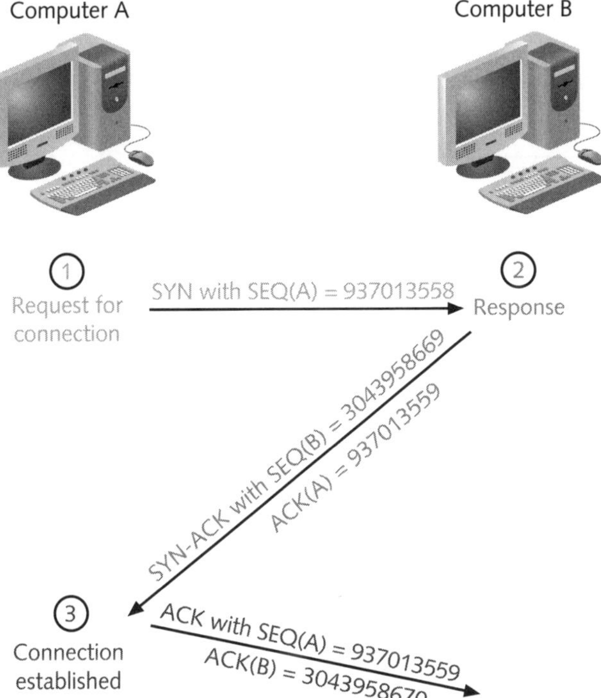

Figure 4-3 Establishing a TCP connection

TCP is not the only core protocol at the transport layer. A similar but less complex protocol, UDP, is discussed next.

Net+ UDP (User Datagram Protocol)

1.1   UDP (User Datagram Protocol), like TCP, belongs to the transport layer of the OSI model. Unlike TCP, however, UDP is a connectionless transport service. In other words, UDP offers no assurance that packets will be received in the correct sequence. In fact, this protocol does not guarantee that the packets will be received at all. Furthermore, it provides no error checking or sequencing. Nevertheless, UDP's lack of sophistication makes it more efficient than TCP. It can be useful when a great volume of data must be transferred quickly, such as for live audio or video transmissions over the Internet. In these cases, TCP—with its acknowledgments, checksums, and flow control mechanisms—would only add more overhead to the transmission. UDP is also more efficient for carrying messages that fit within one data packet.

In contrast to a TCP header's 10 fields, the UDP header contains only 4 fields: Source port, Destination port, Length, and Checksum. Use of the Checksum field in UDP is optional. Figure 4-4 depicts a UDP segment. Contrast its header with the much larger TCP segment header shown in Figure 4-1.

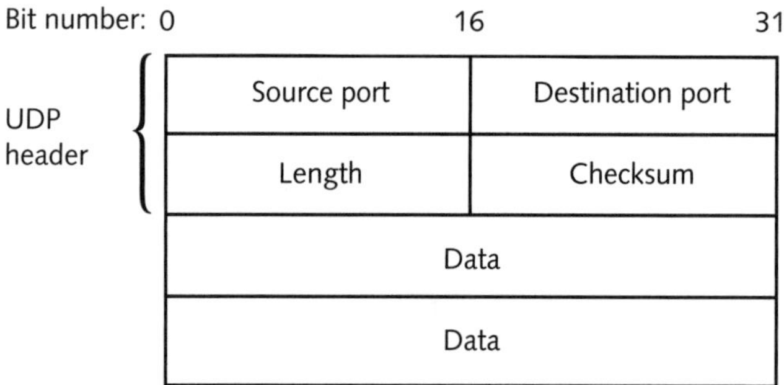

Figure 4-4 A UDP segment

Now that you understand the functions of and differences between TCP and UDP, you are ready to learn more about IP (Internet Protocol).

IP (Internet Protocol)

IP (Internet Protocol) belongs to the network layer of the OSI model. It provides information about how and where data should be delivered, including the data's source and destination addresses. IP is the subprotocol that enables TCP/IP to **internetwork**—that is, to traverse more than one LAN segment and more than one type of network through a router.

This section describes the IP subprotocol as it is used in **IPv4 (IP version 4)**, the original version that has been used for 25 years and is still used by many networks today. Later in this chapter you'll learn about the newer version, IPv6.

As you know, at the network layer of the OSI model, data is formed into packets. In the context of TCP/IP, a packet is also known as an **IP datagram**. The IP datagram acts as an envelope for data and contains information necessary for routers to transfer data between different LAN segments. IP is an unreliable, connectionless protocol, which means that it does not guarantee delivery of data. Higher-level protocols of the TCP/IP suite, however, use IP to ensure that data packets are delivered to the right addresses. Note that the IP datagram does contain one reliability component, the Header checksum, which verifies only the integrity of the routing information in the IP header. If the checksum accompanying the message does not have the proper value when the packet is received, the packet is presumed to be corrupt and is discarded; at that point, a new packet is sent.

Figure 4-5 depicts the format of an IP datagram. Its fields are described in the following list:

- *Version*—Identifies the version number of the protocol—for example, IPv4 or IPv6. The receiving workstation looks at this field first to determine whether it can read the incoming data. If it cannot, it will reject the packet. Rejection rarely occurs, however, because most TCP/IP-based networks use IPv4. This field is 4 bits long.

- *Internet header length (IHL)*—Identifies the number of 4-byte (or 32-bit) blocks in the IP header. The most common header length is composed of five groupings, as the minimum length of an IP header is 20 4-byte blocks. This field is important because it indicates to the receiving node where data will begin (immediately after the header ends). The IHL field is 4 bits long.

- *Differentiated Services (DiffServ) field*—Informs routers what level of precedence they should apply when processing the incoming packet. This field is 8 bits long. It used to be called the Type of Service (ToS) field, and its purpose was the same as the redefined Differentiated Services field. However, the ToS specification allowed only eight different values regarding the precedence of a datagram, and the field was rarely used. Differentiated Services allows up to 64 values and a greater range of priority-handling options.

- *Total length*—Identifies the total length of the IP datagram, including the header and data, in bytes. An IP datagram, including its header and data, cannot exceed 65,535 bytes. The Total length field is 16 bits long.

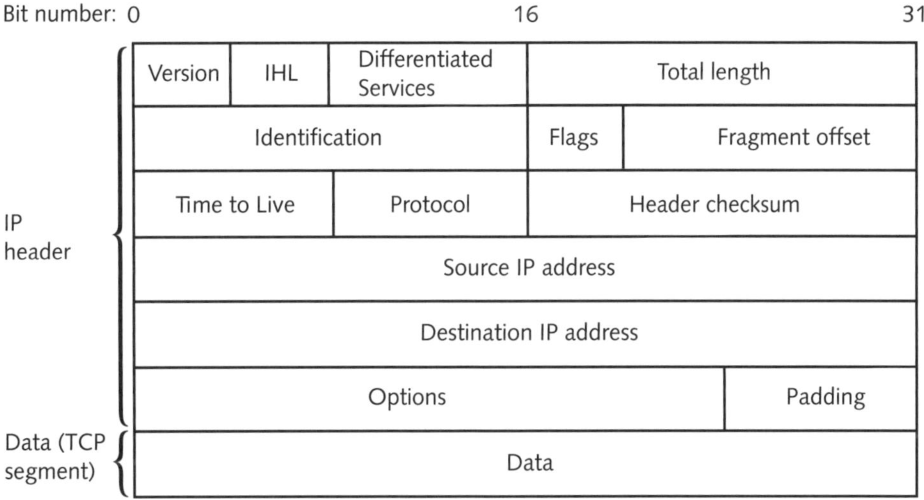

Figure 4-5 An IP datagram

1.1

- *Identification*—Identifies the message to which a datagram belongs and enables the receiving node to reassemble fragmented messages. This field and the following two fields, Flags and Fragment offset, assist in reassembly of fragmented packets. The Identification field is 16 bits long.

- *Flags*—Indicates whether a message is fragmented and, if it is fragmented, whether this datagram is the last in the fragment.

- *Fragment offset*—Identifies where the datagram fragment belongs in the incoming set of fragments. This field is 13 bits long.

- ***Time to Live (TTL)***—Indicates the maximum time that a datagram can remain on the network before it is discarded. Although this field was originally meant to represent units of time, on modern networks it represents the number of times a datagram has been forwarded by a router, or the number of router **hops** it has endured. The TTL for datagrams is variable and configurable but is usually set at 32 or 64. Each time a datagram passes through a router, its TTL is reduced by 1. When a router receives a datagram with a TTL equal to 1, it discards that datagram (or more precisely, the frame to which it belongs). The TTL field in an IP datagram is 8 bits long.

- *Protocol*—Identifies the type of transport layer protocol that will receive the datagram (for example, TCP or UDP). This field is 8 bits long.

- *Header checksum*—Allows the receiving node to calculate whether the IP header has been corrupted during transmission. This field is 16 bits long.

- *Source IP address*—Identifies the full IP address (or network layer address) of the source node. This field is 32 bits long.

- *Destination IP address*—Indicates the full IP address (or network layer address) of the destination node. This field is 32 bits long.

- *Options*—May contain optional routing and timing information. The Options field varies in length.

- *Padding*—Contains filler bits to ensure that the header is a multiple of 32 bits. The length of this field varies.

- *Data*—Includes the data originally sent by the source node, plus information added by TCP in the transport layer. The size of the Data field varies.

In the Chapter 2 discussion of the network layer functions, you were introduced to IP and the data contained in its packets. You also saw an example of IP packet data from an actual HTTP request. However, you might not have understood what all of the data meant. Now that you are familiar with the fields of an IP datagram, you can interpret its contents. Figure 4-6 offers another look at the IP packet, with an interpretation following the figure.

Begin interpreting the datagram with the Version field, which indicates that this transmission relies on version 4 of the Internet Protocol. Next, notice that the datagram has a header length of 20 bytes. Because this is the minimum size for an IP header, you can deduce that the datagram contains no options or padding. In the Differentiated Services field, no options for priority handling are set, which is not unusual in routine data exchanges such as retrieving a Web page. The total length of the datagram is given as 44 bytes. This makes sense when you consider that its header is 20 bytes, and the TCP segment that it encapsulates (discussed previously) is 24 bytes. Considering that the maximum size of an IP packet is 65,535 bytes, this is a very small packet.

```
⊟Internet Protocol, Src Addr: 140.147.249.7 (140.147.249.7), Dst Addr: 10.11.11.51 (10.11.11.51)
      Version: 4
      Header length: 20 bytes
   ⊞Differentiated Services Field: 0x00 (DSCP 0x00: Default; ECN 0x00)
      Total Length: 44
      Identification: 0x0000 (0)
   ⊟Flags: 0x04
         .1.. = Don't fragment: Set
         ..0. = More fragments: Not set
      Fragment offset: 0
      Time to live: 64
      Protocol: TCP (0x06)
      Header checksum: 0x9ff3 (correct)
      Source: 140.147.249.7 (140.147.249.7)
      Destination: 10.11.11.51 (10.11.11.51)
```

Figure 4-6 IP datagram data

Next in the IP datagram is the Identification field, which uniquely identifies the packet. This packet, the first one issued from Computer B to Computer A in the TCP connection exchange, is identified in hexadecimal notation as 0x0000. In the Flags field, which indicates whether this packet is fragmented, the Don't fragment option is set with a value of 1. So you know that this packet is not fragmented. And because it's not fragmented, the fragment offset field does not apply and is set to 0.

This datagram's TTL (Time to Live) is set to 64. That means that if the packet were to keep traveling across a network, it would be allowed 64 more hops before it was discarded. The Protocol field is next. It indicates that encapsulated within the IP datagram is a TCP segment. TCP is always indicated by the hexadecimal string of *0x06*. The next field provides the correct header checksum answer, which is used by the recipient of this packet to determine whether the IP datagram's header was damaged in transit. Finally, the last two fields in the datagram show the logical addresses for the packet's source and destination.

In the next section, you learn about another protocol that operates in the network layer of the OSI model—ICMP.

ICMP (Internet Control Message Protocol)

Whereas IP helps direct data to its correct destination, **ICMP (Internet Control Message Protocol)** is a network layer protocol that reports on the success or failure of data delivery. It can indicate when part of a network is congested, when data fails to reach its destination, and when data has been discarded because the allotted time for its delivery (its TTL) expired. ICMP announces these transmission failures to the sender, but ICMP cannot correct any of the errors it detects; those functions are left to higher-layer protocols, such as TCP. However, ICMP's announcements provide critical information for troubleshooting network problems.

IGMP (Internet Group Management Protocol)

Another key subprotocol in the TCP/IP suite is **IGMP (Internet Group Management Protocol** or **Internet Group Multicast Protocol)**. IGMP operates at the network layer and manages multicasting. **Multicasting** is a transmission method that allows one node to send data to a defined group of nodes (not necessarily the entire network segment, as is the case in a broadcast transmission). Whereas most data transmission occurs on a point-to-point basis, multicasting is a

1.1
1.4

point-to-multipoint method. Multicasting can be used for teleconferencing or videoconferencing over the Internet, for example. Routers use IGMP to determine which nodes belong to a certain multicast group and to transmit data to all nodes in that group. Network nodes use IGMP to join or leave multicast groups at any time.

ARP (Address Resolution Protocol)

1.1
1.4
5.1

ARP (Address Resolution Protocol) is a network layer protocol that obtains the MAC (physical) address of a host, or node, and then creates a database that maps the MAC address to the host's IP (logical) address. If one node needs to know the MAC address of another node on the same network, the first node issues a broadcast message to the network, using ARP, that essentially says, "Will the computer with the IP address 1.2.3.4 please send me its MAC address?" In the context of networking, a broadcast is a transmission that is simultaneously sent to all nodes on a particular network segment. The node that has the IP address 1.2.3.4 then broadcasts a reply that contains the physical address of the destination host.

To make ARP more efficient, computers save recognized MAC-to-IP address mappings on their hard disks in a database known as an **ARP table** (also called an **ARP cache**). After a computer has saved this information, the next time it needs the MAC address for another device, it finds the address in its ARP table and does not need to broadcast another request. Although the precise format of ARP tables may vary from one operating system to another, the essential contents of the table and its purpose remain the same. An example ARP table might resemble Figure 4-7.

An ARP table can contain two types of entries: dynamic and static. **Dynamic ARP table entries** are created when a client makes an ARP request that cannot be satisfied by data already in the ARP table. **Static ARP table entries** are those that someone has entered manually using the ARP utility. The ARP utility, accessed via the `arp` command from a Windows command prompt or a UNIX or Linux shell prompt, provides a way of obtaining information from and manipulating a device's ARP table. For example, you can view a Windows XP or Windows Vista workstation's ARP table by typing `arp -a` at the command line and pressing Enter. ARP can be a valuable troubleshooting tool for discovering the identity of a machine whose IP address you know, or for identifying the problem of two machines trying to use the same IP address.

RARP (Reverse Address Resolution Protocol)

1.1

If a device doesn't know its own IP address, it cannot use ARP. This is because without an IP address, a device cannot issue an ARP request or receive an ARP reply. One solution to this problem is to allow the client to send a broadcast message with its MAC address and receive an IP address in reply. This process, which is the reverse of ARP, is made possible by **RARP (Reverse Address Resolution Protocol)**. A RARP server maintains a table of MAC addresses and their associated IP addresses (similar to an ARP table). After the RARP server receives

```
IP Address          Hardware Address     Type

123.45.67.80        60:23:A6:F1:C4:D2    Static
123.45.67.89        20:00:3D:21:E0:11    Dynamic
123.45.67.73        A0:BB:77:C2:25:FA    Dynamic
```

Figure 4-7 Example ARP table

Net+
1.1

the client's request, it consults the RARP table to find the IP address that matches the client's MAC address. The RARP server then transmits the IP address information to the client.

RARP was originally developed as a means for **diskless workstations**—workstations that do not contain hard disks, but rely on a small amount of read-only memory to connect to a network—to obtain IP addresses from a server before more sophisticated protocols emerged to perform this function.

IPv4 Addressing

Net+
1.1
1.3

You have learned that networks recognize two kinds of addresses: logical (or network layer) and physical (or MAC, or hardware) addresses. MAC addresses are assigned to a device's NIC at the factory by its manufacturer. Logical addresses can be manually or automatically assigned and must follow rules set by the protocol standards. In the TCP/IP protocol suite, IP is the core protocol responsible for logical addressing. For this reason, addresses on TCP/IP-based networks are often called IP addresses. IP addresses are assigned and used according to very specific parameters.

Each IP address is a unique 32-bit number, divided into four **octets**, or sets of 8 bits, that are separated by periods. (Because 8 bits equals 1 byte, each octet is a byte, and an IP address is thus composed of 4 bytes.) An example of a valid IP address is 144.92.43.178. An IP address contains two types of information: network and host. From the first octet, you can determine the **network class**. In traditional IP addressing, three types of network classes are used for LANs: Class A, Class B, and Class C. (In Chapter 10, however, you'll learn about developments that allow networks to circumvent such class designations.) Table 4-1 summarizes characteristics of the three commonly used classes of TCP/IP-based networks.

In addition, Class D and Class E addresses do exist, but they are rarely used. Class D addresses, which begin with an octet whose value is between 224 and 239, are reserved for multicasting. IETF (Internet Engineering Task Force) reserves Class E addresses, which begin with an octet whose value is between 240 and 254, for experimental use. You should never assign Class D or Class E addresses to devices on your network.

Although 8 bits have 256 possible combinations, only the numbers 1 through 254 can be used to identify networks and hosts in an IP address. The number 0 is reserved as a placeholder when referring to an entire group of computers on a network—for example, 10.0.0.0 represents all of the devices whose first octet is 10. The number 255 is reserved for broadcast transmissions. For example, sending a message to the address 255.255.255.255 sends a message to all devices connected to your network segment.

Table 4-1 Commonly Used TCP/IP Classes

Network Class	Beginning Octet	Number of Networks	Maximum Addressable Hosts per Network
A	1–126	126	16,777,214
B	128–191	>16,000	65,534
C	192–223	>2,000,000	254

Net+

1.1

1.3

A portion of each IP address contains clues about the network class. An IP address whose first octet is in the range of 1–126 belongs to a Class A network. All IP addresses for devices on a Class A segment share the same first octet, or bits 0 through 7, as shown in Figure 4-8. For example, nodes with the following IP addresses may belong to the same Class A network: 23.78.110.109, 23.164.32.97, 23.48.112.43, and 23.108.37.22. In this example, 23 is the **network ID**. The second through fourth octets (bits 8 through 31) in a Class A address identify the host.

An IP whose first octet is in the range of 128–191 belongs to a Class B network. All IP addresses for devices on a Class B segment share the first two octets, or bits 0 through 15. For example, nodes with the following IP addresses may belong to the same Class B network: 168.34.88.29, 168.34.55.41, 168.34.73.49, and 168.34.205.113. In this example, 168.34 is the network ID. The third and fourth octets (bits 16 through 31) on a Class B network identify the host, as shown in Figure 4-8.

An IP address whose first octet is in the range of 192–223 belongs to a Class C network. All IP addresses for devices on a Class C segment share the first three octets, or bits 0 through 23. For example, nodes with the following addresses may belong to the same Class C network: 204.139.118.7, 204.139.118.54, 204.139.118.14, and 204.139.118.31. In this example, 204.139.118 is the network ID. The fourth octet (bits 24 through 31) on a Class C network identifies the host, as shown in Figure 4-8.

Internet founders intended the use of network classes to provide easy organization and a sufficient quantity of IP addresses on the Internet. However, their goals haven't necessarily been met. Class A addresses were distributed liberally to large companies and government organizations who were early users of the Internet, such as IBM. Some organizations reserved many more addresses than they had devices. Class B addresses were distributed to midsized organizations and Class C addresses to smaller organizations, such as colleges. Today, many Internet addresses go unused, but they cannot be reassigned because an organization has reserved them. Although potentially more than 4.3 billion Internet addresses are available, the demand

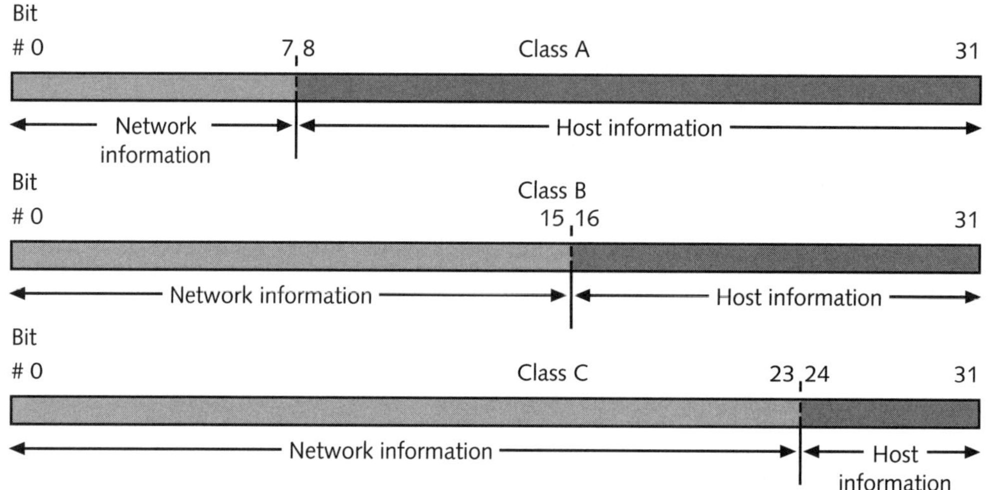

Figure 4-8 IP addresses and their classes

Net+

1.1

1.3

for such addresses grows exponentially every year. To respond to this demand, a new addressing scheme was developed that can supply the world with enough addresses to last well into this century. **IP version 6 (IPv6)**, also known as the next-generation IP, incorporates this new addressing scheme.

In addition, some IP addresses are reserved for special functions, like broadcasts, and cannot be assigned to machines or devices. Notice that 127 is not a valid first octet for any IP address. The range of addresses beginning with 127 is reserved for a device communicating with itself or performing loopback communication. Thus, the IP address 127.0.0.1 is called a **loopback address**. Attempting to contact this IP number—in other words, attempting to contact your own machine—is known as a **loopback test**. (In fact, when you transmit to any IP address beginning with the 127 octet, you are communicating with your own machine.) A loopback test can prove useful when troubleshooting problems with a workstation's TCP/IP communications. If you receive a positive response from a loopback test, you know that the TCP/IP core protocols are installed and in use on your workstation.

The command used to view IP information on a Windows XP or Windows Vista workstation is `ipconfig`. To view your current IP information on a Windows XP or Windows Vista workstation:

1. Click the Start button, select **All Programs**, select **Accessories**, and then select **Command Prompt**. The Command Prompt window opens.

2. At the command prompt, type `ipconfig /all` and press **Enter**. Your workstation's IP address information is displayed, similar to the information shown in Figure 4-9.

3. Type `exit` and press **Enter** to close the Command Prompt window.

To view and edit IP information on a computer running a version of the UNIX or Linux operating system, use the `ifconfig` command. (Note that ipconfig and ifconfig differ by only one letter.) Simply type ifconfig -a at the shell prompt to view all the information about your TCP/IP connections and addresses, as shown in Figure 4-10. In this figure, the IP address is labeled "inet addr."

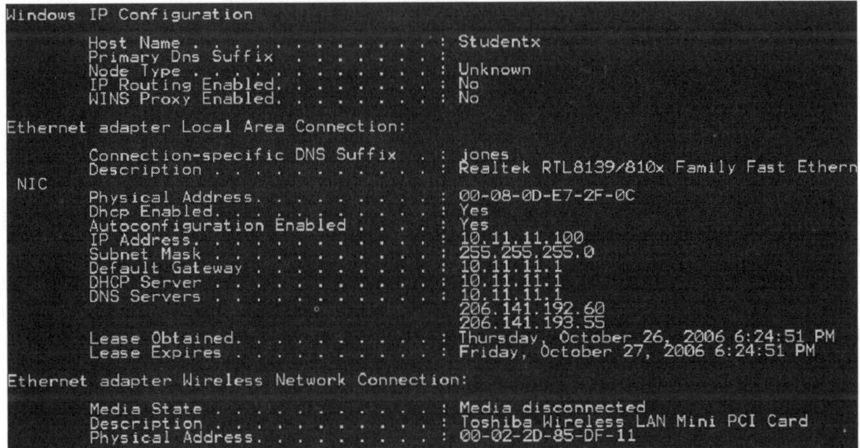

Figure 4-9 Results of the `ipconfig /all` command on a Windows XP or Windows Vista workstation

```
bash-3.00% ifconfig -a
eth0      Link encap:Ethernet   HWaddr 00:02:8A:A4:F8:C8
          inet addr:10.1.1.100  Bcast:10.1.1.255  Mask:255.255.255.0
          UP BROADCAST NOTRAILERS RUNNING MULTICAST  MTU:1500  Metric:1
          RX packets:0 errors:0 dropped:0 overruns:0 frame:0
          TX packets:0 errors:0 dropped:0 overruns:0 carrier:0
          collisions:0 txqueuelen:1000
          RX bytes:0 (0.0 b)  TX bytes:0 (0.0 b)

lo        Link encap:Local Loopback
          inet addr:127.0.0.1  Mask:255.0.0.0
          UP LOOPBACK RUNNING  MTU:16436  Metric:1
          RX packets:0 errors:0 dropped:0 overruns:0 frame:0
          TX packets:0 errors:0 dropped:0 overruns:0 carrier:0
          collisions:0 txqueuelen:0
          RX bytes:0 (0.0 b)  TX bytes:0 (0.0 b)

bash-3.00%
```

Figure 4-10 Results of the `ifconfig -a` command on a UNIX workstation

Now that you have learned the most important characteristics of IP addresses, you are ready to learn more about how computers interpret these addresses.

Binary and Dotted Decimal Notation

So far, all of the IP addresses in this section have been represented in dotted decimal notation. **Dotted decimal notation**, the most common way of expressing IP addresses, refers to the "shorthand" convention used to represent IP addresses and make them easy for people to read. In dotted decimal notation, a decimal number between 0 and 255 represents each binary octet (for a total of 256 possibilities). A period, or dot, separates each decimal. An example of a dotted decimal IP address is 131.65.10.18.

Each number in a dotted decimal address has a binary equivalent. In Chapter 3, you learned how to convert decimal numbers to their binary equivalents. Converting a dotted decimal address to its binary equivalent is simply a matter of converting each octet and removing the decimal points. For example, in the dotted decimal address 131.65.10.36, the binary equivalent of the first octet, 131, is 10000011, the binary equivalent of the second octet, 65, is 01000001, the binary equivalent of the third octet, 10, is 00001010, and the binary equivalent of the fourth octet, 36, is 00100100. Therefore, the binary value for 131.65.10.36 is 10000011 01000001 00001010 00100100.

Subnet Mask

In addition to an IP address, every device on a TCP/IP-based network is identified by a subnet mask. A **subnet mask** is a special 32-bit number that, when combined with a device's IP address, informs the rest of the network about the segment or network to which the device is attached. That is, it identifies the device's **subnet**. Like IP addresses, subnet masks are composed of four octets (32 bits) and can be expressed in either binary or dotted decimal notation. Subnet masks are assigned in the same way that IP addresses are assigned—either manually, within a device's TCP/IP configuration, or automatically, through a service such as DHCP (described in detail later in this chapter). A more common term for subnet mask is **net mask,** and sometimes simply **mask** (as in "a device's mask").

You might wonder why a network node even needs a subnet mask, given that the first octet of its IP address indicates its network class. The answer lies with **subnetting**, a process of subdividing a single class of networks into multiple, smaller logical networks, or segments.

1.1

1.3
Network managers create subnets to control network traffic and to make the best use of a limited number of IP addresses. Methods of subnetting are discussed in detail in Chapter 10. For now, it is enough to know that regardless of whether a network is subnetted, its devices are assigned a subnet mask.

On networks that use subnetting, the subnet mask varies depending on the way the network is subnetted. On networks that do not use subnetting, however, the subnet masks take on a default value, as shown in Table 4-2. To qualify for Network+ certification, you should be familiar with the default subnet masks associated with each network class.

Table 4-2 Default Subnet Masks

Network Class	Beginning Octet	Default Subnet Mask
A	1–126	255.0.0.0
B	128–191	255.255.0.0
C	192–223	255.255.255.0

Assigning IP Addresses

1.1

1.4
You have learned that several government-sponsored organizations—including IANA, ICANN, and RIRs—cooperate to dole out IP addresses to ISPs and other network providers around the world. You also learned that most companies and individuals obtain IP addresses from their ISPs and not directly from the government's higher authorities. This section describes how an organization assigns its group of IP addresses to networked devices so that they can communicate over the Internet.

Whether connecting to the Internet or to another computer within a LAN, every node on a network must have a unique IP address. If you add a node to a network and its IP address is already in use by another node on the same subnet, an error message is generated on the new client and its TCP/IP services are disabled. The existing host may also receive an error message, but it can continue to function normally.

Recall that a host is any machine on a network that enables resource sharing. All individual computers connected through a TCP/IP-based network can be called hosts. This idea represents a slightly different interpretation of the term *host*, because probably not all computers on a TCP/IP-based network facilitate resource sharing (though theoretically, they could).

You can assign IP addresses manually, by modifying the client workstation's TCP/IP properties. A manually assigned IP address is called a **static IP address** because it does not change automatically. It changes only when you reconfigure the client's TCP/IP properties. Unfortunately, due to human error, static IP addressing can easily result in the duplication of address assignments. So rather than assigning IP addresses manually, most network administrators rely on a network service to automatically assign them. The following sections discuss two methods of automatic IP addressing: BOOTP and DHCP.

Net+ **BOOTP (Bootstrap Protocol)**

1.1

1.4

On the earliest TCP/IP-based networks, each device was manually assigned a static IP address through a configuration file stored on the hard disk of every computer that needed to communicate on the network. As networks grew larger, however, these configuration files became more difficult to manage. Imagine the arduous task faced by a network administrator who must visit each of 3,000 workstations, printers, and hosts on a company's LAN to assign IP addresses and ensure that no single IP address is used twice. Now imagine how much extra work would be required to revamp the company's IP addressing scheme or to move an entire department's machines to a different or new network.

To facilitate IP address management, a service called the Bootstrap Protocol was developed in the mid-1980s. **BOOTP (Bootstrap Protocol)**, an application layer protocol, uses a central list of IP addresses and their associated devices' MAC addresses to assign IP addresses to clients dynamically. An IP address that is assigned to a device upon request and is changeable is known as a **dynamic IP address**.

When a client that relies on BOOTP first connects to the network, it sends a broadcast message to the network asking to be assigned an IP address. This broadcast message includes the MAC address of the client's NIC. The BOOTP server recognizes a BOOTP client's request, looks up the client's MAC address in its BOOTP table, and responds to the client with the following information: the client's IP address, the IP address of the server, the host name of the server, and the IP address of a default router. Using BOOTP, a client does not have to remember its own IP address, and, therefore, network administrators do not have to go to each workstation on a network to assign its IP address manually.

You might recognize that the BOOTP process resembles the way RARP issues IP addresses to clients. The main difference between the two protocols is that RARP requests and responses are not routable. Thus, if you wanted to use RARP to issue IP addresses, you would have to install a separate RARP server for every LAN. BOOTP, on the other hand, can traverse LANs. Also, RARP is only capable of issuing an IP address to a client; BOOTP has the potential to issue additional information, such as the client's subnet mask.

In most cases, BOOTP has been surpassed by the more sophisticated IP addressing utility, DHCP (Dynamic Host Configuration Protocol). DHCP requires little intervention, whereas BOOTP requires network administrators to enter every IP and MAC address manually into the BOOTP table. Because of this requirement, the BOOTP table can be difficult to maintain on large networks. You may still encounter BOOTP in existing networks, but most likely it will support only diskless workstations, which are not capable of using DHCP.

DHCP (Dynamic Host Configuration Protocol)

DHCP (Dynamic Host Configuration Protocol) is an automated means of assigning a unique IP address to every device on a network. DHCP, like BOOTP, belongs to the application layer of the OSI model. It was developed by the IETF as a replacement for BOOTP. DHCP operates in a similar manner to BOOTP, but unlike BOOTP, DHCP does not require the network administrator to maintain a table of IP and MAC addresses on the server. Thus, the administrative burden of running DHCP is much lower. DHCP does, however, require the network administrator in charge of IP address management to install and configure the DHCP service on a DHCP server.

 Reasons for implementing DHCP include the following:

1.1

1.4

- *To reduce the time and planning spent on IP address management*—Central management of IP addresses eliminates the need for network administrators to edit the TCP/IP configuration on every network workstation, printer, or other device.

- *To reduce the potential for errors in assigning IP addresses*—With DHCP, almost no possibility exists that a workstation will be assigned an invalid address or that two workstations will attempt to use the same IP address. (Occasionally, the DHCP server software may make a mistake.)

- *To enable users to move their workstations and printers without having to change their TCP/IP configuration*—As long as a workstation is configured to obtain its IP address from a central server, the workstation can be attached anywhere on the network and receive a valid address.

- *To make IP addressing transparent for mobile users*—A person visiting your office, for example, could attach to your network and receive an IP address without having to change his laptop's configuration.

In some instances, BOOTP and DHCP may appear together under the same category or service. For example, if you are configuring a Hewlett-Packard LaserJet that uses a JetDirect print server card, you can select BOOTP/DHCP from the printer's TCP/IP Configuration menu. BOOTP and DHCP are not always distinguished as separate services because they appear the same to the client.

DHCP Leasing Process With DHCP, a device borrows, or **leases**, an IP address while it is attached to the network. In other words, it uses the IP address on a temporary basis for a specified length of time. On most modern networks, a client obtains its DHCP-assigned address as soon as it logs on to a network. The length of time a lease remains in effect depends on DHCP server and client configurations. Leases that expire must be renegotiated for the client to remain on the network. Alternatively, users can force a lease termination at the client, or a network administrator can force lease terminations at the server.

Configuring the DHCP service involves specifying a range of addresses that can be leased to any network device on a particular segment and a list of excluded addresses (if any). As a network administrator, you configure the duration of the lease to be as short or as long as necessary, from a matter of minutes to forever. After the DHCP server is running, the client and server take the following steps to negotiate the client's first lease. (Note that this example applies to a workstation, but devices such as networked printers may also take advantage of DHCP.)

1. When the client workstation is powered on and its NIC detects a network connection, it sends out a DHCP discover packet in broadcast fashion via the UDP protocol to the DHCP/BOOTP server.

2. Every DHCP server on the same subnet as the client receives the broadcast request. Each DHCP server responds with an available IP address, while simultaneously withholding that address from other clients. The response message includes the available IP address, subnet mask, IP address of the DHCP server, and lease duration. (Because the

client doesn't have an IP address, the DHCP server cannot send the information directly to the client.)

3. The client accepts the first IP address that it receives, responding with a broadcast message that essentially confirms to the DHCP server that it wants to accept the address. Because this message is broadcast, all other DHCP servers that might have responded to the client's original query see this confirmation and return the IP addresses they had reserved for the client to their pool of available addresses.

4. When the selected DHCP server receives the confirmation, it replies to the client with an acknowledgment message. It also provides more information, such as DNS, subnet mask, or gateway addresses that the client might have requested.

The preceding steps involve the exchange of only four packets and, therefore, do not usually increase the time it takes for a client to log on to the network. Figure 4-11 depicts the DHCP leasing process. The client and server do not have to repeat this exchange until the lease is terminated. The IP address remains in the client's TCP/IP settings so that even after the client shuts down and reboots, it can use this information and not have to request a new address. However, if the device is moved to another network, it will be assigned different IP address information suited to that network.

Terminating a DHCP Lease A DHCP lease may expire based on the period established for it in the server configuration, or it may be manually terminated at any time from either the client's TCP/IP configuration or the server's DHCP configuration. In some instances, a user must terminate a lease. For example, if a DHCP server fails and another is installed to replace it, the clients that relied on the first DHCP server need to release their old leases (and obtain new leases from the new server). In Windows terms, this event is called a **release** of the TCP/IP settings.

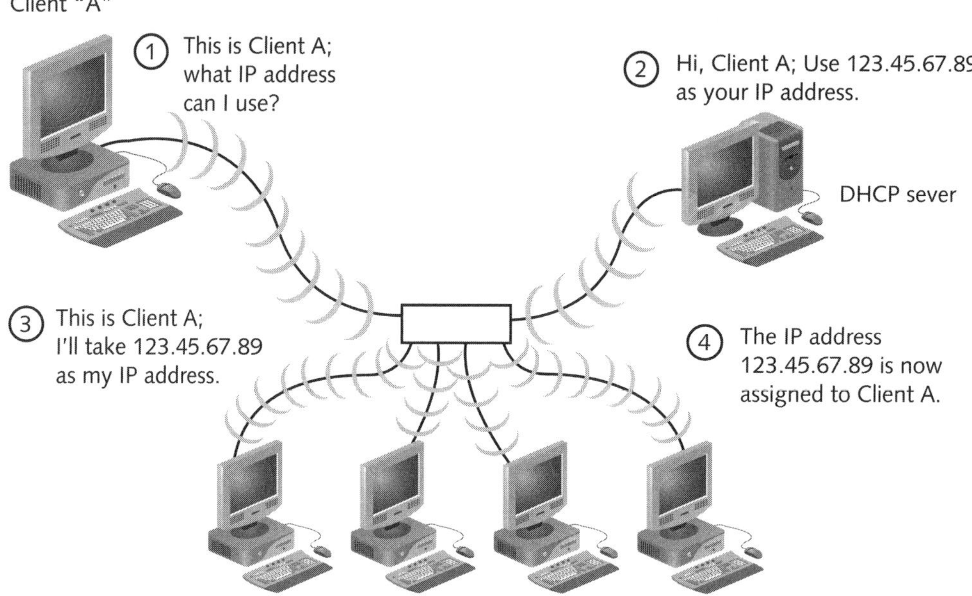

Figure 4-11 The DHCP leasing process

Net+   To release TCP/IP settings on a computer running the Windows XP operating system:

1.1
1.4

1. Click **Start**, point to **All Programs**, point to **Accessories**, and then click **Command Prompt**. The Command Prompt window opens.

2. At the command prompt, type **ipconfig /release** and then press **Enter**. Your TCP/IP configuration values are cleared, and both the IP address and subnet mask revert to 0.0.0.0.

3. Type **exit** and press **Enter** to close the Command Prompt window.

Releasing old DHCP information is the first step in the process of obtaining a new IP address. To obtain a new IP address on a Windows XP workstation:

1. If you are not already at a command prompt, click **Start**, point to **All Programs**, point to **Accessories**, and then click **Command Prompt**. The Command Prompt window opens.

2. At the command prompt, type **ipconfig /renew** and then press **Enter**. Your client follows the DHCP leasing process, which reestablishes its TCP/IP configuration values. These values will be appropriate for the network to which you are attached.

3. Type **exit** and press **Enter** to close the Command Prompt window.

With TCP/IP being the protocol of choice on most networks, you will most certainly have to work with DHCP—either at the client, the server, or both. DHCP services run on several types of servers. The installation and configurations for each type of server vary; for specifics, refer to the DHCP server software or NOS manual. To qualify for Network+ certification, you need not know the intricacies of installing and configuring DHCP server software. You do, however, need to know what DHCP does and how it accomplishes it. You also need to understand the advantages of using DHCP rather than other means of assigning IP addresses.

APIPA (Automatic Private IP Addressing)

By now, you understand that as long as DHCP is operating correctly, a client will obtain a valid IP address from the DHCP server and use that address to communicate over the network. But what if the DHCP server is unreachable? Even if everything else on the network is functioning properly, a client cannot communicate without a valid IP address. To address the possibility that the computer might be configured to use DHCP but be unable to find a DHCP server, Microsoft offers Automatic Private IP Addressing for its Windows 98, Me, 2000, XP, Vista, Windows Server 2003, and Windows Server 2008 operating systems. As its name implies, **APIPA (Automatic Private IP Addressing)** provides a computer with an IP address automatically. Specifically, it assigns the computer's network adapter an IP address from a predefined pool of addresses, 169.254.0.0 through 169.254.255.255, that IANA (Internet Assigned Numbers Authority) has reserved for this purpose. It also assigns a subnet mask of 255.255.0.0, the default subnet mask for a Class B network. Because APIPA is part of a computer's operating software, the assignment happens without the need to register or check with a central authority. In the case of a network whose DHCP is temporarily unavailable, when the DHCP server is available once again, APIPA releases its assigned IP address and allows the client to receive a DHCP-assigned address.

After APIPA assigns an address, a computer can then communicate across a LAN. However, it can only communicate with other nodes using addresses in the APIPA range. It cannot

1.1

1.4

communicate with nodes on other subnets. That means, for example, that clients with APIPA-assigned addresses cannot send or receive data to or from the Internet or any other WAN. Therefore, APIPA is best suited to small networks that do not use DHCP servers, in which case it makes IP address management very easy. But it is unsuitable for networks that must communicate with other subnets or over a WAN.

APIPA is enabled by default upon installing the operating system software. To check whether a computer running a Windows operating system is using APIPA:

1. Click the **Start** button, point to **All Programs**, point to **Accessories**, and then select **Command Prompt**. The Command Prompt window opens.

2. At the command prompt, type **`ipconfig /all`** and then press **Enter**. If the Autoconfiguration Enabled option is set to Yes, your computer is using APIPA.

Even if your network does not need or use APIPA, leaving it enabled is not necessarily problematic, because APIPA is designed to first check for the presence of a DHCP server and allow the DHCP server to assign addresses. In addition, if a computer's IP address has been assigned statically, APIPA does not reassign a new address. It only works with clients configured to use DHCP. APIPA can be disabled, however, by editing the Windows operating system's registry.

IPv6 Addressing

1.1

1.3

Up to this point, you have learned about IP addressing according to the IPv4 scheme. This section introduces you to addressing in IPv6 and explains the differences between addressing in IPv4 and addressing in IPv6. For Network+ certification, you will need to understand both addressing schemes.

As you have learned, IPv6 (IP version 6)—also known as **IP next generation**, or **IPng**—is gradually replacing IPv4. Most new applications, servers, and network devices support IPv6. However, due to the cost of upgrading infrastructure, some organizations might hesitate to upgrade from IPv4, which is the addressing scheme still used on the majority of LANs and WANs. Switching to IPv6 has advantages. IPv6 offers a more efficient header, better security, and better prioritization provisions than IPv4, plus automatic IP address configuration. But perhaps the most valuable advantage IPv6 offers is its promise of billions and billions of additional IP addresses through its new addressing scheme.

The most notable difference between IP addresses in IPv4 and IPv6 is their size. While IPv4 addresses are composed of 32 bits, IPv6 addresses are composed of eight 16-bit fields, for a total of 128 bits. The added fields and the larger address size result in an increase of 2^{96} (or 4 billion times 4 billion times 4 billion) available IP addresses in the IPv6 addressing scheme. The addition of more IP addresses not only allows every interface on every Internet-connected device to have a unique number, but it also eliminates the need for IP address conservation. With the increasing number of network-enabled devices, including handheld computers, telephones, home security systems, traffic cameras, and even pet tracking systems, the limited quantity of IPv4 addresses posed a serious bottleneck.

A second difference between IPv4 and IPv6 addresses is the way they are represented. While each octet in an IPv4 address contains binary numbers separated by a period (for example,

123.45.67.89), each field in an IPv6 address is typically represented in hexadecimal numbers separated by a colon. (Keep in mind that the computer still reads the binary version of this address, and if you wanted, you could also write an IPv6 address in binary format.) An example of a valid IPv6 address is F:F:0:0:0:0:3012:0CE3. Because many IPv6 addresses will contain multiple fields that have values of 0, a shorthand for representing these fields has been established. This shorthand substitutes "::" for any number of multiple, zero-value fields. Thus, the preceding IPv6 address example can also be written as F:F::3012:0CE3. An interesting, easily shortened address is the IPv6 loopback address. Recall that in IPv4 the loopback address has a value of 127.0.0.1. In IPv6, however, the loopback address has a value of 0:0:0:0:0:0:0:1. Abbreviated, the IPv6 loopback address becomes ::1. The substitution of multiple zero value fields can only be performed once within an address; otherwise, you cannot tell how many fields the "::" symbol represents. For example, the IPv6 address F:F:0:0:3012:0:0:0CE could *not* be abbreviated FF::3012::CE. It could instead be abbreviated FF::3012:0:0:0CE.

A third difference between the two types of IP addresses is that in IPv6, addresses can reflect the scope of a transmission's recipients—for example, a single node, a group, or a special kind of group. One type of IPv6 address is a **unicast address,** or an address that represents a single interface on a device. A unicast address is the type of address that would be assigned, for example, to a workstation's network adapter. If you wanted to save a file from your laptop onto your company's server using IPv6, that transmission would call for a unicast address. Also, the loopback address is a unicast address.

A **multicast address** represents multiple interfaces (often on multiple devices). Multicast addresses are useful for transmitting the same data to many different devices simultaneously, as in point-to-multipoint communications. IPv6 allows for the specification of several types of multicast groups. For example, the global multicast group, which directs data to all reachable nodes, is akin to the broadcast transmission in IPv4. The link-local multicast group includes computers that share the same link as the transmitting node.

An **anycast address** represents any one interface from a group of interfaces (often on multiple nodes), any one of which (usually the first available) can accept a transmission. Anycast addresses could be useful for identifying all of the routers that belong to one ISP, for example. In this instance, an Internet transmission destined for one of that ISP's servers could be accepted by the first available router in the anycast group. The result is that the transmission finishes faster than if it had to wait for one specific router interface to become available. At this time, anycast addresses are not designed to be assigned to hosts, such as servers or workstations.

A fourth significant difference between IPv4 and IPv6 addressing is that in IPv6, each address contains a **Format Prefix,** or a variable-length field at the beginning of the address that indicates what type of address it is—unicast, multicast, or anycast. A unicast or anycast address begins with one of the two following hexadecimal strings: FEC0 or FE80. A multicast address begins with the following hexadecimal string: FF0x, where x is a character that corresponds to a group scope ID. For example, the Format Prefix for a link-local multicast address is FF02, while the Format Prefix for a global multicast address is FF0E.

Although IPv6 has been defined since the mid-1990s, organizations have been slow to adopt it. However, the use of IPv6 is predicted to grow. Virtually all new devices and operating systems support IPv6 out of the box. For example, operating systems, including Windows Vista and Windows Server 2008, can transmit and receive data using both IPv4 and IPv6 without

1.1

1.3

requiring any configuration changes to their standard installation. More network administrators are realizing that the advantages of using IPv6 outweigh the hassle and cost of changing existing equipment. During this transition phase, IPv4 and IPv6 will coexist. To function in this environment, modern connectivity devices typically embed IPv4 addresses inside IPv6 addresses for transmission over the Internet, padding the extra fields with zeros to fill IPv6's 128-bit address space.

Sockets and Ports

1.2

Just as a device requires a unique address to send and receive information over the network, a process also requires a unique address. Every process on a machine is assigned a port number. If you compare IP addressing with the addressing system used by the postal service, and you equate a host's IP address to the address of a building, a port number is similar to an apartment number within that building. A process's port number plus its host machine's IP address equals the process's **socket**. For example, the standard port number for the Telnet service is 23. On a host whose IPv4 address is 10.43.3.87, the socket address for Telnet is 10.43.3.87:23. In other words, the host assumes that any requests coming into port number 23 are Telnet requests (that is, unless you reconfigure the host to change the default Telnet port). Notice that a port number is expressed as a number following a colon after an IP address. In this example, 23 is not considered an additional octet, but simply a pointer to a port. Sockets form virtual connections between a process on one computer and the same process running on another computer.

Because port numbers are used by transport layer protocols, they apply whether your network uses IPv4 or IPv6.

The use of port numbers simplifies TCP/IP communications and ensures that data is transmitted to the correct application. When a client requests communications with a server and specifies port 23, for example, the server knows immediately that the client wants a Telnet session. No extra data exchange is necessary to define the session type, and the server can initiate the Telnet service without delay. The server will connect to the client's Telnet port—by default, port 23—and establish a virtual circuit. Figure 4-12 depicts this process.

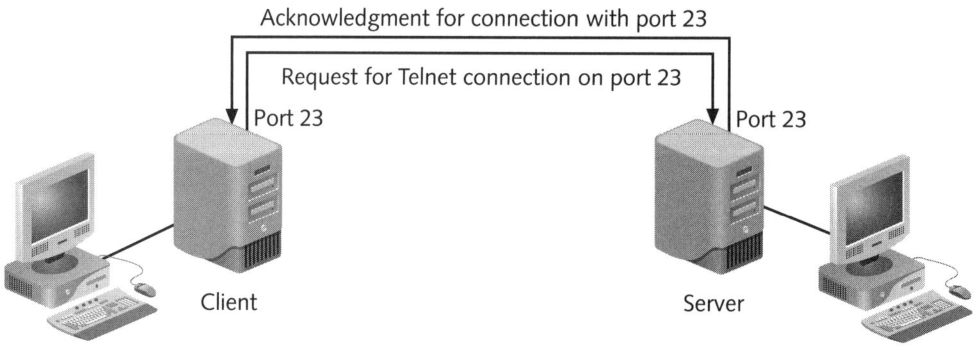

Figure 4-12 A virtual connection for the Telnet service

1.2

Port numbers range from 0 to 65535 and are divided by IANA into three types: Well Known Ports, Registered Ports, and Dynamic and/or Private Ports. **Well Known Ports** are in the range of 0 to 1023 and are assigned to processes that only the operating system or an administrator of the system can access. These were the first ports assigned to processes, and so the earliest TCP/IP protocols, such as TCP, UDP, Telnet, and FTP, use Well Known Ports. Table 4-3 lists some of these Well Known Ports. **Registered Ports** are in the range of 1024 to 49151. These ports are accessible to network users and processes that do not have special administrative privileges. Default assignments of these ports (for example, by a software program) must be registered with IANA. **Dynamic Ports** and/or **Private Ports** are those ranging from 49152 through 65535 and are open for use without restriction.

Although you do not need to memorize every port number for the Network+ certification exam, you may be asked about the port numbers associated with common services, such as Telnet, FTP, and HTTP. Knowing them will also help you in configuring and troubleshooting networks using TCP/IP.

Port numbers are assigned either by the operating system or by software programs that rely on them. Servers maintain an editable, text-based file of port numbers and their associated services. With administrative (unlimited) privileges, you are free to change any port numbers a device uses. For example, you could change the default port number for the Telnet service on your server from 23 to 2330. Changing a default port number is rarely a good idea, however, because it violates the standard and means that processes programmed to use a standard port will not be able to communicate with your machine. Nevertheless, some network administrators who are preoccupied with security may change their servers' port numbers in an attempt to confuse people with malicious intent who try connecting to their devices through conventional sockets.

Table 4-3 Commonly Used TCP/IP Port Numbers

Port Number	Process Name	Protocol Used	Description
20	FTP-DATA	TCP	File transfer—data
21	FTP	TCP	File transfer—control
22	SSH	TCP	Secure Shell
23	TELNET	TCP	Telnet
25	SMTP	TCP	Simple Mail Transfer Protocol
53	DNS	TCP and UDP	Domain Name System
69	TFTP	UDP	Trivial File Transfer Protocol
80	HTTP	TCP and UDP	Hypertext Transfer Protocol
110	POP3	TCP	Post Office Protocol 3
123	NTP	TCP	Network Time Protocol
143	IMAP	TCP	Internet Message Access Protocol
443	HTTPS	TCP	Secure implementation of HTTP

Host Names and DNS (Domain Name System)

Net+

1.1

Much of TCP/IP addressing involves numbers—often long, complicated numbers. Computers can manage numbers easily. However, most people can remember words better than numbers. Imagine if you had to identify your friends' and families' Social Security numbers whenever you wanted to write a note or talk to them. Communication would be frustrating at the very least, and perhaps even impossible—especially if you're the kind of person who has trouble remembering even your own Social Security number. Similarly, people prefer to associate names with networked devices rather than remember IP addresses. For this reason, the Internet authorities established a naming system for all nodes on the Internet.

Every device on the Internet is technically known as a host. Every host can take a **host name**, a name that describes the device. For example, someone named Jasmine McDonald might name her workstation "Jasmine." If the computer is reserved for a specific purpose, you may want to name it accordingly. For example, a company that offers free software downloads through the FTP service might call its host machine "ftpserver."

Domain Names

Every host is a member of a **domain**, or a group of computers that belongs to the same organization and has part of their IP addresses in common. A domain is identified by its domain name. Usually, a **domain name** is associated with a company or other type of organization, such as a university, government organization, or company. For example, IBM's domain name is ibm.com, and the United States Library of Congress's domain name is loc.gov.

Often, when networking professionals refer to a machine's host name, they in fact mean its local host name *plus* its domain name—in other words, its **fully qualified host name**. If you worked at the Library of Congress and gave your workstation the host name Jasmine, your fully qualified host name might be jasmine.loc.gov.

A domain name is represented by a series of character strings, called **labels**, separated by dots. Each label represents a level in the domain naming hierarchy. In the domain name www.google.com, *com* is the **top-level domain** (TLD), *google* is the second-level domain, and *www* is the third-level domain. Each second-level domain can contain multiple third-level domains. For instance, in addition to www.google.com, Google owns the following domains: *news.google.com*, *maps.google.com*, and *mail.google.com*.

Domain names must be registered with an Internet naming authority that works on behalf of ICANN. ICANN has established conventions for domain naming so that certain TLDs apply to every type of organization that uses the Internet. Table 4-4 lists ICANN-approved TLDs. The first eight TLDs listed in this table were established in the mid-1980s. Of these, no restrictions exist on the use of the .com, .org, and .net TLDs, but ICANN does restrict what type of hosts can be associated with the .arpa, .mil, .int, .edu, and .gov TLDs. Over the past few years, ICANN has responded to requests from various organizations and approved the next seven TLDs in Table 4-4. Additional efforts are underway to open up even more TLDs.

In addition to those listed in Table 4-4, ICANN has approved over 240 **country code TLDs** to represent different countries and territories across the globe. For example, .ca is the country code TLD assigned to Canada, and .jp is the country code TLD assigned to Japan. Organizations are not required to use country code TLDs. For example, although Cisco's headquarters are located in the United States, the company's domain name is *www.cisco.com*, not *www.cisco.us*. On the other hand, some United States organizations do use the .us

1.1

Table 4-4 Top-Level Domains

Domain Suffix	Type of Organization
ARPA	Reverse lookup domain (special Internet function)
COM	Commercial
EDU	Educational
GOV	Government
ORG	Noncommercial organization (such as a nonprofit agency)
NET	Network (such as an ISP)
INT	International Treaty Organization
MIL	United States military organization
BIZ	Businesses
INFO	Unrestricted use
AERO	Air-transport industry
COOP	Cooperatives
MUSEUM	Museums
NAME	Individuals
PRO	Professionals such as doctors, lawyers, and engineers

suffix. For example, the domain name for the Garden City, New York, public school district is *www.gardencity.k12.ny.us*.

After an organization reserves a domain name, the rest of the world's computers know to associate that domain name with the organization to which it is assigned, and no other organization can legally use it. For example, you might apply for the domain name called freeflies.com; not only would the rest of the Internet associate that name with your network, but also, no other parties in the world could use freeflies.com in naming computers on their network that connects to the Internet.

Host and domain names are subject to some restrictions. They may consist of any alphanumeric combination up to a maximum of 63 characters, and they can include hyphens, underscores, or periods in the name, but no other special characters. The interesting part of host and domain naming relates to how all Internet-connected machines in the world know which names belong to which machines. Before tackling the entire world, however, you can start by thinking about how one company might deal with its local host names, as explained in the following section.

Host Files

The first incarnation of the Internet (ARPAnet) was used by fewer than 1,000 hosts. The entire network relied on one ASCII text file called HOSTS.TXT to associate host names with IP addresses. This file was generically known as a **host file**. Growth of the Internet soon made this simple arrangement impossible to maintain—the host file would require constant changes, searching through one file from all over the nation would strain the Internet's bandwidth capacity, and the entire Internet would fail if the file were accidentally deleted.

However, within a company or university, you may still encounter this older system of using a text file to associate (internal) host names with their IP addresses. Figure 4-13 provides an example of such a file. Notice that each host is matched by one line identifying the host's name and IP address. In addition, a third field, called an **alias**, provides a nickname for the host. An alias allows a user within an organization to address a host by a shorter name than the full host name. Typically, the first line of a host file begins with a pound sign and contains comments about the file's columns. A pound sign may precede comments anywhere in the host file.

```
# IP address          host name             alias
132.55.78.109         bingo.games.com       bingo
132.55.78.110         parcheesi.games.com   parcheesi
132.55.78.111         checkers.games.com    checkers
132.55.78.112         darts.games.com       darts
```

Figure 4-13 Example host file

On a UNIX- or Linux-based computer, a host file is called **hosts** and is located in the /etc directory. On a Windows 9x, NT, 2000, XP, or Vista computer, a host file is also called hosts (with no file extension) and is located in the %systemroot%\system32\drivers\etc folder (where %systemroot% is the directory in which the operating system is installed). If you are using hosts files, you should not only master the syntax of this file, but you should also research the implications of using a static host file on your network.

DNS (Domain Name System)

A simple host file can satisfy the needs of a small organization; however, it is not sufficient for large organizations, much less for the Internet. Instead, a more automated solution has become mandatory. In the mid-1980s, computer scientists responsible for the Internet's growth devised a hierarchical way of associating domain names with IP addresses, called the **DNS (Domain Name System** or **Domain Name Service)**. *DNS* refers to both the application layer service that accomplishes this association and the organized system of computers and databases that makes this association possible. The DNS service does not rely on one file or even one server, but rather on many computers across the globe. These computers are related in a hierarchical manner, with 13 computers, known as **root servers**, acting as the ultimate authorities. Because it is distributed, DNS will not fail catastrophically if one or a handful of servers experience errors.

To direct traffic efficiently, the DNS service is divided into three components: resolvers, name servers, and namespace. **Resolvers** are any hosts on the Internet that need to look up domain name information. The resolver client is built into TCP/IP applications such as HTTP. If you point your Web browser to *http://www.loc.gov*, your HTTP client software initiates the resolver service to find the IP address for *www.loc.gov*. If you have visited the site before, the information may exist in temporary memory and may be retrieved very quickly. Otherwise, the resolver service queries your machine's designated name server to find the IP address for *www.loc.gov*.

Name servers, or **DNS servers,** are servers that contain databases of associated names and IP addresses and provide this information to resolvers on request. If one name server cannot resolve the domain name to its IP address, it passes the query to a higher-authority name

server. For example, suppose you are trying to open the *www.loc.gov* Web page from a workstation on your company's network. Further, suppose this is the first time you've visited the Library of Congress online. Upon discovering it does not have the information saved locally, your client's resolver service queries the closest name server for the IP address associated with *www.loc.gov*. That name server is probably connected to your LAN. If your LAN's name server cannot supply the IP address for *www.loc.gov*, it queries a higher-level name server. In other words, your company's name server sends a request to the name server at the company's Internet service provider (ISP). If that name server does not have the information in its database, it queries a name server elsewhere on the Internet that acts as the ISP's naming authority. This process, depicted in Figure 4-14, continues until the request is granted.

Figure 4-14 Domain name resolution

Net+
1.1

The term *namespace* refers to the database of Internet IP addresses and their associated names. Namespace is not a database that you can open and view like a store's inventory database. Rather, this abstract concept describes how the name servers of the world share DNS information. Pieces of it are tangible, however, and are stored on a name server in a **resource record**, which is a single record that describes one piece of information in the DNS database. For example, an **address resource record** is a type of resource record that maps the IP address of an Internet-connected device to its domain name. By storing resource records, every name server holds a piece of the DNS namespace.

Resource records come in many different types, depending on their function. Each resource record contains a name field to identify the domain name of the machine to which the record refers, a type field to identify the type of resource record involved, a class field to identify the class to which the record belongs (usually "IN" or "Internet"), a Time to Live field to identify how long the record should be saved in temporary memory, a data length field to identify how much data the record contains, and the actual record data. Approximately 20 types of resource records are currently used.

In the following fictitious address resource record, knight.chess.games.com is the host domain name, IN stands for the Internet record class, A identifies the record type as "address," and 203.99.120.76 is the host's IP address:

```
knight.chess.games.com IN A 203.99.120.76
```

At one time, network administrators manually maintained resource records for their networks' hosts. Now, however, most modern clients update their resource records dynamically. This saves time and eliminates the possibility for human error in modifying DNS information. Clients can be configured to trigger a DNS update when they receive a new IP address (for example, through DHCP), when their host names change, or when they connect to a network. Alternatively, a user can force a DNS record update by issuing a command. For example, typing `ipconfig /registerdns` at a Windows XP or Windows Vista command prompt forces an update of the client's registered DNS information.

Configuring DNS

Any host that must communicate with other hosts on the Internet needs to know how to find its name server. Although some organizations use only one name server, large organizations often maintain two name servers—a primary and a secondary name server—to help ensure Internet connectivity. If the primary name server experiences a failure, all devices on the network attempt to use the secondary name server. Each device on the network relies on the name server and, therefore, must know how to find it.

On most networks, the DHCP service automatically assigns clients the appropriate addresses for its primary and secondary name servers. However, on occasion you might need to manually configure these values in a workstation's TCP/IP properties.

To view or change the name server information on a Windows XP workstation:

1. Click **Start**, and then click **My Network Places**. The My Network Places window opens.

2. From the Network Tasks list, click **View network connections**. The Network Connections window opens.

1.1

3. Right-click the icon that represents your network adapter, and click **Properties** in the shortcut menu. The network adapter's Properties dialog box opens.

4. Under the This connection uses the following items heading, select **Internet Protocol (TCP/IP)**, and then click **Properties**. The Internet Protocol (TCP/IP) Properties dialog box opens, as shown in Figure 4-15.

5. If you want to specify the DNS server your workstation relies on, rather than allowing DHCP to supply the DNS server address, verify that the General tab is still selected, and then click the **Use the following DNS server addresses** button.

6. Enter the IP address for your primary DNS server in the Preferred DNS server space and the address for your secondary DNS server in the Alternate DNS server space.

7. Click **OK**, click **Close** to save your changes, and then close the Network Connections window.

To view or change name server information on a Windows Vista workstation:

1. Click the **Start** button, and then click **Control Panel**. The Control Panel window opens.

2. If your Control Panel window is displayed in Classic View, select **Control Panel Home** in the left pane. You see the Control Panel home page view.

3. Click **Network and Internet**. The Network and Internet window opens.

4. Click **Network and Sharing Center**. The Network and Sharing Center window opens.

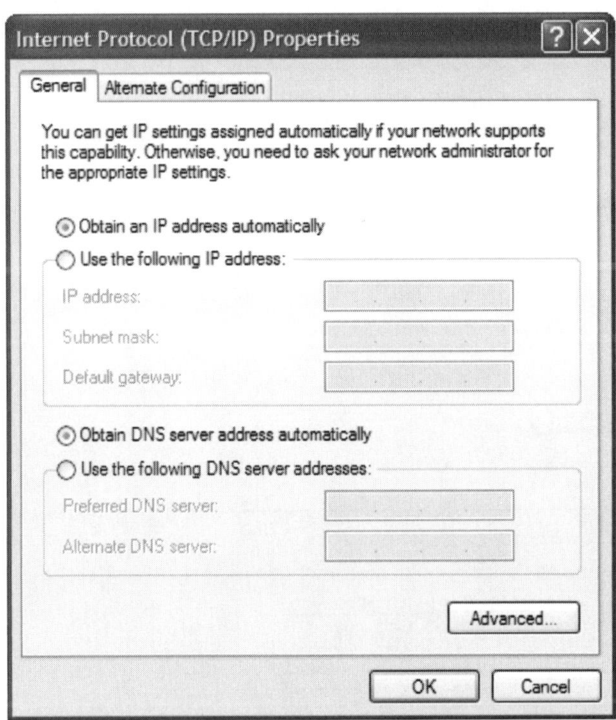

Figure 4-15 Windows XP Internet Protocol (TCP/IP) Properties dialog box

1.1

5. Click **Manage network connections** from the list of options on the left side of the window. The Network Connections window opens, showing your network interfaces and their connection status. (For example, an interface that is not connected to a network will be marked with a red X.)

6. Right-click a network interface, and then click **Properties** from the shortcut menu.

7. A User Account Control window appears. Click **Continue** to access the network interface properties.

8. The Network Connection Properties window opens, showing a list of the network services used by that connection. In that list, click **Internet Protocol Version 4 (TCP/IPv4)** to highlight this service, and then click **Properties**. The Internet Protocol Version 4 (TCP/IPv4) Properties dialog box opens, as shown in Figure 4-16.

9. If you want to specify the DNS server your workstation relies on, rather than allowing DHCP to supply the DNS server address, verify that the General tab is selected, and then click the **Use the following DNS server addresses** button.

10. Enter the IP address for your primary DNS server in the Preferred DNS server space and the address for your secondary DNS server in the Alternate DNS server space.

11. Click **OK**, and then click **Close** to save your changes.

12. Finally, close the Network Connections and Network and Sharing Center windows.

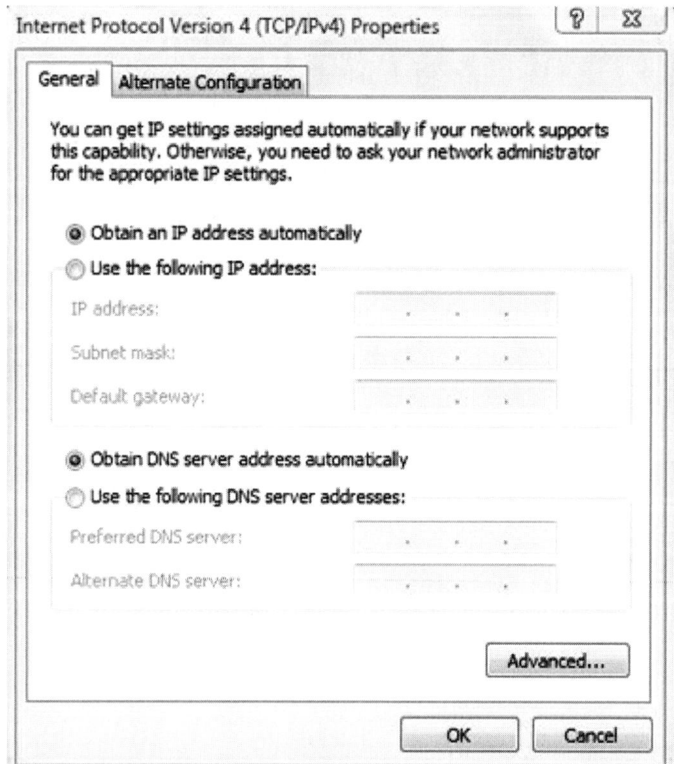

Figure 4-16 Windows Vista Internet Protocol Version 4 (TCP/IPv4) Properties dialog box

1.1

For Network+ certification, you should know the purpose of DNS and host files, understand the hierarchical nature of DNS, and be able to specify name servers on a client workstation.

DDNS (Dynamic DNS)

DNS is a reliable way of locating a host as long as the host's IP address remains relatively constant over time—that is, if it's static. However, many Internet users subscribe to a type of Internet service in which their IP address changes periodically. For a user who only wants to send and receive e-mail and surf the Web, frequently changing IP addresses is not problematic. But for a user who wants to host a Web site, for example, it can be. To maintain the association between his Web site's host or domain name and an IP address, such a user must change his computer's DNS record and propagate this change across the Internet each time the IP address changes. When IP addresses change frequently, manually changing DNS records becomes unmanageable.

A solution is to use **DDNS (Dynamic DNS)**. In DDNS, a service provider runs a program on the user's computer that notifies the service provider when the user's IP address changes. Upon notification, the service provider's server launches a routine that automatically updates the DNS record for that user's computer. The DNS record update becomes effective throughout the Internet in a matter of minutes.

Note that DDNS does not take the place of DNS but is an additional service, available for a small fee. DDNS is a good option for home or small office users who maintain Web sites but do not want to pay the additional (often high) cost of reserving a static IP address. However, because of the slight delay in DNS record propagation caused each time an IP address changes, larger organizations typically prefer to pay more for a statically assigned IP address.

Associating host and domain names with computers on a TCP/IP-based network is performed by the application layer protocol DNS. The following section describes other important application layer protocols.

Zeroconf (Zero Configuration)

Zeroconf (Zero Configuration) is a collection of protocols designed by the IETF to simplify the setup of nodes on a TCP/IP network. Zeroconf assigns a node an IP address, resolves the node's host name and IP address without requiring a DNS server, and discovers services, such as print services, available to the node, also without requiring a DNS server. Zeroconf enables two workstations directly connected (using a crossover cable, for example) to communicate without relying on static IP addressing, DHCP servers, or DNS servers. Before Zeroconf, this type of communication could take place among Windows systems using NetBIOS or Macintosh systems using AppleTalk, but not between the two different systems. Zeroconf functions identically on multiple different operating systems, and it comes with Macintosh OS 9 and X, Windows 98, Me, 2000, XP, Vista, Server 2003, Server 2008, and most implementations of Linux. Apple's version of Zeroconf is called **Rendezvous**.

With Zeroconf, IP addresses are assigned through **IPv4LL (IP version 4 Link Local)**, a protocol that manages automatic address assignment among locally connected nodes. In IPv4LL, when Computer A joins the network, it randomly chooses an IP address in the range of 169.254.1.0 to 169.254.254.255, which is reserved for IPv4LL use. Before using its chosen address to communicate, Computer A sends a message, via the ARP protocol, to the rest of its subnet indicating its desire to use that IP address. But suppose Computer B is already using the address. In that case, Computer B will respond to Computer A's message with a broadcast that alerts every other node on the subnet that the IP address is already in use. Computer A will then randomly select a different IP address. However, if, after a brief period of time, no other node responds to the first node's announcement, Computer A will issue a broadcast message that informs the rest of the subnet that it has assigned itself the address it chose initially.

Note that IPv4LL-assigned addresses are reserved for communication among locally linked nodes. Because they are not globally unique, they cannot be used on larger networks, like the Internet. (Advanced TCP/IP addressing techniques, such as those discussed in Chapter 10, can be used to allow these nodes to communicate with the Internet, however.) IPv4LL is especially useful with network printers. Most printers don't come with interfaces that enable a network administrator to easily configure TCP/IP variables. If they support Zeroconf and use IPv4LL, printers can be connected to the network and ready to communicate with no human intervention. Most printers manufactured today come with Zeroconf support.

Application Layer Protocols

1.1

In addition to the core transport and Internet layer protocols, the TCP/IP suite encompasses several application layer protocols. These protocols work over TCP or UDP plus IP, translating user requests into a format the network can read. In Chapter 2 you learned about an application layer protocol central to using the Web, HTTP. And earlier in this chapter you learned about two application layer protocols used for automatic address assignment, BOOTP and DHCP. The following sections describe some additional application layer protocols. Throughout this book, and especially in Chapter 10, you'll encounter even more TCP/IP application layer protocols.

Telnet

Telnet is a terminal emulation protocol used to log on to remote hosts using the TCP/IP protocol suite. Using Telnet, a TCP connection is established and keystrokes on the user's machine act like keystrokes on the remotely connected machine. Often, Telnet is used to connect two dissimilar systems (such as PCs and UNIX machines). Through Telnet, you can control a remote host over LANs and WANs such as the Internet. For example, network managers can use Telnet to log on to a router from a computer elsewhere on their LAN and modify the router's configuration. Telnet, however, is notoriously insecure (meaning that someone with malicious intent could easily falsify the credentials Telnet requires to log on to a device successfully), so telnetting to a router across a public network would not be wise. Other, more secure methods of remotely connecting to a host have replaced Telnet for that reason. A popular alternative, known as SSH, is described in Chapter 12, which focuses on security.

FTP (File Transfer Protocol)

FTP (File Transfer Protocol) is an application layer protocol used to send and receive files via TCP/IP. In FTP exchanges, a host running the FTP server portion accepts commands from another host running the FTP client portion. FTP clients come with a set of simple commands that make up its user interface. To exchange data, the client depends on an FTP server that is always waiting for requests. After a client connects to the FTP server, FTP data is exchanged via TCP, which means that FTP provides some assurance of delivery.

FTP commands will work from your operating system's command prompt; they do not require special client software. As a network professional, you may need to use these commands to download software (such as NOS patches or client updates) from hosts. For example, if you need the latest version of the Fedora Linux distribution, you can use FTP from your workstation's command prompt to download the compressed software from a Fedora-authorized FTP server to your hard disk. To do so, you can start the FTP utility by typing `ftp` from your operating system command (or shell) prompt. The command prompt turns into the FTP prompt, `FTP>`. From there, you can run FTP commands. Alternatively, if you know what operation you want to perform, you can connect directly to an FTP server. For example, to connect directly to the Fedora FTP server at Boston University (one of several that provides the software via FTP), type `ftp fedora.bu.edu`, and then press Enter. If the host is running, it responds with a greeting and a request for you to log on.

Many FTP hosts, especially those whose purpose is to provide software updates, accept anonymous logons. This means that when prompted for a user name, you need only type the word `anonymous` (in all small letters). When prompted for a password on an anonymous FTP site, you can typically use your e-mail address. The host's logon screen should indicate whether this is acceptable. On the other hand, if you are logging on to a private FTP site, you must obtain a valid user name and password from the site's network administrator to make a successful connection.

After you have successfully connected to a host, additional commands allow you to manage the connection and manipulate files. For example, after you have connected to one of Fedora's FTP sites, you could type `ls` and press Enter to view a directory listing. Next, you could type `cd pub` and press Enter to change your working directory to the pub directory, where files are made available for public access. Then you could type `cd releases` and press Enter to change your working directory to the releases directory, where the latest version of the Fedora Linux software is kept. Once in that directory, you could download a file by typing `get`*XXX*, where *XXX* is the name of the file you want to download. To terminate the connection, simply type `quit`. The following list summarizes a handful of useful FTP commands and their syntax. To learn more about these and other FTP commands, type `help` after starting the FTP utility.

- `ascii`—Sets the file transfer mode to ASCII. Most FTP hosts store two types of files: ASCII and binary. Text files are typically ASCII-based and contain formatting characters, such as carriage returns. Binary files (for example, executable programs) typically contain no formatting characters. Before downloading files from an FTP host, you must understand what type of file you are downloading. If you download a file while in the wrong mode (ASCII if the file is binary or vice versa), your file will appear as gibberish when you open it. If the file you want to download is an ASCII file, type `ascii` at the FTP prompt and press Enter before starting your file transfer.

- `binary`—Sets the file transfer mode to binary. If the file you want to download from an FTP site is binary (for example, an executable program or a compressed software patch), type `binary` at the FTP prompt and press Enter before starting your file transfer.

- `cd`—Changes your working directory on the host machine.

- delete—Deletes a file on the host machine (provided you have permissions to do so).

- get—Transfers a file from the host machine to the client. For example, to transfer the file called update.exe from the host to your workstation, you can type get update.exe. Unless you specify a target directory and file name, the file is saved to your hard disk in the directory where you started the FTP utility. Therefore, if you want to save the update.exe file to your C:\download\patches directory, you type: get update.exe "c:\download\patches" (Make sure to include the quotation marks.)

- help—Provides a list of commands when issued from the FTP prompt. When used in conjunction with a command, help provides information on the purpose of that command. For example, after typing help ls, you learn that the ls command lists the contents of a remote directory.

- ls—Provides a directory listing of files and subdirectories.

- mget—Transfers multiple files from the FTP site to your workstation simultaneously. For example, to transfer all the text files within one directory, you could type: mget .txt at the FTP> prompt.

- mput—Transfers multiple files from your workstation to the FTP host.

- open—Creates a connection with an FTP host.

- put—Transfers a file from your workstation to the FTP host.

- quit—Terminates your FTP connection and closes the FTP utility.

Graphical FTP clients, such as MacFTP, WS_FTP, CuteFTP, and SmartFTP, have rendered this command-line method of FTPing files less common. In many cases you can also accomplish FTP file transfers directly from a modern Web browser. To do this, you need only point your browser to the FTP host. From there, you can move through directories and exchange files just as you would navigate the files and directories on your desktop or LAN server.

As with Telnet, a more secure version of the FTP protocol has been developed. This protocol, known as SFTP, is discussed in Chapter 12.

FTP and Telnet share some similarities, including their reliance on TCP and their ability to log on to a remote host and perform commands on that host. However, they differ in that, when you use Telnet, the commands you type require a syntax that is relative to your local workstation. When you use FTP, the commands you type require a syntax that is relative to the remote host to which you have logged on. Also, Telnet has no built-in commands for transferring files between the remote host and your workstation.

TFTP (Trivial File Transfer Protocol)

TFTP (Trivial File Transfer Protocol) is another TCP/IP application layer protocol that enables file transfers between computers, but it is simpler (or more trivial) than FTP. A significant difference between FTP and TFTP is that TFTP relies on UDP at the transport layer. Its use of UDP means that TFTP is connectionless and does not guarantee reliable delivery of data. Also, TFTP does not require users to log on to the remote host with an ID and password to gain access to a directory and transfer files. Instead, when you enter the TFTP command, your computer issues a simple request to access the host's files. The remote host responds with an acknowledgment, and then the two computers begin transferring data. Each time a packet

of data is transmitted to the host, the local workstation waits for an acknowledgment from the host before issuing another packet. In this way, TFTP overcomes some of the limitations of relying on a connectionless transport layer protocol. A final difference between FTP and TFTP is that the latter does not allow directory browsing. In FTP, you can connect to a host and navigate through all the directories you've been granted access to view.

TFTP is useful when you need to load data or programs on a diskless workstation. For example, suppose a TFTP server holds Microsoft Excel. When a client issues a TFTP request for that program, the server would transmit the program files to the workstation's memory. After the user completes his Excel work, the program files would be released from his workstation's memory. In this situation, the fact that TFTP does not require a user to log on to a host is an advantage. It makes the transfer of program files quick and easy. As you can imagine, however, not requiring a logon also presents a security risk, so TFTP servers must be carefully placed and monitored on a network.

NTP (Network Time Protocol)

NTP (Network Time Protocol) is a simple application layer protocol used to synchronize the clocks of computers on a network. NTP depends on UDP for transport layer services. Although it is simple, it is also important. Time is critical in routing to determine the most efficient path for data over a network. Time synchronization across a network is also important for time-stamped security methods and maintaining accuracy and consistency between multiple storage systems. NTP is a protocol that benefits from UDP's quick, connectionless nature at the transport layer. NTP is time sensitive and cannot wait for the error checking that TCP would require.

NNTP (Network News Transfer Protocol)

Another application layer protocol in the TCP/IP suite is **NNTP (Network News Transfer Protocol** or **Network News Transport Protocol)**, which facilitates the exchange of newsgroup messages between multiple servers and users. A **newsgroup** is similar to e-mail, in that it provides a means of conveying messages; it differs from e-mail in that it distributes messages to a wide group of users at once rather than from one user to another. Newsgroups have been formed to discuss every conceivable topic, such as political issues, professional affiliations, entertainment interests, or sports clubs. To join a newsgroup, a user subscribes to the server that hosts the newsgroup. From that point forward, the user receives all messages that other newsgroup members post to the group. To send a message to the group, a user only has to address the message to the newsgroup's e-mail address.

Newsgroups require news servers that act as a central collection and distribution point for newsgroup messages. News servers are organized hierarchically across the Internet, similar to the way DNS servers are organized. Clients can use e-mail, Internet browsers, or special newsgroup reading software to receive newsgroup messages. NNTP supports the process of reading newsgroup messages, posting new messages, and transferring news files between news servers.

PING (Packet Internet Groper)

PING (Packet Internet Groper) is a utility that can verify that TCP/IP is installed, bound to the NIC, configured correctly, and communicating with the network. It is often employed simply to determine whether a host is responding (or "up"). PING uses ICMP services to send echo request and echo reply messages that determine the validity of an IP address. These two types of messages work in much the same way that sonar operates. First, a signal, called an **echo request**, is sent out to another computer. The other computer then rebroadcasts the signal, in the form of an **echo reply**, to the sender. The process of sending this signal back and forth is known as **pinging**.

You can ping either an IP address or a host name. For example, to determine whether the *www.loc.gov* site is responding, you could type `ping www.loc.gov` and press Enter. Alternately, you could type `ping 140.147.249.7` (the IP address of this site at the time this book was written) and press Enter. If the site is operating correctly, you will receive a response that includes multiple replies from that host. If the site is not operating correctly, you will receive a response indicating that the request timed out or that the host was not found. You could also receive a "request timed out" message if your workstation is not properly connected to the network, or if the network is malfunctioning. Figure 4-17 gives examples of a successful and an unsuccessful ping test.

By pinging the loopback address, 127.0.0.1, you can determine whether your workstation's TCP/IP services are running. By pinging a host on another subnet, you can determine whether the problem lies with a connectivity device between the two subnets.

For example, suppose that you have recently moved your computer from the Accounting department to the Advertising department, and now you cannot access the Web. The first test you should perform is pinging the loopback address. If that test is successful, then you know that your workstation's TCP/IP services are running correctly. Next, you might try pinging your neighbor's machine. If you receive a positive response, you know that your network connection is working. You should then try pinging a machine on another subnet that you know is connected to the network—for example, a computer in the IT department. If this test is unsuccessful, you can safely conclude that you do not have the correct settings in

```
C:\>ping 140.147.249.7

Pinging 140.147.249.7 with 32 bytes of data:

Reply from 140.147.249.7: bytes=32 time=47ms TTL=243
Reply from 140.147.249.7: bytes=32 time=46ms TTL=243
Reply from 140.147.249.7: bytes=32 time=46ms TTL=243
Reply from 140.147.249.7: bytes=32 time=48ms TTL=243

Ping statistics for 140.147.249.7:
    Packets: Sent = 4, Received = 4, Lost = 0 (0% loss),
Approximate round trip times in milli-seconds:
    Minimum = 46ms, Maximum = 48ms, Average = 46ms

C:\>ping 22.34.129.87

Pinging 22.34.129.87 with 32 bytes of data:

Request timed out.
Request timed out.
Request timed out.
Request timed out.

Ping statistics for 22.34.129.87:
    Packets: Sent = 4, Received = 0, Lost = 4 (100% loss),

C:\>
```

Figure 4-17   Output from successful and unsuccessful PING tests your TCP/IP configuration or that something is wrong with your network's connectivity (for example, a router may be malfunctioning).

As with other TCP/IP commands, PING can be used with a number of different options, or **switches,** and the syntax of the command may vary depending on the operating system. But a ping command always begins with the word *ping* followed by a hyphen (-) and a switch, followed by a variable pertaining to that switch. The following are some useful PING switches:

- -?—Displays the help text for the `ping` command, including its syntax and a full list of switches.

- -a—When used with an IP address, resolves the address to a host name.

- -n—Allows you to specify a number of echo requests to send. For example, if you want to ping the Library of Congress site with only two echo requests (rather than the standard four that a Windows operating system uses), you could type the following command: `ping -n 2 www.loc.gov`.

- -r—When used with a number from 1 to 9, displays the route taken during ping hops.

To view the proper syntax and a list of switches available for PING, type `ping` at the command prompt on a Windows-based computer or at the shell prompt on a UNIX or Linux system.

Chapter Summary

- Protocols define the standards for communication between nodes on a network. The term *protocol* can refer to a group, or suite, of individual protocols that work together to accomplish data translation, data handling, error checking, and addressing.

- Protocols vary by transmission efficiency, utilization of resources, ease of setup, compatibility, and ability to travel between one LAN segment and another. Protocols that can span more than one LAN are routable, which means they carry network layer addressing information that can be interpreted by a router.

- TCP/IP is the most popular protocol suite because of its low cost, open nature, ability to communicate between dissimilar platforms, and the fact that it is routable. It is a de facto standard on the Internet and is commonly the protocol of choice on LANs.

- TCP (Transmission Control Protocol) belongs to the transport layer of the OSI model. TCP is a connection-oriented subprotocol; it requires a connection to be established between communicating nodes before it will transmit data. TCP provides reliability through checksum, flow control, and sequencing information.

- UDP (User Datagram Protocol), like TCP, is a transport layer protocol. UDP is a connectionless service and offers no delivery guarantees. But UDP is more efficient than TCP and useful in applications that require fast data transmission, such as videoconferencing.

- IP (Internet Protocol) belongs to the network layer of the OSI model and provides information about how and where data should be delivered.

- ARP (Address Resolution Protocol) belongs to the network layer of the OSI model. It obtains the MAC (physical) address of a host, or node, and then creates a local database that maps the MAC address to the host's IP (logical) address. RARP (Reverse Address Resolution Protocol) performs the opposite function; it maps IP addresses to MAC addresses.

- In IPv4, each IP address is a unique 32-bit number, divided into four octets (or bytes). Every IP address contains two types of information: network and host.

- In traditional IPv4 addressing, all nodes on a Class A network share the first octet of their IP numbers, a number between 1 and 126. Nodes on a Class B network share the first two octets, and all their IP addresses begin with a number between 128 and 191. Class C network IP numbers share the first three octets, with their first octet being a number between 192 and 223.

- Although computers read IPv4 addresses in binary form, humans usually read them in dotted decimal notation, in which a decimal number represents each octet and every number is separated by a period.

- A subnet mask is a 32-bit number that indicates whether and how a network has been subnetted—that is, subdivided into multiple smaller networks—and indicates the difference between network and host information in an IPv4 address. Subnetting is implemented to control network traffic and conserve a limited number of IPv4 addresses.

- IP addresses assigned manually are called static IP addresses; however, using static IP addresses allows for the possibility of assigning the same address to more than one device.

- Dynamic IP address assignment can be achieved using BOOTP or the more sophisticated DHCP (Dynamic Host Configuration Protocol). DHCP, though not foolproof, essentially eliminates duplicate-addressing problems.

- If a computer runs the Windows 98, Me, 2000, XP, Vista, Server 2003, or Server 2008 operating system, is configured to use DHCP, and cannot locate a DHCP server, it can be assigned an IP address and subnet mask through APIPA (Automatic Private IP Addressing). This configuration allows the computer to communicate with other computers on the same subnet only.

- IPv6 (IP version 6) is the latest version of IP. Its addresses are composed of eight 16-bit fields and total 128 bits. The larger address size results in an additional 2^{96} available IP addresses compared to IPv4. IPv6 provides several other benefits over IPv4, including a more efficient header, better overall security, better prioritization allowances, and automatic IP address configuration. IPv6 is not yet widely implemented.

- A socket is a logical address assigned to a specific process running on a host. It forms a virtual circuit between the processes on two networked hosts. The socket's address represents a combination of the host's IP address and the port number associated with a process.

- Every host is identified by a host name and belongs to a domain. A domain is a group of hosts that share a domain name and have part of their IP addresses in common.

- Every domain is identified by its domain name. Usually, a domain name is associated with a company or other type of organization, such as a university or military unit. Domain names must be reserved with an ICANN-approved domain registrar.

- DNS (Domain Name System or Domain Name Service) is a hierarchical way of tracking domain names and their addresses. The DNS database does not rely on one file or even one server, but rather is distributed over several key computers across the Internet to prevent catastrophic failure if one or a few computers go down.

- Name servers or DNS servers contain databases of names and their associated IP addresses. If one name server cannot resolve the IP address, the query passes to a higher-level name server. Each name server manages a group of machines called a zone. DNS relies on the hierarchical zones to distribute naming information.

- When one host needs to communicate with another host, it must first find its name server. Large organizations often maintain a primary and a secondary name server to help ensure Internet connectivity. You need to specify a name server's IP address in the TCP/IP properties of a workstation so that the workstation will know which machine to query when looking up a name.

- Some key TCP/IP application layer protocols include Telnet (for logging on to hosts), FTP and TFTP (for transferring files between hosts), NTP (for synchronizing time between hosts), NNTP (for storage and distribution of newsgroup messages), and PING (for sending echo requests and echo replies that can indicate whether a host is responding).

Key Terms

Address Resolution Protocol   *See* ARP.

address resource record   A type of DNS data record that maps the IP address of an Internet-connected device to its domain name.

alias   A nickname for a node's host name. Aliases can be specified in a local host file.

anycast address   A type of address specified in IPv6 that represents a group of interfaces, any one of which (and usually the first available of which) can accept a transmission. At this time, anycast addresses are not designed to be assigned to hosts, such as servers or workstations, but rather to routers.

APIPA (Automatic Private IP Addressing)   A service available on computers running the Windows 98, Me, 2000, XP, Vista, Server 2003, or Server 2008 operating system that automatically assigns the computer's network interface an IP address from the range of 169.254.0.0 to 169.254.255.255 if an IP address hasn't been assigned to that interface.

ARP (Address Resolution Protocol)   A core protocol in the TCP/IP suite that belongs in the network layer of the OSI model. ARP obtains the MAC (physical) address of a host, or node, and then creates a local database that maps the MAC address to the host's IP (logical) address.

ARP cache   *See* ARP table.

ARP table   A database of records that maps MAC addresses to IP addresses. The ARP table is stored on a computer's hard disk where it is used by the ARP utility to supply the MAC addresses of network nodes, given their IP addresses.

Automatic Private IP Addressing   *See* APIPA.

BOOTP (Bootstrap Protocol)   An application layer protocol in the TCP/IP suite that uses a central list of IP addresses and their associated devices' MAC addresses to assign IP addresses to clients dynamically. BOOTP was the precursor to DHCP.

Bootstrap Protocol   *See* BOOTP.

country code TLD   A top-level domain that corresponds to a country. For example, the country code TLD for Canada is .ca, and the country code TLD for Japan is .jp.

DDNS (Dynamic DNS)   A method of dynamically updating DNS records for a host. DDNS client computers are configured to notify a service provider when their IP addresses change; then the service provider propagates the DNS record change across the Internet automatically.

DHCP (Dynamic Host Configuration Protocol)   An application layer protocol in the TCP/IP suite that manages the dynamic distribution of IP addresses on a network. Using DHCP to assign IP addresses can nearly eliminate duplicate-addressing problems.

diskless workstation   A workstation that doesn't contain a hard disk but instead relies on a small amount of read-only memory to connect to a network and to pick up its system files.

DNS (Domain Name System or Domain Name Service)   A hierarchical way of tracking domain names and their addresses, devised in the mid-1980s. The DNS database does not rely on one file or even one server, but rather is distributed over several key computers across the Internet to prevent catastrophic failure if one or a few computers go down. DNS is a TCP/IP service that belongs to the application layer of the OSI model.

DNS server   *See* name server.

domain   A group of computers that belong to the same organization and have part of their IP addresses in common.

domain name   The symbolic name that identifies a domain. Usually, a domain name is associated with a company or other type of organization, such as a university or military unit.

Domain Name Service   *See* DNS.

Domain Name System   *See* DNS.

dotted decimal notation   The shorthand convention used to represent IPv4 addresses and make them more easily readable by humans. In dotted decimal notation, a decimal number between 0 and 255 represents each binary octet. A period, or dot, separates each decimal.

dynamic ARP table entry   A record in an ARP table that is created when a client makes an ARP request that cannot be satisfied by data already in the ARP table.

Dynamic DNS   *See* DDNS.

Dynamic Host Configuration Protocol   *See* DHCP.

dynamic IP address   An IP address that is assigned to a device upon request and may change when the DHCP lease expires or is terminated. BOOTP and DHCP are two ways of assigning dynamic IP addresses.

Dynamic Ports   TCP/IP ports in the range of 49152 through 65535, which are open for use without requiring administrative privileges on a host or approval from IANA.

echo reply   The response signal sent by a device after another device pings it.

echo request   The request for a response generated when one device pings another device.

File Transfer Protocol   *See* FTP.

Format Prefix   A variable-length field at the beginning of an IPv6 address that indicates what type of address it is (for example, unicast, anycast, or multicast).

FTP (File Transfer Protocol)   An application layer protocol used to send and receive files via TCP/IP.

fully qualified host name   A host name plus domain name. For example, a host belonging to the loc.gov domain might be called Jasmine, making its fully qualified host name Jasmine.loc.gov.

hop   A term used to describe each trip a unit of data takes from one connectivity device to another. Typically, *hop* is used in the context of router-to-router communications.

host file   A text file that associates TCP/IP host names with IP addresses.

host name   A symbolic name that describes a TCP/IP device.

hosts   The name of the host file used on UNIX, Linux, and Windows systems. On a UNIX- or Linux-based computer, hosts is found in the /etc directory. On a Windows-based computer, it is found in the %systemroot%\system32\drivers\etc folder.

ICMP (Internet Control Message Protocol)   A core protocol in the TCP/IP suite that notifies the sender that something has gone wrong in the transmission process and that packets were not delivered.

ifconfig   A TCP/IP configuration and management utility used with UNIX and Linux systems.

IGMP (Internet Group Management Protocol or Internet Group Multicast Protocol)   A TCP/IP protocol used to manage multicast transmissions. Routers use IGMP to determine which nodes belong to a multicast group, and nodes use IGMP to join or leave a multicast group.

Internet Control Message Protocol   *See* ICMP.

Internet Group Management Protocol   *See* IGMP.

Internet Group Multicast Protocol   *See* IGMP.

internetwork   To traverse more than one LAN segment and more than one type of network through a router.

IP datagram   The IP portion of a TCP/IP frame that acts as an envelope for data, holding information necessary for routers to transfer data between subnets.

IP next generation   *See* IPv6.

IP version 4 Link Local   *See* IPv4LL.

ipconfig   The utility used to display TCP/IP addressing and domain name information in the Windows NT, Windows 2000, Windows XP, and Windows Vista client operating systems.

IPng   *See* IPv6.

IPv4 (IP version 4)   The current standard for IP addressing that specifies 32-bit addresses composed of four octets.

IPv4LL (IP version 4 Link Local)   A protocol that manages automatic address assignment among locally connected nodes. IPv4LL is part of the Zeroconf group of protocols.

IPv6 (IP version 6)   A newer standard for IP addressing that will replace the current IPv4 (IP version 4). Most notably, IPv6 uses a newer, more efficient header in its packets and allows for 128-bit source and destination IP addresses. The use of longer addresses will allow for many more IP addresses to be in circulation.

label   A character string that represents a domain (either top-level, second-level, or third-level).

lease   The agreement between a DHCP server and client on how long the client can use a DHCP-assigned IP address. DHCP services can be configured to provide lease terms equal to any amount of time.

loopback address   An IP address reserved for communicating from a node to itself (used mostly for troubleshooting purposes). The IPv4 loopback address is always cited as 127.0.0.1, although in fact, transmitting to any IP address whose first octet is 127 will contact the originating device. In IPv6, the loopback address is represented as ::1.

loopback test   An attempt to contact one's own machine for troubleshooting purposes. In TCP/IP-based networking, a loopback test can be performed by communicating with an IPv4 address that begins with an octet of 127. Usually, this means pinging the address 127.0.0.1.

mask   *See* subnet mask.

multicast address   A type of address in the IPv6 that represents multiple interfaces, often on multiple nodes. An IPv6 multicast address begins with the following hexadecimal field: FF0x, where x is a character that identifies the address's group scope.

multicasting   A means of transmission in which one device sends data to a specific group of devices (not necessarily the entire network segment) in a point-to-multipoint fashion.

name server   A server that contains a database of TCP/IP host names and their associated IP addresses. A name server supplies a resolver with the requested information. If it cannot resolve the IP address, the query passes to a higher-level name server.

namespace   The database of Internet IP addresses and their associated names distributed over DNS name servers worldwide.

net mask   *See* subnet mask.

network class   A classification for TCP/IP-based networks that pertains to the network's potential size and is indicated by an IP address's network ID and subnet mask. Network Classes A, B, and C are commonly used by clients on LANs; network Classes D and E are reserved for special purposes.

network ID   The portion of an IP address common to all nodes on the same network or subnet.

Network News Transport Protocol   *See* NNTP.

Network Time Protocol   *See* NTP.

newsgroup   An Internet-based forum for exchanging messages on a particular topic. Newsgroups rely on NNTP for the collection and dissemination of messages.

NNTP (Network News Transfer Protocol or Network News Transport Protocol)   An application layer protocol in the TCP/IP suite that facilitates the exchange of newsgroup messages, or articles, between multiple servers and users.

NTP (Network Time Protocol)   A simple application layer protocol in the TCP/IP suite used to synchronize the clocks of computers on a network. NTP depends on UDP for transport layer services.

octet   One of the 4 bytes that are separated by periods and together make up an IPv4 address.

Packet Internet Groper *See* PING.

ping To send an echo request signal from one node on a TCP/IP-based network to another, using the PING utility. *See also* PING.

PING (Packet Internet Groper) A TCP/IP troubleshooting utility that can verify that TCP/IP is installed, bound to the NIC, configured correctly, and communicating with the network. PING uses ICMP to send echo request and echo reply messages that determine the validity of an IP address.

port number The address on a host where an application makes itself available to incoming data.

Private Port *See* Dynamic Port.

RARP (Reverse Address Resolution Protocol) A core protocol in the TCP/IP suite that belongs in the network layer of the OSI model. RARP relies on a RARP table to associate the IP (logical) address of a node with its MAC (physical) address. RARP can be used to supply IP addresses to diskless workstations.

Registered Ports The TCP/IP ports in the range of 1024 to 49151. These ports are accessible to network users and processes that do not have special administrative privileges. Default assignments of these ports must be registered with IANA.

release The act of terminating a DHCP lease.

Rendezvous Apple Computer's implementation of the Zeroconf group of protocols.

resolver Any host on the Internet that needs to look up domain name information.

resource record The element of a DNS database stored on a name server that contains information about TCP/IP host names and their addresses.

Reverse Address Resolution Protocol *See* RARP.

root server A DNS server maintained by ICANN and IANA that is an authority on how to contact the top-level domains, such as those ending with .com, .edu, .net, .us, and so on. ICANN oversees the operation of 13 root servers around the world.

routable The protocols that can span more than one LAN because they carry network layer and addressing information that can be interpreted by a router.

socket A logical address assigned to a specific process running on a computer. Some sockets are reserved for operating system functions.

static ARP table entry A record in an ARP table that someone has manually entered using the ARP utility. Static ARP table entries remain the same until someone manually modifies them with the ARP utility.

static IP address An IP address that is manually assigned to a device and remains constant until it is manually changed.

subnet A part of a network in which all nodes share a network addressing component and a fixed amount of bandwidth.

subnet mask In IPv4 addressing, a 32-bit number that, when combined with a device's IP address, indicates what kind of subnet the device belongs to.

subnetting The process of subdividing a single class of network into multiple, smaller networks.

subprotocols   The specialized protocols that work together and belong to a protocol suite.

switch   The letters or words added to a command that allow you to customize a utility's output. Switches are usually preceded by a hyphen or forward slash character.

TCP (Transmission Control Protocol)   A core protocol of the TCP/IP suite. TCP belongs to the transport layer and provides reliable data delivery services.

TCP/IP (Transmission Control Protocol/Internet Protocol)   A suite of networking protocols that includes TCP, IP, UDP, and many others. TCP/IP provides the foundation for data exchange across the Internet.

TCP/IP core protocols   The major subprotocols of the TCP/IP suite, including IP, TCP, and UDP.

Telnet   A terminal emulation protocol used to log on to remote hosts using the TCP/IP protocol. Telnet resides in the application layer of the OSI model.

TFTP (Trivial File Transfer Protocol)   A TCP/IP application layer protocol that enables file transfers between computers. Unlike FTP, TFTP relies on UDP at the transport layer and does not require a user to log on to the remote host.

Time to Live   *See* TTL.

TLD (top-level domain)   The highest-level category used to distinguish domain names—for example, .org, .com, and .net. A TLD is also known as the domain suffix.

top-level domain   *See* TLD.

Transmission Control Protocol   *See* TCP.

Transmission Control Protocol/Internet Protocol   *See* TCP/IP.

Trivial File Transfer Protocol   *See* TFTP.

TTL (Time to Live)   A number that indicates the maximum time that a datagram or packet can remain on the network before it is discarded. Although this field was originally meant to represent units of time, on modern networks it represents the number of router hops a datagram has endured. The TTL for datagrams is variable and configurable, but it is usually set at 32 or 64. Each time a datagram passes through a router, its TTL is reduced by 1. When a router receives a datagram with a TTL equal to 1, the router discards that datagram.

UDP (User Datagram Protocol)   A core protocol in the TCP/IP suite that sits in the transport layer of the OSI model. UDP is a connectionless transport service.

unicast address   A type of IPv6 address that represents a single interface on a device. An IPv6 unicast address begins with either FFC0 or FF80.

User Datagram Protocol   *See* UDP.

Well Known Ports   The TCP/IP port numbers 0 to 1023, so named because they were long ago assigned by Internet authorities to popular services (for example, FTP and Telnet), and are, therefore, well known and frequently used.

Zero Configuration   *See* Zeroconf.

Zeroconf (Zero Configuration)   A collection of protocols designed by the IETF to simplify the setup of nodes on a TCP/IP network. Zeroconf assigns a node an IP address, resolves the node's host name and IP address without requiring a DNS server, and discovers services, such as print services, available to the node, also without requiring a DNS server.

Review Questions

1. Which TCP/IP core protocol operates in the network layer of the OSI model as a connectionless protocol?

   a. TCP

   b. UDP

   c. IP

   d. ICMP

2. Which IPv4 network class address contains a first octet in the range of 128 to 191?

   a. Class A

   b. Class B

   c. Class C

   d. Class D

3. How many bits are in an IPv6 address?

   a. 32

   b. 64

   c. 128

   d. 256

4. In the domain name `www.google.com`, which of the following describes the label for `com`?

   a. Top-level domain (TLD)

   b. Second-level domain

   c. Third-level domain

   d. Host-level domain

5. Which TCP/IP application protocol allows users to log on to remote hosts?

   a. Ping

   b. FTP

   c. NNTP

   d. Telnet

6. True or false? RARP maps MAC addresses to host IP addresses.

7. True or false? BOOTP provides a way to manually assign static IP addresses.

8. True or false? In IPv6, the loopback address has a value of 0:0:0:0:0:0:0:1.

9. True or false? The term namespace refers to the database of Internet IP addresses and their associated names.

10. True or false? DNS (Domain Name System or Domain Name Service) is a hierarchical way of tracking domain names and their addresses.

11. A(n) _____ protocol carries network layer addressing information that can be interpreted by a router.

12. In the IPv4 _____, a decimal number between 0 and 255 represents each binary octet and a period, or dot, separates each decimal.

13. A(n) _____ is a special 32-bit number that, when combined with a device's IP address, informs the rest of the network about the segment or network to which the device is attached.

14. _____ provides a Microsoft Windows 98, Me, 2000, XP, Vista, Windows Server 2003, and Windows Server 2008 operating systems computer with an IP address automatically if a DHCP server is unavailable.

15. A process's port number plus its host machine's IP address equals the process's _____.

Topologies and Ethernet Standards

After reading this chapter and completing the exercises, you will be able to:

- Describe the basic and hybrid LAN physical topologies and their uses, advantages, and disadvantages

- Describe the backbone structures that form the foundation for most LANs

- Understand the transmission methods underlying Ethernet networks

- Compare the different types of switching used in data transmission

On the Job

I work as a systems and network administrator for a large university. The environment at my university is more like a collection of small- to medium-size businesses, each funded by grants (public and private) awarded to individual researchers. The researchers are largely autonomous in their decision-making process. In the networking world, this sometimes results in a diverse mix of technologies, and you rarely have an opportunity to design a network from scratch.

One such mix occurred when a research center combined two networks in an effort to streamline operations. One of them was an Ethernet network used for research activities and included a variety of UNIX workstations and servers. The other was a token ring network that handled the center's business and accounting functions. It soon became clear that Ethernet would ultimately be the best network topology for our environment, so we took the approach of adopting Ethernet for all new purchases and allowing the token ring system to phase out as equipment was replaced.

One afternoon, the token ring network started "beaconing," meaning it was no longer able to deliver traffic. After checking a few basic issues (cabling, server, and workstation configurations), we disconnected half of the network to isolate the fault to one of the halves. We eventually isolated a failed concentrator.

Needless to say, we did not want to repeat this process. After looking more closely at the situation, we found that we had only a few machines (about 40) left on the token ring. The problem was that they were older machines with a proprietary peripheral bus. Ethernet cards based on that bus cost $700 at a time when typical Ethernet cards cost $40. Fortunately, the University's "swap shop," which disposes of old inventory, had many of those cards available for $1 apiece, so we bought our way out of the token ring for about $40.

Steve Barnet
University of Wisconsin

Just as an architect of a house must decide where to place walls and doors, where to install electrical and plumbing systems, and how to manage traffic patterns through rooms to make a house more livable, a network architect must consider many factors, both seen and unseen, when designing a network. This chapter details some basic elements of network architecture: physical and logical topologies. These elements are crucial to understanding networking design, troubleshooting, and management, all of which are discussed later in this book.

In this chapter, you will also learn about the most commonly used network access method, Ethernet, including its many physical layer standards. After you master the physical and logical fundamentals of network architecture, you will have all the tools necessary to design a network as elegant as the Taj Mahal.

Simple Physical Topologies

Net+

2.3

A **physical topology** is the physical layout, or pattern, of the nodes on a network. It depicts a network in broad scope; that is, it does not specify device types, connectivity methods, or addressing schemes for the network. Physical topologies are divided into three fundamental geometric shapes: bus, ring, and star. These shapes can be mixed to create hybrid topologies. Before you design a network, you need to understand physical topologies because they are integral to the type of network (for example, Ethernet), cabling infrastructure, and transmission media you use. You must also understand a network's physical topology to troubleshoot its problems or change its infrastructure. A thorough knowledge of physical topologies is necessary to obtain Network+ certification.

Physical topologies and logical topologies (discussed later) are two different networking concepts. You should be aware that when used alone, the word *topology* often refers to a network's *physical* topology.

Bus

A **bus topology** consists of a single cable, called the **bus,** that connects all nodes on a network without intervening connectivity devices. A bus topology can support only one channel for communication; as a result, every node shares the bus's total capacity. Most bus networks—for example, Thinnet and Thicknet—use coaxial cable as their physical medium. Bus networks rely on a **passive topology,** or one in which each node passively listens for, and then accepts, data directed to it. When one node wants to transmit data to another node, it broadcasts an alert to the entire network, informing all nodes that a transmission is being sent; the destination node then picks up the transmission. Nodes other than the sending and receiving nodes ignore the message.

For example, suppose that you want to send an instant message to your friend Diane, who works across the hall, asking whether she wants to have lunch with you. You click the Send button after typing your message, and the data stream that contains your message is sent to your NIC. Your NIC then sends a message across the shared wire that essentially says, "I have a message for Diane's computer." The message passes by every NIC between your computer and Diane's computer until Diane's computer recognizes that the message is meant for it and responds by accepting the data.

The fact that all nodes connected to a bus network can communicate directly via broadcast transmissions makes them part of a single **broadcast domain.** Similarly, all nodes connected to a single hub or switch belong to a broadcast domain (that is, unless the switch is specially configured to separate broadcast domains). Routers and other devices that operate at Layer 3 separate broadcast domains. Recall that the TCP/IP subprotocol ARP, for example, uses broadcast transmissions to discover which MAC address it should associate with an IP address. On a bus network, every client would receive ARP queries, even if the request for information wasn't meant for them.

Net+

2.3

4.7

At the ends of each bus network are 50-ohm resistors known as **terminators.** Terminators stop signals after they have reached the end of the wire. Without these devices, signals on a bus network would travel endlessly between the two ends of the network—a phenomenon known as **signal bounce**—and new signals could not get through. To understand this concept, imagine

Net+
2.3
4.7

that you and a partner, standing at opposite sides of a canyon, are yelling to each other. When you call out, your words echo; when your partner replies, his words also echo. Now imagine that the echoes never fade. After a short while, you could not continue conversing because all of the previously generated sound waves would still be bouncing around, creating too much noise for you to hear anything else. On a network, terminators prevent this problem by halting the transmission of old signals. In some cases, a hub provides termination for one end of a segment. A bus network must also be grounded at one end to help remove static electricity that could adversely affect the signal. Figure 5-1 depicts a terminated bus network.

Net+
2.3

Although networks based on a bus topology are relatively inexpensive to set up, they do not scale well. As you add more nodes, the network's performance degrades. Because of the single-channel limitation, the more nodes on a bus network, the more slowly the network will transmit and deliver data. For example, suppose a bus network in your small office supports two workstations and a server, and saving a file to the server takes two seconds. During that time, your NIC first checks the communication channel to ensure it is free, and then it issues data directed to the server. When the data reaches the server, the server accepts it. Suppose, however, that your business experiences tremendous growth, and you add five workstations during one weekend. The following Monday, when you attempt to save a file to the server, the save process might take five seconds, because the new workstations may also be using the communications channel, and your workstation may have to wait for a chance to transmit. As this example illustrates, a bus topology is rarely practical for networks with more than a dozen workstations.

Bus networks are also difficult to troubleshoot because it is a challenge to identify fault locations. To understand why, think of the game called "telephone," in which one person whispers a phrase into the ear of the next person, who whispers the phrase into the ear of another person, and so on, until the final person in line repeats the phrase aloud. The vast majority of the time, the phrase recited by the last person bears little resemblance to the original phrase. When the game ends, it's hard to determine precisely where in the chain the individual errors cropped up. Similarly, errors may occur at any intermediate point on a bus network, but at the receiving end it's possible to tell only that an error occurred. Finding the source of the error can prove very difficult.

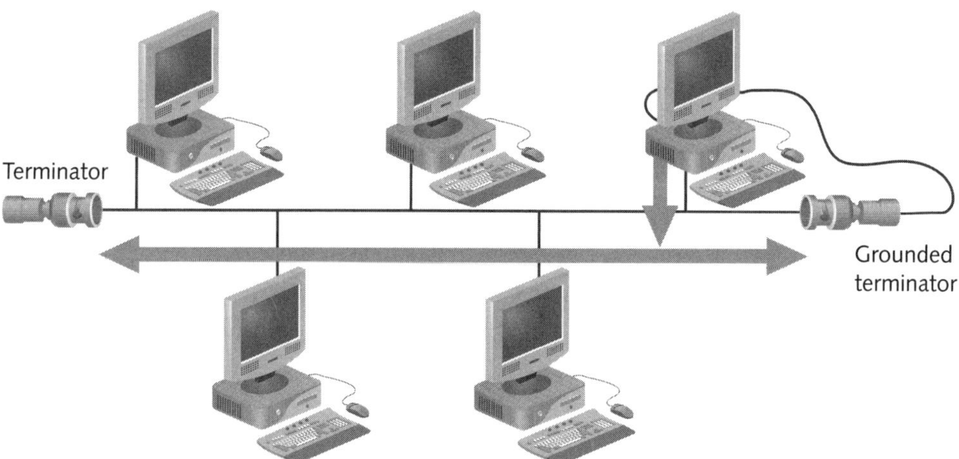

Figure 5-1 A terminated bus topology network

Net+
2.3

A final disadvantage to bus networks is that they are not very fault tolerant. **Fault tolerance** is the capability for a component or system to continue functioning despite damage or malfunction. On bus networks, any single break or a defect affects the entire network. As a result, and because of the other disadvantages associated with this topology, you will rarely see a network run on a pure bus topology. You may, however, encounter hybrid topologies that include a bus component.

Ring

In a **ring topology**, each node is connected to the two nearest nodes so that the entire network forms a circle, as shown in Figure 5-2. Data is transmitted clockwise, in one direction (unidirectionally), around the ring. Each workstation accepts and responds to packets addressed to it, and then it forwards the other packets to the next workstation in the ring. Each workstation acts as a repeater for the transmission. The fact that all workstations participate in delivery makes the ring topology an **active topology**. This is one way a ring topology differs from a bus topology. A ring topology also differs in that it has no "ends" and data stops at its destination. In most ring networks, twisted pair or fiber-optic cabling is used as the physical medium.

The drawback of a simple ring topology is that a single malfunctioning workstation can disable the network. For example, suppose that you and five colleagues share a pure ring topology LAN in your small office. You decide to send an instant message to Thad, who works three offices away, telling him you found his lost glasses. Between your office and Thad's office are two other offices, and two other workstations on the ring. Your instant message must pass through the two intervening workstations' NICs before it reaches Thad's computer. If one of these workstations has a malfunctioning NIC, your message will never reach Thad.

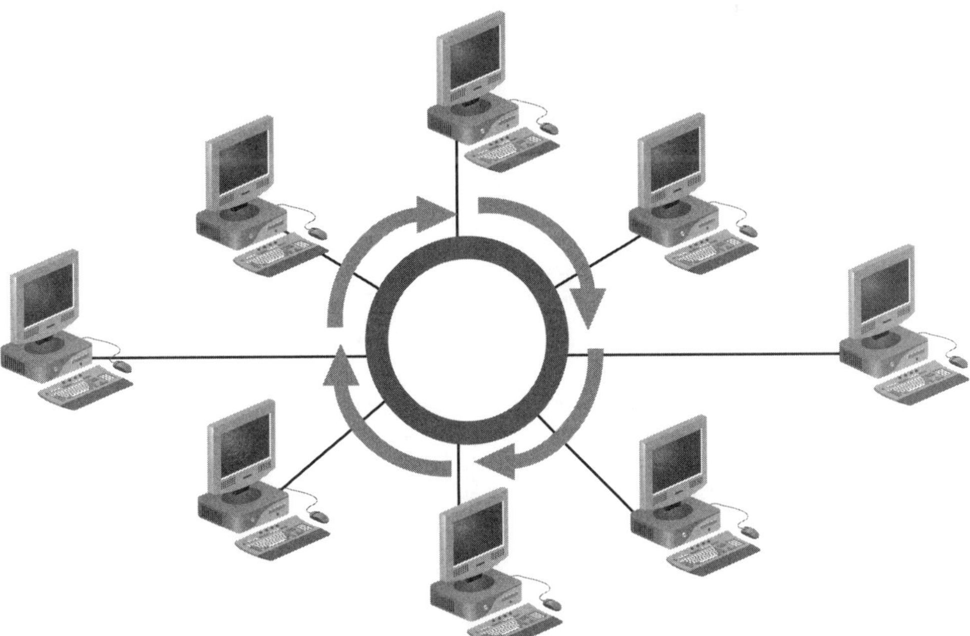

Figure 5-2 A typical ring topology network

In addition, just as in a bus topology, the more workstations that must participate in data transmission, the slower the response time. Consequently, pure ring topologies are not very flexible or scalable. Contemporary LANs rarely use pure ring topologies.

Star

In a **star topology**, every node on the network is connected through a central device, such as a hub, router, or switch. Figure 5-3 depicts a typical star topology. Star topologies are usually built with twisted pair or fiber-optic cabling. Any single cable on a star network connects only two devices (for example, a workstation and a hub), so a cabling problem will affect two nodes at most. Devices such as workstations or printers transmit data to the hub, router, or switch, which then retransmits the signal to the network segment containing the destination node.

Star topologies require more cabling than ring or bus networks. They also require more configuration. However, because each node is separately connected to a central connectivity device, star topologies are more fault tolerant. A single malfunctioning workstation cannot disable an entire star network. A failure in the central connectivity device can take down a LAN segment, though.

Because they include a centralized connection point, star topologies can easily be moved, isolated, or interconnected with other networks; they are, therefore, scalable. For this reason, and because of their fault tolerance, the star topology has become the most popular fundamental layout used in contemporary LANs. Single star networks are commonly interconnected with other networks through switches or routers to form more complex topologies. Most Ethernet networks are based on the star topology.

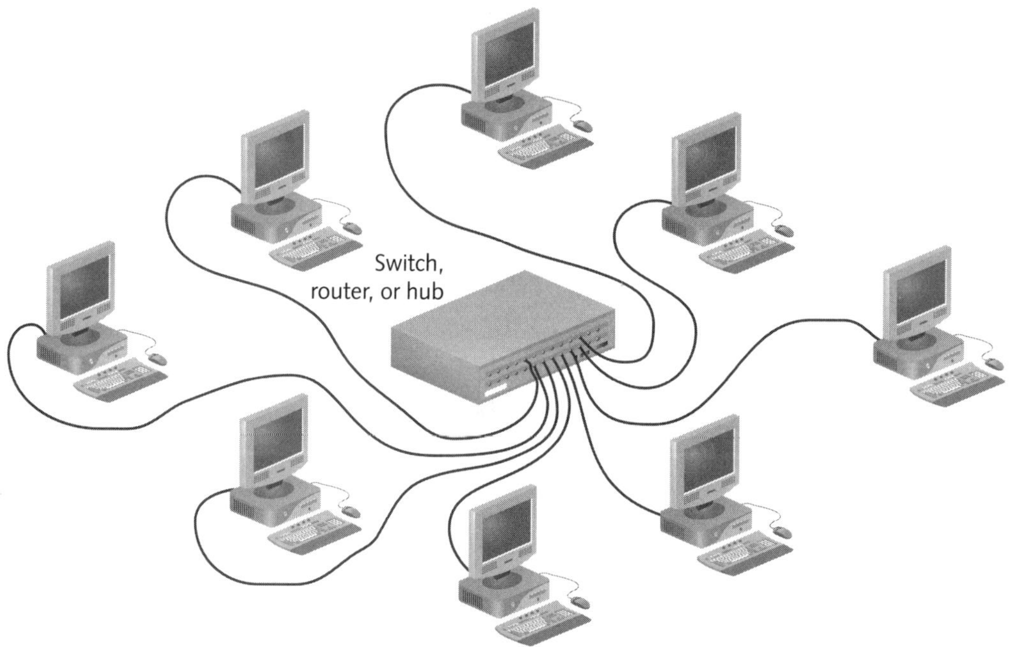

Figure 5-3 A typical star topology network

Net+
2.3
Star networks can support a maximum of only 1,024 addressable nodes on a logical network. For example, if you have a campus with 3,000 users, hundreds of networked printers, and scores of other devices, you must strategically create smaller logical networks. Even if you had 1,000 users and *could* put them on the same logical network, you wouldn't, because doing so would result in poor performance and difficult management. Instead, you would use routers to subdivide clients and peripherals into many separate broadcast domains.

Logical Topologies

The term **logical topology** refers to the way in which data is transmitted between nodes, rather than the physical layout of the paths that data takes. A network's logical topology will not necessarily match its physical topology.

The most common logical topologies are bus and ring. In a bus logical topology, signals travel from one network device to all other devices on the network (or network segment). They may or may not travel through an intervening connectivity device (as in a star topology network). A network that uses a bus physical topology also uses a bus logical topology. In addition, networks that use either the star or star-wired bus physical topologies also result in a bus logical topology.

In contrast, in a ring logical topology, signals follow a circular path between sender and receiver. Networks that use a pure ring topology use a ring logical topology. The ring logical topology is also used by the star-wired ring hybrid physical topology because signals follow a circular path, even as they travel through a connectivity device (as shown by the dashed lines in Figure 5-4). Different types of networks are characterized by one of the two main logical topologies. For example, Ethernet networks use the bus logical topology, whereas token ring networks use the ring logical topology.

Understanding logical topologies is useful when troubleshooting and designing networks. For example, on Ethernet networks, it is necessary to understand that all of a segment's traffic is transmitted to all nodes in the manner of a bus logical topology. Thus, for example, if one device has a malfunctioning NIC that is issuing bad or excessive packets, those packets will be detected by the NICs of all devices on the same segment. The result is a waste of available bandwidth and potential transmission errors.

Hybrid Physical Topologies

Net+
2.3
Except in very small networks, you will rarely encounter a network that follows a pure bus, ring, or star topology. Simple topologies are too restrictive, particularly if the LAN must accommodate a large number of devices. More likely, you will work with a complex combination of these topologies, known as a **hybrid topology**. Several kinds of hybrid topologies are explained in the following sections.

Star-Wired Ring

The **star-wired ring topology** uses the physical layout of a star in conjunction with the ring logical topology. In Figure 5-4, which depicts this architecture, the solid lines represent a physical connection and the dotted lines represent the flow of data. Data is sent around the

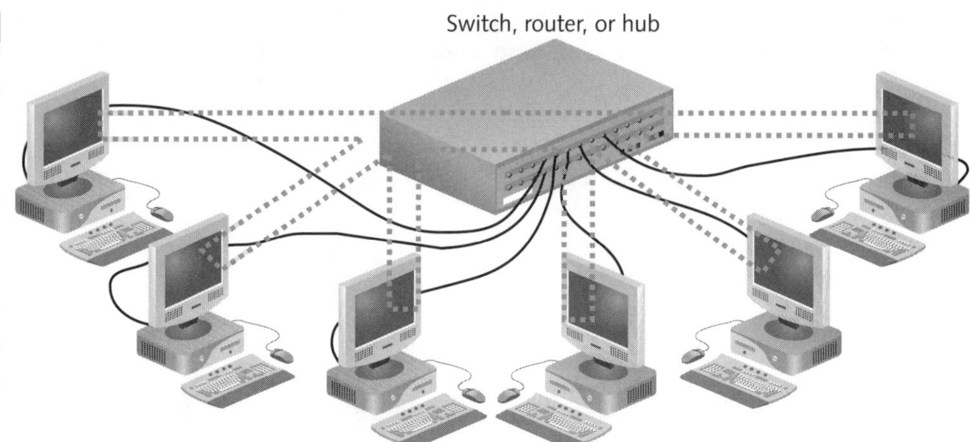

Figure 5-4 A star-wired ring topology network

star in a circular pattern. This hybrid topology benefits from the fault tolerance of the star topology (data transmission does not depend on each workstation to act as a repeater). Token ring networks, as specified in IEEE 802.5, use this hybrid topology.

Star-Wired Bus

Another popular hybrid topology combines the star and bus formations. In a **star-wired bus topology**, groups of workstations are star-connected to connectivity devices and then networked via a single bus, as shown in Figure 5-5. With this design, you can cover longer distances and easily interconnect or isolate different network segments. One drawback is that this option is more expensive than using either the star or, especially, the bus topology alone

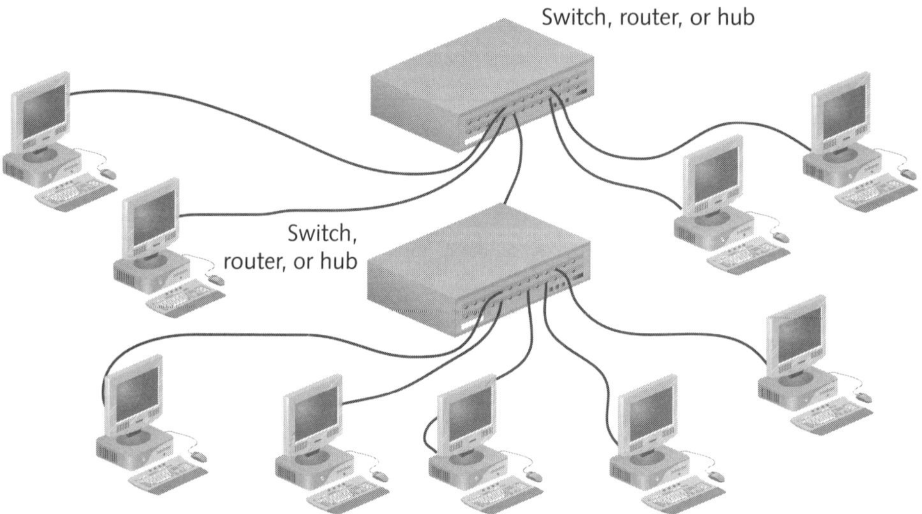

Figure 5-5 A star-wired bus topology network

Net+
2.3

because it requires more cabling and potentially more connectivity devices. However, compared to the benefits, these drawbacks are negligible. The star-wired bus topology forms the basis for modern Ethernet networks, which commonly use switches or routers as the connectivity devices.

Backbone Networks

A network backbone is the cabling that connects the hubs, switches, and routers on a network. Backbones usually are capable of more throughput than the cabling that connects workstations to hubs. This added capacity is necessary because backbones carry more traffic than any other cabling in the network. For example, LANs in large organizations commonly rely on a fiber-optic backbone but continue to use Cat 5 or better UTP to connect hubs or switches with workstations.

Although even the smallest LAN technically has a backbone, on an enterprise-wide network, backbones are more complex and more difficult to plan. In networking, the term **enterprise** refers to an entire organization, including its local and remote offices, a mixture of computer systems, and a number of departments. Enterprise-wide computing must, therefore, take into account the breadth and diversity of a large organization's computer needs. The backbone is the most significant building block of enterprise-wide networks. It may take one of several different shapes, as described in the following sections.

Serial Backbone

A **serial backbone** is the simplest kind of backbone. It consists of two or more internetworking devices connected to each other by a single cable in a daisy-chain fashion. In networking, a **daisy chain** is simply a linked series of devices. Hubs and switches are often connected in a daisy chain to extend a network. For example, suppose you manage a small star-wired bus topology network in which a single hub serves a workgroup of eight users. When new employees are added to that department and you need more network connections, you could connect a second hub to the first hub in a daisy-chain fashion. The new hub would offer open ports for new users. Because the star-wired hybrids provide for modular additions, daisy-chaining is a logical solution for growth. Also, because hubs can easily be connected through cables attached to their ports, a LAN's infrastructure can be expanded with little additional cost.

Hubs are not the only devices that can be connected in a serial backbone. In fact, more commonly, gateways, routers, switches, and bridges form part of the backbone. Figure 5-6 illustrates a serial backbone network, in which the backbone is indicated by a dashed line.

Bear in mind that if you do use hubs in a serial fashion, the distance you can span between connected hubs is limited. Later in this chapter you will learn about the maximum number of repeating devices (such as hubs) and segments for each type of Ethernet network. Using more hubs than the standard suggests (in other words, exceeding the maximum network length) will adversely affect the performance of a LAN. If you extend a LAN beyond its recommended size, intermittent and unpredictable data transmission errors will result. Similarly, if you daisy-chain a topology with limited bandwidth, you risk overloading the channel and generating still more data errors.

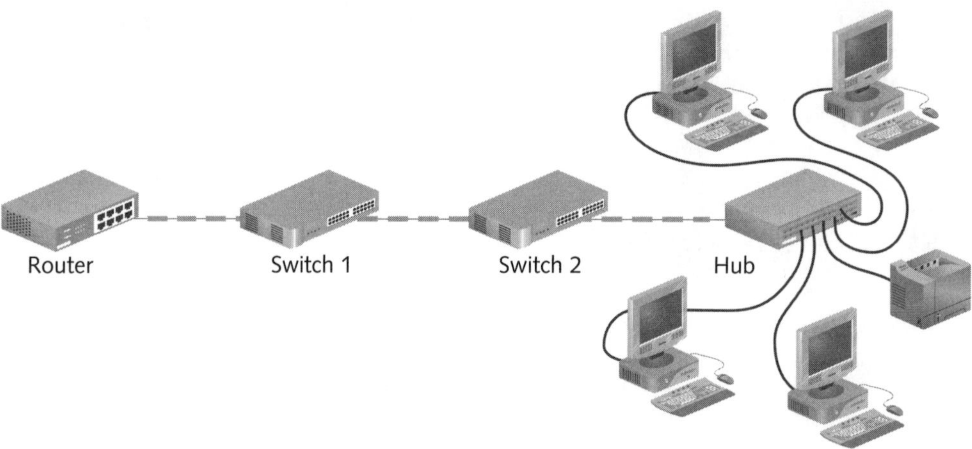

Figure 5-6 A serial backbone

Distributed Backbone

A **distributed backbone** consists of a number of connectivity devices connected to a series of central connectivity devices, such as hubs, switches, or routers, in a hierarchy, as shown in Figure 5-7. In Figure 5-7, the dashed lines represent the backbone. This kind of topology allows for simple expansion and limited capital outlay for growth, because more layers of devices can be added to existing layers. For example, suppose that you are the network administrator for a small publisher's office. You might begin your network with a distributed backbone consisting of two switches that supply connectivity to your 20 users, 10 on each switch. When your company hires more staff, you can connect another switch to one of the existing switches, and you can use the new switch to connect the new staff to the network.

A more complicated distributed backbone connects multiple LANs or LAN segments using routers, as shown in Figure 5-8. In this example, the routers form the highest layer of the backbone to connect the LANs or LAN segments.

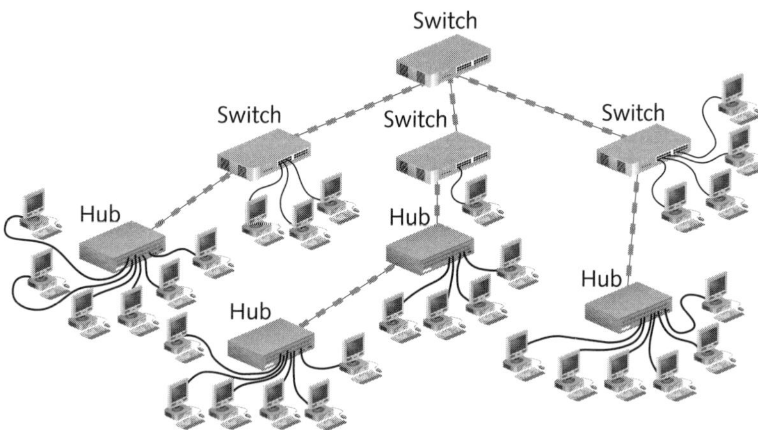

Figure 5-7 A simple distributed backbone

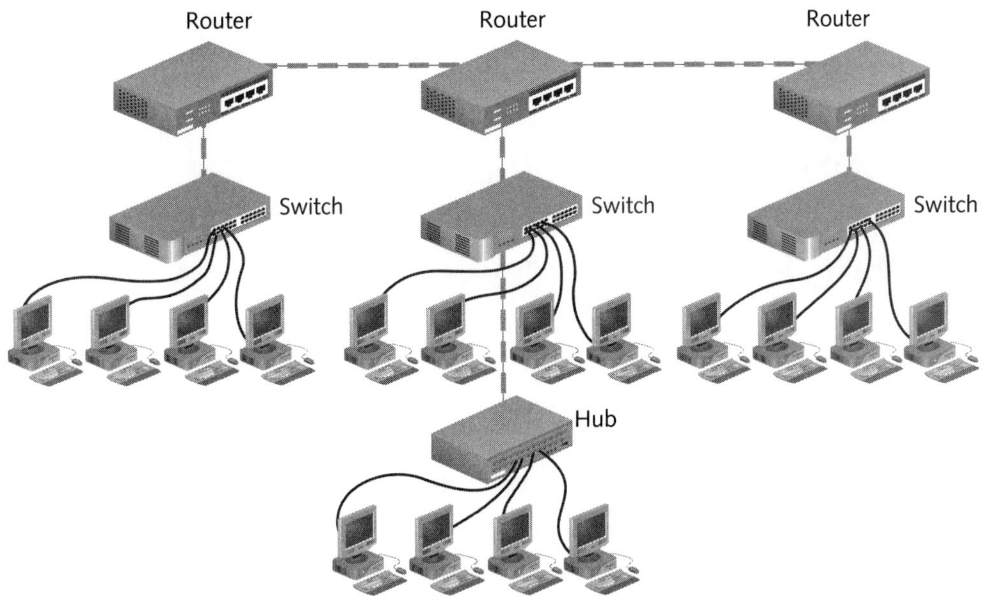

Figure 5-8 A distributed backbone connecting multiple LANs

A distributed backbone also provides network administrators with the ability to segregate workgroups and, therefore, manage them more easily. It adapts well to an enterprise-wide network confined to a single building, in which certain hubs or switches can be assigned according to the floor or department. Note that distributed backbones may include hubs linked in a daisy-chain fashion. This arrangement requires the same length considerations that serial backbones demand. Another possible problem in this design relates to the potential single points of failure, such as the devices at the uppermost layers. Despite these potential drawbacks, implementing a distributed backbone network can be relatively simple, quick, and inexpensive.

Collapsed Backbone

The **collapsed backbone** topology uses a router or switch as the single central connection point for multiple subnetworks, as shown in Figure 5-9. Contrast Figure 5-9 with Figure 5-8, in which multiple LANs are connected via a distributed backbone. In a collapsed backbone, a single router or switch is the highest layer of the backbone. The router or switch that makes up the collapsed backbone must contain multiprocessors to handle the heavy traffic going through it. This is risky because a failure in the central router or switch can bring down the entire network. In addition, because routers cannot move traffic as quickly as hubs or switches, using a router may slow data transmission.

Nevertheless, a collapsed backbone topology offers substantial advantages. Most significantly, this arrangement allows you to interconnect different types of subnetworks. You can also centrally manage maintenance and troubleshooting chores.

Parallel Backbone

A **parallel backbone** is the most robust type of network backbone. This variation of the collapsed backbone arrangement consists of more than one connection from the central router

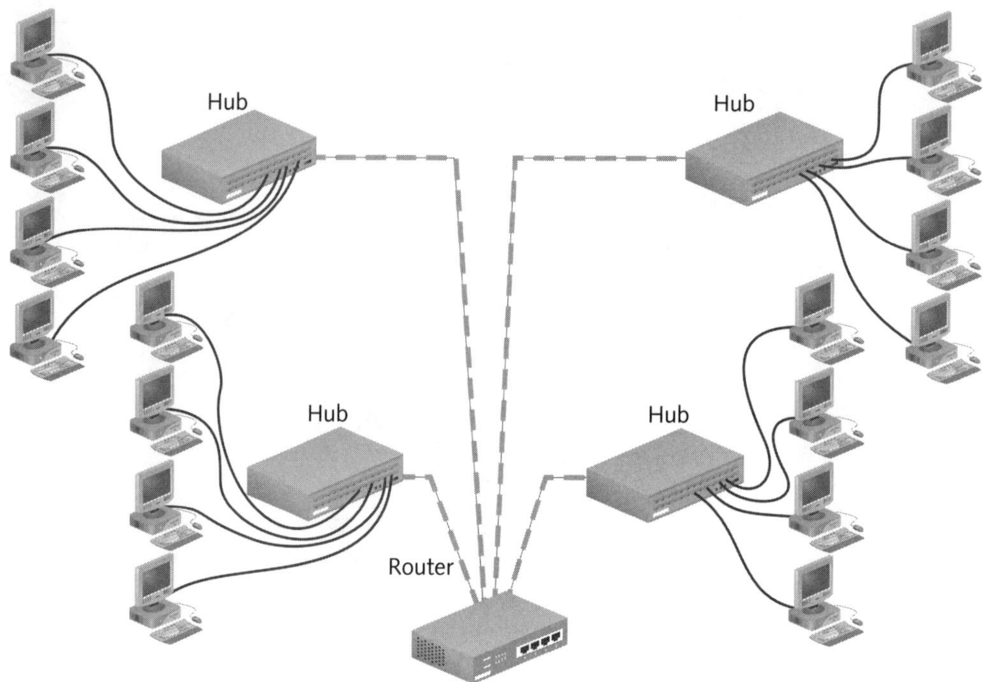

Figure 5-9 A collapsed backbone

or switch to each network segment. In a network with more than one router or switch, the parallel backbone calls for duplicate connections between those connectivity devices as well. Figure 5-10 depicts a simple parallel backbone topology. As you can see, each switch is connected to the router by two cables, and the two routers are also connected by two cables. The most significant advantage of using a parallel backbone is that its redundant (duplicate) links ensure network connectivity to any area of the enterprise. Parallel backbones are more expensive than other enterprise-wide topologies because they require much more cabling than the others. However, they make up for the additional cost by offering increased performance and better fault tolerance.

As a network administrator, you might choose to implement parallel connections to only some of the most critical devices on your network. For example, if the first and second switches in Figure 5-10 connected your Facilities and Payroll departments to the rest of the network, and your organization could never afford to lose connectivity with those departments, you might use a parallel structure for those links. If the third and fourth hubs in Figure 5-10 connected your organization's Recreation and Training departments to the network, you might decide that parallel connections were unnecessary for these departments. By selectively implementing the parallel structure, you can lower connectivity costs and leave available additional ports on the connectivity devices.

Bear in mind that an enterprise-wide LAN or WAN may include different combinations of simple physical topologies and backbone designs. Now that you understand how networks

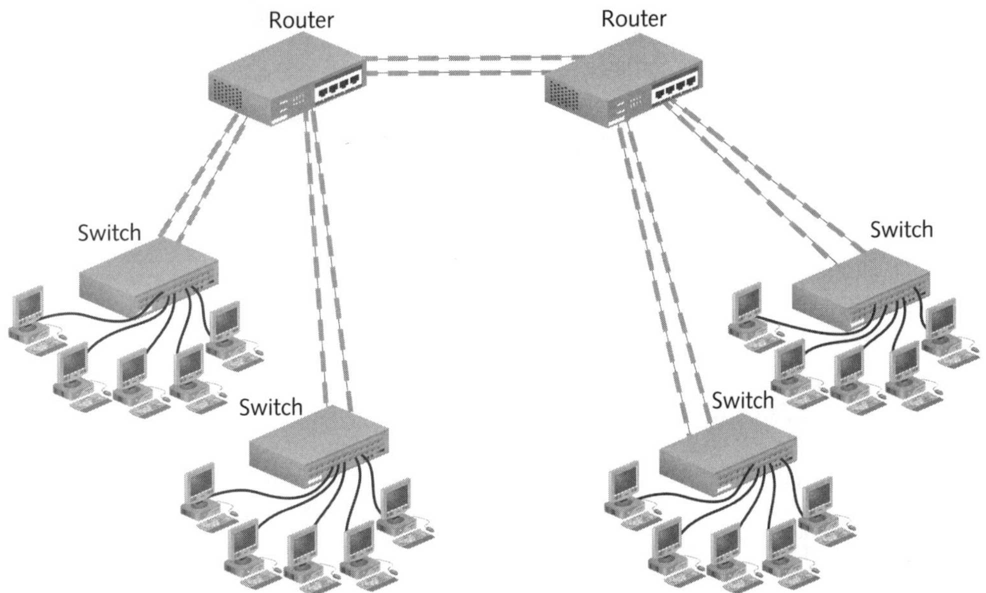

Figure 5-10 A parallel backbone

may be arranged, both physically and logically, you are ready to learn more about how connections between nodes are established.

Switching

Switching is a component of a network's logical topology that determines how connections are created between nodes. There are three methods for switching: circuit switching, message switching, and packet switching.

2.5

Circuit Switching

In **circuit switching**, a connection is established between two network nodes before they begin transmitting data. Bandwidth is dedicated to this connection and remains available until the users terminate communication between the two nodes. While the nodes remain connected, all data follows the same path initially selected by the switch. Traditional telephone calls—that is, calls not carried over TCP/IP networks—for example, typically use a circuit-switched connection.

Because circuit switching monopolizes its piece of bandwidth while the two stations remain connected (even when no actual communication is taking place), it can result in a waste of available resources. However, some network applications benefit from such a "reserved" path. For example, live audio or videoconferencing might not tolerate the time delay it would take to reorganize data packets that have taken separate paths through another switching method. Another example of circuit switching occurs if you connect your home PC via modem to an ISP's access server. WAN technologies, such as ISDN T1 services, and ATM (described in Chapter 7) also use circuit switching.

Message Switching

Message switching establishes a connection between two devices, transfers the information to the second device, and then breaks the connection. The information is stored and forwarded from the second device after a connection between that device and a third device on the path is established. This store-and-forward routine continues until the message reaches its destination. All information follows the same physical path; unlike with circuit switching, however, the connection is not continuously maintained. Message switching requires that each device in the data's path has sufficient memory and processing power to accept and store the information before passing it to the next node. None of the network transmission technologies discussed in this chapter use message switching.

Net+ Packet Switching

2.5   A third and, by far, the most popular method for connecting nodes on a network is packet switching. **Packet switching** breaks data into packets before it is transported. Packets can travel any path on the network to their destination, because, as you learned in Chapter 4, each packet contains the destination address and sequencing information. Consequently, packets can attempt to find the fastest circuit available at any instant. They need not follow each other along the same path, nor must they arrive at their destination in the same sequence as when they left their source.

To understand this technology, imagine that you work in Washington, D.C., and you organized a field trip for 50 colleagues to the National Air and Space Museum. You gave the museum's exact address to your colleagues and told them to leave precisely at 7:00 a.m. from your office building several blocks away. You did not tell your coworkers which route to take. Some might choose the subway, others might hail a taxicab, and still others might choose to drive their own cars or even walk. All of them will attempt to find the fastest route to the museum. But if a group of six decide to take a taxicab and only four people fit in that taxi, the next two people have to wait for another taxi. Or, a taxi might get caught in rush hour traffic and be forced to find an alternate route. Thus, the fastest route might not be obvious the moment everyone departs. But no matter which transportation method your colleagues choose, all will arrive at the museum and reassemble as a group. This analogy illustrates how packets travel in a packet-switched network.

When packets reach their destination node, the node reassembles them based on their control information. Because of the time it takes to reassemble the packets into a message, packet switching requires speedy connections if it's used for live audio or video transmission. Even connections as slow as a dial-up Internet service, however, are sufficiently fast to send and receive typical network data, such as e-mail messages, spreadsheet files, or even software programs from a server to client. The greatest advantage to packet switching lies in the fact that it does not waste bandwidth by holding a connection open until a message reaches its destination, as circuit switching does. And unlike message switching, it does not require devices in the data's path to process information. Ethernet networks and the Internet are the most common examples of packet-switched networks.

Net+ MPLS (Multiprotocol Label Switching)

2.5   A fourth type of switching, **MPLS (multiprotocol label switching)**, was introduced by the IETF in 1999. As its name implies, MPLS enables multiple types of Layer 3 protocols to travel over any one of several connection-oriented Layer 2 protocols. As you have learned,

Net+
2.5

IP is the most commonly used Layer 3 protocol, so MPLS most often supports IP. MPLS can operate over Ethernet frames (discussed in detail later in this chapter), but it is more often used with other Layer 2 protocols, like those designed for WANs (discussed in Chapter 7). In fact, one of its benefits is the ability to use packet-switched technologies over traditionally circuit-switched networks. MPLS can also create end-to-end paths that act like circuit-switched connections.

In addition, MPLS addresses some limitations of traditional packet switching. For example, on an IP-based network, each router along the data's path must interpret the IP datagram's header to discover its destination address, and then it must perform a route lookup to determine where to forward the packet next. As you can imagine, stopping to process this information at every router slows transmission. In MPLS the first router that receives a packet adds one or more labels to the Layer 3 datagram. Then the network's Layer 2 protocol header is added, as shown in Figure 5-11. (Collectively, the MPLS labels are sometimes called a shim, because of their placement between Layer 3 and Layer 2 information. Also, MPLS is sometimes said to belong to "Layer 2.5.") These labels include special addressing and, sometimes, prioritization information. Routers then need only interpret the MPLS labels, which can point to exclusive, predefined data paths. Network engineers have significant control in setting these paths. Consequently, MPLS offers potentially faster transmission than traditionally packet-switched or circuit-switched networks. Because it can add prioritization information, MPLS can also offer better **QoS (quality of service)**. QoS is a specification that guarantees delivery of data within a certain time frame. These advantages make MPLS especially well suited to WANs.

Now that you are familiar with the various methods of establishing paths between nodes, you are ready to investigate Ethernet, a Layer 2 standard used on nearly every LAN.

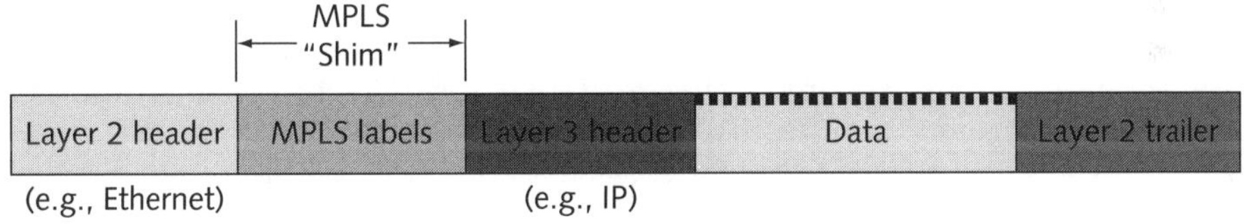

Figure 5-11 MPLS shim within a frame

Ethernet

Net+
2.6

As you have learned, Ethernet is a network technology originally developed by Xerox in the 1970s and later improved by Digital Equipment Corporation (DEC), Intel, and Xerox (DIX). This flexible technology can run on a variety of network media and offers excellent throughput at a reasonable cost. Ethernet is, by far, the most popular network technology used on modern LANs.

Ethernet has evolved through many variations, and its speed and reliability continue to improve. As a result of this history, it supports many different versions—so many, in fact, that you might find the many variations a little confusing. However, all Ethernet networks have at least one thing in common—their access method, which is known as CSMA/CD.

Net+ CSMA/CD (Carrier Sense Multiple Access with Collision Detection)

2.6   A network's **access method** is its method of controlling how network nodes access the communications channel. In comparing a network to a highway, the on-ramps would be one part of the highway's access method. A busy highway might use stoplights at each on-ramp to allow only one person to merge into traffic every five seconds. After merging, cars must drive within lanes, and each lane is limited as to how many cars it can hold at one time. All of these highway controls are designed to avoid collisions and help drivers get to their destinations. On networks, similar restrictions apply to the way in which multiple computers share a finite amount of bandwidth on a network. These controls make up the network's access method.

All Ethernet networks, independent of their speed or frame type, use an access method called **CSMA/CD (Carrier Sense Multiple Access with Collision Detection)**. To understand Ethernet, you must first understand CSMA/CD. Take a minute to think about the full name *Carrier Sense Multiple Access with Collision Detection*. The term *Carrier Sense* refers to the fact that Ethernet NICs listen on the network and wait until they detect (or sense) that no other nodes are transmitting data over the signal (or carrier) on the communications channel before they begin to transmit. The term *Multiple Access* refers to the fact that several Ethernet nodes can be connected to a network and can monitor traffic, or access the media, simultaneously.

In CSMA/CD, when a node wants to transmit data, it must first access the transmission media and determine whether the channel is free. If the channel is not free, it waits and checks again after a very brief amount of time. If the channel is free, the node transmits its data. Any node can transmit data after it determines that the channel is free. But what if two nodes simultaneously check the channel, determine that it's free, and begin to transmit? When this happens, their two transmissions interfere with each other; this is known as a **collision**.

The last part of CSMA/CD, the term *Collision Detection*, refers to the way nodes respond to a collision. In the event of a collision, the network performs a series of steps known as the collision detection routine. If a node's NIC determines that its data has been involved in a collision, it immediately stops transmitting. Next, in a process called **jamming**, the NIC issues a special 32-bit sequence that indicates to the rest of the network nodes that its previous transmission was faulty and that those data frames are invalid. After waiting, the NIC determines if the line is again available; if it is available, the NIC retransmits its data.

On heavily trafficked network segments, collisions are fairly common. It is not surprising that the more nodes there are transmitting data on a segment, the more collisions that will take place (although a collision rate greater than 5 percent of all traffic is unusual and may point to a problematic NIC or poor cabling on the network). When an Ethernet segment grows to include a particularly large number of nodes, you may see performance suffer as a result of collisions. This "critical mass" number depends on the type and volume of data that the network regularly transmits. Collisions can corrupt data or truncate data frames, so it is important that the network detect and compensate for them. Figure 5-12 depicts the way CSMA/CD regulates data flow to avoid and, if necessary, detect collisions.

On an Ethernet network, a **collision domain** is the portion of a network in which collisions occur if two nodes transmit data at the same time. When designing an Ethernet network, it's important to note that because repeaters simply regenerate any signal they receive, they repeat collisions just as they repeat data. Thus, connecting multiple parts of a network with repeaters or hubs results in a larger collision domain. Switches and routers, however, separate collision domains. Note that collision domains differ from broadcast domains in that

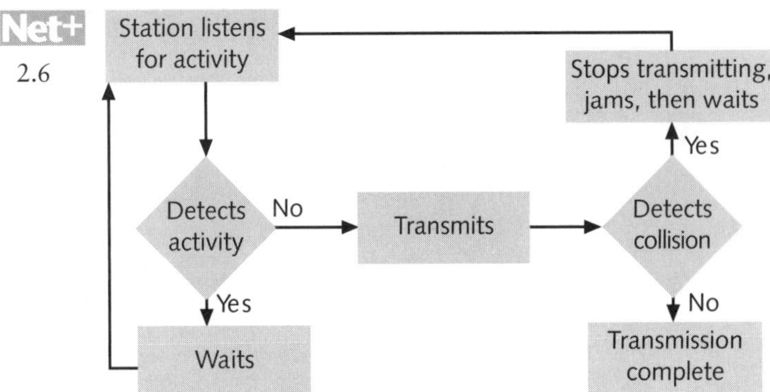

Figure 5-12 CSMA/CD process

they define a logically shared space for Layer 2 communications. Also, by default, switches do not separate broadcast domains.

Collision domains play a role in the Ethernet cabling distance limitations. For example, if two nodes on the same segment are positioned beyond the maximum recommended segment length, data propagation delays will be too long for CSMA/CD to be effective. A **data propagation delay** is the length of time data takes to travel from one point on the segment to another point. When data takes a long time, CSMA/CD's collision detection routine cannot identify collisions accurately. In other words, one node on the segment might begin its CSMA/CD routine and determine that the channel is free even though a second node has begun transmitting because the second node's data is taking so long to reach the first node.

At rates of 100 or 1,000Mbps, data travels so quickly that NICs can't always keep up with the collision detection and retransmission routines. For example, because of the speed employed on a 100Mbps Ethernet network, the window of time for the NIC to both detect and compensate for the error is much less than that of a 10Mbps network. To minimize undetected collisions, 100Mbps networks can support only a maximum of three network segments connected with two hubs, whereas 10Mbps buses can support a maximum of five network segments connected with four hubs. This shorter path reduces the highest potential propagation delay between nodes.

Net+ Ethernet Standards for Copper Cable

2.6   Recall that IEEE physical layer standards specify how signals are transmitted to the media. The following sections describe the standards for several types of Ethernet networks. Bear in mind that the technologies described by IEEE standards differ significantly in how they encode signals at the physical layer. The specifics of encoding methods are beyond the scope of this book. However, encoding methods affect a standard's maximum throughput, segment length, and wiring requirements—and these are the details you need to understand for designing networks and installing cable.

In Ethernet technology, the most common theoretical maximum data transfer rates are 10Mbps, 100Mbps, 1Gbps, and 10Gbps. Actual data transfer rates on a network will vary, just as you might average 22 miles per gallon (mpg) driving your car to work and back, even though the manufacturer rates the car's gas mileage at 28mpg.

10Base-T 10Base-T was a popular Ethernet networking standard that replaced the older Thicknet and Thinnet technologies (mentioned in Chapter 3). In 10Base-T, the *10* represents its maximum throughput of 10Mbps, the *Base* indicates that it uses baseband transmission, and the *T* stands for *twisted pair*, the medium it uses. On a 10Base-T network, one pair of wires in the UTP cable is used for transmission, while a second pair of wires is used for reception. These two pairs of wires allow 10Base-T networks to provide full-duplex transmission. A 10Base-T network requires Cat 3 or higher UTP.

Nodes on a 10Base-T Ethernet network connect to a central network device in a star fashion. As is typical of a star topology, a single network cable connects only two devices. This characteristic makes 10Base-T networks more fault tolerant than 10Base-2 or 10Base-5, both of which use the bus topology. Use of the star topology also makes 10Base-T networks easier to troubleshoot, because you can isolate problems more readily when every device has a separate connection to the LAN.

10Base-T follows the **5-4-3 rule** of networking. This rule says that, between two communicating nodes, the network cannot contain more than five network segments connected by four repeating devices, and no more than three of the segments may be populated (at least two must be unpopulated). The maximum distance that a 10Base-T segment can traverse is 100 meters. To go beyond that distance, Ethernet star segments must be connected by additional hubs or switches to form more complex topologies. This arrangement can connect a maximum of five sequential network segments, for an overall distance between communicating nodes of 500 meters. Figure 5-13 depicts a 10Base-T Ethernet network with maximum segment lengths.

100Base-T (Fast Ethernet) As networks expanded and handled heavier traffic, Ethernet's long-standing 10Mbps limitation proved a bottleneck. The need for faster LANs that could use the same infrastructure as the popular 10Base-T technology was met by **100Base-T,**

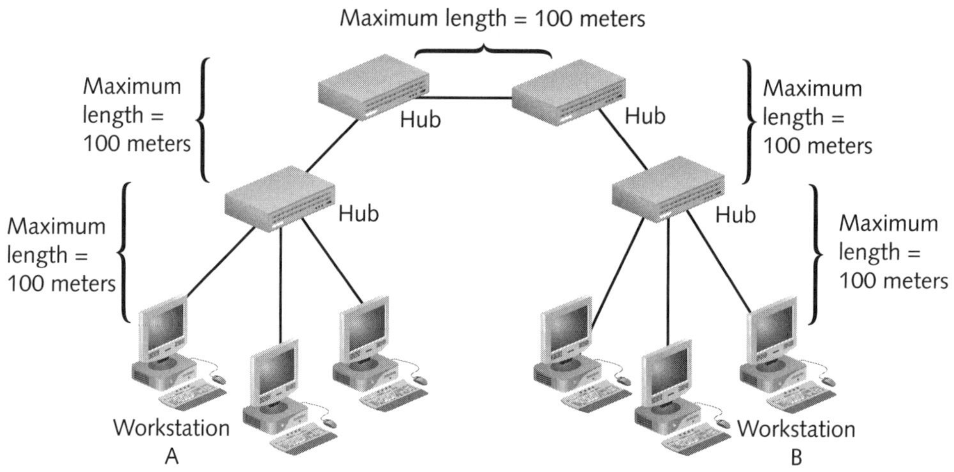

Figure 5-13 A 10Base-T network

Net+

2.6

also known as **Fast Ethernet**. 100Base-T, specified in the IEEE **802.3u** standard, enables LANs to run at a 100Mbps data transfer rate, a tenfold increase from that provided by 10Base-T, without requiring a significant investment in new infrastructure. 100Base-T uses baseband transmission and the same star topology as 10Base-T. It also uses the same RJ-45 modular connectors. Depending on the type of 100Base-T technology used, it may require Cat 3, Cat 5, or higher UTP.

As with 10Base-T, nodes on a 100Base-T network are configured in a star topology. However, unlike 10Mbps Ethernet networks, 100Base-T networks do not follow the 5-4-3 rule. Because of their faster response requirements, to avoid data errors, they require communicating nodes to be even closer. 100Base-T buses can support a maximum of three network segments connected with two repeating devices. Each segment length is limited to 100 meters. Thus, the overall maximum length between nodes is limited to 300 meters, as shown in Figure 5-14.

The most common standard for achieving 100Mbps throughput over twisted pair is **100Base-TX**. Compared to 10Base-T, it sends signals 10 times faster and condenses the time between digital pulses as well as the time a station must wait and listen for a signal. 100Base-TX requires Cat 5 or higher unshielded twisted pair cabling. Within the cable, it uses the same two pairs of wire for transmitting and receiving data that 10Base-T uses. Therefore, like 10Base-T, 100Base-TX is also capable of full-duplex transmission. Full duplexing can potentially double the effective bandwidth of a 100Base-T network to 200Mbps.

1000Base-T Because of increasing volumes of data and numbers of users who need to access this data quickly, even 100Mbps has not met the throughput demands of many networks. Ethernet technologies designed to transmit data at 1Gbps are collectively known as **Gigabit Ethernet**. **1000Base-T** is a standard for achieving throughputs 10 times faster than Fast Ethernet over copper cable, as described in IEEE's **802.3ab** standard. In *1000Base-TX*, *1000* represents *1000 megabits per second (Mbps)*, or 1 gigabit per second (Gbps). *Base* indicates that it uses baseband transmission, and *T* indicates that it relies on twisted pair wiring. 1000Base-T achieves its higher throughput by using all four pairs of wires in a Cat 5 or higher cable to both transmit and receive signals, whereas 100Base-T uses only two of

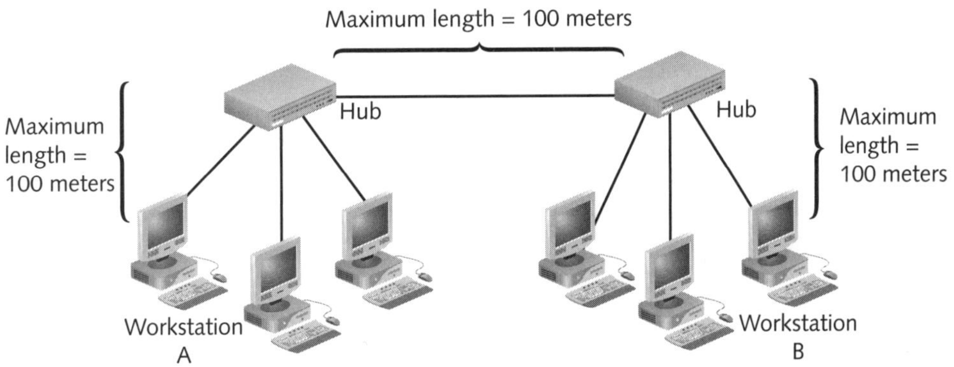

Figure 5-14 A 100Base-T network

the four pairs. 1000Base-T also uses a different data encoding scheme than 100Base-T networks use. However, the standards can be combined on the same network, and you can purchase NICs that support 10Mbps, 100Mbps, and 1Gbps via the same connector jack. Because of this compatibility and the fact that 1000Base-T can use existing Cat 5 cabling, the 1-gigabit technology can be added gradually to an existing 100Mbps network with minimal interruption of service. The maximum segment length on a 1000Base-T network is 100 meters. It allows for only one repeater. Therefore, the maximum distance between communicating nodes on a 1000Base-T network is 200 meters.

10GBase-T In 2006 IEEE released its **802.3an** standard for transmitting 10Gbps over twisted pair, **10GBase-T**. This standard was a breakthrough in pushing the limits of the twisted pair medium. To achieve such dramatic data transmission rates, however, 10GBase-T segments require Cat 6 or Cat 7 cabling. Still, as with other twisted pair Ethernet standards, the maximum segment length for 10GBase-T is 100 meters. The primary benefit of the 10GBase-T standard is that it makes very fast data transmission available at a much lower cost than using fiber-optic cable. 10GBase-T would probably not be used to connect two office locations across town, because of its distance limitations. However, it could be used to connect network devices or to connect servers or workstations to a LAN. This type of implementation would easily allow the use of converged services, such as video and voice, at every desktop.

Yet long before IEEE developed a 10GBase-T standard for twisted pair cable, it had established standards for achieving high data rates over fiber-optic cable. In fact, fiber optic is the best medium for delivering high throughput. The following section details the IEEE standards that apply to these high-speed networks.

Just as with twisted pair and coaxial cabling, IEEE has established physical layer standards for networks that use fiber-optic cable. Commonly used standards are described in the following sections.

Ethernet Standards for Fiber-Optic Cable

100Base-FX The 100Base-FX standard specifies a network capable of 100Mbps throughput that uses baseband transmission and fiber-optic cabling. 100Base-FX requires multimode fiber containing at least two strands of fiber. In half-duplex mode, one strand is used for data transmission while the other strand is used for reception. In full-duplex implementations, both strands are used for sending and receiving data. 100Base-FX has a maximum segment length of 412 meters if half-duplex transmission is used and 2,000 meters if full-duplex is used. The standard allows for a maximum of one repeater to connect segments. The 100Base-FX standard uses a star topology, with its repeaters connected in a bus fashion.

100Base-FX, like 100Base-T, is also considered Fast Ethernet and is described in IEEE's 802.3u standard. Organizations switching, or migrating, from UTP to fiber media can combine 100Base-TX and 100Base-FX within one network. To do this, transceivers (for example, NICs) in computers and connectivity devices must have both RJ-45 and SC, ST, LC, or MT-RJ ports. Alternatively, a 100Base-TX to 100Base-FX media converter may be used at any point in the network to interconnect the different media and convert the signals of one standard to signals that work with the other standard.

1000Base-LX   IEEE has specified three different types of 1000Base, or 1-Gigabit, Ethernet technologies for use over fiber-optic cable in its **802.3z** standard.

2.6

Probably the most common 1-Gigabit Ethernet standard in use today is **1000Base-LX**. The *1000* in 1000Base-LX stands for *1,000Mbps*—or 1Gbps—throughput. *Base* stands for *baseband transmission*, and *LX* represents its reliance on long wavelengths of 1,300 nanometers. (A nanometer equals 0.000000001 meters, or about the width of six carbon atoms in a row.) 1000Base-LX has a longer reach than any other 1-gigabit technology available today. It relies on either single-mode or multimode fiber. With multimode fiber (62.5 microns in diameter), the maximum segment length is 550 meters. When used with single-mode fiber (8 microns in diameter), 1000Base-LX can reach 5,000 meters. 1000Base-LX networks can use one repeater between segments. Because of its potential length, 1000Base-LX is an excellent choice for long backbones—connecting buildings in a MAN, for example, or connecting an ISP with its telecommunications carrier.

1000Base-SX   1000Base-SX is similar to 1000Base-LX in that it has a maximum throughput of 1Gbps. However, it relies on only multimode fiber-optic cable as its medium. This makes it less expensive to install than 1000Base-LX. Another difference is that 1000Base-SX uses short wavelengths of 850 nanometers—thus, the *SX*, which stands for *short*. The maximum segment length for 1000Base-SX depends on two things: the diameter of the fiber and the modal bandwidth used to transmit signals. **Modal bandwidth** is a measure of the highest frequency of signal a multimode fiber can support over a specific distance and is measured in MHz-km. It is related to the distortion that occurs when multiple pulses of light, although issued at the same time, arrive at the end of a fiber at slightly different times. The higher the modal bandwidth, the longer a multimode fiber can carry a signal reliably.

When used with fibers whose diameters are 50 microns each, and with the highest possible modal bandwidth, the maximum segment length on a 1000Base-SX network is 550 meters. When used with fibers whose diameters are 62.5 microns each, and with the highest possible modal bandwidth, the maximum segment length is 275 meters. Only one repeater may be used between segments. Therefore, 1000Base-SX is best suited for shorter network runs than 1000Base-LX—for example, connecting a data center with a telecommunications closet in an office building.

10-Gigabit Fiber-Optic Standards

2.6

As you have learned, the throughput potential for fiber-optic cable is extraordinary, and scientists continue to push its limits. In 2002 IEEE published its **802.3ae** standard for fiber-optic Ethernet networks transmitting data at 10Gbps. Several variations were described by the standard, but all share some characteristics in common. For example, all of the fiber-optic 10-gigabit options rely on a star topology and allow for only one repeater. (As you will learn in later chapters, however, switches, and not repeaters, are more commonly used with high-speed data links.) In addition, all 10-gigabit standards operate under full-duplex mode only. The 10-gigabit fiber optic standards differ significantly in the wavelength of light each uses to issue signals and, as a result, their maximum allowable segment length differs also.

10GBase-SR and 10GBase-SW   The 10-gigabit options with the shortest segment length are **10GBase-SR** and **10GBase-SW**. By now you can guess that the *10G* stands for the standard's maximum throughput of 10 gigabits per second and *Base* stands for

2.6

baseband transmission. S stands for *short reach*. The fact that one of the standards ends with *R* and the other ends with *W* reflects the type of physical layer encoding each uses. Simply put, 10GBase-SR is designed to work with fiber connections on LANs, and 10GBase-SW is designed to work with WAN links that use a highly reliable fiber-optic ring technology called SONET. You'll learn more about SONET in Chapter 7.

10GBase-SR and 10GBase-SW rely on multimode fiber and transmit signals with wavelengths of 850 nanometers. As with the 1-gigabit standards, the maximum segment length on a 10GBase-SR or 10GBase-SW network depends on the diameter of the fibers used. It also depends on the modal bandwidth used. For example, if 50-micron fiber is used with the maximum possible modal bandwidth, the maximum segment length is 300 meters. If 62.5-micron fiber is used with the maximum possible modal bandwidth, a 10GBase-SR or 10GBase-SW segment can be 66 meters long. Either way, this 10-Gigabit Ethernet technology is best suited for connections within a data center or building, as its distance is the most limited.

10GBase-LR and 10GBase-LW Another standard defined in IEEE 802.3ae is 10GBase-LR and 10GBase-LW, in which the *10G* stands for *10 gigabits per second*, *Base* stands for *baseband transmission*, and *L* stands for *long reach*. 10GBase-LR and 10GBase-LW networks carry signals with wavelengths of 1,310 nanometers through single-mode fiber. Their maximum segment length is 10,000 meters. As is the case with the previously described 10-gigabit standard, in 10GBase-LW the *W* reflects its unique method of encoding that allows it to work over SONET WAN links. 10GBase-LR and 10GBase-LW technology is suited to WAN or MAN implementations.

10GBase-ER and 10GBase-EW For the longest fiber-optic segments, network administrators choose **10GBase-ER** or **10GBase-EW**. In this standard, *E* stands for *extended reach*. 10GBase-ER and 10GBase-EW require single-mode fiber, through which they transmit signals with wavelengths of 1,550 nanometers. These standards allow for segments up to 40,000 meters, or nearly 25 miles, long. The 10GBase-EW standard specifies encoding that makes it compatible with the SONET transmission format. Given their long-distance capabilities, 10GBase-ER and 10GBase-EW are best suited for use on WANs.

At the time of this writing, only those organizations with the highest demand for fast data transfer—for example, ISPs—were using 10-Gigabit Ethernet on their networks. As with any new technology, however, as it becomes more economical, more organizations will adopt it. In fact, IEEE is looking ahead and working on standards for 100-Gigabit Ethernet.

Summary of Common Ethernet Standards

2.6

To obtain Network+ certification, you must be familiar with the different characteristics and limitations of each type of network discussed in this chapter. To put this information in context, Table 5-1 summarizes the characteristics and limitations for common physical layer networking standards, including Ethernet networks that use twisted pair cable and fiber-optic cable. In addition to the varying specifications that follow, remember that all of these standards rely on a star or star-bus hybrid network topology.

Table 5-1 Common Ethernet Standards

Standard	Maximum Transmission Speed (Mbps)	Maximum Distance per Segment (m)	Physical Media
10Base-T	10	100	Cat 3 or higher UTP
100Base-TX	100	100	Cat 5 or higher UTP
1000Base-T	1,000	100	Cat 5 or higher UTP (Cat 5e is preferred)
10GBase-T	10,000	100	Cat 6 or Cat 7 (preferred)
100Base-FX	100	2,000	MMF
1000Base-LX	1,000	Up to 550, depending on wavelength and fiber core diameter 5,000	MMF SMF
1000Base-SX	1,000	Up to 500, depending on modal bandwidth and fiber core diameter	MMF
10GBase-SR and 10GBase-SW	10,000	Up to 300, depending on modal bandwidth and fiber core diameter	MMF
10GBase-LR and 10GBase-LW	10,000	10,000	SMF
10GBase-ER and 10GBase-EW	10,000	40,000	SMF

Ethernet Frames

Chapter 2 introduced you to data frames, the packages that carry higher-layer data and control information that enables data to reach its destinations without errors and in the correct sequence. Ethernet networks may use one (or a combination) of four kinds of data frames: Ethernet_802.2 (Raw), Ethernet_802.3 (Novell proprietary), Ethernet_II (DIX), and Ethernet_SNAP. This variety of Ethernet frame types came about as different organizations released and revised Ethernet standards during the 1980s, changing as LAN technology evolved. Each frame type differs slightly in the way it codes and decodes packets of data traveling from one device to another.

Physical layer standards, such as 100Base-T, have no effect on the type of framing that occurs in the data link layer. Thus, Ethernet frame types have no relation to the topology or cabling characteristics of the network. Framing also takes place independently of the higher-level layers. Theoretically, all frame types could carry any one of many higher-layer protocols. For example, a single Ethernet_II data frame may carry either TCP/IP or AppleTalk data (but not both simultaneously). But as you'll learn in the following discussion, not all frame types are well suited to carrying all kinds of traffic.

Using and Configuring Frames A node's data link layer services must be properly configured to expect the types of frames it might receive. You can use multiple frame types on a network, but a node configured to use only one frame type cannot communicate with another node that uses a different frame type. If a node receives an unfamiliar frame type, it will not be able to decode the data contained in the frame, nor will it be able to communicate with nodes configured to use that frame type. For this reason, it is important for LAN administrators to ensure that all devices use the same, correct frame type. These days, virtually all networks use the Ethernet_II frame type. But in the 1990s, before this uniformity evolved, the use of different NOSs or legacy hardware often required managing devices to interpret multiple frame types.

Frame types are typically specified through a device's NIC configuration software. To make matters easier, most NICs can automatically sense what types of frames are running on a network and adjust themselves to that specification. This feature is called autodetect, or autosense. Workstations, networked printers, and servers added to an existing network can all take advantage of autodetection. Even if your devices use the autodetect feature, you should nevertheless know what frame types are running on your network so that you can troubleshoot connectivity problems. Although it is easy to configure, the autodetect feature is not infallible.

Frame Fields All Ethernet frame types share many fields in common. For example, every Ethernet frame contains a 7-byte preamble and a 1-byte start-of-frame delimiter. The **preamble** signals to the receiving node that data is incoming and indicates when the data flow is about to begin. The **SFD (start-of-frame delimiter)** identifies where the data field begins. Preambles and SFDs are not included, however, when calculating a frame's total size.

Each Ethernet frame also contains a 14-byte header, which includes a destination address, a source address, and an additional field that varies in function and size, depending on the frame type. The destination address and source address fields are each 6 bytes long. The destination address identifies the recipient of the data frame, and the source address identifies the network node that originally sent the data. Recall that any network device can be identified by its physical address, also known as a hardware address or MAC (Media Access Control) address. The source address and destination address fields of an Ethernet frame use the MAC address to identify where data originated and where it should be delivered.

Also, all Ethernet frames contain a 4-byte FCS (Frame Check Sequence) field. Recall that the function of the FCS field is to ensure that the data at the destination exactly matches the data issued from the source using the CRC (Cyclic Redundancy Check) algorithm. Together, the FCS and the header make up the 18-byte "frame" for the data. The data portion of an Ethernet frame may contain from 46 to 1,500 bytes of information (and recall that this includes the network layer datagram). If fewer than 46 bytes of data are supplied by the higher layers, the source node fills out the data portion with extra bytes until it totals 46 bytes. The extra bytes are known as **padding** and have no significance other than to fill out the frame. They do not affect the data being transmitted.

Adding the 18-byte framing portion plus the smallest possible data field of 46 bytes equals the minimum Ethernet frame size of 64 bytes. Adding the framing portion plus the largest possible data field of 1,500 bytes equals the maximum Ethernet frame size of 1,518 bytes. No matter what frame type is used, the size range of 64 to 1,518 total bytes applies to all Ethernet frames.

Net+

2.6

Because of the overhead present in each frame and the time required to perform CSMA/CD, the use of larger frame sizes on a network generally results in faster throughput. To some extent, you cannot control your network's frame sizes. You can, however, help improve network performance by properly managing frames. For example, network administrators should strive to minimize the number of broadcast frames on their networks because broadcast frames tend to be very small and, therefore, inefficient. Also, running more than one frame type on the same network can result in inefficiencies because it requires devices to examine each incoming frame to determine its type. Given a choice, it's most efficient to support only one frame type on a network.

Ethernet_II (DIX) Ethernet_II is an Ethernet frame type developed by DEC, Intel, and Xerox (abbreviated as DIX) before the IEEE began to standardize Ethernet. The Ethernet_II frame type (or DIX, as it is sometimes called) is similar to the older Ethernet_802.3 and Ethernet_802.2 frame types, but it differs in one field. Where the other types contain a 2-byte length field, the Ethernet_II frame type contains a 2-byte type field. This type field identifies the network layer protocol (such as IP, ARP, RARP, or IPX) contained in the frame. For example, if a frame were carrying an IP datagram, its type field would contain 0x0800, the type code for IP. Because Ethernet_802.2 and Ethernet_802.3 frames do not contain a type field, they are only capable of transmitting data over a single network layer protocol (for example, only IP and not both IP and ARP) across the network. For TCP/IP networks, which commonly use multiple network layer protocols, these frame types are unsuitable.

Like Ethernet_II, the Ethernet_SNAP frame type also provides a type field. However, the Ethernet_SNAP standard calls for additional control fields, so that compared to Ethernet_II frames, the Ethernet_SNAP frames allow less room for data. Therefore, because of its support for multiple network layer protocols and because it uses fewer bytes as overhead, Ethernet_II is the frame type most commonly used on contemporary Ethernet networks. Figure 5-15 depicts an Ethernet_II frame.

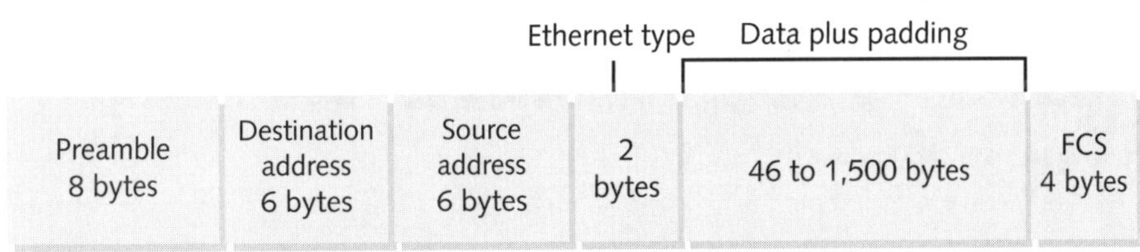

Figure 5-15 Ethernet_II (DIX) frame

Net+

3.3

PoE (Power over Ethernet)

Recently, IEEE has finalized the **802.3af** standard, which specifies a method for supplying electrical power over Ethernet connections, also known as **PoE (Power over Ethernet)**. Although the standard is relatively new, the concept is not. In fact, your home telephone receives power from the telephone company over the lines that enter your residence. This power is necessary for dial tone and ringing. On an Ethernet network, carrying power over signaling connections can be useful for nodes that are far from traditional power receptacles or need a constant, reliable power source. For example, a wireless access point at an outdoor theater, a telephone used to receive digitized voice signals, an Internet gaming station in the center of a mall, or a critical router at the core of a network's backbone can all benefit from PoE.

The PoE standard specifies two types of devices: PSE (power sourcing equipment) and PDs (powered devices). **PSE (power sourcing equipment)** refers to the device that supplies the power; usually this device depends on backup power sources (in other words, not the electrical grid maintained by utilities). **PDs (powered devices)** are those that receive the power from the PSE. PoE requires Cat 5 or better copper cable. In the cable, electric current may run over an unused pair of wires or over the pair of wires used for data transmission in a 10Base-T, 100Base-TX, 1000Base-T, or 10GBase-T network. The standard allows for both approaches; however, on a single network, the choice of current-carrying pairs should be consistent between all PSE and PDs.

Not all connectivity devices are capable of issuing power. To use PoE, you must purchase a switch or router that supports it, like the switch shown in Figure 5-16. Also, not all end nodes are capable of receiving PoE. The IEEE standard has accounted for that possibility by requiring all PSE to first determine whether a node is PoE-capable before attempting to supply it with power. That means that PoE is compatible with current 802.3 installations.

On networks that demand PoE but don't have PoE-capable equipment, you can add PoE adapters, like the ones shown in Figure 5-17. One type of adapter connects to a switch or router to allow it to supply power. The other adapter attaches to a client, such as an outdoor camera, to receive Power over the Ethernet connection.

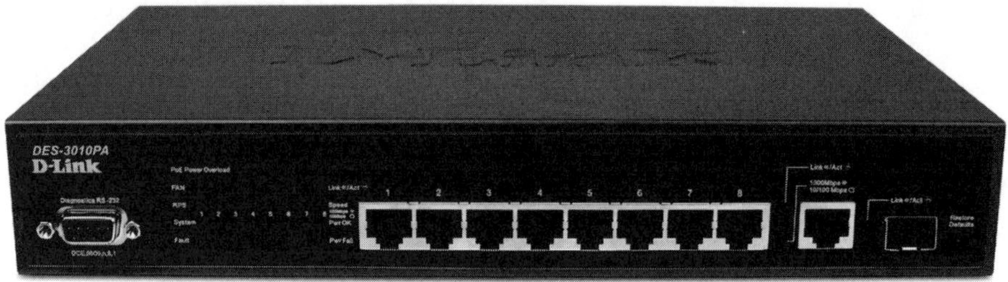

Figure 5-16 PoE-capable switch

Figure 5-17 PoE adapters

Chapter Summary

- A physical topology is the basic physical layout of a network; it does not specify devices, connectivity methods, or addresses on the network. Physical topologies are categorized into three fundamental geometric shapes: bus, ring, and star.

- A bus topology consists of a single cable connecting all nodes on a network without intervening connectivity devices. At either end of a bus network, 50-ohm resistors (terminators) stop signals after they have reached their destination. Without terminators, signals on a bus network experience signal bounce and LAN performance suffers. In a ring topology, each node is connected to the two nearest nodes so that the entire network forms a circle. Data is transmitted in one direction around the ring. Each workstation accepts and responds to packets addressed to it, and then it forwards the other packets to the next workstation in the ring.

- In a star topology, every node on the network is connected through a central device, such as a switch, router, or hub. Any single cable on a star network connects only two devices, so a cabling problem will affect only two nodes. Nodes transmit data to the hub, which then retransmits the information to the rest of the network segment where the destination node can pick it up.

- Star topology networks are more fault tolerant than bus topology networks, because a failure in one part of the network will not necessarily affect transmission on the entire network.

- Network logical topologies describe how signals travel over a network. The two main types of logical topologies are bus and ring. Ethernet networks use a bus logical topology, and token ring networks use a ring logical topology.

- Few LANs use the simple physical topologies in their pure form. More often, LANs employ a hybrid of more than one simple physical topology. The star-wired ring topology uses the physical layout of a star and the token-passing data transmission method. Data is sent around the star in a circular pattern. Token ring networks, as specified in IEEE 802.5, use this hybrid topology.

- In a star-wired bus topology, groups of workstations are connected to a switch, router, or hub in a star formation; all the hubs are networked via a single bus. This design can cover longer distances than a simple star topology and easily interconnect or isolate different network segments, although it is more expensive than using either the star or bus topology alone. The star-wired bus topology commonly forms the basis for Ethernet and Fast Ethernet networks.

- Switches, routers, or hubs that service star-wired bus or star-wired ring topologies can be daisy-chained to form a more complex hybrid topology. However, daisy-chaining can only extend a network so far before data errors are apt to occur. In this case, maximum segment and network length limits must be carefully maintained.

- Network backbones may follow serial, distributed, collapsed, or parallel topologies. In a serial topology, two or more internetworking devices are connected to each other by a single cable in a daisy chain. This is the simplest type of backbone. Hubs or switches are often connected in this way to extend a network.

- A distributed backbone consists of a number of connectivity devices connected to a series of central devices in a hierarchy. This topology allows for easy network management and scalability.

- The collapsed backbone topology uses a router or switch as the single central connection point for multiple subnetworks. This is risky because an entire network could fail if the central device fails. Also, if the central connectivity device becomes overtaxed, performance on the entire network suffers.

- A parallel backbone is the most fault-tolerant backbone topology. It is a variation of the collapsed backbone arrangement that consists of more than one connection from the central router or switch to each network segment and parallel connections between routers and switches, if more than one is present. Parallel backbones are the most expensive type of backbone to implement.

- Switching manages the filtering and forwarding of packets between nodes on a network. Every network relies on one or more types of switching: circuit switching, message switching, packet switching, or MPLS (multiprotocol label switching).

- Ethernet employs a network access method called CSMA/CD (Carrier Sense Multiple Access with Collision Detection). All Ethernet networks, independent of their speed or frame type, use CSMA/CD.

- On heavily trafficked Ethernet segments, collisions are common. The more nodes that are transmitting data on a network segment, the more collisions will take place. When an Ethernet segment grows to a particular number of nodes, performance may suffer as a result of collisions.

- Switching can separate a network segment into smaller logical segments, each independent of the other and supporting its own traffic. The use of switched Ethernet increases the effective bandwidth of a network segment because at any given time fewer workstations vie for the access to a shared channel.

- 10Base-T is a physical layer specification for an Ethernet network that is capable of 10Mbps throughput and uses baseband transmission and twisted pair media. It has a maximum segment length of 100 meters. It follows the 5-4-3 rule, which allows up to five segments between two communicating nodes, permits up to four repeating devices, and allows up to three of the segments to be populated.

- 100Base-T (also called Fast Ethernet) is a physical layer specification for an Ethernet network that is capable of 100Mbps throughput and uses baseband transmission and twisted pair media. It has a maximum segment length of 100 meters and allows up to three segments connected by two repeating devices.

- 1000Base-T (also called Gigabit Ethernet) is a physical layer specification for an Ethernet network that is capable of 1000Mbps (1Gbps) throughput and uses baseband transmission and twisted pair media. It has a maximum segment length of 100 meters and allows only one repeating device between segments.

- 10GBase-T is physical layer specification for transmitting 10Gbps over twisted pair cable. It relies on Cat 6 or better wiring and has a maximum segment length of 100 meters.

- 100Base-FX is a physical layer specification for a network that can achieve 100Mbps throughput using baseband transmission running on multimode fiber. Its maximum segment length is 2,000 meters.

- 1Gbps physical layer standards for fiber-optic networks include 1000Base-SX and 1000Base-LX. Because 1000Base-LX reaches farther and uses a longer wavelength, it is the more popular of the two. 1000Base-LX can use either single-mode or multimode fiber-optic cable; its segments can be up to 550 or 5,000 meters, respectively. 1000Base-SX uses only multimode fiber and can span up to 500 meters.

- 10Gbps physical layer standards include 10GBase-SR and 10GBase-SW (short reach), which rely on multimode fiber-optic cable and can span a maximum of 300 meters; 10GBase-LR and 10GBase-LW (long reach), which rely on single-mode fiber and can span a maximum of 10,000 meters; and 10GBaseER and 10GBase-EW (extended reach), which also use single-mode fiber and can span up to 40,000 meters. Standards marked with a *W* mean they are specially encoded to operate over SONET WAN links.

- Networks may use one (or a combination) of four kinds of Ethernet data frames. Each frame type differs slightly in the way it codes and decodes packets of data from one device to another. Most modern networks rely on Ethernet_II (DIX) frames.

Key Terms

5-4-3 rule A guideline for 10Mbps Ethernet networks stating that between two communicating nodes, the network cannot contain more than five network segments connected by four repeating devices, and no more than three of the segments may be populated.

10Base-T A physical layer standard for networks that specifies baseband transmission, twisted pair media, and 10Mbps throughput. 10Base-T networks have a maximum segment length of 100 meters and rely on a star topology.

10GBase-ER A physical layer standard for achieving 10Gbps data transmission over single-mode, fiber-optic cable. In 10GBase-ER, the *ER* stands for *extended reach*. This standard specifies a star topology and segment lengths up to 40 kilometers.

10GBase-EW A variation of the 10GBase-ER standard that is specially encoded to operate over SONET WAN links.

10GBase-LR A physical layer standard for achieving 10Gbps data transmission over single-mode, fiber-optic cable using wavelengths of 1,310 nanometers. In 10GBase-LR, the *LR* stands for *long reach*. This standard specifies a star topology and segment lengths up to 10 kilometers.

10GBase-LW A variation of the 10GBase-LR standard that is specially encoded to operate over SONET WAN links.

10GBase-SR A physical layer standard for achieving 10Gbps data transmission over multimode fiber using wavelengths of 850 nanometers. The maximum segment length for 10GBase-SR can reach up to 300 meters, depending on the fiber core diameter and modal bandwidth used.

10GBase-SW A variation of the 10GBase-SR standard that is specially encoded to operate over SONET WAN links.

10GBase-T A physical layer standard for achieving 10Gbps data transmission over twisted pair cable. Described in its 2006 standard 802.3an, IEEE specifies Cat 6 or Cat 7 cable as the appropriate medium for 10GBase-T. The maximum segment length for 10GBase-T is 100 meters.

100Base-FX   A physical layer standard for networks that specifies baseband transmission, multimode fiber cabling, and 100Mbps throughput. 100Base-FX networks have a maximum segment length of 2,000 meters. 100Base-FX may also be called Fast Ethernet.

100Base-T   A physical layer standard for networks that specifies baseband transmission, twisted pair cabling, and 100Mbps throughput. 100Base-T networks have a maximum segment length of 100 meters and use the star topology. 100Base-T is also known as Fast Ethernet.

100Base-TX   A type of 100Base-T network that uses two wire pairs in a twisted pair cable but uses faster signaling to achieve 100Mbps throughput. It is capable of full-duplex transmission and requires Cat 5 or higher twisted pair media.

802.3ab   The IEEE standard that describes 1000Base-T, a 1-Gigabit Ethernet technology that runs over four pairs of Cat 5 or better cable.

802.3ae   The IEEE standard that describes 10-Gigabit Ethernet technologies, including 10GBase-SR, 10GBase-SW, 10GBase-LR, 10GBase-LW, 10GBase-ER, and 10GBase-EW.

802.3af   The IEEE standard that specifies a way of supplying electrical Power over Ethernet (PoE). 802.3af requires Cat 5 or better UTP or STP cabling and uses power sourcing equipment to supply current over a wire pair to powered devices. PoE is compatible with existing 10Base-T, 100Base-TX, 1000Base-T, and 10GBase-T implementations.

802.3an   The IEEE standard published in 2006 that describes 10GBase-T, a 10Gbps Ethernet technology that runs on Cat 6 or Cat 7 twisted pair cable.

802.3u   The IEEE standard that describes Fast Ethernet technologies, including 100Base-TX.

802.3z   The IEEE standard that describes 1000Base (or 1-Gigabit) Ethernet technologies, including 1000Base-LX and 1000Base-SX.

1000Base-LX   A physical layer standard for networks that specifies 1Gbps transmission over fiber-optic cable using baseband transmission. 1000Base-LX can run on either single-mode or multimode fiber. The *LX* represents its reliance on long wavelengths of 1,300 nanometers. 1000Base-LX can extend to 5,000-meter segment lengths using single-mode, fiber-optic cable. 1000Base-LX networks can use one repeater between segments.

1000Base-SX   A physical layer standard for networks that specifies 1Gbps transmission over fiber-optic cable using baseband transmission. 1000Base-SX runs on multimode fiber. Its maximum segment length is 550 meters. The *SX* represents its reliance on short wavelengths of 850 nanometers. 1000Base-SX can use one repeater.

1000Base-T   A physical layer standard for achieving 1Gbps over UTP. 1000Base-T achieves its higher throughput by using all four pairs of wires in a Cat 5 or higher twisted pair cable to both transmit and receive signals. 1000Base-T also uses a different data encoding scheme than that used by other UTP physical layer specifications.

access method   A network's method of controlling how nodes access the communications channel. For example, CSMA/CD (Carrier Sense Multiple Access with Collision Detection) is the access method specified in the IEEE 802.3 (Ethernet) standard.

active topology   A topology in which each workstation participates in transmitting data over the network. A ring topology is considered an active topology.

broadcast domain   Logically grouped network nodes that can communicate directly via broadcast transmissions. For example, all nodes connected to a single hub and all nodes that participate in a bus-topology network belong to a single broadcast domain.

bus   The single cable connecting all devices in a bus topology.

bus topology   A topology in which a single cable connects all nodes on a network without intervening connectivity devices.

Carrier Sense Multiple Access with Collision Detection   *See* CSMA/CD.

circuit switching   A type of switching in which a connection is established between two network nodes before they begin transmitting data. Bandwidth is dedicated to this connection and remains available until users terminate the communication between the two nodes.

collapsed backbone   A type of backbone that uses a router or switch as the single central connection point for multiple subnetworks.

collision   In Ethernet networks, the interference of one node's data transmission with the data transmission of another node sharing the same segment.

collision domain   The portion of an Ethernet network in which collisions can occur if two nodes transmit data at the same time.

CSMA/CD (Carrier Sense Multiple Access with Collision Detection)   A network access method specified for use by IEEE 802.3 (Ethernet) networks. In CSMA/CD, each node waits its turn before transmitting data to avoid interfering with other nodes' transmissions. If a node's NIC determines that its data has been involved in a collision, it immediately stops transmitting. Next, in a process called jamming, the NIC issues a special 32-bit sequence that indicates to the rest of the network nodes that its previous transmission was faulty and that those data frames are invalid. After waiting, the NIC determines if the line is again available; if it is available, the NIC retransmits its data.

daisy chain   A group of connectivity devices linked in a serial fashion.

data propagation delay   The length of time data takes to travel from one point on the segment to another point. On Ethernet networks, CSMA/CD's collision detection routine cannot operate accurately if the data propagation delay is too long.

distributed backbone   A type of backbone in which a number of connectivity devices (usually hubs) are connected to a series of central connectivity devices, such as hubs, switches, or routers, in a hierarchy.

enterprise   An entire organization, including local and remote offices, a mixture of computer systems, and a number of departments. Enterprise-wide computing takes into account the breadth and diversity of a large organization's computer needs.

Ethernet_II   The original Ethernet frame type developed by Digital, Intel, and Xerox, before the IEEE began to standardize Ethernet. Ethernet_II contains a 2-byte type field to identify the upper-layer protocol contained in the frame. It supports TCP/IP and other higher-layer protocols.

Fast Ethernet   A type of Ethernet network that is capable of 100Mbps throughput. 100Base-T and 100Base-FX are both examples of Fast Ethernet.

fault tolerance   The capability for a component or system to continue functioning despite damage or malfunction.

Gigabit Ethernet   A type of Ethernet network that is capable of 1000Mbps, or 1Gbps, throughput.

hybrid topology   A physical topology that combines characteristics of more than one simple physical topology.

jamming   A part of CSMA/CD in which, upon detecting a collision, a station issues a special 32-bit sequence to indicate to all nodes on an Ethernet segment that its previously transmitted frame has suffered a collision and should be considered faulty.

logical topology   A characteristic of network transmission that reflects the way in which data is transmitted between nodes (which may differ from the physical layout of the paths that data takes). The most common logical topologies are bus and ring.

message switching   A type of switching in which a connection is established between two devices in the connection path; one device transfers data to the second device and then breaks the connection. The information is stored and forwarded from the second device after a connection between that device and a third device on the path is established.

modal bandwidth   A measure of the highest frequency of signal a multimode fiber-optic cable can support over a specific distance. Modal bandwidth is measured in MHz-km.

MPLS (multiprotocol label switching)   A type of switching that enables any one of several Layer 2 protocols to carry multiple types of Layer 3 protocols. One of its benefits is the ability to use packet-switched technologies over traditionally circuit-switched networks. MPLS can also create end-to-end paths that act like circuit-switched connections.

multiprotocol label switching   *See* MPLS.

packet switching   A type of switching in which data is broken into packets before it is transported. In packet switching, packets can travel any path on the network to their destination, because each packet contains a destination address and sequencing information.

padding   The bytes added to the data (or information) portion of an Ethernet frame to ensure this field is at least 46 bytes in size. Padding has no effect on the data carried by the frame.

parallel backbone   A type of backbone that consists of more than one connection from the central router or switch to each network segment.

passive topology   A network topology in which each node passively listens for, and then accepts, data directed to it. A bus topology is considered a passive topology.

PD (powered device)   On a network using Power over Ethernet, a node that receives power from power sourcing equipment.

physical topology   The physical layout of a network. A physical topology depicts a network in broad scope; it does not specify devices, connectivity methods, or addresses on the network. Physical topologies are categorized into three fundamental geometric shapes: bus, ring, and star. These shapes can be mixed to create hybrid topologies.

PoE (Power over Ethernet)   A method of delivering current to devices using Ethernet connection cables.

Power over Ethernet   *See* PoE.

power sourcing equipment   *See* PSE.

powered device   *See* PD.

preamble   The field in an Ethernet frame that signals to the receiving node that data is incoming and indicates when the data flow is about to begin.

PSE (power sourcing equipment)   On a network using Power over Ethernet, the device that supplies power to end nodes.

QoS (quality of service)   The result of specifications for guaranteeing data delivery within a certain period of time after their transmission.

quality of service   *See* QoS.

ring topology   A network layout in which each node is connected to the two nearest nodes so that the entire network forms a circle. Data is transmitted unidirectionally around the ring. Each workstation accepts and responds to packets addressed to it and then forwards the other packets to the next workstation in the ring.

serial backbone   A type of backbone that consists of two or more internetworking devices connected to each other by a single cable in a daisy chain. Hubs are often connected in this way to extend a network.

SFD (start-of-frame delimiter)   A 1-byte field that indicates where the data field begins in an Ethernet frame.

signal bounce   A phenomenon, caused by improper termination on a bus-topology network, in which signals travel endlessly between the two ends of the network, preventing new signals from getting through.

star topology   A physical topology in which every node on the network is connected through a central device, such as a hub. Any single physical wire on a star network connects only two devices, so a cabling problem will affect only two nodes. Nodes transmit data to the hub, which then retransmits the data to the rest of the network segment where the destination node can pick it up.

star-wired bus topology   A hybrid topology in which groups of workstations are connected in a star fashion to hubs that are networked via a single bus.

star-wired ring topology   A hybrid topology that uses the physical layout of a star and the token-passing data transmission method.

start-of-frame delimiter   *See* SFD.

switching   A component of a network's logical topology that manages how packets are filtered and forwarded between nodes on the network.

terminator   A resistor that is attached to each end of a bus-topology network and that causes the signal to stop rather than reflect back toward its source.

Review Questions

1. Which of the following describes a ring topology?

    a. A single cable connects all nodes on a network without intervening connectivity devices.

    b. Each node is connected to the two nearest nodes so that the entire network forms a circle.

    c. Every node on the network is connected through a central device, such as a hub, router, or switch.

    d. Signals follow a circular path between sender and receiver.

2. A star-wired bus is referred to as which of the following topology types?

   a. Physical

   b. Logical

   c. Hybrid

   d. Backbone

3. Which of the following has a backbone network topology that uses a router or switch as the single central connection point for multiple subnetworks?

   a. Serial

   b. Distributed

   c. Collapsed

   d. Parallel

4. What switching technique establishes a connection between two network nodes before transmitting data?

   a. Circuit switching

   b. Message switching

   c. Packet switching

   d. MPLS (Multiple Label Switching)

5. Which of the following is a 10-Gigabyte Fiber-optic Ethernet standard?

   a. 10GBase-LR

   b. 10Base-T

   c. 10GBase-T

   d. 100Base-FX

6. True or false? The most common logical topologies are bus and ring.

7. True or false? Connecting two or more internetworking devices by a single cable in a daisy-chain fashion makes the serial network backbone complex.

8. True or false? The most popular method for connecting nodes on a network is packet switching.

9. True or false? On heavily trafficked Ethernet network segments, collisions are fairly common.

10. True or false? The various Ethernet standards for copper cable utilize encoding methods that affect maximum throughput, segment length, and wiring requirements.

11. A physical ____ is the physical layout, or pattern, of the nodes on a network.

12. The term ____ refers to the way in which data is transmitted between nodes.

13. All Ethernet networks use the ____ access method.

14. Most modern networks rely on ____ frames.

15. The IEEE 802.3af standard, which specifies a method for supplying electrical power over Ethernet connections, is also known as ____.

Network Hardware

After reading this chapter and completing the exercises, you will be able to:

- Identify the functions of LAN connectivity hardware

- Install, configure, and differentiate between network devices such as NICs, hubs, bridges, switches, routers, and gateways

- Explain the advanced features of a switch and understand popular switching techniques, including VLAN management

- Explain the purposes and properties of routing

- Describe common IPv4 and IPv6 routing protocols

On the Job

Every now and then we have one of those days I live for at work, when we get an especially thorny troubleshooting problem. For example, one day something came up with one of the Cisco 2611 routers that we use as terminal servers. These servers give us access to the console serial ports on our remote servers. As we were in the process of updating all our remote router configurations, I found that we couldn't telnet to one of the terminal servers the way we could the other terminal servers. We couldn't even ping the loopback device IP address. I guess it had been a while since we last tried to access any of those servers' serial ports.

We tried to access the terminal server from different points on the network, to no avail. Then one of my coworkers suggested logging in to the router that is the next hop from the terminal server. Voila! We could get in to the terminal server. I verified the running configuration and it looked fine, but sure enough, we couldn't ping an IP address that was on a network different from the network the terminal server was physically connected to. I double-checked the default gateway, and it was correct:

```
ip default-gateway 192.168.0.1
```

I rebooted the terminal server to see if something had changed without us noticing. I started running a continuous ping while the terminal server was rebooting, and it did respond. But it responded to only 5 packets. I rebooted again to see if I imagined that the terminal server responded to a handful of pings. There it was again: the terminal server replied to six ICMP echo requests, and then it was unreachable.

I checked the Cisco documentation to see if there was a bug with the IOS version that was running on that terminal server, but I didn't see anything that would apply. Scratching my head, I went home for the evening. But I couldn't let it rest. I Googled "IOS default gateway" later that evening and learned that when a router is not being used for routing, the "ip default-gateway" statement is ignored. I added a static default route to the configuration first thing the next morning:

```
ip route 0.0.0.0 0.0.0.0 192.168.0.1
```

Thanks to this one change, the server was able to get to all those remote hosts that it couldn't see before. The only remaining mystery is how it ever worked before!

Elena Velasquez
Castle Ridge Computing

In Chapter 3, you learned how data is transmitted. Now you need to know how data arrives at its destination. To understand this process, it's helpful to compare data transmission to the means by which the United States Postal Service delivers mail: Mail trucks, airplanes, and delivery staff serve as the transmission system that moves information from place to place. Machines and personnel at the post office interpret addresses on the envelopes and either deliver the mail to a transfer point or to your home. Inefficiencies in mail delivery, such as letters being misdirected to the wrong transfer point, frustrate both the sender and the receiver of the mail and increase the overall cost of delivery.

In data networks, the task of directing information efficiently to the correct destination is handled by hubs, routers, bridges, and switches. In this chapter, you will learn about these devices and their roles in managing data traffic. Material in this chapter relates mostly to functions occurring in the data link and network layers of the OSI model. Some material also relates to the physical layer. You will learn the concepts involved in moving data from place to place, including issues related to switching and routing protocols. You will also see pictures of the hardware—hubs, switches, bridges, and routers—that make data transfer possible. (It's important for you to have an accurate mental image of this equipment because, in a cluttered data closet, it may prove difficult to identify the hardware underneath the wiring.) In addition, you will learn all about network interface cards, which serve as the workstation's link to the network and are often the source of connectivity problems.

NICs (Network Interface Cards)

Net+

3.1

NICs (network interface cards, also called network adapters or network cards) are connectivity devices that enable a workstation, server, printer, or other node to receive and transmit data over the network media. Nearly all NICs contain a data transceiver, the device that transmits and receives data signals. NICs belong to both the physical layer and data link layer of the OSI model because they issue data signals to a wire or into the atmosphere and assemble or disassemble data frames. They also interpret physical addressing information to ensure data is delivered to its proper destination. In addition, they perform the routines that determine which node has the right to transmit data over a network at any given instant—CSMA/CD on an Ethernet network, for example.

Advances in NIC technology are making this hardware smarter than ever. Many NICs can also perform prioritization, network management, buffering, and traffic-filtering functions. On most networks, NICs do not, however, analyze information added by the protocols in Layers 3 through 7 of the OSI model. For example, they could not determine whether the frames they transmit and receive use IP datagrams or a different Layer 2 protocol. Nor could they determine whether the presentation layer has encrypted the data in those packets.

As you learn about installing, configuring, and troubleshooting NICs, you should concentrate first on generalities and then move on to special situations. Because NICs are common to every networking device and every network, knowing as much as possible about them may prove to be the most useful tool you have at your disposal.

Types of NICs

Before you order or install a NIC in a network device, you need to know which type of interface the device uses. NICs come in a variety of types depending on the following:

- The access method (for example, Ethernet versus token ring)
- Network transmission speed (for example, 100Mbps versus 1Gbps)
- Connector interfaces (for example, RJ-45 versus SC)
- Type of compatible motherboard or device (for example, PCI)
- Manufacturer (popular NIC manufacturers include 3Com, Adaptec, D-Link, IBM, Intel, Kingston, Linksys, NETGEAR, SMC, and Western Digital, to name just a few)

Net+
3.1

The following section describes one category of NICs: those that are installed on an expansion board inside a computer.

Internal Bus Standards If you have worked with PCs or studied for CompTIA's A+ exam, you are probably familiar with the concept of a bus. A computer's **bus** is the circuit, or signaling pathway, used by the motherboard to transmit data to the computer's components, including its memory, processor, hard disk, and NIC. (A computer's bus may also be called its **system bus** or **main bus**.) Buses differ according to their capacity. The capacity of a bus is defined principally by the width of its data path (expressed in bits) and its clock speed (expressed in MHz). A data path size equals the number of bits that it can transmit in parallel at any given time. In the earliest PCs, buses had an 8-bit data path. Later, manufacturers expanded buses to handle 16 bits of data, then 32 bits. Most new desktop computers use buses capable of exchanging 64 bits of data, and some are even capable of 128 bits. As the number of bits of data that a bus can handle increases, so too does the speed of the devices attached to the bus.

A computer's bus can be expanded to include devices other than those found on the motherboard. The motherboard contains **expansion slots,** or openings with multiple electrical contacts, that allow devices such as NICs, modems, or sound cards to connect to the computer's expanded bus. The devices are found on a circuit board called an **expansion card** or **expansion board**. Inserting an expansion board into an expansion slot establishes an electrical connection between the expansion board and the motherboard. Thus, the device connected to the expansion board becomes connected to the computer's main circuit and part of its bus. With expansion boards connected to its main circuit, a computer can centrally control the device.

Multiple bus types exist, and to become part of a computer's bus, an expansion board must use the same bus type. By far, the most popular expansion board NIC is one that uses a PCI bus. **PCI (Peripheral Component Interconnect)** is a 32- or 64-bit bus with clock speeds rated at 33, 66, or 133MHz whose maximum data transfer rate is 1Gbps. Intel introduced the first version of PCI in 1992. The latest official version, 3.0, was released in 2004 and became the expansion card type used for nearly all NICs in new PCs and Macintosh computers. Figure 6-1 depicts a typical PCI NIC.

A PCI bus is characterized by a shorter connector length and a much faster data transmission capability than previous bus types such as **ISA (Industry Standard Architecture)**, the original PC bus type, developed in the early 1980s to support an 8-bit and later a 16-bit

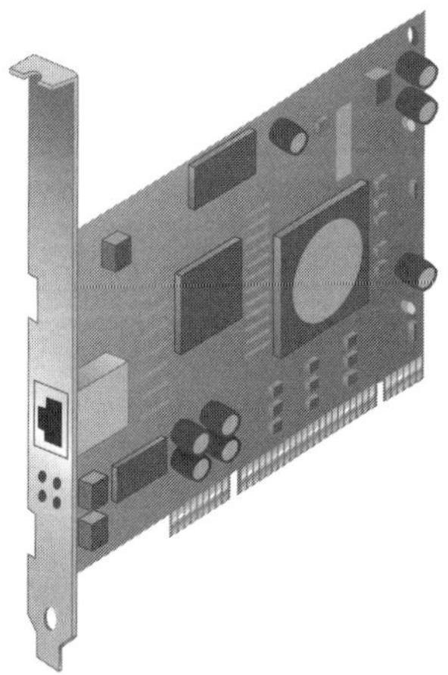

Figure 6-1 PCI NIC

data path and a 4.77MHz clock speed. Another advantage to PCI adapters is that they work with both PCs and Macintosh computers, allowing an organization to standardize on one type of NIC for use with all of its workstations.

Newer, faster variations on the PCI standard exist, however. One example is **PCIe (PCI Express)**, which specifies a 32- or 64-bit bus with a maximum 133MHz clock speed capable of transferring data at up to 500Mbps per data path, or lane, in full-duplex transmission. PCI Express, which was introduced in 2002 and has continued to evolve ever since, follows a different type of bus design from traditional PCI and offers several advantages: more efficient data transfer, support for quality of service distinctions, error reporting and handling, and compatibility with the current PCI software. Because of their unique design, PCIe cards cannot be inserted into a conventional PCI slot. PCIe slots vary depending on the number of lanes they support: An x1 slot supports a single lane, an x2 slot supports two lanes, and so on. Each lane offers a full-duplex throughput of 500Mbps. A PCIe slot can support up to 16 lanes, and an x16 slot can provide 8Gbps throughput. Computers such as servers that must perform fast data transfer use the PCIe standard. Figure 6-2 depicts a PCIe NIC.

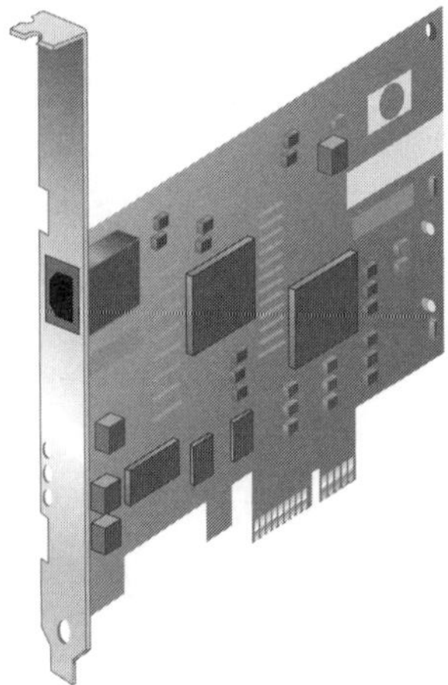

Figure 6-2 PCIe NIC

You can easily determine the type of bus your PC uses by reading the documentation that came with the computer. Someday, however, you may need to replace a NIC on a PC whose documentation is missing. To verify the type of bus a PC uses, you can look inside the PC case. (Later in this chapter, you will learn how to open a computer case, check the computer's bus, and install a NIC safely.) Most PCs have at least two different types of bus connections on the same motherboard. Figure 6-3 illustrates a motherboard with PCI and PCIe expansion slots.

If a motherboard supports more than one kind of expansion slot, refer to the NIC and PC manufacturers' guidelines (either in print or on the Web) for information on the preferred type of NIC. If possible, you should choose a NIC that matches the most modern bus on the motherboard. For example, if a PC supports both ISA and PCI, attempt to use a PCI NIC. Although you may be able to use the older bus and NIC types without adverse effects, some NICs will not work in an older bus if a faster, newer bus is available on the motherboard.

Peripheral Bus Standards Some peripheral devices, such as modems or NICs, are attached to the computer's bus externally rather than internally. PCMCIA (Personal Computer Memory Card International Association), USB (universal serial bus), CompactFlash, and

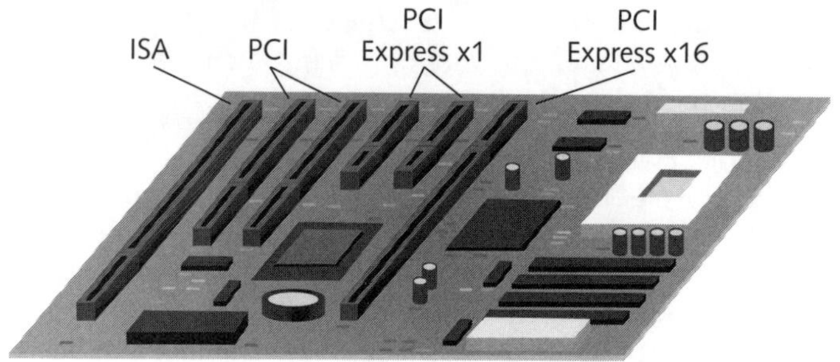

Figure 6-3 A motherboard with multiple expansion slots

FireWire (IEEE 1394) slots can all be used to connect peripherals such as NICs. One advantage to externally attached NICs is their simple installation. Typically, an externally attached adapter needs only to be plugged into the port to be physically installed. An expansion board NIC, on the other hand, requires the user to turn off the computer, remove its cover, insert the board into an expansion slot, fasten the board in place, replace the cover, and turn on the computer. The oldest externally attached type of NIC still in use today is the PCMCIA adapter.

In 1989, a group of PC system and computer manufacturers formed the **Personal Computer Memory Card International Association,** or **PCMCIA.** The group's original goal was to establish a standard method for connecting external memory to a portable computer. Later, seeing the potential for many other uses, PCMCIA revised the standard and offered cards that could connect virtually any type of external device. Now, PCMCIA slots may be used to connect external modems, NICs (for either wire-bound or wireless networks), printers, and external storage drives to most laptop computers.

The first standard PCMCIA-standard adapter to be released, called **PC Card,** specified a 16-bit interface running at 8MHz. However, the PC Card standard was hampered by its slow data transfer rates. In the 1990s, recognizing the need for a faster standard, the PCMCIA group developed CardBus. **CardBus** specifies a 32-bit interface running at 33MHz, which matches the PCI expansion board standard. Some modern laptops are equipped with CardBus slots. Figure 6-4 depicts a typical CardBus NIC.

As demand for more and faster data transfer grows, PCMCIA has continued to improve its standards. In 2003, it released the ExpressCard standard. **ExpressCard** allows many different external devices to connect to portable computers through a 26-pin interface, and it offers data transfer rates of 250Mbps in each direction (for a total of 500Mbps). It uses the same data transfer standards as those specified in the PCIe specification. ExpressCard modules come in two sizes: 34mm (40% smaller than current CardBus modules) and 54mm wide (the same width as CardBus modules). At the time this was written, PCMCIA hinted that it would soon release an ExpressCard 2.0 standard, which promises significantly faster data transfer speeds than the original ExpressCard standard. Figure 6-5 shows examples of the two types of ExpressCard modules.

PCMCIA-standard adapters are often called "credit card adapters" because they are approximately the same size as a credit card.

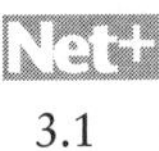

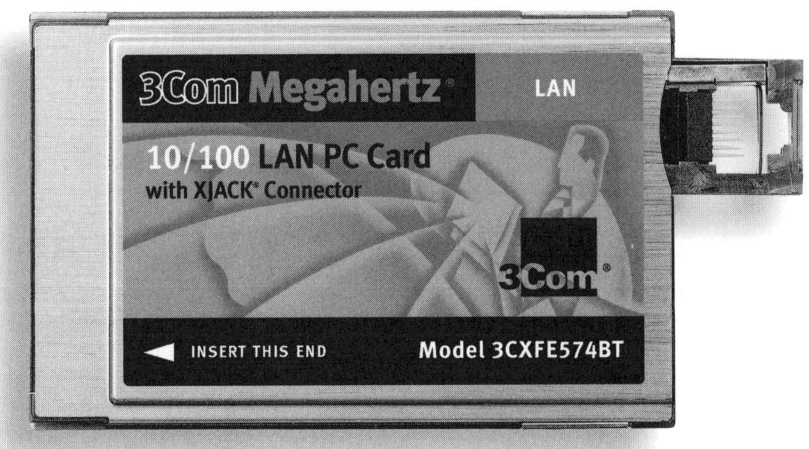

Figure 6-4 A CardBus NIC

Another type of externally attached NIC is one that relies on a **USB (universal serial bus) port**. USB is a standard interface used to connect multiple types of peripherals, including modems, mice, audio players, and NICs. The original USB standard was developed in 1995 by a group of computer manufacturers working to make a low-cost, simple-to-install method of connecting peripheral devices to any make or model of computer. Since 1998, USB ports have been supplied on the motherboards of most modern laptop and desktop computers.

USB adapters may follow one of two USB standards: USB 1.1 or USB 2.0. The primary difference between the two standards is speed. The USB 1.1 standard has a maximum data transfer rate of 12Mbps. The 2.0 standard can reach 480Mbps, if the correct transfer

Figure 6-5 ExpressCard modules

options are selected and if the attached device is capable of supporting that speed. Most new PCs are shipped with USB 2.0 ports. The release of an even faster USB standard, USB 3.0 (or SuperSpeed USB), which will be able to transfer data as fast as 4.8Gbps, is expected soon. Figure 6-6 shows an example of a USB NIC, which has a USB connector on one end and an RJ-45 receptacle on the other end.

Yet another peripheral bus type is called **FireWire**. Apple Computer began developing the FireWire standard in the 1980s, and it was codified by the IEEE as the **IEEE 1394** standard in 1995. It has been included on the motherboards of Macintosh computers for many years but has become common on PCs only in the past few years. As with PCMCIA and USB standards, FireWire has undergone several improvements since its inception. Traditional FireWire connections support a maximum throughput of 400Mbps. A newer version of the standard supports potential throughput rates of over 3Gbps.

FireWire can connect most any type of peripheral, such as a digital camera, VCR, external hard disk, or CD-ROM drive, to a desktop or laptop computer. It can also connect two or more computers on a small network using a bus topology—that is, by linking one computer to another in a daisy-chain fashion. On such a network, FireWire supports a maximum of 63 devices per segment, allows for up to 4.5 meters between nodes, and the chain of FireWire-linked computers can extend no farther than 72 meters from end to end. If your computer doesn't come with a FireWire port, you can install a FireWire adapter, which is a card (usually PCI or PCMCIA) that contains a FireWire port, to allow for this type of network.

FireWire-connected peripherals are similar to USB- and PCMCIA-connected peripherals in that they are simple to install and are supported by most modern operating systems. Connectors come in two varieties: 4-pin and 6-pin. The 6-pin connector contains two pins that can be used to supply power to a peripheral. The 6-pin connector is also the one most frequently used for interconnecting computers. FireWire has distinctively small connectors and a thin cable, as shown in Figure 6-7.

A fourth external bus standard is the **CompactFlash** standard. The original group of 12 electronics companies that formed the CompactFlash Association (CFA) designed CompactFlash

Figure 6-6 A USB NIC

Figure 6-7 FireWire connectors (4-pin and 6-pin)

as an ultrasmall, removable data and input/output device that would connect to many kinds of peripherals. If you have used a digital camera recently, chances are you've saved photos on a CompactFlash storage card. However, CompactFlash slots can also be used to connect to a network. The latest CompactFlash standard, 4.0, provides a data transfer rate of 133Mbps. Note that this is slower than any of the current external adapter standards discussed previously. Because of their relatively slower speed, CompactFlash NICs are most likely to be found connecting devices too small to handle PCMCIA slots (for example, PDAs or computers embedded into other devices, such as defibrillators or heart monitors). They are often used in wireless connections, although CompactFlash NICs with RJ-45 connectors do exist, as shown in Figure 6-8.

Figure 6-8 A CompactFlash NIC

Net+
3.1
On-Board NICs Not all peripheral devices are connected to a computer's motherboard via an expansion slot or peripheral bus. Some are connected directly to the motherboard using **on-board ports**. For example, the electrical connection that controls a computer's mouse operates through an on-board port, as does the connection for its keyboard and monitor. Many new computers, especially laptops, also use **on-board NICs**, or NICs that are integrated into the motherboard. The advantage to using an on-board NIC is that it saves space and frees expansion slots for additional peripherals. When a computer contains an on-board network adapter, its RJ-45 port is located on the back or side of the computer.

Wireless NICs NICs are designed for use with either wired or wireless networks. Wireless NICs, which contain antennas to send and receive signals, can be found for all of the bus types discussed in this chapter. One disadvantage to using wireless NICs is that currently they are somewhat more expensive than wire-bound NICs using the same bus type. (Other reasons for choosing wire-bound NICs over wireless, if the choices are equally convenient, are the bandwidth and security limitations of wireless transmission. These limitations are discussed elsewhere in the book.) Figure 6-9 depicts wireless PCI, CardBus, and USB NICs.

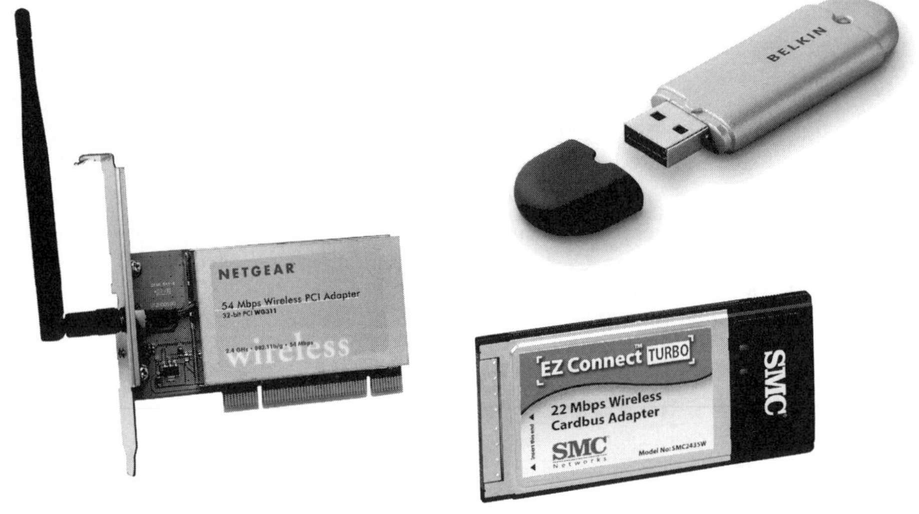

Figure 6-9 Wireless NICs

Installing NICs

You probably won't have to install a NIC on a brand-new PC or server. However, someday you might want to upgrade the NIC in your desktop to one that can handle faster transmission speeds or add NICs to your server, for example. In that case, you need to know how to install NICs properly.

To install a NIC, you must first install the hardware, and then install the software that shipped with it. In some cases, you may also have to perform a third step: configuring the

3.1

firmware, a set of data or instructions that has been saved to a ROM (read-only memory) chip (which is on the NIC). The ROM's data can be changed by a configuration utility program provided with the NIC. Because its data can be erased or changed by applying electrical charges to the chip (via the software program), this particular type of ROM is called **EEPROM (electrically erasable programmable read-only memory).** You'll learn more about a NIC's firmware later in the chapter. The following sections explain how to install and configure NICs.

Installing and Configuring NIC Hardware

It's always advisable to start by reading the manufacturer's documentation that accompanies the NIC hardware. The following steps generally apply to any kind of expansion card NIC installation in a desktop computer, but your experience may vary.

To install an expansion card NIC:

1. Make sure that your toolkit includes a Phillips-head screwdriver, a ground strap, and a ground mat to protect the internal components from electrostatic discharge. Also, make sure that you have ample space in which to work, whether it be on the floor, a desk, or table.

2. Turn off the computer's power switch, and then unplug the computer. In addition to endangering you, opening a PC while it's turned on can damage the PC's internal circuitry. Also unplug attached peripherals and the network cable, if necessary.

3. Attach the ground strap to your wrist and make sure that it's connected to the ground mat underneath the computer.

4. Open the computer's case. Desktop computer cases are attached in several different ways. They might use four or six Phillips-head screws to attach the housing to the back panel, or they might not use any screws and slide off instead. Remove all necessary screws and then remove the computer's case.

5. Select a slot on the computer's motherboard where you will insert the NIC. Make sure that the slot matches the type of expansion card you have. Remove the metal slot cover for that slot from the back of the PC. Some slot covers are attached with a single Phillips-head screw; after removing the screw, you can lift out the slot cover. Other slot covers are merely metal parts with perforated edges that you can punch or twist out with your hands.

6. Insert the NIC by lining up its slot connector with the slot and pressing it firmly into the slot. Don't be afraid to press down hard, but make sure the expansion card is properly aligned with the slot when you do so. If you have correctly inserted the NIC, it should not wiggle near its base. (Depending on the card's size and thickness, it may have some inherent flexibility, however.) A loose NIC causes connectivity problems. Figure 6-10 shows a close-up of a NIC firmly seated in its slot.

7. The metal bracket at the end of the NIC should now be positioned where the metal slot cover was located before you removed the slot cover. Attach the bracket with a Phillips-head screw to the back of the computer cover to secure the NIC in place.

8. Make sure that you have not loosened any cables or cards inside the PC or left any screws or debris inside the computer.

Figure 6-10 A properly inserted NIC

9. Replace the cover on the computer and reinsert the screws that you removed in step 4, if applicable. Also reinsert any cables you removed.

10. Plug in the computer and turn it on. Proceed to configure the NIC's software, as discussed later in this chapter.

Physically installing a PCMCIA-standard NIC is much easier than installing an expansion card NIC. In general, you simply insert the card into the PCMCIA slot, as shown in Figure 6-11.

Figure 6-11 Installing a PCMCIA-standard NIC

Most modern operating systems allow you to insert and remove the PCMCIA-standard adapter without restarting the machine. Make sure that the card is firmly inserted. If you can wiggle it, you need to realign it or push it in farther. Installing other types of external NICs, such as USB, ExpressCard, and CompactFlash adapters, is similar. All you need to do is insert the device into the computer's port, making sure that it's securely attached.

On servers and other high-powered computers, you may need to install multiple NICs. For the hardware installation, you can simply repeat the installation process for the first NIC, choosing a different slot. The trick to using multiple NICs on one machine lies in correctly configuring the software for each NIC. Simple NIC configuration is covered in the following section. The precise steps involved in configuring NICs on servers will depend on the server's networking operating system.

Installing and Configuring NIC Software Even if your computer runs an operating system with plug-and-play technology, you must ensure that the correct device driver is installed for the NIC and that it is configured properly. A **device driver** (sometimes called, simply, a **driver**) is software that enables an attached device to communicate with the computer's operating system. When you purchase a computer that already contains an attached peripheral (such as a sound card), the device drivers should already be installed. However, when you add hardware, you must install the device drivers. Most operating systems come with a multitude of built-in device drivers. In that case, after you physically install new hardware and restart, the operating system automatically recognizes the hardware and installs the device's drivers. Each time a computer starts up, the device drivers for all its connected peripherals are loaded into RAM so that the computer can communicate with those devices at any time.

In other cases, the operating system might not contain appropriate device drivers for the hardware you have added. This section describes how to install and configure NIC software on a Windows Vista operating system that does not already use the correct and current device driver. For other operating systems with plug-and-play capability, the process will be similar. Regardless of which operating system you use, you should first refer to the NIC's documentation, because your situation may vary. Read the NIC documentation carefully before installing the relevant drivers, and make sure you are installing the appropriate drivers. Installing a device driver designed for Windows Vista on a Windows XP computer, for example, probably won't work.

To install NIC software from a Windows Vista interface, you need access to the Windows Vista software (via either a Windows Vista CD or hard disk) and the device drivers specific to the NIC. These drivers can be found on a CD-ROM or DVD shipped with the NIC. If you do not have the CD-ROM or DVD that shipped with the NIC and the Windows Vista software does not recognize your NIC and suggest the appropriate device driver, you can usually download the NIC software from the manufacturer's Web site. If you choose this option, make sure that you get the appropriate drivers for your operating system and NIC type. Also, make sure that the drivers you download are the most current version (sometimes called "shipping drivers") and not beta-level (unsupported) drivers.

To install and configure NIC software:

1. Physically install the NIC, and then restart the computer. Log on to the computer as a user with administrator privileges.

Net+

3.1

2. As long as you haven't disabled the plug-and-play capabilities, Windows Vista should automatically detect the new hardware. Upon detecting the NIC, it should also install the NIC's driver. In many cases, you need not install any other software or adjust the configuration for the NIC to operate properly.

3. There are certain situations in which you might want to change or update the device driver that the operating system has chosen. To do this, click **Start,** and then select **Control Panel.** The Control Panel window opens.

4. Click **System and Maintenance.** The System and Maintenance window appears.

5. Click **System.** The System window appears.

6. Under the Tasks list, click **Device Manager.** A User Account Control window appears, requesting your permission to continue.

7. Click **Continue.** The Device Manager window opens, displaying a list of installed devices.

8. Double-click the **Network adapters** icon. A list of installed NICs appears.

9. Double-click the adapter for which you want to install new device drivers. The NIC's Properties dialog box opens.

10. Click the **Driver** tab. Details about your NIC's current driver appear.

11. Click **Update Driver.** The Update Driver Software window appears, prompting you to choose whether to search automatically for updated driver software or browse your computer for driver software.

12. Make sure that the disk with the correct driver on it is inserted or that you know where on your hard disk you saved the driver. Click **Browse my computer for driver software.** The Update Driver Software dialog box appears, as shown in Figure 6-12.

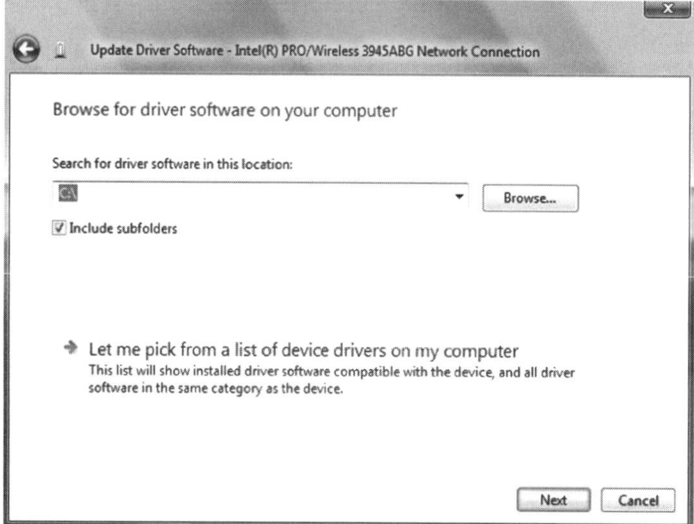

Figure 6-12 Windows Vista Update Driver Software dialog box

3.1

13. In the Search for driver software in this location text box, enter the drive and directory information for your driver. For example, if your driver is located on a DVD and your DVD drive is E:, enter **E:**.

14. Click **Next** to continue. Wait while Windows Vista searches your drive for a driver that matches your network card. (If the disk sent with the NIC contains drivers for more than one type of NIC, you are asked to select the precise model you are using. After making your choice, click **OK**.)

15. Windows Vista will find the appropriate driver for your NIC and install it onto your hard disk. Later, it informs you that it has successfully updated your driver software. To continue, click **Close**. Then close all windows.

The procedures outlined in this section work in most situations. Because every situation is different, however, you should always read the manufacturer's documentation and follow the installation instructions. Some manufacturers supply setup programs that automatically install and register NIC software as soon as you run them, thereby eliminating the need to follow the steps outlined previously.

Installing NIC drivers on a UNIX or Linux workstation depends somewhat on the version you are running. For example, a recent version of Linux from Red Hat, which supports plug-and-play technology, normally detects a connected NIC and automatically installs the correct drivers. The first NIC the operating system detects is called, by default, eth0. If a second NIC is present, it is called eth1. Because they provide the network interface, eth0 and eth1 are called, in UNIX and Linux terminology, simply, interfaces.

Interpreting LED Indicators After you have installed a NIC, you can test it by attempting to transmit data over the network. But even before such a test, you can learn about your NIC's functionality simply by looking at it. Most NICs have LEDs that indicate whether they are communicating with the network. The precise location, type, and meaning of LED indicators vary from one manufacturer to another. The following are some general guidelines that apply more often to expansion-card NICs. However, the only way to know for certain what your NIC's LEDs are trying to tell you is to read the documentation. Your NIC might have one or more of the following lights, and they might not be labeled:

- *ACT*—If blinking, this LED indicates that the NIC is either transmitting or receiving data (in other words, experiencing activity) on the network. If steady, it indicates that the NIC is experiencing heavy traffic volume.

- *LNK*—If lit, this LED indicates that the NIC is functional. Further, if the NIC drivers are properly installed, a lit LNK LED indicates that the NIC has a connection to the network (but is not necessarily transmitting or receiving data). In some models, if this LED is blinking, it means the NIC detects the network but cannot communicate with it (for example, in the case of a 100Base-T NIC deployed on a 10Base-T network).

- *TX*—If blinking, this LED indicates that the NIC is functional and transmitting frames to the network.

- *RX*—If blinking, this LED indicates that the NIC is functional and receiving frames from the network.

The next sections describe the variable settings you should understand when configuring NICs. Depending on your computer's use of resources, NIC configuration might not be necessary after installation. For troubleshooting purposes, however, you need to understand how to view and adjust these variables.

IRQ (Interrupt Request) When a device attached to a computer's bus, such as a keyboard or floppy disk drive, requires attention from the computer's processor, it issues an interrupt request. An **IRQ (interrupt request)** is a message to the computer that instructs it to stop what it is doing and pay attention to something else. An **interrupt** is the circuit board wire over which a device issues voltage to signal this request. Each interrupt must have a unique IRQ number, a number that uniquely identifies that component to the main bus. An **IRQ number** is the means by which the bus understands which device to acknowledge. The term *IRQ* is frequently substituted for *IRQ number* in casual conversation, even though they are technically two different things.

IRQ numbers range from 0 to 15. Many computer devices reserve the same IRQ number by default no matter what type of system they are installed on. For example, on every type of computer, a floppy disk controller claims IRQ 6 and a keyboard controller takes IRQ 1. On the other hand, some IRQ numbers are not reserved by default but are available to additional devices such as sound cards, graphics cards, modems, and NICs. Most often, NICs use IRQ 9, 10, or 11. Table 6-1 lists all of the IRQ numbers and their default device assignments, if they have any.

Table 6-1 IRQ Assignments

IRQ Number	Default Device Assignment
0	System timer (only)
1	Keyboard controller (only)
2	Access to IRQs 8–15
3	COM2 (second serial port) or COM4 (fourth serial port)
4	COM1 (first serial port) or COM3 (third serial port)
5	Sound card or LPT2 (second parallel port)
6	Floppy disk drive controller
7	LPT1 (parallel port 1)
8	Real-time clock (only)
9	No default assignment
10	No default assignment
11	No default assignment
12	PS/2 mouse
13	Math coprocessor (only)
14	IDE channel (for example, an IDE hard disk drive)
15	Secondary IDE channel

Net+
3.1

Normally, the BIOS and the operating system manage IRQ assignment without problems. But if two devices attempt to use the same interrupt, resource conflicts and performance problems result. Any of the following symptoms could indicate that two devices are attempting to use the same IRQ:

- The computer might lock up or "hang" either upon starting or when the operating system is loading.

- The computer might run much more slowly than usual.

- Although the computer's NIC might work properly, other devices—such as USB or parallel ports—may stop working.

- Video or sound card problems might occur. For example, after the operating system loads, you may see an error message indicating that the video settings are incorrect, or your sound card may stop working.

- The computer might fail to connect to the network (as evidenced by an error message after you attempt to log on to a server, for example).

- The computer might experience intermittent data errors during transmission.

If IRQ conflicts do occur, you must reassign a device's IRQ. NIC IRQs can be changed through the operating system, through the adapter's EEPROM configuration utility, or through the computer's CMOS configuration utility. **CMOS (complementary metal oxide semiconductor)** is a type of microchip that requires very little energy to operate. In a PC, the CMOS stores settings pertaining to a computer's devices, among other things. These settings are saved even after you turn off a PC because the CMOS is powered by a tiny battery in your computer. Information saved in CMOS is used by the computer's **BIOS (basic input/output system)**. The BIOS is a simple set of instructions that enables a computer to initially recognize its hardware. When you turn on a computer, the BIOS performs its start-up tasks. After a computer is up and running, the BIOS provides an interface between the computer's software and hardware, allowing it to recognize which device is associated with each IRQ.

Although you can usually modify IRQ settings in the CMOS configuration utility, whether you can change them via the operating system software depends on the type of NIC involved. For example, on a PCI NIC, which requires a PCI bus controller, the PCI controller's settings will dictate whether this type of modification is possible.

Memory Range The **memory range** indicates, in hexadecimal notation, the area of memory that the NIC and CPU use for exchanging, or buffering, data. As with IRQs, some memory ranges are reserved for specific devices—most notably, the motherboard. Reserved address ranges should never be selected for new devices.

NICs typically use a memory range in the high memory area, which in hexadecimal notation equates to the A0000–FFFFF range. As you work with NICs, you will notice that some manufacturers prefer certain ranges. For example, a 3Com PC Card adapter might, by default, choose a range of C8000–C9FFF.

Memory range settings are less likely to cause resource conflicts than IRQ settings, mainly because there are more available memory ranges than IRQs. Nevertheless, you might run

3.1

into situations in which you need to change a NIC's memory address. In such an instance, you might not be able to change the memory range from the operating system. Refer to the manufacturer's guidelines for instructions.

Base I/O Port The **base I/O port** setting specifies, in hexadecimal notation, which area of memory will act as a channel for moving data between the NIC and the CPU. Like its IRQ, a device's base I/O port cannot be used by any other device. Most NICs use two memory ranges for this channel, and the base I/O port settings identify the beginning of each range. Although a NIC's base I/O port varies depending on the manufacturer, some popular addresses (in hexadecimal notation) are 300 (which means that the range is 300–30F), 310, 280, or 2F8.

You will probably not need to change a NIC's base I/O port. If you do, bear in mind that, as with IRQ settings, base I/O port settings for PCI cards can be changed in the computer's CMOS setup utility or sometimes through the operating system.

Firmware Settings After you have adjusted the NIC's system resources, you might need to modify its transmission characteristics—for example, whether it uses full duplexing, whether it can detect a network's speed, or even its MAC address. These settings are held in the adapter's firmware. As mentioned earlier, firmware constitutes the combination of an EEPROM chip on the NIC and the data it holds. When you change the firmware, you are actually writing to the EEPROM chip on the NIC. You are not writing to the computer's hard disk. Although most configurable settings can be changed in the operating system or NIC setup software, you may encounter complex networking problems that require a change to firmware settings.

To change a NIC's firmware, you need a bootable CD-ROM containing the configuration or install utility that shipped with the NIC. If you don't have the utility, you can usually download it from the manufacturer's Web site. To run the utility, you must start the computer with this CD-ROM inserted. The NIC configuration utility might not run if an operating system or memory management program is already running.

Configuration utilities differ slightly, but all should allow you to view the IRQ, I/O port, base memory, and node address. Some might allow you to change settings such as the NIC's CPU utilization, its ability to handle full duplexing, or its capability to be used with only 10Base-T or 100Base-T media, for example (although many of these can also be changed through the NIC's properties from the operating system interface). The changeable settings vary depending on the manufacturer. Again, read the manufacturer's documentation to find out the details for your hardware.

NIC configuration utilities also allow you to perform diagnostics—tests of the NIC's physical components and connectivity. Most of the tests can be performed without additional hardware. However, to perform the entire group of the diagnostic tests on the NIC's utility disk, you must have a loopback plug. A **loopback plug** (also called a **loopback adapter**) is a connector that plugs into a port, such as a serial or parallel or an RJ-45 port, and crosses over the transmit line to the receive line so that outgoing signals can be redirected into the computer for testing. One connectivity test, called a loopback test, requires you to install a loopback plug into the NIC's media connector. Note that none of the connectivity tests should be performed on a computer connected to a live network. If a NIC fails its connectivity tests, it is probably configured incorrectly. If a NIC fails a physical component test, it might need to be replaced.

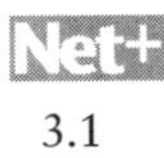

3.1

The word loopback implies that signals are routed back toward their source, rather than toward an external destination. When used in the context of NICs, the loopback test refers to a check of the adapter's ability to transmit and receive signals. Recall that the term loopback is also used in the context of TCP/IP protocol testing. In that context, pinging the loopback address provides you with information on TCP/IP functionality.

Choosing the Right NIC

You'll undoubtedly consider several factors when choosing a NIC for your workstation or server. Of course, the most critical factor is compatibility with your existing system. The adapter must match the network's bus type, access method, connector types, and transmission speed. You also need to ensure that drivers available for that NIC will work with your operating system and hardware.

Beyond these considerations, however, you should examine more subtle differences, such as those that affect network performance. Table 6-2 lists some features available on NICs that specifically influence performance and ease of use. As you review this table, keep in mind that performance is especially important if the NIC will be installed in a server.

Table 6-2 NIC Characteristics

NIC Feature	Function	Benefit
Automatic speed selection	Enables NICs to sense and adapt to a network's speed and mode (half- or full-duplex) automatically	Aids configuration and performance
One or more on-board CPUs	Allows the card to perform some data processing independently of the PC's CPU	Improves performance
Direct memory access (DMA)	Enables the card to transfer data to the computer's memory directly	Improves performance
Diagnostic LEDs (lights on the NIC)	Indicates traffic, connectivity, and, sometimes, speed	Aids in troubleshooting
Dual channels	Effectively creates two NICs in one slot	Improves performance; suited to servers
Load balancing	Allows the NIC's processor to determine when to switch traffic between internal cards	Improves performance for heavily trafficked networks; suited to servers
"Look Ahead" transmit and receive	Allows the NIC's processor to begin processing data before it has received the entire packet	Improves performance
Management capabilities (SNMP)	Allows the NIC to perform its own monitoring and troubleshooting, usually through installed application software	Aids in troubleshooting; can find a problem before it becomes dire
Power management capabilities	Allows a NIC to participate in the computer's power-saving measures; found on PCMCIA-based adapters	Increases the life of the battery for laptop computers
RAM buffering	Provides additional memory on the NIC, which, in turn, provides more space for data buffering	Improves performance
Upgradeable (flash) ROM	Allows on-board chip memory to be upgraded	Improves ease of use and performance

3.1

The quality of the printed documentation that you receive from a manufacturer about its NICs might be lacking. What's more, this documentation might not apply to the kinds of computers or networking environments you are using. To find out more about the type of NIC you are installing or troubleshooting, visit the manufacturer's Web site.

Repeaters and Hubs

3.1

Now that you have learned about the many types of NICs and how to install and configure them, you are ready to learn about connectivity devices. As you'll recall, the telecommunications closet is the area containing the connectivity equipment for work areas and sometimes, entire floors of a building. Within the telecommunications closet, horizontal cabling from the workstations attaches to punch-down blocks, patch panels, hubs, switches, routers, and bridges. In addition, telecommunications closets may house repeaters. Repeaters are the simplest type of connectivity devices that regenerate a digital signal.

Repeaters operate in the physical layer of the OSI model and, therefore, have no means to interpret the data they retransmit. For example, they cannot improve or correct a bad or erroneous signal; they merely repeat it. In this sense, they are not "intelligent" devices. Since they cannot read higher-layer information in the data frames, repeaters cannot direct data to their destination. Instead, repeaters simply regenerate a signal over an entire segment. It is up to the receiver to recognize and accept its data.

A repeater is limited not only in function, but also in scope. A repeater contains one input port and one output port, so it is capable only of receiving and repeating a single data stream. Furthermore, repeaters are suited only to bus topology networks. The advantage to using a repeater is that it allows you to extend a network inexpensively. However, because of repeaters' limitations and the decreasing costs of other connectivity devices, repeaters are rarely used on modern networks. Instead, clients in a workgroup area are more likely to be connected by switches, which are discussed later in this chapter.

At its most primitive, a **hub** is a repeater with more than one output port. A hub typically contains multiple **data ports** into which the patch cables for network nodes are connected. Like repeaters, hubs operate at the physical layer of the OSI model. A hub accepts signals from a transmitting node and repeats those signals to all other connected nodes in a broadcast fashion. Most hubs also contain one port, called an **uplink port**, that allows the hub to connect to another hub or other connectivity device. On Ethernet networks, hubs can serve as the central connection point for branches of a star or star-based hybrid topology.

In addition to connecting Macintosh and PC workstations, hubs can connect print servers, switches, file servers, or other devices to a network. As you learned in Chapter 5, all devices connected to a hub share the same amount of bandwidth and the same collision domain. The more nodes participating in the same collision domain, the higher the likelihood of transmission errors and slower performance.

Placement of hubs in a network design can vary. The simplest structure would employ a stand-alone workgroup hub that is connected to another connectivity device, such as a switch

Net+
3.1

or router. Some networks assign a different hub to each small workgroup, thereby benefiting from not having a single point of failure. No matter what the network design, when using hubs, adhering to a network's maximum segment and network length limitations is essential. Figure 6-13 suggests how hubs can fit into the overall design of a network.

Dozens of types of hubs exist. They vary according to the type of media and data transmission speeds they support. Some hubs allow for multiple media connector types or multiple data transmission speeds. The simplest type of hubs—known as **passive hubs**—do nothing but repeat signals. Like NICs, however, some hubs possess internal processing capabilities. For example, they may permit remote management, filter data, or provide diagnostic information about the network. Hubs that can perform any of these functions are known as **intelligent hubs**. Intelligent hubs are also called **managed hubs**, because they can be managed from anywhere on the network. **Stand-alone hubs**, as their name implies, are hubs that serve a group of computers that are isolated from the rest of the network or that form their own small network. They are best suited to small organizations or home offices. They can be passive or intelligent, and they are simple to install and connect for a small group of users. Stand-alone hubs may also be called **workgroup hubs**. Figure 6-14 depicts a small stand-alone hub.

Hubs have been a mainstay of network connectivity since the first small networks of the 1980s. However, because of their limited features and the fact that they merely repeat signals within a single collision domain, most network administrators have replaced their hubs with switches or routers. To understand how switches operate, it is helpful to learn about bridges first.

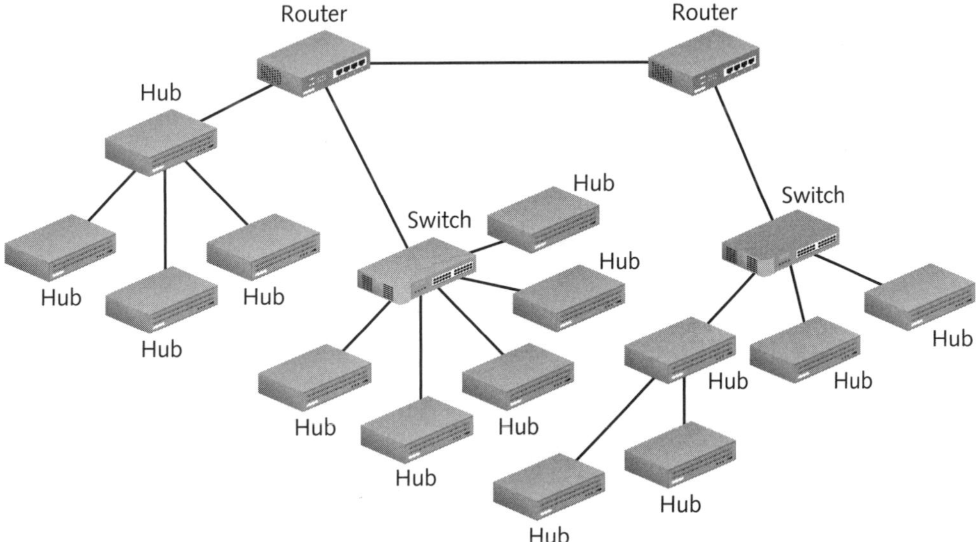

Figure 6-13 Hubs in a network design

3.1

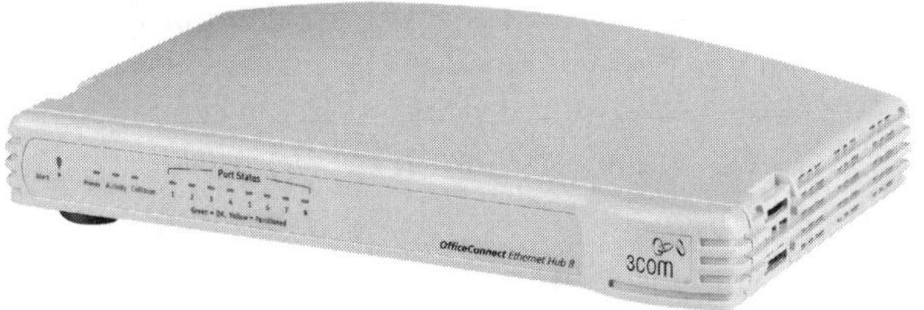

Figure 6-14 A stand-alone hub

Bridges

3.1

Bridges are devices that connect two network segments by analyzing incoming frames and making decisions about where to direct them based on each frame's MAC address. They operate at the data link layer of the OSI model. Bridges look like repeaters, in that they have a single input and a single output port. They differ from repeaters in that they can interpret physical addressing information.

A significant advantage to using bridges over repeaters or hubs is that bridges are protocol independent. For instance, all bridges can connect an Ethernet segment carrying IP-based traffic with an Ethernet segment carrying traffic that uses a different network layer protocol. Some bridges can also connect two segments using different data link and physical layer protocols—for example, an Ethernet segment with a token ring segment, or a wire-bound Ethernet segment with a wireless Ethernet segment.

Because they are protocol ignorant, bridges can move data more rapidly than traditional routers, for example, which do care about network layer protocol information. On the other hand, bridges take longer to transmit data than either repeaters or hubs, because bridges actually analyze each packet, whereas repeaters and hubs do not.

Another advantage to using bridges is that they can extend an Ethernet network without further extending a collision domain, or segment. In other words, by inserting a bridge into a network, you can add length beyond the maximum limits that apply to segments. Finally, bridges can help improve network performance because they can be programmed to filter out certain types of frames (for example, unnecessary broadcast frames, whose transmissions squander bandwidth).

To translate between two segment types, a bridge reads a frame's destination MAC address and decides to either forward or filter it. If the bridge determines that the destination node is on another segment on the network, it forwards (retransmits) the packet to that segment. If the destination address belongs to the same segment as the source address, the bridge filters (discards) the frame. As nodes transmit data through the bridge, the bridge establishes a **filtering database** (also known as a **forwarding table**) of known MAC addresses and their locations on the network. The bridge uses its filtering database to determine whether a packet should be forwarded or filtered, as illustrated in Figure 6-15.

Using Figure 6-15 as an example, imagine that you sit at workstation 1 on segment A of the LAN, and your colleague Cory sits at workstation 2 on segment A. When you attempt to send

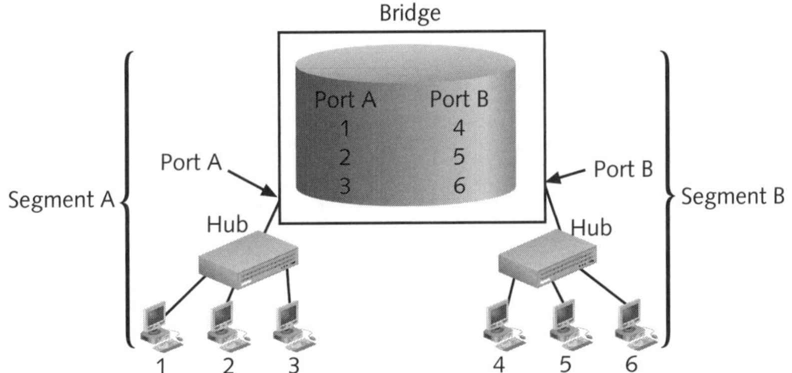

Figure 6-15 A bridge's use of a filtering database

data to Cory's computer, your transmission goes through your segment's hub and then to the bridge. The bridge reads the MAC address of Cory's computer. It then searches its filtering database to determine whether that MAC address belongs to the same segment you are on or whether it belongs to a different segment. The bridge can determine only that the MAC address of Cory's workstation is associated with its port A. If the MAC address belongs to a different segment, the bridge forwards the data to that segment, whose corresponding port identity is also in the filtering database. In this case, however, your workstation and Cory's workstation reside on the same LAN segment, so the data is filtered (that is, ignored) and your message is delivered to Cory's workstation through segment A's hub.

Conversely, if you want to send data to your supervisor's computer, which is workstation 5 in Figure 6-15, your transmission first passes through segment A's hub and then on to the bridge. The bridge reads the MAC address for your supervisor's machine (the destination address in your data stream) and searches for the port associated with that machine. In this case, the bridge recognizes workstation 5 as being connected to port B, and it forwards the data to that port. Subsequently, the segment B hub ensures delivery of the data to your supervisor's computer.

After you install a new bridge, it uses one of several methods to learn about the network and discover the destination address for each packet it handles. After it discovers this information, it records the destination node's MAC address and its associated port in its filtering database. Over time, it discovers all nodes on the network and constructs database entries for each.

Stand-alone bridges became popular in the 1980s and early 1990s; since then, bridging technology has evolved to create more sophisticated bridge devices. But devices other than bridges have also evolved. Equipment manufacturers have improved the speed and functionality of routers and switches while lowering their cost, leaving bridges to become nearly extinct. Although bridges are less common than switches on modern LANs, understanding the concept of bridging is essential to understanding how switches work. For example, the bridging process pictured in Figure 6-15 applies to every port on a switch. The next section introduces switches and explains their functions.

Switches

Net+

3.1

Switches are connectivity devices that subdivide a network into smaller logical pieces, or segments. Traditional switches operate at the data link layer of the OSI model, while more modern switches can operate at Layer 3 or even Layer 4. As with bridges, switches interpret MAC address information. In fact, they can be described as multiport bridges. Figure 6-16 depicts two switches. On the right is a 24-port switch, useful for connecting nodes in a workgroup, and on the left is a high-capacity switch that contains multiple redundant features (such as two NICs) and offers security, automated traffic management, and even routing functions. Switches vary greatly in size and function, so there's no such thing as a "typical" switch. Most switches have at least an internal processor, an operating system, memory, and several ports that enable other nodes to connect to them.

Because they have multiple ports, switches can make better use of limited bandwidth and prove more cost-efficient than bridges. Each port on the switch acts like a bridge, and each device connected to a switch effectively receives its own dedicated channel. In other words, a switch can turn a shared channel into several channels. From the Ethernet perspective, each dedicated channel represents a collision domain. Because a switch limits the number of devices in a collision domain, it limits the potential for collisions.

Switches have historically been used to replace hubs and ease traffic congestion in LAN workgroups. Some network administrators have replaced backbone routers with switches, because switches provide at least two advantages: better security and better performance. By their

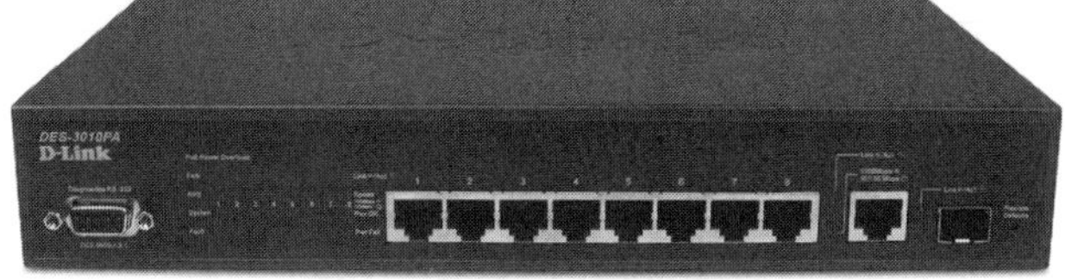

Figure 6-16 Switches

3.1

nature, switches provide better security than many other devices because they isolate one device's traffic from other devices' traffic. And because switches provide separate channels for (potentially) every device, performance stands to gain. Applications that transfer a large amount of traffic and are sensitive to time delays, such as videoconferencing applications, benefit from the full use of the channel's capacity. In addition, hardware and software in a switch are optimized for fast data forwarding.

Switches have their disadvantages, too. Although they contain buffers to hold incoming data and accommodate bursts of traffic, they can become overwhelmed by continuous, heavy traffic. In that event, the switch cannot prevent data loss. Also, although higher-layer protocols, such as TCP, detect the loss and respond with a timeout, others, such as UDP, do not. For packets using such protocols, the number of collisions mounts, and eventually all network traffic grinds to a halt. Therefore, plan placement of switches carefully to match backbone capacity and traffic patterns.

Switches have also replaced workgroup hubs on many small and home office networks because their cost has decreased dramatically, they have become easier to install and configure, and they offer the benefit of separating traffic according to port. You might need to install such a switch on a home or office network. The next section describes how to install a simple switch.

Installing a Switch

As with any networking equipment, the best way to ensure that you install a switch properly is to follow the manufacturer's guidelines. Small workgroup switches are normally simple to install. Many operate properly upon being added to a network. The following steps describe, in general, how to connect multiple nodes to a small switch, and then how to connect that switch to another connectivity device. These instructions assume you're using Cat 5 or better UTP cables to connect devices to the switch.

1. Make sure the switch is situated where you are going to keep it after all the cables are connected.

2. Before connecting any cables to the switch's ports, plug it in and turn it on. Also, when connecting a node to a switch, the node should not be turned on. Otherwise, data irregularities can occur, forcing you to reset the switch.

3. The switch's power light should illuminate. Most switches perform self-tests when turned on, and blinking lights indicate that these tests are in progress. Wait until the tests are completed (as indicated by a steady, green power light).

4. If you are using a small, inexpensive switch, you might not have to configure it and you can skip to step 5. However, you might need to assign an IP address to the switch, change the administrator password, or set up management functions. Configuring a switch usually requires connecting it to a PC and then running a configuration utility from a CD-ROM that came with the switch. Refer to your switch's instructions to find out how to configure it.

5. Using a straight-through patch cable, connect the node's NIC to one of the switch's ports, as shown in Figure 6-17. If you intend to connect this switch to another

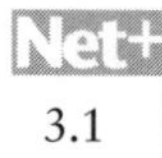

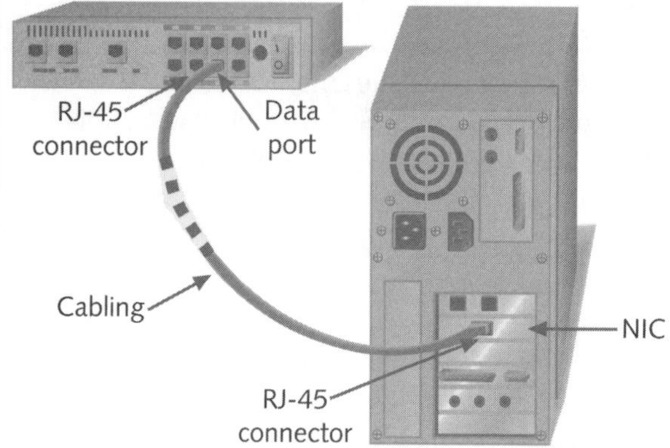

Figure 6-17 Connecting a workstation to a switch

connectivity device, do not connect patch cables from nodes to the uplink port or to the port adjacent to the uplink port. On most hubs and switches, the uplink port is directly wired to its adjacent port inside the device.

6. After all the nodes have been connected to the switch, if you do not plan to connect the switch to another connectivity device, you can turn on the nodes. After the nodes connect to the network through the newly installed switch, check to verify that the switch's link and traffic lights for each port act as they should, according to the switch's documentation. Then make sure the nodes can access the network as planned.

7. To connect the switch to a larger network, you can insert one end of a crossover patch cable into the switch's uplink port and then insert the other end of the cable into a data port on the other connectivity device. Alternately, you can insert one end of a straight-through cable into one of the switch's data ports and then insert the other end of the straight-through cable into another device's data port. If you are connecting one switch's uplink port to another switch's uplink port, you must use a crossover cable. After you connect the switch to another device, the switch senses the activity on its uplink port, evidenced by its blinking traffic light.

Figure 6-18 illustrates a typical way of using a small switch on a small office or home network. In this example, the switch connects a group of nodes, including workstations, server, and printer, with each other and with an Internet connection.

Now that you understand the purposes and placement of switches in a network, you are ready to learn more about how they perform their functions.

Switching Methods

Switches differ in how they interpret incoming frames and determine what to do with the frames. Although four switching modes exist, the two basic methods discussed in the following sections are most popular.

Cut-Through Mode   A switch running in **cut-through mode** reads a frame's header and decides where to forward the data before it receives the entire packet. Recall that the first 14 bytes of a frame constitute its header, which contains the destination MAC address.

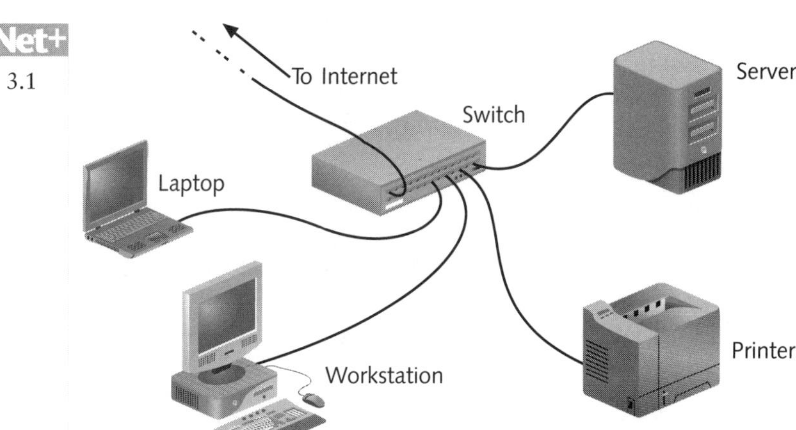

Figure 6-18 A switch on a small network

This information is sufficient for the switch to determine which port should get the frame and begin transmitting the frame (without bothering to read the rest of the frame and check its accuracy).

What if the frame becomes corrupt? Because the cut-through mode does not allow the switch to read the frame check sequence before it begins transmitting, it can't verify data integrity in that way. On the other hand, cut-through switches can detect **runts**, or erroneously shortened packets. Upon detecting a runt, the switch waits to transmit that packet until it determines its integrity. It's important to remember, however, that runts are only one type of data flaw. Cut-through switches *cannot* detect corrupt packets; indeed, they may increase the number of errors found on the network by propagating flawed packets.

The most significant advantage of the cut-through mode is its speed. Because it does not stop to read the entire data packet, a cut-through switch can forward information much more rapidly than a store and forward switch can (as described in the next section). The time-saving advantages to cut-through switching become insignificant, however, if the switch is flooded with traffic. In this case, the cut-through switch must buffer (or temporarily hold) data, just like a store-and-forward switch. Cut-through switches are best suited to small workgroups in which speed is important and the relatively low number of devices minimizes the potential for errors.

Store-and-Forward Mode In **store-and-forward mode,** a switch reads the entire data frame into its memory and checks it for accuracy before transmitting the information. Although this method is more time consuming than the cut-through method, it allows store-and-forward switches to transmit data more accurately. Store-and-forward mode switches are more appropriate for larger LAN environments because they do not propagate data errors. In contrast, cut-through mode switches do forward errors, so they may contribute to network congestion if a particular segment is experiencing a number of collisions. In large environments, a failure to check for errors can result in problematic traffic congestion.

Store-and-forward switches can also transfer data between segments running different transmission speeds. For example, a high-speed network printer that serves 50 students could be attached to a 100Mbps port on the switch, thereby allowing all of the student workstations to connect to 10Mbps ports on the same switch. With this scheme, the printer can quickly service multiple jobs. This characteristic makes store-and-forward mode switches preferable in mixed-speed environments.

 VLANs and Trunking

In addition to improving bandwidth usage compared to lower-layer devices, switches can create **VLANs (virtual local area networks)**, or logically separate networks within networks, by grouping a number of ports into a broadcast domain. A **broadcast domain** is a combination of ports that make up a Layer 2 segment. Ports in a broadcast domain rely on a Layer 2 device, such as a switch, to forward broadcast frames among them. In contrast to a collision domain, ports in the same broadcast domain do not share a single channel. (Recall that switches separate collision domains.) In the context of TCP/IP networking, a broadcast domain is also known as a subnet. Figure 6-19 illustrates a simple VLAN design.

Network engineers value VLANs for their flexibility. They can include ports from more than one switch or segment. Any type of end node can belong to one or more VLANs. VLANs can link geographically distant users over a WAN, and they can create small workgroups within LANs. Reasons for using VLANs include:

- Separating groups of users who need special security or network functions
- Isolating connections with heavy or unpredictable traffic patterns
- Identifying groups of devices whose data should be given priority handling
- Containing groups of devices that rely on legacy protocols incompatible with the majority of the network's traffic.

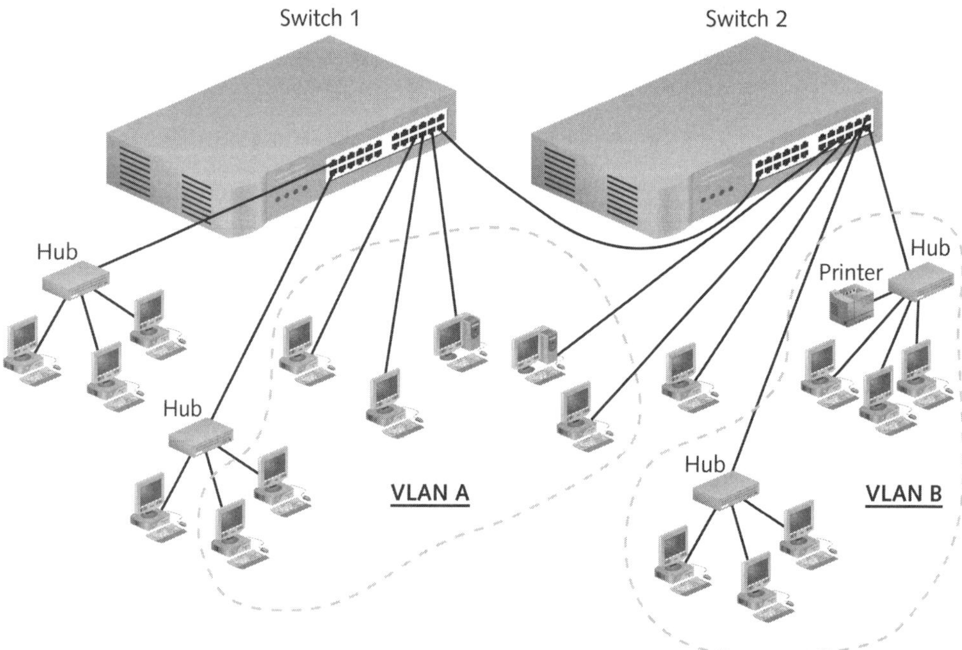

Figure 6-19 A simple VLAN design

One case in which a company might want to implement a VLAN is to allow visitors access to minimal network functions—for example, an Internet connection—without allowing the possibility of access to the company's data stored on servers. In another example, companies that use their packet-switched networks to carry telephone calls often group all of the voice traffic on a separate VLAN to prevent this unique and potentially heavy traffic from adversely affecting routine client/server tasks.

You create a VLAN by properly configuring a switch's software. You can do this manually through the switch's configuration utility (or through its command line interface) or automatically using a VLAN software tool. The critical step is to indicate to which VLAN each port belongs. In addition, network managers can specify security parameters, filtering instructions (if the switch should not forward any frames from a certain segment, for example), performance requirements for certain ports, and network addressing and management options. Options vary according to the switch manufacturer and model.

Once you create a VLAN, you maintain it via the switch's software. Figure 6-20 illustrates the result of a `show vlans` command on a Cisco switch on a large enterprise-wide network. The `show vlans` command is used to list the current VLANs recognized by a switch, and it is unique to Cisco-brand switches (and a few others that mimic that company's conventions). Other manufacturers' switch software includes similar maintenance commands.

Figure 6-20 shows 13 VLANs configured on the network. (VLAN number 1 and VLANs 1002 through 1005 are defaults that were preestablished on the Cisco switch but were not actually used.) The first half of the command output shows each VLAN's number, name, and status. In addition, the fourth column shows which ports belong to each VLAN. The second half of the command output provides additional information about each VLAN, including the type of network it operates on. (In this example, all active VLANs use Ethernet.)

One potential problem in creating VLANs is that by grouping certain nodes, you are not merely including those nodes—you are also excluding another group. This means you can potentially cut off a group from the rest of the network. For example, suppose your company's IT director demands that you assign all executive workstations to their own VLAN, and that you configure the network's switch to group these users' computers into a VLAN. After this change, users would be able to exchange data with each other, but they would not be able to download data from the file server or download mail from the mail server, because these servers are not included in their VLAN. To allow different VLANs to exchange data, you need to connect those VLANs with a router.

A single switch can manage traffic belonging to several VLANs. In fact, one switch's interface can carry the traffic of multiple VLANs, thanks to a technique known as **trunking**. The term *trunk* originated in the telephony field, where it referred to an aggregation of logical connections over one physical connection. For instance, a trunk carried signals for many residential telephone lines in the same neighborhood over one cable. Similarly, in the context of switching, a trunk is a single physical connection between devices through which many logical VLANs can transmit and receive data. To keep the data belonging to each VLAN separate, each frame is identified with a VLAN identifier, or tag, added to its header. Trunking protocols assign and interpret these tags, thereby managing the distribution of frames through a trunk.

One advantage of VLAN trunking is its economical use of interfaces. For example, if you establish five different VLANs that span two switches, you can connect these VLANs using only one interface on each switch, rather than five separate interfaces. Trunking also allows

```
VLAN Name                             Status    Ports
---- -------------------------------- --------- -------------------------------
1    default                          active    Te1/1, Te1/2, Gi1/5, Gi1/6
                                                Te2/1, Te2/2, Gi2/5, Gi2/6
                                                Gi4/3, Gi5/12, Gi6/12, Gi6/19
                                                Gi8/11, Gi8/19, Gi9/4
5    VLAN0005                         active
13   VLAN0013                         active    Gi3/2, Gi3/3, Gi3/4, Gi8/12
14   VLAN0014                         active    Gi4/1, Gi4/2, Gi4/4, Gi9/12
16   VLAN0016                         active    Gi5/8
18   VLAN0018                         active    Gi1/3, Gi2/3
19   VLAN0019                         active    Gi5/11, Gi6/11
104  VLAN0104                         active    Gi1/4, Gi2/4, Gi3/5, Gi3/6
                                                Gi4/5, Gi4/6, Gi5/1, Gi5/2
                                                Gi5/3, Gi5/4, Gi5/5, Gi5/6
                                                Gi5/7, Gi5/9, Gi5/10, Gi5/13
                                                Gi5/14, Gi5/15, Gi5/16, Gi5/17
                                                Gi5/18, Gi5/19, Gi5/20, Gi5/21
                                                Gi5/22, Gi5/23, Gi5/24, Gi6/1
                                                Gi6/2, Gi6/3, Gi6/4, Gi6/5
                                                Gi6/6, Gi6/7, Gi6/9, Gi6/10
                                                Gi6/13, Gi6/14, Gi6/15, Gi6/16
                                                Gi6/17, Gi6/18, Gi6/20, Gi6/21
                                                Gi6/22, Gi6/23, Gi6/24, Gi7/6
                                                Gi7/8, Gi7/11, Gi7/12, Gi7/19
                                                Gi8/8, Gi8/24, Gi9/1, Gi9/2
                                                Gi9/3, Gi9/13
105  VLAN0105                         active    Gi7/24, Gi9/5, Gi9/6, Gi9/7
                                                Gi9/8, Gi9/10, Gi9/11, Gi9/14
                                                Gi9/16, Gi9/18, Gi9/19, Gi9/20
                                                Gi9/21, Gi9/22, Gi9/23, Gi9/24
                                                Gi10/1, Gi10/2, Gi10/4, Gi10/5
                                                Gi10/6, Gi10/8, Gi10/9, Gi10/10
                                                Gi10/11, Gi10/12, Gi10/13
                                                Gi10/14, Gi10/15, Gi10/16
                                                Gi10/17, Gi10/18, Gi10/19
                                                Gi10/20, Gi10/21, Gi10/22
                                                Gi10/23, Gi10/24
106  VLAN0106                         active    Gi6/8
107  VLAN0107                         active    Gi7/1, Gi7/2, Gi7/3, Gi7/4
                                                Gi7/5, Gi7/7, Gi7/9, Gi7/10
                                                Gi7/13, Gi7/14, Gi7/16, Gi7/17
                                                Gi7/18, Gi7/21, Gi7/22, Gi8/1
                                                Gi8/2, Gi8/3, Gi8/4, Gi8/5
                                                Gi8/6, Gi8/7, Gi8/9, Gi8/10
                                                Gi8/13, Gi8/14, Gi8/16, Gi8/17
                                                Gi8/18, Gi8/21, Gi8/22
108  VLAN0108                         active    Gi7/15, Gi7/20, Gi7/23, Gi8/15
                                                Gi8/20, Gi8/23
109  VLAN0109                         active
601  VLAN0601                         active
1002 fddi-default                     act/unsup
1003 token-ring-default               act/unsup
1004 fddinet-default                  act/unsup
1005 trnet-default                    act/unsup

VLAN Type  SAID       MTU   Parent RingNo BridgeNo Stp  BrdgMode Trans1 Trans2
---- ----- ---------- ----- ------ ------ -------- ---- -------- ------ ------
1    enet  100001     1500  -      -      -        -    -        0      0
5    enet  100005     1500  -      -      -        -    -        0      0
13   enet  100013     1500  -      -      -        -    -        0      0
14   enet  100014     1500  -      -      -        -    -        0      0
16   enet  100016     1500  -      -      -        -    -        0      0
18   enet  100018     1500  -      -      -        -    -        0      0
19   enet  100019     1500  -      -      -        -    -        0      0
104  enet  100104     1500  -      -      -        -    -        0      0
105  enet  100105     1500  -      -      -        -    -        0      0
106  enet  100106     1500  -      -      -        -    -        0      0
107  enet  100107     1500  -      -      -        -    -        0      0
108  enet  100108     1500  -      -      -        -    -        0      0
109  enet  100109     1500  -      -      -        -    -        0      0
601  enet  100601     1500  -      -      -        -    -        0      0
1002 fddi  101002     1500  -      -      -        -    -        0      0
1003 tr    101003     1500  -      -      -        -    -        0      0
1004 fdnet 101004     1500  -      -      -        ieee -        0      0
1005 trnet 101005     1500  -      -      -        ibm  -        0      0
```

Figure 6-20 Result of the `show vlans` command on a Cisco switch

3.1

3.3

switches to make efficient use of their processing capabilities. As when creating VLANs, you configure trunking through the switch's operating system software.

VLAN configuration can be complex. It requires careful planning to ensure that all users and devices that need to exchange data can do so after the VLAN is in operation. It also requires contemplating how the VLAN switch will interact with other devices. For example, in a large office building, you probably would still use hubs or small switches (not configured for a VLAN) as a means of connecting groups of end users to the VLAN switch. If you want users from different VLANs to be able to communicate, you need to connect those VLANs through a Layer 3 device, such as a router or a higher-layer switch, like the ones discussed later in this chapter.

STP (Spanning Tree Protocol)

Suppose you design an enterprise-wide network with several switches interconnected via their uplink ports in a hybrid star-bus topology. To make the network more fault tolerant, you install multiple, or redundant, switches at critical junctures. Redundancy allows data the option of traveling through more than one switch toward its destination and makes your network less vulnerable to hardware malfunctions. For example, if one switch suffers a power supply failure, traffic can reroute through a second switch. Your network might look something like the one pictured in Figure 6-21. (In reality, of course, it would have many more nodes connected to the switches.)

A potential problem with the network shown in Figure 6-21 has to do with traffic loops. What if the server attached to Switch A issues a broadcast frame, which Switch A then reissues to all of its ports (other than the port to which the server is attached)? In that case, Switch A will issue the broadcast frame to Switches B, C, and D, which will then reissue the broadcast frame back to Switch A and to each other, and so on. If no mechanism exists to stop this broadcast storm, the high traffic volume will severely impair network performance. To eliminate the possibility of this and other types of traffic loops, switches and bridges use **STP (Spanning Tree Protocol)**.

STP is defined in IEEE standard **802.1D** and functions in the data link layer. It prevents traffic loops by calculating paths that avoid potential loops and by artificially blocking the links that would complete a loop. In addition, STP can adapt to changes in the network. For instance, if a switch is removed, STP will recalculate the best loop-free data paths between the remaining switches.

In the following explanation of STP, you can substitute **switch** wherever the word *bridge* is used. (As you have learned, a switch is really just a glorified bridge.) STP terminology refers to a Layer 2 device as a *bridge*.

First, STP selects a **root bridge,** or master bridge, which will provide the basis for all subsequent path calculations. The term *root bridge* makes sense when you consider the protocol's method, "spanning tree." Only one root bridge exists on a network, and from it a series of logical branches, or data paths, emanate. STP selects the root bridge based on its **BID (Bridge ID)**, which is a combination of a 2-byte priority field and the bridge's MAC address. To begin with, all bridges on the network share the same priority number, so the bridge with the lowest MAC address becomes the root bridge.

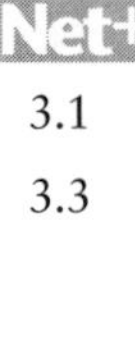

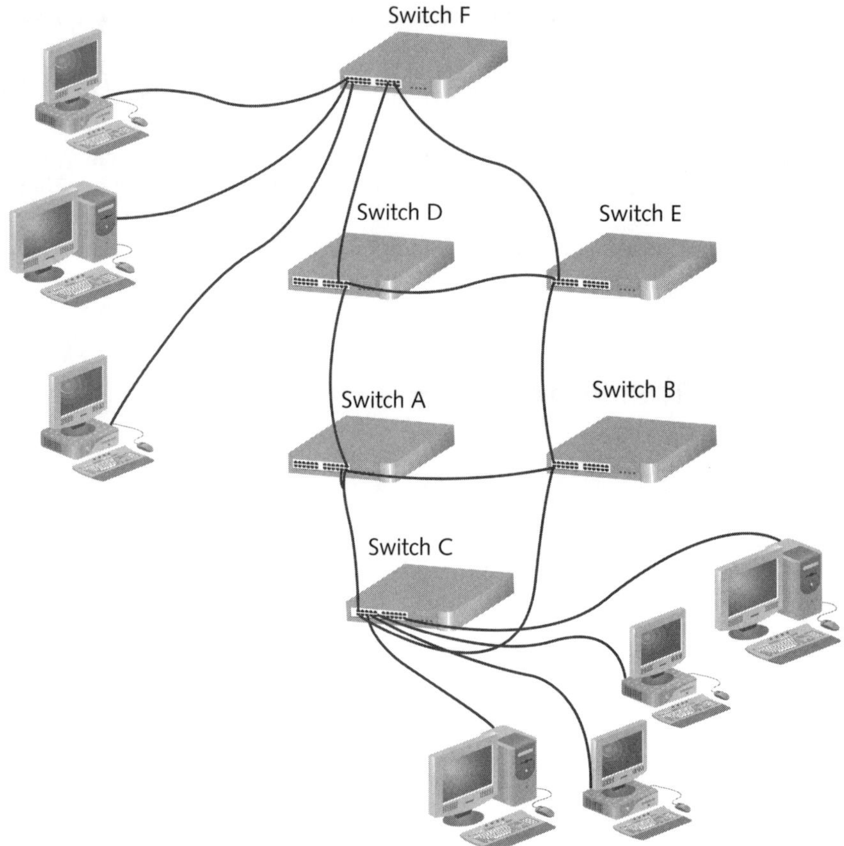

Figure 6-21 Enterprise-wide switched network

Next, on every other bridge on the network, STP examines the possible paths between that bridge and the root bridge. Then it chooses the shortest of these paths—that is, the path that will carry data to its target fastest. Furthermore, STP stipulates that only one port and one intermediary bridge can forward frames from the root bridge to the destination bridge.

Finally, STP disables links that are not part of the shortest path. To do so, it blocks all ports other than the designated forwarding port from transmitting or receiving network traffic. (The ports can, however, continue to receive information from STP.) Figure 6-22 illustrates a switched network with certain paths selected and others blocked by STP. In this drawing, for example, traffic from the root bridge would only be forwarded to Switch D via Switch A. Even though Switch D is physically connected to Switches E, F, and A, STP has limited the logical pathway to go through Switch A. If Switch A were to fail, STP would choose a different logical pathway for frames destined for Switch D.

STP was introduced in the 1980s, and since then, network developers have repeatedly modified it to improve and customize its functioning. The original STP is considered too slow for today's networks. For instance, it could take up to two minutes to detect and account for a link failure. With that kind of lag time, older versions of STP would bog down network transmissions, especially where high-volume, speed-dependent traffic, like telephone or video

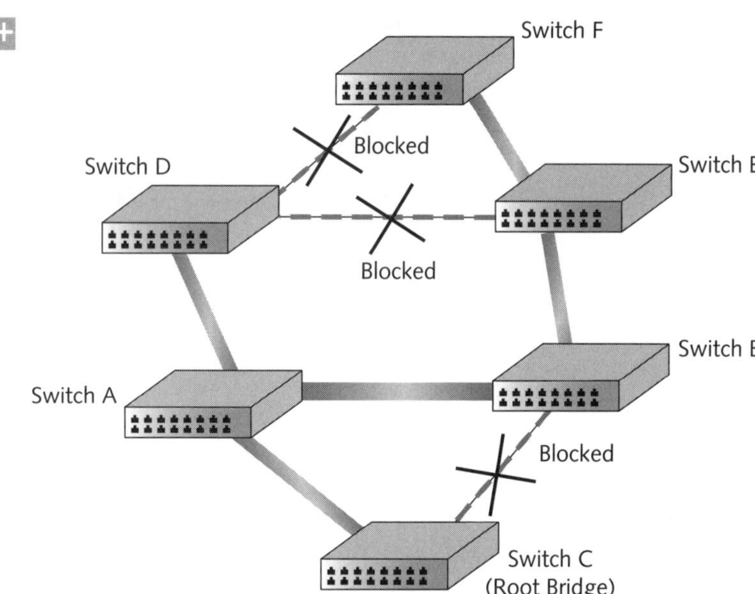

Figure 6-22 STP-selected paths on a switched network

signals, is involved. Newer versions of STP, such as **RSTP (Rapid Spanning Tree Protocol)**, defined in IEEE's **802.1w** standard, can detect and correct for link failures in milliseconds. Some switch manufacturers, such as Cisco and Extreme Networks, have designed proprietary versions of STP that are optimized to work most efficiently on their equipment.

When installing switches on your network, you do not need to enable or configure STP (or the more current version that came with your switch). It will come with the switch's operating software and should function smoothly by default and without intervention. However, if you want to designate preferred paths between bridges or choose a special root bridge, for example, STP allows you to alter its default prioritization.

Content and Multilayer Switches

You have learned that switches operate in Layer 2 of the OSI model, routers operate in Layer 3, and hubs operate in Layer 1. You have also learned that the distinctions between bridges, switches, and routers are blurring. Indeed, many networks already use switches that can operate at Layer 3 (network layer), similar to a router. Manufacturers have also made switches that operate at Layer 4 (transport layer). A switch capable of interpreting Layer 3 data is called a **Layer 3 switch** (and sometimes called a **routing switch**). Similarly, a switch capable of interpreting Layer 4 data is called a **Layer 4 switch**. Switches that operate anywhere between Layer 4 and Layer 7 are also known as **content switches** or **application switches**.

Among other things, the ability to interpret higher-layer data enables switches to perform advanced filtering, statistics keeping, and security functions. But the features of Layer 3 and Layer 4 switches vary widely depending on the manufacturer and the price. (This variability

3.2

is exacerbated by the fact that key players in the networking trade have not agreed on standards for these switches.) In fact, it's often hard to distinguish between a Layer 3 switch and a router. In some cases the difference comes down to what the manufacturer has decided to call the device to sell more of it. But in general, Layer 3 and Layer 4 switches, similar to Layer 2 switches, are optimized for fast Layer 2 data handling.

Higher-layer switches can cost three times more than Layer 2 switches and are typically used as part of a network's backbone. They would not be appropriate for use on a small, contained LAN or to connect a group of end users to the network.

Despite the fact that the boundaries between switches and routers blur, it's important to understand the key functions of traditional routers, which are still used on most WANs and many enterprise-wide networks today. The following section discusses routers and routing in detail.

Routers

3.1

A **router** is a multiport connectivity device that directs data between nodes on a network. Routers can integrate LANs and WANs running at different transmission speeds and using a variety of protocols. Simply put, when a router receives an incoming packet, it reads the packet's logical addressing information. Based on this, it determines to which network the packet must be delivered. Then it determines the shortest path to that network. Finally, it forwards the packet to the next hop in that path. Routers operate at the network layer (Layer 3) of the OSI model. They can be devices dedicated to routing, or they can be off-the-shelf computers configured to perform routing services.

Recall that network layer protocols direct data from one segment or type of network to another. Logical addressing, using protocols such as IP, also occurs at this layer. Consequently, unlike bridges and Layer 2 switches, routers are protocol dependent. In other words, they must be designed or configured to recognize a certain network layer protocol before they can forward data transmitted using that protocol. Broadly speaking, routers are slower than switches or bridges because they take time to interpret information in Layers 3 and higher.

Traditional stand-alone LAN routers are being replaced by Layer 3 switches that support the routing functions. However, despite competition from Layer 3 switches, routers are finding niches in specialized applications such as linking large Internet nodes or completing digitized telephone calls. The concept of routing, and everything described in the remainder of this section, applies to both routers and Layer 3 switches.

Router Characteristics and Functions

A router's strength lies in its intelligence. Not only can routers keep track of the locations of certain nodes on the network, as switches can, but they can also determine the shortest, fastest path between two nodes. For this reason, and because they can connect dissimilar network types, routers are powerful, indispensable devices on large LANs and WANs. The Internet, for example, relies on a multitude of routers across the world.

A typical router has an internal processor, an operating system, memory, input and output jacks for different types of network connectors (depending on the network type), and, usually, a management console interface. Three examples of routers are shown in Figure 6-23, with the most complex on the left and the simplest on the right. High-powered, multiprotocol routers may have several slot bays to accommodate multiple network interfaces. A router with multiple slots that can hold different interface cards or other devices is called a **modular router**. At the other end of the scale are simple, inexpensive routers often used in small offices and homes. As with the simple switches described in the previous section, these simple routers can be added to a network and function properly without significant configuration.

A router is a very flexible device. Although any one can be specialized for a variety of tasks, all routers can do the following:

- Connect dissimilar networks.

- Interpret Layer 3 addressing and other information (such as quality of service indicators).

- Determine the best path for data to follow from point A to point B.

- Reroute traffic if a primary path is down but another path is available.

In addition to performing these basic functions, routers may perform any of the following optional functions:

- Filter out broadcast transmissions to alleviate network congestion.

- Prevent certain types of traffic from getting to a network, enabling customized segregation and security.

- Support simultaneous local and remote connectivity.

- Provide high network fault tolerance through redundant components such as power supplies or network interfaces.

Figure 6-23 Routers

3.1

- Monitor network traffic and report statistics.

- Diagnose internal or other connectivity problems and trigger alarms.

1.6

3.1

Routers are often categorized according to the scope of the network they serve. A router that directs data between nodes on an autonomous LAN (or one owned and operated by a single organization) is known as an **interior router**. Such routers do not direct data between an employee's workstation and a Web server on the Internet. They can, however, direct data between an employee's workstation and his supervisor's workstation in an office down the hall. Another type of router is an **exterior router**. Exterior routers direct data between nodes external to a given autonomous LAN. Routers that operate on the Internet backbone are exterior routers. Between interior and exterior routers are **border routers** (or **gateway routers**). Such routers connect an autonomous LAN with a WAN. For example, the router that connects a business with its ISP is a border router.

Routers may use one of two methods for directing data on the network: static or dynamic routing. **Static routing** is a technique in which a network administrator programs a router to use specific paths between nodes. Because it does not account for occasional network congestion, failed connections, or device moves, static routing is not optimal. If a router or a segment connected to a router is moved, the network administrator must reprogram the static router's tables. Static routing requires human intervention, so it is less efficient and accurate than dynamic routing. **Dynamic routing**, on the other hand, automatically calculates the best path between two nodes and accumulates this information in a routing table. If congestion or failures affect the network, a router using dynamic routing can detect the problems and reroute data through a different path. As a part of dynamic routing, by default, when a router is added to a network, routing protocols update its routing tables. Most networks primarily use dynamic routing, but they may include some static routing to indicate, for example, a router of last resort, the router that accepts all unroutable packets.

On small office or home LANs, routers are simple to install. Setting up the hardware connections is similar to installing a workgroup switch, as described earlier in this chapter. A router, however, requires additional configuration. For small office and home routers, a CD or DVD inserted into a workstation connected to the router leads you through the setup process.

However, because of their customizability, routers can be a challenge to install on sizable networks. Typically, an engineer must be very familiar with routing technology to figure out how to place and configure a router to best advantage. Figure 6-24 gives you some idea of how routers fit into a LAN environment. If you plan to specialize in network design or router configuration, you should research router technology further. You might begin with Cisco System's online documentation at *www.cisco.com/univercd/home/home.htm*. Cisco Systems currently provides the majority of networking routers installed in the world.

In the setup depicted in Figure 6-24, if a workstation in workgroup A wants to print to the printer in workgroup B, it creates a transmission containing the address of the workgroup B printer. Then it sends its packets to hub A. Hub A simply retransmits the message to switch A. When switch A receives the transmission, it checks the MAC address for the printer and determines that the message needs to be forwarded. It forwards the message to router A, which examines the destination network address in each packet and determines the most efficient way of delivering the message. In this example, it sends the data to router B. Before it forwards the data, however, router A increments (increases) the number of hops tallied in all

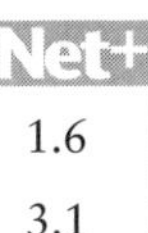

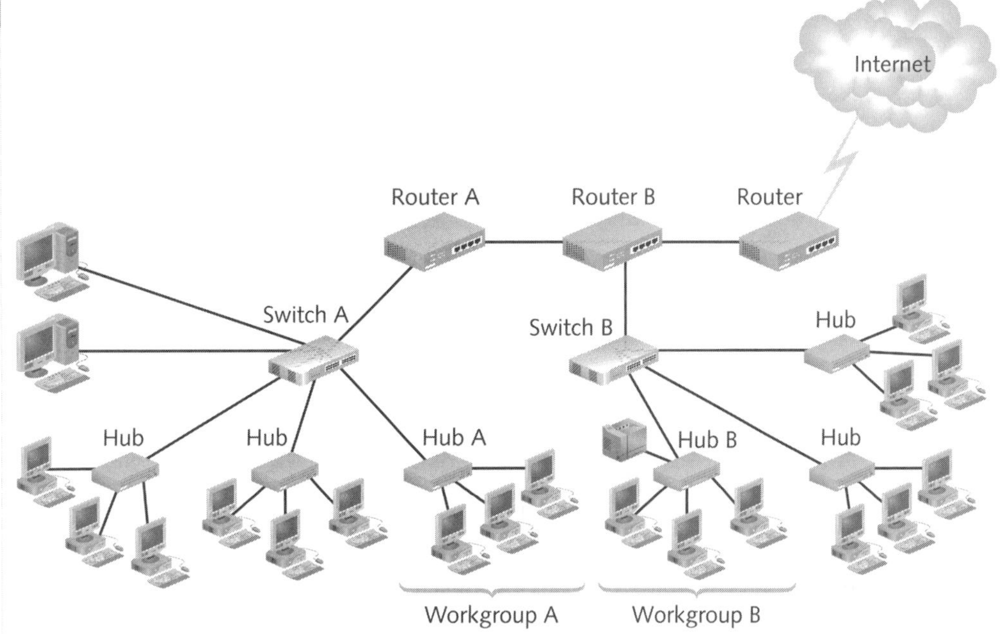

Figure 6-24 The placement of routers on a LAN

the packets. Each time a packet passes through a router, it has made a hop. Packets can only take a certain number of hops before they are discarded.

After it increments the number of hops tallied in each packet, router A forwards the data to router B. Router B increments each packet's hop count, reads each packet's destination network address, and sends them to switch B. Based on the destination MAC address in the packets, switch B decides to forward the message to hub B, which then broadcasts the transmission to workgroup B. The printer picks up the message and then begins printing.

Routing Protocols

Finding the best route for data to take across the network is one of the most valued and sophisticated functions performed by a router. The term **best path** refers to the most efficient route from one node on a network to another. The best path in a particular situation depends on the number of hops between nodes, the current network activity, the unavailable links, the network transmission speed, and the topology. To determine the best path, routers communicate with each other through **routing protocols**. Keep in mind that routing protocols are *not* the same as routable protocols, such as TCP/IP, although routing protocols may piggyback on routable protocols. Routing protocols are used only to collect data about current network status and contribute to the selection of the best paths. From this data, routers create routing tables, which act as a type of road map for future packet forwarding. You'll learn more about routing tables in Chapter 10.

In addition to its ability to find the best path, a routing protocol can be characterized according to its router **convergence time**, the time it takes for a router to recognize a best path in

1.5

3.1

the event of a change or network outage. Its overhead, or the burden placed on the underlying network to support the routing protocol, is also a distinguishing feature.

To attain Network+ certification, you should be familiar with the most common routing protocols: RIP, RIPv2, BGP, OSPF, IS-IS, and EIGRP. (Additional routing protocols exist, but a discussion of these exceeds the scope of this book.) These six common routing protocols are described in the following sections.

Distance-Vector: RIP, RIPv2, BGP Routing protocols can be divided into three types: distance-vector, link-state, or a hybrid of distance-vector and link-state. The types differ in how they learn and share information about data routes. **Distance-vector** routing protocols determine the best route for data based on the distance to a destination. Some distance-vector routing protocols only factor in the number of hops to the destination, while others take into account latency and other network traffic characteristics. Furthermore, distance-vector routing protocols periodically exchange their route information with neighboring routers. However, routers relying on this type of routing protocol must accept the data they receive from their neighbors. They cannot, for example, independently assess network conditions two hops away.

RIP (Routing Information Protocol), a distance-vector routing protocol, is the oldest routing protocol. RIP factors in only the number of hops between nodes when determining the best path from one point to another. It does not consider network congestion or link speed, for example. RIP is an interior routing protocol, meaning that it is used on interior or border routers.

Routers using RIP broadcast their routing tables every 30 seconds to other routers, regardless of whether the tables have changed. This broadcasting creates excessive network traffic, especially if a large number of routes exist. If the routing tables change, it may take several minutes before the new information propagates to routers at the far reaches of the network; thus, the convergence time for RIP is poor. However, one advantage to RIP is its stability. For example, RIP prevents routing loops from continuing indefinitely by limiting the number of hops a packet can take between its source and its destination to 15. If the number of hops in a path exceeds 15, the network destination is considered unreachable. Thus, RIP does not work well in very large network environments in which data may have to travel through more than 15 routers to reach its destination (for example, on the Internet). Also, compared with other routing protocols, RIP is slower and less secure.

Developers have improved RIP since its release in 1988 and informally renamed the original RIP RIPv1 (Routing Information Protocol Version 1). The latest version, **RIPv2 (Routing Information Protocol Version 2)**, generates less broadcast traffic and functions more securely than RIPv1. Still, RIPv2 cannot exceed 15 hops, and it is less commonly used than some link-state routing protocols discussed later.

A distance-vector routing protocol suited to WANs is **BGP (Border Gateway Protocol)**. Unlike RIP, BGP communicates using BGP-specific messages that travel between routers over TCP sessions. Using BGP, routers can determine best paths based on many different factors. In addition, network administrators can configure BGP to follow policies that might, for example, avoid a certain router or instruct a group of routers to prefer one particular route over other available routes. BGP is the most complex of the routing protocols mentioned in this chapter. It is the routing protocol of choice for Internet traffic, and it is used by border and exterior routers (but not interior routers). If you maintain networks for an ISP or large telecommunications company, you will need to understand BGP.

Link-State: OSPF, IS-IS A **link-state** routing protocol is one that enables routers across a network to share information, after which each router can independently map the network and determine the best path between itself and a packet's destination node. (By contrast, recall that distance-vector routing protocols require routers to rely on their neighbors for data path information.)

OSPF (Open Shortest Path First) is a link-state routing protocol used on interior or border routers. It was introduced as an improvement to RIP and can coexist with RIP (or RIPv2) on a network. Unlike RIP, OSPF imposes no hop limits on a transmission path. Also, OSPF uses a more complex algorithm for determining best paths than RIP uses. Under optimal network conditions, the best path is the most direct path between two points. If excessive traffic levels or an outage precludes data from following the most direct path, a router may determine that the most efficient path actually goes through additional routers. Because OSPF is a link-state routing protocol, each router running OSPF maintains a database of the other routers' links. If OSPF learns of the failure of a given link, the router can rapidly compute an alternate path. This calculation demands more memory and CPU power than RIP would, but it keeps network bandwidth to a minimum and provides a very fast convergence time, often invisible to the users. OSPF is supported by all modern routers. Therefore, it is commonly used on LANs that rely on a mix of routers from different manufacturers.

Another link-state routing protocol, which uses a best-path algorithm similar to OSPF's, is **IS-IS (Intermediate System to Intermediate System)**. IS-IS was originally codified by ISO, which referred to routers as "intermediate systems," thus the protocol's name. Unlike OSPF, however, IS-IS is designed for use on interior routers only. Also, it differs in that it supports two Layer 3 protocols: IP or an ISO-specific protocol. IS-IS is much less common than OSPF.

Hybrid: EIGRP Some routing protocols reflect characteristics of both link-state and distance-vector routing protocols and are known as hybrid routing protocols. The most popular example is **EIGRP (Enhanced Interior Gateway Routing Protocol)**. This routing protocol, used on interior or border routers, was developed in the mid-1980s by Cisco Systems. It has a fast convergence time and a low network overhead, and it is easier to configure and less CPU-intensive than OSPF. EIGRP also offers the benefits of supporting multiple protocols and limiting unnecessary network traffic between routers. It accommodates very large and heterogeneous networks but is only supported by Cisco routers. On LANs that use exclusively Cisco routers, EIGRP is generally preferred over OSPF.

You have learned about a router's essential features, including how it functions, how it fits into a network, and how it communicates with other routers. Because routers are such critical backbone devices, this book discusses them in more detail in several chapters. For example, you will learn about routers in the context of wireless networks in Chapter 8 and about the roles routers play in transmitting voice and video signals in Chapter 11. The following section introduces gateways, which share some similarities with routers and may even exist on routers.

Gateways and Other Multifunction Devices

Net+

3.2

Gateway is a term that can refer to one of many similar kinds of devices or interfaces in networking, so it's important to understand the context in which the term is used. In broad terms, **gateways** are combinations of networking hardware and software that connect two dissimilar kinds of networks. Specifically, they may connect two systems that use different formatting, communications protocols, or architecture. Unlike the connectivity hardware discussed earlier in this chapter, gateways actually repackage information so that it can be read by another system. To accomplish this task, gateways must operate at multiple layers of the OSI model. They communicate with an application, establish and manage sessions, translate encoded data, and interpret logical and physical addressing data.

Gateways can reside on servers, microcomputers, connectivity devices (such as routers), or mainframes. They are almost always designed for one category of gateway functions. In addition, they transmit data more slowly than bridges or routers (which are not acting as gateways) because of the complex translations they conduct. At a slower speed, gateways have the potential to cause extreme network congestion. In certain situations, however, only a gateway will suffice.

During your networking career, you will most likely hear gateways discussed in the context of Internet connections and e-mail systems. Popular types of gateways, including e-mail gateways, are described in the following list:

- *E-mail gateway*—A gateway that translates messages from one type of e-mail system to another. For example, an e-mail gateway allows networks that use Sendmail mail server software to exchange mail with networks that use Microsoft Exchange Server software.

- *Internet gateway*—A gateway that allows and manages access between LANs and the Internet. An Internet gateway can restrict the kind of access LAN users have to the Internet, and vice versa.

- *LAN gateway*—A gateway that allows segments of a LAN running different protocols or different network models to communicate with each other. A router, a single port on a router, or even a server may act as a LAN gateway. The LAN gateway category might also include remote access servers that allow dial-up connectivity to a LAN.

- *Voice/data gateway*—A gateway that connects the part of a network that handles data traffic with the part of a network that handles voice traffic. Voice applications have drastically different requirements from data applications. For example, before a voice signal can be transmitted over a data network, it needs to be digitized and compressed. When it reaches a voice receiver, such as a telephone, it has to be uncompressed and regenerated as recognizable speech, without delays. All these functions require specialized protocols and processes. A voice/data gateway can translate between these unique network segments and traditional data network segments.

- *Firewall*—A gateway that selectively blocks or filters traffic between networks. As with any other type of gateway, **firewalls** may be devices optimized for performing their tasks or computers installed with software necessary to accomplish those tasks. Because firewalls are integral to network security, they are discussed in detail in Chapter 12.

Chapter Summary

- Network adapters come in a variety of types depending on access method (Ethernet versus token ring), network transmission speed (for example, 100Mbps versus 1Gbps), connector interfaces (for example, SC versus RJ-45), type of compatible motherboard or device, and manufacturer.

- Desktops or tower PCs may use an expansion card NIC, which must match the system's bus. A bus is the type of circuit used by the motherboard to transmit data to components. New desktop computers almost always use PCI or PCIe buses.

- NICs may also be externally attached, through the PCMCIA-standard (PC Card, CardBus, or ExpressCard), USB, FireWire, or CompactFlash peripheral bus types.

- Some NICs are integrated into a computer's motherboard. These are also known as on-board NICs.

- NICs are designed to be used with either wire-bound or wireless connections. A wireless NIC uses an antenna to exchange signals with the network. This type of connectivity suits environments in which cabling cannot be installed or where roaming clients must be supported.

- To install a NIC, you must physically attach it to the bus (or port), install the NIC device drivers, and configure its settings.

- Firmware combines hardware and software. The hardware component of firmware is an EEPROM (electrically erasable programmable read-only memory) chip that stores data established at the factory. On a NIC, the EEPROM chip contains information about the adapter's transmission characteristics, plus its MAC address. You can change this data via a configuration utility.

- An IRQ is the means by which a device can request attention from the CPU. IRQ numbers range from 0 to 15. The BIOS attempts to assign free IRQ numbers to new devices. Typically, it assigns IRQ numbers 9, 10, or 11 to NICs. If conflicts occur, you must change a device's IRQ number rather than accept the default suggested by the BIOS or operating system.

- Repeaters are the connectivity devices that perform the regeneration of a digital signal. They belong to the physical layer of the OSI model; therefore, they do not have any means to interpret the data they are retransmitting.

- At its most primitive, a hub is a multiport repeater. A hub contains multiple data ports into which the patch cables for network nodes are connected. The hub accepts signals from a transmitting node and repeats those signals to all other connected nodes in a broadcast fashion, thereby creating a single collision domain. Most hubs also contain one port, called an uplink port, that allows the hub to connect to another hub or other connectivity device.

- Bridges resemble repeaters in that they have a single input and a single output port, but they can interpret the data they retransmit. Bridging occurs at the data link layer of the OSI model. Bridges read the destination (MAC) address information and decide whether to forward (retransmit) a packet to another segment on the network or, if the destination address belongs to the same segment as the source address, filter (discard) it.

- As nodes transmit data through the bridge, the bridge establishes a filtering database of known MAC addresses and their locations on the network. The bridge uses its filtering database to determine whether a packet should be forwarded or filtered.

- Switches subdivide a network into smaller, logical pieces. They operate at the data link layer (Layer 2) of the OSI model and can interpret MAC address information. In this respect, switches resemble bridges.

- Switches are generally secure because they isolate one device's traffic from other devices' traffic. Because switches provide separate channels for (potentially) every device, they allow applications that transfer a large amount of traffic and that are sensitive to time delays, such as video conferencing, to make full use of the network's capacity.

- A switch running in cut-through mode reads a frame's header and decides where to forward the data before it receives the entire packet. In store-and-forward mode, switches read the entire data frame into their memory and check it for accuracy before transmitting it. Although this method is more time consuming than the cut-through method, it allows store-and-forward switches to transmit data more accurately.

- Switches can create VLANs (virtual local area networks) by logically grouping several ports into a broadcast domain. The ports do not have to reside on the same switch or even on the same network segment. VLANs can isolate nodes and their traffic for security, convenience, or better performance. Multiple VLANs can be carried over single switch interfaces using VLAN trunking.

- On networks with several interconnected switches, STP (Spanning Tree Protocol) prevents traffic loops (and, as a consequence, broadcast storms) by calculating paths that avoid potential loops and by artificially blocking the links that would complete a loop.

- Manufacturers are producing switches that can operate at Layer 3 (network layer) and Layer 4 (transport layer) of the OSI model, making them act more like routers. The ability to interpret higher-layer data enables switches to perform advanced filtering, statistics keeping, and security functions.

- A router is a multiport device that can connect dissimilar LANs and WANs running at different transmission speeds, using a variety of protocols. Routers operate at the network layer (Layer 3) or higher of the OSI model. They interpret logical addresses and determine the best path between nodes. The best path depends on the number of hops between nodes, network activity, available links, transmission speed, and topology. To determine the best path, routers communicate with each other through routing protocols.

- Unlike bridges and traditional switches, routers are protocol dependent. They must be designed or configured to recognize a certain protocol before they can forward data transmitted using that protocol.

- Static routing is a technique in which a network administrator programs a router to use specific paths between nodes. Dynamic routing automatically calculates the best path between two nodes and accumulates this information in a routing table. If congestion or failures affect the network, a router using dynamic routing can detect the problems and reroute data through a different path. Most modern networks use dynamic routing.

- Routing protocols provide rules for communication between routers and help them determine the best path between two nodes. Some popular routing protocols include RIP, RIPv2, BGP, OSPF, IS-IS, and EIGRP.

- Distance-vector routing protocols determine the best route for data based on the distance to a destination. Some distance-vector routing protocols only factor in the number of hops to the destination, while others take into account latency and other network traffic characteristics.

- A link-state routing protocol enables routers across a network to share information, after which each router can independently map the network and determine the best path between itself and a packet's destination node.

- Some routing protocols reflect characteristics of both link-state and distance-vector routing protocols and are known as hybrid routing protocols.

- RIP, a distance-vector routing protocol, is the slowest and least secure and limits transmissions to 15 hops. RIPv2 makes up for some of the original RIP's overhead and security limitations, but its forwarding remains limited to 15 hops.

- BGP, used primarily for routing over Internet backbones, uses the most complex best-path calculation of all the commonly used routing protocols. It's considered a border routing protocol.

- OSPF (Open Shortest Path First) is a link-state routing protocol used on interior or border routers. It was introduced as an improvement to RIP and can coexist with RIP (or RIPv2) on a network. Unlike RIP, OSPF imposes no hop limits on a transmission path. Also, OSPF uses a more complex algorithm for determining best paths than RIP uses.

- IS-IS uses virtually the same methods as OSPF to calculate best paths, is less common, and is limited to interior routers.

- EIGRP is a Cisco standard commonly used on LANs that use exclusively Cisco routers.

- Gateways are combinations of networking hardware and software that connect two dissimilar kinds of networks. Specifically, they may connect two systems that use different formatting, communications protocols, or architecture. To accomplish this task, they must operate at multiple layers of the OSI model.

- Several different network devices can perform functions at multiple layers of the OSI model, including e-mail gateways, Internet gateways, LAN gateways, firewalls, and voice/data gateways.

Key Terms

802.1D   The IEEE standard that describes, among other things, bridging and STP (Spanning Tree Protocol).

802.1w   The IEEE standard that describes RSTP (Rapid Spanning Tree Protocol), which evolved from STP (Spanning Tree Protocol).

application switch   A switch that provides functions between Layer 4 and Layer 7 of the OSI model.

base I/O port   A setting that specifies, in hexadecimal notation, which area of memory will act as a channel for data traveling between the NIC and the CPU. Like its IRQ, a device's base I/O port cannot be used by any other device.

basic input/output system   *See* BIOS.

best path   The most efficient route from one node on a network to another. Under optimal network conditions, the best path is the most direct path between two points. However, when traffic congestion, segment failures, and other factors create obstacles, the most direct path may not be the best path.

BGP (Border Gateway Protocol)   A complex routing protocol used on border and exterior routers. BGP is the routing protocol used on Internet backbones.

BID (bridge ID)   A combination of a 2-byte priority field and a bridge's MAC address, used in STP (Spanning Tree Protocol) to select a root bridge.

BIOS (basic input/output system)   The firmware attached to a computer's motherboard that controls the computer's communication with its devices, among other things.

Border Gateway Protocol   *See* BGP.

border router   A router that connects an autonomous LAN with an exterior network—for example, the router that connects a business to its ISP.

bridge   A connectivity device that operates at the data link layer (Layer 2) of the OSI model and reads header information to forward packets according to their MAC addresses. Bridges use a filtering database to determine which packets to discard and which to forward. Bridges contain one input and one output port and separate network segments.

bridge ID   *See* BID.

broadcast domain   A combination of ports on a switch (or multiple switches) that make up a Layer 2 segment. To be able to exchange data with each other, broadcast domains must be connected by a Layer 3 device, such as a router or Layer 3 switch. A VLAN is one type of broadcast domain.

bus   The type of circuit used by a computer's motherboard to transmit data to components. Most new Pentium computers use buses capable of exchanging 32 or 64 bits of data. As the number of bits of data a bus handles increases, so too does the speed of the device attached to the bus.

CardBus   A PCMCIA standard that specifies a 32-bit interface running at 33MHz, similar to the PCI expansion board standard. Most modern laptops are equipped with CardBus slots for connecting external modems and NICs, among other things.

CMOS (complementary metal oxide semiconductor)   A type of microchip that requires very little energy to operate. In a PC, the CMOS stores settings pertaining to a computer's devices, among other things.

CompactFlash   The standard for an ultrasmall removable data and input/output device capable of connecting many kinds of external peripherals to workstations, PDAs, and other computerized devices. CompactFlash was designed by the CompactFlash Association (CFA), a consortium of computer manufacturers.

complementary metal oxide semiconductor   *See* CMOS.

content switch   A switch that provides functions between Layer 4 and Layer 7 of the OSI model.

convergence time   The time it takes for a router to recognize a best path in the event of a change or network outage.

cut-through mode   A switching mode in which a switch reads a frame's header and decides where to forward the data before it receives the entire packet. Cut-through mode is faster, but less accurate, than the other switching method, store-and-forward mode.

data port   A port on a connectivity device to which network nodes are connected.

device driver   The software that enables an attached device to communicate with the computer's operating system.

distance-vector   The simplest type of routing protocols, these determine the best route for data based on the distance to a destination. Some distance-vector routing protocols, like RIP, only factor in the number of hops to the destination, while others take into account latency and other network traffic characteristics.

driver   *See* device driver.

dynamic routing   A method of routing that automatically calculates the best path between two nodes and accumulates this information in a routing table. If congestion or failures affect the network, a router using dynamic routing can detect the problems and reroute data through a different path. Modern networks primarily use dynamic routing.

EEPROM (electrically erasable programmable read-only memory)   A type of ROM that is found on a circuit board and whose configuration information can be erased and rewritten through electrical pulses.

EIGRP (Enhanced Interior Gateway Routing Protocol)   A routing protocol developed in the mid-1980s by Cisco Systems that has a fast convergence time and a low network overhead but is easier to configure and less CPU-intensive than OSPF. EIGRP also offers the benefits of supporting multiple protocols and limiting unnecessary network traffic between routers.

electrically erasable programmable read-only memory   *See* EEPROM.

Enhanced Interior Gateway Routing Protocol   *See* EIGRP.

expansion board   A circuit board used to connect a device to a computer's motherboard.

expansion card   *See* expansion board.

expansion slot   A receptacle on a computer's motherboard that contains multiple electrical contacts into which an expansion board can be inserted.

ExpressCard   A PCMCIA standard that allows external devices to connect to portable computers through a 26-pin interface, with data transfer rates of 250Mbps in each direction (for a total of 500Mbps), similar to the PCI Express expansion board specification. ExpressCard modules come in two sizes: 34mm and 54mm wide. Over time, PCMCIA expects the ExpressCard standard to replace the CardBus standard.

exterior router   A router that directs data between nodes outside a given autonomous LAN, for example, routers used on the Internet's backbone.

filtering database   A collection of data created and used by a bridge that correlates the MAC addresses of connected workstations with their locations. A filtering database is also known as a forwarding table.

firewall A device (either a router or a computer running special software) that selectively filters or blocks traffic between networks. Firewalls are commonly used to improve data security.

FireWire A peripheral bus standard developed by Apple Computer and codified by the IEEE as the IEEE 1394 standard. Traditional FireWire connections support a maximum throughput of 400Mbps, but a newer version supports potential throughput rates of over 3Gbps. In addition to connecting peripherals, FireWire can be used to network computers directly in a bus fashion.

firmware A combination of hardware and software. The hardware component of firmware is a ROM (read-only memory) chip that stores data established at the factory and possibly changed by configuration programs that can write to ROM.

forwarding table *See* filtering database.

gateway A combination of networking hardware and software that connects two dissimilar kinds of networks. Gateways perform connectivity, session management, and data translation, so they must operate at multiple layers of the OSI model.

gateway router *See* border router.

hub A connectivity device that retransmits incoming data signals to its multiple ports. Typically, hubs contain one uplink port, which is used to connect to a network's backbone.

IEEE 1394 *See* FireWire.

Industry Standard Architecture *See* ISA.

intelligent hub A hub that possesses processing capabilities and can therefore monitor network traffic, detect packet errors and collisions, poll connected devices for information, and gather the data in database format.

interior router A router that directs data between nodes on an autonomous LAN.

Intermediate System to Intermediate System *See* IS-IS.

interrupt A circuit board wire through which a device issues voltage, thereby signaling a request for the processor's attention.

interrupt request *See* IRQ.

IRQ (interrupt request) A message sent to the computer that instructs it to stop what it is doing and pay attention to something else. *IRQ* is often used (informally) to refer to the interrupt request number.

IRQ number The unique number assigned to each interrupt in a computer. Interrupt request numbers range from 0 to 15, and many PC devices reserve specific numbers for their use alone.

IS-IS (Intermediate System to Intermediate System) A link-state routing protocol that uses a best-path algorithm similar to OSPF's. IS-IS was originally codified by ISO, which referred to routers as "intermediate systems," thus the protocol's name. Unlike OSPF, IS-IS is designed for use on interior routers only.

ISA (Industry Standard Architecture) The original PC bus type, developed in the early 1980s to support an 8-bit and later a 16-bit data path and a 4.77MHz clock speed.

Layer 3 switch A switch capable of interpreting data at Layer 3 (network layer) of the OSI model.

Layer 4 switch A switch capable of interpreting data at Layer 4 (transport layer) of the OSI model.

link-state A type of routing protocol that enables routers across a network to share information, after which each router can independently map the network and determine the best path between itself and a packet's destination node.

loopback adapter *See* loopback plug.

loopback plug A connector used for troubleshooting that plugs into a port (for example, a serial, parallel, or RJ-45 port) and crosses over the transmit line to the receive line, allowing outgoing signals to be redirected back into the computer for testing.

main bus *See* bus.

managed hub *See* intelligent hub.

memory range A hexadecimal number that indicates the area of memory that the NIC and CPU will use for exchanging, or buffering, data. As with IRQs, some memory ranges are reserved for specific devices—most notably, the motherboard.

modular router A router with multiple slots that can hold different interface cards or other devices so as to provide flexible, customizable network interoperability.

on-board NIC A NIC that is integrated into a computer's motherboard, rather than connected via an expansion slot or peripheral bus.

on-board port A port that is integrated into a computer's motherboard.

Open Shortest Path First *See* OSPF.

OSPF (Open Shortest Path First) A routing protocol that makes up for some of the limitations of RIP and can coexist with RIP on a network.

passive hub A hub that simply retransmits signals over the network.

PC Card A PCMCIA standard that specifies a 16-bit interface running at 8MHz for externally attached devices. PC Cards' characteristics match those of the ISA expansion card. And like the ISA standard, the PC Card standard suffered from its lower data transfer rates, compared to other PCMCIA standards.

PCI (Peripheral Component Interconnect) A 32- or 64-bit bus that can run at 33 or 66MHz, introduced in its original form in the 1990s. The PCI bus is the NIC connection type used for nearly all new PCs. It's characterized by a shorter length than ISA or EISA cards, but it has a much faster data transmission capability.

PCI Express *See* PCIe.

PCIe (PCI Express) A 32- or 64-bit bus standard capable of transferring data at up to 4.26Gbps in full-duplex transmission. PCI Express was introduced in 2002 and offers several advantages over traditional PCI. Its expansion cards can fit into older PCI slots, with some modifications to the motherboard.

PCMCIA (Personal Computer Memory Card International Association) A group of computer manufacturers who developed an interface for connecting any type of device to a portable computer. PCMCIA slots may hold memory, modem, network interface, external hard disk, or CD-ROM cards. PCMCIA-standard cards include PC Card, CardBus, and the newest, ExpressCard.

Peripheral Component Interconnect *See* PCI.

Personal Computer Memory Card International Association *See* PCMCIA.

Rapid Spanning Tree Protocol *See* RSTP.

RIP (Routing Information Protocol) The oldest routing protocol that is still widely used, RIP does not work in very large network environments in which data may have to travel through more than 15 routers to reach its destination (for example, on the Internet). And, compared to other routing protocols, RIP is slower and less secure.

RIPv2 (Routing Information Protocol version 2) An updated version of the original RIP routing protocol that makes up for some of its predecessor's overhead and security flaws. However, RIPv2's packet forwarding is still limited to a maximum 15 hops.

root bridge The single bridge on a network selected by the Spanning Tree Protocol to provide the basis for all subsequent path calculations.

router A multiport device that operates at Layer 3 of the OSI model and uses logical addressing information to direct data between networks or segments. Routers can connect dissimilar LANs and WANs running at different transmission speeds and using a variety of network layer protocols. They determine the best path between nodes based on traffic congestion, available versus unavailable routes, load balancing targets, and other factors.

Routing Information Protocol *See* RIP.

Routing Information Protocol Version 2 *See* RIPv2.

routing protocols The means by which routers communicate with each other about network status. Routing protocols determine the best path for data to take between nodes.

routing switch *See* Layer 3 switch.

RSTP (Rapid Spanning Tree Protocol) As described in IEEE's 802.1w standard, a newer version of the Spanning Tree Protocol that can detect and correct for network changes much more quickly.

runt An erroneously shortened packet.

Spanning Tree Protocol *See* STP.

stand-alone hub A type of hub that serves a workgroup of computers that are separate from the rest of the network, also known as a workgroup hub.

static routing A technique in which a network administrator programs a router to use specific paths between nodes. Because it does not account for occasional network congestion, failed connections, or device moves, static routing is not optimal.

store-and-forward mode A method of switching in which a switch reads the entire data frame into its memory and checks it for accuracy before transmitting it. Although this method is more time consuming than the cut-through method, it allows store-and-forward switches to transmit data more accurately.

STP (Spanning Tree Protocol) A switching protocol defined in IEEE 802.1D. STP operates in the data link layer to prevent traffic loops by calculating paths that avoid potential loops and by artificially blocking links that would complete a loop. Given changes to a network's links or devices, STP recalculates its paths.

switch A connectivity device that logically subdivides a network into smaller, individual collision domains. A switch operates at the data link layer of the OSI model and can interpret MAC address information to determine whether to filter (discard) or forward packets it receives.

system bus *See* bus.

trunking The aggregation of multiple logical connections in one physical connection between connectivity devices. In the case of VLANs, trunking allows data from multiple VLANs to share a single interface on a switch.

uplink port A port on a connectivity device, such as a hub or switch, used to connect it to another connectivity device.

USB (universal serial bus) port A standard external bus that can be used to connect multiple types of peripherals, including modems, mice, and NICs, to a computer. Two USB standards exist: USB 1.1 and USB 2.0. USB 3.0 promises to be released soon. Most modern computers support the USB 2.0 standard.

virtual local area network *See* VLAN.

VLAN (virtual local area network) A network within a network that is logically defined by grouping its devices' switch ports in the same broadcast domain. A VLAN can consist of any type of network node in any geographic location and can incorporate nodes connected to different switches.

workgroup hub *See* stand-alone hub.

Review Questions

1. Which bus type allows a NIC to be attached externally?

    a. PCI

    b. PCIe

    c. PCMCIA

    d. ISA

2. Which device acts most like a router?

    a. OSI model Layer 1 repeater

    b. OSI model Layer 2 hub

    c. OSI model Layer 2 bridge

    d. OSI model Layer 3 switch

3. Which term identifies a router category that directs data between nodes on an autonomous LAN?

    a. Interior

    b. Exterior

    c. Border

    d. Gateway

4. Which routing technique is used to program a router to use specific paths between nodes?

    a. Dynamic routing

    b. Static routing

    c. Interior routing

    d. Exterior routing

5. Which routing protocol is commonly used on LANs that use exclusively Cisco routers?

    a. RIPv2

    b. OSPF

    c. BGP

    d. EIGRP

6. True or false? When choosing a NIC for your workstation or server, the most critical factor is transmission speed.

    a. True

    b. False

7. True or false? EEPROM is a particular type of ROM with data that can be erased or changed by applying electrical charges to the chip.

8. True or false? Bridges can move data more rapidly than traditional routers.

9. True or false? Routers are protocol dependent.

10. True or false? Routing protocols are the same as routable protocols, such as TCP/IP.

11. A(n) _____ is the simplest type of connectivity device that simply regenerates a digital signal.

12. A(n) _____ is a repeater with more than one output port.

13. A(n) _____ is a device that connects two network segments by analyzing incoming frames and making decisions about where to direct them based on each frame's MAC address.

14. A switch running in _____ mode reads a frame's header and decides where to forward the data before it receives the entire packet.

15. _____ are combinations of networking hardware and software that connect two dissimilar kinds of networks.

WANs and Remote Connectivity

After reading this chapter and completing the exercises, you will be able to:

- Identify a variety of uses for WANs

- Explain different WAN topologies, including their advantages and disadvantages

- Compare the characteristics of WAN technologies, including their switching type, throughput, media, security, and reliability

- Describe several WAN transmission and connection methods, including PSTN, ISDN, T-carriers, DSL, broadband cable, ATM, and SONET

- Describe multiple methods for remotely connecting to a network

On the Job

My most unusual experience occurred while I was working on our company's wide area network (WAN). We were bringing up a new site and couldn't make the connection function. It was the last step before we opened the new branch of our bank. In fact, on the day the connection was scheduled to go live, the general manager at the new location was holding an open house that featured a remote videoconference with the bank's president at our corporate headquarters.

We had ordered the T1 circuit from the provider several months prior to the opening of the branch. We had received the router and CSU/DSU module for the router well in advance of the opening. In fact, we had even configured the equipment with the required IP address and line settings, and we had already shipped the equipment to the branch. The last step was to visit the new branch and hook everything up.

The new branch was our most remote location up to that point, so I booked a flight and made a hotel reservation well in advance of the occasion. The day I left for the trip, I checked with the T1 provider on the remote end to make sure the circuit was ready to be installed. On arriving, I was surprised to see that a major party was scheduled for the grand opening of the bank. I was a little nervous because we hadn't had a chance to test the video quality back to HQ.

I prepared to hook up all the gear and got on the phone with my coworker at HQ to verify that the other end of the circuit was up. I went to plug in the T1 line and found that the cable had the wrong connector on it. I hastily put a new end on the cable. Then I plugged the cable in to the serial interface on the router and checked in my terminal session to see whether the interface would come up. I got a little more nervous when the interface didn't come up right away, but I had seen other circuits take some time to show active on the router console.

Ten minutes later I decided to call the provider to see whether there were any alarms on their end of the circuit. After the usual trip through the customer support phone system, I got a technician on the phone. He said there were no alarms on his end, but that the circuit did appear to be down.

He checked the line using many of his tools, but I couldn't get the line to show up as active. After several hours, he said he'd drive over to our bank to try a different course of action. I waited for another hour (the drive was supposed to be only 20 minutes away) before I heard from the technician again. He thought he was at our location, and wondered why the bank was closed up when we were supposed to be having an open house. What? To make a long story short, in the original order for the service, someone had transposed the location's address, and the technician

(continued)

had installed the line at our competitor's bank. The technician made a heroic effort to reprovision the T1 to our location, and we had video running over the T1 only 15 minutes late for the new branch open house.

The moral? Never underestimate the dedication of phone service providers and their technicians.

Selim Mansur
Coastal Federated Bank

Now that you understand the basic transmission media, network models, and networking hardware associated with LANs (local area networks), you need to expand that knowledge to encompass WANs (wide area networks). As you have learned, a WAN is a network that connects two or more geographically distinct LANs. You might assume that WANs are the same as LANs, only bigger. Although a WAN is based on the same principles as a LAN, including reliance on the OSI model, its distance requirements affect its entire infrastructure. As a result, WANs differ from LANs in nearly every respect.

To understand the difference between a LAN and WAN, think of the hallways and stairs of your house as LAN pathways. These interior passages allow you to go from room to room. To reach destinations outside your house, however, you need to use sidewalks and streets. These public thoroughfares are analogous to WAN pathways—except that WAN pathways are not necessarily public.

This chapter discusses the technical differences between LANs and WANs and describes in detail WAN transmission media and methods. It also notes the potential pitfalls in establishing and maintaining WANs. In addition, it introduces you to remote connectivity for LANs—a technology that, in some cases, can be used to extend a LAN into a WAN. Remote connectivity and WANs are significant concerns for organizations attempting to meet the needs of telecommuting workers, global business partners, and Internet-based commerce. To pass the Network+ certification exam, you must be familiar with the variety of WAN and remote connectivity options.

WAN Essentials

A WAN is a network that traverses some distance and usually connects LANs, whether across the city or across the nation. You are probably familiar with at least one WAN—the Internet, which is the largest WAN in existence today. However, the Internet is not a typical WAN. Many WANs arise from the simple need to connect one location to another. As an organization grows, the WAN might grow to connect more and more sites, located across a city or around the world. Only an organization's information technology budget and aspirations limit the dimensions of its WAN.

Any business or government institution with sites scattered over a wide geographical area needs a way to exchange data between those sites. Each of the following scenarios demonstrates a need for a WAN:

- A bank with offices around the state needs to connect those offices to gather transaction and account information into a central database. Furthermore, it needs to connect with global financial clearinghouses to, for example, conduct transactions with other institutions.

- Regional sales representatives for a national pharmaceutical company need to submit their sales figures to a file server at the company's headquarters and receive e-mail from the company's mail server.

- An automobile manufacturer in Detroit contracts out its plastic parts manufacturing to a Delaware-based company. Through WAN links, the auto manufacturer can video-conference with the plastics manufacturer, exchange specification data, and even examine the parts for quality from a remote location.

- A clothing manufacturer sells its products over the Internet to customers throughout the world.

Although all of these businesses need WANs, they may not need the same kinds of WANs. Depending on the traffic load, budget, geographical breadth, and commercially available technology, each might implement a different transmission method. For every business need, a few (or possibly only one) appropriate WAN connection types might exist. However, many WAN technologies can coexist on the same network.

WANs and LANs have several fundamental properties in common. Both are designed to enable communication between clients and hosts for resource sharing. In general, both use the same protocols from Layers 3 and higher of the OSI model. And both networks typically carry digitized data via packet-switched connections.

However, LANs and WANs often differ at Layers 1 and 2 of the OSI model in access methods, topologies, and sometimes, media. They also differ in the extent to which the organization that uses the network is responsible for the network. LANs use a building's internal cabling, such as twisted pair, that runs from work area to the wall, through plenum areas, and to a telecommunications closet. Such wiring is private; it belongs to the building owner. In contrast, WANs typically send data over publicly available communications networks, which are owned by local and long-distance telecommunications carriers. Such carriers, which are privately owned corporations, are also known as **NSPs (network service providers)**. Some large NSPs based in the United States include AT&T, Verizon, and Sprint. Customers lease connections from these carriers, paying based on the amount of bandwidth they need. For best throughput and quality, organizations lease **dedicated** lines, or continuously available communications channels, from a telecommunications provider, such as a local telephone company or ISP. Dedicated lines come in a variety of types that are distinguished by their capacity and transmission characteristics.

The individual geographic locations connected by a WAN are known as WAN sites. A **WAN link** is a connection between one WAN site (or point) and another site (or point). Most WAN links are point-to-point, connecting one site to only one other site. That is, the link does not connect one site to several other sites, in the way that LAN hubs or switches connect multiple segments or workstations. Nevertheless, one location may be connected to more than one location by multiple WAN links. Figure 7-1 illustrates the difference between WAN and LAN connectivity.

The following section describes different topologies used on WANs.

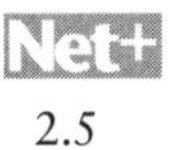

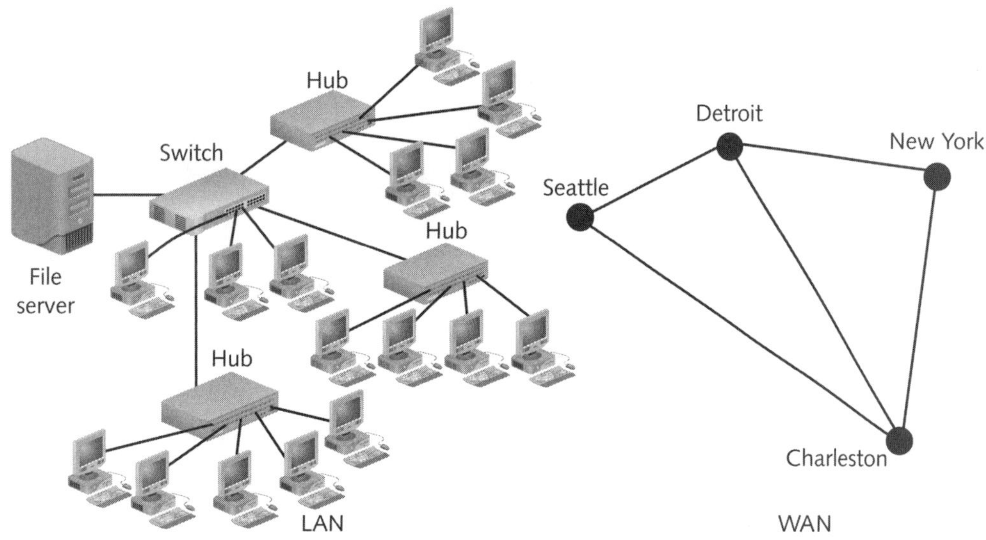

Figure 7-1 Differences in LAN and WAN connectivity

WAN Topologies

WAN topologies resemble LAN topologies, but their details differ because of the distance they must cover, the larger number of users they serve, and the heavy traffic they often handle. For example, WAN topologies connect sites via dedicated and, usually, high-speed links. As a consequence, WANs use different connectivity devices. For example, to connect two buildings via high-speed T1 carrier lines, each location must use a special type of terminating device, a multiplexer, plus a router. And because WAN connections require routers or other Layer 3 devices to connect locations, their links are not capable of carrying nonroutable protocols. The following sections describe common WAN topologies and special considerations for using each.

Bus

A WAN in which each site is directly connected to no more than two other sites in a serial fashion is known as a **bus topology WAN**. A bus topology WAN is similar to a bus topology LAN in that each site depends on every other site in the network to transmit and receive its traffic. However, bus topology LANs use computers with shared access to one cable, whereas the WAN bus topology uses different locations, each one connected to another one through point-to-point links.

A bus topology WAN is often the best option for organizations with only a few sites and the capability to use dedicated circuits. Some examples of dedicated circuits include T1, DSL, and ISDN connections, all of which are detailed later in this chapter. Dedicated circuits make it possible to transmit data regularly and reliably. Figure 7-2 depicts a bus topology WAN using T1 and DSL connections.

Bus WAN topologies are suitable for only small WANs. Because all sites between the sending and receiving location must participate in carrying traffic, this model does not scale well. The

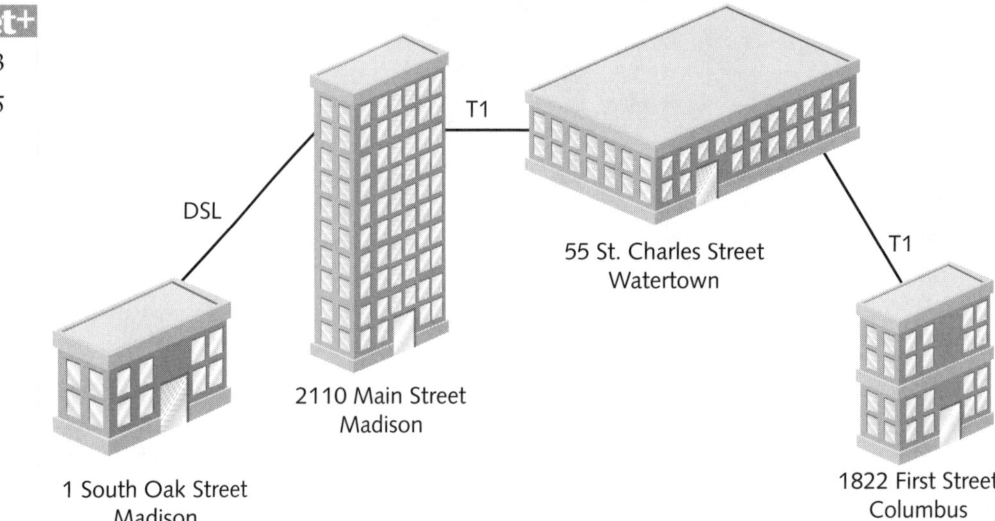

Figure 7-2 A bus topology WAN

addition of more sites can cause performance to suffer. Also, a single failure on a bus topology WAN can take down communications between all sites.

Ring

In a **ring topology WAN,** each site is connected to two other sites so that the entire WAN forms a ring pattern, as shown in Figure 7-3. This architecture is similar to the simple ring topology used on a LAN, except that a WAN ring topology connects locations rather than local nodes. Also, on most modern WANs, a ring topology relies on redundant rings to carry data. Using redundant rings means that a ring topology WAN cannot be taken down

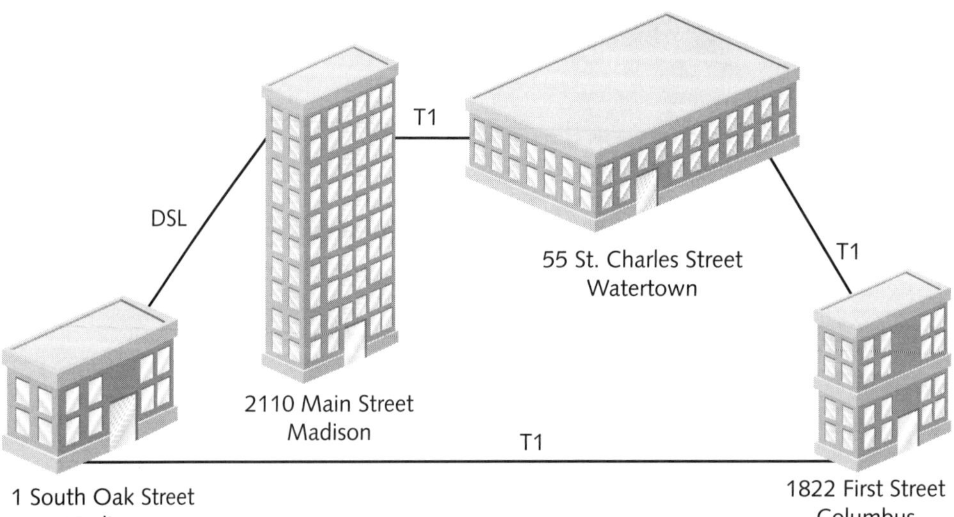

Figure 7-3 A ring topology WAN

Net+

2.3

2.5

by the loss of one site; instead, if one site fails, data can be rerouted around the WAN in a different direction. On the other hand, expanding ring-configured WANs can be difficult, and it is more expensive than expanding a bus topology WAN. For these reasons, WANs that use the ring topology are only practical for connecting fewer than four or five locations.

Star

The **star topology WAN** mimics the arrangement of a star topology LAN. A single site acts as the central connection point for several other points, as shown in Figure 7-4. This arrangement provides separate routes for data between any two sites. That means that if a single connection fails, only one location loses WAN access. For example, if the T1 link between the Oak Street and Main Street locations fails, the Watertown and Columbus locations can still communicate with the Main Street location because they use different routes. In a bus or ring topology, however, a single connection failure would halt all traffic between all sites. Another advantage of a star WAN is that when all of its dedicated circuits are functioning, a star WAN provides shorter data paths between any two sites.

Extending a star WAN is relatively simple and less costly than extending a bus or ring topology WAN. For example, if the organization that uses the star WAN pictured in Figure 7-4 wanted to add a Maple Street, Madison, location to its topology, it could simply lease a new dedicated circuit from the Main Street office to its Maple Street office. None of the other offices would be affected by the change. If the organization were using a bus or ring WAN topology, however, two separate dedicated connections would be required to incorporate the new location into the network.

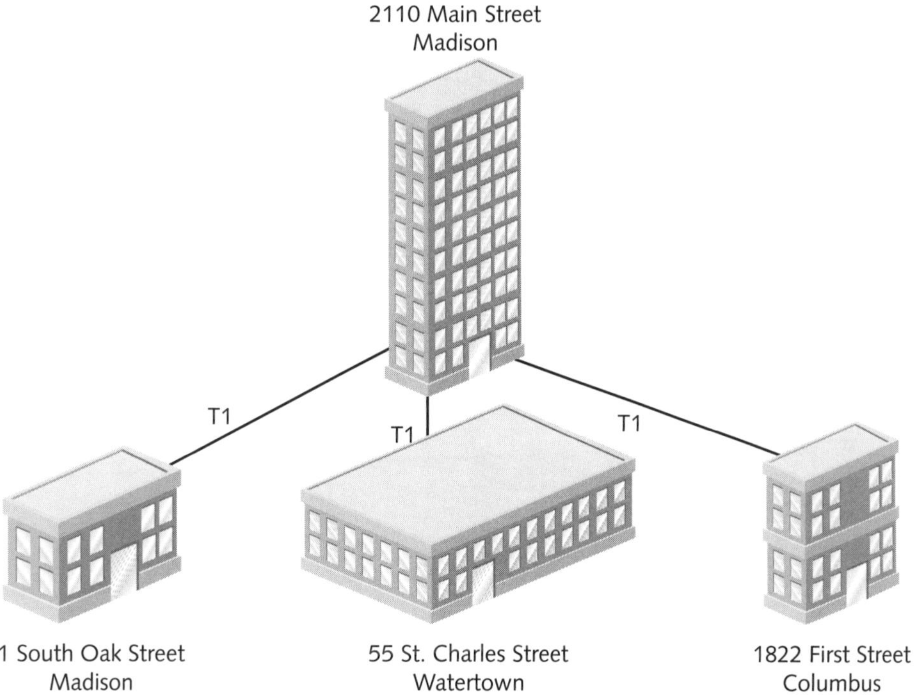

Figure 7-4 A star topology WAN

2.3

2.5

As with star LAN topologies, the greatest drawback of a star WAN is that a failure at the central connection point can bring down the entire WAN. In Figure 7-4, for example, if the Main Street office suffered a catastrophic fire, the entire WAN would fail. Similarly, if the central connection point is overloaded with traffic, performance on the entire WAN will be adversely affected.

Mesh

A **mesh topology WAN** incorporates many directly interconnected sites. Because every site is interconnected, data can travel directly from its origin to its destination. If one connection suffers a problem, routers can redirect data easily and quickly. Mesh WANs are the most fault-tolerant type of WAN because they provide multiple routes for data to follow between any two points. For example, if the Madison office in Figure 7-5 suffered a catastrophic fire, the Dubuque office could still send and transmit data to and from the Detroit office by going directly to the Detroit office. If both the Madison and Detroit offices failed, the Dubuque and Indianapolis offices could still communicate.

The type of mesh topology in which every WAN site is directly connected to every other site is called a **full-mesh WAN**. One drawback to a full-mesh WAN is the cost. If more than a few sites are involved, connecting every site to every other requires leasing a large number of dedicated circuits. As WANs grow larger, the expense multiplies. To reduce costs, a network administrator might choose to implement a **partial-mesh WAN**, in which only critical WAN sites are directly interconnected and secondary sites are connected through star or ring topologies, as shown in Figure 7-5. Partial-mesh WANs are more common in today's business world than full-mesh WANs because they are more economical.

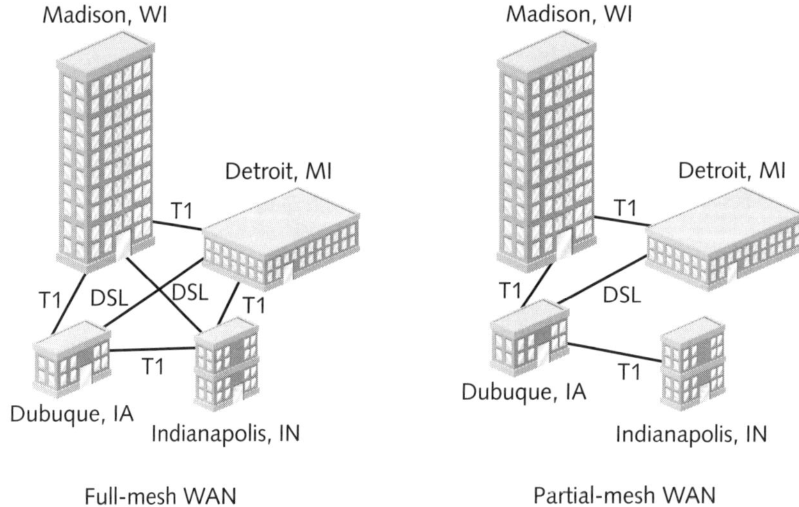

Figure 7-5 Full-mesh and partial-mesh WANs

Tiered

In a **tiered topology WAN**, sites connected in star or ring formations are interconnected at different levels, with the interconnection points being organized into layers to form hierarchical groupings. Figure 7-6 depicts a tiered WAN. In this example, the Madison, Detroit, and

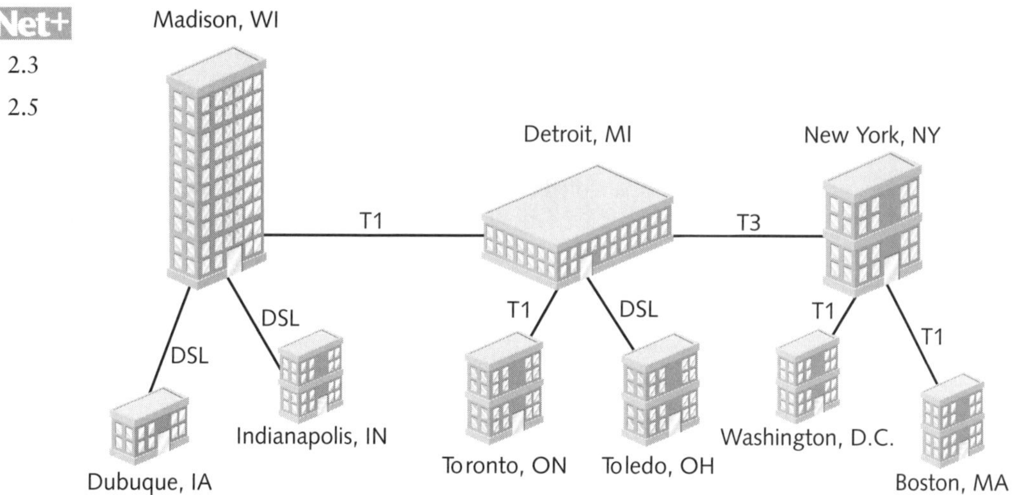

Figure 7-6 A tiered topology WAN

New York offices form the upper tier, and the Dubuque, Indianapolis, Toronto, Toledo, Washington, and Boston offices form the lower tier. If the Detroit office suffers a failure, the Toronto and Toledo offices cannot communicate with any other nodes on the WAN, nor can the Washington, Boston, and New York locations exchange data with the other six locations. Yet the Washington, Boston, and New York locations can still exchange data with each other, as can the Indianapolis, Dubuque, and Madison locations.

Variations on this topology abound. Indeed, flexibility makes the tiered approach quite practical. A network architect can determine the best placement of top-level routers based on traffic patterns or critical data paths. In addition, tiered systems allow for easy expansion and inclusion of redundant links to support growth. On the other hand, their enormous flexibility means that creation of tiered WANs requires careful consideration of geography, usage patterns, and growth potential.

Now that you understand the fundamental shapes that WANs may take, you are ready to learn about specific technologies and types. WAN technologies discussed in the following sections differ in terms of speed, reliability, cost, distance covered, and security. Also, some are defined by specifications at the data link layer, whereas others are defined by specifications at the physical layer of the OSI model. As you learn about each technology, pay attention to its characteristics and think about its possible applications. To qualify for Network+ certification, you must be familiar with the variety of WAN connection types and be able to identify the networking environments that each suits best.

PSTN

PSTN, which stands for **Public Switched Telephone Network,** refers to the network of lines and carrier equipment that provides telephone service to most homes and businesses. PSTN may also be called **POTS (plain old telephone service).** The PSTN encompasses the entire telephone system, from the wires that enter homes and businesses to the network centers that connect different regions of a country.

2.5

Originally, the PSTN carried only analog traffic. All of its lines were copper wires, and switching was handled by operators who manually connected calls upon request. Today, switching is computer controlled, and nearly all of the PSTN uses digital transmission. Signals may deliver voice, video, or data traffic and travel over fiber-optic or twisted pair copper cable, microwave, and satellite connections.

This chapter includes many examples of PSTN-based network technologies, including dial-up networking and dedicated Internet connections, that enable users to connect to WANs. In Chapter 11 you'll learn about computer networking technologies that have replaced the PSTN's original function as a voice carrier. Boundaries between the PSTN and computer networks have blurred. To appreciate how these spheres overlap, it's helpful to understand how the PSTN provided WAN connectivity when the Internet first became popular in the 1990s. At that time, most home users logged on to the Internet via a dial-up connection.

A **dial-up** connection is one in which a user connects her computer, via a modem, to a distant network and stays connected for a finite period of time. Unlike other types of WAN connections, dial-up connections provide a fixed period of access to the network, just as the phone call you make to a friend has a fixed length, determined by when you initiate and terminate the call. The term *dial-up* usually refers to a connection that uses a PSTN line.

When computers connect to a public or private data network via the PSTN, modems are almost always necessary, because even today, certain elements of the PSTN can't handle digital transmission. Recall that a modem converts a computer's digital pulses into analog signals before it issues them to the telephone line, and then it converts the analog signals back into digital pulses at the receiving computer's end. Between the modems at either end, a signal travels through a carrier's network of switches and, possibly, long-distance connections.

Tracing the path of a dial-up connection is one good way to learn about the traditional PSTN. Imagine you are vacationing at a cabin in Alaska and the only way to connect to the Internet is via the phone line. You decide to dial into your ISP to pick up e-mail using your laptop's 56Kbps modem. To do so, you first initiate a call through your computer's dial-up software, which instructs your modem to dial the number for your ISP's remote access server. Next, your modem attempts to establish a connection. It converts the digital signal from your laptop into an analog signal that travels over the phone line to the local telephone company's network until it reaches the **CO** (**central office**). A CO is the place where a telephone company terminates lines and switches calls between different locations. Between your vacation cabin and the nearest CO, signals might go through one or more of the telephone company's remote switching facilities. Modern remote switching facilities (sometimes called pedestals, because of their shape) usually contain digital equipment to convert the analog signal back to a digital signal before forwarding it to the CO.

Whether at a remote switching facility or at the CO, your signal is converted back to digital pulses. If your cabin and your ISP share the same CO, the signal is switched from your incoming connection directly to your ISP. In most cases, the ISP would have a dedicated connection to a CO. If so, your signal is issued over this dedicated connection multiplexed together with many other signals.

Yet it's likely that your vacation cabin doesn't share the same CO as your ISP. In that case, the first part of the process is the same as if you were at home—you initiate a call and connect to the local telephone company's CO, and along the way, your signal is converted to digital pulses. However, this time your signal cannot go straight to your ISP because your ISP doesn't have a connection in that carrier's CO. Instead, the local telephone company that serves the

Net+
2.5

cabin's geographical area forwards the signal from its local CO to a regional CO through a dedicated connection between the two. This regional office most likely connects to a much larger regional or national WAN. The signal travels over the WAN to the regional CO closest to your ISP. That regional office directs the signal to your ISP's local CO, or straight to the ISP's network. Figure 7-7 illustrates the path a signal might take in a long-distance dial-up connection. Notice that in this figure, the WAN to which regional offices connect is represented as a cloud. On networking diagrams, packet-switched networks (including the Internet) are depicted as clouds, because of the indeterminate nature of their traffic patterns.

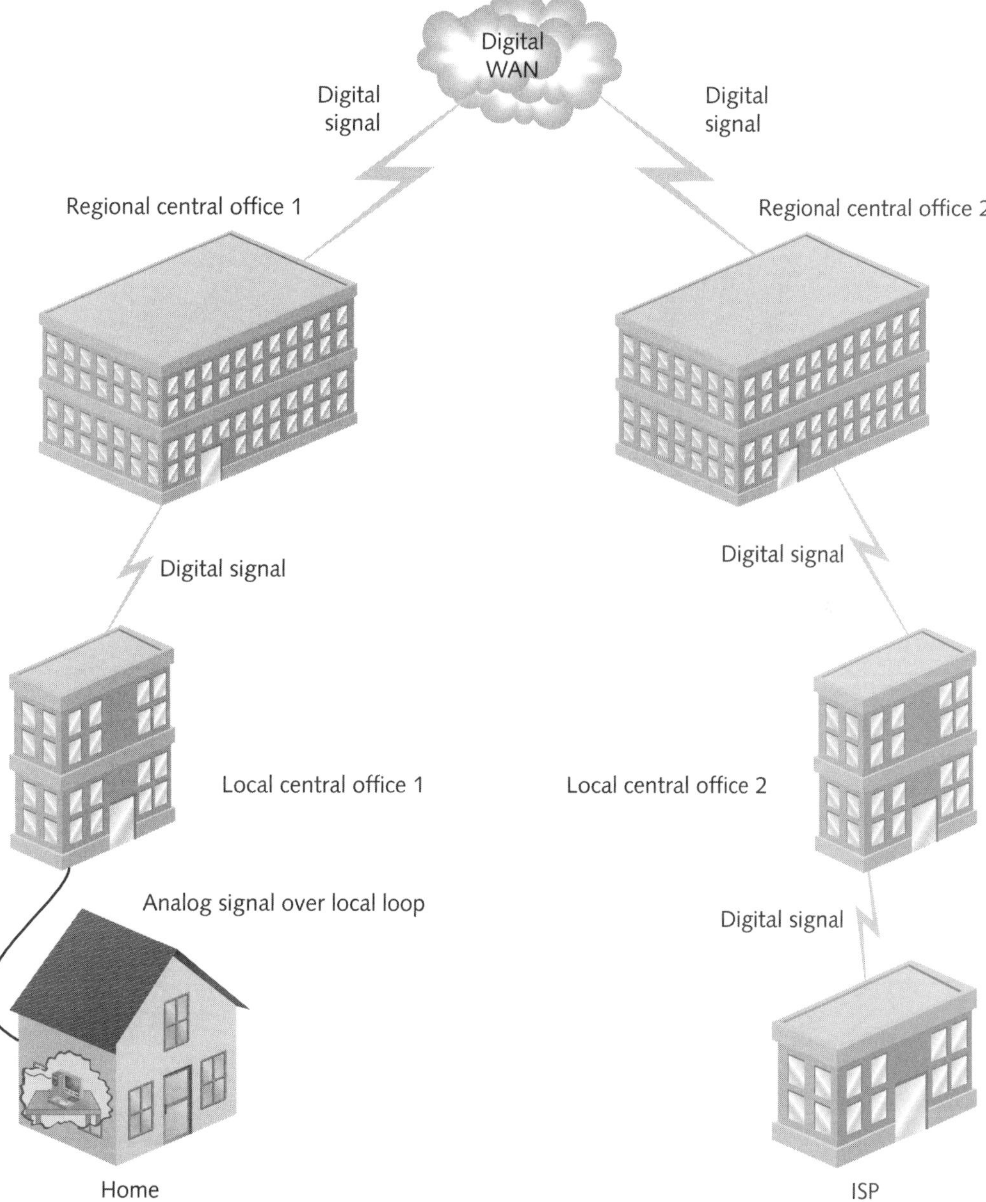

Figure 7-7 A long-distance dial-up connection

Net+
2.5

The portion of the PSTN that connects any residence or business to the nearest CO is known as the **local loop**, or the **last mile**, and is illustrated in Figure 7-8. It's the part of the PSTN most likely to still use copper wire and carry analog signals. That's because extending fiber-optic cable or high-speed wireless connections to every residence and business is very costly. However, fully digital connections, though less common, do exist. One example is **fiber to the home,** which simply means that a telephone company connects residential users to its network with fiber-optic cable. As you can imagine, this dramatically increases the range of services and potential throughput available to customers. But no matter what kind of media is used, the end of the local loop, and also the end of the carrier's responsibility for the network, is the customer's demarcation point, where wires terminate at an **NIU (network interface unit)**.

The advantages to using the PSTN for an Internet connection are its ubiquity, ease of use, and low cost. You can access a phone line virtually anywhere in the world and, thereby gain remote access to the network of your choice (as detailed later in this chapter).

Although nearly all COs in the PSTN handle digitized data, some still use circuit switching rather than the more efficient packet switching. Recall that in circuit switching, data travels over a point-to-point connection that is reserved by a transmission until all of its data has been transferred. You might think that circuit switching makes the PSTN more secure than other types of WAN connections; in fact, the PSTN offers only marginal security. Because it is a public network, PSTN presents many points at which communications can be intercepted and interpreted on their way from sender to receiver. For example, an eavesdropper could tap into the connection where your local telephone company's line enters your house.

The PSTN is not limited to servicing workstation dial-up WAN connections. Following sections describe other, more sophisticated WAN technologies that also rely on the public telephone network.

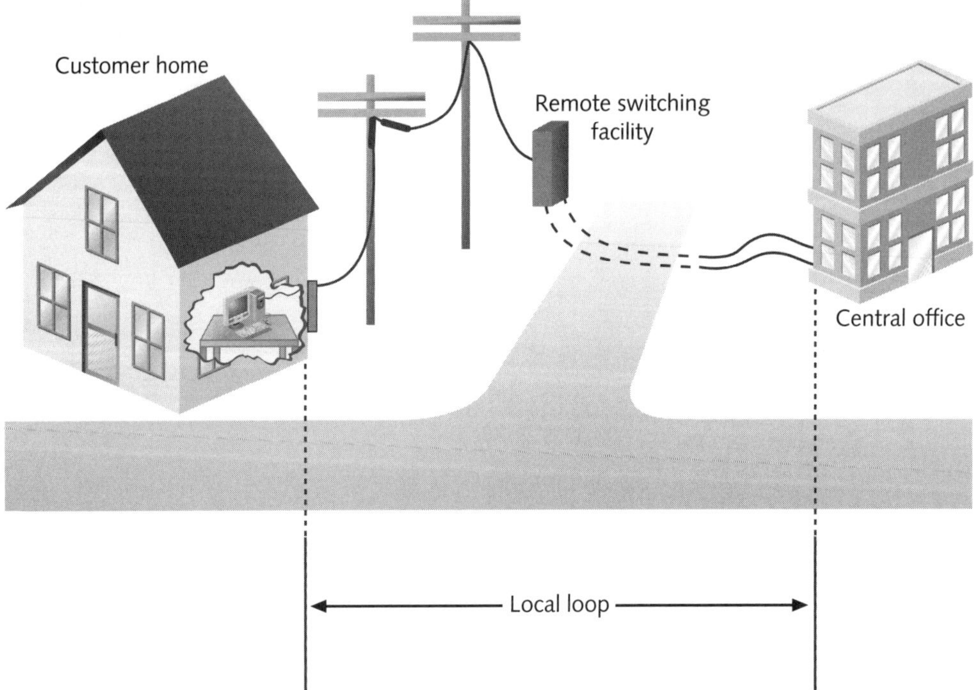

Figure 7-8 Local loop portion of the PSTN

X.25 and Frame Relay

Net+
2.5

X.25 is an analog, packet-switched technology designed for long-distance data transmission and standardized by the ITU in the mid-1970s. The original standard for X.25 specified a maximum of 64Kbps throughput, but by 1992 the standard was updated to include maximum throughput of 2.048Mbps. It was originally developed as a more reliable alternative to the voice telephone system for connecting mainframe computers and remote terminals. Later, it was adopted as a method of connecting clients and servers over WANs.

The X.25 standard specifies protocols at the physical, data link, and network layers of the OSI model. It provides excellent flow control and ensures data reliability over long distances by verifying the transmission at every node. Unfortunately, this verification also renders X.25 comparatively slow and unsuitable for time-sensitive applications, such as audio or video. On the other hand, X.25 benefits from being a long-established, well-known, and low-cost technology. X.25 was never widely adopted in the United States, but it was accepted by other countries and was for a long time the dominant packet-switching technology used on WANs around the world.

Recall that, in packet switching, packets belonging to the same data stream may follow different, optimal paths to their destination. As a result, packet switching uses bandwidth more efficiently and allows for faster transmission than if each packet in the data stream had to follow the same path, as in circuit switching. Packet switching is also more flexible than circuit switching because packet sizes may vary.

Frame relay is an updated, digital version of X.25 that also relies on packet switching. ITU and ANSI standardized frame relay in 1984. However, because of a lack of compatibility with other WAN technologies at the time, frame relay did not become popular in the United States and Canada until the late 1980s. Frame relay protocols operate at the data link layer of the OSI model and can support multiple different network and transport layer protocols. The name is derived from the fact that data is separated into frames, which are then relayed from one node to another without verification or processing.

An important difference between frame relay and X.25 is that frame relay does not guarantee reliable delivery of data. X.25 checks for errors and, in the case of an error, either corrects the damaged data or retransmits the original data. Frame relay, on the other hand, simply checks for errors. It leaves the error correction up to higher-layer protocols. Partly because it doesn't perform the same level of error correction that X.25 performs (and, thus, has less overhead), frame relay supports higher throughput than X.25. It offers throughputs between 64Kbps and 45Mbps. A frame relay customer chooses the amount of bandwidth he requires and pays for only that amount.

Both X.25 and frame relay rely on virtual circuits. **Virtual circuits** are connections between network nodes that, although based on potentially disparate physical links, logically appear to be direct, dedicated links between those nodes. One advantage to virtual circuits is their configurable use of limited bandwidth, which can make them more efficient. Several virtual circuits can be assigned to one length of cable or even to one channel on that cable. A virtual circuit uses the channel only when it needs to transmit data. Meanwhile, the channel is available for use by other virtual circuits.

X.25 and frame relay may be configured as SVCs (switched virtual circuits) or PVCs (permanent virtual circuits). **SVCs** are connections that are established when parties need to transmit, and then they are terminated when the transmission is complete. **PVCs** are connections that are established before data needs to be transmitted and maintained after the transmission is complete. Note that in a PVC, the connection is established only between the two points (the sender and receiver); the connection does not specify the exact route the data will travel. Thus, in a PVC, data may follow any number of paths from point A to point B. For example, a transmission traveling over a PVC from Baltimore to Phoenix might go from Baltimore to Washington, D.C., to Chicago, and then to Phoenix; the next transmission over that PVC, however, might go from Baltimore to Boston to St. Louis to Denver to Phoenix.

PVCs are *not* dedicated, individual links. When you lease an X.25 or frame relay circuit from your local carrier, your contract reflects the endpoints you specify and the amount of bandwidth you require between those endpoints. The service provider guarantees a minimum amount of bandwidth, called the **CIR (committed information rate)**. Provisions usually account for bursts of traffic that occasionally exceed the CIR. When you lease a PVC, you share bandwidth with the other X.25 and frame relay users on the backbone. PVC links are best suited to frequent and consistent data transmission.

The advantage to leasing a frame relay circuit over leasing a dedicated service is that you pay for only the amount of bandwidth required. Another advantage is that frame relay is less expensive than some other WAN technologies, depending on your location and its network availability. Also, frame relay is a long-established worldwide standard. Figure 7-9 illustrates a WAN using frame relay.

On the other hand, because frame relay and X.25 use shared lines, their throughput remains at the mercy of variable traffic patterns. In the middle of the night, data over your frame relay network may zip along at 1.544Mbps; during midday, when everyone is surfing the Web, it may slow down to less than your CIR. In addition, frame relay circuits are not as private (and potentially not as secure) as dedicated circuits. Nevertheless, because they use the same connectivity equipment as T-carriers, they can easily be upgraded to T-carrier dedicated lines. In all but the most remote locations, frame relay connections have been replaced with newer WAN technologies such as those described in the next section.

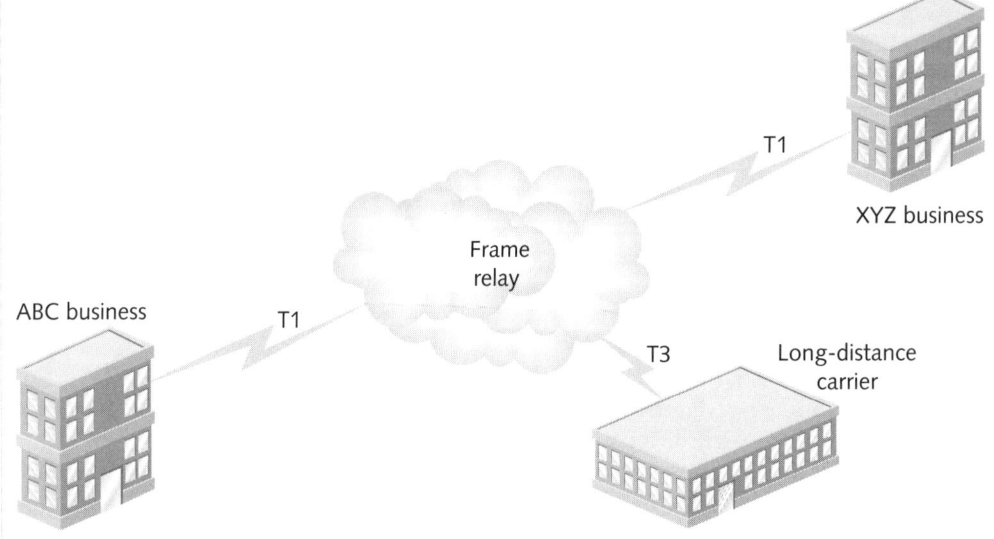

Figure 7-9 A WAN using frame relay

ISDN

ISDN (Integrated Services Digital Network) is an international standard, originally established by the ITU in 1984, for transmitting digital data over the PSTN. In North America, a standard ISDN implementation wasn't finalized until 1992, because telephone switch manufacturers couldn't agree on compatible technology for supporting ISDN. The technology's uncertain start initially made telephone companies reluctant to invest in it, and ISDN didn't catch on as quickly as predicted. However, in the 1990s ISDN finally became a popular method of connecting WAN locations to exchange both data and voice signals.

ISDN specifies protocols at the physical, data link, and transport layers of the OSI model. These protocols handle signaling, framing, connection setup and termination, routing, flow control, and error detection and correction. ISDN relies on the PSTN for its transmission medium. Connections can be either dial-up or dedicated. Dial-up ISDN is distinguished from the workstation dial-up connections discussed previously because it relies exclusively on digital transmission. In other words, it does not convert a computer's digital signals to analog before transmitting them over the PSTN. Also, ISDN is distinguished because it can simultaneously carry as many as two voice calls and one data connection on a single line. Therefore, ISDN can eliminate the need to pay for separate phone lines to support faxes, modems, and voice calls at one location.

All ISDN connections are based on two types of channels: B channels and D channels. The **B channel** is the "bearer" channel, employing circuit-switching techniques to carry voice, video, audio, and other types of data over the ISDN connection. A single B channel has a maximum throughput of 64Kbps (although it is sometimes limited to 56Kbps by the ISDN provider). The number of B channels in a single ISDN connection may vary. The **D channel** is the "data" channel, employing packet-switching techniques to carry information about the call, such as session initiation and termination signals, caller identity, call forwarding, and conference calling signals. A single D channel has a maximum throughput of 16 or 64Kbps, depending on the type of ISDN connection. Each ISDN connection uses only one D channel.

In North America, two types of ISDN connections are commonly used: BRI (Basic Rate Interface) and PRI (Primary Rate Interface). **BRI** uses two B channels and one D channel, as indicated by the notation 2B+D. The two B channels are treated as separate connections by the network and can carry voice and data or two data streams simultaneously and separate from each other. In a process called **bonding**, these two 64Kbps B channels can be combined to achieve an effective throughput of 128Kbps—the maximum amount of data traffic that a BRI connection can accommodate. Most consumers who subscribe to ISDN from home use BRI, which is the most economical type of ISDN connection.

Figure 7-10 illustrates how a typical BRI link supplies a home consumer with an ISDN link. From the telephone company's lines, the ISDN channels connect to a Network Termination 1 device at the customer's site. The **NT1 (Network Termination 1)** device connects the twisted pair wiring at the customer's building with the ISDN terminal equipment via RJ-11 (standard telephone) or RJ-45 data jacks. The ISDN **TE (terminal equipment)** may include cards or stand-alone devices used to connect computers to the ISDN line (similar to a network adapter used on Ethernet or token ring networks).

So that the ISDN line can connect to analog equipment, the signal must first pass through a terminal adapter. A **TA (terminal adapter)** converts digital signals into analog signals for use with ISDN phones and other analog devices. (Terminal adapters are sometimes called ISDN modems, though they are not, technically, modems.) Typically, telecommuters who want

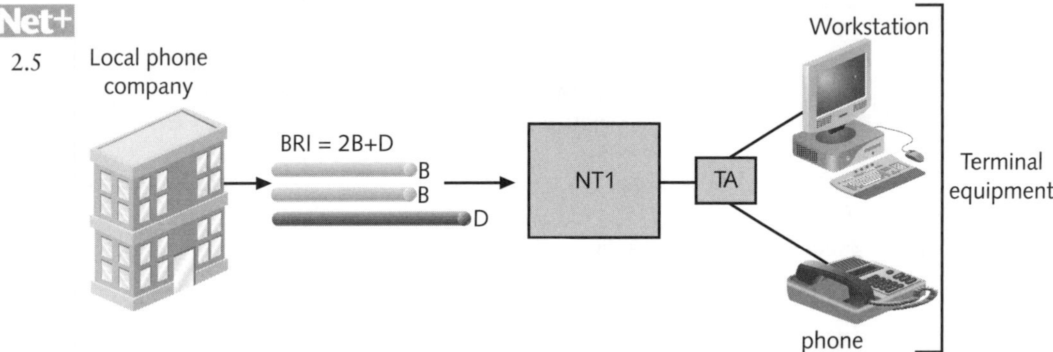

Figure 7-10 A BRI link

more throughput than their analog phone line can offer choose BRI as their ISDN connection. For a home user, the terminal adapter would most likely be an ISDN router, whereas the terminal equipment could be an Ethernet card in the user's workstation plus, perhaps, a phone.

The BRI configuration depicted in Figure 7-10 applies to installations in North America only. Because transmission standards differ in Europe and Asia, different numbers of B channels are used in ISDN connections in those regions.

PRI (Primary Rate Interface) uses 23 B channels and one 64Kbps D channel, as represented by the notation 23B+D. PRI is less commonly used by individual subscribers than BRI is, but it may be selected by businesses and other organizations that need more throughput. As with BRI, the separate B channels in a PRI link can carry voice and data, independently of each other or bonded together. The maximum potential throughput for a PRI connection is 1.544Mbps.

PRI and BRI connections may be interconnected on a single network. PRI links use the same kind of equipment as BRI links but require the services of an extra network termination device, called an **NT2 (Network Termination 2)**, to handle the multiple ISDN lines. Figure 7-11 depicts a typical PRI link as it would be installed in North America.

Individual customers who need to transmit more data than a typical modem can handle or who want to use a single line for both data and voice may use ISDN lines. ISDN, although not available in every location of the United States, can be purchased from most local

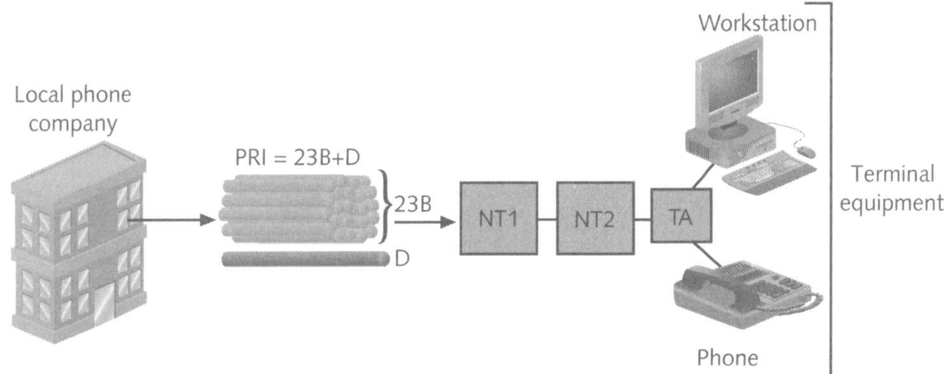

Figure 7-11 A PRI link

2.5

telephone companies. Costs vary depending on the customer's location. PRI and B-ISDN are significantly more expensive than BRI. Dial-up ISDN service is less expensive than dedicated ISDN service. In some areas, ISDN providers charge customers additional usage fees based on the total length of time they remain connected. One disadvantage of ISDN is that it can span a distance of only 18,000 linear feet before repeater equipment is needed to boost the signal. For this reason, it is only feasible to use for the local loop portion of the WAN link.

T-Carriers

2.5

Another WAN transmission method that grew from a need to transmit digital data at high speeds over the PSTN is T-carrier technology, which includes T1s, fractional T1s, and T3s. **T-carrier** standards specify a method of signaling, which means they belong to the physical layer of the OSI model. A T-carrier uses TDM (time division multiplexing) over two wire pairs (one for transmitting and one for receiving) to divide a single channel into multiple channels. For example, multiplexing enables a single T1 circuit to carry 24 channels, each capable of 64Kbps throughput; thus, a T1 has a maximum capacity of 24 × 64Kbps, or 1.544Mbps. Each channel may carry data, voice, or video signals. The medium used for T-carrier signaling can be ordinary telephone wire, fiber-optic cable, or wireless links.

AT&T developed T-carrier technology in 1957 in an effort to digitize voice signals and thereby enable such signals to travel longer distances over the PSTN. Before that time, voice signals, which were purely analog, were expensive to transmit over long distances because of the number of connectivity devices needed to keep the signal intelligible. In the 1970s, many businesses installed T1s to obtain more voice throughput per line. In the 1990s, with increased data communication demands, such as Internet access and geographically dispersed offices, T1s became a popular way to connect WAN sites.

The next section describes the various types of T-carriers; then the chapter moves on to T-carrier connectivity devices.

Types of T-Carriers

A number of T-carrier varieties are available to businesses today, as shown in Table 7-1. The most common T-carrier implementations are T1 and, for higher bandwidth needs, T3. A **T1** circuit can carry the equivalent of 24 voice or data channels, giving a maximum data

Table 7-1 Carrier Specifications

Signal Level	Carrier	Number of T1s	Number of Channels	Throughput (Mbps)
DS0	—	1/24	1	.064
DS1	T1	1	24	1.544
DS1C	T1C	2	48	3.152
DS2	T2	4	96	6.312
DS3	T3	28	672	44.736
DS4	T4	168	4,032	274.176
DS5	T5	240	5,760	400.352

throughput of 1.544Mbps. A **T3** circuit can carry the equivalent of 672 voice or data channels, giving a maximum data throughput of 44.736Mbps. (Its throughput is typically rounded up to 45Mbps for the purposes of discussion.)

The speed of a T-carrier depends on its signal level. The **signal level** refers to the T-carrier's physical layer electrical signaling characteristics as defined by ANSI standards in the early 1980s. **DS0 (digital signal, level 0)** is the equivalent of one data or voice channel. All other signal levels are multiples of DS0.

You may hear *signal level* and *carrier* terms used interchangeably—for example, DS1 and T1. In fact, T1 is the implementation of the DS1 standard used in North America and most of Asia. In Europe, the standard high-speed carrier connections are **E1** and **E3**. Like **T1s** and **T3s**, E1s and E3s use time division multiplexing. However, an E1 allows for 30 channels and offers 2.048Mbps throughput. An E3 allows for 480 channels and offers 34.368Mbps throughput. In Japan, the equivalent carrier standards are **J1** and **J3**. Like a T1, a J1 connection allows for 24 channels and offers 1.544Mbps throughput. A J3 connection allows for 480 channels and offers 32.064Mbps throughput. Using special hardware, T1s can interconnect with E1s or J1s and T3s with E3s or J3s for international communications.

As a networking professional, you are most likely to work with T1 or T3 lines. In addition to knowing their capacity, you should be familiar with their costs and uses. T1s are commonly used by businesses to connect branch offices or to connect to a carrier, such as an ISP. Telephone companies also use T1s to connect their smaller COs. ISPs may use one or more T1s or T3s, depending on the provider's size, to connect to their Internet carriers.

Because a T3 provides 28 times more throughput than a T1, many organizations may find that multiple T1s—rather than a single T3—can accommodate their throughput needs. For example, suppose a university research laboratory needs to transmit molecular images over the Internet to another university, and its peak throughput need (at any given time) is 10Mbps. The laboratory would require seven T1s (10Mbps divided by 1.544Mbps equals 6.48 T1s). Leasing seven T1s would prove much less expensive for the university than leasing a single T3.

The cost of T1s varies from region to region. On average, leasing a full T1 might cost approximately $500 to install, plus an additional $300 to $800 per month in access fees. The longer the distance between the provider (such as an ISP or a telephone company) and the subscriber, the higher a T1's monthly charge. For example, a T1 between Houston and New York will cost more than a T1 between Washington, D.C., and New York. Similarly, a T1 from a suburb of New York to the city center will cost more than a T1 from the city center to a business three blocks away.

For organizations that do not need as much as 1.544Mbps throughput, a fractional T1 might be a better option. A **fractional T1** lease allows organizations to use only some of the channels on a T1 line and be charged according to the number of channels they use. Thus, fractional T1 bandwidth can be leased in multiples of 64Kbps. A fractional T1 is best suited to businesses that expect their traffic to grow and that may require a full T1 eventually, but can't currently justify leasing a full T1.

T3s are more expensive than T1s and are used by more data-intensive businesses—for example, computer consulting firms that provide online data backups and warehousing for a number of other businesses or large long-distance carriers. A T3 might cost as much as $1,000 to install, plus monthly service fees based on usage. If a customer uses the full T3 bandwidth of

Net+
2.5

45Mbps, for example, the monthly charges might be as high as $10,000. Of course, T3 costs will vary depending on the carrier, your location, and the distance covered by the T3.

T-Carrier Connectivity

The approximate costs mentioned previously include monthly access and installation, but not connectivity hardware. Every T-carrier line requires connectivity hardware at both the customer site and the local telecommunications provider's switching facility. Connectivity hardware may be purchased or leased. If your organization uses an ISP to establish and service your T-carrier line, you will most likely lease the connectivity equipment. If you lease the line directly from the local carrier and you anticipate little change in your connectivity requirements over time, however, you might want to purchase the hardware.

T-carrier lines require specialized connectivity hardware that cannot be used with other WAN transmission methods. In addition, T-carrier lines require different media, depending on their throughput. In the following sections, you will learn about the physical components of a T-carrier connection between a customer site and a local carrier.

Wiring As mentioned earlier, the T-carrier system is based on AT&T's original attempt to digitize existing long-distance PSTN lines. T1 technology can use UTP or STP (unshielded or shielded twisted pair) copper wiring—in other words, plain telephone wire—coaxial cable, microwave, or fiber-optic cable as its transmission media. Because the digital signals require a clean connection (that is, one less susceptible to noise and attenuation), STP is preferable to UTP. For T1s using STP, repeaters must regenerate the signal approximately every 6,000 feet. Twisted pair wiring cannot adequately carry the high throughput of multiple T1s or T3 transmissions. Thus, for multiple T1s, coaxial cable, microwave, or fiber-optic cabling may be used. For T3s, microwave or fiber-optic cabling is necessary.

Net+
2.5
2.8

Smart Jack At the customer's demarc (demarcation point), either inside or outside the building, T-carrier wire pairs terminate with a **smart jack**. (Smart jacks are one type of NIU.) In addition to terminating the line, a smart jack functions as a monitoring point for the connection. If the line between the carrier and customer experiences significant data errors, the smart jack will report this fact to the carrier. Technicians can also check the status of the line at the smart jack. Most include LEDs associated with transmitted and received signals. For example, a steady green light on the display indicates no connectivity problems, while a flickering light indicates data errors. A power light indicates whether or not the smart jack is receiving any signal. Figure 7-12 shows a smart jack (or network interface) designed to be used with a T1.

The smart jack is not capable of interpreting data, however. For that, the T-carrier signals depend on a CSU/DSU.

Net+
2.5
3.2

CSU/DSU (Channel Service Unit/Data Service Unit) Although CSUs (channel service units) and DSUs (data service units) are actually two separate devices, they are typically combined into a single stand-alone device or an interface card called a **CSU/DSU**. The CSU/DSU is the connection point for a T1 line at the customer's site. The **CSU** provides termination for the digital signal and ensures connection integrity through error correction and line monitoring. The **DSU** converts the T-carrier frames into frames the LAN can interpret and vice versa. It also connects T-carrier lines with terminating equipment. Finally, a DSU usually incorporates a multiplexer. (In some T-carrier installations, the multiplexer can be a separate device connected to the DSU.) For an incoming T-carrier line, the multiplexer

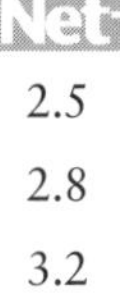

2.5

2.8

3.2

Figure 7-12 A T1 smart jack

separates its combined channels into individual signals that can be interpreted on the LAN. For an outgoing T-carrier line, the multiplexer combines multiple signals from a LAN for transport over the T-carrier. After being demultiplexed, an incoming T-carrier signal passes on to devices collectively known as terminal equipment. Examples of terminal equipment include switches, routers, or telephone exchange devices that accept only voice transmissions (such as a telephone switch).

Figure 7-13 shows a stand-alone CSU/DSU.

Figure 7-14 depicts a typical use of smart jacks and CSU/DSUs with a point-to-point T1-connected WAN. In the following sections, you will learn how routers and switches integrate with CSU/DSUs and multiplexers to connect T-carriers to a LAN.

Terminal Equipment On a typical T1-connected data network, the terminal equipment consists of switches, routers, or bridges. Usually, a router or Layer 3 or higher switch is the best option because these devices can translate between different Layer 3 protocols that might be used on the WAN and LAN. The router or switch accepts incoming signals

Figure 7-13 A CSU/DSU

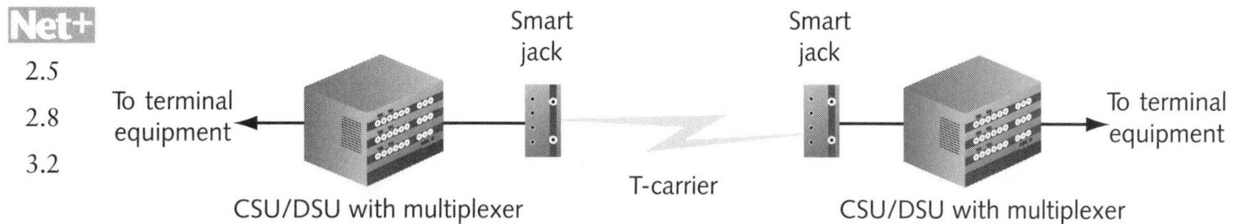

Figure 7-14 A point-to-point T-carrier connection

from a CSU/DSU and, if necessary, translates network layer protocols and then directs data to its destination exactly as it does on any LAN.

On some implementations, the CSU/DSU is not a separate device but is integrated with the router or switch as an expansion card. Compared to a stand-alone CSU/DSU, which must connect to the terminal equipment via a cable, an integrated CSU/DSU offers faster signal processing and better network performance. In most cases, it is also a less expensive and lower-maintenance solution than using a separate CSU/DSU device. Figure 7-15 illustrates one way a router with an integrated CSU/DSU can be used to connect a LAN with a T1 WAN link.

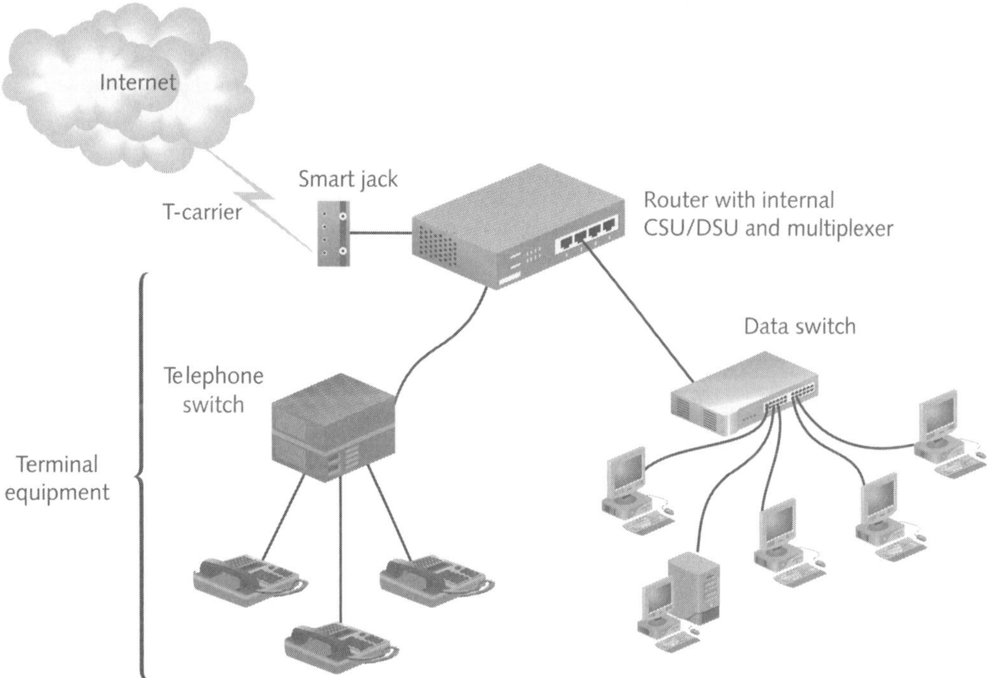

Figure 7-15 A T-carrier connecting to a LAN through a router

DSL

DSL (digital subscriber line) is a WAN connection method introduced by researchers at Bell Laboratories in the mid-1990s. It operates over the PSTN and competes directly with ISDN and T1 services. Like ISDN, DSL can span only limited distances without the help of repeaters

and is, therefore, best suited to the local loop portion of a WAN link. Also, like its competitors, DSL can support multiple data and voice channels over a single line.

DSL uses advanced data modulation techniques (at the physical layer of the OSI model) to achieve extraordinary throughput over regular telephone lines. To understand how DSL and voice signals can share the same line, it's helpful to recall that telephone lines carry voice signals over a very small range of frequencies, between 300 and 3,300Hz. This leaves higher, inaudible frequencies unused and available for carrying data. Also recall that in data modulation, a data signal alters the properties of a carrier signal. Depending on its version, DSL connection may use a modulation technique based on amplitude or phase modulation. However, in DSL, modulation follows more complex patterns than the modulation you learned about earlier in this book. The details of DSL modulation techniques are beyond the scope of this book. However, you should understand that the types of modulation used by a DSL version affect its throughput and the distance its signals can travel before requiring a repeater. The following section describes the different versions of DSL.

Types of DSL

The term **xDSL** refers to all DSL varieties, of which at least eight currently exist. The better-known DSL varieties include ADSL (Asymmetric DSL), G.Lite (a version of ADSL), HDSL (High Bit-Rate DSL), SDSL (Symmetric or Single-Line DSL), VDSL (Very High Bit-Rate DSL), and SHDSL (Single-Line High Bit-Rate DSL)—the *x* in *xDSL* is replaced by the variety name. DSL types can be divided into two categories: asymmetrical and symmetrical.

To understand the difference between these two categories, you must understand the concepts of downstream and upstream data transmission. The term **downstream** refers to data traveling from the carrier's switching facility to the customer. **Upstream** refers to data traveling from the customer to the carrier's switching facility. In some types of DSL, the throughput rates for downstream and upstream traffic differ. In other words, if you were connected to the Internet via a DSL link, you could download images from the Internet more rapidly than you could upload them because the downstream throughput would be greater. A technology that offers more throughput in one direction than in the other is considered **asymmetrical**. In asymmetrical communications, downstream throughput is higher than upstream throughput. Asymmetrical communication is well suited to users who receive more information from the network than they send to it—for example, people watching videoconferences or people surfing the Web. ADSL and VDSL are examples of **asymmetrical DSL**.

Conversely, **symmetrical** technology provides equal capacity for data traveling both upstream and downstream. Symmetrical transmission is suited to users who both upload and download significant amounts of data—for example, a bank's branch office that sends large volumes of account information to the central server at the bank's headquarters and, in turn, receives large amounts of account information from the central server at the bank's headquarters. HDSL, SDSL, and SHDSL are examples of **symmetrical DSL**.

DSL versions also differ in the type of modulation they use. Some, such as the popular full-rate ADSL and VDSL, create multiple narrow channels in the higher frequency range to carry more data. For these versions, a splitter must be installed at the carrier and at the customer's premises to separate the data signal from the voice signal before it reaches the terminal equipment (for example, the phone or the computer). G.Lite, a slower and less expensive version of ADSL, eliminates the splitter but requires the use of a filter to prevent high-frequency DSL signals from reaching the telephone. Other types of DSL, such as HDSL and SDSL, cannot use the same wire pair that is used for voice signals. Instead, these types of DSL use the extra pair of wires contained in a telephone cable (that are otherwise typically unused).

The types of DSL also vary in terms of their capacity and maximum line length. A VDSL line that carries as much as 52Mbps in one direction and as much as 6.4Mbps in the opposite direction can extend only a maximum of 1,000 feet between the customer's premises and the carrier's switching facility. This limitation might suit businesses located close to a telephone company's CO (for example, in the middle of a metropolitan area), but it won't work for most individuals. The most popular form of DSL, ADSL, provides a maximum of 6.144Mbps downstream and a maximum of 640Kbps upstream. However, the distance between the customer and the central office affects the actual throughput a customer experiences. Close to the central office, DSL achieves its highest maximum throughput. The farther away the customer's premises, the lower the throughput. In the case of ADSL, a customer 9,000 feet from the central office can potentially experience ADSL's maximum potential throughput of 6.144Mbps downstream. At 18,000 feet away, the farthest allowable distance, the customer will experience as little as 1.544Mbps throughput. Still, this throughput and this distance (approximately 3.4 miles) renders ADSL suitable for most telecommuters. Table 7-2 compares current specifications for six DSL types.

Published distance limitations and throughput can vary from one service provider to another, depending on how far the provider is willing to guarantee a particular level of service. In addition, service providers may limit each user's maximum throughput based on terms of the service agreement.

In addition to their data modulation techniques, capacity, and distance limitations, DSL types vary according to how they use the PSTN. Next, you will learn about how DSL connects to a business or residence over the PSTN.

DSL Connectivity

This section follows the path of an ADSL connection from a home computer, through the local loop, and to the telecommunications carrier's switching facility. Although variations exist, this describes the most common implementation of DSL.

Table 7-2 Comparison of DSL Types

DSL Type	Maximum Upstream Throughput (Mbps)	Maximum Downstream Throughput (Mbps)	Distance Limitation (Feet)
ADSL ("full rate")	0.640	6.144	18,000
G.Lite (a type of ADSL)	0.512	1.544	25,000
HDSL or HDSL-2	1.544 or 2.048	1.544 or 2.048	18,000 or 12,000
SDSL	1.544	1.544	12,000
SHDSL	2.36 or 4.7	2.36 or 4.7	26,000 or 18,000
VDSL	1.6, 3.2, or 6.4	12.9, 25.9, or 51.8	1,000–4,500

Net+

2.5

Suppose you have an ADSL connection at home. One evening you open your Web browser and request the home page of your favorite sports team to find the last game's score. As you know, the first step in this process is establishing a TCP connection with the team's Web server. Your TCP request message leaves your computer's NIC and travels over your home network to a DSL modem. A **DSL modem** is a device that modulates outgoing signals and demodulates incoming DSL signals. Thus, it contains receptacles to connect both to your incoming telephone line and to your computer or network connectivity device. Because you are using ADSL, the DSL modem also contains a splitter to separate incoming voice and data signals. The DSL modem may be external or internal (as an expansion card, for example) to the computer. If external, it may connect to a computer's NIC via an RJ-45, USB, or wireless interface. If your home network contains more than one computer and you want all computers to share the DSL bandwidth, the DSL modem must connect to a device such as a hub, switch, or router, instead of just one computer. In fact, rather than using two separate devices, you could buy a router that combines DSL modem functionalities with the ability to connect multiple computers and share DSL bandwidth. A DSL modem is shown in Figure 7-16.

When your request arrives at the DSL modem, it is modulated according to the ADSL specifications. Then the DSL modem forwards the modulated signal to your local loop—the lines that connect your home with the rest of the PSTN. For the first stretch of the local loop, the signal continues over four-pair UTP wire. At some distance less than 18,000 feet, it is combined with other modulated signals in a telephone switch, usually at a remote switching facility. (To accept DSL signals, your telecommunications carrier must have newer digital switching equipment. In the few remaining locales where carriers have not updated their switching equipment, DSL service is not available.)

Inside the carrier's remote switching facility, a splitter separates your line's data signal from any voice signals that are also carried on the line. Next, your request is sent to a device called a **DSLAM (DSL access multiplexer)**, which aggregates multiple DSL subscriber lines and connects them to the carrier's CO. Finally, your request is issued from your carrier's network to the Internet backbone, as pictured in Figure 7-17. The request travels over the Internet until it reaches your sports team's Web server. Barring line problems and Internet congestion, the entire journey happens in a fraction of a second. After your team's Web server accepts the connection request, the data follows the same path, but in reverse.

Telecommunications carriers and manufacturers have positioned DSL as a competitor for T1, ISDN, and broadband cable services. The installation, hardware, and monthly access costs for DSL are slightly less than those for ISDN lines and significantly less than the cost for T1s. (At the time of this writing, ADSL costs approximately $30 per month in the United States.)

One drawback to DSL is that it is not available in all areas of the United States, either because carriers have not upgraded their switching equipment or because customers do not

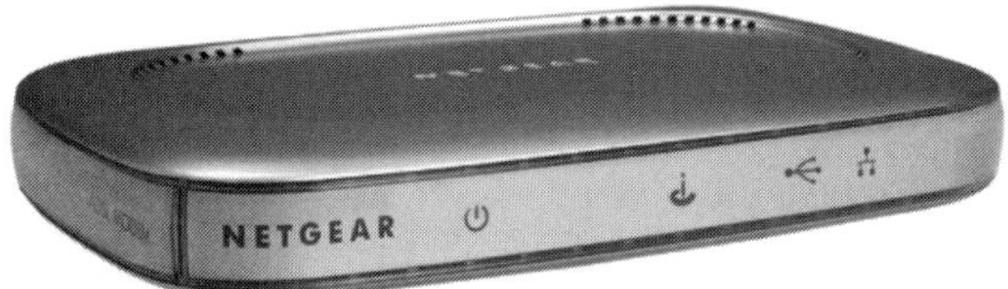

Figure 7-16 A DSL modem

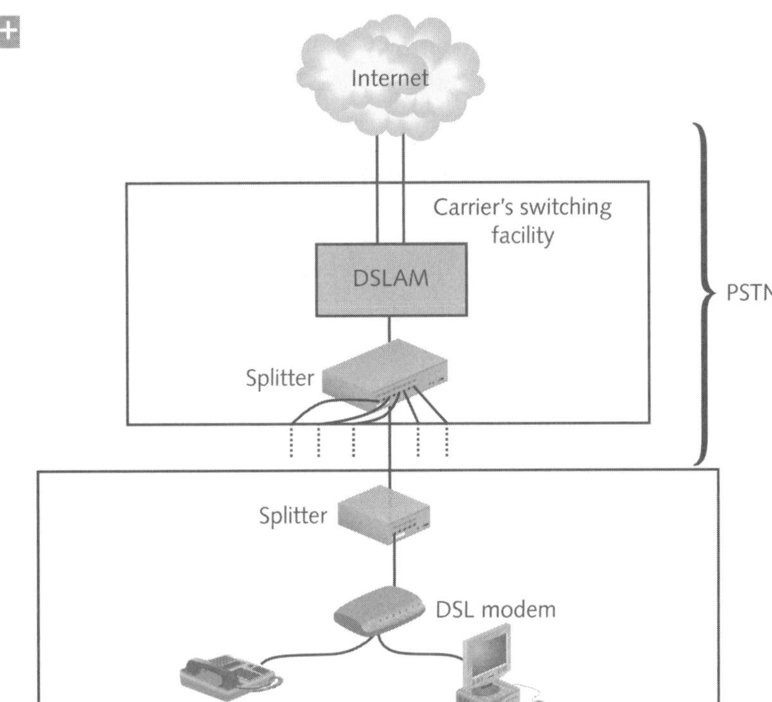

Figure 7-17 A DSL connection

reside within the service's distance limitations. Also, generally speaking, DSL throughput rates, especially upstream, are lower than broadband cable, its main competition among residential customers. For these reasons, more consumers in the United States use cable for broadband Internet access service.

Broadband Cable

While local and long-distance phone companies strive to make DSL the preferred method of Internet access for consumers, cable companies are pushing their own connectivity option. This option, called **broadband cable** or **cable modem access**, is based on the coaxial cable wiring used for TV signals. Such wiring can theoretically transmit as much as 150Mbps downstream and as much as 10Mbps upstream. Thus, broadband cable is an asymmetrical technology. However, actual broadband cable throughput is typically limited (or throttled) by the cable companies and further diminished by the fact that physical connections are shared. Customers might be allowed, at most, 10Mbps downstream and 2Mbps upstream throughput. During peak times of use, they might see data rates of 3Mbps downstream and 1Mbps upstream, for example. The asymmetry of broadband cable makes it a logical choice for users who want to surf the Web or download data from a network.

Broadband cable connections require that the customer use a special **cable modem,** a device that modulates and demodulates signals for transmission and reception via cable wiring.

Net+
2.5

Cable modems operate at the physical and data link layer of the OSI model, and, therefore, do not manipulate higher-layer protocols, such as IP. The cable modem then connects to a customer's PC via an RJ-45, USB, or wireless interface to a NIC. Alternately, the cable modem could connect to a connectivity device, such as a hub, switch, or router, thereby supplying bandwidth to a LAN rather than to just one computer. It's also possible to use a device that combines cable modem functionality with a router; this single device can then provide both the broadband cable connection and the capability of sharing the bandwidth between multiple nodes. Figure 7-18 provides an example of a cable modem.

Before customers can subscribe to broadband cable, however, their local cable company must have the necessary infrastructure. Traditional cable TV networks supply the infrastructure for downstream communication (the TV programming), but not for upstream communication. To provide Internet access through its network, the cable company must have upgraded its equipment to support bidirectional, digital communications. For starters, the cable company's network wiring must be replaced with **HFC (hybrid fiber-coax)**, an expensive fiber-optic link that can support high frequencies. The HFC connects the cable company's offices to a node location near the customer. Most large cable companies, such as Comcast and Charter, long ago upgraded their infrastructure to use HFC. Either fiber-optic or coaxial cable may connect the node to the customer's business or residence via a connection known as a **cable drop**. All cable drops for the cable subscribers in the same neighborhood connect to the local node. These nodes then connect to the cable company's central office, which is known as its **head-end**. At the head-end, the cable company can connect to the Internet through a variety of means (often via fiber-optic cable), or it can pick up digital satellite or microwave transmissions. The head-end can transmit data to as many as 1,000 subscribers, in a one-to-many communication system. Figure 7-19 illustrates the infrastructure of a cable system.

Like DSL, broadband cable provides a dedicated, or continuous, connection that does not require dialing up a service provider. Unlike DSL, broadband cable requires many subscribers to share the same local line, thus raising concerns about security and actual (versus theoretical) throughput. For example, if your cable company supplied you and five of your neighbors with broadband cable services, your neighbors could, with some technical prowess, capture the data that you transmit to the Internet. (Modern cable networks provide encryption for data traveling to and from customer premises; however, these encryption schemes can be thwarted.) Moreover, the throughput of a cable line is fixed. As with any fixed resource, the

Figure 7-18 A cable modem

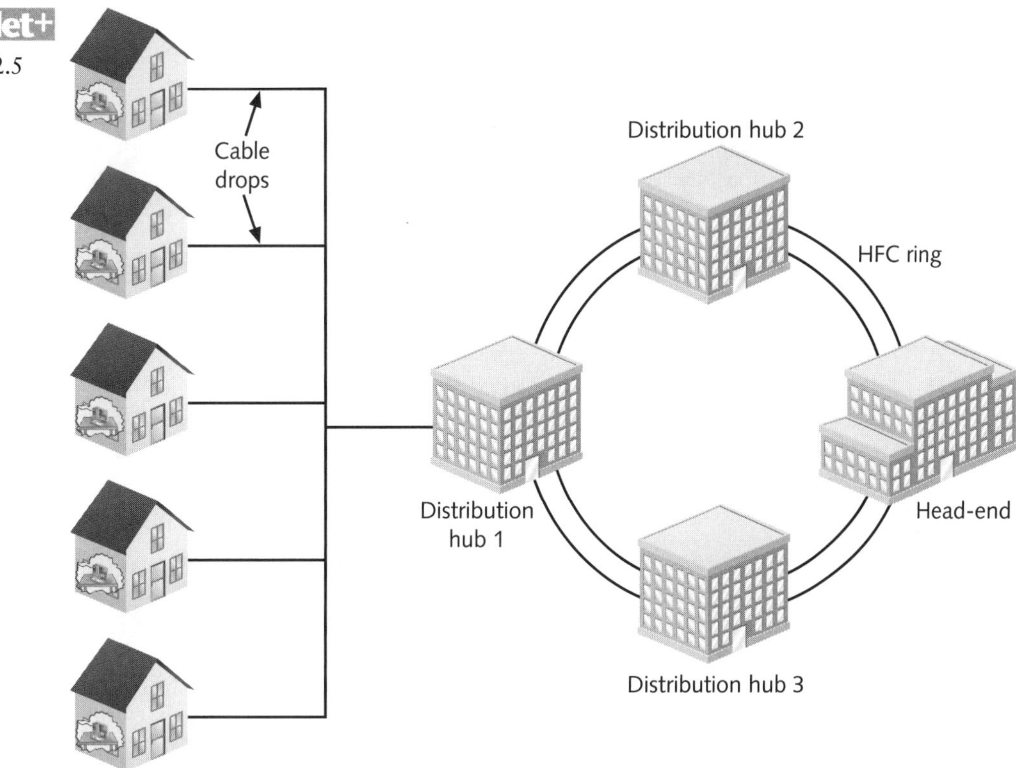

Figure 7-19 Cable infrastructure

more one claims, the less that is left for others. In other words, the greater the number of users sharing a single line, the less throughput available to each user. Cable companies counter this perceived disadvantage by rightly claiming that at some point (for example, at a remote switching facility or at the DSLAM interface), a telecommunications carrier's DSL bandwidth is also fixed and shared among a group of customers.

As mentioned earlier, cable broadband access continues to service the majority of residential customers, whereas DSL is more popular among business customers. Now, however, since the cost of DSL has decreased, the rate of new DSL and broadband cable installations is nearly identical. In the United States, broadband cable access costs approximately $45 per month for customers who already subscribe to cable TV service. Broadband cable is less often used in businesses than DSL, primarily because most office buildings do not contain a coaxial cable infrastructure.

ATM (Asynchronous Transfer Mode)

So far you have learned about several WAN transmission methods, such as ISDN, T-carriers, and DSL, that achieve high throughput by manipulating signals at the physical layer. You also learned about some, such as X.25 and frame relay, that operate at the data link layer. **ATM**

(Asynchronous Transfer Mode) is a third WAN technology that functions in the data link layer. Its ITU standard prescribes both network access and signal multiplexing techniques. **Asynchronous** refers to a communications method in which nodes do not have to conform to any predetermined schemes that specify the timing of data transmissions. In asynchronous communications, a node can transmit at any instant, and the destination node must accept the transmission as it comes. To ensure that the receiving node knows when it has received a complete frame, asynchronous communications provide start and stop bits for each character transmitted. When the receiving node recognizes a start bit, it begins to accept a new character. When it receives the stop bit for that character, it ceases to look for the end of that character's transmission. Asynchronous data transmission, therefore, occurs in random stops and starts.

ATM was first conceived by researchers at Bell Labs in the early 1980s, but it took a dozen years before standards organizations could reach an agreement on its specifications. ATM may run over fiber-optic cable or Cat 5 or higher UTP or STP cable. Though less popular now than in the late 1990s, ATM may still be found on WANs, particularly those owned by large, public telecommunication carriers.

Like Ethernet, ATM specifies data link layer framing techniques. But what sets ATM apart from Ethernet is its fixed packet size. In ATM, a packet is called a **cell** and always consists of 48 bytes of data plus a 5-byte header. This fixed-sized, 53-byte packet allows ATM to provide predictable network performance. However, recall that a smaller packet size requires more overhead. In fact, ATM's smaller packet size does decrease its potential throughput, but the efficiency of using cells compensates for that loss.

Like X.25 and frame relay, ATM relies on virtual circuits. On an ATM network, switches determine the optimal path between the sender and receiver and then establish this path before the network transmits data. Because ATM packages data into cells before transmission, each of which travels separately to its destination, ATM is typically considered a packet-switching technology. At the same time, the use of virtual circuits means that ATM provides the main advantage of circuit switching—that is, a point-to-point connection that remains reliably available to the transmission until it completes, making ATM a connection-oriented technology.

Establishing a reliable connection allows ATM to guarantee a specific QoS (quality of service) for certain transmissions. ATM networks can supply four QoS levels, from a "best effort" attempt for noncritical data to a guaranteed, real-time transmission for time-sensitive data. This is important for organizations using networks for time-sensitive applications, such as video and audio transmissions. For example, a company that wants to use its physical connection between two offices located at opposite sides of a state to carry voice phone calls might choose the ATM network technology with the highest possible QoS. On the other hand, the company might assign a low QoS to routine e-mail messages exchanged between the two offices. Without QoS guarantees, cells belonging to the same message may arrive in the wrong order or too slowly to be properly interpreted by the receiving node.

ATM's developers have made certain it is compatible with other leading network technologies. Its cells can support multiple types of higher-layer protocols. In addition, the ATM networks can be integrated with Ethernet or token ring networks through the use of **LANE (LAN Emulation)**. LANE encapsulates incoming Ethernet or token ring frames and then converts them into ATM cells for transmission over an ATM network.

2.5

ATM's throughput potential rivals any other described in this chapter, ranging from 25Mbps to 622Mbps. When leasing ATM connections, you can choose to pay for only as much throughput as you think you'll need. This also allows you to tailor your desired QoS.

Currently, ATM is relatively expensive, is rarely used on small LANs, and is almost never used to connect typical workstations to a network. Gigabit Ethernet, a cheaper technology, has replaced ATM on many networks. In addition to its lower cost, Gigabit Ethernet is a more natural upgrade for the multitude of Fast Ethernet users. It overcomes the QoS issue by simply providing a larger pipe for the greater volume of traffic using the network. Although ATM caught on among the very largest carriers in the late 1990s, most networking professionals have followed the Gigabit Ethernet standard rather than spending extra dollars on ATM infrastructure.

Where ATM is still used, it's often deployed over the popular SONET WAN technology, discussed next.

SONET (Synchronous Optical Network)

2.5

SONET (Synchronous Optical Network) is a high-bandwidth WAN signaling technique developed by Bell Communications Research in the 1980s and later standardized by ANSI and ITU. SONET specifies framing and multiplexing techniques at the physical layer of the OSI model. Its four key strengths are that it can integrate many other WAN technologies, it offers fast data transfer rates, it allows for simple link additions and removals, and it provides a high degree of fault tolerance. (The word **synchronous** as used in the name of this technology means that data being transmitted and received by nodes must conform to a timing scheme. A clock maintains time for all nodes on a network. A receiving node in synchronous communications recognizes that it should be receiving data by looking at the time on the clock.)

Perhaps the most important SONET advantage is that it provides interoperability. Before SONET, telecommunications carriers that used different signaling techniques (or even the same technique but different equipment) could not be assured that their networks could communicate. Now, SONET is often used to aggregate multiple T1s, T3s, or ISDN lines. SONET is also used as the underlying technology for ATM transmission. Furthermore, because it can work directly with the different standards used in different countries, SONET has emerged as the best choice for linking WANs between North America, Europe, and Asia. Internationally, SONET is known as **SDH (Synchronous Digital Hierarchy)**.

SONET's extraordinary fault tolerance results from its use of a double-ring topology over fiber-optic cable. In this type of layout, one ring acts as the primary route for data, transmitting in a clockwise direction. The second ring acts as a backup, transmitting data counterclockwise around the ring. If, for example, a backhoe operator severs the primary ring, SONET would automatically reroute traffic to the backup ring without any loss of service. This characteristic, known as **self-healing**, makes SONET very reliable. (To lower the potential for a single accident to sever both rings, the cables that make up each ring should not lay adjacent to each other.) Figure 7-20 illustrates a SONET ring and its dual-fiber connections.

A SONET ring begins and ends at the telecommunications carrier's facility. In between, it connects an organization's multiple WAN sites in a ring fashion. It may also connect with

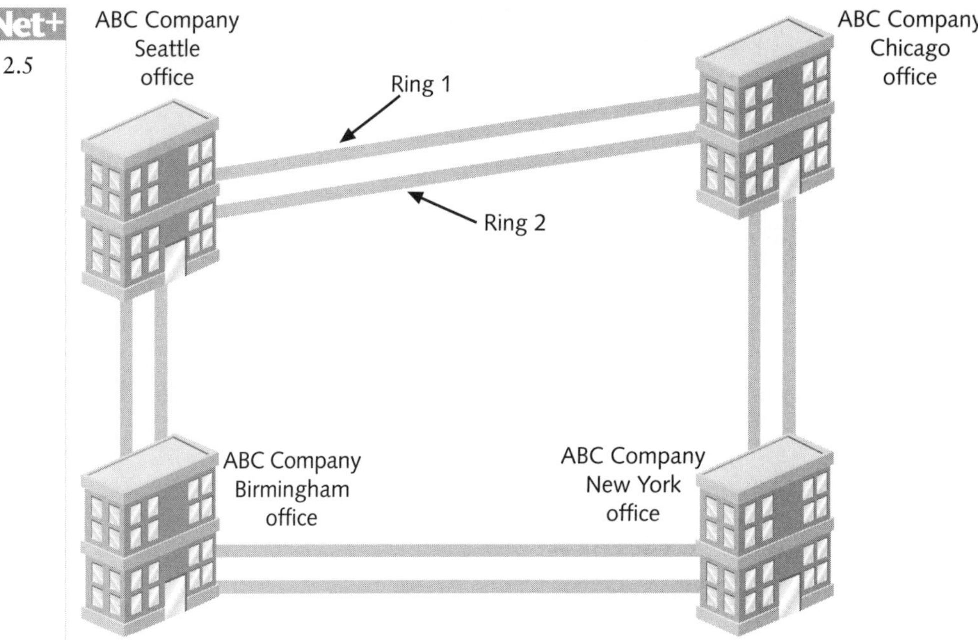

Figure 7-20 A SONET ring

multiple carrier facilities for additional fault tolerance. Companies can lease an entire SONET ring from a telecommunications carrier, or they can lease part of a SONET ring—for example, a circuit that offers T1 throughput—to take advantage of SONET's reliability.

At both the carrier and the customer premises, a SONET ring terminates at a multiplexer. A multiplexer combines individual SONET signals on the transmitting end, and another multiplexer separates combined signals on the receiving end. On the transmitting end, multiplexers accept input from different network types (for example, a T1 or ISDN line) and format the data in a standard SONET frame. That means that many different devices might connect to a SONET multiplexer, including, for example, a private telephone switch, a T1 multiplexer, and an ATM data switch. On the receiving end, multiplexers translate the incoming signals back into their original format. Most SONET multiplexers allow for easy additions or removals of connections to the SONET ring, which makes this technology easily adaptable to growing and changing networks. Figure 7-21 shows the devices necessary to connect a WAN site with a SONET ring. This is the simplest type of SONET connection; however, variations abound.

The data rate of a particular SONET ring is indicated by its **OC (Optical Carrier)** level, a rating that is internationally recognized by networking professionals and standards organizations. OC levels in SONET are analogous to the digital signal levels of T1s. Table 7-3 lists the OC levels and their maximum throughput.

SONET technology is typically not implemented by small or medium-sized businesses because of its high cost. It is commonly used, for example, by large companies; long-distance companies linking metropolitan areas and countries; ISPs that want to guarantee fast, reliable

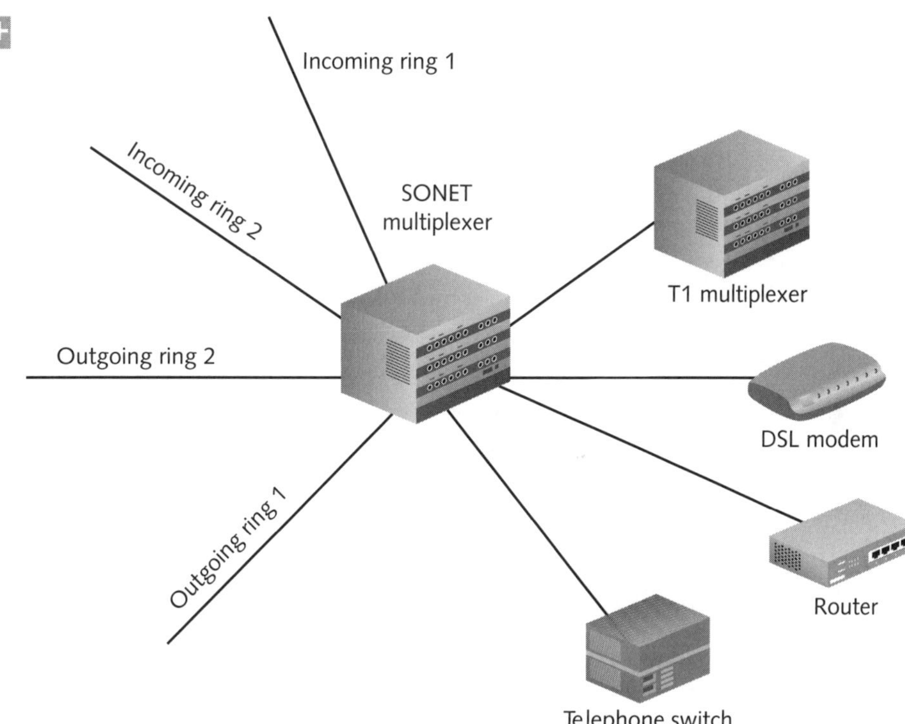

Figure 7-21 SONET connectivity

Table 7-3 SONET OC Levels

OC Level	Throughput (Mbps)
OC1	51.84
OC3	155.52
OC12	622
OC24	1,244
OC48	2,488
OC96	4,976
OC192	9,953
OC768	39,813

access to the Internet; or telephone companies connecting their COs. SONET is particularly suited to audio, video, and imaging data transmission. As you can imagine, given its reliance on fiber-optic cable and its redundancy requirements, SONET technology is expensive to implement.

2.5

WAN Technologies Compared

You have learned that WAN links offer a wide range of throughputs, from 56Kbps for a PSTN dial-up connection to potentially 39.8Gbps for a full-speed SONET connection. Table 7-4 summarizes the media and throughputs offered by each technology discussed in this chapter. Bear in mind that each technology's transmission techniques (for example, switching for frame relay versus point-to-point for T1) will affect real throughput, so the maximum transmission speed is a theoretical limit. Actual transmission speeds will vary. In addition, this table omits wireless and satellite WAN technologies, which are discussed in the next chapter.

Table 7-4 A Comparison of WAN Technology Throughputs

WAN Technology	Typical Media	Maximum Throughput
Dial-up over PSTN	UTP or STP	56Kbps theoretical; actual limit is 53Kbps
X.25	UTP/STP (DS1 or DS3)	64Kbps or 2.048Mbps
Frame relay	UTP/STP (DS1 or DS3)	45Mbps
BRI (ISDN)	UTP/STP (PSTN)	128Kbps
PRI (ISDN)	UTP/STP (PSTN)	1.544Mbps
T1	UTP/STP (PSTN), microwave, or fiber-optic cable	1.544Mbps
Fractional T1	UTP/STP (PSTN), microwave, or fiber-optic cable	n times 64Kbps (where n = number of channels leased)
T3	Microwave link or fiber-optic cable	45Mbps
xDSL	UTP/STP (PSTN)	Theoretically, 1.544Mbps–52Mbps (depending on the type), but typical residential DSL throughputs are limited to 1.5Mbps
Broadband cable	Hybrid fiber-coaxial cable	Theoretically, 56Mbps downstream, 10Mbps upstream, but actual throughputs are approximately 1.5–3Mbps upstream and 256–768Kbps downstream
ATM	Fiber-optic cable, UTP/STP (PSTN)	25Mbps to 622Mbps (depending on the customer's preferred bit rate)
SONET	Fiber-optic cable	51, 155, 622, 1,244, 2,488, 4,976, 9,952, or 39,813Mbps (depending on the OC level)

2.5

Remote Connectivity

Most of the connectivity examples you've learned about thus far assume that a WAN site has continuous, dedicated access to the WAN. For example, when a user in Phoenix wants to open a document on a server in Dallas, she needs only to find the Dallas server on her network, open a directory on the Dallas server, and then open the file. The server is available to her at any time, because the Phoenix and Dallas offices are always connected and sharing resources over the WAN. However, this is not the only way to share resources over a WAN. For remote users (such as employees on the road, off-campus students, telecommuters, or staff in small, branch offices), intermittent access with a choice of connectivity methods is often more appropriate.

As a remote user, you can connect to a LAN via **remote access**, a service that allows a client to connect with and log on to a LAN or WAN in a different geographical location. After connecting, a remote client can access files, applications, and other shared resources, such as printers, like any other client on the LAN or WAN. To communicate via remote access, the client and host need a transmission path plus the appropriate software to complete the connection and exchange data.

Many remote access methods exist, and they vary according to the type of transmission technology, clients, hosts, and software they can or must use. Popular remote access techniques, including dial-up networking, Microsoft's RAS (Remote Access Service) or RRAS (Routing and Remote Access Service), and VPNs (virtual private networks), are described in the following sections. You will also learn about common remote access protocols.

Dial-Up Networking

Dial-up networking refers to dialing directly into a private network's or ISP's remote access server to log on to a network. Dial-up clients can use PSTN, X.25, or ISDN transmission methods. As discussed earlier in this chapter, however, the term *dial-up networking* usually refers to a connection between computers using the PSTN—that is, regular telephone lines. To accept client connections, the remote access server is attached to a group of modems, all of which are associated with one phone number. The client must run dial-up software (normally available with the operating system) to initiate the connection. At the same time, the remote access server runs specialized software to accept and interpret the incoming signals. When it receives a request for connection, the remote access server software presents the remote user with a prompt for his **credentials**—typically, his user name and password. The server compares his credentials with those in its database, in a process known as **authentication**. If the credentials match, the user is allowed to log on to the network. Thereafter, the remote user can perform the same functions he could perform while working at a client computer in the office. With the proper server hardware and software, a remote access server can offer multiple users simultaneous remote access to the LAN. Though less popular than it was in the 1990s, some Internet subscribers still use dial-up networking to connect to their ISP.

Advantages to using dial-up networking are that the technology is well understood and its software comes with virtually every operating system. Within the United States, the dial-up configuration for one location differs little from the dial-up configuration in another location. And nearly all mobile personal computers contain a modem, the only peripheral hardware a computer requires to establish this type of connection.

However, a dial-up connection via the PSTN comes with significant disadvantages, with the worst being its low throughput. Currently, manufacturers of PSTN modems advertise a connection speed of 56Kbps. But the 56Kbps maximum is only a *theoretical* threshold that

2.5

assumes a pristine connection between the initiator and the receiver. Splitters, fax machines, or other devices that a signal must navigate between the sender and receiver all reduce the actual throughput. The number of switching facilities and modems through which your phone call travels also affects throughput. Each time the signal passes through a switch or is converted from analog to digital or digital to analog, it loses a little throughput. If you're surfing the Web, for example, by the time a Web page returns to you, the connection may have lost from 5 to 30Kbps, and your effective throughput might have been reduced to 30Kbps or less. In addition, the FCC (Federal Communications Commission), the regulatory agency that sets standards and policy for telecommunications transmission and equipment in the United States, limits the use of PSTN lines to 53Kbps to reduce the effects of cross talk. Thus, you will never actually achieve full 56Kbps throughput using a dial-up connection over the PSTN.

Nor can dial-up networking provide the quality required by many network applications. The quality of a WAN connection is largely determined by how many data packets that it loses or that become corrupt during transmission, how quickly it can transmit and receive data, and whether it drops the connection altogether. To improve this quality, most protocols employ error-checking techniques. For example, TCP/IP depends on acknowledgments of the data it receives. In addition, many (though not all) PSTN links are now digital, and digital lines are more reliable than the older analog lines. Such digital lines reduce the quality problems that once plagued purely analog PSTN connections.

From a network administrator's point of view, dial-up networking also requires a significant amount of maintenance to make sure clients can always connect to a pool of modems. One way to limit the maintenance burden is for an organization to contract with an ISP to supply remote access services. In this arrangement, clients dial into the ISP's remote access server, and then the ISP connects the incoming clients with the organization's network.

2.5

6.3

The dial-up networking software that Microsoft provided with its Windows 95, 98, NT, and 2000 client operating systems is called **RAS (Remote Access Service)**. For the Network+ exam, you will need to be familiar with the term *RAS* and be aware that, as with other dial-up networking services, RAS requires software installed on both the client and server, a server configured to accept incoming clients, and a client with sufficient privileges (including user name and password) on the server to access its resources. In the Windows 2000 Server, XP, Vista, Server 2003, and Server 2008 operating systems, RAS is part of a more comprehensive remote access package called the RRAS (Routing and Remote Access Service). RRAS is described in the following section.

Remote Access Servers

The previous section described dial-up networking, a type of remote access method defined by its direct, PSTN-based connection method. However, users who previously depended on dial-up connections are increasingly adopting broadband connections, such as DSL and cable. This section and following sections describe services that can accept remote access connections from a client, no matter what type of Internet access it uses.

As you have learned, remote access allows a client that is not directly attached to a LAN or WAN to connect and log on to that network. A remote client attempting to connect to a LAN or WAN requires a server to accept its connection and grant it privileges to the network's resources. Many types of remote access servers exist. Some are devices dedicated

Net+

2.5

6.3

to this task, such as Cisco's AS5800 access servers. These devices run software that, in conjunction with their operating system, performs authentication for clients and communicates via dial-up networking protocols. Other types of remote access servers are computers installed with special software that enables them to accept incoming client connections and grant them access to resources.

RRAS (Routing and Remote Access Service) is Microsoft's remote access software available with the Windows Server 2003 and Server 2008 network operating systems and the Windows XP and Vista client operating systems. RRAS enables a computer to accept multiple remote client connections over any type of transmission path. It also enables the server to act as a router, determining where to direct incoming packets across the network. Further, RRAS incorporates multiple security provisions to ensure that data cannot be intercepted and interpreted by anyone other than the intended recipient and to ensure that only authorized clients can connect to the remote access server.

Figure 7-22 illustrates how clients connect with a remote access server to log on to a LAN.

Remote access servers depend on several types of protocols to communicate with clients, as described in the following section.

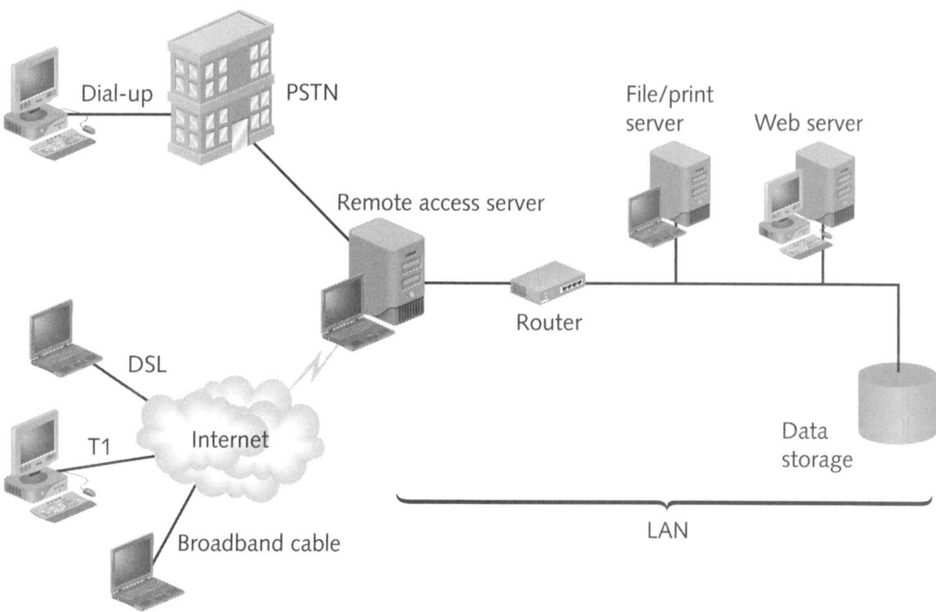

Figure 7-22 Clients connecting with a remote access server

Net+ Remote Access Protocols

6.3

To exchange data, remote access servers and clients require special protocols. The **SLIP (Serial Line Internet Protocol)** and **PPP (Point-to-Point Protocol)** are two protocols that enable a workstation to connect to another computer using a serial connection. (In the case of dial-up networking, *serial connection* refers to a modem.) Such protocols are necessary to transport network layer traffic over serial interfaces, which belong to the data link layer of the OSI model. Both SLIP and PPP encapsulate higher-layer networking protocols, such as TCP and IP, in their lower-layer data frames.

SLIP is an earlier and much simpler version of the protocol than PPP. For example, SLIP can carry only IP packets, whereas PPP can carry many different types of network layer packets. Because of its primitive nature, SLIP requires significantly more setup than PPP. When using SLIP, you typically must specify the IP addresses for both your client and your server in your dial-up networking profile. PPP, on the other hand, can automatically obtain this information as it connects to the server. PPP also performs error correction and data compression, but SLIP does not. In addition, SLIP does not support data encryption, which makes it less secure than PPP. For all these reasons, PPP is the preferred communications protocol for remote access communications.

Another difference between SLIP and PPP is that SLIP supports only asynchronous data transmission, and PPP supports both asynchronous and synchronous transmission. As you learned earlier, in synchronous transmission, data must conform to a timing scheme, while asynchronous transmission may stop and start sporadically. In fact, asynchronous transmission was designed for communication that happens at random intervals, such as sending the keystrokes of a person typing on a remote keyboard. Thus, it is well suited to use on modem connections.

When PPP is used over an Ethernet network (no matter what the connection type), it is known as **PPPoE (PPP over Ethernet)**. PPPoE is the standard for connecting home computers to an ISP via DSL or broadband cable. When you sign up for broadband cable or DSL service, the ISP supplies you with connection software that is configured to use PPPoE. Figure 7-23 illustrates how the protocols discussed in this section and commonly used to establish a broadband Internet connection fit in the OSI model. (The application layer protocol RDP, discussed in the following section, is only used when remotely controlling computers. Several different application layer protocols, including HTTP or FTP, could be substituted for RDP in Figure 7-23.)

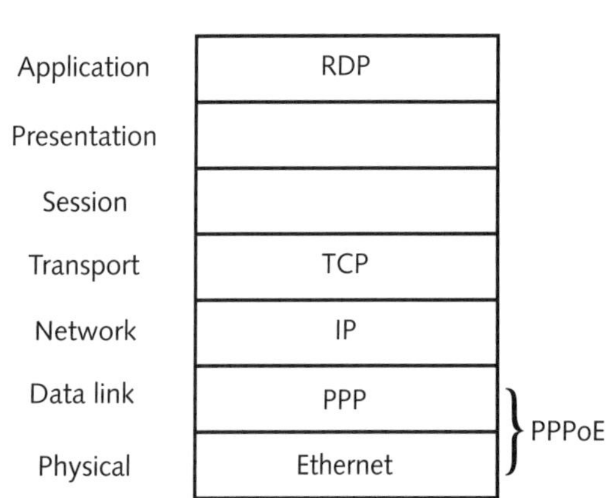

Figure 7-23 Protocols used in a remote access Internet connection

Net+ **Remote Virtual Computing**

6.3   So far you have learned about dial-up networking and remote access servers, which are designed to allow many clients to log onto a network from afar. Sometimes, however, it's necessary for one workstation to remotely access and control another workstation. For example, suppose a traveling salesperson must submit weekly sales figures to her home office every Friday afternoon. While out of town, she discovers a problem with her spreadsheet program, which should automatically calculate her sales figures (for example, the percentage of a monthly quota she's reached for any given product) after she enters the raw data. She calls the home office, and a support technician attempts to resolve her issue on the phone. When this doesn't work, the technician may decide to run a remote virtual computing program and "take over" the salesperson's laptop (via a WAN link) to troubleshoot the spreadsheet problem. Every keystroke and mouse click the technician enters on his workstation is then issued to the salesperson's laptop. After the problem is resolved, the technician can disconnect from the salesperson's laptop.

Remote virtual computing allows a user on one computer, called the client, to control another computer, called the host or server, across a network connection. The connection could be a dedicated WAN link (such as a T1), an Internet connection, or even a dial-up connection established directly between the client's modem and the host's modem. Also, the host must be configured to allow access from the client by setting user name or computer name and password credentials. A host may allow clients a variety of privileges, from merely viewing the screen to running programs and modifying data files on the host's hard disk. After connecting, if the remote user has sufficient privileges, she can send keystrokes and mouse clicks to the host and receive screen output in return. In other words, to the remote user, it appears as if she is working on the LAN- or WAN-connected host. Remote virtual computing software is specially designed to require little bandwidth. A workstation that uses such software to access a LAN is often called a **thin client**, because very little hard disk space or processing power is required of the workstation.

Advantages to using the remote virtual computing are its simplicity to configure and its ability to run over any type of connection. This benefits anyone who must use dial-up connections or who must run processor-intensive applications such as databases. In this scenario, the data processing occurs on the host without the data having to traverse the connection to the remote workstation. Another advantage to remote virtual computing is that a single host can accept simultaneous connections from multiple clients. A presenter can use this feature to establish a virtual conference, for example, in which several attendees log on to the host and watch the presenter manipulate the host computer's screen and keyboard.

Many types of remote virtual computing software exist, and they differ marginally in their capabilities, security mechanisms, and supported platforms. Three popular programs, discussed next, are: Microsoft's Remote Desktop, VNC (virtual network computing), and Citrix's ICA (Independent Computing Architecture).

Remote Desktop   Remote Desktop is the remote virtual computing software that comes with Windows client and server operating systems. Remote Desktop relies on **RDP (Remote Desktop Protocol)**, which is an application layer protocol that uses TCP/IP to transmit graphics and text quickly. RDP also carries session, licensing, and encryption information. RDP clients also exist for other operating systems, such as Linux, so you can connect from those clients to a Windows computer running Remote Desktop. Note that Home editions of

Net+

6.3

Windows client operating systems, such as Windows XP and Windows Vista, do not offer the Remote Desktop feature.

To enable your Windows XP Professional computer as a Remote Desktop host:

1. First log on to the computer as Administrator or another user name with administrator-level privileges.

2. Click **Start** and then click **Control Panel**. If necessary, click **Switch to Category View**. The Control Panel window opens in Category view.

3. Click **Performance and Maintenance,** and then click the **System** icon. The System Properties dialog box opens.

4. Click the **Remote** tab. Options for remote connections to your computer appear, as shown in Figure 7-24.

5. Check the **Allow users to connect remotely to this computer** option.

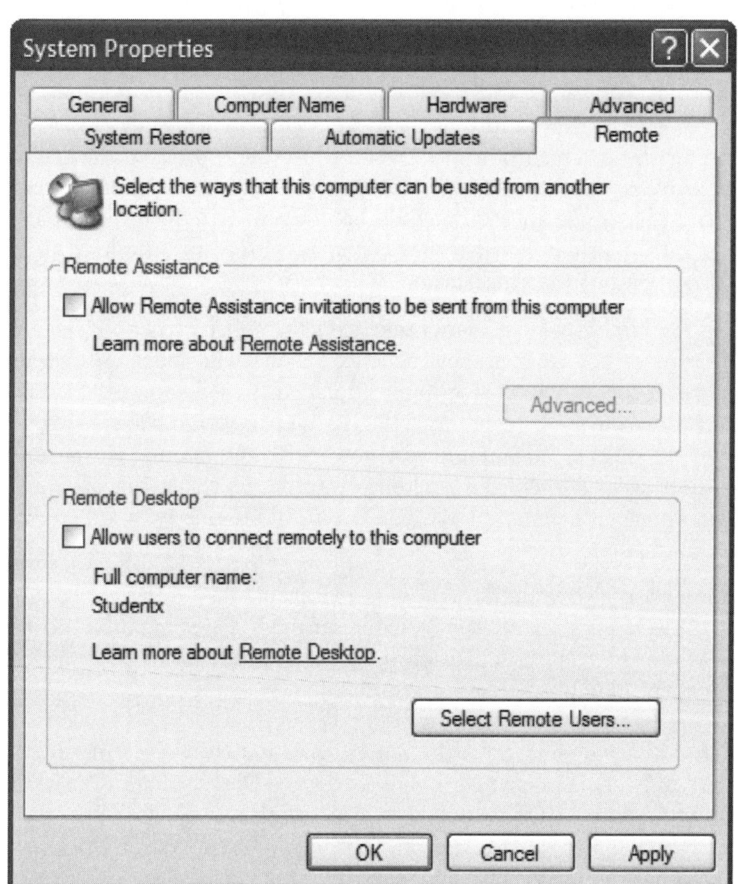

Figure 7-24 Remote tab in the Windows XP System Properties window

6. If this is the first time you've enabled remote services, the Remote Sessions window opens, alerting you that accounts used for remote access must have passwords to connect to your computer. Click **OK**.

7. Click **Select Remote Users** to choose from a list of users who you will allow to connect to your computer. The **Remote Desktop Users** dialog box opens.

8. Click **Add** to add a user to the list. The **Select Users** dialog box opens. If you have created multiple user accounts on your computer, these accounts will be listed under "Enter the object names to select (examples)."

9. Check the user names that will have access to your computer, and then click **OK**.

10. Click **OK** again to close the Remote Desktop Users dialog box.

11. Click **OK** once more to close the System Properties dialog box and save your changes.

12. The previous steps describe how to establish your computer as a host. To start a Remote Desktop session from a Windows XP client:

13. Make sure the Remote Desktop client software has been installed on the computer. Also make sure that the host and remote computers are connected to networks that can exchange data. (For example, the host might be a desktop on a company's office WAN, and the remote client might be a home computer that can connect to that WAN over the Internet.)

14. Click **Start**, point to **All Programs**, point to **Accessories**, point to **Communications**, and then click **Remote Desktop Connection**. The Remote Desktop Connection window opens, as shown in Figure 7-25.

15. In the Computer text box, enter the name of the host computer to which you want to connect. The host computer must be running the Remote Desktop software, and you must have permission to log on to it.

16. Click **Connect**.

17. In the **Log On to Windows** dialog box, type your user name, password, and domain (if necessary), and then click **OK** to log on to this host.

18. The Remote Desktop window opens, showing you the desktop of the host computer. At this point, your keystrokes and mouse clicks will act on the host computer, not on your client computer.

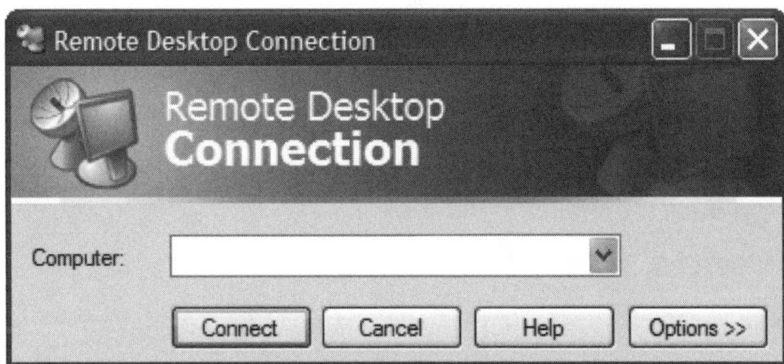

Figure 7-25 Windows XP Remote Desktop Connection window

With the release of Windows Vista, Microsoft enhanced the capabilities of RDP, including the option for stronger authentication requirements. The newer version of RDP is not currently backward-compatible with RDP software that came with Windows 95, NT, and XP operating systems, but Microsoft has plans to make it so. Officially, even the newest release of Remote Desktop supports only one concurrent session between a client and host. A remote virtual computing program that supports multiple concurrent sessions, VNC, is discussed next.

VNC (Virtual Network Computing) VNC (**virtual network computing**) is an open source system designed to allow one workstation to remotely manipulate and receive screen updates from another workstation. **Open source** is the term for software that is developed and packaged by individuals and made available to anyone for free—that is, no one must pay licensing fees to use it. Open source software is not owned by any one company. As a result, anyone can modify the software to enhance it or fix problems and share their modified version with others.

VNC's protocols, like Remote Desktop's, operate at the application layer. VNC packages have been developed for multiple computer platforms, including all modern versions of Windows, UNIX, Linux, and Mac OS X. In addition, VNC functions across platforms. That is, you can use a VNC client (or viewer, as it's known in VNC terms) on a Windows Vista workstation to access a VNC server running Ubuntu Linux. VNC is unique among remote virtual networking systems in this ability.

Besides its open source status, VNC boasts the ability to support multiple sessions on a single computer. One drawback of VNC compared to Remote Desktop is that its screen refresh rate is somewhat slower. However, software engineers have modified VNC to use compression techniques that expedite its data transmission. In addition, security has historically been a concern with VNC, but techniques have also evolved to mitigate this concern. Some popular versions of VNC include RealVNC, TightVNC, and UltraVNC.

ICA (Independent Computing Architecture) Another system for remote virtual computing that supports multiple simultaneous server connections is Citrix System's Presentation Server. With the Citrix option, remote workstations rely on proprietary software known as an **ICA (Independent Computing Architecture) client** to connect with a remote access server and exchange keystrokes, mouse clicks, and screen updates. Running Presentation Server, the remote access server makes applications available to clients and manages their connections. Citrix's ICA client can work with virtually any operating system or application. Its ease of use and broad compatibility make the ICA client a popular method for supplying widespread remote access across an organization. Potential drawbacks to this method include the relatively high cost of Citrix's products and the complex nature of its server software configuration.

(VPNs) Virtual Private Networks

VPNs (**Virtual private networks**) are wide area networks that are logically defined over public transmission systems. To allow access to only authorized users, traffic on a VPN is isolated from other traffic on the same public lines. For example, a national insurance provider could

Net+

2.7

6.3

establish a private WAN that uses Internet connections but serves only its agent offices across the country. By relying on the public transmission networks already in place, VPNs provide a way of constructing a convenient and relatively inexpensive WAN. In the example of a national insurance provider, the company gains significant savings by having each office connect to the Internet separately rather than leasing point-to-point connections between each office and the national headquarters.

The software required to establish VPNs is usually inexpensive, and in some cases is being included with other widely used software. For example, in Windows Server 2003 and Server 2008, RRAS allows you to create a simple VPN. It turns a Windows server into a remote access server and allows clients to dial into it. Alternately, clients could dial into an ISP's remote access server and then connect with the VPN managed by RRAS. Third-party software companies also provide VPN programs that work with Windows, UNIX, Linux, and Macintosh OS X Server network operating systems. Or VPNs can be created simply by configuring special protocols on the routers or firewalls that connect each site in the VPN. This is the most common implementation of VPNs on UNIX-based networks.

Figure 7-26 depicts one possible VPN layout. The beauty of VPNs is that they are tailored to a customer's distance and bandwidth needs, so, of course, every one is different.

Two important considerations when designing a VPN are interoperability and security. To ensure a VPN can carry all types of data in a private manner over any kind of connection, special VPN protocols encapsulate higher-layer protocols in a process known as **tunneling**. You can say that these protocols create the virtual connection, or **tunnel**, between two VPN nodes. One endpoint of the tunnel is the client. The other endpoint may be a connectivity device (for example, a router, firewall, or gateway) or a remote access server that allows

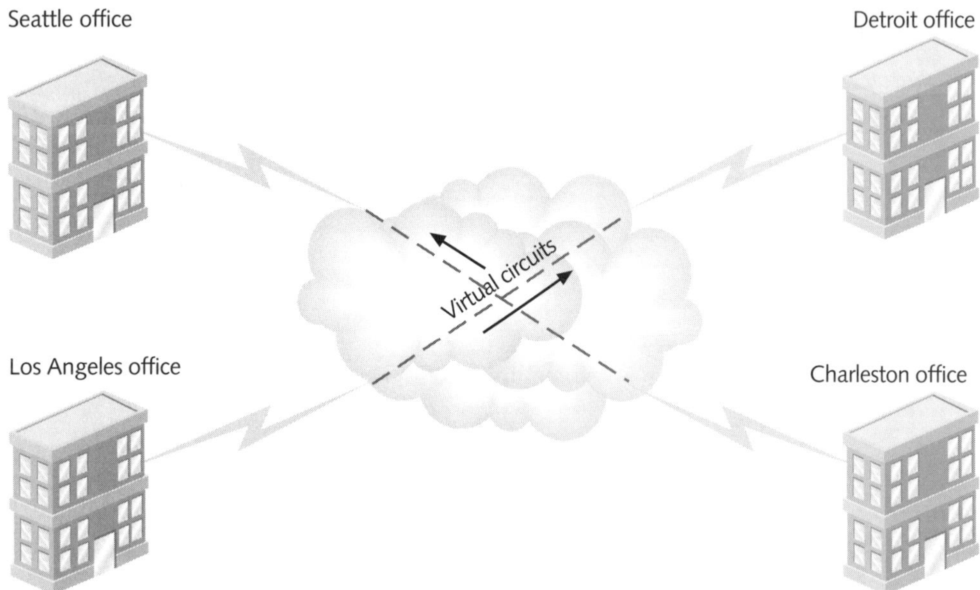

Figure 7-26 An example of a VPN

2.7

6.3

clients to log on to the network. As you have learned, encapsulation involves one protocol adding a header to data received from a higher-layer protocol. A VPN tunneling protocol operates at the data link layer and encapsulates network layer packets, no matter what network layer protocol is used. Two major types of tunneling protocols are used on contemporary VPNs: PPTP or L2TP.

PPTP (Point-to-Point Tunneling Protocol) is a protocol developed by Microsoft that expands on PPP by encapsulating it so that any type of PPP data can traverse the Internet masked as an IP transmission. PPTP supports the encryption, authentication, and access services provided by the Windows Server 2003 and Server 2008 RRAS (and previous versions of this remote access software). Users can either dial directly into an RRAS access server that's part of the VPN, or they can dial into their ISP's remote access server and then connect to a VPN. Either way, data is transmitted from the client to the VPN using PPTP. Windows, UNIX, Linux, and Macintosh clients are all capable of connecting to a VPN using PPTP. PPTP is easy to install and is available at no extra cost with Microsoft networking services. However, it provides less stringent security than other tunneling protocols.

Another VPN tunneling protocol is **L2TP (Layer 2 Tunneling Protocol)**, based on technology developed by Cisco and standardized by the IETF. It encapsulates PPP data in a similar manner to PPTP but differs in a few key ways. Unlike PPTP, L2TP is a standard accepted and used by multiple different vendors, so it can connect a VPN that uses a mix of equipment types—for example, a 3Com router, a Cisco router, and a NETGEAR router. Also, L2TP can connect two routers, a router and a remote access server, or a client and a remote access server.

Another important advantage to L2TP is that tunnel endpoints do not have to reside on the same packet-switched network. In other words, an L2TP client could connect to a router running L2TP on an ISP's network. The ISP could then forward the L2TP frames to another VPN router, without interpreting the frames. This L2TP tunnel, although not direct from node to node, remains isolated from other traffic. Because of its many advantages, L2TP is more commonly used than PPTP.

PPTP and L2TP are not the only protocols that can be used to carry VPN traffic. For networks in which security is critical, it is advisable to use protocols that can provide both tunneling and data encryption. Such protocols are discussed in detail in Chapter 12, which focuses on network security.

Chapter Summary

- WANs are distinguished from LANs by the fact that WANs traverse a wider geographical area. They usually employ point-to-point, dedicated communications rather than point-to-multipoint communications. They also use different connectivity devices, depending on the WAN technology in use.

- A WAN in which each site is connected in a serial fashion to no more than two other sites is known as a bus topology WAN. This topology often provides the best solution for organizations with only a few sites and access to dedicated circuits.

- In a ring topology WAN, each site is connected to two other sites so that the entire WAN forms a ring pattern. This architecture is similar to the LAN ring topology, except that most ring topology WANs have the capability to reverse the direction data travels to avoid a failed site.

- In the star topology WAN, a single site acts as the central connection point for several other points. This arrangement allows one connection to fail without affecting other connections. Therefore, star topology WANs are more fault-tolerant than bus or ring WANs.

- A mesh topology WAN consists of many directly interconnected sites. In partial-mesh WANs, only some of the WAN sites are directly interconnected. In full-mesh WANs, every site is directly connected to every other site. The full-mesh topology is the most fault tolerant and also the most expensive WAN topology to implement.

- A tiered topology WAN is one in which sites that are connected in star or ring formations are interconnected at different levels, with the interconnection points being organized into layers to form hierarchical groupings.

- The PSTN (Public Switched Telephone Network) is the network of lines and carrier equipment that provides telephone service to most homes and businesses. It was originally composed of analog lines alone, but now it also uses digital transmission over fiber-optic or copper twisted pair cable, microwave, and satellite connections. The local loop portion of the PSTN is still primarily UTP; it is this portion that limits throughput on the PSTN. The PSTN provides the foundation for several types of WAN connections, including dial-up networking, X.25, frame relay, T-carriers, and DSL.

- X.25 is an analog, packet-switched technology optimized for reliable, long-distance data transmission. It can support 2Mbps throughput. X.25 was originally developed and used for communications between mainframe computers and remote terminals.

- Frame relay, like X.25, relies on packet switching, but it carries digital signals. It does not analyze frames to check for errors but simply relays them from node to node, so frame relay supports higher bandwidth than X.25, offering a maximum of 45Mbps throughput.

- Both X.25 and frame relay are configured as PVCs (permanent virtual circuits), or point-to-point connections over which data may follow different paths. When leasing an X.25 or frame relay circuit from a telecommunications carrier, a customer specifies endpoints and the amount of bandwidth required between them.

- ISDN (Integrated Services Digital Network) is an international standard for protocols at the physical, data link, and transport layers that allows the PSTN to carry digital signals. ISDN lines may carry voice and data signals simultaneously but require an ISDN phone to carry voice traffic and an ISDN router and ISDN terminal adapter to carry data.

- Two types of ISDN connections are commonly used by consumers in North America: BRI (Basic Rate Interface) and PRI (Primary Rate Interface). Both use a combination of bearer channels (B channels) and data channels (D channels). The B channel transmits and receives data or voice from point to point. The D channel carries information about the call, such as session initiation and termination signals, caller identity, call forwarding, and conference calling signals.

- BRI uses two 64Kbps circuit-switched B channels and a 16Kbps D channel. The maximum throughput for a BRI connection is 128Kbps. PRI uses 23 B channels and one 64Kbps D channel. The maximum potential throughput for a PRI connection is 1.544Mbps. Individual subscribers rarely use PRI, preferring BRI instead, but PRI may be used by businesses and other organizations that need more throughput.

- T-carrier technology uses TDM (time division multiplexing) to divide a single channel into multiple channels for carrying voice, data, video, or other signals. Devices at the sending end arrange the data streams (multiplex), and then devices at the receiving end filter them back into separate signals (demultiplex).

- The most common T-carrier implementations are T1 and T3. A T1 circuit can carry the equivalent of 24 voice channels, giving a maximum data throughput of 1.544Mbps. A T3 circuit can carry the equivalent of 672 voice channels, giving a maximum data throughput of 44.736Mbps.

- The signal level of a T-carrier refers to its physical layer electrical signaling characteristics, as defined by ANSI standards. DS0 is the equivalent of one data or voice channel. All other signal levels are multiples of DS0.

- T1 technology can use UTP or STP. However, twisted pair wiring cannot adequately carry the high throughput of multiple T1s or T3 transmissions. For T3 transmissions, fiber-optic cable or microwave connections are necessary.

- Incoming T-carrier lines terminate at a smart jack at the customer's demarc. Next, signals are processed by a CSU/DSU. The CSU/DSU ensures connection integrity through error correction and line monitoring and converts the T-carrier frames into frames the LAN can interpret, and vice versa. It also connects T-carrier lines with terminating equipment. A CSU/DSU often includes a multiplexer.

- DSL (digital subscriber line) is a WAN connection method that uses advanced phase or amplitude modulation in the higher (inaudible) frequencies on a phone line to achieve throughputs of up to 51.8Mbps. DSL comes in eight different varieties, each of which is either asymmetrical or symmetrical. In asymmetrical transmission, more data can be sent in one direction than in the other direction. In symmetrical transmission, throughput is equal in both directions. The most popular form of DSL is ADSL.

- DSL technology creates a dedicated circuit. At the consumer end, a DSL modem connects computers and telephones to the DSL line. At the carrier end, a DSLAM (DSL access multiplexer) aggregates multiple incoming DSL lines before connecting them to the Internet or to larger carriers.

- Broadband cable is a dedicated service that relies on the cable wiring used for TV signals. The service can theoretically provide as much as 36Mbps downstream and 10Mbps upstream throughput, though actual throughput is much lower.

- Broadband cable connections require that the customer use a special cable modem to transmit and receive signals over coaxial cable wiring. In addition, cable companies must have replaced their coaxial cable plant with hybrid fiber-coax cable to support bidirectional, digital communications.

- ATM (Asynchronous Transfer Mode) is a data link layer standard that relies on fixed packets, called cells, consisting of 48 bytes of data plus a 5-byte header. It's a connection-oriented technology based on virtual circuits. Having a reliable connection enables ATM to guarantee QoS (quality of service) levels for designated transmissions.

- SONET (Synchronous Optical Network) is a high-bandwidth WAN signaling technique that specifies framing and multiplexing techniques at the physical layer of the OSI model. Its four key strengths are that it can integrate many other WAN technologies (for example, T-carriers, ISDN, and ATM technology), it offers fast data transfer rates, it allows for simple link additions and removals, and it provides a high degree of fault tolerance. Internationally, SONET is known as SDH.

- SONET depends on fiber-optic transmission media and uses multiplexers to connect to network devices (such as routers or telephone switches) at the customer's end. A typical SONET network takes the form of a dual-ring topology. If one ring breaks, SONET technology automatically reroutes traffic along a backup ring. This characteristic, known as self-healing, makes SONET very reliable.

- As a remote user, you can connect to a LAN or WAN in one of several ways: dial-up networking, connecting to a remote access server, remote virtual computing, or through a VPN (virtual private network).

- Dial-up networking involves a remote client dialing into a remote access server and connecting via a PSTN, X.25, or ISDN connection. The client must run dial-up software to initiate the connection, and the server runs specialized remote access software to accept and interpret the incoming signals.

- Remote access servers accept incoming connections from remote clients, authenticate users, allow them to log on to a LAN or WAN, and exchange data by encapsulating higher-layer protocols, such as TCP and IP in specialized protocols such as PPP. The Microsoft RRAS (Routing and Remote Access Service) is the remote access software that comes with the Windows XP, Vista, Server 2003, and Server 2008 operating systems.

- To exchange data, remote access servers and clients must communicate through special data link layer protocols, such as PPP (Point-to-Point Protocol) or SLIP (Serial Line Internet Protocol), that encapsulate higher-layer protocols, such as TCP and IP. PPP is the preferred protocol. When PPP is used on an Ethernet network, as is the case with most modern broadband Internet connections, it is called PPP over Ethernet, or PPPoE.

- Remote virtual computing uses specialized client and host software to allow a remote user to connect via modem to a LAN-attached workstation and control that host. After connecting, the remote user can perform functions just as if she were directly connected to the LAN.

- Remote Desktop is a remote virtual computing client and server package that comes with Windows operating systems. VNC (virtual network computing) refers to an open source system that enables a remote client (or viewer) workstation to manipulate and receive screen updates from a host. ICA (Independent Computing Architecture) provides the basis for Citrix Systems' proprietary remote virtual computing software.

- VPNs (virtual private networks) represent one way to construct a WAN from existing public transmission systems. A VPN offers connectivity only to an organization's users, while keeping the data secure and isolated from other (public) traffic. To accomplish this, VPNs may be software or hardware based. Either way, they depend on secure protocols and transmission methods to keep data private.

- To make sure a VPN can carry all types of data in a private manner over any kind of connection, special VPN protocols encapsulate higher-layer protocols via tunneling. Common tunneling protocols include PPTP (Point-to-Point Tunneling Protocol) and L2TP (Layer 2 Tunneling Protocol). Additional VPN protocols are discussed in Chapter 12, which focuses on network security.

Key Terms

asymmetrical   The characteristic of a transmission technology that affords greater bandwidth in one direction (either from the customer to the carrier, or vice versa) than in the other direction.

asymmetrical DSL   A variation of DSL that offers more throughput when data travels downstream, downloading from a local carrier's switching facility to the customer, than when it travels upstream, uploading from the customer to the local carrier's switching facility.

asynchronous   A transmission method in which data being transmitted and received by nodes does not have to conform to any timing scheme. In asynchronous communications, a node can transmit at any time, and the destination node must accept the transmission as it comes.

Asynchronous Transfer Mode   *See* ATM.

ATM (Asynchronous Transfer Mode)   A data link layer technology originally conceived in the early 1980s at Bell Labs and standardized by the ITU in the mid-1990s. ATM relies on fixed packets, called cells, that each consist of 48 bytes of data plus a 5-byte header. ATM relies on virtual circuits and establishes a connection before sending data. The reliable connection ensured by ATM allows network managers to specify QoS levels for certain types of traffic.

authentication   The process of comparing and matching a client's credentials with the credentials in the NOS user database to enable the client to log on to the network.

B channel   In ISDN, the "bearer" channel, so named because it bears traffic from point to point.

Basic Rate Interface   *See* BRI.

bonding   The process of combining more than one bearer channel of an ISDN line to increase throughput. For example, BRI's two 64Kbps B channels are bonded to create an effective throughput of 128Kbps.

BRI (Basic Rate Interface)   A variety of ISDN that uses two 64Kbps bearer channels and one 16Kbps data channel, as summarized by the notation 2B+D. BRI is the most common form of ISDN employed by home users.

broadband cable   A method of connecting to the Internet over a cable network. In broadband cable, computers are connected to a cable modem that modulates and demodulates signals to and from the cable company's head-end.

bus topology WAN   A WAN in which each location is connected to no more than two other locations in a serial fashion.

cable drop   The fiber-optic or coaxial cable that connects a neighborhood cable node to a customer's house.

cable modem   A device that modulates and demodulates signals for transmission and reception via cable wiring.

cable modem access   *See* broadband cable.

cell   A packet of a fixed size. In ATM technology, a cell consists of 48 bytes of data plus a 5-byte header.

central office   *See* CO.

channel service unit   *See* CSU.

CIR (committed information rate)   The guaranteed minimum amount of bandwidth selected when leasing a frame relay circuit. Frame relay costs are partially based on CIR.

CO (central office)   The location where a local or long-distance telephone service provider terminates and interconnects customer lines.

committed information rate   *See* CIR.

credentials   A user's unique identifying characteristics that enable him to authenticate with a server and gain access to network resources. The most common type of credentials are a user name and password.

CSU (channel service unit)   A device used with T-carrier technology that provides termination for the digital signal and ensures connection integrity through error correction and line monitoring. Typically, a CSU is combined with a DSU in a single device, a CSU/DSU.

CSU/DSU   A combination of a CSU (channel service unit) and a DSU (data service unit) that serves as the connection point for a T1 line at the customer's site. Most modern CSU/DSUs also contain a multiplexer. A CSU/DSU may be a separate device or an expansion card in another device, such as a router.

D channel   In ISDN, the "data" channel is used to carry information about the call, such as session initiation and termination signals, caller identity, call forwarding, and conference calling signals.

data service unit   *See* DSU.

dedicated   A continuously available link or service that is leased through another carrier. Examples of dedicated lines include ADSL, T1, and T3.

dial-up   A type of connection in which a user connects to a distant network from a computer and stays connected for a finite period of time. Most of the time, the term *dial-up* refers to a connection that uses a PSTN line.

dial-up networking   The process of dialing into a remote access server to connect with a network, be it private or public.

digital subscriber line   *See* DSL.

downstream   A term used to describe data traffic that flows from a carrier's facility to the customer. In asymmetrical communications, downstream throughput is usually much higher than upstream throughput. In symmetrical communications, downstream and upstream throughputs are equal.

DS0 (digital signal, level 0)   The equivalent of one data or voice channel in T-carrier technology, as defined by ANSI physical layer standards. All other signal levels are multiples of DS0.

DSL (digital subscriber line)   A dedicated WAN technology that uses advanced data modulation techniques at the physical layer to achieve extraordinary throughput over regular phone lines. DSL comes in several different varieties, the most common of which is asymmetric DSL (ADSL).

DSL access multiplexer   *See* DSLAM.

DSL modem   A device that demodulates an incoming DSL signal, extracting the information and passing it to the data equipment (such as telephones and computers), and modulates an outgoing DSL signal.

DSLAM (DSL access multiplexer)   A connectivity device located at a telecommunications carrier's office that aggregates multiple DSL subscriber lines and connects them to a larger carrier or to the Internet backbone.

DSU (data service unit)   A device used in T-carrier technology that converts the digital signal used by bridges, routers, and multiplexers into the digital signal used on cabling. Typically, a DSU is combined with a CSU in a single device, a CSU/DSU.

E1   A digital carrier standard used in Europe that offers 30 channels and a maximum of 2.048Mbps throughput.

E3   A digital carrier standard used in Europe that offers 480 channels and a maximum of 34.368Mbps throughput.

fiber to the home   A carrier's provision of fiber-optic connections to residential end users for dramatically increased throughput and a better range of services.

fractional T1   An arrangement that allows a customer to lease only some of the channels on a T1 line.

frame relay   A digital, packet-switched WAN technology whose protocols operate at the data link layer. The name is derived from the fact that data is separated into frames, which are then relayed from one node to another without verification or processing. Frame relay offers throughputs between 64Kbps and 45Mbps. A frame relay customer chooses the amount of bandwidth he requires and pays for only that amount.

full-mesh WAN   A version of the mesh topology WAN in which every site is directly connected to every other site. Full-mesh WANs are the most fault-tolerant type of WAN.

head-end   A cable company's central office, which connects cable wiring to many nodes before it reaches customers' sites.

HFC (hybrid fiber-coax)   A link that consists of fiber cable connecting the cable company's offices to a node location near the customer and coaxial cable connecting the node to the customer's house. HFC upgrades to existing cable wiring are required before current TV cable systems can provide Internet access.

hybrid fiber-coax   *See* HFC.

ICA (Independent Computing Architecture) client   The software from Citrix Systems, Inc., that, when installed on a client, enables the client to connect with a host computer and exchange keystrokes, mouse clicks, and screen updates. Citrix's ICA client can work with virtually any operating system or application.

Integrated Services Digital Network   *See* ISDN.

ISDN (Integrated Services Digital Network)   An international standard that uses PSTN lines to carry digital signals. It specifies protocols at the physical, data link, and transport layers of the OSI model. ISDN lines may carry voice and data signals simultaneously. Two types of ISDN connections are used in North America: BRI (Basic Rate Interface) and PRI (Primary Rate Interface). Both use a combination of bearer channels (B channels) and data channels (D channels).

J1   A digital carrier standard used in Japan that offers 24 channels and 1.544Mbps throughput.

J3   A digital carrier standard used in Japan that offers 480 channels and 32.064Mbps throughput.

L2TP (Layer 2 Tunneling Protocol)   A protocol that encapsulates PPP data, for use on VPNs. L2TP is based on Cisco technology and is standardized by the IETF. It is distinguished by its compatibility among different manufacturers' equipment; its ability to connect between clients, routers, and servers alike; and by the fact that it can connect nodes belonging to different Layer 3 networks.

LAN Emulation   *See* LANE.

LANE (LAN Emulation)   A method for transporting token ring or Ethernet frames over ATM networks. LANE encapsulates incoming Ethernet or token ring frames and then converts them into ATM cells for transmission over an ATM network.

last mile   *See* local loop.

Layer 2 Tunneling Protocol   *See* L2TP.

local loop   The part of a phone system that connects a customer site with a telecommunications carrier's switching facility.

mesh topology WAN   A type of WAN in which several sites are directly interconnected. Mesh WANs are highly fault tolerant because they provide multiple routes for data to follow between any two points.

network interface unit   *See* NIU.

network service provider   *See* NSP.

Network Termination 1   *See* NT1.

Network Termination 2   *See* NT2.

NIU (network interface unit)   The point at which PSTN-owned lines terminate at a customer's premises. The NIU is usually located at the demarc.

NSP (network service provider)   A carrier that provides long-distance (and often global) connectivity between major data-switching centers across the Internet. AT&T, Verizon, and Sprint are all examples of network service providers in the United States. Customers, including ISPs, can lease dedicated private or public Internet connections from an NSP.

NT1 (Network Termination 1)   A device used on ISDN networks that connects the incoming twisted pair wiring with the customer's ISDN terminal equipment.

NT2 (Network Termination 2)   An additional connection device required on PRI to handle the multiple ISDN lines between the customer's network termination connection and the local phone company's wires.

OC (Optical Carrier)   An internationally recognized rating that indicates throughput rates for SONET connections.

open source   The term that describes software that is developed and packaged by individuals and made available to anyone, without licensing fees. Open source software is not owned by any one company.

Optical Carrier   *See* OC.

partial-mesh WAN   A version of a mesh topology WAN in which only critical sites are directly interconnected and secondary sites are connected through star or ring topologies. Partial mesh WANs are less expensive to implement than full mesh WANs.

permanent virtual circuit   *See* PVC.

plain old telephone service (POTS)   *See* PSTN.

Point-to-Point Protocol   *See* PPP.

Point-to-Point Protocol over Ethernet   *See* PPPoE.

Point-to-Point Tunneling Protocol   *See* PPTP.

POTS   *See* PSTN.

PPP (Point-to-Point Protocol)   A communications protocol that enables a workstation to connect to a server using a serial connection. PPP can support multiple network layer protocols and can use both asynchronous and synchronous communications. It performs compression and error correction and requires little configuration on the client workstation.

PPPoE (Point-to-Point Protocol over Ethernet)   PPP running over an Ethernet network.

PPTP (Point-to-Point Tunneling Protocol)   A Layer 2 protocol developed by Microsoft that encapsulates PPP data for transmission over VPN connections. PPTP operates with Windows RRAS access services and can accept connections from multiple clients. It is simple, but it is less secure than other modern tunneling protocols.

PRI (Primary Rate Interface)   A type of ISDN that uses 23 bearer channels and one 64Kbps data channel, represented by the notation 23B+D. PRI is less commonly used by individual subscribers than BRI, but it may be used by businesses and other organizations needing more throughput.

PSTN (Public Switched Telephone Network)   The network of lines and carrier equipment that provides telephone service to most homes and businesses. Now, except for the local loop, nearly all of the PSTN uses digital transmission. Its traffic is carried by fiber-optic or copper twisted pair cable, microwave, and satellite connections.

Public Switched Telephone Network   *See* PSTN.

PVC (permanent virtual circuit)   A point-to-point connection over which data may follow any number of different paths, as opposed to a dedicated line that follows a predefined path. X.25, frame relay, and some forms of ATM use PVCs.

RAS (Remote Access Service)   The dial-up networking software provided with Microsoft Windows 95, 98, NT, and 2000 client operating systems. RAS requires software installed on both the client and server, a server configured to accept incoming clients, and a client with sufficient privileges (including user name and password) on the server to access its resources. In more recent versions of Windows, RAS has been incorporated into the RRAS (Routing and Remote Access Service).

RDP (Remote Desktop Protocol)   An application layer protocol that uses TCP/IP to transmit graphics and text quickly over a remote client–host connection. RDP also carries session, licensing, and encryption information.

remote access   A method for connecting and logging on to a LAN from a workstation that is remote, or not physically connected, to the LAN.

Remote Access Service   *See* RAS.

Remote Desktop   A feature of Windows operating systems that allows a computer to act as a remote host and be controlled from a client running another Windows operating system.

Remote Desktop Protocol   *See* RDP.

ring topology WAN   A type of WAN in which each site is connected to two other sites so that the entire WAN forms a ring pattern.

Routing and Remote Access Service (RRAS)   The software included with Windows 2000 Server, XP, Vista, Server 2003, and Server 2008 operating systems that enables a server to act as a router, firewall, and remote access server. Using RRAS, a server can provide network access to multiple remote clients.

RRAS   *See* Routing and Remote Access Service.

SDH (Synchronous Digital Hierarchy)   The international equivalent of SONET.

self-healing   A characteristic of dual-ring topologies that allows them to automatically reroute traffic along the backup ring if the primary ring becomes severed.

Serial Line Internet Protocol   *See* SLIP.

signal level   An ANSI standard for T-carrier technology that refers to its physical layer electrical signaling characteristics. DS0 is the equivalent of one data or voice channel. All other signal levels are multiples of DS0.

SLIP (Serial Line Internet Protocol)   A communications protocol that enables a workstation to connect to a server using a serial connection. SLIP can support only asynchronous communications and IP traffic and requires some configuration on the client workstation. SLIP has been made obsolete by PPP.

smart jack   A termination for T-carrier wire pairs that is located at the customer demark and which functions as a connection protection and monitoring point.

SONET (Synchronous Optical Network)   A high-bandwidth WAN signaling technique that specifies framing and multiplexing techniques at the physical layer of the OSI model. It can integrate many other WAN technologies (for example, T-carriers, ISDN, and ATM technology) and allows for simple link additions and removals. SONET's topology includes a double ring of fiber-optic cable, which results in very high fault tolerance.

star topology WAN   A type of WAN in which a single site acts as the central connection point for several other points. This arrangement provides separate routes for data between any two sites; however, if the central connection point fails, the entire WAN fails.

SVC (switched virtual circuit)   A logical, point-to-point connection that relies on switches to determine the optimal path between sender and receiver. ATM technology uses SVCs.

switched virtual circuit   *See* SVC.

symmetrical A characteristic of transmission technology that provides equal throughput for data traveling both upstream and downstream and is suited to users who both upload and download significant amounts of data.

symmetrical DSL A variation of DSL that provides equal throughput both upstream and downstream between the customer and the carrier.

synchronous A transmission method in which data being transmitted and received by nodes must conform to a timing scheme.

Synchronous Digital Hierarchy *See* SDH.

Synchronous Optical Network *See* SONET.

T1 A digital carrier standard used in North America and most of Asia that provides 1.544Mbps throughput and 24 channels for voice, data, video, or audio signals. T1s rely on time division multiplexing and may use shielded or unshielded twisted pair, coaxial cable, fiber optics, or microwave links.

T3 A digital carrier standard used in North America and most of Asia that can carry the equivalent of 672 channels for voice, data, video, or audio, with a maximum data throughput of 44.736Mbps (typically rounded up to 45Mbps for purposes of discussion). T3s rely on time division multiplexing and require either fiber-optic or microwave transmission media.

T-carrier The term for any kind of leased line that follows the standards for T1s, fractional T1s, T1Cs, T2s, T3s, or T4s.

TA (terminal adapter) A device used to convert digital signals into analog signals for use with ISDN phones and other analog devices. TAs are sometimes called ISDN modems.

TE (terminal equipment) The end nodes (such as computers and printers) served by the same connection (such as an ISDN, DSL, or T1 link).

terminal adapter *See* TA.

terminal equipment *See* TE.

thin client A client that relies on another host for the majority of processing and hard disk resources necessary to run applications and share files over the network.

tiered topology WAN A type of WAN in which sites that are connected in star or ring formations are interconnected at different levels, with the interconnection points being organized into layers to form hierarchical groupings.

tunnel A secured, virtual connection between two nodes on a VPN.

tunneling The process of encapsulating one type of protocol in another. Tunneling is the way in which higher-layer data is transported over VPNs by Layer 2 protocols.

upstream A term used to describe data traffic that flows from a customer's site to a carrier's facility. In asymmetrical communications, upstream throughput is usually much lower than downstream throughput. In symmetrical communications, upstream and downstream throughputs are equal.

virtual circuit A connection between network nodes that, although based on potentially disparate physical links, logically appears to be a direct, dedicated link between those nodes.

virtual network computing *See* VNC.

virtual private network *See* VPN.

VNC (virtual network computing) An open source system that enables a remote client (or viewer) workstation to manipulate and receive screen updates from a host. Examples of VNC software include RealVNC, TightVNC, and UltraVNC.

VPN (virtual private network) A logically constructed WAN that uses existing public transmission systems. VPNs can be created through the use of software or combined software and hardware solutions. This type of network allows an organization to carve out a private WAN through the Internet, serving only its offices, while keeping the data secure and isolated from other (public) traffic.

WAN link A point-to-point connection between two nodes on a WAN.

X.25 An analog, packet-switched WAN technology optimized for reliable, long-distance data transmission and standardized by the ITU in the mid-1970s. The X.25 standard specifies protocols at the physical, data link, and network layers of the OSI model. It provides excellent flow control and ensures data reliability over long distances by verifying the transmission at every node. X.25 can support a maximum of only 2Mbps throughput.

xDSL The term used to refer to all varieties of DSL.

Review Questions

1. Which WAN topology is practical for connecting fewer than four or five locations?

   a. Star

   b. Mesh

   c. Ring

   d. Partial-mesh

2. What is a disadvantage of using the PSTN for an Internet connection?

   a. High cost

   b. Marginal security

   c. Complexity

   d. Lack of availability

3. Which type of DSL would a bank's branch office that sends large volumes of account information to the central server at the bank's headquarters and, in turn, receives large amounts of account information from the central server at the bank's headquarters, require?

   a. ADSL

   b. HDSL

   c. G.Lite

   d. VDSL

4. What advantage is gained from ATM's fixed-size, 53-byte packet?

   a. Increased throughput

   b. Less overhead

   c. Predictable network performance

   d. Low costs for small networks

5. Which WAN technology is the best choice for linking WANs between North America, Europe, and Asia?

   a. SONET

   b. Frame relay

   c. ATM

   d. Broadband

6. True or false? WANs typically send data over publicly available communications networks.

7. True or false? A bus WAN topology scales well.

8. True or false? Broadband cable is a symmetrical technology.

9. True or false? The speed of a T-carrier depends on its signal level.

10. True or false? Remote access is a service that allows a client to connect with and log on to a LAN or WAN in a different geographical location.

11. A(n) _____ topology WAN incorporates many directly interconnected sites such that data can travel directly from its origin to its destination.

12. In a(n) _____ topology WAN, sites connected in star or ring formations are interconnected at different levels, with the interconnection points being organized into layers to form hierarchical groupings.

13. A(n) _____ refers to the network of lines and carrier equipment that provides telephone service to most homes and businesses.

14. The dial-up networking software that Microsoft provided with its Windows 95, 98, NT, and 2000 client operating systems is called _____.

15. _____ allows a user on one computer, called the client, to control another computer, called the host or server, across a network connection.

Wireless Networking

After reading this chapter and completing the exercises, you will be able to:

- Explain how nodes exchange wireless signals

- Identify potential obstacles to successful wireless transmission and their repercussions, such as interference and reflection

- Understand WLAN (wireless LAN) architecture

- Specify the characteristics of popular WLAN transmission methods, including 802.11 a/b/g/n

- Install and configure wireless access points and their clients

- Describe wireless MAN and WAN technologies, including 802.16 and satellite communications

On the Job

When Isthmus Publishing was attempting to gain better bandwidth than its current DSL access allowed, we decided on WiMAX. We acquired and installed hardware that allowed non-line-of-sight connectivity. A solid connection was made and worked flawlessly for several months. We were so pleased with the new access that we canceled our DSL service as being redundant and slow.

At the same time, a new building was being erected directly in the path of our line of sight. Initially, this posed no problems at all. Then, one day, our Internet access was agonizingly slow at best and non-functional at worst. We spent many hours on the rooftop adjusting the radio antenna in an attempt to restore service to the previous levels, all to no avail. Since our previous DSL connection had been shut down, we had little Web access, sporadic e-mail delivery, and no way to process credit card payments in a timely fashion.

We quickly tried to reestablish a DSL subscription; it had become apparent that a secondary backup connection was essential to ensure business operations. In the meantime, we kept working with the supplier of the WiMAX connection.

Eventually, we figured out that the metallic content in the reflective glass of the new building across the street created the disruption. The ISP installed new hardware that allowed us to send our signal to a rooftop 180 degrees in the opposite direction; the signal would then be sent to them from that other customer's antenna. Service was restored, all systems returned to normal, and we have had no problems since.

We still, however, keep DSL around as a backup.

Thom Jones
Isthmus Publishing

The Earth's atmosphere provides an intangible means of transporting data over networks. For decades, radio and TV stations have used the atmosphere to transport information via analog signals. Such analog signals are also capable of carrying data. Networks that transmit signals through the atmosphere via radio frequency (RF) waves are known as **wireless networks** or **WLANs (wireless local area networks)**. Wireless transmission media is now common in business and home networks and necessary in some specialized network environments. For example, inventory control personnel who drive through large warehouses to record inventory data use wireless networking. In addition to RF transmission, microwave and satellite links can be used to transport data through the atmosphere. In this chapter you'll learn how data travels through the air and how to make it happen on your network.

The Wireless Spectrum

All wireless signals are carried through the air by electromagnetic waves. The **wireless spectrum** is a continuum of the electromagnetic waves used for data and voice communication. On the spectrum, waves are arranged according to their frequencies, from lowest to highest. The wireless spectrum (as defined by the FCC, which controls its use) spans frequencies between 9KHz and 300GHz. Each type of wireless service can be associated with one area of the wireless spectrum. AM broadcasting, for example, sits near the low-frequency end of the wireless communications spectrum, using frequencies between 535 and 1,605KHz. Infrared waves belong to a wide band of frequencies at the high-frequency end of the spectrum, between 300GHz and 300,000GHz. Most cordless telephones and many WLANs use frequencies around 2.4GHz. Other WLANs use a range of frequencies near 5GHz. Figure 8-1 shows the wireless spectrum and identifies the major wireless services associated with each range of frequencies.

In the United States, the collection of frequencies available for communication—also known as "the airwaves"—is a natural resource available for public use. The FCC grants organizations in different locations exclusive rights to use each frequency. It also determines what frequency ranges can be used for what purposes. Of course, signals propagating through the air do not necessarily remain within one nation. Therefore, it is important for countries across the world to agree on wireless communications standards. ITU is the governing body that sets standards for international wireless services, including frequency allocation, signaling and protocols used by wireless devices, wireless transmission and reception equipment, satellite orbits, and so on. If governments and companies did not adhere to ITU standards, chances are that a wireless device could not be used outside the country in which it was manufactured.

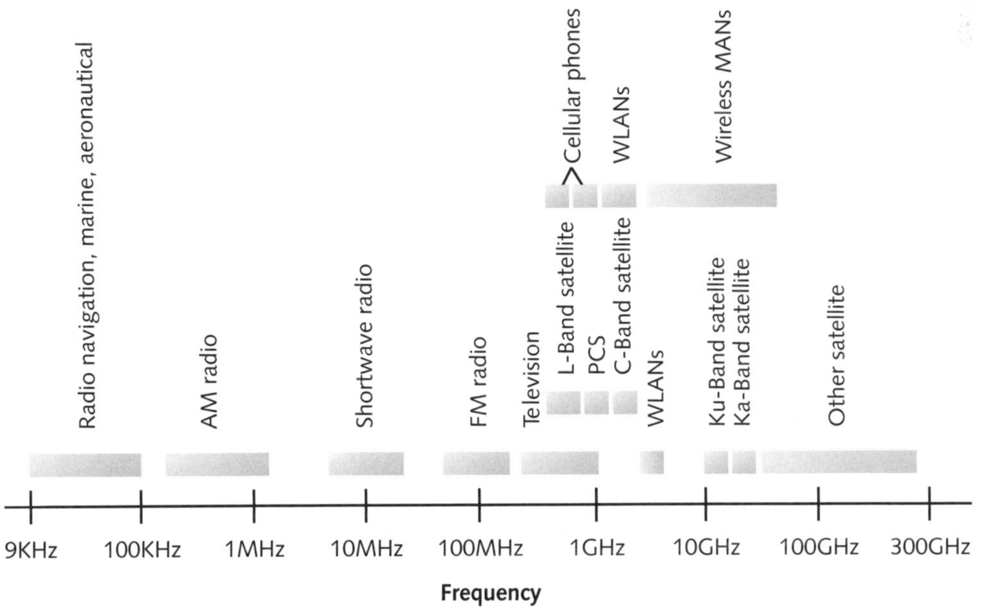

Figure 8-1 The wireless spectrum

Characteristics of Wireless Transmission

In previous chapters you learned about signals that travel over a physical medium, such as a copper or fiber-optic cable. Wired and wireless signals share many similarities, including use of the same Layer 3 and higher protocols, for example. However, the nature of the atmosphere makes wireless transmission vastly different from wired transmission. Because the air provides no fixed path for signals to follow, signals travel without guidance. Contrast this to guided media, such as UTP or fiber-optic cable, which do provide a fixed signal path. The lack of a fixed path requires wireless signals to be transmitted, received, controlled, and corrected differently from wired signals.

Just as with wired signals, wireless signals originate from electrical current traveling along a conductor. The electrical signal travels from the transmitter to an antenna, which then emits the signal, as a series of electromagnetic waves, to the atmosphere. The signal propagates through the air until it reaches its destination. At the destination, another antenna accepts the signal, and a receiver converts it back to current. Figure 8-2 illustrates this process.

Notice that antennas are used for both the transmission and reception of wireless signals. As you would expect, to exchange information, two antennas must be tuned to the same frequency. In communications terminology, this means they share the same channel. Next, you will learn about some fundamental types of antennas and their properties.

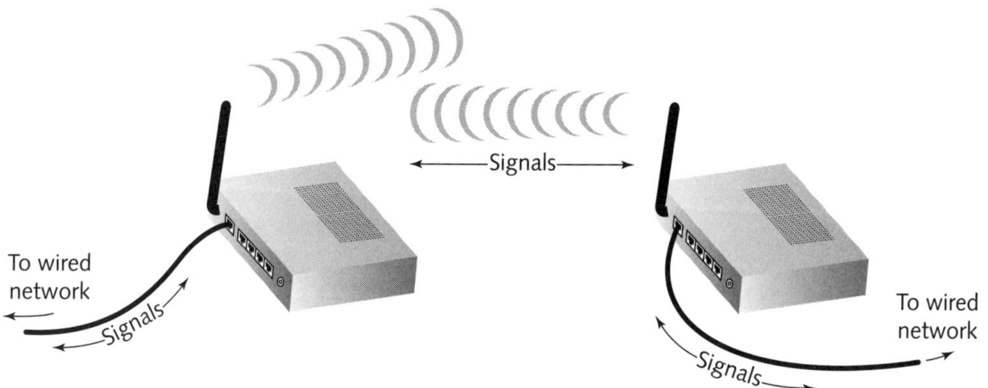

Figure 8-2 Wireless transmission and reception

Antennas

Each type of wireless service requires an antenna specifically designed for that service. The service's specifications determine the antenna's power output, frequency, and radiation pattern. An antenna's **radiation pattern** describes the relative strength over a three-dimensional area of all the electromagnetic energy the antenna sends or receives.

A **directional antenna** issues wireless signals along a single direction. This type of antenna is used when the source needs to communicate with one destination, as in a point-to-point link. A satellite downlink (for example, the kind used to receive digital TV signals) uses directional antennas. In contrast, an **omnidirectional antenna** issues and receives wireless signals with equal strength and clarity in all directions. This type of antenna is used when many different receivers must be able to pick up the signal, or when the receiver's location is highly mobile. TV and radio stations use omnidirectional antennas, as do most towers that transmit cellular telephone signals.

The geographical area that an antenna or wireless system can reach is known as its **range**. Receivers must be within the range to receive accurate signals consistently. Even within an antenna's range, however, signals may be hampered by obstacles and rendered unintelligible.

Signal Propagation

Ideally, a wireless signal would travel directly in a straight line from its transmitter to its intended receiver. This type of propagation, known as **LOS (line-of-sight)**, uses the least amount of energy and results in the reception of the clearest possible signal. However, because the atmosphere is an unguided medium and the path between a transmitter and a receiver is not always clear, wireless signals do not usually follow a straight line. When an obstacle stands in a signal's way, the signal may pass through the object or be absorbed by the object, or it may be subject to any of the following phenomena: reflection, diffraction, or scattering. The object's geometry governs which of these three phenomena occurs.

Reflection in wireless signaling is no different from reflection of other electromagnetic waves, such as light. The wave encounters an obstacle and reflects—or bounces back—toward its source. A wireless signal will bounce off objects whose dimensions are large compared to the signal's average wavelength. In the context of a WLAN, which may use signals with wavelengths between 1 and 10 meters, such objects include walls, floors, ceilings, and the Earth. In addition, signals reflect more readily off conductive materials, like metal, than insulators, like concrete.

In **diffraction**, a wireless signal splits into secondary waves when it encounters an obstruction. The secondary waves continue to propagate in the direction in which they were split. If you could see wireless signals being diffracted, they would appear to be bending around the obstacle. Objects with sharp edges—including the corners of walls and desks—cause diffraction.

Scattering is the diffusion, or the reflection in multiple different directions, of a signal. Scattering occurs when a wireless signal encounters an object that has small dimensions compared to the signal's wavelength. Scattering is also related to the roughness of the surface a wireless signal encounters. The rougher the surface, the more likely a signal is to scatter when it hits that surface. In an office building, objects such as chairs, books, and computers cause scattering of WLAN signals. For signals traveling outdoors, rain, mist, hail, and snow may all cause scattering.

Because of reflection, diffraction, and scattering, wireless signals follow a number of different paths to their destination. Such signals are known as **multipath** signals. Figure 8-3 illustrates multipath signals caused by these three phenomena.

The multipath nature of wireless signals is both a blessing and a curse. On one hand, because signals bounce off obstacles, they have a better chance of reaching their destination. In environments such as an office building, wireless services depend on signals bouncing off walls, ceilings, floors, and furniture so that they may eventually reach their destination. Imagine

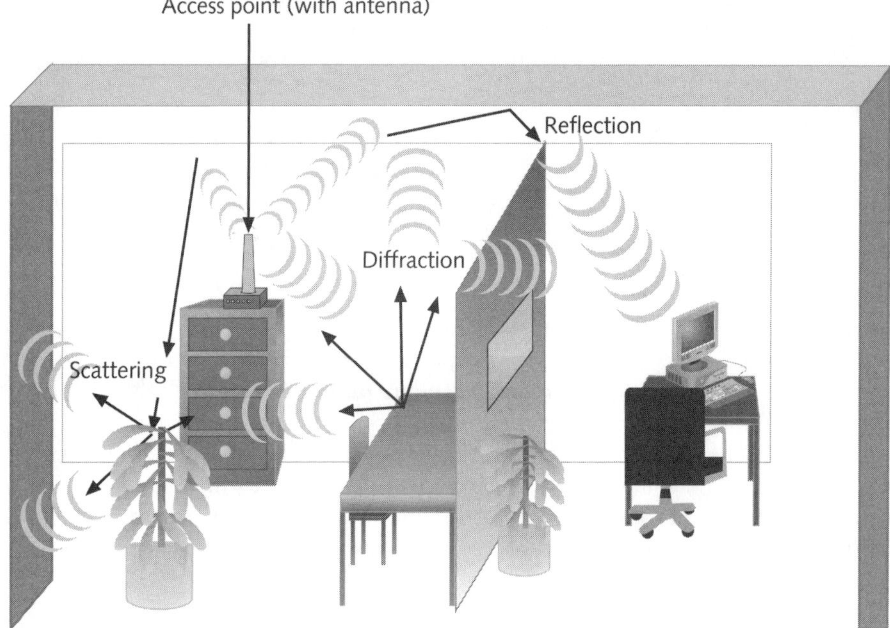

Figure 8-3 Multipath signal propagation

how inconvenient and inefficient it would be, for example, to make sure you were standing within clear view of a transmitter to receive a paging signal.

The downside to multipath signaling is that, because of their various paths, multipath signals travel different distances between their transmitter and a receiver. Thus, multiple instances of the same signal can arrive at a receiver at different times, causing signal delay.

Signal Degradation

No matter what paths wireless signals take, they are bound to run into obstacles. When they do, the original signal issued by the transmitter will experience **fading**, or a change in signal strength as a result of some of the electromagnetic energy being scattered, reflected, or diffracted after being issued by the transmitter. Because of fading, the strength of the signal that reaches the receiver is lower than the transmitted signal's strength. This makes sense because as more waves are reflected, diffracted, or scattered by obstacles, fewer are likely to reach their destination.

As with wired signals, wireless signals also experience attenuation. After a signal is transmitted, the farther it moves away from the transmission antenna the more it weakens. Just as with wired transmission, wireless signals are amplified (if analog) or repeated (if digital) to strengthen the signal so that it can be clearly received. The difference is that the intermediate points through which wireless signals are amplified or repeated are transceivers connected to antennas.

However, attenuation is not the most severe flaw affecting wireless signals. Wireless signals are also susceptible to noise (more often called electromagnetic interference or simply, interference, in the context of wireless communications). Interference is a significant problem for wireless

Net+
4.7
communications because the atmosphere is saturated with electromagnetic waves. For example, WLANs may be affected by cellular phones, mobile phones, or overhead lights.

Interference can distort and weaken a wireless signal in the same way that noise distorts and weakens a wired signal. However, because wireless signals cannot depend on a conduit or shielding to protect them from extraneous EMI, they are more vulnerable to noise. The extent of interference that a wireless signal experiences depends partly on the density of signals within a geographical area. Signals traveling through areas in which many wireless communications systems are in use—for example, the center of a metropolitan area—are the most apt to suffer interference.

Net+ Frequency Ranges

1.7
For many years WLANs have relied on frequencies in the range of 2.4–2.4835GHz, more commonly known as the **2.4GHz band,** to send and receive signals. This band offers 11 communications channels that are unlicensed in the United States. An unlicensed frequency is one for which the FCC does not require users to register their service and reserve it for their sole use. Because the 2.4GHz band also carries cordless telephone and other types of signals, it is highly susceptible to interference. For example, on your home wireless network, your laptop might lose connectivity when your cordless telephone rings. One way to guard against this type of interference is to make sure your access point and cordless telephone use different channels within the 2.4GHz band.

The **5GHz band** is used by newer types of WLANs. The 5GHz band actually comprises four frequency bands: 5.1GHz, 5.3GHz, 5.4GHz, and 5.8GHz. It consists of 24 unlicensed bands, each 20MHz wide. Because the 5GHz band is also used by weather and military radar communications in the United States, WLAN equipment using this range of frequencies must be able to monitor and detect radar signals and, if one is detected, switch to a different channel automatically.

Narrowband, Broadband, and Spread Spectrum Signals

Transmission technologies differ according to how much of the wireless spectrum their signals use. An important distinction is whether a wireless service uses narrowband or broadband signaling. In **narrowband,** a transmitter concentrates the signal energy at a single frequency or in a very small range of frequencies. In contrast to narrowband, broadband uses a relatively wide band of the wireless spectrum. Broadband technologies, as a result of their wider frequency bands, offer higher throughputs than narrowband technologies.

The use of multiple frequencies to transmit a signal is known as **spread-spectrum** technology (because the signal is spread out over the wireless spectrum). In other words, a signal never stays continuously within one frequency range during its transmission. One result of spreading a signal over a wide frequency band is that it requires less power per frequency than narrowband signaling. This distribution of signal strength makes spread-spectrum signals less likely to interfere with narrowband signals traveling in the same frequency band.

Spread-spectrum signaling, originally used with military wireless transmissions in World War II, remains a popular way of making wireless transmissions more secure. Because signals are split across several frequencies according to a sequence known only to the authorized transmitter and receiver, it is much more difficult for unauthorized receivers to capture and decode spread-spectrum signals. To generic receivers, signals issued via spread-spectrum technology appear as unintelligible noise.

One specific implementation of spread spectrum is **FHSS (frequency hopping spread spectrum)**. In FHSS transmission, a signal jumps between several different frequencies within a band in a synchronization pattern known only to the channel's receiver and transmitter. Another type of spread-spectrum signaling is called **DSSS (direct-sequence spread spectrum)**. In DSSS, a signal's bits are distributed over an entire frequency band at once. Each bit is coded so that the receiver can reassemble the original signal upon receiving the bits.

Fixed versus Mobile

Each type of wireless communication falls into one of two categories: fixed or mobile. In **fixed** wireless systems, the locations of the transmitter and receiver do not move. The transmitting antenna focuses its energy directly toward the receiving antenna. This results in a point-to-point link. One advantage of fixed wireless is that because the receiver's location is predictable, energy need not be wasted issuing signals across a large geographical area. Thus, more energy can be used for the signal. Fixed wireless links are used in some data and voice applications. For example, a service provider may obtain data services through a fixed link with a satellite. In cases in which a long distance or difficult terrain must be traversed, fixed wireless links are more economical than cabling.

Many types of communications are unsuited to fixed wireless, however. For example, a waiter who uses a wireless handheld computer to transmit orders to the restaurant's kitchen could not use a service that requires him to remain in one spot to send and receive signals. Instead, WLANs, along with cellular telephone, paging, and many other services, use mobile wireless systems. In **mobile** wireless, the receiver can be located anywhere within the transmitter's range. This allows the receiver to roam from one place to another while continuing to pick up its signal.

Now that you understand some characteristics of wireless transmission, you are ready to learn about the way most WLANs are structured. Later, you'll learn about their access methods and how to install wireless connectivity devices.

WLAN Architecture

3.1

3.4

Because they are not bound by cabling paths between nodes and connectivity devices, wireless networks are not laid out using the same topologies as wired networks. They have their own, different layouts. Smaller wireless networks, in which a small number of nodes closely positioned need to exchange data, can be arranged in an ad hoc fashion. In an **ad hoc** WLAN, wireless nodes, or **stations**, transmit directly to each other via wireless NICs without an intervening connectivity device, as shown in Figure 8-4.

However, an ad hoc arrangement would not work well for a WLAN with many users or whose users are spread out over a wide area, or where obstacles could stand in the way of signals between stations. Instead of communicating directly with each other in ad hoc mode, nearly all WLANs use the infrastructure mode, which depends on an intervening connectivity device called an access point. An **access point (AP)** is a device that accepts wireless signals from multiple

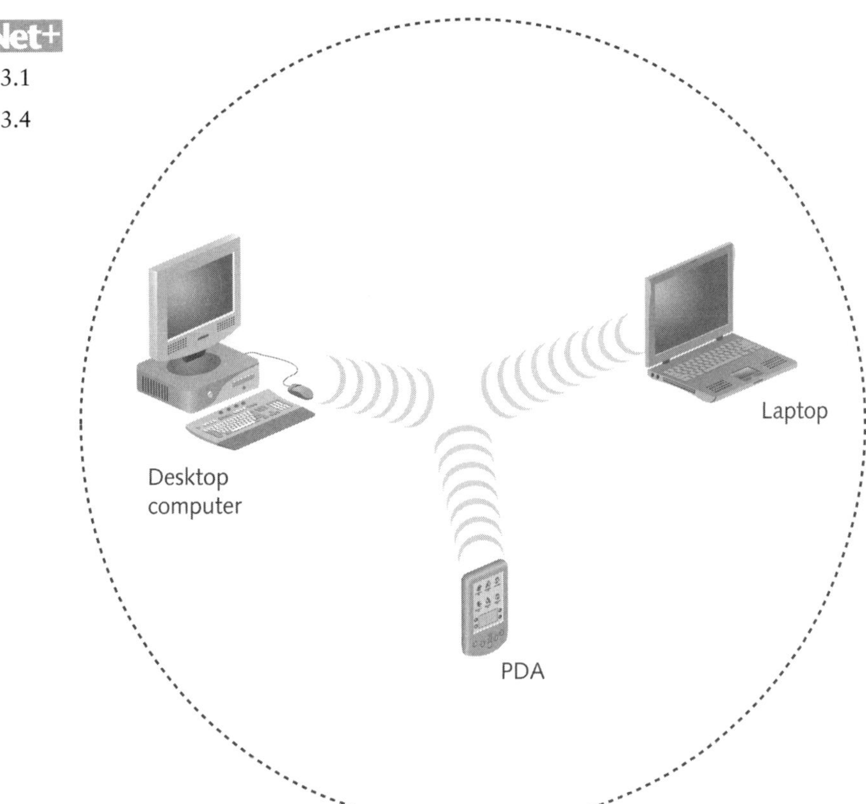

Figure 8-4 An ad hoc WLAN

nodes and retransmits them to the rest of the network. Access points may also be known as **base stations**. Access points for use on small office or home networks often include routing functions. As such, they may also be called **wireless routers** or **wireless gateways**.

To cover its intended range, an access point must have sufficient power and be strategically placed so that stations can communicate with it. For instance, if an access point serves a group of workstations in several offices on one floor in a building, it should probably be located in an open area near the center of that floor. And like other wireless devices, access points contain an antenna connected to their transceivers. An **infrastructure WLAN** is shown in Figure 8-5.

It's common for a WLAN to include several access points. The number of access points depends on the number of stations a WLAN connects. The maximum number of stations each access point can serve varies from 10 to 100, depending on the wireless technology used. Exceeding the recommended maximum leads to a greater incidence of errors and slower overall transmission.

Mobile networking allows wireless nodes to roam from one location to another within a certain range of their access point. This range depends on the wireless access method, the equipment manufacturer, and the office environment. As with other wireless technologies, WLAN signals

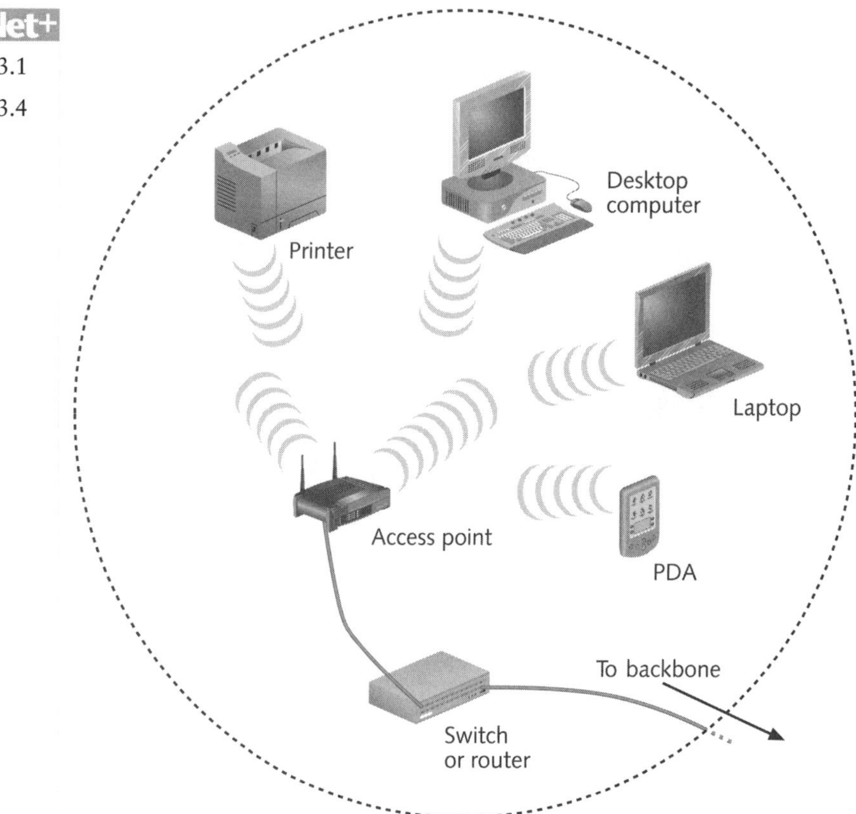

Figure 8-5 An infrastructure WLAN

are subject to interference and obstruction that cause multipath signaling. Therefore, a building with many thick, concrete walls, for example, will limit the effective range of a WLAN more severely than an open area divided into cubicles. In most WLAN scenarios, stations must remain within 300 feet of an access point to maintain optimal transmission speeds.

In addition to connecting multiple nodes within a LAN, wireless technology can be used to connect two different parts of a LAN or two separate LANs. Such connections typically use a fixed link with directional antennas between two access points, as shown in Figure 8-6. Because point-to-point links only have to transmit in one direction, they can apply more energy to signal propagation than mobile wireless links. As a result of applying more energy to the signal, their maximum transmission distance is greater. In the case of connecting two WLANs, access points could be as far as 1,000 feet apart.

WLANs support the same protocols (for example, TCP/IP) and operating systems (for example, UNIX, Linux, or Windows) as wired LANs. This compatibility ensures that wireless and wired transmission methods can be integrated on the same network. Only the signaling techniques differ between wireless and wired portions of a LAN. However, techniques for generating and encoding wireless signals vary from one WLAN standard to another. The following section describes the most popular WLAN physical and data link layer standards.

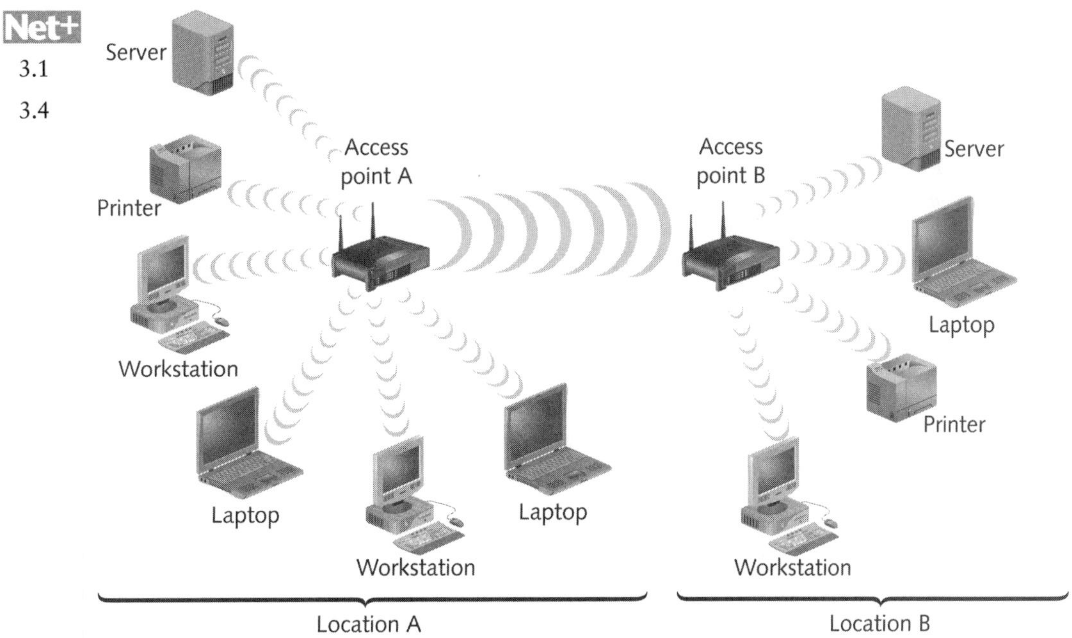

Figure 8-6 WLAN interconnection

802.11 WLANs

Similar to the development of wired network access technologies, the evolution of wireless access methods did not follow one direct and cooperative path, but grew from the efforts of multiple vendors and organizations. Now, the industry accepts a handful of different wireless technologies. Each wireless technology is defined by a standard that describes unique functions at both the physical and the data link layers of the OSI model. These standards differ in their specified signaling methods, geographic ranges, and frequency usages, among other things. Such differences make certain technologies better suited to home networks and others better suited to networks at large organizations. The most popular wireless standards used on contemporary LANs are those developed by IEEE's 802.11 committee.

IEEE released its first wireless network standard in 1997. Since then, its WLAN standards committee, also known as the 802.11 committee, has published several distinct standards related to wireless networking. Each IEEE wireless network access standard is named after the 802.11 task group (or subcommittee) that developed it. The three IEEE 802.11 task groups that have generated notable wireless standards are 802.11b, 802.11a, and 802.11g. In addition, a fourth standard, 802.11n, in draft form at the time this was written, will be ratified in 2009. These four 802.11 standards (also known as **Wi-Fi**, for wireless fidelity) share many characteristics. For example, although some of their physical layer services vary, all three use half-duplex signaling. In other words, a wireless station using one of the 802.11 techniques can either transmit or receive but cannot do both simultaneously (assuming the station has only one transceiver installed, as is usually the case). In addition, all 802.11 networks follow the same access method, as described in the following section.

Net+ Access Method

1.7   In Chapter 2 you learned that the MAC sublayer of the data link layer is responsible for appending physical addresses to a data frame and for governing multiple nodes' access to a single medium. As with 802.3 (Ethernet), the 802.11 MAC services append 48-bit (or 6-byte) physical addresses to a frame to identify its source and destination. The use of the same physical addressing scheme allows 802.11 networks to be easily combined with other IEEE 802 networks, including Ethernet networks. However, because wireless devices are not designed to transmit and receive simultaneously (and, therefore, cannot quickly detect collisions), 802.11 networks use a different access method than Ethernet networks.

802.11 standards specify the use of **CSMA/CA (Carrier Sense Multiple Access with Collision Avoidance)** to access a shared medium. Using CSMA/CA, before a station begins to send data on an 802.11 network, it checks for existing wireless transmissions. If the source node detects no transmission activity on the network, it waits a brief, random amount of time and then sends its transmission. If the source does detect activity, it waits a brief period of time before checking the channel again. The destination node receives the transmission and, after verifying its accuracy, issues an acknowledgment (ACK) packet to the source. If the source receives this acknowledgment, it assumes the transmission was properly completed. However, interference or other transmissions on the network could impede this exchange. If, after transmitting a message, the source node fails to receive acknowledgment from the destination node, it assumes its transmission did not arrive properly, and it begins the CSMA/CA process anew. Compared to CSMA/CD (Carrier Sense Multiple Access with Collision Detection), CSMA/CA minimizes, but does not eliminate, the potential for collisions.

The use of ACK packets to verify every transmission means that 802.11 networks require more overhead than 802.3 networks. Therefore, a wireless network with a theoretical maximum throughput of 10Mbps will, in fact, transmit less data per second than a wired Ethernet network with the same theoretical maximum throughput. In reality, most wireless networks tend to achieve between one-third and one-half of their theoretical maximum throughput. For example, one type of 802.11 network, 802.11g is rated for a maximum of 54Mbps; most 802.11g networks achieve between 20 and 25Mbps. As described later in this chapter, however, the new 802.11n standard includes several techniques for reducing overhead and making the technology's actual throughput match its theoretical throughput.

One way to ensure that packets are not inhibited by other transmissions is to reserve the medium for one station's use. In 802.11, this can be accomplished through the optional **RTS/CTS (Request to Send/Clear to Send)** protocol. RTS/CTS enables a source node to issue an RTS signal to an access point requesting the exclusive opportunity to transmit. If the access point agrees by responding with a CTS signal, the access point temporarily suspends communication with all stations in its range and waits for the source node to complete its transmission. RTS/CTS is not routinely used by wireless stations, but for transmissions involving large packets (those more subject to damage by interference), RTS/CTS can prove more efficient. On the other hand, using RTS/CTS further decreases the overall efficiency of the 802.11 network.

Association

Suppose you have just purchased a new laptop with a wireless NIC that supports one of the 802.11 wireless standards. When you bring your laptop to a local Internet café and turn it on, your laptop soon prompts you to log on to the café's wireless network to gain access to the Internet. This seemingly simple process, known as **association**, involves a number of

Net+
1.7

packet exchanges between the café's access point and your computer. Association is another function of the MAC sublayer described in the 802.11 standard.

As long as a station is on and has its wireless protocols running, it periodically surveys its surroundings for evidence of an access point, a task known as **scanning**. A station can use either active scanning or passive scanning. In **active scanning**, the station transmits a special frame, known as a **probe**, on all available channels within its frequency range. When an access point finds the probe frame, it issues a probe response. This response contains all the information a station needs to associate with the access point, including a status code and station ID number for that station. After receiving the probe response, a station can agree to associate with that access point. The two nodes begin communicating over the frequency channel specified by the access point.

In **passive scanning**, a wireless station listens on all channels within its frequency range for a special signal, known as a **beacon frame**, issued from an access point. The beacon frame contains information that a wireless node requires to associate itself with the access point. For example, the frame indicates the network's transmission rate and the **SSID (service set identifier)**, a unique character string used to identify an access point. After detecting a beacon frame, the station can choose to associate with that access point. The two nodes agree on a frequency channel and begin communicating.

When setting up a WLAN, most network administrators use the access point's configuration utility to assign a unique SSID (rather than the default SSID provided by the manufacturer). This can contribute to better security and easier network management. For example, the access point used by employees in the customer service department of a company could be assigned the SSID "CustSvc". In IEEE terminology, a group of stations that share an access point are said to be part of one **BSS (basic service set)**. The identifier for this group of stations is known as a **BSSID (basic service set identifier)**.

Some WLANs are large enough to require multiple access points. A group of access points connected to the same LAN are known collectively as an **ESS (extended service set)**. BSSs that belong to the same ESS share a special identifier, called an **ESSID (extended service set identifier)**. (In practice, many networking professionals don't distinguish between the terms *SSID* and *ESSID*. They simply configure every access point in a group or LAN with the same SSID.)

Within an ESS, a client can associate with any one of many access points that use the same ESSID. That allows users to roam about an office without losing wireless network service. In fact, **roaming** is the term applied to a station moving from one BSS to another without losing connectivity.

Figure 8-7 illustrates a network with only one BSS; Figure 8-8 shows a network encompassing multiple BSSs that form an ESS.

Net+
1.7

6.6

If a station detects the presence of several access points, it will choose the one with the strongest signal and the lowest error rate compared to other access points. Note that a station does not necessarily choose the *closest* access point. For example, in the case of an Internet café, if another user brought his own access point to the café and his access point had a signal twice as strong as the café's access point, even if the new access point were farther away, your laptop would associate with it instead. Other users' laptops would also associate with his access point. (This assumes that the laptops are not configured to connect to only one specific access point, identified by its SSID in the station's wireless connection properties). This situation can present a security risk for any station within range of this powerful, rogue access point.

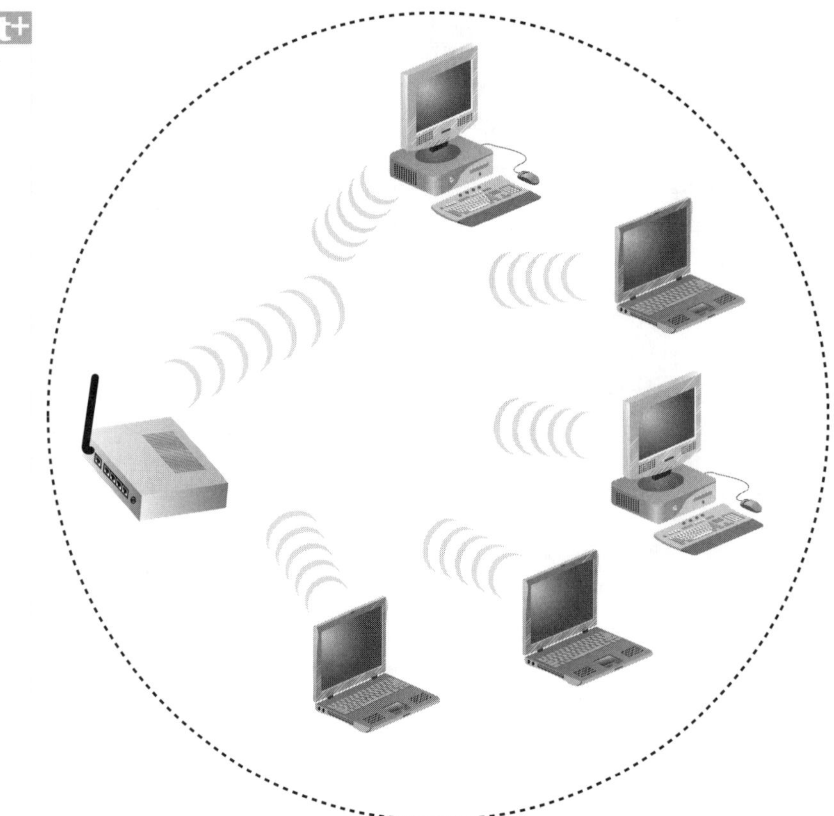

Figure 8-7 A network with a single BSS

On a network with several authorized access points in an ESS, however, a station must be able to associate with any access point while maintaining network connectivity. Suppose that when you begin work in the morning at your desk, your laptop associates with an access point located in a telco room down the hall. Later, you need to give a presentation in the company's main conference room on another floor of your building. Without your intervention, your laptop will choose a different access point as you travel to the conference room (perhaps more than one, depending on the size of your company's building and network).

Connecting to a different access point requires reassociation. **Reassociation** occurs when a mobile user moves out of one access point's range and into the range of another, as described in the previous example. It might also happen if the initial access point is experiencing a high rate of errors. On a network with multiple access points, network managers can take advantage of the stations' scanning feature to automatically balance transmission loads between those access points.

The IEEE 802.11 standard specifies communication between two wireless nodes, or stations, and between a station and an access point. However, it does not specify how two access points should communicate. Therefore, when designing an 802.11 network, it is best to use access points manufactured by the same company, to ensure full compatibility.

Figure 8-8 A network with multiple BSSs forming an ESS

Frames

You have learned about some types of overhead required to manage access to the 802.11 wireless networks—for example, ACKs, probes, and beacons. For each function, the 802.11 standard specifies a frame type at the MAC sublayer. These multiple frame types are divided into three groups: control, management, and data. Management frames are those involved in association and reassociation, such as the probe and beacon frames. Control frames are those related to medium access and data delivery, such as the ACK and RTS/CTS frames. Data frames are those that carry the data sent between stations. An 802.11 data frame is illustrated in Figure 8-9. (Details of control and management frames are beyond the scope of this book.) Glancing at the 802.11 data frame, its significant overhead—that is, the large quantity of fields added to the data field—becomes apparent. These fields are explained next.

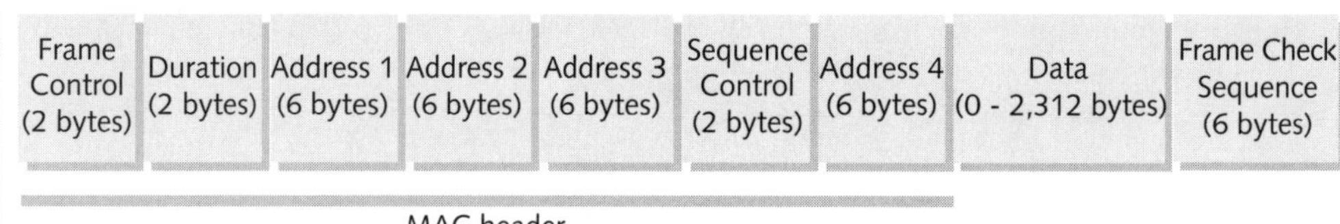

Figure 8-9 Basic 802.11 data frame

Compare the 802.11 data frame with the Ethernet_II data frame pictured earlier in Figure 5-15. Notice that the wireless data frame contains four address fields, rather than two. These four addresses are the source address, transmitter address, receiver address, and destination address. The transmitter and receiver addresses refer to the access point or another intermediary device (if used) on the wireless network. The source and destination addresses have the same meaning as they do in the Ethernet_II frame.

Another unique characteristic of the 802.11 data frame is its Sequence Control field. This field is used to indicate how a large packet is fragmented—that is, subdivided into smaller packets for more reliable delivery. Recall that on wired TCP/IP networks, error checking occurs at the transport layer of the OSI model and packet fragmentation, if necessary, occurs at the network layer. However, in 802.11 networks, error checking and packet fragmentation are handled at the MAC sublayer of the data link layer. By handling fragmentation at a lower layer, 802.11 makes its transmission—which is less efficient and more error prone—transparent to higher layers. This means 802.11 nodes are more easily integrated with 802.3 networks and prevent the 802.11 segments of an integrated network from slowing down the 802.3 segments.

The Frame Control field in an 802.11 data frame holds information about the protocol in use, the type of frame being transmitted, whether the frame is part of a larger, fragmented packet, whether the frame is one that was reissued after an unverified delivery attempt, what type of security the frame uses, and so on. Security is a significant concern with WLANs, because access points are typically more vulnerable than devices on a wired network. Wireless security is discussed in detail along with other network security topics in Chapter 12.

Although 802.11b, 802.11a, 802.11g, and 802.11n share all of the MAC sublayer characteristics described in the previous sections, they differ in their modulation methods, frequency usage, and ranges. In other words, each varies at the physical layer. In addition, 802.11n modifies the way frames are used at the MAC sublayer. The following sections summarize those differences.

802.11b

In 1999, the IEEE released its **802.11b** standard, which is unique among 802.11 standards in its use of DSSS (direct-sequence spread spectrum) signaling. Recall that in DSSS, a signal is distributed over the entire bandwidth of the allocated spectrum. 802.11b uses the 2.4–2.4835GHz frequency range (better known as the 2.4GHz band) and separates it into 22MHz channels. 802.11b provides a theoretical maximum of 11Mbps throughput; actual throughput is typically around 5Mbps. To ensure this throughput, wireless nodes must stay within 100 meters (or approximately 330 feet) of an access point or each other, in the case of an ad hoc network. Among all the 802.11 standards, 802.11b was the first to take hold. It is also the least expensive

1.7

of all the 802.11 WLAN technologies. In recent years, network administrators have replaced 802.11b with the much faster (and backward compatible) 802.11g standard.

802.11a

Although the 802.11a task group began its standards work before the 802.11b group, 802.11a was released after 802.11b. The **802.11a** standard differs from 802.11b and 802.11g in that it uses channels in the 5GHz band and provides a maximum theoretical throughput of 54Mbps, though its effective throughput falls generally between 11 and 18Mbps. 802.11a's high throughput is attributable to its use of higher frequencies, its unique method of modulating data, and more available bandwidth. Perhaps most significant is that the 5GHz band is not as congested as the 2.4GHz band. Thus, 802.11a signals are less likely to suffer interference from microwave ovens, cordless phones, motors, and other (incompatible) WLAN signals. However, higher-frequency signals require more power to transmit, and they travel shorter distances than lower-frequency signals. The average geographic range for an 802.11a antenna is 20 meters, or approximately 66 feet. As a result, 802.11a networks require a greater density of access points between the wired LAN and wireless clients to cover the same distance that 802.11b networks cover. The additional access points, as well as the nature of 802.11a equipment, make this standard more expensive than either 802.11b or 802.11g. Of the three currently ratified 802.11 standards, 802.11a is the least popular.

802.11g

IEEE's **802.11g** WLAN standard is designed to be just as affordable as 802.11b while increasing its maximum theoretical throughput from 11Mbps to 54Mbps through different data modulation techniques. The effective throughput of 802.11g ranges generally from 20 to 25Mbps. An 802.11g antenna has a geographic range of 100 meters (or approximately 330 feet).

802.11g, like 802.11b, uses the 2.4GHz frequency band. In addition to its high throughput, 802.11g benefits from being compatible with 802.11b networks. Thus, if a network administrator installed 802.11b access points on her LAN three years ago, this year she could add 802.11g access points and laptops, and the laptops could roam between the ranges of the 802.11b and 802.11g access points without an interruption in service. 802.11g's compatibility with the more established 802.11b has caused many network managers to choose it over 802.11a, despite 802.11a's comparative advantages.

802.11n

The newest 802.11 standard drafted by IEEE is **802.11n**. At the time this was written, the standard was expected to be ratified in late 2009. However, it has been in development for years, and as early as mid-2007, manufacturers were selling 802.11n-compatible transceivers in their networking equipment. The primary goal of IEEE's 802.11n committee was to create a wireless standard that provided much higher effective throughput than the other 802.11 standards. By all accounts, they succeeded. 802.11n boasts a maximum throughput of 600Mbps, making it a threat to Fast Ethernet and a realistic platform for telephone and video signals. IEEE also specified that the 802.11n standard must be backward compatible with the 802.11a, b, and g standards.

802.11n may use either the 2.4GHz or 5GHz frequency range. It employs the same data modulation techniques used by 802.11a and 802.11g. However, it differs dramatically from

Net+
1.7
the other three 802.11 standards in how it manages frames, channels, and encoding. These differences, which allow 802.11n to achieve its high throughput, include the following innovations:

- *MIMO (multiple input-multiple output)*—In 802.11n, multiple antennas on an access point may issue a signal to one or more receivers. As you learned earlier, signals issued by an omnidirectional antenna will propagate in a multipath fashion. Therefore, multiple signals cannot be expected to arrive at the same receiver in concert. To account for this, in MIMO the phases of these signals are adjusted when they reach a receiving station, and the strength of the multiple signals are summed. To properly adjust phases, MIMO requires stations to update access points with information about their location. Among 802.11 equipment, this function is only available with 802.11n-capable transceivers. In addition to increasing the network's throughput, MIMO can increase an access point's range. Figure 8-10 shows an 802.11n access point with three antennas.

- *Channel bonding*—In 802.11n, two adjacent 20MHz channels can be combined, or bonded, to make a 40MHz channel. In fact, bonding two 20MHz channels more than doubles the bandwidth available in a single 20MHz channel. That's because the small amount of bandwidth normally reserved as buffers against interference at the top and

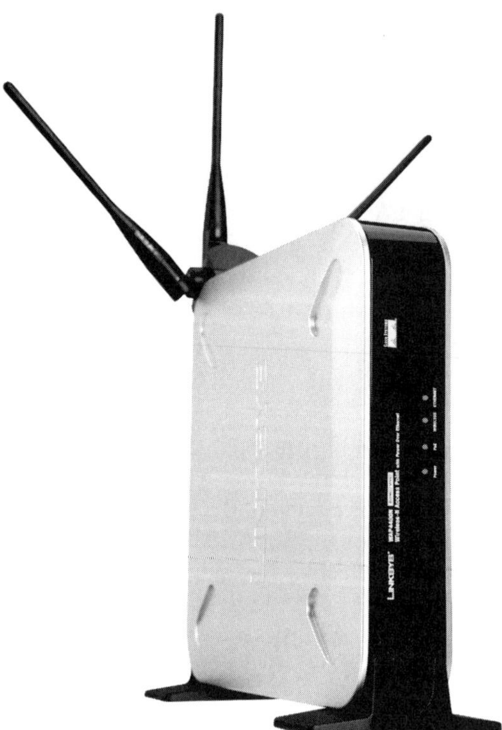

Figure 8-10 802.11n access point with three antennas

1.7

bottom of the 20MHz channels can be assigned to carry data instead. Channel bonding is not recommended for use in the 2.4GHz band, however. In that range, the probability of interference is too high to make channel bonding practical. Because the 5GHz band contains more channels and is less crowded (at least, for now), it's better suited to channel bonding.

- *Higher modulation rates*—As mentioned earlier, 802.11n uses the same type of data modulation used by 802.11a and 802.11g. This modulation technique allows for a single channel to be subdivided into multiple, smaller channels. Simply put, 802.11n makes more efficient use of these smaller channels and is capable of choosing from different encoding methods. 802.11n also allows for shortening the period of time transceivers wait between issuing each bit of data (which is necessary to prevent interference).

- *Frame aggregation*—802.11n networks can use one of two techniques for combining multiple frames (of the type shown in Figure 8-9) into one larger frame. Combining multiple frames reduces overhead. Suppose four small data frames are combined into one larger frame. Each larger frame will have only one copy of the same addressing information that would appear in the smaller frames. Proportionally, the data field takes up more of the aggregated frame's space. In addition, replacing four small frames with one large frame means an access point and station will have to exchange one-quarter the number of statements to negotiate media access and error control. To take advantage of frame aggregation, the maximum frame size for 802.11n is 64KB, compared to the maximum 802.11a, b, and g frame size of 4KB. The potential disadvantage with using larger frames is the increased probability of errors when transmitting larger blocks of data. Figure 8-11 illustrates the relatively low overhead of an aggregated 802.11n frame.

Note that not all of the techniques listed here will be used in every 802.11n implementation. Further, reaching maximum throughput depends on the number and type of these strategies used. It also depends on whether the network uses the 2.4GHz or 5GHz band. Considering these factors, an 802.11n network's actual throughputs will vary between 65 to 600Mbps.

As mentioned earlier, 802.11n is compatible with all three earlier versions of the 802.11 standard. However, in mixed environments, some of the new standard's techniques for improving throughput will not be possible. To ensure the fastest data rates on your 802.11n LAN, it's optimal to use only 802.11n-compatible devices.

To qualify for Network+ certification, you need to understand the differences between the 802.11 wireless standards. The next section describes the Bluetooth wireless standard, which, though less common and not included on the Network+ exam, is still used on some networks.

Figure 8-11 Aggregated 802.11n frame

Bluetooth Networks

In the early 1990s, Ericsson began developing a wireless networking technology for use between multiple devices, including cordless telephones, PDAs, computers, printers, keyboards, telephone headsets, and pagers, in a home. It was designed to carry voice, video, and data signals over the same communications channels. Besides being compatible with a variety of devices, this technology was also meant to require little power and cover short ranges. In 1998, Intel, Nokia, Toshiba, and IBM joined Sony Ericsson to form the **Bluetooth Special Interest Group (SIG)** (its members currently number over 9,000 companies), whose aim was to refine and standardize this technology. The resulting standard was named **Bluetooth**. Bluetooth is a mobile wireless networking standard that uses FHSS (frequency hopping spread spectrum) RF signaling in the 2.4GHz band. Recall that in FHSS, a signal hops between multiple frequencies within a band in a synchronization pattern known only to the channel's receiver and transmitter.

Bluetooth was named after King Harald I of Denmark, who ruled in the 10th century. One legend has it that he was so fond of eating blueberries that his teeth were discolored, earning him the nickname "Bluetooth." This king was also famous for unifying hostile tribes from Denmark, Norway, and Sweden, just as Bluetooth can unify disparate network nodes.

The original Bluetooth standard, version 1.1, was designed to achieve a maximum theoretical throughput of 1Mbps. However, its effective throughput is 723Kbps, with error correction and control data consuming the remaining bandwidth. The latest version of the standard, version 2.0, was released in 2004. This version uses different encoding schemes that allow Bluetooth to achieve up to 2.1Mbps throughput. (The newer version of Bluetooth is backward compatible, meaning that devices running version 2.0 can communicate with devices running earlier versions of Bluetooth.) The Bluetooth 1.1 and 1.2 standards recommend that communicating nodes be spaced no farther than 10 meters (or approximately 33 feet) apart. When using Bluetooth version 2.0, communicating nodes can be as far as 30 meters (or approximately 100 feet) apart.

Bluetooth was designed to be used on small networks composed of personal communications devices, also known as **PANs (personal area networks)**. However, due to Bluetooth's relatively low throughput and short range, it proved impractical for business LANs. Nevertheless, it has become a popular wireless technology for communicating among cellular telephones, phone headsets, computer peripherals (such as mice and keyboards), and PDAs.

Summary of WLAN Standards

 To summarize what you have learned about wireless network standards, Table 8-1 offers comparisons of the common wireless networking standards, their ranges, and throughputs.

1.7

The actual geographic range of any wireless technology depends on several factors, including the power of the antenna, physical barriers or obstacles between sending and receiving nodes, and interference in the environment. Therefore, although a technology is rated for a certain average geographic range, it may actually transmit signals in a shorter or longer range.

1.7

Table 8-1 Wireless Standards

Standard	Frequency Range	Theoretical Maximum Throughput	Effective Throughput (Approximate)	Average Geographic Range
802.11b	2.4GHz	11Mbps	5Mbps	100 meters (or approximately 330 feet)
802.11a	5GHz	54Mbps	11–18Mbps	20 meters (or approximately 66 feet)
802.11g	2.4GHz	54Mbps	20–25Mbps	100 meters (or approximately 330 feet)
802.11n	2.4GHz or 5GHz	65 to 600Mbps	65 to 600Mbps	Up to 400 meters (or approximately 1,310 feet) if MIMO used
Bluetooth ver. 1.x	2.4GHz	1Mbps	723Kbps	10 meters (or approximately 33 feet)
Bluetooth ver. 2.0	2.4GHz	2.1Mbps	1.5Mbps	30 meters (or approximately 100 feet)

3.4

Implementing a WLAN

Now that you understand how wireless signals are exchanged, what can hinder them, and which physical and data link layer standards they may follow, you are ready to put these ideas into practice. This section first describes how to design small WLANs, the types you might use at home or in a small office. It also describes how larger, enterprise-wide WANs are formed. Next it walks you through installing and configuring access points and clients. Finally, it details the pitfalls of implementing WLANs and how to avoid them. Generally speaking, the material in this section applies to the most popular WLAN standards, 802.11b and 802.11g. However, some aspects of WLAN implementation hold true no matter which standard you follow.

Determining the Design

You have learned that WLANs may be arranged as ad hoc or infrastructure networks. You also know that infrastructure WLANs are far more common. This section assumes your WLAN follows the infrastructure model, and as such, will include access points.

A home or small office network might call for only one access point. In this case the access point, often combined with switching and routing functions, connects wireless clients to the LAN and acts as their gateway to the Internet. Note that the access point functions independently from the Internet access technology. In other words, configuring your home or small office WLAN follows the same principles no matter whether you connect to the Internet using broadband cable or DSL.

Figure 8-12 illustrates the typical arrangement of a home or small office WLAN. Notice that the access point (or wireless router) is connected to the cable or DSL modem using an RJ-45 cable. The cable is inserted into the access point's WAN port, which is set apart from the other data ports (and might be labeled "Internet" or remain unlabeled). The additional ports on the access point allow for wired access to the router. An access point that does not include routing or switching functions would lack these extra ports and act much like a wireless hub.

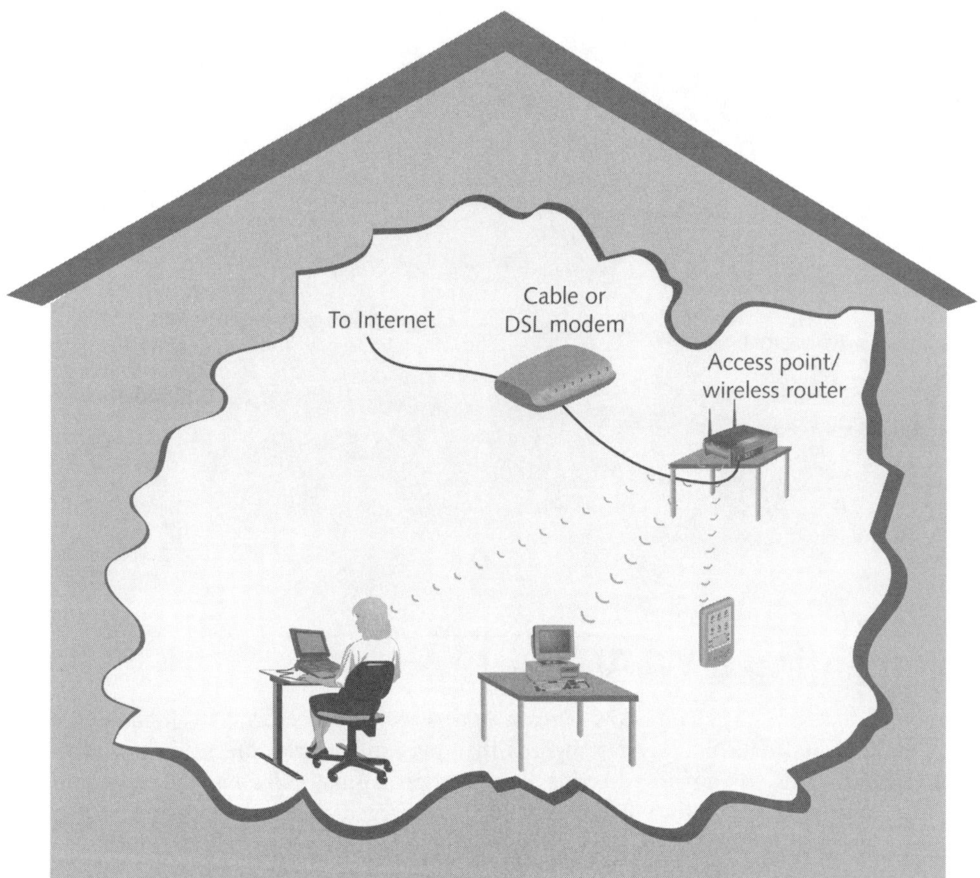

Figure 8-12 Home or small office WLAN arrangement

Placement of an access point on a WLAN must take into account the typical distances between the access point and its clients. If your small office spans three floors, for instance, and clients are evenly distributed among the floors, you might choose to situate the access point on the second floor. Recall that 802.11a, b, and g signals can extend a maximum of 330 feet and still deliver data reliably. Also consider the type and number of obstacles between the access point and clients. For example, if your three-story building is constructed like a bunker with massive concrete floors, you might consider installing a separate access point on each floor. For best signal coverage, place the access point in a high spot, such as on a shelf or rack or in a drop ceiling. Also, make sure it's not close to potential sources of interference, including cordless phones and microwave ovens.

Larger WLANs warrant a more systematic approach to access point placement. Before placing access points in every telco room, it's wise to conduct a site survey. A **site survey** assesses client requirements, facility characteristics, and coverage areas to determine an access point arrangement that will ensure reliable wireless connectivity within a given area. For example, suppose you are the network manager for a large organization whose wireless clients are distributed over six floors of a building. On two floors, your organization takes up 2,000 square feet of office space, but on the other four floors, your offices are limited to only 200 square feet. In addition, clients move between floors regularly. Other building occupants are also

Net+
3.4

running wireless networks. As part of a site survey, you should study building blueprints to help identify potential obstacles and clarify the distances your network needs to span on each floor. The site survey will indicate whether certain floors require multiple access points. Visually inspecting the floors will also help determine coverage areas and best access point locations. Measuring the signal coverage and strength from other WLANs will inform your decision about the optimal strength and frequency for your wireless signals.

A site survey also includes testing proposed access point locations. In testing, a "dummy" access point is carried from location to location while a wireless client connects to it and measures its range and throughput. (Some companies sell software specially designed to conduct such testing.) Most important is testing wireless access from the farthest corners of your space. Also, testing will reveal unforeseen obstacles, such as EMI issued from lights or heavy machinery.

After a site survey has identified and verified the optimal quantity and location of access points, you are ready to install them. Recall that to ensure seamless connectivity from one coverage area to another, all access points must belong to the same ESS and share an ESSID. Configuring access points, including assigning ESSIDs, is described in the next section.

Figure 8-13 shows an example of an enterprise-wide WLAN.

When designing an enterprise-wide WLAN, you must consider how the wireless portions of the LAN will integrate with the wired portions. Access points connect the two. But an access point may perform other functions as well. It may provide security features, by, for example, including and excluding certain clients. It may participate in VLANs, allowing mobile clients to move from one access point's range to another while belonging to the same virtual LAN. Every wireless client's MAC address can be associated with an access point, and each access point can be associated with a port on a switch. When these ports are grouped in a VLAN, it

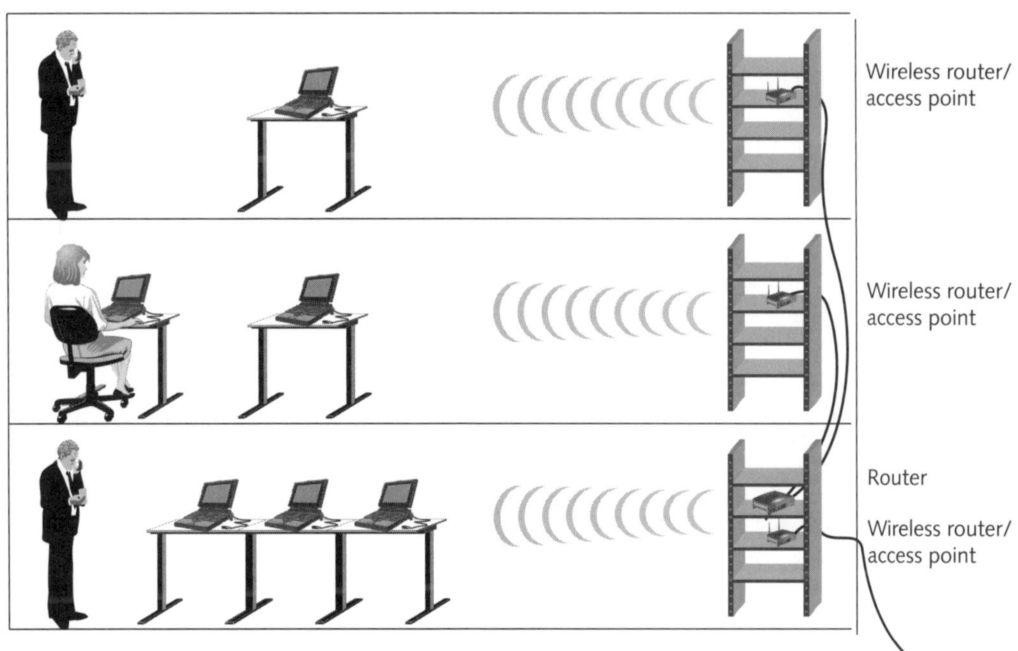

Figure 8-13 Enterprise-wide WLAN

 doesn't matter with which access point a client associates. Because the client stays in the same grouping, it can continue to communicate with the network as if it had remained in one spot.

3.4

Configuring Wireless Connectivity Devices

3.1

3.4

You have learned that access points provide wireless connectivity for mobile clients on an infrastructure WLAN. Access points vary in which wireless standards they support, antenna strength, and optional features such as support for voice signals or the latest security measures. You can find a small access point or wireless router suitable for home or small-office use for less than $30. More sophisticated or specialized access points—for example, those designed for rugged outdoor use, as on city streets or at train platforms—cost much more. However, as wireless networking has become commonplace, sophistication in even the least expensive devices has increased.

In this section, you'll learn how to configure one popular, low-cost access point, a NETGEAR WGR614 (v7). This access point comes with four switch ports and routing capabilities. It supports 802.11b and 802.11g transmission. Configuration steps on other small wireless connectivity devices will differ somewhat, but you'll follow a similar process and modify the same variables.

For initial configuration, it's best to connect to an access point or wireless router directly using a patch cable. Most wireless routers come with installation software designed to guide you through the configuration process step-by-step. After connecting your workstation to the wireless router, you can insert the CD-ROM or DVD that came with the router into your workstation's CD-ROM or DVD drive, and then follow the prompts. Alternatively, you could point your browser to the device's default IP address or Web address. For example, on many routers this address is 192.168.1.1. On the NETGEAR WGR614, it's *www.routerlogin.net/basicsetting.htm* (though, in fact, pointing your browser to 192.168.1.1 will also work on this model). The following steps assume that your workstation is only connected to the wireless router and not connected to a LAN or WLAN when you begin.

To configure the essential properties on a NETGEAR WGR614 access point and wireless router from a workstation running the Windows XP or Windows Vista operating system:

1. Plug in the router's power adapter and then use an RJ-45 patch cable to connect your workstation's LAN port to one of the wireless router's data ports.

2. Click the **Start** button, select **Run**, and then type **www.routerlogin.net/basicsetting.htm** in the Open text box.

3. Click **OK**. Your browser opens, and the Prompt dialog box appears. Under User Name, enter **admin**. Under Password, enter **password**. These are the default values set by the manufacturer.

After you have launched the NETGEAR router setup program, you might be prompted to log in again when attempting to change a setting. This occurs when a certain period of time has passed during which you have not interacted with the setup program.

4. Click **OK**. The NETGEAR router Basic Settings page appears, as shown in Figure 8-14.

5. Notice that the Basic Settings page allows you to do the following: enter your login ID and password given to you by your ISP; choose whether you want to assign the wireless device a static IP address or accept a dynamic address from your ISP; choose your DNS

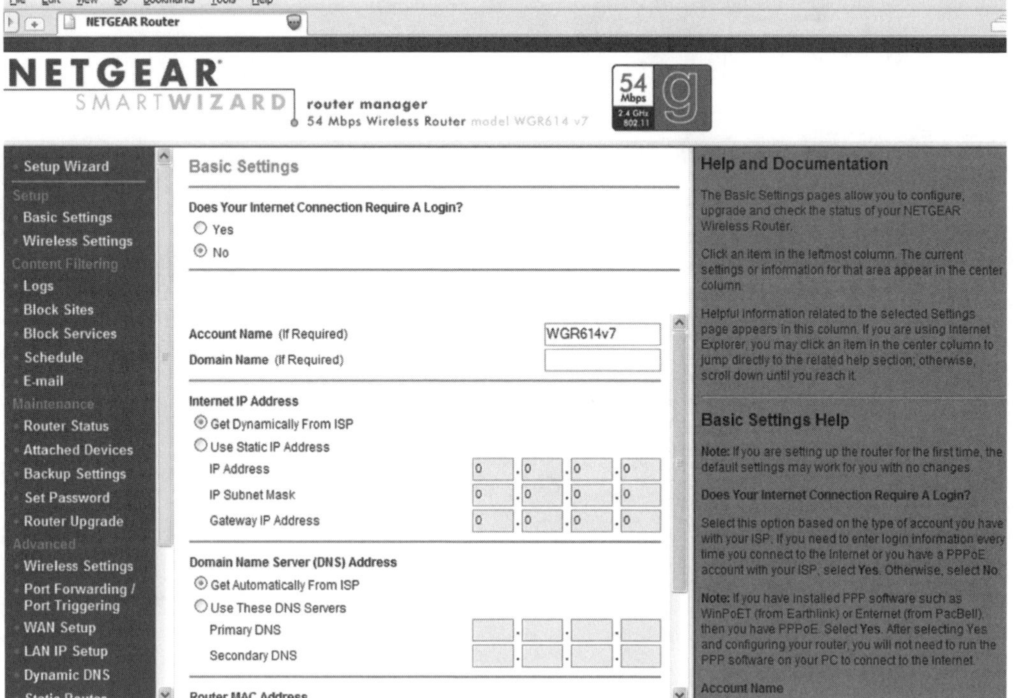

Figure 8-14 The NETGEAR router Basic Settings page

server; and, finally, change the router's MAC address. If your wireless router will connect your WLAN with the Internet, you must at least indicate that your ISP requires a login and enter your ISP account information here.

6. Under the Setup heading in the navigation menu on the left, select **Wireless Settings**. The NETGEAR router Wireless Settings page appears, as shown in Figure 8-15.

7. In the Name (SSID) text box, you can (and should) change the access point's SSID. As mentioned earlier in this chapter, many network administrators change the SSID to reflect the BSS or ESS it serves. For example, an access point that serves your company's finance department might have the SSID "Finance_Dept." Suppose the finance department were spread across four floors, each requiring its own access point. In that case, every access point would have an SSID of "Finance_Dept." Note that an SSID may contain numbers, letters, and special characters and is case sensitive. Change the SSID from NETGEAR to **CLASS_1**, and then click **Apply** to save your changes. Wait while the setup program reconfigures your wireless router.

8. The Region choice is preselected, based on the country your router was manufactured to operate in, and cannot be changed.

9. You can, however, change the Channel and Mode settings. You might want to change the channel if you suspect other wireless devices near your WLAN are communicating over the preselected channel. (After changing an access point's channel, you needn't change channel settings on wireless clients; as described earlier in this chapter, they will scan and find the access point's channel.) For now, keep the default channel, 11.

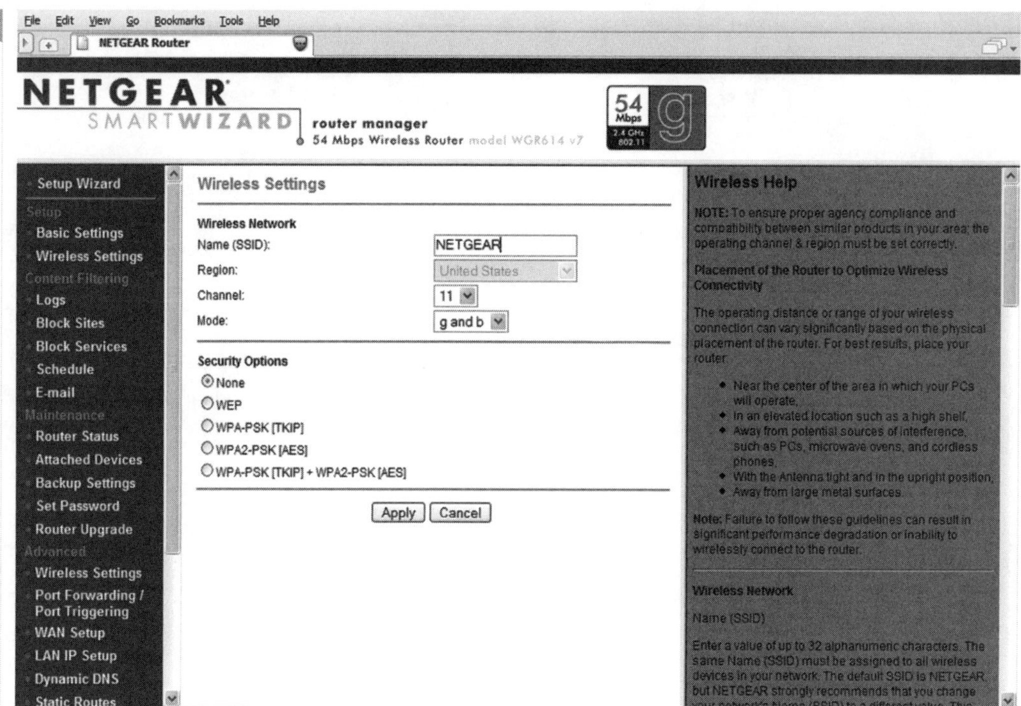

Figure 8-15 NETGEAR router Wireless Settings page

10. The default Mode setting for this router is "g and b." With this setting, the wireless router can communicate using either the 802.11b or 802.11g standard. Other options are "b" or "g" alone, in case you want the device to communicate using only the 802.11b or 802.11g standards. For now, leave the Mode setting at "g and b".

11. Next, you need to choose a Security Option. Each of these options is described in detail in Chapter 12. It's essential to implement some type of security to protect your WLAN from malicious intruders. After selecting a Security Option, you'll be prompted to enter security keys or passphrases that clients must supply to communicate with this router. For now, leave the Security Option at its default selection (None).

12. For security purposes, you will want to change the device's password before you allow it to serve clients on your WLAN. Under the Maintenance heading in the left part of the page, click **Set Password**. The NETGEAR router Set Password page appears. Here you can change the default password that grants access to the wireless router's configuration.

13. Type **password** in the Old Password text box; then type **!@#$%12345** in the New Password text box. Type **!@#$%12345** again in the Repeat New Password text box; then click **Apply**.

14. Before the password change is saved, you will be prompted to enter your User name and Password twice. Enter **admin** and the new password, **!@#$%12345**.

15. Also, for security reasons, you might want to restrict which clients may access the wireless router. You can accomplish this by first choosing the **Wireless Settings** option under the Advanced heading on the left side of the window. The NETGEAR router Advanced Wireless Settings page appears, as shown in Figure 8-16.

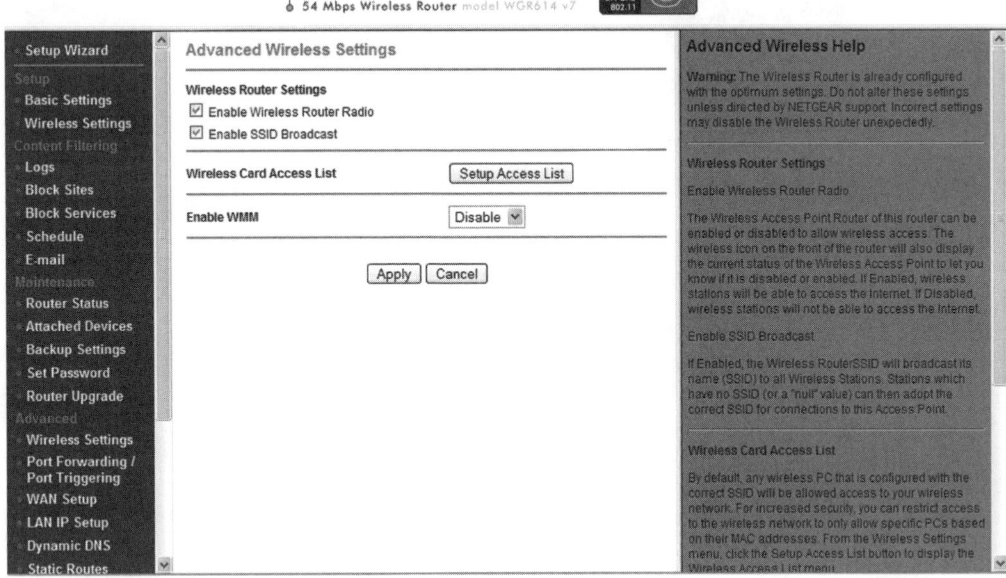

Figure 8-16 The NETGEAR router Advanced Wireless Settings page

16. On this page, you may choose whether your wireless router's radio (i.e., transceiver) is enabled and whether it broadcasts its SSID. If the radio is disabled, it cannot communicate with clients, so for now, leave that option selected. (This option could be temporarily deselected if you were performing maintenance on the wireless router and wanted to prevent clients from accessing it. It could also be deselected if you wanted to use the device as a wired router or switch.)

17. Deselect **Enable SSID Broadcast**; then click **Apply** and wait for the change to be completed. This will prevent the access point from broadcasting its SSID. Consequently, the SSID will not automatically appear in a client's list of available wireless networks. Instead, a client must know and specify this access point's SSID when attempting to connect to it.

18. By choosing Setup Access List on the Advanced Wireless Settings page, you can specify that only certain clients, based on their MAC addresses, can access the wireless router. You will learn about access lists in Chapter 12.

19. To change the TCP/IP settings for your WLAN, select the **LAN IP Setup** option under the Advanced heading on the left side of the page. The NETGEAR router LAN IP Setup page appears, as shown in Figure 8-17.

20. On this page you can do the following: assign your wireless router an IP address that will be used on your LAN (this is different from the IP address that your ISP provider assigns to your connection); modify the RIP characteristics of the router; choose to use the router as a DHCP server for wireless clients; and reserve IP addresses for certain clients on your WLAN. Many network administrators choose to reset their routers' IP addresses as part of systematic, networkwide address management. You will learn

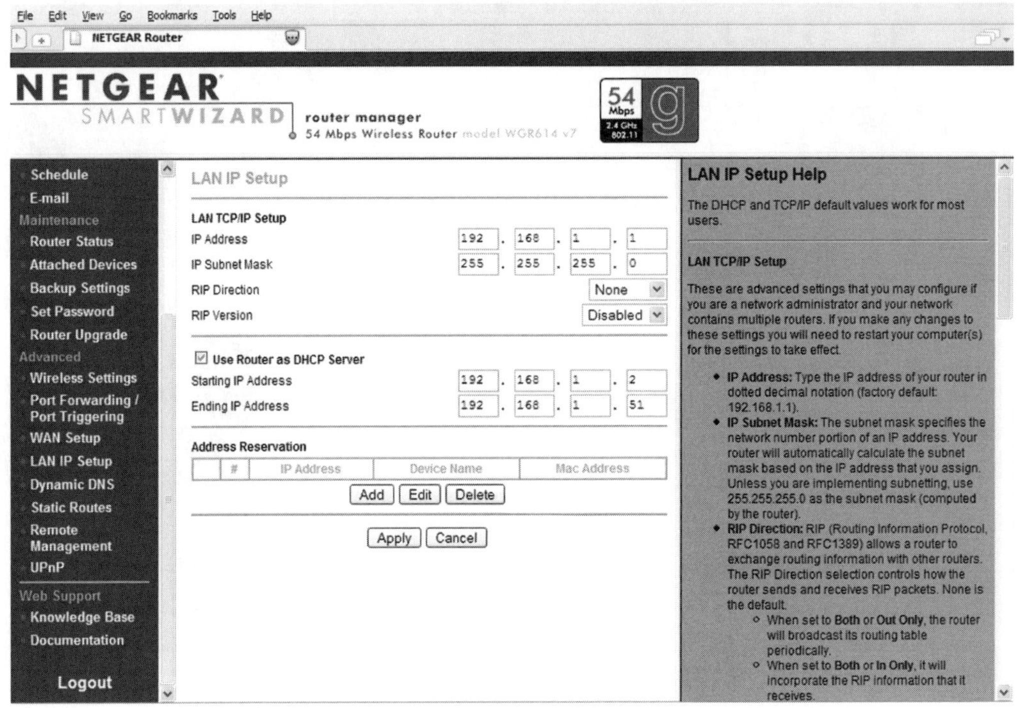

Figure 8-17 The NETGEAR router LAN IP Setup page

more about such practices in Chapter 10. In this case, replace the default IP address of 192.168.1.1 with **10.2.1.1**. If necessary, the subnet mask value will automatically change to match the new IP address you've entered. Click **Apply** to save your change.

21. Keep the Use Router as DHCP Server option selected, and enter **10.2.1.12** as the Starting IP Address.

22. Enter **10.2.1.32** as the Ending IP Address. This will allow clients using this wireless router as a DHCP server to obtain any IP address in the range between 10.2.1.12 and 10.2.1.32. Click **Apply** to save your changes.

23. A message appears, alerting you that to communicate with the router after changing its IP address and DHCP range, you must release and renew your client's IP address information before you can access the setup program again. Click **OK** to continue.

24. Click the **Start** button, select **All Programs**, select **Accessories,** and then select **Command Prompt.** A command window opens.

25. At the command prompt, type **`ipconfig /renew`** and press **Enter**. Notice that the IP address now assigned to your client falls within the range of IP addresses you instructed the wireless router to dole out. Also notice that your Default gateway address, 10.2.1.1, matches the address you assigned to the wireless router. That's because the wireless router will act as your client's gateway to external networks or segments.

Net+

3.1

3.4

26. To return to the NETGEAR router configuration program, click the **Start** button, select **Run** and then type **www.routerlogin.com/basicsetting.htm** in the Open text box. (Alternatively, you could now point your browser to the 10.2.1.1 address.)

27. Click **OK**. Your browser opens, and the Prompt dialog box appears. Enter **admin** as the user name and **!@#$%12345** as the password. The NETGEAR router Basic Settings page appears.

28. Continue to explore the router setting options as you wish. When you have finished, view many of the changes you've made by selecting **Router Status** under the Maintenance heading. The NETGEAR router Router Status page appears, as shown in Figure 8-18. In the future, viewing this page will prove useful when troubleshooting problems with your wireless router.

If something goes awry during your wireless router configuration, you can force all of the variables you changed to be reset. Wireless routers feature a reset button on their back panel. To reset the wireless router, first unplug it. Then, using the end of a paperclip, depress the reset button while you plug it in. Continue holding down the button for at least 30 seconds. (This time period varies among manufacturers; check your wireless router's documentation for the duration yours requires.) At the end of this period, the wireless router's values will be reset to the manufacturer's defaults.

After successfully configuring your access point/wireless router, you are ready to introduce it to the network. In the case of a small office or home WLAN, this means using a patch cable

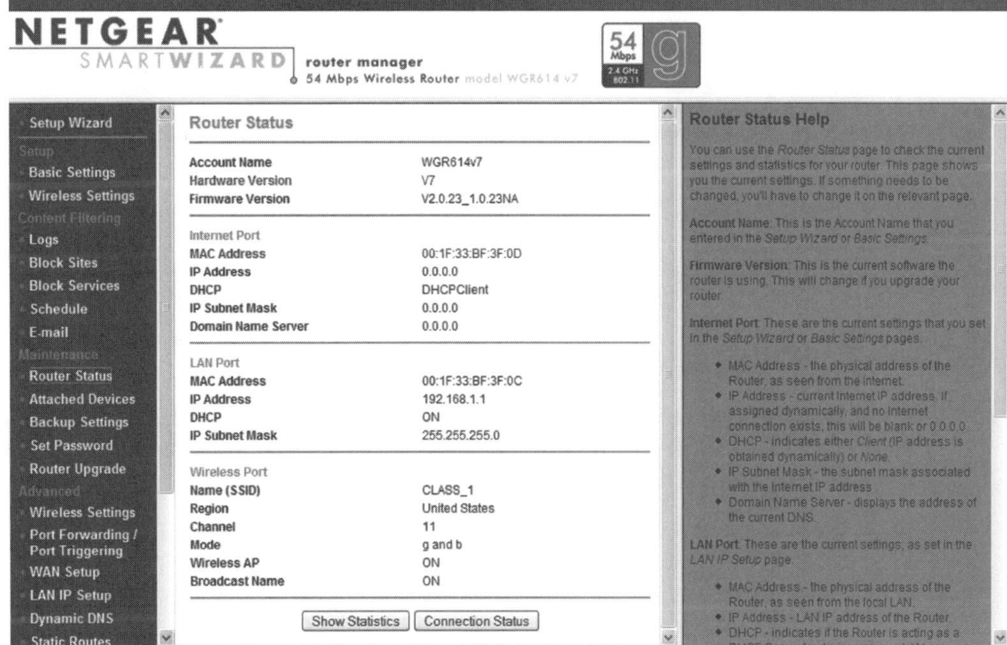

Figure 8-18 The NETGEAR router Router Status page

to connect the device's WAN port and your cable or DSL modem's LAN port. Afterward, clients should be able to associate with the access point and gain Internet access. The following section describes how to configure clients to connect to your WLAN.

Configuring Wireless Clients

Wireless access configuration varies from one type of client to another. In this section you'll learn how to establish access between a workstation running Windows XP, and then you'll learn how Linux and UNIX clients handle wireless interface configuration. (Note that these steps assume that your computer allows Windows XP to manage wireless network connections.)

To configure your Windows XP client to access a WLAN:

1. Turn off your Windows XP workstation if it is currently on.

2. Turn on the access point and place it somewhere within view of your workstation. Then turn on your Windows XP workstation.

3. If your wireless card is properly installed and enabled, your workstation should be available to associate with an access point. (Note that some workstations with built-in wireless NICs require you to manually flip a toggle switch on the computer to turn on the antenna. If your computer has this type of NIC, be certain to turn on the NIC's antenna before continuing.) However, if you have configured your access point to not broadcast its SSID, your client will not automatically find it. Instead, you must provide your access point's information during wireless configuration.

4. Click **Start** on the menu bar, and then click **Control Panel.** (If your Control Panel window is not displayed in Category view, click **Switch to Category View.**) Select **Network and Internet Connections**, and then select **Network Connections.**

5. Right-click the **Wireless Network Connection** icon, and then select **Properties** from the shortcut menu that appears. The Wireless Network Connection Properties dialog box opens.

6. Select the **Wireless Networks** tab to access options pertaining to your wireless connection, as shown in Figure 8-19.

7. Verify that the **Use Windows to configure my wireless network settings** option is selected.

8. Under Preferred networks, click **Add.** The Wireless Network Properties dialog box opens, as shown in Figure 8-20.

9. In the Network name (SSID) text box, enter the SSID of the access point to which your client should associate. For example, if, as in the previous section, you changed your SSID to *CLASS_1* enter **CLASS_1.**

10. Choose **Disabled** from the drop-down menu next to Data encryption. (By default, WEP is selected. If you were using WEP security, you could enter the security key here. You'll learn how to configure clients for wireless security in Chapter 12.)

11. Click **OK** to save CLASS_1 as your default access point. Notice that it now appears under the Preferred networks section of the Wireless Network Connection Properties dialog box.

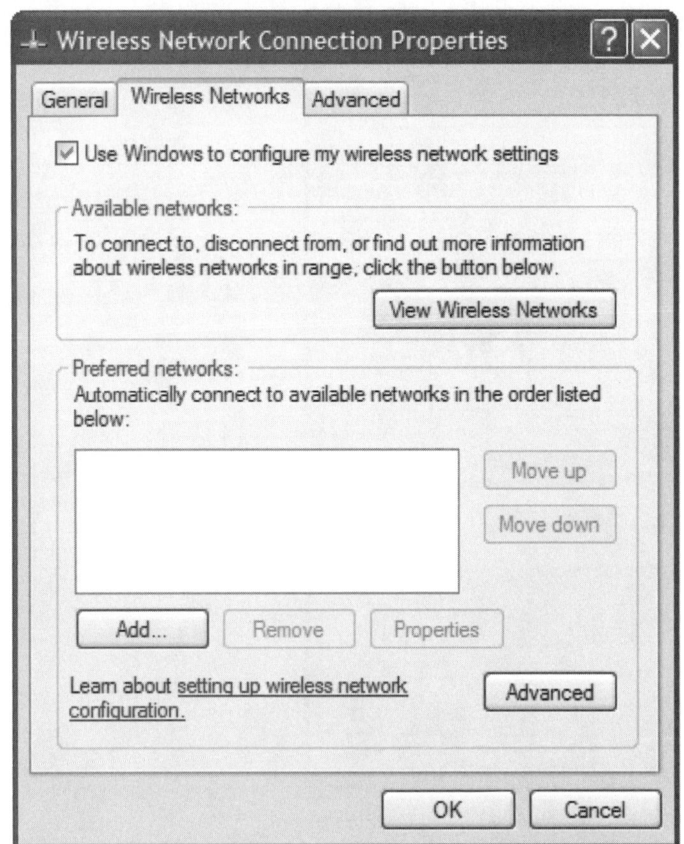

Figure 8-19 Windows XP Wireless Network Connection Properties dialog box

12. Click **Advanced**. The Advanced dialog box opens. Select the **Access point (infrastructure) networks only** option.

13. Click **OK** again to save your changes. You have now learned the basics of configuring a wireless client connection.

14. If your access point/wireless router is acting as a gateway to the Internet, open your browser software and attempt to access a Web page to verify that your connection via the access point to the Internet works.

As with Windows XP, most Linux and UNIX clients provide a graphical interface for configuring their wireless interfaces. Because each version differs somewhat from the others, describing the steps required for each graphical interface is beyond the scope of this book. However, **iwconfig**, a command-line function for viewing and setting wireless interface parameters, is common to nearly all versions of Linux and UNIX. Following is a basic primer for using the iwconfig command. For more detailed information, you may type man iwconfig at any Linux or UNIX command-line prompt.

Before using iwconfig, make sure your wireless NIC is installed and that your Linux or UNIX workstation is within range of a working access point. You must also be logged in as

Figure 8-20 Windows XP Wireless Network Properties dialog box

root or a user with root-equivalent privileges. Next, open a terminal session (i.e., command prompt window), type iwconfig at the prompt, and then press Enter. The iwconfig output should look similar to that shown in Figure 8-21. Notice that in this example, "eth0" represents an interface that is not wireless (that is, a wired NIC), while "eth1" represents the wireless interface. (The "lo" portion of the output indicates the loopback interface.) On your computer, the

```
% iwconfig
lo        no wireless extensions.

eth0      no wireless extensions.

eth1      IEEE 802.11g  ESSID:"CLASS_1"
          Mode:Managed  Frequency:2.412 GHz  Access Point: 00:0F:66:8E:19:89
          Bit Rate:54 Mb/s   Tx-Power:15 dBm
          Retry limit:15   RTS thr:off   Fragment thr:off
          Power Management:off
          Link Quality=89/100  Signal level=-44 dBm  Noise level=-45 dBm
          Rx invalid nwid:0  Rx invalid crypt:0  Rx invalid frag:0
          Tx excessive retries:0  Invalid misc:2   Missed beacon:0
```

Figure 8-21 Output from iwconfig command

3.4

wireless NIC might have a different designation. Also notice that `iwconfig` reveals character-istics of your access point's signal, including its frequency, power, and signal and noise levels.

Using the `iwconfig` command, you can modify the SSID of the access point you choose to associate with, as well as many other variables. Some examples are detailed next. The syntax of the following examples assumes your workstation regards your wireless NIC as "eth1":

- `iwconfig eth1 essid CLASS_1`—This command instructs the wireless interface to associate with an access point whose SSID (or ESSID, as shown in this command) is CLASS_1.

- `iwconfig eth1 mode Managed`—This command instructs the wireless interface to operate in infrastructure mode (as opposed to ad hoc mode).

- `iwconfig eth1 channel auto`—This command instructs the wireless interface to automatically select the best channel for wireless data exchange.

- `iwconfig eth1 freq 2.422G`—This command instructs the wireless interface to communicate on the 2.422GHz frequency.

- `iwconfig eth1 key 6e225e3931`—This command instructs the wireless interface to use the hexadecimal number 6e225e3931 as its key for secure authentication with the access point. (6e225e3931 is only an example; on your network you will choose your own key.)

In this and the previous section, you have learned how to configure wireless clients and access points. The following section summarizes some key points about setting up wireless networks properly.

Avoiding Pitfalls

3.4

4.7

You might have had the frustrating experience of not being able to log on to a network, even though you were sure you'd typed in your user name and password correctly. Maybe it turned out that your Caps Lock key was on, changing your case-sensitive password. Or maybe you were trying to log on to the wrong server. On every type of network, many vari-ables must be accurately set on clients, servers, and connectivity devices for communication to succeed. Wireless networks add a few more variables. As a reminder, following are some wireless configuration pitfalls to avoid:

- *SSID mismatch*—Your wireless client must specify the same SSID as the access point it's attempting to associate with. As you have learned, you may instruct clients to search for any available access point (or clients might be configured to do this by default). However, if the access point does not broadcast its SSID, or if your worksta-tion is not configured to look for access points, you will have to enter the SSID during client configuration. Also bear in mind that SSIDs are case sensitive. That is, CLASS_1 does not equal Class_1. SSID mismatch will result in failed association.

- *Incorrect encryption*—Your wireless client must be configured to (a) use the same type of encryption as your access point, and (b) use a key or passphrase that matches the access point's. If either of these is incorrect, your client cannot authenticate with the access point.

- *Incorrect channel or frequency*—You have learned that the access point establishes the channel and frequency over which it will communicate with clients. Clients, then,

3.4

4.7

automatically sense the correct channel and frequency. However, if you have instructed your client to use only a channel or frequency different from the one your access point uses, association will fail to occur.

- *Standard mismatch (802.11 a/b/g/n)*—If your access point is set to communicate only via 802.11g, even if the documentation says it supports 802.11b and 802.11g, clients must also follow the 802.11g standard. Clients configured to follow a different wireless standard will never find the access point.

- *Incorrect antenna placement*—On a network, many factors can cause data errors and a resulting decrease in performance. As you have learned, the most popular WLAN standards require clients to be within 330 feet of an access point's antenna for reliable data delivery. Beyond that distance, communication might occur, but data errors become more probable. Also remember to place your antenna in a high spot for best signal reception.

- *Interference*—If intermittent and difficult-to-diagnose wireless communication errors occur, interference might be the culprit. Check for sources of EMI, such as fluorescent lights, heavy machinery, cordless phones, and microwaves in the data transmission path.

Wireless WANs and Internet Access

2.5

Wireless WANs can be created using many types of transmission technologies. Some of the oldest technologies were developed by telephone companies to provide their customers with an alternative to wired local loops. Other wireless WANs use another technology from the 20th century—satellite transmission—which was originally developed in the late 1950s for military purposes and then adopted commercially for TV and radio broadcasts. But the latest wireless WAN technologies, collectively known as **wireless broadband**, are designed specifically for high-throughput, long-distance digital data exchange. The following sections describe a variety of ways wireless clients can access the Internet.

802.11 Internet Access

In the previous section, you learned how access points figure into home networks and enterprise wide LANs. Access points are also used by airports, libraries, universities, hotels, cafés, and restaurants to provide the public with wireless Internet access. Currently, most use the 802.11b or 802.11g access methods.

Places where wireless Internet access is available to the public are called **hot spots**. Some organizations, such as T-Mobile, have established a network of hot spots across the nation. Other organizations, such as a local coffee shop, might have only one hot spot. In some cases, Internet access is free. In other cases, the organization running the hot spot requires users to pay based on their usage or subscribe to a service. An average subscription costs $20 to $30 per month.

When users subscribe to a wireless Internet service, they are usually required to log on via a Web page to gain access to the service. Alternatively, the service provider might supply users with client software that manages the client's connection to the wireless service. This software allows the user to log on to the network and secures data exchanged between the client computer and the access point, where transmissions are most vulnerable to eavesdropping. As an added security measure, a wireless access provider might configure its access point to accept a user's connection based on his computer's MAC address, in addition to the user's logon ID and password. Wireless security measures are discussed in detail in Chapter 12.

At each hot spot, the access point available for public use is connected to the Internet using technology other than 802.11. For example, a local coffee shop might lease a DSL line that terminates at a combined access point and router behind the counter. That device can connect the coffee shop with its ISP while allowing patrons within the access point's range to log on to the Internet. At T-Mobile hot spots, access points are connected (via routers) to T1 links. In general, to configure your client to access the Internet from an 802.11 hot spot, follow the same process you would for associating with your WLAN access point, as described earlier in this chapter.

As you know, IEEE created the 802.11 wireless standards specifically for LANs. Next, you will learn about an IEEE wireless transmission that was designed for MANs and WANs.

802.16 (WiMAX) Internet Access

In 2001, IEEE standardized a new wireless technology under its **802.16** (wireless MAN) committee. Since that time, IEEE has released several versions of the 802.16 standard. Collectively, the 802.16 standards are known as **WiMAX**, which stands for **Worldwide Interoperability for Microwave Access**, the name of a group of manufacturers, including Intel and Nokia, who banded together to promote and develop 802.16 products and services. The currently favored IEEE 802.16 version is **802.16e**, which was approved in 2005. With 802.16e, IEEE improved the mobility and QoS characteristics of WiMAX, making it better suited to carrying digital voice signals and serving mobile phone users.

On the wireless spectrum, WiMAX functions in ranges between 2 and 66GHz, on either licensed or nonlicensed frequencies. (In fact, it could operate at lower frequencies, including those formerly used for broadcast television signals.) It may use line-of-sight paths between antennas—in which case throughput potential is maximized—or non-line-of-sight paths, as 802.11 does. In non-line-of-sight mode, WiMAX antennas can exchange signals with multiple stations at once, just as with 802.11. Line-of-sight transmissions, on the other hand, occur between only two antennas.

WiMAX offers two distinct advantages over Wi-Fi. First, it can provide much greater throughput than 802.11a, b, or g—up to 70Mbps. Second, its range extends much farther than any of the 802.11 standards, topping out at 50 kilometers (or approximately 30 miles). For these reasons, WiMAX is considered more appropriate for use on MANs and WANs. As you would expect, the highest throughput is possible only over the shortest distances between transceivers. For example, WiMAX will not achieve its maximum 70Mbps across a 30-mile span.

WiMAX offers an alternative to DSL and broadband cable for business and residential customers who want high-speed Internet access. It's well suited to rural users, for example, who might be in an area lacking cable infrastructure and far from their telecommunications carrier's switching facility. WiMAX also provides Internet access to mobile computerized devices, including cell phones, laptops, and PDAs in metropolitan areas.

In residential WiMAX, the carrier installs a small antenna on the homeowner's roof or chimney or even inside the house. This antenna is connected to a device similar to a cable or DSL modem for clients to access the LAN. The connectivity device could be incorporated along with the antenna in the same housing or might be separate. If separate, the device typically attaches to the antenna with coaxial cable. It's often combined with a router. The homeowner's antenna communicates in a non-line-of-sight fashion with the service provider's antenna. If the service provider's facility is far away, it might use multiple antennas on towers that communicate in a line-of-sight manner, as shown in Figure 8-22. In Figures 8-23 and 8-24, you'll see

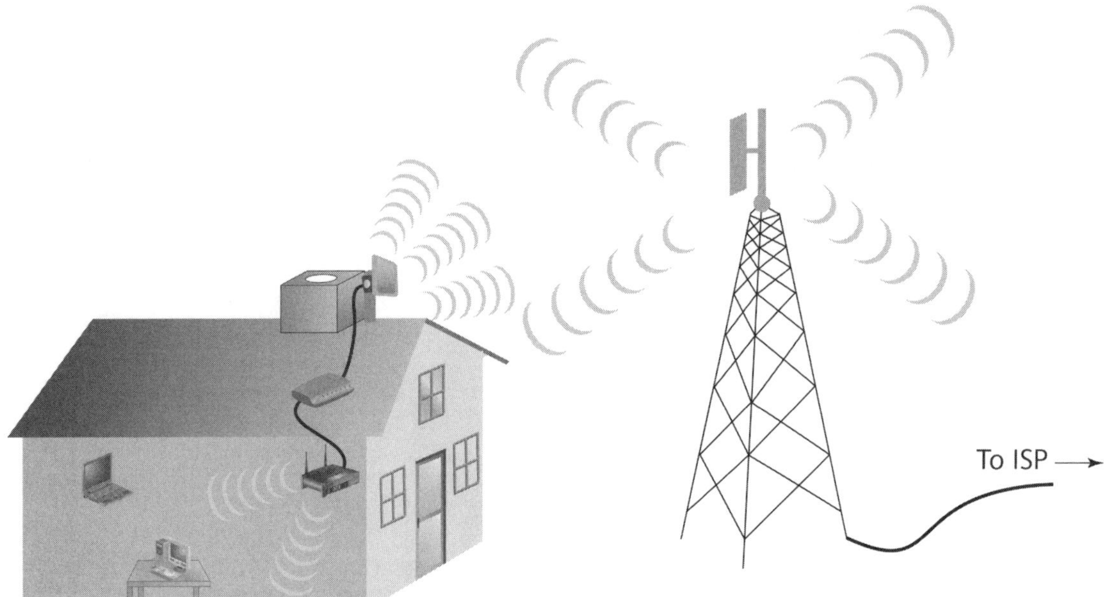

Figure 8-22 WiMAX residential service installation

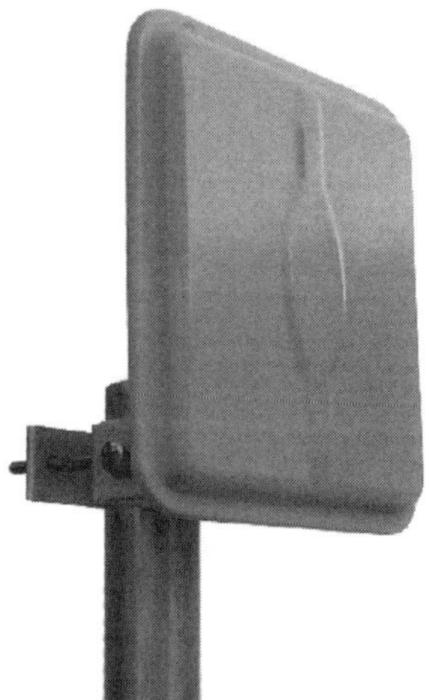

Figure 8-23 WiMAX residential antenna

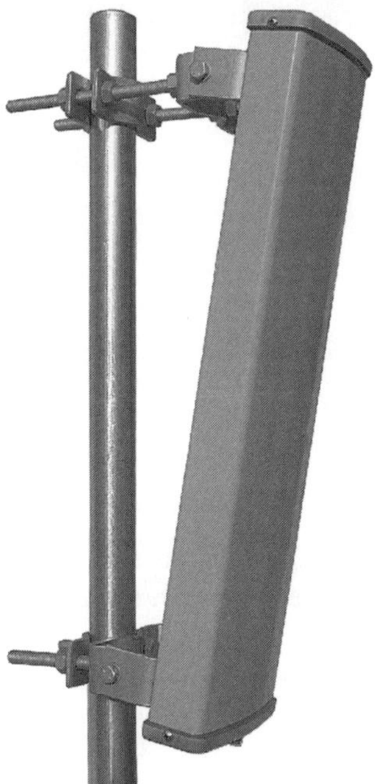

Figure 8-24 WiMAX service provider's antenna

photos of the type of antenna used at a customer's location and the type of antenna used by service providers on their towers.

In some installations, as when a WiMAX provider serves a metropolitan area, the home antenna and connectivity device is eliminated. Instead, each computer communicates directly via its on-board WiMAX transceiver with an antenna such as the one shown in Figure 8-24.

Imagine being able to pick up your e-mail from your laptop, phone, or PDA whether in your living room, waiting in traffic, or lounging on the beach, without ever having to adjust your client's wireless properties or subscribe to multiple services. WiMAX MANs promise this type of connectivity. Not only that, but they offer download data rates faster than your home broadband connection. (Prominent service providers' estimates are between 2–4Mbps. Upload throughput is estimated at 400Kbps to 1Mbps.) However, since WiMAX is a shared service, and service providers will apportion bandwidth so that everyone can gain access, an individual subscriber cannot expect to experience the highest throughput rates of 70Mbps advertised for WiMAX.

In the United States, companies such as Clearwire have established WiMAX networks in several cities using licensed frequency bands. For example, Clearwire has registered with the FCC for the sole use of channels in the 2.5GHz band in the Chicago metropolitan area. Because the band is licensed, it suffers little interference, and Clearwire can guarantee a certain level of service. On a citywide network, WiMAX makes more sense than Wi-Fi. Besides its higher throughput and longer range, it doesn't rely on multiple hot spots.

As is the case with most new technologies, WiMAX is currently more expensive than existing options, both for residential Internet access and MAN connectivity. In addition, factor in the

cost of adding an external WiMAX-capable transceiver, if your device, like most, isn't equipped with the very latest wireless technology.

Another, less expensive way to access the Internet without wires is to use satellite signals, as described next.

Satellite Internet Access

In 1945, Arthur C. Clarke (the author of *2001: A Space Odyssey*) wrote an article in which he described the possibility of communication between manned space stations that continually orbited the Earth. Other scientists recognized the worth of using satellites to convey signals from one location on Earth to another. By the 1960s, the United States was using satellites to transmit telephone and television signals across the Atlantic Ocean. Since then, the proliferation of this technology and reductions in its cost have made satellite transmission appropriate and available for more regional (or even local) consumer voice and data services.

You are probably familiar with satellites used to present live broadcasts of events happening around the world. Satellites are also used to deliver digital television and radio signals, voice and video signals, and cellular and paging signals. And they provide homes and businesses—most notably in rural or hard-to-reach locations—with Internet access. This following sections describe how satellite technology works.

Satellite Orbits Most satellites circle the Earth 22,300 miles above the equator in a geosynchronous orbit. **Geosynchronous orbit** (also called **geostationary orbit**, or **GEO**) means that satellites orbit the Earth at the same rate that the Earth turns. Consequently, at every point in their orbit, the satellites maintain a constant distance from a specific point on the Earth's equator. Because satellites are generally used to relay information from one point on Earth to another, information sent to Earth from a satellite first has to be transmitted to the satellite from Earth in an uplink. An **uplink** is the creation of a communications channel for a transmission from an Earth-based transmitter to an orbiting satellite. Often, the uplink signal information is scrambled (in other words, its signal is encoded) before transmission to prevent unauthorized interception. At the satellite, a **transponder** receives the uplink signal and then transmits it to an Earth-based receiver in a **downlink**. A typical satellite contains 24 to 32 transponders. Each satellite uses unique frequencies for its downlink. These frequencies, as well as the satellite's orbit location, are assigned and regulated by the FCC. Back on Earth, the downlink is picked up by a dish-shaped antenna. The dish shape concentrates the signal so that it can be interpreted by a receiver. Figure 8-25 provides a simplified view of satellite communication.

An alternative to geosynchronous satellites are **LEO (low Earth orbiting)** satellites. LEO satellites orbit the Earth with an altitude as low as 100 miles and up to 1,240 miles, not above the equator but closer to the Earth's poles. Because their altitude is lower, LEO satellites cover a smaller geographical range than GEO satellites. However, less power is required to issue signals between Earth and an LEO satellite versus a GEO satellite.

In between the altitudes of LEO and GEO satellites lie **MEO (medium Earth orbiting)** satellites. MEO satellites orbit the Earth between 6,000 and 12,000 miles above its surface. As with LEO satellites, MEO satellites are not positioned over the equator, but over a latitude between the equator and the poles. MEOs have the advantage of covering a larger area of the Earth's surface than LEO satellites while at the same time using less power and causing less signal delay than GEO satellites.

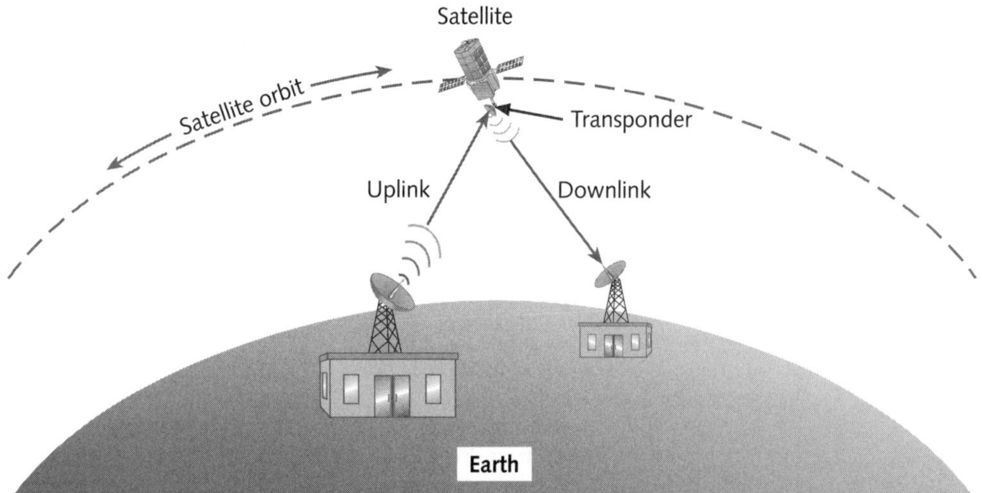

Figure 8-25 Satellite communication

Geosynchronous orbiting satellites are the type used by the most popular satellite Internet access service providers. This technology is well established and is the least expensive of all satellite technology. Also, because they remain in a fixed position relative to the Earth's surface, stationary receiving dishes on Earth can be counted on to receive satellite signals reliably.

Satellite Frequencies Satellites transmit and receive signals in any of the following five frequency bands, which are roughly defined as:

- *L-band*—1.5–2.7GHz
- *S-band*—2.7–3.5GHz
- *C-band*—3.4–6.7GHz
- *Ku-band*—12–18GHz
- *Ka-band*—18–40GHz

Within each band, frequencies used for uplink and downlink transmissions differ. This variation helps ensure that signals traveling in one direction (for example from a satellite to the Earth) do not interfere with signals traveling in the other direction (for example, signals from the Earth to a satellite). Satellite Internet access providers typically use frequencies in the C- or Ku-bands. Newer satellite Internet access technologies are currently being developed for the Ka-band.

Satellite Internet Services A handful of companies offer high-bandwidth Internet access via GEO satellite links. Each subscriber uses a small satellite dish antenna and receiver to exchange signals with the service provider's satellite network. Subscribers can choose one of two types of satellite Internet access service: dial return or satellite return. In a **dial return** arrangement, a subscriber receives data from the Internet via a satellite downlink transmission but sends data to the satellite via an analog modem (dial-up) connection. With dial return, service providers advertise downstream (or downlink) throughputs of 400–500Kbps, though in practice, they may be as high as 1Mbps. However, upstream (or uplink) throughputs are practically limited to 53Kbps and are usually lower. Therefore, dial return satellite Internet access is an asymmetrical technology. In a **satellite return** arrangement, a subscriber sends and receives data to and from the Internet using a satellite uplink and downlink. This is a symmetrical technology, in which both upstream and downstream throughputs are advertised to reach 400–500Kbps. In reality, throughputs are often higher.

To establish a satellite Internet connection, each subscriber must have a dish antenna, which is approximately two feet high by three feet wide, installed in a fixed position. In North America, these dish antennas are pointed toward the southern hemisphere (because the geosynchronous satellites travel over the equator). The dish antenna's receiver is connected, via cable, to a modem. This modem uses either a PCI or USB interface to connect with the subscriber's computer. In a dial return system, an analog modem is also connected to the subscriber's computer to handle upstream communications.

Figure 8-26 illustrates how a home user with dial return satellite Internet access service connects with a satellite Internet service provider.

Costs for popular Internet access services in the United States are approximately $200 for installation (which must be performed by a professional) plus a monthly service fee of $20 to $30.

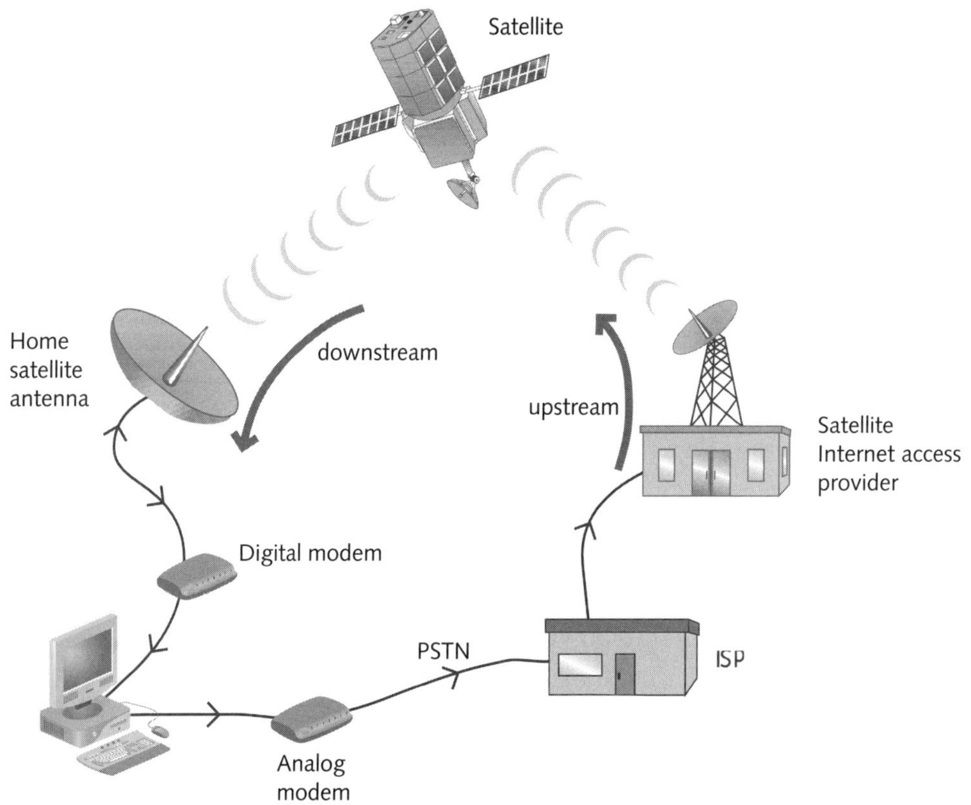

Figure 8-26 Dial return satellite Internet service

Chapter Summary

- The wireless spectrum is a continuum of the electromagnetic waves used for data and voice communication. Each type of wireless service can be associated with one area, or frequency band, of the wireless spectrum.

- Most cordless telephones and many WLANs (wireless LANs) use frequencies in the 2.4GHz band. Other WLANs use a range of frequencies near 5GHz. The 5GHz band offers more unlicensed channels and less potential interference.

- Wireless signals originate from electrical current traveling along a conductor. The electrical signal travels from the transmitter to an antenna, which then emits the signal, as a series of electromagnetic waves, to the atmosphere. The signal propagates through the air until it reaches its destination. At the destination, another antenna accepts the signal, and a receiver converts it back to current.

- To exchange information, two antennas must be tuned to the same frequency. In communications terminology, this means they share the same channel.

- The geographical area that an antenna or wireless system can reach is known as its range. Receivers must be within the range to receive accurate signals consistently.

- Wireless transmission is susceptible to interference from EMI. Signals are also affected by obstacles in their paths, which cause them to reflect, diffract, or scatter. A large number of obstacles can prevent wireless signals from reaching their destination.

- Because of reflection, diffraction, and scattering, wireless signals follow a number of different paths to their destination. Such signals are known as multipath signals.

- Each type of wireless communication falls into one of two categories: fixed or mobile. In fixed wireless systems, the locations of the transmitter and receiver do not move. In mobile wireless, the receiver can be located anywhere within the transmitter's range. This allows the receiver to roam from one place to another while continuing to pick up its signal.

- In an ad hoc WLAN, wireless nodes, or stations, transmit directly to each other via wireless NICs without an intervening connectivity device.

- Modern WLANs operate in infrastructure mode. They rely on access points that transmit and receive signals to and from wireless stations and connectivity devices. Access points may connect stations to a LAN or multiple network segments to a backbone. They are often combined with routers.

- Wireless standards vary by frequency, methods of signal, and geographic range. The IEEE 802.11 committee has ratified three notable wireless standards: 802.11b, 802.11a, and 802.11g. A fourth standard, 802.11n, is expected to be ratified in late 2009.

- All four 802.11 standards share characteristics at the MAC sublayer level, including the CSMA/CA access method, frame formats, and methods of association between access points and stations.

- 802.11b operates in the 2.4GHz band, uses DSSS (direct-sequence spread spectrum), and is characterized by a maximum theoretical throughput of 11Mbps (though actual throughput is typically half of that). It was popular on WLANs until the faster 802.11g became common.

- 802.11a, ratified after 802.11b, operates in the 5GHz band and is incompatible with 802.11b or g. It's characterized by a maximum theoretical throughput of 54Mbps, though actual throughput is much less.

- 802.11g, which operates in the 2.4GHz band and is compatible with 802.11b, is characterized by a maximum theoretical throughput of 54Mbps, though actual throughput is much less.

- 802.11n, which is due to be ratified by IEEE in late 2009, provides for significantly faster throughput than any previously adopted 802.11 standard. Techniques such as MIMO (multiple input-multiple output), channel bonding, frame aggregation, and higher modulation rates allow 802.11n to achieve between 65 and 600Mbps actual throughput. MIMO also dramatically increases the range of 802.11n access points. 802.11n is backward compatible with 802.11b, a, and g, though mixed environments cannot take advantage of all of 802.11n's speed enhancements.

- Home networks might use Bluetooth technology, whose ranges are shorter and throughputs are lower than those of 802.11 networks.

- Most home and small office WLANs depend on a single access point, which should be centrally located to provide reliable wireless service to clients at any location.

- Designing an enterprise-wide WLAN involves choosing the appropriate quantity of access points and knowing where to position them. A site survey helps by assessing the network's client requirements, facility characteristics, and coverage areas.

- You can install and configure an access point using setup software provided by the manufacturer, or by directly connecting to the device's operating software. At a minimum, you should change the access point's SSID (service set identifier) and administrator password. If the access point acts as a router, or Internet gateway, you must provide your Internet account credentials. In addition, you probably want to choose a method of secure authentication, modify the LAN TCP/IP properties, and perhaps change the channel and mode of communication.

- Client setup for WLANs can be very simple, if you allow the client to find an access point and choose default values for associating with it. If the access point requires secure authentication, you must at least configure the client to meet those credentials.

- For correct functioning on your WLAN, make sure clients and access points agree on an SSID, security settings, and channels. Also make sure access points are positioned far from sources of interference and that client locations do not exceed the maximum range for the type of wireless technology you use.

- Wireless Internet access can be achieved through one of several technologies. Libraries, universities, coffee shops, and airports might offer access by allowing the public to connect with their IEEE 802.11-compatible access points. These organizations, in turn, connect their access points to dedicated, high-speed Internet connections such as T1 links.

- IEEE 802.16 (WiMAX) is a wireless Internet access technology designed for residential or business Internet access and MANs with mobile users. The currently favored 802.16e standard can use frequencies from 2–66GHz and may issue signals in a line-of-sight or non-line-of-sight manner. WiMAX can achieve throughputs of up to 70Mbps at the shortest ranges. Its signals can travel up to 30 miles.

- Geosynchronous satellites are used to provide Internet access. This type of setup requires a stationary antenna at the customer's premises, which is connected to a modem connected to the customer's computer. Downstream throughput for satellite Internet access is advertised at throughputs of 400Kbps but is often higher. In the case of a dial return arrangement, upstream throughputs are limited by the analog telephone line's 53Kbps maximum throughput.

Key Terms

2.4GHz band   The range of radio frequencies from 2.4 to 2.4835GHz. The 2.4GHz band, which allows for 11 unlicensed channels, is used by WLANs that follow the popular 802.11b and 802.11g standards. However, it is also used for cordless telephone and other transmissions, making the 2.4GHz band more susceptible to interference than the 5GHz band.

5GHz band   A range of frequencies that comprises four frequency bands: 5.1GHz, 5.3GHz, 5.4GHz, and 5.8GHz. It consists of 24 unlicensed bands, each 20MHz wide. The 5GHz band is used by WLANs that follow the 802.11a and 802.11n standards.

802.11a   The IEEE standard for a wireless networking technique that uses multiple frequency bands in the 5GHz frequency range and provides a theoretical maximum throughput of 54Mbps. 802.11a's high throughput, compared with 802.11b, is attributable to its use of higher frequencies, its unique method of encoding data, and more available bandwidth.

802.11b   The IEEE standard for a wireless networking technique that uses DSSS (direct-sequence spread spectrum) signaling in the 2.4–2.4835GHz frequency range (also called the 2.4GHz band). 802.11b separates the 2.4GHz band into 14 overlapping 22MHz channels and provides a theoretical maximum of 11Mbps throughput.

802.11g   The IEEE standard for a wireless networking technique designed to be compatible with 802.11b while using different encoding techniques that allow it to reach a theoretical maximum capacity of 54Mbps. 802.11g, like 802.11b, uses the 2.4GHz frequency band.

802.11n   The IEEE standard for a wireless networking technique that may issue signals in the 2.4- or 5GHz band and can achieve actual data throughput between 65 and 600Mbps. It accomplishes this through several means, including MIMO, channel bonding, and frame aggregation. 802.11n is backward compatible with 802.11a, b, and g.

802.16   An IEEE standard for wireless MANs. 802.16 networks may use frequencies between 2 and 66GHz. Their antennas may operate in a line-of-sight or non-line-of-sight manner and cover 50 kilometers (or approximately 30 miles). 802.16 connections can achieve a maximum throughput of 70Mbps, though actual throughput diminishes as the distance between transceivers increases. Several 802.16 standards exist. Collectively, they are known as WiMAX.

802.16e   Currently, the most popular version of WiMAX. With 802.16e, IEEE improved the mobility and QoS characteristics of the technology, making it better suited to VoIP and mobile phone users.

access point   A device used on WLANs that transmits and receives wireless signals to and from multiple nodes and retransmits them to the rest of the network segment. Access points can connect a group of nodes with a network or two networks with each other. They may use directional or omnidirectional antennas.

active scanning   A method used by wireless stations to detect the presence of an access point. In active scanning, the station issues a probe to each channel in its frequency range and waits for the access point to respond.

ad hoc   A type of WLAN in which stations communicate directly with each other (rather than using an access point).

AP   *See* access point.

association   In the context of wireless networking, the communication that occurs between a station and an access point to enable the station to connect to the network via that access point.

base station   *See* access point.

basic service set   *See* BSS.

basic service set identifier   *See* BSSID.

beacon frame   In the context of wireless networking, a frame issued by an access point to alert other nodes of its existence.

Bluetooth   A wireless networking standard that uses FHSS (frequency hopping spread spectrum) signaling in the 2.4GHz band to achieve a maximum throughput of either 723Kbps or 2.1Mbps, depending on the version. Bluetooth was designed for use primarily with small office or home networks in which multiple devices (including cordless phones, computers, and pagers) are connected.

Bluetooth Special Interest Group (SIG)   A consortium of companies, including Sony Ericsson, Intel, Nokia, Toshiba, and IBM, that formally banded together in 1998 to refine and standardize Bluetooth technology.

BSS (basic service set)   In IEEE terminology, a group of stations that share an access point.

BSSID (basic service set identifier)   In IEEE terminology, the identifier for a BSS (basic service set).

Carrier Sense Multiple Access with Collision Avoidance   *See* CSMA/CA.

channel bonding   In the context of 802.11n wireless technology, the combination of two 20MHz frequency bands to create one 40MHz frequency band that can carry more than twice the amount of data that a single 20MHz band could. It's recommended for use only in the 5GHz range, because this band has more available channels and suffers less interference than the 2.4GHz band.

CSMA/CA (Carrier Sense Multiple Access with Collision Avoidance)   A network access method used on 802.11 wireless networks. In CSMA/CA, before a node begins to send data, it checks the medium. If it detects no transmission activity, it waits a brief, random amount of time, and then it sends its transmission. If the node does detect activity, it waits a brief period of time before checking the channel again. CSMA/CA does not eliminate, but minimizes, the potential for collisions.

dial return   A method of satellite Internet access in which a subscriber receives data via a satellite downlink transmission but sends data to the satellite via an analog modem (dial-up) connection.

diffraction   In the context of wireless signal propagation, the phenomenon that occurs when an electromagnetic wave encounters an obstruction and splits into secondary waves. The secondary waves continue to propagate in the direction in which they were split. If you could see wireless signals being diffracted, they would appear to be bending around the obstacle. Objects with sharp edges—including the corners of walls and desks—cause diffraction.

direct-sequence spread spectrum   *See* DSSS.

directional antenna   A type of antenna that issues wireless signals along a single direction, or path.

downlink   A connection from an orbiting satellite to an Earth-based receiver.

DSSS (direct-sequence spread spectrum)   A transmission technique in which a signal's bits are distributed over an entire frequency band at once. Each bit is coded so that the receiver can reassemble the original signal upon receiving the bits.

ESS (extended service set)   A group of access points and associated stations (or basic service sets) connected to the same LAN.

ESSID (extended service set identifier)   A special identifier shared by BSSs that belong to the same ESS.

extended service set   *See* ESS.

extended service set identifier   *See* ESSID.

fading   A change in a wireless signal's strength as a result of some of the electromagnetic energy being scattered, reflected, or diffracted after being issued by the transmitter.

FHSS (frequency hopping spread spectrum)   A wireless signaling technique in which a signal jumps between several different frequencies within a band in a synchronization pattern known to the channel's receiver and transmitter.

fixed   A type of wireless system in which the locations of the transmitter and receiver are static. In a fixed connection, the transmitting antenna focuses its energy directly toward the receiving antenna. This results in a point-to-point link.

frequency hopping spread spectrum   *See* FHSS.

GEO (geosynchronous orbit or geostationary orbit)   The term used to refer to a satellite that maintains a constant distance from a point on the equator at every point in its orbit. Geosynchronous orbit satellites are the type used to provide satellite Internet access.

geostationary orbit   *See* GEO.

geosynchronous   *See* GEO.

hot spot   An area covered by a wireless access point that provides visitors with wireless services, including Internet access.

infrastructure WLAN   A type of WLAN in which stations communicate with an access point and not directly with each other.

`iwconfig`   A command-line utility for viewing and setting wireless interface parameters on Linux and UNIX workstations.

LEO (low Earth orbiting)   A type of satellite that orbits the Earth with an altitude between 100 and 900 miles, closer to the Earth's poles than the orbits of either GEO or MEO satellites. LEO satellites cover a smaller geographical range than GEO satellites and require less power.

line-of-sight   *See* LOS.

LOS (line-of-sight)   A wireless signal or path that travels directly in a straight line from its transmitter to its intended receiver. This type of propagation uses the least amount of energy and results in the reception of the clearest possible signal.

low Earth orbiting   *See* LEO.

medium Earth orbiting   *See* MEO.

MEO (medium Earth orbiting)   A type of satellite that orbits the Earth roughly 6,000 to 12,000 miles above its surface, positioned between the equator and the poles. MEO satellites can cover a larger area of the Earth's surface than LEO satellites while using less power and causing less signal delay than GEO satellites.

MIMO (multiple input-multiple output)   In the context of 802.11n wireless networking, the ability for access points to issue multiple signals to stations, thereby multiplying the signals' strength and increasing their range and data-carrying capacity. Because the signals follow multipath propagation, they must be phase-adjusted when they reach their destination.

mobile   A type of wireless system in which the receiver can be located anywhere within the transmitter's range. This allows the receiver to roam from one place to another while continuing to pick up its signal.

multipath   The characteristic of wireless signals that follow a number of different paths to their destination (for example, because of reflection, diffraction, and scattering).

multiple input-multiple output   *See* MIMO.

narrowband   A type of wireless transmission in which signals travel over a single frequency or within a specified frequency range.

omnidirectional antenna   A type of antenna that issues and receives wireless signals with equal strength and clarity in all directions. This type of antenna is used when many different receivers must be able to pick up the signal, or when the receiver's location is highly mobile.

PAN (personal area network)   A small (usually home) network composed of personal communications devices.

passive scanning   In the context of wireless networking, the process in which a station listens to several channels within a frequency range for a beacon issued by an access point.

personal area network   *See* PAN.

probe   In 802.11 wireless networking, a type of frame issued by a station during active scanning to find nearby access points.

radiation pattern   The relative strength over a three-dimensional area of all the electromagnetic energy an antenna sends or receives.

range   The geographical area in which signals issued from an antenna or wireless system can be consistently and accurately received.

reassociation   In the context of wireless networking, the process of a station establishing a connection (or associating) with a different access point.

reflection   In the context of wireless, the phenomenon that occurs when an electromagnetic wave encounters an obstacle and bounces back toward its source. A wireless signal will bounce off objects whose dimensions are large compared to the signal's average wavelength.

Request to Send/Clear to Send   *See* RTS/CTS.

roaming   In wireless networking, the process that describes a station moving between BSSs without losing connectivity.

RTS/CTS (Request to Send/Clear to Send) An exchange in which a wireless station requests the exclusive right to communicate with an access point and the access point confirms that it has granted that request.

satellite return A type of satellite Internet access service in which a subscriber sends and receives data to and from the Internet over the satellite link. This is a symmetrical technology, in which both upstream and downstream throughputs are advertised to reach 400–500Kbps; in reality, throughput is often higher.

scanning The process a wireless station undergoes to find an access point. *See also* active scanning and passive scanning.

scattering The diffusion of a wireless signal that results from hitting an object that has smaller dimensions compared to the signal's wavelength. Scattering is also related to the roughness of the surface a wireless signal encounters. The rougher the surface, the more likely a signal is to scatter when it hits that surface.

service set identifier *See* SSID.

site survey In the context of wireless networking, an assessment of client requirements, facility characteristics, and coverage areas to determine an access point arrangement that will ensure reliable wireless connectivity within a given area.

spread spectrum A type of wireless transmission in which lower-level signals are distributed over several frequencies simultaneously. Spread-spectrum transmission is more secure than narrowband.

SSID (service set identifier) A unique character string used to identify an access point on an 802.11 network.

station An end node on a network; used most often in the context of wireless networks.

transponder The equipment on a satellite that receives an uplinked signal from Earth, amplifies the signal, modifies its frequency, and then retransmits it (in a downlink) to an antenna on Earth.

uplink A connection from an Earth-based transmitter to an orbiting satellite.

Wi-Fi *See* 802.11.

WiMAX *See* 802.16.

wireless The signals made of electromagnetic energy that travel through the atmosphere.

wireless broadband The term used to describe the recently released standards for high-throughput, long-distance digital data exchange over wireless connections. WiMAX (IEEE 802.16) is one example of a wireless broadband technology.

wireless gateway An access point that provides routing functions and is used as a gateway.

wireless LAN *See* WLAN.

wireless router An access point that provides routing functions.

wireless spectrum A continuum of electromagnetic waves used for data and voice communication. The wireless spectrum (as defined by the FCC, which controls its use) spans frequencies between 9KHz and 300FGHz. Each type of wireless service can be associated with one area of the wireless spectrum.

WLAN (wireless LAN) A LAN that uses wireless connections for some or all of its transmissions.

Worldwide Interoperability for Microwave Access (WiMAX) *See* 802.16a.

Review Questions

1. Which antenna type issues and receives wireless signals with equal strength and clarity in all directions?

   a. Radiant

   b. Omnidirectional

   c. Directional

   d. Unidirectional

2. Which wireless frequency band do the newer types of WLANs use?

   a. 1.2GHz

   b. 2.4GHz

   c. 5GHz

   d. 50GHz

3. Which term describes the use of multiple frequencies to transmit a signal?

   a. Spread-spectrum technology

   b. Broadband

   c. Narrowband

   d. Full-duplexing

4. What innovation in the 802.11n standard combines two adjacent 20MHz channels to make a 40MHz channel that achieves high throughput?

   a. MIMO (multiple input-multiple output)

   b. Channel bonding

   c. Higher modulation rates

   d. Frame aggregation

5. Which Internet service type makes more sense on a citywide network?

   a. Satellite

   b. Wi-Fi

   c. WiMAX

   d. Broadband

6. True or false? Attenuation is the most severe flaw affecting wireless signals.

7. True or false? As long as a receiver is within the range to receive accurate signals consistently, signals will remain intelligible.

8. True or false? In most WLAN scenarios, stations must remain within 600 feet of an access point to maintain optimal transmission speeds.

9. True or false? WiMAX is not available to residential customers.

10. True or false? In satellite return Internet access service, a subscriber sends and receives data to and from the Internet using a satellite uplink and downlink.

11. In _____ wireless, the receiver can be located anywhere within the transmitter's range.

12. _____ is a mobile wireless networking standard that uses FHSS (frequency hopping spread spectrum) RF signaling in the 2.4GHz band.

13. A(n) _____ assesses client requirements, facility characteristics, and coverage areas to determine an access point arrangement that will ensure reliable wireless connectivity within a given area.

14. Collectively, the 802.16 standards are known as _____.

15. _____ orbiting satellites are the type used by the most popular satellite Internet access service providers.

Network Operating Systems

After reading this chapter and completing the exercises, you will be able to:

- Describe characteristics common to all NOSs (network operating systems)

- Compare and evaluate NOSs to select the right one for your network

- Define the requirements for and features of the Windows Server 2008 NOS

- Define the requirements for and features of UNIX and Linux NOSs

- Create users and groups and assign file permissions on systems running Windows Server 2008 and UNIX

On the Job

I'm the UNIX systems administrator for a large data services company. One day I was on my usual, casual morning walk through the data center, keeping an eye on the racks filled with servers. Many customers house servers in our data center, but my primary customer had 128 of them in an eight-rack cluster. Green LEDs flashed, indicating that all was well. But wait! A flashing amber LED? I made a mental note of the server number and headed to my desk. My pager started buzzing on my way. I must have walked by just when that LED flipped to amber.

Checking the logging server, the kernel log file showed that the server was throwing network errors on the primary network interface. Out of transmit buffers. It seemed odd, since we'd long ago tuned the network parameters on these systems to handle extreme amounts of traffic. I SSH'd to the server and ran a couple diagnostics: `dmesg` (yup, there were the errors), `ip link show eth0` (nothing unusual with the driver side of the interface), `ethtooli—show-ring eth0` (the usual number of ring buffers allocated). Something else must be causing trouble.

I returned to the kernel log file and studied the log messages. I noted that the time stamps on the messages were regular, eight seconds apart. It seemed odd to me, since I knew that the network traffic from the customer's application was far less regular than that.

I decided to connect a network traffic analyzer to the interface in question. I configured the upstream switch to monitor traffic on the port connected to the node's primary interface. I fired up my analyzer, connected it to the switch's monitor port, and let it run for a minute to collect some traffic. Sure enough, there they were, corrupted packets at the data link layer. The packets appeared to have random data in the Ethernet destination address bytes. But only at 8-second intervals.

Back on the troubled node, I ran tcpdump on the interface to see whether the application or the kernel driver was causing the trouble. No, the driver was showing the proper data being sent, even at the Ethernet layer.

It seemed like it must be a hardware problem. I replaced the primary NIC in the cluster node and kept an eye on the server for a couple days. I haven't seen a problem since.

Eleanor Wu
Chimera Data Solutions

You have learned that an NOS (network operating system) enables a server to share resources with clients. NOSs also facilitate other services, such as communications, security, and user management. NOSs do not fit neatly into one layer of the OSI model. Some of their functions—those that facilitate communication between computers on a network—belong in the application layer of the OSI model. However, many of their functions—those that interact with users—take place above the application layer. Consequently, the OSI model does not completely describe all aspects of NOSs.

During your career as a networking professional, you will probably work with more than one NOS and possibly several versions of the same NOS. This chapter introduces the basic concepts related to NOSs. It also discusses features of the most popular NOSs: Windows Server 2008, UNIX, and Linux.

Characteristics of Network Operating Systems

2.7

Recall that most modern networks are based on a client/server architecture, in which a server enables multiple clients to share resources. Such sharing is managed by the NOS. However, that's not all an NOS provides. Among other things, an NOS must do the following:

- Centrally manage network resources, such as programs, data, and devices (for example, printers).
- Secure access to a network.
- Allow remote users to connect to a network.
- Allow users to connect to other networks (for example, the Internet).
- Back up data and make sure it's always available.
- Allow for simple additions of clients and resources.
- Monitor the status and functionality of network elements.
- Distribute programs and software updates to clients.
- Ensure efficient use of a server's capabilities.
- Provide fault tolerance in case of a hardware or software problem.

Not all of these functions are built in to every NOS installation; some are optional. When installing an NOS, you can accept the default settings or customize your configuration to more closely meet your needs. You can also take advantage of special services or enhancements that come with a basic NOS. For example, if you install Linux with only its minimum components, you may later choose to install the clustering service, which enables multiple servers to act as a single server, sharing the burden of NOS functions. The components included in each NOS and every version of a particular NOS vary. This variability is just one reason why you should plan your NOS installation carefully.

In this chapter, the word *server* refers to the hardware on which an NOS runs. In the field of networking, the word *server* may also refer to an application that runs on this hardware to provide a dedicated service. For example, although you may use a Compaq server as your hardware, you could run the Sendmail application as your mail server on that hardware. Some specialized server programs come with an NOS—for example, many versions of Linux include a Web server program called Apache.

Although each NOS discussed in this book supports file and print sharing, plus a host of other services, NOSs differ in how they achieve those functions, what type of environment

they suit, and how they are administered. In the next section, you will learn how to evaluate an NOS for use on your network.

Network Operating Systems and Servers

Most networks rely on servers that exceed the minimum hardware requirements suggested by the software vendor. Every situation will vary, but to determine the optimal hardware for your servers, be sure to ask the following questions:

- What kinds of applications will run on the server?
- How many clients will connect to the server?
- How much storage space will each user need?
- How much downtime, if any, is acceptable?
- What can the organization afford?

The first question in this list is perhaps the most important. For example, you can purchase an inexpensive, low-end server that runs Linux adequately and suffices for resource sharing and simple application services. However, to perform more advanced functions and run resource-intensive applications on your network, you would need to invest in a server that has significantly more processing power and memory. Every application comes with different processor, RAM, and storage requirements. Before purchasing or upgrading a server, consult the installation guide for each application you intend to run.

The way an application uses resources may also influence your choice of software and hardware. Applications might not provide the option of sharing the processing burden between the client and server. For example, you might install a group scheduling and messaging package that requires every client to run executable files from a network drive, thereby almost exclusively using the server's processing resources. Alternately, you might install the program files on each client workstation and use the server only to distribute messages. The latter solution puts the processing burden on the client.

If your server assumes most of the application-processing burden, or if you have a large number of services and clients to support, you will need to add more hardware than the minimum NOS requirements. For example, you might add multiple processors, more RAM, multiple NICs, fault-tolerant hard drives, and a backup drive. Each of these components will enhance network reliability or performance. Carefully analyze your current situation and plans for growth before making a hardware purchasing decision. Whereas high-end servers with massive processing and storage resources plus fault-tolerant components can cost as much as $10,000, your department may need only a $1,000 server.

No matter what your needs, ensure that your hardware vendor has a reputation for high quality, dependability, and excellent technical support. Although you might be able to trim your costs on workstation hardware by using generic models, you should spend as much as necessary for a reliable server. A component failure in a server can cause problems for many people, whereas a workstation problem will probably affect only one person.

Client Support

The primary reason for using networks is to enable clients to communicate and share resources efficiently. Therefore, client support is one of the most important functions an NOS provides. Client support includes the following tasks:

- Creating and managing client accounts
- Enabling clients to connect to the network
- Allowing clients to share resources
- Managing clients' access to shared resources
- Facilitating communication between clients

You are already familiar with the way lower-layer protocols assist clients and servers in communication. The following discussion provides a general view of client/server communication from the higher layers of the OSI model.

Client/Server Communication Both the client software and the NOS participate in logging a client on to the server. Although clients and their software may differ, the process of logging on is similar in all NOSs, no matter what clients are involved. First, the user launches the client software from his desktop. Then he enters his credentials (normally, a user name and password) and presses the Enter key. At this point, a service on the client workstation, called the **redirector**, intercepts the request to determine whether it should be handled by the client or by the server. A redirector belongs to the presentation layer of the OSI model. It's a service of both the NOS and the client's desktop operating system. After the client's redirector decides that the request is meant for the server, the client transmits this data over the network to the server. (If the redirector had determined that the request was meant for the client, rather than the server, it would have issued the request to the client's processor.) For security's sake, most modern clients will encrypt user name and password information before transmitting it to the network media. Encryption is another presentation layer function.

At the server, the NOS receives the client's request for service and decrypts it, if necessary. Next, it attempts to authenticate the user's credentials. If authentication succeeds, the NOS responds to the client by granting it access to resources on the network, according to limitations specified for this client. Figure 9-1 depicts the process of a client connecting to an NOS.

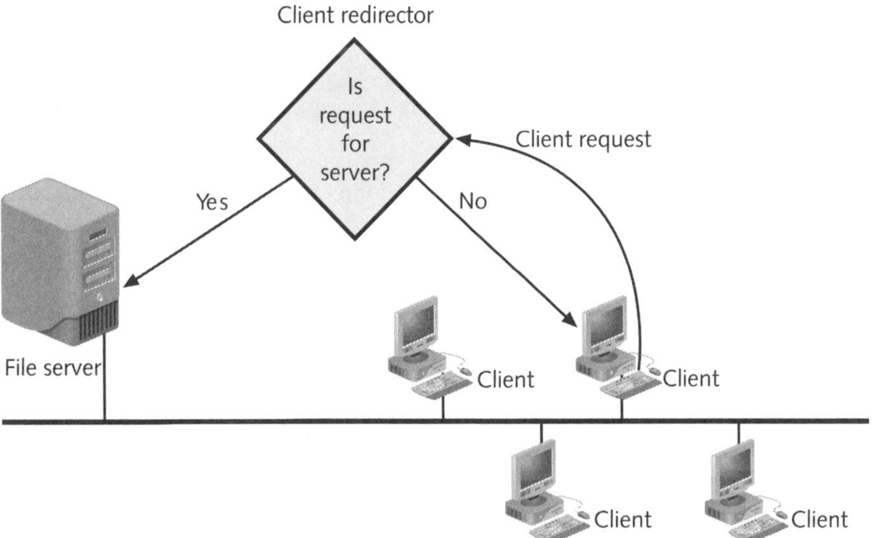

Figure 9-1 A client connecting to an NOS

You should understand the logon process for troubleshooting purposes. For example, if after entering her name and password, a user receives an error message indicating that the server was not found, you can conclude that the request never made it to the server's NOS. In this case, a physical connection problem may be at fault. However, if after entering her name and password, a user receives an error message indicating that the user name or password is invalid, you know that at least the physical connection is working because the request reached the NOS and the NOS attempted to verify the user name. In this case, the password or user name may have been typed incorrectly.

After the client has successfully logged on, the client software communicates with the NOS each time the client requests services from the server. For example, if you wanted to open a file on the server's hard drive, you would interact with your workstation's operating system to make the file request; the file request would then be intercepted by the redirector and passed to the server via the client software. To expedite access to directories whose files you frequently require, you can **map** a drive to that directory. Mapping involves associating a letter, such as *M* or *T*, with a disk, directory, or other resource (such as a CD-ROM tower). Logon scripts, which run automatically after a client authenticates, often map drives to directories on the server that contain files required by client applications.

In the early days of networking, client software from one manufacturer could not always communicate with network software from another manufacturer. One difference between NOSs is the **file access protocol** that enables one system to access resources stored on another system on the network. For example, a Windows XP client communicates with a Windows Server 2008 server using the **CIFS (Common Internet File System)** file access protocol. CIFS was developed by Microsoft as a way for clients to request file and print services from servers. It's a more recent version of an older client/server communications protocol, **SMB (Server Message Block)**, which originated at IBM and then was adopted and further developed by Microsoft.

Thanks in part to broader support of multiple file access protocols, most every type of client can authenticate and access resources via any NOS. Usually, the NOS manufacturer supplies a preferred client software package for each popular type of client. For example, Microsoft requires Windows workstations connecting to its Windows Server 2003 or Server 2008 NOSs to have Client for Microsoft Networks running. Client software other than that recommended by the NOS manufacturer might work, but it's wise to follow the NOS manufacturer's guidelines.

In some instances a piece of software called **middleware** is necessary to translate requests and responses between the client and server. Middleware prevents the need for a shared application to function differently for each different type of client. It stands between the client and the server and performs some of the tasks that an application in a simple client/server relationship would otherwise perform. Typically, middleware runs as a separate service—and sometimes on a separate physical server—from the NOS. To interact with the middleware, a client issues a request to the middleware. Middleware reformats the request in such a way that the application on the server can interpret it. When the application responds, middleware translates the response into the client's preferred format and issues the response to the client. Middleware may be used as a messaging service between clients and servers, as a universal query language for databases, or as a means of coordinating processes between multiple servers that need to work together in servicing clients.

Net+
2.7

For example, suppose a library's database of materials is contained on a UNIX server. Some library workstations run the Macintosh desktop operating system, while others run Windows Vista and Linux. Each workstation must be able to access the database of materials. Ideally, all client interfaces would look similar, so that a patron who uses a Macintosh workstation one day could use a Linux workstation the next day without even noticing the difference. Further, the library can only manage one large database; it cannot maintain a separate database for each type of client. In this case, a server running the database middleware can accept the queries from each type of client. When a Linux workstation submits a query, the database middleware interprets the Linux instruction, reformats it, and then issues the standardized query to the database. The database middleware server might next accept a query from a Macintosh computer, which it then reformats into a standardized query for the database. In this way, the same database can be used by multiple clients.

A client/server environment that incorporates middleware in this fashion is said to have a **3-tier architecture** because of its three layers: client, middleware, and server. To take advantage of a 3-tier architecture, a client workstation requires the appropriate client software, for example, a Web browser or remote terminal services client. Figure 9-2 illustrates the concept of middleware.

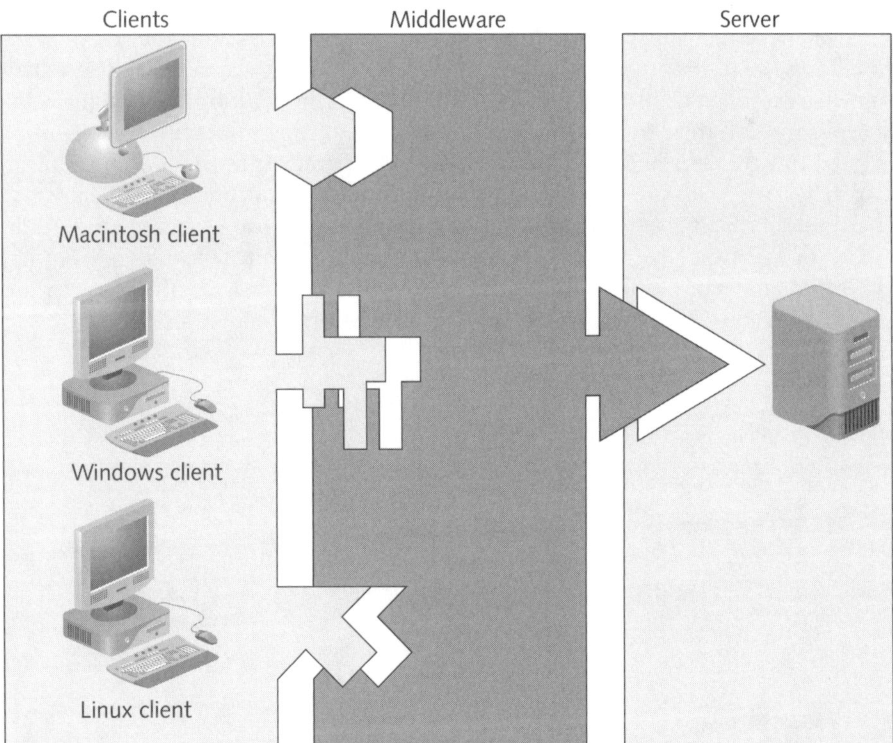

Figure 9-2 Middleware between clients and a server

Users and Groups   After an NOS authenticates a client, it grants the client access to the services and resources it manages. The type of access a client (or user) has depends on her user account and the groups to which she's assigned. The most privileged user account on a system is the **administrator**. The administrator has unlimited rights to resources and objects managed by a server or domain. When you install an NOS, this account is created by default. And on a UNIX or Linux system, the account is also known as **root**. In this section, you will learn about other users and groups.

You have probably worked with enough computers and networks to know why user names are necessary: to grant each user on a network access to files and other shared resources. Imagine that you are the network administrator for a large college campus with 20,000 user names. Assigning directory, file, printer, and other resource rights for each user name would consume all of your time, especially if the user population changed regularly. To manage network access more easily, you can combine users with similar needs and restrictions into **groups**.

In every NOS, groups form the basis for resource and account management. Many network administrators create groups according to department or, even more specifically, according to job function within a department. They then assign different file or directory access rights to each group. For example, on a high school's network, the administrator may create a group called Students for the students and a group called Teachers for the teachers. The administrator could then easily grant the Teachers group rights to view all attendance and grade records on the server, but deny the same access to the Students group.

To better understand the role of groups in resource sharing, first consider their use on a relatively small scale. Suppose you are the network administrator for a public elementary school. You might want to give all teachers and students access to run instructional programs from a network directory called PROGRAMS. In addition, you might want to allow teachers to install their own instructional programs in this same directory. Meanwhile, you need to allow teachers and administrators to record grade information in a central database called GRADES. Of course, you don't want to allow students to read information from this database. Finally, you might want administrators to use a shared drive called STAFF to store the teachers' performance review information, which should not be accessible to teachers or students. Table 9-1 illustrates how you can provide this security by dividing separate users into three groups: teachers, students, and administrators.

Table 9-1 Providing Security through Groups

Group	Rights to PROGRAMS	Rights to GRADES	Rights to STAFF
Teachers	Read, modify	Full control	No access
Students	Read	No access	No access
Administrators	No access	Read, modify	Full control

Plan your groups carefully. Creating many groups (for example, a separate group for every job classification in your organization) might impose as much of an administrative burden as not using any groups.

After an NOS authenticates a user, it checks the user name against a list of resources and their access restrictions list. If the user name is part of a group with specific access permissions or restrictions, the system will apply those same permissions and restrictions to the user's account.

For simpler management, groups can be nested (one within another) or arranged hierarchically (multiple levels of nested groups) according to the type of access required by different types of users. The way groups are arranged will affect the permissions granted to each group's members. For example, if you created a group called Temps within the Administrators group for temporary office assistants, the Temps group would be nested within the Administrators group and would, by default, share the same permissions as the Administrators group. Such permissions are called **inherited** because they are passed down from the parent group (Administrators) to the child group (Temps). If you wanted to restrict the Temps users from seeing the staff performance reviews, you would have to separately assign restrictions to the Temps group for that purpose. After you assign different rights to the Temps group, you have begun creating a hierarchical structure of groups. NOSs differ slightly in how they treat inherited permissions, and enumerating these differences is beyond the scope of this book. However, if you are a network administrator, you must thoroughly understand the implications of hierarchical group arrangements.

After the user and group restrictions are applied, the client is allowed to share resources on the network, including data, data storage space, applications, and peripherals. To understand how NOSs enable resource sharing, it's useful to first understand how they identify and organize network elements.

Identifying and Organizing Network Elements

Modern NOSs follow similar patterns for organizing information about network elements, such as users, printers, servers, data files, and applications. This information is kept in a directory. A **directory** is a list that organizes resources and associates them with their characteristics. One example of a directory is a file system directory, which organizes files and their characteristics, such as file size, owner, type, and permissions. You may be familiar with this type of directory from manipulating or searching for files on your workstation. NOSs do use file system directories. However, these directories are different from and unrelated to the directories used to manage network clients, servers, and shared resources.

Recent versions of all popular NOSs use directories that adhere to standard structures and naming conventions set forth by **LDAP (Lightweight Directory Access Protocol)**. LDAP is a protocol used to access information stored in a directory. By following the same directory standard, different NOSs can easily share information about their network elements.

According to the LDAP standard, a thing or person associated with the network is represented by an **object**. Objects may include users, printers, groups, computers, data files, and applications. Each object may have a multitude of **attributes**, or properties, associated with it. For example, a user object's attributes may include a first and last name, location, mail address, group membership, access restrictions, and so on. A printer object's attributes may include a location, model number, printing preferences (for example, double-sided printing), and so on.

In LDAP-compatible directories, a **schema** is the set of definitions of the kinds of objects and object-related information that the directory can contain. For example, one type of object is a printer, and one type of information associated with that object is the location of the printer. Thus, "printer" and "location of printer" would be definitions contained within the schema.

A directory's schema may contain two types of definitions: classes and attributes. **Classes** (also known as **object classes**) identify what type of objects can be specified in a directory. User account is an example of an object class. Another object class is Printer. As you learned previously, an attribute is a characteristic associated with an object. For example, Home Directory is the name of an attribute associated with the User account object, whereas Location is an attribute associated with the Printer object. Classes are composed of many attributes. When you create an object, you also create a number of attributes that store information about that object. The object class and its attributes are then saved in the directory. Figure 9-3 illustrates some schema elements associated with a User account object.

To better organize and manage objects, a network administrator places objects in **containers,** or **OUs (organizational units)**. OUs are logically defined receptacles that serve only to assemble similar objects. Returning to the example of a school network, suppose each student, teacher, and administrator were assigned a user name and password for the network. Each of these users would be considered an object, and each would require an account. (An **account** is the record of a user that contains all of his properties, including rights to

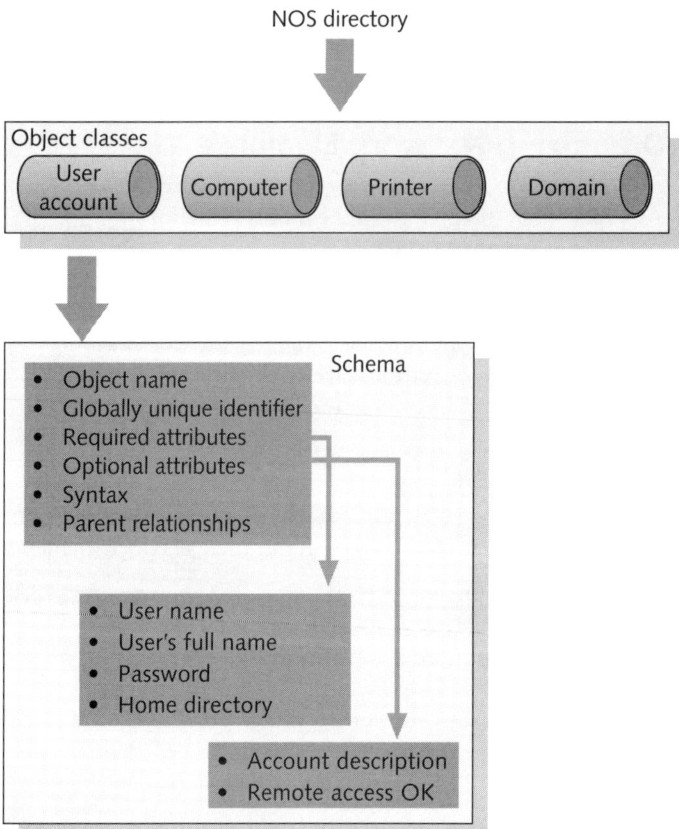

Figure 9-3 Schema elements associated with a User account object

resources, password, name, and so on.) One way of organizing these objects is to put all the user objects in one OU called "Users." But suppose the school provided a server and a room of workstations strictly for student use. The use of these computers would be restricted to applications and Internet access during only certain hours of the day. As the network administrator, you could gather the student user names (or the Students group), the student server, the student printers, and the student applications in an OU called Students. You could associate the restricted network access (an attribute) with this OU so that these students could access the school's applications and the Internet only during certain hours of the day. An OU can hold multiple objects. Also, an OU is a logical construct—that is, a means of organizing other things; it does not represent something real. An OU is different from a group because it can hold and apply parameters for many different types of objects, not only users.

In the LDAP standard, directories and their contents form trees. A **tree** is a logical representation of multiple, hierarchical levels within a directory. The term *tree* is drawn from the fact that the whole structure shares a common starting point (the root) and from that point extends **branches** (or containers), which may extend additional branches, and so on. Objects are the last items in the hierarchy connected to the branches and are sometimes called **leaf objects**. Figure 9-4 depicts a simple directory tree.

Before you install an NOS, be sure to plan the directory tree with current and future needs in mind. For example, suppose you work at a new manufacturing firm, called Circuits Now, which produces high-quality, inexpensive circuit boards. You might decide to create a simple tree that branches into three OUs: users, printers, and computers. But if Circuits Now plans to open new manufacturing facilities sometime in the future (for instance, one devoted to making memory chips and another for transistors), you might want to call the first OU in the tree "circuit boards." This would separate the existing circuit board business from the new businesses, which would employ different people and require different resources. Figure 9-5 shows both possible trees.

Directory trees are very flexible, and as a result, are usually more complex than the examples in Figure 9-5. Chances are that you will enter an organization that has already established its

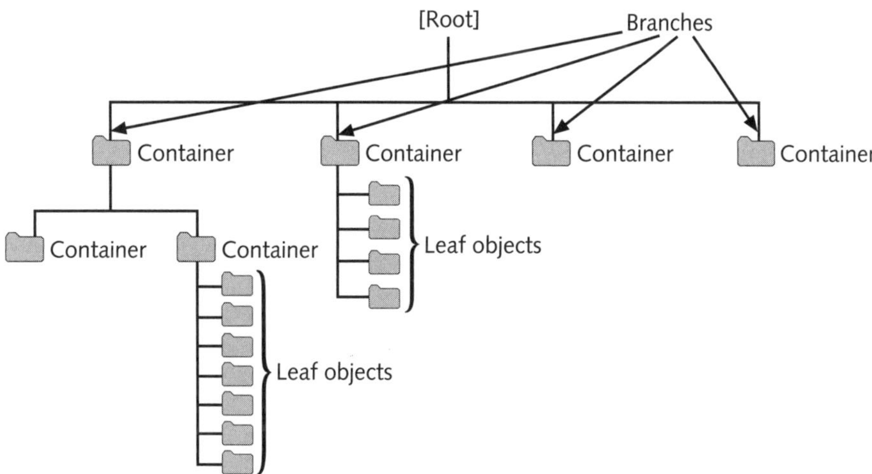

Figure 9-4 A directory tree

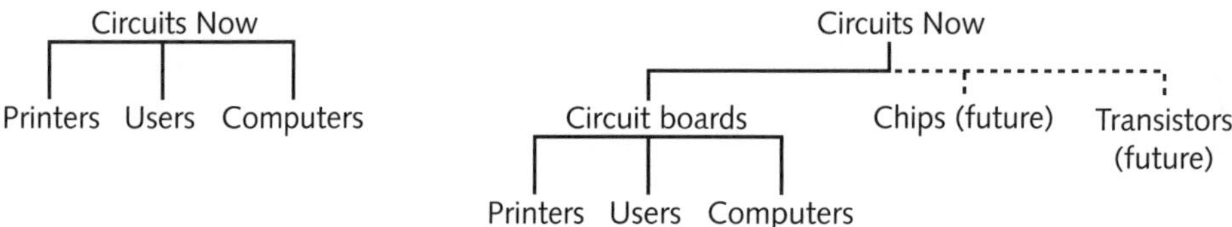

Figure 9-5 Two possible directory trees for the same organization

tree, and you will need to understand the logic of that tree to perform your tasks. Later in this chapter, you will learn about Active Directory, which is the LDAP-compatible directory used by the Windows Server 2003 and Server 2008 NOSs.

Sharing Applications

As you have learned, one of the significant advantages of the client/server architecture is the ability to share resources, thereby reducing costs and the time required to manage the resources. In this section, you will learn how an NOS enables clients to share applications.

Shared applications are often installed on a file server that is specifically designed to run applications. In a small organization, however, they might be installed on the same server that provides other functions, such as Internet, security, and remote access services. As a network administrator, you must purchase a license for the application that allows it to be shared among clients. In other words, you cannot legally purchase one licensed copy of Microsoft Word, install it on a server, and allow hundreds of your users to share it.

Software licensing practices vary from one vendor to another. A software vendor might sell an organization a fixed quantity of licenses, which allows only that number of clients to use the application simultaneously. This type of licensing is known as **per user** licensing. For example, suppose a life sciences library purchases a 20-user license for a database of full-text articles from a collection of *Biology* journals. If 20 users are running the database, the 21st person who attempts to access the database will receive a message announcing that access to the database is prohibited because all of the licenses are currently in use. Other software vendors sell a separate license for each *potential* user. Regardless of whether the user is accessing an application, a license is reserved so that the user will not be denied access. This practice is commonly known as **per seat** licensing. For example, if the life sciences library wanted to make sure each of its 15 employees could access the *Biology* journal database at any time, it would choose to purchase licenses for each of the employees. The application on the server could verify the user through a logon ID or the workstation's network address, for example. A third licensing option is the **site license**, which for a fixed price allows an unlimited number of users to legally access an application. In general, a site license is most economical for applications shared by many people (for example, if the life sciences library shared its *Biology* journal database with all of the students on a university campus), whereas for small numbers of users, per seat or per user licenses are more economical.

After you have purchased the appropriate type and number of licenses, you are ready to install the application on a server. Before doing so, however, make sure your server has enough free hard drive space, memory, and processing power to run the application. Then follow the software manufacturer's guidelines for a server installation. Depending on the application, this process might be the same as installing the application on a workstation, or it might be much different.

After installing the software on a server, you are ready to make it available to clients. Through the NOS, assign users rights to the directories where the application's files are installed. Users will at least need rights to access and read files in those directories. For some applications, you might also need to give users rights to create, delete, or modify files associated with the application. For example, a database program may create a small temporary file on the server when a user launches the program to indicate to other potential users that the database is open. If this is the case, users must have rights to create files in the directory where this temporary file is kept. An application's installation guidelines will indicate the rights you need to assign users for each of the application's directories.

Next, you will need to provide users with a way to access the application. On nearly all types of clients, you can create an icon on the user's desktop that is associated with the application file. When the user double-clicks the icon, her client software issues a request for the server to open the application. In response, the NOS sends a part of the program to her workstation, where it will be held in RAM. This allows the user to interact with the program quickly, without having to relay every command over the network to the server. As the user works with the application, the amount of processing that occurs on her workstation versus the amount of processing that the server handles will vary according to the network architecture.

You might wonder how an application can operate efficiently or accurately when multiple users are simultaneously accessing its files. After all, an application's program file is a single resource. If two or more network users double-click their application icons simultaneously, how does the application know which client to respond to? In fact, the NOS is responsible for arbitrating access to these files. In the case of multiple users simultaneously launching a network application from their desktop icons, the NOS will respond to one request, then the next, then the next, each time issuing a copy of the program to the client's RAM. In this way, each client is technically working with a separate instance of the application.

Shared access becomes more problematic when multiple users are simultaneously accessing the same data files as well as the same program files. For example, consider an online auction site, which accepts bids on many items from many Internet users. Imagine that an auction is nearing a close with three users simultaneously bidding on the same large-screen TV. How does the auction site's database accept bid data for that TV from multiple sources? One solution to this problem is middleware. The three Internet bidders cannot directly modify the database located on the auction site's server. Instead, a middleware program on the server accepts data from the clients. If the database is not busy, the middleware passes a bid to the database. If the database is busy (or open), the middleware queues the bids (forces them to wait) until the database is ready to rewrite its existing data, then passes one bid, then another, and another, to the database until its queue is empty. In this way, only one client's data can be written to the database at any point in time.

Sharing Printers

Sharing peripherals, such as printers, can increase the efficiency of managing resources and reduce costs for an organization. In this section, you will learn how networks enable clients to share printers. Sharing other peripheral devices, such as fax machines, works in a similar manner.

In most cases, an organization designates a server as the print server—that is, as the server in charge of managing print services. A printer may be directly attached to the print server or, more likely, be attached to the network in a location convenient for the users. A printer directly attached to the network requires its own NIC and network address, as with any network node. In other cases, shared printers may be attached to networked workstations. For these printers to be accessible, the workstation must be turned on and functioning properly. Figure 9-6 depicts multiple ways to share printers on a network.

After the printer is physically connected to the network, it needs to be recognized and managed by the NOS before users can access it. Different NOSs present different interfaces for managing printers, but all NOSs can do the following:

- Create an object that identifies the printer to the rest of the network.
- Assign the printer a unique name.
- Install drivers associated with the printer.
- Set printer attributes, such as location and printing preferences.
- Establish or limit access to the printer.
- Remotely test and monitor printer functionality.
- Update and maintain printer drivers.
- Manage print jobs, including modifying a job's priority or deleting jobs from the queue.

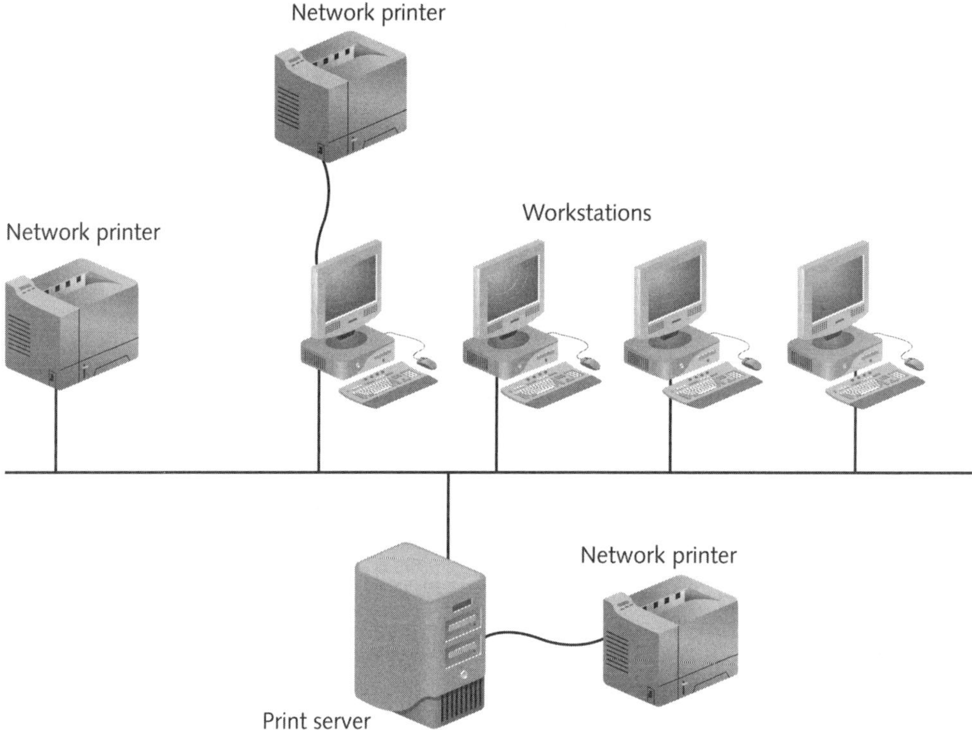

Figure 9-6 Shared printers on a network

As a network administrator, you should establish a plan for naming printers before you install them. Because the names you assign the printers will appear in lists of printers available to clients, you should choose names that users can easily decipher. For example, an HP Color LaserJet 3600 in the Engineering department may be called "ENG_HP3600." Whatever convention you choose, remain consistent to avoid user confusion and to make your own job easier.

As you create a new printer, the NOS will require you to install a printer driver, unless one is already installed on the server. This makes the printer's device driver files accessible to users who want to send jobs to that printer. Before users can access the printer, however, you must ensure that they have proper rights to the printer's queue. The **printer queue** (or *share*, as it is known in Microsoft terminology) is a logical representation of the printer's input and output. That is, a queue does not physically exist, but rather acts as a sort of virtual in-box for the printer. When a user prints a document (whether by clicking a button or selecting a menu command), he sends the document to the printer queue. To send it to the printer queue, he must have rights to access that queue. As with shared data, the rights to shared printers can vary. Users might have minimal privileges that allow them to simply send jobs to the printer, or they might have advanced privileges that allow them to change the priority of print jobs in the queue, or even (in the case of an administrator) change the name of the queue.

Networked printers appear as icons in the Printers folder on Windows and Macintosh workstations, just as local printers would appear. After they have found a networked printer, users can send documents to that printer just as they would send documents to a local printer. When a user chooses to print, the client redirector determines whether the request should be transmitted to the network or remain at the workstation. On the network, the user's request gets passed to the print server, which puts the job into the appropriate printer queue for transmission to the printer.

Managing System Resources

Because a server's system resources (for example, memory and processor) are limited and are required by multiple users, it is important to make the best use of them. Modern NOSs have capabilities that maximize the use of a server's memory, processor, bus, and hard drive. The result is that a server can accommodate more client requests faster—thus improving overall network performance. In the following sections, you will learn about some NOS techniques for managing a server's resources.

Memory From working with computers, you might already be familiar with the technique of using virtual memory to boost the total memory available to a system. Servers can use both physical and virtual memory, too, as this section describes.

Before learning about virtual memory, you should understand physical memory. The term **physical memory** refers to the RAM chips that are installed on the computer's system board and whose sole function is to provide memory to that machine. The amount of physical memory required by your server varies depending on the tasks that it performs. For example, the minimum amount of physical memory required to run the Standard Edition of Windows Server 2008 (the version of Windows Server 2008 designed to meet the needs of most businesses) is 512MB. However, if you intend to run file and print sharing, Internet, and remote access services on one server, additional physical memory will ensure better performance. Microsoft recommends using at least 2GB for optimal performance.

Another type of memory may be logically carved out of space on the hard drive for temporary use. In this arrangement, both the space on the hard drive and the RAM together form **virtual memory**. Virtual memory is stored on the hard drive as a **page file** (also known as a **paging file** or a **swap file**), the use of which is managed by the operating system. Each time the system exceeds its available RAM, blocks of information, called pages, are moved out of RAM and into virtual memory on disk. This technique is called **paging**. When the processor requires the information moved to the page file, the blocks are moved back from virtual memory into RAM.

Virtual memory is both a blessing and a curse. On the one hand, if your server has plenty of hard drive space, you can use virtual memory to easily expand the memory available to server applications. This is a great advantage when a process temporarily needs more memory than the physical memory can provide. Virtual memory is typically engaged by default; it requires no user or administrator intervention and is accessed without the clients' knowledge. (However, as a network administrator, you can modify the amount of hard drive space available for virtual memory.) On the other hand, using virtual memory slows operations because accessing a hard drive takes longer than accessing physical memory. Therefore, an excessive reliance on virtual memory will cost you in terms of performance.

Multitasking   Another technique that helps servers use their system resources more efficiently is **multitasking**, which is the execution of multiple tasks at one time. The ability to multitask enables a processor to perform many different operations in a very brief period of time. If you have used multiple programs on a desktop computer, you have taken advantage of your operating system's multitasking capability. All of the major NOSs are capable of multitasking. If they weren't, network performance would be considerably slower, because busy servers are continually receiving and responding to multiple requests.

Note that multitasking does not mean performing more than one operation simultaneously. (A computer can only process multiple operations simultaneously if it has more than one processor.) In UNIX, Linux, Windows Server 2003, and Windows Server 2008, the server performs one task at a time, allowing one program to use the processor for a certain period of time, and then suspending that program to allow another program to use the processor. Thus, each program has to take turns loading and running. Because no two tasks are ever actually performed at one time, this capability is more accurately referred to as **preemptive multitasking**—or, in UNIX terms, **time sharing**. Preemptive multitasking happens so quickly, however, that the average user would probably think that multiple tasks were occurring simultaneously.

Multiprocessing   Before you learn about the next method of managing system resources, you need to understand the terms used when discussing data processing. A **process** is a routine of sequential instructions that runs until it has achieved its goal. When it is running, a word-processing program's executable file is an example of a process. A **thread** is a self-contained, well-defined task within a process. A process may contain many threads, each of which may run independently of the others. All processes have at least one thread—the main thread. For example, to eliminate the waiting time when you save a file in your word processor, the programmer who wrote the word-processor program might have designed the file save operation as a separate thread. That is, the file save part of the program happens in a thread that is independent of the main thread. This independent execution allows you to continue typing while a document is being written to the disk, for example.

On systems with only one processor, only one thread can be handled at any time. Thus, if a number of programs are running simultaneously, no matter how fast the processor, a number of processes and threads will be left to await execution. Using multiple processors allows different threads to run on different processors. The support and use of multiple processors to handle multiple threads is known as **multiprocessing**. Multiprocessing is often used on servers as a technique to improve response time. To take advantage of more than one processor on a computer, its operating system must be capable of multiprocessing. Depending on the edition, a Windows Server 2008 computer may support up to 64 processors.

Multiprocessing splits tasks among more than one processor to expedite the completion of any single instruction. To understand this concept, think of a busy metropolitan freeway during rush hour. If five lanes are available for traffic, drivers can pick any lane—preferably the fastest lane—to get home as soon as possible. If traffic in one lane slows, drivers may choose another, less congested lane. This ability to move from lane to lane allows all traffic to move faster. If the same amount of traffic had to pass through only one lane, everyone would go slower and get home later. In the same way, multiple processors can handle more instructions more rapidly than a single processor could.

Modern NOSs support a special type of multiprocessing called **symmetric multiprocessing**, which splits all operations equally among two or more processors. Another type of multiprocessing, **asymmetric multiprocessing**, assigns each subtask to a specific processor. Continuing the freeway analogy, asymmetric multiprocessing would assign all semitrucks to the far-right lane, all pickup trucks to the second-to-the right lane, all compact cars to the far-left lane, and so on. The efficiency of each multiprocessing model is open to debate, but, in general, symmetric processing completes operations more quickly because the processing load is more evenly distributed.

Multiprocessing offers a great advantage to servers with high processor usage—that is, servers that perform numerous tasks simultaneously. If an organization uses its server merely for occasional file and print sharing, however, multiple processors may not be necessary. Therefore, carefully assess your processing needs before purchasing a server with multiple processors. Some processing bottlenecks are not actually caused by the processor—but rather by the time it takes to access the server's hard drives or by problems related to cabling or connectivity devices.

Windows Server 2008

Windows Server 2008 is the latest version of Microsoft's NOS, released in February 2008. It's an enhancement of its predecessor, Windows Server 2003, though many of the older NOS's features remain in the newer version. Windows-based NOSs are known for their intuitive graphical user interface, multitasking capabilities, and compatibility with a huge array of applications. A **GUI** (**graphical user interface**; pronounced "gooey") is a pictorial representation of computer functions that, in the case of NOSs, enables administrators to manage files, users, groups, security, printers, and so on. Windows Server 2008 carries on many of the advantages of Windows Server 2003, plus enhances its security, reliability, support for remote clients, and performance. In addition, with Windows Server 2008, Microsoft has added new features that make server management even easier.

As with Windows Server 2003, Server 2008 comes in several editions. The most commonly installed are Standard Edition, Web Edition, Enterprise Edition, and Datacenter Edition. Differences between the 64-bit Server 2008 editions can be summarized as follows:

- *Standard Edition*—Provides the basic resource sharing and management features necessary for most businesses, including support for up to 32GB of RAM and four processors performing symmetric multiprocessing.
- *Web Edition*—Provides added services for Web site hosting, Web development, and Web-based applications and includes support for up to 32GB of RAM and four processors performing symmetric multiprocessing.
- *Enterprise Edition*—Provides support for up to eight processors performing symmetric multiprocessing, up to 2TB (terabytes, or 1,000 gigabytes) of RAM, and clustering. Designed for environments that need a high level of reliability and performance. (Clustering is a fault-tolerance technique discussed in Chapter 14.)
- *Datacenter Edition*—Provides support for up to 64 processors, up to 2TB of RAM, clustering, and unlimited virtualization. **Virtualization** refers to the capability for operating multiple logical servers—or virtual servers—on a single machine. This edition is designed for environments that need the highest degree of reliability and performance.

Windows Server 2003 and Server 2008 are popular NOSs because they address most of a network administrator's needs very well. Microsoft is, of course, a well-established vendor, and many devices and programs are compatible with its systems. Its large market share guarantees that technical support—whether through Microsoft, private developer groups, or third-party newsgroups—is readily available. If you become MCSE-certified, you will be eligible to receive enhanced support directly from Microsoft. This enhanced support will help you solve problems more quickly and accurately. Because Windows operating systems are so widely used, you can also search newsgroups on the Web and will probably find someone who has encountered and solved a problem like yours.

Some general benefits of the Windows Server 2008 NOSs include:

- Support for multiple processors, multitasking, and symmetric multiprocessing
- A comprehensive system for organizing and managing network objects, called Active Directory
- Simple centralized management of multiple clients, resources, and services
- Centralized management of all server functions through a single interface known as the Server Manager.
- Multiple, integrated Web development and delivery services that incorporate a high degree of security and an easy-to-use administrator interface
- Support for modern protocols and security standards
- Excellent integration with other NOSs and support for many different client operating systems

- Integrated remote client services—for example, automatic software updates and client assistance

- Provisions for monitoring and improving server performance

- Support for high-performance, large-scale storage devices

Although Microsoft NOSs have long been appreciated for their simple user interfaces, some network administrators have criticized their performance and security. With the release of Windows Server 2008, Microsoft has implemented new security measures and enhanced those they included with Server 2003. Bear in mind that performance greatly depends on the type of routines and commands tested. The only sure way to find out how an NOS will perform on your network is to compare it against another NOS using your applications, clients, and infrastructure.

This chapter gives a broad overview of how Windows Server 2008, Standard Edition, fits into a network environment. It does not attempt to give exhaustive details of the process of installing, maintaining, or optimizing Windows Server 2008 networks. For this in-depth knowledge (and particularly if you plan to pursue MCSE certification), you should invest in books devoted to Windows Server 2008.

Hardware Requirements

You have learned that servers generally require more processing power, memory, and hard drive space than do client workstations. In addition, servers may contain redundant components, such as multiple hard drives, self-monitoring firmware, multiple processors and NICs, or peripherals other than the common DVD-ROM drives. The type of servers you choose for your network will depend partly on your NOS. Each NOS demands specific server hardware.

An important resource for determining what kind of hardware to purchase for your Windows server is the Windows Server Catalog. The Windows Server Catalog lists all computer components proven to be compatible with Windows Server 2008, and it can be found online at *www.windowsservercatalog.com*. Always consult this list before buying new hardware. Although hardware that is *not* listed on the Web site might work with Windows Server 2008, Microsoft's technical support won't necessarily help you solve problems related to such hardware.

Table 9-2 lists Microsoft's minimum server requirements for Windows Server 2008, Standard Edition.

Minimum requirements specify the least amount of RAM, hard drive space, and processing power you must have to run the NOS. Your applications and performance demands, however, may require more resources. Some of the minimum requirements listed in Table 9-2 (for example, the 1.4GHz processor) may apply to the smallest test system but not to a realistic networking environment. Be sure to assess the optimal configuration for your network's server based on your environment's needs before you purchase new hardware. For instance, you should make a list of every application and utility you expect the server to run in addition to the NOS. Then look up the processor, memory, and hard drive requirements for each of those programs and estimate how significantly their requirements will affect your server's overall hardware requirements. It is easier and more efficient to perform an analysis before you install the server than to add hardware after your server is up and running.

Table 9-2 Minimum Hardware Requirements for Windows Server 2008, Standard Edition

Component	Requirement
Processor	1GHz (×86) or 1.4GHz (×64) processor (2GHz or faster processor recommended); Windows Server 2008, Standard Edition, supports up to four CPUs in one server.
Memory	512MB of RAM is the absolute minimum, but at least 2GB is recommended. A computer running Windows Server 2008 may hold a maximum of 32GB of memory for a 64-bit system.
Hard drive	A hard drive supported by Windows Server 2008 (as specified in the Windows Server Catalog) with a minimum of 10GB of free space available for system files. (40GB or more is recommended.)
NIC	Although a NIC is not required by Windows Server 2008, it is required to connect to a network. Use a NIC found in the Windows Server Catalog. The NOS can support the use of more than one NIC.
DVD-ROM	A DVD-ROM drive found in the Windows Server Catalog is required unless the installation will take place over the network.
Pointing device	A mouse or other pointing device found in the Windows Server Catalog.

Memory Model

Earlier, you learned that Windows Server 2008, Standard Edition, can use up to four processors and, further, that it employs a type of multiprocessing called symmetric multiprocessing. In addition, Windows Server 2008 can use virtual memory. This section provides more information on how Windows Server 2008 optimizes its use of a server's memory to juggle many complex tasks.

Some versions of Windows Server 2008 use a 32-bit addressing scheme, whereas others use a 64-bit addressing scheme (which also requires a different type of processor). Essentially, the larger the addressing size, the more efficiently instructions can be processed.

The Windows Server 2008, Standard Edition, memory model also assigns each application (or process) its own 32-bit memory area. This memory area is a logical subdivision of the entire amount of memory available to the server. Assigning separate areas to processes helps prevent one process from interfering with another's operations, even though the processor is handling both instructions.

Another important feature of the Windows Server 2008 memory model is that it allows you to install more physical memory on the server than previous versions of Windows did, which, in turn, means that the server can process more instructions faster.

Finally, as you have learned, Windows Server 2008 can use virtual memory. To find out how much virtual memory your Windows Server 2008 computer uses, perform these steps:

1. While logged in as administrator or a user with equivalent privileges, click **Start,** and then select **Control Panel.** The Control Panel window opens.

2. Double-click the **System** icon. The System window opens.

3. Under the list of Tasks, click **Advanced system settings.** The System Properties dialog box appears.

4. Click the **Advanced** tab.

5. Under Performance, click **Settings**. The Performance Options dialog box appears.

6. Click the **Advanced** tab, as shown in Figure 9-7.

7. To change the amount of virtual memory the server uses, click the **Change** button. This opens the Virtual Memory dialog box, where you can increase or decrease the paging file size. If you suspect that your server's processing is being degraded because it relies on virtual memory too often, you should invest in additional physical memory (RAM).

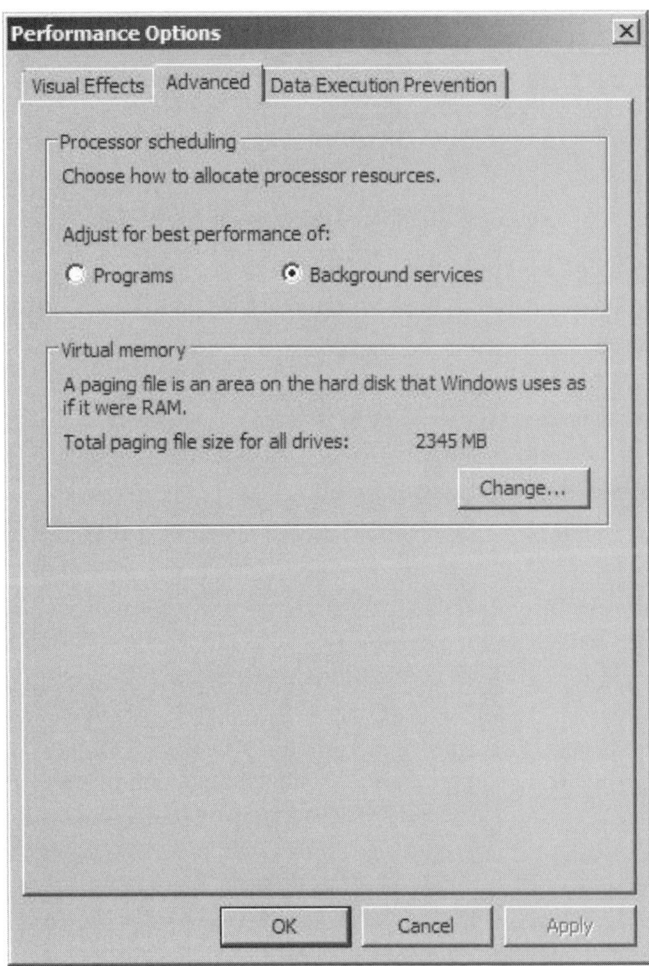

Figure 9-7 The Windows Server 2008 Performance Options Advanced tab

NTFS (New Technology File System)

Windows Server 2008 supports several **file systems,** or methods of organizing, managing, and accessing its files through logical structures and software routines. By default, however, this NOS establishes **NTFS (New Technology File System)** when installed on a server. Microsoft designed NTFS expressly for its Windows NT platform, which preceded Windows 2000 Server and Windows Server 2003.

To understand file systems, you must first understand the distribution of data on a disk. Disks are divided into allocation units (also known as clusters). Each allocation unit represents a small portion of the disk's space; depending on your operating system, the allocation unit's size may or may not be customizable. A number of allocation units combine to form a **partition,** which is a logically separate area of storage on the hard drive. Each partition can be installed with any type of file system that your NOS can interpret.

NTFS is secure, reliable, and makes it possible to compress files so they take up less space. At the same time, NTFS can handle massive files and allows fast access to data, programs, and other shared resources. It has been used on all versions of the Windows operating system since Windows NT. If you are working with Windows Server 2008, Microsoft recommends choosing NTFS for your server's file system. Therefore, you should familiarize yourself with the following NTFS features:

- NTFS filenames can be a maximum of 255 characters long.
- NTFS stores file size information in 64-bit fields.
- NTFS files or partitions can theoretically be as large as 16 exabytes (2^{64} bytes).
- NTFS is required for Macintosh connectivity.
- NTFS incorporates sophisticated, customizable compression routines. These compression routines reduce the space taken by files by as much as 40 percent. A 10GB database file, for example, could be squeezed into 6GB of disk space.
- NTFS keeps a log of file system activity to facilitate recovery if a system crash occurs.
- NTFS is required for encryption and advanced access security for files, user accounts, and processes.
- NTFS improves fault tolerance through RAID and system file redundancy. (RAID is discussed in detail in Chapter 14.)

One potential drawback to using an NTFS partition is that it cannot be read by older operating systems, such as Windows 95, Windows 2000 Professional, and early versions of UNIX. However, owing to all the benefits listed previously, the only instance in which you should not use NTFS is if one of your server's applications is incompatible with this file system.

Active Directory

Early in this chapter, you learned about directories, the methods for organizing and managing objects on the network. Windows Server 2008 uses a directory service called **Active Directory,** which was originally designed for Windows 2000 Server networks and enhanced with Windows Server 2008. This section provides an overview of how Active Directory is structured and how it uses standard naming conventions to better integrate with other networks. You'll also learn how Active Directory stores information for Windows domains.

Workgroups A Windows Server 2008 network can be set up in a workgroup model or a domain model. This section describes the workgroup model. In the next section, you will learn about the more popular domain model.

A **workgroup** is a group of interconnected computers that share each other's resources without relying on a central server. In other words, a workgroup is a type of peer-to-peer network. As in any peer-to-peer network, each computer in the workgroup has its own database of user accounts and security privileges.

Because each computer maintains its own database, each user must have a separate account on each computer he wants to access. This decentralized management results in significantly more administration effort than a client/server Windows Server 2008 network would require. In addition, workgroups are only practical for small networks with very few users. On the other hand, peer-to-peer networks such as a Windows Server 2008 workgroup are simple to design and implement and may be the best solution for home or small office networks in which security concerns are minimal.

Domains In Windows Server 2008 terminology, the term **domain model** refers to a type of client/server network that relies on domains rather than on workgroups. A **domain** is a group of users, servers, and other resources that share a centralized database of account and security information. The database that domains use to record their objects and attributes is contained within Active Directory. Domains are established on a network to make it easier to organize and manage resources and security. For example, a university might create separate domains for each of the following colleges: Life Sciences, Humanities, Communications, and Engineering. Within the Engineering domain, additional domains such as Chemical Engineering, Industrial Engineering, Electrical Engineering, and Mechanical Engineering may be created, as shown in Figure 9-8. In this example, all users, workstations, servers, printers, and other resources within the Engineering domain would share a distinct portion of the Active Directory database.

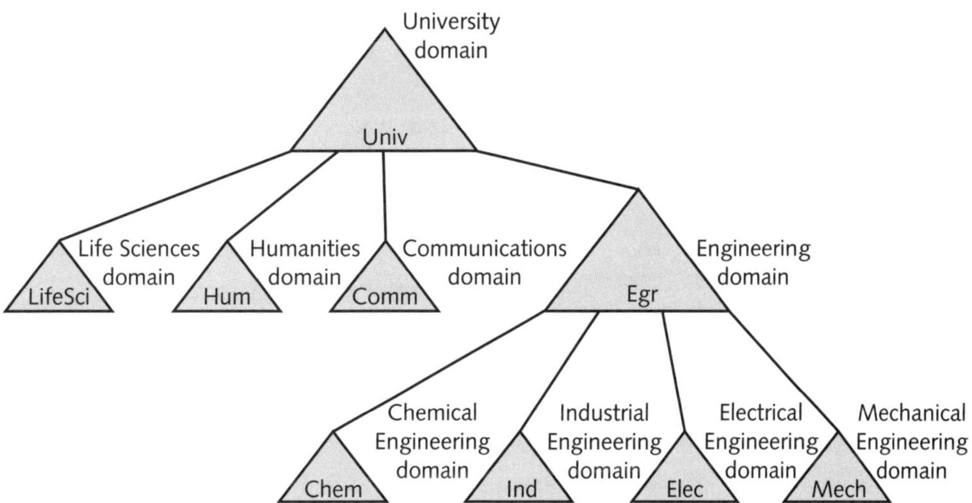

Figure 9-8 Multiple domains in one organization

Keep in mind that a domain is not confined by geographical boundaries. Computers and users belonging to the university's Engineering domain may be located at five different campuses across a state, or even across the globe. No matter where they are located, they obtain their object, resource, and security information from the same database and the same portion of Active Directory.

Depending on the network environment, an administrator can define domains according to function, location, or security requirements. For example, if you worked at a large hospital whose WAN connected the city's central healthcare facility with several satellite clinics, you could create separate domains for each WAN location, or you could create separate domains for each clinical department, no matter where they are located. Alternatively, you might choose to use only one domain and assign the different locations and specialties to different organizational units within the domain.

The directory containing information about objects in a domain resides on computers called **domain controllers**. A Windows Server 2008 network may use multiple domain controllers. In fact, you should use at least two domain controllers on each network so that if one domain controller fails, the other will continue to retain your domains' databases. Windows Server 2008 computers that do not store directory information are known as **member servers**. Because member servers do not contain a database of users and their associated attributes (such as password or permissions to files), member servers cannot authenticate users. Only domain controllers can do that. Every server on a Windows Server 2008 network is either a domain controller or a member server.

When a network uses multiple domain controllers, a change to the database contained on one domain controller is copied to the databases on other domain controllers so that their databases are always identical. The process of copying directory data to multiple domain controllers is known as **replication**. Replication ensures redundancy so that, in case one of the domain controllers fails, another can step in to allow clients to log on to the network, be authenticated, and access resources. Figure 9-9 illustrates a Windows Server 2008 network built using the domain model.

OUs (Organizational Units)   Earlier, you learned that NOSs use OUs (organizational units) to hold multiple objects that have similar characteristics. In Windows Server 2008, an OU can contain several million objects. And each OU can contain multiple OUs. For example, suppose you were the network administrator for the university described previously, which has the following domains: Life Sciences, Humanities, Communications, and Engineering. You could choose to make additional domains within each college's domain. But suppose instead that the colleges weren't diverse or large enough to warrant separate domains. In that case, you might decide to group objects according to organizational units. For the Life Sciences domain, you might create the following OUs that correspond to the Life Sciences departments: Biology, Geology, Zoology, and Botany. In addition, you might want to create OUs for the buildings associated with each department. For example, Schroeder and Randall for Biology, Morehead and Kaiser for Geology, Randall and Arthur for Zoology, and Thorne and Grieg for Botany. The tree in Figure 9-10 illustrates this example. Notice that Randall belongs to both the Biology and Zoology OUs.

Collecting objects in organizational units allows for simpler, more flexible administration. For example, suppose you want to restrict access to the Zoology printers in the Arthur building so that the devices are only available between 8 a.m. and 6 p.m. To accomplish this, you could apply this policy to the OU that contains the Arthur building's printer objects.

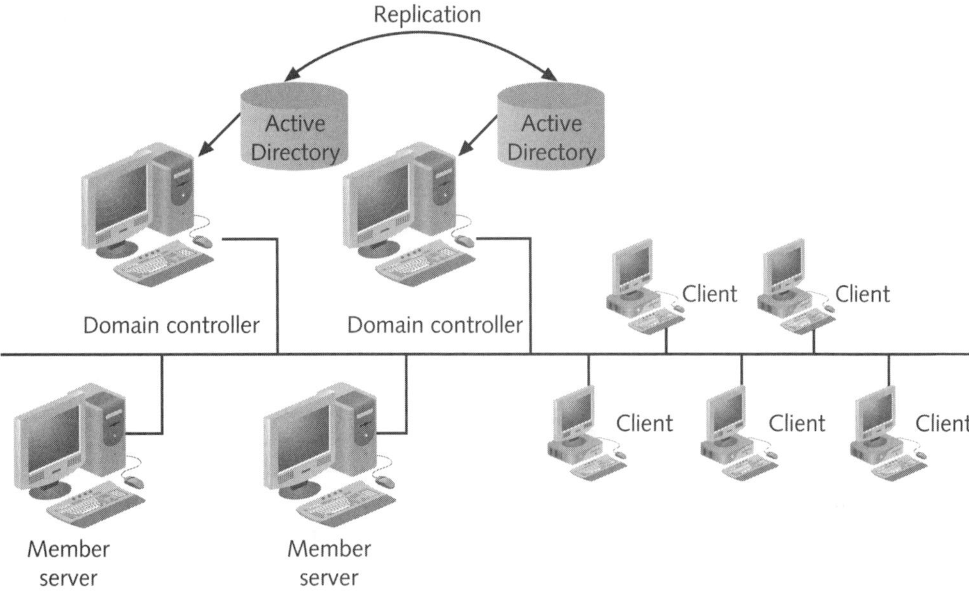

Figure 9-9 Domain model on a Windows Server 2008 network

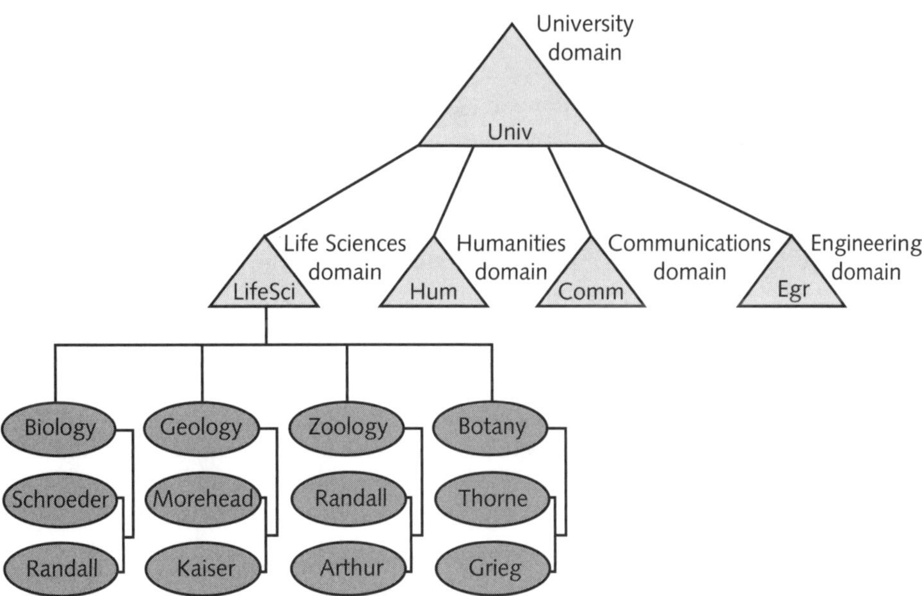

Figure 9-10 A tree with multiple domains and OUs

Trees and Forests Now that you understand how an NOS directory can contain multiple levels of domains and organizational units, you are ready to learn the structure of the directory that exists above domains. It is common for large organizations to use multiple domains in their Windows Server 2008 networks. Active Directory organizes multiple domains hierarchically in a **domain tree** (or simply, tree). (Recall that NOS trees were introduced earlier in the chapter. Active Directory's domain tree is an example of a typical NOS tree.) At the base of the Active Directory tree is the **root domain**. From the root domain, **child domains** branch out to separate groups of objects with the same policies, as you saw in Figure 9-8. Underneath the child domains, multiple organizational units branch out to further subdivide the network's systems and objects.

A collection of one or more domain trees is known as a **forest**. All trees in a forest share a common schema. Domains within a forest can communicate, but only domains within the same tree share a common Active Directory database. In addition, objects belonging to different domain trees are named separately, even if they are in the same forest. You will learn more about naming later in this chapter.

Trust Relationships For your network to work efficiently, you must give some thought to the relationships between the domains in a domain tree. A relationship between two domains in which one domain allows another domain to authenticate its users is known as a **trust relationship**. Active Directory supports two types of trust relationships: two-way transitive trusts and explicit one-way trusts. Each child and parent domain within a domain tree and each top-level domain in a forest share a **two-way transitive trust** relationship. This means that a user in domain A is recognized by and can be authenticated by domain B, and vice versa. In addition, a user in domain A may be granted rights to any of the resources managed by domain B, and vice versa.

When a new domain is added to a tree, it immediately shares a two-way trust with the other domains in the tree. These trust relationships allow a user to log on to and be authenticated by a server in any domain within the domain tree. However, this does not necessarily mean that the user has privileges to access any resources in the tree. A user's permissions must be assigned separately for the resources in each different domain. For example, suppose Irina is a research scientist in the Mechanical Engineering department. Her user account belongs to the Engineering domain at the university. One day, due to construction in her building, she has to temporarily work in an office in the Zoology department's building across the street. The Zoology department OU and all its users and workstations belong to the Life Sciences domain. When Irina sits down at the computer in her temporary office, she can log on to the network from the Life Sciences domain, which happens to be the default selection on her logon screen. She can do this because the Life Sciences and Engineering domains have a two-way trust. After she is logged on, she can access all her usual data, programs, and other resources in the Engineering domain. But even though the Life Sciences domain authenticated Irina, she will not automatically have privileges for the resources in the Life Sciences domain. For example, she can retrieve her research reports from the Mechanical Engineering department's server, but unless a network administrator grants her rights to access the Zoology department's printer, she cannot print the document to the networked printer outside her temporary office.

Figure 9-11 depicts the concept of a two-way trust between domains in a tree.

The second type of trust relationship supported by Active Directory is an **explicit one-way trust**. In this scenario, two domains that are not part of the same tree are assigned a trust relationship. The explicit one-way trust does not apply to other domains in the tree, however. Figure 9-12 shows how an explicit one-way trust can enable domains from different trees to share resources. In this figure, notice that the Engineering domain in the University tree and the Research domain in the Science Corporation tree share a one-way trust. However, this trust does not apply to parent or child domains associated with the Engineering or

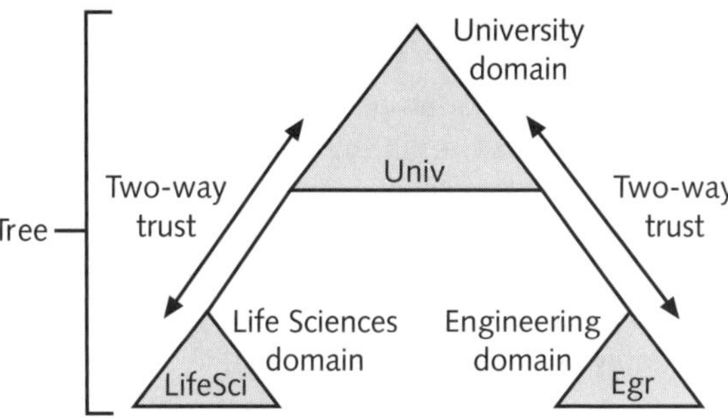

Figure 9-11 Two-way trusts between domains in a tree

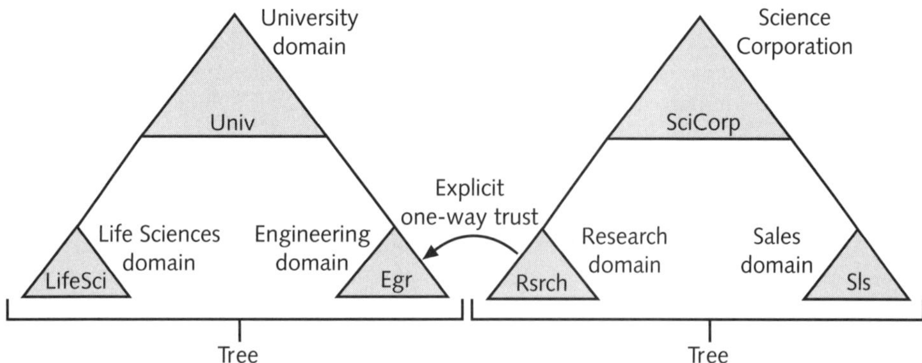

Figure 9-12 Explicit one-way trust between domains in different trees

Research domains. In other words, the Research domain could not have access to the entire University domain (including its child domains such as Life Sciences).

This section introduced you to the basic concepts of a Windows Server 2008 network structure. If you are charged with establishing a new network that relies on Windows Server 2003 or Server 2008, you will need to learn a lot more about Active Directory. In that case, you'll want to buy a book on the topic and perhaps take a class exclusively devoted to Active Directory.

Naming Conventions In the preceding section, you learned to think about domains in terms of their hierarchical relationships. Getting to know the structure of a network by studying its domain tree is similar to understanding your ancestry by studying a genealogical chart. Another way to look at ancestors is to consider their names and their relationship to you. For example, suppose a man named John Smith walks into a room full of relatives. The various people in the room will refer to him in various ways, depending on their relationship to him. One person might refer to him as "Uncle John," another as "Grandpa John," and another as "My husband, John." In the same way, different types of names, depending on where in the domain they are located, may be used to identify objects in a domain.

Naming (or addressing) conventions in Active Directory are based on the LDAP naming conventions. Because it is a standard, LDAP allows any application to access the directory of any system according to a single naming convention. Naming conventions on the Internet also follow LDAP standards. In Internet terminology, the term **namespace** refers to the complete database of hierarchical names used to map IP addresses to their hosts' names. The Internet namespace is not contained on just one computer. Instead, it is divided into many smaller pieces on computers at different locations on the Internet. In the genealogy analogy, this would be similar to having part of your family records in your home file cabinet, part of them in the state historical archives, part of them in your country's immigration files, and part of them in the municipal records of the country of your ancestors' origins. Somewhere in the Internet's vast, decentralized database of names and IP addresses (its namespace), your office workstation's IP address indicates that it can be located at your organization and, further, that it is associated with your computer.

In Active Directory, the term *namespace* refers to a collection of object names and their associated places in the Windows Server 2003 or Server 2008 network. In the genealogy analogy, this would be similar to having one relative (the Active Directory) who knows the names of each family member and how everyone is related. If this relative recorded the information about every relative in a database (for instance, Mary Smith is the wife of John Smith and the mother of Steve and Jessica Smith), this would be similar to what Active Directory does through its namespace.

Because the Active Directory namespace follows the conventions of the Internet's namespace, when you connect your Windows Server 2008 network to the Internet, these two namespaces are compatible. For example, suppose you work for a company called Trinket Makers, and it contracted with a Web development firm to create a Web site. Further, suppose that the firm chose the Internet domain name trinketmakers.com to uniquely identify your company's location on the Internet. When you plan your Windows Server 2008 network, you will want to call your root domain trinketmakers to match its existing Internet domain name. (The .com part is assumed to be a domain.) That way, objects within the Active Directory namespace can be assigned names related to the trinketmakers.com domain name, and they will match the object's name in the Internet namespace, should that be necessary.

Each object on a Windows Server 2008 network can have three different names. The following list describes the formats for these names, which follow LDAP specifications:

- **DN (distinguished name)**—A long form of the object name that explicitly indicates its location within a tree's containers and domains. A distinguished name includes a **DC (domain component)** name, the names of the domains to which the object belongs, an OU (organizational unit) name, the names of the organizational units to which the object belongs, and a **CN (common name)**, or the name of the object. A common name must be unique within a container. In other words, you could have a user called "Msmith" in the Legal container and a user called "Msmith" in the Accounting container, but you could not have two users called "Msmith" in the Legal container. Distinguished names are expressed with the following notation: DC=domain name, OU=organizational unit name, CN=object name. For example, the user Mary Smith in the Legal OU of the trinketmakers domain would have the following distinguished name: DC=com, DC=trinketmakers, OU=legal, CN=msmith. Another way of expressing this distinguished name would be trinketmakers.com/legal/msmith.

- **RDN (relative distinguished name)**—A name that uniquely identifies an object within a container. For most objects, the relative distinguished name is the same as its CN in the distinguished name convention. A relative distinguished name is an attribute that belongs to the object. This attribute is assigned to the object when the administrator creates the object. Figure 9-13 provides an example of an object, its distinguished name, and its relative distinguished name.

- **UPN (user principal name)**—The preferred naming convention for users in e-mail and related Internet services. A user's UPN looks like a familiar Internet address, including the positioning of the domain name after the @ sign. When you create a user account, the user's logon name is added to a **UPN suffix**, the portion of the user's UPN that follows the @ sign. A user's default UPN suffix is the domain name of her root domain. For example, if Mary Smith's user name is msmith and her root domain is trinketmakers.com, her UPN suffix is trinketmakers.com, and her UPN is *msmith@trinketmakers.com.*

In addition to these names, each object has a **GUID (globally unique identifier)**, a 128-bit number that ensures that no two objects have duplicate names. The GUID is generated and assigned to an object upon its creation. Rather than use any of the alphabetical names, network applications and services communicate with an object via the object's GUID.

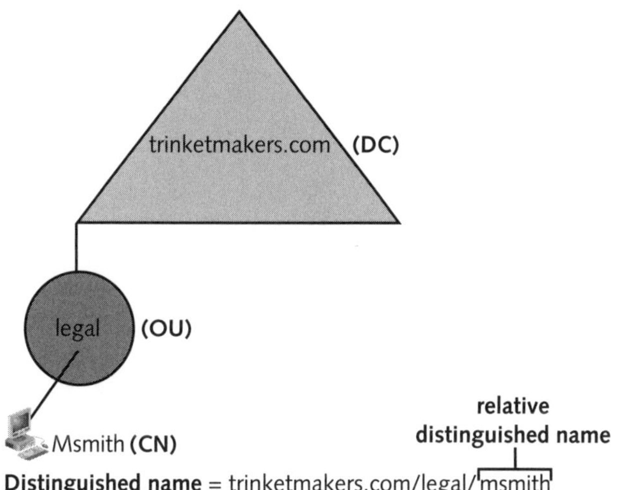

Figure 9-13 Distinguished name and relative distinguished name

Server Management

With the release of Windows Server 2008, Microsoft simplified the process of setting up and managing a server running its NOS. To begin, upon installing Windows Server 2008, you are asked to choose roles for your server. In Microsoft terminology, a **role** reflects a server's primary purpose. For example, a large business might designate one server as its fax server, another as its file server, and a third to manage its Active Directory domain services. It follows that the services a server runs will depend on its role. A designated print server would run print services, for instance, but wouldn't run Web services.

After you have installed Windows 2008 and assigned your server at least one role, you can conduct virtually any server management task through a GUI tool known as **Server Manager**.

Server Manager includes the functions that, in Windows Server 2003, were part of the **MMC (Microsoft Management Console)**. However, it's more comprehensive than MMC. Using Server Manager, you may:

- Assign, remove, or change roles assigned to your server.
- Add, remove, or modify services (or features) operating on your server.
- Diagnose problems related to security, software, or hardware.
- Manage user accounts and groups.
- Manage shared and local resources.

To access Server Manager, simply click **Start,** point to **Administrative Tools,** and then click **Server Manager.** The Server Manager window appears, as shown in Figure 9-14.

Within Server Manager, you click Roles to add, remove, or modify a role assigned to your server, as well as to manage print and file sharing services. The Features option allows you to add, remove, or modify services your server runs. The Diagnostics option allows you to view logs of system events, monitor server performance, and view and modify hardware properties. For example, to view the extent to which your processor, hard drive, memory, and network connection resources are utilized, click Reliability and Performance under the Diagnostics option. The Reliability and Performance window appears, as shown in Figure 9-15.

Also in Server Manager, the Configuration option is what allows you to manage users and groups, as well as to schedule tasks and stop or start processes. Finally, the Storage option allows you to manage your server's disks, including setting up server backups and scanning disks.

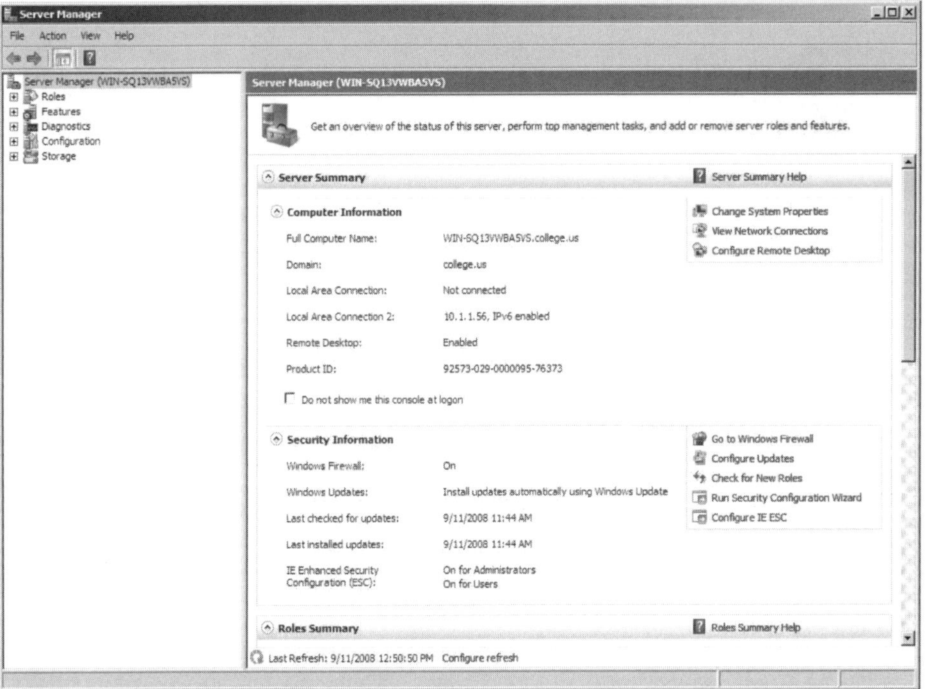

Figure 9-14 Windows Server 2008 Server Manager

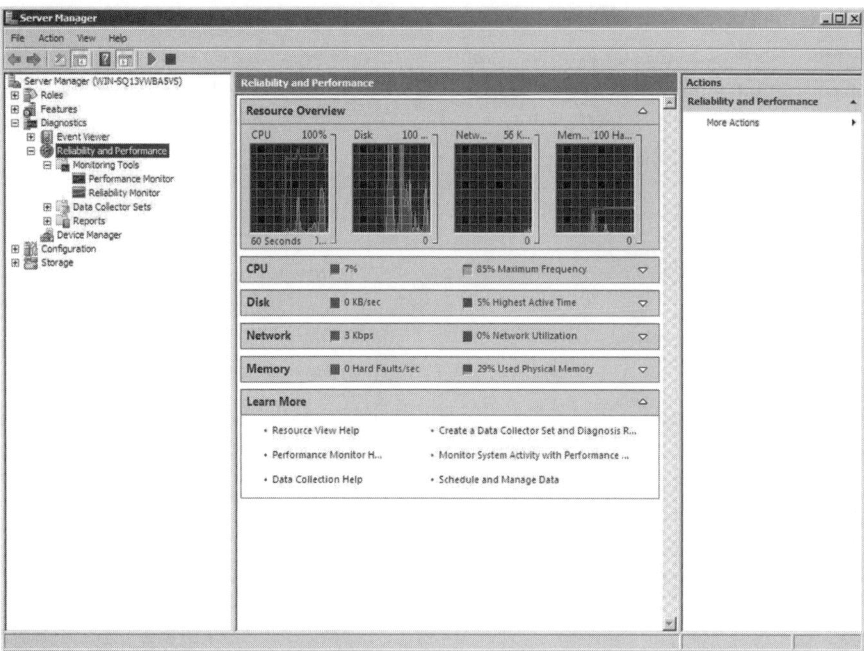

Figure 9-15 Server Manager's Reliability and Performance window

Now that you have learned about the fundamental aspects of Windows Server 2008, you are ready to learn about two other popular NOSs: UNIX and Linux.

UNIX and Linux

Along with Microsoft's Windows Server 2003 and Server 2008, **UNIX** is one of the most popular NOSs. All of these operating systems enable servers to provide resource sharing, but UNIX differs in fundamental ways from Windows. Researchers at AT&T Bell Laboratories developed UNIX in 1969; thus, it is much older than Windows. In fact, UNIX preceded and led to the development of the TCP/IP protocol suite in the early 1970s. Today, most Internet servers run UNIX. Reflecting this operating system's efficiency and flexibility, the number of installed UNIX systems continues to grow. Many local and wide area networks include UNIX servers. You should familiarize yourself with UNIX so you can set up and maintain these networks.

Mastering UNIX can be difficult because, unlike Windows, it is not controlled and distributed by a single software manufacturer. Instead, numerous vendors sell their own UNIX varieties. In addition, you may install operating systems that share many of UNIX's characteristics but are nonproprietary and freely distributed. The most popular example is **Linux**. Fortunately, the differences between UNIX and Linux varieties are relatively minor, and, if you understand how to use one, with a little effort you can understand how to use another. The following sections introduce the UNIX operating system in general and then describes two varieties— Solaris and Linux—in more detail.

A Brief History of UNIX

In the late 1960s, a few programmers grew dissatisfied with the existing programming environments. In particular, they didn't like the cumbersome nature of systems that required a programmer to write a set of instructions, submit them all at once, and then wait for the results. Instead, programmers desired a more interactive operating environment that allowed them to build and test their programs piece by piece. In addition, the programmers sought a system that imposed as few predetermined structures as possible on the users. For example, they preferred to let programmers decide how data should be formatted within a data file or how to structure filenames. With this in mind, Ken Thompson and Dennis Ritchie, two employees of Bell Labs (which was then part of AT&T), decided to create an entirely new programming environment. To properly design this new environment, they decided to start at the lowest level—the operating system. This environment ultimately evolved into the UNIX operating system.

Antitrust law prohibited AT&T from profiting from the sale of computers and software during the 1970s. Thus, for a nominal licensing fee, anyone could purchase the **source code**—that is, the form of a computer program that can be read by people—to the work produced at Bell Labs. The word spread rapidly, and researchers in educational institutions and large corporations all over the world soon had this new software running on their lab computers. Versions of UNIX that come from Bell Labs are known as **System V**. Researchers at the University of California at Berkeley were among the first enthusiastic supporters of early versions of UNIX. They added many useful features to the operating system, including the TCP/IP network subsystem. Berkeley versions of UNIX are known as **BSD (Berkeley Software Distribution)**.

The 1980s saw the breakup of AT&T and the removal of some of its antitrust restrictions. This enabled the company to begin marketing the UNIX system to other computer manufacturers. However, AT&T eventually sold its rights to the UNIX system, and these rights changed hands a number of times during the early 1990s. At the time this was written, courts were still teasing out which organizations share ownership of the UNIX system. The most current ruling awards Novell rights to the UNIX source code, or the raw materials for creating a UNIX system. Anyone could try writing a UNIX operating system from scratch, but the effort required to do so is prohibitive. Most organizations choose to start with the existing source code by licensing it from Novell and then make modifications for their specific computer hardware.

In addition, a nonprofit industry association called **the Open Group** owns the UNIX trademark. After a vendor changes the code licensed from Novell, its modified system must pass Novell's verification tests before the operating system may be called UNIX. IBM, for example, pays source code licensing fees to Novell and verification and trademark use fees to the Open Group so that it can refer to its AIX operating system as UNIX.

Now that you understand some of the history of UNIX, you are better prepared to learn about its many varieties and how these varieties are related.

Varieties of UNIX

Today, the UNIX operating system comes in many varieties, or, as they are more casually called, **flavors** or **distributions**. Before learning about their differences, however, you should know that all flavors of the UNIX operating system share the following features:

- The ability to support multiple, simultaneously logged-on users
- The ability to coordinate multiple, simultaneously running tasks (or programs)

- The ability to **mount**—or to make available—disk partitions upon demand

- The ability to apply permissions for file and directory access and modification

- A uniform method of issuing data to or receiving data from hardware devices, files, and running programs

- The ability to start a program without interfering with a currently running program

- Hundreds of subsystems, including dozens of programming languages

- Source code portability, or the ability to extract code from one UNIX system and use it on another

- Window interfaces that the user can configure, the most popular of which is the **X Window system**

Types of the UNIX operating system can be divided into two main categories: proprietary and open source. The following sections describe characteristics of each category and offer examples of UNIX versions in both categories. Note that some flavors of UNIX will operate only on certain types of computers. Examples of such UNIX varieties and their unique hardware requirements are also described next.

Proprietary UNIX Many companies market both hardware and software based on the UNIX operating system. An implementation of UNIX for which the source code is either unavailable or available only by purchasing a licensed copy from Novell (costing as much as millions of dollars) is known as **proprietary UNIX**. By most counts, the three most popular vendors of proprietary UNIX are Apple Computer, Sun Microsystems, and IBM. Apple's proprietary version of UNIX, **Mac OS X Server**, runs on computers that use Intel processors. Sun's proprietary version of UNIX, called **Solaris**, runs on the company's proprietary **SPARC**-based (the CPU invented by Sun Microsystems) workstations and servers, as well as Intel-based Pentium-class workstations and servers. IBM's proprietary version, **AIX**, runs on its **PowerPC**-based computers. Many other organizations have licensed the UNIX source code and created proprietary UNIX versions that run on highly customized computers (that is, computers that are appropriate for very specific tasks).

Choosing a proprietary UNIX system has several advantages:

- *Accountability and support*—An organization might choose a proprietary UNIX system so that when something doesn't work as expected, it has a resource on which to call for assistance.

- *Optimization of hardware and software*—Workstation vendors who include proprietary UNIX with the computers they sell invest a great deal of time in ensuring that their software runs as well and as fast as possible on their hardware.

- *Predictability and compatibility*—Purveyors of proprietary UNIX systems strive to maintain backward-compatibility with new releases. They schedule new releases at somewhat regular, predictable intervals. Customers usually know when and how things will change with proprietary UNIX systems.

One drawback of choosing a proprietary UNIX system, however, relates to the fact that the customer has no access to the system's source code and, thus, cannot customize the operating system. Open source UNIX solves this problem.

Open Source UNIX An interesting factor in the UNIX marketplace in recent years has been the emergence of UNIX or Linux systems that are not owned by any one company. This software is developed and packaged by a few individuals and made available to anyone, without licensing fees. Often referred to as **open source software,** or **freely distributable software,** this category includes UNIX versions such as **GNU** (an acronym that stands for GNU's Not UNIX), BSD, and Linux. These systems, in turn, come in a variety of implementations, each of which incorporates slightly different features and capabilities. As mentioned, these packages are often referred to as the different flavors of the open source software. For example, the different flavors of Linux include Red Hat, **Fedora,** SUSE, Ubuntu, and a host of others.

The key difference between freely distributable UNIX and proprietary implementations relates to the software license. Proprietary UNIX includes agreements that require payment of royalties for each system sold and that forbid redistribution of the source code. A primary advantage of open source UNIX and Linux is that users can modify their code and thereby add functionality not provided by a proprietary version of UNIX. For example, a manufacturing company that uses computer-controlled robotic spot welders might combine open source UNIX or Linux with custom software to control its robots. In contrast, it might be very difficult or costly to integrate the robotic control software with a proprietary UNIX system.

Another potential advantage of using a freely distributable version of UNIX or Linux is that, in general, these varieties run on a wider range of systems.

Two Flavors of UNIX

The rest of this chapter focuses on two operating systems: Solaris and Linux.

Solaris, the UNIX system Sun Microsystems uses on its SPARC-based servers, offers users all the benefits of commercially supported operating systems. It has seen numerous revisions and improvements over the years, and now it runs behind the scenes of some of the most intensive applications in the world. Some examples include large, multiterabyte databases, weather prediction systems, and large economic modeling applications.

Linux follows standard UNIX conventions, is highly stable, and is free. Linus Torvalds developed it in 1991 when he was a second-year computer science student in Finland. After developing Linux, Torvalds posted it on the Internet and recruited other UNIX aficionados and programmers to help enhance it. Today, Linux is used for file, print, and Web servers across the globe. Its popularity has even convinced large corporations that own proprietary UNIX versions, such as IBM, Hewlett-Packard, and Sun Microsystems, to publicly embrace and support Linux.

All versions of UNIX and Linux offer a host of features, including the TCP/IP protocol suite and all applications necessary to support the networking infrastructure as a part of the basic operating system. UNIX and Linux also support non-IP protocols. In addition, when you use one of these NOSs, you get the programs necessary for routing, firewall protection, DNS services, and DHCP services. Like Windows Server 2003 and Server 2008, UNIX may operate over many different network topologies and physical media.

UNIX and Linux systems efficiently and securely handle the growth, change, and stability requirements of today's diverse networks. The source code on which UNIX and Linux systems are based has been used and thoroughly debugged by thousands of developers for many years.

Now that you have been introduced to two popular versions of UNIX and Linux, you are ready to learn more details about these NOSs, beginning with the hardware requirements for each.

Hardware Requirements

Hardware requirements for UNIX and Linux systems are very similar to those for Windows Server 2003 and Server 2008. One key difference, however, is that any UNIX or Linux operating system can act as a workstation or server operating system (whereas Microsoft sells different operating systems for workstations and servers). Therefore, the computer's minimum hardware requirements depend partly on which version of UNIX or Linux you are installing and partly on how you intend to use the system.

A further difference is that in all flavors of UNIX, the use of a GUI (graphical user interface) remains optional—that is, you can choose to use the GUI, a command-line interface, or a combination of the two. By contrast, in Windows Server 2003 and with most versions of Server 2008, you *must* use the GUI for many operations (so a mouse is required). Many people regard the choice of using a GUI or a command-line interface in UNIX and Linux as an advantage. For example, you might choose to use the GUI for operations that require a great deal of interaction, such as adding new users or configuring services. However, for server operations that run unattended, it often makes sense to use the command-line interface (which consumes less of the computer's memory and other resources). Note that in Windows Server 2008, Microsoft added the ability to perform many common administrative functions from a command-line interface.

As you have learned, no single "right" server configuration exists. You might need to add more memory and more disk space according to your networking environment and users' needs. Unfortunately, you sometimes cannot learn the memory requirements of an application until you actually run it on the server. In these instances, it is always better to overestimate your needs than to underestimate them. However, you can get an idea of what additional hardware your server may require by answering the questions in the following sections. The following sections provide rough guidelines for choosing the hardware you will need to run Solaris and Linux.

Solaris Hardware Requirements Solaris runs on computers containing Sun SPARC processors or on Intel-based processors. Table 9-3 lists the minimum hardware requirements

Table 9-3 Minimum Hardware Recommendations for Solaris 10

Component	Requirement	Notes
Platform	Sun UltraSPARC and Fujitsu SPARC64	Solaris also supports AMD and Intel Pentium-class processors
Memory	512MB RAM	Consider adding more RAM for better system performance
Hard drive	2 to 6GB	
NIC	A NIC supported by Solaris (included with SPARC systems)	
CD-ROM/DVD-ROM	A CD-ROM or DVD-ROM drive supported by Solaris (included with SPARC systems)	

for the most recent Solaris operating system release, version 10. Components on SPARC workstations and servers have been tested to ensure their compatibility with Solaris. To determine which components on an Intel-based system will be compatible with Solaris, refer to Sun Microsystems' Intel Hardware Compatibility List (HCL) at *www.sun.com/software/ solaris/specs.html*.

The hardware requirements listed in Table 9-3 reflect the *minimum* amount of memory and hard drive space recommended to run Solaris 10. However, for better performance, you should consider using more than the minimum recommendation. For example, for application support, most systems need at least 10GB of hard drive space.

Linux Hardware Requirements

Linux hardware requirements vary to some extent based on the version of Linux you are installing. However, all Linux servers adhere to certain minimum hardware requirements, as shown in Table 9-4. You may find more current lists of supported hardware on the HCL at *www.tldp.org/HOWTO/HOWTO-INDEX/hardware.html*.

Table 9-4 Minimum Hardware Recommendations for a Linux Server

Component	Requirement	Notes
Processor	Intel-compatible x86	Recent versions of the Linux kernel (2.0 and later) include support for as many as 32 Intel processors
Memory	64MB RAM	Consider adding more RAM for better performance; most network administrators opt for 2GB of RAM or more for servers
Hard drive	A hard drive supported by Linux with a minimum of 2GB of free space	Most server implementations require additional free hard drive space; 10GB of free space is recommended
NIC	A NIC supported by Linux	
CD-ROM	A CD-ROM drive listed on the HCL	Recent versions of Linux support SCSI, IDE, and ATAPI CD-ROM drives
Floppy disk	One or two 3.5-inch disks, if no bootable CD-ROM drive is available	3.5-inch disks can be useful for creating emergency repair disks during installation
Pointing device	Optional	A pointing device is only necessary if you install the GUI component

Adding high-performance video cards, sound cards, and other I/O devices to your Linux server is also optional.

UNIX Multiprocessing

As you have learned, a process represents an instance of a program running in memory (RAM). In addition to processes, UNIX and Linux also support threads, which, as you have learned, are self-contained subsets of a process. Any modern NOS must handle multiple processes and threads in an efficient manner. UNIX and Linux allocate separate resources (such as memory space) to each process as it is created. They also manage all programs' access to these resources. This approach enables partitioning of processes in memory, thereby preventing one program from disrupting the operation of the entire system. When one program ends unexpectedly on a UNIX or Linux system, it doesn't cause the whole computer to crash.

As with Windows Server 2003 and Server 2008, modern UNIX and Linux systems support SMP (symmetric multiprocessing). Different flavors of UNIX support different numbers of processors. For example, Solaris supports up to 128 processors per server (although Sun does not make hardware containing that many processors). Linux supports SMP using a maximum of 32 processors per server.

You must know how your servers will be used and plan for multiprocessing servers according to your estimated application-processing loads.

The UNIX Memory Model

From early on, UNIX systems were created to use both physical and virtual memory efficiently. Similar to Windows Server 2003 and Server 2008, UNIX and Linux allocate a memory area for each application. All of these operating systems attempt to decrease the inefficiency of this practice, however, by sharing memory between programs wherever they can. For example, if five people are using FTP on your UNIX server, five instances of the FTP program will run. In reality, only a small part of each FTP program (called the private data region—the part that stores the user name, for example) will receive its own memory space; most of the program will remain in a region of memory shared by all five instances of the program. In this case, rather than using five times the memory required by one instance of the program, a UNIX or Linux system sets aside only a little more memory for five FTP users than it does for one FTP user.

Most current UNIX and Linux systems use a 32-bit addressing scheme that enables programs to access 4GB of memory. Most of these systems also run on CPUs that employ 64-bit addresses, enabling programs to access more than 18 exabytes (2^{64} bytes) of memory. That's more than 18 billion billion bytes of data—by one estimate, three times the total number of words ever spoken by human beings! Virtual memory in a UNIX server can take the form of a disk partition, or it can be in a file (much like the virtual memory file pagefile.sys in Windows Server 2003 and Server 2008).

The UNIX Kernel

The core of all UNIX and Linux systems is called the **kernel**. The kernel is loaded into memory and runs when you turn on your computer. Its primary function is to coordinate access to all your computer's hardware, such as the disks, memory, keyboard, and monitor. You can add or remove functionality on a running UNIX or Linux system by loading and unloading kernel modules. A UNIX **kernel module** is a file that contains instructions for performing a specific task such as reading data from and writing data to a hard drive. The Solaris kernel is derived from the original AT&T UNIX software from Bell Labs. The Linux kernel is the software Linus Torvalds wrote and released to the public in 1991.

UNIX System File and Directory Structure

UNIX was one of the first operating systems to implement a **hierarchical file system** (a method of organizing files and directories on a disk in which directories may contain files and other directories). The notion of a file system organized in this way was considered revolutionary at the time of UNIX's inception. Today, most operating systems, including all

Microsoft operating systems, use hierarchical file systems. Figure 9-16 shows a typical UNIX file system hierarchy.

On a UNIX or Linux system, the /boot directory contains the kernel and other system initialization files. Applications and services are stored in the /bin and /sbin directories. (The applications and services in the /sbin directory support the system initialization process; you'll rarely use these programs.) The /var directory holds variable data (such as log files, users' unread e-mail, and print jobs waiting to be printed). The file /var/log/messages, for example, stores system log messages, such as a notification of a disk drive that is running out of space. Users' login directories typically appear in /home. When you create a new user account, the system assigns a directory in /home to that user. The login (or home) directory matches the account's user name. Thus, /home/jones is the login (or home) directory for the user name jones on a UNIX system.

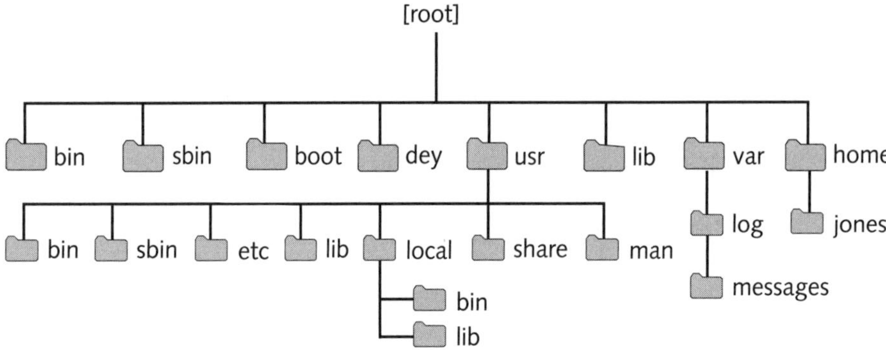

Figure 9-16 UNIX file system hierarchy

UNIX File Systems

UNIX file systems fall into two broad categories: disk file systems and network file systems. Disk file systems are used to organize the information on a hard drive. Network file systems enable users to access files on other servers via the network.

Disk File Systems   The UNIX disk file system is the operating system's facility for organizing, managing, and accessing files through logical structures and software routines. Just as Windows Server 2003 and Server 2008 support NTFS and other file systems, UNIX and Linux systems also support multiple file system types. The native file system type on Linux, called *ext3*, is the "third extended" file system for Linux. Solaris employs the file system called UFS (UNIX file system) for its native file system type.

On UNIX and Linux systems, you can access disk partitions formatted with NTFS file systems. This applies to partitions on disks that are physically attached to computers that are running a UNIX or Linux system. Over a network, UNIX systems have access to nonnative file system types, using network file systems, as described next.

Network File Systems   Computers running UNIX or Linux also make use of network file systems, which are analogous to Windows shares. From a UNIX host, the network file system allows you to attach shared file systems (or drives) from Windows or other UNIX servers and share files with users on other computers. Sun Microsystems' **NFS (Network File System)** is a popular remote file system type supported by UNIX and Linux. Sun Microsystems published the specification for NFS, and most vendors of UNIX and Linux systems include NFS applications for sharing and accessing files over a network. Another network file system, called **Samba,** is an open source application that implements the Windows SMB and CIFS file system protocols. Samba is included with Solaris and most Linux distributions by default.

A UNIX and Linux Command Sampler

For many years, the command line was the primary method of interacting with a computer running the UNIX or Linux NOS, and to this day, many system administrators prefer this method. Even when you're running a GUI, the GUI merely executes commands in response to your mouse clicks. This section discusses the basics of the UNIX user interface and provides a sample of fundamental UNIX commands.

The program that accepts the commands you type on the keyboard and runs the commands for you is called a **command interpreter.** Also known as a **shell,** a command interpreter translates your typed commands into machine instructions that a UNIX or Linux system can understand. In other words, the command interpreter is a program that runs other programs. UNIX command interpreters also perform file globbing (described later) and keep track of what commands you've entered previously. The primary UNIX command interpreter is the file /bin/sh. To use the shell effectively, you should be familiar with at least some basic commands.

Every UNIX and Linux system contains full documentation of UNIX commands in the **man pages** (or **manual pages**). The man pages describe each command's function and proper execution. Although their organization differs slightly in various flavors of UNIX, man pages are typically arranged in nine sections:

- *Section 1*—Covers the commands that you most typically enter while typing in a command window
- *Sections 2 through 5*—Document the programmer's interface to the UNIX system
- *Section 6*—Documents some of the amusements and games that are included in the UNIX system
- *Section 7*—Describes the device drivers for the system.
- *Section 8*—Covers the commands used by administrators to manage the system
- *Section 9*—Documents the UNIX kernel functions that programmers use when writing device drivers

You access man pages by entering the man command in a UNIX command window. For example, to read the man page entry for the telnet command, you would type man telnet in a command window, and then press Enter.

Although the UNIX man pages are accurate and complete, UNIX newcomers often complain that they can't find the appropriate man page if they don't know the name of the command they want to use. That's why the apropos command exists. It enables you to find possible man page entries for the command you want to use. For example, you might type apropos list to search for a command that lists files. The apropos command would then display all commands and programming functions that include the keyword list in their man page entries.

Type man *<command>* (where *<command>* is a command name displayed by apropos), and press Enter when you find a command name that looks like it might do what you want.

Commands function in much the same way as sentences in ordinary language. Some of these sentences are one-word directives to the system requesting that it perform a simple task on your behalf (such as date for "tell me the current date and time"). Other sentences are detailed instructions to the system containing the equivalent of nouns, adjectives, and adverbs and creating a precise description of the task you want the system to perform. For example, to instruct the system to "display the names of all files in the current directory that have been accessed in the past five days," you would type:

```
find . -type f -atime -5 -print.
```

All commands, command options, and filenames in UNIX and Linux are case sensitive. Be certain to use uppercase and lowercase as appropriate each time you type a command in a UNIX or Linux command window.

A few rules exist to guide your use of UNIX commands and, as you might expect, exceptions to most of the rules also exist. Most commands (though not all) are lowercase alphabetic characters. Using the analogy of a sentence, the command itself would be the verb—that is, the action you want the system to take (for example, ls to list information about files). The things on which you want the system to operate (often files) would be the nouns. (So, for example, you would type ls index.html to list a file named index.html.) Options to the commands are analogous to adjectives and adverbs—that is, modifiers that give more specifics about the command. To specify an option, you usually type a hyphen (-) followed by a letter. (For example, if you want to list files in a directory and also list details about the files, such as their size and creation date, you type ls -l.) You can make commands even more specific by using **file globbing**—the equivalent to using wildcards in Windows and DOS. On a UNIX or Linux system, this operation is also called filename substitution. (For example, ls -l a* would produce a detailed listing of all files beginning with the letter "a".)

A significant (and perhaps initially confusing) difference between the UNIX and Windows command-line interfaces relates to the character you use to separate directory names when you type in a command window. The Windows separator character is (\ ) (backslash). The equivalent UNIX directory separator character is (/) (forward slash). For example, in a Windows Command Prompt window, you type the telnet command as \windows\system32\telnet.exe. The telnet command in UNIX is /usr/bin/telnet.

Table 9-5 lists some common UNIX commands and provides a brief description of each.

The developers of the original UNIX system worked at AT&T, then the largest public corporation in the world. Two features of communication within large corporations are a tendency to abbreviate words and a reliance on acronyms. The command names in the UNIX system reflect this culture in that they drop vowels and syllables (*cp* for *copy*, *cat* for *concatenate*, and so on), and they name commands with the initials of their intended use (*grep* for *general regular expression parser* and *ftp* for *File Transfer Protocol*). Refer to the relevant man pages when you encounter command names that you don't understand. The synopsis section usually indicates the origin of the command name.

Table 9-5 Commonly Used UNIX Commands

Command	Function
date	Display the current date and time
ls –la	Display with details all the files in the current directory
ps –ef	Display details of the current running programs
find *dir filename- print*	Search for *filename* in the directory *dir* and display the path to the filename on finding the file
cat *file*	Display the contents of *file*
cd */d1/d2/d3*	Change the current directory to *d3*, located in */d1/d2*
cp *file1 file2*	Make a copy of *file1*, named *file2*
rm *file*	Remove (delete) *file* (Note that this is a permanent deletion; there is no trash can or recycle bin from which to recover the deleted file.)
mv *file1 file2*	Move (or rename) *file1* to *file2*
mkdir *dir*	Make a new directory named *dir*
rmdir *dir*	Remove the directory named *dir*
who	Display a list of users currently logged on
vi *file*	Use the "visual" editor named *vi* to edit *file*
lpr *file*	Print *file* using the default printer; **lpr** actually places *file* in the printer queue. The file is actually printed by **lpd (line printer daemon)**, the UNIX printer service.
grep "*string*" *file*	Search for the string of characters in *string* in the file named *file*
ifconfig	Display the network interface configuration, including the IP address, MAC address, and usage statistics for all NICs in the system
netstat -r	Display the system's TCP/IP network routing table
sort *filename*	Sort alphabetically the contents of *filename*
man *command*	Display the man page entry for "*command*"
chmod *rights file*	Change the access rights (the mode) of *file* to *rights*
chgrp *group file*	Change the group to which the *file* belongs to *group*
telnet *host*	Start a virtual terminal connection to *host* (where *host* may be an IP address or a host name)
ftp *host*	Start an interactive file transfer to (or from) *host* using the FTP protocol (where *host* may be an IP address or a host name)
startx	Start the X Window system
kill *process*	Attempt to stop a running program with the process ID *process*
tail *file*	Display the last 10 lines of *file*
exit	Stop the current running command interpreter. Log off the system if this is the initial command interpreter started when logging is on

The most frequently used UNIX command is `ls`. By entering `ls` (and specifying `-l`, the detailed listing option), you learn everything about a file except its contents. UNIX and Linux systems maintain the following information about each file:

- The filename
- The file size (in bytes)
- The date and time that the file was created
- The date and time that the file was last accessed (viewed or printed)
- The date and time that the file contents were last modified (created, edited, or changed in any way)
- The number of "aliases" or links to the file
- The numeric identifier of the user who owns the file
- The numeric identifier of the group to which the file belongs
- The access rights for the owner, the group, and all others

For each file, the system stores all of this information (except the filename) in a file **inode** (**information node**). The beginning of each disk partition contains reserved space for all inodes on that partition. Inodes also contain pointers to the actual file contents on the disk. The file's name is stored in the directory that contains the file. To learn about the inode information, use the ls command. Figure 9-17 shows a sample list generated by `ls -l`.

In Figure 9-17, the letters in the far-left column (for example, `drwxr-xr-x`) make up the access permissions field. The first character in the access permissions field (on the far left) indicates the file type. Files type designations include the following:

- d for directories
- `(-)`, a hyphen, for regular files, such as word-processing files or spreadsheet files—that is, those which, as far as the operating system is concerned, contain unstructured data

```
% ls -l
total 154
drwxr-xr-x   2 root root  4096 Nov 14 15:31 bin
drwxr-xr-x   4 root root  1024 Nov 14 15:21 boot
drwxr-xr-x   9 root root  3920 Nov 20 19:55 dev
drwxr-xr-x  74 root root 12288 Nov 20 20:16 etc
drwxr-xr-x   3 root root  4096 Nov 19 15:35 home
drwxr-xr-x   2 root root  4096 Aug 12 12:02 initrd
drwxr-xr-x  11 root root  4096 Nov 14 15:28 lib
drwx------   2 root root 16384 Nov 14 09:03 lost+found
drwxr-xr-x   3 root root  4096 Nov 20 19:55 media
drwxr-xr-x   2 root root  4096 Oct 15 19:21 misc
drwxr-xr-x   2 root root  4096 Aug 12 12:02 mnt
drwxr-xr-x   2 root root  4096 Aug 12 12:02 opt
dr-xr-xr-x  67 root root     0 Nov 20 13:49 proc
drwxr-x---   7 root root  4096 Nov 20 20:11 root
drwxr-xr-x   2 root root 12288 Nov 14 15:26 sbin
drwxr-xr-x   1 root root     0 Nov 20 13:49 selinux
drwxr-xr-x   2 root root  4096 Aug 12 12:02 srv
drwxr-xr-x   9 root root     0 Nov 20 13:49 sys
drwxrwxrwt   5 root root  4096 Nov 20 20:13 tmp
drwxr-xr-x  14 root root  4096 Nov 14 15:19 usr
drwxr-xr-x  20 root root  4096 Nov 14 15:23 var
% _
```

Figure 9-17   Example of output from ls -l

- l for symbolic link files (much like Windows shortcuts)
- b for block device files (such as disk partitions)
- c for character device files (such as serial ports)

The remaining letters in the access permissions field (for example, rwxr-xr-x) represent the permissions that users and groups have to access each file. The meaning of these letters is described in the output of ls - l shown in Figure 9-18.

Windows and UNIX systems share the powerful ability to direct output from one command to the input of another command. In UNIX, you combine commands using a **pipe**, which is entered as a vertical bar (|). (Think of data "flowing" through a pipe from one command to another.) Two or more commands connected by a pipe are called a **pipeline**. UNIX pipes make it possible to create sequences of commands that might require custom programming on other systems. For example, you can learn the process ID number assigned to a running program by combining two simple UNIX commands as follows: ps -ef|grep "/bin/sh". In UNIX, most commands that display output in a command window allow you to direct the output to another command. Most commands that accept typing from your keyboard also accept input from other commands.

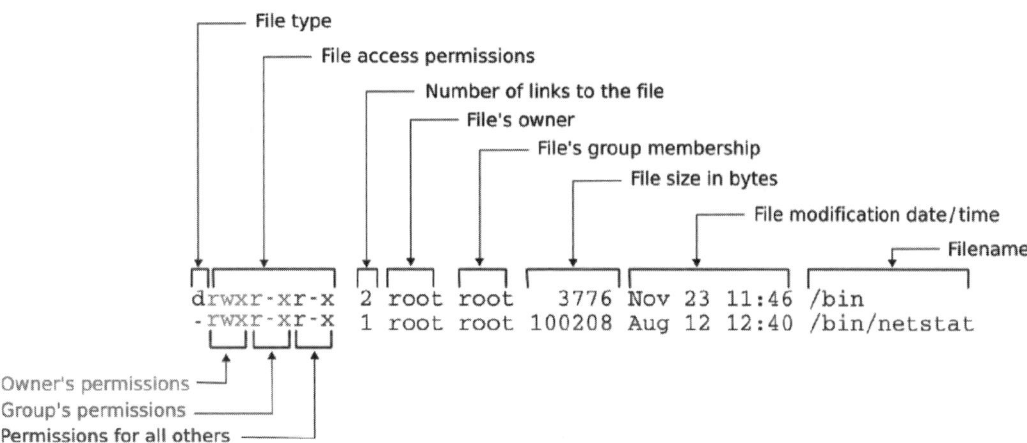

Figure 9-18 Anatomy of ls -l output

Chapter Summary

- NOSs are entirely software-based and can run on a number of different hardware platforms and network topologies.

- Network administrators choose an appropriate NOS according to what is compatible with the existing infrastructure; whether it supports the applications, services, and security required by the environment; whether it will grow with the organization; whether the vendor will provide reliable technical support; and whether it fits in the budget.

- A redirector, which belongs to the presentation layer of the OSI model, is inherent in both the NOS and the client operating system. On the client side, it intercepts client communications and decides whether the request is meant for the server or for the client.

- When a client attempts to log on, the NOS receives the client's request for service and tries to match the user name and password with the name and password in its user database. If the passwords match, the NOS grants the client access to resources on the network, according to limitations. This process is known as authentication.

- A directory is an NOS's method of organizing and managing objects, such as users, printers, server volumes, and applications. It is sometimes compared to a tree because it has one common starting point and branches into multiple containers, which may branch into additional containers.

- A file system is an operating system's method of organizing, managing, and accessing its files through logical structures and software routines.

- For clients to share a server application, the network administrator must assign users rights to the directories where the application's files are installed. Users will need at least the rights to access and read files in those directories. For some applications, users may also need rights to create, erase, or modify files associated with the application. Users are organized into groups to streamline administration.

- For clients to share a network printer, the printer must be created as an object, assigned a name and properties, and then shared among clients. Users or groups may be assigned different levels of privileges to operate printers.

- The type of multitasking supported by most NOSs performs one task at a time, allowing one program to use the processor for a certain period of time, and then suspending that program to allow another program to use the processor. This is called preemptive multitasking.

- Multiprocessing splits tasks among multiple processors to expedite the completion of any single instruction. It's a great advantage for servers with high CPU utilization because it improves performance.

- Windows Server 2008 requires the following minimum hardware: 1GHz processor, 512MB of RAM, at least 10GB free hard drive space for system files, and a pointing device.

- The Windows Server 2008 memory model assigns each process its own 32-bit (or in some versions, 64-bit) memory area. This memory area is a logical subdivision of the entire amount of memory available to the server. Assigning processes separate areas makes the processes less prone to interfering with each other when they run simultaneously.

- NTFS (New Technology File System) is the default file system installed on Windows Server 2008 servers. It's secure, reliable, and makes it possible to compress files so they take up less space. Also, NTFS can handle massive files and allows fast access to data, programs, and other shared resources. It's been used on all versions of the Windows operating system since Windows NT.

- In Windows Server 2008, the Server Manager application provides a centralized GUI for managing server roles, features, devices, resources, users, and groups.

- The description of object types, or classes, and their required and optional attributes that are stored in Active Directory is known as a schema.

- Domains define a group of systems and resources that share common security and management policies. The database that domains use to record their objects and attributes is contained within Active Directory. Domains are established on a network to make it easier to organize and manage resources and security.

- To collect domains into logical groups, Windows Server 2008 uses a domain tree (or simply, tree). At the base of the tree is the root domain. From the root domain, child domains branch out to separate objects with the same policies. Underneath the child domains, multiple organizational units branch out to further logically subdivide the network's systems and objects. A collection of domain trees is known as a forest.

- Each tree, domain, container, and object has a unique name that becomes part of the namespace. The names of these elements may be used in one of three different ways to uniquely identify an object in a Windows Server 2008 tree: as a distinguished name, as a relative distinguished name, and as a user principal name.

- UNIX is a stable, flexible, and efficient NOS. It relies on TCP/IP and forms the basis of much of the Internet. Despite the preponderance of proprietary implementations of UNIX, the differences between the various versions—or distributions—are relatively minor.

- UNIX was developed at AT&T Bell Laboratories, when a few programmers grew dissatisfied with the programming environments available in the late 1960s and decided to devise their own flexible operating system from scratch.

- Many varieties of UNIX exist, and each of these belong to one of two categories: proprietary and open source. Proprietary UNIX operating systems are those for which the source code is either unavailable or available only by purchasing a licensed copy from Novell. Apple Computer, Sun Microsystems, and IBM sell the three most popular proprietary versions of UNIX—Mac OS X Server, Solaris, and AIX.

- In the past few years, open source implementations of UNIX-type systems have grown in popularity. Open source means that the source code is freely available to anyone. This category includes BSD, GNU, and Linux. Popular varieties of Linux include Red Hat, Fedora, SUSE, and Ubuntu.

- Characteristics of UNIX and Linux include the ability to support multiple, simultaneous users; hierarchical files; a uniform method for interacting with files, devices, and programs; hundreds of subsystems and dozens of programming languages; and source code portability between different implementations of the system.

- Minimum hardware requirements for a Solaris 10 server include a SPARC system or Intel-based system with a Pentium-class processor, 512MB RAM, 5 to 7GB of disk space, a Solaris-supported NIC, and a Solaris-supported CD-ROM or DVD-ROM drive.

- Minimum hardware requirements for a Linux server include an Intel-compatible x86 processor, 64MB RAM, 2GB of hard drive space, a NIC compatible with the rest of your network, and a CD-ROM drive.

- UNIX and Linux use virtual memory and allocate a memory area for each application. These systems attempt to decrease the inefficiency of this practice, however, by sharing memory between programs wherever they can.

- Most current UNIX or Linux systems use a 32-bit addressing scheme that enables programs to access 4GB of memory. They may run on systems with 64-bit CPUs.

- The UNIX kernel, the core of the operating system, is loaded into memory from disk and runs when you turn on your computer. The kernel's primary function is to coordinate access to all the computer's hardware. You can add or remove functionality on a running UNIX or Linux system by loading and unloading UNIX kernel modules.

- Like other NOSs, UNIX and Linux support multiple file system types. The native file system type for Linux, called *ext3*, is the "third extended" file system for Linux. The default file system for Solaris is UFS (UNIX file system).

- UNIX and Linux support network file systems that are analogous to Windows shares. Common UNIX file systems include NFS and Samba.

- Most UNIX commands are lowercase alphabetic characters. To specify an option, you usually type a hyphen (-) followed by a letter. The letter is often (but not always) a mnemonic abbreviation for the option (such as -l for a long file listing).

- Command names are usually acronyms or abbreviations. Consult the command's manual (man) page by typing man *command* at the shell prompt and pressing Enter to learn more about a command.

- The UNIX ls command is the most frequently used. When you use ls with the -l option, it allows you to learn everything about a file except its contents. ls -l reports the filename, the file size, the date and time that the file was last accessed, the number of "aliases" or links to the file, the user who owns the file, the group to which the file belongs, and the access rights for the owner, the group, and all others.

Key Terms

3-tier architecture   A client/server environment that uses middleware to translate requests between the client and server.

account   A record of a user that contains all of her properties, including rights to resources, password, user name, and so on.

Active Directory   The method for organizing and managing objects associated with the network in the Windows Server 2003 and Server 2008 NOSs.

administrator   A user account that has unlimited privileges to resources and objects managed by a server or domain. The administrator account is created during NOS installation.

AIX   A proprietary implementation of the UNIX system distributed by IBM.

asymmetric multiprocessing   A multiprocessing method that assigns each subtask to a specific processor.

attribute   A variable property associated with a network object. For example, a restriction on the time of day a user can log on is an attribute associated with that user object.

Berkeley Software Distribution   *See* BSD.

branch   A part of the organizational structure of an operating system's directory that contains objects or other organizational units.

BSD (Berkeley Software Distribution)   A UNIX distribution that originated at the University of California at Berkeley. The BSD suffix differentiates these distributions from AT&T distributions. No longer being developed at Berkeley, the last public release of BSD UNIX was version 4.4.

child domain   A domain established within another domain in a Windows Server 2003 or Server 2008 domain tree.

CIFS (Common Internet File System)   A file access protocol. CIFS runs over TCP/IP and is the standard file access protocol used by Windows operating systems.

class   A type of object recognized by an NOS directory and defined in an NOS schema. Printers and users are examples of object classes.

CN (common name)   In LDAP naming conventions, the name of an object.

command interpreter   A program (usually text-based) that accepts and executes system programs and applications on behalf of users. Often, it includes the ability to execute a series of instructions that are stored in a file.

Common Internet File System   *See* CIFS.

common name   *See* CN.

container   *See* organizational unit.

DC (domain component)   In LDAP naming conventions, the name of any one of the domains to which an object belongs.

directory   In general, a listing that organizes resources and correlates them with their properties. In the context of NOSs, a method for organizing and managing objects.

distinguished name   *See* DN.

distribution   The term used to refer to the different implementations of a particular UNIX or Linux system. For example, different distributions of Linux include Fedora, SUSE, and Ubuntu.

DN (distinguished name)   A long form of an object's name in Active Directory that explicitly indicates the object name, plus the names of its containers and domains. A distinguished name includes a DC (domain component), OU (organizational unit), and CN (common name). A client uses the distinguished name to access a particular object, such as a printer.

domain   A group of users, servers, and other resources that share account and security policies through a Windows Server 2003 or Server 2008 NOS.

domain component   *See* DC.

domain controller   A Windows Server 2003 or Server 2008 computer that contains a replica of the Active Directory database.

domain model   In Microsoft terminology, the type of client/server network that relies on domains, rather than workgroups.

domain tree   A group of hierarchically arranged domains that share a common namespace in the Windows Server 2003 or Server 2008 Active Directory.

explicit one-way trust   A type of trust relationship in which two domains that belong to different NOS directory trees are configured to trust each other.

ext3   The name of the primary file system used in most Linux distributions.

Fedora   A version of Linux packaged and distributed by Red Hat.

file access protocol   A protocol that enables one system to access files on another system.

file globbing   A form of filename substitution, similar to the use of wildcards in Windows and DOS.

file system   An operating system's method of organizing, managing, and accessing its files through logical structures and software routines.

flavor   *See* distribution.

forest   In the context of Windows Server 2003 or Server 2008, a collection of domain trees that use different namespaces. A forest allows trust relationships to be established between trees.

freely distributable software   *See* open source software.

globally unique identifier   *See* GUID.

GNU   The name given to the public software project to implement a complete, free source code implementation of UNIX. It also refers to the collection of UNIX-inspired utilities and tools that are included with Linux distributions. The term *GNU* is an acronym within an acronym that stands for "GNU's Not UNIX."

graphical user interface   *See* GUI.

group   A means of collectively managing users' permissions and restrictions applied to shared resources. Groups form the basis for resource and account management for every type of NOS. Many network administrators create groups according to department or, even more specifically, according to job function within a department.

GUI (graphical user interface)   A pictorial representation of computer functions and elements that, in the case of NOSs, enables administrators to more easily manage files, users, groups, security, printers, and other issues.

GUID (globally unique identifier)   A 128-bit number generated and assigned to an object upon its creation in Active Directory. Network applications and services use an object's GUID to communicate with it.

hierarchical file system   The organization of files and directories (or folders) on a disk in which directories may contain files and other directories. When displayed graphically, this organization resembles a treelike structure.

information node   *See* inode.

inherited   A type of permission, or right, that is passed down from one group (the parent) to a group within that group (the child).

inode (information node)   A UNIX or Linux file system information storage area that holds all details about a file. This information includes the size, the access rights, the date and time of creation, and a pointer to the actual contents of the file.

kernel   The core of a UNIX or Linux system. This part of the operating system is loaded and run when you turn on your computer. It mediates between user programs and the computer hardware.

kernel module   A portion of the kernel that you can load and unload to add or remove functionality on a running UNIX or Linux system.

LDAP (Lightweight Directory Access Protocol)   A standard protocol for accessing network directories.

leaf object   An object in an operating system's directory, such as a printer or user, that does not contain other objects.

Lightweight Directory Access Protocol   *See* LDAP.

line printer daemon   *See* lpd.

Linux   A freely distributable implementation of a UNIX-type of system. Finnish computer scientist Linus Torvalds originally developed it.

lpd   (line printer daemon) A UNIX service responsible for printing files placed in the printer queue by the lpr command.

lpr   A UNIX command that places files in the printer queue. The files are subsequently printed with lpd, the print service.

Mac OS X Server   A proprietary NOS from Apple Computer that is based on a version of UNIX.

man pages (manual pages)   The online documentation for any variety of the UNIX operating system. This documentation describes the use of the commands and the programming interface.

manual pages   *See* man pages.

map   The action of associating a disk, directory, or device with a drive letter.

member server   A type of server on a Windows Server 2003 or Server 2008 network that does not hold directory information and, therefore, cannot authenticate users.

Microsoft Management Console   *See* MMC.

middleware   The software that sits between the client and server in a 3-tier architecture. Middleware may be used as a messaging service between clients and servers, as a universal query language for databases, or as means of coordinating processes between multiple servers that need to work together in servicing clients.

MMC (Microsoft Management Console)   A customizable, graphical network management interface introduced with Windows Server 2003 and incorporated in Window Server 2008's Server Manager.

mount   The process of making a disk partition available.

multiprocessing   The technique of splitting tasks among multiple processors to expedite the completion of any single instruction.

multitasking   The ability of a processor to perform multiple activities in a brief period of time (often seeming simultaneous to the user).

namespace   The complete database of hierarchical names (including host and domain names) used to resolve IP addresses with their hosts.

Network File System   *See* NFS.

New Technology File System   See *NTFS*.

NFS (Network File System)   A popular remote file system created by Sun Microsystems and available for UNIX and Linux operating systems.

NTFS (New Technology File System)   A file system developed by Microsoft and used with its Windows NT, Windows 2000 Server, Windows Server 2003, and Windows 2008 operating systems.

object   A representation of a thing or person associated with the network that belongs in the NOS directory. Objects include users, printers, groups, computers, data files, and applications.

object class   *See* class.

Open Group, the   A nonprofit industry association that owns the UNIX trademark.

open source software   The term used to describe software that is distributed with few restrictions and whose source code is freely available.

organizational unit   *See* OU.

OU (organizational unit)   A logical receptacle for holding objects with similar characteristics or privileges in an NOS directory. Containers form the branches of the directory tree.

page file   A file on the hard drive that is used for virtual memory.

paging   The process of moving blocks of information, called pages, between RAM and into a page file on disk.

paging file   *See* page file.

partition   An area of a computer's hard drive that is logically defined and acts as a separate disk drive.

per seat   In the context of applications, a licensing mode that limits access to an application to specific users or workstations.

per user   A licensing mode that allows a fixed quantity of clients to use one software package simultaneously.

physical memory   The RAM chips installed on the computer's system board that provide dedicated memory to that computer.

pipe   A character that enables you to combine existing commands to form new commands. The pipe symbol is the vertical bar (|).

pipeline   A series of two or more commands in which the output of prior commands is sent to the input of subsequent commands.

PowerPC   The brand of computer central processing unit invented by Apple Computer, IBM, and Motorola, Inc., and used in IBM servers.

preemptive multitasking   The type of multitasking in which tasks are actually performed one at a time, in very brief succession. In preemptive multitasking, one program uses the processor for a certain period of time and then is suspended to allow another program to use the processor.

printer queue   A logical representation of a networked printer's functionality. To use a printer, clients must have access to the printer queue.

process   A routine of sequential instructions that runs until it has achieved its goal. For example, a spreadsheet program is a process.

proprietary UNIX   Any implementation of UNIX for which the source code is either unavailable or available only by purchasing a licensed copy from Novell (costing as much as millions of dollars). Redistribution of proprietary UNIX versions requires paying royalties to Novell.

RDN (relative distinguished name)   An attribute of an object that identifies the object separately from its related container(s) and domain. For most objects, the relative distinguished name is the same as its common name (CN) in the distinguished name convention.

redirector   A service that runs on a client workstation and determines whether the client's request should be handled by the client or the server.

relative distinguished name   *See* RDN.

replication   The process of copying Active Directory data to multiple domain controllers. This ensures redundancy so that in case one of the domain controllers fails, clients can still log on to the network, be authenticated, and access resources.

role   In Microsoft terminology, the primary purpose of a Windows Server 2008 server.

root   A highly privileged user ID that has all rights to create, delete, modify, move, read, write, or execute files on a UNIX or Linux system.

root domain   In Windows Server 2003 or Server 2008 networking, the single domain from which child domains branch out in a domain tree.

Samba   An open source software package that provides complete Windows-style file- and printer-sharing capabilities.

schema   The description of object types, or classes, and their required and optional attributes that are stored in an NOS's directory.

Server Manager   A GUI tool provided with Windows Server 2008 that enables network administrators to manage server roles, features, resources, and users from a single interface.

Server Message Block   *See* SMB.

shell   Another term for the UNIX command interpreter.

site license   A type of software license that, for a fixed price, allows any number of users in one location to legally access a program.

SMB (Server Message Block)   A protocol for communications and resource access between systems, such as clients and servers. SMB originated at IBM and then was adopted and further developed by Microsoft for use on its Windows operating systems. The current version of SMB is known as the CIFS (Common Internet File System) protocol.

Solaris   A proprietary implementation of the UNIX operating system by Sun Microsystems.

source code   The computer instructions written in a programming language that is readable by humans. Source code must be translated into a form that is executable by the machine, typically called binary code (for the sequence of zeros and ones) or target code.

SPARC   The brand of computer central processing unit invented by and used in Sun Microsystems servers.

swap file   *See* page file.

symmetric multiprocessing   A method of multiprocessing that splits all operations equally among two or more processors.

System V   The proprietary version of UNIX that comes from Bell Labs.

thread   A well-defined, self-contained subset of a process. Using threads within a process enables a program to efficiently perform related, multiple, simultaneous activities. Threads are also used to enable processes to use multiple processors on SMP systems.

time-sharing   *See* preemptive multitasking.

tree   A logical representation of multiple, hierarchical levels in a directory. It is called a tree because the whole structure shares a common starting point (the root), and from that point extends branches (or containers), which may extend additional branches, and so on.

trust relationship   The relationship between two domains on a Windows Server 2003 or Server 2008 network that allows a domain controller from one domain to authenticate users from the other domain.

two-way transitive trust   The security relationship between domains in the same domain tree in which one domain grants every other domain in the tree access to its resources and, in turn, that domain can access other domains' resources. When a new domain is added to a tree, it immediately shares a two-way trust with the other domains in the tree.

UNIX   A client or server operating system originally developed by researchers at AT&T Bell Laboratories in 1969. UNIX is a proprietary operating system, but similar operating systems, such as Linux, are freely distributable.

UPN (user principal name)   The preferred Active Directory naming convention for objects when used in informal situations. This name looks like a familiar Internet address, including the positioning of the domain name after the @ sign. UPNs are typically used for e-mail and related Internet services.

UPN (user principal name) suffix   The portion of a universal principal name (in Active Directory's naming conventions) that follows the @ sign.

user principal name   *See* UPN.

virtual memory   The memory that is logically carved out of space on the hard drive and added to physical memory (RAM).

virtualization   The capability for operating multiple logical servers—or virtual servers—on a single machine.

workgroup   In Microsoft terminology, a group of interconnected computers that share each others' resources without relying on a central file server.

X Window system   The GUI environment for UNIX and Linux systems.

Review Questions

1. Which item identifies one of the most important functions of an NOS?

   a. Client support

   b. Remote user connectivity

   c. Network element monitoring

   d. Data backup and recovery

2. Which type of licensing allows an unlimited number of users to legally access an application for a fixed price?

   a. Per seat

   b. Site

   c. Per user

   d. Per system

3. Which is the minimum processor requirement for the Windows 2008 Server Standard Edition?

   a. 1GHz processor

   b. 2GHz processor

   c. Intel-based system with a Pentium-class processor

   d. Intel-compatible x86 processor

4. What is the minimum amount of RAM required for a Linux server?

   a. 64MB

   b. 512MB

   c. 1,024MB

   d. 2,048MB

5. Which operating system is proprietary?

   a. Red Hat

   b. Fedora

   c. Solaris

   d. Ubuntu

6. True or false? The components included in each NOS and every version of a particular NOS vary.

7. True or false? One difference between NOSs is the file access protocol that enables one system to access resources stored on another system on the network.

8. True or false? In most cases, an organization designates an administrator as the print server in charge of managing print services.

9. True or false? A process is a self-contained, well-defined task within a thread.

10. True or false? In all flavors of UNIX, the use of a GUI (graphical user interface) remains optional.

11. A service on the client workstation, called the ____, intercepts requests to determine whether they should be handled by the client or by the server.

12. In some instances, a piece of software called ____ is necessary to translate requests and responses between the client and server.

13. In LDAP-compatible directories, a(n) ____ is the set of definitions of the kinds of objects and object-related information that the directory can contain.

14. To better organize and manage objects, a network administrator places objects in containers, or ____, which are logically defined receptacles that serve only to assemble similar objects.

15. Computers running UNIX or Linux also make use of network file systems, which are analogous to Windows ____.

In-Depth TCP/IP Networking

After reading this chapter and completing the exercises, you will be able to:

- Understand methods of network design unique to TCP/IP networks, including subnetting, CIDR, and address translation
- Explain the differences between public and private TCP/IP networks
- Describe protocols used between mail clients and mail servers, including SMTP, POP3, and IMAP4
- Employ multiple TCP/IP utilities for network discovery and troubleshooting

On the Job

My company provided a full networking kit so I could work from my home office through a VPN. Everything worked well for over a year, until a newly hired coworker came to my location for on-the-job training.

I had wired my laptop and printer to two of the four available switched ports on the router, which also offered wireless access. The coworker's laptop had built-in wireless, so we turned it on, tested it (perfect!) and both went to work. The problems began almost immediately.

The first problem we noticed was that our previously smooth-running applications began to pause for random lengths of time, and then resume. As we became busier, the pauses became freezes and time-outs. Work became impossible. The training session switched to network troubleshooting.

Whenever a previously functioning network becomes unreliable, even from apparently trivial changes like adding a new host, my initial troubleshooting approach is to return to the previous configuration. I switched off the new laptop's wireless radio, and everything returned to normal. With the radio on, the intermittent problems returned.

I quickly ruled out obvious potential conflicts, such as a duplicate IP address. I switched the second laptop to a wired connection. No improvement. The router's error log showed no errors.

My suspicions now turned to the VPN. With a single VPN session, or no VPN sessions, simultaneous access to random sites on the Internet worked perfectly. The second VPN session triggered the problems. I contacted the IT department head, who agreed we had encountered a router limitation. Namely, its NAT (network address translation) capabilities were not sophisticated enough to maintain the proper status and state of two simultaneous VPN sessions.

Any VPN-capable router can support a single worker in a home office. A second (or subsequent) VPN session can only be reliably established if the router has been designed to support it. We solved the problem by replacing the router with a model from a different manufacturer.

David Butcher
Client Services Director

In Chapter 4, you learned about core protocols and subprotocols in the TCP/IP protocol suite, addressing schemes, and host and domain naming. You also learned that TCP/IP is a complex and highly customizable protocol suite. This chapter builds on these basic concepts, examining how TCP/IP-based networks are designed and analyzed. It also describes the services and applications that TCP/IP-based networks commonly support. If you are unclear about the concepts related to IP addressing or binary-to-decimal conversion, take time to review Chapter 4 before reading this chapter.

Designing TCP/IP-Based Networks

By now, you understand that most modern networks rely on the TCP/IP protocol suite, not only for Internet connectivity, but also for transmitting data over private connections. Before proceeding with TCP/IP network design considerations, it's useful to briefly review some TCP/IP fundamentals. For example, you have learned that IP is a routable protocol, and that on a network using TCP/IP, each interface is associated with a unique IP address. Some nodes may use multiple IP addresses. For example, on a router that contains two NICs, each NIC can be assigned a separate IP address. Or, on a Web server that hosts multiple Web sites—such as one managed by an ISP—each Web service associated with a site can have a different IP address.

In Chapter 4 you learned about two versions of IP: IPv4 and IPv6. This chapter's discussions of IP addressing concentrate on IPv4 because, though older, it is still more common on today's networks. Recall that IPv4 addresses consist of four 8-bit octets (or bytes) that can be expressed in either binary (for example, 10000011 01000001 00001010 00100100) or dotted decimal (for example, 131.65.10.36) notation. Many networks assign IP addresses and host names dynamically, using DHCP, rather than statically. In addition, every IPv4 address can be associated with a network class—A, B, C, D, or E (though Class D and E addresses are reserved for special purposes). A node's network class provides information about the segment or network to which the node belongs. The following sections explain how network and host information in an IPv4 address can be manipulated to subdivide networks into smaller segments.

Subnetting

Subnetting separates a network into multiple logically defined segments, or subnets. Networks are commonly subnetted according to geographic locations (for example, the floors of a building connected by a LAN, or the buildings connected by a WAN), departmental boundaries, or technology types (for example, Ethernet or token ring). Where subnetting is implemented, each subnet's traffic is separated from every other subnet's traffic. A network administrator might separate traffic to accomplish the following:

- *Enhance security*—Subnetworks must be connected via routers or other Layer 3 devices. As you know, these devices do not retransmit incoming frames to all other nodes on the same segment (as a hub does). Instead, they forward frames only as necessary to reach their destination. Because every frame is not indiscriminately retransmitted, the possibility for one node to tap into another node's transmissions is reduced.

- *Improve performance*—For the same reason that subnetting enhances security, it also improves performance on a network. When data is selectively retransmitted, unnecessary transmissions are kept to a minimum. Subnetting is useful for limiting the amount of broadcast traffic—and, therefore, the amount of potential collisions on Ethernet networks—by decreasing the size of each broadcast domain. The more efficient use of bandwidth results in better overall network performance.

- *Simplify troubleshooting*—For example, a network administrator might subdivide an organization's network according to geography, assigning a separate subnet to the nodes in the downtown office, west-side office, and east-side office of her company. Suppose one day the network has trouble transmitting data only to a certain group of

1.4

IP addresses—those located on the west-side office subnet. When troubleshooting, rather than examining the whole network for errors or bottlenecks, the network administrator needs only to see that the faulty transmissions are all associated with addresses on the west-side subnet to know that she should zero in on that subnet.

To understand how subnetting is implemented, it's useful to first review IPv4 addressing conventions on a network that does not use subnetting.

Subnetting is also possible in IPv6. However, most challenges that subnetting addresses, such as improving security and creating smaller broadcast domains, are solved by IPv6 features, such as selective multicasting. This chapter concentrates on subnetting techniques for IPv4 networks.

1.3

1.4

Classful Addressing in IPv4   In Chapter 4, you learned about the first and simplest type of IPv4 addressing, which is known as **classful addressing** because it adheres to network class distinctions. In classful addressing, only Class A, Class B, and Class C addresses are recognized. Recall that all IPv4 addresses consist of network and host information. In classful addressing, the network information portion of an IPv4 address (the network ID) is limited to the first 8 bits in a Class A address, the first 16 bits in a Class B address, and the first 24 bits in a Class C address. Host information is contained in the last 24 bits for a Class A address, the last 16 bits in a Class B address, and the last 8 bits in a Class C address. Refer to Figure 4-8 to review the bit separation between network and host information in classful addressing. Figure 10-1 offers some example IPv4 addresses separated into network and host information according to the classful addressing convention.

```
Example Class A network address: 114.56.204.33
        network information = 114
        host information = 56.204.33


Example Class B network address: 147.12.38.81
        network information = 147.12
        host information = 38.81


Example Class C network address: 214.57.42.7
        network information = 214.57.42
        host information = 7
```

Figure 10-1 Example IPv4 addresses with classful addressing

Adhering to a fixed network ID size ultimately limits the number of hosts a network can include. For example, leasing an entire Class C network of addresses gives you only 254 usable IPv4 addresses. In addition, using classful addressing makes it difficult to separate traffic from various parts of a network. As you have learned, separating traffic offers many practical benefits. For example, if an organization used an entire Class B network of addresses, it could have up to 65,534 hosts all on one network segment. Imagine the challenges involved in managing such a highly populated network, not to mention the poor performance that would result. In 1985, because of the difficulty of managing a whole network class of addresses and the dwindling supply of usable IPv4 addresses, computer scientists introduced subnetting.

Depending on the source, you may find the term *network ID* used interchangeably with the terms *network number* or *network prefix*.

IPv4 Subnet Masks Subnetting depends on the use of subnet masks to identify how a network is subdivided. A subnet mask indicates where network information is located in an IPv4 address. The *1* bits in a subnet mask indicate that corresponding bits in an IPv4 address contain network information. The *0* bits in a subnet mask indicate that corresponding bits in an IP address contain host information.

Each network class is associated with a default subnet mask, as shown in Table 10-1. For example, by default, a Class A address's first octet (or eight bits) represents network information and is composed of all *1*s. (Recall that an octet composed of all *1*s in binary notation equals *255* in decimal notation. An octet composed of all *0*s in binary notation equals *0* in decimal notation.) That means that if you work on a network whose hosts are configured with a subnet mask of 255.0.0.0, you know that the network is using Class A addresses and, furthermore, that it is not using subnetting, because 255.0.0.0 is the default subnet mask for a Class A network.

Table 10-1 Default IPv4 Subnet Masks

Network Class	Default Subnet Mask (Binary)	Number of Bits Used for Network Information	Default Subnet Mask (Dotted Decimal)
A	11111111 00000000 00000000 00000000	8	255.0.0.0
B	11111111 11111111 00000000 00000000	16	255.255.0.0
C	11111111 11111111 11111111 00000000	24	255.255.255.0

To calculate a host's network ID given its IPv4 address and subnet mask, you follow a logical process of combining bits known as **ANDing**. In ANDing, a bit with a value of 1 plus another bit with a value of 1 results in a 1. A bit with a value of 0 plus any other bit results in a 0. If you think of 1 as "true" and 0 as "false," the logic of ANDing makes sense. Adding a true statement to a true statement still results in a true statement. But adding a true statement to a false statement results in a false statement. ANDing logic is demonstrated in Table 10-2, which provides every possible combination of having a 1 or 0 bit in an IPv4 address or subnet mask.

Table 10-2 ANDing

IP address bit	1	1	0	0
Subnet mask bit	1	0	1	0
Resulting bit	1	0	0	0

An example IPv4 host address, its default subnet mask, and its network ID are shown in Figure 10-2 in both binary and dotted decimal notation. Notice that the address's fourth

	IP address:	11000111	01000100	00100010	01111111	199.34.89.127
and	Subnet mask:	11111111	11111111	11111111	00000000	255.255.255.0
Equals	Network ID:	11000111	01000100	00100010	00000000	199.34.89.0

Figure 10-2 Example of calculating a host's network ID

octet could have been composed of any combination of *1*s and *0*s, and the network ID's fourth octet would still be all *0*s.

At this point, you should understand how to determine a host's network ID given its IPv4 address and subnet mask. This section explained how to apply ANDing logic to an IPv4 address plus a *default* subnet mask, but it works just the same way for networks that are subnetted and have different subnet masks, as you will soon learn. Before learning how to create subnets, however, it is necessary to understand the types of addresses that cannot be used as subnet masks or host addresses.

Reserved Addresses   Certain types of IP addresses cannot be assigned to a network interface on a node or used as subnet masks. Instead, these IP addresses are reserved for special functions. One type of reserved address should be familiar to you already—that is, the network ID. In a network ID, as you know, bits available for host information are set to 0. Therefore, a workstation on the example network used in Figure 10-2 could not be assigned the IP address 199.34.89.0, because that address is the network ID. When using classful IPv4 addressing, a network ID always ends with an octet of 0 (and may have additional, preceding octets equal to 0). However, when subnetting is applied and a default subnet mask is no longer used, a network ID may have other decimal values in its last octet(s).

Another reserved IP address is the broadcast address for a network or segment. In a broadcast address, the octet(s) that represent the host information are set to equal all *1*s, or in decimal notation, 255. In the example in Figure 10-2, the broadcast address would be 199.34.89.255. If a workstation on that network sent a message to the address 199.34.89.255, it would be issued to every node on the segment.

Because the octets equal to 0 and 255 are reserved, only the numbers 1 through 254 can be used for host information in an IPv4 address. Thus, on a network that followed the example in Figure 10-2, the usable host addresses would range from 199.34.89.1 to 199.34.89.254. If you subnetted this network, the range of usable host addresses would be different. The next section describes how subnets are created and how you can determine the range of usable host addresses on a subnet.

IPv4 Subnetting Techniques   Subnetting breaks the rules of classful IPv4 addressing. To create subnets, some of an IP address's bits that in classful addressing would represent host information are changed to represent network information instead. By making bits that previously were used for host information represent network information, you reduce the number of bits available for identifying hosts. Consequently, you reduce the number of usable host addresses per subnet. The number of hosts and subnets available after subnetting is related to how many host information bits you use (or borrow, as network professionals like to say) for network information. Table 10-3 illustrates the numbers of subnets and hosts that can be created by subnetting a Class B network. Notice the range of subnet masks that can be used instead of the default Class B subnet mask of 255.255.0.0. Also compare the

Table 10-3 IPv4 Class B Subnet Masks

Subnet Mask	Number of Subnets on Network	Number of Hosts per Subnet
255.255.192.0 or 11111111 11111111 11000000 00000000	2	16,382
255.255.224.0 or 11111111 11111111 11100000 00000000	6	8,190
255.255.240.0 or 11111111 11111111 11110000 00000000	14	4,094
255.255.248.0 or 11111111 11111111 11111000 00000000	30	2,046
255.255.252.0 or 11111111 11111111 11111100 00000000	62	1,022
255.255.254.0 or 11111111 11111111 11111110 00000000	126	510
255.255.255.0 or 11111111 11111111 11111111 00000000	254	254
255.255.255.128 or 11111111 11111111 11111111 10000000	510	126
255.255.255.192 or 11111111 11111111 11111111 11000000	1,022	62
255.255.255.224 or 11111111 11111111 11111111 11100000	2,046	30
255.255.255.240 or 11111111 11111111 11111111 11110000	4,094	14
255.255.255.248 or 11111111 11111111 11111111 11111000	8,190	6
255.255.255.252 or 11111111 11111111 11111111 11111100	16,382	2

listed numbers of hosts per subnet to the 65,534 hosts available on a Class B network that does not use subnetting.

Table 10-4 illustrates the numbers of subnets and hosts that can be created by subnetting a Class C network. Notice that a Class C network allows for fewer subnets than a Class B network. This is because Class C addresses have fewer host information bits that can be borrowed for network information. In addition, fewer bits are left over for host information, which leads to a lower number of hosts per subnet than the number available to Class B subnets.

Table 10-4 IPv4 Class C Subnet Masks

Subnet Mask	Number of Subnets on Network	Number of Hosts per Subnet
255.255.255.192 or 11111111 11111111 11111111 1100000	2	62
255.255.255.224 or 11111111 11111111 11111111 1110000	6	30
255.255.255.240 or 11111111 11111111 11111111 1111000	14	14
255.255.255.248 or 11111111 11111111 11111111 1111100	30	6
255.255.255.252 or 11111111 11111111 11111111 1111110	62	2

Calculating IPv4 Subnets Now that you have seen the results of subnetting, you are ready to try subnetting an IPv4 network. Suppose you have leased the Class C network whose network ID is 199.34.89.0 and you want to divide it into six subnets to correspond to the six different departments in your company. The formula for determining how to modify a default subnet mask is:

$$2^n - 2 = Y$$

where n equals the number of bits in the subnet mask that must be switched from 0 to 1, and Y equals the number of subnets that result.

Notice that this formula subtracts 2 from the total number of possible subnets—that is, from the calculation of 2 to the power of the number of the bits that equal 1. That's because in traditional subnetting, bit combinations of all 0s or all 1s are not allowed for identifying subnets—just as host addresses ending in all 0s or all 1s are not allowed because of addresses reserved for the network ID and broadcast transmissions. (However, in the next section of this chapter, you learn why this equation doesn't apply to all modern networks.)

Because you want six separate subnets, the equation becomes $6 = 2^n - 2$. Because $6 + 2 = 8$ and $8 = 2^3$, you know that the value of n equals 3. Thus, you need to change three additional subnet mask bits from 0 to 1. That means that rather than using the default subnet mask, in which the first 24 bits indicate the position of network information, you would use a subnet mask of 11111111 11111111 11111111 11100000, in which the first 27 bits indicate the position of network information. Converting from binary to the more familiar dotted decimal notation, this subnet mask becomes 255.255.255.224. When you configure the TCP/IP properties of clients on your network, you would specify this subnet mask.

Now that you have calculated the subnet mask, you still need to assign IP addresses to nodes based on your new subnetting scheme. Recall that you have borrowed three bits from what used to be host information in the IP address. That leaves five bits available in the last octet of your Class C addresses to identify hosts. Adding the values of the last five bits, 16 + 8 + 4 + 2 + 1, equals 31, for a total of 32 potential addresses (0 through 31). However, as you have learned, one address is reserved for the network ID and cannot be used. Another address is reserved for the broadcast ID and cannot be used. Thus, using five bits for host information allows a maximum of 30 different host addresses for each of the six subnets. So, in this example, you can have a maximum of 6 × 30, or 180, unique host addresses on the network.

Table 10-5 lists the network ID, broadcast address, and usable host addresses for each of the six subnets in this example Class C network. Together, the additional bits used for subnet information plus the existing network ID are known as the **extended network prefix**.

Table 10-5 Subnet Information for Six Subnets in an Example IPv4 Class C Network

Subnet Number	Extended Network Prefix	Broadcast Address	Usable Host Addresses
1	199.34.89.32 or 11000111 00100010 01011001 00100000	199.34.89.63 or 11000111 00100010 01011001 00111111	199.34.89.33 through 199.34.89.62
2	199.34.89.64 or 11000111 00100010 01011001 01000000	199.34.89.95 or 11000111 00100010 01011001 01011111	199.34.89.65 through 199.34.89.94
3	199.34.89.96 or 11000111 00100010 01011001 01100000	199.34.89.127 or 11000111 00100010 01011001 01111111	199.34.89.97 through 199.34.89.126
4	199.34.89.128 or 11000111 00100010 01011001 10000000	199.34.89.159 or 11000111 00100010 01011001 10011111	199.34.89.129 through 199.34.89.158
5	199.34.89.160 or 11000111 00100010 01011001 10100000	199.34.89.191 or 11000111 00100010 01011001 10111111	199.34.89.161 through 199.34.89.190
6	199.34.89.192 or 11000111 00100010 01011001 11000000	199.34.89.223 or 11000111 00100010 01011001 11011111	199.34.89.193 through 199.34.89.222

Net+
1.4

The extended network prefix for each subnet is based on which of the additional (borrowed) network information bits are set to equal 1. For example, in subnet number 1, only the third bit of the three is set to 1, making the last octet of the extended network prefix 00100000, or in decimal notation, 32. In subnet number 2, only the second bit is set to 1, making the last octet of the extended network prefix 01000000, or 64. In Table 10-5, the three bits borrowed from the host information portion of the Class C address (to indicate network information) are underlined.

Class A, Class B, and Class C networks can all be subnetted. But because each class reserves a different number of bits for network information, each class has a different number of host information bits that can be used for subnet information. The number of hosts and subnets on your network will vary depending on your network class and the way you use subnetting. Enumerating the dozens of subnet possibilities based on different arrangements and network classes is beyond the scope of this book. However, several Web sites provide excellent tools that help you calculate subnet information. One such site is *www.subnetmask.info*.

If you use subnetting on your LAN, only your LAN's devices need to interpret your devices' subnetting information. Routers external to your LAN, such as those on the Internet, pay attention to only the network portion of your devices' IP addresses when transmitting data to them. As a result, devices external to a subnetted LAN (such as routers on the Internet) can direct data to those LAN devices without interpreting the LAN's subnetting information.

Figure 10-3 illustrates a situation in which a LAN running IPv4 has been granted the Class C range of addresses that begin with 199.34.89. The network administrator has subnetted this Class C network into six smaller networks with the network IDs listed in Table 10-5. As you know, routers connect different network segments via their physical interfaces. In the case of subnetting, a router must interpret IP addresses from different subnets and direct data from one subnet to another. Each subnet corresponds to a different port on the router.

When a router on the internal LAN needs to direct data from a machine with the IP address of 199.34.89.73 to a machine with the IP address of 199.34.89.114, its interpretation of the workstations' subnet masks (255.255.255.224) plus the host information in the IP addresses tell the router that they are on different subnets. The router forwards data between the two subnets (or ports). In this figure, the devices connecting subnets to the router are labeled switches, but they could also be routers, bridges, or hubs. Alternatively, nodes having different extended network prefixes could be directly connected to the router so that each subnet is associated with only one device, though this is an unlikely configuration.

When a server on the Internet attempts to deliver a Web page to the machine with IP address 199.34.89.73, however, the Internet router does not use the subnet mask information. It only knows that the machine is on a Class C network beginning with a network ID of 199.34.89. That's all the information it needs to reach the organization's router. After the data enters the organization's LAN, the LAN's router then interprets the subnet mask information as if it were transmitting data internally to deliver data to the machine with IP address 199.34.89.73. Because subnetting does not affect how a device is addressed by external networks, a network administrator does not need to inform Internet authorities about new segments created via subnetting.

You have learned how to subdivide a network into multiple smaller segments through subnetting. Next, you'll learn about more contemporary variations on this method.

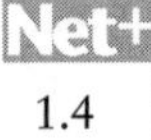

Figure 10-3 showing the network diagram:

Figure 10-3 A router connecting several subnets

CIDR (Classless Interdomain Routing)

By 1993, the Internet was growing exponentially, and the demand for IP addresses was growing with it. The IETF (Internet Engineering Task Force) recognized that additional measures were necessary to increase the availability and flexibility of IP addresses. In response to this need, the IETF devised **CIDR (Classless Interdomain Routing)**, which is sometimes called **classless routing** or **supernetting**. CIDR is not exclusive of subnetting; it merely provides additional ways of arranging network and host information in an IP address. In CIDR, conventional network class distinctions do not exist.

CIDR is pronounced *cider*.

NOTE

Net+

1.4

For example, the previous section described subdividing a Class C network into six subnets of 30 addressable hosts each. To achieve this, the subnet boundary (or length of the extended network prefix) was moved to the right—from the default 24th bit to the 27th bit—into what used to be the host information octet. In CIDR, a subnet boundary can move to the left. Moving the subnet boundary to the left allows you to use more bits for host information and, therefore, generate more usable IP addresses on your network. A subnet created by moving the subnet boundary to the left is known as a **supernet**. Figure 10-4 contrasts examples of a Class C **supernet mask** with a subnet mask.

Example subnet mask:

```
Bit# 0            8            16          24
     11111111     11111111     11111111    11100000
```

or

255.255.255.224

Example supernet mask:

```
Bit# 0            8            16          24
     11111111     11111111     11111100    00000000
```

or

255.255.252.0

Figure 10-4 Subnet mask and supernet mask

Notice that in Figure 10-4, 27 bits are used for network information in the subnet mask, whereas only 22 bits are used for network information in the supernet mask.

Suppose that you have leased the Class C range of IPv4 addresses that shares the network ID 199.34.89.0 and, because of growth in your company, you need to greatly increase the number of host addresses this network allows by default. By changing the default subnetmask of 255.255.255.0 (11111111 11111111 11111111 00000000) to 255.255.252.0 (11111111 11111111 11111100 00000000), as shown in Figure 10-4, you can make available two extra bits for host information. Adding the values of the last 10 bits, 512 + 256 + 128 + 64 + 32 + 16 + 8 + 4 + 2 + 1, equals 1,023, which leads to 1,024 (0 through 1,023) potential host addresses on each subnet. However, as you know, two addresses are reserved and, therefore, are unusable as host addresses. Thus, the actual number of host addresses available on this subnet is 1,022.

In this example, you have subtracted information from the host portion of the IP address. Therefore, the IP addresses that result from this subnetting scheme will be different from the IP addresses you would use if you had left the network ID untouched (as in the subnetting example used in the previous section). The calculation for the new network ID is shown in Figure 10-5. For this example subnetted Class C network, the potential host addresses fall in the range of 199.34.88.1 to 199.34.91.254. The broadcast address is 199.34.91.255.

With CIDR also came a new shorthand for denoting the position of subnet boundaries, known as **CIDR notation** (or **slash notation**). CIDR notation takes the form of the network ID followed by a forward slash (/), followed by the number of bits that are used for the extended

Net+		IP address:	11000111	01000100	01011001	01111111	199.34.89.127
1.4	and	Subnet mask:	11111111	11111111	11111100	00000000	255.255.252.0
	Equals	Network ID:	11000111	01000100	01011000	00000000	199.34.88.0

Figure 10-5 Calculating a host's network ID on a supernetted network

network prefix. For example, for the Class C network whose network ID is 199.34.89.0 and which was divided into six subnets, the slash notation would be 199.34.89.0/27, because 27 bits of the subnets' addresses are used for the extended network prefix. The CIDR notation for the Class C network used as an example of supernetting earlier in this section would be 199.34.89.0/22. In CIDR terminology, the forward slash, plus the number of bits used for the extended network prefix—for example, /22—is known as a **CIDR block**.

To take advantage of classless routing, your network's routers must be able to interpret IP addresses that don't adhere to conventional network class parameters. Routers that rely on older routing protocols, such as RIP, are not capable of interpreting classless IP addresses.

Net+ Internet Gateways

1.4

1.6

3.2

As you have learned, gateways are a combination of software and hardware that enable two different network segments to exchange data. A gateway facilitates communication between different networks or subnets. Because one device on the network cannot send data directly to a device on another subnet, a gateway must intercede and hand off the information. Every device on a TCP/IP-based network has a **default gateway**—that is, the gateway that first interprets its outbound requests to other subnets and then interprets its inbound requests from other subnets.

A gateway is analogous to your local post office, which gathers your outbound mail and decides where to forward it. It also handles your inbound mail on its way to your mailbox. Just as a large city has several local post offices, a large organization will have several gateways to route traffic for different groups of devices. Each node on the network can have only one default gateway; that gateway is assigned either manually or automatically (in the latter case, through a service such as DHCP). Of course, if your network includes only one segment and you do not connect to the Internet, your devices would not need a default gateway because traffic would not need to cross the network's boundary.

In many cases, a default gateway is not a separate device, but rather a network interface on a router. For this reason, you may hear the term **default router** used to refer to a default gateway. By using a router's network interfaces as gateways, one router can supply multiple gateways. Each default gateway is assigned its own IP address. In Figure 10-6, workstation 10.3.105.23 (workstation A) uses the 10.3.105.1 gateway to process its requests, and workstation 10.3.102.75 (workstation B) uses the 10.3.102.1 gateway for the same purpose.

On a network running IPv4, an Internet gateway is usually assigned an IP address that ends with an octet of .1.

Default gateways may connect multiple internal networks, or they may connect an internal network with external networks, such as WANs or the Internet. As you have learned, routers that connect multiple networks must maintain a routing table to determine where to forward information. When a router is used as a gateway, it must maintain routing tables as well.

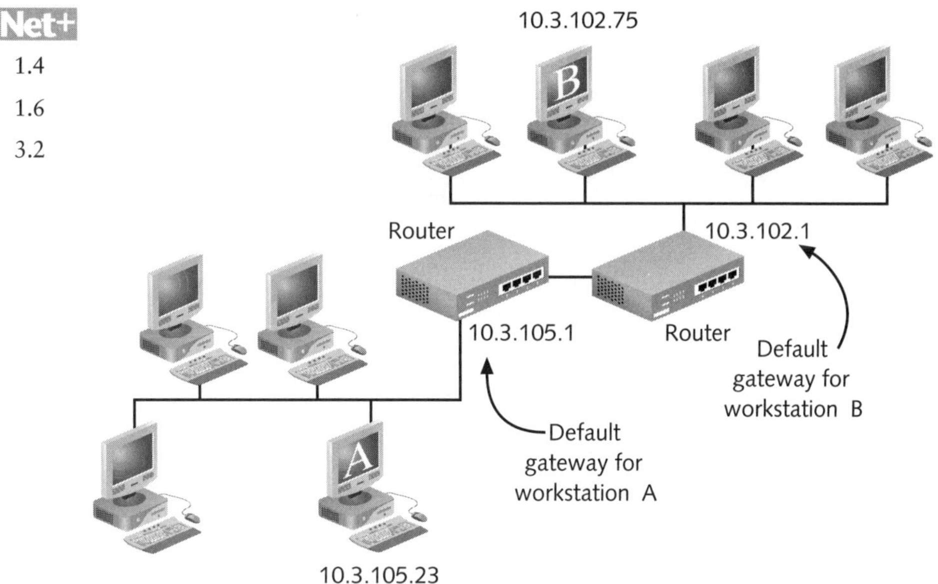

Figure 10-6 The use of default gateways

The Internet contains a vast number of routers and gateways. If each gateway had to track addressing information for every other gateway on the Internet, it would be overtaxed. Instead, each handles only a relatively small amount of addressing information, which it uses to forward data to another gateway that knows more about the data's destination. Like routers on an internal network, Internet gateways maintain default routes to known addresses to expedite data transfer. The gateways that make up the Internet backbone are called **core gateways**.

Address Translation

An organization's default gateway can also be used to "hide" the organization's internal IP addresses and keep them from being recognized on a public network. A **public network** is one that any user may access with little or no restrictions. The most familiar example of a public network is the Internet. A citywide kiosk system may also be considered a public network. Conversely, a **private network** is a network whose access is restricted to only clients or machines with proper credentials. Virtually all business LANs and WANs are private networks.

On private networks, hiding IP addresses allows network managers more flexibility in assigning addresses. Clients behind a gateway may use any IP addressing scheme, regardless of whether it is recognized as legitimate by the Internet authorities. But as soon as those clients need to connect to the Internet, they must have a legitimate IP address to exchange data. When the client's transmission reaches the default gateway, the gateway opens the IP datagram and replaces the client's private IP address with an Internet-recognized IP address. This process is known as **NAT (Network Address Translation)**. A few types of NAT are available to network administrators. Before learning how each works, though, it's helpful to know more about the reasons for address translation.

One reason for using address translation is to overcome the limitations of a low quantity of IPv4 addresses. In the early days of the Internet, businesses could lease large blocks of IP addresses, enough to assign a separate Internet-routable address to each device and client on their WAN. However, as more hosts joined the Internet, the scarcity of IPv4 addresses became a problem. Today a small business with 25 hosts, for example, might only be able to lease one IP address from its ISP. Yet the business still needs to allow all its hosts access to the Internet. With address translation, all 25 hosts can share a single Internet-routable IP address.

Another reason for using address translation is to add a marginal amount of security to a private network when it is connected to a public network. Because a transmission is assigned a new IP address each time it reaches the public sphere, those outside an organization cannot trace the origin of the transmission back to the specific network node that sent it. However, the IP address assigned to a transmission by the gateway must be an Internet-authorized IP address; thus, it can be traced back to the organization that leased the address.

A third reason for using address translation is to enable a network administrator to develop her own network addressing scheme that does not conform to a scheme dictated by ICANN. For example, suppose you are the network administrator for a private elementary school. You maintain the school's entire network, which, among other things, includes 50 client workstations. Suppose half of these clients are used by students in the classrooms or library and half are used expressly by staff. To make your network management easier, you might decide to assign each student workstation an IPv4 address whose first octet begins with the number 10 and whose second octet is the number of the classroom where the computer is located.

For example, a student workstation in room 235 might have an IP address of 10.235.1.12. You might then assign each staff workstation an IP address whose first octet is the number 50 and whose second octet is the number of the employee's office or classroom. For example, the principal's workstation, which is located in his office in Room 135, might have an IP address of 50.135.1.10. These IP addresses would be used strictly for communication between devices on the school's network. When staff or students wanted to access the Internet, however, they would need to have at least some IP addresses that would be legitimate for use on the Internet.

If you have leased at least 50 Internet-valid IP addresses from your ISP, you can assign each client a corresponding IP address for use on the Internet. For example, the student workstation in room 235 with a private IP address of 10.235.1.12 might be assigned an Internet-valid IP address of 168.11.124.110. The principal's workstation might be assigned an Internet-valid IP address of 168.11.124.113. This type of address translation is known as **SNAT (Static Network Address Translation)**. It is considered static, because each client is associated with one private IP address and one public IP address that never changes. SNAT is useful when operating a mail server, for example, whose address must remain the same for clients to reach it at any time. Figure 10-7 illustrates SNAT.

Now suppose that, because the school has limited funds and does not require that all clients be connected to the Internet at all times, you decide to lease only eight IP numbers from your ISP. You then configure your gateway to translate the school's private IP addresses to addresses that can be used on the Internet. Each time a client attempts to reach the Internet, the gateway would replace its source address field in the datagram with one of the eight legitimate IP addresses. Because any Internet-valid IP address might be assigned to any client's outgoing transmission, this technique is known as **DNAT (Dynamic Network Address Translation)**. It may also be called **IP masquerading**.

You might wonder how an Internet host can respond to a client on a private network using DNAT, if all the clients on that network share a small pool of addresses. For example, when a student at the elementary school opens a browser and requests the Library of Congress Web

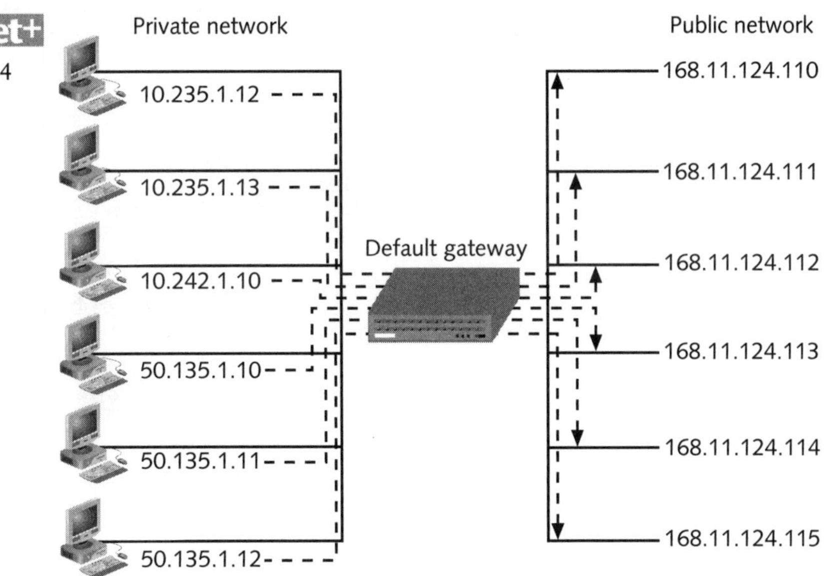

Figure 10-7 SNAT (Static Network Address Translation)

page, how will the Web server know which student workstation should receive the response? In fact, to accomplish DNAT, a gateway performs **PAT (Port Address Translation)**. With PAT, each client session with a server on the Internet is assigned a separate TCP port number. When the client issues a request to the server, its datagram's source address includes this port number. When the Internet server responds, its datagram's destination address includes the same port number. This allows the gateway to send the response to the appropriate client. PAT is the most common type of address translation used on small office and home networks.

Figure 10-8 illustrates the use of PAT where one Internet-recognized IP address is shared by four clients.

You have learned that NAT separates private and public transmissions on a TCP/IP network. Further, you have learned that gateways conduct the network translation. On most networks, this refers to a router acting as a gateway. However, the gateway might instead operate on a network host. For example, on Windows operating systems, **ICS (Internet Connection Sharing)** can be used to translate network addresses and allow clients to share an Internet connection. Using ICS, a computer with Internet access, called the **ICS host**, is configured to translate requests to and from the Internet on behalf of other computers on the network. To do this, it acts as a DHCP server, DNS resolver, and NAT gateway for clients on its LAN. The ICS host requires two network connections: one that connects to the Internet, which could be dial-up, DSL, ISDN, or broadband cable; and one that connects to the LAN. If the network uses a dial-up connection to the Internet, the ICS host connects to the Internet on demand—that is, when other computers on the network issue a request to the Internet.

When ICS is enabled on a LAN, the network adapter on the ICS host that connects to the LAN is assigned an IP address of 192.168.0.1. Clients on the small office or home office LAN must be set up to obtain IP addresses automatically. The ICS host then assigns clients IP addresses in the range of 192.168.0.2 through 192.168.0.255. If you are already using this range of addresses on your network (for example, in a NAT scheme), you might experience problems establishing or using ICS.

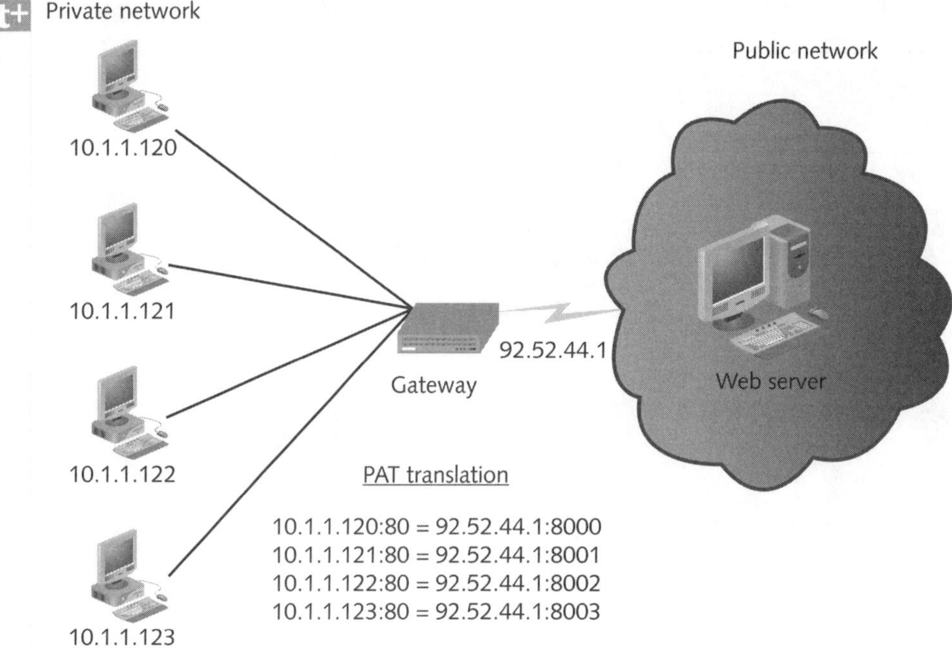

Figure 10-8 PAT (Port Address Translation)

When designing a network to share an Internet connection, most network administrators prefer using a router or switch rather than ICS, because ICS typically requires more configuration. It also requires the ICS host to be available whenever other computers need Internet access. However, in the unlikely event that a router or switch is not available, ICS is an adequate alternative for sharing an Internet connection among multiple clients.

TCP/IP Mail Services

E-mail is one of the most frequently used Internet services you will manage as a network administrator. You need to understand how mail services work so that you can set up and support mail clients or install and configure a mail server.

All Internet mail services rely on the same principles of mail delivery, storage, and pickup, though they may use different types of software to accomplish these functions. You have learned that mail servers communicate with other mail servers to deliver messages across the Internet. They send, receive, and store messages. They may also filter messages according to content, route messages according to configurable conditions such as timing or priority, and make available different types of interfaces for different mail clients. Hundreds of different software packages for mail servers exist. The most popular are Sendmail and Microsoft Exchange Server.

Mail clients send messages to and retrieve messages from mail servers. They may also provide ways of organizing messages (using folders or mailboxes), filter messages according to content or sender information, set message priority, create and use distribution lists, send file attachments, and interpret graphic and HTML content. Hundreds of different types of mail clients exist. Examples of popular mail client software include Eudora and Microsoft Outlook. Many companies that provide Internet access, such as AOL, provide mail client software with their access software. However, subscribers may use a mail client other than the package supplied by their Internet access provider.

E-mail servers and clients communicate through special TCP/IP application layer protocols. These protocols, all of which operate on Macintosh, Windows, UNIX, and Linux systems, are discussed in the following sections.

Net+ SMTP (Simple Mail Transfer Protocol)

1.1

1.2

SMTP (Simple Mail Transfer Protocol) is the protocol responsible for moving messages from one mail server to another over TCP/IP-based networks. SMTP belongs to the application layer of the OSI model and relies on TCP at the transport layer. It operates from port 25. (That is, requests to receive mail and send mail go through port 25 on the SMTP server.) SMTP, which provides the basis for Internet e-mail service, relies on higher-level programs for its instructions. Although SMTP comes with a set of human-readable (text) commands that you could conceivably use to transport mail from machine to machine, this method would be laborious, slow, and prone to error. Instead, other services, such as the Sendmail software for UNIX and Linux systems, provide more friendly and sophisticated mail interfaces that rely on SMTP as their means of transport.

SMTP is a simple subprotocol, incapable of doing anything more than transporting mail or holding it in a queue. In the post office analogy of data communications, SMTP is like the mail carrier who picks up his day's mail load at the post office and delivers it to the homes on his route. The mail carrier does not worry about where the mail is stored overnight or how it gets from another city's post office to his post office. If a piece of mail is undeliverable, he simply holds onto it; the mail carrier does not attempt to figure out what went wrong. In Internet e-mail transmission, higher-level mail protocols such as POP and IMAP, which are discussed later in this chapter, take care of these functions.

When you configure clients to use e-mail, you need to identify the user's SMTP server. (Sometimes, this server is called the mail server.) Each e-mail program specifies this setting in a different place. Assuming that your client uses DNS, you do not have to identify the IP address of the SMTP server—only the name. For example, if a user's e-mail address is *jdoe@usmail.com*, his SMTP server is probably called "*usmail.com.*" You do not have to specify the TCP/IP port number used by SMTP because both the client workstation and the server assume that SMTP requests and responses flow through port 25.

MIME (Multipurpose Internet Mail Extensions)

The standard message format specified by SMTP allows for lines that contain no more than 1000 ASCII characters. That means if you relied solely on SMTP, you couldn't include pictures or even formatted text in an e-mail message. SMTP sufficed for mail transmissions in the early days of the Internet. However, its limitations prompted IEEE to release **MIME (Multipurpose Internet Mail Extensions)** in 1992. MIME is a standard for encoding and interpreting binary files, images, video, and non-ASCII character sets within an e-mail message. MIME identifies each element of a mail message according to content type. Some content types are text, graphics, audio, video, and multipart. The multipart content type indicates that a message contains more than non-ASCII element; for example, some of the message's content is formatted as text, some as a binary file, and some as a graphics file.

MIME does not replace SMTP but works in conjunction with it. It encodes different content types so that SMTP is fooled into thinking it is transporting an ASCII message stream. Most modern e-mail clients and servers support MIME.

Net+ POP (Post Office Protocol)

1.1

1.2

POP (Post Office Protocol) is an application layer protocol used to retrieve messages from a mail server. The most current and commonly used version of the POP protocol is **POP3 (Post Office Protocol, version 3)**, which relies on TCP and operates over port 110. With POP3, mail is delivered and stored on a mail server until a user connects—via an e-mail client—to the server to retrieve his messages. As the user retrieves his messages, the messages are downloaded to his workstation. After they are downloaded, the messages are typically deleted from the mail server. You can think of POP3 as a store-and-forward type of service. Mail is stored on the POP3 server and forwarded to the client on demand. One advantage to using POP3 is that it minimizes the use of server resources because mail is deleted from the server after retrieval. Another advantage is that virtually all mail server and client applications support POP3. However, the fact that POP3 downloads messages rather than keeping them on the server can be a drawback for some users.

POP3's design makes it best suited to users who retrieve their mail from the same workstation all the time. Users who move from machine to machine are at a disadvantage, because POP3 does not normally allow users to keep the mail on the server after they retrieve it. Thus, the mail is not accessible from other workstations. For example, suppose a consultant begins his day at his company's office and retrieves his e-mail on the workstation at his desk. Then he spends the rest of the day at a client's office, where he retrieves messages on his laptop. When he comes home, he checks his e-mail from his home computer. Using POP3, his messages would be stored on three different computers. A few options exist for circumventing this problem (such as downloading messages from the mail server to a file server on a LAN), but a more thorough solution has been provided by a new, more sophisticated e-mail protocol called IMAP, described next.

IMAP (Internet Message Access Protocol)

IMAP (Internet Message Access Protocol) is a mail retrieval protocol that was developed as a more sophisticated alternative to POP3. The most current version of IMAP is version 4, or, **IMAP4**. IMAP4 can replace POP3 without the user having to change e-mail programs. The single biggest advantage IMAP4 has over POP3 is that users can store messages on the mail server, rather than always having to download them to a local machine. This feature benefits users who may check mail from different workstations. In addition, IMAP4 provides the following features:

- *Users can retrieve all or only a portion of any mail message*—The remainder can be left on the mail server. This feature benefits users who move from machine to machine and users who have slow connections to the network or minimal free hard drive space.

- *Users can review their messages and delete them while the messages remain on the server*—This feature preserves network bandwidth, especially when the messages are long or contain attached files, because the data need not travel over the wire from the server to the client's workstation. For users with a slow modem connection, deleting messages without having to download them represents a major advantage over POP3.

- *Users can create sophisticated methods of organizing messages on the server*—A user might, for example, build a system of folders to contain messages with similar content. Also, a user might search through all of the messages or only those that contain one particular keyword or subject line.

1.1

1.2

- *Users can share a mailbox in a central location*—For example, if several maintenance personnel who use different workstations need to receive the same messages from the Facilities department head but do not need e-mail for any other purpose, they can all log on with the same ID and share the same mailbox on the server. If POP3 were used in this situation, only one maintenance staff member could read the message; she would then have to forward or copy it to her colleagues.

Although IMAP4 provides significant advantages over POP3, it also comes with a few disadvantages. For instance, IMAP4 servers require more storage space and usually more processing resources than POP servers do. By extension, network managers must keep a closer watch on IMAP4 servers to ensure that users are not consuming more than their fair share of space on the server. In addition, if the IMAP4 server fails, users cannot access the mail left there. (IMAP4 does allow users to download messages to their own workstations, however.)

Now that you have learned more about e-mail, the most frequently used TCP/IP service, you are ready to learn about utilities that will help you analyze TCP/IP-based networks.

Additional TCP/IP Utilities

As with any type of communication, many potential points of failure exist in the TCP/IP transmission process, and these points increase with the size of the network and the distance of the transmission. Fortunately, TCP/IP comes with a complete set of utilities that can help you track down most TCP/IP-related problems without using expensive software or hardware to analyze network traffic. You should be familiar with the use of the following tools and their switches, not only because the Network+ certification exam covers them, but also because you will regularly need these diagnostics in your work with TCP/IP networks.

In Chapter 4, you learned about three very important TCP/IP utilities—Telnet, ARP, and ping. The following sections present additional TCP/IP utilities that can help you discover information about your node and network.

Nearly all TCP/IP utilities can be accessed from the command prompt on any type of server or client running TCP/IP. However, the syntax of these commands may differ, depending on your client's operating system. For example, the default command that traces the path of packets from one host to another is known as `traceroute` in UNIX, as `tracepath` in some modern versions of Linux, and as `tracert` in the Windows operating systems. Similarly, the options used with each command may differ according to the operating system. For example, when working on a UNIX or Linux system, you can limit the maximum number of router hops the `traceroute` command allows by using the -m switch. On a Windows-based system, the -h switch accomplishes the same thing. The following sections cover the proper command syntax for Windows, UNIX, and Linux systems.

Ipconfig

5.1

Earlier in this book, you used the ipconfig utility to determine the TCP/IP configuration of a Windows Vista workstation. Ipconfig is the TCP/IP administration utility for use with Windows NT, 2000, XP, Vista, Server 2003, and Server 2008 operating systems. If you work with these operating systems, you will frequently use this tool to view a computer's TCP/IP settings. Ipconfig is a command-line utility that provides information about a network adapter's IP address, subnet mask, and default gateway.

To use the ipconfig utility from a Windows Vista workstation, for example, click Start, point to All Programs, click Accessories, and then click Command Prompt to open the Command Prompt window. At the command prompt, type `ipconfig` and press Enter. You should see TCP/IP information for your computer, similar to the output shown in Figure 10-9.

In addition to being used alone to list information about the TCP/IP configuration, the ipconfig utility can be used with switches to manage a computer's TCP/IP settings. For example, if you wanted to view complete information about your TCP/IP settings, including your MAC address, when your DHCP lease expires, the address of your WINS server, and so on, you could type: `ipconfig /all`. Note that the syntax of this command differs slightly from other TCP/IP utilities. With `ipconfig`, a forward slash (/) precedes the command switches, rather than a hyphen. The following list describes some popular switches that can be used with the `ipconfig` command:

- `/?`—Displays a list of switches available for use with the `ipconfig` command
- `/all`—Displays complete TCP/IP configuration information for each network interface on that device

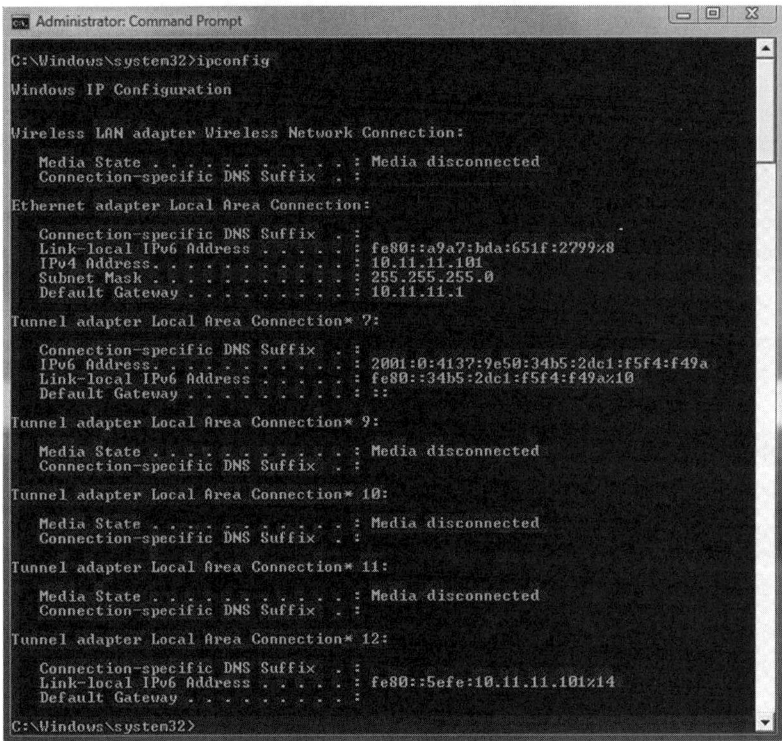

Figure 10-9 Output of an `ipconfig` command on a Windows Vista workstation

- /release—Releases DHCP-assigned addresses for all of the device's network interfaces
- /renew—Renews DHCP-assigned addresses for all of the device's network interfaces

When using the ipconfig command in Windows Vista, you must be logged in as an administrator to change your workstation's IP configuration.

Ifconfig

Chapter 4 also introduced you to the ifconfig utility, which is the TCP/IP configuration and management utility used on UNIX and Linux systems. As with ipconfig on Windows systems, ifconfig enables you to modify TCP/IP settings for a network interface, release and renew DHCP-assigned addresses, or simply check the status of your machine's TCP/IP settings. Ifconfig is also a utility that runs when a UNIX or Linux system starts, to establish the TCP/IP configuration for that computer.

Similar to the TCP/IP configuration utilities used with other operating systems, ifconfig can be used alone or with switches to reveal more customized information. For example, if you want to view the TCP/IP information associated with every interface on a device, you could type: ifconfig -a. The output would resemble the output shown in Figure 10-10. Notice that the syntax of the ifconfig command uses a hyphen (-) before some of the switches and no preceding character for other switches. The following list describes some of the popular switches you can use with ifconfig. To view a complete list of options, read the ifconfig man pages.

- -a—Applies the command to all interfaces on a device; can be used with other switches
- down—Marks the interface as unavailable to the network
- up—Reinitializes the interface after it has been taken "down," so that it is once again available to the network

Other ifconfig switches, such as those that apply to DHCP settings, vary according to the type and version of the UNIX or Linux system you use. Refer to your operating system's man pages for more information.

```
% ifconfig -a
eth0      Link encap:Ethernet  HWaddr 00:10:A4:B6:24:82
          inet addr:10.1.1.10  Bcast:10.1.1.255  Mask:255.255.255.0
          UP BROADCAST RUNNING MULTICAST  MTU:1500  Metric:1
          RX packets:38130 errors:1 dropped:0 overruns:0 frame:0
          TX packets:36103 errors:0 dropped:0 overruns:0 carrier:0
          collisions:0 txqueuelen:100
          RX bytes:32055118 (30.5 Mb)  TX bytes:3424759 (3.2 Mb)
          Interrupt:11 Base address:0x200

lo        Link encap:Local Loopback
          inet addr:127.0.0.1  Mask:255.0.0.0
          UP LOOPBACK RUNNING  MTU:16436  Metric:1
          RX packets:374 errors:0 dropped:0 overruns:0 frame:0
          TX packets:374 errors:0 dropped:0 overruns:0 carrier:0
          collisions:0 txqueuelen:0
          RX bytes:29705 (29.0 Kb)  TX bytes:29705 (29.0 Kb)
%
```

Figure 10-10 Detailed information available through ifconfig

Net+ Netstat

 The **netstat** utility displays TCP/IP statistics and details about TCP/IP components and connections on a host. Information that can be obtained from the `netstat` command includes the port on which a particular TCP/IP service is running, regardless of whether a remote node is logged on to a host; which network connections are currently established for a client; how many packets have been handled by a network interface since it was activated; and how many data errors have occurred on a particular network interface. As you can imagine, with so much information available, the netstat utility makes a powerful diagnostic tool.

For example, suppose you are a network administrator in charge of maintaining file, print, Web, and Internet servers for an organization. You discover that your Web server, which has multiple processors, sufficient hard disk space, and multiple NICs, is suddenly taking twice as long to respond to HTTP requests. Of course, you would want to check the server's memory resources as well as its Web server software to determine that nothing is wrong with either of those. In addition, you can use the netstat utility to determine the characteristics of the traffic going into and out of each NIC. You may discover that one network card is consistently handling 80 percent of the traffic, even though you had configured the server to share traffic equally among the two. This fact may lead you to run hardware diagnostics on the NIC, and perhaps discover that its on-board processor has failed, making it much slower than the other NIC. Netstat provides a quick way to view traffic statistics, without having to run a more complex traffic analysis program, such as Wireshark.

If you use the `netstat` command without switches, it will display a list of all the active TCP/IP connections on your machine, including the transport layer protocol used (UDP or TCP), the packets sent and received, the IP address, and the state of those connections.

However, like other TCP/IP commands, `netstat` can be used with a number of different switches. A `netstat` command begins with the word `netstat` followed by a space, then a hyphen and a switch, followed by a variable pertaining to that switch, if required. For example, `netstat -a` displays all current TCP and UDP connections from the issuing device to other devices on the network, as well as the source and destination service ports. The `netstat -r` command allows you to display the routing table on a given machine. The following list describes some of the most common switches used with the netstat utility:

- `-a`—Provides a list of all available TCP and UDP connections, even if they are simply listening and not currently exchanging data

- `-e`—Displays details about all the packets that have been sent over a network interface

- `-n`—Lists currently connected hosts according to their port and IP address (in numerical form)

- `-p`—Allows you to specify what type of protocol statistics to list; this switch must be followed by a protocol specification (TCP or UDP)

- `-r`—Provides a list of routing table information

- `-s`—Provides statistics about each packet transmitted by a host, separated according to protocol type (IP, TCP, UDP, or ICMP)

Figure 10-11 illustrates the output of a `netstat -a` command run at the command prompt on a Windows XP computer.

Figure 10-11 Output of a `netstat -a` command

Nbtstat

NetBIOS is a protocol that runs in the session and transport layers of the OSI model and associates NetBIOS names with workstations. NetBIOS alone is not routable because it does not contain network layer information. However, when encapsulated in another protocol such as TCP/IP, it can be routed. On networks that run NetBIOS over TCP/IP, the **nbtstat** utility can provide information about NetBIOS statistics and resolve NetBIOS names to their IP addresses. In other words, if you know the NetBIOS name of a workstation, you can use nbtstat to determine its IP address.

Nbtstat is useful only on networks that run Windows-based operating systems and NetBIOS. UNIX and Linux systems do not use NetBIOS, so nbtstat is not useful on these computers. Since most networks run pure TCP/IP (and not NetBIOS over TCP/IP), nbtstat has limited use as a TCP/IP diagnostic utility.

As with netstat, nbtstat offers a variety of switches that you can use to tailor the output of the command. For example, you can type `nbtstat-A ip_address` to determine what machine is registered to a given IP address. The following list details popular switches used with the `nbtstat` command. Notice that they are case sensitive; the `-a` switch has a different meaning than the `-A` switch.

- `-a`—Displays a machine's name table given its NetBIOS name; the name of the machine must be supplied after the `-a` switch
- `-A`—Displays a machine's name table given its IP address; the IP address of the machine must be supplied after the `-A` switch

- -r—Lists statistics about names that have been resolved to IP addresses by broadcast and by WINS; this switch is useful for determining whether a workstation is resolving names properly or for determining whether WINS is operating correctly

- -s—Displays a list of all the current NetBIOS sessions for a machine; when used with this switch, the `nbtstat` command attempts to resolve IP addresses to NetBIOS names in the listing; if the machine has no current NetBIOS connections, the result of this command will indicate that fact

Hostname, Host, and Nslookup

In Chapter 4 you learned that each client on a network is identified by a host name. If you aren't sure what host name has been assigned to a client, you can discover it by using the **hostname** utility. At the command prompt of a computer running Windows, UNIX, or Linux, type `hostname` and then press Enter. The utility responds with the client's host name. If you have administrator privileges on a client, you may also use the hostname utility to change its host name as follows: type `hostname` *new_hostname*, where *new_hostname* is the name you want to assign to the host, and then press Enter.

If you already know a host's name and want to learn its IP address, you can use the **host** utility. When used without switches, `host` simply returns either the IP address of a host if its host name is specified or its host name if its IP address is specified. For example, on a Linux workstation, you can type `/usr/bin/host www.cengage.com` and press Enter to discover the IP address associated with the host whose name is *www.cengage.com*. Or, you could type `/usr/bin/host 69.32.134.163` and press Enter to discover that the host name associated with this IP address is *www.cengage.com*. The host command comes with Linux and UNIX distributions. If your computer uses a Windows operating system, you'll need to download a third-party version of host.

A utility that is similar to host but has more flexibility is nslookup. **Nslookup** allows you to query the DNS database from any computer on the network and find the host name of a device by specifying its IP address, or vice versa. This ability is useful for verifying that a host is configured correctly or for troubleshooting DNS resolution problems. For example, if you wanted to find out whether the host whose name is *ftp.netscape.com* is operational, you could type: `nslookup` *ftp.netscape.com* and press Enter. Figure 10-12 shows the result of running a simple `nslookup` command at a Linux shell prompt.

Notice that the command provides not only the host's IP address, but also the primary DNS server name and address that holds the record for this name. To find the host name of a device whose IP address you know, type: `nslookup` *ip_address* and press Enter. In this case, the response would include not only the host name for that device, but also its IP address and the IP address and host name of its primary DNS server.

```
% nslookup ftp.netscape.com
Server:   proxy1.mdsn1.wi.home.com
Address:  24.6.204.15

Non-authoritative answer:
Name:    ftp.netscape.com
Address: 64.12.168.249

% 
```

Figure 10-12 Output of a simple `nslookup` command

Net+

5.1

Nslookup can reveal much more than just the IP address or host name of a device. Typing just `nslookup` (without switches) and then pressing Enter starts the nslookup utility, and the command prompt changes to a >. You can then use additional commands to find out more about the contents of the DNS database. For example, on a computer running UNIX, you could view a list of all the host name and IP address correlations on a particular DNS server by typing `ls`. Or you could specify five seconds as the period to wait for a response by typing `timeout=5`. (The default is 10 seconds.) Many other nslookup options exist. On a UNIX or Linux system, you can find the complete list of the nslookup options in the nslookup man pages. On a Windows-based system, you can view them by typing `nslookup ?` at the command prompt. To exit the nslookup utility and return to the normal command prompt, type `exit`.

Dig

A TCP/IP utility similar to nslookup is **dig**, which stands for **domain information groper**. As with nslookup, dig allows you to query a DNS database and find the host name associated with a specific IP address or vice versa. Also similar to nslookup, dig is useful for helping network administrators diagnose DNS problems. However, both in its simplest form and when used with one or more of its multiple switches, the dig utility can provide more detailed information than nslookup. An example of a simple dig command is `dig ftp.netscape.com`, the output of which is shown in Figure 10-13. Compare this output to the simple `nslookup` command output shown in Figure 10-12. Whereas the simple nslookup command returned the IP address for the host name, the simple dig command returned specifics about the resource records associated with the host name *ftp.netscape.com*. The domain name is in the first column, followed by the record's Time to Live, its type code (for example, A for an address record or MX for a mail record), and finally, a data field indicating the IP address or other domain name with which the primary domain name is associated. A summary of this particular query, including the time it took for the `dig` command to return the data, is shown at the bottom of the output.

```
% dig ftp.netscape.com

; <<>> DiG 9.4.1 <<>> ftp.netscape.com
;; global options:  printcmd
;; Got answer:
;; ->>HEADER<<- opcode: QUERY, status: NOERROR, id: 62444
;; flags: qr rd ra; QUERY: 1, ANSWER: 2, AUTHORITY: 2, ADDITIONAL: 2

;; QUESTION SECTION:
;ftp.netscape.com.                   IN      A

;; ANSWER SECTION:
ftp.netscape.com.          10        IN      CNAME    ftp.gftp.netscape.com.
ftp.gftp.netscape.com.     10        IN      A        205.188.212.121

;; AUTHORITY SECTION:
gftp.netscape.com.         1412      IN      NS       mtc-gdns001.ns.aol.com.
gftp.netscape.com.         1412      IN      NS       dtc-gdns001.ns.aol.com.

;; ADDITIONAL SECTION:
dtc-gdns001.ns.aol.com. 2340         IN      A        205.188.139.67
mtc-gdns001.ns.aol.com. 1464         IN      A        64.12.182.67

;; Query time: 132 msec
;; SERVER: 10.1.1.28#53(10.1.1.28)
;; WHEN: Thu Oct 26 18:34:28 2006
;; MSG SIZE  rcvd: 164

%
```

Figure 10-13 Output of a simple `dig` command

5.1

The dig utility comes with over two dozen switches, making it much more flexible than nslookup. For example, in a dig command you can specify the DNS server to query and the type of DNS record(s) for which you want to search, a timeout period for the query, a port (other than the default port 53) on the DNS server to query, and many other options. Look for the complete list of dig command switches and the syntax needed to use each in the `dig` man pages. The dig utility is included with UNIX and Linux operating systems. If your computer runs a Windows-based operating system, however, you must obtain the code for the dig utility from a third party and install it on your system.

Whois

You have learned about the process of domain name resolution and how individuals must register domain names with the Internet authority ICANN. When you register a domain name with ICANN, you provide contact information for yourself, the technical person responsible for the domain (for example, an engineer at an ISP who maintains DNS services there), and information about the hosting entity (usually an ISP) and the DNS server addresses. This information is stored in a database maintained by your RIR (Regional Internet Registry). The utility that allows you to query this DNS registration database and obtain information about a domain is called **whois**.

Using whois can help troubleshoot network problems. For example, if you noticed your network received a flood of messages that originated from *www.trinketmakers.com*, you could find out who leases the *trinketmakers.com* domain and contact them about the problem.

Syntax of the `whois` command is whois *xxx.yy*, where *xxx.yy* is the second-level domain name for which you want to know DNS registration information. For example, you could type whois `trinketmakers.com` at a UNIX shell prompt to obtain the registration information for *www.trinketmakers.com*. On a computer running one of the Windows operating systems, you need to install additional network utilities before you can run the `whois` command at a command prompt.

Rather than type `whois` at the shell or command prompt, however, you might prefer to use one of the many Web sites that provide simple, Web-based interfaces for running the `whois` command. For example, you could go straight to the source of the whois database, ARIN, at *www.arin.net*. There you will find a whois search prompt on the organization's home page. Many ICANN-authorized domain registrars will also provide whois search capabilities. They may also provide interfaces for running nslookup, ping, and other TCP/IP utilities.

A simple whois command does not work with all types of domains, because in some cases, a special server must be queried for some domain information. For example, domains registered with an RIR outside of North America and domains ending in .gov or .mil necessitate querying a server that holds DNS registration information only for these types of domains.

Traceroute (Tracert)

Suppose you work in technical support for a large company and one afternoon you receive calls from several employees complaining about slow Internet connections. With only that knowledge, you can't say whether the problem lies with your company's LAN (for example, a workgroup or backbone switch or router), default gateway, WAN connection, your service provider's CO, or a major ISP. However, simply by using one of the commands listed in this section, you can better assess where network performance is degraded.

The **traceroute** utility (known as **tracert** on Windows-based systems and **tracepath** on some Linux systems) uses ICMP ECHO requests to trace the path from one networked node to another, identifying all intermediate hops between the two nodes. To find the route, the traceroute utility transmits a series of UDP datagrams to a specified destination, using either the IP address or the host name to identify the destination. The first three datagrams that traceroute transmits have their TTL (Time to Live) set to 1. Because the TTL determines how many more network hops a datagram can make, datagrams with a TTL of 1 expire as they hit the first router. When they expire, they are returned to the source—in this case, the node that began the traceroute. In this way, traceroute obtains the identity of the first router. After it learns about the first router in the path, traceroute transmits a series of datagrams with a TTL of 2. The process continues for the next router in the path, and then the third, fourth, and so on, until the destination node is reached. Traceroute also returns the amount of time it took for the datagrams to reach each router in the path.

A traceroute test might stop before reaching the destination, however. This happens for one of two reasons: Either the device that traceroute is attempting to reach is down, or it does not accept ICMP transmissions. The latter is usually the case with firewalls. Therefore, if you are trying to trace a route to a host situated behind a firewall, your efforts will be thwarted. (Because ping uses ICMP transmissions, the same limitations exist for that utility.) Furthermore, traceroute cannot detect router configuration problems or detect whether a router uses different send and receive interfaces. In addition, routers might not decrement the TTL value correctly at each stop in the path. Therefore, traceroute is best used on a network with which you are already familiar. If you are reasonably certain that devices in the path between your host and a destination host do not block ICMP transmissions, traceroute can help you diagnose network congestion or network failures. You can then use your judgment and experience to compare the actual test results with what you anticipate the results should be.

The simplest form of the `traceroute` command (on a UNIX or Linux system) is `traceroute` *ip_address* or `traceroute` *host_name*. On some versions of Linux, it's `tracepath` *ip_address* or `tracepath` *host_name*. On computers that use a Windows-based operating system, the proper syntax is `tracert` *ip_address* or `tracert` *host_name*.

When run on a UNIX system, the command will return a list as shown in Figure 10-14. Tracert and tracepath output looks virtually identical.

```
% traceroute www.networksolutions.com
traceroute to www.networksolutions.com (216.168.224.69), 30 hops max, 38 byte packets
 1  * * *

% traceroute -I www.networksolutions.com
traceroute to www.networksolutions.com (216.168.224.69), 30 hops max, 38 byte packets
 1  * * *
 2  10.75.149.1 (10.75.149.1)  21.171 ms  21.026 ms  11.883 ms
 3  bb1-ge2-0.mdsn1.wi.home.net (24.6.204.1)  13.249 ms  14.739 ms  9.679 ms
 4  c2-se3-0-9.chcgil1.home.net (24.7.76.49)  13.511 ms  12.596 ms  18.576 ms
 5  aads.agis.net (206.220.243.19)  18.310 ms  26.789 ms  20.132 ms
 6  at-100100.inindrr01.us.telia.net (206.185.201.6)  68.421 ms  92.255 ms *
 7  at-0001.dcwdcrr01.us.telia.net (206.84.253.14)  97.508 ms  106.618 ms  100.920 ms
 8  ga011.herndon1.us.telia.net (206.84.235.249)  110.407 ms  108.272 ms  106.386 ms
 9  tii-internic.herndon1.us.telia.net (206.84.235.26)  96.980 ms  95.273 ms  92.744 ms
10  www.networksolutions.com (216.168.224.69)  93.718 ms  89.265 ms  88.828 ms
%
```

Figure 10-14 Output of a `traceroute` command

As with other TCP/IP commands, `traceroute` has a number of switches that may be used with it. The command begins with either `traceroute`, `tracert`, or `tracepath` (depending on the operating system your computer uses), followed by a hyphen, a switch, and a variable pertaining to a particular switch, if required. For example, on a Windows-based system, `tracert -4` forces the utility to use only IPv4 transmission. The following list describes some of the popular tracert switches:

- `-d`—Instructs the `tracert` command not to resolve IP addresses to host names

- `-h`—Specifies the maximum number of hops the packets should take when attempting to reach a host (the default is 30); this switch must be followed by a specific number of hops (for example, `tracert -h 12` would indicate a maximum of 12 hops)

- `-w`—Identifies a timeout period for responses; this switch must be followed by a variable to indicate the number of milliseconds the utility should wait for a response

Mtr (my traceroute)

Mtr (my traceroute) is a route discovery and analysis utility that comes with UNIX and Linux operating systems. It combines the functions of the ping and traceroute utilities and delivers an easy-to-read chart as its output. By issuing the `mtr` command, you instruct your computer to first determine the path between your client and the host you specify, and then you successively send ICMP ECHO requests to every hop on the route. In return, you learn about the devices in the path and whether and how promptly they respond. After letting the command run for a while, you also learn the devices' shortest, longest, and average response times and the extent of packet loss for each hop. This can reveal what portions of a network are suffering poor performance or even faults.

The simplest form of the `mtr` command is `mtr` *ip_address* or `mtr` *host_name*. After you enter the command, `mtr` will run continuously until you stop it by pressing Ctrl+C or unless you add an option to the command to limit its number of probes.

As you might guess, `mtr` can be used with a number of switches to refine the command's functioning and output. The command begins with `mtr`, followed by a hyphen, a switch, and a variable pertaining to a particular switch, if required. For example, entering `mtr - c 2` limits the number of ICMP ECHO requests to two. The following list defines some `mtr` switches:

- `-c`—Specifies how many ICMP ECHO requests to issue (in this case *c* stands for count).

- `-r`—Used with the `-c` switch, `-r` instructs mtr to generate a report and then exit after a certain number of probes.

- `-n`—Instructs mtr to not use DNS—that is, to display only IP addresses and not host names.

- `-i`—Used with a specific number of seconds to specify the period of time between ICMP ECHO requests; the default value is one second.

Figure 10-15 illustrates the output of the command `mtr -c 100 -r www.cengage.com`—in other words, an `mtr` command that will send 100 ICMP ECHO requests along the path to the host *www.cengage.com* and will issue the results in report format. Notice that the "Snt" column displays the quantity of ICMP ECHO requests sent.

```
Net+  HOST: Work_1                              Loss%   Snt   Last   Avg  Best   Wrst StDev

5.1   1. my.office.com                          0.0%    100    1.4   1.3   0.8    2.6   0.4

      2. adsl-12-34-56-254.dsl.chcgil.net       0.0%    100    9.5   9.6   8.8   11.5   0.5

      3. dist1-vlan62.chcgil.sbcglobal.net      5.0%    100    9.4   9.6   8.8   12.0   0.5

      4. bb1-g7-0.chcgil.ameritech.net          0.0%    100   10.3  28.7   8.5  210.0  45.3

      5. ex2-p1-0.eqchil.sbcglobal.net          0.0%    100    9.3  25.1   8.8  222.2  47.8

      6. asn209-qwest.eqchil.sbcglobal.net      0.0%    100    9.2  31.2   9.0  266.5  55.6

      7. cer-core-01.inet.qwest.net             3.0%    100    9.7  10.8   9.0   26.5   3.1

      8. jfk-edge-23.inet.qwest.net             0.0%    100   32.1  32.3  31.1   35.0   0.6

      9. 65.115.48.146                          0.0%    100   71.1  72.5  69.1  261.4  19.4

      10. academic.cengage.com                  0.0%    100   70.0  70.3  69.4   73.0   0.6
```

Figure 10-15 Output of the `mtr` command

Bear in mind that as with traceroute, mtr results might be misleading if certain devices on the network are prevented from responding to ICMP traffic. Even if a router does accept ICMP traffic, it will likely assign such requests lowest priority. A small percentage of packet loss in the middle of a route might merely reflect the fact that a router is busy and therefore slower at handling less-important traffic. In addition, beware that mtr generates a significant amount of traffic on a network. By running the mtr utility, you might slow network performance.

A program similar to mtr, **pathping**, is available as a command-line utility in Windows XP, Vista, Server 2003, and Server 2008. The switches available for use with `pathping` are similar to those available with `mtr`. However, the `pathping` output differs slightly. `Pathping` displays the path first and then issues hundreds of ICMP ECHO requests before revealing any reply or packet loss statistics.

Net+ Route

1.6

5.1

In Chapter 6 you learned that a routing table is a file on a networked host (for example, a workstation or router) that contains information about the paths that data will take between that host and other network nodes. When a client or connectivity device is added to a network, it discovers best paths and adds them to its routing table. (Recall that in dynamic routing, routers gather information about the network and incorporate that information in their routing tables even as the network changes.)

The **route** utility allows you to view a host's routing table. On a UNIX or Linux system, type `route` and then press Enter at the command prompt to view the routing table. On a Windows-based system, type `route print` and then press Enter. On a Cisco-brand router (or another brand that uses Cisco command conventions), type `show ip route` and press Enter. Routing tables on network clients typically have no more than a few unique entries, including the default gateway and loopback address. However, routing tables on Internet backbone routers, such as those operated by ISPs, maintain hundreds of thousands of entries.

The routing table in Figure 10-16 is an example of one that might be found on a UNIX host.

```
Kernel IP routing table
Destination      Gateway         Genmask          Flags Metric Ref  Use   Iface
223.37.128.0     0.0.0.0         255.255.255.0     U      0     0   4580  eth0
127.0.0.1        0.0.0.0         255.0.0.0         U      0     0   1360  lo
0.0.0.0          223.37.128.1    0.0.0.0           UG     0     0   3780  eth0
```

Figure 10-16 Example routing table

Table 10-6 explains the fields belonging to routing tables on UNIX or Linux systems.

The `route print` command used on a computer running a Windows operating system does not provide as much information and displays it in a different format.

In fact, the `route` command allows you to do much more than simply view a host's routing table. With it you may also add, delete, or modify routes. Following are some options available for use with the `route` command:

- `add`—Adds a route to the routing table; this switch must be followed by information about the route, for example, `route add default gw 123.45.67.1 eth1` instructs the host to add a route that uses the gateway with an address of 123.45.67.1 on the eth1 interface.

- `del`—Deletes a route from the routing table; this option must be followed by information about the route.

- `change`—Changes an existing route; this switch must be followed by information about the route to be changed (available on Windows systems only).

- `-p`—Makes a route persistent, or makes it reappear after a system is restarted (available on Windows systems only).

To learn about more `route` command options and the correct syntax for each, type `man route` and press Enter on a UNIX or Linux system. On a Windows system, type `route ?` and press Enter.

Table 10-6 Fields in Routing Table on a UNIX Host

Field	Explanation
Destination	The destination host's identity
Gateway	The destination host's gateway
Genmask	The destination host's netmask number
Flags	Additional information about the route, including whether it's usable (U), whether it's a gateway (G), and whether, as is the case with the loopback entry, only a single host can be reached via that route (H)
Metric	The cost of the route—that is, how efficiently it carries traffic
Ref	The number of references to the route that exist—that is, the number of routes that rely on this route
Use	The number of packets that have traversed the route
Iface	The type of interface the route uses

Most routers and other types of hosts optimize their routing tables without human intervention. If you choose to modify a routing table, be careful not to eliminate or damage a necessary route or cause routing loops. You risk degrading network performance or even cutting off network access to some or all clients.

Chapter Summary

- Subnetting separates one network or segment into multiple logically defined segments, or subnets. A network administrator might subnet a network to achieve simpler troubleshooting, enhanced security, improved performance, and easier network management.

- A subnet mask provides clues about the location of network information in an IP address. Bits in a subnet mask that equal 1 indicate that corresponding bits in an IP address contain network information. Bits in a subnet mask that equal 0 indicate that corresponding bits in an IP address contain host information.

- To create subnets, some of an IP address's bits (which by default represent host information) are changed to represent network information instead. The change is indicated by a change in the subnet mask's bits.

- If you use subnetting on your LAN, only your LAN's devices need to interpret your devices' subnetting information. External routers, such as those on the Internet, pay attention to only the network portion of your devices' IP addresses—not their subnet masks—when transmitting data to them.

- A newer variation on traditional subnetting is provided by CIDR (Classless Interdomain Routing). CIDR offers additional ways of arranging network and host information in an IP address. In CIDR, conventional network class distinctions do not exist.

- CIDR allows the creation of supernets, or subnets established by using bits that normally would be reserved for network class information. By moving the subnet boundary to the left, more bits are made available for host information, thus increasing the number of usable host addresses on a subnetted network.

- Gateways facilitate communication between different subnets. Because one device on the network cannot send data directly to a device on another subnet, a gateway (usually in the form of a router interface) must intercede and hand off the information.

- Every device on a TCP/IP-based network has a default gateway, the gateway that first interprets its outbound requests to other subnets, and then interprets its inbound requests from other subnets.

- Internet gateways maintain default routes to known addresses to expedite data transfer. The gateways that make up the Internet backbone are called core gateways.

- NAT (Network Address Translation) allows a network administrator to "hide" IP addresses assigned to nodes on a private network. In NAT, gateways assign transmissions valid Internet IP addresses when the transmission is sent to the Internet.

- SNAT (Static Network Address Translation) establishes a one-to-one correlation between each private IP address and Internet-recognized IP address.

- DNAT (Dynamic Network Address Translation) allows one or more Internet-recognized IP addresses to be shared by multiple clients. To achieve this type of address translation, a gateway assigns ports to each client's sessions, in a technique known as PAT (Port Address Translation). This is the most common type of address translation on small office and home networks.

- ICS (Internet Connection Sharing) is a service included with Windows 98, Me, 2000, XP, and Vista operating systems that allows a network of computers to share a single Internet connection through an ICS host computer.

- All Internet mail services rely on the same principles of mail delivery, storage, and pickup, though they may use different types of software to accomplish these functions.

- Mail client software can communicate with various types of mail server software, because the TCP/IP application layer protocols used for this communication are standard.

- SMTP (Simple Mail Transfer Protocol) is responsible for moving messages from one e-mail server to another over TCP/IP-based networks. SMTP operates through port 25, with requests to receive mail and send mail going through that port on the SMTP server. SMTP is used in conjunction with either POP or IMAP. MIME operates over SMTP to enable mail messages to contain non-ASCII content, such as graphics, audio, video, and binary files. Most modern e-mail clients support MIME encoding.

- POP (Post Office Protocol) is a mail retrieval protocol. The most current and commonly used version of POP is called POP3. Using POP3, messages are downloaded from the mail server to a client workstation each time the user retrieves messages.

- IMAP (Internet Message Access Protocol) is another mail retrieval protocol. Its most current version is IMAP4. IMAP4 differs from POP3 in that it allows users to store messages on the mail server, rather than always having to download them to the local machine. This is an advantage for users who do not always check mail from the same computer.

- Typing `ipconfig` at the command prompt of a system running Windows NT, 2000, XP, Vista, Server 2003, or Server 2008 reveals the TCP/IP settings for that computer.

- Ifconfig is the utility that establishes and allows management of TCP/IP settings on a UNIX or Linux system. The netstat utility displays TCP/IP statistics and the state of current TCP/IP components and connections. It also displays ports, which can signal whether services are using the correct ports.

- The nbtstat utility provides information about NetBIOS names and their addresses. If you know the NetBIOS name of a workstation, you can use nbtstat to determine the workstation's IP address.

- The hostname utility allows you to view or change a client's host name.

- The host utility, which comes with Linux and UNIX operating systems, allows you to find out either the host name of a node given its IP address or the IP address of a node given its host name.

- The nslookup utility is a more flexible version of the `host` command. It allows you to look up the DNS host name of a network node by specifying the node's IP address, or vice versa. Nslookup is useful for troubleshooting host configuration and DNS resolution problems.

- The dig utility, similar to nslookup, queries the network's DNS database to return information about a host given its IP address, or vice versa. In its simplest form, or when used with one of its many switches, dig provides more information than nslookup.

- The whois utility allows you to obtain DNS registration information for a second-level domain.

- The traceroute utility, known as tracert on Windows-based systems and tracepath on some Linux systems, uses ICMP to trace the path from one networked node to another, identifying all intermediate hops between the two nodes. This utility is useful for determining router or subnet connectivity problems.

- Mtr is a TCP/IP utility that combines the functions of traceroute and ping to reveal not only the path data takes between two hosts, but also statistics about the path, such as how promptly router interfaces respond and the extent of packet loss at each hop.

- The route command allows you to view a host's routing table and add, delete, or modify preferred routes.

Key Terms

ANDing   A logical process of combining bits. In ANDing, a bit with a value of 1 plus another bit with a value of 1 results in a 1. A bit with a value of 0 plus any other bit results in a 0.

CIDR (Classless Interdomain Routing)   An IP addressing and subnetting method in which network and host information is manipulated without adhering to the limitations imposed by traditional network class distinctions. CIDR is also known as classless routing or supernetting. Older routing protocols, such as RIP, are not capable of interpreting CIDR addressing schemes.

CIDR block   In CIDR notation, the number of bits used for an extended network prefix. For example, the CIDR block for 199.34.89.0/22 is /22.

CIDR notation   In CIDR, a method of denoting network IDs and their subnet boundaries. Slash notation takes the form of the network ID followed by a slash (/), followed by the number of bits that are used for the extended network prefix.

classful addressing   An IP addressing convention that adheres to network class distinctions, in which the first 8 bits of a Class A address, the first 16 bits of a Class B address, and the first 24 bits of a Class C address are used for network information.

Classless Interdomain Routing   *See* CIDR.

classless routing   *See* CIDR.

core gateway   A gateway that operates on the Internet backbone.

default gateway   The gateway that first interprets a device's outbound requests and then interprets its inbound requests to and from other subnets. In a Postal Service analogy, the default gateway is similar to a local post office.

default router   *See* default gateway.

dig (domain information groper)   A TCP/IP utility that queries the DNS database and provides information about a host given its IP address or vice versa. Dig is similar to the nslookup utility but provides more information, even in its simplest form, than nslookup can.

DNAT (Dynamic Network Address Translation)   A type of address translation in which a limited pool of Internet-valid IP addresses is shared by multiple private network hosts.

domain information groper   *See* dig.

Dynamic Network Address Translation   *See* DNAT

extended network prefix   The combination of an IP address's network ID and subnet information. By interpreting the address's extended network prefix, a device can determine the subnet to which an address belongs.

host   A TCP/IP utility that at its simplest returns either the IP address of a host if its host name is specified or its host name if its IP address is specified.

hostname   A TCP/IP utility used to show or modify a client's host name.

ICS (Internet Connection Sharing)   A service provided with Windows 98, Me, 2000, and 32-bit versions of XP operating systems that allows one computer, the ICS host, to share its Internet connection with other computers on the same network.

ICS host   On a network using the Microsoft Internet Connection Sharing service, the computer whose Internet connection other computers share. The ICS host must contain two network interfaces: one that connects to the Internet and one that connects to the LAN.

IMAP (Internet Message Access Protocol)   A mail retrieval protocol that improves on the shortcomings of POP. The single biggest advantage IMAP4 has relative to POP is that it allows users to store messages on the mail server, rather than always having to download them to the local machine. The most current version of IMAP is version 4 (IMAP4).

IMAP4 (Internet Message Access Protocol, version 4)   The most commonly used form of the Internet Message Access Protocol (IMAP).

Internet Connection Sharing   *See* ICS.

Internet Message Access Protocol   *See* IMAP.

Internet Message Access Protocol, version 4   *See* IMAP4.

IP masquerading   *See* DNAT.

MIME (Multipurpose Internet Mail Extensions)   A standard for encoding and interpreting binary files, images, video, and non-ASCII character sets within an e-mail message.

mtr (my traceroute)   A route discovery and analysis utility that comes with UNIX and Linux operating systems. Mtr combines the functions of the `ping` and `traceroute` commands and delivers an easily readable chart as its output.

Multipurpose Internet Mail Extensions   *See* MIME.

NAT (Network Address Translation)   A technique in which IP addresses used on a private network are assigned a public IP address by a gateway when accessing a public network.

nbtstat   A TCP/IP troubleshooting utility that provides information about NetBIOS names and their addresses. If you know the NetBIOS name of a workstation, you can use nbtstat to determine its IP address.

NetBIOS   A protocol that runs in the session and transport layers of the OSI model and associates NetBIOS names with workstations. NetBIOS alone is not routable because it does not contain network layer information. However, when encapsulated in another protocol such as TCP/IP, it can be routed.

netstat   A TCP/IP troubleshooting utility that displays statistics and the state of current TCP/IP connections. It also displays ports, which can signal whether services are using the correct ports.

Network Address Translation   *See* NAT.

nslookup   A TCP/IP utility that allows you to look up the DNS host name of a network node by specifying its IP address, or vice versa. This ability is useful for verifying that a host is configured correctly and for troubleshooting DNS resolution problems.

PAT (Port Address Translation)   A form of address translation that uses TCP port numbers to distinguish each client's transmission, thus allowing multiple clients to share a limited number of Internet-recognized IP addresses.

pathping   A command-line utility that combines the functionality of the `tracert` and `ping` commands (similar to UNIX's `mtr` command) and comes with Windows XP, Vista, Windows Server 2003, and Server 2008.

POP (Post Office Protocol)   An application layer protocol used to retrieve messages from a mail server. When a client retrieves mail via POP, messages previously stored on the mail server are downloaded to the client's workstation and then deleted from the mail server.

POP3 (Post Office Protocol, version 3)   The most commonly used form of the Post Office Protocol.

Port Address Translation   *See* PAT.

Post Office Protocol   *See* POP.

Post Office Protocol, version 3   *See* POP3.

private network   A network whose access is restricted to only clients or machines with proper credentials.

public network   A network that any user can access with no restrictions. The most familiar example of a public network is the Internet.

route   A utility for viewing or modifying a host's routing table.

Simple Mail Transfer Protocol   *See* SMTP.

slash notation   *See* CIDR notation.

SMTP (Simple Mail Transfer Protocol)   The application layer TCP/IP subprotocol responsible for moving messages from one e-mail server to another.

SNAT (Static Network Address Translation)   A type of address translation in which each private IP address is correlated with its own Internet-recognized IP address.

Static Network Address Translation   *See* SNAT.

supernet   A type of subnet that is created using bits that normally would be reserved for network class information—by moving the subnet boundary to the left.

supernet mask   A 32-bit number that, when combined with a device's IP address, indicates the kind of supernet to which the device belongs.

supernetting   *See* CIDR.

tracepath   A version of the traceroute utility found on some Linux distributions.

traceroute (tracert)   A TCP/IP troubleshooting utility that uses ICMP to trace the path from one networked node to another, identifying all intermediate hops between the two nodes. Traceroute is useful for determining router or subnet connectivity problems. On Windows-based systems, the utility is known as tracert.

whois   The utility that allows you to query ICANN's DNS registration database and find information about a domain.

Review Questions

1. What is a disadvantage of classful addressing?

   a. Security

   b. Poor performance

   c. Troubleshooting mechanisms

   d. Network traffic separation

2. Which term describes an IP address that cannot be assigned to a network interface on a node or used as subnet mask?

   a. Host ID

   b. MAC ID

   c. Router ID

   d. Network ID

3. Which term describes a network that any user may access with little or no restrictions?

   a. Open source

   b. Public

   c. Proprietary

   d. Private

4. Which mail retrieval protocol allows users to store messages on the mail server, rather than always having to download them to the local machine?

   a. SMTP (Simple Mail Transfer Protocol)

   b. IMAP (Internet Message Access Protocol)

   c. POP (Post Office Protocol)

   d. MIME

5. Which Windows command is used to reveal a computer's TCP/IP settings?

   a. `ifconfig`

   b. `ipconfig`

   c. `nbtstat`

   d. `nslookup`

6. True or false? In classful addressing, only Class A and Class B addresses are recognized.

7. True or false? Class A, Class B, and Class C networks can all be subnetted.

8. True or false? E-mail is one of the most frequently used Internet services an administrator manages.

9. True or false? The `nbtstat` command is useful on networks that run UNIX and Linux operating systems and NetBIOS.

10. True or false? The `route` utility is useful for determining router or subnet connectivity problems.

11. ____ separates a network into multiple logically defined segments, or subnets.

12. ____ is not exclusive of subnetting; it merely provides additional ways of arranging network and host information in an IP address.

13. The ____ process occurs when the client's transmission reaches the default gateway; the gateway opens the IP datagram and replaces the client's private IP address with an Internet-recognized IP address.

14. The ____ host is configured to translate requests to and from the Internet on behalf of other computers on the network.

15. ____ is a standard for encoding and interpreting binary files, images, video, and non-ASCII character sets within an e-mail message.

After reading this chapter and completing the exercises, you will be able to:

- Use terminology specific to converged networks

- Explain VoIP (voice over IP) services and their user interfaces

- Explain video over IP services and their user interfaces

- Describe VoIP and video over IP signaling and transport protocols, including SIP, H.323, and RTP

- Understand QoS (quality of service) assurance methods critical to converged networks, including RSVP and DiffServ

On the Job

The critical element in a stroke is time. Doctors have three hours from the onset of a stroke to deliver a lifesaving drug called tPA. Neurologists can cut this time by seeing patients through videoconferencing.

I provide support for the WAN and H.323 videoconferencing systems for Utah Telehealth Network's 49 sites. We recently installed a new H.323 videoconferencing codec in a doctor's home. Unlike the old unit, it kept randomly losing the far end's image. A second codec had the same problem. The troubleshooting process quickly turned interesting.

First, we made sure the network cable was secure by recrimping the ends. Next, we checked the router and switch for a data link. We also verified that speed and duplex were set correctly. No errors appeared in the counters.

Videoconferencing is often prone to IP addressing issues when using network address translation, so we verified that both the private and public IP addresses were correct. When the problem continued, we applied a sniffer capture to the Internet side of the firewall. Its log showed that the firewall was not correctly converting private IP addresses to public addresses. Sessions would establish but then fail because the far end was trying to contact the private IP address rather than the near end's public address. We also tried changing the H.323 firewall's application layer gateway settings. The adjustments let calls stay up, but we now lost far-end camera control. This indicated that the firewall was affecting the application layer as well.

I sent the packet captures to the firewall vendor, who claimed that Layer 3 routing caused the problem. However, thanks to those valuable logs, we proved that the firewall was not properly processing the H.323 application. Ultimately, we discovered that the firewall's firmware did not support the latest H.323 standards.

We chose to replace the firewall with a newer model that used the latest H.323 standards. The replacement worked fine with the codec. The increased maintenance costs taught us the hard way to evaluate every potential purchase in a test environment before putting it in production.

Jeff Shuckra
Network Engineer, Utah Telehealth Network

In Chapter 1 you learned that convergence is the use of one network to simultaneously carry voice, video, and data communications. Traditionally, separate networks served voice and data signals. Through most of the 20th century, the PSTN (public switched telephone network), based on Alexander Graham Bell's circuit-switched model, carried telephone calls and fax transmissions. Packet-switched networks, such as the Internet, took care of e-mail, Web pages, file transfers, and access to other data resources. In the latter part of the 20th century, the two types of networks began intersecting. For example, today, when an Internet user dials into his ISP, he is using the PSTN to connect to a data network. However, this intersection is not seamless or efficient. As you have learned, it requires modems to convert digital data into analog signals and vice versa. Networks achieve more unified integration, however, by packetizing voice—that is, digitizing the voice signal and issuing it as a stream of packets over the network.

In the past 15 years, telecommunications carriers, network service providers, data equipment manufacturers, and standards organizations have concentrated on ways to deliver voice, video, and data over the same networks. These converged networks, as they are called, may be cheaper and more convenient, but they also require new technology. This chapter describes a variety of voice and video over IP applications, plus the protocols and infrastructure necessary to deliver them.

Terminology

In discussions of convergence, the use of multiple terms to refer to the same or similar technologies is common. This is partly a result of a market that developed rapidly while many different vendors touted their own solutions and applied their preferred terminology. The terms used throughout this chapter are those most frequently cited by standards organizations that focus on converged network technology, such as the ITU and IETF. Before you learn how voice and video over IP services work, it's useful to understand the meaning of these terms.

One important term is **IP telephony**, the use of any network (either public or private) to carry voice signals using the TCP/IP protocol. IP telephony is more commonly known as **VoIP (voice over IP)**. VoIP can run over any packet-switched network. When an ATM network is used to transport packetized voice signals, the service is called **VoATM (voice over ATM)**. Similarly, when a DSL connection is used to carry packetized voice signals, the service is known as **VoDSL (voice over DSL)**. (Note, however, that these terms are not mutually exclusive. For example, VoIP is considered VoDSL if the packets travel over a DSL connection.) Virtually any type of data connection can carry VoIP signals, including T-carriers, ISDN, broadband cable, satellite connections, WiFi, WiMAX, and cellular telephone networks.

When VoIP relies on the Internet, it is often called **Internet telephony**. But not all VoIP calls are carried over the Internet. In fact, VoIP over private lines is an effective and economical method of completing calls between two locations within an organization. And because the line is private, its network congestion can be easily controlled, which often translates into better sound quality than an Internet telephone call can provide. But given the Internet's breadth and low cost, it is appealing to consider the Internet for carrying conversations that we currently exchange over the PSTN.

Voice is not the only nondata application that can be carried on a converged network. **FoIP (fax over IP)** uses packet-switched networks to transmit faxes from one node on the network to another. Other applications include **IPTV (IP television)**, in which television signals from broadcast or cable networks travel over packet-switched networks. **Videoconferencing**, which allows multiple participants to communicate and collaborate at once through audiovisual means, is another example of using networks to carry video information. **Streaming video** refers to video signals that are compressed and delivered in a continuous stream. For example, when you choose to watch a television show episode on the Web, you are requesting a streaming video service. You don't have to download the entire episode before you begin to see and hear it. When streaming videos are supplied via the Web, they are often called **Webcasts**.

One way to distribute video signals over IP is multicasting. As you learned in Chapter 4, in multicasting, one node transmits the same content to every client in a defined group of nodes, such as a subnet. IPTV, videoconferencing, streaming video, and IP multicasting belong to the range of services known as **video over IP**.

Over time, voice and video services over packet-switched networks have matured, and as a result more users rely on them. These users, in turn, have demanded better integration with traditional data services, such as e-mail and Web browsing. In Chapter 1 you learned that unified communications (sometimes called **unified messaging**) is a service that makes several forms of communication available from a single user interface. In unified communications, a user can, for example, access the Web; send and receive faxes, e-mail messages, voice mail messages, instant messages, or telephone calls; and participate in videoconference calls—all from one console.

This overview of the terms used when discussing converged services gives you a sense of the breadth of these applications. Now you are ready to learn how they work.

VoIP (Voice over IP) Applications and Interfaces

VoIP (pronounced "voyp") has existed in various forms for over a decade. Although organizations were slow to adopt it at first, as networks became faster, more reliable, and more accessible, use of VoIP increased dramatically. Significant reasons for implementing VoIP include the following:

- *Lower costs for voice calls*—In the case of long-distance calling, using VoIP over a WAN allows an organization to avoid paying long-distance telephone charges, a benefit known as **toll bypass**. For example, an organization that already leases T3s between its offices within a region can use the T3s to carry voice traffic between colleagues.

- *Supply new or enhanced features and applications*—VoIP runs over TCP/IP, an open protocol suite, whereas the PSTN runs over proprietary protocols. This means developers with enough skill and interest can develop their own VoIP applications, making the possibilities for new VoIP features and services endless. It also means that off-the-shelf VoIP applications can be modified to suit a particular organization's needs.

- *Centralize voice and data network management*—When voice and data transmissions use the same infrastructure, a network manager needs only to design, maintain, and troubleshoot a single network. Furthermore, on that network, VoIP devices can provide detailed information about voice transmissions, such as the date, time, and duration of calls, in addition to their originating number and caller names.

Voice and data can be combined on a network in several configurations. VoIP callers can use either a traditional telephone, which sends and receives analog signals, a telephone specially designed for TCP/IP transmission, or a computer equipped with a microphone, speaker, and VoIP client software. And on any VoIP network, a mix of these three types of clients is possible.

The following sections explain how analog and digital voice networks are integrated and describe equipment necessary to accomplish such integration.

Analog Telephones

If a VoIP caller uses a traditional telephone, signals issued by the telephone must be converted to digital form before being transmitted on a TCP/IP-based network. In fact, even if the entire VoIP connection is digital, voice signals still need to be converted from their natural, analog form into bits. This conversion involves first compressing and encoding analog signals, functions that occur at the presentation layer of the OSI model. Any method for accomplishing this conversion is known as a codec (a word that derives from its function as a *cod*er/*dec*oder). Detailing the wide variety of voice and video codecs is beyond the scope of this book. However, to successfully implement converged networks, you should understand what types of equipment are necessary to accomplish analog-to-digital conversion.

One possibility is to connect an analog telephone to a VoIP adapter, sometimes called an **ATA (analog telephone adapter)**. The ATA might be a card within a computer workstation or an externally attached device that allows for one or more telephone connections. The traditional telephone line connects to an RJ-11 port on the adapter. The ATA, along with its device drivers and software on the computer, converts analog voice signals to IP packets and vice versa. Figure 11-1 shows an ATA that supports two telephone connections.

A second way to achieve this conversion is by connecting an analog telephone line to a switch, router, or gateway capable of accepting analog voice signals, converting them into packets, issuing the packets to a data network—and vice versa. Like the switches, routers, and gateways you learned about earlier in this book, VoIP-enabled devices come with a variety of features, including support for NAT, VPN protocols, encryption, and more. Figure 11-2

Figure 11-1 ATA (analog telephone adapter)

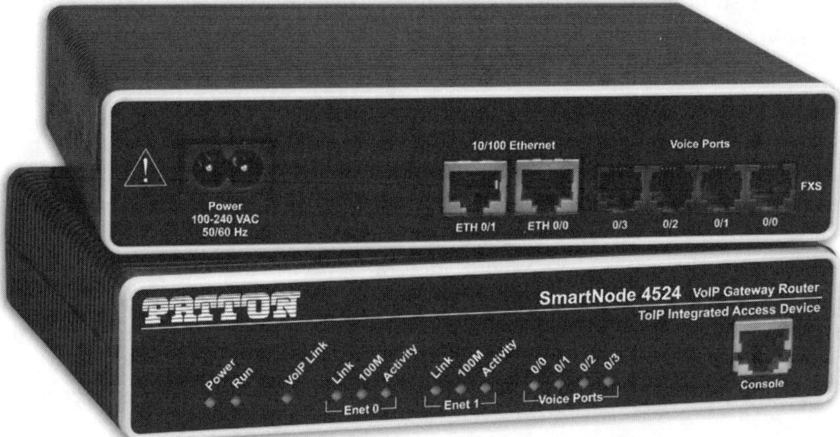

Figure 11-2 VoIP router

shows a VoIP router that accepts up to four telephone lines. Next to the bank of eight RJ-11 ports for incoming analog lines are two RJ-45 ports to connect the router to an Ethernet network.

A third example of an analog-to-digital voice conversion device is a **digital PBX** or, more commonly, an **IP-PBX**. (**PBX** stands for **private branch exchange**, which is the term used to describe a telephone switch that connects calls within a private organization.) In general, an IP-PBX is a private switch that accepts and interprets both analog and digital voice signals. Thus, it can connect with both traditional PSTN lines and data networks. An IP-PBX transmits and receives IP-based voice signals to and from other network connectivity devices, such as routers or gateways. Most IP-PBX systems are packaged with sophisticated software that allows network managers to configure and maintain an organization's phone system. Figure 11-3 shows an IP-PBX capable of managing up to 60 calls at once.

In a fourth scenario, the traditional telephone connects to an analog PBX, which then connects to a voice-data gateway. In this case, the gateway connects the traditional telephone circuits with a TCP/IP network (such as the Internet or a private WAN). The gateway digitizes incoming analog voice signals, compresses the data, assembles the data into packets, and then issues the packets to the packet-switched network. When transferring calls from a packet-switched network to a circuit-switched network (for example, if you call your home telephone number from your office's IP telephone), the gateway performs the same functions in the reverse order.

Figure 11-4 depicts the four different ways analog telephones can be used to access a VoIP network.

Figure 11-3 IP-PBX

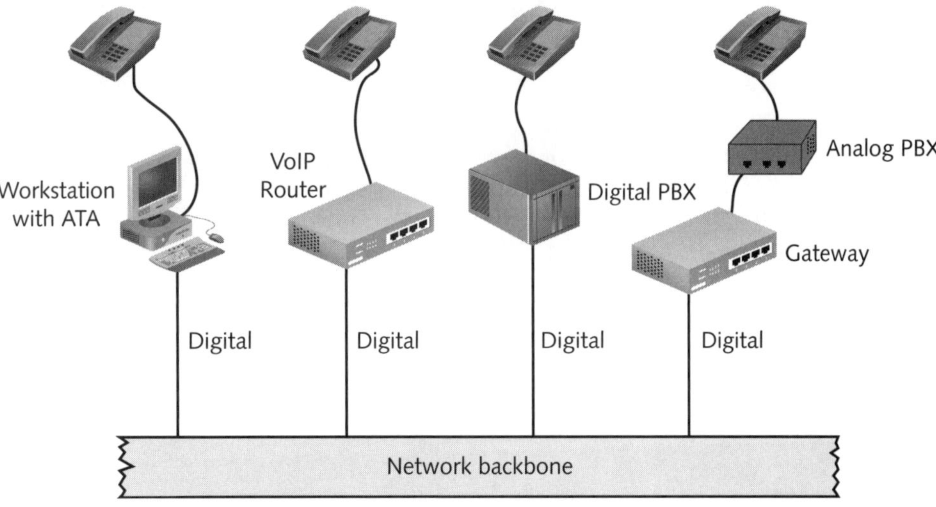

Figure 11-4 Integrating VoIP networks and analog telephones

IP Telephones

Most new VoIP installations use **IP telephones** (or **IP phones**), which, unlike traditional phones, transmit and receive only digital signals. When a caller uses an IP telephone, her voice is immediately digitized and issued from the telephone to the network in packet form. To communicate on the network, each IP telephone must have a unique IP address, just as any client connected to the network has a unique IP address. The IP telephone looks like a traditional touch-tone phone but connects to an RJ-45 wall jack, like a computer workstation. Its connection may then pass through a connectivity device, such as a switch or router, before reaching the IP-PBX. An IP-PBX may contain its own voice-data gateway, or it may connect to a separate voice-data gateway, which is then connected to the network backbone. Figure 11-5 illustrates different ways IP telephones can connect with a data network.

IP telephones act much like traditional telephones. For example, they feature speed-dialing, call hold, transfer, and forwarding buttons, conference calling, voice mail access, speakers and microphones, and an LCD screen that displays caller ID and call hold information. IP telephones come in both mobile and wired styles. More sophisticated IP telephones offer features not available with traditional telephones. Because IP telephones are essentially network clients, like workstations, the number and types of customized features that can be programmed for use with these phones is limitless. Some popular features unique to IP telephones are listed below.

- Screens on IP telephones can act as Web browsers, allowing a user to open HTTP encoded pages, and, for example, click a telephone number link to complete a call to that number.

- IP telephones may connect to a user's PDA (personal digital assistant) wirelessly, enabling the user to, for example, view his phone directory and touch a number on the IP telephone's LCD screen to call that number.

- Some IP telephones have speech recognition capabilities, which means that rather than pushing a button, a caller can say aloud the number he wishes to call, and the telephone will dial that number. Or, if the caller has activated a browser screen on his

IP telephone, he can open a Web page by speaking the name of the URL or an alias he has programmed the telephone to recognize.

- If a line is busy, an IP telephone can offer the caller the option to leave an instant message on the called party's IP telephone screen.

- An IP telephone can be programmed to accept emergency messages when they are broadcast to all IP telephones in an organization, even as the user is talking over the phone. In this case, the audio signal for the emergency message is combined with the audio signal of the user's call.

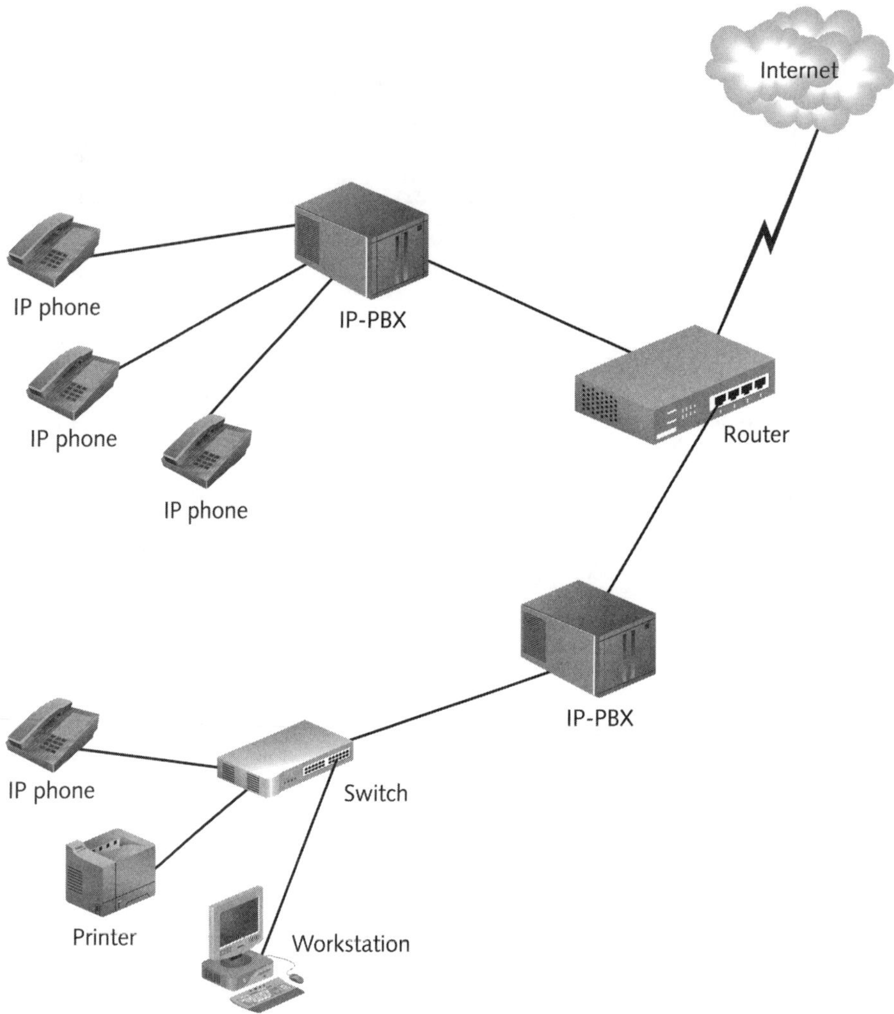

Figure 11-5 Accessing a VoIP network from IP phones

Another benefit of IP telephones is their mobility. Because IP telephones are addressable over a network, they can be moved from one office to another office, connected to a wall jack, and be ready to accept or make calls. Compare this to the traditional method of moving telephone extensions, which requires reprogramming the extension's location in a PBX database. A user would have to wait for the network administrator to perform this change before her telephone extension would work in a new location. With IP telephones, however, the user is free to move to any point on the network without missing a call.

One issue that faces IP telephones is the need for electric current. A conventional analog telephone obtains current from the local loop. This is necessary for signaling—for example, to make your phone ring and to provide a dial tone. However, IP telephones are not directly connected to the local loop. Instead, most obtain electric current from a separate power supply. This makes IP telephones susceptible to power outages in a way that analog telephones are not. It also points to the need for assured backup power sources in organizations that rely on IP telephones. In some VoIP installations, IP telephones obtain current via their Ethernet connection using PoE (power over Ethernet).

In the United States, an IP telephone can cost between $150 and $750. A typical IP phone is shown in Figure 11-6.

Using IP telephones is not the only way to benefit from a fully digital voice connection. Instead, an off-the-shelf workstation can be programmed to act like an IP telephone, as described in the next section.

Figure 11-6 An IP phone

Softphones

Rather than using traditional telephones or IP telephones, a third option is to use a computer programmed to act like an IP telephone, otherwise known as a **softphone**. Softphones and IP telephones provide the same calling functions; they simply connect to the network and deliver services differently. Before it can be used as a softphone, a computer must meet minimum hardware requirements (which any new workstation purchased at an electronics store would likely meet), be installed with an IP telephony client, and communicate with a digital telephone switch. In addition, softphone computers must have a sound card capable of full-duplex transmission, so that both the caller and the called party can speak at the same time. Finally, a softphone requires a microphone and speakers or a headset. Skype, the popular Internet telephony software, is one type of softphone.

After a user starts the softphone client software, she is typically presented with a graphical representation of a telephone dial pad, as shown in Figure 11-7. The interface might also present a list of telephone numbers in the caller's address book, so that the caller can click on the number she wishes to call. And like IP telephones, the program features buttons for call forwarding, speed dialing, conferencing, and so on—except that on a softphone, these buttons are clickable icons.

Unlike many types of phones, softphones allow the user to customize her graphical interface. For example, an administrative assistant who spends most of his time calling clients and vendors on behalf of his supervisor can position a list of clickable, frequently called numbers in the foreground of his default interface.

One difference between IP telephones and softphones is that a softphone's versatile connectivity makes it an optimal VoIP solution for traveling employees and telecommuters. For example, suppose you are a district sales manager with a home office and you supervise 32 sales representatives throughout the Pacific Northwest. Your company uses VoIP, with an IP-PBX connected to the company headquarters' LAN. At your home office, you have a desktop workstation equipped with a sound card, headset, and softphone software. You also lease a DSL connection to your local carrier, which allows you to log on to your company's LAN from home. After logging onto the LAN, you initiate the softphone client and then log into the company's IP-PBX. By logging onto the IP-PBX, you access your personal call profile and indicate to the IP-PBX that your calls should be routed to your home computer. However, because you are a district sales manager, you only spend half of the time working from home. The other half of the time you travel to visit your sales representatives across the region. During that time you use a laptop that, like your home workstation, is equipped with a sound card, a headset, and the softphone client software. While on the road, you use remote connectivity software to access your company's LAN, and then you initiate your softphone client. Now your calls are directed to your laptop computer, rather than your home

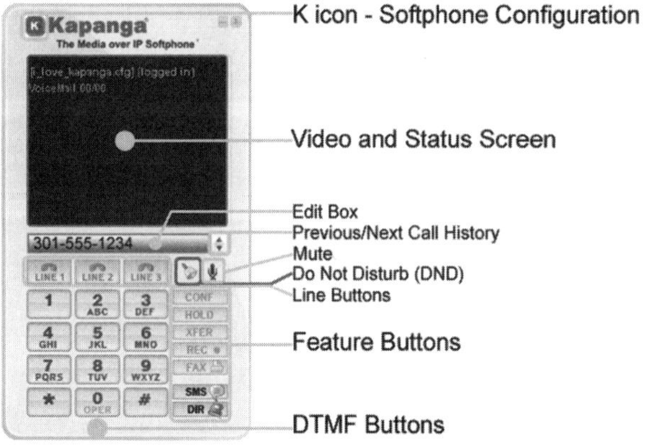

Figure 11-7 Softphone interface

workstation. No matter where you are, you can establish a remote telephone extension, if the computer has the appropriate software and hardware installed. Figure 11-8 depicts the use of softphones on a converged network.

Besides their extreme mobility, another advantage to softphones is the capability for convenient, localized call management. Like IP phones, softphone clients can easily track the date, time, and duration of calls, in addition to their originating number and caller names. A softphone user can also, for example, export call information to a billing or accounting program on the same workstation. This feature simplifies recordkeeping and billing for professionals—such as lawyers or consulting engineers—who bill their customers by the hour.

Now that you understand the variety of ways that VoIP services may be implemented, you are ready to learn about the different types of video services that packet-switched networks may carry.

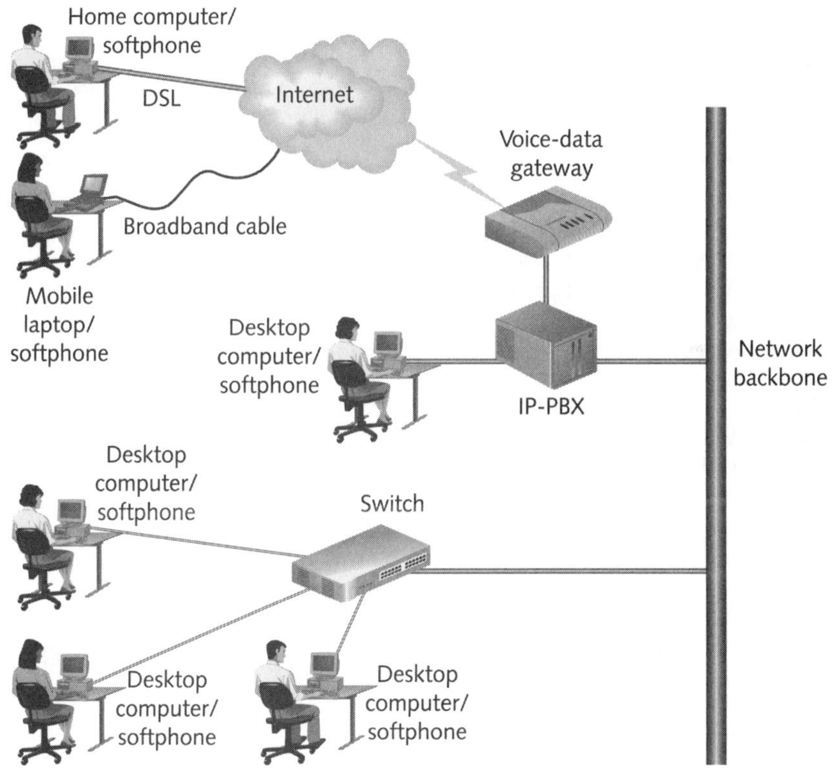

Figure 11-8 Connecting softphones to a converged network

Video over IP Applications and Interfaces

Cisco Systems, the largest supplier of networking hardware in the world, estimates that by 2011, 60 percent of the traffic carried by the Internet will be video traffic. Currently, however, video services are less common on TCP/IP networks than voice services. For Cisco's prediction to come true, the price of video over IP hardware must continue to drop. At the same time, networks must further augment their capacities and reliability. Many networking professionals confidently assert that both are already underway. Therefore, you should understand the types of video services that TCP/IP networks may carry and the hardware and software they rely on.

The following sections divide video over IP services into three categories: streaming video, IPTV, and videoconferencing. However, divisions between these services are not always clear, as you'll learn. Also bear in mind that no matter what the application or distribution method, every video over IP transmission begins with digitizing the audio and visual signals using one of several popular video codecs, such as MPEG-4. Details of video codecs are beyond the scope of this book.

Streaming Video

You have already learned that streaming video is a service in which audiovisual signals are compressed and delivered over the Internet in a continuous stream. If you have watched a YouTube video on the Internet, you have used streaming video. Because most networks are TCP/IP-based, most streaming video belongs to the category of video over IP.

Among all video over IP applications, streaming video is perhaps the simplest. A user needs only to have a computer with sufficient processing and caching resources, plus the appropriate audiovisual hardware and software to view encoded video. On the transmission end, video can be delivered by any computer with sufficient capabilities to capture, encode, and send the video. In many cases, this will be a streaming server dedicated to the task, but it could also be a workstation that performs video streaming, among other tasks. Streaming video can traverse any type of TCP/IP network, though it often relies on the Internet.

One popular way of providing video streams is to make them available as stored files (saved in any one of a number of popular video formats) on a video streaming server. The viewer then chooses to watch the video at his convenience, typically from a Web browser. Upon receiving a request, the streaming server delivers the video to the viewer. This type of service, in which the video file remains on the server until it is specifically requested by the user, is known as **video-on-demand**. When you choose to watch a news report from your local TV channel's Web page, for example, you are making use of video-on-demand.

In another form of streaming video, the video is issued live—that is, directly from the source to the user as the camera captures it. For example, suppose you wanted to watch a Senate subcommittee hearing that's being broadcast on CSPAN. You could access CSPAN's Web site and watch the hearing as it happens using live streaming video. One drawback to live streaming is that content may not be edited before it's distributed. Another potential drawback is that viewers must connect with the stream when it's issued, whereas they can use video-on-demand at their convenience. In addition, video-on-demand allows viewers to control their viewing experience, for example, by pausing, rewinding, or fast-forwarding.

Figure 11-9 illustrates video-on-demand and live streaming video services.

The distinction between on-demand video and live streaming video is just the beginning. You also need to consider the number of clients receiving each service. For example, an IT manager in one office might use his laptop and its built-in camera to capture and issue a video

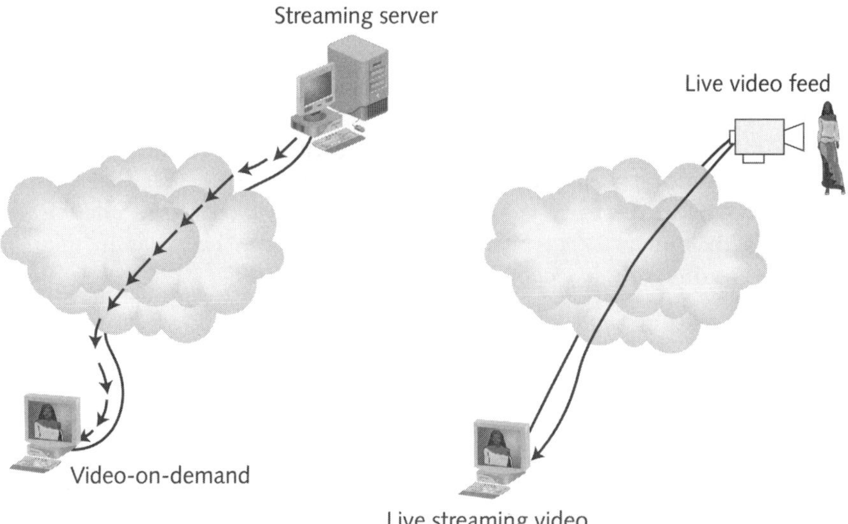

Figure 11-9 Video-on-demand and live streaming video

of himself explaining a technical topic to one of his employees in another office. This is an example of point-to-point video over IP. Or he might issue the video stream to a whole group of employees in a point-to-multipoint manner.

You might recall the terms *unicast* and *multicast* from Chapter 4 and assume that point-to-multipoint streaming video means multicast transmission. That's not necessarily the case. Recall that in IP multicasting, a source issues data to a defined group of IP addresses. In fact, many streaming video services—and nearly all of those issued over a public network, such as the Internet—are examples of unicast transmissions. As you have learned, in a unicast transmission, a single node issues a stream of data to one other node. In a VoIP call, for example, one IP phone addresses another in unicast fashion. If many Internet users watch CSPAN's streaming video on the Web simultaneously, the CSPAN source would issue encoded audiovisual signals to each viewer via separate unicast transmissions. In the example of an IT manager sharing a video discussion with his employees in another office, the transmission might be unicast or multicast, depending on how he configured it.

Finally, streaming video services may also be classified according to the type of network they use: private or public. YouTube videos or TV episodes on *Hulu.com* are obviously cases of streaming video issued over a public network, the Internet. Examples of streaming video on private networks include educational videos delivered over the private networks of schools, businesses, or other organizations. For example, a guest speaker's presentation at a college's main campus auditorium could be filmed and transmitted via live streaming to classrooms in the college's satellite campuses, all without ever leaving the college's private network.

Most, though not all, examples of streaming video take place over public networks. The following section describes a video over IP service that typically makes use of private networks.

IPTV (IP Television)

In Chapter 7 you learned about the networks that telecommunications carriers and cable companies have established to deliver high-bandwidth Internet connections to their customers. These networks are now being used to deliver digital television signals using IPTV. In fact, because of digital video's value as an added service, your local telephone company is likely investing significant sums into the hardware and software that make IPTV possible. Because telecommunications carriers are leading the way with IPTV installation, this section concentrates on their network architecture and components, but bear in mind that cable companies are investing in this technology, too.

Several elements come together to deliver digital video to consumers, as shown in Figure 11-10. Each element and its role is described next.

To begin, a telco accepts video content at a head end. The content may include signals captured from satellite video feeds, national or regional broadcasts, or local content, such as live feeds of city council meetings. Typically, this content arrives in analog format, and at the head end, an encoder converts it to digital format.

At the telco's CO (central office), one or more servers manage customer subscription information, encrypt video to comply with digital rights regulations, publish channel listing information, and associate each video input with its own channel, among other things. Also at the CO, each video channel is assigned to a multicast group.

Multicasting makes sense for delivering IPTV. First, it's a simple way of managing content delivery. For example, 2,000 of the telco's customers might choose to watch a Monday night football game. Rather than supply the video via 2,000 separate unicast transmissions, the carrier can issue one multicast transmission to the entire group of 2,000 subscribers. The second advantage to using multicasting has to do with local loop capacity. As you know,

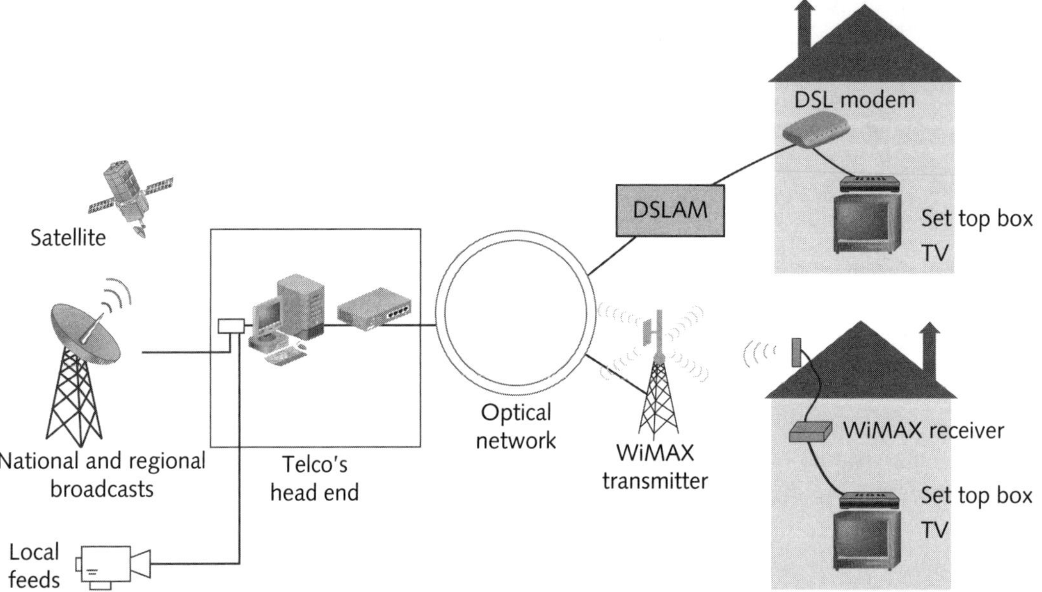

Figure 11-10 A telecommunications carrier's IPTV network

fiber to the home is still rare in the United States, and most local loops rely on copper cabling. Therefore, throughput is limited. In an environment where customers may choose from hundreds of channels, supplying all the choices to every customer at all times would overwhelm the local loop's capacity. Even supplying more than a few channels would be too much. Instead, the telco transmits only the content a subscriber has chosen. When an IPTV user changes the channel, therefore, she is merely opting out of one IP multicast group and opting into another.

Recall from Chapter 4 that multicasting is managed by IGMP (Internet Group Management Protocol). Therefore, IGMP underlies all IPTV implementations at the network layer of the OSI model. However, IGMP can only identify group members. To ensure efficient content delivery to a multicast group, routers communicate using a multicast routing protocol. Several multicast routing protocols exist. Which protocol the network uses is less important than the fact that all Layer 3 devices communicate using the same multicast routing protocol.

A compressed, digital video signal travels over the telco's network just as a data signal would. For example, if a subscriber obtains DSL service from the carrier, the signal would go from the telco's router to a DSLAM (DSL access multiplexer), either at the CO or at a remote switching facility, and then to the subscriber's DSL modem. If the subscriber obtains WiMAX service, the signal would be issued from the carrier's router to an antenna on a tower, and then to an antenna and WiMAX connectivity device at the subscriber's home. After passing through the DSL modem or home WiMAX device, the video signal is decoded and issued to a television by a **set top box**. Besides decoding the video signal, set top boxes communicate with content servers to manage video delivery. For example, the set top box delivers TV program schedules from the content server to subscribers and sends a subscriber's channel request to the content server. In cases where IPTV providers allow pay-per-view or video-on-demand programming, set top boxes manage requesting and delivering those services. Set top boxes may also allow a user to browse the Internet from his TV. Figure 11-11 shows one type of set top box.

A significant advantage of delivering video services over a telecommunications carrier's or cable company's network is that those firms control the connection end to end; this means they can better monitor and adjust its QoS (quality of service). Later in this chapter you'll

Figure 11-11 IPTV set top box

learn some techniques for controlling the QoS of voice and video transmissions. The next section describes a third popular video over IP service: videoconferencing.

Videoconferencing

So far in this chapter, you have learned about unidirectional video over IP services—that is, video delivered to a user who only watches the content but does not respond with her own. In most examples of videoconferencing, connections are full-duplex, and participants may send and receive audiovisual signals. This allows two or more people in different locations to see and hear each other in real time. As you can imagine, the cost savings and convenience of such a service make it especially attractive to organizations with offices, clients, or consultants scattered across the nation or the globe. Besides replacing face-to-face business meetings and allowing collaboration, uses for videoconferencing include the following:

- Telemedicine, or the provision of medical services from a distance. For example, a physician can view and listen to a patient in another location. Often, the patient is accompanied by a nurse or physician's assistant, who might administer tests and supply information about the patient's condition. For patients who live far from major medical facilities, this saves the cost, time, and potential health risks of having to travel long distances. NASA is developing telemedicine capabilities for diagnosing patients in space.

- Tele-education, or the exchange of information between one or more participants for the purposes of training and education. A significant benefit of tele-education is the capability for one or a few experts to share their knowledge with many students.

- Judicial proceedings, in which judges, lawyers, and defendants can conduct arraignments, hearings, or even trials while in different locations. This not only saves costs, but it may minimize potential security risks of transporting prisoners.

- Surveillance, or remotely monitoring events happening at one or more distant locations. Unlike previously mentioned videoconferencing applications, surveillance is typically unidirectional. In other words, security personnel watch (and perhaps also listen to) live video feeds from multiple locations around a building or campus, but they do not send audiovisual signals to those locations.

Hardware and software requirements for videoconferences include, at minimum, a means for each participant to generate, send, and receive audiovisual signals. This may be accomplished by workstations that have sufficient processing resources, plus cameras, microphones, and videoconferencing software to capture, encode, and transmit audiovisual signals. Instead of a workstation, viewers may use a video terminal or a **video phone**, a type of phone that includes a screen, such as the one shown in Figure 11-12. These devices can decode compressed video and interpret transport and signaling protocols necessary for conducting videoconference sessions.

When more than two people participate in a videoconference, for example, in a point-to-multipoint or multipoint-to-multipoint scenario, a **video bridge** is required. A video bridge manages multiple audiovisual sessions so that participants can see and hear each other. Video bridges may exist as a piece of hardware or as software, in the form of a conference server. For an organization that only occasionally uses videoconferencing, Internet-accessible video bridging services can be leased for a predetermined period. Organizations such as universities

Figure 11-12 Video phone

that frequently rely on videoconferencing might maintain their own conference servers or supply each auditorium, for example, with its own video bridge.

To establish and manage videoconferencing sessions, video bridges depend on signaling protocols, which are described in the following section.

Signaling Protocols

In VoIP and video over IP transmission, **signaling** is the exchange of information between the components of a network or system for the purposes of establishing, monitoring, or releasing connections as well as controlling system operations. Simply put, signaling protocols set up and manage sessions between clients. Some functions performed by signaling protocols include the following:

- Requesting a call or videoconference setup
- Locating clients on the network and determining the best routes for calls or video transmissions to follow
- Acknowledging a request for a call or videoconference setup and setting up the connection
- Managing ringing, dial tone, call waiting, and in some cases, caller ID and other telephony features
- Detecting and reestablishing dropped calls or video transmissions
- Properly terminating a call or videoconference

In the early days of VoIP, vendors developed their own, proprietary signaling protocols, which meant that if you wanted to use the Internet to call your neighbor, you and your neighbor had to use hardware or software from the same manufacturer. Now, however, most VoIP and video over IP clients and gateways use standardized signaling protocols. The following sections describe the most common of these.

On the circuit-switched portions of the PSTN, a set of standards established by the ITU known as *SS7 (Signaling System 7)* typically handles call signaling. You should be familiar with this term, as it might appear in discussions of interconnecting the PSTN with networks running VoIP.

H.323

H.323 is an ITU standard that describes an architecture and a group of protocols for establishing and managing multimedia sessions on a packet-switched network. H.323 protocols may support voice or video over IP services. Before learning about H.323 protocols, it's helpful to understand the set of terms unique to H.323 that ITU has designated. Elements of VoIP and video over IP networks you have already learned about have special names in H.323 parlance. Following are five key elements identified by H.323:

- *H.323 terminal*—Any node that provides audio, visual, or data information to another node. An IP phone, video phone, or server issuing streaming video could be considered an H.323 terminal.

- *H.323 gateway*—A device that provides translation between network devices running H.323 signaling protocols and devices running other types of signaling protocols (for example, SS7 on the PSTN).

- *H.323 gatekeeper*—The nerve center for networks that adhere to H.323. Gatekeepers authorize and authenticate terminals and gateways, manage bandwidth, and oversee call routing, accounting, and billing. Gatekeepers are optional on H.323 networks.

- *MCU (multipoint control unit)*—A computer that provides support for multiple H.323 terminals (for example, several workstations participating in a videoconference) and manages communication between them. In videoconferencing, a video bridge serves as an MCU.

- *H.323 zone*—A collection of H.323 terminals, gateways, and MCUs that are managed by a single H.323 gatekeeper. Figure 11-13 illustrates an H.323 zone comprising four terminals, one gateway, and one MCU.

Now that you understand the elements that belong to an H.323 network, you are ready to learn about the H.225 and H.245 signaling protocols, which are specified in the H.323 standard. Both protocols operate at the session layer of the OSI model. However, each performs a different function. **H.225** is the H.323 protocol that handles call or videoconference signaling. For instance, when an IP telephone user wants to make a call, the IP telephone requests a call setup (from the H.323 gateway) via H.225. The same IP telephone would use the H.225 protocol to announce its presence on the network, to request the allocation of additional bandwidth, and to indicate when it wants to terminate a call.

Another H.323 session layer protocol, **H.245**, ensures that the type of information—whether voice or video—issued to an H.323 terminal is formatted in a way that the H.323 terminal can interpret. To perform this task, H.245 first sets up logical channels between the sending

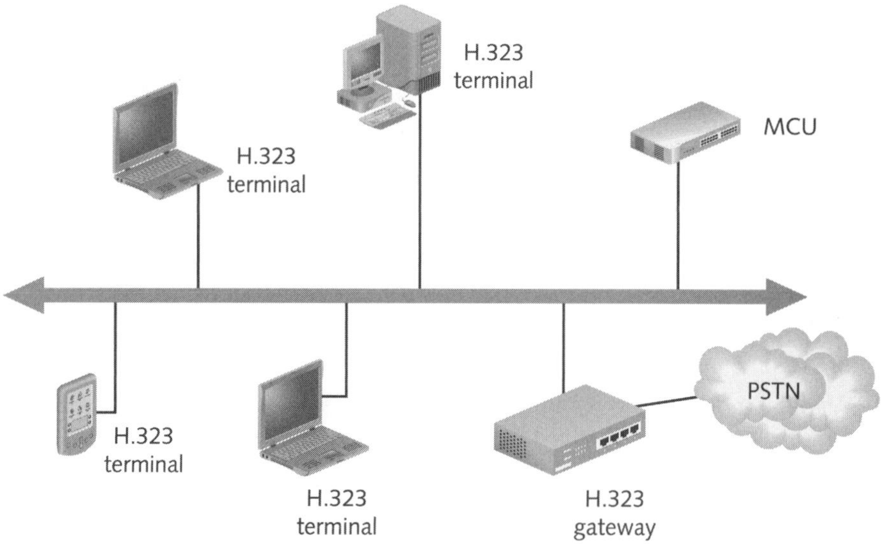

Figure 11-13 An H.323 zone

and receiving nodes. On a VoIP or video over IP network, these logical channels are identified as port numbers at each IP address. One logical channel is assigned to each transmission direction. Thus, for a call between two IP telephones, H.245 would use two separate control channels. Note that these channels are distinct from the channels used for H.225 call signaling. They are also different from channels used to exchange the actual voice or video signals (for example, the words you speak during a conversation or the pictures transmitted in a videoconference).

In addition to the H.225 and H.245 signaling protocols, the H.323 standard specifies interoperability with certain protocols at the presentation layer, such as those responsible for coding and decoding signals, and at the transport layer. Later in this chapter you'll learn about the transport layer protocols used with voice and video services.

ITU codified H.323 as an open protocol for multiservice signaling in 1996. Early versions of the H.323 protocol suffered from slow call setup, due to the volume of messages exchanged between nodes. Since that time, ITU has revised and improved H.323 standards twice. The second version of H.323, known as H.323.2, was a popular call signaling protocol on VoIP networks. The third version of H.323 has yet to be widely accepted. And after H.323 was released, another protocol for VoIP call signaling, SIP, emerged and attracted the attention of network administrators.

SIP (Session Initiation Protocol)

SIP (Session Initiation Protocol) is a protocol that performs functions similar to those performed by H.323. The version of SIP most popular today, 2.0, was codified by the IETF (in RFC 2543) in 1999 as an application layer signaling and control protocol for multiservice, packet-based networks. SIP's developers modeled it on the HTTP protocol. For example, the text-based messages that clients exchange to initiate a VoIP call are formatted like an HTTP request and rely on URL-style addresses. Developers also aimed to reuse as many existing

TCP/IP protocols as possible for managing sessions and providing enhanced services. Furthermore, they wanted SIP to be modular and specific. SIP's capabilities are limited to the following:

- Determining the location of an **endpoint**, which in SIP terminology refers to any client, server, or gateway communicating on a network; this means SIP translates the endpoint's name into its current network address

- Determining the availability of an endpoint; if SIP discovers that a client is not available, it returns a message indicating whether the client was already connected to a call or simply didn't respond

- Establishing a session between two endpoints and managing calls by adding (inviting), dropping, or transferring participants

- Negotiating features of a call or videoconference when it's established—for example, agreeing on the type of encoding both endpoints will employ

- Changing features of a call or videoconference while it's connected

SIP's functions are more limited than those performed by the protocols in the H.323 group. For example, SIP does not supply some enhanced features, such as caller ID, that H.323 does. Instead, it depends on other protocols and services to supply them.

As with H.323, a SIP network uses terms and follows a specific architecture mapped out in the standard. Components of a SIP network include the following:

- *User agent*—This is any node that initiates or responds to SIP requests.

- *User agent client*—These are end-user devices, which may include workstations, PDAs, cell phones, or IP telephones. A user agent client initiates a SIP connection.

- *User agent server*—This type of server responds to user agent clients' requests for session initiation and termination. Practically speaking, a device such as an IP telephone can act as a user agent client and server, thus allowing it to directly contact and establish sessions with other clients in a peer-to-peer fashion. As you have learned, however, peer-to-peer arrangements are undesirable because they become difficult to manage when more than a few users participate. User agent clients and user agent servers are considered user agents.

- *registrar server*—This type of server maintains a database containing information about the locations (network addresses) of each user agent in its domain. When a user agent joins a SIP network, it transmits its location information to the SIP registrar server.

- *proxy server*—This type of server accepts requests for location information from user agents, and then it queries the nearest registrar server on behalf of those user agents. If the recipient user agent is in the SIP proxy server's domain, that server will also act as a go-between for calls established and terminated between the requesting user agent and the recipient user agent. If the recipient user agent is not in the SIP proxy server's domain, the proxy server will pass on session information to a SIP redirect server. Proxy servers are optional on a SIP network.

- *redirect server*—This type of server accepts and responds to requests from user agents and SIP proxy servers for location information on recipients that belong to external domains. A redirect server does not get involved in establishing or maintaining sessions. Redirect servers are optional on SIP networks.

Net+

1.1

Figure 11-14 shows how the elements of a SIP system may be arranged on a network. In this example, user agents connect to proxy servers, which accept and forward addressing requests and make use of redirect servers to learn about user agents on other domains. For purposes of illustration, the registrar server, proxy server, and redirect server are shown as separate computers in Figure 11-14. However, on a SIP network, all might be installed on a single computer.

Many VoIP vendors prefer SIP because of its simplicity, which makes SIP easier to maintain than H.323. And because it requires fewer instructions to control a call, SIP consumes fewer processing resources than H.323. Some network engineers believe SIP also has the potential to adapt more easily to growing and changing network environments. In many cases, SIP is more flexible than H.323. For example, it is designed to work with many types of transport layer protocols, not just one. One popular system based on SIP is Asterisk, an open-source IP-PBX software package. Companies that provide telephone equipment, such as 3Com, Avaya, Cisco, and Nortel, also supply SIP software with their hardware.

SIP and H.323 regulate call signaling and control for VoIP or video over IP clients and servers. However, they do not account for communication between media gateways. This type of communication is governed by one of two protocols, MGCP or MEGACO, which are discussed in the following sections.

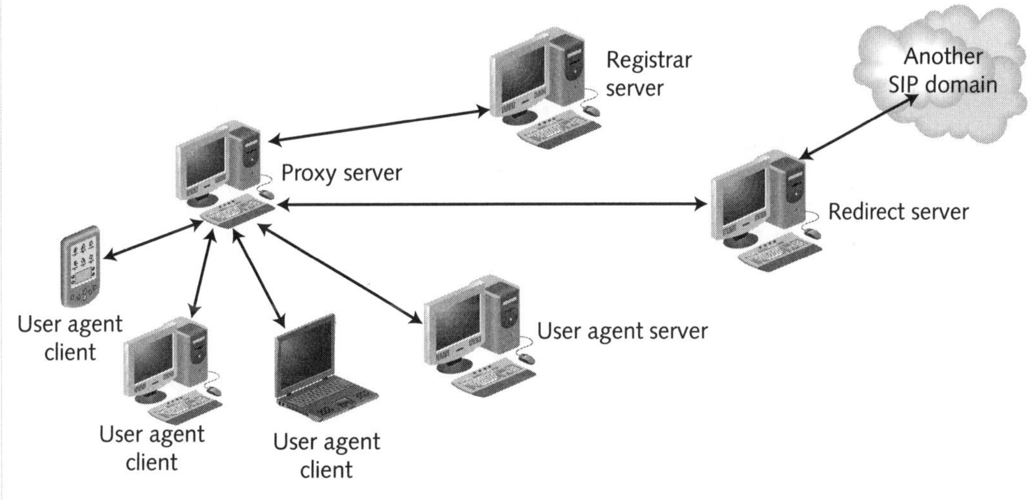

Figure 11-14 A SIP network

MGCP (Media Gateway Control Protocol) and MEGACO (H.248)

Gateways are integral to converged networks. For example, a **media gateway** accepts PSTN lines, converts the analog signals into VoIP format, and translates between SS7, the PSTN signaling protocol suite, and VoIP signaling protocols, such as H.323 or SIP. In another example, to send a real-time fax from one TCP/IP network to another, a sending fax gateway must communicate with a receiving fax gateway. A **fax gateway** is a gateway that can translate IP fax data into analog fax data and vice versa. A fax gateway can also emulate and interpret conventional fax signaling protocols when communicating with a conventional fax machine.

You have also learned that information (or "payload," such as the speech carried by a VoIP network) uses different channels from and may take different logical or physical paths than control signals. In fact, to expedite information handling, the use of separate physical paths is often preferable. The reason for this is that if media gateways are freed from having to process control signals, they can dedicate their resources (for example, ports and processors) to encoding, decoding, and translating data. As a result, they process information faster. And as you have learned, faster data processing on a converged network is particularly important, given quality and reliability concerns.

However, gateways still need to exchange and translate signaling and control information with each other so that voice and video packets are properly routed through the network. To do so, gateways rely on an intermediate device known as an **MGC (media gateway controller)**. As its name implies, an MGC is a computer that manages multiple media gateways. This means that it facilitates the exchange of call signaling information between these gateways. It also manages and disseminates information about the paths that voice or video signals take between gateways. Because it is software that performs call switching functions, an MGC is sometimes called a **softswitch**.

For example, suppose a network has multiple media gateways, all of which accept thousands of connections from both the PSTN and from private TCP/IP WAN and LAN links. When a media gateway receives a call, rather than attempting to determine how to handle the call, the gateway simply contacts the media gateway controller with a message that essentially says, "I received a signal. You figure out what to do with it next." The media gateway controller then determines which of the network's media gateways should translate the information carried by the signal. It also figures out which physical media the call should be routed over, according to what signaling protocols the call must be managed, and to what devices the call should be directed. After the media gateway controller has processed this information, it instructs the appropriate media gateways how to handle the call. The media gateways simply follow orders from the media gateway controller.

MGCs are especially advantageous on large VoIP networks—for example, at a telecommunications carrier's CO (central office). In such an environment, they make a group of media gateways appear to the outside world as one large gateway. This centralizes call control functions, which can simplify network management. Figure 11-15 illustrates this model. (Note that in this figure, as on most large networks, the media gateways supply access services.)

MGCs communicate with media gateways according to one of several protocols. The older protocol is **MGCP (Media Gateway Control Protocol)**. MGCP was developed by IETF and is now described in RFC 3435. It's commonly used on multiservice networks that support a number of media gateways. MGCP can operate in conjunction with either H.323 or SIP call signaling and control protocols.

A newer gateway control protocol is **MEGACO**. MEGACO performs the same functions as MGCP, but using different commands and processes. Like MGCP, MEGACO can operate with H.323 or SIP. Many network engineers consider MEGACO superior to MGCP because it

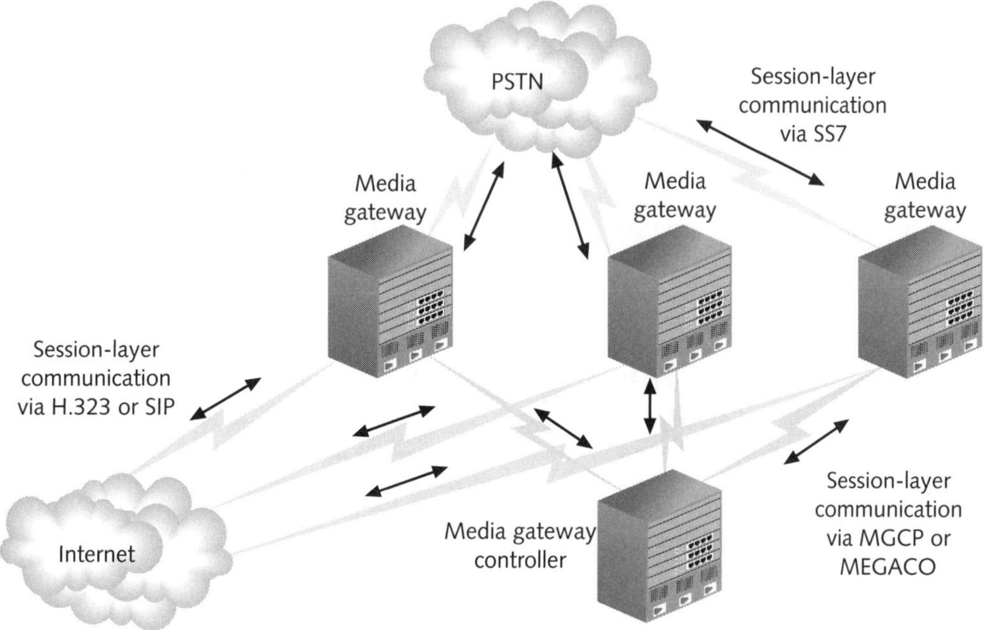

Figure 11-15 Use of an MGC (media gateway controller)

supports a broader range of network technologies, including ATM. MEGACO was developed by cooperative efforts of the ITU and IETF, and the ITU has codified the MEGACO protocol in its **H.248** standard.

Bear in mind that this chapter describes only some of the signaling protocols used on converged networks. In fact, some softphones, VoIP servers, and videoconferencing software packages (for example, Skype) use proprietary protocols, which means that these devices or applications will only work with other devices or applications that use the same proprietary protocols.

Now that you are familiar with the most popular session control protocols used on converged networks, you are ready to learn about the transport protocols that work in tandem with those session control protocols.

Transport Protocols

The protocols you just learned about only communicate information about a voice or video *session*. At the transport layer, a different set of protocols is used to actually deliver the voice or video payload—for example, the bits of encoded voice that together make up words spoken into an IP telephone.

4.5

Recall that on a TCP/IP network, the UDP and TCP protocols operate at the transport layer of the OSI model. Also recall that TCP is connection oriented; therefore, it provides some measure of delivery guarantees. UDP, on the other hand, is connectionless and does not pay attention to the order in which packets arrive or how quickly they arrive. Despite this lack of accountability, UDP is preferred over TCP for real-time applications such as telephone conversations and videoconferences because it requires less overhead and, as a result, can transport packets more quickly. In transporting voice and video signals, TCP's slower delivery of packets is intolerable. However, UDP's occasional loss of packets is tolerable—that is, as long as additional protocols are used in conjunction with UDP to make up for its faults.

RTP (Real-Time Transport Protocol)

1.1

One protocol that helps voice and video networks overcome UDP's shortcomings is the **RTP (Real-time Transport Protocol)**. RTP, which is standardized in RFC 1889, operates at the application layer of the OSI model (despite its name) and relies on UDP at the transport layer. It applies sequence numbers to indicate the order in which packets should be assembled at their destination. Sequence numbers also help to indicate whether packets were lost during transmission. In addition, RTP assigns each packet a timestamp that corresponds to when the data in the packet was sampled from the voice or video stream. This timestamp helps the receiving node to compensate for network delay and to synchronize the signals it receives.

RTP alone does not, however, provide mechanisms to detect whether or not it's successful. For that, it relies on a companion protocol, RTCP.

RTCP (Real-Time Transport Control Protocol)

RTCP (Real-time Transport Control Protocol), defined in RFC 3550 by the IETF, provides feedback on the quality of a call or videoconference to its participants. RTCP packets are transmitted periodically to all session endpoints. RTCP allows for several types of messages. For example, each sender issues information about its transmissions' NTP (Network Time Protocol) timestamps, RTP timestamps, number of packets, and number of bytes. Recipients of RTP data use RTCP to issue information about the number and percentage of packets lost and delay suffered between the sender and receiver. RTCP also maintains identifying information for RTP sources.

The value of RTCP lies in what clients and their applications do with the information that RTCP supplies. For example, if a call participant's software uses RTCP to report that an excessive number of packets are being delayed during transmission, the sender's software can adjust the rate at which it issues RTP packets.

RTCP is not mandatory on networks that use RTP. In fact, on large networks running high-bandwidth services, such as IPTV, RTCP might not be able to supply useful feedback in a timely manner. Some network administrators prefer not to use it.

It's important to realize that although RTP and RTCP can provide information about packet order, loss, and delay, they cannot do anything to correct transmission flaws. Attempts to correct these flaws, and thus improve the quality of a voice or video signal, are handled by QoS protocols, which are discussed in the following section.

QoS (Quality of Service) Assurance

Net+

4.5

Despite all the advantages to using VoIP and video over IP, it is more difficult to transmit these types of signals over a packet-switched network than it is to transmit data signals. First, more so than data transmissions, voice and video can easily be distorted by a connection's inconsistent QoS. When you talk with your friend, you need to hear his syllables in the order in which he uttered them, and preferably, without delay. When you watch a movie over the Web, you want to see the scenes sequentially and without interruption. In general, to prevent delays, disorder, and distortion, a voice or video connection requires more dedicated bandwidth than a data connection. In addition, it requires the use of techniques that ensure high QoS.

As you learned earlier, QoS is a measure of how well a network service matches its expected performance. From the point of view of a person using VoIP or video over IP, high QoS translates into an uninterrupted, accurate, and faithful reproduction of audio or visual input. Low, or poor, QoS is often cited as a key disadvantage to using VoIP or video over IP. But although early attempts at converged services sounded and looked dreadful, thanks to technology improvements, these services now achieve quality comparable to the PSTN (in the case of VoIP) and cable television (in the case of video over IP).

Network engineers have developed several techniques to overcome the QoS challenges inherent in delivering voice and video over IP. The following sections describe three of these techniques, all of which are standardized by IETF.

RSVP (Resource Reservation Protocol)

RSVP (Resource Reservation Protocol), specified in RFC 2205, is a transport layer protocol that attempts to reserve a specific amount of network resources for a transmission before the transmission occurs. In other words, assuming it is successful, RSVP will create a path between the sender and receiver that provides sufficient bandwidth for the signal to arrive without suffering delay. You can think of RSVP as a technique that addresses the QoS problem by emulating a circuit-switched connection.

To establish the path, the sending node issues a PATH statement via RSVP to the receiving node. This PATH message indicates the amount of bandwidth the sending node requires for its transmission, as well as the level of service it expects. RSVP allows for two service types: guaranteed service and controlled-load service. Guaranteed service assures that the transmission will not suffer packet losses and that it will experience minimal delay. Controlled-load service provides the type of QoS a transmission would experience if the network carried little traffic.

Each router that the PATH message traverses marks the transmission's path by noting which router the PATH message came from. This process continues until the PATH message reaches its destination. But the reservation is not yet complete. After the destination node receives the PATH message, it responds with a Reservation Request (RESV) message. The RESV message follows the same path taken by the PATH message, but in reverse. It reiterates information about bandwidth requirements that the sending node transmitted in its PATH message. It also includes information about the type of service the sending node requested. Upon receiving the RESV message, each router between the destination node and the sender allocates the requested bandwidth to the message's path. This assumes that each router is

4.5

capable of interpreting RSVP messages and has sufficient bandwidth to allocate to the transmission. If routers do not have sufficient bandwidth to allocate, they reject the reservation request.

After each router in the established path has agreed to allocate the specified amount of bandwidth to the transmission, the sending node transmits its data. It's important to note that RSVP messaging is separate from the data transmission. In other words, RSVP does not modify the packets that carry voice or video signals. Another characteristic about RSVP is that it can only specify and manage unidirectional transmission. Therefore, for two users to participate in a VoIP call or a videoconference, the resource reservation process must take place in both directions.

Because it emulates a circuit-switched path, RSVP provides excellent QoS. However, one drawback to RSVP is its high overhead. It requires a series of message exchanges before data transmission can occur. Thus, RSVP consumes more network resources than some other QoS techniques. Although RSVP might be acceptable on small networks, it is less popular on large, heavily trafficked networks. Instead, these networks use more streamlined QoS techniques, such as DiffServ.

DiffServ (Differentiated Service)

DiffServ (Differentiated Service) is a simple technique that addresses QoS issues by prioritizing traffic. It differs significantly from RSVP in that it modifies the actual IP datagrams that contain payload data. Also, it takes into account all types of network traffic, not just the time-sensitive services such as voice and video. That way, it can assign voice streams a high priority and at the same time assign unessential data streams (for example, an employee surfing the Internet on his lunch hour) a low priority. This technique offers more protection for the time-sensitive voice and video services.

To prioritize traffic, DiffServ places information in the DiffServ field in an IPv4 datagram. (For a review of the fields in an IP datagram, refer to Chapter 4.) In IPv6 datagrams, DiffServ uses a similar field known as the Traffic Class field. This information indicates to the network routers how the data stream should be forwarded. DiffServ defines two types of forwarding: **EF (Expedited Forwarding)** or **AF (Assured Forwarding)**. In EF, a data stream is assigned a minimum departure rate from a given node. This technique circumvents delays that slow normal data from reaching its destination on time and in sequence. In AF, different levels of router resources can be assigned to data streams. AF prioritizes data handling but provides no guarantee that on a busy network packets will arrive on time and in sequence. This description of DiffServ's prioritization mechanisms is oversimplified, but a deeper discussion is beyond the scope of this book.

Because of its simplicity and relatively low overhead, DiffServ is better suited to large, heavily trafficked networks than RSVP.

MPLS (Multiprotocol Label Switching)

2.5

4.5

Another QoS technique that modifies data streams at the network layer is MPLS (multiprotocol label switching). As you learned in Chapter 5, to indicate where data should be forwarded, MPLS replaces the IP datagram header with a label at the first router a data stream encounters. The MPLS label contains information about where the router should forward the packet next. Each router in the data stream's path revises the label to indicate the data's next

Net+

2.5

hop. In this manner, routers on a network can take into consideration network congestion, QoS indicators assigned to the packets, plus other criteria.

4.5

MPLS forwarding is also fast. This is because, in MPLS, a router knows precisely where to forward a packet. On a typical packet-switched network, routers compare the destination IP address to their routing tables and forward data to the node with the closest matching address. With MPLS, data streams are more likely to arrive without delay. On a network supplying clients with voice and video services, fast transmission is desirable.

A network's connectivity devices and clients must support the same set of protocols to achieve their QoS benefits. However, networks can—and often do—combine multiple QoS techniques.

Chapter Summary

- The use of a network (either public or private) to carry voice signals using the TCP/IP protocol is commonly known as VoIP (voice over IP). VoIP services can operate over any type of transmission medium and access method that support TCP/IP.

- When VoIP relies on the Internet, it is often called Internet telephony. But not all VoIP calls are carried over the Internet. In fact, VoIP over private lines is an effective and economical method of completing calls between two locations within an organization.

- An organization might use VoIP to save money on telephone calls, centralize management of voice and data services, or take advantage of customizable call features.

- Many types of clients and network designs are available with VoIP networks. Clients can be traditional analog telephones, IP telephones, or softphones (a computer running telephony software and connected to a microphone and headphones). In each case, analog voice signals are first converted to digital signals by a voice codec (coder/decoder).

- Analog VoIP clients may connect to IP networks in one of four ways: using an internal or external ATA (analog telephone adapter); connecting directly to a router or to a voice-data gateway that digitizes call information; connecting directly to an IP-PBX capable of handling both analog and digital voice connections; or connecting to an analog PBX, which then connects to a voice-data gateway.

- Digital VoIP clients typically connect to a digital PBX or other connectivity device with VoIP capabilities.

- Rather than analog telephones, most new VoIP installations use IP telephones, which transmit and receive only digital signals. To communicate on the network, each IP telephone must have a unique IP address. The IP telephone connects to an RJ-45 wall jack, like a computer workstation.

- One significant benefit to using IP telephones is their mobility. Because IP telephones are addressable over a network, they can be moved from one office to another office, connected to a wall jack, and be ready to accept or make calls.

- Rather than using traditional telephones or IP telephones, a third option is to use a computer programmed to act like an IP telephone, otherwise known as a softphone. Softphones and IP telephones provide the same calling functions; they simply connect to the network and deliver services differently. A softphone's versatile connectivity makes it an optimal VoIP solution for traveling employees and telecommuters.

- Streaming video refers to video signals that are compressed and delivered in a continuous stream. It may be made available as files stored on a streaming server for video-on-demand or as real-time feeds in live streaming. Streaming video may be delivered in a point-to-point or point-to-multipoint fashion, though both types typically use unicast transmission.

- In IPTV (IP television), television signals from broadcast or cable networks travel over packet-switched connections. Telecommunications carriers and cable companies supply IPTV over their existing networks. They accept video content from satellite feeds, national or regional broadcasters, and local sources at a head end. IPTV channels are delivered in multicast fashion to consumers, where they are decoded and issued to televisions by set top boxes.

- Videoconferencing allows multiple participants to communicate and collaborate at once through audiovisual means. To view a videoconference, each participant must have at least a video terminal or video phone that can decode compressed video and interpret signaling protocols. To send and receive audiovisual signals, participants must also have a device equipped with a camera, microphone, and video-encoding capabilities.

- Videoconferences that are point to multipoint or multipoint to multipoint rely on video bridges to manage communication among participants. Video bridges may be hardware devices dedicated to this task or software running on conference servers.

- In VoIP and video over IP transmission, signaling is the exchange of information between the components of a network or system for the purposes of establishing, monitoring, or releasing connections as well as controlling system operations.

- Voice and video over IP services depend on signaling protocols to request a call or videoconference setup, locate clients on the network and determine the best routes for calls to follow, and acknowledge a request for a call or videoconference setup. Voice and video over IP services also depend on signaling protocols to set up the connection; manage ringing, dial tone, and other telephony features; detect and reestablish dropped calls or video transmissions; and properly terminate a call or videoconference.

- H.323 is an ITU standard that describes an architecture and a group of protocols for establishing and managing multimedia sessions on a packet-switched network.

- H.225 is the protocol specified by the H.323 standard that handles call or videoconference signaling. For instance, when an IP telephone user wants to make a call, the IP telephone requests a call setup (from the H.323 gateway) via H.225.

- Another H.323 session layer protocol, H.245, ensures that the type of information—whether voice or video—issued to an H.323 terminal is formatted in a way that the H.323 terminal can interpret.

- SIP (Session Initiation Protocol) is a protocol codified by the IETF in 1999 as an application layer signaling and control protocol for multiservice, packet-based networks. SIP's developers modeled it on the HTTP protocol and aimed to reuse as many existing TCP/IP protocols as possible for managing sessions and providing enhanced services.

- SIP does not attempt to perform and control as many functions as the H.323 protocols. Its capabilities are limited to determining the location of an endpoint; determining the availability of an endpoint; establishing a session between two endpoints; managing calls by adding (inviting), dropping, or transferring participants; negotiating features of a call or videoconference when it's established; and changing features of a call or videoconference while it's connected.

- Many VoIP vendors prefer SIP because of its simplicity, which makes SIP easier to maintain than H.323. And because it requires fewer instructions to control a call, SIP consumes fewer processing resources than H.323.

- Media gateways rely on an intermediate device known as an MGC (media gateway controller) to exchange and translate signaling and control information with each other. An MGC facilitates the exchange of call signaling information between these gateways and manages and disseminates information about the paths that voice or video signals take between gateways.

- MGCs communicate with media gateways according to one of several protocols. The older protocol is MGCP (Media Gateway Control Protocol). MGCP was developed by IETF and is now described in RFC 3435.

- MEGACO performs the same functions as MGCP but uses different commands and processes. Many network engineers consider MEGACO superior to MGCP because it supports a broader range of network technologies, including ATM. The ITU has codified the MEGACO protocol in its H.248 standard.

- RTP (Real-time Transport Protocol) operates at the application layer of the OSI model and relies on UDP at the transport layer. It applies sequence numbers to indicate the order in which packets should be assembled at their destination and assigns each packet a timestamp that corresponds to when the data in the packet was sampled from the voice or video stream. This timestamp helps the receiving node to compensate for network delay and to synchronize the signals it receives.

- RTCP (Real-time Transport Control Protocol) provides feedback on the quality of a call or videoconference, such as the extent of delay or packet loss in a transmission.

- Network engineers have developed several techniques to overcome the QoS challenges inherent in delivering voice and video over IP. One, RSVP (Resource Reservation Protocol), is a transport layer protocol that attempts to reserve a specific amount of network resources for a transmission before the transmission occurs.

- DiffServ (Differentiated Service) is a simple technique that addresses QoS issues by prioritizing traffic. DiffServ places information in the DiffServ field in an IPv4 datagram. In IPv6 datagrams, DiffServ uses a similar field known as the Traffic Class field. This information indicates to the network routers how the data stream should be forwarded.

- Another QoS technique that modifies data streams at the network layer is MPLS (multiprotocol label switching). To indicate where data should be forwarded, MPLS replaces the IP datagram header with a label at the first router a data stream encounters. The MPLS label contains information about where the router should forward the packet next. Each router in the data stream's path revises the label to indicate the data's next hop. In this manner, routers on a network can take into consideration network congestion, QoS indicators assigned to the packets, plus other criteria.

Key Terms

AF (Assured Forwarding)   In the DiffServ QoS technique, a forwarding specification that allows routers to assign data streams one of several prioritization levels. AF is specified in the DiffServ field in an IPv4 datagram.

analog telephone adapter   *See* ATA.

Assured Forwarding   *See* AF.

ATA (analog telephone adapter)   An internal or externally attached adapter that converts analog telephone signals into packet-switched voice signals and vice versa.

Differentiated Service   *See* DiffServ.

DiffServ (Differentiated Service)   A technique for ensuring QoS by prioritizing traffic. DiffServ places information in the DiffServ field in an IPv4 datagram. In IPv6 datagrams, DiffServ uses a similar field known as the Traffic Class field. This information indicates to the network routers how the data stream should be forwarded.

digital PBX   *See* IP-PBX.

EF (Expedited Forwarding)   In the DiffServ QoS technique, a forwarding specification that assigns each data stream a minimum departure rate from a given node. This technique circumvents delays that slow normal data from reaching its destination on time and in sequence. EF information is inserted in the DiffServ field of an IPv4 datagram.

endpoint   In SIP terminology, any client, server, or gateway communicating on the network.

Expedited Forwarding   *See* EF.

fax gateway   A gateway that can translate IP fax data into analog fax data and vice versa. A fax gateway can also emulate and interpret conventional fax signaling protocols when communicating with a conventional fax machine.

fax over IP   *See* FoIP.

FoIP (fax over IP)   A service that transmits faxes over a TCP/IP network.

H.225   A session layer call signaling protocol defined as part of ITU's H.323 multiservice network architecture. H.225 is responsible for call or videoconference setup between nodes on a VoIP or video over IP network, indicating node status, requesting additional bandwidth and call termination.

H.245   A session layer control protocol defined as part of ITU's H.323 multiservice network architecture. H.245 is responsible for controlling a session between two nodes. For example, it ensures that the two nodes are communicating in the same format.

H.248   *See* MEGACO.

H.323   An ITU standard that describes an architecture and a suite of protocols for establishing and managing multimedia services sessions on a packet-switched network.

H.323 gatekeeper   The nerve center for networks that adhere to H.323. Gatekeepers authorize and authenticate terminals and gateways, manage bandwidth, and oversee call routing, accounting, and billing. Gatekeepers are optional on H.323 networks.

H.323 gateway   On a network following the H.323 standard, a gateway that provides translation between network devices running H.323 signaling protocols and devices running other types of signaling protocols (for example, SS7 on the PSTN).

H.323 terminal   On a network following the H.323 standard, any node that provides audio, visual, or data information to another node.

H.323 zone   A collection of H.323 terminals, gateways, and MCUs that are managed by a single H.323 gatekeeper.

Internet telephony   The provision of telephone service over the Internet.

IP-PBX   A private switch that accepts and interprets both analog and digital voice signals (although some IP-PBXs do not accept analog lines). It can connect with both traditional PSTN lines and data networks. An IP-PBX transmits and receives IP-based voice signals to and from other network connectivity devices, such as routers and gateways.

IP phone   *See* IP telephone.

IP telephone   A telephone used for VoIP on a TCP/IP-based network. IP telephones are designed to transmit and receive only digital signals.

IP telephony   *See* voice over IP.

IP television   *See* IPTV.

IPTV (IP television)   A service in which television signals from broadcast or cable networks travel over packet-switched networks.

MCU (multipoint control unit)   A computer that provides support for multiple H.323 terminals (for example, several workstations participating in a videoconference) and manages communication between them. An MCU is also known as a video bridge.

media gateway   A gateway capable of accepting connections from multiple devices (for example, IP telephones, traditional telephones, IP fax machines, traditional fax machines, and so on) and translating analog signals into packetized, digital signals, and vice versa.

Media Gateway Control Protocol   *See* MGCP.

media gateway controller   *See* MGC.

MEGACO   A protocol used between media gateway controllers and media gateways. MEGACO is poised to replace MGCP on modern converged networks, as it supports a broader range of network technologies, including ATM. Also known as H.248.

MGC (media gateway controller)   A computer that manages multiple media gateways and facilitates the exchange of call control information between these gateways.

MGCP (Media Gateway Control Protocol)   A protocol used for communication between media gateway controllers and media gateways. MGCP is defined in RFC 2507, but it was never officially adopted as a standard. MGCP is currently the most popular media gateway control protocol used on converged networks.

multipoint control unit   *See* MCU.

PBX (private branch exchange)   A telephone switch used to connect calls within a private organization.

private branch exchange   *See* PBX.

proxy server   On a SIP network, a server that accepts requests for location information from user agents and then queries the nearest registrar server on behalf of those user agents. If the recipient user agent is in the SIP proxy server's domain, that server will also act as a go-between for calls established and terminated between the requesting user agent and the recipient user agent.

Real-time Transport Control Protocol   *See* RTCP.

Real-time Transport Protocol   *See* RTP.

redirect server   On a SIP network, a server that accepts and responds to requests from user agents and SIP proxy servers for location information on recipients that belong to external domains.

registrar server   On a SIP network, a server that maintains a database containing information about the locations (network addresses) of each user agent in its domain. When a user agent joins a SIP network, it transmits its location information to the SIP registrar server.

Resource Reservation Protocol   *See* RSVP.

RSVP (Resource Reservation Protocol)   As specified in RFC 2205, a QoS technique that attempts to reserve a specific amount of network resources for a transmission before the transmission occurs.

RTCP (Real-time Transport Control Protocol)   A companion protocol to RTP, defined in RFC 3550 by the IETF, RTCP provides feedback on the quality of a call or videoconference to its participants.

RTP (Real-time Transport Protocol)   A transport layer protocol used with voice and video transmission. RTP operates on top of UDP and provides information about packet sequence to help receiving nodes detect delay and packet loss. It also assigns packets a timestamp that corresponds to when the data in the packet was sampled from the voice or video stream. This timestamp helps the receiving node synchronize incoming data.

RTP Control Protocol   *See* RTCP.

Session Initiation Protocol   *See* SIP.

set top box   In the context of IPTV, a device that decodes digital video signals and issues them to the television. Set top boxes also communicate with content servers to manage video delivery.

signaling   The exchange of information between the components of a network or system for the purposes of establishing, monitoring, or releasing connections as well as controlling system operations.

Signaling System 7   *See* SS7.

SIP (Session Initiation Protocol)   A protocol suite codified by the IETF (in RFC 2543) as a set of session layer signaling and control protocols for multiservice, packet-based networks. With few exceptions, SIP performs much the same functions as the H.323 signaling protocols perform. SIP was developed as a more efficient alternative to H.323 before H.323 was revised to expedite its call setup functions. But although SIP is more efficient, because it was released later, it has never enjoyed the same widespread usage as H.323.

softphone A computer configured to act like an IP telephone. Softphones present the caller with a graphical representation of a telephone dial pad and can connect to a network via a LAN, WAN, PPP dial-up connection, or leased line.

softswitch *See* MGC.

SS7 (Signaling System 7) A set of standards established by the ITU for handling call signaling on the PSTN (public switched telephone network).

streaming video A service in which video signals are compressed and delivered over the Internet in a continuous stream so that a user can watch and listen even before all the data has been transmitted.

toll bypass A cost-savings benefit that results from organizations completing long-distance telephone calls over their packet-switched networks, thus bypassing tolls charged by common carriers on comparable PSTN calls.

unified messaging The centralized management of multiple types of network-based communications, such as voice, video, fax, and messaging services.

user agent In SIP terminology, a user agent client or user agent server.

user agent client In SIP terminology, end-user devices such as workstations, PDAs, cell phones, or IP telephones. A user agent client initiates a SIP connection.

user agent server In SIP terminology, a server that responds to user agent clients' requests for session initiation and termination.

video bridge *See* MCU.

video-on-demand A service in which a video stored as an encoded file is delivered to a viewer upon his request.

video over IP Any type of video service, including IPTV, videoconferencing, and streaming video, that delivers video signals over packet-switched networks using the TCP/IP protocol suite.

video phone A type of phone that includes a screen and can decode compressed video and interpret transport and signaling protocols necessary for conducting videoconference sessions.

videoconferencing The real-time reception and transmission of images and audio among two or more locations.

VoATM (voice over ATM) A service that uses the ATM network access method (and ATM cells) to transmit voice signals over a network.

VoDSL (voice over DSL) A service that relies on a DSL connection to transmit packetized voice signals.

voice over ATM *See* VoATM.

voice over DSL *See* VoDSL.

voice over IP *See* VoIP.

VoIP (voice over IP) The provision of telephone service over a packet-switched network running the TCP/IP protocol suite.

Webcast A streaming video, either on demand or live, that is delivered via the Web.

Review Questions

1. Which VoIP phone type allows the exporting of call information to a billing or accounting program on the same workstation?

   a. Digital PBX

   b. Softphone

   c. Traditional telephone

   d. IP telephone

2. Which video over IP service is useful in telemedicine applications?

   a. Video-on-demand

   b. IPTV (IP television)

   c. Videoconferencing

   d. Streaming video

3. Which H.323 key element provides translation between network devices running H.323 signaling protocols and devices running other types of signaling protocols?

   a. H.323 gateway

   b. H.323 gatekeeper

   c. H.323 terminal

   d. H.323 zone

4. Which signaling protocol ensures that the type of information—whether voice or video—issued to an H.323 terminal is formatted in a way that the H.323 terminal can interpret?

   a. H.232

   b. H.325

   c. H.225

   d. H.245

5. Which transport protocol applies sequence numbers to indicate the order in which packets should be assembled at their destination?

   a. RTCP (Real-time Transport Control Protocol)

   b. RTP (Real-time Transport Protocol)

   c. RSVP (Resource Reservation Protocol)

   d. MGCP (Media Gateway Control Protocol)

6. True or false? All VoIP calls are carried over the Internet.

7. True or false? Every video over IP transmission begins with digitizing the audio and visual signals.

8. True or false? Because each IP telephone must have a unique IP address, they are stationary devices.

9. True or false? The newer MEGACO (Media Gateway Control Protocol) gateway control protocol can operate with H.323 or SIP.

10. True or false? Although RTP and RTCP can provide information about packet order, loss, and delay, they cannot do anything to correct transmission flaws.

11. ____ is the use of any network (either public or private) to carry voice signals using the TCP/IP protocol.

12. ____ is an ITU standard that describes an architecture and a group of protocols for establishing and managing multimedia sessions on a packet-switched network.

13. ____ is a VoIP call signaling protocol operating as an application layer signaling and control protocol for multiservice, packet-based networks.

14. An intermediate device, known as a(n) ____, is used to exchange and translate gateway signaling and control information so that voice and video packets are properly routed through the network.

15. ____, specified in RFC 2205, is a transport layer protocol that attempts to reserve a specific amount of network resources for a transmission before the transmission occurs.

Network Security

After reading this chapter and completing the exercises, you will be able to:

- Identify security risks in LANs and WANs and design security policies that minimize risks

- Explain how physical security contributes to network security

- Discuss hardware- and design-based security techniques

- Understand methods of encryption, such as SSL and IPSec, that can secure data in storage and in transit

- Describe how popular authentication protocols, such as RADIUS, TACACS, Kerberos, PAP, CHAP, and MS-CHAP, function

- Use network operating system techniques to provide basic security

- Understand wireless security protocols, such as WEP, WPA, and 802.11i

On the Job

Security often involves synthesizing tidbits of information from many disparate sources to form an accurate picture of what has happened. My team once responded to a report that desktop computers at a biomedical corporation were crashing, with their hard drives erased, apparently, by a virus that circumvented the company's anti-virus protections.

While examining an affected PC, we noticed that a few processes were still running—thanks to the fact that the operating system generally won't allow the deletion of files that are in use. Among these processes were several instances of svchost.exe. Closer examination revealed that one of these had the same name as the legitimate Windows executable, but was in fact an impostor: a saboteur was at work.

Using a disassembler, we determined that, every minute, the Trojan checked a folder on a server for the presence of a command file, whose contents it would execute. We built a program to monitor that directory and archive copies of any files that appeared; our program also recorded the user account that put the file there, and the name of the system from which this was done.

The account had domain administrator privileges, and this led us to examine the domain's login scripts, where we found the code that installed the Trojan on users' workstations. We wrote a second program to record the MAC address of the system when it registered its name with the DHCP server, and inspect the ARP tables from the network's switches to find the physical port to which it was connected. Then, with a building wiring diagram, we were able to track the culprit to a specific cubicle.

Finding the source of this problem involved knowledge about network infrastructure, operating systems, administration techniques, programming, and reverse-engineering. This is an extreme example, to be sure, but real-world security problems seldom confine themselves to a single technical area of specialization.

Peyton Engel
Technical Architect, CDW Corporation

In the early days of computing, when secured mainframes acted as central hosts and data repositories that were accessed only by dumb terminals with limited rights, network security was all but unassailable. As networks have become more geographically distributed and heterogeneous, however, the risk of their misuse has also increased. Consider the largest, most heterogeneous network in existence: the Internet. Because it contains millions of points of entry, millions of servers, and millions of miles of transmission paths, it is vulnerable to millions of break-ins. Because so many networks connect to the Internet, the threat of an outsider accessing an organization's network via the Internet, and then stealing or destroying data, is very real. In this chapter, you will learn how to assess your network's risks, how to manage those risks, and, perhaps most important, how to convey the importance of network security to the rest of your organization through an effective security policy.

Security Audits

Before spending time and money on network security, you should examine your network's security risks. As you learn about each risk facing your network, consider the effect that a loss or breach of data, programs, or access would have on your network. The more serious the potential consequences, the more attention you need to pay to the security of your network.

Different types of organizations have different levels of network security risk. For example, if you work for a large savings and loan institution that allows its clients to view their current loan status online, you must consider a number of risks associated with data and access. If someone obtained unauthorized access to your network, all of your customers' personal financial data could be vulnerable. On the other hand, if you work for a local car wash that is not connected to the Internet and uses its internal LAN only to track assets and sales, you may be less concerned if someone gains access to your network, because the implications of unauthorized access to your data are less dire. When considering security risks, the fundamental questions are: "What is at risk?" and "What do I stand to lose if it is stolen, damaged, or eradicated?"

Every organization should assess its security risks by conducting a **security audit**, which is a thorough examination of each aspect of the network to determine how it might be compromised. Security audits should be performed at least annually and preferably quarterly. They should also be performed after making any significant changes to the network. For each threat listed in the following sections, your security audit should rate the severity of its potential effects, as well as its likelihood. A threat's consequences may be severe, potentially resulting in a network outage or the dispersal of top-secret information, or they may be mild, potentially resulting in a lack of access for one user or the dispersal of a relatively insignificant piece of corporate data. The more devastating a threat's effects and the more likely the threat is to happen, the more rigorously your security measures should address it.

If your IT department has sufficient skills and time for routine security audits, the audits can be performed in-house. A qualified consulting company can also conduct security audits for your network. The advantage of having an objective third party, such as a consultant, analyze your network is that she might find risks that you overlooked because of your familiarity with your environment. Third-party audits may seem expensive, but if your network hosts confidential and critical data, they are well worth their cost.

In the next section, you will learn about security risks associated with people, hardware, software, and Internet access.

Security Risks

To understand how to manage network security, you first need to know how to recognize threats that your network could suffer. Not all security breaches result from a manipulation of network technology. Instead, some occur when staff members purposely or inadvertently reveal their passwords; others result from undeveloped security policies.

6.6

Many terms are used to describe those who break into data networks. A **hacker**, in the original sense of the word, is someone who masters the inner workings of computer hardware and software in an effort to better understand them. To be called a hacker used to be a compliment, reflecting extraordinary computer skills. Those who use their computer skills to destroy data or systems are technically considered **crackers**. Today, many people use the words "hacker" and "cracker" interchangeably, and many networking professionals have settled on "hacker" as a general term for hackers and crackers alike. For simplicity's sake, this chapter uses "hacker" to describe individuals who gain unauthorized access to voice or data networks, with or without malicious intent.

As you read about each security threat, think about how it could be prevented, whether it applies to your network (and if so, how damaging it might be), and how it relates to other security threats. Keep in mind that malicious and determined intruders may use one technique, which then allows them to use a second technique, which then allows them to use a third technique, and so on. For example, a hacker might discover someone's user name by watching her log on to the network; the hacker might then use a password-cracking program to access the network, where he might plant a program that generates an extraordinary volume of traffic that essentially disables the network's connectivity devices.

Risks Associated with People

By some estimates, human errors, ignorance, and omissions cause more than half of all security breaches sustained by networks. One of the most common methods by which an intruder gains access to a network is to simply ask a user for his password. For example, the intruder might pose as a technical support analyst who needs to know the password to troubleshoot a problem. This strategy is commonly called **social engineering** because it involves manipulating social relationships to gain access. A related practice is **phishing**, in which a person attempts to glean access or authentication information by posing as someone who needs that information. For example, a hacker might send an e-mail asking you to submit your user ID and password to a Web site whose link is provided in the message, claiming that it's necessary to verify your account with a particular online retailer. Following are some additional risks associated with people:

- Intruders or attackers using social engineering or snooping to obtain user passwords

- An administrator incorrectly creating or configuring user IDs, groups, and their associated rights on a file server, resulting in file and logon access vulnerabilities

- Network administrators overlooking security flaws in topology or hardware configuration

- Network administrators overlooking security flaws in the operating system or application configuration

- Lack of proper documentation and communication of security policies, leading to deliberate or inadvertent misuse of files or network access

- Dishonest or disgruntled employees abusing their file and access rights

- An unused computer or terminal being left logged on to the network, thereby providing an entry point for an intruder

- Users or administrators choosing easy-to-guess passwords

- Authorized staff leaving computer room doors open or unlocked, allowing unauthorized individuals to enter

6.6

- Staff discarding disks or backup tapes in public waste containers

- Administrators neglecting to remove access and file rights for employees who have left the organization

- Users writing their passwords on paper and then placing the paper in an easily accessible place (for example, taping it to their monitor or keyboard)

Human errors account for so many security breaches because taking advantage of them is the easiest way to circumvent network security. Imagine a man named Isaac, who was recently fired from his job at a local bank. Isaac felt he was unfairly treated, so he wants to take revenge on his employer. He still has a few friends at the bank. Even though the bank's network administrator was wise enough to deactivate Isaac's user account upon his termination, and even though the bank has a policy prohibiting employees from sharing their passwords, Isaac knows his friends' user names and passwords. Nevertheless, the bank's policy prevents former employees from walking into its offices.

How might Isaac attain his goal of deleting a month's worth of client account activity statements? Although the bank has a network security policy, employees such as Isaac's friends probably don't pay much attention to it. Isaac might walk into the bank's offices, ostensibly to meet one of his friends for lunch. While in the offices, Isaac could either sit down at a machine where his friend was still logged on or log on as his friend because he knows his friend's password. Once in the system, he could locate the account activity statements and delete them. Alternatively, if the bank allows employees to access the network remotely, Isaac might use a friend's user name and password to log on to the bank's LAN from home.

Risks Associated with Transmission and Hardware

6.5

6.6

This section describes security risks inherent in the physical, data link, and network layers of the OSI model. Recall that the transmission media, NICs, hubs, network access methods (for example, Ethernet), bridges, switches, and routers reside at these layers. At these levels, security breaches require more technical sophistication than those that take advantage of human errors. For instance, to eavesdrop on transmissions passing through a switch, an intruder must use a device such as a protocol analyzer, connected to one of the switch's ports. In the middle layers of the OSI model, it is somewhat difficult to distinguish between hardware and software techniques. For example, because a router acts to connect one type of network to another, an intruder might take advantage of the router's security flaws by sending a flood of TCP/IP transmissions to the router, thereby disabling it from carrying legitimate traffic. You will learn about software-related risks in the following section.

The following risks are inherent in network hardware and design:

- Transmissions can be intercepted. One type of attack that relies on intercepted transmissions is known as a **man-in-the-middle attack**. It can take one of several forms, but in all cases a person redirects or captures secure transmissions as they occur. For example, suppose a hacker gains control of an access point at a café that offers free Wi-Fi Internet access. She could intercept transmissions between café visitors and the access point, and, for instance, learn users' passwords or even supply users with a phony Web site that looks valid but presents clickable options capable of harming their systems. Spread-spectrum wireless and fiber-based transmissions are more difficult to intercept than wireless transmissions using only one frequency band and copper cable-based transmissions.

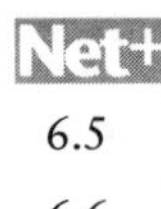

6.5

6.6

- Networks that use leased public lines, such as T1 or DSL connections to the Internet, are vulnerable to eavesdropping at a building's demarc (demarcation point), at a remote switching facility, or in a central office.

- Network hubs broadcast traffic over the entire segment, thus making transmissions more widely vulnerable to sniffing. By contrast, switches provide logical point-to-point communications, which limit the availability of data transmissions to the sending and receiving nodes. Still, intruders could physically connect to a switch or router and intercept the traffic it receives and forwards.

- Unused hub, switch, router, or server ports can be exploited and accessed by hackers if they are not disabled. A router's configuration port, accessible by Telnet, might not be adequately secured. Network administrators can test how vulnerable their servers, routers, switches, and other devices are by using a **port scanner**, or software that searches the node for open ports. The network administrator can then secure those ports revealed by the scan to be vulnerable.

- If routers are not properly configured to mask internal subnets, users on outside networks (such as the Internet) can read the private addresses.

- If routers aren't configured to drop packets that match certain, suspicious characteristics, they are more vulnerable to attack.

- Modems attached to network devices may be configured to accept incoming calls, thus opening security holes if they are not properly protected.

- Dial-in access servers used by telecommuting or remote staff might not be carefully secured and monitored.

- Computers hosting very sensitive data might coexist on the same subnet with computers open to the general public.

- Passwords for switches, routers, and other devices might not be sufficiently difficult to guess, changed frequently, or worse, might be left at their default value.

Imagine that a hacker wants to bring a library's database and mail servers to a halt. Suppose also that the library's database is public and can be searched by anyone on the Web. The hacker might begin by scanning ports on the database server to determine which ones have no protection. If she found an open port on the database server, the hacker might connect to the system and deposit a program that would, a few days later, damage operating system files. Or, she could launch a heavy stream of traffic that overwhelms the database server and prevents it from functioning. She might also use her newly discovered access to determine the root password on the system, gain access to other systems, and launch a similar attack on the library's mail server, which is attached to the database server. In this way, even a single mistake on one server (not protecting an open port) can open vulnerabilities on multiple systems.

Risks Associated with Protocols and Software

Like hardware, networked software is only as secure as you configure it to be. This section describes risks inherent in the higher layers of the OSI model, such as the transport, session, presentation, and application layers. As noted earlier, the distinctions between hardware and software risks are somewhat blurry because protocols and hardware operate in tandem. For example, if a router is improperly configured, a hacker could exploit the openness of TCP/IP to gain access to a network. NOSs (network operating systems) and application software present different risks. In many cases, their security is compromised by a poor understanding

Net+

6.5

6.6

of file access rights or simple negligence in configuring the software. Remember—even the best encryption, computer room door locks, security policies, and password rules make no difference if you grant the wrong users access to critical data and programs.

The following are some risks pertaining to networking protocols and software:

- TCP/IP contains several security flaws. For example, IP addresses can be falsified easily, checksums can be thwarted, UDP requires no authentication, and TCP requires only weak authentication.

- Trust relationships between one server and another might allow a hacker to access the entire network because of a single flaw.

- NOSs might contain "back doors" or security flaws that allow unauthorized users to gain access to the system. Unless the network administrator performs regular updates, a hacker may exploit these flaws.

- If the NOS allows server operators to exit to a command prompt, intruders could run destructive command-line programs.

- Administrators might accept the default security options after installing an operating system or application. Often, defaults are not optimal. For example, the default user name that enables someone to modify anything in Windows Server 2008 is *administrator*. This default is well known, so if you leave the default user name as *administrator*, you have given a hacker half the information he needs to access and obtain full rights to your system.

- Transactions that take place between applications, such as databases and Web-based forms, might allow interception.

To understand the risks that arise when an administrator accepts the default settings associated with a software program, consider the following scenario. Imagine that you have invited a large group of computer science students to tour your IT department. While you're in the computer room talking about subnetting, a bored student standing next to a Windows Vista workstation that is logged on to the network decides to find out which programs are installed on the workstation. He discovers that this workstation has the SQL Server administrator software installed. Your organization uses a SQL Server database to hold all of your employees' salaries, addresses, and other confidential information. The student knows a little about SQL Server, including the facts that the default administrator user ID is called *sa*, and that, by default, no password is created for this ID when someone installs SQL Server. He tries connecting to your SQL Server database with the *sa* user ID and no password. Because you accepted the defaults for the program during its installation, within seconds the student is able to gain access to your employees' information. He could then change, delete, or steal any of the data.

Risks Associated with Internet Access

Although the Internet has brought computer crime, such as hacking, to the public's attention, network security is more often compromised "from the inside" than from external sources. Nevertheless, the threat of outside intruders is very real.

Users need to be careful when they connect to the Internet. Even the most popular Web browsers sometimes contain bugs that permit scripts to access their systems while they're connected to the Internet, potentially for the purpose of causing damage. Users must also be careful about providing information while browsing the Web. Some sites will capture that information to use

6.5

6.6

when attempting to break into systems. Bear in mind that hackers are creative and typically revel in devising new ways of breaking into systems. As a result, new Internet-related security threats arise frequently. By keeping software current, staying abreast of emerging security threats, and designing your Internet access wisely, users can prevent most of these threats.

Common Internet-related security issues include the following:

- A firewall may not provide adequate protection if it is configured improperly. For example, it may allow outsiders to obtain internal IP addresses, and then use those addresses to pretend that they have authority to access your internal network from the Internet—a process called **IP spoofing**. Alternatively, a firewall may not be configured correctly to perform even its simplest function—preventing unauthorized packets from entering the LAN from outside. (You will learn more about firewalls later in this chapter.) Correctly configuring a firewall is one of the best means to protect your internal LAN from Internet-based attacks.

- When a user Telnets or FTPs to your site over the Internet, her user ID and password are transmitted in plain text—that is, unencrypted. Anyone monitoring the network (that is, running a network monitor program or a hacking program specially designed to capture logon data) can pick up the user ID and password and use it to gain access to the system.

- Hackers may obtain information about your user ID from newsgroups, mailing lists, or forms you have filled out on the Web.

- While users remain logged on to Internet chat sessions, they may be vulnerable to other Internet users who might send commands to their machines that cause the screen to fill with garbage characters and require them to terminate their chat sessions. This type of attack is called **flashing**.

- After gaining access to your system through the Internet, a hacker may launch denial-of-service attacks. A **denial-of-service attack** occurs when a system becomes unable to function because it has been deluged with data transmissions or otherwise disrupted. This incursion is a relatively simple attack to launch. (For example, a hacker could create a looping program that sends thousands of e-mail messages to your system per minute.) One specific type of denial-of-service attack, known as a **smurf attack**, occurs when a hacker issues a flood of broadcast ping messages. In this case, the originating source address of the attack is spoofed to appear as a known host on the network. Because it's a broadcast transmission, all hosts on the subnet receive the ping messages and then generate more ICMP traffic by responding to it. Denial-of-service attacks can also result from malfunctioning software. Regularly upgrading software is essential to maintaining network security.

Now that you understand the variety of risks facing networks, you are ready to learn about policies that help mitigate these risks.

An Effective Security Policy

6.6

Network security breaches can be initiated from within an organization, and many depend on human errors. This section describes how to minimize the risk of break-ins by communicating with and managing the users in your organization via a thoroughly planned security policy.

A **security policy** identifies your security goals, risks, levels of authority, designated security coordinator and team members, responsibilities for each team member, and responsibilities for each employee. In addition, it specifies how to address security breaches. It should not state exactly which hardware, software, architecture, or protocols will be used to ensure security, nor how hardware or software will be installed and configured. These details change from time to time and should be shared only with authorized network administrators or managers.

Security Policy Goals

Before drafting a security policy, you should understand why the security policy is necessary and how it will serve your organization. Typical goals for security policies are as follows:

- Ensure that authorized users have appropriate access to the resources they need.

- Prevent unauthorized users from gaining access to the network, systems, programs, or data.

- Protect sensitive data from unauthorized access, both from within and from outside the organization.

- Prevent accidental damage to hardware or software.

- Prevent intentional damage to hardware or software.

- Create an environment in which the network and systems can withstand and, if necessary, quickly respond to and recover from any type of threat.

- Communicate each employee's responsibilities with respect to maintaining data integrity and system security.

A company's security policy need not pertain exclusively to computers or networks. For example, it might state that each employee must shred paper files that contain sensitive data or that each employee is responsible for signing in his visitors at the front desk and obtaining a temporary badge for them. Noncomputer-related aspects of security policies are beyond the scope of this chapter, however.

After defining the goals of your security policy, you can devise a strategy to attain them. First, you might form a committee composed of managers and interested parties from a variety of departments, in addition to your network administrators. The more decision-making people you can involve, the more supported and effective your policy will be. This committee can assign a security coordinator, who will then drive the creation of a security policy.

To increase the acceptance of your security policy in your organization, tie security measures to business needs and clearly communicate the potential effects of security breaches. For example, if your company sells clothes over the Internet and a two-hour outage (as could be caused by a hacker who uses IP spoofing to gain control of your systems) could cost the company $1 million in lost sales, make certain that users and managers understand this fact. If they do, they are more likely to embrace the security policy.

A security policy must address an organization's specific risks. To understand your risks, you should conduct a security audit that identifies vulnerabilities and rates both the severity of each threat and its likelihood of occurring, as described earlier in this chapter. After risks

are identified, the security coordinator should assign one person the responsibility for addressing that threat.

Security Policy Content

After you have identified risks and assigned responsibilities for managing them, you are ready to outline the policy's content. Subheadings for the policy outline might include the following: Password policy; Software installation policy; Confidential and sensitive data policy; Network access policy; E-mail use policy; Internet use policy; Modem use policy; Remote access policy; Policies for connecting to remote locations, the Internet, and customers' and vendors' networks; Policies for use of laptops and loaner machines; and Computer room access policy. Although compiling all of this information might seem daunting, the process ensures that everyone understands the organization's stance on security and the reasons it is so important.

The security policy should explain to users what they can and cannot do and how these measures protect the network's security. Clear and regular communication about security policies makes them more acceptable and better understood. One idea for making security policies more sustainable is to distribute a "security newsletter" that keeps security issues fresh in everyone's mind. Perhaps the newsletter could highlight industry statistics about significant security breaches and their effect on the victimized organizations.

Another tactic is to create a separate section of the policy that applies only to users. Within the users' section, divide security rules according to the particular function or part of the network to which they apply. This approach makes the policy easier for users to read and understand; it also prevents them from having to read through the entire document. For example, in the "Passwords" section, guidelines might include: "Users may not share passwords with friends or relatives"; "users must choose passwords that exceed six characters and are composed of both letters and numbers"; and "users should choose passwords that bear no resemblance to a spouse's name, pet's name, birth date, anniversary, or other widely available information."

A security policy should also define what *confidential* means to the organization. In general, information is confidential if it could be used by other parties to impair an organization's functioning, decrease customers' confidence, cause a financial loss, damage an organization's status, or give a significant advantage to a competitor. However, if you work in an environment such as a hospital, where most data is sensitive or confidential, your security policy should classify information in degrees of sensitivity that correspond to how strictly its access is regulated. For example, top-secret data may be accessible only by the organization's CEO and vice presidents, whereas confidential data may be accessible only to those who must modify or create it (for example, doctors or hospital accountants).

Response Policy

Finally, a security policy should provide for a planned response in the event of a security breach. The response policy should identify the members of a response team, all of whom should clearly understand the security policy, risks, and measures in place. Each team member should accept a role with certain responsibilities. The security response team should regularly rehearse its defense by participating in a security threat drill. Suggested team roles include:

- *Dispatcher*—The person on call who first notices or is alerted to the problem. The dispatcher notifies the lead technical support specialist and then the manager. She creates a record for the incident, detailing the time it began, its symptoms, and any other

6.6

pertinent information about the situation. The dispatcher remains available to answer calls from clients or employees or to assist the manager.

- *Manager*—This team member coordinates the resources necessary to solve the problem. If in-house technicians cannot handle the break-in, the manager finds outside assistance. The manager also ensures that the security policy is followed and that everyone within the organization is aware of the situation. As the response ensues, the manager continues to monitor events and communicate with the public relations specialist.

- *Technical support specialist*—This team member focuses on only one thing: solving the problem as quickly as possible. After the situation has been resolved, the technical support specialist describes in detail what happened and helps the manager find ways to avert such an incident in the future. Depending on the size of the organization and the severity of the incident, this role may be filled by more than one person.

- *Public relations specialist*—If necessary, this team member learns about the situation and the response and then acts as the official spokesperson for the organization to the public.

After resolving a problem, the team reviews what happened, determines how the problem might have been prevented, and then implements those measures to prevent future problems. A security policy alone can't guard against intruders. Network administrators must also attend to physical, network design, and NOS vulnerabilities, as described in the following sections.

Physical Security

6.5

An important element in network security is restricting physical access to its components. At the very least, only authorized networking personnel should have access to computer rooms. If computer rooms are not locked, intruders may steal equipment or sabotage software and hardware. For example, a malicious visitor could slip into an unsecured computer room and take control of a server where an administrator is logged on, and then he could steal data or reformat the server's hard disk. Although a security policy defines who has access to the computer room, locking the computer room is necessary to keep unauthorized individuals out.

It isn't only the computer room that must be secured. Think of all the points at which your systems or data could be compromised: switches in a wiring closet, an unattended workstation at someone's desk, an equipment room or entrance facility where your leased line to the Internet terminates, or a storage room for archived data and backup tapes. If a wiring closet is left unlocked, for example, a prankster could easily enter, grab a handful of wires, and pull them out of the patch panels.

Locks may be either physical or electronic. Many large organizations require authorized employees to wear electronic access badges. These badges can be programmed to allow their owner access to some, but not all, rooms in a building. Figure 12-1 depicts a typical badge access security system.

A less expensive alternative to the electronic badge access system consists of locks that require entrants to punch a numeric code to gain access. For added security, these electronic locks can be combined with key locks. A more expensive solution involves **bio-recognition access**, in which a device scans an individual's unique physical characteristics, such as the color patterns in her iris or the geometry of her hand, to verify her identity. On a larger scale, organizations

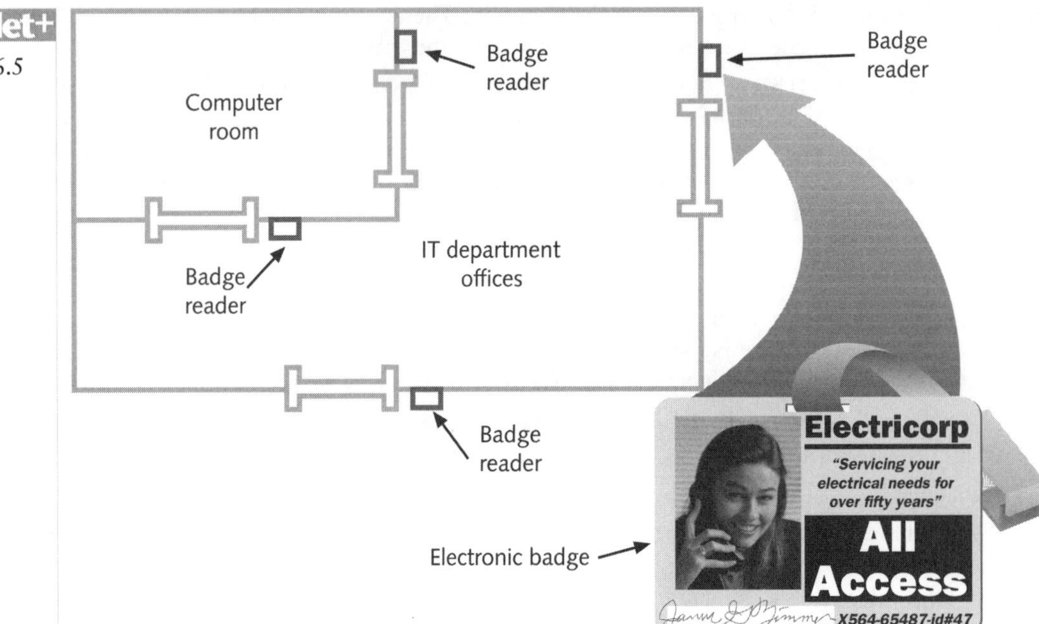

Figure 12-1 Badge access security system

may regulate entrance through physical barriers to their campuses, such as gates, fences, walls, or landscaping.

Many IT departments also use closed-circuit TV systems to monitor activity in secured rooms. Surveillance cameras can be placed in computer rooms, telco rooms, supply rooms, and data storage areas, as well as facility entrances. A central security office might display several camera views at once, or it might switch from camera to camera. The video footage generated from these cameras is usually saved for a time in case it's needed in a security breach investigation or prosecution.

As with other security measures, the most important way to ensure physical security is to plan for it. You can begin your planning by asking questions related to physical security checks in your security audit. Relevant questions include the following:

- Which rooms contain critical systems or data and must be secured?

- Through what means might intruders gain access to the facility, computer room, telecommunications room, wiring closet, or data storage areas (including doors, windows, adjacent rooms, ceilings, temporary walls, hallways, and so on)?

- How and to what extent are authorized personnel granted entry? (Do they undergo background or reference checks? Is their need for access clearly justified? Are their hours of access restricted? Who ensures that lost keys or ID badges are reported?)

- Are employees instructed to ensure security after entering or leaving secured areas (for example, by not propping open doors)?

- Are authentication methods (such as ID badges) difficult to forge or circumvent?

- Do supervisors or security personnel make periodic physical security checks?

6.5

- Are all combinations, codes, or other access means to computer facilities protected at all times, and are these combinations changed frequently?

- Do you have a plan for documenting and responding to physical security breaches?

Also consider what you might stand to lose if someone salvaged computers you discarded. To guard against the threat of information being stolen from a decommissioned hard disk, you can run a specialized disk sanitizer program to not only delete the hard drive's contents but also make file recovery impossible. Alternatively, you can remove the disk from the computer and erase its contents using a magnetic hard disk eraser. Some security professionals even advise physically destroying a disk by pulverizing or melting it to be certain data is unreadable.

Security in Network Design

6.3

6.5

Addressing physical access to hardware and connections is just one part of a comprehensive security approach. Even if you restrict access to computer rooms, teach employees how to select secure passwords, and enforce a security policy, breaches may still occur due to poor LAN or WAN design. In this section, you will learn how to address some security risks via intelligent network design.

The optimal way to prevent external security breaches from affecting your LAN is not to connect your LAN to the outside world. This option is impractical in today's business environment, however. The next best protection is to restrict access at every point where your LAN connects to the rest of the world. This principle forms the basis of hardware- and design-based security.

Router Access Lists

Before a malicious intruder on another network can gain access to files on your network's server, he must traverse a switch or router. Although devices such as firewalls, described later in this chapter, provide more security than any simple switch or router configuration, manipulating these configurations affords a small degree of security. This section describes a fundamental way to control traffic through routers.

A router's main function is to examine packets and determine where to direct them based on their network layer addressing information. Thanks to a router's **ACL** (**access control list**, also known as an **access list**), routers can also decline to forward certain packets. An ACL instructs the router to permit or deny traffic according to one or more of the following variables:

- Network layer protocol (for example, IP or ICMP)

- Transport layer protocol (for example, TCP or UDP)

- Source IP address

- Source netmask

- Destination IP address

- Destination netmask

- TCP or UDP port number

Each time a router receives a packet, it examines the packet and refers to its ACL to determine whether the packet meets criteria for permitting or denying travel on the network. If a

6.3
6.5

packet's characteristics match a variable that's flagged as "deny" in the ACL, the router drops the packet. Otherwise, it forwards the packet.

An access list may contain many different statements. For example, it might include a statement to deny all traffic from source addresses whose netmask is 255.255.255.255 and another statement to deny all traffic destined for TCP port 23. If a router contains several interfaces, each interface can be assigned a separate ACL. In addition, different ACLs may be associated with inbound and outbound traffic. Naturally, the more statements a router must scan (in other words, the longer the ACL), the more time it takes a router to act, and, therefore, the slower the router's overall performance.

Intrusion Detection and Prevention

5.2
6.1

While a router's access list can block certain types of traffic, a more proactive security measure involves detecting suspicious network activity. In the world outside of computer networks, a business owner might install closed-circuit TV cameras above her business's entrance and electrical sensors on its doors to monitor attempts to enter the building. Similarly, a network administrator might use techniques to monitor and flag any unauthorized attempt to access an organization's secured network resources using an **IDS (intrusion-detection system)**. An IDS exists as software running on a dedicated IDS device or on another device, such as a server or switch, that also performs other functions. Major vendors of networking hardware, such as Cisco, HP, Juniper Networks, and Lucent, sell IDS devices. Examples of popular open-source IDS software, which can run on virtually any network-connected machine, include TripWire and Snort.

3.3

One technique that an IDS may use to monitor traffic traveling by a switch is port mirroring. In **port mirroring**, one port is configured to send a copy of all its traffic to a second port on the switch. The second port issues the copied traffic to a monitoring program.

5.2
6.1

An IDS is one example of traffic monitoring. In Chapter 13 you'll learn about other examples.

IDS software can be configured to detect many types of suspicious traffic patterns, including those typical of denial-of-service or smurf attacks, for example. For detecting unauthorized attempts to access a network, its sensors are installed at the edges of the network, the places where a protected, internal network intersects with a public network. A network's protective perimeter is known as the **DMZ**, or **demilitarized zone**. Alternatively, an IDS can operate on a host to monitor suspicious attempts to log on or access the host's resources.

One drawback to using an IDS at a network's DMZ is the number of false positives it can log. For instance, it might interpret multiple logon attempts of a legitimate user who's forgotten his password as a security threat. If the IDS is configured to alert the network manager each time such an event occurs, the network manager might be overwhelmed with such warnings and eventually ignore all the IDS's messages. Therefore, to be useful, IDS software must be thoughtfully customized. In addition, to continue to guard against new threats, IDS software must be updated and rules of detection reevaluated regularly.

While an IDS can only detect and log suspicious activity, an **IPS (intrusion-prevention system)** can react when alerted to such activity. For example, if a hacker's attempt to flood the network with traffic is detected, the IPS can detect the threat and prevent that traffic, based on its originating IP address, from flowing to the network. Thereafter the IPS will quarantine that malicious user. At the same time, the IPS continues to allow valid traffic to pass. An IPS can protect entire networks or only certain hosts. Many vendors sell devices that integrate both IDS and IPS functions. As with an IDS, an IPS must be carefully configured to avoid an abundance of false alarms.

Figure 12-2 illustrates the placement of an IDS/IPS device on a private network that's connected to the Internet. Note that such a device may be positioned between the firewall and the external network, as shown in Figure 12-2, or behind the firewall.

Intrusion-protection systems were originally designed as a more comprehensive traffic analysis and protection tool than firewalls, which are discussed next. However, firewalls have evolved, and as a result, the differences between a firewall and an IPS have diminished.

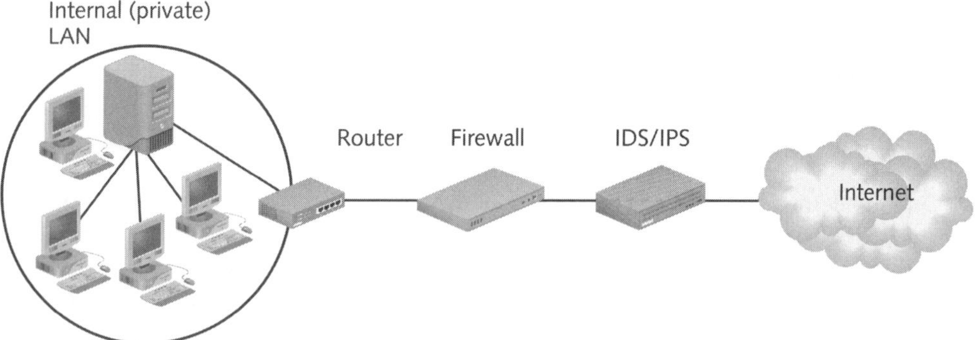

Figure 12-2 Placement of an IDS/IPS on a network

Firewalls

A firewall is a specialized device, or a computer installed with specialized software, that selectively filters or blocks traffic between networks. A firewall typically involves a combination of hardware and software and may reside between two interconnected private networks or, more typically, between a private network and a public network (such as the Internet), as shown in Figure 12-3. This is an example of a **network-based firewall**, so named because it protects an entire network. Figure 12-4 shows a firewall designed for use in a business with

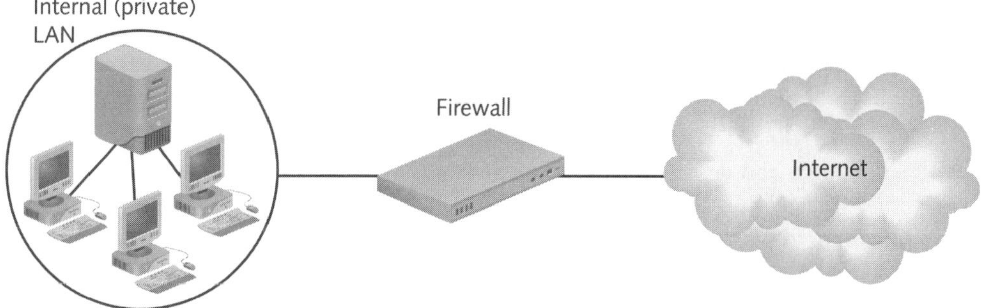

Figure 12-3 Placement of a firewall between a private network and the Internet

6.1

6.2

Figure 12-4 Firewall

many users. Other types of firewalls, known as **host-based firewalls,** only protect the computer on which they are installed.

Many types of firewalls exist, and they can be implemented in different ways. To understand secure network design and to qualify for Network+ certification, you should recognize which functions firewalls can provide, where they can appear on a network, and how to determine what features you need in a firewall.

The simplest form of a firewall is a **packet-filtering firewall,** which is a router (or a computer installed with software that enables it to act as a router) that examines the header of every packet of data it receives to determine whether that type of packet is authorized to continue to its destination. If a packet does not meet the filtering criteria, the firewall prevents the packet from continuing. However, if a packet does meet filtering criteria, the firewall allows that packet to pass through to the network connected to the firewall. Packet-filtering firewalls are also called **screening firewalls.** (In fact, nearly all routers can be configured to act as packet-filtering firewalls.) Examples of software that enables a computer to act as a packet-filtering firewall include IP Tables (for Linux systems), Checkpoint Firewall Technologies' Firewall-1, and Symantec Enterprise Firewall.

In addition to blocking traffic on its way *into* a LAN, packet-filtering firewalls can block traffic attempting to *exit* a LAN. One reason for blocking outgoing traffic is to stop worms from spreading. For example, if you are running a Web server, which in most cases only needs to respond to incoming requests and does not need to initiate outgoing requests, you could configure a packet-filtering firewall to block certain types of outgoing transmissions initiated by the Web server. In this way, you help prevent spreading worms that are designed to attach themselves to Web servers and propagate themselves to other computers on the Internet.

Often, firewalls ship with a default configuration designed to block the most common types of security threats. In other words, the firewall may be preconfigured to accept or deny certain types of traffic. However, many network administrators choose to customize the firewall settings, for example, blocking additional ports or adding criteria for the type of traffic that may travel in or out of ports. Some common criteria a packet-filtering firewall might use to accept or deny traffic include the following:

- Source and destination IP addresses
- Source and destination ports (for example, ports that supply TCP/UDP connections, FTP, Telnet, ARP, ICMP, and so on)
- Flags set in the IP header (for example, SYN or ACK)
- Transmissions that use the UDP or ICMP protocols

6.1

6.2

6.3

- A packet's status as the first packet in a new data stream or a subsequent packet

- A packet's status as inbound to or outbound from your private network

Based on these options, a network administrator could configure his firewall, for example, to prevent any IP address that does not begin with "196.57," the network ID of the addresses on his network, from accessing the network's router and servers. Furthermore, he could disable—or block—certain well-known ports, such as the FTP ports (20 and 21), through the router's configuration. Blocking ports prevents *any* user from connecting to and completing a transmission through those ports. This technique is useful to further guard against unauthorized access to the network. In other words, even if a hacker could spoof an IP address that began with *196.57*, he could not access the FTP ports (which are notoriously insecure) on the firewall. Ports can be blocked not only on firewalls, but also on routers, servers, or any device that uses ports. For example, if you established a Web server for testing but did not want anyone in your organization to connect to your Web pages through his or her browsers, you could block port 80 on that server.

For greater security, you can choose a firewall that performs more complex functions than simply filtering packets. Among the factors to consider when making your decision are the following:

- Does the firewall support encryption? (You will learn more about encryption later in this chapter.)

- Does the firewall support user authentication?

- Does the firewall allow you to manage it centrally and through a standard interface (for example, by using SNMP)?

- How easily can you establish rules for access to and from the firewall?

- Does the firewall support filtering at the highest layers of the OSI model, not just at the data link and transport layers? For example, **content-filtering firewalls** can block designated types of traffic based on application data contained within packets. A school might configure its firewall to prevent responses from a Web site with questionable content from reaching the client that requested the site.

- Does the firewall provide logging and auditing capabilities, such as IDS or IPS?

- Does the firewall protect the identity of your internal LAN's addresses from the outside world?

- Can the firewall monitor a data stream from end to end, rather than simply examine each packet individually? If it can view a data stream, it's known as a **stateful firewall**. If not, it's known as a **stateless firewall**. Stateless firewalls perform more quickly than stateful firewalls, but they are not as sophisticated.

You will recognize examples of firewall placement in most VPN architectures. For example, you might design a VPN that uses the Internet to connect your Houston and Denver offices. To ensure that only traffic from Houston can access your Denver LAN through an external connection, you could install a packet-filtering firewall between the Denver LAN and the Internet. Further, you could configure the firewall to accept incoming traffic only from IP addresses that match the IP addresses on your Houston LAN. In a way, the firewall acts like a bouncer at a private club who checks everyone's ID and ensures that only club members enter through the door. In the case of the Houston-Denver VPN, the firewall discards any

6.1

6.2

6.3

data packets that arrive at the Denver firewall and *do not* contain source IP addresses that match those of Houston's LAN.

Because you must tailor a firewall to your network's needs, you cannot simply purchase one, install it between your private LAN and the Internet, and expect it to offer much security. Instead, you must consider what type of traffic you want to filter and then configure the firewall accordingly. It may take weeks to achieve the best configuration—not so strict that it prevents authorized users from transmitting and receiving necessary data, yet not so lenient that you risk security breaches. Further complicating the matter is that you may need to create exceptions to the rules. For example, suppose that your human resources manager is working from a conference center in Salt Lake City while recruiting new employees and needs to access the Denver server that stores payroll information. In this instance, the Denver network administrator might create an exception to allow transmissions from the human resources manager's workstation's IP address to reach that server. In the networking profession, creating an exception to the filtering rules is called "punching a hole" in the firewall.

Because packet-filtering firewalls operate at the network layer of the OSI model and examine only network addresses, they cannot distinguish between a user who is trying to breach the firewall and a user who is authorized to do so. For example, your organization might host a Web server, which necessitates accepting requests for port 80 on that server. In this case, a packet-filtering firewall, because it only examines the packet header, could not distinguish between a harmless Web browser and a hacker attempting to manipulate his way through the Web site to gain access to the network. For higher-layer security, a firewall that can analyze data at higher layers is required. The next section describes this kind of device.

Proxy Servers

3.2

One approach to enhancing the security of the network and transport layers provided by firewalls is to combine a packet-filtering firewall with a proxy service. A **proxy service** is a software application on a network host that acts as an intermediary between the external and internal networks, screening all incoming and outgoing traffic. The network host that runs the proxy service is known as a **proxy server**. (A proxy server may also be called an **application layer gateway**, an **application gateway**, or simply, a **proxy**.) Proxy servers manage security at the application layer of the OSI model. To understand how they work, think of the secure data on a server as the president of a country and the proxy server as the secretary of state. Rather than have the president risk her safety by leaving the country, the secretary of state travels abroad, speaks for the president, and gathers information on the president's behalf. In fact, foreign leaders may never actually meet the president. Instead, the secretary of state acts as her proxy. In a similar way, a proxy server represents a private network to another network (usually the Internet).

Although a proxy server appears to the outside world as an internal network server, in reality it is merely another filtering device for the internal LAN. One of its most important functions is preventing the outside world from discovering the addresses of the internal network. For example, suppose your LAN uses a proxy server, and you want to send an e-mail message from your workstation to your mother via the Internet. Your message would first go to the proxy server. (Depending on the configuration of your network, you may or may not have to log on separately to the proxy server first.) The proxy server would repackage the data frames that make up the message so that, rather than your workstation's IP address being the source, the proxy server inserts its own IP address as the source. Next, the proxy server passes your repackaged data to the packet-filtering firewall. The firewall verifies that the source IP address in your packets is valid (that it came from the proxy server) and then sends your message to the Internet. Examples of proxy server software include Squid (for use on UNIX or Linux systems) and Microsoft Internet Security and Acceleration (ISA) Server 2000, an optional service for Windows 2000 Server and Windows Server 2003 servers. Microsoft's proxy server software for Windows Server 2008, called Microsoft Forefront Threat Management Gateway, was still under development at the time this was written. Figure 12-5 depicts how a proxy server might fit into a WAN design.

Proxy servers can also improve performance for users accessing resources external to their network by caching files. For example, a proxy server situated between a LAN and an external Web server can be configured to save recently viewed Web pages. The next time a user on the LAN wants to view one of the saved Web pages, content is provided by the proxy server. This eliminates the time required to travel over a WAN and retrieve the content from the external Web server.

Often, firewall and proxy server features are combined in one device. In other words, you might purchase a firewall and be able to configure it not only to block certain types of traffic from entering your network but also to modify the addresses in the packets leaving your network.

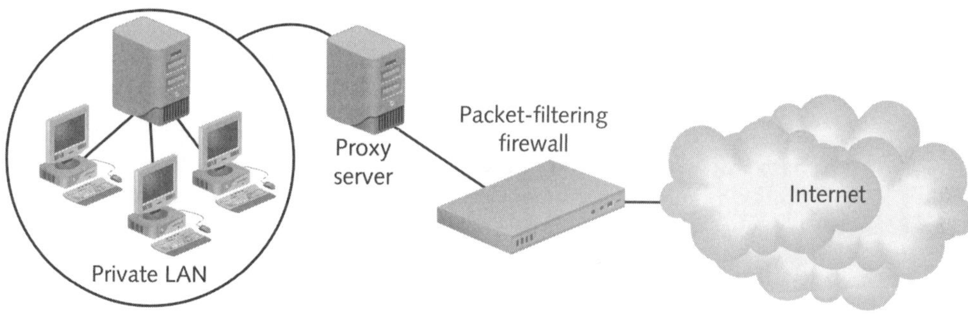

Figure 12-5 A proxy server used on a WAN

NOS (Network Operating System) Security

Regardless of whether you run your network on a Microsoft, Macintosh, Linux, or UNIX NOS, you can implement basic security by restricting what users are authorized to do on a network. Every network administrator should understand which resources on the server all users need to access. The rights conferred to all users are called public rights, because anyone can have them, and exercising them presents no security threat to the network. In most cases, public rights are very limited. They may include privileges to view and execute programs from the server and to read, create, modify, delete, and execute files in a shared data directory.

In addition, network administrators need to group users according to their security levels and assign additional rights that meet the needs of those groups. As you know, creating groups simplifies the process of granting rights to users. For example, if you work in the IT department at a large college, you will most likely need more than one person to create new user

IDs and passwords for students and faculty. Naturally, the staff in charge of creating new user IDs and passwords needs the rights to perform this task. You could assign the appropriate rights to each staff member individually, but a more efficient approach is to put all of the personnel in a group and then assign the appropriate rights to the group as a whole.

Logon Restrictions

In addition to restricting users' access to files and directories on the server, a network administrator can constrain the ways in which users can access the server and its resources. The following is a list of additional restrictions that network administrators can use to strengthen the security of their networks:

- *Time of day*—Some user accounts may be valid only during specific hours—for example, between 8:00 a.m. and 5:00 p.m. Specifying valid hours for an account can increase security by preventing any account from being used by unauthorized personnel after hours.

- *Total time logged on*—Some user accounts may be restricted to a specific number of hours per day of logged-on time. Restricting total hours in this way can increase security in the case of temporary user accounts. For example, suppose that your organization offers an Adobe Photoshop training class to a group of high school students one afternoon, and the Photoshop program and training files reside on your staff server. You might create accounts that could log on for only four hours on that day.

- *Source address*—You can specify that user accounts may log on only from certain workstations or certain areas of the network (that is, domains or segments). This restriction can prevent unauthorized use of user names from workstations outside the network.

- *Unsuccessful logon attempts*—Hackers might repeatedly attempt to log on under a valid user name for which they do not know the password. As the network administrator, you can set a limit on how many consecutive unsuccessful logon attempts from a single user ID the server will accept before blocking that ID from even attempting to log on.

Another security technique that can be enforced by a network administrator through the NOS is the selection of secure passwords. The following section discusses the importance and characteristics of choosing a secure password.

Passwords

Choosing a secure password is one of the easiest and least expensive ways to guard against unauthorized access. Unfortunately, too many people prefer to use an easy-to-remember password. If your password is obvious to you, however, it may also be easy for a hacker to figure out. The following guidelines for selecting passwords should be part of your organization's security policy. It is especially important for network administrators to choose difficult passwords, to keep passwords confidential, and to change them frequently.

Tips for making and keeping passwords secure include the following:

- Always change system default passwords after installing new programs or equipment. For example, after installing a router, the default administrator's password on the router might be set by the manufacturer to be "1234" or the router's model number.

- Do not use familiar information, such as your name, nickname, birth date, anniversary, pet's name, child's name, spouse's name, user ID, phone number, address, or any other words or numbers that others might associate with you.

Net+

6.5

- Do not use any word that might appear in a dictionary. Hackers can use programs that try a combination of your user ID and every word in a dictionary to gain access to the network. This is known as a **dictionary attack,** and it is typically the first technique a hacker uses when trying to guess a password (besides asking the user for her password).

- Make the password longer than eight characters—the longer, the better. Some operating systems require a minimum password length (often, eight characters), and some might also restrict the password to a maximum length.

- Choose a combination of letters and numbers; add special characters, such as exclamation marks or hyphens, if allowed. Also, if passwords are case sensitive, use a combination of uppercase and lowercase letters.

- Do not write down your password or share it with others.

- Change your password at least every 60 days, or more frequently, if desired. If you are a network administrator, establish controls through the NOS to force users to change their passwords at least every 60 days. If you have access to sensitive data, change your password even more frequently.

- Do not reuse passwords after they have expired.

- Use different passwords for different applications. For example, choose separate passwords for your e-mail program, online banking, remote access connection, dial-up connection, and so on. That way, if someone learns one of your passwords, she won't necessarily be able to access all of your secured accounts.

Password guidelines should be clearly communicated to everyone in your organization through your security policy. Although users might grumble about choosing a combination of letters and numbers and changing their passwords frequently, you can assure them that the company's financial and personnel data is safer as a result. No matter how much your colleagues protest, do not back down from your password requirements. Many companies mistakenly require employees only to use a password, and don't help them choose a good one. This oversight increases the risk of security breaches.

Encryption

Net+

6.3

Encryption is the use of an algorithm to scramble data into a format that can be read only by reversing the algorithm—that is, by decrypting the data. The purpose of encryption is to keep information private. Many forms of encryption exist, with some being more secure than others. Even as new forms of encryption are developed, new ways of cracking their codes emerge, too.

Encryption is the last means of defense against data theft. In other words, if an intruder has bypassed all other methods of access, including physical security (for instance, he has broken into the telecommunications room) and network design security (for instance, he has defied a firewall's packet-filtering techniques), data may still be safe if it is encrypted. Encryption can protect data stored on a medium, such as a hard disk, or in transit over a communications channel. To protect data, encryption provides the following assurances:

- Data was not modified after the sender transmitted it and before the receiver picked it up.

- Data can only be viewed by its intended recipient (or at its intended destination).

- All of the data received at the intended destination was truly issued by the stated sender and not forged by an intruder.

The following sections describe data encryption techniques used to protect data stored on or traveling across networks.

Key Encryption

The most popular kind of encryption algorithm weaves a **key**, or a random string of characters, into the original data's bits—sometimes several times in different sequences—to generate a unique data block. The scrambled data block is known as **ciphertext**. The longer the key, the less easily the ciphertext can be decrypted by an unauthorized system. For example, a 128-bit key allows for 2^{128} possible character combinations, whereas a 16-bit key allows for 2^{16} possible character combinations. Hackers may attempt to crack, or discover, a key by using a **brute force attack**, which means simply trying numerous possible character combinations to find the key that will decrypt encrypted data. (Typically, a hacker runs an application to carry out the attack.) Through a brute force attack, a hacker could discover a 16-bit key quickly and without using sophisticated computers but would have difficulty discovering a 128-bit key.

Adding 1 bit to an encryption key makes it twice (2^1 times) as hard to crack. For example, a 129-bit key would be twice as hard to crack as a 128-bit key. Similarly, a 130-bit key would be four (2^2) times harder to crack than a 128-bit key.

The process of key encryption is similar to what happens when you finish a card game, place your five-card hand into the deck, and then shuffle the deck numerous times. After shuffling, it might take you a while to retrieve your hand. If you shuffled your five cards into four decks of cards at once, it would be even more difficult to find your original hand. In encryption, theoretically only the user or program authorized to retrieve the data knows how to unshuffle the ciphertext and compile the data in its original sequence. Figure 12-6 provides a

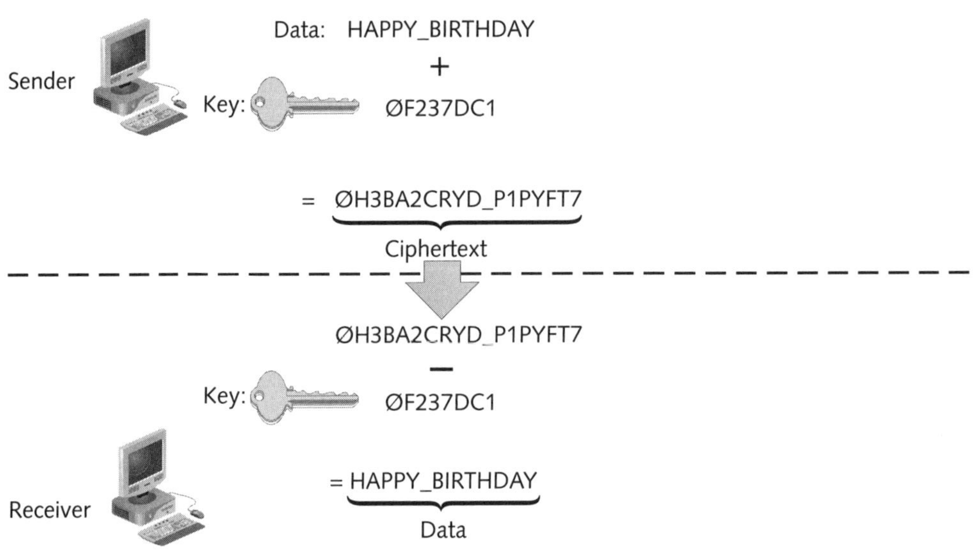

Figure 12-6 Key encryption and decryption

Net+
6.3

simplified view of key encryption and decryption. Note that actual key encryption does not simply weave a key into the data once, but rather inserts the key, shuffles the data, shuffles the key, inserts another copy of the shuffled key into the shuffled data, shuffles the data again, and so on for several iterations.

Keys are randomly generated, as needed, by the software that manages the encryption. For example, an e-mail program or a Web browser program may be capable of generating its own keys to encrypt data. In other cases, special encryption software is used to generate keys. This encryption software works with other types of software, such as word-processing or spreadsheet programs, to encrypt data files before they are saved or transmitted.

Private Key Encryption Key encryption can be separated into two categories: private key and public key encryption. In **private key encryption**, data is encrypted using a single key that only the sender and the receiver know. Private key encryption is also known as **symmetric encryption**, because the same key is used during both the encryption and decryption of the data.

Suppose Leon wants to send a secret message to Mia via private encryption. Assume he has chosen a private key. Next, he must share his private key with Mia, as shown in step 1 of Figure 12-7. Then Leon runs a program that encrypts his message by combining it with his private key, as shown in step 2. Next, Leon sends Mia the encrypted message, as shown in step 3. After Mia receives Leon's encrypted message, she runs a program that uses Leon's private key to decrypt the message, as shown in step 4. The result is that Mia can read the original message Leon wrote.

The most popular private, or symmetric, key encryption is based on **DES** (pronounced *dez*), which stands for **Data Encryption Standard**. DES, which uses a 56-bit key, was developed by IBM in the 1970s. When DES was released, a 56-bit key was secure; however, now such a key could be cracked within days, given sufficient computer power. For greater security,

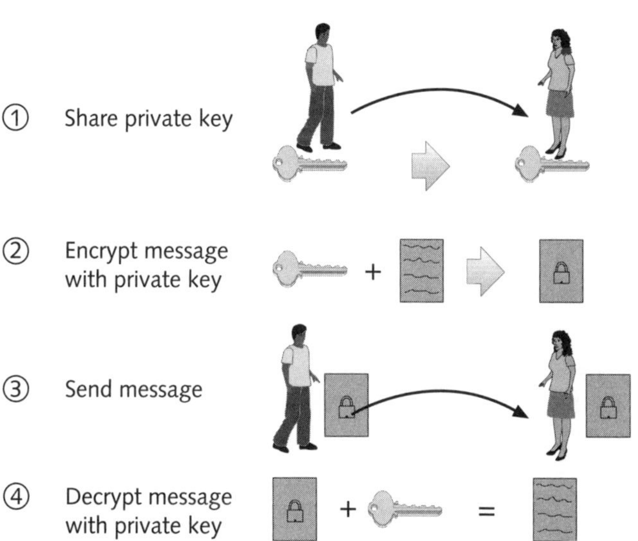

Figure 12-7 Private key encryption

the modern implementation of DES weaves a 56-bit key through data three times, using two or three different keys. This implementation is known as **Triple DES (3DES)**.

A more recent private key encryption standard is the **AES (Advanced Encryption Standard)**, which weaves keys of 128, 160, 192, or 256 bits through data multiple times. The algorithm used in the most popular form of AES is known as **Rijndael**, after its two Belgian inventors, Dr. Vincent Rijmen and Dr. Joan Daemen. AES is considered more secure than DES and much faster than Triple DES. AES has replaced DES in situations such as military communications, which must have the highest level of security.

The problem with private key encryption is that the sender must somehow share his key with the recipient. For example, Leon could call Mia and tell her his key, or he could send it to her in an e-mail message. But neither of these methods is very secure. To overcome this potential vulnerability, a method of associating publicly available keys with private keys was developed. This method is called public key encryption.

Public Key Encryption In **public key encryption**, data is encrypted using two keys: One is a key known only to a user (that is, a private key), and the other is a public key associated with the user. A user's public key can be obtained the old-fashioned way—by asking that user—or it can be obtained from a third-party source, such as a public key server. A **public key server** is a publicly accessible host (such as a server on the Internet) that freely provides a list of users' public keys, much as a telephone book provides a list of peoples' phone numbers.

Figure 12-8 illustrates the process of public key encryption.

For example, suppose that Mia wants to use public key encryption to send Leon a message via the Internet. Assume Leon already established a private and a public key, as shown in step 1 of Figure 12-8. He stores his public key on a key server on the Internet, as shown in step 2, and keeps his private key to himself. Before Mia can send Leon a message, she must know his public key. Leon tells Mia where she can find his public key, as shown in step 3. Next, Mia writes Leon a message, retrieves his public key from the public key server, and then uses her encryption software to scramble her message with Leon's public key, as shown in step 4. Mia sends her encrypted message to Leon over the Internet, as shown in step 5. When Leon receives the message, his software recognizes that the message has been encrypted with his public key. In other words, the public key has an association with the private key. A message that has been encrypted with Leon's public key can only be decrypted with his private key. The program then prompts Leon for his private key to decrypt the message, as shown in step 6. To respond to Mia in a publicly encrypted message, Leon must obtain Mia's public key. Then the steps illustrated in Figure 12-8 are repeated, with Leon and Mia's roles reversed.

The combination of a public key and a private key is known as a **key pair**. In the private key encryption example discussed previously, Leon has a key pair, but only he knows his private key, whereas the public key is available to people, like Mia, who want to send him encrypted messages. Because public key encryption requires the use of two different keys, it is also known as **asymmetric encryption**.

Due to their semipublic nature, public keys are more vulnerable than private keys, and, therefore, public key algorithms generally use longer keys. The first public, or asymmetric, key algorithm, called **Diffie-Hellman**, was released in 1975 by its creators, Whitfield Diffie

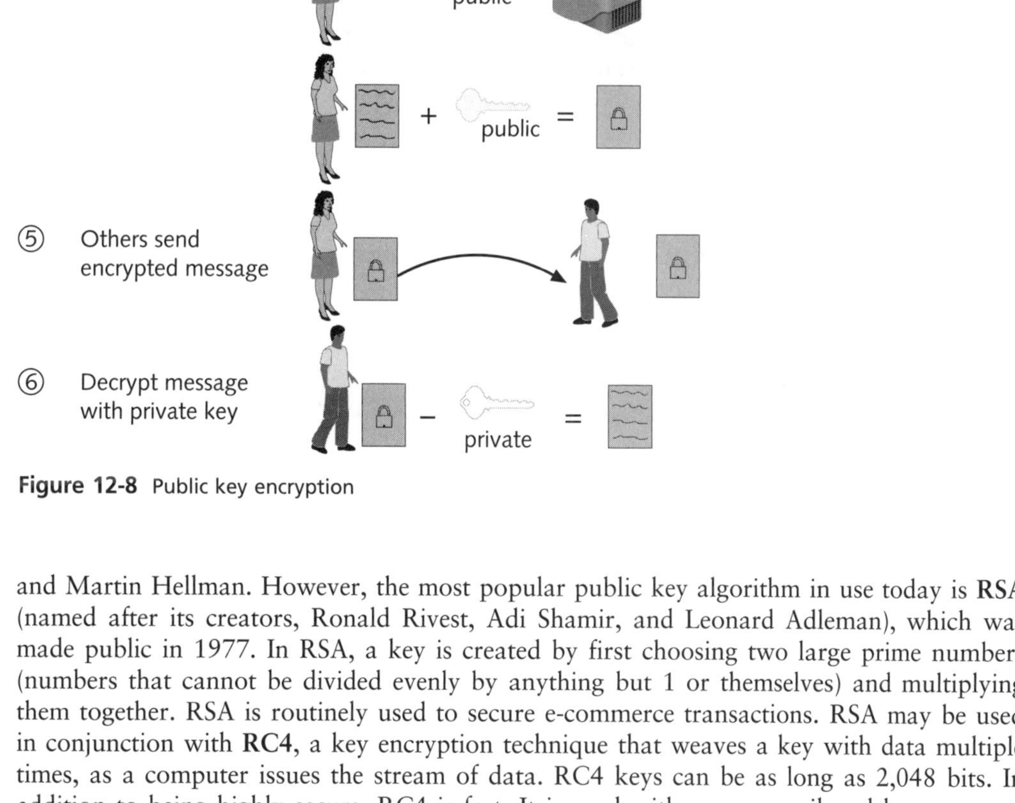

Figure 12-8 Public key encryption

and Martin Hellman. However, the most popular public key algorithm in use today is **RSA** (named after its creators, Ronald Rivest, Adi Shamir, and Leonard Adleman), which was made public in 1977. In RSA, a key is created by first choosing two large prime numbers (numbers that cannot be divided evenly by anything but 1 or themselves) and multiplying them together. RSA is routinely used to secure e-commerce transactions. RSA may be used in conjunction with **RC4**, a key encryption technique that weaves a key with data multiple times, as a computer issues the stream of data. RC4 keys can be as long as 2,048 bits. In addition to being highly secure, RC4 is fast. It is used with many e-mail and browser programs, including Lotus Notes and Netscape.

With the abundance of private and public keys, not to mention the number of places where each may be kept, users need easier key management. One answer to this problem is using digital certificates. A **digital certificate** is a password-protected and encrypted file that holds an individual's identification information, including a public key. In the context of digital

6.3

certificates, the individual's public key verifies the sender's digital signature. An organization that issues and maintains digital certificates is known as a **CA (certificate authority)**. For example, on the Internet, certificate authorities such as VeriSign will, for a fee, keep your digital certificate on their server and ensure to all who want to send encrypted messages to you (for example, an order via your e-commerce site) that the certificate is indeed yours. The use of certificate authorities to associate public keys with certain users is known as **PKI (public key infrastructure)**.

The following sections detail specific methods of encrypting data as it is transmitted over a network. These methods use one or more of the encryption algorithms discussed in this section.

PGP (Pretty Good Privacy)

You have probably exchanged e-mail messages over the Internet without much concern for what happens with your message between the time you send it and when your intended recipient picks it up. In addition, you have probably picked up e-mails from friends without thinking that they might *not* be from your friends, but rather from other users who are impersonating your friends over the Internet. In fact, typical e-mail communication is a highly insecure form of data exchange. The contents of a message are usually sent in clear (that is, unencrypted) text, which makes it readable by anyone who can capture the message on its way from you to your recipient. In addition, a person with malicious intentions can easily pretend he is someone else. For example, if your e-mail address is *joe@trinketmakers.com*, someone else could assume your address and send messages that appear to be sent by *joe@trinketmakers.com*. To secure e-mail transmissions, a computer scientist named Phil Zimmerman developed PGP in the early 1990s. **PGP (Pretty Good Privacy)** is a public key encryption system that can verify the authenticity of an e-mail sender and encrypt e-mail data in transmission. PGP, which is now administered at MIT, is freely available as both an open source and a proprietary software package. Since its release, it has become the most popular tool for encrypting e-mail. However, PGP can also be used to encrypt data on storage devices (for example, a hard disk) or with applications other than e-mail (for example, IP telephony).

SSL (Secure Sockets Layer)

SSL (Secure Sockets Layer) is a method of encrypting TCP/IP transmissions—including Web pages and data entered into Web forms—en route between the client and server using public key encryption technology. If you trade stocks or purchase goods on the Web, for example, you are most likely using SSL to transmit your order information. SSL is popular and used widely. The most recent versions of Web browsers, such as Firefox and Internet Explorer, include SSL client support in their software.

If you have used the Web, you have probably noticed that URLs for most Web pages begin with the HTTP prefix, which indicates that the request is handled by TCP/IP port 80 using the HTTP protocol. When Web page URLs begin with the prefix **HTTPS** (which stands for **HTTP over Secure Sockets Layer or HTTP Secure**), they require that their data be transferred from server to client and vice versa using SSL encryption. HTTPS uses the TCP port number 443, rather than port 80. After an SSL connection has been established between a Web server and client, the client's browser indicates this by showing a padlock in the lower-right corner of the screen in the browser's status bar, in the URL text box, or elsewhere. (Some older browser versions might not display the padlock, but almost all popular contemporary browsers do.)

Each time a client and server establish an SSL connection, they also establish a unique **SSL session**, or an association between the client and server that is defined by an agreement on a specific set of encryption techniques. An SSL session allows the client and server to continue to exchange data securely as long as the client is still connected to the server. An SSL session is created by the SSL handshake protocol, one of several protocols within SSL, and perhaps the most significant. As its name implies, the **handshake protocol** allows the client and server to authenticate (or introduce) each other and establishes terms for how they will securely exchange data. For example, when you are connected to the Web and you decide to open your bank's account access URL, your browser initiates an SSL connection with the handshake protocol. The handshake protocol sends a special message to the server, called a **client_hello** message, which contains information about what level of security your browser is capable of accepting and what type of encryption your browser can decipher (for example, RSA or Diffie-Hellman). The client_hello message also establishes a randomly generated number that uniquely identifies your client and another number that identifies your SSL session. The server responds with a **server_hello** message that confirms the information it received from your client and agrees to certain terms of encryption based on the options your client supplied. Depending on the Web server's preferred encryption method, the server may choose to issue your browser a public key or a digital certificate at this time. After the client and server have agreed on the terms of encryption, they begin exchanging data.

SSL was originally developed by Netscape. Since that time, the IETF has attempted to standardize SSL in a protocol called **TLS (Transport Layer Security)**. Besides standardizing SSL for use with software from multiple vendors, IETF aims to create a version of SSL that encrypts UDP as well as TCP transmissions. TLS, which is supported by modern Web browsers, uses slightly different encryption algorithms than SSL, but otherwise it is very similar to the most recent version of SSL.

SSH (Secure Shell)

Earlier in this book, you learned about Telnet, the TCP/IP utility that provides remote connections to hosts. For example, if you were a network administrator working at one of your company's satellite offices and had to modify the configuration on a router at the home office, you could telnet to the router (over a VPN, for example) and run commands to modify its configuration. However, Telnet provides little security for establishing a connection (authenticating) and no security for transmitting data (encryption). **SSH (Secure Shell)** is a collection of protocols that does both. With SSH, you can securely log on to a host, execute commands on that host, and copy files to or from that host. SSH encrypts data exchanged throughout the session. It guards against a number of security threats, including unauthorized access to a host, IP spoofing, interception of data in transit (even if it must be transferred via intermediate hosts), and **DNS spoofing**, in which a hacker forges name server records to falsify his host's identity. Depending on the version, SSH may use DES, Triple DES, RSA, Kerberos, or another, less common encryption algorithm or method.

SSH was developed by SSH Communications Security, and use of their SSH implementation requires paying for a license. However, open source versions of the protocol suite, such as **OpenSSH**, are available for most computer platforms. To form a secure connection, SSH must be running on both the client and server. Like Telnet, the SSH client is a utility that can be run at the shell prompt on a UNIX or Linux system or at the command prompt on a Windows-based system. Other versions of the program come with a graphical interface. The SSH suite of protocols is included with all modern UNIX and Linux distributions and with

Mac OS X Server and Mac OS X client operating systems. For Windows-based computers, you need to download a freeware SSH client, such as PuTTY.

Before you can establish a secure SSH connection, you must generate a public key and a private key on your client workstation by running the `ssh keygen` command (or by choosing the correct menu options in a graphical SSH program). The keys are saved in two different, encrypted files on your hard disk. Next, you must transfer the public key to an authorization file on the host to which you want to connect. Finally, you are ready to connect to the host via SSH. On a computer running UNIX or Linux, this is accomplished by running the `slogin -l` *username hostname* command, where *username* is your client user name and *hostname* is the name of the host to which you are trying to connect. The client and host then exchange public keys, and if both can be authenticated, the connection is completed. On a Windows-based computer, follow the menu options in the SSH client application.

SSH is highly configurable. For example, it can be configured to use one of several types of encryption for data en route between the client and host. It can be configured to require that the client enter a password in addition to a key. It can also be configured to perform **port forwarding**, which means it can redirect traffic that would normally use an insecure port (such as FTP) to an SSH-secured port. This allows you to use SSH for more than simply logging on to a host and manipulating files. With port forwarding you could, for example, exchange HTTP traffic with a Web server via a secured SSH connection.

SCP (Secure CoPy) and SFTP (Secure File Transfer Protocol)

An extension to OpenSSH is the **SCP (Secure CoPy)** utility, which allows you to copy files from one host to another securely. SCP replaces insecure file copy protocols such as FTP, which do not encrypt user names, passwords, or data while transferring them. Most modern OpenSSH packages, such as those supplied with the UNIX, Linux, and Macintosh OS X (client and server version) operating systems, include the SCP utility. Not all freeware SSH programs available for Windows include SCP, but separate, freeware SCP applications, such as WinSCP, exist.

SCP is simple to use. At the shell prompt of a UNIX or Linux system, type `scp` *filename1 filename2*, where *filename1* is the name of the file on the source host and *filename2* is the name of the file on the target host. Suppose you are copying a file from a server to your client workstation. In that case, you also need to include your user name on the server and the server's host name in the command, as follows:

`scp` *userid@hostname:filename1 filename2*

In this command, *userid* is your user name on the server, *hostname* is the server's fully qualified host name, *filename1* is the name of the file on the server, and *filename2* is what you want to call the file on your client workstation. On a Windows-based system, follow the menu options in your SSH or SCP client for copying files with SCP.

If your system uses the proprietary version of SSH, available from SSH Communications Security, you need to use **SFTP (Secure File Transfer Protocol)** to copy files rather than SCP. SFTP is slightly different from SCP, in that it does more than copy files. Like FTP, SFTP first establishes a connection with a host and then allows a remote user to browse directories, list files, and copy files. To open an SFTP connection from a UNIX or Linux system, type `sftp` *hostname* at a shell prompt, where *hostname* is the fully qualified host name of the computer to which you want to connect. To copy a file, type `get` *filename1*

Net+
6.5

filename2, where *filename1* is the name of the file on the source computer and *filename2* is what you want to call the file on the target computer. To close the SFTP connection, type `quit` and then press Enter. On a Windows-based system, follow the menu options in the SSH or SFTP client for copying files with SFTP.

The following section describes another technique for encrypting data in transit on a network.

Net+ IPSec (Internet Protocol Security)

6.3

The **IPSec (Internet Protocol Security)** protocol defines encryption, authentication, and key management for TCP/IP transmissions. It is an enhancement to IPv4 and is native to the newer IPv6 standard. IPSec is somewhat different from other methods of securing data in transit. Rather than apply encryption to a stream of data, IPSec actually encrypts data by adding security information to the header of all IP packets. In effect, IPSec transforms the data packets. To do so, IPSec operates at the network layer (Layer 3) of the OSI model.

IPSec accomplishes authentication in two phases. The first phase is key management, and the second phase is encryption. **Key management** refers to the way in which two nodes agree on common parameters for the keys they will use. IPSec relies on **IKE (Internet Key Exchange)** for its key management. IKE is a service that runs on UDP port 500. After IKE has established the rules for the type of keys two nodes will use, IPSec invokes its second phase, encryption. In this phase, two types of encryption may be used: **AH (authentication header)** and **ESP (Encapsulating Security Payload)**. It is not important to know the inner workings of these services to qualify for Network+ certification, but you should be aware that both types of encryption provide authentication of the IP packet's data payload through public key techniques. In addition, EPS encrypts the entire IP packet for added security.

Net+
6.1
6.3

IPSec can be used with any type of TCP/IP transmission. However, it most commonly runs on routers or other connectivity devices in the context of VPNs. As you learned in Chapter 7, VPNs are used to transmit private data over public networks. Therefore, they require strict encryption and authentication to ensure that data is not compromised. On networks where more than a few simultaneous VPN connections must be maintained, a specialized device known as a **VPN concentrator** can be positioned at the edge of the private network to establish VPN connections, as shown in Figure 12-9. VPN concentrators authenticate VPN clients

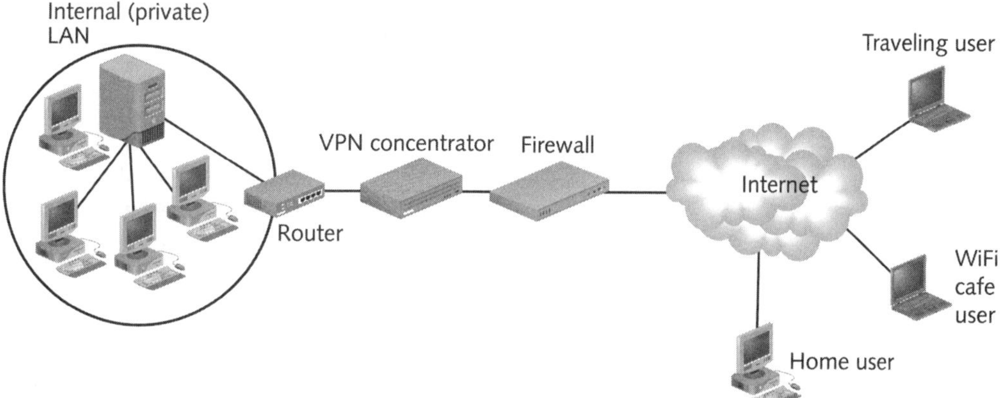

Figure 12-9 Placement of a VPN concentrator on a WAN

6.3

and establish tunnels for VPN connections. Their support of specific tunneling protocols, authentication mechanisms, and encryption algorithms varies from one manufacturer and model to another. Some support only IPSec or SSL, while others support both, for example. Some also provide enhanced features such as packet filtering.

Authentication Protocols

6.4

You have learned that authentication is the process of verifying a user's credentials (typically a user name and password) to grant the user access to secured resources on a system or network. **Authentication protocols** are the rules that computers follow to accomplish authentication. Several types of authentication protocols exist. They vary according to which encryption schemes they rely on and the steps they take to verify credentials. The following sections describe some common authentication protocols in more detail.

RADIUS and TACACS

In environments in which many simultaneous dial-up connections must be supported and their user IDs and passwords managed, a service called **RADIUS (Remote Authentication Dial-In User Service)** might be used to authenticate users. RADIUS is a service defined by the IETF that runs over UDP and provides centralized network authentication and accounting for multiple users. RADIUS can operate as a software application on a remote access server or on a computer dedicated to this type of authentication, called a **RADIUS server**. A RADIUS server does not replace functions performed by the remote access server, but communicates with the access server to manage user logons. RADIUS is frequently used with dial-up networking connections.

RADIUS servers are highly scalable, as they can attach to pools containing hundreds of modems. Many Internet service providers use a RADIUS server to allow their subscribers to dial in to their network and gain access to the Internet. Other organizations employ it as a central authentication point for mobile or remote users. RADIUS is also more secure than a simple remote access solution because its method of authentication prevents users' IDs and passwords from traveling across the connection in clear text format.

Figure 12-10 illustrates these two methods for allowing remote users to connect using RADIUS authentication. RADIUS can run on UNIX, Linux, Windows, or Macintosh networks. A similar, but earlier version of a centralized authentication system is **TACACS (Terminal Access Controller Access Control System)**.

RADIUS and TACACS belong to a category of protocols known as **AAA (authentication, authorization, and accounting)**. This reflects the fact that such protocols establish a client's identity; examine the client's credentials and, based on their validity, allow or deny access to a system or network; and finally, track the client's system or network usage. Each of the protocols described in the following sections also plays a role in AAA.

PAP (Password Authentication Protocol)

In Chapter 7's discussion of remote access protocols, you were introduced to PPP (Point-to-Point Protocol), which belongs to the data link layer of the OSI model and provides the foundation for connections between remote clients and hosts. PPP alone, however, does not secure connections. For this it requires an authentication protocol.

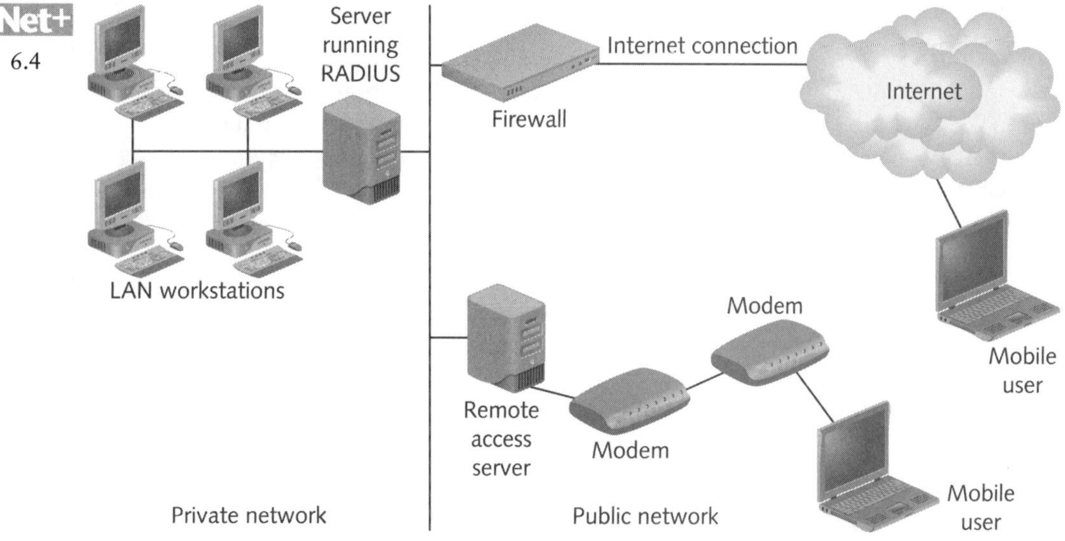

Figure 12-10 A RADIUS server providing centralized authentication

In fact, several types of authentication protocols can work over PPP. One is **PAP (Password Authentication Protocol)**. After establishing a link with a server through PPP, a client uses PAP to send an authentication request that includes its credentials—usually a user name and password. The server compares the credentials to those in its user database. If the credentials match, the server responds to the client with an acknowledgment of authentication and grants the client access to secured resources. If the credentials do not match, the server denies the request to authenticate. Figure 12-11 illustrates PAP's two-step authentication process.

Thus, PAP is a simple authentication protocol, but it is not very secure. It sends the client's credentials in clear text, without encryption, and this opens the way for eavesdroppers to capture a user name and password. In addition, PAP does not protect against the possibility of a malicious intruder attempting to guess a user's password through a brute force attack. For these reasons, PAP is rarely used on modern networks. Instead, more sophisticated protocols, such as those described in the following sections, are preferred.

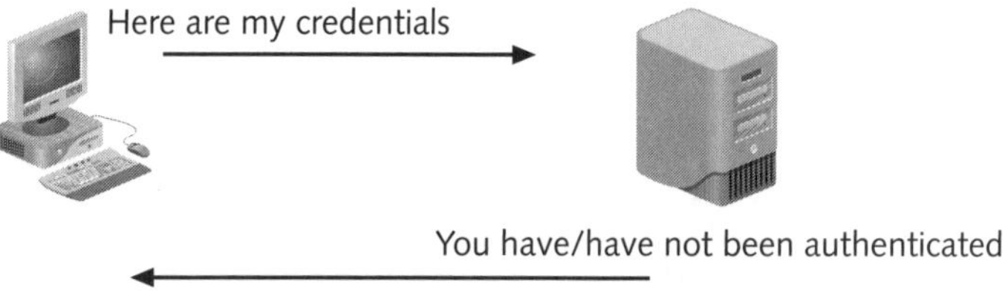

Figure 12-11 Two-step authentication used in PAP

CHAP and MS-CHAP

CHAP (Challenge Handshake Authentication Protocol) is another authentication protocol that operates over PPP. Unlike PAP, CHAP encrypts user names and passwords for transmission.

Net+

6.4

It also differs from PAP in that it requires three steps to complete the authentication process. Together, these steps are known as a **three-way handshake**.

In CHAP, the authenticating device (for example, the remote access server in a dial-up scenario) takes the first step in authentication after PPP establishes a connection between it and the computer requesting authentication (for example, a dial-up client). The server sends the client a randomly generated string of characters called the **challenge**. In the second step, the client adds its password to the challenge and encrypts the new string of characters. It sends this new string of characters in a response to the server. Meanwhile, the server also concatenates the user's password with the challenge and encrypts the new character string, using the same encryption scheme the client used. In the third step of the three-way handshake, the server compares the encrypted string of characters it received from the client with the encrypted string of characters it has generated. If the two match, it authenticates the client. But if the two differ, it rejects the client's request for authentication. Figure 12-12 illustrates the three-way handshake used in CHAP.

The benefit of CHAP over PAP is that in CHAP, a password is never transmitted alone, and never as clear text. This same type of security is offered in **MS-CHAP (Microsoft Challenge Authentication Protocol)**, a similar authentication protocol from Microsoft used with Windows-based computers. One potential flaw in CHAP and MS-CHAP authentication is that someone eavesdropping on the network could capture the string of characters that is encrypted with the password, decrypt that string, and obtain the client's password. To address this, Microsoft released **MS-CHAPv2 (Microsoft Challenge Authentication Protocol, version 2)**, which uses stronger encryption, does not use the same encryption strings for transmission and reception, and requires mutual authentication. In **mutual authentication**, both computers verify the credentials of the other—for example, the client authenticates the server just as the server authenticates the client. This is more secure than requiring only one of the communicating computers to authenticate the other.

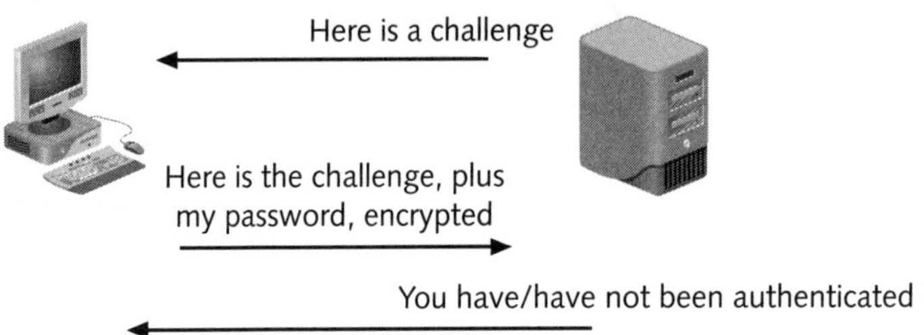

Figure 12-12 Three-way handshake used in CHAP

MS-CHAPv2 is available for use with VPN and dial-up connections in the Windows 2000, XP, Vista, Server 2003, and Server 2008 operating systems. Windows XP and Vista clients support the use of PAP, CHAP, or MS-CHAPv2 when making dial-up connections.

To modify the dial-up connection's supported authentication protocols on a Windows XP client:

1. Click **Start** and then click **My Network Places**. The My Network Places window opens.

2. Under Network Tasks, click **View network connections**. The Network Connections window opens.

6.4

3. Right-click the dial-up connection and click **Properties** from the shortcut menu. The dial-up connection's Properties dialog box opens.

4. Click the **Security** tab to view security options for this connection.

5. Click the **Advanced (custom settings)** option, and then click the **Settings** button. The Advanced Security Settings dialog box opens, as shown in Figure 12-13.

6. Notice that, by default, the Data encryption variable is set to the Optional encryption (connect even if no encryption) option, and under Allow these protocols, all available authentication protocols are selected. In this dialog box, you could choose, for example, to require encryption for your dial-up connection by selecting the Require encryption (disconnect if server declines) option under the Data encryption heading. Or, you could choose to support only certain authentication protocols by deselecting some of the protocols listed under the Allow these protocols heading.

7. Click **OK** to save your changes, if you made any. If you chose to require encryption and did not deselect PAP, SPAP (the Shiva Password Authentication Protocol, which is used with remote access servers using the Shiva software), or CHAP, you will receive a message alerting you that if one of these authentication protocols is negotiated, data encryption will not occur.

8. Click **Yes** to continue. Thereafter, you will not be able to connect to a server that supports only PAP, SPAP, or CHAP. If you deselected MS-CHAP and did not select EAP, you will receive a message telling you that you must choose one of these. In that case, click **OK** to return to the Advanced Security Settings dialog box, select at least one of the more secure authentication protocols, and then click **OK** to continue.

9. Click **OK** to close the dial-up connection Properties dialog box.

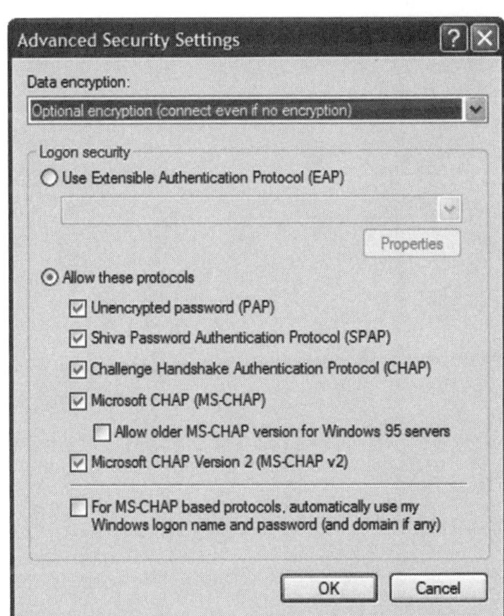

Figure 12-13 Windows XP Advanced Security Settings dialog box

Net+
6.4

To modify the dial-up connection's supported authentication protocols on a Windows Vista client:

1. Click **Start,** and then click **Control Panel.** The Control Panel window appears.

2. In the left pane, click **Control Panel Home,** and then click **Network and Internet.** The Network and Internet window appears.

3. Click **Network and Sharing Center.** The Network and Sharing Center window appears.

4. Click **Manage network connections** on the left side of the Network and Sharing Center window.

5. Right-click the dial-up connection and choose **Properties** from the shortcut menu. The dial-up connection's Properties dialog box opens.

6. Click the **Security** tab to view security options for this connection.

7. Click the **Advanced (custom settings)** option, and then click the **Settings** button. The Advanced Security Settings dialog box opens, as shown in Figure 12-14.

8. By default, the Data encryption variable is set to the Optional encryption (connect even if no encryption) option, and under Allow these protocols, all available authentication protocols are selected. In this dialog box, you could choose, for example, to require encryption for your dial-up connection by selecting the Require encryption (disconnect if server declines) option or the Maximum strength encryption (disconnect if server declines) option under the Data encryption heading. You could also choose to support only certain authentication protocols by deselecting some of the protocols listed under the Allow these protocols heading.

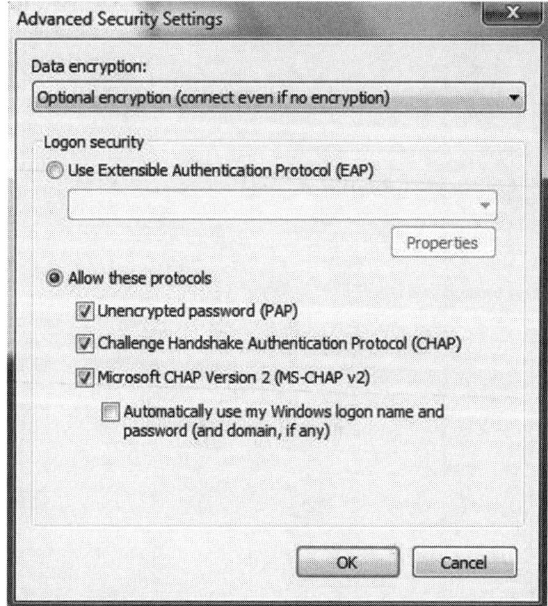

Figure 12-14 Windows Vista Advanced Security Settings dialog box

6.4

9. Click **OK** to save any changes you made.

10. If you chose to require encryption and selected PAP or CHAP, you will receive a message alerting you that if one of these authentication protocols is negotiated, data encryption will not occur. Click **Yes** to confirm that you want to keep these settings.

11. Click **OK** to close the dial-up connection Properties dialog box.

An authentication protocol that is more secure than CHAP or MS-CHAP and is supported by multiple operating systems is EAP, discussed next.

EAP (Extensible Authentication Protocol)

EAP (Extensible Authentication Protocol) is another extension to the PPP protocol suite. It differs from the authentication protocols discussed previously in that it is only a mechanism for authenticating clients and servers; it does not perform encryption or authentication on its own. Instead, it works with other encryption and authentication schemes to verify the credentials of clients and servers.

Like CHAP, EAP requires the authenticator (for example, the server) to initiate the authentication process by asking the connected computer (for example, the client) to verify itself. In EAP, the server usually sends more than one request. In its first request, it asks the client's identity and indicates what type of authentication to use. In subsequent requests, it asks the client for authentication information to prove the client's identity. The client responds to each of the servers' requests in the required format. If the responses match what the server expects, the server authenticates the client.

One of EAP's advantages is its flexibility. It is supported by nearly all modern operating systems and can be used with any authentication method. For example, although the typical network authentication involves a user ID and password, EAP also works with biorecognition methods, such as retina or hand scanning. EAP is also adaptable to new technology. Therefore, no matter what future wireless encryption schemes are developed, EAP will support them.

In the case of wireless LANs, EAP is used with older encryption and authentication protocols to form a new, more secure method of connecting to networks from wireless stations. A distinct implementation of EAP, described next, forms the basis of one of the most secure wireless authentication techniques.

802.1x (EAPoL)

The **802.1x** standard, codified by IEEE, specifies the use of one of many authentication methods, plus EAP, to grant access to and dynamically generate and update authentication keys for transmissions to a particular port. Although it's primarily used with wireless networks now, it was originally designed for wired LANs; thus, it's also known as **EAPoL (EAP over LAN)**. 802.1x only defines a process for authentication. It does not specify the type of authentication or encryption protocols that clients and servers must use. However, 802.1x is commonly used with RADIUS authentication. As you might expect, for nodes to communicate using 802.1x, they must agree on the same authentication method.

What distinguishes 802.1x from other authentication standards is the fact that it applies to communication with a particular port—for example, a physical switch port or a logically defined port on an access point. When a client wants to access the network, a port on the authenticator (such as a switch or access point) challenges the client to prove its identity. If the client is running the proper 802.1x software, the client will supply the authenticator with its credentials. The authenticator next passes on the client's credentials to an authentication server—for example, a RADIUS server. Only after the authentication server has verified a client's legitimacy will the switch or access point port be opened to the client's Layer 3 traffic. For this reason, 802.1x is sometimes also called **port authentication**, or **port-based authentication**. After the port is opened, the client and network communicate using EAP and an agreed-upon encryption scheme. Figure 12-15 illustrates the process followed by 802.1x when used with a WLAN (wireless LAN). You'll learn more about wireless network security techniques later in this chapter.

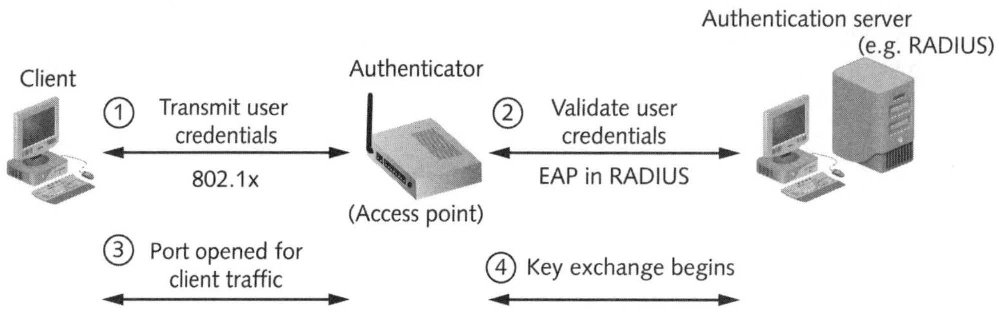

Figure 12-15 802.1x authentication process

Kerberos

Kerberos is a cross-platform authentication protocol that uses key encryption to verify the identity of clients and to securely exchange information after a client logs on to a system. It is an example of a private key encryption service. Kerberos provides significant security advantages over simple NOS authentication. Whereas an NOS client/server logon process assumes that clients are who they say they are and only verifies a user's name against the password in the NOS database, Kerberos does not automatically trust clients. Instead, it requires clients to prove their identities through a third party. This is similar to what happens when you apply for a passport. The government does not simply believe that you are "Leah Torres," but instead requires you to present proof, such as your birth certificate. In addition to checking the validity of a client, Kerberos communications are encrypted and unlikely to be deciphered by any device on the network other than the client. Contrast this type of transmission to the normally unencrypted and vulnerable communication between an NOS and a client.

To understand specifically how a client uses Kerberos, you need to understand some of the terms used when discussing this protocol. In Kerberos terminology, the server that issues keys to clients during initial client authentication is known as the **KDC (Key Distribution Center)**. To authenticate a client, the KDC runs an **AS (authentication service)**. An AS issues a **ticket**, which is a temporary set of credentials that a client uses to prove that its identity has been validated. (Note that a ticket is not the same as a key, which is used to initially validate its identity.) A Kerberos client, or user, is known as a **principal**.

Net+
6.4

Now that you have learned the terms used by Kerberos, you can follow the process it requires for client/server communication. Bear in mind that the purpose of Kerberos is to connect a valid user with the *service* that user wants to access. To accomplish this, both the user and the service must register their keys with the authentication service. Suppose the principal is Jamal Sayad and the service is called "inventory." Jamal first logs on to his network as usual. Next, he attempts to log on to the "inventory" service with his Kerberos principal name and password. (On a Windows 2000 Server, Windows Server 2003, or Windows Server 2008 network, the KDC is, by default, the user's domain controller, and, therefore, a user may not need to separately log on to a Kerberos-authenticated service.) The KDC confirms that Jamal Sayad is in its database and that he has provided the correct password. Then, the AS running on the KDC randomly generates two copies of a new key, called the **session key**. The AS issues one copy to Jamal's computer and the other copy to the inventory service. Further, it creates a ticket that allows Jamal to use the inventory service. This ticket contains the inventory service key and can only be decrypted using Jamal Sayad's key. The AS sends the ticket to Jamal Sayad. Jamal's computer decrypts the session key with Jamal's personal key. It then creates a time stamp associated with his request and encrypts this time stamp with the session key. The encrypted time stamp is known as the **authenticator**. This time stamp helps the service verify that the ticket is indeed associated with Jamal Sayad's request to use the inventory service. Next, Jamal's computer sends his ticket and authenticator to the service. The service decrypts the ticket using its own key and decrypts the authenticator using its session key. Finally, the service verifies that the principal requesting its use is truly Jamal Sayad as the KDC indicated.

The preceding events illustrate the original version of the Kerberos authentication process. The problem with the original version was that a user had to request a separate ticket each time he wanted to use a different service. To alleviate this inconvenience, Kerberos developers created the **TGS (Ticket Granting Service)**, an application separate from the AS that also runs on the KDC. So that the client does not need to request a new ticket from the TGS each time it wants to use a different service on the network, the TGS issues the client a **TGT (Ticket Granting Ticket)**. After receiving the TGT, anytime the user wants to contact a service, he requests a ticket not from the AS, but from the TGS. Furthermore, the reply is encrypted not with the user's personal key, but with the session key that the AS provided for use with the TGS. Inside that reply is the new session key for use with the regular service. The rest of the exchange continues as described previously.

Kerberos, which is named after the three-headed dog in Greek mythology who guarded the gates of Hades, was designed at MIT (Massachusetts Institute of Technology). MIT still provides free copies of the Kerberos code. In addition, many software vendors have developed their own versions of Kerberos.

Wireless Network Security

Net+
1.7

Wireless transmissions are particularly susceptible to eavesdropping. For example, a hacker could search for unprotected wireless networks by driving around with a laptop configured to receive and capture wireless data transmissions—a practice known as **war driving**. (The term is derived from the term *war dialing*, which is a similar tactic involving modems.) War driving is surprisingly effective for obtaining private information. Years ago, the hacker community publicized the vulnerabilities of a well-known store chain, which were discovered while war driving. The retailer used wireless cash registers to help customers make purchases when the regular, wired cash registers were busy. However, the wireless cash registers transmitted purchase information, including credit card numbers and customer names, to network access points in clear text. By chance, a person in the parking lot who was running a protocol analyzer program on his laptop obtained several credit card numbers in a very short time. The person alerted the retailer to the security risk (rather than exploiting the information he gathered). Needless to say, after the retailer discovered its error, it abandoned the use of wireless cash registers until after a thorough evaluation of its data security.

WEP (Wired Equivalent Privacy)

As you have learned, most organizations use one of the 802.11 protocol standards on their WLANs. By default, the 802.11 standard does not offer security. In addition, most access points do not require a client to authenticate before it can communicate with the AP. The client only needs to know the access point's SSID, which most access points broadcast. Smart network administrators prevent their access points from broadcasting the SSIDs, making them harder to detect. However, this does not provide true security.

For some measure of security, 802.11 allows for optional encryption using the **WEP (Wired Equivalent Privacy)** standard. WEP uses keys both to authenticate network clients and to encrypt data in transit. When configuring WEP, you establish a character string required to associate with the access point, also known as the **network key**. When the client detects the presence of the access point, the user is prompted to provide a network key before the client can gain access to a network via the access point. On a Windows XP computer, the network key can be saved as part of the wireless connection's properties.

To edit or add a WEP key for a wireless connection on your Windows XP client:

1. Click **Start** and then click **My Network Places**. The My Network Places window opens.

2. Under Network Tasks, click **View network connections**. The Network Connections window opens.

3. Right-click the **Wireless Network Connection** icon, and then choose **Properties** from the shortcut menu. The Wireless Network Connection Properties dialog box opens.

4. Select the **Wireless Networks** tab.

5. Under Preferred networks, click the network (or the SSID) for which you want to establish a WEP key, and then click **Properties**. Your wireless network's properties dialog box opens, with the Association tab selected by default.

6. In the drop-down menu next to Data encryption, choose **WEP**.

7. Uncheck the check box next to the **The key is provided for me automatically** option.

8. Enter your WEP key in the Network key text box. You must enter precisely the same key that your AP is configured to use, in either ASCII or hexadecimal form.

9. Enter your WEP key again in the Confirm network key text box. As shown in Figure 12-16, the network key will not appear on the screen, so that anyone peering over your shoulder cannot discover it.

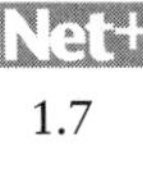

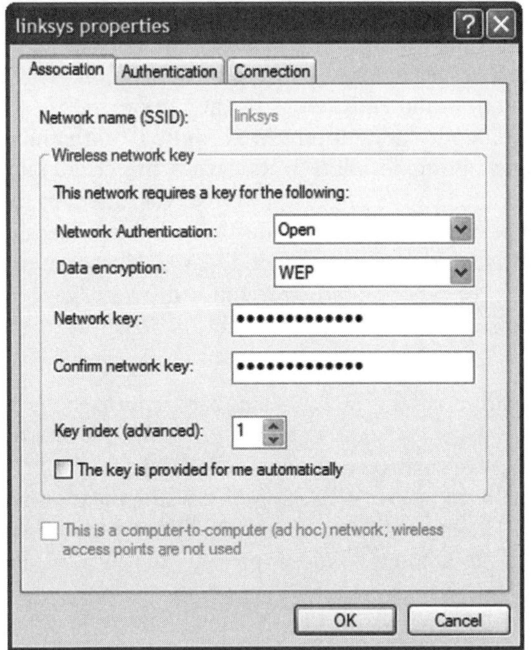

Figure 12-16 Entering a WEP key in the Windows XP wireless network properties dialog box

10. Click **OK** to save your changes and close the wireless network properties dialog box.

11. Click **OK** again to close the Wireless Network Connection Properties dialog box.

The first implementation of WEP allowed for 64-bit network keys, and current versions of WEP allow for more secure, 128-bit or even 256-bit network keys. Still, WEP's use of the shared key for authenticating all users and for exchanging data makes it more susceptible to discovery than a dynamically generated, random, or single-use key. Even 128-bit network keys can be cracked in a matter of minutes. Moreover, because WEP operates in the physical and data link layers of the OSI model, it does not offer end-to-end data transmission security. A better wireless security technique is 802.11i, which is discussed next.

IEEE 802.11i and WPA (Wi-Fi Protected Access)

Because of WEP's relative insecurity, IEEE devised a new wireless security protocol, called **802.11i**, that uses 802.1x (EAPoL) to authenticate devices and dynamically assign every transmission its own key. 802.11i often relies on an encryption key generation and management scheme known as **TKIP** (**Temporal Key Integrity Protocol**, pronounced *tee-kip*).

As you can imagine, EAP makes logging on to a wireless network more complex than it is with WEP. In 802.11i, a wireless station first issues a request to the access point. The access point functions as a proxy between the remote access server and station until the station has successfully authenticated with a remote access server. Meanwhile, the access point prevents

Net+

1.7

any direct exchange of data between the two. After obtaining data from an unknown station, the access point repackages the data and then transmits it to the remote access server. It also repackages data from the remote access server before issuing it to the station. Thus, 802.11i requires mutual authentication—the station authenticates with the remote access server, and the remote access server authenticates with the station. After mutual authentication, the remote access server instructs the access point to allow traffic from the client into the network without first having to be repackaged. Next, the client and server agree on the encryption key they will use with the encryption scheme. Following that, they exchange data that has been encrypted through the mutually agreed-upon method. 802.11i specifies the AES encryption method and mixes each packet in a data stream with a different key. Because of its impressive security, 802.11i is poised to replace the less-secure WEP as the preferred means for protecting wireless transmissions from intruders.

WPA (Wi-Fi Protected Access) is a subset of the 802.11i standard endorsed by the **Wi-Fi Alliance,** an international, nonprofit organization dedicated to ensuring the interoperability of 802.11-capable devices. In fact, the Wi-Fi Alliance released WPA before 802.11i was ratified to quickly provide a more secure alternative to WEP. In WPA, authentication follows the same mechanism specified in 802.11i. The main difference is that WPA specifies RC4 encryption rather than AES. Since the 802.11i standard was approved, the Wi-Fi Alliance has released an updated version called **WPA2.** WPA2 includes support for the previously released WPA protocol. In all other ways, it is identical to 802.11i.

To support 802.11i, WPA, and WPA2, most currently installed APs and wireless NICs require driver, if not firmware, upgrades.

Chapter Summary

- Every organization should assess its security risks by conducting a security audit, at least annually and preferably quarterly. For each threat, the security audit should rate the severity of its potential consequences, as well as its likelihood.

- One of the most common methods by which an intruder gains access to a network is to simply ask a user for his password. This strategy is commonly called social engineering because it involves manipulating social relationships to gain access. Phishing, a related tactic, involves luring users into revealing information that would allow intruders to gain access to secured network resources.

- Security risks that a network administrator must guard against include incorrectly configuring user accounts or groups and their privileges; overlooking security flaws in topology or hardware configuration; overlooking security flaws in operating system or application configuration; improperly documenting or communicating security policies; and leaving system settings (such as a program's administrator user name or the administrator's password on a router) at their default values.

- Some risks inherent in network transmission and design include leased public lines that may allow for eavesdropping; hubs that broadcast traffic over the entire segment; unused hub, router, or server ports that can be exploited and accessed by hackers if not disabled; a router's configuration port, accessible by Telnet, that might not be adequately secured; routers that may not be properly configured to mask internal subnets or to deny access to certain hosts; modems attached to network devices that might be configured to accept incoming calls; and dial-in access servers used by telecommuting or remote staff that might not be carefully secured and monitored.

- Some risks pertaining to networking protocols and software include the following: inherent TCP/IP security flaws; trust relationships between one server and another; NOS "back doors" or security flaws; an NOS that allows server operators to exit to a command prompt; administrators who accept default operating system security; and transactions that take place between applications left open to interception.

- A security policy identifies an organization's security goals, risks, levels of authority, designated security coordinator and team members, responsibilities for each team member, responsibilities for each employee, and strategies for addressing security breaches.

- At the very least, computer rooms should allow access only to authorized networking personnel. If computer rooms or wiring closets remain unlocked, intruders may easily enter and steal equipment, or sabotage software and hardware.

- A router's ACL (access control list, also known as an access list) instructs it to decline to forward certain packets according to source IP address, source netmask, destination IP address, destination netmask, or TCP or UDP port, among other things.

- An IDS (intrusion-detection system) monitors traffic on a network or host for unauthorized attempts to access a network's resources. An IPS (intrusion-protection system) can detect such attempts and automatically react to them—for example, by denying access to a host whose traffic triggers an alert.

- A firewall is a specialized device (typically a router, but possibly only a desktop computer running special software) that selectively filters or blocks traffic between networks. It can be placed between two interconnected private networks or, more typically, between a private network and a public network (such as the Internet).

- The most common form of firewall is a packet-filtering firewall, which examines the header of every packet of data that it receives to determine whether that type of packet is authorized to continue to its destination.

- A proxy service is a software application on a network host that acts as an intermediary between the external and internal networks, screening all incoming and outgoing traffic. The host that runs the proxy service is known as a proxy server. A proxy server appears to external machines as a network server, but it is actually another filtering device for the internal LAN.

- Every NOS provides at least some security by allowing you to limit users' access to files and directories on the network. In addition, network administrators can constrain how those with different types of user IDs can use the network by setting restrictions on, for example, time of day, total time logged on, source address, and number of unsuccessful logon attempts.

- Choosing secure passwords is one of the easiest and least expensive ways to guard against unauthorized access.

- Encryption is the use of an algorithm to scramble data into a format that can be read only by reversing the algorithm—or decrypting the data—to keep the information private. Many forms of encryption exist, with some being more secure than others.

- The most popular kind of encryption algorithm weaves a key (a random string of characters) into the original data's bits, sometimes several times in different sequences, to generate a unique data block. The longer the key, the less easily the encrypted data can be decrypted by an unauthorized system.

- Key encryption comes in two forms: public and private key encryption. Popular private (symmetric) key encryption algorithms include DES (Data Encryption Standard), Triple DES (3DES), and AES (Advanced Encryption Standard). Popular public (asymmetric) key encryption algorithms include Diffie-Hellman, RSA, and RC4.

- Popular methods of encryption include PGP (Pretty Good Privacy), SSL (Secure Sockets Layer), SSH (Secure Shell) and OpenSSH, and IPSec (Internet Protocol Security). IPSec is the protocol used on many modern VPNs.

- SCP (Secure CoPy) and SFTP (Secure File Transfer Protocol) are ways of copying files securely via SSH or OpenSSH.

- Authentication protocols used with PPP connections include RADIUS (Remote Authentication Dial-In User Service), TACACS (Terminal Access Controller Access Control System), PAP (Password Authentication Protocol), CHAP (Challenge Handshake Authentication Protocol), and MS-CHAP (Microsoft Challenge Handshake Authentication Protocol). Other authentication protocols include EAP (Extensible Authentication Protocol), 802.1x (or EAPoL), and Kerberos.

- Wireless networks can use the WEP (Wired Equivalent Privacy) method of encrypting data in transit between stations and access points. WEP allows for keys as long as 256 bits. However, because WEP uses the same key for all stations attaching to an access point and for all transmissions, it is not very secure.

- A better wireless security solution than WEP is provided by IEEE's 802.11i standard, also known as TKIP (Temporal Key Integrity Protocol). In 802.11i, the 802.1x authentication method is combined with AES encryption. Each 802.11i transmission is dynamically assigned its own key for encryption.

- The Wi-Fi Alliance has released two wireless security standards: WPA and WPA2. WPA follows the same authentication and encryption processes as 802.11i but uses RC4 encryption. WPA2 is identical to 802.11i but provides backward compatibility for clients running WPA.

Key Terms

3DES *See* Triple DES.

802.11i The IEEE standard for wireless network encryption and authentication that uses the EAP authentication method, strong encryption, and dynamically assigned keys, which are different for every transmission. 802.11i specifies AES encryption and weaves a key into each packet.

802.1x A vendor-independent IEEE standard for securing transmission between nodes according to the transmission's port, whether physical or logical. 802.1x, also known as EAPoL, is the authentication standard followed by wireless networks using 802.11i.

AAA (authentication, authorization, and accounting) The name of a category of protocols that establish a client's identity; check the client's credentials and, based on those, allow or deny access to a system or network; and finally, track the client's system or network usage.

access control list   *See* ACL.

access list   *See* ACL.

ACL (access control list)   A list of statements used by a router to permit or deny the forwarding of traffic on a network based on one or more criteria.

Advanced Encryption Standard   *See* AES.

AES (Advanced Encryption Standard)   A private key encryption algorithm that weaves keys of 128, 160, 192, or 256 bits through data multiple times. The algorithm used in the most popular form of AES is known as Rijndael. AES has replaced DES in situations such as military communications, which require the highest level of security.

AH (authentication header)   In the context of IPSec, a type of encryption that provides authentication of the IP packet's data payload through public key techniques.

application gateway   *See* proxy server.

application layer gateway   *See* proxy server.

AS (authentication service)   In Kerberos terminology, the process that runs on a KDC (Key Distribution Center) to initially validate a client who's logging on. The authentication service issues a session key to the client and to the service the client wants to access.

asymmetric encryption   A type of encryption (such as public key encryption) that uses a different key for encoding data than is used for decoding the ciphertext.

authentication, authorization, and accounting   *See* AAA.

authentication header   *See* AH.

authentication protocol   A set of rules that govern how servers authenticate clients. Several types of authentication protocols exist.

authentication service   *See* AS.

authenticator   In Kerberos authentication, the user's time stamp encrypted with the session key. The authenticator is used to help the service verify that a user's ticket is valid.

biorecognition access   A method of authentication in which a device scans an individual's unique physical characteristics (such as the color patterns in her iris or the geometry of her hand) to verify the user's identity.

brute force attack   An attempt to discover an encryption key or password by trying numerous possible character combinations. Usually, a brute force attack is performed rapidly by a program designed for that purpose.

CA (certificate authority)   An organization that issues and maintains digital certificates as part of the public key infrastructure.

certificate authority   *See* CA.

challenge   A random string of text issued from one computer to another in some forms of authentication. It is used, along with the password (or other credential), in a response to verify the computer's credentials.

Challenge Handshake Authentication Protocol   *See* CHAP.

CHAP (Challenge Handshake Authentication Protocol)   An authentication protocol that operates over PPP and that requires the authenticator to take the first step by offering the other computer a challenge. The requestor responds by combining the challenge with its password, encrypting the new string of characters and sending it to the authenticator. The authenticator matches to see if the requestor's encrypted string of text matches its own encrypted string of characters. If so, the requestor is authenticated and granted access to secured resources.

ciphertext   The unique data block that results when an original piece of data (such as text) is encrypted (for example, by using a key).

client_hello   In the context of SSL encryption, a message issued from the client to the server that contains information about what level of security the client's browser is capable of accepting and what type of encryption the client's browser can decipher (for example, RSA or Diffie-Hellman). The client_hello message also establishes a randomly generated number that uniquely identifies the client, plus another number that identifies the SSL session.

content-filtering firewall   A firewall that can block designated types of traffic from entering a protected network.

cracker   A person who uses his knowledge of operating systems and utilities to intentionally damage or destroy data or systems.

Data Encryption Standard   *See* DES.

demilitarized zone   *See* DMZ.

denial-of-service attack   A security attack caused by a deluge of traffic that disables the victimized system.

DES (Data Encryption Standard)   A popular private key encryption technique that was developed by IBM in the 1970s.

dictionary attack   A technique in which attackers run a program that tries a combination of a known user ID and, for a password, every word in a dictionary to attempt to gain access to a network.

Diffie-Hellman   The first commonly used public, or asymmetric, key algorithm. Diffie-Hellman was released in 1975 by its creators, Whitfield Diffie and Martin Hellman.

digital certificate   A password-protected and encrypted file that holds an individual's identification information, including a public key and a private key. The individual's public key is used to verify the sender's digital signature, and the private key allows the individual to log on to a third-party authority who administers digital certificates.

DMZ (demilitarized zone)   The perimeter of a protected, internal network where users, both authorized and unauthorized, from external networks can attempt to access it. Firewalls and IDS/IPS systems are typically placed in the DMZ.

DNS spoofing   A security attack in which an outsider forges name server records to falsify his host's identity.

EAP (Extensible Authentication Protocol)   A data link layer protocol defined by the IETF that specifies the dynamic distribution of encryption keys and a preauthentication process in which a client and server exchange data via an intermediate node (for example, an access point on a wireless LAN). Only after they have mutually authenticated can the client and server exchange encrypted data. EAP can be used with multiple authentication and encryption schemes.

EAP over LAN   *See* EAPoL.

EAPoL (EAP over LAN)   *See* 802.1x.

Encapsulating Security Payload   *See* ESP.

encryption   The use of an algorithm to scramble data into a format that can be read only by reversing the algorithm—decrypting the data—to keep the information private. The most popular kind of encryption algorithm weaves a key into the original data's bits, sometimes several times in different sequences, to generate a unique data block.

ESP (Encapsulation Security Payload)   In the context of IPSec, a type of encryption that provides authentication of the IP packet's data payload through public key techniques. In addition, ESP encrypts the entire IP packet for added security.

Extensible Authentication Protocol   *See* EAP.

flashing   A security attack in which an Internet user sends commands to another Internet user's machine that cause the screen to fill with garbage characters. A flashing attack causes the user to terminate her session.

hacker   A person who masters the inner workings of operating systems and utilities in an effort to better understand them. A hacker is distinguished from a cracker in that a cracker attempts to exploit a network's vulnerabilities for malicious purposes.

handshake protocol   One of several protocols within SSL, and perhaps the most significant. As its name implies, the handshake protocol allows the client and server to authenticate (or introduce) each other and establishes terms for how they securely exchange data during an SSL session.

host-based firewall   A firewall that only protects the computer on which it's installed.

HTTP over Secure Sockets Layer   *See* HTTPS.

HTTP Secure   *See* HTTPS.

HTTPS (HTTP over Secure Sockets Layer)   The URL prefix that indicates that a Web page requires its data to be exchanged between client and server using SSL encryption. HTTPS uses the TCP port number 443, rather than port 80 (the port that normal HTTP uses).

IDS (intrusion-detection system)   A dedicated device or software running on a host that monitors and flags (and sometimes logs) any unauthorized attempt to access an organization's secured resources on a network or host.

IKE (Internet Key Exchange)   The first phase of IPSec authentication, which accomplishes key management. IKE is a service that runs on UDP port 500. After IKE has established the rules for the type of keys two nodes use, IPSec invokes its second phase, encryption.

Internet Key Exchange   *See* IKE.

Internet Protocol Security   *See* IPSec.

intrusion-detection system   *See* IDS.

intrusion-prevention system   *See* IPS.

IP spoofing   A security attack in which an outsider obtains internal IP addresses and then uses those addresses to pretend that he has authority to access a private network from the Internet.

IPS (intrusion-prevention system)   A dedicated device or software running on a host that automatically reacts to any unauthorized attempt to access an organization's secured resources on a network or host. IPS is often combined with IDS.

IPSec (Internet Protocol Security)   A Layer 3 protocol that defines encryption, authentication, and key management for TCP/IP transmissions. IPSec is an enhancement to IPv4 and is native to IPv6. IPSec is unique among authentication methods in that it adds security information to the header of all IP packets.

KDC (Key Distribution Center)   In Kerberos terminology, the server that runs the authentication service and the Ticket Granting Service to issue keys and tickets to clients.

Kerberos   A cross-platform authentication protocol that uses key encryption to verify the identity of clients and to securely exchange information after a client logs on to a system. It is an example of a private key encryption service.

key   A series of characters that is combined with a block of data during that data's encryption. To decrypt the resulting data, the recipient must also possess the key.

Key Distribution Center   *See* KDC.

key management   The method whereby two nodes using key encryption agree on common parameters for the keys they will use to encrypt data.

key pair   The combination of a public and private key used to decipher data that was encrypted using public key encryption.

man-in-the-middle attack   A security threat that relies on intercepted transmissions. It can take one of several forms, but in all cases a person redirects or captures secure data traffic while in transit.

Microsoft Challenge Handshake Authentication Protocol   *See* MS-CHAP.

Microsoft Challenge Handshake Authentication Protocol, version 2   *See* MS-CHAPv2.

MS-CHAP (Microsoft Challenge Handshake Authentication Protocol)   An authentication protocol offered by Microsoft with its Windows clients and servers. Similar to CHAP, MS-CHAP uses a three-way handshake to verify a client's credentials and encrypts passwords with a challenge text.

MS-CHAPv2 (Microsoft Challenge Authentication Protocol, version 2)   An authentication protocol provided with Windows XP, 2000, and Server 2003 operating systems that follows the CHAP model but uses stronger encryption, uses different encryption keys for transmission and reception, and requires mutual authentication between two computers.

mutual authentication   An authentication scheme in which both computers verify the credentials of each other.

network-based firewall   A firewall configured and positioned to protect an entire network.

network key   A key (or character string) required for a wireless station to associate with an access point using WEP.

OpenSSH   An open source version of the SSH suite of protocols.

packet-filtering firewall   A router that operates at the data link and transport layers of the OSI model, examining the header of every packet of data that it receives to determine whether that type of packet is authorized to continue to its destination. Packet-filtering firewalls are also called screening firewalls.

PAP (Password Authentication Protocol)   A simple authentication protocol that operates over PPP. Using PAP, a client issues its credentials in a request to authenticate, and the server responds with a confirmation or denial of authentication after comparing the credentials to those in its database. PAP is not very secure and is, therefore, rarely used on modern networks.

Password Authentication Protocol   *See* PAP.

PGP (Pretty Good Privacy)   A key-based encryption system for e-mail that uses a two-step verification process.

phishing   A practice in which a person attempts to glean access or authentication information by posing as someone who needs that information.

PKI (public key infrastructure)   The use of certificate authorities to associate public keys with certain users.

port authentication   A technique in which a client's identity is verified by an authentication server before a port, whether physical or logical, is opened for the client's Layer 3 traffic. *See also* 802.1x.

port-based authentication   *See* port authentication.

port forwarding   The process of redirecting traffic from its normally assigned port to a different port, either on the client or server. In the case of using SSH, port forwarding can send data exchanges that are normally insecure through encrypted tunnels.

port mirroring   A monitoring technique in which one port on a switch is configured to send a copy of all its traffic to a second port.

port scanner   Software that searches a server, switch, router, or other device for open ports, which can be vulnerable to attack.

Pretty Good Privacy   *See* PGP.

principal   In Kerberos terminology, a user or client.

private key encryption   A type of key encryption in which the sender and receiver use a key to which only they have access. DES (Data Encryption Standard), which was developed by IBM in the 1970s, is a popular example of a private key encryption technique. Private key encryption is also known as symmetric encryption.

proxy   *See* proxy server.

proxy server   A network host that runs a proxy service. Proxy servers may also be called gateways.

proxy service   A software application on a network host that acts as an intermediary between the external and internal networks, screening all incoming and outgoing traffic and providing one address to the outside world, instead of revealing the addresses of internal LAN devices.

public key encryption   A form of key encryption in which data is encrypted using two keys: One is a key known only to a user, and the other is a key associated with the user and that can be obtained from a public source, such as a public key server. Some examples of public key algorithms include RSA and Diffie-Hellman. Public key encryption is also known as asymmetric encryption.

public key infrastructure   *See* PKI.

public key server   A publicly available host (such as an Internet host) that provides free access to a list of users' public keys (for use in public key encryption).

RADIUS (Remote Authentication Dial-In User Service)   A protocol that runs over UDP and provides centralized network authentication and accounting for multiple users. RADIUS is commonly used with dial-up networking, VPNs, and wireless connections.

RADIUS server   A server that offers centralized authentication services to a network's access server, VPN server, or wireless access point via the RADIUS protocol.

RC4   An asymmetric key encryption technique that weaves a key with data multiple times as a computer issues the stream of data. RC4 keys can be as long as 2,048 bits. In addition to being highly secure, RC4 is fast.

Remote Authentication Dial-In User Service   *See* RADIUS.

Rijndael   The algorithm used for AES encryption.

RSA   An encryption algorithm that creates a key by randomly choosing two large prime numbers and multiplying them together. RSA is named after its creators, Ronald Rivest, Adi Shamir, and Leonard Adleman. RSA was released in 1977 but remains popular today for e-commerce transactions.

SCP (Secure CoPy)   A method for copying files securely between hosts. SCP is part of the OpenSSH package, which comes with modern UNIX and Linux operating systems. Third-party SCP applications are available for Windows-based computers.

screening firewall   *See* packet-filtering firewall.

Secure CoPy   *See* SCP.

Secure File Transfer Protocol   *See* SFTP.

Secure Shell   *See* SSH.

Secure Sockets Layer   *See* SSL.

security audit   An assessment of an organization's security vulnerabilities. A security audit should be performed at least annually and preferably quarterly—or sooner if the network has undergone significant changes. For each risk found, it should rate the severity of a potential breach, as well as its likelihood.

security policy   A document or plan that identifies an organization's security goals, risks, levels of authority, designated security coordinator and team members, responsibilities for each team member, and responsibilities for each employee. In addition, it specifies how to address security breaches.

server_hello   In the context of SSL encryption, a message issued from the server to the client that confirms the information the server received in the client_hello message. It also agrees to certain terms of encryption based on the options the client supplied. Depending on the Web server's preferred encryption method, the server may choose to issue your browser a public key or a digital certificate at this time.

session key   In the context of Kerberos authentication, a key issued to both the client and the server by the authentication service that uniquely identifies their session.

SFTP (Secure File Transfer Protocol)   A protocol available with the proprietary version of SSH that copies files between hosts securely. Like FTP, SFTP first establishes a connection with a host and then allows a remote user to browse directories, list files, and copy files. Unlike FTP, SFTP encrypts data before transmitting it.

smurf attack A threat to networked hosts in which the host is flooded with broadcast ping messages. A smurf attack is a type of denial-of-service attack.

social engineering The act of manipulating personal relationships to circumvent network security measures and gain access to a system.

SSH (Secure Shell) A connection utility that provides authentication and encryption. With SSH, you can securely log on to a host, execute commands on that host, and copy files to or from that host. SSH encrypts data exchanged throughout the session.

SSL (Secure Sockets Layer) A method of encrypting TCP/IP transmissions—including Web pages and data entered into Web forms—en route between the client and server using public key encryption technology.

SSL session In the context of SSL encryption, an association between the client and server that is defined by an agreement on a specific set of encryption techniques. An SSL session allows the client and server to continue to exchange data securely as long as the client is still connected to the server. SSL sessions are established by the SSL handshake protocol.

stateful firewall A firewall capable of monitoring a data stream from end to end.

stateless firewall A firewall capable only of examining packets individually. Stateless firewalls perform more quickly than stateful firewalls but are not as sophisticated.

symmetric encryption A method of encryption that requires the same key to encode the data as is used to decode the ciphertext.

TACACS (Terminal Access Controller Access Control System) A centralized authentication system for remote access servers that is similar to, but older than, RADIUS.

Temporal Key Integrity Protocol *See* TKIP.

Terminal Access Controller Access Control System *See* TACACS.

TGS (Ticket Granting Service) In Kerberos terminology, an application that runs on the KDC that issues Ticket Granting Tickets to clients so that they need not request a new ticket for each new service they want to access.

TGT (Ticket Granting Ticket) In Kerberos terminology, a ticket that enables a user to be accepted as a validated principal by multiple services.

three-way handshake An authentication process that involves three steps.

ticket In Kerberos terminology, a temporary set of credentials that a client uses to prove that its identity has been validated by the authentication service.

Ticket Granting Service *See* TGS.

Ticket Granting Ticket *See* TGT.

TKIP (Temporal Key Integrity Protocol) An encryption key generation and management scheme used by 802.11i.

TLS (Transport Layer Security) A version of SSL being standardized by the IETF (Internet Engineering Task Force). With TLS, the IETF aims to create a version of SSL that encrypts UDP as well as TCP transmissions. TLS, which is supported by new Web browsers, uses slightly different encryption algorithms than SSL, but otherwise it is very similar to the most recent version of SSL.

Transport Layer Security *See* TLS.

Triple DES (3DES) The modern implementation of DES, which weaves a 56-bit key through data three times, each time using a different key.

VPN concentrator A specialized device that authenticates VPN clients and establishes tunnels for VPN connections.

war driving The act of driving while running a laptop configured to detect and capture wireless data transmissions.

WEP (Wired Equivalent Privacy) A key encryption technique for wireless networks that uses keys both to authenticate network clients and to encrypt data in transit.

Wi-Fi Alliance An international, nonprofit organization dedicated to ensuring the interoperability of 802.11-capable devices.

Wi-Fi Protected Access *See* WPA.

Wired Equivalent Privacy *See* WEP.

WPA (Wi-Fi Protected Access) A wireless security method endorsed by the Wi-Fi Alliance that is considered a subset of the 802.11i standard. In WPA, authentication follows the same mechanism specified in 802.11i. The main difference between WPA and 802.11i is that WPA specifies RC4 encryption rather than AES.

WPA2 The name given to the 802.11i security standard by the Wi-Fi Alliance. The only difference between WPA2 and 802.11i is that WPA2 includes support for the older WPA security method.

Review Questions

1. Which strategy is most commonly used by an intruder to gain access to a network?

   a. Using malware

   b. Social engineering

   c. Man-in the middle attacks

   d. Circumventing network hardware and design flaws

2. What is the type of risk when an administrator accepts the default security options after installing an operating system or application?

   a. Risks associated with Internet access

   b. Risks associated with people

   c. Risks inherent in network hardware and design

   d. Risks associated with protocols and software

3. Which response team member is the person on call who first notices or is alerted to the problem?

   a. Dispatcher

   b. Technical support specialist

   c. Manager

   d. Public relations specialist

4. Which authentication protocol encrypts user names and passwords for transmission?

    a. CHAP

    b. PAP

    c. EAP

    d. PPP

5. By default, which standard does not offer security?

    a. WPA

    b. WEP

    c. 802.11i

    d. 802.11

6. True or false? SSL (Secure Sockets Layer) is a method of encrypting TCP/IP transmissions—including Web pages and data entered into Web forms—en route between the client and server using public key encryption technology.

7. True or false? An IDS can detect, react to, and log suspicious activity.

8. True or false? When a firewall can view a data stream, it is known as a stateless firewall.

9. True or false? Encryption is the last means of defense against data theft.

10. True or false? RADIUS and TACACS belong to a category of protocols known as AAA (authentication, authorization, and accounting.)

11. A(n) _____ is a thorough examination of each aspect of the network to determine how it might be compromised.

12. A(n) _____ identifies your security goals, risks, levels of authority, designated security coordinator and team members, responsibilities for each team member, and responsibilities for each employee.

13. A(n) _____ is a software application on a network host that acts as an intermediary between the external and internal networks, screening all incoming and outgoing traffic.

14. In _____ encryption, data is encrypted using two keys.

15. _____ is a key encryption technique for wireless networks that uses keys both to authenticate network clients and to encrypt data in transit.

After reading this chapter and completing the exercises, you will be able to:

- Describe the steps involved in an effective troubleshooting methodology

- Follow a systematic troubleshooting process to identify and resolve networking problems

- Document symptoms, solutions, and results when troubleshooting network problems

- Use a variety of software and hardware tools to diagnose problems

On the Job

A customer called the managed security services firm I worked for and asked why one of their subnets was unable to reach the HTTP proxy service that was running on the inside interface of the Linux-based firewall we managed for them. I dutifully fired up tcpdump, an open source network diagnostic utility, and watched packets arriving from the subnet in question. The packets didn't look obviously malformed, and they were correctly addressed for the proxy service on the firewall. Usually this sort of customer call resulted from a poorly configured automatic proxy configuration file, but not this time.

Puzzled, I watched as the customer removed the proxy address specification on a workstation in the affected network and was suddenly able to reach the world. This suggested that the problem was somehow related to the firewall. In each case, though, I would see the packets arrive on the inside interface of the firewall.

If the firewall were dropping the packet, I would have seen it in the logging. So I watched the socket state with netstat and saw that the proxy service never received the connection initiation segments (TCP SYN) from the problem subnet. Though I could see the packets arriving, the IP stack seemed to be ignoring them.

After examining the packet traces at various layers using tcpdump and Wireshark, I asked for another pair of eyes to help me. He noticed something I had overlooked. The 10th byte of the Ethernet frame destination address on the frame bound for the proxy service was wrong. This was the smoking gun. It meant that when packets passed through their switch to the Internet as a whole, the frame destination address was not mangled. But when packets passed through to the inside interface on the firewall, the switch was corrupting the frame destination address.

Our customer's network equipment vendor confirmed that the problem was the electronics on one of the switch ports. Sometimes another pair of eyes is all it takes.

Martin A. Brown
Renesys Corporation

By now, you know how networks should work. Like other complex systems, however, they don't always work as planned. Many things can go wrong on a network, just as many things can go wrong with your car, your house, or a project at work. In fact, a network professional probably spends more time fixing network problems than designing or upgrading a network. Some breakdowns (such as an overtaxed processor) come with plenty of warning, but others (such as a hard disk controller failure) can strike instantly.

The best defense against problems is prevention. Just as you maintain your car regularly, you should monitor the health of your network regularly. Of course, even the most well-monitored network will sometimes experience unexpected problems. For example, a utility company could dig a new hole for its cable and accidentally cut your dedicated link to the Internet. In such a situation, your network can go from perfect to disastrous performance in an instant. In this chapter, you will learn how to diagnose and solve network problems in a logical, step-by-step fashion, using a variety of tools.

Troubleshooting Methodology

Net+

4.6

Successful troubleshooters proceed logically and methodically. This section introduces a basic troubleshooting methodology, leading you through a series of general problem-solving steps. These steps follow the recommendations specified in CompTIA's Network+ exam objectives. Bear in mind that experience in your network environment may prompt you to follow the steps in a different order or to skip certain steps entirely. For example, if you know that one segment of your network is poorly cabled, you might try replacing a section of cable in that area to solve a connectivity problem before attempting to verify the physical and logical integrity of the workstation's NIC. In general, however, it's best to follow each step in the order shown. Such a logical approach can save you from undertaking wasteful, time-consuming efforts such as unnecessary software or hardware replacements.

Steps for troubleshooting network problems are as follows:

- Identify the symptoms and problems. Record what you learn from people or systems that alerted you to the problems, and keep that documentation handy.

- Identify the affected area. Are users across the entire network experiencing the problem at all times? Or, is the problem limited to a specific geographic area of the network, to a specific demographic group of users, or to a particular period of time? Are all of the symptoms related to a single problem, or are you dealing with multiple problems?

- Determine what has changed. Recent hardware or software changes could be causing the symptoms.

- Establish the most probable cause. To find the probable cause, you might need to do the following:

  - Verify user competency.

  - Re-create the problem, and ensure that you can reproduce it reliably.

  - Verify the physical integrity of the network connection (such as cable connections, NIC installations, and power to devices), starting at the affected nodes and moving outward toward the backbone.

  - Verify the logical integrity of the network connection (such as addressing, protocol bindings, software installations, and so on).

- Determine whether escalation is necessary. If a problem appears to affect a large group of clients and you suspect a router is involved, for example, you might need to contact one of the engineers responsible for maintaining routers on your network.

- Create an action plan and solution and be prepared for all potential effects. For example, if you have to reassign IP addresses, how will the change of an IP address on a server affect its clients? Or, in another case, if you upgrade the type of client software used on a workstation, how will that affect a user's daily routine?

- Implement the solution and test the result. Has your solution solved the problem?

- Identify the results and effects of the solution. For example, if you had to replace a switch, did the new switch affect network performance, VLAN status, or client access to the network?

- Document the solution and process. Make sure that both you and your colleagues understand the cause of the problem and how you solved it. This information should be kept in a centrally available repository, such as an online database.

In addition to the organized method of troubleshooting described in this section, a good, general rule for troubleshooting can be stated as follows: Pay attention to the obvious! Although some questions may seem too simple to bother asking, don't discount them. You can often save much time by checking cable connections first. Every networking professional can tell a story about spending half a day trying to figure out why a computer wouldn't connect to the network, only to discover that the network cable was not plugged into the wall jack or the device's NIC.

Identify the Symptoms and Problems

When troubleshooting a network problem, your first step is to identify the problem and its symptoms. After you identify the problem and its symptoms, you can begin to deduce their cause. For example, suppose a user complains that he cannot save a file to a network drive. That's a symptom of a problem, which might be that he cannot access the network drive. At that point, you can list several potential causes, including a faulty NIC, cable, switch, or router; an incorrect client software configuration; a server failure; or a user error. On the other hand, you can probably rule out a power failure, a printer failure, an Internet connectivity failure, an e-mail server failure, and a host of other problems.

Answering the following questions may help you identify symptoms of a network problem that aren't immediately obvious:

- Is access to the LAN or WAN affected?

- Is network performance affected?

- Are data or programs affected? Or are both affected?

- Are only certain network services (such as printing) affected?

- If programs are affected, does the problem include one local application, one networked application, or multiple networked applications?

- What specific error messages do users report?

- Is one user or are multiple users affected?

- Do the symptoms manifest themselves consistently?

Net+
4.6

One danger in troubleshooting technical problems is jumping to conclusions about the symptoms. For example, you might field 12 questions from users one morning about a problem printing to the network printer in the Facilities department. You might have already determined that the problem is an addressing conflict with the printer and be in the last stages of resolving the problem. Minutes later, when a 13th caller says, "I'm having problems printing," you might immediately conclude that she is another facilities staff member and that her inability to print results from the same printer addressing problem. In fact, this user may be in the Administration department, and her inability to print could represent a symptom of a larger network problem.

Take time to pay attention to the users, system and network behaviors, and any error messages. Treat each symptom as unique (but potentially related to others). In this way, you avoid the risk of ignoring problems or—even worse—causing more problems.

Take note of the error messages reported by users. If you aren't near the users, ask them to read the messages to you directly off their screens or, better yet, print the screens that contain the error messages. (On some computers, pressing the Print Screen button—which is sometimes labeled "Print Scrn" or "PrtSc"—will issue a copy of what's on the screen to the computer's clipboard, after which it can be printed or saved as a file. On other computers, you can use the Shift+Print Screen or Alt+Print Screen keystroke combinations.) Keep a record of these error messages along with your other troubleshooting notes for that problem.

Identify the Affected Area

After you have identified the problem and its symptoms, you should determine whether the problem affects only a certain group of users or certain areas of the organization, or if the problem occurs at certain times. For example, if a problem affects only users on a wireless network segment, you might deduce that the problem lies with that segment's access point. On the other hand, if symptoms are limited to one user, you can typically narrow down the cause of the problem to a single piece of hardware (for example, a workstation's NIC), software configuration, or user.

As you learned in Chapter 4, a quick way to confirm that a node's network interface is responding and that its core TCP/IP protocols are properly installed is to ping the loopback address, 127.0.0.1. To perform this test on a host running IPv4, type `ping 127.0.0.1` and press Enter at a command prompt. If you receive a positive response, you can expand the scope of your troubleshooting. If not, begin to determine why the node's network interface doesn't respond.

To begin, you must ascertain how many users or network segments are affected. For example, do the symptoms apply to:

- One user or workstation?
- A workgroup?
- A department?

4.6

- One location within an organization?
- An entire organization?

In addition, it is useful to narrow down the time frame during which the problem occurred. The following questions can help you determine the chronological scope of a problem:

- When did the problem begin?
- Has the network, server, or workstation ever worked properly?
- Did the symptoms appear in the last hour or day?
- Have the symptoms appeared intermittently for a long time?
- Do the symptoms appear only at certain times of the day, week, month, or year?

Similar to identifying symptoms, narrowing down the area affected by a problem can eliminate some causes and point to others. In particular, it can help distinguish workstation (or user) problems from network problems. If the problem affects only a department or floor of your organization, for example, you probably need to examine that network segment, its router interface, its cabling, or a server that provides services to those users. Or, you might trace a problem to a single user in that area—for example, an employee who watches video news reports from the Internet on his lunch hour, thereby consuming much of that segment's shared bandwidth. If a problem affects users at a remote location, you should examine the WAN link or its router interfaces. If a problem affects all users in all departments and locations, a catastrophic failure has occurred, and you should assess critical devices such as central switches and backbone connections.

With all network problems, including catastrophic ones, you should take the time to troubleshoot them correctly by asking specific questions designed to identify their scope. For example, suppose a user complains that his mail program isn't picking up e-mail. You should begin by asking when the problem began, whether it affects only that user or everyone in his department, and what error message (or messages) the user receives when he attempts to pick up mail. In answering your questions, he might say, "The problem began about 10 minutes ago. Both my neighbors are having problems with e-mail, too. And as a matter of fact, a network technician was working on my machine this morning and installed a new graphics program."

As you listen to the user's response, you may need to politely filter out information that is unlikely to be related to the problem. In this situation, the user relayed two significant pieces of information: (1) The scope of the problem includes a group of users, and (2) the problem began 10 minutes ago. With this knowledge, you can then delve further in your troubleshooting. In this example, you would proceed by focusing on the network segment rather than on one workstation.

Discovering the time or frequency with which a problem occurs can reveal more subtle network problems. For example, if multiple users throughout the organization experience poor performance when attempting to log on to the server at 8:05 a.m., you might deduce that the server needs additional resources to handle the processing burden of accepting so many requests. If a network fails at noon every Tuesday, you might be able to correlate this problem with a test of your building's power system, which causes a power dip that affects the servers, routers, and other devices.

Net+
4.6

Identifying the affected area of a problem leads you to your next troubleshooting steps. The path might not always be clear-cut, but as the flowcharts in Figures 13-1 and 13-2 illustrate, some direction can be gained from narrowing both the demographic (or geographic) and the chronological scopes of a problem. Notice that these flowcharts end with the process of further troubleshooting. In the following sections, you will learn more about these subsequent troubleshooting steps.

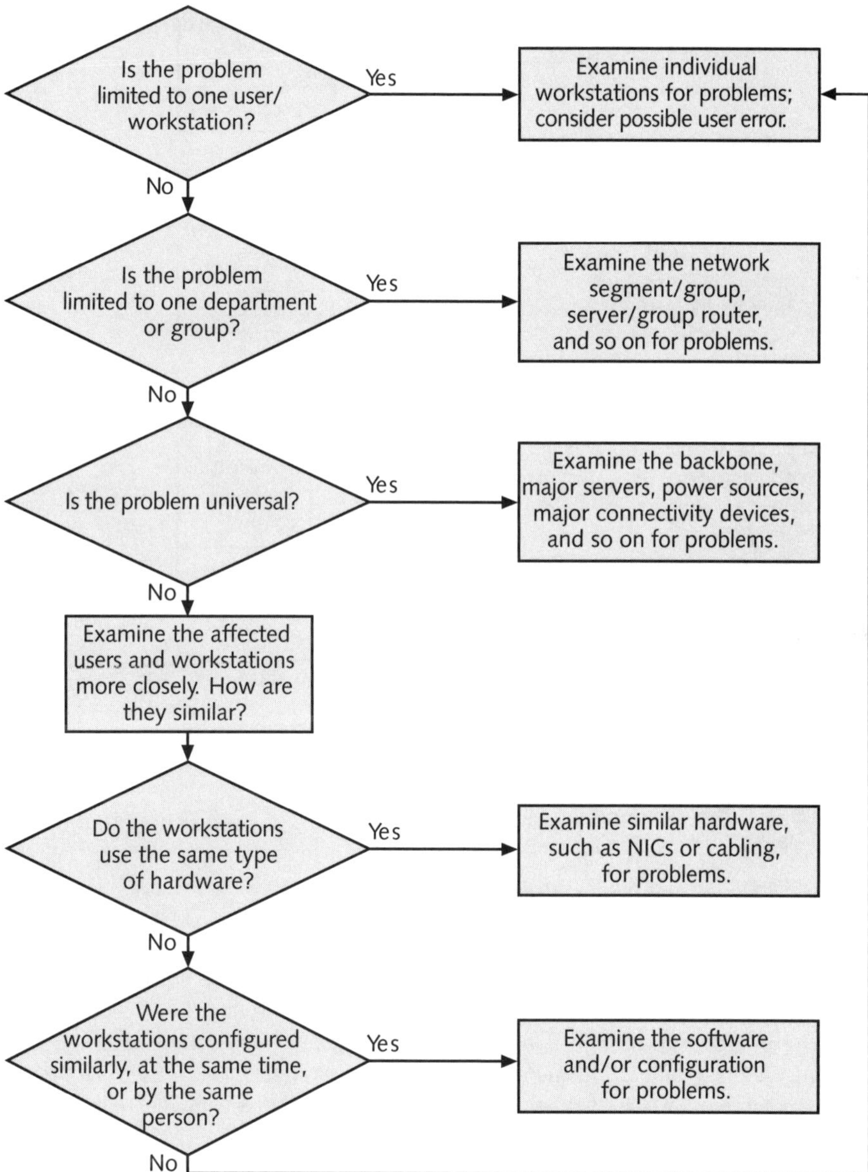

Figure 13-1 Identifying the area affected by a problem

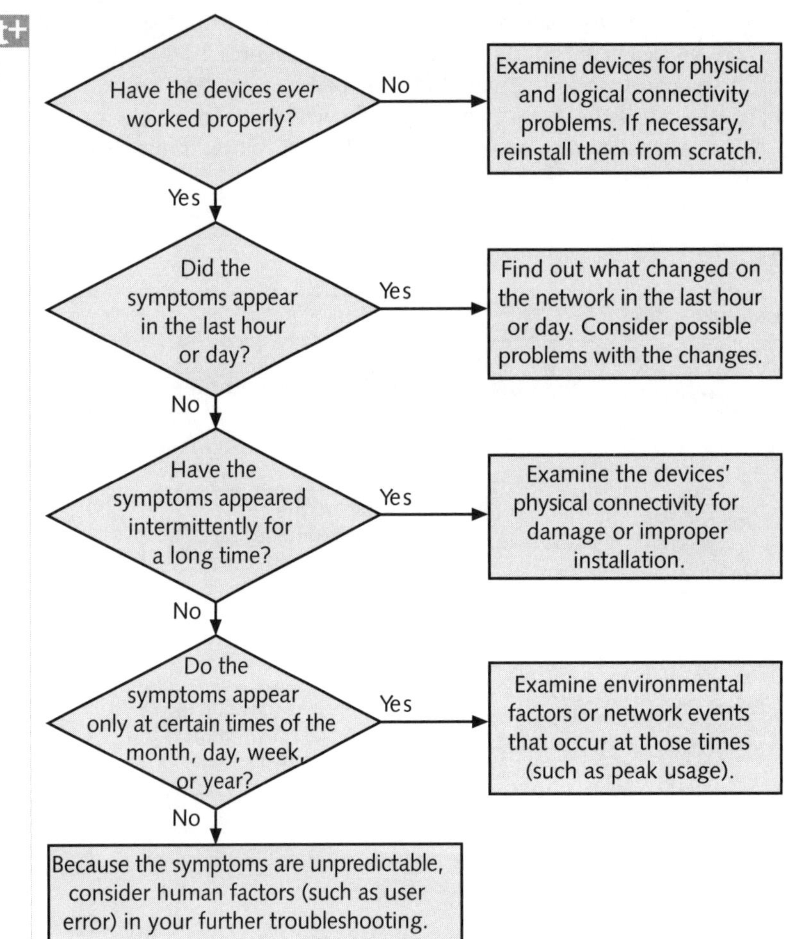

Figure 13-2 Identifying the chronological scope of a problem

One fascinating example of troubleshooting that began with determining a problem's chronological scope was experienced by a wireless networking engineer working on a small metropolitan area network. His spread-spectrum RF network links, which connected businesses to a carrier's facility via a transmitter and receiver on a hospital's roof, worked perfectly all day but failed when the sun went down. When the sun came up the next morning, the wireless links worked again. The engineer confirmed that the equipment was fully operational (as he suspected) and then talked with the hospital personnel. The hospital's director informed him that the hospital had installed security cameras on the outside of the building. The cameras used the same RF frequency as the network's wireless links. When the security cameras were activated at sunset, their signals interfered with the wireless network's signals, preventing data from reaching its destination.

Determine What Has Changed

One could argue that considering recent network changes is not a separate step, but rather a continual and integral part of the troubleshooting process. As you begin troubleshooting, you

4.6 should be aware of any recent changes to your network. The following questions could help you pinpoint a problem that results from a network change:

- Did the operating system or configuration on a server, workstation, or connectivity device change?
- Were new components added to a server, workstation, or connectivity device?
- Were old components removed from a server, workstation, or connectivity device?
- Were new users or segments added to the network?
- Was a server, workstation, or connectivity device moved from its previous location to a new location?
- Was a server, workstation, or connectivity device replaced?
- Was new software installed on a server, workstation, or connectivity device?
- Was old software removed from a server, workstation, or connectivity device?

If you suspect that a network change has generated a problem, you can react in two ways: You can attempt to correct the problem that resulted from the change, or you can attempt to reverse the change and restore the hardware or software to its previous state. Both options come with hazards. Of the two, reverting to a previous state is probably less risky and less time consuming.

However, correcting the problem is sometimes the best solution. For example, if you immediately suspect that a change-related problem can be fixed easily, try correcting the problem first. If it is impossible to restore a software or hardware configuration to its previous state, your only choice is to solve the problem.

Before changing a network device or configuration, develop a plan and gather the proper resources for reversing the change in case things go wrong. For example, if you upgrade the memory module in a server, you should keep the old memory module handy in case the new one has flaws. In another situation, you might keep a backup of device or application configurations—perhaps by making a copy of the directory that stores the target configuration.

To track what has changed on a network, you and your colleagues in the IT department should keep complete network change records. The more precisely you describe a change, its purpose, and the time and date when it occurred in your records, the easier your troubleshooting will be if the change subsequently causes problems.

In addition to keeping thorough records, you must make them available to staff members who might need to reference them. For example, you might want to keep a record of changes in a database on a file server, and then use a Web-based form to retrieve and submit information from and to the database. That way, no matter where a network technician works in the organization, she can retrieve the information from any Web-enabled workstation. A simpler alternative is to keep a clipboard in the computer room with notes about changes.

Often, network changes cause unforeseen problems. For example, if you have narrowed a connectivity problem to a group of six users in the Marketing department, you might refer to your network's change log and find that a switch in the Marketing department's telecommunications closet was recently moved from one end of the closet to another. Reviewing the

4.6

record of this change can help you more quickly pinpoint the switch as a possible cause of the problem. Perhaps the switch was incorrectly reconnected to the backbone after the move, or perhaps it became damaged in the move or lost its configuration.

Establish the Most Probable Cause

After you have identified the scope of the problem and analyzed recent changes to the network, you are close to determining the problem's cause. The following sections provide techniques on how to zero in on the most likely cause among several plausible scenarios.

Verify User Competency You have probably experienced a moment in your dealings with computers in which you were certain you were doing everything correctly but still couldn't access the network, save a file, or pick up your e-mail. For example, you might have typed your case-sensitive network password without realizing that the Caps Lock function was turned on. Even though you were certain that you typed the right password, you received a "password incorrect" error message each time you tried to enter it. All users experience such problems from time to time.

It's natural for human beings to make mistakes. Thus, as a troubleshooter, one of your first steps is to ensure that human error is not the source of the problem. This approach saves you time and worry. In fact, a problem caused by human error is usually simple to solve. It's much quicker and easier to assist a user in remapping a network drive, for example, than to perform diagnostics on the file server.

Sometimes, an inability to log on to the network results from a user error. Users become so accustomed to typing their passwords every morning and logging on to the network that, if something changes in the logon process, they don't know what to do. In fact, some users might never log out, so they don't know how to log on properly. Although these kinds of problems may seem simple to solve, unless a user receives training in the proper procedures and understands what might go wrong, she will never know how to solve a logon problem without assistance. Even if the user took a computer class that covered logging on, she might not remember what to do in unfamiliar situations.

The best way to verify that a user is performing network tasks correctly is to watch her. If this tactic isn't practical, the next best way is to connect to her computer using remote desktop software that allows you to view everything that appears on the user's screen or even control the computer from afar. If that isn't possible, talk with the user by phone while she tries to replicate the error. At every step, calmly ask the user to explain what appears on the screen and what, exactly, she is doing. Urge the user to proceed slowly, according to your prompts, so that she doesn't rush ahead. After every keystroke or command, ask the user again what appears on the screen. With this methodical approach, you will have a good chance at catching user-generated mistakes. At the same time, if the problem does not result from human error, you will gain important clues for further troubleshooting.

Re-Create the Problem An excellent way to learn more about the causes of a problem is to try to re-create the symptoms yourself. If you cannot reproduce the symptoms, you might suspect that a problem was a one-time occurrence or that a user performed an operation incorrectly.

Net+
4.6

You should try to reproduce symptoms both while logged on as the user who reported the problem and while logged on under a privileged account (such as an administrator-equivalent user name). If the symptoms appear only when you're logged on as the user, the problem might relate to the user's limited rights on the network. For example, suppose a user complains that he could edit a particular spreadsheet in the Accounting directory on the file server on Friday but was unable to open the file on Monday. When you visit his workstation, you verify this sequence of events while logged on with his user name. When you then log on as administrator, however, you are able to open and edit the file. The difference in your experiences points to a user rights problem. At that point, you should check the user's privileges—especially whether they have changed since he could last retrieve the file. Perhaps someone removed him from a group that had Read and Modify rights to the Accounting directory.

Answering the following questions may help you determine whether a problem's symptoms are truly reproducible and, if so, to what extent:

- Can you make the symptoms recur every time? If symptoms recur, are they consistent?

- Can you make the symptoms recur some of the time?

- Do the symptoms happen only under certain circumstances? For instance, if you log on under a different user name or try the operation from a different machine, do the symptoms still appear?

- In the case of software malfunctions, are the symptoms consistent no matter how many and which programs or files the user has open?

- Do the symptoms *ever* happen when you try to repeat them?

When attempting to reproduce the symptoms of a problem, you should follow the same steps that the person reporting the symptoms followed. As you know, many computer functions can be achieved through different means. For example, in a word-processing program, you might save a file by using the menu bar, using a keystroke combination, or clicking a button on a toolbar. All three methods result in the same outcome. Similarly, you might log on to the network from a command prompt, from a predefined script inside a batch file, or from a window presented by the client software. If you attempt to reproduce a problem by performing different functions than those employed by the user, you might not be able to reproduce a legitimate problem and, thus, might assume that the symptoms resulted from user error. In fact, you might be missing a crucial clue to solving the problem.

To reproduce a symptom reliably, ask the user precisely what she did before the error appeared. For example, if a user complains that her network connection mysteriously drops when she's in the middle of surfing the Web, try to replicate the problem at her workstation; also, find out what else was running on the user's workstation or what kind of Web sites she was surfing.

Use good judgment when attempting to reproduce problems. In some cases, reproducing a problem could wreak havoc on the network, its data, and its devices; you should not attempt to reproduce such a problem. An obvious example involves a power outage in which your backup power source failed to supply power. After your network equipment comes back online, you would not cut the power again simply to verify that the problem derived from a faulty backup power source.

Net+ **Verify Physical Layer Connectivity** By some estimates, more than half of all network problems occur at the physical layer of the OSI model, which includes cabling, network
4.6 adapters, repeaters, and hubs. The physical layer also controls signaling—both wired and wireless. Because physical layer faults are so common (and are often easily fixed), you should be
4.7 thoroughly familiar with the symptoms of such problems.

Symptoms of Physical Layer Problems Often, physical connectivity problems manifest
as a continuous or intermittent inability to connect to the network and perform network-
related functions. Causes of unreliable network connectivity can include the following:

- Segment or network lengths that exceed the IEEE maximum standards (for example,
  an Ethernet 100Base-TX segment that exceeds 100 meters)
- Noise affecting a wireless or wire-bound signal (from EMI sources, improper grounding, or cross talk)
- Improper terminations, faulty connectors, loose connectors, or poorly crimped connections
- Damaged cables (for example, crushed, bent, nicked, or partially severed)
- Faulty NICs

Physical connectivity problems do not typically (but occasionally can) result in software
application anomalies, the inability to use a single application, poor network performance,
protocol errors, software licensing errors, or software usage errors. Some software errors,
however, point to a physical connectivity problem. For example, a user might be able to log
on to his file server without problems. When he chooses to run a query on a database, however, his report software might produce an error message indicating that the database is
unavailable or not found. If the database resides on a separate server, this symptom could
point to a physical connectivity problem with the database server.

Diagnosing Physical Layer Problems Answering the following questions may help you
identify a problem pertaining to physical connectivity:

- Is the device turned on?
- Is the NIC properly inserted?
- In the case of wireless NICs, is the antenna turned on?
- Is a device's network cable properly (that is, not loosely) connected to both its NIC
  and the wall jack?
- Do patch cables properly connect punch-down blocks to patch panels and patch
  panels to hubs or switches?
- Is the hub, router, or switch properly connected to the backbone?
- Are all cables in good condition (without signs of wear or damage)?
- Are all connectors (for example, RJ-45) in good condition and properly seated?
- Do network (maximum and segment) lengths conform to the IEEE 802 specifications?
- Are all devices configured properly to work with your network type or speed?

4.6

4.7

A first step in verifying the physical integrity of a connection is to follow the cabling from one endpoint on the network to the other. For example, if a workstation user cannot log on to the network, and you have verified that he is typing his password correctly, check the physical connectivity from his workstation's NIC and patch cable. Follow his connection all the way through the network to the server that he cannot reach. Recently moved computers, recently recabled workgroups or nodes, and computers with cables in busy areas that could be unseated by bumping or pulling are prime candidates for errors caused by faulty connections.

In addition to verifying the connections between devices, you must verify the soundness of the hardware used in those connections. A sound connection means that cables are inserted firmly in ports, NICs, and wall jacks; NICs are seated firmly in the system board; connectors are not broken; and cables are not damaged. Damaged or improperly inserted connectivity elements may result in only occasional (and, therefore, difficult-to-troubleshoot) errors.

Swapping Equipment If you suspect a problem lies with a network component, one of the easiest ways to test your theory is to exchange that component for a functional one. In many cases, such a swap resolves the problem very quickly, so you should try this tactic early in your troubleshooting process. It won't always work, of course, but with experience you will learn what types of problems are most likely caused by component failure.

For example, if a user cannot connect to the network, and you have checked to make sure all the connections are secure and the logical connectivity elements are sound, you might consider swapping the user's network cable with a functional one. As you know, network cables must meet specific standards to operate properly. If one becomes damaged (for example, by a chair repeatedly rolling over it), it will prevent a user from connecting to the network. Swapping an old network cable with a new one is a quick test that could save you further troubleshooting.

In addition to swapping network cables, you might need to change a patch cable from one port in a switch to another, or from one data jack to another. Ports and data jacks can be operational one day and faulty the next. You might also swap a network adapter from one machine to another, or try installing a new network adapter, making sure it's compatible with the client. Obviously, it's more difficult to swap a switch or router because of the number of nodes serviced by these components and the potentially significant configuration they require; if network connectivity has failed for an entire segment or network, however, this approach may provide a quicker answer than attempting to troubleshoot the faulty device.

A better—albeit more expensive—alternative to swapping parts is to have redundancy built in to your network. For example, you might have a server that contains two network adapters, allowing one network adapter to take over for the other if one adapter should fail. If properly installed and configured, this arrangement results in no downtime; in contrast, swapping parts requires at least a few minutes of service disruption. In the case of swapping a router, the downtime might last for several hours.

Before swapping any network component, make sure that the replacement has the same specifications as the original part. By installing a component that's different from the original device, you risk thwarting your troubleshooting efforts because the new component might not work in the environment. In the worst case, you may damage existing equipment by installing a component that isn't rated for it.

Net+

4.6

4.7

The flowchart in Figure 13-3 illustrates how logically assessing physical layer elements can help you solve a network problem. The steps in this flowchart apply to a typical problem: a user's inability to log on to the network. They assume that you have already ruled out user error and that you have successfully reproduced the problem under both your and the user's logon ID.

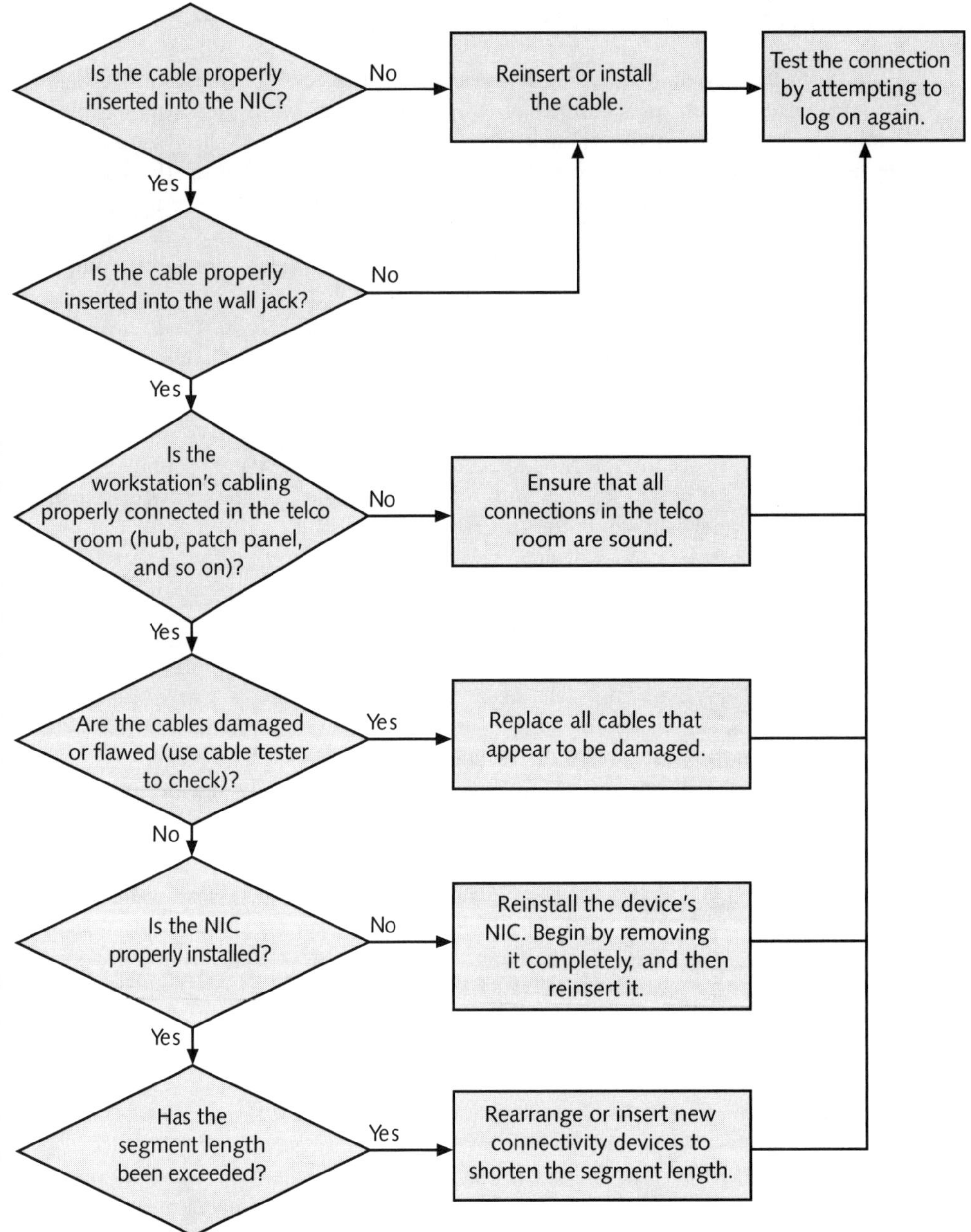

Figure 13-3 Verifying physical connectivity

 **Verify Logical Connectivity** After you have verified the physical connections, you must examine the firmware and software configurations, settings, installations, and privileges. Depending on the type of symptoms, you might need to investigate networked applications, the network operating system, or hardware configurations. All of these elements belong in the category of "logical connectivity."

4.6

4.7

Answering the following questions may help you identify a problem with logical connectivity:

- Do error messages reference damaged or missing files or device drivers?
- Do error messages reference malfunctioning or insufficient resources (such as memory)?
- Has an operating system, configuration, or application been recently changed, introduced, or deleted?
- Does the problem occur with only one application or a few, similar applications?
- Does the problem happen consistently?
- Does the problem affect a single user or one group of users?

Logical connectivity problems often prove more difficult to isolate and resolve than physical connectivity problems because they can be more complex. For example, a user might complain that she has been unable to connect to the network for the past two hours. After you go to her workstation and find that you can reproduce the symptoms while logged on under both her user name and your user name, you check the physical connections. Everything seems to be in order. Next, you may ask the user whether anything changed on her machine approximately two hours ago. She tells you that she didn't do a thing to the machine—it just stopped working.

At this point, you might investigate the workstation's logical connectivity. Some possible software-based causes for a failure to connect to the network include (but are not limited to) the following: resource conflicts with the NIC's configuration, an improperly configured NIC (for example, it may be set to the wrong data rate), improperly installed or configured client software, and improperly installed or configured network protocols or services. In this example, you may take another look at the client logon screen and notice that the wrong server is selected as the default. After you change the default server setting in the user's client software, she will likely be able to log on to the network.

Determine Whether Escalation Is Necessary

4.6

Many staff members can contribute to troubleshooting a network problem. Often, the division of duties is formalized, with a help desk acting as a single point of contact for users. A help desk is typically staffed with **help desk analysts**—people proficient in basic (but not usually advanced) workstation and network troubleshooting. Larger organizations might group their help desk analysts into teams based on their expertise. For example, a company that provides users with word processing, spreadsheet, project planning, scheduling, and graphics software might assign different technical support personnel at the help desk to answer questions pertaining to each application.

The help desk analysts are often considered **first-level support**, because they provide the first level of troubleshooting. When a user calls with a problem, a help desk analyst typically creates a record for the incident and attempts to diagnose the problem. The help desk analyst might be able to solve a common problem over the phone within minutes by explaining something to the user. On other occasions, the problem could be rare or complex. In such cases, the first-level support analyst will refer, or **escalate**, the problem to a second-level support analyst.

A **second-level support** analyst is someone who has specialized knowledge in one or more aspects of a network. For example, if a user complains that she can't connect to a server, and the first-level support person narrows down the problem to a failed file server, that first-level support analyst would then refer the problem to the second-level support person. Some organizations also have **third-level support** personnel who are highly skilled in one area of networking. Second-level analysts escalate only the most severe or complex issues to third-level support personnel. Such staff are typically not part of the help desk, but specialists in another area, such as routing and switching, server management, or security.

In addition to having first- and second-level support analysts, most help desks include a help desk coordinator. The **help desk coordinator** ensures that analysts are divided into the correct teams, schedules shifts at the help desk, and maintains the infrastructure to enable analysts to better perform their jobs. They might also serve as third-level support personnel, taking responsibility for troubleshooting a problem when the second-level support analyst is unable to solve it.

When you're part of a troubleshooting team, you need to know when and how to escalate problems. For guidance, you might turn to a procedure that lists specific conditions under which escalation is critical. For example, suppose you work for an ISP with one large corporate customer whose income depends largely on Internet sales that are handled by servers and connections in your data center. Your organization might deem that anytime one of that company's servers fails to respond, a second-level support analyst is assigned to troubleshoot it. In other cases, you will have to use your judgment to determine whether a situation warrants escalation. You'll base your decision on several factors, including the number of users affected, the importance of the access or service affected, the familiarity of the problem, and your technical skills.

Create an Action Plan and Solution Including Potential Effects

After you have thoroughly analyzed a network problem, you will be able to devise an action plan and implement your solution. First, however, you must consider how your solution might affect users and network functionality.

Scope One of the most important aspects to consider is the breadth, or scope, of your change. For example, replacing a cable that connects a workstation to a switch may affect only one user, but replacing a cable that connects a server to a switch affects all users who access that server. Assess the scope of your solution—whether it is a single workstation, a workgroup, a location, or the entire network—before implementing that solution. If the problem does not pose an emergency, wait until no one is on the network before implementing solutions that affect many users. That way, you will have time to assess the solution's effects systematically and fix any new problems that might arise.

Trade-Offs Along with the scope, another factor to consider is the trade-off your solution might impose. In other words, your solution might restore functionality for one group of users but remove it for others. For example, let's say you are a network technician at a stationery company that uses specialized software to program custom logos and control its embossing machines. When you add a group of new Windows Vista workstations to your network, you

Net+

4.6

discover that these new workstations can't run the embossing control software properly. The software vendor tells you that to be compatible with Windows Vista, you must install a new, Vista-compatible version of the software on your file server. You might be thrilled to hear of such a simple solution and install the updated embossing control software immediately. In the next half hour, you receive numerous phone calls from employees using Windows XP workstations who cannot properly use the embossing control software. You have solved one problem but created another. In this situation, it would have been wise to ask the software vendor about its upgrade's compatibility with all the other operating systems your company uses. If the vendor told you about a problem with Windows XP workstations, you could have kept the old installation on the server for these users and then installed the new version of the software in another directory for use by Windows Vista users.

Security Be aware of the security implications of your solution because it may inadvertently result in the addition or removal of network access or resource privileges for a user or group of users. One consequence may be that a user can no longer access a data file or application he is accustomed to accessing. But a worse consequence is that you could create a security vulnerability that allows unauthorized people to access your network. Before installing a software upgrade or patch, for example, be sure to understand how it could change access for both authorized and unauthorized users.

Scalability Also consider the scalability of the solution you intend to implement. Does it position the network for additions and enhancements later on, or is it merely a temporary fix that the organization will outgrow in a year? Ideally, your solution would be perfectly suited to your network and allow for future growth. But a temporary fix is not necessarily wrong, depending on the scenario. For example, suppose you walk into the office one day to find that none of your users can access the network. You track down the problem as an internal hardware problem with your Internet gateway. Because the gateway is under warranty, you quickly call the manufacturer to get the gateway replaced or fixed immediately. The manufacturer tells you that although it doesn't have the identical gateway available in its local office, it can substitute a different, smaller model to get your users reconnected today, and meanwhile order the identical gateway that you can install when you have more time. In this situation, it's probably preferable to take the temporary gateway and restore functionality than to wait for the ideal solution.

Cost Another factor to consider when implementing your solution is cost. Obviously, replacing one patch cable or faulty network adapter is a fairly inexpensive proposition, and you don't need to analyze cost in these cases. But if the solution you have proposed requires significant dollars for either software or hardware, weigh your options carefully. For example, suppose you discover a problem with performance on your network. After some investigation, you determine that the best solution is to replace all 400 workstations' network adapters with newer, faster network adapters. If you purchase quality NICs, this solution could cost over $5,000 for the hardware alone, not to mention the time it will take technicians to replace the devices, which would cost more. Also, you should consider when these workstations will be replaced and if you will have to either discard or remove the network adapters you just installed. It might be more prudent to identify where the network's performance is poor and address those areas separately—for example, by adding a switch to a busy segment or adding a more powerful server for a heavily used application.

4.6

Use Vendor Information Some networking professionals pride themselves in being able to install, configure, and troubleshoot devices without reading the instructions—or at least exhausting all possibilities before they submit to reading a manual. Although some manufacturers provide better documentation than others, you have nothing to lose by referring to the manual, except a little time. Chances are you will find exactly what you need—configuration commands for a router or switch, recommendations for remote access server setup, or troubleshooting tips for a network operating system function, to name a few examples.

In addition to the documentation that comes with hardware and software, most vendors provide free online troubleshooting information. For example, Microsoft, Red Hat, and Apple offer searchable databases in which you can type your error message or a description of your problem and receive lists of possible solutions. Reputable equipment manufacturers, such as 3Com, Compaq, Cisco, IBM, and Intel, also offer sophisticated Web interfaces for troubleshooting their equipment. If you cannot find the documentation for a networking component, you should try looking for information on the Web.

Call the vendor's technical support phone number only after you have read the product documentation and searched the vendor's Web page. With some manufacturers, you can talk to a technical support agent only if you have established and paid for a support agreement. With others, you must pay per phone call. Each vendor has a different pricing structure for technical support, so before you agree to pay for technical support, you should find out whether the vendor charges on a per-hour or per-problem basis.

Keep a list handy of the hardware and software vendors for your networking equipment; the list should include the company's name, its technical support phone number, a contact name (if available), its technical support Web site address, its policies for technical support, and the type of agreement you currently have with the vendor. Make sure the list is updated regularly and available to all IT personnel who might need it.

If you are uncertain whether your proposed solution is the *best* solution, even after your thorough diagnosis and research, you should consult with others, either within or outside your organization. Colleagues or consultants might share an experience that leads you to prefer one solution to another.

Implement and Test the Solution

Finally, after you have researched the effects of your proposed solution, you are ready to implement the solution. This step might be very brief (such as correcting the default server designation in a user's client logon screen), or it might take a long time (such as replacing the hard disk of a server). In either case, implementing a solution requires foresight and patience. As with finding the problem, the more methodically and logically you can approach the solution, the more efficient the correction process will be. If a problem is causing catastrophic outages, however, you should solve it as quickly as possible.

The following steps will help you implement a safe and reliable solution:

- Collect all the documentation you have about a problem's symptoms from your investigation, and keep it handy while solving the problem.

- If you are reinstalling software on a device, make a backup of the device's existing software installation. If you are changing hardware on a device, keep the old parts handy in case the solution doesn't work. If you are changing the configuration of a program or device, take the time to print the program or device's current configuration. Even if the change seems minor, jot down notes about the original state. For example, if you intend to add a user to a privileged group to allow her access to the accounting spreadsheets, first write down the groups to which she currently belongs.

- Perform the change, replacement, move, or addition that you believe will solve the problem. Record your actions in detail so that you can later enter the information into a database.

- Test your solution. (Details follow this list.)

- Before leaving the area in which you were working, clean it up. For instance, if you created a new patch cable for a telecommunications room, remove the debris left from cutting and crimping the cable.

- If the solution fixes the problem, record the details you have collected about the symptoms, the problem, and the solution in your organization's troubleshooting database.

- If your solution involved a significant change or addressed a significant problem (one that affected more than a few users), revisit the solution a day or two later to verify that the problem has, indeed, been solved and that it hasn't created additional problems.

In the case of large-scale fixes—for example, applying new configurations on a global VPN's routers because of a security threat—it's often best to roll out changes in stages. This approach allows you to find and correct any problem that occurs during the upgrade before it affects all users. It also allows you to test whether you're implementing the solution in the best possible way. In the example of reconfiguring routers, you could log on to the routers and apply configurations from a remote office, but in some cases this creates additional security concerns. You might prefer instead to visit the offices and apply the changes yourself or talk to a local IT employee who can make the changes on site.

After implementing your solution, you must test its result and verify that you have solved the problem properly. Obviously, the type of testing you perform depends on your solution. For example, if you replaced a patch cable between a switch port and a patch panel, a quick test of your solution would be to determine whether you could connect to the network from the device that relies on that patch cable. If the device does not successfully connect to the network, you might have to try another cable or reconsider whether the problem stems from physical or logical connectivity or some other cause. In that case, using the hardware and software troubleshooting tools discussed later in this chapter might lead to a more efficient evaluation of your solution.

Testing the results of your solution will also depend on the area affected by the problem. Suppose you replaced a switch that served four different departments in an organization. To test the result of your solution, you would need to verify connectivity from workstations in each of the four departments.

You might not be able to test your solution immediately after implementing it. In some cases, you might wait days or weeks before you know for certain whether it worked. For example, suppose you discovered that a server was sometimes running out of processor capacity when handling clients' database queries, causing users to experience unacceptably slow response times. To solve this problem, you add two processors and enable the server's symmetric

multiprocessing capabilities. The timing of the database usage is unpredictable, however. As a result, you don't find out whether the added processors eliminated the problem until a certain number of users attempt the operations that push the server to its peak processor usage.

Identify the Results and Effects of the Solution

Upon testing your solution, you should be able to determine how and why the solution was successful and what effects it had on users and functionality. For example, suppose you identified a symptom of excessively slow performance when saving and retrieving files to and from a server on your LAN. You determined that all users were affected by the problem and that it had worsened steadily in the past month. Your proposed solution was to replace the server with one that contained a faster processor, more memory, greater hard disk capacity, and dual NICs. You implemented the solution and then tested its outcome to make sure all users could save and retrieve files to and from the new server. If all went well, the effect of the solution might be an 80 percent increase in performance between clients and the server.

Most importantly, you want to avoid creating unintended, negative consequences as a result of your solution. For example, in the process of diagnosing a problem with a user's access to a mail directory, you might have reconfigured his mail settings to log on with your own user name to rule out the possibility of a physical connectivity error. After discovering that the problem was actually due to an IP addressing conflict, you might fix the IP addressing problem but forget that you changed the user's e-mail configuration. Having the user test your solution would reveal this oversight—and prevent you from having to return to the workstation to solve another problem.

After you have implemented and tested your solution and identified its results and effects, communicate your solution to your colleagues, thus adding to the store of knowledge about your network. The next section discusses how best to document your troubleshooting efforts and notify others of changes you've made.

Document the Solution and Process

Whether you are a one-person network support team or one of 100 network technicians at your organization, you should always record the symptoms and cause (or causes) of a problem and your solution. Given the volume of problems you and other analysts will troubleshoot, it will be impossible to remember the circumstances of each incident. In addition, networking personnel frequently change jobs, and everyone appreciates clear, thorough documentation. An effective way to document problems and solutions is in a centrally located database to which all networking personnel have online access.

Document the Solution and Process For documenting problems, some organizations use a software program known as a **call tracking system** (also informally known as help desk software). Such programs provide user-friendly graphical interfaces that prompt the user for every piece of information associated with the problem. They assign unique identifying numbers to each problem, in addition to identifying the caller, the nature of the problem, the time necessary to resolve it, and the nature of the resolution.

Most call tracking systems are highly customizable, so you can tailor the form fields to your particular computing environment. For example, if you work for an oil refinery, you might add fields for identifying problems with the plant's flow-control software. In addition, most call tracking systems allow you to enter free-form text explanations of problems and solutions. Some also offer Web-based interfaces.

4.6

If your organization does not have a call tracking system, you should at least keep records in a simple electronic form. A typical problem record form should include at least the following fields:

- The name, department, and phone number of the problem originator (the person who first noticed the problem)
- Information regarding whether the problem is software or hardware related
- If the problem is software related, the package to which it pertains; if the problem is hardware-related, the device or component to which it pertains
- Symptoms of the problem, including when it was first noticed
- The name and telephone number of the network support contact
- The amount of time spent troubleshooting the problem
- The resolution of the problem

As discussed earlier in this chapter, many organizations operate a help desk staffed with personnel who have only basic troubleshooting expertise and who record problems called in by users. To effectively field network questions, an organization's help desk staff must maintain current and accurate records for network support personnel. Your department should take responsibility for managing a supported services list that help desk personnel can use as a reference. A **supported services list** is a document (preferably online) that lists every service and software package supported within an organization, plus the names of first- and second-level support contacts for those services or software packages. Anything else you or your department can do to increase communication and availability of support information will expedite troubleshooting.

In addition to communicating problems and solutions to your peers whenever you work on a network problem, you should follow up with the user who reported the problem. Make sure that the client understands how or why the problem occurred, what you did to resolve the problem, and whom to contact should the problem recur. This type of education helps your clients make better decisions about the type of support or training they need, and also improves their understanding of and respect for your department.

Notify Others of Changes After solving a particularly thorny network problem, you should record its resolution in your call tracking system and notify others of your solution and what, if anything, you needed to change to fix the problem. This communication serves two purposes: (1) It alerts others about the problem and its solution, and (2) it notifies others of network changes you made, in case they affect other services.

The importance of recording changes cannot be overemphasized. Imagine that you are the network manager for a group of five network technicians who support a WAN consisting of 3 different offices and 150 users. One day, the company's CEO travels from headquarters to a branch office for a meeting with an important client. At the branch office, she needs to print a financial statement but encounters a printing problem. Your network technician discovers that her user account does not have rights to that office's printer, because users on your WAN do not have rights to printers outside the office to which they belong. The network technician quickly takes care of the problem by granting all users rights to all printers across the WAN. What are the implications of this change? If your technician tells no one about this change, at best users may incorrectly print to a printer in Duluth from the St. Paul office. In a worst-case scenario, a "guest" user account may gain rights to a networked printer, potentially creating a security hole in your network.

4.6

Large organizations often implement change management systems to methodically track changes on the network. A **change management system** is a process or program that provides support personnel with a centralized means of documenting changes to the network. In smaller organizations, a change management system may be as simple as one document on the network to which networking personnel continually add entries to mark their changes. In larger organizations, the system might consist of a database package complete with graphical interfaces and customizable fields tailored to the computing environment. Whatever form your change management system takes, the most important element is participation. If networking personnel do not record their changes, even the most sophisticated software is useless.

The types of changes that network personnel should record in a change management system include the following:

- Adding or upgrading software on network servers or other devices
- Adding or upgrading hardware components on network servers or other devices
- Adding new hardware on the network (for example, a new server)
- Changing the properties or configurations of network devices (for example, changing the IP address or host name of a server or creating a new VLAN)
- Increasing or decreasing rights for a group of users
- Physically moving networked devices
- Moving user accounts and their files and directories from one server to another
- Making changes in processes (for example, a new backup schedule or a new contact for DNS support)
- Making changes in vendor policies or relationships (for example, a new hard disk supplier)

It's generally not necessary to record minor modifications, such as changing a user's password, creating a new group for users, creating new directories, or changing a network drive mapping for a user. Each organization will have unique requirements for its change management system, and analysts who record change information should clearly understand these requirements.

Help to Prevent Future Problems

If you review the troubleshooting questions and examples in this chapter, you can predict how some network problems can be averted by network maintenance, documentation, security, or upgrades. Although not all network problems are preventable, many can be avoided. Just as with your body's health, the best prescription for network health is prevention.

For example, to avoid problems with users' access levels for network resources, you can comprehensively assess users' needs, set policies for groups, use a variety of groups, and communicate to others who support the network why those groups exist. To prevent overusing network segments, you should perform regular network health checks—perhaps even continual network monitoring (discussed in the next section), with filters that isolate anomalous occurrences—and ensure that you have the means to either redesign the network to distribute traffic or purchase additional bandwidth well before utilization reaches critical levels. With experience, you will be able to add more suggestions for network problem prevention. When planning or upgrading a network, you should consciously think about how good network designs and policies can prevent later problems—not to mention, make your job easier and more fun.

Troubleshooting Tools

5.3

You have already learned about some utilities that can help you troubleshoot network problems. For example, you can learn many things about a user's workstation connection by attempting to ping different hosts on the network from that workstation. However, in some cases, the most efficient troubleshooting approach is to use a tool specifically designed to analyze and isolate network problems. Several tools are available, ranging from simple continuity testers that indicate whether a cable is faulty, to sophisticated protocol analyzers that capture and interpret all types of data traveling over the network. The tool you choose depends on the particular problem you need to investigate and the characteristics of your network. The following sections describe a variety of network troubleshooting tools, their functions, and their relative costs.

Crossover Cable

As you have learned, in a crossover cable the transmit and receive wire pairs in one of the connectors are reversed. This reversal enables you to use a crossover cable to directly interconnect two nodes without using an intervening connectivity device. A crossover cable is useful for quickly and easily verifying that a node's NIC is transmitting and receiving signals properly. For example, suppose you are a network technician on your way to fix urgent network problems. A user flags you down and says that over the last week he occasionally had problems connecting to the network and, as of this morning, he hasn't been able to connect at all. He's very frustrated, so you kindly say that if you can help him in 10 minutes, you will; otherwise, he'll have to call the help desk. You follow him to his workstation and, by asking around, you determine that he is the only one suffering this problem. Thus, you can probably narrow the problem down to his workstation (either hardware or software) or his cabling (or less likely, his port on the hub in the telecommunications closet). Because you have your laptop and troubleshooting gear in your bag, you quickly connect one plug of the crossover cable to his workstation's network adapter and the other plug to your laptop's network adapter. You then try logging on to your laptop from his workstation. Because this process is successful, you suggest that the problem lies with his network cable, and not with his workstation's software or hardware. You quickly hand him a new patch cable to replace his old one and rush off to your original destination.

Tone Generator and Tone Locator

Ideally, you and your networking colleagues would label each port and wire termination in a telecommunications closet so that problems and changes can be easily managed. However, because of personnel changes and time constraints, a telecommunications closet might be disorganized and poorly documented. If this is the case where you work, you might need a tone generator and a tone locator to determine where one pair of wires (out of possibly hundreds) terminates.

A **tone generator** (or **toner**) is a small electronic device that issues a signal on a wire pair. A **tone locator** (or **probe**) is a device that emits a tone when it detects electrical activity on a wire pair. They are sold together as a set, often called a toner and probe kit. By placing the tone generator at one end of a wire and attaching a tone locator to the other end, you can verify the location of the wire's termination. Figure 13-4 depicts the use of a tone generator and a tone locator. Of course, you must work by trial and error, guessing which termination

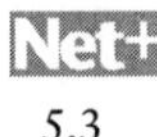

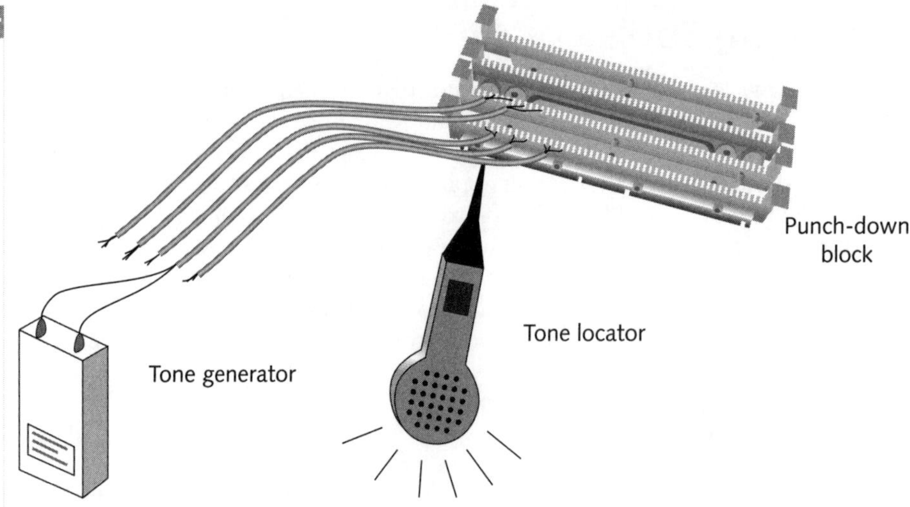

Figure 13-4 Use of a tone generator and tone locator

corresponds to the wire over which you've generated a signal until the tone locator indicates the correct choice. This combination of devices is also known as a **fox and hound,** because the locator (the hound) chases the generator (the fox).

Tone generators and tone locators cannot be used to determine characteristics about a cable, such as whether it's defective or whether its length exceeds IEEE standards for a certain type of network. They are only used to determine where a wire pair terminates.

A tone generator should never be used on a wire that's connected to a device's port or network adapter. Because a tone generator transmits electricity over the wire, it could damage the device or network adapter.

Net+ Multimeter

Cable testing tools are essential for both cable installers and network troubleshooters, as faulty cables are often the cause of network problems. Symptoms of cabling problems can be as elusive as occasional lost packets or as obvious as a break in network connectivity. You can easily test cables for faults with specialized tools. In this section and in the ones following, you will learn about different tools that can help isolate problems with network cables. The first device you will learn about is a **multimeter,** a simple instrument that can measure many characteristics of an electric circuit, including its resistance and voltage.

If you have taken an introductory electronics class, you are probably familiar with a **voltmeter,** the instrument that measures the pressure, or voltage, of an electric current. Recall that voltage is used to create signals over a network wire. Thus, every time data travels over a wire, the wire carries a small voltage. In addition, each wire has a certain amount of resistance, or opposition to electric current. Resistance is a fundamental property of wire that depends on a wire's molecular structure and size. Every type of wire has different resistance characteristics. Resistance is measured in ohms, and the device used to measure resistance is called an **ohmmeter.** Another characteristic of electrical circuits is impedance—the resistance that contributes to controlling the signal. Impedance is also measured in ohms. Impedance is the telltale factor for ascertaining where faults in a cable lie. A certain amount of impedance is required for a signal to be properly transmitted and interpreted. However, very high or low levels of impedance can signify a damaged wire, incorrect pairing, or a termination point. In other words, changes in impedance can indicate where current is stopped or inhibited.

Although you could use separate instruments for measuring impedance, resistance, and voltage on a wire, it is more convenient to have one instrument that accomplishes all of these functions. The multimeter is such an instrument. Figure 13-5 shows a multimeter.

As a network professional, you might use a multimeter to do the following:

- Verify that a cable is properly conducting electricity—that is, whether its signal can travel unimpeded from one node on the network to another.

- Check for the presence of noise on a wire (by detecting extraneous voltage).

- Verify that the amount of resistance presented by terminators on coaxial cable networks is appropriate, or whether terminators are actually present and functional.

- Test for short or open circuits in the wire (by detecting unexpected resistance or loss of voltage).

Multimeters vary in their degree of sophistication and features. Some merely show voltage levels, for example, whereas others can measure the level of noise on a circuit at any moment with extreme precision. Costs for multimeters also vary; some, such as those available at any home electronics store, cost as little as $30, while others cost as much as $4,000. Multimeters capable of the greatest accuracy are most useful to electronics engineers. As a network technician, you won't often need to know the upper limit of noise on a cable within a small fraction of a decibel, for example. However, you do need to know how to check whether a cable is conducting current. Another instrument that can perform such a test is a continuity tester, which is discussed next.

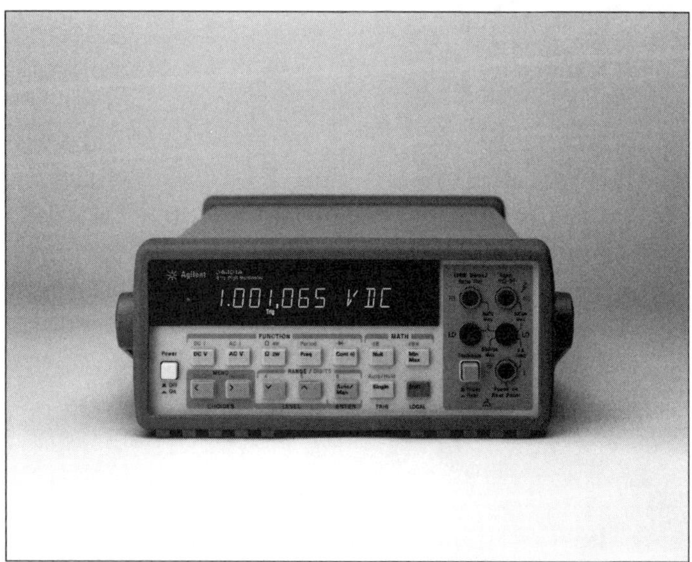

Figure 13-5 A multimeter

Net+ Cable Continuity Testers

4.7

5.3

In troubleshooting a physical layer problem, you may find the cause of a problem by simply testing whether your cable is carrying a signal to its destination. Tools used to make this determination are said to be testing the continuity of the cable and may be called **cable checkers** or **continuity testers**. They may also be called cable testers. The term **cable tester**, however, is a general term that also includes more sophisticated tools that can measure cable performance, as discussed in the following section.

When used on a copper-based cable, a continuity tester applies a small amount of voltage to each conductor at one end of the cable, and then checks whether that voltage is detectable at the other end. That means that a continuity tester consists of two parts: the base unit that generates the voltage and the remote unit that detects the voltage. Most cable checkers provide a series of lights that signal pass/fail. Some also indicate a cable pass/fail with an audible tone. A pass/fail test provides a simple indicator of whether a component can perform its stated function.

In addition to checking cable continuity, some continuity testers will verify that the wires in a UTP or STP cable are paired correctly and that they are not shorted, exposed, or crossed. Recall that different network models use specific wire pairings and follow cabling standards set forth in TIA/EIA 568. Make sure that the cable checker you purchase can test the type of network you use—for example, 10Base-T, 100Base-TX, or 1000Base-T Ethernet.

Continuity testers for fiber-optic networks also exist. Rather than issuing voltage on a wire, however, these testers issue light pulses on the fiber and determine whether they reached the other end of the fiber. Some continuity testers offer the ability to test both copper and fiber-optic cable.

Figure 13-6 depicts a basic continuity tester and a more sophisticated continuity tester.

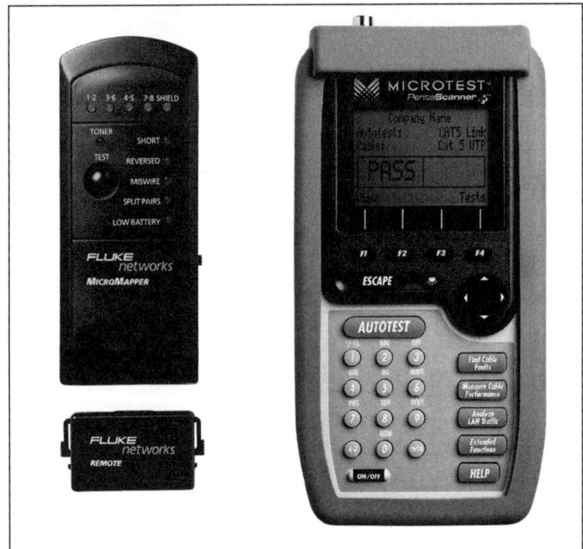

Figure 13-6 Cable continuity testers

Whether you make your own cables or purchase cabling from a reputable vendor, test the cable to ensure that it meets your network's required standards. Just because a cable is labeled "Cat 6," for example, does not necessarily mean that it will live up to that standard. Testing cabling before installing it could save many hours of troubleshooting after the network is in place.

Do not use a continuity tester on a live network cable. Disconnect the cable from the network, and then test its continuity.

NOTE

For convenience, most continuity testers are portable and lightweight and typically use one 9-volt battery. A continuity tester can cost between $30 and $500 and can save many hours of work. Popular manufacturers of these cable testing devices include Belkin, Fluke, Microtest, and Paladin.

Cable Performance Testers

If you need to know more than whether a cable is simply carrying current, you can use a **cable performance tester**. The difference between continuity testers and performance testers lies in their sophistication and price. A performance tester accomplishes the same continuity and fault tests as a continuity tester, but it can also perform the following tasks:

- Measure the distance to a connectivity device, termination point, or cable fault.
- Measure attenuation along a cable.
- Measure near end cross talk between wires.
- Measure termination resistance and impedance.
- Issue pass/fail ratings for Cat 3, Cat 5, Cat 5e, Cat 6, or Cat 7 standards.
- Store and print cable testing results or directly save data to a computer database.
- Graphically depict a cable's attenuation and cross talk characteristics over the length of the cable.

A sophisticated performance tester will include a **TDR (time domain reflectometer)**. A TDR issues a signal on a cable and then measures the way the signal bounces back (or reflects) to the TDR. Connectors, crimps, bends, short circuits, cable mismatches, or other defects modify the signal's amplitude before it returns to the TDR, thus changing the way it reflects. The TDR then accepts and analyzes the return signal, and based on its condition and the amount of time the signal took to return, determines cable imperfections. In the case of a coaxial cable network, a TDR can indicate whether terminators are properly installed and functional. A TDR can also indicate the distance between nodes and segments.

In addition to performance testers for coaxial and twisted-pair connections, you can find performance testers for fiber-optic connections. Such performance testers use **OTDRs (optical time domain reflectometers)**. Rather than issue an electrical signal over the cable as twisted-pair cable testers do, an OTDR transmits light-based signals of different wavelengths over the fiber. Based on the type of return light signal, the OTDR can accurately measure the length of the fiber; determine the location of faulty splices, breaks, connectors, or bends; and measure attenuation over the cable.

4.7

5.3

Because of their sophistication, performance testers for both copper and fiber-optic cables cost significantly more than continuity testers. A high-end unit could cost up to $30,000, and a low-end unit could sell for less than $4,000. Popular performance tester manufacturers include Fluke and Microtest. Figure 13-7 shows an example of a high-end cable performance tester that is capable of measuring the characteristics of both copper and fiber-optic cables.

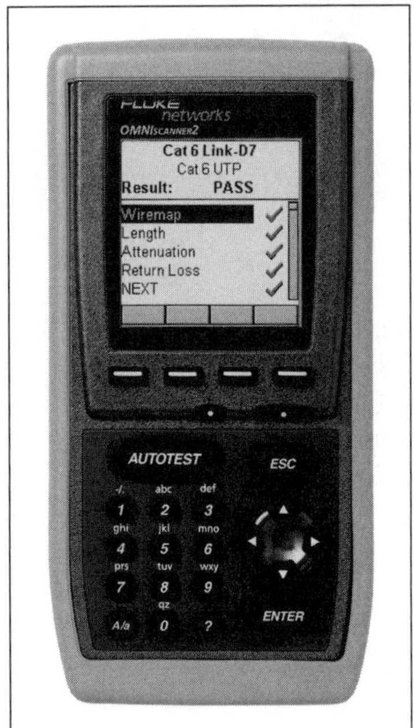

Figure 13-7 A cable performance tester

Voltage Event Recorders

Hardware depends on a steady flow of electricity to function properly. The term **voltage event** refers to any condition in which voltage exceeds or drops below predefined levels. In Chapter 14 you will learn how inconsistent or insufficient power can cause problems for network devices. In this chapter, you will focus on a device that allows you to monitor the electricity flowing to their servers, routers, and switches with a voltage event recorder.

This device, called a **voltage event recorder**, collects data about power quality. Left plugged into the same outlet that will be used by a network node, it gathers data about the power that outlet will provide to the node. This data is then downloaded to a workstation and analyzed by software that comes with the voltage event recorder. The software can check for and report on any voltage anomalies that exceed preset parameters. For example, you can configure the software to highlight any occasion on which the frequency of the power supplied by an outlet dips below 60Hz (the standard for North American electrical outlets).

Voltage event recorders such as the one shown in Figure 13-8 can cost up to $5,000.

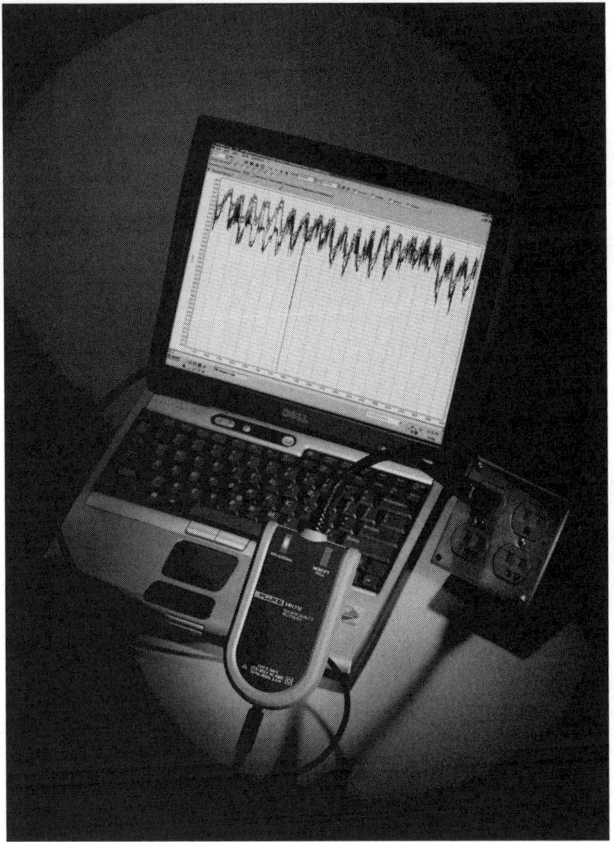

Figure 13-8 Voltage event recorder

Butt Set

If you have seen telephone technicians on the job, you have probably noticed the oversized telephone-like devices they carry. This device is known as a **lineman's handset,** a **telephone test set,** or more commonly, a **butt set,** because it can be used to butt into a telephone conversation. A butt set is essentially a rugged and sophisticated telephone. It helps a telephone technician working in the field to determine whether a line is functioning, not only by receiving the signal, but also by picking up any noise that might affect the signal. Some sophisticated butt sets can also perform rudimentary cable testing. For the most part, however, the butt set is a simple means of detecting dial tone on a line.

A butt set contains clips that fasten onto telephone transmission wires, thereby attaching to the local loop just as a telephone would. This connection can occur at the demarc, where a telephone line enters a residence, for example, or at a remote switching facility or at a CO (central office). However, it can only function on lines that have already been demultiplexed. For example, you could not attach a butt set to the ends of a line carrying multiple channels and expect to test one of those channels.

A butt set is shown in Figure 13-9.

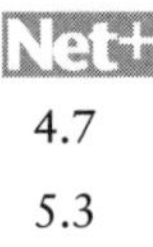

4.7

5.3

Figure 13-9 Butt set

Network Monitors

4.3

4.7

5.3

A **network monitor** is a software-based tool that continually monitors network traffic from a server or workstation attached to the network. Network monitors typically can interpret up to Layer 3 of the OSI model. They can determine the protocols passed by each frame, but they can't interpret the data inside the frame. By capturing data, they provide either a snapshot of network activity at one point in time or a historical record of network activity over a period of time.

Some NOSs come with network monitoring tools. Microsoft's **Network Monitor** is the tool that ships with Windows Server 2008 as well as with Windows 2000 Server and Windows Server 2003. You can also download and install Network Monitor for your Windows XP or Vista workstation. In addition, you can purchase or download for free network monitoring tools developed by other software companies. Hundreds of such programs exist. After you have worked with one network monitoring tool, you will find that other products work in much the same way. Most even use very similar graphical interfaces.

To take advantage of network monitoring and analyzing tools, the network adapter installed in the machine running the software must support promiscuous mode. In **promiscuous mode**, a device driver directs the NIC to pick up all frames that pass over the network—not just those destined for the node served by the card. You can determine whether your network adapter supports promiscuous mode by reading its manual or checking with the manufacturer. Some network monitoring software vendors may even suggest which network adapters to use with their software.

All network monitoring tools can perform at least the following functions:

- Continuously monitor network traffic on a segment
- Capture network data transmitted on a segment
- Capture frames sent to or from a specific node
- Reproduce network conditions by transmitting a selected amount and type of data
- Generate statistics about network activity (for example, what percentage of the total frames transmitted on a segment are broadcast frames)

Some network monitoring tools can also:

- Discover all network nodes on a segment.
- Establish a **baseline**, or a record of how the network operates under normal conditions, including its performance, collision rate, utilization rate, and so on.
- Store traffic data and generate reports.
- Trigger alarms when traffic conditions meet preconfigured conditions (for example, if usage exceeds 50 percent of capacity).

How can capturing data help you solve a problem? Imagine that traffic on a segment of the network you administer suddenly grinds to a halt one morning at about 8:00. You no sooner step in the door than everyone from the help desk calls to tell you how slowly the network is running. Nothing has changed on the network since last night, when it ran normally, so you can think of no obvious reasons for problems.

At the workstation where you have previously installed a network monitoring tool, you capture all data transmissions for approximately five minutes. You then sort the frames in the network monitoring software, arranging the nodes in order based on the volume of traffic each has generated. You might find that one workstation appears at the top of the list with an inordinately high number of bad transmissions. Or, you might discover that a server has been compromised by a hacker and is generating a flood of data over the network.

Before adopting a network monitor or protocol analyzer, you should be aware of some of the data errors that these tools can distinguish. The following list defines some commonly used terms for abnormal data patterns and packets, along with their characteristics:

- *Local collisions*—Collisions that occur when two or more stations are transmitting simultaneously. A small number of collisions are normal on an Ethernet network. Excessively high collision rates within the network usually result from cable or routing problems.
- *Late collisions*—Collisions that take place outside the window of time in which they would normally be detected by the network and redressed. Late collisions are usually caused by one of two problems: (1) a defective station (for example, a card or transceiver) that is transmitting without first verifying line status, or (2) failure to observe the configuration guidelines for cable length, which results in collisions being recognized too late.

Net+

4.3

4.7

5.3

- *Runts*—Packets that are smaller than the medium's minimum packet size. For instance, any Ethernet packet that is smaller than 64 bytes is considered a runt. Runts are often the result of collisions.

- *Giants*—Packets that exceed the medium's maximum packet size. For example, an Ethernet packet larger than 1,518 bytes is considered a giant.

- *Jabber*—A device that handles electrical signals improperly, usually affecting the rest of the network. A network analyzer will detect a jabber as a device that is always retransmitting, effectively bringing the network to a halt. A jabber usually results from a bad NIC. Occasionally, it can be caused by outside electrical interference.

- *Negative frame sequence checks*—The result of the CRC (cyclic redundancy check) generated by the originating node not matching the checksum calculated from the data received. It usually indicates noise or transmission problems on the LAN interface or cabling. A high number of negative CRCs usually result from excessive collisions or a station transmitting bad data.

- *Ghosts*—Frames that are not actually data frames, but aberrations caused by a device misinterpreting stray voltage on the wire. Unlike true data frames, ghosts have no starting delimiter.

Network monitors are typically simple tools to master. The following section describes a similar type of tool that provides even more information about a network's traffic.

Protocol Analyzers

Similar to a network monitor, a **protocol analyzer** (or **network analyzer**) captures traffic. But a protocol analyzer can also analyze frames, typically all the way to Layer 7 of the OSI model. For example, it can identify that a frame uses TCP/IP and, more specifically, that it is an ARP request from one particular workstation to a server. Analyzers can also interpret the payload portion of frames, translating from binary or hexadecimal code to human-readable form. As a result, network analyzers can capture passwords going over the network, if their transmission is not encrypted. Some protocol analyzer software packages can run on a standard workstation, but others require computers equipped with special network adapters and operating system software.

As with network monitoring software, a variety of protocol analyzer software is available. One popular example is the free program called Wireshark. Essentially, a protocol analyzer performs the same features as the network monitor software discussed previously, plus a few extras. It can also generate traffic in an attempt to reproduce a network problem and monitor multiple network segments simultaneously. Protocol analyzers typically support a multitude of protocols and network topologies. Those programs with graphical interfaces are especially helpful for revealing the traffic flow across the network.

Figure 13-10 illustrates the distribution of traffic captured by a protocol analyzer.

Before many companies developed protocol analyzing software, a hardware device dedicated to this task, sold by the company Sniffer Technologies and known under the brand name Sniffer, was popular. Just as the brand name Kleenex has become a substitute for the term *facial tissue*, network engineers today might call any protocol analyzer tool a **sniffer** or **packet sniffer**. And now, even the company that bought Sniffer Technologies, NetScout, only sells software-based protocol analyzers.

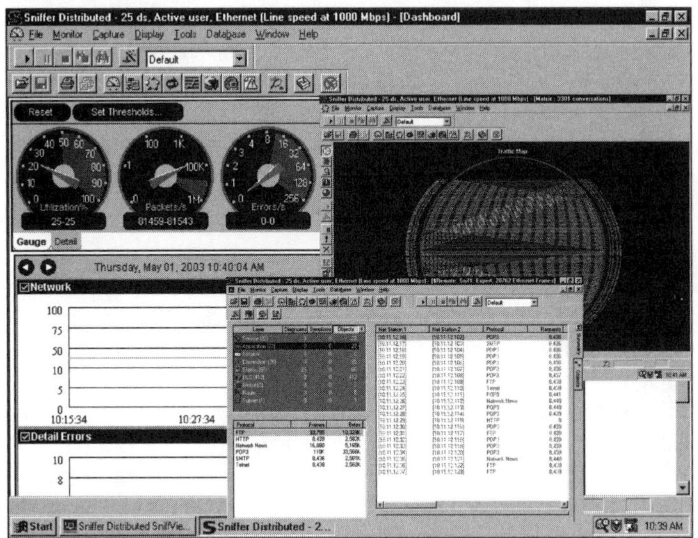

Figure 13-10 Traffic captured by a protocol analyzer

Protocol analyzers offer a great deal of versatility in the type and depth of information they can reveal. The danger in using this type of tool is that it could collect more information than you or the machine can reasonably process, thus rendering your exercise futile. To avoid this problem, you should set filters on the data gathered. For example, if you suspect that a certain workstation is causing a traffic problem, you should filter the data collection to accept only frames to or from that workstation's MAC address. If you suspect that you have a gateway-related TCP/IP problem, you should set a filter to capture only TCP/IP frames and to ignore other protocols from the gateway's MAC address.

Recall that using a switch logically separates a network into different segments. If a network is fully switched (that is, if every node is connected to its own switch port), your protocol analyzer can capture only frames destined for the port to which your node is connected. The increasing use of switches has made network monitoring more difficult, but not impossible. One solution to this problem is to reconfigure the switch to reroute the traffic so that your network analyzer can pick up all traffic—that is, to set up port mirroring.

Before using a network monitor or protocol analyzer on a network, it's important to know what traffic on your network normally looks like. To obtain this information, you can run the program and capture data for a period of time on a regular basis—for example, every weekday between 8:00 a.m. and noon. You'll generate a lot of data, but you'll also learn a lot about your network. From this data, you can establish a baseline to use as a comparison with future traffic analyses.

Wireless Network Testers

Cable continuity testers and performance testers, of course, will tell you nothing about the wireless connections, stations, or access points on a network. For that, you need tools that contain wireless NICs and run wireless protocols. In fact, you can learn some things about a

3.4

4.7

5.3

wireless environment by viewing the wireless network connection properties on your workstation. For example, after establishing a wireless connection in Windows Vista, click Start, and then click Control Panel. In the Control Panel window, click View network status and tasks. Then, in the line that represents your wireless network connection, click View status. The Wireless Network Connection Status dialog box opens. This dialog box shows you the duration of your connection, the speed and strength of your signal, and the number of packets that have been exchanged. (For an example, see Figure 8-30.)

However, viewing the status of the wireless connection on your workstation tells you only a little about your wireless environment—and this information only applies to one workstation. Many programs exist that can scan for wireless signals over a certain geographical range and discover all the access points and wireless stations transmitting in the area. This is useful for determining whether an access point is functioning properly, whether it is positioned correctly so that all the stations it serves are within its range, and whether stations and access points are communicating over the proper channels within a frequency band. Some programs can also capture the data transmitted between stations and access points. This information is useful for troubleshooting wireless connection problems (for example, poor performance or intermittent faults) after you've verified that connectivity is present. And some programs contain a **spectrum analyzer,** a tool that can assess the quality of the wireless signal. Spectrum analysis is useful, for example, to ascertain where noise (or interference) is greatest.

Software that can perform wireless network assessment is often available for free and may be provided by the access point's manufacturer. Following is a list of specific capabilities common to wireless network testing tools:

- Identify transmitting access points and stations and the channels over which they are communicating.
- Measure signal strength from and determine the range of an access point.
- Indicate the effects of attenuation, signal loss, and noise.
- Interpret signal strength information to rate potential access point locations (from "excellent" to "poor").
- Ensure proper association and reassociation when moving between access points.
- Capture and interpret traffic exchanged between wireless access points and stations.
- Measure throughput and assess data transmission errors.
- Analyze the characteristics of each channel within a frequency band to indicate the clearest channels.

Some companies have created testing instruments whose sole purpose is to assess the status of wireless networks. These tools can perform the same detection, data capture, and spectrum analysis functions as the software tools described previously. One advantage to using such devices, however, is that they are typically more portable than a laptop or desktop workstation. Second, they come installed with all the wireless network analysis tools you'll need, and these are usually accessible from one simple, graphical interface. A third advantage is that most wireless testing tools contain more powerful antennas than a workstation NIC. A more powerful antenna could mean the difference between assessing the wireless network for an entire building from your desk versus walking around to each floor with your laptop. Figure 13-11 shows one example of such a wireless network testing tool.

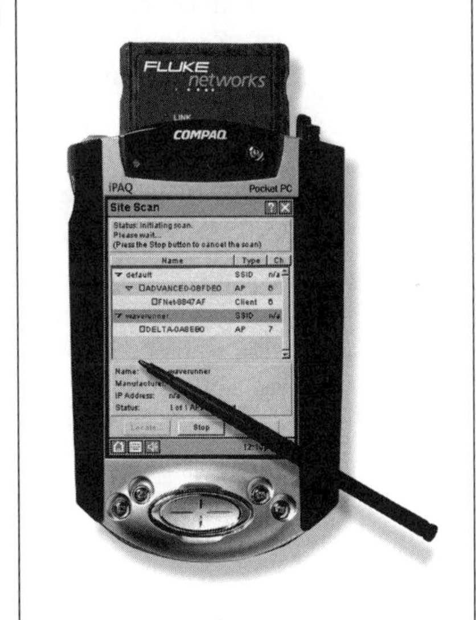

Figure 13-11 Wireless network testing tool

Wireless testing tools—both software- and hardware-based—are not only used for troubleshooting, but are also critical for wireless site selection, or determining the optimal placement for access points on a wireless LAN.

Chapter Summary

- The key to solving network problems is to approach them methodically and logically, using your experience to inform your decisions, and knowing when to ask for someone else's help.

- The first step in troubleshooting is identifying the problem and its symptoms. Symptoms can include error messages, the inability to perform certain functions on the network, or the inability to connect to a network. Record what you learn about symptoms.

- Next identify the affected area. In general, a network problem may be limited to one user; all users on a segment; all users on a network; certain types of users, departments, or locations; or to certain times of the day or week.

- At each point in the troubleshooting process, stop to consider what kind of changes have occurred on the network that might have created a problem. Changes pertaining to hardware may include the addition of a new device, the removal of an old device, a component upgrade, a cabling upgrade, or an equipment move. Changes pertaining to software may include an operating system upgrade, a device driver upgrade, a new application, or a changed configuration.

- Based on an analysis of the symptoms and how changes might have affected the network, establish a probable cause for the problem. First ensure that the user is performing all functions correctly, and then attempt to reproduce the problem's symptoms, check the physical connectivity of clients and devices involved in the problem, and determine whether software and hardware are configured correctly.

- Next, based on what you believe to be the problem's cause, determine whether the troubleshooting process warrants escalation. That is, decide whether you and other first-level support personnel can solve the problem or whether it should be transferred to second- or third-level support personnel.

- After determining whether the problem should be escalated, the appropriate troubleshooting personnel should create an action plan and solution, while considering the potential effects of the solution. Consider the number of users affected, costs, potential down time, and scalability of your solution. Collect documentation about the hardware or software configuration you are working with, and keep this handy while implementing your solution.

- After implementing a solution, test its result to ensure that you solved the problem and haven't created new problems. The type of testing you perform will depend on your solution. If the solution required significant network changes, revisit the solution a day or two after you implement it to verify that it has truly worked and not caused additional problems.

- Next, identify the effects and results of your solution. Verify that you have solved the problem you set out to solve and that you have not created new problems inadvertently as a result.

- Finally, document the solution and the process of solving the problem. Some organizations use a software program for documenting problems, known as a call tracking system (or help desk software). These programs provide a user-friendly graphical interface that prompts the user for every piece of information associated with the problem.

- When troubleshooting, record the following details about a problem: the originator's name, department, and phone number; whether the problem is software or hardware related; if the problem is software related, the package to which it pertains; if the problem is hardware related, the device or component to which it pertains; the symptoms of the problem, including when it was first noticed; the name and telephone number of the network support contact; the amount of time spent troubleshooting the problem; and the resolution of the problem.

- A tone generator and tone locator are used to identify the terminating location of a wire pair. This combination of devices may also be known as a toner and probe or a fox and hound.

- A multimeter is a simple device that can measure the voltage, resistance, impedance, and other characteristics of an electrical circuit. On a network, it can, among other things, verify proper cable terminations and detect noise that might adversely affect a connection.

- Basic cable continuity testers determine whether your cabling can provide connectivity. In the case of copper-based cables, they apply a small voltage to each conductor at one end of the cable and then check whether that voltage is detectable at the other end. They may also verify that voltage cannot be detected on other conductors in the cable. A good cable checker will also verify that the wires are paired correctly and that they are not shorted, exposed, or crossed.

- A cable performance tester accomplishes the same continuity and fault tests as a continuity tester, but it also ensures that the cable length is not too long, measures the distance to a cable fault, measures attenuation along a cable, measures near end cross talk between wires, measures termination resistance and impedance, issues pass/fail ratings for Cat 3, Cat 5, Cat 6, and Cat 7 standards, and stores and prints test results.

- A voltage event recorder captures information about power quality. The data captured by the voltage event recorder can then be analyzed using the accompanying software (installed on any workstation). Analyzing the data allows you to pinpoint any power anomalies, such as excessive current or drops in voltage.

- A butt set is a common term for a telephone test set or lineman's handset, a tool that resembles an oversized telephone and allows technicians to access and test a local loop telephone connection.

- A network monitor is a software-based tool that monitors network traffic from a server or workstation attached to the network. Network monitors typically can interpret up to Layer 3 of the OSI model. They can determine the protocols passed by each packet, but they can't interpret the data inside the packet.

- Network Monitor is the name of the network monitoring software that comes with Windows Server 2008 (and earlier versions of the Windows NOS).

- Protocol analyzers can typically interpret data up to Layer 7 of the OSI model. They can also interpret the payload portion of packets, translating from binary or hexadecimal code to human-readable form. Protocol analyzers may be software programs or devices dedicated to protocol analysis. Wireless network testing tools can be dedicated instruments or software that runs on a workstation (usually a laptop). They can discover wireless access points and stations, measure signal strength and interference, capture and interpret wireless data, measure throughput and identify data errors, and ensure proper association and reassociation between stations and access points.

Key Terms

baseline A record of how a network operates under normal conditions (including its performance, collision rate, utilization rate, and so on). Baselines are used for comparison when conditions change.

butt set A tool for accessing and testing a telephone company's local loop. The butt set, also known as a telephone test set or lineman's handset, is essentially a telephone handset with attached wires that can be connected to local loop terminations at a demarc or switching facility.

cable checker *See* continuity tester.

cable performance tester A troubleshooting tool that tests cables for continuity but can also measure cross talk, attenuation, and impedance; identify the location of faults; and store or print cable testing results.

cable tester A device that tests cables for one or more of the following conditions: continuity, segment length, distance to a fault, attenuation along a cable, near end cross talk, and termination resistance and impedance. Cable testers may also issue pass/fail ratings for wiring standards or store and print cable testing results.

call tracking system A software program used to document technical problems and how they were resolved (also known as help desk software).

change management system A process or program that provides support personnel with a centralized means of documenting changes made to the network.

continuity tester An instrument that tests whether voltage (or light, in the case of fiber-optic cable) issued at one end of a cable can be detected at the opposite end of the cable. A continuity tester can indicate whether the cable will successfully transmit a signal.

escalate In network troubleshooting, to refer a problem to someone with deeper knowledge about the subject. For example, a first-level support person might escalate a router configuration issue to a second- or third-level support person.

first-level support In network troubleshooting, the person or group who initially fields requests for help from users.

fox and hound Another term for the combination of devices known as a tone generator and a tone locator. The tone locator is considered the hound because it follows the tone generator (the fox).

ghost A frame that is not actually a data frame, but rather an aberration caused by a device misinterpreting stray voltage on the wire. Unlike true data frames, ghosts have no starting delimiter.

giant A packet that exceeds the medium's maximum packet size. For example, any Ethernet packet that is larger than 1,518 bytes is considered a giant.

help desk analyst A person who's proficient in basic (but not usually advanced) workstation and network troubleshooting. Help desk analysts are part of first-level support.

help desk coordinator A person who ensures that help desk analysts are divided into the correct teams, schedules shifts at the help desk, and maintains the infrastructure to enable analysts to better perform their jobs. They might also serve as third-level support personnel, taking responsibility for troubleshooting a problem when the second-level support analyst is unable to solve it.

jabber A device that handles electrical signals improperly, usually affecting the rest of the network. A network analyzer will detect a jabber as a device that is always retransmitting, effectively bringing the network to a halt. A jabber usually results from a bad NIC. Occasionally, it can be caused by outside electrical interference.

late collision A collision that takes place outside the normal window in which collisions are detected and redressed. Late collisions are usually caused by a defective station (such as a card, or transceiver) that is transmitting without first verifying line status or by failure to observe the configuration guidelines for cable length, which results in collisions being recognized too late.

lineman's handset *See* butt set.

local collision A collision that occurs when two or more stations are transmitting simultaneously. Excessively high collision rates within the network can usually be traced to cable or routing problems.

multimeter A simple instrument that can measure multiple characteristics of an electric circuit, including its resistance and voltage.

negative frame sequence check The result of the CRC (cyclic redundancy check) generated by the originating node not matching the checksum calculated from the data received. It usually indicates noise or transmission problems on the LAN interface or cabling. A high number of (nonmatching) CRCs usually results from excessive collisions or a station transmitting bad data.

network analyzer *See* protocol analyzer.

network monitor A software-based tool that monitors traffic on the network from a server or workstation attached to the network. Network monitors typically can interpret up to Layer 3 of the OSI model.

Network Monitor A network monitoring program from Microsoft that comes with Windows Server 2003 and Server 2008 (as well as with Windows NT and Windows 2000 Server).

ohmmeter A device used to measure resistance in an electrical circuit.

optical time domain reflectometer *See* OTDR.

OTDR (optical time domain reflectometer) A performance testing device for use with fiber-optic networks. An OTDR works by issuing a light-based signal on a fiber-optic cable and measuring the way in which the signal bounces back (or reflects) to the OTDR. By measuring the length of time it takes the signal to return, an OTDR can determine the location of a fault.

packet sniffer *See* protocol analyzer.

probe *See* tone locator.

promiscuous mode The feature of a network adapter that allows it to pick up all frames that pass over the network—not just those destined for the node served by the card.

protocol analyzer A software package or hardware-based tool that can capture and analyze data on a network. Protocol analyzers are more sophisticated than network monitoring tools, as they can typically interpret data up to Layer 7 of the OSI model.

runt A packet that is smaller than the medium's minimum packet size. For instance, any Ethernet packet that is smaller than 64 bytes is considered a runt.

second-level support In network troubleshooting, a person or group with deeper knowledge about a subject and to whom first-level support personnel escalate problems.

sniffer *See* protocol analyzer.

spectrum analyzer A tool that assesses the characteristics (for example, frequency, amplitude, and the effects of interference) of wireless signals.

supported services list A document that lists every service and software package supported within an organization, plus the names of first- and second-level support contacts for those services or software packages.

TDR (time domain reflectometer) A high-end instrument for testing the qualities of a cable. It works by issuing a signal on a cable and measuring the way in which the signal bounces back (or reflects) to the TDR. Many performance testers rely on TDRs.

telephone test set *See* butt set.

third-level support In network troubleshooting, a person or group with deep knowledge about specific networking topics to whom second-level support personnel escalate challenging problems.

time domain reflectometer *See* TDR.

tone generator   A small electronic device that issues a signal on a wire pair. When used in conjunction with a tone locator, it can help locate the termination of a wire pair.

tone locator   A small electronic device that emits a tone when it detects electrical activity on a wire pair. When used in conjunction with a tone generator, it can help locate the termination of a wire pair.

toner   *See* tone generator.

voltage event   Any condition in which voltage exceeds or drops below predefined levels.

voltage event recorder   A device that, when plugged into the same outlet that will be used by a network node, gathers data about the power that the outlet will provide the node.

voltmeter   A device used to measure voltage (or electrical pressure) on an electrical circuit.

Review Questions

1. Which step in the troubleshooting methodology involves the task of identifying the affected areas?

   a. Step 1

   b. Step 2

   c. Step 3

   d. Step 4

2. In determining the most probable cause of a problem, which step should be conducted first?

   a. Review and analyze recent changes

   b. Determine what areas are affected

   c. Identity the symptoms

   d. Ensure that human error is not the source of the problem

3. Which type of personnel are highly skilled in one area of networking?

   a. First-level support

   b. Second-level support

   c. Third-level support

   d. Help desk coordinator

4. Which troubleshooting tool is useful for quickly and easily verifying that a node's NIC is transmitting and receiving signals properly?

   a. Tone generator

   b. Crossover cable

   c. Tone locator

   d. Butt set

5. Which data error describes a packet that is smaller than the medium's minimum packet size?

    a. Jabber

    b. Ghosts

    c. Runts

    d. Bot

6. True or false? When attempting to reproduce the symptoms of a problem, you should follow the same steps that the person reporting the symptoms followed.

7. True or false? By some estimates, more than half of all network problems occur at the logical layer of the OSI model.

8. True or false? Logical connectivity problems often prove more difficult to isolate and resolve than physical connectivity problems.

9. True or false? Tone generators and tone locators can be used to determine characteristics about a cable.

10. True or false? The difference between continuity testers and performance testers lies in their sophistication and price.

11. A software program known as a(n) _____ system is used in many organizations for documenting problems.

12. A(n) _____ is a simple instrument that can measure many characteristics of an electric circuit, including its resistance and voltage.

13. A(n) _____ is a software-based tool that continually monitors network traffic from a server or workstation attached to the network.

14. A(n) _____ analyzer (or network analyzer) captures traffic and can analyze frames, typically all the way to Layer 7 of the OSI model.

15. A(n) _____ is a tool that can assess the quality of the wireless signal.

After reading this chapter and completing the exercises, you will be able to:

- Identify the characteristics of a network that keep data safe from loss or damage

- Protect an enterprise-wide network from viruses

- Explain network- and system-level fault-tolerance techniques

- Discuss issues related to network backup and recovery strategies

- Describe the components of a useful disaster recovery plan and the options for disaster contingencies

On the Job

Net+

4.2

4.5

I wanted my data to be safe, so I created a RAID 5 array. But somewhere along the way, my array went into a degraded state. Unbeknownst to me, one of the drives timed out and was dropped from the array.

The other drives took over, and my RAID 5 array continued to work. But because I didn't use the management software that came with my RAID controller, I didn't know that this had happened. So I used my system for weeks with the array in degraded mode (which, at that point, was equivalent to an unprotected RAID 0 array).

One day the disk attached to port 2 on my controller started to click. I powered my computer down, removed the port 2 drive, and ran the manufacturer's diagnostic utilities on it. My worst fear was realized: the port 2 drive was dead. I lost everything!

I called the technical support team for the company that made my RAID controller. To my surprise, they didn't tell me I was out of luck. They told me to run a diagnostic script on the drives that I had remaining and to send the output to the tech support team.

After examining the script output, tech support was able to send me a "repair script." I ran the script, and my array was back, with almost all the files intact. But how?

This is how they did it. While the port 1 drive timed out, causing the array to degrade, it was not physically bad--probably just a bad data block somewhere. That drive still contained all the data that it had before it was dropped from the array. The repair script put the original port 1 data drive back into the array, leaving the clicking port 2 drive as the only degraded drive left. The data written while that drive was out of the array was lost, but everything else was there.

I now back up on a regular basis, and I also check my RAID management software from time to time.

Patrick Pejack
Applied Micro Circuits Corporation

Because networks are a vital part of keeping an organization running, you must pay attention to measures that keep LANs and WANs safe and secure. You can never assume that data is safe on the network until you have taken explicit measures to protect the information. In this book, you have learned about building scalable, reliable enterprise-wide networks as well as selecting the most appropriate hardware and network operating systems to operate your network. You have also learned about security measures to guard network access and resources. In this chapter you learn about protecting networks and their resources from the adverse effects of power flaws, hardware or system failures, malware, and natural disasters.

What Are Integrity and Availability?

Net+

4.2

4.5

In the world of networking, the term **integrity** refers to the soundness of a network's programs, data, services, devices, and connections. To ensure a network's integrity, you must protect it from anything that might render it unusable. Closely related to the concept of integrity is availability. The term **availability** refers to how consistently and reliably a file or system can be accessed by authorized personnel. For example, a server that allows staff to log on and use its programs and data 99.99% of the time is considered highly available, whereas one that is functional only 98% of the time is less available. To guarantee high availability, you need a well-planned and well-configured network, as well as data backups, redundant devices, and protection from malicious intruders who could potentially immobilize the network.

A number of phenomena can compromise both integrity and availability, including security breaches, natural disasters (such as tornadoes, floods, hurricanes, and ice storms), malicious intruders, power flaws, and human error. Every network administrator should consider these possibilities when designing a sound network. You can readily imagine the importance of integrity and availability of data in a hospital, for example, in which the network stores patient records and provides quick medical reference material, video displays for surgical cameras, and perhaps even control of critical care monitors.

If you have ever supported computer users, you know that they sometimes unintentionally harm data, applications, software configurations, or even hardware. Networks can also be intentionally harmed by users unless network administrators take precautionary measures and pay regular, close attention to systems and networks to protect them. This section reminds you of common sense approaches to data integrity and availability. Later in this chapter, you will learn about more specific or formal (and potentially more expensive) approaches to data protection.

Although you can't predict every type of vulnerability, you can take measures to guard against most damaging events. Following are some general guidelines for protecting your network:

- *Allow only network administrators to create or modify NOS and application system files*—Pay attention to the permissions assigned to regular users (including the groups "users" or "everyone" and the user name "guest"). Bear in mind that the worst consequence of applying overly stringent file restrictions is an inconvenience to users. In contrast, the worst consequence of applying overly lenient file restrictions could be a failed network.

- *Monitor the network for unauthorized access or changes*—You can install programs that routinely check whether and when the files you've specified have changed. Such monitoring programs are typically inexpensive and easy to customize. Some enable the system to page or e-mail you when a system file changes.

- *Record authorized system changes in a change management system*—You have learned about the importance of change management when troubleshooting networks. Routine changes should also be documented in a change management system. Recording system changes enables you and your colleagues to understand what's happening to your network and protect it from harm. For example, suppose that the remote access service on a Linux server has stopped accepting connections. Before taking troubleshooting steps that may create more problems and further reduce the availability of the system, you could review the change management log. It might indicate that a colleague

Net+

4.2

4.5

recently installed an update to the Linux NOS. With this information in hand, you could focus on the update as a likely source of the problem.

- *Install redundant components*—The term **redundancy** refers to an implementation in which more than one component is installed and ready to use for storing, processing, or transporting data. Redundancy is intended to eliminate single points of failure. To maintain high availability, you should ensure that critical network elements, such as your connection to the Internet or your file server's hard disk, are redundant. Some types of redundancy—for example, redundant sources of electrical power for a building—require large investments, so your organization should weigh the risks of losing connectivity or data against the cost of adding duplicate components.

- *Perform regular health checks on the network*—Prevention is the best weapon against network downtime. By establishing a baseline and regular network monitoring, you can anticipate problems before they affect availability or integrity. For example, if your network monitor alerts you to rapidly rising utilization on a critical network segment, you can analyze the network to discover where the problem lies and perhaps fix it before it takes down the segment.

Net+

4.4

4.5

- *Check system performance, error logs, and the system log book regularly*—By keeping track of system errors and trends in performance, you have a better chance of correcting problems before they cause a hard disk failure and potentially damage your system files. By default, all NOSs keep error logs. On a Linux server, for example, a file called "messages" located in the /var/log directory collects error messages from system services, such as DNS, and other programs also save log files in the /var/log directory. It's important that you know where these error logs reside on your server and understand how to interpret them.

Net+

4.2

4.5

- *Keep backups, boot disks, and emergency repair disks current and available*—If your file system or critical boot files become corrupted by a system crash, you can use the emergency or boot disks to recover the system. Otherwise, you might need to reinstall the software before you can start the system. If you ever face the situation of recovering from a system loss or disaster, you must recover in the quickest manner possible. For this effort, you need backup devices and a backup strategy tailored to your environment.

- *Implement and enforce security and disaster recovery policies*—Everyone in your organization should know what he is allowed to do on the network. For example, if you decide that it's too risky for employees to download games off the Internet because of the potential for virus infection, you should inform them of a ban on downloading games. You might enforce this policy by restricting users' ability to create or change files (such as executable files) that are copied to the workstation during the downloading of games. Making such decisions and communicating them to staff should be part of your IT policy. Likewise, key personnel in your organization should be familiar with your disaster recovery plan, which should detail your strategy for restoring network functionality in case of an unexpected failure. Although such policies take time to develop and may be difficult to enforce, they can directly affect your network's availability and integrity.

These measures are merely first steps to ensuring network integrity and availability, but they are essential. The following sections describe what types of policies, hardware, and software you can implement to achieve availability and integrity, beginning with malware detection and prevention.

Malware

Malware refers to any program or piece of code designed to intrude upon or harm a system or its resources. The term *malware* is derived from a combination of the words malicious and software. Included in this category are viruses, Trojan horses, worms, and bots, all of which are described in this section.

Strictly speaking, a **virus** is a program that replicates itself with the intent to infect more computers, either through network connections or through the exchange of external storage devices (such as floppy disks, CD-ROMs, or CompactFlash cards). Viruses are typically copied to a computer's storage device without the user's knowledge. A virus might damage files or systems, or it might simply annoy users by flashing messages or pictures on the screen or by causing the computer to beep. In fact, some viruses cause no harm and can remain unnoticed on a system indefinitely.

Many other unwanted and potentially destructive programs are often called viruses, but technically do not meet the criteria used to define a virus. For example, a program that disguises itself as something useful but actually harms your system is called a **Trojan horse** (or simply, **Trojan**), after the famous wooden horse in which soldiers were hidden. Because Trojan horses do not replicate themselves, they are not considered viruses. An example of a Trojan horse is an executable file that someone sends you over the Internet, promising that the executable will install a great new game, when in fact it erases data on your hard disk or mails spam to all the users in your e-mail program's address book.

In this section, you will learn about the different viruses and other malware that can infect your network, their methods of distribution, and, most important, protection against them. Malware can harm computers running any type of operating system—Macintosh, Windows, Linux, or UNIX—at any time. As a network administrator, you must take measures to guard against them.

Types of Malware

Symantec, one of the largest vendors of anti-malware software, predicted that in 2008 more malware would be written and released than legitimate software. Among the high volume of potentially harmful programs, however, only a small number cause the majority of damage. Malware can be classified into different categories based on where it resides on a computer and how it propagates itself. All malware belongs to one of the following categories:

- *Boot sector viruses*—**Boot sector viruses** position their code in the boot sector of a computer's hard disk so that when the computer boots up, the virus runs in place of the computer's normal system files. Boot sector viruses are commonly spread from external storage devices to hard disks. This can happen, for example, if a floppy disk is left in the drive when a computer boots up and the computer is configured to boot first from a floppy disk when a floppy disk is present (rather than from the hard disk). Boot sector viruses vary in their destructiveness. Some merely display a screen advertising the virus's presence when you boot the infected computer. Others do not advertise themselves but stealthily destroy system files or make it impossible for the file system to access at least some of the computer's files. Examples of boot sector viruses include Michelangelo and the Stoned virus, which was widespread in the early 1990s (in fact, it disabled U.S. military computers during the 1991 Persian Gulf War) and

persists today in many variations. Until you disinfect a computer that harbors a boot sector virus, the virus propagates to every external disk to which that computer writes information. Removing a boot sector virus first requires rebooting the computer from an uninfected, write-protected disk with system files on it. Only after the computer is booted from a source other than the infected hard disk can you run software to remove the boot sector virus.

- *Macro viruses*—**Macro viruses** take the form of a macro (such as the kind used in a word-processing or spreadsheet program), which may be executed as the user works with a program. For example, you might send a Microsoft Word document as an attachment to an e-mail message. If that document contains a macro virus, when the recipient opens the document, the macro runs, and all future documents created or saved by that program are infected. Macro viruses were the first type of virus to infect data files rather than executable files. They are quick to emerge and spread because they are easy to write and because users share data files more frequently than execut-able files. Although the earliest versions of macro viruses were annoying but not harmful, currently circulating macro viruses may threaten data files. Examples of macro viruses include W97M/Kukudro and its variants; W97M/Wazzu and its var-iants, which can be transmitted as Microsoft Word macros; and X97M/Jal and its variants, which can be transmitted as Microsoft Excel macros. Symptoms of macro virus infection vary widely but may include missing options from application menus; damaged, changed, or missing data files; or strange pop-up messages that appear when you use an application.

- *File-infector viruses*—**File-infector viruses** attach themselves to executable files. When an infected executable file runs, the virus copies itself to memory. Later, the virus attaches itself to other executable files. Some file-infector viruses attach themselves to other programs even while their "host" executable runs a process in the background, such as a printer service or screen saver program. Because they stay in memory while you continue to work on your computer, these viruses can have devastating conse-quences, infecting numerous programs and requiring that you disinfect your computer, as well as reinstall virtually all software. Symptoms of virus infection can include damaged program files, inexplicable file size increases, changed icons for programs, strange messages that appear when you attempt to run a program, or the inability to run a program. Examples of file-infector viruses include Vacsina and WoodGoblin (both of which are dangerous because they overwrite files on a computer's hard disk), and Harmony.A, which is harmless but increases the size of and adds a message to all executable files on a hard disk installed with a Windows operating system.

- *Worms*—**Worms** are programs that run independently and travel between computers and across networks. They may be transmitted by any type of file transfer, including e-mail attachments. Worms do not alter other programs in the same way that viruses do, but they can carry viruses. Because they can transport (and hide) viruses, you should be concerned about picking up worms when you exchange files from the Inter-net, via e-mail, or through disks. Examples of worms include Pyskse.A, which spreads via instant messaging exchanges; VBS/Gedza.B, which spreads via e-mail attachments; and Korgo and its variants, which spread through unprotected TCP and UDP ports on Windows computers when a user is connected to a network. Symptoms of worm infection may include almost any type of anomaly, ranging from strange pop-up messages to file damage.

6.6

- *Trojan horse*—As mentioned earlier, a Trojan horse (or Trojan) is a program that claims to do something useful but instead harms the computer or system. Trojan horses range from being nuisances to causing significant system destruction. Anti-malware programs recognize known Trojan horses and eradicate them. Examples of Trojan horses include W32/Gimmiv.A, which is one of many Trojan horses that install programs to spy on a user by capturing his keystrokes, and Konov, which operates on any cellular telephone capable of running Java applications and will issue messages to premium rate numbers. The best way to guard against Trojan horses is to refrain from downloading an executable file whose origins you can't confirm. Suppose, for example, that you needed to download a new driver for a NIC on your network. Rather than going to a generic "network support site" on the Internet, you should download the file from the NIC manufacturer's Web site. Most important, never run an executable file that was sent to you over the Internet as an attachment to a mail message whose sender or origins you cannot verify.

- *Network viruses*—**Network viruses** propagate themselves via network protocols, commands, messaging programs, and data links. Although all viruses can theoretically travel across network connections, network viruses are specially designed to take advantage of network vulnerabilities. For example, a network virus may attach itself to FTP transactions to and from your Web server. Another type of network virus may spread through Microsoft Outlook messages only. Because network viruses are characterized by their transmission method, their symptoms may include almost any type of anomaly, ranging from strange pop-up messages to file damage.

- *Bots*—Another malware category defined by its propagation method is a bot. In networking, the term **bot** (short for robot) means a program that runs automatically, without requiring a person to start or stop it. One type of bot is a virus that propagates itself automatically between systems. It does not require an unsuspecting user to download and run an executable file or to boot from an infected disk, for example. Many bots spread through the **IRC (Internet Relay Chat)**, a protocol that enables users running IRC client software to communicate instantly with other participants in a chat room on the Internet. Chat rooms require an IRC server, which accepts messages from an IRC client and either broadcasts the messages to all other chat room participants (in an open chat room) or sends the message to select users (in a restricted chat room). Malicious bots take advantage of IRC to transmit data, commands, or executable programs from one infected participant to others. (Consequently, a malware-spreading bot can also be considered a worm or Trojan.) After a bot has copied files on a client's hard disk, these files can be used to damage or destroy a computer's data or system files, issue objectionable content, and further propagate the malware. Bots are especially difficult to contain because of their fast, surreptitious, and distributed dissemination.

Malware Characteristics

Certain characteristics can make malware harder to detect and eliminate. Some of these characteristics, which can be found in any type of malware, include:

- *Encryption*—Some viruses, worms, and Trojan horses are encrypted to prevent detection. Most anti-malware software searches files for a recognizable string of characters that identify the virus. However, an **encrypted virus**, for example, might thwart the antivirus program's attempts to detect it.

6.6

- *Stealth*—Some malware hides itself to prevent detection. For example, **stealth viruses** disguise themselves as legitimate programs or replace part of a legitimate program's code with their destructive code.

- *Polymorphism*—**Polymorphic viruses** change their characteristics (such as the arrangement of their bytes, size, and internal instructions) every time they are transferred to a new system, making them harder to identify. Some polymorphic viruses use complicated algorithms and incorporate nonsensical commands to achieve their changes. Polymorphic viruses are considered the most sophisticated and potentially dangerous type of virus.

- *Time dependence*—Some viruses, worms, and Trojan horses are programmed to activate on a particular date. This type of malware can remain dormant and harmless until its activation date arrives. Like any other malware, time-dependent malware can have destructive effects or might cause some innocuous event periodically. For example, viruses in the "Time" family cause a PC's speaker to beep approximately once per hour. Time-dependent malware can include **logic bombs**, or programs designed to start when certain conditions are met. (Although logic bombs can also activate when other types of conditions, such as a specific change to a file, are met, and they are not always malicious.)

Malware can exhibit more than one of the preceding characteristics. The Natas virus, for example, combines polymorphism and stealth techniques to create a very destructive virus.

Hundreds of new viruses, worms, Trojan horses, and bots are unleashed on the world's computers each month. Although it is impossible to keep abreast of every virus in circulation, you should at least know where you can find out more information about malware. An excellent resource for learning about new viruses, their characteristics, and ways to get rid of them is McAfee's Virus Information Library at *us.mcafee.com/virusInfo/default.asp*.

Malware Protection

You might think that you can simply install a virus-scanning program on your network and move to the next issue. In fact, protection against harmful code involves more than just installing anti-malware software. It requires choosing the most appropriate anti-malware program for your environment, monitoring the network, continually updating the anti-malware program, and educating users.

Anti-Malware Software Even if a user doesn't immediately notice malware on her system, the harmful software generally leaves evidence of itself, whether by changing the operation of the machine or by announcing its signature characteristics in the malware code. Although the latter can be detected only via anti-malware software, users can typically detect the operational changes without special software. For example, you might suspect a virus on your system if any of the following symptoms appear:

- Unexplained increases in file sizes

- Significant, unexplained decline in system performance (for example, a program taking much longer than usual to start or to save a file)

- Unusual error messages appearing without probable cause

- Significant, unexpected loss of system memory

6.6

- Periodic, unexpected rebooting
- Fluctuations in display quality

Often, however, you don't notice malware until it has already damaged your files.

Although malware programmers have become more sophisticated in disguising their software (for example, using encryption and polymorphism), anti-malware software programmers have kept pace with them. The anti-malware software you choose for your network should at least perform the following functions:

- Detect malware through **signature scanning**, a comparison of a file's content with known malware signatures (that is, the unique identifying characteristics in the code) in a signature database. This signature database must be frequently updated so that the software can detect new viruses as they emerge. Updates can be downloaded from the anti-malware software vendor's Web site. Alternatively, you can configure such updates to be copied from the Internet to your computer automatically, with or without your consent.

- Detect malware through **integrity checking**, a method of comparing current characteristics of files and disks against an archived version of these characteristics to discover any changes. The most common example of integrity checking involves using a checksum, though this tactic may not prove effective against malware with stealth capabilities.

- Detect malware by monitoring unexpected file changes or viruslike behaviors.

- Receive regular updates and modifications from a centralized network console. The vendor should provide free upgrades on a regular (at least monthly) basis, plus technical support.

- Consistently report only valid instances of malware, rather than reporting false alarms. Scanning techniques that attempt to identify malware by discovering "malware-like" behavior, also known as **heuristic scanning**, are the most fallible and most likely to emit false alarms. On the other hand, heuristic scanning successfully detected the SoBig worm that affected thousands of users in 2003 before the worm could be added to vendors' signature databases. Heuristic scanning worked in this case because of the way SoBig propagated itself.

Occasionally, shrink-wrapped, off-the-shelf software or software pre-installed on hardware includes malware. In 2007, for example, laptops from a German reseller that came with Windows Vista installed also came with the boot sector virus Stoned.Angelina. Therefore, it's always a good idea to scan authorized software from known sources just as you would scan software from unknown sources.

Your implementation of anti-malware software depends on your computing environment's needs. For example, you might use a desktop security program on every computer on the network that prevents users from copying executable files to their hard disks or to network drives. In this case, it might be unnecessary to implement a program that continually scans each machine; in fact, this approach might be undesirable because the continual scanning adversely affects performance. On the other hand, if you are the network administrator for a student computer lab where potentially thousands of different users bring their own disks

6.6

for use on the computers, you will want to scan the machines thoroughly at least once a day and perhaps more often.

When implementing anti-malware software on a network, one of your most important decisions is where to install the software. If you install anti-malware software only on every desktop, you have addressed the most likely point of entry but ignored the most important files that might be infected—those on the server. If the anti-malware software resides on the server and checks every file and transaction, you will protect important files but slow your network performance considerably. To find a balance between sufficient protection and minimal impact on performance, you must examine your network's vulnerabilities and critical performance needs.

Obviously, the anti-malware package you choose should be compatible with your network and desktop operating systems. Popular anti-malware packages include F-Secure's Anti-Virus, McAfee's VirusScan, Computer Associates' eTrust Antivirus Scanner, and Symantec's Norton AntiVirus.

In addition to using specialized anti-malware software to guard against malware infection, you might find that your applications can help identify malware. Microsoft Word and Excel programs, for example, warn you when you attempt to open a file that contains macros. You then have the option of disabling the macros (thereby preventing any macro viruses from working when you open the file) or allowing the macros to remain usable. In general, it's a good idea to disable the macros in a file that you have received from someone else, at least until after you have checked the file for viruses with your virus-scanning software.

Anti-Malware Policies Anti-malware software alone will not keep your network safe from malicious code. Because most malware can be prevented by applying a little technology and forethought, it's important that all network users understand how to prevent the spread of malware. An anti-malware policy provides rules for using anti-malware software, as well as policies for installing programs, sharing files, and using external disks such as flash drives. To be most effective, anti-malware policy should be authorized and supported by the organization's management. Suggestions for anti-malware policy guidelines include the following:

- Every computer in an organization should be equipped with malware detection and cleaning software that regularly scans for malware. This software should be centrally distributed and updated to stay current with newly released malware.

- Users should not be allowed to alter or disable the anti-malware software.

- Users should know what to do in case their anti-malware program detects malware. For example, you might recommend that the user stop working on his computer and instead call the help desk to receive assistance in disinfecting the system.

- An anti-malware team should be appointed to focus on maintaining the anti-malware measures. This team would be responsible for choosing anti-malware software, keeping the software updated, educating users, and responding in case of a significant malware outbreak.

- Users should be prohibited from installing any unauthorized software on their systems. This edict may seem extreme, but in fact users downloading programs (especially

6.6

games) from the Internet are a common source of malware. If your organization permits game playing, you might institute a policy in which every game must be first checked for malware and then installed on a user's system by a technician.

- Systemwide alerts should be issued to network users notifying them of a serious malware threat and advising them how to prevent infection, even if the malware hasn't been detected on your network yet.

When drafting an anti-malware policy, bear in mind that these measures are not meant to restrict users' freedom, but rather to protect the network from damage and downtime. Explain to users that the anti-malware policy protects their own data as well as critical system files. If possible, automate the anti-malware software installation and operation so that users barely notice its presence. Do not rely on users to run their anti-malware software each time they insert a disk or download a new program, because they will quickly forget to do so.

Hoaxes

As in any other community, rumors spread through the Internet user community. One type of rumor consists of a false alert about a dangerous, new virus or other type of malware that could cause serious damage to your workstation. Such an alert is known as a **hoax**. Hoaxes usually have no realistic basis and should be ignored, as they merely attempt to create panic. Hoaxes also typically demand that you pass the alert to everyone in your Internet address book, thus propagating the rumor. However, hoaxes should not be passed on. If you receive a message that you suspect is a hoax, you can confirm your suspicion by looking up the message on a Web page that lists virus hoaxes. A good resource for verifying hoaxes is *www.f-secure.com/virus-info/hoax/*. This Web site also teaches you more about the phenomenon of hoaxes.

If you receive a hoax, simply ignore it. Educate your colleagues to do the same, explaining why hoaxes should not cause alarm. Remember, however, that even a hoax message could potentially contain an *attached* file that does cause damage if executed. Once again, the best policy is to refrain from running any program whose origins you cannot verify.

Fault Tolerance

4.5

Besides guarding against malware, another key factor in maintaining the availability and integrity of data is fault tolerance. You have learned that fault tolerance is the capacity for a system to continue performing despite an unexpected hardware or software malfunction. To better understand the issues related to fault tolerance, you must recognize the difference between failures and faults as they apply to networks. In broad terms, a **failure** is a deviation from a specified level of system performance for a given period of time. In other words, a failure occurs when something doesn't work as promised or as planned. For example, if your car breaks down on the highway, you can consider the breakdown to be a failure. A **fault**, on the other hand, involves the malfunction of one component of a system. A fault can result in a failure. For example, the fault that caused your car to break down might be a leaking water pump. The goal of fault-tolerant systems is to prevent faults from progressing to failures.

Fault tolerance can be realized in varying degrees; the optimal level of fault tolerance for a system depends on how critical its services and files are to productivity. At the highest level of

4.5

fault tolerance, a system remains unaffected by even the most drastic problem, such as a regional power outage. In this case, a backup power source, such as an electrical generator, is necessary to ensure fault tolerance. However, less dramatic faults, such as a malfunctioning NIC on a router, can still cause network outages, and you should guard against them.

The following sections describe network aspects that must be monitored and managed to ensure fault tolerance.

Environment

As you consider sophisticated fault-tolerance techniques for servers, routers, and WAN links, remember to analyze the physical environment in which your devices operate. Part of your data protection plan involves protecting your network from excessive heat or moisture, break-ins, and natural disasters. For example, you should make sure that your telecommunications closets and equipment rooms have locked doors and are air-conditioned and maintained at a constant humidity, according to the hardware manufacturer's recommendations. You can purchase temperature and humidity monitors that trip alarms if specified limits are exceeded. These monitors can prove very useful because the temperature can rise rapidly in a room full of equipment, causing overheated equipment to function poorly or fail outright.

Power

No matter where you live, you have probably experienced a complete loss of power (a blackout) or a temporary dimming of lights (a brownout). Such fluctuations in power are frequently caused by forces of nature, such as hurricanes, tornadoes, or ice storms. They might also occur when a utility company performs maintenance or construction tasks. The following section describes the types of power fluctuations that network administrators should prepare for. The next two sections describe alternate power sources, such as a UPS (uninterruptible power supply) or an electrical generator, that can compensate for power loss.

Power Flaws Whatever the cause, power loss or less than optimal power cannot be tolerated by networks. The following list describes power flaws that can damage your equipment:

- *Surge*—A momentary increase in voltage due to lightning strikes, solar flares, or electrical problems. Surges might last only a few thousandths of a second, but they can degrade a computer's power supply. Surges are common. You can guard against them by making sure every computer device is plugged into a **surge protector**, which redirects excess voltage away from the device to a ground, thereby protecting the device from harm. Without surge protectors, systems would be subjected to multiple surges each year.

- *Noise*—Fluctuation in voltage levels caused by other devices on the network or electromagnetic interference. Some noise is unavoidable on an electrical circuit, but excessive noise can cause a power supply to malfunction, immediately corrupting program or data files and gradually damaging motherboards and other computer circuits. If you've ever turned on fluorescent lights or a laser printer and noticed the lights dim, you have probably introduced noise into the electrical system. Power that is free from noise is called "clean" power. To make sure power is clean, a circuit must pass through an electrical filter.

Net+
4.5

- *Brownout*—A momentary decrease in voltage; also known as a **sag**. An overtaxed electrical system can cause brownouts, which you might recognize in your home as a dimming of the lights. Such decreases in voltage can cause significant problems for computer devices.

- *Blackout*—A complete power loss. A blackout could cause significant damage to your network. For example, if you are performing an NOS upgrade when a blackout occurs and you have not protected the server, its NOS might be damaged so extensively that the server cannot restart and its operating system must be reinstalled from scratch. If the file server is idle when a blackout occurs, however, it might recover very easily.

Each of these power problems can adversely affect network devices and their availability. It is not surprising then, that network administrators spend a great deal of money and time ensuring that power remains available and problem free. The following sections describe devices and ways of dealing with unstable power.

UPSs (Uninterruptible Power Supplies) A popular way to ensure that a network device does not lose power is to install a UPS (**uninterruptible power supply**). A UPS is a battery-operated power source directly attached to one or more devices and to a power supply (such as a wall outlet) that prevents undesired features of the wall outlet's A/C power from harming the device or interrupting its services.

UPSs vary widely in the type of power aberrations they can rectify, the length of time they can provide power, and the number of devices they can support. Of course, they also vary widely in price. Some UPSs are intended for home use, designed merely to keep your workstation running long enough for you to properly shut it down in case of a blackout. Other UPSs perform sophisticated operations such as line filtering or conditioning (which includes the elimination of noise to ensure clean power), power supply monitoring, and error notification. The type of UPS you choose depends on your budget, the number and size of your systems, and the critical nature of those systems.

UPSs are classified into two general categories: standby and online. A **standby UPS** provides continuous voltage to a device by switching virtually instantaneously to the battery when it detects a loss of power from the wall outlet. Upon restoration of the power, the standby UPS switches the device back to A/C power. The problem with standby UPSs is that, in the brief amount of time that it takes the UPS to discover that power from the wall outlet has faltered, a device may have already detected the power loss and shut down or restarted. Technically, a standby UPS doesn't provide continuous power; for this reason, it is sometimes called an **offline UPS**. Nevertheless, standby UPSs may prove adequate even for critical network devices, such as servers, routers, and gateways. They cost significantly less than online UPSs.

An **online UPS** uses the A/C power from the wall outlet to continuously charge its battery, while providing power to a network device through its battery. In other words, a server connected to an online UPS always relies on the UPS battery for its electricity. Because the server never needs to switch from the wall outlet's power to the UPS's power, there is no risk of momentarily losing service. Also, because the UPS always provides the power, it can handle noise, surges, and sags before the power reaches the attached device. As you can imagine, online UPSs are more expensive than standby UPSs. Figure 14-1 shows standby and online UPSs.

Figure 14-1 Standby and online UPSs

How do you decide which UPS is right for your network? Consider a number of factors:

- *Amount of power needed*—The more power required by your device, the more power-ful the UPS must be. Suppose that your organization decides to cut costs and purchase a UPS that cannot supply the amount of power required by a device. If the power to your building ever fails, this UPS will not support your device—you might as well not have a UPS.

- *Electrical power is measured in volt-amps*—A **volt-amp** (**VA**) is the product of the volt-age and current (measured in amps) of the electricity on a line. To determine approxi-mately how many VAs your device requires, you can use the following conversion: 1.4 volt-amps = 1 watt (W). A desktop computer, for example, may use a 200 W power supply, and, therefore, require a UPS capable of at least 280 VA to keep the CPU run-ning in case of a blackout. If you want backup power for your entire home office, how-ever, you must account for the power needs for your monitor and any peripherals, such as printers, when purchasing a UPS. A medium-sized server with a monitor and external tape drive might use 402 W, thus requiring a UPS capable of providing at least 562 VA power. Determining your power needs can be a challenge. You must account for your existing equipment and consider how you might upgrade the supported device(s) over the next several years. Consider consulting with your equipment manufacturer to obtain recommendations on power needs.

- *Period of time to keep a device running*—The longer you anticipate needing a UPS to power your device, the more powerful your UPS must be. For example, the medium-sized server that relies on a 574 VA UPS to remain functional for 20 minutes needs a

1100 VA UPS to remain functional for 90 minutes. To determine how long your device might require power from a UPS, research the length of typical power outages in your area.

- *Line conditioning*—A UPS should also offer surge suppression to protect against surges and line conditioning, or filtering, to guard against line noise. Line conditioners and UPS units include special noise filters that remove line noise. The manufacturer's technical specifications should indicate the amount of filtration required for each UPS. Noise suppression is expressed in decibel levels (dB) at a specific frequency (KHz or MHz). The higher the decibel level, the greater the protection.

- *Cost*—Prices for good UPSs vary widely, depending on the unit's size and extra features. A relatively small UPS that can power one server for five to 10 minutes might cost between $100 and $300. A large UPS that can power a sophisticated router for three hours might cost up to $5,000. Still larger UPSs, which can power an entire data center for several hours, can cost hundreds of thousands of dollars. On a critical system, you should not try to cut costs by buying an off-brand, potentially unreliable, or weak UPS.

As with other large purchases, you should research several UPS manufacturers and their products before selecting a UPS. Make sure the manufacturer provides a warranty and lets you test the UPS with your equipment. Testing UPSs with your equipment is an important part of the decision-making process. Popular UPS manufacturers are APC, Falcon, Liebert, and Tripp Lite.

Generators If your organization cannot withstand a power loss of any duration, either because of its computer services or other electrical needs, you might consider investing in an electrical generator for your building. Generators can be powered by diesel, liquid propane gas, natural gas, or steam. They do not provide surge protection, but they do provide electricity that's free from noise. In highly available environments, such as an ISP's or telecommunications carrier's data center, generators are common. In fact, in those environments, they are typically combined with large UPSs to ensure that clean power is always available. In the event of a power failure, the UPS supplies electricity until the generator starts and reaches its full capacity, typically no more than three minutes. If your organization relies on a generator for backup power, be certain to check fuel levels and quality regularly. Figure 14-2 illustrates the power infrastructure of a network (such as a data center's) that uses both a generator and dual UPSs.

Before choosing a generator, calculate your organization's crucial electrical demands to determine the generator's optimal size. Also estimate how long the generator may be required to power your building. Depending on the amount of power draw, a high-capacity generator can supply power for several days. Gas or diesel generators may cost between $10,000 and $3,000,000 (for the largest industrial types). For a company such as a network service provider that stands to lose up to $1,000,000 per minute if its data facilities fail completely, a multi-million-dollar investment to ensure available power is a wise choice. Smaller businesses, however, might choose the more economical solution of renting an electrical generator. To find out more about options for renting or purchasing generators in your area, contact your local electrical utility.

Net+
4.5

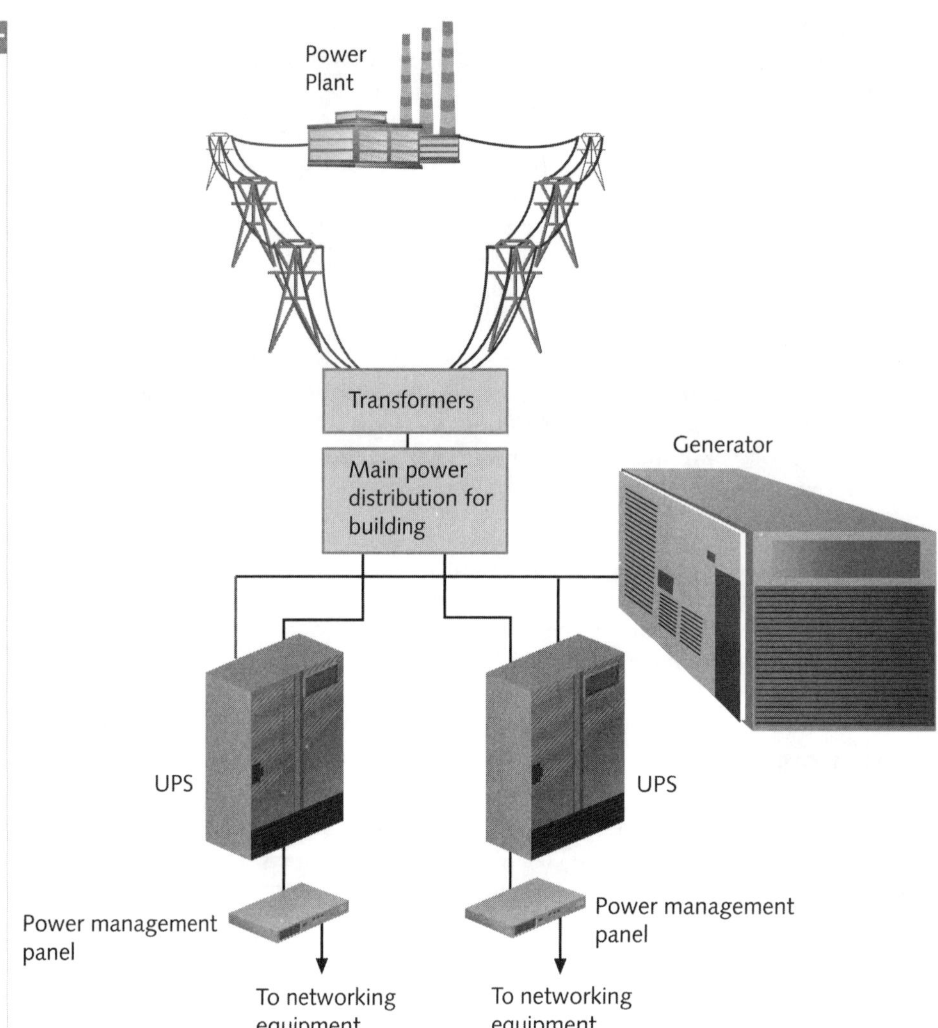

Figure 14-2 UPSs and a generator in a network design

Net+ Topology and Connectivity

2.3

4.5

You read about topology and architecture fault tolerance in previous chapters of this book. Recall that each physical topology offers certain advantages and disadvantages, and you need to assess your network's needs before designing your data links.

The key to fault tolerance in network design is supplying multiple paths that data can use to travel from any one point to another. Therefore, if one connection fails, data can be rerouted over an alternate path. On a LAN, a star topology and a parallel backbone provide the greatest fault tolerance. On a WAN, a full-mesh topology offers the best fault tolerance. A partial-mesh topology offers some redundancy, but it is not as fault tolerant as a full-mesh WAN because it offers fewer alternate routes for data. Refer to Figure 7-5 to refresh your memory on the comparison between partial-mesh and full-mesh WAN topologies.

Another highly fault-tolerant network is one based on SONET technology, which relies on a dual, fiber-optic ring for its transmission. Recall that because it uses two fiber rings for every

2.3

4.5

connection, a SONET network can easily recover from a fault in one of its links. Refer to Figure 7-20 to refresh your memory on SONET's dual-ring topology.

Mesh topologies and SONET rings are good choices for highly available enterprise networks. But what about connections to the Internet or data backup connections? You might need to establish more than one of these links.

As an example, imagine that you work for a data services firm called PayNTime that processes payroll checks for a large oil company in the Houston area. Every day, you receive updated payroll information over a T1 link from your client, and every Thursday you compile this information and then cut 2,000 checks that you ship overnight to the client's headquarters. What would happen if the T1 link between PayNTime and the oil company suffered damage in a flood and became unusable on a Thursday morning? How would you ensure that the employees received their pay? If no redundant link to the oil company existed, you would probably need to gather and input the data into your system at least partially by hand. Even then, chances are that you wouldn't process the payroll checks in time to be shipped overnight.

In this type of situation, you would want a duplicate connection between PayNTime and the oil company's site for redundancy. You might contract with two different service carriers to ensure the redundancy. Alternatively, you might arrange with one service carrier to provide two different routes. However you provide redundancy in your network topology, you should make sure that the critical data transactions can follow more than one possible path from source to target.

Redundancy in your network offers the advantage of reducing the risk of lost functionality, and potentially lost profits, from a network fault. As you might guess, however, the main disadvantage of redundancy is its cost. If you subscribed to two different service providers for two T1 links in the PayNTime example, you would probably double your monthly leasing costs of approximately $400. Multiply that amount times 12 months, and then times the number of clients for which you need to provide redundancy, and the extra layers of protection quickly become expensive. Redundancy is like a homeowner's insurance policy: You might never need to use it, but if you don't get it, the cost when you do need it can be much higher than your premiums. As a general rule, you should invest in connection redundancies where they are absolutely necessary.

Now suppose that PayNTime provides services not only to the oil company, but also to a temporary agency in the Houston area. Both links are critical because both companies need their payroll checks cut each week. To address concerns of capacity and scalability, the company may want to consider partnering with an ISP and establishing secure VPNs (virtual private networks) with its clients. With a VPN, PayNTime could shift the costs of redundancy and network design to the service provider and concentrate on the task it does best—processing payroll. Figure 14-3 illustrates this type of arrangement.

But what about the devices that connect one segment of a LAN or WAN to another? What happens when they experience a fault? Previously, you learned how connectivity devices work and how dedicated lines terminate at a customer's premises and in a service provider's data center. Next, consider how to fundamentally increase the fault tolerance of connectivity devices and a LAN's or WAN's connecting links.

To understand how to increase the fault tolerance of not just the topology, but also the network's connectivity, let's return to the example of PayNTime. Suppose that the company's network administrator decides to establish a VPN agreement with a national ISP. PayNTime's bandwidth analysis indicates that a T1 link is sufficient to transport the data of five customers

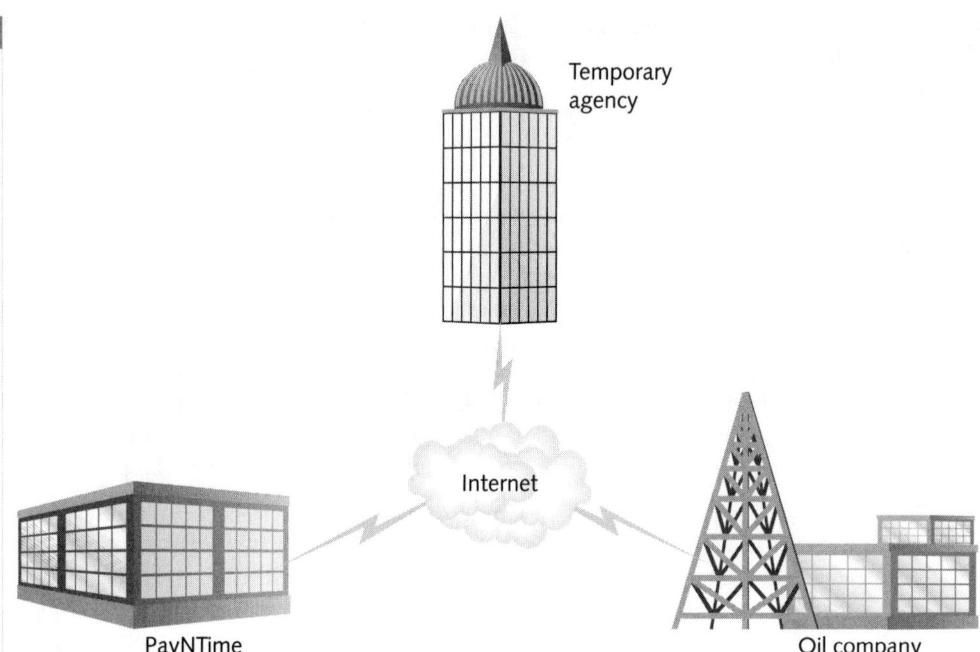

Figure 14-3 VPNs linking multiple customers

from the ISP's office to PayNTime's data room. Figure 14-4 provides a detailed representation of this arrangement.

Notice the many single points of failure in the arrangement depicted in Figure 14-4. As mentioned earlier, the T1 connection could incur a fault. In addition, the firewall, router, CSU/DSU, multiplexer, or switch might suffer faults in its power supplies, NICs, or circuit boards. In a critical component such as a router or switch, the utmost fault tolerance necessitates the use of redundant NICs, power supplies, cooling fans, interfaces, and I/O modules, all of which should ideally be able to immediately assume the duties of an identical component, a capability known as automatic **failover**. Even if one router's NIC fails, for example, failover ensures that the router's other NIC can automatically handle the first server's responsibilities.

In cases in which it's impractical to have failover capable components, you can provide some level of fault tolerance by using hot swappable parts. The term **hot swappable** refers to identical components that can be changed (or swapped) while a machine is still running (hot). A hot swappable component assumes the functions of its counterpart if one suffers a fault.

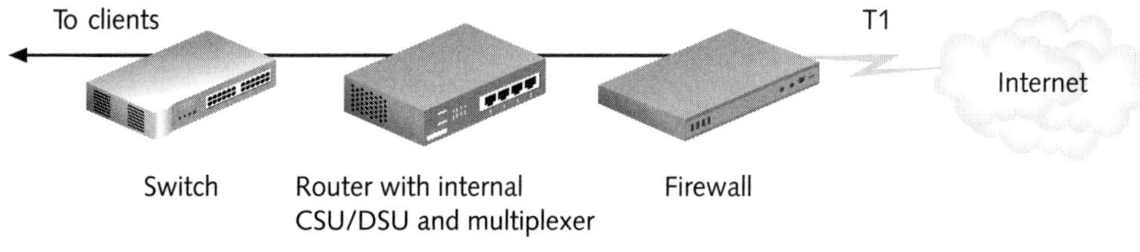

Figure 14-4 Single T1 connectivity

Net+
2.3
4.5

When you purchase switches or routers to support critical links, look for those that contain failover capable or hot swappable components. As with other redundancy provisions, these features add to the cost of your device purchase.

Purchasing connectivity devices with hot swappable or failover capable components does not address all faults that can occur on a connection. Faults might also affect the connecting links. For example, if you connect two offices with a dedicated T1 connection and the T1 cable is severed during a construction mishap, it doesn't matter whether your router has redundant NICs. The connection will still be down. Because a fault in the T1 link has the same effect as a bad T1 interface in a router, a fully redundant system might be a better option. Such a system is depicted in Figure 14-5.

The preceding scenario utilizes the most reliable option for providing network redundancy for PayNTime. In addition, leasing redundant T1s allows for **load balancing,** or an automatic distribution of traffic over multiple links or processors to optimize response. Load balancing would maximize the throughput between PayNTime and its ISP, because the aggregate traffic flowing between the two points could move over either T1 link, avoiding potential bottlenecks on a single T1 connection. Although one company might be willing to pay for such complete redundancy, another might prefer a less expensive solution. A less expensive redundancy option might be to use a dial-back WAN link. For example, a company that depends on an ATM WAN might also have an access server with a DSL or dial-up link that automatically connects to the remote site when it detects a failure of the primary link.

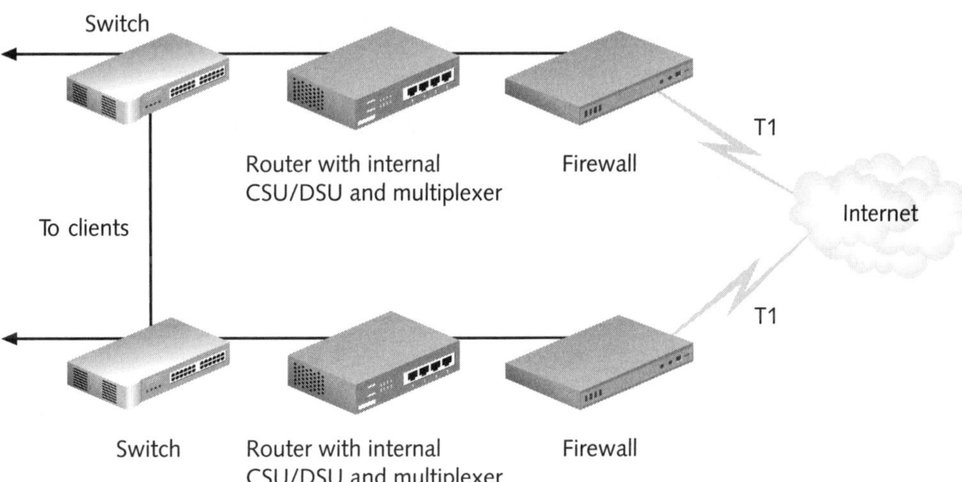

Figure 14-5 Fully redundant T1 connectivity

Net+ Servers

4.5

As with other devices, you can make servers more fault tolerant by supplying them with redundant components. Critical servers (such as those that perform user authentication for an entire LAN, or those that run important, enterprise-wide applications such as an electronic catalog in a library) often contain redundant NICs, processors, and hard disks. These redundant components provide assurance that if one item fails, the entire system won't fail; at the same time, they enable load balancing.

For example, a server with two 100Mbps NICs might receive and transmit traffic at a rate of 46Mbps during a busy time of the day. With additional software provided by either the NIC manufacturer or a third party, the redundant NICs can work in tandem to distribute the load, ensuring that approximately half the data travels through the first NIC and half through the second. This approach improves response time for users accessing the server. If one NIC fails, the other NIC automatically assumes full responsibility for receiving and transmitting all data to and from the server. Although load balancing does not technically fall under the category of fault tolerance, it helps justify the purchase of redundant components that do contribute to fault tolerance.

The following sections describe more sophisticated ways of providing server fault tolerance, beginning with server mirroring.

Server Mirroring Mirroring is a fault-tolerance technique in which one device or component duplicates the activities of another. In **server mirroring**, one server continually duplicates the transactions and data storage of another. The servers involved must be identical machines using identical components. As you would expect, mirroring requires a high-speed link between the servers. It also requires software running on both servers that allows them to synchronize their actions continually and, in case of a failure, that permits one server to take over for the other. Server mirroring is considered to be a form of **replication**, a term that refers to the dynamic copying of data from one location to another.

To illustrate the concept of mirroring, suppose that you give a presentation to a large group of people, and the audience is allowed to interrupt you to ask questions at any time. You might talk for two minutes, wait while someone asked a question, answer the question, begin lecturing again, take another question, and so on. In this sense, you act like a primary server, busily transmitting and receiving information. Now imagine that your identical twin is standing in the next room and can hear you over a loudspeaker. Your twin was instructed to say exactly what you say as quickly as possible after you spoke, but to an empty room containing only a tape recorder. Of course, your twin must listen to you before imitating you. It takes time for the twin to digest everything you say and repeat it, so you must slow down your lecture and your room's question-and-answer process. A mirrored server acts in much the same way. The time it takes to duplicate the incoming and outgoing data detrimentally affects network performance if the network handles a heavy traffic load. But if you should faint during your lecture, for example, your twin can step into your room and take over for you in very short order. The mirrored server also stands ready to assume the responsibilities of its counterpart.

One advantage to mirroring is that the servers involved can stand side by side or be positioned in different locations—perhaps in two different buildings of a company's headquarters, or possibly even on opposite sides of a continent. One potential disadvantage to mirroring, however, is the time it takes for a mirrored server to assume the functionality of the failed server. This delay could last 15 to 90 seconds. Obviously, this downtime makes mirroring imperfect. When a server fails, users lose network service, and any data in transit at the moment of the failure is susceptible to corruption. Another disadvantage to mirroring is its toll on the network as data is copied between sites.

Although server mirroring software can be expensive, the hardware costs of mirroring also mount, because you must devote an entire server to simply acting as a "tape recorder" for all data in case the other server fails. Depending on the potential cost of losing a server's functionality for any period of time, however, the expense involved may be justifiable.

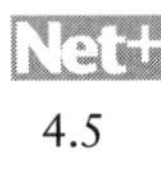 

4.5

You might be familiar with the term *mirroring* as it refers to Web sites on the Internet. Mirrored Web sites are locations on the Internet that dynamically duplicate other locations on the Internet, to ensure their continual availability. They are similar to, but not necessarily the same as, mirrored servers.

Clustering Clustering is a fault-tolerance technique that links multiple servers to act as a single server. In this configuration, clustered servers share processing duties and appear as a single server to users. If one server in the cluster fails, the other servers in the cluster automatically take over its data transaction and storage responsibilities. Because multiple servers can perform services independently of other servers, as well as ensure fault tolerance, clustering is more cost-effective than mirroring for large networks.

To understand the concept of clustering, imagine that you and several colleagues (who are not exactly like you) are simultaneously giving separate talks in different rooms in the same conference center. All of your colleagues are constantly aware of your lecture, and vice versa. If you should faint during your lecture, one of your colleagues can immediately jump into your spot and pick up where you left off, without the audience ever noticing. (At the same time, your colleague must continue to present his own lecture, which means that he must split his time between these two tasks.)

To detect failures, clustered servers regularly poll each other on the network, asking, "Are you still there?" They then wait a specified period of time before again asking, "Are you still there?" If they don't receive a response from one of their counterparts, the clustering software initiates the failover. This process can take anywhere from a few seconds to a minute, because all information about a failed server's shared resources must be gathered by the cluster. Unlike with mirroring, users will not notice the switch. Later, when the other servers in the cluster detect that the missing server has been replaced, they automatically relinquish that server's responsibilities. The failover and recovery processes are transparent to network users.

Often, clustering is implemented among servers located in the same data room. However, some clusters can contain servers that are geographically distant from each other. One factor to consider when separating clustered servers is the time required for the servers to communicate. For example, Microsoft recommends ensuring a return-trip latency of less than 500 milliseconds for requests to clustered servers. Thus, clusters that must appear as a single storage entity to LAN clients depend on fast WAN or MAN connections. They also require close attention to their setup and configuration, as they are more complex to install than clusters of servers on the same LAN.

Clustering offers many advantages over mirroring. Each server in the cluster can perform its own data processing; at the same time, it is always ready to take over for a failed server if necessary. Not only does this ability to perform multiple functions reduce the cost of ownership for a cluster of servers, but it also improves performance.

Like mirroring, clustering is implemented through a combination of software and hardware. Microsoft Windows Server 2003 and Windows Server 2008 incorporate options for server clustering. Clustering has been part of UNIX-type operating systems since the early 1990s.

Storage

Related to the availability and fault tolerance of servers is the availability and fault tolerance of data storage. In the following sections, you learn about different methods for making sure shared data and applications are never lost or irretrievable.

Net+
4.5

RAID (Redundant Array of Independent [or Inexpensive] Disks)

RAID (Redundant Array of Independent [or Inexpensive] Disks) refers to a collection of disks that provide fault tolerance for shared data and applications. A group of hard disks is called a disk **array** (or a drive). The collection of disks that work together in a RAID configuration is often referred to as the *RAID drive* or *RAID array*. To the system, the multiple disks in a RAID drive appear as a single logical drive. One advantage of using RAID is that a single disk failure will not cause a catastrophic loss of data. Other advantages are increased storage capacity and potentially better disk performance. Although RAID comes in many different forms (or levels), all types use shared, multiple physical or logical hard disks to ensure data integrity and availability.

RAID can be implemented as a hardware or software solution. **Hardware RAID** includes a set of disks and a separate disk controller. The hardware RAID array is managed exclusively by the RAID disk controller, which is attached to a server through the server's controller interface. To the server's NOS, a hardware RAID array appears as just another storage device.

Software RAID relies on software to implement and control RAID techniques over virtually any type of hard disk (or disks). Software RAID is less expensive overall than hardware RAID, because it does not require special controller or disk array hardware. With today's fast processors, software RAID performance rivals that of hardware RAID, which was formerly regarded as faster. The software may be a third-party package, or it may exist as part of the NOS. On a Windows Server 2008 server, for example, RAID drives are configured through the Disk Management snap-in, which is accessed through the Server Manager or Computer Management tool.

Several different types of RAID are available. The following sections describe the four types that are most common and supported by modern NOSs.

RAID Level 0—Disk Striping

RAID level 0 (otherwise known as **disk striping**) is a very simple implementation of RAID in which data is written in 64KB blocks equally across all disks in the array. Disk striping is not a fault-tolerant method, because if one disk fails, the data contained in it is inaccessible. Thus, RAID level 0 does not provide true redundancy. Nevertheless, it does use multiple disk partitions effectively, and it improves performance by utilizing multiple disk controllers. The multiple disk controllers allow several instructions to be sent to the disks simultaneously. Of the four types of RAID discussed in this chapter, RAID level 0 has the best performance.

Figure 14-6 illustrates how data is written to multiple disks in RAID level 0. Notice how each 64KB piece of data is written to one discrete area of the disk array. For example, if you saved a 128KB file, the file would be separated into two pieces and saved in different areas of the drive. Although RAID level 0 is easy to implement, it should not be used on mission-critical servers because of its lack of fault tolerance.

RAID Level 1—Disk Mirroring

RAID level 1 provides redundancy through a process called **disk mirroring**, in which data from one disk is copied to another disk automatically as the information is written. Because data is continually saved to multiple locations, disk mirroring provides a dynamic data backup. If one disk in the array fails, the disk array controller automatically switches to the disk that was mirroring the failed disk. Users do not even notice the failure. After repairing the failed disk, the network administrator must perform a resynchronization to return the disk to the array. Because the failed disk's twin has been saving all of its data while it was out of service, this task is rarely difficult.

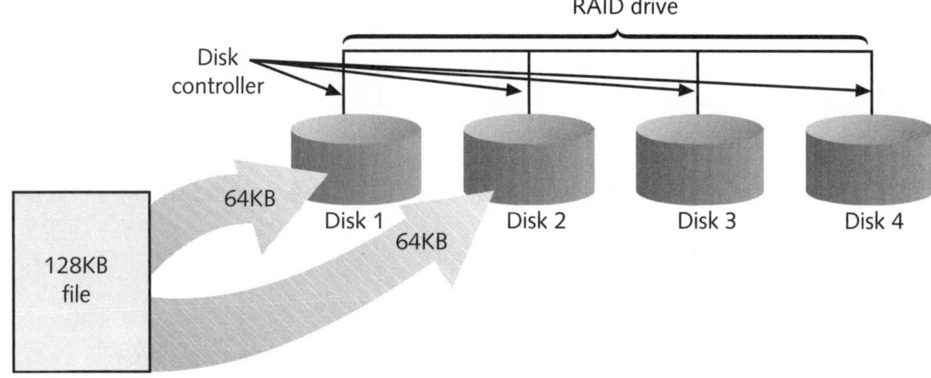

Figure 14-6 RAID level 0—disk striping

The advantages of RAID level 1 derive from its simplicity and its automatic and complete data redundancy. On the other hand, because it requires two identical disks instead of just one, RAID level 1 is somewhat costly. In addition, it is not the most efficient means of protecting data, as it usually relies on system software to perform the mirroring, which taxes CPU resources. Figure 14-7 depicts a 128KB file being written to a disk array using RAID level 1.

Although they are not covered in this chapter, RAID levels 2, 4, and higher also exist, in addition to RAID installations that combine multiple RAID levels. These versions of RAID are rarely used, however, because they are less reliable, less economical, or less efficient than Levels 0, 1, 3, and 5.

The concept of disk duplexing is related to disk mirroring. In **disk duplexing**, data is continually copied from one disk to another when it is saved, just as in disk mirroring. In duplexing, however, a separate disk controller is used for each disk. This provides added fault tolerance, because a disk controller failure will not render data inaccessible. Conversely, if a RAID 1 disk controller fails, all of the data on the storage device becomes inaccessible.

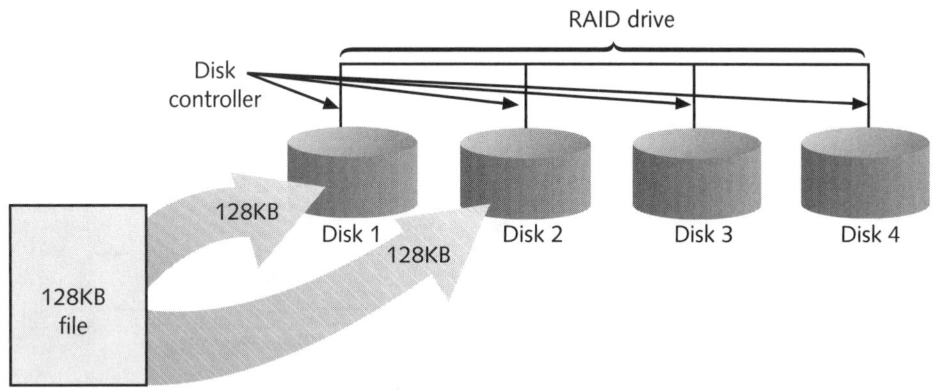

Figure 14-7 RAID level 1—disk mirroring

Net+
4.5

RAID Level 3—Disk Striping with Parity ECC **RAID** level 3 involves disk striping with a special ECC (**error correction code**), or algorithm used to detect and correct errors, known as parity error correction code. The term **parity** refers to the mechanism used to verify the integrity of data by making the number of bits in a byte sum to either an odd or even number. To accomplish parity, a parity bit (equal to either 0 or 1) is added to the bits' sum. Table 14-1 expresses how the sums of many bits achieve even parity through a parity bit. Notice that the numbers in the fourth column are all even. If the summed numbers in the fourth column were odd, an odd parity would be used. A system may use either even parity or odd parity, but not both.

Table 14-1 The Use of Parity Bits to Achieve Parity

Original Data	Sum of Data Bits	Parity Bit	Sum of Data Plus Parity Bits
01110010	4	0	4
00100010	2	0	2
00111101	5	1	6
10010100	3	1	4

Parity tracks the integrity of data on a disk. It does not reflect the data type, protocol, transmission method, or file size. A parity bit is assigned to each data byte when it is transmitted or written to a disk. When data is later read from the disk, the data's bits plus the parity bit are summed again. If the parity does not match (for example, if the end sum is odd but the system uses even parity), then the system assumes that the data has suffered some type of damage. The process of comparing the parity of data read from a disk with the type of parity used by the system is known as **parity error checking**.

In RAID level 3, parity error checking occurs when data is written across the disk array. If the parity error checking indicates an error, the RAID level 3 system can automatically correct it. The advantage of using RAID 3 is that it provides a high data transfer rate when reading from or writing to the disks. This quality makes RAID 3 particularly well suited to applications that require high speed in data transfers, such as video editing. A disadvantage of RAID 3 is that the parity information appears on a single disk, which represents a potential single point of failure in the system. Figure 14-8 illustrates how RAID level 3 works.

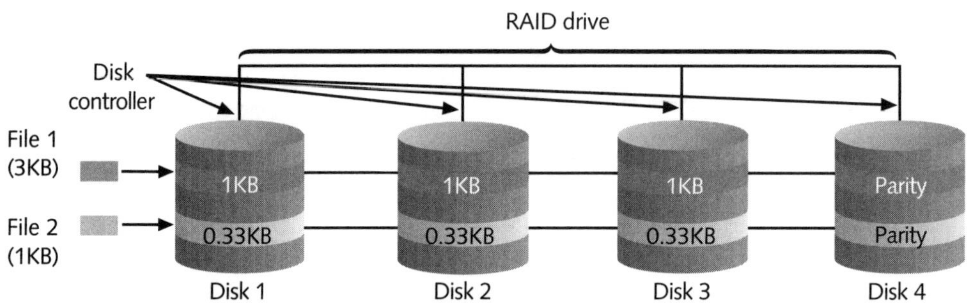

Figure 14-8 RAID level 3—disk striping with parity ECC

Net+
4.5

RAID Level 5—Disk Striping with Distributed Parity The highly fault-tolerant **RAID level 5** is the most popular data storage technique in use today. In RAID level 5, data is written in small blocks across several disks. At the same time, parity error checking information is distributed among the disks. Figure 14-9 depicts two files being written over several disks via RAID level 5.

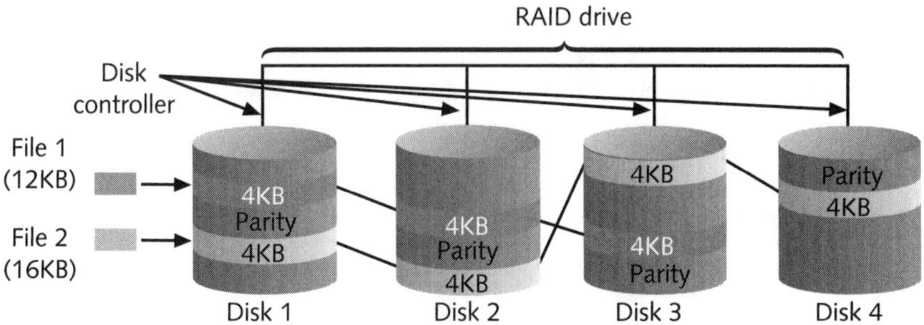

Figure 14-9 RAID level 5—disk striping with distributed parity

RAID level 5 is similar to, but has several advantages over, RAID level 3. First, it can write data more rapidly because the parity information can be written by any one of the several disk controllers in the array. Unlike RAID level 3, RAID level 5 uses several disks for parity information, making it more fault tolerant. Also, RAID level 5 allows you to replace a failed disk with a good one with little interruption of service. This is because, using parity information and the parts of a file that remain on the good disks, RAID controlling software can regenerate the parts of the file that were on the failed disk after that disk is replaced. To take advantage of this feature, some network administrators equip their RAID 5 systems with a **hot spare**, a disk or partition that is part of the array, but used only in case one of the RAID disks fails. More generally, the term *hot spare* is used as a synonym for a hot swappable component, which, as you learned earlier, is a duplicate component installed in a device that can assume the original component's functions in case that component fails. In contrast, **cold spare** refers to a duplicate component that is not installed but can be installed in case of a failure. Replacing a component with a cold spare requires an interruption of service.

NAS (Network Attached Storage) NAS (**network attached storage**) is a specialized storage device or group of storage devices that provides centralized fault-tolerant data storage for a network. NAS differs from RAID in that it maintains its own interface to the LAN rather than relying on a server to connect it to the network and control its functions. In fact, you can think of NAS as a unique type of server dedicated to data sharing. The advantage to using NAS over a typical file server is that a NAS device contains its own file system that is optimized for saving and serving files (as opposed to also managing printing, authenticating logon IDs, and so on). Because of this optimization, NAS reads and writes from its disk significantly faster than other types of servers could.

Another advantage to using NAS is that it can be easily expanded without interrupting service. For instance, if you purchased a NAS device with 400GB of disk space and then six months later realized you need three times as much storage space, you could add the new 800GB of disk space to the NAS device without requiring users to log off the network or taking down the NAS device. After physically installing the new disk space, the NAS device

14

would recognize the added storage and add it to its pool of available reading and writing space. Compare this process to adding hard disk space to a typical server, for which you would have to take the server down, install the hardware, reformat the drive, integrate it with your NOS, and then add directories, files, and permissions as necessary.

Although NAS is a separate device with its own file system, it still cannot communicate directly with clients on the network. When using NAS, the client requests a file from its usual file server over the LAN. The server then requests the file from the NAS device on the network. In response, the NAS device retrieves the file and transmits it to the server, which transmits it to the client. Figure 14-10 depicts how a NAS device physically connects to a LAN.

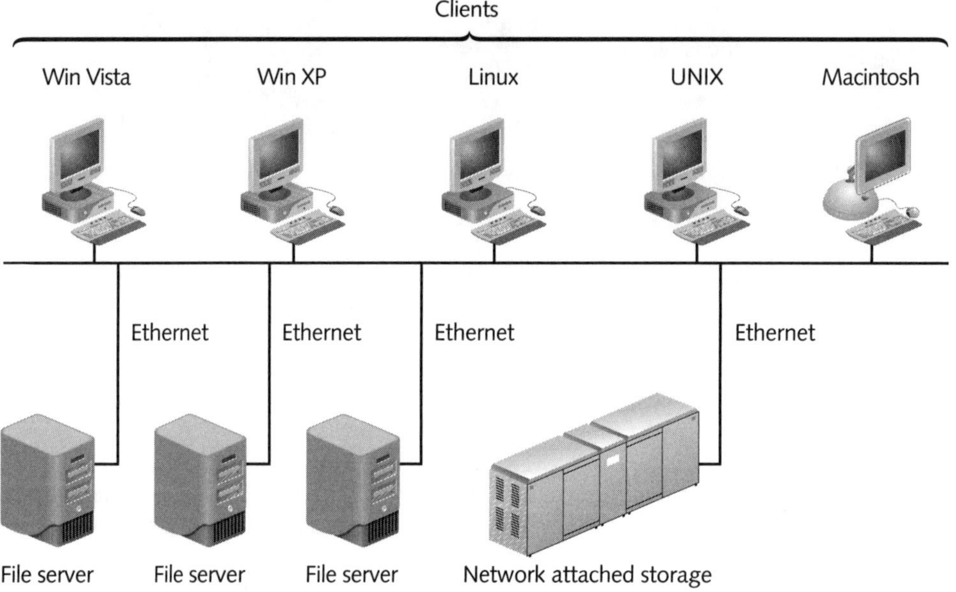

Figure 14-10 Network attached storage on a LAN

NAS is appropriate for enterprises that require not only fault tolerance, but also fast access for their data. For example, an ISP might use NAS to host its customers' Web pages. Because NAS devices can store and retrieve data for any type of client (providing it can run TCP/IP), NAS is also appropriate for organizations that use a mix of different operating systems on their desktops.

Large enterprises that require even faster access to data and larger amounts of storage might prefer storage area networks over NAS. You will learn about storage area networks in the following section.

SANs (Storage Area Networks) As you have learned, NAS devices are separate storage devices, but they still require a file server to interact with other devices on the network. In contrast, SANs (**storage area networks**) are distinct networks of storage devices that communicate directly with each other and with other networks. In a typical SAN, multiple storage devices are connected to multiple, identical servers. This type of architecture is similar to the mesh topology in WANs, the most fault-tolerant type of topology possible. If one storage device within a SAN suffers a fault, data is automatically retrieved from elsewhere in the SAN. If one server in a SAN suffers a fault, another server steps in to perform its functions.

Not only are SANs extremely fault tolerant, but they are also extremely fast. Much of their speed can be attributed to the use of a special transmission method that relies on fiber-optic media and its own proprietary protocols. One popular SAN transmission method is called **Fibre Channel**. Fibre Channel connects devices within the SAN and connects the SAN to other networks. Fibre Channel is capable of up to 2Gbps throughput. Because it depends on Fibre Channel and not on a traditional network transmission method (for example, 1GBase-T), a SAN is not limited to the speed of the client/server network for which it provides data storage. In addition, because the SAN does not belong to the client/server network, it does not have to contend with the normal overhead of that network, such as broadcasts and acknowledgments. Likewise, a SAN frees the client/server network from the traffic-intensive duties of backing up and restoring data.

Figure 14-11 shows a SAN connected to a traditional Ethernet network.

Another advantage to using SANs is that a SAN can be installed in a location separate from the LAN it serves. Being in a separate location provides added fault tolerance. For example, if an organization's main offices suffered a fire or flood, the SAN and the data it stores would still be safe. Remote SANs can be kept in an ISP's data center, which can provide

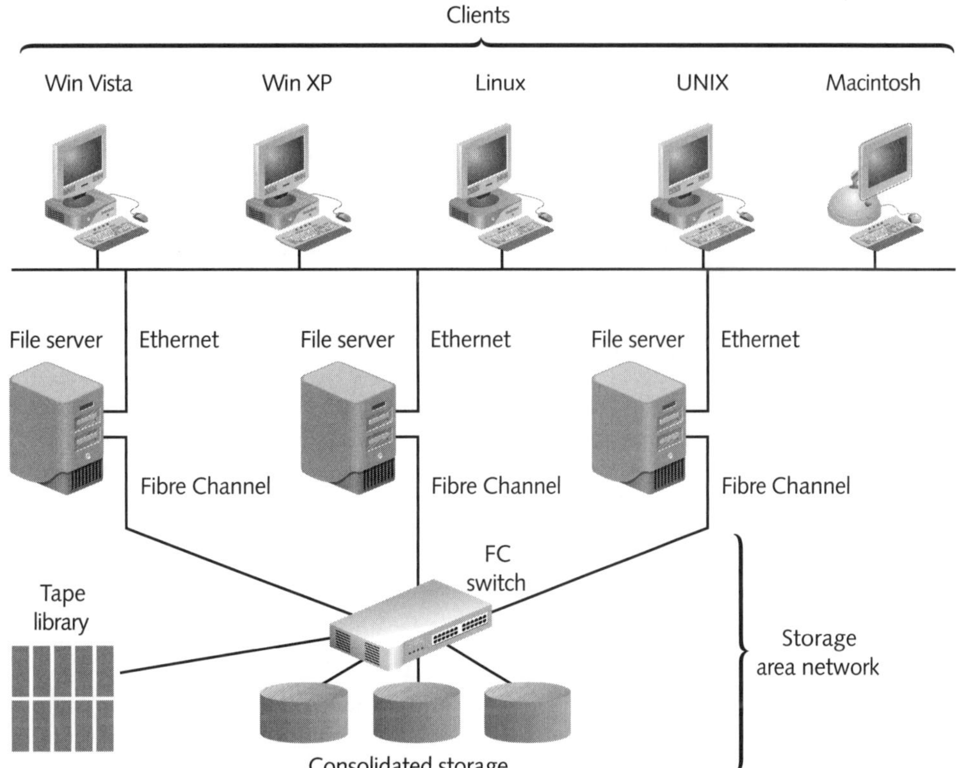

Figure 14-11 A storage area network

Net+
4.5

greater security and fault tolerance and allows an organization to outsource the management of its storage, in case its own staff don't have the time or expertise.

Like NAS, SANs provide the benefit of being highly scalable. After establishing a SAN, you can easily add further storage and new devices to the SAN without disrupting client/server activity on the network. Finally, SANs use a faster, more efficient method of writing data than do both NAS devices and typical client/server networks.

SANs are not without drawbacks, however. One noteworthy disadvantage to implementing SANs is their high cost. A small SAN can cost $100,000, while a large SAN costs several millions of dollars. In addition, because SANs are more complex than NAS or RAID systems, investing in a SAN means also investing in long hours of training for technical staff before installation, plus significant administration efforts to keep the SAN functional (that is, unless an organization outsources its storage management).

Due to their very high fault tolerance, massive storage capabilities, and speedy data access, SANs are best suited to environments with huge quantities of data that must always be quickly available. Usually, such an environment belongs to a very large enterprise. A SAN is typically used to house multiple databases—for example, inventory, sales, safety specifications, payroll, and employee records for an international manufacturing company.

Data Backup

You have probably heard or even spoken the axiom, "Make regular backups!" A **backup** is a copy of data or program files created for archiving or safekeeping. If you don't back up your data, you risk losing everything through a hard disk fault, fire, flood, or malicious or accidental erasure or corruption. No matter how reliable and fault tolerant you believe your server's hard disk (or disks) to be, you still risk losing everything unless you make backups on separate media and store them off site.

Elsewhere in this book, the term *media* refers to the elements, physical or atmospheric, that make up a path for data transmission (for example, fiber-optic cable). In the context of data backups, *media* refers to the objects on which data is stored (for example, CD-ROMs).

To fully appreciate the importance of backups, imagine coming to work one morning to find that everything disappeared from the server: programs, configurations, data files, user IDs, passwords, and the network operating system. It doesn't matter how it happened. What matters is how long it will take to reinstall the network operating systems; how long it will take to duplicate the previous configuration; and how long it will take to figure out which IDs should reside on the server, in which groups they should belong, and which permissions each group should have. What will you say to your colleagues when they learn that all of the data that they have worked on for the last year is irretrievably lost? When you think about this scenario, you quickly realize that you can't afford *not* to perform regular backups.

Many different options exist for making backups. They can be performed by different types of software and hardware combinations and use different types of media for storage. They can be controlled by NOS utilities or third-party software. In this section, you will learn about the most common backup media, methods of performing data backups, ways to schedule them, and methods for determining what you must back up.

Backup Media and Methods

When selecting backup media and methods, you can choose from several approaches, each of which comes with certain advantages and disadvantages. To select the appropriate solution for your network, consider the following questions:

- Does the backup drive or media provide sufficient storage capacity?
- Are the backup software and hardware proven to be reliable?
- Does the backup software use data error checking techniques?
- Is the system efficient enough to complete the backup process before daily operations resume?
- How much do the hardware, software, and media cost, relative to the amount of data they can store?
- Will the backup hardware and software be compatible with existing network hardware and software?
- Does the backup system require frequent manual intervention? (For example, must staff members become involved in inserting media or filing it in a library?)
- Will the backup hardware, software, and media accommodate your network's growth?

To help you answer these questions for your own situation, the following sections compare the most popular backup media and methods available today.

Optical Media A simple way to save data is by copying it to **optical media,** which is a type of media capable of storing digitized data and that uses a laser to write data to it and read data from it. Examples of optical media include all types of CDs and DVDs. Backing up data to optical media requires only a computer with the appropriate recordable CD or DVD drive and a utility for writing data to the media. Such utilities often come with a computer's operating system. If not, they are inexpensive and easy to find. A **CD-R (compact disc-recordable)** can be written to once and can store about 650MB of data. A **CD-RW (compact disc-rewriteable)** also stores about 650MB of data, but it can be used more than once for backing up data. Besides being simple to create, CD backups are simple to restore from, because their formats are standard and can be read by any computer with a matching drive. However, they suffer from a relatively low storage capacity.

A **recordable DVD** can hold up to 4.7GB on one single-layered side, and both sides of the disc can be used. In addition, each side can have up to two layers. Thus, in total, a double-layered, two-sided DVD can store up to 17GB of data. Recordable DVDs, which are not the same as the video DVD that you rent from a movie store, come in several different formats. DVD manufacturers, such as Dell, Hewlett-Packard, Hitachi, Panasonic, Philips, Pioneer, and Sony, are competing to make their version of the recordable DVD format the most popular. Therefore, if you decide to back up media to DVDs, be sure to standardize on one manufacturer's equipment.

One potential disadvantage to using CD-R and recordable DVDs for backups is that writing your data to these optical media usually takes longer than saving your data to another type of media, such as a tape or disk drive. In addition, this method requires more human intervention than other backup methods, such as tape backups, which are discussed next.

Tape Backups   In the early days of networking, the most popular method for backing up networked systems was **tape backup**, or copying data to a magnetic tape. This method is relatively simple and capable of storing very large amounts of data. Tape backups require the use of a tape drive connected to the network (via a system such as a file server or dedicated, networked workstation), software to manage and perform backups, and, of course, backup media. The tapes used for tape backups resemble small cassette tapes, but they are higher quality, specially made to reliably store data. Figure 14-12 depicts typical tape backup media.

Figure 14-12 Tape backup media

On a relatively small network, stand-alone tape drives might be attached to each server. On a large network, one large, centralized tape backup device might manage all of the subsystems' backups. This tape backup device usually is connected to a computer other than a busy file server to reduce the possibility that backups might cause traffic bottlenecks. Extremely large environments (for example, global manufacturers with several terabytes of inventory and product information to safeguard) may require robots to retrieve and circulate tapes from a tape storage library, also known as a **vault**, that may be as large as a warehouse.

Although many network administrators appreciate the durability and ease of tape backups, a faster and increasingly less expensive option is to use disk drives.

External Disk Drives   An **external disk drive** is a storage device that can be attached temporarily to a computer via its USB, PCMCIA, FireWire, or CompactFlash port. External disk drives are also known as **removable disk drives**. Small external disk drives are frequently used by laptop or desktop computer users to save and share data. After being connected to the computer, the external disk drives appear as any other drive, and the user can copy files directly to them. For backing up large amounts of data, however, network administrators are likely to use an external disk drive with backup control features, higher storage capacity, and faster read-write access. One example is the Iomega REV drive, which uses a cartridge containing a small hard disk that can hold up to 120GB of data. The REV drive operates faster than tape backups or optical media. It can connect to a computer via several bus types and comes with proprietary software that automates the backup, manages the backup schedule, identifies data to be backed up, compresses files, and verifies that the backup completed successfully. Another disk manufacturer, LaCie, makes external drives that can hold up to 1TB of data.

One advantage to using external disk drives is that they are simple to use. Also, they provide faster data transfer rates than optical media or tape backups. However, on most networks, backing up data to a fixed disk elsewhere on the network, as explained in the next section, is faster.

Network Backups Instead of saving data to a removable disk or media, you might choose to save data to another place on the network. For example, you could copy all the user data from your organization's mail server to a different server on the network. If you choose this option, be certain to back up data to a different disk than where it was originally stored, because if the original disk fails, you will lose both the original data and its backup. (Although disk locations on workstations are typically obvious, on a network they might not be.) If your organization operates a WAN, it's best to back up data to disks at another location. That way, if one location suffers an outage or catastrophe, the data will remain safe at the other location on the WAN. A sophisticated network backup solution would use software to automate and manage backups and save data to a SAN or NAS storage device. Most NOSs provide utilities for automating and managing network backups.

If your organization does not have a WAN or a high-end storage solution, you might consider online backups. An **online backup** saves data across the Internet to another company's storage array. Usually, online backup providers require you to install their client software. You also need a (preferably high-speed) connection to the Internet. Online backups implement strict security measures to protect the data in transit, as the information traverses public carrier links. Most online backup providers allow you to retrieve your data at any time of day or night, without calling a technical support number. Both the backup and restoration processes are entirely automated. In case of a disaster, the online backup company might offer to create CDs containing your servers' data. When evaluating an online backup provider, you should test its speed, accuracy, security, and, of course, the ease with which you can recover the backed-up data. Be certain to test the service before you commit to a long-term contract for online backups.

Backup Strategy

After selecting the appropriate tool for performing your servers' data backups, devise a backup strategy to guide you and your colleagues in performing reliable backups that provide maximum data protection. This strategy should be documented in a common area where all IT staff can access it. The strategy should address at least the following questions:

- What data must be backed up?
- What kind of rotation schedule will backups follow?
- At what time of day or night will the backups occur?
- How will you verify the accuracy of the backups?
- Where and for how long will backup media be stored?

- Who will take responsibility for ensuring that backups occurred?
- How long will you save backups?
- Where will backup and recovery documentation be stored?

Different backup methods provide varying levels of certainty and corresponding labor and cost. An important concept to understand before learning about different backup methods is the archive bit. An **archive bit** is a file attribute that can be checked (or set to "on") or unchecked (or set to "off") to indicate whether the file must be archived. When a file is created or changed, the operating system automatically sets the file's archive bit to "on." Various backup methods use the archive bit in different ways to determine which files should be backed up, as described in the following list:

- *Full backup*—All data on all servers is copied to storage media, regardless of whether the data is new or changed. After backing up the files, a full backup unchecks—or turns off—the files' archive bits.

- *Incremental backup*—Only data that has changed since the last full or incremental backup is copied to a storage medium. An incremental backup saves only files whose archive bit is checked. After backing up files, an incremental backup unchecks the archive bit for every file it has saved.

- *Differential backup*—Only data that has changed since the last backup is copied to a storage medium, and that information is then marked for subsequent backup, regardless of whether it has changed. In other words, a differential backup does not uncheck the archive bits for files it backs up.

When managing network backups, you need to determine the best possible **backup rotation scheme**—you need to create a plan that specifies when and how often backups will occur. The aim of a good backup rotation scheme is to provide excellent data reliability without overtaxing your network or requiring a lot of intervention. For example, you might think that backing up your entire network's data every night is the best policy because it ensures that everything is completely safe. But what if your network contains 2TB of data and is growing by 100GB per month? Would the backups even finish by morning? How many tapes would you have to purchase? Also, why should you bother backing up files that haven't changed in three weeks? How much time will you and your staff need to devote to managing the tapes? How would the transfer of all of the data affect your network's performance? All of these considerations point to a better alternative than the "tape-a-day" solution—that is, an option that promises to maximize data protection but reduce the time and cost associated with backups.

When planning your backup strategy, you can choose from several standard backup rotation schemes. The most popular of these schemes, called **Grandfather-Father-Son**, uses daily (son), weekly (father), and monthly (grandfather) backup sets. As depicted in Figure 14-13, in the Grandfather-Father-Son scheme, three types of backups are performed each month: daily incremental (every Monday through Thursday), weekly full (every Friday), and monthly full (last day of the month).

In this scheme, backup tapes are reused regularly. For example, week 1's Monday tape also serves as week 2's and week 3's Monday tape. One day each week, a full backup, called Father, is recorded in place of an incremental one and labeled for the week to which it corresponds— for example, "week 1," "week 2," and so on. This Father tape is reused monthly—for example, October's week 1 tape is reused for November's week 1 tape. The final set of media is labeled

	Monday	Tuesday	Wednesday	Thursday	Friday
Week 1	A	A	A	A	B
Week 2	A	A	A	A	B
Week 3	A	A	A	A	B
Week 4	A	A	A	A	B
Week 5	A	A	C		

One month of backups

A = Incremental "son" backup (daily)
B = Full "father" backup (weekly)
C = Full "grandfather" backup (monthly)

Figure 14-13 The Grandfather-Father-Son backup rotation scheme

"month 1," "month 2," and so on, according to which month of the quarter the tapes are used. This Grandfather medium records full backups on the last business day of each month and is reused quarterly. Each of these media may consist of a single tape or a set of tapes, depending on the amount of data involved. A total of 12 media sets are required for this basic rotation scheme, allowing for a history of two to three months.

After you have determined your backup rotation scheme, you should ensure that backup activity is recorded in a backup log. Information that belongs in a backup log includes the backup date, tape identification (day of week or type), type of data backed up (for example, Accounting department spreadsheets or a day's worth of catalog orders), type of the backup (full, incremental, or differential), files that were backed up, and site at which the tape is stored. Having this information available in case of a server failure greatly simplifies data recovery.

Finally, after you begin to back up network data, you should establish a regular schedule of verification. From time to time (depending on how often your data changes and how critical the information is), you should attempt to recover some critical files from your backup media. Many network administrators attest that the darkest hour of their career was when they were asked to retrieve critical files from a backup tape and found that no backup data existed because their backup system never worked in the first place!

Disaster Recovery

Disaster recovery is the process of restoring your critical functionality and data after an enterprise-wide outage that affects more than a single system or a limited group of users. Disaster recovery must take into account the possible extremes, rather than relatively minor outages, failures, security breaches, or data corruption.

Disaster Recovery Planning

A disaster recovery plan accounts for the worst-case scenarios, from a far-reaching hurricane to a military or terrorist attack. It should identify a disaster recovery team (with an appointed coordinator) and provide contingency plans for restoring or replacing computer systems, power, telephony systems, and paper-based files. Sections of the plan related to computer systems should include the following:

- Contact names and phone and pager numbers for emergency coordinators who will execute the disaster recovery response in case of disaster, as well as roles and responsibilities of other staff

- Details on which data and servers are being backed up, how frequently backups occur, where backups are kept (off site), and, most important, how backed-up data can be recovered in full

- Details on network topology, redundancy, and agreements with national service carriers, in case local or regional vendors fall prey to the same disaster

- Regular strategies for testing the disaster recovery plan

- A plan for managing the crisis, including regular communications with employees and customers. Consider the possibility that regular communications modes (such as phone lines) might be unavailable.

Having a comprehensive disaster recovery plan lessens the risk of losing critical data in case of extreme situations and makes potential customers and your insurance providers look more favorably on your organization.

Disaster Recovery Contingencies

An organization can choose from several options for recovering from a disaster. The options vary by the amount of employee involvement, hardware, software, planning, and investment each involves. They also vary according to how quickly they will restore network functionality in case a disaster occurs. As you would expect, every contingency necessitates a site other than the building where the network's main components normally reside. An organization might maintain its own disaster recovery sites—for example, by renting office space in a different city—or contract with a company that specializes in disaster recovery services to provide the site. Disaster recovery contingencies are commonly divided into three categories: cold site, warm site, and hot site.

A **cold site** is a place where the computers, devices, and connectivity necessary to rebuild a network exist, but they are not appropriately configured, updated, or connected. Therefore, restoring functionality from a cold site could take a long time. For example, suppose your small business network consists of a file and print server, mail server, backup server, Internet gateway/DNS/DHCP server, 25 clients, four printers, a router, a switch, two access points, and a connection to your local ISP. At your cold site, you might store four server computers on which your company's NOS is not installed and that do not possess the appropriate configurations and data necessary to operate in your environment. The 25 client machines stored there might be in a similar state. In addition, you might have a router, a switch, and two access points at the cold site, but these might also require configuration to operate in your environment. Finally, the cold site would not necessarily have Internet connectivity, or at least not the same type that your network used. Supposing you followed good backup practices and stored your backup media at the cold site, you would then need to restore operating systems, applications, and data to your servers and clients, reconfigure your connectivity devices, and arrange with your ISP to have your connectivity restored to the cold site. Even for a small network, this process could take weeks.

A **warm site** is a place where the computers, devices, and connectivity necessary to rebuild a network exist, with some appropriately configured, updated, or connected. For example, a service provider that specializes in disaster recovery might maintain a duplicate of each of your servers in its data center. You might arrange to have the service provider update those duplicate servers with your backed-up data on the first of each month, because updating the servers daily is much more expensive. In that case, if a disaster occurs in the middle of the month, you would still need to update your duplicate servers with your latest weekly or daily backups before they could stand in for the downed servers. Recovery from a warm site can take hours or days, compared to the weeks a cold site might require. Maintaining a warm site costs more than maintaining a cold site, but not as much as maintaining a hot site.

A **hot site** is a place where the computers, devices, and connectivity necessary to rebuild a network exist, and all are appropriately configured, updated, and connected to match your network's current state. For example, you might use server mirroring to maintain identical copies of your servers at two WAN locations. In a hot site contingency plan, both locations would also contain identical connectivity devices and configurations, and thus be able to stand in for the other at a moment's notice. As you can imagine, hot sites are expensive and potentially time consuming to maintain. For organizations that cannot tolerate downtime, however, hot sites provide the best disaster recovery option.

Chapter Summary

- Integrity refers to the soundness of your network's files, systems, and connections. To ensure their integrity, you must protect them from anything that might render them unusable, such as corruption, tampering, natural disasters, and malware. Availability refers to how consistently and reliably a file or system can be accessed by authorized personnel.

- Several basic measures can be employed to protect data and systems on a network: (1) Prevent anyone other than a network administrator from opening or changing the system files; (2) monitor the network for unauthorized access or changes; (3) record authorized system changes in a change management system; (4) use redundancy for critical servers, cabling, routers, switches, gateways, NICs, hard disks, power supplies, and other components; (5) perform regular health checks on the network; (6) monitor system performance, error logs, and the system log book regularly; (7) keep backups, boot disks, and emergency repair disks current and available; and (8) implement and enforce security and disaster recovery policies.

- Malware is any type of code that aims to intrude upon or harm a system or its resources. Malware includes viruses, worms, bots, and Trojan horses.

- A virus is a program that replicates itself to infect more computers, either through network connections or through external storage devices passed among users. Viruses may damage files or systems, or they may simply annoy users by flashing messages or pictures on the screen or by causing the computer to beep.

- Any type of malware can have additional characteristics that make it harder to detect and eliminate. Such malicious code might be encrypted, stealth, polymorphic, or time dependent.

- A good anti-malware program should be able to detect malware through signature scanning, integrity checking, and heuristic scanning. It should also be compatible with your network environment, centrally manageable, easy to use (transparent to users), and not prone to false alarms.

- Anti-malware software is merely one piece of the puzzle in protecting your network from harmful programs. An anti-malware policy is another essential component. It should provide rules for using anti-malware software, as well as policies for installing programs, sharing files, and using floppy disks.

- A failure is a deviation from a specified level of system performance for a given period of time. A fault, on the other hand, is the malfunction of one component of a system. A fault can result in a failure. The goal of fault-tolerant systems is to prevent faults from progressing to failures.

- Fault tolerance is a system's capacity to continue performing despite an unexpected hardware or software malfunction. It can be achieved in varying degrees. At the highest level of fault tolerance, a system is unaffected by even a drastic problem, such as a power failure.

- As you consider sophisticated fault-tolerance techniques for servers, routers, and WAN links, remember to address the environment in which your devices operate. Protecting your data also involves protecting your network from excessive heat or moisture, break-ins, and natural disasters.

- Networks cannot tolerate power loss or less than optimal power and may suffer downtime or reduced performance due to blackouts, brownouts (sags), surges, and line noise.

- A UPS (uninterruptible power supply) is a battery power source directly attached to one or more devices and to a power supply that prevents undesired features of the power source from harming the device or interrupting its services. UPSs vary in the type of power aberrations they can rectify, the length of time they can provide power, and the number of devices they can support.

- A standby UPS provides continuous voltage to a device by switching virtually instantaneously to the battery when it detects a loss of power from the wall outlet. Upon restoration of the power, the standby UPS switches the device to use A/C power again.

- An online UPS uses the A/C power from the wall outlet to continuously charge its battery, while providing power to a network device through its battery. In other words, a server connected to an online UPS always relies on the UPS battery for its electricity.

- The most certain way to guarantee power to your network is to rely on a generator. Generators can be powered by diesel, liquid propane gas, natural gas, or steam. They do not provide surge protection, but they do provide noise-free electricity.

- Network topologies such as a full-mesh WAN or a star-based LAN with a parallel backbone offer the greatest fault tolerance. A SONET ring also offers high fault tolerance, because of its dual-ring topology.

- When components are hot swappable, they have identical functions and can automatically assume the functions of their counterpart if it suffers a fault. They can be changed (or swapped) while a machine is still running (hot). Hot swappable components are sometimes called hot spares.

- Critical servers often contain redundant NICs, processors, and/or hard disks to provide better fault tolerance. These redundant components provide assurance that if one fails, the whole system won't fail, and they enable load balancing.

- A fault-tolerance technique that involves utilizing a second, identical server to duplicate the transactions and data storage of one server is called server mirroring. Mirroring can take place between servers that are either side by side or geographically distant. Mirroring requires not only a link between the servers, but also software running on both servers to enable the servers to continually synchronize their actions and to permit one to take over in case the other fails.

- Clustering is a fault-tolerance technique that links multiple servers to act as a single server. In this configuration, clustered servers share processing duties and appear as a single server to users. If one server in the cluster fails, the other servers in the cluster automatically take over its data transaction and storage responsibilities.

- An important storage redundancy feature is a RAID (Redundant Array of Independent [or Inexpensive] Disks). All types of RAID use shared, multiple physical or logical hard disks to ensure data integrity and availability; some designs also increase storage capacity and improve performance. RAID is either hardware or software based. Software RAID can be implemented through operating system utilities.

- RAID level 0 is a simple version of RAID in which data is written in 64KB blocks equally across all of the disks in the array, a technique known as disk striping. Disk striping is not a fault-tolerant method, because if one disk fails, the data contained in it will be inaccessible.

- RAID level 1 provides redundancy through a process called disk mirroring, in which data from one disk is automatically copied to another disk as the information is written. This option is considered a dynamic data backup. If one disk in the array fails, the disk array controller automatically switches to the disk that was mirroring the failed disk.

- RAID level 3 involves disk striping with parity error correction code. Parity refers to the integrity of the data as expressed in the number of 1s contained in each group of correctly transmitted bits. In RAID level 3, parity error checking takes place when the data is written across the disk array.

- RAID level 5 is the most popular fault-tolerant data storage technique in use today. In RAID level 5, data is written in small blocks across several disks; parity error checking information is also distributed among the disks.

- NAS (network attached storage) is a dedicated storage device attached to a client/server network. It uses its own file system but relies on a traditional network transmission method such as Ethernet to interact with the rest of the client/server network.

- A SAN (storage area network) is a distinct network of multiple storage devices and servers that provides fast, highly available, and highly fault-tolerant access to large quantities of data for a client/server network. A SAN uses a proprietary network transmission method (such as Fibre Channel) rather than Ethernet.

- A backup is a copy of data or program files created for archiving or safekeeping. If you do not back up your data, you risk losing everything through a hard disk fault, fire, flood, or malicious or accidental erasure or corruption. Backups should be stored on separate media (other than the backed-up server), and these media should be stored off site.

- Backups can be saved to optical media (such as CDs and DVDs), tapes, external disk drives, or to another location on a network. Of these, tape backups remain popular because of their reliability, storage capacity, and speed. Tape backups require a tape drive connected to the network, software to manage and perform backups, and backup media.

- A full backup copies all data on all servers to a storage medium, regardless of whether the data is new or changed. An incremental backup copies only data that has changed since the last full or incremental backup, and unchecks the archive bit for files it backs up. A differential backup copies only data that has changed since the last full or incremental backup, but it does not uncheck the archive bit for files it backs up.

- The aim of a good backup rotation scheme is to provide excellent data reliability but not to overtax your network or require much intervention. The most popular backup rotation scheme is called Grandfather-Father-Son. This scheme combines daily (son), weekly (father), and monthly (grandfather) backup sets.

- Disaster recovery is the process of restoring your critical functionality and data after an enterprise-wide outage that affects more than a single system or a limited group of users. It must account for the possible extremes, rather than relatively minor outages, failures, security breaches, or data corruption. In a disaster recovery plan, you should consider the worst-case scenarios, from a hurricane to a military or terrorist attack.

- Every organization should have a disaster recovery team (with an appointed coordinator) and a disaster recovery plan. The plan should address not only computer systems, but also power, telephony, and paper-based files.

- To prepare for recovery after a potential disaster, you can maintain (or hire a service to maintain for you) a cold site, warm site, or hot site. A cold site contains the elements necessary to rebuild a network, but none are appropriately configured and connected. Therefore, restoring functionality from a cold site can take a long time. A warm site contains the elements necessary to rebuild a network, and only some of them are appropriately configured and connected. A hot site is a precise duplicate of the network's elements, all properly configured and connected. This allows an organization to regain network functionality almost immediately.

Key Terms

archive bit A file attribute that can be checked (or set to "on") or unchecked (or set to "off") to indicate whether the file needs to be archived. An operating system checks a file's archive bit when it is created or changed.

array A group of hard disks.

availability How consistently and reliably a file, device, or connection can be accessed by authorized personnel.

backup A copy of data or program files created for archiving or safekeeping.

backup rotation scheme A plan for when and how often backups occur, and which backups are full, incremental, or differential.

blackout A complete power loss.

boot sector virus A virus that resides on the boot sector of a floppy disk and is transferred to the partition sector or the DOS boot sector on a hard disk. A boot sector virus can move from a floppy to a hard disk only if the floppy disk is left in the drive when the machine starts.

bot   A program that runs automatically. Bots can spread viruses or other malicious code between users in a chat room by exploiting the IRC protocol.

brownout   A momentary decrease in voltage, also known as a *sag*. An overtaxed electrical system may cause brownouts, recognizable as a dimming of the lights.

CD-R (compact disc-recordable)   A type of compact disc that can be written to only once. It can store about 650MB of data.

CD-RW (compact disc-rewriteable)   A type of compact disc that can be written to more than once. It can store about 650MB of data.

clustering   A fault-tolerance technique that links multiple servers to act as a single server. In this configuration, clustered servers share processing duties and appear as a single server to users. If one server in the cluster fails, the other servers in the cluster automatically take over its data transaction and storage responsibilities.

cold site   A place where the computers, devices, and connectivity necessary to rebuild a network exist, but they are not appropriately configured, updated, or connected to match the network's current state.

cold spare   A duplicate component that is not installed but can be installed in case of a failure.

compact disc-recordable   *See* CD-R.

compact disc-rewriteable   *See* CD-RW.

differential backup   A backup method in which only data that has changed since the last full or incremental backup is copied to a storage medium, and in which that same information is marked for subsequent backup, regardless of whether it has changed. In other words, a differential backup does not uncheck the archive bits for files it backs up.

disaster recovery   The process of restoring critical functionality and data to a network after an enterprise-wide outage that affects more than a single system or a limited group of users.

disk duplexing   A storage fault-tolerance technique in which data is continually copied from one disk to another when it is saved, just as in disk mirroring. In duplexing, however, a separate disk controller is used for each disk.

disk mirroring   A RAID technique in which data from one disk is automatically copied to another disk as the information is written.

disk striping   A simple implementation of RAID in which data is written in 64KB blocks equally across all disks in the array.

ECC (error correction code)   An algorithm used to detect and correct errors. In RAID levels 3 and 5, for example, a type of ECC known as parity error checking is used.

encrypted virus   A virus that is encrypted to prevent detection.

error correction code   *See* ECC.

external disk drive   A storage device that can be attached temporarily to a computer.

failover   The capability for one component (such as a NIC or server) to assume another component's responsibilities without manual intervention.

failure   A deviation from a specified level of system performance for a given period of time. A failure occurs when something doesn't work as promised or as planned.

fault   The malfunction of one component of a system. A fault can result in a failure.

Fibre Channel   A distinct network transmission method that relies on fiber-optic media and its own proprietary protocol. Fibre Channel is capable of up to 2Gbps throughput.

file-infector virus   A virus that attaches itself to executable files. When the infected executable file runs, the virus copies itself to memory. Later, the virus attaches itself to other executable files.

full backup   A backup in which all data on all servers is copied to a storage medium, regardless of whether the data is new or changed. A full backup unchecks the archive bit on files it has backed up.

Grandfather-Father-Son   A backup rotation scheme that uses daily (son), weekly (father), and monthly (grandfather) backup sets.

hardware RAID   A method of implementing RAID that relies on an externally attached set of disks and a RAID disk controller, which manages the RAID array.

heuristic scanning   A type of virus scanning that attempts to identify viruses by discovering viruslike behavior.

hoax   A rumor, or false alert, about a dangerous, new virus that could supposedly cause serious damage to your workstation.

hot site   A place where the computers, devices, and connectivity necessary to rebuild a network exist, and all are appropriately configured, updated, and connected to match your network's current state.

hot spare   In the context of RAID, a disk or partition that is part of the array but is used only in case one of the RAID disks fails. More generally, *hot spare* is used as a synonym for a hot swappable component.

hot swappable   A characteristic that enables identical components to be interchanged (or swapped) while a machine is still running (hot). After being installed, a hot swappable component automatically assumes the functions of its counterpart.

incremental backup   A backup in which only data that has changed since the last full or incremental backup is copied to a storage medium. After backing up files, an incremental backup unchecks the archive bit for every file it has saved.

integrity   The soundness of a network's files, systems, and connections. To ensure integrity, you must protect your network from anything that might render it unusable, such as corruption, tampering, natural disasters, and viruses.

integrity checking   A method of comparing the current characteristics of files and disks against an archived version of these characteristics to discover changes. The most common example of integrity checking involves a checksum.

Internet Relay Chat   *See* IRC.

IRC (Internet Relay Chat)   A protocol that enables users running special IRC client software to communicate instantly with other participants in a chat room on the Internet.

load balancing   An automatic distribution of traffic over multiple links, hard disks, or processors intended to optimize responses.

logic bomb   A program designed to start when certain conditions are met.

macro virus   A virus that takes the form of an application (for example, a word-processing or spreadsheet) program macro, which may execute when the program is in use.

malware A program or piece of code designed to harm a system or its resources.

mirroring A fault-tolerance technique in which one component or device duplicates the activity of another.

NAS (network attached storage) A device or set of devices attached to a client/server network, dedicated to providing highly fault-tolerant access to large quantities of data. NAS depends on traditional network transmission methods such as Ethernet.

network attached storage *See* NAS.

network virus A virus that takes advantage of network protocols, commands, messaging programs, and data links to propagate itself. Although all viruses could theoretically travel across network connections, network viruses are specially designed to attack network vulnerabilities.

noise The unwanted signals, or interference, from sources near network cabling, such as electrical motors, power lines, and radar.

offline UPS *See* standby UPS.

online backup A technique in which data is backed up to a central location over the Internet.

online UPS A power supply that uses the A/C power from the wall outlet to continuously charge its battery, while providing power to a network device through its battery.

optical media A type of media capable of storing digitized data, which uses a laser to write data to it and read data from it.

parity The mechanism used to verify the integrity of data by making the number of bits in a byte sum equal to either an odd or even number.

parity error checking The process of comparing the parity of data read from a disk with the type of parity used by the system.

polymorphic virus A type of virus that changes its characteristics (such as the arrangement of its bytes, size, and internal instructions) every time it is transferred to a new system, making it harder to identify.

RAID (Redundant Array of Independent [or Inexpensive] Disks) A server redundancy measure that uses shared, multiple physical or logical hard disks to ensure data integrity and availability. Some RAID designs also increase storage capacity and improve performance. *See also* disk mirroring, disk striping.

RAID level 0 An implementation of RAID in which data is written in 64KB blocks equally across all disks in the array.

RAID level 1 An implementation of RAID that provides redundancy through disk mirroring, in which data from one disk is automatically copied to another disk as the information is written.

RAID level 3 An implementation of RAID that uses disk striping for data and writes parity error correction code on a separate parity disk.

RAID level 5 The most popular fault-tolerant data storage technique in use today, RAID level 5 writes data in small blocks across several disks. At the same time, it writes parity error checking information among several disks.

recordable DVD An optical storage medium that can hold up to 4.7GB on one single-layered side. Both sides of the disc can be used, and each side can have up to two layers. Thus, in total, a double-layered, two-sided DVD can store up to 17GB of data. Recordable DVDs come in several formats.

redundancy The use of more than one identical component, device, or connection for storing, processing, or transporting data. Redundancy is the most common method of achieving fault tolerance.

Redundant Array of Independent (or Inexpensive) Disks *See* RAID.

removable disk drive *See* external disk drive.

replication A fault-tolerance technique that involves dynamic copying of data (for example, an NOS directory or an entire server's hard disk) from one location to another.

sag *See* brownout.

SAN (storage area network) A distinct network of multiple storage devices and servers that provides fast, highly available, and highly fault-tolerant access to large quantities of data for a client/server network. A SAN uses a proprietary network transmission method (such as Fibre Channel) rather than a traditional network transmission method such as Ethernet.

server mirroring A fault-tolerance technique in which one server duplicates the transactions and data storage of another, identical server. Server mirroring requires a link between the servers and software running on both servers so that the servers can continually synchronize their actions and one can take over in case the other fails.

signature scanning The comparison of a file's content with known virus signatures (unique identifying characteristics in the code) in a signature database to determine whether the file is a virus.

software RAID A method of implementing RAID that uses software to implement and control RAID techniques over virtually any type of hard disk(s). RAID software may be a third-party package or utilities that come with an operating system NOS.

standby UPS A power supply that provides continuous voltage to a device by switching virtually instantaneously to the battery when it detects a loss of power from the wall outlet. Upon restoration of the power, the standby UPS switches the device to use A/C power again.

stealth virus A type of virus that hides itself to prevent detection. Typically, stealth viruses disguise themselves as legitimate programs or replace part of a legitimate program's code with their destructive code.

storage area network *See* SAN.

surge A momentary increase in voltage caused by distant lightning strikes or electrical problems.

surge protector A device that directs excess voltage away from equipment plugged into it and redirects it to a ground, thereby protecting the equipment from harm.

tape backup A relatively simple and economical backup method in which data is copied to magnetic tapes.

Trojan *See* Trojan horse.

Trojan horse A program that disguises itself as something useful but actually harms your system.

uninterruptible power supply   *See* UPS.

UPS (uninterruptible power supply)   A battery-operated power source directly attached to one or more devices and to a power supply (such as a wall outlet) that prevents undesired features of the power source from harming the device or interrupting its services.

vault   A large tape storage library.

virus   A program that replicates itself to infect more computers, either through network connections or through floppy disks passed among users. Viruses might damage files or systems or simply annoy users by flashing messages or pictures on the screen or by causing the keyboard to beep.

volt-amp (VA)   A measure of electrical power. A volt-amp is the product of the voltage and current (measured in amps) of the electricity on a line.

warm site   A place where the computers, devices, and connectivity necessary to rebuild a network exist, though only some are appropriately configured, updated, or connected to match the network's current state.

worm   An unwanted program that travels between computers and across networks. Although worms do not alter other programs as viruses do, they can carry viruses.

Review Questions

1. Which type of malware is a program that claims to do something useful but instead harms the computer or system?

   a. Bot

   b. Worm

   c. Boot sector virus

   d. Trojan horse

2. Which factor is the most important decision to consider when implementing anti-malware software on a network?

   a. Where to install the software

   b. Ease of use for end-users

   c. Portability

   d. Disk space usage

3. Which type of power flaw is caused by a momentary decrease in voltage?

   a. Brownout

   b. Blackout

   c. Surge

   d. Noise

4. Which type of RAID allows you to replace a failed disk with a good one with little interruption of service?

   a. RAID level 5

   b. RAID level 3

   c. RAID level 1

   d. RAID level 0

5. Which type of backup does not uncheck the archive bits for files it backs up?

   a. Full

   b. Incremental

   c. Partial

   d. Differential

6. True or false? Macro viruses were the first type of virus to infect data files rather than executable files.

7. True or false? On a LAN, a star topology and a parallel backbone provide the greatest fault tolerance.

8. True or false? Clustering is a fault-tolerance technique that links multiple servers to act as a single server.

9. True or false? SANs (storage area networks) are distinct networks of storage devices that communicate directly with each other and with other networks.

10. True or false? A hot site is a place where the computers, devices, and connectivity necessary to rebuild a network exist, with some appropriately configured, updated, or connected.

11. The term _____ refers to the soundness of a network's programs, data, services, devices, and connections.

12. The term _____ refers to how consistently and reliably a file or system can be accessed by authorized personnel.

13. _____ viruses change their characteristics (such as the arrangement of their bytes, size, and internal instructions) every time they are transferred to a new system, making them harder to identify.

14. A(n) _____ provides rules for using anti-malware software, as well as policies for installing programs, sharing files, and using external disks such as flash drives.

15. A(n) _____ UPS provides continuous voltage to a device by switching virtually instantaneously to the battery when it detects a loss of power from the wall outlet.

Network Management

After reading this chapter and completing the exercises, you will be able to:

- Understand network management and the importance of documentation, baseline measurements, policies, and regulations to assess and maintain a network's health

- Manage a network's performance using SNMP-based network management software, system and event logs, and traffic-shaping techniques

- Identify the reasons for and elements of an asset management system

- Plan and follow regular hardware and software maintenance routines

On the Job

I used to work for a service provider whose shared network supplied switching, content distribution, and firewall protection for many medium-sized customer Web servers in our data center. We'd assigned one of our best network engineers a project that required a change to every firewall port opening statement on the network. That sort of work did appear on our list of preapproved routine changes, as long as the customer had provided written authorization for the security port opening. Notifying all customers five days before the change, scheduling the change after hours, and management approval of a change record were not required.

But the network engineer had a complex project in mind. He was going to modify hundreds of lines of configuration at once on a redundant set of network devices that supported dozens of customers, and those lines of configuration were security related. Of course, this wasn't what I'd had in mind when I allowed this activity to be put on the preapproved changes list.

The network engineer had never done this kind of project before, so he mocked it up and tested it in our test lab. The lab maintained equipment and configurations for that purpose, but not a perfect copy of the production system with traffic.

During the middle of the day, the network engineer went ahead and implemented this "routine" change. It took down the whole network, including every one of those dozens of customers, for about 30 minutes. Worse, there was a brief period where some security rules at the firewall weren't working, exposing some ports.

Today, in networks for which I'm responsible for change management standards, I always include the following caveats for any preauthorization of routine changes:

1. If it's the first time we've done it, it isn't routine.

2. If it's not the version of the change that we do regularly, it isn't routine.

3. If it requires testing before performance, it isn't routine.

This network engineer and I both learned a lot after that change.

Brooke Guthrie
CDW Hosting and Managed Services

In this book, you have learned the technologies and techniques necessary to design an efficient, fault tolerant, and secure network. However, your work isn't finished once all the clients, servers, switches, routers, and gateways have been installed. After a network is in place, it requires continual review and adjustment. A network, like any other complex system, is in a constant state of flux. Whether the changes are caused by internal factors, such as increased demand on the server's processor, or external factors, such as the obsolescence of a router, you should count on spending a significant amount of time investigating, performing, and verifying changes to your network. In this chapter, you will learn about changes dictated by immediate needs as well as those required to enhance the network's functionality, growth, performance, or security. You'll also learn how best to implement those changes.

Fundamentals of Network Management

Network management is a general term that means different things to different networking professionals. At its broadest, **network management** refers to the assessment, monitoring, and maintenance of all aspects of a network. It can include checking for hardware faults, ensuring high QoS (quality of service) for critical applications, maintaining records of network assets and software configurations, and determining what time of day is best for upgrading a router.

The scope of network management techniques differs according to the network's size and importance. On some large networks, for example, administrators run network management applications that continually check devices and connections to make certain they respond within an expected performance threshold. If a device doesn't respond quickly enough or at all, the application automatically issues an alert that pages the network administrator responsible for that device. On a small network, however, comprehensive network management might not be economically feasible. Instead, such a network might run an inexpensive application that periodically tests devices and connections to determine only whether they are still functioning.

Several disciplines fall under the heading of network management (including topics discussed in previous chapters, such as security audits and change management), but all share the goals of enhancing efficiency and performance while preventing costly downtime or loss. Ideally, network management accomplishes this by helping the administrator predict problems before they occur. For example, a trend in network usage could indicate when a switch will be overwhelmed with traffic. In response, the network administrator could increase the switch's processing capabilities (or replace the switch) before users begin experiencing slow or dropped connections. Before you can assess and make predictions about a network's health, however, you must understand its logical and physical structure and how it functions under typical conditions.

Net+ Documentation

4.2 Throughout this book, you have witnessed and read about different types of network documentation. For example, in Chapter 13's discussion of troubleshooting, you learned that keeping a record of a problem and its solution helps to prevent similar problems from recurring, or at least helps technicians deal with it if it does recur. In this section and in the rest of this chapter, you'll learn about other types of documentation that contribute to sound network management.

The way you format and store your documentation can vary, but to adequately manage your network, you should at least record the following:

- *Physical topology*—Which types of LAN and WAN topologies does your network use: bus, star, ring, hybrid, mesh, or a combination of these? Which type of backbone does your network use—collapsed, distributed, parallel, serial, or a combination of these? Which type and grade of cabling does your network use?

- *Access method*—Does your network use Ethernet (802.3), token ring (802.5), Wi-Fi (802.11), WiMAX (802.16), or a mix of transmission methods? What transmission speed(s) does it provide? Is it switched?

- *Protocols*—Which protocols are used by servers, nodes, and connectivity devices?

- *Devices*—How many of the following devices are connected to your network—switches, routers, hubs, gateways, firewalls, access points, servers, UPSs, printers, backup devices, and clients? Where are they located? What are their model numbers and vendors?

- *Operating systems*—Which network and desktop operating systems appear on the network? Which versions of these operating systems are used by each device? Which type and version of operating systems are used by connectivity devices such as routers?

- *Applications*—Which applications are used by clients and servers? Where do you store the applications? From where do they run?

- *Configurations*—What versions of operating systems and applications does each workstation, server, and connectivity device run? How are these programs configured? How is hardware configured? The collection, storage, and assessment of such information belongs to a category of network management known as **configuration management**. Ideally, you would rely on configuration management software to gather and store the information in a database, where those who need it can easily access and analyze the data.

If you have not already collected and centrally stored the answers to the preceding questions, it could take the efforts of several people and several weeks to compile them, depending on the size and complexity of your network. This evaluation involves visits to the telecommunications and equipment rooms, an examination of servers and desktops, a review of receipts for software and hardware purchases, and, potentially, the use of a protocol analyzer or network management software package. Though it requires effort, documenting all aspects of your network promises to save work in the future. After you have compiled the information, organize it into a format (such as a database) that can be easily updated and searched. That way, staff can access the information in a timely manner and keep it current.

Understanding conventions for network documentation can make your task easier. In this book you have seen many instances of **network diagrams**, which are graphical representations of a network's devices and connections. Network diagrams can be as varied as the engineers who create them. Some adhere strictly to the network's physical layout and label each connection. Some represent only the logical topology. Others, like many of the figures in this book, are more general or designed to highlight one critical part of a network, such as its perimeter. These might depict an internal network of hundreds of clients with only a few clients within a circle labeled "internal network," for example.

You could sketch your network diagram on the back of a napkin or draw it on your computer using a graphics program. However, many people use software designed for mapping networks, such as Microsoft Visio, ConceptDraw, or eDraw. Such applications come with icons that represent different types of devices and connections. Soon after entering the world of network engineering, you'll recognize certain icons that Cisco Systems has created and made popular. Because of its status in the networking world and the volume of networking hardware it sells, Cisco has set trends for network diagramming. Like the "Walk" or "Don't Walk" signs that are understood on street corners around the globe, Cisco's symbols for routers, switches, firewalls, and other devices are widely accepted and understood in the

Net+

4.2

4.3

networking field. Figure 15-1 shows a simplified network diagram that uses Cisco's iconography, with each device labeled. Notice that a router is represented by a hockey-puck shape with two arrows pointing inward and two arrows pointing outward. A wireless router looks the same but has two antennas attached. A workgroup switch is represented by a small rectangular box, which also contains two arrows pointing inward and two arrows pointing outward.

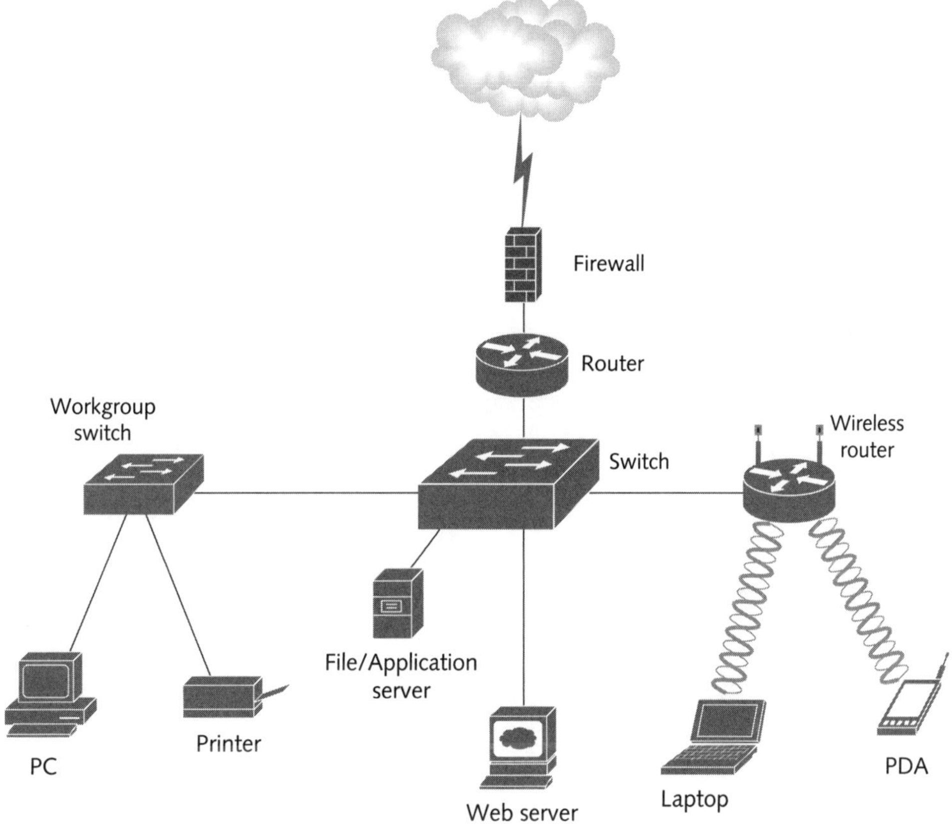

Figure 15-1 Network diagram using Cisco symbols

Most network diagrams provide broad snapshots of a network's physical or logical topology. This type of view is useful for planning where to insert a new switch or determining how a particular router, gateway, and firewall interact. However, if you're a technician who needs to find a fault in a client's wired connection to the LAN, a broad overview might be too general. Instead, you need a wiring schematic. A **wiring schematic** is a graphical representation of a network's wired infrastructure. In its most detailed form, it shows every wire necessary to interconnect network devices. Some less detailed wiring schematics might use a single line to represent the group of wires necessary to connect several clients to a switch. Figure 15-2 provides an example of a detailed wiring schematic for a small office network connection that relies on cable broadband service to access the Internet.

Documenting and capturing an accurate picture of your network's physical and logical elements are initial steps in understanding the network. Next you need to know how it routinely performs.

15

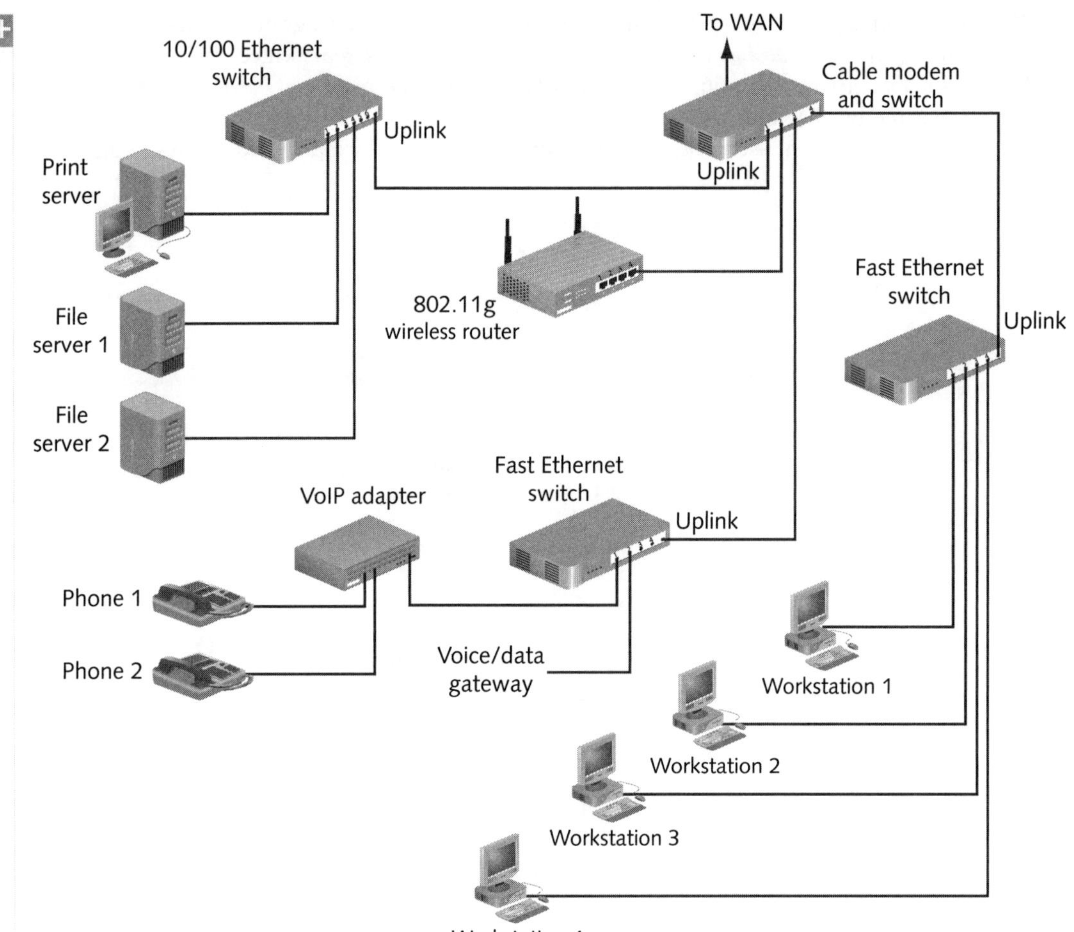

Figure 15-2 Wiring schematic

Baseline Measurements

As you learned in Chapter 13, a baseline is a report of the network's current state of operation. Baseline measurements might include the utilization rate for your network backbone, number of users logged on per day or per hour, number of protocols that run on your network, statistics about errors (such as runts, collisions, jabbers, or giants), frequency with which networked applications are used, or information regarding which users take up the most bandwidth. The graph in Figure 15-3 shows an example baseline for daily network traffic over a six-week period.

Baseline measurements allow you to compare future performance increases or decreases caused by network changes or events with past network performance. Obtaining baseline measurements is the only way to know for certain whether a pattern of usage has changed (and requires attention) or, later, whether a network upgrade made a difference. Each network requires its own approach. The elements you measure depend on which functions are most critical to your network and its users.

For instance, suppose that your network currently serves 500 users and that your backbone traffic exceeds 50% at 10:00 a.m. and 2:00 p.m. each business day. That pattern constitutes

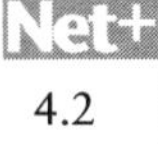

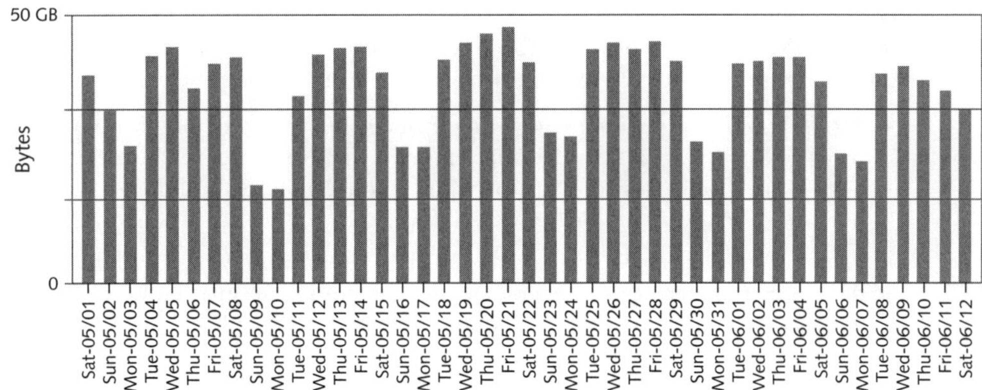

Figure 15-3 Baseline of daily network traffic

your baseline. Now suppose that your company decides to add 200 users who perform the same types of functions on the network. The added number of users equals 40% of the current number of users (200/500). Therefore, you can estimate that your backbone's capacity should increase by approximately 40% to maintain your current service levels.

The more data you gather while establishing your network's baseline (in other words, the longer you gather data), the more accurate your prediction will be. Network traffic patterns might be difficult to forecast, because you cannot predict users' habits, effects of new technology, or changes in demand for resources over a given period of time. For instance, the preceding example assumed that all new users would share the same network usage habits as the current users. In fact, however, the new users may generate a great deal more, or a great deal less, network traffic.

How do you gather baseline data on your network? Although you could theoretically use a network monitor or network analyzer and record its output at regular intervals, several software applications can perform the baselining for you. These applications range from freeware available on the Internet to expensive, customizable hardware and software combination products. Before choosing a network-baselining tool, you should determine how you will use it. If you manage a small network that provides only one critical application to users, an inexpensive tool may suffice. If you work on a WAN with several critical links, however, you should investigate purchasing a more comprehensive package. The baseline measurement tool should also be capable of collecting the statistics needed. For example, only a sophisticated tool can measure traffic generated by each node on a network, filter traffic according to types of protocols and errors, and simultaneously measure statistics from several network segments.

Policies, Procedures, and Regulations

Imagine you are the network administrator for a large enterprise network and that you supervise eight network technicians who are responsible for day-to-day installations, upgrades, and troubleshooting. Unless you and your technicians agree on policies for adding new users, for example, you might discover that some users have fewer access restrictions than they ought to have or that logon IDs don't follow a standard naming convention. The former could cause security vulnerabilities, and the latter could make future user management more challenging.

4.2

Following rules helps limit chaos, confusion, and possibly downtime for you and your users. Several previous chapters of this book have described policies, procedures, and regulations that make for sound network management. They are summarized here:

- *Media installation and management*—Includes designing the physical layout of a cable or wireless infrastructure, choosing and following best practices for cable management, testing the effectiveness of cable or wireless infrastructure, and documenting cable layouts; see Chapters 3 and 8 for more information.

- *Network addressing policies*—Includes choosing and applying an addressing scheme, determining the use and limits of subnets, integrating an internal network's addressing with an external network's, and configuring gateways for NAT; see Chapters 4 and 10 for more information.

- *Resource sharing and naming conventions*—Includes establishing rules for logon IDs, setting up users and groups and applying access restrictions, designing directory trees and assigning objects, and configuring resource-sharing relationships between domains and servers; see Chapter 9 for more information.

- *Security-related policies*—Includes establishing rules for passwords, limiting access to physical spaces such as the data center, limiting access to shared resources on the network, imposing restrictions on the types of files that are saved to networked computers, monitoring computers for malware, and conducting regular security audits; see Chapters 12 and 14 for more information.

- *Troubleshooting procedures*—Includes following a methodology for troubleshooting network problems and documenting their solutions; see Chapter 13 for more information.

- *Backup and disaster recovery procedures*—Includes establishing a method and schedule for making backups, regularly testing the effectiveness of backups, assigning a disaster recovery team and defining each member's role, and choosing a disaster recovery strategy and testing it; see Chapter 14 for more information.

In addition to internal policies, a network manager must consider state and federal regulations that might affect her responsibilities. In the United States, one such federal regulation is **CALEA (Communications Assistance for Law Enforcement Act)**, which requires telecommunications carriers and equipment manufacturers to provide for surveillance capabilities. CALEA was passed by Congress in 1994 after pressure from the FBI, which worried that networks relying solely on digital communications would circumvent traditional wiretapping strategies. In other words, a phone call made using VoIP over a private WAN cannot be intercepted as easily as a phone call made via the PSTN. Therefore, if you work at an ISP, for example, your switches and routers must provide an interface for electronic eavesdropping, and your staff must be ready to allow authorities access to those devices when presented with a warrant.

A second significant federal regulation in the United States is **HIPAA (Health Insurance Portability and Accountability Act)**, which was passed by Congress in 1996. One aspect of this regulation addresses the security and privacy of medical records, including those stored or transmitted electronically. If you work at any organization that handles medical records, such as an insurance company, hospital, or transcription service, you must understand and follow federal standards for protecting the security and privacy of these records. HIPAA rules are very specific. They govern not only the way medical records are stored and

transmitted, but also the policies for authorizing access and even the placement and orientation of workstations where such records might be viewed.

Many of the policies and procedures mentioned in this section are not laws, but best practices aimed at preventing network problems before they occur. The next section describes techniques for detecting and managing network problems before they significantly impair access or performance.

Fault and Performance Management

After documenting every aspect of your network and following policies and best practices, you are ready to assess your network's status on an ongoing basis. This process includes both **performance management**, or monitoring how well links and devices are keeping up with the demands placed on them, and **fault management**, or the detection and signaling of device, link, or component faults.

Network Management Software

To accomplish both fault and performance management, organizations often use enterprise-wide network management software. Some popular applications include IBM's Tivoli NetView and Cisco's CiscoWorks, but hundreds of other such tools exist. All rely on a similar architecture, in which at least one network management console (which may be a server or workstation, depending on the size of the network) collects data from multiple networked devices at regular intervals, in a process called **polling**. Each managed device runs a network management **agent**, a software routine that collects information about the device's operation and provides it to the network management application running on the console. So as not to affect the performance of a device while collecting information, agents do not demand significant processing resources.

A managed device may contain several objects that can be managed, including components such as processor, memory, hard disk, NIC, or intangibles such as performance or utilization. For example, on a server, an agent can measure how many users are connected to the server or what percentage of the processor's resources are used at any time. The definition of managed devices and their data is collected in an **MIB (Management Information Base)**.

Agents communicate information about managed devices via any one of several application layer protocols. On modern networks, most agents use **SNMP (Simple Network Management Protocol)**. SNMP is part of the TCP/IP suite of protocols and typically runs over UDP on port 161 (though it can be configured to run over TCP).

Figure 15-4 illustrates the relationship between a network management application and managed devices on a network.

After data is collected, the network management application can present an administrator with several ways to view and analyze the data. For example, a popular way to view data is in the form of a map that shows fully functional links or devices in green, partially (or less than optimally) functioning links or devices in yellow, and failed links or devices in red. One type of network status map generated by SolarWinds' Orion network management software is shown in Figure 15-5.

Because of their flexibility, sophisticated network management applications are also challenging to configure and fine-tune. You have to be careful to collect only useful data and not an

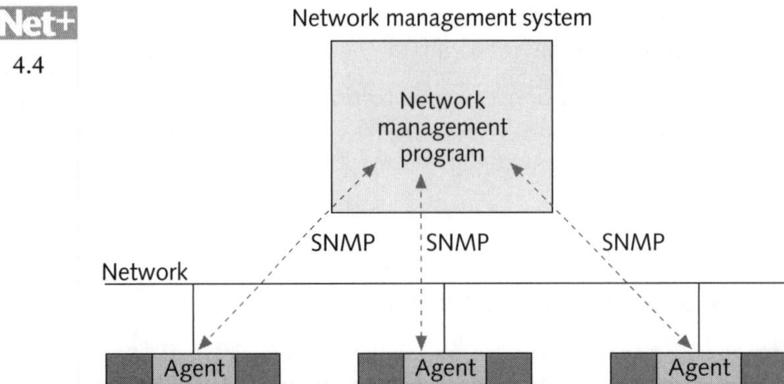

Figure 15-4 Network management architecture

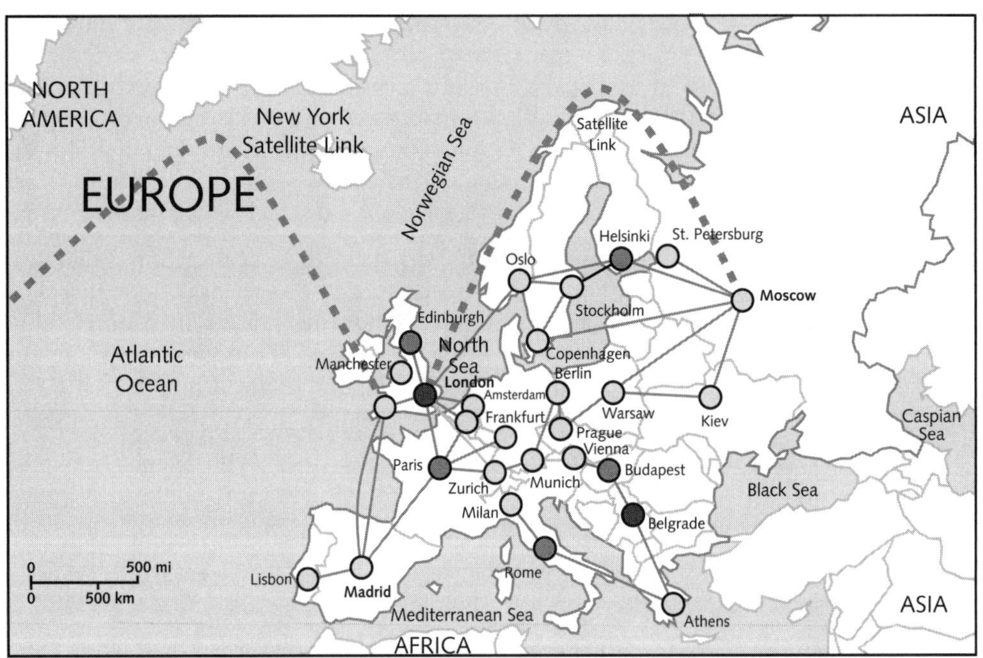

Figure 15-5 Map showing network status

excessive amount of routine information. For example, on a network with dozens of routers, collecting SNMP-generated messages that essentially say "I'm still here" every five seconds would result in massive amounts of insignificant data. A glut of information makes it difficult to ascertain when a router in fact requires attention. Instead, when configuring a network management application to poll a router, you might choose to generate an SNMP-based message only when the router's processor is operating at 75% of its capacity or to measure only the amount of traffic passing through a NIC every five minutes.

Performance and fault management monitoring does not necessarily require a complex application. One of the most common network management tools used on WANs is **MRTG (Multi Router Traffic Grapher)**. MRTG is a command-line utility that uses SNMP to poll devices, collects data in a log file, and then generates HTML-based views of the data. MRTG is freely distributed software originally written by Tobias Oetiker, a networking professional who in the early 1990s saw a need for a tool to regularly measure the status of his organization's WAN link. The software has undergone many enhancements since then but retains its simple interface. MRTG can be used with UNIX, Linux, and Windows operating systems and can collect and graph data from any type of device that uses SNMP. Figure 15-6 provides examples of two MRTG-generated graphs. One shows the amount of traffic traversing a WAN link in one day, and the other shows the amount of traffic on the same WAN link over eight days' time.

Faults and conditions that exceed certain thresholds can trigger alarms in network management software. They can also be recorded by system and event logs, as described next.

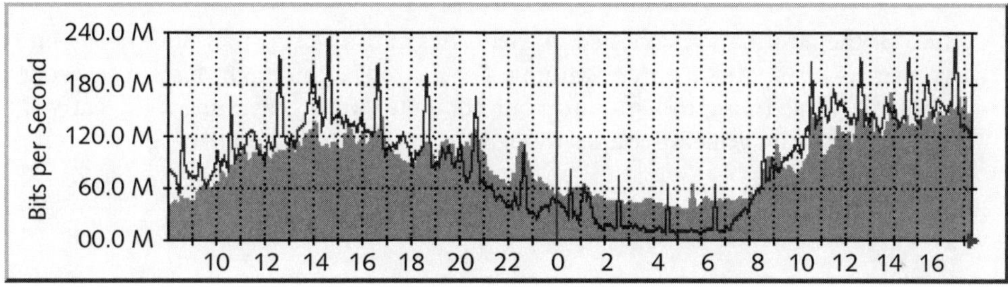

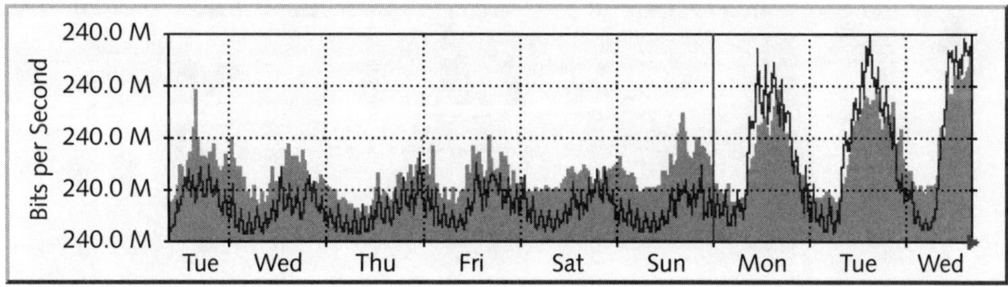

Figure 15-6 Graphs generated by MRTG

System and Event Logs

Virtually every condition recognized by an operating system can be recorded on your computer. Records of such activity are kept in a log. For example, each time your computer requests an IP address from the DHCP server and doesn't receive a response, this can be recorded in a log. Each time it attempts and fails to find a domain controller on a Windows-based network, this situation can also be recorded. In addition to predefined events, developers can customize logs by defining conditions under which new entries are created. For example, an engineer might want to know when the relative humidity in a data center exceeds 60%. If a device can monitor this information, the results can be written to a log. On Windows-based computers, including those running Windows Vista or Windows Server 2008, such a log is known as an **event log** and can be easily viewed with the GUI **Event Viewer** application. Figure 15-7 provides an example of data collected in the event log on a workstation running the Windows Vista operating system.

Similar information is routinely recorded by computers running Linux or UNIX in a **system log**. In general, newer versions of Linux typically write their system logs to the file /var/log/messages, while older versions of UNIX often write to a system log in the file /var/logs/syslog and Solaris versions of UNIX write to a system log in the file /var/adm/messages. To find out where various logs are kept on your UNIX or Linux system, view the /etc/syslog.conf file (on some systems this is the /etc/rsyslog.conf file). The /etc/syslog.conf file is also where you can configure the types of events to log and what priority to assign each event (where "0" indicates an emergency situation and "7" simply points to very specific information that might help in debugging a problem). Bear in mind that the syslog function doesn't alert you to any problems. It only records messages issued by the system. It's up to you to monitor the syslog file for errors. Most UNIX and Linux operating systems provide a GUI application for easily viewing and filtering the information in syslog files. Other applications are available for sifting through syslog data and generating alerts.

Much of the information collected in event logs and syslog files does not point to a problem, even if it is marked with a warning. For example, you might have typed your password incorrectly while trying to log on to your computer, thus generating a log entry. Using these logs for fault management requires thoughtful data filtering and sorting.

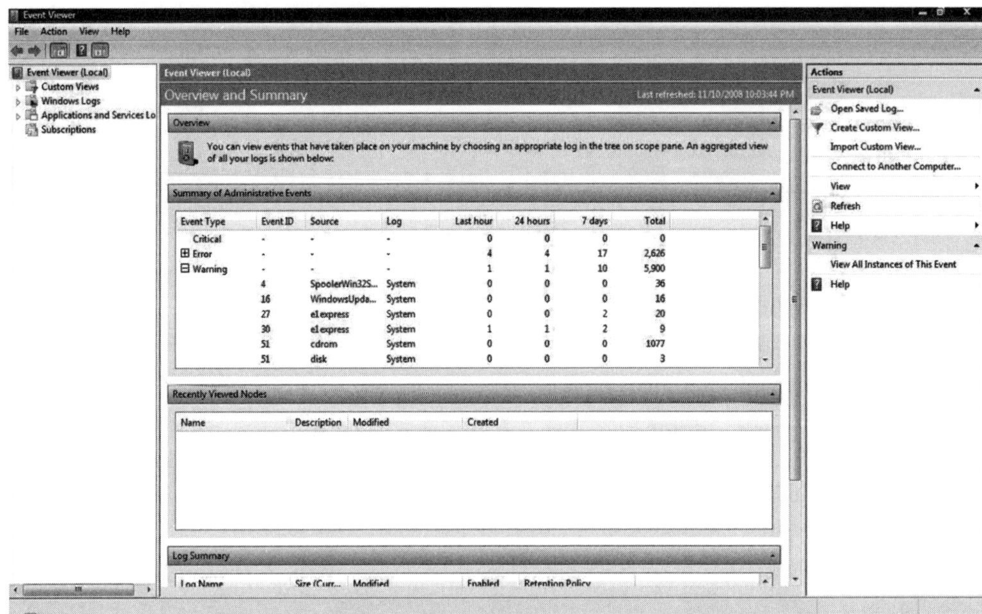

Figure 15-7 Event log on a workstation running Windows Vista

Net+ Traffic Shaping

4.5   When a network must handle high volumes of network traffic, users benefit from a performance management technique known as traffic shaping. **Traffic shaping** involves manipulating certain characteristics of packets, data streams, or connections to manage the type and amount of traffic traversing a network or interface at any moment. Its goals are to assure timely delivery of the most important traffic while offering the best possible performance for all users.

Traffic shaping can involve delaying less important traffic, increasing the priority of more important traffic, limiting the volume of traffic flowing in or out of an interface during a specified time period, or limiting the momentary throughput rate for an interface. The last two techniques belong to a category of traffic shaping known as **traffic policing**. An ISP might impose a maximum on the capacity it will grant a certain customer. That way, it ensures that the customer does not tie up more than a certain amount of the network's overall capacity. Traffic policing helps the service provider predict how much capacity it must purchase from its network provider. It also holds down costs, because the ISP doesn't have to plan for every client using all the throughput he could at all times (an unlikely scenario). An ISP that imposes traffic policing might allow customers to choose their preferred maximum daily traffic volume or momentary throughput and pay commensurate fees. A more sophisticated instance of traffic policing is dynamic and takes into account the network's traffic patterns. For example, the service provider might allow certain customers to exceed their maximums when few other customers are using the network.

Figure 15-8 illustrates how traffic volume might appear on an interface without limits compared to an interface subject to traffic policing.

A controversial example of traffic shaping came to light in 2007. Comcast, one of the largest Internet service providers in the United States, was found to be clandestinely discriminating against certain types of traffic. For users uploading files to P2P (peer-to-peer) networks such as BitTorrent, Comcast was interjecting TCP packets with the RST (reset) field set. These packets were spoofed to appear as if they originated from the accepting site, and they cut the connection as the user attempted to upload files. Soon customers figured out the pattern and used packet analyzers such as Wireshark to reveal the forged TCP RST packets. They complained to authorities that Comcast had violated their user agreement. The FCC investigated,

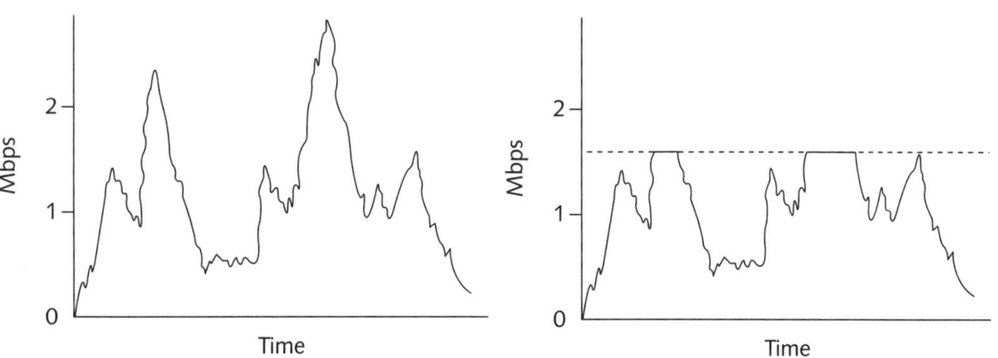

Figure 15-8 Traffic volume before and after applying limits

4.5

upheld the customers' claims, and ordered Comcast to stop this practice. Now Comcast has chosen a different method of traffic shaping. It will assign a lower priority to data from customers who generate a high volume of traffic when the network is at risk of congestion.

Several types of traffic prioritization—that is, treating more important traffic preferentially—exist. Software running on a router, multilayer switch, gateway, server, or even a client workstation can prioritize traffic according to any of the following characteristics:

- Protocol
- IP address
- User group
- DiffServ (Differentiated Services) flag or TOS (type of service) field in an IP datagram
- VLAN tag in a data link layer frame
- Service or application

Depending on the traffic prioritization software, different types of traffic might be assigned priority classes, such as "high," "normal," "low," or "slow;" alternatively, it can be rated on a prioritization scale from 1 (lowest priority) to 7 (highest priority). For example, traffic generated by time-sensitive VoIP applications might be assigned high priority, while online gaming might be assigned low priority. Traffic prioritization is needed most when the network is busiest. It ensures that during peak usage times, the most important data gets through quickly, while less important data waits. When network usage is low, however, prioritization might have no noticeable effects.

Caching

In addition to traffic shaping, a network or host might use caching to improve performance. **Caching** is the local storage of frequently needed files that would otherwise be obtained from an external source. By keeping files close to the requestor, caching allows the user to access those files quickly. As you'll learn, it can also save money for ISPs.

The most common type of caching is **Web caching**, in which Web pages are stored locally, either on a host or network, and then delivered to requestors. You might be familiar with the term *cache* from browsing the Web on your computer. A locally stored cache will keep copies of the Web pages you have viewed on your computer's hard drive. Later, when you want to view the page again, the browser will attempt to retrieve the page from your cache if the page hasn't changed since the last time you viewed it. Local caching is highly customizable. You can choose the size of your cache, the rules it uses to refresh its contents, and the conditions under which it clears its contents.

To an ISP, however, caching is much more than just a convenience. It prevents a significant volume of WAN traffic, thus improving performance and saving money. For example, if dozens of an ISP's subscribers read a popular news Web site each morning, the ISP can keep the entire Web site on its **cache engine**, a network device devoted to storage and delivery of frequently requested files. When the ISP's network receives a request for that Web site, the network examines the request and redirects it to a cache engine. The cache engine searches its files for the news Web site. If the cache engine doesn't have a current copy of the Web site, it requests the site from the news organization's server. In that case, the cache engine receives and stores the Web site for later delivery. When another user subsequently requests the same site, the network redirects the request to the cache engine, which delivers the Web

Net+
4.5

site without having to request it from the originating server. The ISP need not spend any of its bandwidth to retrieve the site again until it has changed.

Asset Management

Another key component in managing networks is identifying and tracking its hardware and software through **asset management**. The first step in asset management is to take an inventory of each node on the network. This inventory should include the total number of components on the network and each device's configuration files, model number, serial number, location on the network, and technical support contact. You will also want to keep records of every piece of software purchased by your organization, its version number, vendor, licensing, and technical support contact.

The asset management tool you choose depends on your organization's needs. You might purchase an application that can automatically discover all devices on the network and then save that information in a database, or you might use a simple spreadsheet to save the data. In either case, your asset management records should be comprehensive and accessible to all personnel who may become involved in maintaining or troubleshooting the network. In addition, ensure that the asset management database is regularly updated, either manually or automatically, as changes to network hardware and software occur. The information you retain is useful only while it is current.

Asset management simplifies maintaining and upgrading the network chiefly because you know what the system includes. For example, if you discover that a router purchased two years ago requires an upgrade to its operating system software to fix a security flaw, you need to know how many routers are installed, where they are installed, and whether any have already received the software upgrade. An up-to-date asset management system allows you to avoid searching through old invoices and troubleshooting records to answer these questions.

In addition, asset management provides network administrators with information about the costs and benefits of certain types of hardware or software. For example, if you conclude that 50% of your staff's troubleshooting time is spent on one flawed brand of NIC, an asset management system can reveal how many NICs you would need to replace if you chose to replace those cards, and whether it would make sense to replace the entire installed base. Some asset management applications can even track the length of equipment leases and alert network managers when leases will expire.

The term "asset management" originally referred to an organization's system for keeping tabs on every piece of equipment it owned. This function was usually handled through the Accounting department. Some of the accounting-related tasks included under the original definition for asset management, such as managing the depreciation on network equipment or tracking the expiration of leases, apply to asset management in networking as well.

Change Management

If you have ever worked on a network, you realize that conditions are always in a state of flux. Technology advances, vendors come and go, and users' needs change. Managing change while maintaining your network's efficiency and availability requires good planning. The following sections describe how to approach the most common types of software and hardware changes, from installing patches to replacing a network backbone.

Software Changes

If you have ever supported desktop computers professionally or even maintained your own computer at home, you know that an important part of keeping a system running optimally is upgrading its software.

You are most likely to implement the following types of software changes on your network: patches (improvements or enhancements to a particular piece of a software application), upgrades (major changes to the existing code), and revisions (a general term for minor or major changes to the existing code). Although the specifics vary for each type of software change, the general steps involved can be summarized as follows:

1. Determine whether the change (whether it be a patch, revision, or upgrade) is necessary.

2. Research the purpose of the change and its potential effects on other applications. Also determine whether and how the change can be reversed, in case troubles arise.

3. Determine whether the change should apply to some or all users and whether it will be distributed centrally or machine by machine.

4. If you decide to implement the change, notify system administrators, help desk personnel, and users. Schedule the change for completion during off-hours (unless it is an emergency).

5. Back up the current system or software before making modifications.

6. Prevent users from accessing the system or part of the system being altered (for example, disable logons).

7. Keep the upgrade instructions handy, and follow them during installation of the patch or revision.

8. Make the change.

9. Test the system fully after the change, preferably exercising the software as a typical user would. Note any unintended or unanticipated consequences of the modification.

10. If the change was successful, reenable access to the system. If it was unsuccessful, revert to the previous version of the software.

11. Inform system administrators, help desk personnel, and users when the change is complete. If you had to reverse it, explain why.

12. Record your change in the change management system.

As a general rule, upgrading or patching software according to a vendor's recommendations is a good idea and can often prevent network problems. For example, a vendor might issue an alert to its customers regarding a security flaw in its Web browser product. To fix this flaw, it might supply a patch. At other times, you might have to search for product upgrades on your own. Whatever your means of finding patches and upgrades, you should take responsibility for this task and make the necessary changes to your network's software. Bear in mind, however, that such changes can sometimes create new troubles on your system. You should, therefore, be prepared to reverse software upgrades or patches, just in case.

In the following sections, you will learn about the types of software changes associated with sensible network maintenance. You will also see the best way to approach these changes.

Patches A **patch** is a correction, improvement, or enhancement to a particular piece of a software application. It differs from a revision or software upgrade in that it changes only part of an application, leaving most of the code untouched. Patches are often distributed at no charge by software vendors in an attempt to fix a bug in their code or to add slightly more functionality.

You'll encounter patches in all areas of routine networking maintenance. Among other things, network maintenance sometimes entails patching the server's NOS. For example, if your server runs Windows Server 2008, you might need to apply a patch to close a security hole that allows remote users to hack into your server.

Microsoft calls its significant patches for its Windows operating systems **service packs**. You may see them abbreviated as "SP1," "SP2," and "SP3" for Service Pack 1, Service Pack 2, and Service Pack 3, respectively.

Keep in mind that a patch is not a replacement for an entire software package; instead, a patch is installed on top of the existing software. Patches apply to more than just NOS software. For example, you might have to patch the software on your Cisco switch to allow it to handle IP multicasts over a token ring network. Alternatively, you might patch the application that allows you to centrally control your printers across the network.

Patch installations are no more difficult than installations of new software applications. The patch itself should come with installation instructions and a description of its purpose, at the very least, in the form of a text file. It's advisable to back up the system before installing a patch. Although patches ought to be fully tested by the vendor before release, you cannot assume that they will work flawlessly on your system. This consideration is especially important when you patch an NOS. Some patch installation utilities automatically make a backup of the system before installation begins, but you should not rely on this method. Always make sure you have a way to reverse a software change if it does more harm than good.

In addition, try to perform software patches during a time when users cannot and will not attempt to access the network. Even if you suspect that a patch can be implemented quickly and without adverse effects on current users, don't take a chance by applying it during normal business hours. If the patch does create problems, you will need extra time to reverse the process. Depending on how complicated or comprehensive the patch is, you may want to alert users to stay off the system for only a few hours or perhaps overnight.

After applying the patch, test the system to verify that its desired enhancements have taken effect. At this time, you should review the vendor's documentation to ensure that you correctly understood the patch's purpose and installed it correctly. For some patches to take effect, you have to change system configuration files and restart the system. Test the software to verify that the patch hasn't caused any unintentional, undesired effects. After you are certain that the patch worked successfully, you can allow users to access the system again.

To stay apprised of patches released by your vendors, check the vendor's technical support Web site regularly or subscribe to its mailing list. Manufacturers usually attempt to bundle a number of bug fixes into one large patch; if you're a registered user, they will alert you about the release of significant patches. News about patches from vendors as large as Microsoft, Sun, Apple, and Red Hat will also probably appear in trade magazines. Smaller vendors may only occasionally need to release a patch that fixes a single problem with their application.

Make it a policy to keep informed about patches to your network software, whether it involves the operating system, an application, or the client software. If you work in a large organization with several servers, routers, and other devices, you may want to assign one network administrator to manage patches for the servers, one to manage patches for the printers, and so on.

Client Upgrades A software **upgrade** is a major change to a software package's existing code. Vendors might or might not offer upgrades for free. Also, the upgrade might or might not be comprehensive enough to substitute for the original application. In general, upgrades are designed to add functionality and fix bugs in the previous version of the client. For example, an upgrade to a newer version of Firefox might incorporate features to protect you from Web sites that launch phishing attempts. The scope and purpose of client upgrades vary widely, depending on whether the upgrade is a redesign or simply a bug fix.

The term **bug** is frequently used to describe a flaw in a software application that causes some part of the application to malfunction. Less frequently, this term may also be used to describe a hardware defect. Legend has it that the term originated when a moth became trapped inside the electrical workings of the first digital computer.

Before upgrading client software, carefully read the documentation accompanying the upgrade. It should reveal how best to install the software, whether the upgrade requires you to install any previous upgrades first, whether the upgrade requires any special preparation, and how its changes will affect users.

A client upgrade might be transparent to users, or it might completely change the appearance of the network logon interface. Client upgrades typically overwrite some system files on the workstation, so their installation may affect other applications adversely. They might even prevent other applications from working as they did in the past. For example, a user who receives an upgrade to his Windows XP Dial-Up Networking client may later experience problems with an older version of AOL software that worked perfectly for the last two years. In this case, the best solution might be to upgrade the AOL software as well.

As with all upgrades, test a client upgrade on a single workstation before distributing it to all users. Also, prepare a way to reverse the process. Because most client upgrades do not back up the previous version automatically, you should keep the old client software close at hand, either on the network or on disk, in case you need to reinstall it.

You may either perform client upgrades on a workstation-by-workstation basis or use a software distribution application to upgrade multiple workstations simultaneously from the network. Although the latter approach is more efficient, it might not be appropriate in all situations. Consider a network of 500 users who have different software, hardware, and usage requirements. Can you be certain that the client upgrade will be compatible with each workstation's hardware and software? Can you be certain that the client upgrade will not adversely affect any user's current software setup? Can you be certain that every user will log on to the network to receive her upgrade? (For instance, what happens if many users are mobile?)

In general, you need to plan carefully and become familiar with your client characteristics before allowing a software distribution application to upgrade client software. In addition, you should notify clients about the upgrade and explain how their workstation might change as a result. If you don't, users might become alarmed at the changes and flood the help desk with questions.

Shared Application Upgrades Like client upgrades, application upgrades represent modifications to all or part of an application that are designed to enhance functionality or fix problems related to software. Shared application upgrades, however, apply to software shared by clients on the network. Bear in mind that changes to shared applications affect all users at once. You should, therefore, take extra precautions to ensure that the application upgrade does not cause unanticipated problems. It's essential to test it fully before allowing users to access the new version.

The principles underlying the modification of shared applications on the network are the same as those for the modification of client software. Before applying the change, you should determine the need for it and its potential effects. Also back up the current software before upgrading it, prevent users from accessing the software during the implementation process, and keep users and system administrators informed of all changes.

Applications are usually designed to enhance the application's functionality. For this reason, an application upgrade may be more a matter of convenience than necessity. Therefore, the time, cost, and effort involved in application upgrades should be weighed against the necessity of performing operating system or client upgrades. This consideration is especially important if a networking professional's time is limited (as it usually is).

For a significant application upgrade, you might also need to provide (or suggest classes for) user training. If you choose to refer your users to an outside training facility, make sure they will learn about the particulars of the application in your networking environment. For instance, if you make it a policy never to install the foreign language support for a word-processing application, make sure your users know about this constraint. Likewise, if you have limited the functionality of an application (for example, preventing users from accessing video content on the Web using the network's browser application), you should publicize this policy. The better you prepare and inform your users, the fewer support calls your help desk will have to field.

NOS (Network Operating System) Upgrades Perhaps the most critical type of software upgrade you'll perform is an upgrade to your NOS (network operating system). It usually involves significant, potentially drastic, changes to the way your servers and clients operate. As such, it requires plenty of forethought, product research, and rigorous testing before you implement it. In fact, for any network with more than a few users, you should create and follow a project plan for this undertaking. This plan should include all of the precautions typically associated with other software upgrades. In addition, you should consider the following:

- How will the upgrade affect user IDs, groups, rights, and policies?
- How will the upgrade affect file, printer, and directory access on the server?
- How will the upgrade affect applications or client interactions on the server?

- How will the upgrade affect configuration files, protocols, and services running on the server?

- How will the upgrade affect the server's interaction with other devices on the network?

- How accurately can you test the upgrade software in a simulated environment?

- How can you take advantage of the new operating system to make your system more efficient?

- What is your technical support arrangement with the operating system's manufacturer if you need help in the midst of the upgrade?

- Have you allotted enough time to perform the upgrade? (For example, would it be more appropriate to do it over a weekend than overnight?)

- During the upgrade, will old NOS files be saved, and can you reverse the installation if troubles arise?

- Have you ensured that the users, help desk personnel, and system administrators understand how the upgrade will affect their daily operations and support burdens?

These are only some of the critical questions you need to ask before embarking on an NOS upgrade. Your networking environment might warrant additional considerations. For example, suppose that you are the network administrator for a company that is merging with a second company. Your two companies might use dissimilar NOSs, and the IT director might ask you to upgrade your NOS to match the other company's version. In this situation, you would have not only the previous list of questions to consider, but also a list of questions pertaining to the other company's operating system—for instance, how its NOS directories are organized. By addressing these questions before you upgrade your own NOS, you ensure that the merger of the two networks goes more smoothly.

An NOS upgrade is a complex and far-reaching change. It should not be undertaken with severe budgetary, resource, or time constraints. The following steps demonstrate how careful planning and a methodical process can help you accomplish an NOS upgrade. (Depending on your situation, the order and complexity of the steps could vary.)

1. *Research*—Gather information about the NOS from the manufacturer and from other sources, including reputable Internet bulletin boards, reputable magazines, and other networking professionals. Evaluate the costs involved in upgrading. Also list the benefits and risks involved in embarking on this NOS upgrade.

2. *Project plan*—Before you have committed significant time and money to the project, devise a project plan. This plan should include the steps to follow, task assignments for staff, and a rough budget and timeline. Even if you decide not to upgrade the NOS after all, you must commit resources to proposing and evaluating the option.

3. *Proposal*—Write a proposal to evaluate the product, including a plan to purchase and implement it if the proposal is accepted. A proposal should include the following elements:

   - Questions to answer during evaluation (for example, "Will the NOS work with my current network monitoring software?")

   - Names of personnel who will assist with evaluation and final approval

   - A rough timeline and plan for implementing the change if it is approved

- A rough project plan for implementing the change if it is approved

- Cost considerations

- A review of the short- and long-term benefits and risks of the upgrade

- A recommendation for or against performing the upgrade

- A plan for purchasing the software and implementing the change

4. *Evaluation*—Assuming that the proposal indicates that you should proceed with an upgrade and that your superiors approve your recommendation, you are ready to begin the evaluation phase. First order an evaluation copy of the NOS. Then install the software on an unused server whose hardware is similar to the hardware of your production servers (making sure that the test server meets the NOS manufacturer's recommended hardware requirements). On the test system, create several mock user IDs and groups to simulate the real network environment. Also install the applications and services that the server will support if it goes into production.

5. *Testing*—Next, as part of your evaluation, distribute updated client software to a team of technical staff and project stakeholders and ask them to use the mock IDs and groups to test the system. Over a given time period, they can test the system and keep notes on how the system meets the requirements specified in your proposal. The test team should pay particular attention to the new user interface for clients, the way in which your company's applications operate, the system's response time, and any new features provided by the upgrade. Meet regularly with the team during the evaluation period to discuss and compare experiences.

6. *Training*—If the results of the initial stages of evaluation lead you to decide to purchase the upgrade, make sure you and other networking staff are trained on how to work with the new NOS. Schedule training to take place only weeks before the anticipated implementation date so that your new skills are fresh when you begin the conversion.

7. *Preimplementation*—Before implementing the change, expand on the rough project plan for the upgrade. Ensure that your plan for transferring user accounts, groups, and their rights to the new system is sound. Decide how you want to reorganize the NOS directory, if necessary, and what types of volumes to create. In addition, review the existing servers to determine which applications, files, and directories should be transferred and which can be archived.

    Weeks before upgrading, inform users, help desk personnel, and other networking staff of the timeline and explain what changes to expect. Recommend that users clean up their data directories on the server and discard any unnecessary files. Similarly, ask networking staff to remove any nonessential applications or services they have installed on the server. If necessary, arrange to upgrade the client software on all workstations that will be affected by the operating system upgrade. A few days before the upgrade, issue a final warning to staff specifying when and for how long the server will be down to accomplish the upgrade.

8. *Implementation*—Perform the upgrade when few or no users will be on the network. Before beginning the upgrade, gather the software documentation and your project plan, along with the software CDs or DVDs and a bootable disk for the server (making certain that the CD-ROM or DVD-ROM device driver is on the bootable disk). Just before taking the system down, broadcast a warning to all users on the network that the server is going down soon. Then disable all logons to the network. Next, back up

the entire server's hard disk. When the backup is complete, use your backup software to verify that critical files were successfully copied. Finally, perform the upgrade according to the manufacturer's instructions and your network's specifications.

9. *Postimplementation*—Test functions and applications on the upgraded server to verify the success of your upgrade. After you are satisfied that the upgrade is successful, reenable logons to the network and inform staff that the system is running again. Later, you can review the upgrade process with other networking staff to find out whether you learned any lessons that could make future server upgrades more efficient and less troublesome. Work with the help desk personnel to understand the kinds of support calls generated by the upgrade. Also continue testing the new operating system, fine-tuning when necessary, to fix problems or find errors before they become problems for users.

Reversing a Software Upgrade If the software upgrade you perform creates problems in your existing system, you should be prepared to reverse the process. The process of reverting to a previous version of software after attempting to upgrade it is known as **backleveling**. Every network professional has been forced to backlevel at some point in her career. The steps that constitute this process differ, depending on the complexity of the upgrade and the network environment involved.

Although no hard-and-fast rules for backleveling exist, Table 15-1 summarizes some basic suggestions. Bear in mind that you must always refer to the software vendor's documentation to reverse an upgrade. If you must backlevel a network operating system upgrade, you should also consult with experienced professionals about the best approach for your network environment.

Table 15-1 Reversing a Software Upgrade

Type of Upgrade	Options for Reversing
Operating system patch	Use the patch's automatic uninstall utility.
Client software upgrade	Use the upgrade's automatic uninstall utility, or reinstall the previous version of the client on top of the upgrade.
Shared application upgrade	Use the application's automatic uninstall utility, or maintain a complete copy of the previous installation of the application and reinstall it over the upgrade.
Operating system upgrade	Prior to the upgrade, make a complete backup of the system; to backlevel, restore the entire system from the backup; uninstall an operating system upgrade only as a last resort.

Hardware and Physical Plant Changes

Hardware and physical plant changes might be required when a network component fails or malfunctions, but more often they are performed as part of an upgrade to increase capacity, improve performance, or add functionality to the network. In this section, you will learn about the simplest and most popular form of hardware change—adding more of what you already use, such as adding four more switches to the backbone or adding 10 new networked printers. You'll also learn about more complex hardware changes, such as replacing the entire network backbone with a more robust system.

Many of the same issues apply to hardware changes as apply to software changes. In particular, proper planning is the key to a successful upgrade. When considering a change to your network hardware, use the following steps as a guide:

1. Determine whether the change is necessary.

2. Research the upgrade's potential effects on other devices, functions, and users.

3. If you decide to implement the change, notify system administrators, help desk personnel, and users, and schedule it during off-hours (unless it is an emergency).

4. If possible, back up the current hardware's configuration. Ideally, you would have stored this information in a configuration management program. If that isn't the case, or if you want to be certain you have the most current information, you should collect it now. Most hardware (for example, routers, switches, and servers) has a configuration that you can easily copy to a disk. In other cases (for example, networked printers), you might have to print the hardware's configuration.

5. Prevent users from accessing the system or the part of the system that you are changing.

6. Keep the installation instructions and hardware documentation handy.

7. Implement the change.

8. Test the hardware fully after the change, preferably putting a higher load on the device than it would incur during normal use in your organization. Note any unintended or unanticipated consequences of the change.

9. If the change was successful, reenable access to the device. If it was unsuccessful, isolate the device or reinsert the old device, if possible.

10. Inform system administrators, help desk personnel, and users when the change is complete. If it was not successful, explain why.

11. Record your change in the change management system.

Adding or Upgrading Equipment The difficulty involved in adding or upgrading hardware on your network depends largely on whether you have used the hardware in the past. For instance, if your organization always uses Cisco switches, adding one more Cisco switch to your second-floor telecommunications closet might take only a few minutes and cause absolutely no disruption of service to your users. On the other hand, even if your company uses Cisco switches, adding a Cisco VPN router to your network might be an entirely new experience. Therefore, take time to research, evaluate, and test any unfamiliar piece of equipment that you intend to add or upgrade on your network, even if it is manufactured by a vendor that supplies much of your other hardware.

With the rapid changes in the hardware industry, you might not be able to purchase identical hardware even from one quarter to the next. If consistency is a concern—for example, if your technical staff is familiar with only one brand and model of printer, and you do not have the time or money to retrain personnel—you would be wise to purchase as much hardware as possible in a single order. If this approach is not feasible, purchase equipment from vendors with familiar products and solid reputations.

Each type of device that you add or upgrade on the network will have different preparation and implementation requirements. Knowing exactly how to handle the changes requires not only a close reading of the manufacturer's instructions, but also some experience with the type of networking equipment at hand. The following list provides a very general overview of how you might approach adding or upgrading devices on the network, from the least disruptive to the most complex types of equipment. The devices at the bottom of the list are not only the most disruptive and complex to add or upgrade, but also the most difficult to remove or backlevel.

- *Networked workstation*—A networked workstation is perhaps the simplest device to add. It directly affects only a few users and does not alter network access for anyone else. If your organization has a standard networked workstation configuration (for example, a disk image—a compressed snapshot of the workstation's contents—on the server), adding a networked workstation will be a quick operation as well. You can successfully add a networked workstation without notifying users or support staff and without worrying about downtime.

- *Networked printer*—A networked printer is easy to add to your network, too. Adding this equipment is slightly more complex than adding a networked workstation, however, because of its unique configuration process and because it is shared. Although it affects multiple users, a networked printer does not typically perform a mission-critical function in an organization, so the length of time required to install one does not usually affect productivity. Thus, although you should notify the affected users of a networked printer addition, you do not need to notify all users and support staff. Likewise, you do not need to restrict access to the network or worry about downtime in this instance.

- *Hub or access point*—A single hub or access point might service as few as one or as many as 64 users. You do not have to worry about downtime or notifying users when *adding* a new hub or access point, because it cannot affect anyone until it is actually in use. However, if you are upgrading or swapping out an existing hub or access point, you must notify the affected users, because the upgrade or swap will create downtime. In addition, consider the traffic and addressing implications of adding or upgrading a hub or access point. For example, if you need to expand the capacity of a TCP/IP-based network segment from 24 users to 60 users, you can easily enough swap your 24-port hub with a 64-port hub. But before doing so, make sure that the segment has been allotted enough free IP addresses to service 60 users; otherwise, these users will not be able to access the network.

- *Server*—A server addition or upgrade can be tricky. Typically, this type of change (unless it is the replacement of a minor component) requires a great deal of foresight and planning. Before installing a new server, you need to consider the hardware and connectivity implications of the change, as well as issues relating to the NOS. Even if you are adding a server that will not be used immediately, you still need to plan for its installation. It's preferable to add the server while network traffic is low or nonexistent. Also, restrict access to the new server; otherwise, one of your users could find the server while browsing the network and try to save files to it or run an application from it.

  Upgrading the hardware (such as a NIC or memory) on an existing server may require nearly as much planning as adding an entirely new server. Schedule upgrades to an existing server for off-hours so that you can shut down the server without inconveniencing users who rely on it.

- *Switches and routers*—Changing or adding switches or routers to a network design can be complicated for several reasons. First, this type of change can be physically disruptive—for example, it might require the installation of new racks or other support frames in your telecommunications room. Second, switches and routers usually affect many users—and might affect all users—on the network. For instance, if you must replace the Internet gateway for your organization's headquarters, you will cut every user's access to the Internet in the process (unless you have redundant gateways, which is the optimal setup if you rely on the Internet for mission-critical services). You should notify all users on the network about the impending change, even if you don't think they will be affected—a router or switch might affect segments of the network other than the one it services. In addition, you should plan at least weeks in advance for switch or router changes and expect at least several hours of downtime. Because enterprise switches and routers are expensive, take extraordinary care when handling and configuring this type of equipment. Also, because switches and routers serve different purposes, rely on the manufacturer's documentation to guide you through the installation process.

Bear in mind that adding a new processor to a server, a new NIC to a router, or more memory to a printer may affect your service or warranty agreement with the manufacturer. Before purchasing any components to add or replace in your network devices, check your agreement for stipulations that might apply. You may be allowed to add only components made by the same manufacturer, or risk losing all support from that manufacturer.

Above all, keep safety in mind when you upgrade or install hardware on a network. Never tinker with the insides of a device that is turned on. Make sure that all cords and devices are stowed safely out of the way and cannot cause trips or falls. Avoid wearing jewelry, scarves, or very loose clothing when you work on equipment; if you have long hair, tie it back. Not only will you prevent injury this way, but you will also be less distracted. By removing metal jewelry, you could prevent damage to the equipment caused by a short if the metal touches a circuit. If the equipment is heavy (such as a large switch or server), do not try to lift it by yourself. Finally, to protect the equipment from damage, follow the manufacturer's temperature, ventilation, antistatic, and moisture guidelines.

Cabling Upgrades Cabling upgrades (unless they involve the replacement of a single faulty patch cable) can require significant planning and time to implement, depending on the size of your network. Bear in mind that troubleshooting cabling problems can be made easier by maintaining current, accurate wiring schematics. If the network's cable layout is undocumented and poorly planned, particularly if it was installed years before and survived intact despite building changes and network growth, cabling changes will be more difficult. The best way to ensure that future upgrades go smoothly is to carefully document the existing cable *before* making upgrades. If this assessment is not possible, you might have to compile your documentation as you upgrade the existing cabling.

Because a change of this magnitude affects all users on the network, consider upgrading the network cabling in phases. For example, schedule an upgrade of the first-floor east wing of your building one weekend, and then the first-floor west wing of your building the next, and so on. Weigh the importance of the upgrade against its potential for disruption. For example, if the Payroll department is processing end-of-month checks and having no difficulties other than somewhat slow response time, it is not critical to take away its access to install Cat 6 wiring. On the other hand, if the building maintenance staff needs a 1Gbps connection to run a new HVAC control system, you will probably make it a priority to take down this access temporarily and replace the wiring. In this case, not only must you replace the wiring, but you might also need to replace switches and NICs.

For the most part, organizations that run very small networks are able to upgrade or install their own network cabling. Many other organizations rely on contractors who specialize in this service. Nevertheless, as a networking professional, you should know how to run a cable across a room, either under a raised floor or through a ceiling plenum, to connect a device to the network.

Backbone Upgrades The most comprehensive and complex upgrade involving network hardware is a backbone upgrade. Recall that the network backbone represents the main conduit for data on LANs and WANs, connecting major routers, servers, and switches. A backbone upgrade requires not only a great deal of planning, but also the efforts of several personnel (and possibly contractors) and a significant investment. You may upgrade parts of the backbone—a NIC in a router or a section of cabling, for example—at any time, but upgrading the entire backbone changes the whole network.

Examples of backbone upgrades include migrating from token ring to Ethernet, migrating from a slower technology to a faster one, and replacing routers with switches (to make use of VLANs, for example). Such upgrades may satisfy a variety of needs: a need for faster throughput, a physical move or renovation, a more reliable network, greater security, more consistent standards, support of a new application, or greater cost-effectiveness. For example, the need for faster throughput may prompt an upgrade from an older Ethernet technology to Gigabit Ethernet. Likewise, the need to support videoconferencing may require a backbone upgrade from Cat 5 to fiber-optic cable.

If you recall the cabling and hardware required for different networking technologies (as explained in Chapters 3 and 6), you get an idea of how far-reaching a backbone upgrade can be. For example, to convert from token ring to Ethernet, you must replace or upgrade connectivity equipment such as hubs, switches, and routers. In addition, you must replace the NIC in every workstation and printer on the network and change the configuration for each device so that it works with Ethernet rather than token ring. For a small network, this effort may not be more than a weekend's work. For a network of thousands of users, such an upgrade requires the services of a dedicated team.

Because backbone upgrades are expensive and time consuming, the first step in approaching such a project is to justify it. Will the benefits outweigh the costs? Can the upgrade wait a year or more? If so, you might be wise to wait and find out whether a cheaper or better technical solution becomes available later. Don't plan to wait until the technology "settles down," because networking progress never stands still. On the other hand, do wait to implement brand-new technology until you can find out how it has worked on other networks similar to your own or until the manufacturer eliminates most of the bugs.

The second step is to determine which kind of backbone design to implement. To make this decision, you must analyze the future capacity needs of your network, decide whether you want a distributed or collapsed backbone, determine whether you want to rely on switches or routers, decide whether to use subnetting and to what extent, and so on. Although some of these predictions will be guesswork, you can minimize the variables by examining the history of your organization's growth and needs.

After designing your backbone upgrade, develop a project plan to accomplish the upgrade. Given that you don't upgrade your backbone every day, you might want to contract this work to a firm that specializes in network design and upgrades. In that case, you will draft an RFP (request for proposal) to specify what that contractor should do. Regardless of whether you employ specialists, your project plan should include a logical process for upgrading the backbone one section at a time (if possible). Because this process causes network outages, determine how best to proceed based on users' needs. Choose a time when usage is low (such as over a holiday) to perform your upgrade.

Reversing Hardware Changes As with software changes, you should provide a way to reverse the hardware upgrade and reinstall the old hardware if necessary. If you are replacing a faulty component or device, this restoration, of course, is not possible. If you are upgrading a component in a device, on the other hand, keep the old component safe (for example, keep NICs in static-resistant containers) and nearby. Not only might you need to put it back in the device, but you might also need to refer to it for information. Even if the device seems to be operating well with the new component, keep the old component for a while, especially if it is the only one of its kind at your organization.

Chapter Summary

- Network management involves assessing, monitoring, and maintaining network devices and connections.

- Documenting all aspects of your network promises to save work in the future. Information to track includes, but is not limited to: physical topology, access method, protocols, devices, operating systems, applications, and configurations.

- Configuration management refers to the collection of information related to the versions of software installed on every network device and every device's hardware configuration.

- Network diagrams provide broad snapshots of a network's physical or logical topology. A wiring schematic is a graphical representation of a network's wired infrastructure. In its most detailed form, it shows every wire necessary to interconnect network devices. Both are helpful for assessing a network's status and planning for its expansion. Baselining includes keeping a history of network performance and provides the basis for determining what types of changes might improve the network. It also allows for later evaluating how successful the improvements were.

- Policies, procedures, and regulations are important elements of sound network management. Elsewhere in this book you have learned about media installation and management best practices, network addressing policies, resource sharing and naming conventions, security-related policies, troubleshooting procedures, and backup and disaster recovery procedures.

- CALEA (Communications Assistance for Law Enforcement Act) is a federal regulation that requires telecommunications carriers and equipment manufacturers to provide for surveillance capabilities. HIPAA (Health Insurance Portability and Accountability Act)

addresses, among other things, the security and privacy of medical records, including those stored or transmitted electronically. These are just two laws that, depending on where you work, might affect your responsibilities as a network professional.

- Assessing a network's status on an ongoing basis includes performance management, or monitoring how well links and devices are keeping up with the demands placed on them, and fault management, or the detection and signaling of device, link, or component faults.

- Network management applications typically use SNMP (Simple Network Management Protocol) to communicate with agents running on managed devices. Agents can report information on a device's components or status (such as utilization or performance).

- System logs and event logs keep a record of conditions reported by operating systems and applications. On a Windows-based computer, the Event Viewer allows you to review the computer's event log. UNIX and Linux systems typically come with a GUI application for viewing the system log. To find out where your computer's system log is kept, view the `/etc/syslog.conf` file.

- Traffic shaping helps ensure acceptable overall network performance by limiting the throughput or volume of traffic that may traverse certain network interfaces or by assigning variable priority levels to different types of traffic.

- Caching stores files locally that would otherwise be obtained from a remote source, such as a Web server across the country. An ISP uses cache engines on its network to store frequently accessed content and deliver it directly to requestors. In this way, the ISP improves response time and reduces WAN traffic and costs.

- An asset management system includes an inventory of the total number of components on the network as well as each device's configuration files, model number, serial number, location on the network, and technical support contact. In addition, it records every piece of software purchased by your organization, its version number, vendor, and technical support contact.

- A patch is an enhancement or improvement to a part of a software application, often distributed at no charge by software vendors to fix a bug in their code or to add slightly more functionality. Patches differ from revisions and software upgrades because they change only part of the software application, leaving most of the code untouched.

- Make it a policy to keep informed about patches to your network software, whether they involve the operating system, an application, or a client software. If you work in a large organization with several servers, routers, and other devices, you might want to assign one network administrator to manage patches for the servers, another to manage patches for the printers, and so on.

- A software upgrade represents a major change to the existing code, which may or may not be offered free from a vendor and may or may not be comprehensive enough to substitute for the original application. An upgrade to the client software replaces the existing client software to add functionality and fix bugs found in the previous version.

- Before upgrading client software, carefully read the instructions that accompany the upgrade to find out how best to apply it, whether it depends on any previous upgrades, whether it requires any special preparation, and how its changes will affect users. Client upgrades typically overwrite some system files on the workstation, so their installation may affect other applications adversely.

- Like client upgrades, application upgrades consist of modifications to all or part of an application that are designed to enhance functionality or fix problems with the software. Application upgrades, however, affect software applications shared by clients on the network.

- Perhaps the most critical type of software upgrade you'll perform is an upgrade to your network operating system. This effort usually involves significant, potentially drastic, changes to the operation of your servers and clients. As such, it requires plenty of forethought, product research, and rigorous testing before you implement it. In fact, for any network with more than a few users, create and follow a project plan for this undertaking.

- The process of upgrading an NOS should include research, proposal, evaluation, training, preimplementation, implementation, and postimplementation phases.

- Plan for the possibility that a software upgrade might harm your existing system (or systems), and be prepared to reverse the process. The restoration of a previous version of software after an attempted upgrade is known as backleveling.

- Hardware and physical plant changes might be required when your network has problems. More often, however, they are performed as part of a move to increase capacity, improve performance, or add functionality to the network.

- Research, evaluate, and test any unfamiliar piece of equipment you intend to add or upgrade on your network, even if it is manufactured by a vendor that supplies much of your other hardware. The process of implementing a hardware upgrade is very similar to that of carrying out a software upgrade, including notifying users and preparing to bring the system down during the change.

- Cabling upgrades are simpler and less error prone if a network's cable plant is well documented. Also make sure to document new cable infrastructure after making changes. When embarking on a major cabling upgrade, such as a backbone replacement, it is advisable to upgrade the infrastructure in phases.

- The most comprehensive and complex upgrade involving network hardware is a backbone upgrade. The network backbone serves as the main conduit for data on LANs and WANs, connecting major routers, servers, and/or switches. A backbone upgrade not only requires a great deal of time to plan, but also the efforts of several staff members (and possibly contractors) and a significant investment.

- Allow for a way to reverse a hardware upgrade and replace it with the old hardware. If you are upgrading a component in a device, keep the old component safe (for example, keep NICs in static-resistant containers) and nearby. Not only might you need to put it back in the device, but you might also need to refer to it for information.

Key Terms

agent   A software routine that collects data about a managed device's operation and provides it to the network management application running on the console.

asset management   The process of identifying and tracking an organization's assets, such as hardware and software.

backleveling   The process of reverting to a previous version of a software application after attempting to upgrade it.

bug   A flaw in software or hardware that causes it to malfunction.

cache engine   A network device devoted to storage and delivery of frequently requested files.

caching   The local storage of frequently needed files that would otherwise be obtained from an external source.

CALEA (Communications Assistance for Law Enforcement Act)   A United States federal regulation that requires telecommunications carriers and equipment manufacturers to provide for surveillance capabilities. CALEA was passed by Congress in 1994 after pressure from the FBI, which worried that networks relying solely on digital communications would circumvent traditional wiretapping strategies.

Communications Assistance for Law Enforcement Act   *See* CALEA.

configuration management   The collection, storage, and assessment of information related to the versions of software installed on every network device and every device's hardware configuration.

event log   The service on Windows-based operating systems that records events, or the ongoing record of such events.

Event Viewer   A GUI application that allows users to easily view and sort events recorded in the event log on a computer running a Windows-based operating system.

fault management   The detection and signaling of device, link, or component faults.

Health Insurance Portability and Accountability Act   *See* HIPAA.

HIPAA (Health Insurance Portability and Accountability Act)   A federal regulation in the United States, enacted in 1996. One aspect of this regulation addresses the security and privacy of medical records, including those stored or transmitted electronically.

Management Information Base   *See* MIB.

MIB (Management Information Base)   A database used in network management that contains a device's definitions of managed objects and their data.

MRTG (Multi Router Traffic Grapher)   A command-line utility that uses SNMP to poll devices, collects data in a log file, and then generates HTML-based views of the data. MRTG is freely distributed software originally written by Tobias Oetiker, a networking professional who in the early 1990s saw a need for a tool to regularly measure the status of his organization's WAN link.

Multi Router Traffic Grapher   *See* MRTG.

network diagram   A graphical representation of a network's devices and connections.

network management   The assessment, monitoring, and maintenance of the devices and connections on a network.

patch   A correction, improvement, or enhancement to part of a software application, often distributed at no charge by software vendors to fix a bug in their code or to add slightly more functionality.

performance management   The ongoing assessment of how well network links, devices, and components keep up with demands on them.

polling   A network management application's regular collection of data from managed devices.

service pack   A significant patch to one of the Microsoft Windows operating systems.

Simple Network Management Protocol   *See* SNMP.

SNMP (Simple Network Management Protocol)   An application layer protocol in the TCP/IP suite used to convey data regarding the status of managed devices on a network.

system log   On a computer running a UNIX or Linux operating system, the record of monitored events, which can range in priority from 0 to 7 (where "0" indicates an emergency situation and "7" simply points to information that might help in debugging a problem). You can view and modify system log locations and configurations in the file /etc/syslog.conf file on most systems (on some systems this is the /etc/rsyslog.conf file).

traffic policing   A traffic-shaping technique in which the volume or rate of traffic traversing an interface is limited to a predefined maximum.

traffic shaping   Manipulating certain characteristics of packets, data streams, or connections to manage the type and amount of traffic traversing a network or interface at any moment.

upgrade   A major change to the existing code in a software application, which may or may not be offered free from a vendor, and may or may not be comprehensive enough to substitute for the original application.

Web caching   A technique in which Web pages are stored locally, either on a host or network, and then delivered to requestors more quickly than if they had been obtained from the original source.

wiring schematic   A graphical representation of a network's wired infrastructure.

Review Questions

1. Which document is a graphical representation of a network's devices and connections?

    a. Wiring schematic

    b. Network diagram

    c. Traffic shaping report

    d. Configuration management documentation

2. Which category of network management tools is used to know for certain whether a pattern of usage has changed?

    a. Performance management

    b. Configuration management

    c. Policies, procedures, and regulations

    d. Baseline measurements

3. Which category of network management tools does resource sharing and naming conventions fall under?

    a. Performance management

    b. Asset management

    c. Policies, procedures, and regulations

    d. Baseline reporting

4. Which device is the least disruptive type of equipment to add or upgrade?

    a. Networked printer

    b. Hub or access point

    c. Networked workstation

    d. Switch

5. On modern networks, most agents use ____ to communicate information about managed devices.

    a. TCP

    b. SNMP

    c. MIB

    d. MRTG

6. True or false? The scope of network management techniques may differ between organizations.

7. True or false? On Windows-based computers, device monitor results are sent to a log known as a system log.

8. True or false? To an ISP, caching is simply a convenience.

9. True or false? Good planning is necessary to manage change while maintaining a network's efficiency and availability.

10. True or false? The most comprehensive and complex upgrade involving network hardware is a backbone upgrade.

11. ____ management involves assessing, monitoring, and maintaining network devices and connections.

12. ____ involves manipulating certain characteristics of packets, data streams, or connections to manage the type and amount of traffic traversing a network or interface at any moment.

13. ____ is the local storage of frequently needed files that would otherwise be obtained from an external source.

14. A(n) ____ differs from a revision or software upgrade in that it changes only part of an application, leaving most of the code untouched.

15. The process of reverting to a previous version of software after attempting to upgrade it is known as ____.

Network+ Examination Objectives

This book covers all of the Network+ examination objectives, which were released by CompTIA (the Computing Technology Industry Association) in 2009. The official list of objectives is available at CompTIA's Web site, *www.comptia.org*. For your reference, the following table lists each exam objective and the chapter of this book that explains the objective, plus the percentage of the exam that will cover each certification domain. Each objective belongs to one of six domains (or main topics) of networking expertise. For example, the objective of recognizing an RJ-45 connector belongs to the "Network Media and Topologies" domain, which accounts for 20% of the exam's content.

Domain 1.0 Network Technologies – 20% of Examination

Network+ Examination Objectives—Network Technologies

Objective	Chapter
1.1 Explain the function of common networking protocols	
TCP	2, 4, 10
FTP	4
UDP	2, 4, 10
TCP/IP suite	2, 4, 10
DHCP	4
TFTP	4
DNS	4, 10
HTTP(S)	2, 4, 10, 12
ARP	4
SIP (VoIP)	11
RTP (VoIP)	11
SSH	12
POP3	10

Objective	Chapter
NTP	4
IMAP4	10
Telnet	4
SMTP	10
SNMP2/3	15
ICMP	4
IGMP	10
TLS	12
1.2 Identify commonly used TDP and UDP default ports	
TCP ports	
FTP – 20, 21	4
SSH – 22	4
Telnet – 23	4
SMTP – 25	4
DNS – 53	4
HTTP – 80	4
POP3 – 110	4
NTP – 123	4
IMAP4 – 143	4
HTTPS – 443	4
UDP ports	
TFTP – 69	4
DNS – 53	4
BOOTP/DHCP – 67	4
SNMP – 161	15
1.3 Identify the following address formats	
IPv6	4, 10
IPv4	2, 4, 10
MAC addressing	2, 6
1.4 Given a scenario, evaluate the proper use of the following addressing technologies and addressing schemes	
Addressing Technologies	
Subnetting	10
Classful vs. classless (e.g. CIDR, Supernetting)	10
NAT	10

Objective	Chapter
PAT	10
SNAT	10
Public vs. private	10
DHCP (static, dynamic APIPA)	4
Addressing schemes	
Unicast	4, 10, 11
Multicast	4, 10, 11
Broadcast	4, 10, 11
1.5 Identify common IPv4 and IPv6 routing protocols	
Link state	
OSPF	6
IS-IS	6
Distance vector	
RIP	6
RIPv2	6
BGP	6
Hybrid	
EIGRP	6
1.6 Explain the purpose and properties of routing	
IGP vs. EGP	6
Static vs. dynamic	6
Next hop	6
Understanding routing tables and how they pertain to path selection	6
Explain convergence (steady state)	6
1.7 Compare the characteristics of wireless communication standards	
802.11 a/b/g/n	8
Speeds	8
Distance	8
Channels	8
Frequency	8
Authentication and Encryption	7, 8, 12
WPA	12
WEP	12
RADIUS	12
TKIP	12

Domain 2.0 Network Media and Topologies – 20% of Examination

Network+ Examination Objectives—Network Media and Topologies

Objective	Chapter
2.1 Categorize standard cable types and their properties:	
Type:	
Cat 3, Cat 5, Cat 5e, Cat 6	3
STP, UTP	3
Multimode fiber, single-mode fiber	3
Coaxial	3
RG-59	3
RG-6	3
Serial	3
Plenum vs. Non-plenum	3
Properties:	
Transmission speeds	3, 5
Distance	3, 5
Duplex	3
Noise immunity (security, EMI)	3, 12
Frequency	3
2.2 Identify common connector types	
RJ-11	3, Appendix C
RJ-45	3, Appendix C
BNC	3, Appendix C
SC	3, Appendix C
ST	3, Appendix C
LC	3, Appendix C
RS-232	3, Appendix C
2.3 Identify common physical network topologies	
Star	5
Mesh	5
Bus	5
Ring	5

Objective	Chapter
Point-to-point	3
Point-to-multipoint	3
Hybrid	5
2.4 Given a scenario, differentiate and implement appropriate wiring standards	
568A	3
568B	3
Straight vs. cross-over	3
Rollover	3
Loopback	3
2.5 Categorize WAN technology types and properties	
Type:	
Frame relay	7
E1/T1	7
ADSL	7
SDSL	7
VDSL	7
Cable modem	7
Satellite	8
E3/T3	7
OC-x	7
Wireless	8
ATM	7
SONET	7
MPLS	6, 11
ISDN BRI	7
ISDN PRI	7
POTS	7
PSTN	7
Properties:	
Circuit switch	7
Packet switch	7
Speed	7, 8
Transmission media	7, 8
Distance	7, 8

Objective	Chapter
2.6 Categorize LAN technology types and properties	
Types:	
Ethernet	5
10BaseT	5
100BaseTX	5
100BaseFX	5
1000BaseT	5
1000BaseX	5
10GBaseSR	5
10GBaseLR	5
10GBaseER	5
10GBaseSW	5
10GBaseLW	5
10GBaseEW	5
10GBaseT	5
Properties:	
CSMA/CD	5
Broadcast	5
Collision	5
Bonding	5
Speed	5
Distance	5
2.7 Explain common logical network topologies and their characteristics	
Peer to peer	1
Client/server	1, 9
VPN	7
VLAN	6
2.8 Install components of wiring distribution	
Vertical and horizontal cross-connects	3
Patch panels	3
66 block	3
MDFs	3
IDFs	3
25 pair	3
100 pair	3

Objective	Chapter
110 block	3
Demarc	3
Demarc extension	3
Smart jack	7
Verify wiring installation	3
Verify wiring termination	3

Domain 3.0 Network Devices – 17% of Examination

Network+ Examination Objectives—Network Devices

Objective	Chapter
3.1 Install, configure, and differentiate between common network devices	
Hub	6
Repeater	6
Modem	6
NIC	6
Media converters	3
Basic switch	6
Bridge	6
Wireless access point	8
Basic router	6
Basic firewall	12
Basic DHCP server	4
3.2 Identify the functions of specialized network devices	
Multilayer switch	6
Content switch	6
IDS/IPS	12
Load balancer	14
Multifunction network devices	6, 10
DNS server	4
Bandwidth shaper	15
Proxy server	12

Objective	Chapter
CSU/DSU	7
3.3 Explain the advanced features of a switch	
PoE	6
Spanning tree	6
VLAN	6
Trunking	6
Port mirroring	6
Port authentication	12
3.4 Implement a basic wireless network	
Install client	8
Access point placement	8
Install access point	8
Configure appropriate encryption	8
Configure channels and frequencies	8
Set ESSID and beacon	8
Verify installation	8

Domain 4.0 Network Management – 20% of Examination

Network+ Examination Objectives—Network Management

Objective	Chapter
4.1 Explain the function of each layer of the OSI model	
Layer 1 – physical	2
Layer 2 – data link	2
Layer 3 – network	2
Layer 4 – transport	2
Layer 5 – session	2
Layer 6 – presentation	2
Layer 7 – application	2
4.2 Identify types of configuration management documentation	
Wiring schematics	15
Physical and logical network diagrams	15
Baselines	13, 15
Policies, procedures, and configurations	13, 15

Objective	Chapter
Regulations	15
4.3 Given a scenario, evaluate the network based on configuration management documentation	
Compare wiring schematics, physical and logical network diagrams, baselines, policies and procedures, and configurations to network devices and infrastructure	15
Update wiring schematics, physical and logical network diagrams, configurations, and job logs as needed	15
4.4 Conduct network monitoring to identify performance and connectivity issues using the following:	
Network monitoring utilities (e.g. packet sniffers, connectivity software, load testing, throughput testers)	13, 15
System logs, history logs, event logs	14, 15
4.5 Explain different methods and rationales for network performance optimization	14
Methods:	
QoS	7, 11
Traffic shaping	15
Load balancing	14
High availability	14
Caching engines	15
Fault tolerance	14
Reasons:	
Latency sensitivity	11
High-bandwidth applications	11
VoIP	11
Video applications	11
Uptime	11
4.6 Given a scenario, implement the following network troubleshooting methodology	
Information gathering – identify symptoms and problems	13
Identify the affected areas of the network	13
Determine if anything has changed	13
Establish the most probable cause	13
Determine if escalation is necessary	13
Create an action plan and solution identifying potential effects	13
Implement and test the solution	13
Identify the results and effects of the solution	13
Document the solution and the entire process	13

Objective	Chapter
4.7 Given a scenario, troubleshoot common connectivity issues and select an appropriate solution	
Physical issues:	
Cross talk	3
Nearing cross talk	3
Near end cross talk	3
Attenuation	3
Collisions	5, 13
Shorts	13
Open impedance mismatch (echo)	3
Interference	3, 8, 13
Logical issues:	
Port speed	6
Port duplex mismatch	6
Incorrect VLAN	6
Incorrect IP address	4
Wrong gateway	4, 10
Wrong DNS	4
Wrong subnet mask	10
Issues that should be identified but escalated:	
Switching loop	6, 13
Routing loop	6
Route problems	6
Proxy ARP	10
Broadcast storms	6
Wireless issues:	
Interference (bleed, environmental factors)	8, 13
Incorrect encryption	8, 12
Incorrect channel	8
Incorrect frequency	8
ESSID mismatch	8
Standard mismatch (802.11 a/b/g/n)	8
Distance	8
Bounce	8
Incorrect antenna placement	8

Domain 5.0 Network Tools – 12% of Examination

Network+ Examination Objectives—Network Tools

Objective	Chapter
5.1 Given a scenario, select the appropriate command line interface tool and interpret the output to verify functionality	
Traceroute	10
Ipconfig	4, 10
Ifconfig	4, 10
Ping	4, 10
ARP ping	4, 10
ARP	4, 10
Nslookup	10
Hostname	10
Dig	10
Mtr	10
Route	10
Nbtstat	10
Netstat	10
5.2 Explain the purpose of network scanners	
Packet sniffers	13
Intrusion detection software	12
Intrusion prevention software	12
Port scanners	12
5.3 Given a scenario, utilize the appropriate hardware tools	
Cable testers	13
Protocol analyzer	13
Certifiers	3
TDR	13
OTDR	13
Multimeter	13
Toner probe	13
Butt set	13
Punch-down tool	3

Objective	Chapter
Cable stripper	3
Snips	3
Voltage event recorder	13
Temperature monitor	14

Domain 6.0 Network Security – 11% of Examination

Network+ Examination Objectives—Network Security

Objective	Chapter
6.1 Explain the function of hardware and software security devices	
Network-based firewall	12
Host-based firewall	12
IDS	12
IPS	12
VPN concentrator	12
6.2 Explain common features of a firewall	
Application layer vs. network layer	12
Stateful vs. stateless	12
Scanning services	12
Content filtering	12
Signature identification	12
Zones	12
6.3 Explain the methods of network access security	
Filtering:	
ACL	12
MAC filtering	12
IP filtering	12
Tunneling and encryption:	
SSL VPN	12
VPN	7
L2TP	7
PPTP	7
IPSec	12

Objective	Chapter
Remote access:	
RAS	7
RDP	7
PPPoE	7
PPP	7
VNC	7
ICA	7
6.4 Explain methods of user authentication	
PKI	12
Kerberos	12
AAA	12
RADIUS	12
TACACS+	12
Network access control	12
802.1x	12
CHAP	12
MS-CHAP	12
EAP	12
6.5 Explain issues that affect device security	
Physical security	12
Restricting local and remote access	7, 9, 12
Secure methods vs. unsecure methods	
SSH, HTTPS, SNMPv3, SFTP, SCP	12, 15
TELNET, HTTP, FTP, RSH, RCP, SNMPv1/2	4, 10, 12, 15
6.6 Identify common security threats and mitigation techniques	
Security threats:	
DoS	12
Viruses	14
Worms	14
Attackers	12
Man in the middle	12
Smurf	12
Rogue access points	8, 12
Social engineering (phishing)	12

Objective	Chapter
Mitigation techniques:	12
Policies and procedures	12
User training	12
Patches and updates	12, 15

Network+ Practice Exam

The following exam contains questions similar in content and format to what you will encounter on CompTIA's Network+ certification exam. The exam consists of 100 questions, all of which are multiple choice. Some questions have more than one answer, and some questions require that you study a figure to determine the right answer. The questions are in no particular order. The number of questions on each topic reflects the weighting that CompTIA assigned to these topics in its 2009 exam objectives. If you want to simulate taking the CompTIA Network+ certification exam, you should allow yourself 90 minutes to answer all of the questions. You can find the answers to these questions in Appendix F, "Answers to Network+ Practice Exam Questions."

1. What TCP/IP utility would you use to determine the number of hops between two routers?

   a. FTP

   b. Nslookup

   c. Nbtstat

   d. Tracert

   e. Telnet

2. Your network manager has purchased a dozen new access points, and all are configured to use the new 802.11n standard in either the 2.4GHz or 5GHz band. These access points will be capable of communicating with older access points that run which of the following standards? (Choose all that apply.)

   a. 802.11g

   b. 802.11a

   c. 802.11.b

   d. Bluetooth

   e. None of the above

3. Which of the following figures reflects the type of physical topology commonly used on a 100Base-TX network?

a.

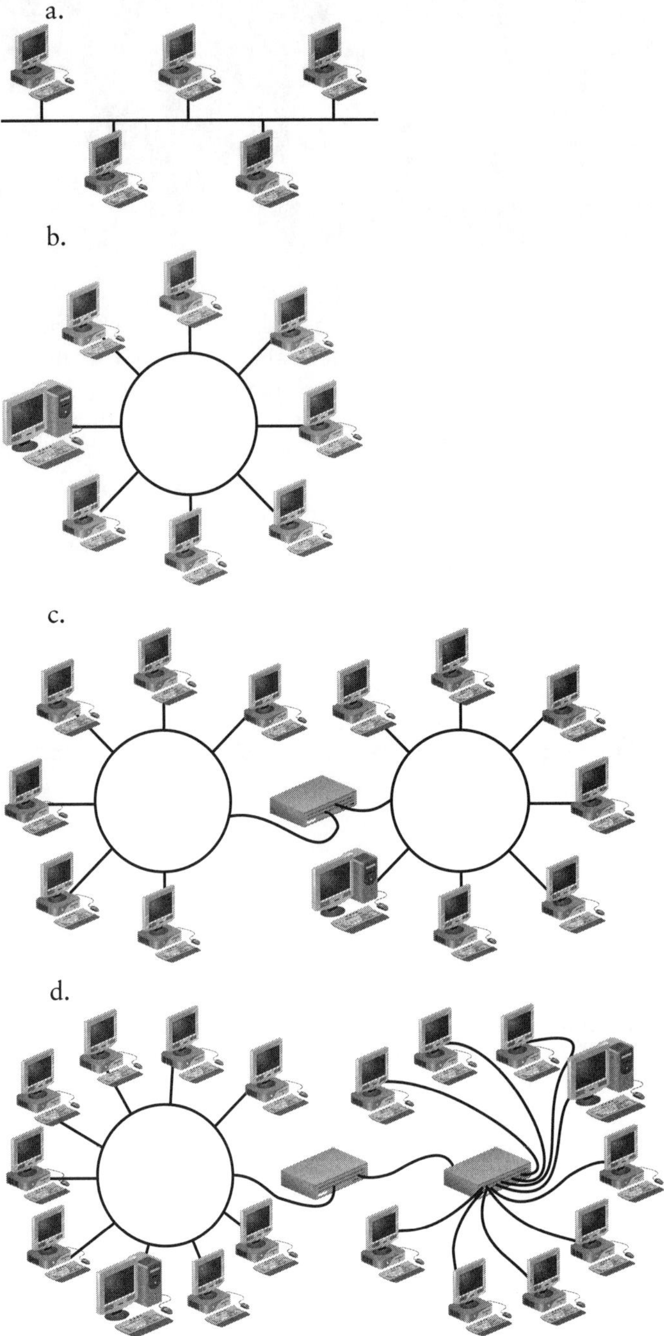

b.

c.

d.

e.

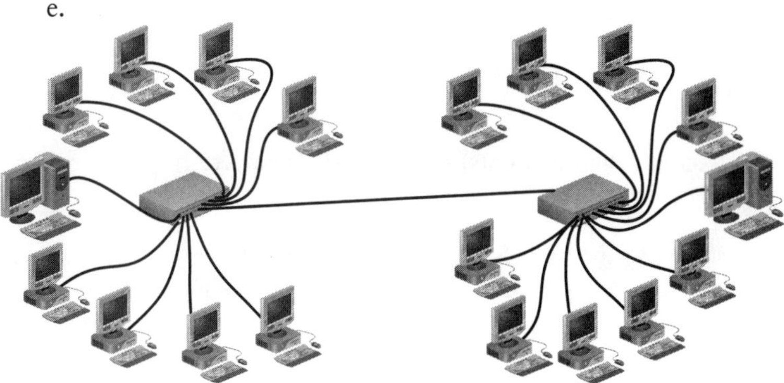

4. You have connected to your bank's home page. Its URL begins with "https://." Based on this information, what type of security can you assume the bank employs for receiving and transmitting data to and from its Web server?

   a. Kerberos

   b. SSL

   c. IPSec

   d. L2TP

   e. Packet-filtering firewall

5. You are a support technician for an ISP (Internet service provider) called Alpha Enterprises. A new customer calls to ask why his dial-up connection to your company's RADIUS access server won't work. After the user double-clicks the ISP dial-up networking connection icon on his Windows XP desktop, you can hear his modem dialing. And even though another machine seems to answer, his connection never gets established. You verify that his phone line is connected properly and that he has entered the correct phone number. You also make sure he is using the correct, case-sensitive user name and password that he just received from your Customer Service department. What do you ask him to check next to get closer to solving his problem?

   a. The type of server specified in his Alpha Enterprises Properties dialog box

   b. The version of Windows XP his system uses

   c. Whether the Save Password check box is checked in his Connect to Alpha Enterprises dialog box

   d. Whether he has disabled the call-waiting feature in his Alpha Enterprises Properties dialog box

   e. The maximum baud rate his modem can handle

6. You are rearranging nodes on your Fast Ethernet network. Due to a necessarily hasty expansion, you have decided to supply power to a wireless router in a makeshift telco room using PoE (power over Ethernet). What is the minimum cabling standard you must use to connect this wireless router to the network's backbone?

   a. Cat 3

   b. RG-59

   c. RG-6

   d. Cat 5

   e. Single mode fiber-optic cable

7. **Which of the following best describes the function(s) of the MAC sublayer?**

   a. It performs data compression, reformatting, and encryption.

   b. It appends a node's physical address to frames before they are transmitted.

   c. It interprets program requests and requirements to provide an interface between applications and the network.

   d. It manages flow control and issues requests for retransmission of data that has suffered errors.

   e. It translates network addresses into their physical counterparts and determines routing.

8. **You are a networking technician in a radiology clinic, where physicians use the network to transmit and store patients' diagnostic results. Shortly after a new wing, which contains X-ray and magnetic resonance imaging (MRI) machines, is added to the building, computers in that area begin having intermittent problems saving data to the file server. After you have identified the symptoms, what is your next step in troubleshooting this problem?**

   a. Determine the number of workstations affected, to which segment the affected workstations belong, and which area of workstations is affected.

   b. Notify colleagues in the clinic's IT department about a change you are going to make while attempting to resolve the problem.

   c. Research the problem on your NOS vendor's technical support Web site.

   d. Identify recent changes to the network to determine whether a hardware or software change may be responsible for the problem.

   e. Identify the potential effects of the solution you are about to apply to make sure that you do not inadvertently create new problems.

9. **As a network administrator, you are most likely to use an RS-232-compatible cable in which of the following instances?**

   a. Connecting a workstation to a hub's uplink port

   b. Connecting a RADIUS server to a router

   c. Connecting a workstation to a router's console port

   d. Connecting a switch to a router's uplink port

   e. Connecting a broadband cable set-top box to the cable company's backbone

10. **In which of the following situations would a crossover cable be useful for troubleshooting a network connectivity problem with a workstation?**

   a. To connect the workstation to a hub

   b. To connect the workstation's hub port to a punch-down block

   c. To connect the workstation to another workstation

   d. To connect the workstation's switch port to its hub port

   e. To connect between the workstation's wall plate and its hub port

11. Which of the following WAN topologies is the most fault tolerant?

    a. Full mesh

    b. Bus

    c. Peer-to-peer

    d. Ring

    e. Hierarchical

12. Which of the following is a valid MAC address?

    a. C3000000FFFF

    b. 111.111.111.111

    c. ::9F53

    d. AEFFG0930110

    e. D0000000

13. What type of network could use the type of connector shown here?

    a. 100Base-FX

    b. 100Base-TX

    c. 10Base-T

    d. 10Base-5

    e. 10Base-2

14. Your organization has just ordered its first T1 connection to the Internet. Prior to that, your organization relied on a DSL connection. Which of the following devices must you now have that your DSL connection didn't require?

    a. Modem

    b. CSU/DSU

    c. Switch

    d. Hub

    e. MAU

15. What type of addresses do bridges read, and to which layer of the OSI model do bridges belong?

    a. IP addresses; the network layer

    b. IP addresses; the transport layer

    c. MAC addresses; the network layer

    d. MAC addresses; the data link layer

    e. IP addresses; the data link layer

16. What is the maximum size of a data unit on an Ethernet network?

    a. 16 bytes

    b. 120 bytes

    c. 1,500 bytes

    d. 6,000 bytes

    e. 16,000 bytes

17. You have been asked to provide a connectivity solution for a small, locally owned franchise of a national restaurant chain. The owners of the franchise want to send their confidential sales figures, personnel information, and inventory updates to the national office, which is 1,200 miles away, once per week. Their total monthly data transfer will amount to almost 50 megabytes. The franchise owners do not plan to use the connection for any other purposes, and they do not have IT staff to support the connection. Also, they do not want to spend more than $75 per month, nor more than $500 to install their connection. Considering cost, speed, reliability, technical expertise, distance, security, and the nature of their environment, what is the best solution for this client?

    a. A T1 that connects to the national office via a router at the local franchise and a router at the national office and that uses IPSec to ensure the security of the data en route

    b. A PSTN connection to a local Internet service provider that uses PPP to dial in to an access server and then sends data via e-mail to the national office

    c. A DSL connection to a local telephone and Internet service provider that uses IPSec to encrypt the data before it is sent to the national office's file server over the Internet

    d. A private SONET ring to connect with two local telephone and Internet service providers that connects to the national office's T3 and sends data via TCP/IP over ATM

    e. An ISDN connection to a local Internet service provider that allows you to copy files to the national office's anonymous FTP site

18. IEEE's physical layer standards for the Ethernet access method are established by which IEEE committee?

    a. 802.2

    b. 802.3

    c. 802.5

    d. 802.7

    e. 802.11

19. You are a software programmer using a development Web server at your office to test your programs. Although your Web server is connected to the Internet for test purposes, you want to ensure that no one on the Internet can access your Web files. To make it more difficult for someone to connect to your Web server from the Internet, which TCP/IP default port number would you change in your Web server software configuration?

    a. 21

    b. 22

    c. 65

    d. 80

    e. 90

20. What is the maximum segment length on a 10Base-T network?

    a. 85 meters

    b. 100 meters

    c. 185 meters

    d. 200 meters

    e. 1,000 meters

21. You are the network administrator for a large college whose network contains nearly 10,000 workstations, over 100 routers, 80 switches, and 2,000 printers. You are researching a proposal to both upgrade the routers and switches on your network and improve the management of your network. What type of protocol should you ensure that the new routers and switches can support to more easily automate your network management?

    a. TFTP

    b. SMTP

    c. NNTP

    d. ICMP

    e. SNMP

22. In the process of troubleshooting an intermittent performance problem with your network's Internet connection, you attempt to run a traceroute test to *www.microsoft.com*. The traceroute response displays the first 12 hops in the route but then presents several "Request timed out" messages in a row. What is the most likely reason for this?

    a. Your network's ISP is experiencing connectivity problems.

    b. The Internet backbone is experiencing traffic congestion.

    c. Your client's TCP/IP service limits the traceroute command to a maximum of 12 hops.

    d. Your IP gateway failed while you were attempting the traceroute test.

    e. Microsoft's network is bounded by firewalls that do not accept incoming ICMP traffic.

23. What is the network ID for a network that contains the group of IP addresses from 194.73.44.1 through 194.73.44.254 and is not subnetted?

    a. 194.1.1.1

    b. 194.73.0.0

    c. 194.73.44.1

    d. 194.73.44.255

    e. 194.73.44.0

24. Which of the following disaster recovery contingencies is the most expensive to maintain?

    a. Hot spare

    b. Warm spare

    c. Hot site

    d. Warm site

    e. Cold site

25. **What type of device is typically used to create a VLAN?**

    a. Hub

    b. Bridge

    c. Switch

    d. Router

    e. Firewall

26. **In NAT, how does an IP gateway ensure that outgoing traffic can traverse public networks?**

    a. It modifies each outgoing frame's Type field to indicate that the transmission is destined for a public network.

    b. It assigns each outgoing packet a masked ID via the Options field.

    c. It interprets the contents of outgoing packets to ensure that they contain no client-identifying information.

    d. It replaces each outgoing packet's Source address field with a valid IP address.

    e. It modifies the frame length to create uniformly sized frames, called cells, which are required for public network transmission.

27. **You have purchased an access point capable of exchanging data via the 802.11b or 802.11g wireless standard. According to these standards, what is the maximum distance from the access point that wireless stations can travel and still exchange data with the access point at the maximum potential throughput?**

    a. 10 feet

    b. 50 feet

    c. 80 feet

    d. 100 feet

    e. 175 feet

28. **Which of the following functions does SIP perform on a VoIP network? (Choose all that apply.)**

    a. Determines the locations of endpoints

    b. Provides call waiting and caller ID services

    c. Prioritizes calls for any single endpoint in a queue

    d. Establishes sessions between endpoints

    e. Encrypts VoIP signals before they are transmitted over the network

29. **At what layer of the OSI model do routers operate?**

    a. Presentation

    b. Session

    c. Network

    d. Data link

    e. Physical

30. **Which of the following is used to resolve NetBIOS names with IP addresses?**

    a. DNS

    b. SMTP

    c. DHCP

    d. WINS

    e. Hosts file

31. **Which of the following figures illustrates a VPN WAN?**

    a.

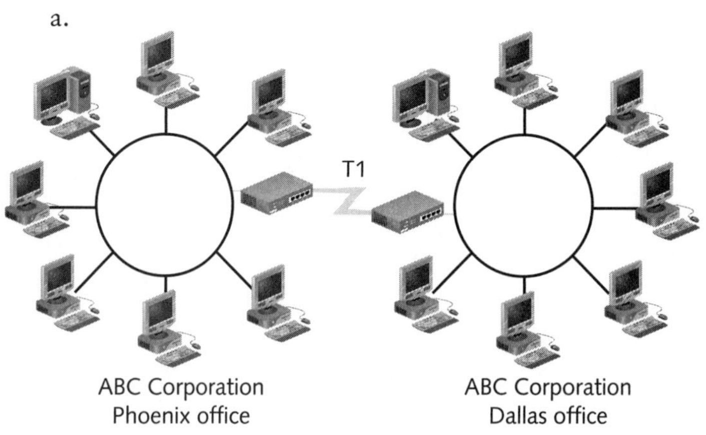

    b.

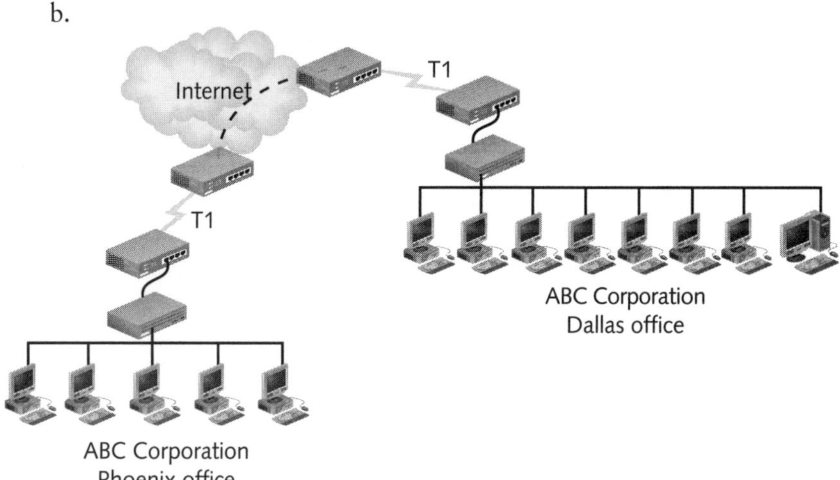

c.

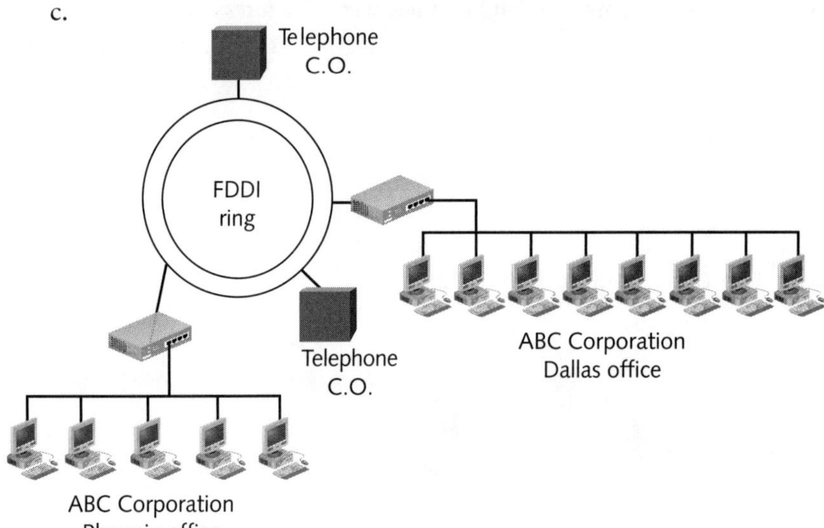

Telephone
C.O.
FDDI
ring
Telephone
C.O.
ABC Corporation
Dallas office
ABC Corporation
Phoenix office

T1
T1
ABC Corporation
Dallas office
DKZ Corporation
Los Angeles office
ABC Corporation
Phoenix office

Internet
T1
ABC Corporation
Phoenix office

d.

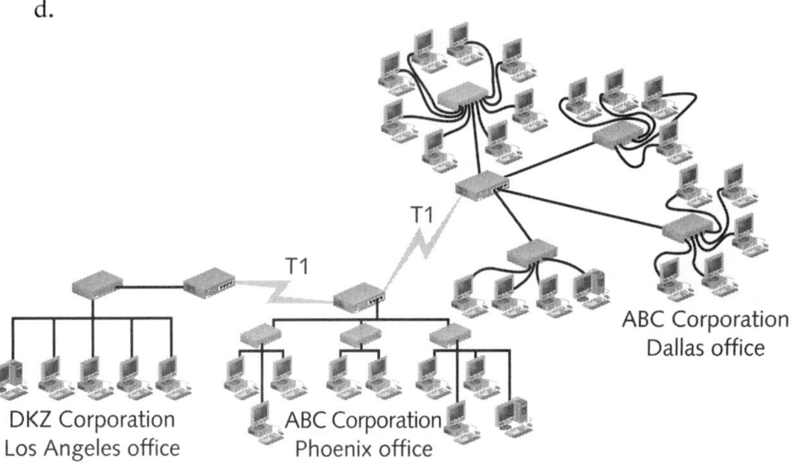

e.

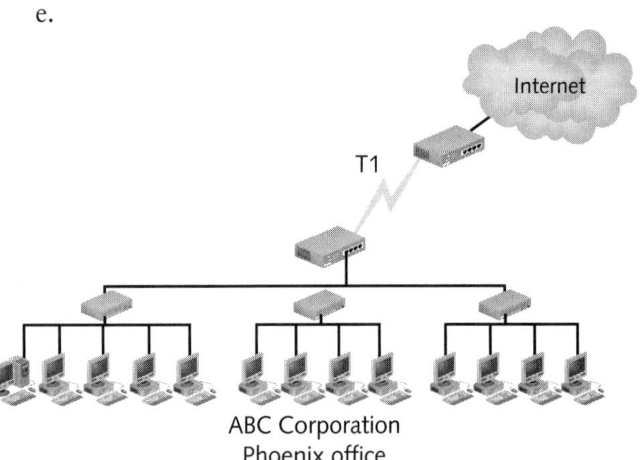

32. Suppose you want to copy files from a Linux server at the office to your home computer, which also runs Linux, across a VPN. Both computers run OpenSSH. Which utility would you use to make sure these files are copied securely?

    a. SCP

    b. SFTP

    c. FTP

    d. TFTP

    e. HTTP

33. What security measure verifies that your user name and password are contained in the NOS directory when you attempt to log on to a server?

    a. Remapping

    b. Encryption

    c. Authentication

    d. Caching

    e. Redirection

34. You are a network administrator for a WAN that connects two regional insurance company offices—one main office and one satellite office—to each other by a T1. The main office is also connected to the Internet using a T1. This T1 provides Internet access for both offices. To ensure that your private network is not compromised by unauthorized access through the Internet connection, you install a firewall between the main office and the Internet. Shortly thereafter, users in your satellite office complain that they cannot access the file server in the main office, but users in the main office can still access the Internet. What two things should you check?

    a. Whether the firewall has been configured to run in promiscuous mode

    b. Whether the firewall is placed in the appropriate location on the network

    c. Whether the firewall has been configured to allow access from IP addresses in the satellite office

    d. Whether the firewall has been configured to receive and transmit UDP-based packets

    e. Whether the firewall has been configured to allow Internet access over the main office's T1

35. What TCP/IP utility was used to generate the following output, and what piece of information does it tell you about the machine on which the utility shown here was used?

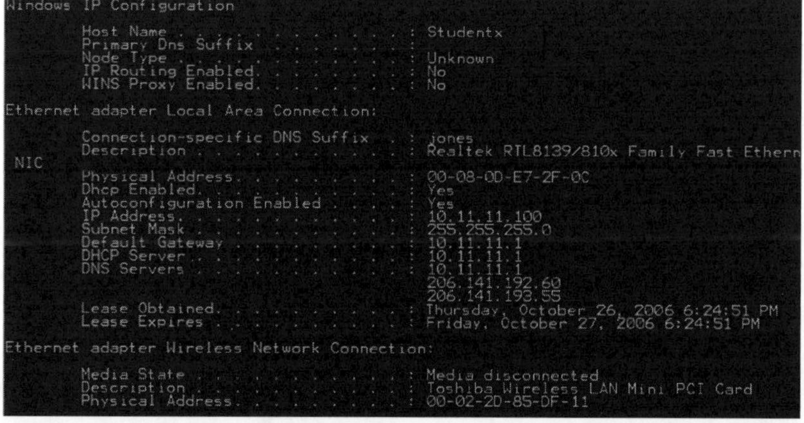

```
Windows IP Configuration

        Host Name . . . . . . . . . . . . : Studentx
        Primary Dns Suffix  . . . . . . . :
        Node Type . . . . . . . . . . . . : Unknown
        IP Routing Enabled. . . . . . . . : No
        WINS Proxy Enabled. . . . . . . . : No

Ethernet adapter Local Area Connection:

        Connection-specific DNS Suffix  . : jones
        Description . . . . . . . . . . . : Realtek RTL8139/810x Family Fast Ethern
        Physical Address. . . . . . . . . : 00-08-0D-E7-2F-0C
        Dhcp Enabled. . . . . . . . . . . : Yes
        Autoconfiguration Enabled . . . . : Yes
        IP Address. . . . . . . . . . . . : 10.11.11.100
        Subnet Mask . . . . . . . . . . . : 255.255.255.0
        Default Gateway . . . . . . . . . : 10.11.11.1
        DHCP Server . . . . . . . . . . . : 10.11.11.1
        DNS Servers . . . . . . . . . . . : 10.11.11.1
                                            206.141.192.60
                                            206.141.193.55
        Lease Obtained. . . . . . . . . . : Thursday, October 26, 2006 6:24:51 PM
        Lease Expires . . . . . . . . . . : Friday, October 27, 2006 6:24:51 PM

Ethernet adapter Wireless Network Connection:

        Media State . . . . . . . . . . . : Media disconnected
        Description . . . . . . . . . . . : Toshiba Wireless LAN Mini PCI Card
        Physical Address. . . . . . . . . : 00-02-2D-85-DF-11
```

a. Ipconfig; the output indicates that the machine has a MAC address of 00080DE72F0C

b. PING; the output indicates that the machine cannot communicate with external hosts

c. ARP; the output indicates that the machine resolves to a name of Studentx

d. Ifconfig; the output indicates that the machine does not rely on DHCP

e. Nbtstat; the output indicates that it is currently connected to the machine with a NetBIOS name of Studentx

36. **While troubleshooting a workstation connectivity problem, you type the following command:** `ping 127.0.0.1`. **The response indicates that the test failed. What can you determine about that workstation?**

a. Its network cable is faulty or not connected to the wall jack.

b. Its TCP/IP protocol is not installed properly.

c. Its IP address has been prevented from transmitting data past the default gateway.

d. Its DHCP settings are incorrect.

e. Its DNS name server specification is incorrect.

37. **You are a support technician working in a telecommunications closet in a remote office. You suspect that a connectivity problem is related to a broken RJ-45 plug on a patch cable that connects a switch to a patch panel. You need to replace that connection, but you forgot to bring an extra patch cable. You decide to install a new RJ-45 connector to replace the broken RJ-45 connector. What two tools should you have to successfully accomplish this?**

a. Punch-down tool

b. Crimping tool

c. Wire stripper

d. Cable tester

e. Multimeter

38. **What types of switches propagate flawed packets and, therefore, can contribute to greater network congestion?**

a. Cut-through switches

b. Transparent bridging switches

c. Store-and-forward switches

d. Layer 3 switches

e. Trunking switches

39. In the IP version 6 addressing scheme, which of the following IP addresses equals the loopback address?

    a. 1.0.0.1

    b. 127:0:0:0:0:0:0:1

    c. 0.0.0.0.0.1

    d. ::1

    e. 127.0.0.1

40. Which two of the following devices operate only at the physical layer of the OSI model?

    a. Hub

    b. Switch

    c. Router

    d. Bridge

    e. Repeater

41. Which of the following is a reason for using subnetting or supernetting?

    a. To facilitate easier migration from IPv4 to IPv6 addressing

    b. To enable a network to use DHCP

    c. To make more efficient use of limited numbers of legitimate IP addresses

    d. To reduce the likelihood for user error when modifying TCP/IP properties

    e. To limit the number of addresses that can be assigned to one network interface

42. In which two of the following switching techniques must multiple data packets that make up the same transmission use identical paths to reach their destination?

    a. Circuit switching

    b. Layer 2 switching

    c. Packet switching

    d. Message switching

    e. Layer 3 switching

43. Which of the following wireless networking technologies can make use of WPA to improve the security of data in transit?

    a. 802.11b

    b. 802.5

    c. Infrared

    d. Bluetooth

    e. 802.3

44. In the following network diagram, which network nodes belong to a private network?

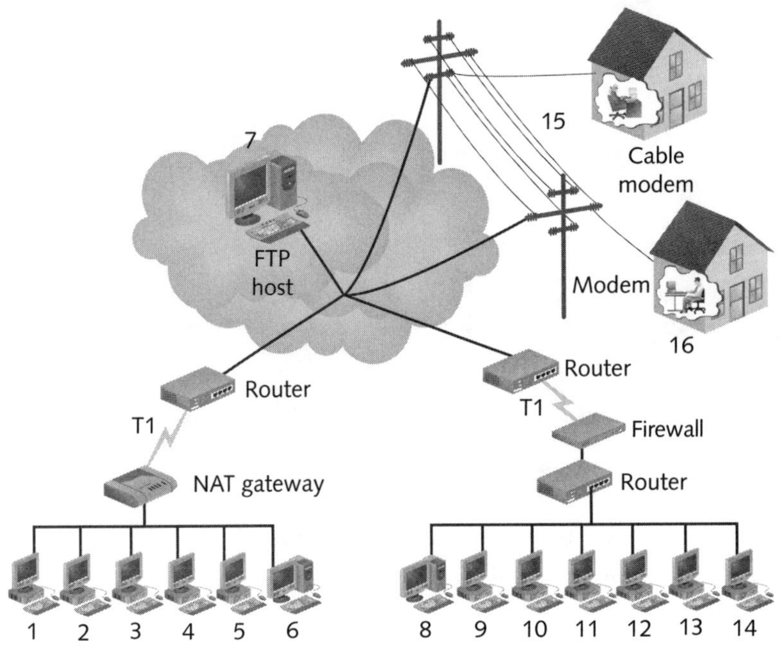

   a. Nodes 1 through 6 and nodes 8 through 14

   b. Nodes 1 through 6 only

   c. Nodes 8 through 14 only

   d. Nodes 1 through 7, plus 15 and 16

   e. All of the nodes

45. You are the network administrator for a law firm whose two primary offices are located five blocks apart in the center of a large city. The two offices have different specialties and, therefore, keep separate file servers. Each file server runs the Windows Server 2003 NOS. A T1 connects the two offices so employees at each office can communicate and share files. To protect the lawyers' records, you currently make regular backups of all the data on both file servers and store the backup tapes in an off-site warehouse. However, one of the firm's partners asked you to do more than simply back up data. In addition, she requests that you implement this added measure within the next week. Which of the following solutions is the best choice to ensure greater data protection in the given time frame?

   a. Contract with an online backup provider to back up data over the Internet using the T1.

   b. Add a UNIX server to the network so that you can establish clustering between all the servers.

   c. Establish mirroring between the two servers using the T1.

   d. Add a RAID level 5 device to one of the file servers.

   e. Connect the T1 to a third office across town, and back up files from the two other locations to the third location.

46. Due to popular demand from employees who need to roam from one floor of your office building to another, you are expanding your wireless network. You want to ensure that mobile users enjoy uninterrupted network connectivity without having to reconfigure their workstations' wireless network connection settings. Which of the following variables must you configure on your new access points to match the settings on existing access points?

    a. Administrator password

    b. Scanning rate

    c. SSID

    d. IP address

    e. Signal strength

47. Which transport protocol and TCP/IP port does the Telnet utility use?

    a. UDP, port 23

    b. TCP, port 21

    c. UDP, port 22

    d. TCP, port 23

    e. UDP, port 21

48. Which two of the following would guarantee that a server continually has power, even if a building's electrical service is interrupted?

    a. RAID level 3

    b. RAID level 5

    c. Online UPS

    d. Standby UPS

    e. Gas-powered generator

49. What protocol is used to transfer mail between a Sendmail server and a Microsoft Exchange server?

    a. SMTP

    b. SNMP

    c. IMAP4

    d. POP3

    e. TFTP

50. What is the function of RARP?

    a. To associate a host name with a given IP address

    b. To associate a MAC address with a given IP address

    c. To associate an IP address with a given MAC address

    d. To associate a NetBIOS name with a given MAC address

    e. To associate a MAC address with a given host name

51. Your 100Base-TX network is wired following the TIA/EIA 568B standard. As you make your own patch cable, which wires do you crimp into pins 1 and 2 of the RJ-45 connector?

    a. White with green stripe and green

    b. White with brown stripe and brown

    c. White with blue stripe and blue

    d. White with red stripe and red

    e. White with orange stripe and orange

52. A regional bank manager asks you to help with an urgent network problem. Because of a sudden and severe network performance decline, the manager worries that the bank's network might be suffering a denial-of-service attack. Viewing which of the following types of network documentation would probably give you the quickest insight into what's causing this problem?

    a. Wiring schematic

    b. Firewall log

    c. Logical network diagram

    d. The main file server's event log

    e. Physical network diagram

53. Which of the following is an application layer protocol used to access information stored in a directory?

    a. LDAP

    b. PPTP

    c. L2TP

    d. PPPoE

    e. ICMP

54. What is the function of protocols and services at the network layer of the OSI model?

    a. To manage the flow of communications over a channel

    b. To add segmentation and assembly information

    c. To encode and encrypt data

    d. To add logical addresses and properly route data

    e. To apply electrical pulses to the wire

55. Which of the following utilities could you use to log on to a UNIX host?

    a. NTP

    b. ARP

    c. PING

    d. Telnet

    e. SNMP

56. **As a networking professional, you might use a multimeter to do which of the following? (Choose all that apply.)**

    a. Determine where the patch cable for a specific server terminates on the patch panel

    b. Verify that the amount of resistance presented by terminators on coaxial cable networks is appropriate

    c. Check for the presence of noise on a wire (by detecting extraneous voltage)

    d. Confirm that a fiber-optic cable can transmit signals from one node to another

    e. Validate the processing capabilities of a new router

57. **On your UNIX workstation, what command(s) would you type at the shell prompt to send a file to the printer queue? (Choose all that apply.)**

    a. `prn` *filename*

    b. `lpr` *filename*

    c. `lpd` *filename*

    d. `ftp` *filename*

    e. `ps` *filename*

58. **What is the default subnet mask for the following IP address: 154.13.44.87?**

    a. 255.255.255.255

    b. 255.255.255.0

    c. 255.255.0.0

    d. 255.0.0.0

    e. 0.0.0.0

59. **Which of the following diagrams illustrates a SONET network?**

    a.

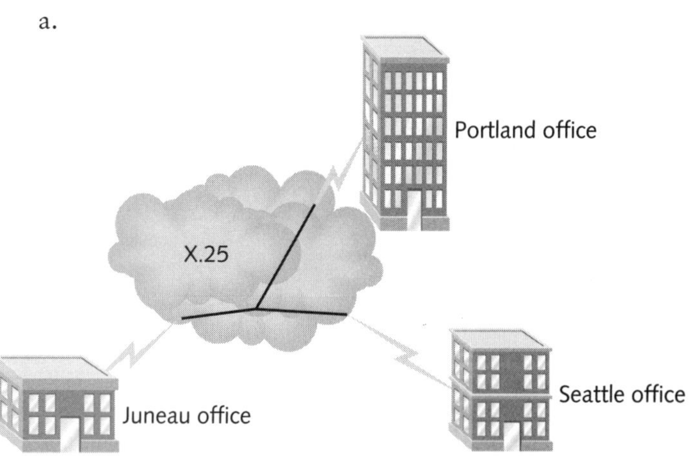

b.

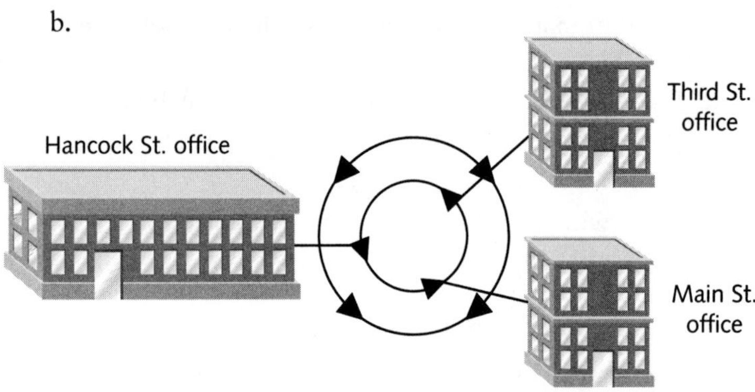

Hancock St. office
Third St. office
Main St. office

Archer St. office
Third St. office
Main St. office
Hancock St. office

Hancock St. office
Third St. office
Main St. office
Archer St. office
Oak St. office
Pine St. office

c.

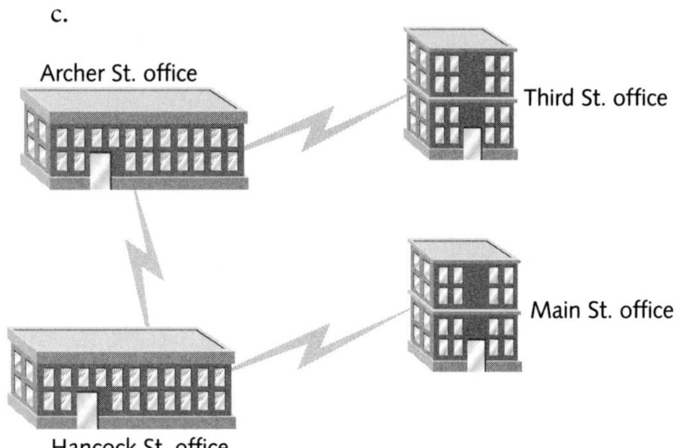

d.

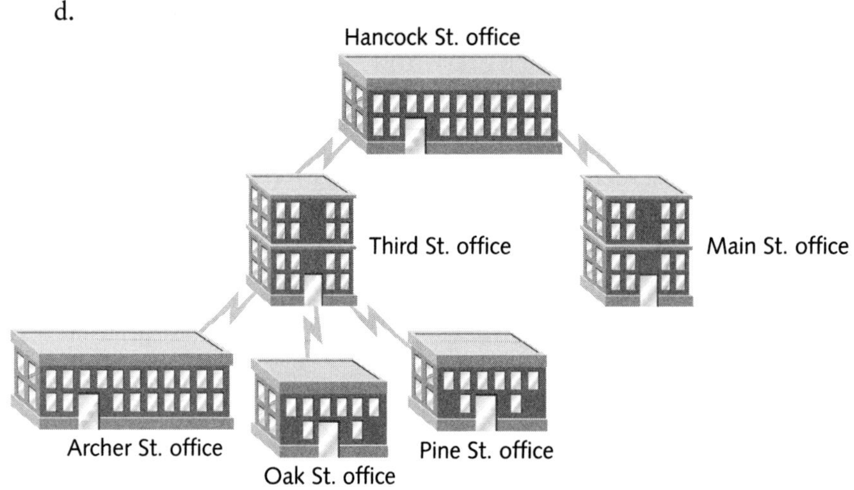

e.

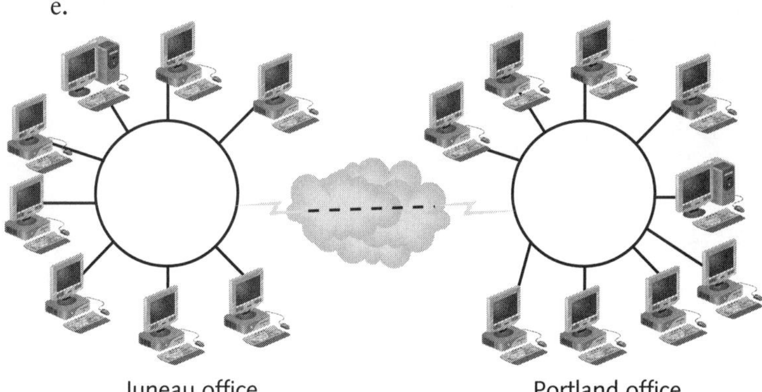

60. You are a support technician installing 13 new Windows Vista workstations on your company's network, which relies on several Windows Server 2008 servers for authentication and file sharing, one Gentoo Linux e-mail server, and one Gentoo Linux proxy server. The network runs the TCP/IP protocol over 100Base-TX Ethernet technology. It also uses DHCP and NAT. Which of the following settings must you manually specify on each workstation so that their users can pick up their Internet e-mail from the Linux e-mail server?

   a. DNS server address

   b. IP address

   c. WINS server name

   d. NTP server address

   e. SMTP server name

61. Which of the following protocols does not operate at the application layer of the OSI model?

   a. POP3

   b. SMTP

   c. ARP

   d. NTP

   e. DNS

62. Which of the following authentication protocols does not issue a challenge or require third-party verification of the computer requesting authentication?

   a. PAP

   b. CHAP

   c. MS-CHAP

   d. EAP

   e. Kerberos

63. You have decided to create two separate VLANs in your office: one for computers on the first floor of your building, and one for computers on the second floor. What type of device will you need for clients on the first floor to communicate with clients on the second floor?

    a. Router

    b. Switch

    c. Bridge

    d. Hub

    e. Repeater

64. You have been asked to help improve network performance on a store's small office network, which relies on two hubs, two access points, and a router to connect its 18 employees to the Internet and other store locations. You decide to determine what type of traffic the network currently handles. In particular, you're interested in the volume of unnecessary broadcast traffic that might be bogging down shared segments. Which of the following tools will help you identify the percentage of traffic that comprises broadcasts?

    a. Butt set

    b. OTDR

    c. Spectrum analyzer

    d. Network monitor

    e. Multimeter

65. What types of files does an incremental backup save?

    a. Data that changed prior to the previous incremental backup

    b. Data that changed since the previous full or incremental backup

    c. All data, regardless of whether it has changed

    d. Data that was backed up exactly a week previously

    e. Data that users have flagged for backup since the last backup occurred

66. You are setting up a new Windows Vista client to connect with your LAN, which relies on DHCP. You made certain that the client has the TCP/IP protocol installed and bound to its NIC. Which of the following must you do next to ensure that the client obtains correct TCP/IP information via DHCP?

    a. Make certain the client's computer name and host name are identical.

    b. Enter the client's MAC address in the DHCP server's ARP table.

    c. Make sure the Client for Microsoft Networks service is bound to the client's NIC.

    d. Enter the DHCP server address in the Windows Vista TCP/IP configuration.

    e. Nothing; in Windows Vista, the DHCP option is selected by default, and the client will obtain IP addressing information upon connecting to the network.

67. You are a support technician trying to help a user configure a new graphics program she installed on her laptop. The laptop runs Ubuntu Linux. After some failed attempts at talking her through the process, you decide to remotely take over her workstation and walk her through the process. Which of the following open source software programs would allow you to do this?

    a. Remote Desktop

    b. RealVNC

    c. OpenConnect

    d. ICA (Independent Computing Architecture) Client

    e. RAS (Remote Access Service)

68. Which of the following devices separates broadcast domains?

    a. Hub

    b. Switch

    c. Bridge

    d. Repeater

    e. Router

69. Which one of the following media is most resistant to EMI?

    a. Coaxial cable

    b. UTP cable

    c. STP cable

    d. Fiber-optic cable

    e. Infrared waves

70. In the following figure, if router B suffers a failure, how will nodes 1 through 9 be affected?

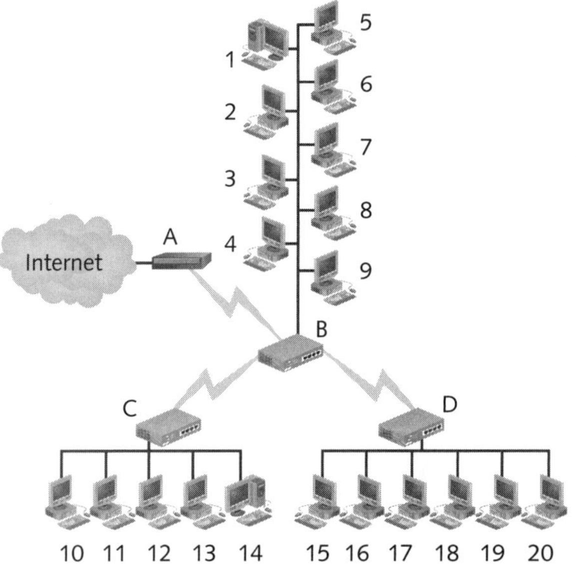

a. They will only be unable to access the Internet.

b. They will be unable to access the Internet and *either* nodes 10 through 14 or 15 through 20.

c. They will be unable to access the Internet, other nodes on the WAN, and other nodes on the LAN.

d. They will be unable to access the Internet and nodes 10 through 20.

e. Their connectivity will not be affected.

71. Which of the following routing protocols has the poorest convergence time?

a. RIP

b. EIGRP

c. OSPF

d. BGP

e. IGRP

72. Which of the following ports would be used during a domain name lookup?

a. 22

b. 23

c. 53

d. 110

e. 443

73. Suppose you have created six subnets on your network, which leases a group of Class C IPv4 addresses. What subnet mask must you specify in your clients' configurations to adhere to your subnetting scheme?

a. 255.255.255.6

b. 255.255.255.128

c. 255.255.255.192

d. 255.255.255.224

e. 255.255.255.252

74. Which of the following protocols encapsulates data for transmission over VPNs?

a. CHAP

b. SNMP

c. L2TP

d. SFTP

e. MPLS

75. You have begun a new job with an ISP, and one of your first tasks is to configure a replacement router for the router that now handles traffic to and from the company's connection to its NSP (network service provider). Which of the following routing protocols will the router likely use?

    a. RIP

    b. BGP

    c. IS-IS

    d. IGRP

    e. RIPv2

76. Which of the following wireless networking standards can reliably transmit data the farthest?

    a. Bluetooth

    b. 802.11a

    c. 802.11b

    d. 802.11c

    e. 802.11n

77. How does STP (Spanning Tree Protocol) prevent or stop broadcast storms?

    a. It examines the source IP address field in each broadcast packet and temporarily blocks traffic from that address.

    b. It enables routers to choose one set of best paths and ensures that alternate paths are used only when the best paths are obstructed.

    c. It enables switches to calculate paths that avoid potential loops and artificially blocks the links that would complete a loop.

    d. It enables firewalls to keep access lists that name hosts known for high-volume broadcast traffic and block those hosts from transmitting to the network.

    e. It helps routers define the boundaries of a broadcast domain.

78. Which of the following standards describes a security technique, often used on wireless networks, in which a port is prevented from receiving traffic until the transmitter's credentials are verified by an authentication server?

    a. EAPoL

    b. SSH

    c. SSL

    d. Kerberos

    e. MS-CHAP

79. If a Windows Vista workstation is configured to use DHCP but cannot find a DHCP server, it will assign itself an address and subnet mask. Which of the following IPv4 addresses might it assign itself?

    a. 129.0.0.1

    b. 255.255.255.255

    c. 123.45.67.89

    d. 169.254.1.120

    e. 987.65.432.1

80. Suppose your Windows Vista workstation's wireless network adapter is configured to use the 802.11b wireless networking standard. Also, suppose a café you visit has an 802.11g access point. Assuming you have the correct SSID and logon credentials, what will happen when you attempt to associate with the café's wireless network?

    a. Your wireless networking client will be able to see the access point but unable to associate with it.

    b. Your wireless networking client will not be able to see the access point.

    c. Your wireless networking client will be able to see the access point and attempt to associate with it, but the incompatible frequencies will prevent successful authentication.

    d. Your wireless networking client will be able to see the access point and attempt to associate with it, but the incompatible security techniques will prevent successful authentication.

    e. Your wireless networking client will be able to see the access point and successfully associate with it.

81. Routers use IGMP to:

    a. Identify nodes belonging to a multicast group

    b. Communicate with other routers about the best path between nodes

    c. Reserve bandwidth for priority transmissions, ensuring high QoS

    d. Filter out potentially harmful packets

    e. Predict the expected round-trip time of a packet over a WAN

82. Which of the following techniques would allow you and eight coworkers to share a single Internet-routable IP address?

    a. IPX/SPX

    b. DNAT

    c. DHCP

    d. SNAT

    e. LLAT

83. You work for a large fashion design firm. Because of a recent TV promotion, your company has received national recognition. At the same time, your WAN has received more security threats. To help fend off these threats, you decide to implement an IPS/IDS. Following is a simplified network diagram that represents your private network and its public network connection. Where on this diagram would you place the IPS/IDS device?

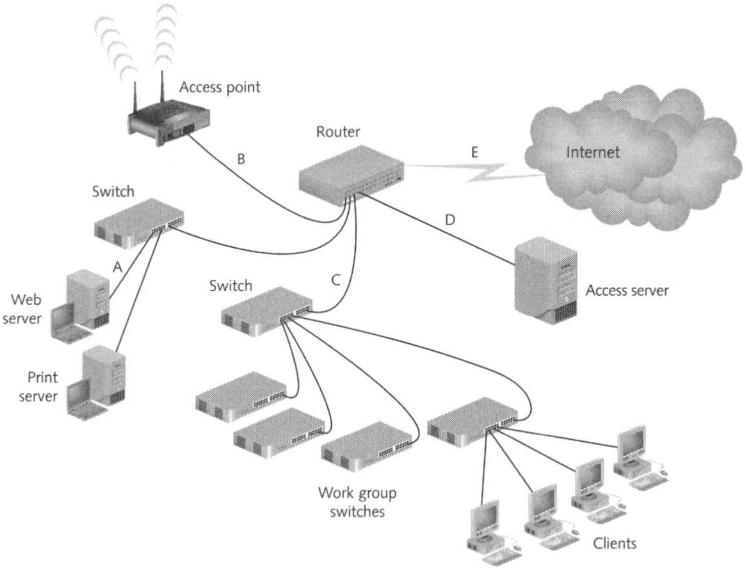

84. A user watching an episode of a popular TV show over the Internet is an example of what type of communication?

   a. Unicast

   b. Multicast

   c. Broadcast

   d. Point-to-multipoint

   e. Multipoint-to-point

85. What's the difference between a rollover cable and a crossover cable?

   a. In a rollover cable, only two wire pairs are reversed, while in a crossover cable, all wire pairs are reversed.

   b. In a rollover cable, no wires are reversed, while in a crossover cable, all wires are reversed.

   c. In a rollover cable, all wires are reversed, while in a crossover cable, only two wire pairs are reversed.

   d. In a rollover cable, one wire pair is reversed, while in a crossover cable, three wire pairs are reversed.

   e. In a rollover cable, three wire pairs are reversed, while in a crossover cable, no wires are reversed.

86. If you use RIP on your LAN, what is the maximum number of hops a packet can take between its source and its destination?

    a. 3

    b. 5

    c. 10

    d. 15

    e. 18

87. You work for a telephone company that provides Internet service via dial-up and DSL connections. One day you have the chance to work in the field with an older telephone technician. You stop at an intersection and open a pedestal where telephone pairs terminate. Which of the following tools does the technician use to determine whether a customer's line is obtaining dial tone from the CO?

    a. OTDR

    b. Network monitor

    c. Protocol analyzer

    d. Butt set

    e. Cable continuity tester

88. Which of the following QoS techniques enables packet-switched technologies to travel over traditionally circuit-switched connections?

    a. ATM

    b. SONET

    c. MPLS

    d. Frame relay

    e. Trunking

89. Every employee in your company receives an e-mail that appears to have been sent from the CEO but wasn't. The message instructs employees to click on a link to update their personnel profile. In fact, the link takes them to a Web site that appears to be a company-sponsored site but is actually one designed by a hacker to capture personal data, such as Social Security numbers and credit card information, from employees. The hacker is using which of the following techniques? (Choose all that apply.)

    a. Denial-of-service attack

    b. Phishing

    c. Spoofing

    d. Flashing

    e. Smurf attack

90. How does a switch know which VLAN a stream of data belongs to?

    a. It reads the FCS in each packet's header.

    b. It keeps a table of source and target MAC addresses and their associated VLANs and refers to that table when examining each datagram.

c. It reads a tag added to each frame's header.

d. It searches for an identifying pattern in the Data field of each frame.

e. The VLAN information is clear from an envelope that encapsulates each packet.

91. **The following graph, which represents traffic activity for an ISP's client, indicates that the ISP is utilizing what traffic-shaping technique?**

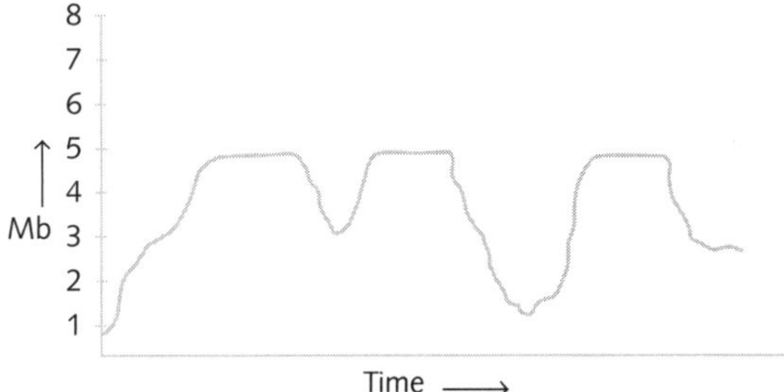

a. Traffic policing

b. Caching

c. Load balancing

d. Access list controls

e. Fault tolerance

92. **Your company's network administrator has told you that you may operate a Web server for employees to access as long as it remains inside the demilitarized zone. What does she mean by this?**

a. You may set up a Web server on your home network.

b. You may set up a Web server on the company's access server, which allows clients from around the globe to connect to your WAN.

c. You may set up a Web server at a hosting facility outside of the company's LAN or WAN.

d. You may set up a Web server on the company's private LAN, which is protected by a firewall.

e. You may not set up a Web server on the company's LAN or WAN.

93. **You are a help desk analyst for a pharmaceutical company whose salespeople travel around the world. One day you receive a call from a sales representative who cannot access the company's VPN. You identify and record the user's symptoms in a help desk database. You verify that he is correctly performing the steps required to connect to the VPN, and you establish that nothing else has changed on his laptop. In addition, you attempt to connect to the VPN and cannot. While you are talking with the sales representative, two other employees call and complain that they cannot access the company's VPN. What is your next step in troubleshooting the problem?**

a. Create an action plan and solution and be prepared for all potential effects.

b. Determine whether escalation is necessary.

c. Implement a solution and test the result.

d. Identify the results and effects of the solution.

e. Establish the most probable cause.

94. If an organization follows structured cabling standards, where would its demarc be located?

    a. Entrance facilities

    b. MDF

    c. IDF

    d. Cross-connect facilities

    e. Backbone

95. You are helping to troubleshoot a recurring problem related to obtaining and keeping a DHCP-distributed IP address on a colleague's Windows Vista workstation. What application would allow you to configure the workstation to tally these errors and send you an e-mail message every time such a problem occurred?

    a. Network and Internet Connections

    b. System Logger

    c. PuTTY

    d. System Manager

    e. Event Viewer

96. What type of satellites are typically used for broadband Internet access?

    a. Low Earth orbiting

    b. Medium Earth orbiting

    c. High Earth orbiting

    d. Multipath

    e. Geosynchronous

97. In IPv6 addressing, which of the following Format Prefixes indicates that an address belongs to a multicast group?

    a. 00FF

    b. 1F3E

    c. FF02

    d. 0001

    e. FEC0

98. Suppose your WAN contained a segment that relied on the 10GBase-EW standard. Which of the following transmission technologies would it use?

    a. SONET

    b. Satellite

    c. Broadband cable

    d. DSL

    e. ISDN

99. To provide some basic security for your small office network, you install software called IP Tables on an old Linux computer. This software examines each incoming datagram. Based on a set of criteria, including source IP address, source and destination ports, and protocols, it blocks or allows traffic. What type of system is this? (Choose all that apply.)

    a. Content-filtering firewall

    b. Stateful firewall

    c. Stateless firewall

    d. Packet-filtering firewall

    e. Application layer firewall

100. Ethernet and ATM both specify data link layer framing techniques. How do they differ?

    a. Ethernet uses CRC fields to confirm the validity of the frame, while ATM uses no error detection.

    b. Ethernet uses variably sized packets, while ATM uses fixed-sized cells.

    c. Ethernet uses synchronous transmission, while ATM uses asynchronous transmission.

    d. Ethernet uses frame headers, while ATM does not.

    e. Ethernet offers no guarantee of timely delivery, while ATM ensures that packets are delivered within 10ms.

Visual Guide to Connectors

Throughout this book, you learned about several cabling and connector options that may be used on networks. Some, such as RJ-45, are very common, whereas others, such as Fiber LC connectors, are used only on newer, high-speed networks. So that you can compare such connectors and ensure that you understand their differences, this Appendix compiles drawings of the connectors and a brief summary of their uses in a simple table. You must be familiar with the most popular types of connectors to qualify for Network+ certification. You can find more detail about these connectors and the networks on which they are used in Chapter 3 and 6.

Table C-1 Network Connectors and Their Uses

Specification	Male Connector (Front View)	Male Connector (Side View)	Female Receptacle (Front View)	Application
BNC				Used with coaxial cable for broadband cable connections; also used on old Ethernet networks such as Thinnet.
RJ-11 (Registered Jack 11)				Used on twisted-pair cabling for telephone systems (and some older twisted-pair networks)
RJ-45 (Registered Jack 45)				Used on twisted-pair cabling for modern networks
F-Type				Used on coaxial cable suitable for use with broadband video and data applications

Table C-1 Network Connectors and Their Uses (*continued*)

Specification	Male Connector (Front View)	Male Connector (Side View)	Female Receptacle (Front View)	Application
ST (Straight Tip)				Used on fiber-optic cabling (for example, on 100Base-FX, Gigabit, and 10Gb Ethernet networks)
SC (Subscriber Connector or Standard Connector)				Used on fiber-optic cabling (for example, on 100Base-FX, Gigabit, and 10Gb Ethernet networks)
Fiber LC (Local Connector), Single-mode				Used on fiber-optic cabling (for example, on 100Base-FX, Gigabit, and 10Gb Ethernet networks)
MT-RJ (Mechanical Transfer-Register Jack)				Used on fiber-optic cabling (for example, on 100Base-FX, Gigabit, and 10Gb Ethernet networks)
DB-9				One of the RS-232 standard connectors used in serial connections; also used on older token ring networks
DB-25				One of the RS-232 standard connectors used in serial connections
USB (Universal Serial Bus)				Used to connect external peripherals, such as modems, mice, audio players, NICs, cameras, PDAs, and smartphones

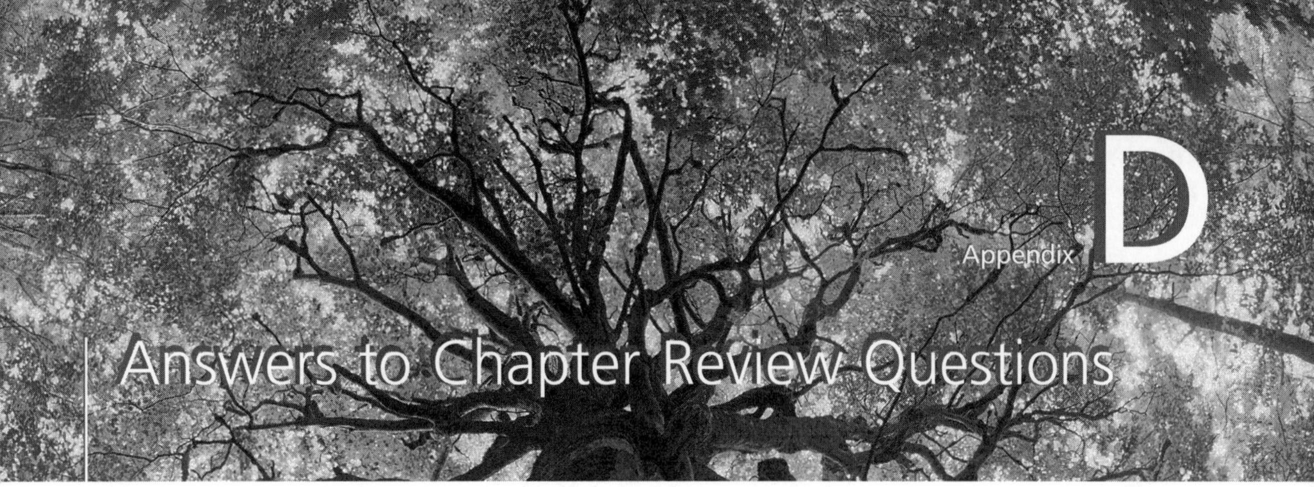

Answers to Chapter Review Questions

Chapter 1

1. d
2. b
3. b
4. b
5. d
6. False
7. True
8. False
9. False
10. False
11. network
12. peer-to-peer
13. scalable
14. network services
15. certification

Chapter 2

1. b
2. c
3. d
4. a
5. d
6. True
7. False
8. False
9. True
10. False
11. voluntary
12. RIR (Regional Internet Registry)
13. OSI (Open Systems Interconnection)
14. application
15. Encapsulation

Chapter 3

1. c
2. c
3. b
4. c
5. d
6. True
7. True
8. False
9. True
10. True
11. Overhead
12. modulation
13. multiplexing
14. straight-through
15. RS-232 (Recommended Standard 232)

Chapter 4

1. c
2. b
3. c
4. a
5. d
6. False
7. False
8. True
9. True
10. True
11. routable
12. dotted decimal notation
13. subnet mask
14. APIPA (Automatic Private IP Addressing)
15. socket

Chapter 5

1. b
2. c
3. c
4. a
5. a
6. True
7. False
8. True
9. True
10. True
11. topology
12. logical topology
13. CSMA/CD (Carrier Sense Multiple Access with Collision Detection)
14. Ethernet_II (DIX)
15. PoE (Power over Ethernet)

Chapter 6

1. c
2. d
3. a
4. b
5. d
6. False
7. True
8. True
9. True
10. False
11. repeater
12. hub
13. bridge
14. cut-through
15. Gateways

Chapter 7

1. c
2. b
3. b
4. c
5. a
6. True
7. False

8. False
9. True
10. True
11. mesh
12. tiered
13. PSTN (Public Switched Telephone Network)
14. RAS (Remote Access Service)
15. Remote virtual computing

Chapter 8

1. b
2. c
3. a
4. b
5. c
6. False
7. False
8. False
9. False
10. True
11. mobile
12. Bluetooth
13. site survey
14. WiMAX (Worldwide Interoperability for Microwave Access)
15. Geosynchronous

Chapter 9

1. a
2. b
3. a
4. a
5. c
6. True
7. True
8. False
9. False
10. True
11. redirector
12. middleware
13. schema
14. OUs (organizational units)
15. shares

Chapter 10

1. d
2. d
3. b
4. b
5. b
6. False
7. True
8. True
9. False
10. True
11. Subnetting
12. CIDR (Classless Interdomain Routing)
13. NAT (Network Address Translation)
14. ICS (Internet Connection Sharing)
15. MIME (Multipurpose Internet Mail Extensions)

Chapter 11

1. b
2. c
3. a
4. d
5. b
6. False
7. True
8. False
9. True
10. True
11. IP telephony
12. H.323
13. SIP (Session Initiation Protocol)
14. MGC (media gateway controller)
15. RSVP (Resource Reservation Protocol)

Chapter 12

1. b
2. d
3. a
4. a
5. d
6. True
7. False

8. False
9. True
10. True
11. security audit
12. security policy
13. proxy service
14. public key
15. WEP (Wired Equivalent Privacy)

Chapter 13

1. b
2. d
3. c
4. b
5. c
6. True
7. False
8. True
9. False
10. True
11. call tracking
12. multimeter
13. network monitor
14. protocol
15. spectrum analyzer

Chapter 14

1. d
2. a
3. a
4. a
5. d
6. True
7. True
8. True
9. True
10. False
11. integrity
12. availability
13. Polymorphic
14. anti-malware policy
15. standby

Chapter 15

1. b
2. d
3. c
4. c
5. b
6. True
7. False
8. False
9. True
10. True
11. Network
12. Traffic shaping
13. Caching
14. patch
15. backleveling

1 gigabit per second (Gbps) 1,000,000,000 bits per second.

1 kilobit per second (Kbps) 1,000 bits per second.

1 megabit per second (Mbps) 1,000,000 bits per second.

1 terabit per second (Tbps) 1,000,000,000,000 bits per second.

2.4GHz band The range of radio frequencies from 2.4 to 2.4835GHz. The 2.4GHz band, which allows for 11 unlicensed channels, is used by WLANs that follow the popular 802.11b and 802.11g standards. However, it is also used for cordless telephone and other transmissions, making the 2.4GHz band more susceptible to interference than the 5GHz band.

3DES *See* Triple DES.

3-tier architecture A client/server environment that uses middleware to translate requests between the client and server.

5GHz band A range of frequencies that comprises four frequency bands: 5.1GHz, 5.3GHz, 5.4GHz, and 5.8GHz. It consists of 24 unlicensed bands, each 20MHz wide. The 5GHz band is used by WLANs that follow the 802.11a and 802.11n standards.

5-4-3 rule A guideline for 10Mbps Ethernet networks stating that between two communicating nodes, the network cannot contain more than five network segments connected by four repeating devices, and no more than three of the segments may be populated.

10Base-2 *See* Thinnet.

10Base-5 *See* Thicknet.

10Base-T A physical layer standard for networks that specifies baseband transmission, twisted pair media, and 10Mbps throughput. 10Base-T networks have a maximum segment length of 100 meters and rely on a star topology.

10GBase-ER A physical layer standard for achieving 10Gbps data transmission over single-mode, fiber-optic cable. In 10GBase-ER, the *ER* stands for *extended reach*. This standard specifies a star topology and segment lengths up to 40 kilometers.

10GBase-EW A variation of the 10GBase-ER standard that is specially encoded to operate over SONET WAN links.

10GBase-LR A physical layer standard for achieving 10Gbps data transmission over single-mode, fiber-optic cable using wavelengths of 1,310 nanometers. In 10GBase-LR, the *LR* stands for *long reach*. This standard specifies a star topology and segment lengths up to 10 kilometers.

10GBase-LW A variation of the 10GBase-LR standard that is specially encoded to operate over SONET WAN links.

10GBase-SR A physical layer standard for achieving 10Gbps data transmission over multimode fiber using wavelengths of 850 nanometers. The maximum segment length for 10GBase-SR can reach up to 300 meters, depending on the fiber core diameter and modal bandwidth used.

10GBase-SW A variation of the 10GBase-SR standard that is specially encoded to operate over SONET WAN links.

10GBase-T A physical layer standard for achieving 10Gbps data transmission over twisted pair cable. Described in its 2006 standard 802.3an, IEEE specifies Cat 6 or Cat 7 cable as the appropriate medium for 10GBase-T. The maximum segment length for 10GBase-T is 100 meters.

25 pair wire UTP supplied by a telecommunications carrier that contains 25 wire pairs.

66 block Part of an organization's cross-connect facilities, a type of punch-down block used for many years to terminate telephone circuits. It does not meet Cat 5 or better standards, so it is infrequently used on data networks.

100 block Part of an organization's cross-connect facilities, a type of punch-down block designed to terminate Cat 5 or better twisted pair wires.

100 pair wire UTP supplied by a telecommunications carrier that contains 100 wire pairs.

100Base-FX A physical layer standard for networks that specifies baseband transmission, multimode fiber cabling, and 100Mbps throughput. 100Base-FX networks have a maximum segment length of 2,000 meters. 100Base-FX may also be called Fast Ethernet.

100Base-T A physical layer standard for networks that specifies baseband transmission, twisted pair cabling, and 100Mbps throughput. 100Base-T networks have a maximum segment length of 100 meters and use the star topology. 100Base-T is also known as Fast Ethernet.

100Base-TX A type of 100Base-T network that uses two wire pairs in a twisted pair cable but uses faster signaling to achieve 100Mbps throughput. It is capable of full-duplex transmission and requires Cat 5 or higher twisted pair media.

802.1D The IEEE standard that describes, among other things, bridging and STP (Spanning Tree Protocol).

802.1w The IEEE standard that describes RSTP (Rapid Spanning Tree Protocol), which evolved from STP (Spanning Tree Protocol).

802.1x A vendor-independent IEEE standard for securing transmission between nodes according to the transmission's port, whether physical or logical. 802.1x, also known as EAPoL, is the authentication standard followed by wireless networks using 802.11i.

802.2 The IEEE standard for error and flow control in data frames.

802.3 The IEEE standard for Ethernet networking devices and data handling (using the CSMA/CD access method).

802.3ab The IEEE standard that describes 1000Base-T, a 1-Gigabit Ethernet technology that runs over four pairs of Cat 5 or better cable.

802.3ae The IEEE standard that describes 10-Gigabit Ethernet technologies, including 10GBase-SR, 10GBase-SW, 10GBase-LR, 10GBase-LW, 10GBase-ER, and 10GBase-EW.

802.3af The IEEE standard that specifies a way of supplying electrical Power over Ethernet (PoE). 802.3af requires Cat 5 or better UTP or STP cabling and uses power sourcing equipment to supply current over a wire pair to powered devices. PoE is compatible with existing 10Base-T, 100Base-TX, 1000Base-T, and 10GBase-T implementations.

802.3an The IEEE standard that describes 10GBase-T, a 10Gbps Ethernet technology that runs on Cat 6 or Cat 7 twisted pair cable.

802.3u The IEEE standard that describes Fast Ethernet technologies, including 100Base-TX.

802.3z The IEEE standard that describes 1000Base (or 1-Gigabit) Ethernet technologies, including 1000Base-LX and 1000Base-SX.

802.5 The IEEE standard for token ring networking devices and data handling.

802.11 The IEEE standard for wireless networking.

802.11a The IEEE standard for a wireless networking technique that uses multiple frequency bands in the 5GHz frequency range and provides a theoretical maximum throughput of 54Mbps. 802.11a's high throughput, compared with 802.11b, is attributable to its use of higher frequencies, its unique method of encoding data, and more available bandwidth.

802.11b The IEEE standard for a wireless networking technique that uses DSSS (direct-sequence spread spectrum) signaling in the 2.4 to 2.4835GHz frequency range (also called the 2.4GHz band). 802.11b separates the 2.4GHz band into 14 overlapping 22MHz channels and provides a theoretical maximum of 11Mbps throughput.

802.11g The IEEE standard for a wireless networking technique designed to be compatible with 802.11b while using different encoding techniques that allow it to reach a theoretical maximum capacity of 54Mbps. 802.11g, like 802.11b, uses the 2.4GHz frequency band.

802.11i The IEEE standard for wireless network encryption and authentication that uses the EAP authentication method, strong encryption, and dynamically assigned keys, which are different for every transmission. 802.11i specifies AES encryption and weaves a key into each packet.

802.11n The IEEE standard for a wireless networking technique that may issue signals in the 2.4 or 5GHz band and can achieve actual data throughput between 65 and 600Mbps. It accomplishes this through several means, including MIMO, channel bonding, and frame aggregation. 802.11n is backward compatible with 802.11a, b, and g.

802.16 An IEEE standard for wireless MANs. 802.16 networks may use frequencies between 2 and 66GHz. Their antennas may operate in a line-of-sight or non-line-of-sight manner and cover 50 kilometers (or approximately 30 miles). 802.16 connections can achieve a maximum throughput of 70Mbps, though actual throughput diminishes as the distance between transceivers increases. Several 802.16 standards exist. Collectively, they are known as WiMAX.

802.16e Currently, the most popular version of WiMAX. With 802.16e, IEEE improved the mobility and QoS characteristics of the technology, making it better suited to VoIP and mobile phone users.

1000Base-LX A physical layer standard for networks that specifies 1Gbps transmission over fiber-optic cable using baseband transmission. 1000Base-LX can run on either single-mode or multimode fiber. The *LX* represents its reliance on long wavelengths of 1,300 nanometers. 1000Base-LX can extend to 5,000-meter segment lengths using single-mode, fiber-optic cable. 1000Base-LX networks can use one repeater between segments.

1000Base-SX A physical layer standard for networks that specifies 1Gbps transmission over fiber-optic cable using baseband transmission. 1000Base-SX runs on multimode fiber. Its maximum segment length is 550 meters. The *SX* represents its reliance on short wavelengths of 850 nanometers. 1000Base-SX can use one repeater.

1000Base-T A physical layer standard for achieving 1Gbps over UTP. 1000Base-T achieves its higher throughput by using all four pairs of wires in a Cat 5 or higher twisted pair cable to both transmit and receive signals. 1000Base-T also uses a different data encoding scheme than that used by other UTP physical layer specifications.

A+ The professional certification established by CompTIA that verifies knowledge about PC operation, repair, and management.

AAA (authentication, authorization, and accounting) The name of a category of protocols that establish a client's identity; check the client's credentials and, based on those, allow or deny access to a system or network; and finally, track the client's system or network usage.

access control list *See* ACL.

access list *See* ACL.

access method A network's method of controlling how nodes access the communications channel. For example, CSMA/CD (Carrier Sense Multiple Access with Collision Detection) is the access method specified in the IEEE 802.3 (Ethernet) standard.

access point A device used on wireless LANs that transmits and receives wireless signals to and from multiple nodes and retransmits them to the rest of the network segment. Access points can connect a group of nodes with a network or two networks with each other. They may use directional or omnidirectional antennas.

access server *See* remote access server.

account A record of a user that contains all of her properties, including rights to resources, password, user name, and so on.

ACK (acknowledgment) A response generated at the transport layer of the OSI model that confirms to a sender that its frame was received. The ACK packet is the third of three in the three-step process of establishing a connection.

acknowledgment *See* ACK.

ACL (access control list) A list of statements used by a router to permit or deny the forwarding of traffic on a network based on one or more criteria.

Active Directory The method for organizing and managing objects associated with the network in the Windows Server 2003 and Server 2008 NOSs.

active scanning A method used by wireless stations to detect the presence of an access point. In active scanning, the station issues a probe to each channel in its frequency range and waits for the access point to respond.

active topology A topology in which each workstation participates in transmitting data over the network. A ring topology is considered an active topology.

ad hoc A type of wireless LAN in which stations communicate directly with each other (rather than using an access point).

address A number that uniquely identifies each workstation and device on a network. Without unique addresses, computers on the network could not reliably communicate.

address management The process of centrally administering a finite number of network addresses for an entire LAN. Usually this task can be accomplished without touching the client workstations.

Address Resolution Protocol *See* ARP.

address resource record A type of DNS data record that maps the IP address of an Internet-connected device to its domain name.

addressing The scheme for assigning a unique identifying number to every workstation and device on the network. The type of addressing used on a network depends on its protocols and network operating system.

administrator A user account that has unlimited privileges to resources and objects managed by a server or domain. The administrator account is created during NOS installation.

Advanced Encryption Standard *See* AES.

AES (Advanced Encryption Standard) A private key encryption algorithm that weaves keys of 128, 160, 192, or 256 bits through data multiple times. The algorithm used in the most popular form of AES is known as Rijndael. AES has replaced DES in situations such as military communications, which require the highest level of security.

AF (Assured Forwarding) In the DiffServ QoS technique, a forwarding specification that allows routers to assign data streams one of several prioritization levels. AF is specified in the DiffServ field in an IPv4 datagram.

agent A software routine that collects data about a managed device's operation and provides it to the network management application running on the console.

AH (authentication header) In the context of IPSec, a type of encryption that provides authentication of the IP packet's data payload through public key techniques.

AIX A proprietary implementation of the UNIX system distributed by IBM.

alias A nickname for a node's host name. Aliases can be specified in a local host file.

alien cross talk EMI interference induced on one cable by signals traveling over a nearby cable.

AM (amplitude modulation) A modulation technique in which the amplitude of the carrier signal is modified by the application of a data signal.

American National Standards Institute *See* ANSI.

American Wire Gauge *See* AWG.

amplifier A device that boosts, or strengthens, an analog signal.

amplitude A measure of a signal's strength.

amplitude modulation *See* AM.

analog A signal that uses variable voltage to create continuous waves, resulting in an inexact transmission.

analog telephone adapter *See* ATA.

ANDing A logical process of combining bits. In ANDing, a bit with a value of 1 plus another bit with a value of 1 results in a 1. A bit with a value of 0 plus any other bit results in a 0.

ANSI (American National Standards Institute) An organization composed of more than 1,000 representatives from industry and government who together determine standards for the electronics industry in addition to other fields, such as chemical and nuclear engineering, health and safety, and construction.

anycast address A type of address specified in IPv6 that represents a group of interfaces, any one of which (and usually the first available of which) can accept a transmission. At this time, anycast addresses are not designed to be assigned to hosts, such as servers or workstations, but rather to routers.

AP *See* access point.

API (application program interface) A set of routines that make up part of a software application.

APIPA (Automatic Private IP Addressing) A service available on computers running the Windows 98, Me, 2000, XP, Vista, Server 2003, or Server 2008 operating system that automatically assigns the computer's network interface an IP address from the range of 169.254.0.0 to 169.254.255.255 if an IP address hasn't been assigned to that interface.

application gateway *See* proxy server.

application layer The seventh layer of the OSI model. Application layer protocols enable software programs to negotiate formatting, procedural, security, synchronization, and other requirements with the network.

application layer gateway *See* proxy server.

application program interface *See* API.

application switch A switch that provides functions between Layer 4 and Layer 7 of the OSI model.

archive bit A file attribute that can be checked (or set to "on") or unchecked (or set to "off") to indicate whether the file needs to be archived. An operating system checks a file's archive bit when it is created or changed.

ARP (Address Resolution Protocol) A core protocol in the TCP/IP suite that belongs in the network layer of the OSI model. ARP obtains the MAC (physical) address of a host, or node, and then creates a local database that maps the MAC address to the host's IP (logical) address.

ARP cache *See* ARP table.

ARP table A database of records that maps MAC addresses to IP addresses. The ARP table is stored on a computer's hard disk where it is used by the ARP utility to supply the MAC addresses of network nodes, given their IP addresses.

array A group of hard disks.

AS (authentication service) In Kerberos terminology, the process that runs on a KDC (Key Distribution Center) to initially validate a client who's logging on. The authentication service issues a session key to the client and to the service the client wants to access.

asset management The process of identifying and tracking an organization's assets, such as hardware and software.

association In the context of wireless networking, the communication that occurs between a station and an access point to enable the station to connect to the network via that access point.

Assured Forwarding *See* AF.

asymmetric encryption A type of encryption (such as public key encryption) that uses a different key for encoding data than is used for decoding the ciphertext.

asymmetric multiprocessing A multiprocessing method that assigns each subtask to a specific processor.

asymmetrical The characteristic of a transmission technology that affords greater bandwidth in one direction (either from the customer to the carrier, or vice versa) than in the other direction.

asymmetrical DSL A variation of DSL that offers more throughput when data travels downstream, downloading from a local carrier's switching facility to the customer, than when it travels upstream, uploading from the customer to the local carrier's switching facility.

asynchronous A transmission method in which data being transmitted and received by nodes does not have to conform to any timing scheme. In asynchronous communications, a node can transmit at any time, and the destination node must accept the transmission as it comes.

Asynchronous Transfer Mode *See* ATM.

ATA (analog telephone adapter) An internal or externally attached adapter that converts analog telephone signals into packet-switched voice signals and vice versa.

ATM (Asynchronous Transfer Mode) A data link layer technology originally conceived in the early 1980s at Bell Labs and standardized by the ITU in the mid-1990s. ATM relies on fixed packets, called cells, that each consist of 48 bytes of data plus a 5-byte header. ATM relies on virtual circuits and establishes a connection before sending data. The reliable connection ensured by ATM allows network managers to specify QoS levels for certain types of traffic.

attenuation The extent to which a signal has weakened after traveling a given distance.

attribute A variable property associated with a network object. For example, a restriction on the time of day a user can log on is an attribute associated with that user object.

authentication The process of comparing and matching a client's credentials with the credentials in the NOS user database to enable the client to log on to the network.

authentication, authorization, and accounting *See* AAA.

authentication header *See* AH.

authentication protocol A set of rules that governs how servers authenticate clients. Several types of authentication protocols exist.

authentication service *See* AS.

authenticator In Kerberos authentication, the user's time stamp encrypted with the session key. The authenticator is used to help the service verify that a user's ticket is valid.

Automatic Private IP Addressing *See* APIPA.

availability How consistently and reliably a file, device, or connection can be accessed by authorized personnel.

AWG (American Wire Gauge) A standard rating that indicates the diameter of a wire, such as the conducting core of a coaxial cable.

B channel In ISDN, the "bearer" channel, so named because it bears traffic from point to point.

backbone The part of a network to which segments and significant shared devices (such as routers, switches, and servers) connect. A backbone is sometimes referred to as "a network of networks," because of its role in interconnecting smaller parts of a LAN or WAN.

backing up The process of copying critical data files to a secure storage area. Often, backups are performed according to a formulaic schedule.

backleveling The process of reverting to a previous version of a software application after attempting to upgrade it.

backup A copy of data or program files created for archiving or safekeeping.

backup rotation scheme A plan for when and how often backups occur, and which backups are full, incremental, or differential.

bandwidth A measure of the difference between the highest and lowest frequencies that a medium can transmit.

base I/O port A setting that specifies, in hexadecimal notation, which area of memory will act as a channel for data traveling between the NIC and the CPU. Like its IRQ, a device's base I/O port cannot be used by any other device.

base station *See* access point.

baseband A form of transmission in which digital signals are sent through direct current pulses applied to a wire. This direct current requires exclusive use of the wire's capacity, so baseband systems can transmit only one signal, or one channel, at a time. Every device on a baseband system shares a single channel.

baseline A record of how a network operates under normal conditions (including its performance, collision rate, utilization rate, and so on). Baselines are used for comparison when conditions change.

basic input/output system *See* BIOS.

Basic Rate Interface *See* BRI.

basic service set *See* BSS.

basic service set identifier *See* BSSID.

beacon frame In the context of wireless networking, a frame issued by an access point to alert other nodes of its existence.

bend radius The radius of the maximum arc into which you can loop a cable before you will cause data transmission errors. Generally, a twisted pair cable's bend radius is equal to or greater than four times the diameter of the cable.

Berkeley Software Distribution *See* BSD.

best path The most efficient route from one node on a network to another. Under optimal network conditions, the best path is the most direct path between two points. However, when traffic congestion, segment failures, and other factors create obstacles, the most direct path may not be the best path.

BGP (Border Gateway Protocol) A complex routing protocol used on border and exterior routers. BGP is the routing protocol used on Internet backbones.

BID (bridge ID) A combination of a 2-byte priority field and a bridge's MAC address, used in STP (Spanning Tree Protocol) to select a root bridge.

binary A system founded on using 1s and 0s to encode information.

biorecognition access A method of authentication in which a device scans an individual's unique physical characteristics (such as the color patterns in her iris or the geometry of her hand) to verify the user's identity.

BIOS (basic input/output system) The firmware attached to a computer's motherboard that controls the computer's communication with its devices, among other things.

bit (binary digit) A bit equals a single pulse in the digital encoding system. It may have only one of two values: 0 or 1.

blackout A complete power loss.

block ID The first set of six characters that make up the MAC address and that are unique to a particular manufacturer.

Bluetooth A wireless networking standard that uses FHSS (frequency hopping spread spectrum) signaling in the 2.4GHz band to achieve a maximum throughput of either 723Kbps or 2.1Mbps, depending on the version. Bluetooth was designed for use primarily with small office or home networks in which multiple devices (including cordless phones, computers, and pagers) are connected.

Bluetooth Special Interest Group (SIG) A consortium of companies, including Sony Ericsson, Intel, Nokia, Toshiba, and IBM, that formally banded together in 1998 to refine and standardize Bluetooth technology.

BNC (Bayonet Neill-Concelman, or British Naval Connector) A standard for coaxial cable connectors named after its coupling method and its inventors.

BNC connector A coaxial cable connector type that uses a twist-and-lock (or bayonet) style of coupling. It may be used with several coaxial cable types, including RG-6 and RG-59.

bonding The process of combining more than one bearer channel of an ISDN line to increase throughput. For example, BRI's two 64Kbps B channels are bonded to create an effective throughput of 128Kbps.

boot sector virus A virus that resides on the boot sector of a floppy disk and is transferred to the partition sector or the DOS boot sector on a hard disk. A boot sector virus can move from a floppy to a hard disk only if the floppy disk is left in the drive when the machine starts.

BOOTP (Bootstrap Protocol) An application layer protocol in the TCP/IP suite that uses a central list of IP addresses and their associated devices' MAC addresses to assign IP addresses to clients dynamically. BOOTP was the precursor to DHCP.

Bootstrap Protocol *See* BOOTP.

Border Gateway Protocol *See* BGP.

border router A router that connects an autonomous LAN with an exterior network—for example, the router that connects a business to its ISP.

bot A program that runs automatically. Bots can spread viruses or other malicious code between users in a chat room by exploiting the IRC protocol.

braiding A braided metal shielding used to insulate some types of coaxial cable.

branch A part of the organizational structure of an operating system's directory that contains objects or other organizational units.

BRI (Basic Rate Interface) A variety of ISDN that uses two 64Kbps bearer channels and one 16Kbps data channel, as summarized by the notation 2B+D. BRI is the most common form of ISDN employed by home users.

bridge A connectivity device that operates at the data link layer (Layer 2) of the OSI model and reads header information to forward packets according to their MAC addresses. Bridges use a filtering database to determine which packets to discard and which to forward. Bridges contain one input and one output port and separate network segments.

bridge ID *See* BID.

broadband A form of transmission in which signals are modulated as radiofrequency analog pulses with different frequency ranges. Unlike baseband, broadband technology does not involve binary encoding. The use of multiple frequencies enables a broadband system to operate over several

channels and, therefore, carry much more data than a baseband system.

broadband cable A method of connecting to the Internet over a cable network. In broadband cable, computers are connected to a cable modem that modulates and demodulates signals to and from the cable company's head-end.

broadcast A transmission that involves one transmitter and multiple, undefined receivers.

broadcast domain A combination of ports on a switch (or multiple switches) that make up a Layer 2 segment and can communicate directly via broadcast transmissions. To be able to exchange data with each other, broadcast domains must be connected by a Layer 3 device, such as a router or Layer 3 switch. A VLAN is one type of broadcast domain.

brownout A momentary decrease in voltage, also known as a *sag*. An overtaxed electrical system may cause brownouts, recognizable as a dimming of the lights.

brute force attack An attempt to discover an encryption key or password by trying numerous possible character combinations. Usually, a brute force attack is performed rapidly by a program designed for that purpose.

BSD (Berkeley Software Distribution) A UNIX distribution that originated at the University of California at Berkeley. The BSD suffix differentiates these distributions from AT&T distributions. No longer being developed at Berkeley, the last public release of BSD UNIX was version 4.4.

BSS (basic service set) In IEEE terminology, a group of stations that share an access point.

BSSID (basic service set identifier) In IEEE terminology, the identifier for a BSS (basic service set).

bug A flaw in software or hardware that causes it to malfunction.

bus 1) The single cable connecting all devices in a bus topology. 2) The type of circuit used by a computer's motherboard to transmit data to components. Most new Pentium computers use buses capable of exchanging 32 or 64 bits of data. As the number of bits of data a bus handles increases, so too does the speed of the device attached to the bus.

bus topology A topology in which a single cable connects all nodes on a network without intervening connectivity devices.

bus topology WAN A WAN in which each location is connected to no more than two other locations in a serial fashion.

butt set A tool for accessing and testing a telephone company's local loop. The butt set, also known as a telephone test set or lineman's handset, is essentially a telephone handset with attached wires that can be connected to local loop terminations at a demarc or switching facility.

byte Eight bits of information. In a digital signaling system, broadly speaking, one byte carries one piece of information.

CA (certificate authority) An organization that issues and maintains digital certificates as part of the public key infrastructure.

cable checker *See* continuity tester.

cable drop The fiber-optic or coaxial cable that connects a neighborhood cable node to a customer's house.

cable modem A device that modulates and demodulates signals for transmission and reception via cable wiring.

cable modem access *See* broadband cable.

cable performance tester A troubleshooting tool that tests cables for continuity but can also measure cross talk, attenuation, and impedance; identify the location of faults; and store or print cable testing results.

cable plant The hardware that constitutes the enterprise-wide cabling system.

cable tester A device that tests cables for one or more of the following conditions: continuity, segment length, distance to a fault, attenuation along a cable, near end cross talk, and termination resistance and impedance. Cable testers may also issue pass/fail ratings for wiring standards or store and print cable testing results.

cache engine A network device devoted to storage and delivery of frequently requested files.

caching The local storage of frequently needed files that would otherwise be obtained from an external source.

CALEA (Communications Assistance for Law Enforcement Act) A United States federal regulation that requires telecommunications carriers and equipment manufacturers to provide for surveillance capabilities. CALEA was passed by Congress in 1994 after pressure from the FBI, which worried that networks relying solely on digital communications would circumvent traditional wiretapping strategies.

call tracking system A software program used to document technical problems and how they were resolved (also known as help desk software).

capacity *See* throughput.

CardBus A PCMCIA standard that specifies a 32-bit interface running at 33MHz, similar to the PCI expansion board standard. Most modern laptops are equipped with CardBus slots for connecting external modems and NICs, among other things.

Carrier Sense Multiple Access with Collision Avoidance *See* CSMA/CA.

Carrier Sense Multiple Access with Collision Detection *See* CSMA/CD.

Cat Abbreviation for the word *category* when describing a type of twisted pair cable. For example, Category 3 unshielded twisted pair cable may also be called Cat 3.

Cat 3 (Category 3) A form of UTP that contains four wire pairs and can carry up to 10Mbps, with a possible bandwidth of 16MHz. Cat 3 has typically been used for 10Mbps Ethernet or 4Mbps token ring networks. Network administrators are gradually replacing Cat 3 cabling with Cat 5 to accommodate higher throughput. Cat 3 is less expensive than Cat 5.

Cat 4 (Category 4) A form of UTP that contains four wire pairs and can support up to 16Mbps throughput. Cat 4 may be used for 16Mbps token ring or 10Mbps Ethernet networks. It is guaranteed for data transmission up to 20MHz and provides more protection against cross talk and attenuation than Cat 1, Cat 2, or Cat 3.

Cat 5 (Category 5) A form of UTP that contains four wire pairs and supports up to 100Mbps throughput and a 100MHz signal rate.

Cat 5e (Enhanced Category 5) A higher-grade version of Cat 5 wiring that contains high-quality copper, offers a high twist ratio, and uses advanced methods for reducing cross talk. Enhanced Cat 5 can support a signaling rate of up to 350MHz, more than triple the capability of regular Cat 5.

Cat 6 (Category 6) A twisted pair cable that contains four wire pairs, each wrapped in foil insulation. Additional foil insulation covers the bundle of wire pairs, and a fire-resistant plastic sheath covers the second foil layer. The foil insulation provides excellent resistance to cross talk and enables Cat 6 to support a signaling rate of 250MHz and at least six times the throughput supported by regular Cat 5.

Cat 6e (Enhanced Category 6) A higher-grade version of Cat 6 wiring that further reduces attenuation and cross talk and allows for potentially exceeding traditional network segment length limits. Cat 6e is capable of a 550MHz signaling rate and can reliably transmit data at multi-gigabit per second rates.

Cat 7 (Category 7) A twisted pair cable that contains multiple wire pairs, each separately shielded and then surrounded by another layer of shielding within the jacket. Cat 7 can support up to a 1GHz signal rate. But because of its extra layers, it is less flexible than other forms of twisted pair wiring.

Category 3 *See* Cat 3.

Category 4 *See* Cat 4.

Category 5 *See* Cat 5.

Category 6 *See* Cat 6.

Category 7 *See* Cat 7.

CCIE (Cisco Certified Internetwork Expert) An elite certification that recognizes expert-level installation, configuration, management, and troubleshooting skills on networks that use a range of Cisco Systems' devices.

CCNA (Cisco Certified Network Associate) A professional certification that attests to one's skills in installing, configuring, maintaining, and troubleshooting medium-sized networks that use Cisco Systems' switches and routers.

CD-R (compact disc-recordable) A type of compact disc that can be written to only once. It can store about 650MB of data.

CD-RW (compact disc-rewriteable) A type of compact disc that can be written to more than once. It can store about 650MB of data.

cell A packet of a fixed size. In ATM technology, a cell consists of 48 bytes of data plus a 5-byte header.

central office *See* CO.

certificate authority *See* CA.

certification The process of mastering material pertaining to a particular hardware system, operating system, programming language, or other software program, and then proving your mastery by passing a series of exams.

challenge A random string of text issued from one computer to another in some forms of authentication. It is used, along with the password (or other credential), in a response to verify the computer's credentials.

Challenge Handshake Authentication Protocol *See* CHAP.

change management system A process or program that provides support personnel with a centralized means of documenting changes made to the network.

channel A distinct communication path between two or more nodes, much like a lane is a distinct transportation path on a freeway. Channels may be separated either logically (as in multiplexing) or physically (as when they are carried by separate wires).

channel bonding In the context of 802.11n wireless technology, the combination of two 20MHz frequency band to create one 40MHz frequency band that can carry more than twice the amount of data that a single 20MHz band could. It's recommended for use only in the 5GHz range, because this band has more available channels and suffers less interference than the 2.4GHz band.

channel service unit *See* CSU.

CHAP (Challenge Handshake Authentication Protocol) An authentication protocol that operates over PPP and that requires the authenticator to take the first step by offering the other computer a challenge. The requestor responds by combining the challenge with its password, encrypting the new string of characters and sending it to the authenticator. The authenticator matches to see if the requestor's encrypted string of text matches its own encrypted string of characters. If so, the requestor is authenticated and granted access to secured resources.

checksum A method of error checking that determines if the contents of an arriving data unit match the contents of the data unit sent by the source.

child domain A domain established within another domain in a Windows Server 2003 or Server 2008 domain tree.

CIDR (Classless Interdomain Routing) An IP addressing and subnetting method in which network and host information is manipulated without adhering to the limitations imposed by traditional network class distinctions. CIDR is also known as classless routing or supernetting. Older routing protocols, such as RIP, are not capable of interpreting CIDR addressing schemes.

CIDR block In CIDR notation, the number of bits used for an extended network prefix. For example, the CIDR block for 199.34.89.0/22 is /22.

CIDR notation In CIDR, a method of denoting network IDs and their subnet boundaries. Slash notation takes the form of the network ID followed by a slash (/), followed by the number of bits that are used for the extended network prefix.

CIFS (Common Internet File System) A file access protocol. CIFS runs over TCP/IP and is the standard file access protocol used by Windows operating systems.

ciphertext The unique data block that results when an original piece of data (such as text) is encrypted (for example, by using a key).

CIR (committed information rate) The guaranteed minimum amount of bandwidth selected when leasing a frame relay circuit. Frame relay costs are partially based on CIR.

circuit switching A type of switching in which a connection is established between two network nodes before they begin transmitting data. Bandwidth is dedicated to this connection and remains available until users terminate the communication between the two nodes.

Cisco Certified Internetwork Expert *See* CCIE.

Cisco Certified Network Associate *See* CCNA.

cladding The glass or plastic shield around the core of a fiber-optic cable. Cladding reflects light back to the core in patterns that vary depending on the transmission mode. This reflection allows fiber to bend around corners without impairing the light-based signal.

class A type of object recognized by an NOS directory and defined in an NOS schema. Printers and users are examples of object classes.

classful addressing An IP addressing convention that adheres to network class distinctions, in which the first 8 bits of a Class A address, the first 16 bits of a Class B address, and the first 24 bits of a Class C address are used for network information.

Classless Interdomain Routing *See* CIDR.

classless routing *See* CIDR.

client A computer on the network that requests resources or services from another computer on a network. In some cases, a client could also act as a server. The term *client* may also refer to the user of a client workstation or a client software application installed on the workstation.

client_hello In the context of SSL encryption, a message issued from the client to the server that contains information about what level of security the client's browser is capable of accepting and what type of encryption the client's browser can decipher (for example, RSA or Diffie-Hellman). The client_hello message also establishes a randomly generated number that uniquely identifies the client, plus another number that identifies the SSL session.

client/server architecture A network design in which clients (typically desktop or laptop computers) use a centrally administered server to share data, data storage space, and devices.

client/server network A network that uses centrally administered computers, known as servers, to enable resource sharing for and to facilitate communication between the other computers on the network.

clustering A fault-tolerance technique that links multiple servers to act as a single server. In this configuration, clustered servers share processing duties and appear as a single server to users. If one server in the cluster fails, the other servers in the cluster automatically take over its data transaction and storage responsibilities.

CMOS (complementary metal oxide semiconductor) A type of microchip that requires very little energy to operate. In a PC, the CMOS stores settings pertaining to a computer's devices, among other things.

CN (common name) In LDAP naming conventions, the name of an object.

CO (central office) The location where a local or long-distance telephone service provider terminates and interconnects customer lines.

coaxial cable A type of cable that consists of a central metal conducting core, which might be solid or stranded and is often made of copper, surrounded by an insulator, a braided metal shielding, called braiding, and an outer cover, called the sheath or jacket. Coaxial cable, called "coax" for short, was the foundation for Ethernet networks in the 1980s. Today it's used to connect cable Internet and cable TV systems.

cold site A place where the computers, devices, and connectivity necessary to rebuild a network exist, but they are not appropriately configured, updated, or connected to match the network's current state.

cold spare A duplicate component that is not installed but can be installed in case of a failure.

collapsed backbone A type of backbone that uses a router or switch as the single central connection point for multiple subnetworks.

collision In Ethernet networks, the interference of one node's data transmission with the data transmission of another node sharing the same segment.

collision domain The portion of an Ethernet network in which collisions could occur if two nodes transmit data at the same time.

command interpreter A program (usually text-based) that accepts and executes system programs and applications on behalf of users. Often, it includes the ability to execute a series of instructions that are stored in a file.

committed information rate *See* CIR.

Common Internet File System *See* CIFS.

common name *See* CN.

Communications Assistance for Law Enforcement Act *See* CALEA.

compact disc-recordable *See* CD-R.

compact disc-rewriteable *See* CD-RW.

CompactFlash The standard for an ultrasmall removable data and input/output device capable of connecting many kinds of external peripherals to workstations, PDAs, and other computerized devices. CompactFlash was designed by the CompactFlash Association (CFA), a consortium of computer manufacturers.

complementary metal oxide semiconductor *See* CMOS.

CompTIA (Computing Technology Industry Association) An association of computer resellers, manufacturers, and training companies that sets industry-wide standards for computer professionals. CompTIA established and sponsors the A+ and Network+ (Net+) certifications.

Computing Technology Industry Association *See* CompTIA.

conduit The pipeline used to contain and protect cabling. Conduit is usually made from metal.

configuration management The collection, storage, and assessment of information related to the versions of software installed on every network device and every device's hardware configuration.

connection oriented A type of transport layer protocol that requires the establishment of a connection between communicating nodes before it will transmit data.

connectionless A type of transport layer protocol that services a request without requiring a verified session and without guaranteeing delivery of data.

connectivity device One of several types of specialized devices that allows two or more networks or multiple parts of one network to connect and exchange data.

connectors The pieces of hardware that connect the wire to the network device, be it a file server, workstation, switch, or printer.

container *See* organizational unit.

content switch A switch that provides functions between Layer 4 and Layer 7 of the OSI model.

content-filtering firewall A firewall that can block designated types of traffic from entering a protected network.

continuity tester An instrument that tests whether voltage (or light, in the case of fiber-optic cable) issued at one end of a cable can be detected at the opposite end of the cable. A continuity tester can indicate whether the cable will successfully transmit a signal.

convergence The use of data networks to carry voice (or telephone), video, and other communications services in addition to data.

convergence time The time it takes for a router to recognize a best path in the event of a change or network outage.

core The central component of a cable designed to carry a signal. The core of a fiber-optic cable, for example, consists of one or several glass or plastic fibers. The core of a coaxial copper cable consists of one large or several small strands of copper.

core gateway A gateway that operates on the Internet backbone.

country code TLD A top-level domain that corresponds to a country. For example, the country code TLD for Canada is .ca, and the country code TLD for Japan is .jp.

cracker A person who uses his knowledge of operating systems and utilities to intentionally damage or destroy data or systems.

CRC (cyclic redundancy check) An algorithm (or mathematical routine) used to verify the accuracy of data contained in a data frame.

credentials A user's unique identifying characteristics that enable him to authenticate with a server and gain access to network resources. The most common type of credentials are a user name and password.

cross talk A type of interference caused by signals traveling on nearby wire pairs infringing on another pair's signal.

crossover cable A twisted pair patch cable in which the termination locations of the transmit and receive wires on one end of the cable are reversed.

CSMA/CA (Carrier Sense Multiple Access with Collision Avoidance) A network access method used on 802.11 wireless networks. In CSMA/CA, before a node begins to send data, it checks the medium. If it detects no transmission activity, it waits a brief, random amount of time and then sends its transmission. If the node does detect activity, it waits a brief period of time before checking the channel again. CSMA/CA does not eliminate, but minimizes, the potential for collisions.

CSMA/CD (Carrier Sense Multiple Access with Collision Detection) A network access method specified for use by IEEE 802.3 (Ethernet) networks. In CSMA/CD, each node waits its turn before transmitting data to avoid interfering with other nodes' transmissions. If a node's NIC determines that its data has been involved in a collision, it immediately stops transmitting. Next, in a process called jamming, the NIC issues a special 32-bit sequence that indicates to the rest of the network nodes that its previous transmission was faulty and that those data frames are invalid. After waiting, the NIC determines if the line is again available; if it is available, the NIC retransmits its data.

CSU (channel service unit) A device used with T-carrier technology that provides termination for the digital signal and ensures connection integrity through error correction and line monitoring. Typically, a CSU is combined with a DSU in a single device, a CSU/DSU.

CSU/DSU A combination of a CSU (channel service unit) and a DSU (data service unit) that serves as the connection point for a T1 line at the customer's site. Most modern CSU/DSUs also contain a multiplexer. A CSU/DSU may be a separate device or an expansion card in another device, such as a router.

cut-through mode A switching mode in which a switch reads a frame's header and decides where to forward the data before it receives the entire packet. Cut-through mode is faster, but less accurate, than the other switching method, store-and-forward mode.

cyclic redundancy check *See* CRC.

D channel In ISDN, the "data" channel is used to carry information about the call, such as session initiation and termination signals, caller identity, call forwarding, and conference calling signals.

daisy chain A group of connectivity devices linked in a serial fashion.

data circuit-terminating equipment *See* DCE.

Data Encryption Standard *See* DES.

data link layer The second layer in the OSI model. The data link layer bridges the networking media with the network layer. Its primary function is to divide the data it receives from the network layer into frames that can then be transmitted by the physical layer.

data link layer address *See* MAC address.

data packet A discrete unit of information sent from one node on a network to another.

data port A port on a connectivity device to which network nodes are connected.

data propagation delay The length of time data takes to travel from one point on the segment to another point. On Ethernet networks, CSMA/CD's collision detection routine cannot operate accurately if the data propagation delay is too long.

data service unit *See* DSU.

data terminal equipment *See* DTE.

DB-25 connector A type of connector with 25 pins that's commonly used in serial communication that conforms to the RS-232 standard.

DB-9 connector A type of connector with nine pins that's commonly used in serial communication that conforms to the RS-232 standard.

DC (domain component) In LDAP naming conventions, the name of any one of the domains to which an object belongs.

DCE (data circuit-terminating equipment) A device, such as a multiplexer or modem, that processes signals. DCE supplies a clock signal to synchronize transmission between DTE and DCE.

DDNS (Dynamic DNS) A method of dynamically updating DNS records for a host. DDNS client computers are configured to notify a service provider when their IP addresses change, and then the service provider propagates the DNS record change across the Internet automatically.

dedicated A continuously available link or service that is leased through another carrier. Examples of dedicated lines include ADSL, T1, and T3.

default gateway The gateway that first interprets a device's outbound requests and then interprets its inbound requests to and from other subnets. In a Postal Service analogy, the default gateway is similar to a local post office.

default router *See* default gateway.

demarcation point (demarc) The point of division between a telecommunications service carrier's network and a building's internal network.

demilitarized zone *See* DMZ.

demultiplexer (demux) A device that separates multiplexed signals once they are received and regenerates them in their original form.

denial-of-service attack A security threat caused by a deluge of traffic that disables the victimized system.

dense wavelength division multiplexing *See* DWDM.

DES (Data Encryption Standard) A popular private key encryption technique that was developed by IBM in the 1970s.

device driver The software that enables an attached device to communicate with the computer's operating system.

device ID The second set of six characters that make up a network device's MAC address. The device ID, which is added at the factory, is based on the device's model and manufacture date.

DHCP (Dynamic Host Configuration Protocol) An application layer protocol in the TCP/IP suite that manages the dynamic distribution of IP addresses on a network. Using DHCP to assign IP addresses can nearly eliminate duplicate-addressing problems.

dial return A method of satellite Internet access in which a subscriber receives data via a satellite downlink transmission but sends data to the satellite via an analog modem (dial-up) connection.

dial-up A type of connection in which a user connects to a distant network from a computer and stays connected for a finite period of time. Most of the time, the term *dial-up* refers to a connection that uses a PSTN line.

dial-up networking The process of dialing into a remote access server to connect with a network, be it private or public.

dictionary attack A technique in which attackers run a program that tries a combination of a known user ID and, for a password, every word in a dictionary to attempt to gain access to a network.

differential backup A backup method in which only data that has changed since the last full or incremental backup is copied to a storage medium, and in which that same information is marked for subsequent backup, regardless of whether it has changed. In other words, a differential backup does not uncheck the archive bits for files it backs up.

Differentiated Service *See* DiffServ.

Diffie-Hellman The first commonly used public, or asymmetric, key algorithm. Diffie-Hellman was released in 1975 by its creators, Whitfield Diffie and Martin Hellman.

diffraction In the context of wireless signal propagation, the phenomenon that occurs when an electromagnetic wave encounters an obstruction and splits into secondary waves. The secondary waves continue to propagate in the direction in which they were split. If you could see wireless signals being diffracted, they would appear to be bending around the obstacle. Objects with sharp edges—including the corners of walls and desks—cause diffraction.

DiffServ (Differentiated Service) A technique for ensuring QoS by prioritizing traffic. DiffServ places information in the DiffServ field in an IPv4 datagram. In IPv6 datagrams, DiffServ uses a similar field known as the Traffic Class field. This information indicates to the network routers how the data stream should be forwarded.

dig (domain information groper) A TCP/IP utility that queries the DNS database and provides information about a host given its IP address or vice versa. Dig is similar to the nslookup utility but provides more information, even in its simplest form, than nslookup can.

digital As opposed to analog signals, digital signals are composed of pulses that can have a value of only 1 or 0.

digital certificate A password-protected and encrypted file that holds an individual's identification information, including a public key and a private key. The individual's public key is used to verify the sender's digital signature, and the private key allows the individual to log on to a third-party authority who administers digital certificates.

digital PBX *See* IP-PBX.

digital subscriber line *See* DSL.

directional antenna A type of antenna that issues wireless signals along a single direction, or path.

directory In general, a listing that organizes resources and correlates them with their properties. In the context of NOSs, a method for organizing and managing objects.

direct-sequence spread spectrum *See* DSSS.

disaster recovery The process of restoring critical functionality and data to a network after an enterprise-wide outage that affects more than a single system or a limited group of users.

disk duplexing A storage fault-tolerance technique in which data is continually copied from one disk to another when it is saved, just as in disk mirroring. In duplexing, however, a separate disk controller is used for each disk.

disk mirroring A RAID technique in which data from one disk is automatically copied to another disk as the information is written.

disk striping A simple implementation of RAID in which data is written in 64KB blocks equally across all disks in the array.

diskless workstation A workstation that doesn't contain a hard disk but instead relies on a small amount of read-only memory to connect to a network and to pick up its system files.

distance-vector The simplest type of routing protocols, these determine the best route for data based on the distance to a destination. Some distance-vector routing protocols, like RIP, only factor in the number of hops to the destination, while others take into account latency and other network traffic characteristics.

distinguished name *See* DN.

distributed backbone A type of backbone in which a number of connectivity devices (usually hubs) are connected to a series of central connectivity devices, such as hubs, switches, or routers, in a hierarchy.

distribution The term used to refer to the different implementations of a particular UNIX or Linux system. For example, different distributions of Linux include Fedora, SUSE, and Ubuntu.

DMZ (demilitarized zone) The perimeter of a protected, internal network where users, both authorized and unauthorized, from external networks can attempt to access it. Firewalls and IDS/IPS systems are typically placed in the DMZ.

DN (distinguished name) A long form of an object's name in Active Directory that explicitly indicates the object name, plus the names of its containers and domains. A distinguished name includes a DC (domain component), OU (organizational unit), and CN (common name). A client uses the distinguished name to access a particular object, such as a printer.

DNAT (Dynamic Network Address Translation) A type of address translation in which a limited pool of Internet-valid IP addresses is shared by multiple private network hosts.

DNS (Domain Name System or Domain Name Service) A hierarchical way of tracking domain names and their addresses, devised in the mid-1980s. The DNS database does not rely on one file or even one server, but rather is distributed over several key computers across the Internet to prevent catastrophic failure if one or a few computers go down. DNS is a TCP/IP service that belongs to the application layer of the OSI model.

DNS server *See* name server.

DNS spoofing A security attack in which an outsider forges name server records to falsify his host's identity.

domain 1) A group of computers that belong to the same organization and have part of their IP addresses in common. 2) A group of users, servers, and other resources that share account and security policies through a Windows Server 2003 or Server 2008 NOS.

domain component *See* DC.

domain controller A Windows Server 2003 or Server 2008 computer that contains a replica of the Active Directory database.

domain information groper *See* dig.

domain model In Microsoft terminology, the type of client/server network that relies on domains, rather than workgroups.

domain name The symbolic name that identifies a domain. Usually, a domain name is associated with a company or other type of organization, such as a university or military unit.

Domain Name Service *See* DNS.

Domain Name System *See* DNS.

domain tree A group of hierarchically arranged domains that share a common namespace in the Windows Server 2003 or Server 2008 Active Directory.

dotted decimal notation The shorthand convention used to represent IPv4 addresses and make them more easily readable by humans. In dotted decimal notation, a decimal number between 0 and 255 represents each binary octet. A period, or dot, separates each decimal.

downlink A connection from an orbiting satellite to an Earth-based receiver.

downstream A term used to describe data traffic that flows from a carrier's facility to the customer. In asymmetrical communications, downstream throughput is usually much higher than upstream throughput. In symmetrical communications, downstream and upstream throughputs are equal.

driver *See* device driver.

DS0 (digital signal, level 0) The equivalent of one data or voice channel in T-carrier technology, as defined by ANSI physical layer standards. All other signal levels are multiples of DS0.

DSL (digital subscriber line) A dedicated WAN technology that uses advanced data modulation techniques at the physical layer to achieve extraordinary throughput over regular phone lines. DSL comes in several varieties, the most common of which is asymmetric DSL (ADSL).

DSL access multiplexer *See* DSLAM.

DSL modem A device that demodulates an incoming DSL signal, extracting the information and passing it to the data equipment (such as telephones and computers), and modulates an outgoing DSL signal.

DSLAM (DSL access multiplexer) A connectivity device located at a telecommunications carrier's office that aggregates multiple DSL subscriber lines and connects them to a larger carrier or to the Internet backbone.

DSSS (direct-sequence spread spectrum) A transmission technique in which a signal's bits are distributed over an entire frequency band at once. Each bit is coded so that the receiver can reassemble the original signal upon receiving the bits.

DSU (data service unit) A device used in T-carrier technology that converts the digital signal used by bridges, routers, and multiplexers into the digital signal used on cabling. Typically, a DSU is combined with a CSU in a single device, a CSU/DSU.

DTE (data terminal equipment) Any end-user device, such as a workstation, terminal (essentially a monitor with little or no independent data-processing capability), or a console (for example, the user interface for a router).

duplex *See* full-duplex.

DWDM (dense wavelength division multiplexing) A multiplexing technique used over single-mode or multimode fiber-optic cable in which each signal is assigned a different wavelength for its carrier wave. In DWDM, little space exists between carrier waves to achieve extraordinary high capacity.

dynamic ARP table entry A record in an ARP table that is created when a client makes an ARP request that cannot be satisfied by data already in the ARP table.

dynamic DNS *See* DDNS.

Dynamic Host Configuration Protocol *See* DHCP.

dynamic IP address An IP address that is assigned to a device upon request and may change when the DHCP lease expires or is terminated. BOOTP and DHCP are two ways of assigning dynamic IP addresses.

Dynamic Network Address Translation *See* DNAT.

Dynamic Ports TCP/IP ports in the range of 49152 through 65535, which are open for use without requiring administrative privileges on a host or approval from IANA.

dynamic routing A method of routing that automatically calculates the best path between two nodes and accumulates this information in a routing table. If congestion or failures affect the network, a router using dynamic routing can detect the problems and reroute data through a different path. Modern networks primarily use dynamic routing.

E1 A digital carrier standard used in Europe that offers 30 channels and a maximum of 2.048Mbps throughput.

E3 A digital carrier standard used in Europe that offers 480 channels and a maximum of 34.368Mbps throughput.

EAP (Extensible Authentication Protocol) A data link layer protocol defined by the IETF that specifies the dynamic distribution of encryption keys and a preauthentication process in which a client and server exchange data via an intermediate node (for example, an access point on a wireless LAN). Only after they have mutually authenticated can the client and server exchange encrypted data. EAP can be used with multiple authentication and encryption schemes.

EAP over LAN *See* EAPoL.

EAPoL (EAP over LAN) *See* 802.1x.

ECC (error correction code) An algorithm used to detect and correct errors. In RAID levels 3 and 5, for example, a type of ECC known as parity error checking is used.

echo reply The response signal sent by a device after another device pings it.

echo request The request for a response generated when one device pings another device.

EEPROM (electrically erasable programmable read-only memory) A type of ROM that is found on a circuit board and whose configuration information can be erased and rewritten through electrical pulses.

EF (Expedited Forwarding) In the DiffServ QoS technique, a forwarding specification that assigns each data stream a minimum departure rate from a given node. This technique circumvents delays that slow normal data from reaching its destination on time and in sequence. EF information is inserted in the DiffServ field of an IPv4 datagram.

EIA (Electronic Industries Alliance) A trade organization composed of representatives from electronics manufacturing firms across the United States that sets standards for electronic equipment and lobbies for legislation favorable to the growth of the computer and electronics industries.

EIGRP (Enhanced Interior Gateway Routing Protocol) A routing protocol developed in the mid-1980s by Cisco Systems that has a fast convergence time and a low network overhead but is easier to configure and less CPU-intensive than OSPF. EIGRP also offers the benefits of supporting multiple protocols and limiting unnecessary network traffic between routers.

electrically erasable programmable read-only memory *See* EEPROM.

electromagnetic interference *See* EMI.

Electronic Industries Alliance *See* EIA.

EMI (electromagnetic interference) A type of interference that may be caused by motors, power lines, televisions, copiers, fluorescent lights, or other sources of electrical activity.

encapsulate The process of wrapping one layer's PDU with protocol information so that it can be interpreted by a lower layer. For example, data link layer protocols encapsulate network layer packets in frames.

Encapsulating Security Payload *See* ESP.

encrypted virus A virus that is encrypted to prevent detection.

encryption The use of an algorithm to scramble data into a format that can be read only by reversing the algorithm—decrypting the data—to keep the information private. The most popular kind of encryption algorithm weaves a key into the original data's bits, sometimes several times in different sequences, to generate a unique data block.

endpoint In SIP terminology, any client, server, or gateway communicating on the network.

enhanced Category 5 *See* Cat 5e.

enhanced Category 6 *See* Cat 6e.

Enhanced Interior Gateway Routing Protocol *See* EIGRP.

enterprise An entire organization, including local and remote offices, a mixture of computer systems, and a number of departments. Enterprise-wide computing takes into account the breadth and diversity of a large organization's computer needs.

entrance facilities The facilities necessary for a service provider (whether it is a local phone company, Internet service provider, or long-distance carrier) to connect with another organization's LAN or WAN.

error correction code *See* ECC.

escalate In network troubleshooting, to refer a problem to someone with deeper knowledge about the subject. For example, a first-level support person might escalate a router configuration issue to a second- or third-level support person.

ESP (Encapsulation Security Payload) In the context of IPSec, a type of encryption that provides authentication of the IP packet's data payload through public key techniques. In addition, ESP encrypts the entire IP packet for added security.

ESS (extended service set) A group of access points and associated stations (or basic service sets) connected to the same LAN.

ESSID (extended service set identifier) A special identifier shared by BSSs that belong to the same ESS.

Ethernet A networking technology originally developed at Xerox in the 1970s and improved by Digital Equipment Corporation, Intel, and Xerox. Ethernet, which is the most common form of network transmission technology, follows the IEEE 802.3 standard.

Ethernet_II The original Ethernet frame type developed by Digital, Intel, and Xerox, before the IEEE began to standardize Ethernet. Ethernet_II contains a 2-byte type field to identify the upper-layer protocol contained in the frame. It supports TCP/IP and other higher-layer protocols.

event log The service on Windows-based operating systems that records events, or the ongoing record of such events.

Event Viewer A GUI application that allows users to easily view and sort events recorded in the event log on a computer running a Windows-based operating system.

expansion board A circuit board used to connect a device to a computer's motherboard.

expansion card *See* expansion board.

expansion slot A receptacle on a computer's motherboard that contains multiple electrical contacts into which an expansion board can be inserted.

Expedited Forwarding *See* EF.

explicit one-way trust A type of trust relationship in which two domains that belong to different NOS directory trees are configured to trust each other.

ExpressCard A PCMCIA standard that allows external devices to connect to portable computers through a 26-pin interface, with data transfer rates of 250Mbps in each direction (for a total of 500Mbps), similar to the PCI Express expansion board specification. ExpressCard modules come in two sizes: 34mm and 54mm wide. Over time, PCMCIA expects the ExpressCard standard to replace the CardBus standard.

ext3 The name of the primary file system used in most Linux distributions.

extended network prefix The combination of an IP address's network ID and subnet information. By interpreting the address's extended network prefix, a device can determine the subnet to which an address belongs.

extended service set *See* ESS.

extended service set identifier *See* ESSID.

Extensible Authentication Protocol *See* EAP.

exterior router A router that directs data between nodes outside a given autonomous LAN, for example, routers used on the Internet's backbone.

external disk drive A storage device that can be attached temporarily to a computer.

fading A change in a wireless signal's strength as a result of some of the electromagnetic energy being scattered, reflected, or diffracted after being issued by the transmitter.

failover The capability for one component (such as a NIC or server) to assume another component's responsibilities without manual intervention.

failure A deviation from a specified level of system performance for a given period of time. A failure occurs when something doesn't work as promised or as planned.

Fast Ethernet A type of Ethernet network that is capable of 100Mbps throughput. 100Base-T and 100Base-FX are both examples of Fast Ethernet.

fault The malfunction of one component of a system. A fault can result in a failure.

fault management The detection and signaling of device, link, or component faults.

fault tolerance The capability for a component or system to continue functioning despite damage or malfunction.

fax gateway A gateway that can translate IP fax data into analog fax data and vice versa. A fax gateway can also emulate and interpret conventional fax signaling protocols when communicating with a conventional fax machine.

fax over IP *See* FoIP.

FCS (frame check sequence) The field in a frame responsible for ensuring that data carried by the frame arrives intact. It uses an algorithm, such as CRC, to accomplish this verification.

FDM (frequency division multiplexing) A type of multiplexing that assigns a unique frequency band to each communications subchannel. Signals are modulated with different carrier frequencies, and then they are multiplexed to simultaneously travel over a single channel.

Fedora A version of Linux packaged and distributed by Red Hat.

ferrule A short tube within a fiber-optic cable connector that encircles the fiber strand and keeps it properly aligned.

FHSS (frequency hopping spread spectrum) A wireless signaling technique in which a signal jumps between several frequencies within a band in a synchronization pattern known to the channel's receiver and transmitter.

fiber to the home A carrier's provision of fiber-optic connections to residential end users for dramatically increased throughput and a better range of services.

fiber-optic cable A form of cable that contains one or several glass or plastic fibers in its core. Data is transmitted via pulsing light sent from a laser or light-emitting diode (LED) through the central fiber (or fibers). Fiber-optic cables offer significantly higher throughput than copper-based cables. They may be single-mode or multimode and typically use wave-division multiplexing to carry multiple signals.

Fibre Channel A distinct network transmission method that relies on fiber-optic media and its own proprietary protocol. Fibre Channel is capable of up to 2Gbps throughput.

file access protocol A protocol that enables one system to access files on another system.

file globbing A form of filename substitution used in UNIX and Linux commands, similar to the use of wildcards in Windows and DOS.

file server A specialized server that enables clients to share applications and data across the network.

file services The functions of a file server that allow users to share data files, applications, and storage areas.

file system An operating system's method of organizing, managing, and accessing its files through logical structures and software routines.

File Transfer Protocol *See* FTP.

file-infector virus A virus that attaches itself to executable files. When the infected executable file runs, the virus copies itself to memory. Later, the virus attaches itself to other executable files.

filtering database A collection of data created and used by a bridge that correlates the MAC addresses of connected workstations with their locations. A filtering database is also known as a forwarding table.

firewall A device (either a router or a computer running special software) that selectively filters or blocks traffic between networks. Firewalls are commonly used to improve data security.

FireWire A peripheral bus standard developed by Apple Computer and codified by the IEEE as the IEEE 1394 standard. Traditional FireWire connections support a maximum throughput of 400Mbps, but a newer version supports potential throughput rates of over 3Gbps. In addition to connecting peripherals, FireWire can be used to network computers directly in a bus fashion.

firmware A combination of hardware and software. The hardware component of firmware is a ROM (read-only memory) chip that stores data established at the factory and possibly changed by configuration programs that can write to ROM.

first-level support In network troubleshooting, the person or group who initially fields requests for help from users.

fixed A type of wireless system in which the locations of the transmitter and receiver are static. In a fixed connection, the transmitting antenna focuses its energy directly toward the receiving antenna. This results in a point-to-point link.

flashing A security attack in which an Internet user sends commands to another Internet user's machine that cause the screen to fill with garbage characters. A flashing attack causes the user to terminate her session.

flavor *See* distribution.

flow control A method of gauging the appropriate rate of data transmission based on how fast the recipient can accept data.

FM (frequency modulation) A method of data modulation in which the frequency of the carrier signal is modified by the application of the data signal.

FoIP (fax over IP) A service that transmits faxes over a TCP/IP network.

forest In the context of Windows Server 2003 or Server 2008, a collection of domain trees that use different namespaces. A forest allows for trust relationships to be established between trees.

Format Prefix A variable-length field at the beginning of an IPv6 address that indicates what type of address it is (for example, unicast, anycast, or multicast).

forwarding table *See* filtering database.

fox and hound Another term for the combination of devices known as a tone generator and a tone locator. The tone locator is considered the hound because it follows the tone generator (the fox).

fractional T1 An arrangement that allows a customer to lease only some of the channels on a T1 line.

fragmentation A network layer service that subdivides segments it receives from the transport layer into smaller packets.

frame A package for data that includes not only the raw data, or "payload," but also the sender's and recipient's addressing and control information. Frames are generated at the data link layer of the OSI model and are issued to the network at the physical layer.

frame check sequence *See* FCS.

frame relay A digital, packet-switched WAN technology whose protocols operate at the data link layer. The name is derived from the fact that data is separated into frames, which are then relayed from one node to another without

verification or processing. Frame relay offers throughputs between 64Kbps and 45Mbps. A frame relay customer chooses the amount of bandwidth he requires and pays for only that amount.

freely distributable software *See* open source software.

frequency The number of times that a signal's amplitude changes over a fixed period of time, expressed in cycles per second, or hertz (Hz).

frequency division multiplexing *See* FDM.

frequency hopping spread spectrum *See* FHSS.

frequency modulation *See* FM.

FTP (File Transfer Protocol) An application layer protocol used to send and receive files via TCP/IP.

F-type connector A connector used to terminate coaxial cable used for transmitting television and broadband cable signals.

full backup A backup in which all data on all servers is copied to a storage medium, regardless of whether the data is new or changed. A full backup unchecks the archive bit on files it has backed up.

full-duplex A type of transmission in which signals may travel in both directions over a medium simultaneously. May also be called, simply, "duplex."

full-mesh WAN A version of the mesh topology WAN in which every site is directly connected to every other site. Full-mesh WANs are the most fault-tolerant type of WAN.

fully qualified host name A host name plus domain name. For example, a host belonging to the loc.gov domain might be called Jasmine, making its fully qualified host name Jasmine.loc.gov.

gateway A combination of networking hardware and software that connects two dissimilar kinds of networks. Gateways perform connectivity, session management, and data translation, so they must operate at multiple layers of the OSI model.

gateway router *See* border router.

GEO (geosynchronous orbit or geostationary orbit) The term used to refer to a satellite that maintains a constant distance from a point on the equator at every point in its orbit. Geosynchronous orbit satellites are the type used to provide satellite Internet access.

geostationary orbit *See* GEO.

geosynchronous orbit *See* GEO.

ghost A frame that is not actually a data frame, but rather an aberration caused by a device misinterpreting stray voltage on the wire. Unlike true data frames, ghosts have no starting delimiter.

giant A packet that exceeds the medium's maximum packet size. For example, any Ethernet packet that is larger than 1,518 bytes is considered a giant.

Gigabit Ethernet A type of Ethernet network that is capable of 1,000Mbps, or 1Gbps, throughput.

globally unique identifier *See* GUID.

GNU The name given to the public software project to implement a complete, free source code implementation of UNIX. It also refers to the collection of UNIX-inspired utilities and tools that are included with Linux distributions. The term *GNU* is an acronym within an acronym that stands for "GNU's Not UNIX."

Grandfather-Father-Son A backup rotation scheme that uses daily (son), weekly (father), and monthly (grandfather) backup sets.

graphical user interface *See* GUI.

group A means of collectively managing users' permissions and restrictions applied to shared resources. Groups form the basis for resource and account management for every type of NOS. Many network administrators create groups according to department or, even more specifically, according to job function within a department.

GUI (graphical user interface) A pictorial representation of computer functions and elements that, in the case of NOSs, enables administrators to more easily manage files, users, groups, security, printers, and other issues.

GUID (globally unique identifier) A 128-bit number generated and assigned to an object upon its creation in Active Directory. Network applications and services use an object's GUID to communicate with it.

H.225 A session layer call signaling protocol defined as part of ITU's H.323 multiservice network architecture. H.225 is responsible for call or videoconference setup between nodes on a VoIP or video over IP network, indicating node status, requesting additional bandwidth and call termination.

H.245 A session layer control protocol defined as part of ITU's H.323 multiservice network architecture. H.245 is responsible for controlling a session between two nodes. For example, it ensures that the two nodes are communicating in the same format.

H.248 *See* MEGACO.

H.323 An ITU standard that describes an architecture and a suite of protocols for establishing and managing multimedia services sessions on a packet-switched network.

H.323 gatekeeper The nerve center for networks that adhere to H.323. Gatekeepers authorize and authenticate terminals and gateways, manage bandwidth, and oversee call routing, accounting, and billing. Gatekeepers are optional on H.323 networks.

H.323 gateway On a network following the H.323 standard, a gateway that provides translation between network devices running H.323 signaling protocols and devices running other types of signaling protocols (for example, SS7 on the PSTN).

H.323 terminal On a network following the H.323 standard, any node that provides audio, visual, or data information to another node.

H.323 zone A collection of H.323 terminals, gateways, and MCUs that are managed by a single H.323 gatekeeper.

hacker A person who masters the inner workings of operating systems and utilities in an effort to better understand them. A hacker is distinguished from a cracker in that a cracker attempts to exploit a network's vulnerabilities for malicious purposes.

half-duplex A type of transmission in which signals may travel in both directions over a medium, but in only one direction at a time.

handshake protocol One of several protocols within SSL, and perhaps the most significant. As its name implies, the handshake protocol allows the client and server to authenticate (or introduce) each other and establishes terms for how they securely exchange data during an SSL session.

hardware address *See* MAC address.

hardware RAID A method of implementing RAID that relies on an externally attached set of disks and a RAID disk controller, which manages the RAID array.

head-end A cable company's central office, which connects cable wiring to many nodes before it reaches customers' sites.

Health Insurance Portability and Accountability Act *See* HIPAA.

help desk analyst A person who's proficient in basic (but not usually advanced) workstation and network troubleshooting. Help desk analysts are part of first-level support.

help desk coordinator A person who ensures that help desk analysts are divided into the correct teams, schedules shifts at the help desk, and maintains the infrastructure to enable analysts to better perform their jobs. They might also serve as third-level support personnel, taking responsibility for troubleshooting a problem when the second-level support analyst is unable to solve it.

hertz (Hz) A measure of frequency equivalent to the number of amplitude cycles per second.

heuristic scanning A type of virus scanning that attempts to identify viruses by discovering viruslike behavior.

HFC (hybrid fiber-coax) A link that consists of fiber cable connecting the cable company's offices to a node location near the customer and coaxial cable connecting the node to the customer's house. HFC upgrades to existing cable wiring are required before current TV cable systems can provide Internet access.

hierarchical file system The organization of files and directories (or folders) on a disk in which directories may contain files and other directories. When displayed graphically, this organization resembles a treelike structure.

HIPAA (Health Insurance Portability and Accountability Act) A federal regulation in the United States, enacted in 1996. One aspect of this regulation addresses the security and privacy of medical records, including those stored or transmitted electronically.

hoax A rumor, or false alert, about a dangerous, new virus that could supposedly cause serious damage to your workstation.

hop A term used to describe each trip a unit of data takes from one connectivity device to another. Typically, *hop* is used in the context of router-to-router communications.

host 1) A computer that enables resource sharing by other computers on the same network. 2) A TCP/IP utility that at its simplest returns either the IP address of a host if its host name is specified or its host name if its IP address is specified.

host file A text file that associates TCP/IP host names with IP addresses.

host name A symbolic name that describes a TCP/IP device.

host-based firewall A firewall that only protects the computer on which it's installed.

hostname A TCP/IP utility used to show or modify a client's host name.

hosts The name of the host file used on UNIX, Linux, and Windows systems. On a UNIX- or Linux-based computer, hosts is found in the /etc directory. On a Windows-based computer, it is found in the %systemroot%\system32 \drivers\etc folder.

hot site A place where the computers, devices, and connectivity necessary to rebuild a network exist, and all are appropriately configured, updated, and connected to match your network's current state.

hot spare In the context of RAID, a disk or partition that is part of the array but used only in case one of the RAID disks fails. More generally, *hot spare* is used as a synonym for a hot swappable component.

hot spot An area covered by a wireless access point that provides visitors with wireless services, including Internet access.

hot swappable A characteristic that enables identical components to be interchanged (or swapped) while a machine is still running (hot). After being installed, a hot swappable component automatically assumes the functions of its counterpart.

HTTP (Hypertext Transfer Protocol) An application layer protocol that formulates and interprets requests between Web clients and servers.

HTTP over Secure Sockets Layer *See* HTTPS.

HTTP Secure *See* HTTPS.

HTTPS (HTTP over Secure Sockets Layer) The URL prefix that indicates that a Web page requires its data to be exchanged between client and server using SSL encryption. HTTPS uses the TCP port number 443, rather than port 80 (the port that normal HTTP uses).

hub A connectivity device that retransmits incoming data signals to its multiple ports. Typically, hubs contain one uplink port, which is used to connect to a network's backbone.

hybrid fiber-coax *See* HFC.

hybrid topology A physical topology that combines characteristics of more than one simple physical topology.

Hypertext Transfer Protocol *See* HTTP.

IAB (Internet Architecture Board) A technical advisory group of researchers and technical professionals responsible for Internet growth and management strategy, resolution of technical disputes, and standards oversight.

IANA (Internet Assigned Numbers Authority) A nonprofit, United States government-funded group that was established at the University of Southern California and charged with managing IP address allocation and the domain name system. The oversight for many of IANA's functions was given to ICANN in 1998; however, IANA continues to perform Internet addressing and domain name system administration.

ICA (Independent Computing Architecture) client The software from Citrix Systems, Inc., that, when installed on a client, enables the client to connect with a host computer and exchange keystrokes, mouse clicks, and screen updates. Citrix's ICA client can work with virtually any operating system or application.

ICANN (Internet Corporation for Assigned Names and Numbers) The nonprofit corporation currently designated by the United States government to maintain and assign IP addresses.

ICMP (Internet Control Message Protocol) A core protocol in the TCP/IP suite that notifies the sender that something has gone wrong in the transmission process and that packets were not delivered.

ICS (Internet Connection Sharing) A service provided with Windows 98, Me, 2000, and 32-bit versions of XP operating systems that allows one computer, the ICS host, to share its Internet connection with other computers on the same network.

ICS host On a network using the Microsoft Internet Connection Sharing service, the computer whose Internet connection other computers share. The ICS host must contain two network interfaces: one that connects to the Internet and one that connects to the LAN.

IDF (intermediate distribution frame) A junction point between the MDF and concentrations of fewer connections—for example, those that terminate in a telecommunications closet.

IDS (intrusion-detection system) A dedicated device or software running on a host that monitors and flags (and sometimes logs) any unauthorized attempt to access an organization's secured resources on a network or host.

IEEE (Institute of Electrical and Electronics Engineers) An international society composed of engineering professionals. Its goals are to promote development and education in the electrical engineering and computer science fields.

IEEE 1394 *See* FireWire.

IETF (Internet Engineering Task Force) An organization that sets standards for how systems communicate over the Internet (for example, how protocols operate and interact).

ifconfig A TCP/IP configuration and management utility used with UNIX and Linux systems.

IGMP (Internet Group Management Protocol or Internet Group Multicast Protocol) A TCP/IP protocol used to manage multicast transmissions. Routers use IGMP to determine which nodes belong to a multicast group, and nodes use IGMP to join or leave a multicast group.

IKE (Internet Key Exchange) The first phase of IPSec authentication, which accomplishes key management. IKE is a service that runs on UDP port 500. After IKE has established the rules for the type of keys two nodes use, IPSec invokes its second phase, encryption.

IMAP (Internet Message Access Protocol) A mail retrieval protocol that improves on the shortcomings of POP. The single biggest advantage IMAP4 has relative to POP is that it allows users to store messages on the mail server, rather than always having to download them to the local machine. The most current version of IMAP is version 4 (IMAP4).

IMAP4 (Internet Message Access Protocol, version 4) The most commonly used form of the Internet Message Access Protocol (IMAP).

impedance The resistance that contributes to controlling an electrical signal. Impedance is measured in ohms.

incremental backup A backup in which only data that has changed since the last full or incremental backup is copied to a storage medium. After backing up files, an incremental backup unchecks the archive bit for every file it has saved.

Industry Standard Architecture *See* ISA.

information node *See* inode.

infrastructure WLAN A type of WLAN in which stations communicate with an access point and not directly with each other.

inherited A type of permission, or right, that is passed down from one group (the parent) to a group within that group (the child).

inode (information node) A UNIX or Linux file system information storage area that holds all details about a file. This information includes the size, the access rights, the date and time of creation, and a pointer to the actual contents of the file.

Institute of Electrical and Electronics Engineers *See* IEEE.

Integrated Services Digital Network *See* ISDN.

integrity The soundness of a network's files, systems, and connections. To ensure integrity, you must protect your network from anything that might render it unusable, such as corruption, tampering, natural disasters, and viruses.

integrity checking A method of comparing the current characteristics of files and disks against an archived version of these characteristics to discover any changes. The most common example of integrity checking involves a checksum.

intelligent hub A hub that possesses processing capabilities and can therefore monitor network traffic, detect packet errors and collisions, poll connected devices for information, and gather the data in database format.

interior router A router that directs data between nodes on an autonomous LAN.

intermediate distribution frame *See* IDF.

Intermediate System to Intermediate System *See* IS-IS.

International Organization for Standardization *See* ISO.

International Telecommunication Union *See* ITU.

Internet A complex WAN that connects LANs and clients around the globe.

Internet Architecture Board *See* IAB.

Internet Assigned Numbers Authority *See* IANA.

Internet Connection Sharing *See* ICS.

Internet Control Message Protocol *See* ICMP.

Internet Corporation for Assigned Names and Numbers *See* ICANN.

Internet Engineering Task Force *See* IETF.

Internet Group Management Protocol *See* IGMP.

Internet Group Multicast Protocol *See* IGMP.

Internet Key Exchange *See* IKE.

Internet Message Access Protocol *See* IMAP.

Internet Message Access Protocol, version 4 *See* IMAP4.

Internet Protocol *See* IP.

Internet Protocol address *See* IP address.

Internet Protocol Security *See* IPSec.

Internet Relay Chat *See* IRC.

Internet service provider *See* ISP.

Internet services The services that enable a network to communicate with the Internet, including World Wide Web servers and browsers, file transfer capabilities, Internet addressing schemes, security filters, and a means for directly logging on to other computers.

Internet Society *See* ISOC.

Internet telephony The provision of telephone service over the Internet.

internetwork To traverse more than one LAN segment and more than one type of network through a router.

interrupt A circuit board wire through which a device issues voltage, thereby signaling a request for the processor's attention.

interrupt request *See* IRQ.

intrusion-detection system *See* IDS.

intrusion-prevention system *See* IPS.

IP (Internet Protocol) A core protocol in the TCP/IP suite that operates in the network layer of the OSI model and provides information about how and where data should be delivered. IP is the subprotocol that enables TCP/IP to internetwork.

IP address (Internet Protocol address) The network layer address assigned to nodes to uniquely identify them on a TCP/IP network. IP addresses consist of 32 bits divided into four octets, or bytes.

IP datagram The IP portion of a TCP/IP frame that acts as an envelope for data, holding information necessary for routers to transfer data between subnets.

IP masquerading *See* DNAT.

IP next generation *See* IPv6.

IP phone *See* IP telephone.

IP spoofing A security attack in which an outsider obtains internal IP addresses and then uses those addresses to pretend that he has authority to access a private network from the Internet.

IP telephone A telephone used for VoIP on a TCP/IP-based network. IP telephones are designed to transmit and receive only digital signals.

IP telephony *See* VoIP.

IP television *See* IPTV.

IP version 4 Link Local *See* IPv4LL.

ipconfig The utility used to display TCP/IP addressing and domain name information in the Windows NT, Windows 2000, Windows XP, and Windows Vista client operating systems.

IPng *See* IPv6.

IP-PBX A private switch that accepts and interprets both analog and digital voice signals (although some IP-PBXs do not accept analog lines). It can connect with both traditional PSTN lines and data networks. An IP-PBX transmits and receives IP-based voice signals to and from other network connectivity devices, such as routers and gateways.

IPS (intrusion-prevention system) A dedicated device or software running on a host that automatically reacts to any unauthorized attempt to access an organization's secured resources on a network or host. IPS is often combined with IDS.

IPSec (Internet Protocol Security) A Layer 3 protocol that defines encryption, authentication, and key management for TCP/IP transmissions. IPSec is an enhancement to IPv4 and is native to IPv6. IPSec is unique among authentication methods in that it adds security information to the header of all IP packets.

IPTV (IP television) A service in which television signals from broadcast or cable networks travel over packet-switched networks.

IPv4 (IP version 4) The current standard for IP addressing that specifies 32-bit addresses composed of four octets.

IPv4LL (IP version 4 Link Local) A protocol that manages automatic address assignment among locally connected nodes. IPv4LL is part of the Zeroconf group of protocols.

IPv6 (IP version 6) A newer standard for IP addressing that will replace the current IPv4 (IP version 4). Most notably, IPv6 uses a newer, more efficient header in its packets and allows for 128-bit source and destination IP addresses. The use of longer addresses allows for many more IP addresses to be in circulation.

IRC (Internet Relay Chat) A protocol that enables users running special IRC client software to communicate instantly with other participants in a chat room on the Internet.

IRQ (interrupt request) A message sent to the computer that instructs it to stop what it is doing and pay attention to something else. *IRQ* is often used (informally) to refer to the interrupt request number.

IRQ number The unique number assigned to each interrupt in a computer. Interrupt request numbers range from 0 to 15, and many PC devices reserve specific numbers for their use alone.

ISA (Industry Standard Architecture) The original PC bus type, developed in the early 1980s to support an 8-bit and later a 16-bit data path and a 4.77MHz clock speed.

ISDN (Integrated Services Digital Network) An international standard that uses PSTN lines to carry digital signals. It specifies protocols at the physical, data link, and transport layers of the OSI model. ISDN lines may carry voice and data signals simultaneously. Two types of ISDN connections are used in North America: BRI (Basic Rate Interface) and PRI (Primary Rate Interface). Both use a combination of bearer channels (B channels) and data channels (D channels).

IS-IS (Intermediate System to Intermediate System) A link-state routing protocol that uses a best-path algorithm similar to OSPF's. IS-IS was originally codified by ISO, which referred to routers as "intermediate systems," thus the protocol's name. IS-IS is designed for use on interior routers only.

ISO (International Organization for Standardization) A collection of standards organizations representing 157 countries with headquarters located in Geneva, Switzerland. Its goal is to establish international technological standards to facilitate the global exchange of information and barrier-free trade.

ISOC (Internet Society) A professional organization with members from 90 chapters around the world that helps to establish technical standards for the Internet.

ISP (Internet service provider) A business that provides organizations and individuals with Internet access and often, other services, such as e-mail and Web hosting.

ITU (International Telecommunication Union) A United Nations agency that regulates international telecommunications and provides developing countries with technical expertise and equipment to advance their technological bases.

iwconfig A command-line utility for viewing and setting wireless interface parameters on Linux and UNIX systems.

J1 A digital carrier standard used in Japan that offers 24 channels and 1.544Mbps throughput.

J3 A digital carrier standard used in Japan that offers 480 channels and 32.064Mbps throughput.

jabber A device that handles electrical signals improperly, usually affecting the rest of the network. A network analyzer will detect a jabber as a device that is always retransmitting, effectively bringing the network to a halt. A jabber usually results from a bad NIC. Occasionally, it can be caused by outside electrical interference.

jamming A part of CSMA/CD in which, upon detecting a collision, a station issues a special 32-bit sequence to indicate to all nodes on an Ethernet segment that its previously transmitted frame has suffered a collision and should be considered faulty.

KDC (Key Distribution Center) In Kerberos terminology, the server that runs the authentication service and the Ticket Granting Service to issue keys and tickets to clients.

Kerberos A cross-platform authentication protocol that uses key encryption to verify the identity of clients and to securely exchange information after a client logs on to a system. It is an example of a private key encryption service.

kernel The core of a UNIX or Linux system. This part of the operating system is loaded and run when you turn on your computer. It mediates between user programs and the computer hardware.

kernel module A portion of the kernel that you can load and unload to add or remove functionality on a running UNIX or Linux system.

key A series of characters that is combined with a block of data during that data's encryption. To decrypt the resulting data, the recipient must also possess the key.

Key Distribution Center *See* KDC.

key management The method whereby two nodes using key encryption agree on common parameters for the keys they will use to encrypt data.

key pair The combination of a public and private key used to decipher data that was encrypted using public key encryption.

L2TP (Layer 2 Tunneling Protocol) A protocol that encapsulates PPP data, for use on VPNs. L2TP is based on Cisco technology and is standardized by the IETF. It is distinguished by its compatibility among different manufacturers' equipment; its ability to connect between clients, routers, and servers alike; and also by the fact that it can connect nodes belonging to different Layer 3 networks.

label A character string that represents a domain (either top-level, second-level, or third-level).

LAN (local area network) A network of computers and other devices that is confined to a relatively small space, such as one building or even one office.

LAN Emulation *See* LANE.

LANE (LAN Emulation) A method for transporting token ring or Ethernet frames over ATM networks. LANE encapsulates incoming Ethernet or token ring frames and then converts them into ATM cells for transmission over an ATM network.

last mile *See* local loop.

late collision A collision that takes place outside the normal window in which collisions are detected and redressed. Late collisions are usually caused by a defective station (such as a card, or transceiver) that is transmitting without first verifying line status or by failure to observe the configuration guidelines for cable length, which results in collisions being recognized too late.

latency The delay between the transmission of a signal and its receipt.

Layer 2 Tunneling Protocol *See* L2TP.

Layer 3 switch A switch capable of interpreting data at Layer 3 (network layer) of the OSI model.

Layer 4 switch A switch capable of interpreting data at Layer 4 (transport layer) of the OSI model.

LC (local connector) A connector used with single-mode or multimode fiber-optic cable.

LDAP (Lightweight Directory Access Protocol) A standard protocol for accessing network directories.

leaf object An object in an operating system's directory, such as a printer or user, that does not contain other objects.

lease The agreement between a DHCP server and client on how long the client can use a DHCP-assigned IP address. DHCP services can be configured to provide lease terms equal to any amount of time.

LEO (low Earth orbiting) A type of satellite that orbits the Earth with an altitude between 100 and 900 miles, closer to the Earth's poles than the orbits of either GEO or MEO satellites. LEO satellites cover a smaller geographical range than GEO satellites and require less power.

license tracking The process of determining the number of copies of a single application that are currently in use on the network and whether the number in use exceeds the authorized number of licenses.

Lightweight Directory Access Protocol *See* LDAP.

line printer daemon *See* lpd.

lineman's handset *See* butt set.

line-of-sight *See* LOS.

link segment *See* unpopulated segment.

link-state A type of routing protocol that enables routers across a network to share information, after which each router can independently map the network and determine the best path between itself and a packet's destination node.

Linux A freely distributable implementation of a UNIX-type system. Finnish computer scientist Linus Torvalds originally developed it.

LLC (logical link control) sublayer The upper sublayer in the data link layer. The LLC provides a common interface and supplies reliability and flow control services.

load balancing An automatic distribution of traffic over multiple links, hard disks, or processors intended to optimize responses.

local area network *See* LAN.

local collision A collision that occurs when two or more stations are transmitting simultaneously. Excessively high collision rates within the network can usually be traced to cable or routing problems.

local connector *See* LC.

local loop The part of a phone system that connects a customer site with a telecommunications carrier's switching facility.

logic bomb A program designed to start when certain conditions are met.

logical address *See* network address.

logical link control sublayer *See* LLC (logical link control) sublayer.

logical topology A characteristic of network transmission that reflects the way in which data is transmitted between nodes (which may differ from the physical layout of the paths that data takes). The most common logical topologies are bus and ring.

loopback adapter *See* loopback plug.

loopback address An IP address reserved for communicating from a node to itself (used mostly for troubleshooting purposes). The IPv4 loopback address is always cited as 127.0.0.1, although in fact, transmitting to any IP address whose first octet is 127 will contact the originating device. In IPv6, the loopback address is represented as ::1.

loopback plug A connector used for troubleshooting that plugs into a port (for example, a serial, parallel, or RJ-45 port) and crosses over the transmit line to the receive line, allowing outgoing signals to be redirected into the computer for testing.

loopback test An attempt to contact one's own machine for troubleshooting purposes. In TCP/IP-based networking, a loopback test can be performed by communicating with an IPv4 address that begins with an octet of 127. Usually, this means pinging the address 127.0.0.1.

LOS (line-of-sight) A wireless signal or path that travels directly in a straight line from its transmitter to its intended receiver. This type of propagation uses the least amount of energy and results in the reception of the clearest possible signal.

low Earth orbiting *See* LEO.

lpd (line printer daemon) A UNIX service responsible for printing files placed in the printer queue by the lpr command.

lpr A UNIX command that places files in the printer queue. The files are subsequently printed with lpd, the print service.

MAC (media access control) sublayer The lower sublayer of the data link layer. The MAC appends the physical address of the destination computer onto the frame.

MAC address A 12-character string that uniquely identifies a network node. The manufacturer hard-codes the MAC address into the NIC. This address is composed of the block ID and device ID.

Mac OS X Server A proprietary NOS from Apple Computer that is based on a version of UNIX.

macro virus A virus that takes the form of an application (for example, a word-processing or spreadsheet) program macro, which may execute when the program is in use.

mail server A server that manages the storage and transfer of e-mail messages.

mail services The network services that manage the storage and transfer of e-mail between users on a network. In addition to sending, receiving, and storing mail, mail services can include filtering, routing, notification, scheduling, and data exchange with other mail servers.

main bus *See* bus.

main cross-connect *See* MDF.

main distribution frame *See* MDF.

malware A program or piece of code designed to harm a system or its resources.

MAN (metropolitan area network) A network that is larger than a LAN, typically connecting clients and servers from multiple buildings, but within a limited geographic area. For example, a MAN could connect multiple city government buildings around a city's center.

man pages (manual pages) The online documentation for any variety of the UNIX operating system. This documentation describes the use of the commands and the programming interface.

managed hub *See* intelligent hub.

Management Information Base *See* MIB.

management services The network services that centrally administer and simplify complicated management tasks on the network. Examples of management services include license tracking, security auditing, asset management, address management, software distribution, traffic monitoring, load balancing, and hardware diagnosis.

man-in-the-middle attack A security threat that relies on intercepted transmissions. It can take one of several forms, but in all cases a person redirects or captures secure data traffic while in transit.

manual pages *See* man pages.

map The action of associating a disk, directory, or device with a drive letter.

mask *See* subnet mask.

maximum transmission unit *See* MTU.

MCSE (Microsoft Certified Systems Engineer) A professional certification established by Microsoft that demonstrates in-depth knowledge about Microsoft products.

MCU (multipoint control unit) A computer that provides support for multiple H.323 terminals (for example, several workstations participating in a videoconference) and manages communication between them. An MCU is also known as a video bridge.

MDF (main distribution frame) Also known as the main cross-connect, the first point of interconnection between an organization's LAN or WAN and a service provider's facility.

mechanical transfer-registered jack *See* MT-RJ.

media access control sublayer *See* MAC (media access control) sublayer.

media converter A device that enables networks or segments using different media to interconnect and exchange signals.

media gateway A gateway capable of accepting connections from multiple devices (for example, IP telephones, traditional telephones, IP fax machines, traditional fax machines, and so on) and translating analog signals into packetized, digital signals, and vice versa.

Media Gateway Control Protocol *See* MGCP.

media gateway controller *See* MGC.

medium Earth orbiting *See* MEO.

MEGACO A protocol used between media gateway controllers and media gateways. MEGACO is poised to replace MGCP on modern converged networks, as it supports a broader range of network technologies, including ATM. Also known as H.248.

member server A type of server on a Windows Server 2003 or Server 2008 network that does not hold directory information and, therefore, cannot authenticate users.

memory range A hexadecimal number that indicates the area of memory that the NIC and CPU will use for exchanging, or buffering, data. As with IRQs, some memory ranges are reserved for specific devices—most notably, the motherboard.

MEO (medium Earth orbiting) A type of satellite that orbits the Earth roughly 6,000 to 12,000 miles above its surface, positioned between the equator and the poles. MEO satellites can cover a larger area of the Earth's surface than LEO satellites while using less power and causing less signal delay than GEO satellites.

mesh topology WAN A type of WAN in which several sites are directly interconnected. Mesh WANs are highly fault tolerant because they provide multiple routes for data to follow between any two points.

message switching A type of switching in which a connection is established between two devices in the connection path; one device transfers data to the second device and then breaks the connection. The information is stored and forwarded from the second device after a connection between that device and a third device on the path is established.

metropolitan area network *See* MAN.

MGC (media gateway controller) A computer that manages multiple media gateways and facilitates the exchange of call control information between these gateways.

MGCP (Media Gateway Control Protocol) A protocol used for communication between media gateway controllers and media gateways. MGCP is defined in RFC 2507, but it was never officially adopted as a standard. MGCP is currently the most popular media gateway control protocol used on converged networks.

MIB (Management Information Base) A database used in network management that contains a device's definitions of managed objects and their data.

Microsoft Certified Systems Engineer *See* MCSE.

Microsoft Challenge Handshake Authentication Protocol *See* MS-CHAP.

Microsoft Challenge Handshake Authentication Protocol, version 2 *See* MS-CHAPv2.

Microsoft Management Console *See* MMC.

middleware The software that sits between the client and server in a 3-tier architecture. Middleware may be used as a messaging service between clients and servers, as a universal query language for databases, or as means of coordinating processes between multiple servers that need to work together in servicing clients.

MIME (Multipurpose Internet Mail Extensions) A standard for encoding and interpreting binary files, images, video, and non-ASCII character sets within an e-mail message.

MIMO (multiple input-multiple output) In the context of 802.11n wireless networking, the ability for access points to issue multiple signals to stations, thereby multiplying the signal's strength and increasing their range and data-carrying capacity. Because the signals follow multipath propagation, they must be phase-adjusted when they reach their destination.

mirroring A fault-tolerance technique in which one component or device duplicates the activity of another.

MMC (Microsoft Management Console) A customizable, graphical network management interface introduced with Windows Server 2003 and incorporated in Window Server 2008's Server Manager.

MMF (multimode fiber) A type of fiber-optic cable that contains a core with a diameter between 50 and 100 microns, through which many pulses of light generated by a light-emitting diode (LED) travel at different angles.

mobile A type of wireless system in which the receiver can be located anywhere within the transmitter's range. This allows the receiver to roam from one place to another while continuing to pick up its signal.

modal bandwidth A measure of the highest frequency of signal a multimode fiber-optic cable can support over a specific distance. Modal bandwidth is measured in MHz-km.

modem A device that modulates analog signals into digital signals at the transmitting end for transmission over telephone lines, and demodulates digital signals into analog signals at the receiving end.

modular router A router with multiple slots that can hold different interface cards or other devices to provide flexible, customizable network interoperability.

modulation A technique for formatting signals in which one property of a simple carrier wave is modified by the addition of a data signal during transmission.

motherboard The main circuit board that controls a computer.

mount The process of making a disk partition available.

MPLS (multiprotocol label switching) A type of switching that enables any one of several Layer 2 protocols to carry multiple types of Layer 3 protocols. One of its benefits is the ability to use packet-switched technologies over traditionally circuit-switched networks. MPLS can also create end-to-end paths that act like circuit-switched connections.

MRTG (Multi Router Traffic Grapher) A command-line utility that uses SNMP to poll devices, collects data in a log file, and then generates HTML-based views of the data. MRTG is freely distributed software originally written by Tobias Oetiker, a networking professional who in the early 1990s saw a need for a tool to regularly measure the status of his organization's WAN link.

MS-CHAP (Microsoft Challenge Handshake Authentication Protocol) An authentication protocol offered by Microsoft with its Windows clients and servers. Similar to CHAP, MS-CHAP uses a three-way handshake to verify a client's credentials and encrypts passwords with a challenge text.

MS-CHAPv2 (Microsoft Challenge Authentication Protocol, version 2) An authentication protocol provided with Windows XP, 2000, and Server 2003 operating systems that follows the CHAP model but uses stronger encryption, uses different encryption keys for transmission and reception, and requires mutual authentication between two computers.

mtr (my traceroute) A route discovery and analysis utility that comes with UNIX and Linux operating systems. Mtr combines the functions of the `ping` and `traceroute` commands and delivers an easily readable chart as its output.

MT-RJ (mechanical transfer-registered jack) A connector used with single-mode or multimode fiber-optic cable.

MTU (maximum transmission unit) The largest data unit a network (for example, Ethernet or token ring) will accept for transmission.

Multi Router Traffic Grapher *See* MRTG.

multicast address A type of address in the IPv6 that represents multiple interfaces, often on multiple nodes. An IPv6 multicast address begins with the following hexadecimal field: FF0*x*, where *x* is a character that identifies the address's group scope.

multicasting A means of transmission in which one device sends data to a specific group of devices (not necessarily the entire network segment) in a point-to-multipoint fashion.

multimeter A simple instrument that can measure multiple characteristics of an electric circuit, including its resistance and voltage.

multimode fiber *See* MMF.

multipath The characteristic of wireless signals that follow a number of different paths to their destination (for example, because of reflection, diffraction, and scattering).

multiple input-multiple output *See* MIMO.

multiplexer (mux) A device that separates a medium into multiple channels and issues signals to each of those subchannels.

multiplexing A form of transmission that allows multiple signals to travel simultaneously over one medium.

multipoint control unit *See* MCU.

multiprocessing The technique of splitting tasks among multiple processors to expedite the completion of any single instruction.

multiprotocol label switching *See* MPLS.

Multipurpose Internet Mail Extensions *See* MIME.

multitasking The ability of a processor to perform multiple activities in a brief period of time (often seeming simultaneous to the user).

mutual authentication An authentication scheme in which both computers verify the credentials of each other.

name server A server that contains a database of TCP/IP host names and their associated IP addresses. A name server supplies a resolver with the requested information. If it cannot resolve the IP address, the query passes to a higher-level name server.

namespace The complete database of hierarchical names (including host and domain names) used to resolve IP addresses with their hosts.

narrowband A type of wireless transmission in which signals travel over a single frequency or within a specified frequency range.

NAS (network attached storage) A device or set of devices attached to a client/server network, dedicated to providing highly fault-tolerant access to large quantities of data. NAS depends on traditional network transmission methods such as Ethernet.

NAT (Network Address Translation) A technique in which IP addresses used on a private network are assigned a public IP address by a gateway when accessing a public network.

nbtstat A TCP/IP troubleshooting utility that provides information about NetBIOS names and their addresses. If you know the NetBIOS name of a workstation, you can use nbtstat to determine its IP address.

near end cross talk *See* NEXT.

negative frame sequence check The result of the CRC (cyclic redundancy check) generated by the originating node not matching the checksum calculated from the data received. It usually indicates noise or transmission problems on the LAN interface or cabling. A high number of (nonmatching) CRCs usually results from excessive collisions or a station transmitting bad data.

net mask *See* subnet mask.

NetBIOS A protocol that runs in the session and transport layers of the OSI model and associates NetBIOS names with workstations. NetBIOS alone is not routable because it does not contain network layer information. However, when encapsulated in another protocol such as TCP/IP, it can be routed.

netstat A TCP/IP troubleshooting utility that displays statistics and the state of current TCP/IP connections. It also displays ports, which can signal whether services are using the correct ports.

network A group of computers and other devices (such as printers) that are connected by and can exchange data via some type of transmission media, such as a cable or the atmosphere.

network adapter *See* NIC.

network address A unique identifying number for a network node that follows a hierarchical addressing scheme and can be assigned through operating system software. Network addresses are added to data packets and interpreted by protocols at the network layer of the OSI model.

Network Address Translation *See* NAT.

network analyzer *See* protocol analyzer.

network attached storage *See* NAS.

network class A classification for TCP/IP-based networks that pertains to the network's potential size and is indicated by an IP address's network ID and subnet mask. Network Classes A, B, and C are commonly used by clients on LANs; network Classes D and E are reserved for special purposes.

network diagram A graphical representation of a network's devices and connections.

Network File System *See* NFS.

network ID The portion of an IP address common to all nodes on the same network or subnet.

network interface card *See* NIC.

network interface unit *See* NIU.

network key A key (or character string) required for a wireless station to associate with an access point using WEP.

network layer The third layer in the OSI model. Protocols in the network layer translate network addresses into their physical counterparts and decide how to route data from the sender to the receiver.

network layer address *See* network address.

network management The assessment, monitoring, and maintenance of the devices and connections on a network.

network monitor A software-based tool that monitors traffic on the network from a server or workstation attached to the network. Network monitors typically can interpret up to Layer 3 of the OSI model.

Network Monitor A network monitoring program from Microsoft that comes with Windows Server 2003 and Server 2008 (as well as with Windows NT and Windows 2000 Server).

Network News Transport Protocol *See* NNTP.

network operating system *See* NOS.

network service provider *See* NSP.

network services The functions provided by a network.

Network Termination 1 *See* NT1.

Network Termination 2 *See* NT2.

Network Time Protocol *See* NTP.

network virus A virus that takes advantage of network protocols, commands, messaging programs, and data links to propagate itself. Although all viruses could theoretically travel across network connections, network viruses are specially designed to attack network vulnerabilities.

Network+ (Net+) The professional certification established by CompTIA that verifies broad, vendor-independent networking technology skills, such as an understanding of protocols, topologies, networking hardware, and network troubleshooting.

network-based firewall A firewall configured and positioned to protect an entire network.

New Technology File System *See* NTFS.

newsgroup An Internet-based forum for exchanging messages on a particular topic. Newsgroups rely on NNTP for the collection and dissemination of messages.

NEXT (near end cross talk) Cross talk, or the impingement of the signal carried by one wire onto a nearby wire, that occurs between wire pairs near the source of a signal.

NFS (Network File System) A popular remote file system created by Sun Microsystems and available for UNIX and Linux operating systems.

NIC (network interface card) The device that enables a workstation to connect to the network and communicate with other computers. NICs are manufactured by several companies and come with a variety of specifications that are tailored to the workstation's and the network's requirements. NICs are also called network adapters.

NIU (network interface unit) The point at which PSTN-owned lines terminate at a customer's premises. The NIU is usually located at the demarc.

NNTP (Network News Transfer Protocol or Network News Transport Protocol) An application layer protocol in the TCP/IP suite that facilitates the exchange of newsgroup messages, or articles, between multiple servers and users.

node A computer or other device connected to a network, which has a unique address and is capable of sending or receiving data.

noise The unwanted signals, or interference, from sources near network cabling, such as electrical motors, power lines, and radar.

nonbroadcast point-to-multipoint transmission A communications arrangement in which a single transmitter issues signals to multiple, defined recipients.

NOS (network operating system) The software that runs on a server and enables it to manage data, users, groups, security, applications, and other networking functions. The most popular network operating systems are Microsoft, and Windows Server 2003, Windows Server 2008, UNIX, Linux, and Novell NetWare.

nslookup A TCP/IP utility that allows you to look up the DNS host name of a network node by specifying its IP address, or vice versa. This ability is useful for verifying that a host is configured correctly and for troubleshooting DNS resolution problems.

NSP (network service provider) A carrier that provides long-distance (and often global) connectivity between major data-switching centers across the Internet. AT&T, Verizon, and Sprint are all examples of network service providers in the United States. Customers, including ISPs, can lease dedicated private or public Internet connections from an NSP.

NT1 (Network Termination 1) A device used on ISDN networks that connects the incoming twisted pair wiring with the customer's ISDN terminal equipment.

NT2 (Network Termination 2) An additional connection device required on PRI to handle the multiple ISDN lines between the customer's network termination connection and the local phone company's wires.

NTFS (New Technology File System) A file system developed by Microsoft and used with its Windows NT, Windows Vista, Windows 2000 Server, Windows Server 2003, and Windows Server 2008 operating systems.

NTP (Network Time Protocol) A simple application layer protocol in the TCP/IP suite used to synchronize the clocks of computers on a network. NTP depends on UDP for transport layer services.

object A representation of a thing or person associated with the network that belongs in the NOS directory. Objects include users, printers, groups, computers, data files, and applications.

object class *See* class.

OC (Optical Carrier) An internationally recognized rating that indicates throughput rates for SONET connections.

octet One of the four bytes that are separated by periods and together make up an IPv4 address.

offline UPS *See* standby UPS.

ohmmeter A device used to measure resistance in an electrical circuit.

omnidirectional antenna A type of antenna that issues and receives wireless signals with equal strength and clarity in all directions. This type of antenna is used when many receivers must be able to pick up the signal, or when the receiver's location is highly mobile.

on-board NIC A NIC that is integrated into a computer's motherboard, rather than connected via an expansion slot or peripheral bus.

on-board port A port that is integrated into a computer's motherboard.

online backup A technique in which data is backed up to a central location over the Internet.

online UPS A power supply that uses the A/C power from the wall outlet to continuously charge its battery, while providing power to a network device through its battery.

Open Group, the A nonprofit industry association that owns the UNIX trademark.

Open Shortest Path First *See* OSPF.

open source The term that describes software that is developed and packaged by individuals and made available to anyone, without licensing fees.

open source software Software that is distributed with few restrictions and whose source code is freely available. Open source software is not owned by any one company.

Open Systems Interconnection model *See* OSI (Open Systems Interconnection) model.

OpenSSH An open source version of the SSH suite of protocols.

Optical Carrier *See* OC.

optical loss The degradation of a light signal on a fiber-optic network.

optical media A type of media capable of storing digitized data, which uses a laser to write data to it and read data from it.

optical time domain reflectometer *See* OTDR.

organizational unit *See* OU.

OSI (Open Systems Interconnection) model A model for understanding and developing computer-to-computer communication developed in the 1980s by ISO. It divides networking functions among seven layers: physical, data link, network, transport, session, presentation, and application.

OSPF (Open Shortest Path First) A routing protocol that makes up for some of the limitations of RIP and can coexist with RIP on a network.

OTDR (optical time domain reflectometer) A performance testing device for use with fiber-optic networks. An OTDR works by issuing a light-based signal on a fiber-optic cable and measuring the way in which the signal bounces back (or reflects) to the OTDR. By measuring the length of time it takes the signal to return, an OTDR can determine the location of a fault.

OU (organizational unit) A logical receptacle for holding objects with similar characteristics or privileges in an NOS directory. Containers form the branches of the directory tree.

overhead The nondata information that must accompany data for a signal to be properly routed and interpreted by the network.

P2P network *See* peer-to-peer network.

Packet Internet Groper *See* PING.

packet sniffer *See* protocol analyzer.

packet switching A type of switching in which data is broken into packets before it is transported. In packet switching, packets can travel any path on the network to their destination, because each packet contains a destination address and sequencing information.

packet-filtering firewall A router that operates at the data link and transport layers of the OSI model, examining the header of every packet of data that it receives to determine whether that type of packet is authorized to continue to its destination. Packet-filtering firewalls are also called screening firewalls.

padding The bytes added to the data (or information) portion of an Ethernet frame to ensure this field is at least 46 bytes in size. Padding has no effect on the data carried by the frame.

page file A file on the hard drive that is used for virtual memory.

paging The process of moving blocks of information, called pages, between RAM and into a page file on disk.

paging file *See* page file.

PAN (personal area network) A small (usually home) network composed of personal communications devices.

PAP (Password Authentication Protocol) A simple authentication protocol that operates over PPP. Using PAP, a client issues its credentials in a request to authenticate, and the server responds with a confirmation or denial of authentication after comparing the credentials to those in its database. PAP is not very secure and is, therefore, rarely used on modern networks.

parallel backbone A type of backbone that consists of more than one connection from the central router or switch to each network segment.

parity The mechanism used to verify the integrity of data by making the number of bits in a byte sum equal to either an odd or even number.

parity error checking The process of comparing the parity of data read from a disk with the type of parity used by the system.

partial-mesh WAN A version of a mesh topology WAN in which only critical sites are directly interconnected and secondary sites are connected through star or ring topologies. Partial mesh WANs are less expensive to implement than full mesh WANs.

partition An area of a computer's hard drive that is logically defined and acts as a separate disk drive.

passive hub A hub that simply retransmits signals over the network.

passive scanning In the context of wireless networking, the process in which a station listens to several channels within a frequency range for a beacon issued by an access point.

passive topology A network topology in which each node passively listens for, and then accepts, data directed to it. A bus topology is considered a passive topology.

Password Authentication Protocol *See* PAP.

PAT (Port Address Translation) A form of address translation that uses TCP port numbers to distinguish each client's

transmission, thus allowing multiple clients to share a limited number of Internet-recognized IP addresses.

patch A correction, improvement, or enhancement to part of a software application, often distributed at no charge by software vendors to fix a bug in their code or to add slightly more functionality.

patch cable A relatively short section (usually between 3 and 25 feet) of cabling with connectors on both ends.

patch panel A wall-mounted panel of data receptors into which cross-connect patch cables from the punch-down block are inserted.

pathping A command-line utility that combines the functionality of the tracert and ping commands (similar to UNIX's mtr command) and comes with Windows XP, Vista, and Windows Server 2003 and Server 2008.

PBX (private branch exchange) A telephone switch used to connect calls within a private organization.

PC Card A PCMCIA standard that specifies a 16-bit interface running at 8MHz for externally attached devices. PC Cards' characteristics match those of the ISA expansion card. And, like the ISA standard, the PC Card standard suffered from its lower data transfer rates, compared to other PCMCIA standards.

PCI (Peripheral Component Interconnect) A 32- or 64-bit bus that can run at 33 or 66MHz, introduced in its original form in the 1990s. The PCI bus is the NIC connection type used for nearly all new PCs. It's characterized by a shorter length than ISA or EISA cards, but it has a much faster data transmission capability.

PCI Express *See* PCIe.

PCIe (PCI Express) A 32- or 64-bit bus standard capable of transferring data at up to 4.26Gbps in full-duplex transmission. PCI Express was introduced in 2002 and offers several advantages over traditional PCI. Its expansion cards can fit into older PCI slots, with some modifications to the motherboard.

PCMCIA (Personal Computer Memory Card International Association) A group of computer manufacturers who developed an interface for connecting any type of device to a portable computer. PCMCIA slots may hold memory, modem, network interface, external hard disk, or CD-ROM cards. PCMCIA-standard cards include PC Card, CardBus, and the newest, ExpressCard.

PD (powered device) On a network using Power over Ethernet, a node that receives power from power-sourcing equipment.

PDU (protocol data unit) A unit of data at any layer of the OSI model.

peer-to-peer network A network in which every computer can communicate directly with every other computer. By default, no computer on a peer-to-peer network has more authority than another. However, each computer can be configured to share only some of its resources and keep other resources inaccessible to other nodes on the network.

per seat In the context of applications, a licensing mode that limits access to an application to specific users or workstations.

per user A licensing mode that allows a fixed quantity of clients to use one software package simultaneously.

performance management The ongoing assessment of how well network links, devices, and components keep up with demands on them.

Peripheral Component Interconnect *See* PCI.

permanent virtual circuit *See* PVC.

personal area network *See* PAN.

Personal Computer Memory Card International Association *See* PCMCIA.

PGP (Pretty Good Privacy) A key-based encryption system for e-mail that uses a two-step verification process.

phase A point or stage in a wave's progress over time.

phishing A practice in which a person attempts to glean access or authentication information by posing as someone who needs that information.

physical address *See* MAC address.

physical layer The lowest, or first, layer of the OSI model. Protocols in the physical layer generate and detect signals to transmit and receive data over a network medium. These protocols also set the data transmission rate and monitor data error rates, but do not provide error correction.

physical memory The RAM chips installed on the computer's system board that provide dedicated memory to that computer.

physical topology The physical layout of a network. A physical topology depicts a network in broad scope; it does not specify devices, connectivity methods, or addresses on the network. Physical topologies are categorized into three fundamental geometric shapes: bus, ring, and star. These shapes can be mixed to create hybrid topologies.

ping To send an echo request signal from one node on a TCP/IP-based network to another, using the PING utility. *See also* PING.

PING (Packet Internet Groper) A TCP/IP troubleshooting utility that can verify that TCP/IP is installed, bound to the NIC, configured correctly, and communicating with the network. PING uses ICMP to send echo request and echo reply messages that determine the validity of an IP address.

pipe A character that enables you to combine existing commands to form new commands. The pipe symbol is the vertical bar (|).

pipeline A series of two or more commands in which the output of prior commands is sent to the input of subsequent commands.

PKI (public key infrastructure) The use of certificate authorities to associate public keys with certain users.

plain old telephone service (POTS) *See* PSTN.

plenum The area above the ceiling tile or below the subfloor in a building.

PoE (Power over Ethernet) A method of delivering current to devices using Ethernet connection cables.

point-to-multipoint A communications arrangement in which one transmitter issues signals to multiple receivers. The receivers may be undefined, as in a broadcast transmission, or defined, as in a nonbroadcast transmission.

point-to-point A data transmission that involves one transmitter and one receiver.

Point-to-Point Protocol *See* PPP.

Point-to-Point Protocol over Ethernet *See* PPPoE.

Point-to-Point Tunneling Protocol *See* PPTP.

polling A network management application's regular collection of data from managed devices.

polymorphic virus A type of virus that changes its characteristics (such as the arrangement of its bytes, size, and internal instructions) every time it is transferred to a new system, making it harder to identify.

POP (Post Office Protocol) An application layer protocol used to retrieve messages from a mail server. When a client retrieves mail via POP, messages previously stored on the mail server are downloaded to the client's workstation and then deleted from the mail server.

POP3 (Post Office Protocol, version 3) The most commonly used form of the Post Office Protocol.

populated segment A network segment that contains end nodes, such as workstations.

Port Address Translation *See* PAT.

port authentication A technique in which a client's identity is verified by an authentication server before a port, whether physical or logical, is opened for the client's Layer 3 traffic. *See also* 802.1x.

port forwarding The process of redirecting traffic from its normally assigned port to a different port, either on the client or server. In the case of using SSH, port forwarding can send data exchanges that are normally insecure through encrypted tunnels.

port mirroring A monitoring technique in which one port on a switch is configured to send a copy of all its traffic to a second port.

port number The address on a host where an application makes itself available to incoming data.

port scanner Software that searches a server, switch, router, or other device for open ports, which can be vulnerable to attack.

port-based authentication *See* port authentication.

Post Office Protocol *See* POP.

Post Office Protocol, version 3 *See* POP3.

POTS *See* PSTN.

Power over Ethernet *See* PoE.

power sourcing equipment *See* PSE.

powered device *See* PD.

PowerPC The brand of computer central processing unit invented by Apple Computer, IBM, and Motorola, Inc., and used in IBM servers.

PPP (Point-to-Point Protocol) A communications protocol that enables a workstation to connect to a server using a serial connection. PPP can support multiple network layer protocols and can use both asynchronous and synchronous communications. It performs compression and error correction and requires little configuration on the client workstation.

PPPoE (Point-to-Point Protocol over Ethernet) PPP running over an Ethernet network.

PPTP (Point-to-Point Tunneling Protocol) A Layer 2 protocol developed by Microsoft that encapsulates PPP data for transmission over VPN connections. PPTP operates with Windows RRAS access services and can accept connections from multiple clients. It is simple, but it is less secure than other modern tunneling protocols.

preamble The field in an Ethernet frame that signals to the receiving node that data is incoming and indicates when the data flow is about to begin.

preemptive multitasking The type of multitasking in which tasks are actually performed one at a time, in very brief succession. In preemptive multitasking, one program uses the processor for a certain period of time and then is suspended to allow another program to use the processor.

presentation layer The sixth layer of the OSI model. Protocols in the presentation layer translate between the application and the network. Here, data is formatted in a schema that the network can understand, with the format varying according to the type of network used. The presentation layer also manages data encryption and decryption, such as the scrambling of system passwords.

Pretty Good Privacy *See* PGP.

PRI (Primary Rate Interface) A type of ISDN that uses 23 bearer channels and one 64Kbps data channel, represented by the notation 23B+D. PRI is less commonly used by individual subscribers than BRI, but it may be used by businesses and other organizations needing more throughput.

principal In Kerberos terminology, a user or client.

print services The network service that allows printers to be shared by several users on a network.

printer queue A logical representation of a networked printer's functionality. To use a printer, clients must have access to the printer queue.

private branch exchange *See* PBX.

private key encryption A type of key encryption in which the sender and receiver use a key to which only they have access. DES (Data Encryption Standard), which was developed by IBM in the 1970s, is a popular example of a private key encryption technique. Private key encryption is also known as symmetric encryption.

private network A network whose access is restricted to only clients or machines with proper credentials.

Private Ports *See* Dynamic Ports.

probe 1) *See* tone locator. 2) In 802.11 wireless networking, a type of frame issued by a station during active scanning to find nearby access points.

process A routine of sequential instructions that runs until it has achieved its goal. For example, a spreadsheet program is a process.

promiscuous mode The feature of a network adapter that allows it to pick up all frames that pass over the network—not just those destined for the node served by the card.

proprietary UNIX Any implementation of UNIX for which the source code is either unavailable or available only by purchasing a licensed copy from Novell (costing as much as millions of dollars). Redistribution of proprietary UNIX versions requires paying royalties to Novell.

protocol A standard method or format for communication between network devices. Protocols ensure that data is transferred whole, in sequence, and without error from one node on the network to another.

protocol analyzer A software package or hardware-based tool that can capture and analyze data on a network. Protocol analyzers are more sophisticated than network monitoring tools, as they can typically interpret data up to Layer 7 of the OSI model.

protocol data unit *See* PDU.

proxy *See* proxy server.

proxy server 1) A network host that runs a proxy service. Proxy servers may also be called gateways. 2) On a SIP network, a server that accepts requests for location information from user agents and then queries the nearest registrar server on behalf of those user agents. If the recipient user agent is in the SIP proxy server's domain, that server will also act as a go-between for calls established and terminated between the requesting user agent and the recipient user agent.

proxy service A software application on a network host that acts as an intermediary between the external and internal networks, screening all incoming and outgoing traffic and providing one address to the outside world, instead of revealing the addresses of internal LAN devices.

PSE (power sourcing equipment) On a network using Power over Ethernet, the device that supplies power to end nodes.

PSTN (Public Switched Telephone Network) The network of lines and carrier equipment that provides telephone service to most homes and businesses. Now, except for the local loop, nearly all of the PSTN uses digital transmission. Its traffic is carried by fiber-optic or copper twisted pair cable, microwave, and satellite connections.

public key encryption A form of key encryption in which data is encrypted using two keys: One is a key known only to a user, and the other is a key associated with the user and that can be obtained from a public source, such as a public key server. Some examples of public key algorithms include RSA and Diffie-Hellman. Public key encryption is also known as asymmetric encryption.

public key infrastructure *See* PKI.

public key server A publicly available host (such as an Internet host) that provides free access to a list of users' public keys (for use in public key encryption).

public network A network that any user can access with no restrictions. The most familiar example of a public network is the Internet.

Public Switched Telephone Network *See* PSTN.

punch-down block A panel of data receptors into which twisted pair wire is inserted, or punched down, to complete a circuit.

PVC (permanent virtual circuit) A point-to-point connection over which data may follow any number of different paths, as opposed to a dedicated line that follows a predefined path. X.25, frame relay, and some forms of ATM use PVCs.

QoS (quality of service) The result of specifications for guaranteeing data delivery within a certain period of time after their transmission.

quality of service *See* QoS.

radiation pattern The relative strength over a three-dimensional area of all the electromagnetic energy an antenna sends or receives.

radiofrequency interference *See* RFI.

RADIUS (Remote Authentication Dial-In User Service) A protocol that runs over UDP and provides centralized network authentication and accounting for multiple users. RADIUS is commonly used with dial-up networking, VPNs, and wireless connections.

RADIUS server A server that offers centralized authentication services to a network's access server, VPN server, or wireless access point via the RADIUS protocol.

RAID (Redundant Array of Independent [or Inexpensive] Disks) A server redundancy measure that uses shared, multiple physical or logical hard disks to ensure data integrity and availability. Some RAID designs also increase storage capacity and improve performance. *See also* disk mirroring, disk striping.

RAID level 0 An implementation of RAID in which data is written in 64KB blocks equally across all disks in the array.

RAID level 1 An implementation of RAID that provides redundancy through disk mirroring, in which data from one disk is automatically copied to another disk as the information is written.

RAID level 3 An implementation of RAID that uses disk striping for data and writes parity error correction code on a separate parity disk.

RAID level 5 The most popular fault-tolerant data storage technique in use today, RAID level 5 writes data in small blocks across several disks. At the same time, it writes parity error checking information among several disks.

range The geographical area in which signals issued from an antenna or wireless system can be consistently and accurately received.

Rapid Spanning Tree Protocol *See* RSTP.

RARP (Reverse Address Resolution Protocol) A core protocol in the TCP/IP suite that belongs in the network layer of the OSI model. RARP relies on a RARP table to associate the IP (logical) address of a node with its MAC (physical) address. RARP can be used to supply IP addresses to diskless workstations.

RAS (Remote Access Service) The dial-up networking software provided with Microsoft Windows 95, 98, NT, and 2000 client operating systems. RAS requires software installed on both the client and server, a server configured to accept incoming clients, and a client with sufficient privileges (including user name and password) on the server to access its resources. In more recent versions of Windows, RAS has been incorporated into the RRAS (Routing and Remote Access Service).

RC4 An asymmetric key encryption technique that weaves a key with data multiple times as a computer issues the stream of data. RC4 keys can be as long as 2,048 bits. In addition to being highly secure, RC4 is fast.

RDN (relative distinguished name) An attribute of an object that identifies the object separately from its related container(s) and domain. For most objects, the relative distinguished name is the same as its common name (CN) in the distinguished name convention.

RDP (Remote Desktop Protocol) An application layer protocol that uses TCP/IP to transmit graphics and text quickly over a remote client–host connection. RDP also carries session, licensing, and encryption information.

Real-time Transport Control Protocol *See* RTCP.

Real-time Transport Protocol *See* RTP.

reassembly The process of reconstructing data units that have been segmented.

reassociation In the context of wireless networking, the process of a station establishing a connection (or associating) with a different access point.

Recommended Standard 232 *See* RS-232.

recordable DVD An optical storage medium that can hold up to 4.7GB on one single-layered side. Both sides of the disc can be used, and each side can have up to two layers. Thus, in total, a double-layered, two-sided DVD can store up to 17GB of data. Recordable DVDs come in several formats.

redirect server On a SIP network, a server that accepts and responds to requests from user agents and SIP proxy servers for location information on recipients that belong to external domains.

redirector A service that runs on a client workstation and determines whether the client's request should be handled by the client or the server.

redundancy The use of more than one identical component, device, or connection for storing, processing, or transporting data. Redundancy is the most common method of achieving fault tolerance.

Redundant Array of Independent (or Inexpensive) Disks *See* RAID.

reflection In the context of wireless transmission, the phenomenon that occurs when an electromagnetic wave encounters an obstacle and bounces back toward its source. A wireless signal will bounce off objects whose dimensions are large compared to the signal's average wavelength.

regeneration The process of retransmitting a digital signal. Regeneration, unlike amplification, repeats the pure signal, with none of the noise it has accumulated.

Regional Internet Registry *See* RIR.

registered jack 11 *See* RJ-11.

registered jack 45 *See* RJ-45.

Registered Ports The TCP/IP ports in the range of 1024 to 49151. These ports are accessible to network users and processes that do not have special administrative privileges. Default assignments of these ports must be registered with IANA.

registrar server On a SIP network, a server that maintains a database containing information about the locations (network addresses) of each user agent in its domain. When a user agent joins a SIP network, it transmits its location information to the SIP registrar server.

relative distinguished name *See* RDN.

release The act of terminating a DHCP lease.

remote access A method for connecting and logging on to a LAN from a workstation that is remote, or not physically connected, to the LAN.

remote access server A server that runs communications services that enable remote users to log on to a network. Also known as an access server.

Remote Access Service *See* RAS.

Remote Authentication Dial-In User Service *See* RADIUS.

Remote Desktop A feature of Windows operating systems that allows a computer to act as a remote host and be controlled from a client running another Windows operating system.

Remote Desktop Protocol *See* RDP.

remote user A person working on a computer on a different network or in a different geographical location from the LAN's server.

removable disk drive *See* external disk drive.

Rendezvous Apple Computer's implementation of the Zeroconf group of protocols.

repeater A device used to regenerate a signal.

replication 1) A fault-tolerance technique that involves dynamic copying of data (for example, an NOS directory or an entire server's hard disk) from one location to another. 2) The process of copying Active Directory data to multiple domain controllers. This ensures redundancy so that in case one of the domain controllers fails, clients can still log on to the network, be authenticated, and access resources.

Request to Send/Clear to Send *See* RTS/CTS.

resolver Any host on the Internet that needs to look up domain name information.

resource record The element of a DNS database stored on a name server that contains information about TCP/IP host names and their addresses.

Resource Reservation Protocol *See* RSVP.

resources The devices, data, and data storage space provided by a computer, whether stand-alone or shared.

restore The process of retrieving files from a backup. It is necessary to restore files if the original files are lost or deleted.

Reverse Address Resolution Protocol *See* RARP.

RFI (radiofrequency interference) A kind of interference that may be generated by broadcast signals from radio or TV towers.

RG-6 A type of coaxial cable with an impedance of 75 ohms and that contains an 18 AWG core conductor. RG-6 is used for television, satellite, and broadband cable connections.

RG-8 A type of coaxial cable characterized by a 50-ohm impedance and a 10 AWG core. RG-8 provided the medium for the first Ethernet networks, which followed the now-obsolete 10Base-5 standard.

RG-58 A type of coaxial cable characterized by a 50-ohm impedance and a 24 AWG core. RG-58 was a popular medium for Ethernet LANs in the 1980s, used for the now-obsolete 10Base-2 standard.

RG-59 A type of coaxial cable characterized by a 75-ohm impedance and a 20 or 22 AWG core, usually made of braided copper. Less expensive but suffering greater attenuation than the more common RG-6 coax, RG-59 is used for relatively short connections.

Rijndael The algorithm used for AES encryption.

ring topology A network layout in which each node is connected to the two nearest nodes so that the entire network forms a circle. Data is transmitted unidirectionally around the ring. Each workstation accepts and responds to packets addressed to it and then forwards the other packets to the next workstation in the ring.

ring topology WAN A type of WAN in which each site is connected to two other sites so that the entire WAN forms a ring pattern.

RIP (Routing Information Protocol) The oldest routing protocol that is still widely used, RIP does not work in very large network environments in which data may have to travel through more than 15 routers to reach its destination (for example, on the Internet). And, compared to other routing protocols, RIP is slower and less secure.

RIPv2 (Routing Information Protocol version 2) An updated version of the original RIP routing protocol that makes up for some of its predecessor's overhead and security flaws. However, RIPv2's packet forwarding is still limited to a maximum 15 hops.

RIR (Regional Internet Registry) A not-for-profit agency that manages the distribution of IP addresses to private and public entities. ARIN is the RIR for North, Central, and South America and sub-Saharan Africa. APNIC is the RIR for Asia and the Pacific region. RIPE is the RIR for Europe and North Africa.

RJ-11 (registered jack 11) The standard connector used with unshielded twisted pair cabling (usually Cat 3 or Level 1) to connect analog telephones.

RJ-45 (registered jack 45) The standard connector used with shielded twisted pair and unshielded twisted pair cabling.

roaming In wireless networking, the process that describes a station moving between BSSs without losing connectivity.

role In Microsoft terminology, the primary purpose of a Windows Server 2003 or 2008 server.

rollover cable A type of cable in which the terminations on one end are exactly the reverse of the terminations on the other end. It is used for serial connections between routers and consoles or other interfaces.

root A highly privileged user ID that has all rights to create, delete, modify, move, read, write, or execute files on a UNIX or Linux system.

root bridge The single bridge on a network selected by the Spanning Tree Protocol to provide the basis for all subsequent path calculations.

root domain In Windows Server 2003 or Server 2008 networking, the single domain from which child domains branch out in a domain tree.

root server A DNS server maintained by ICANN and IANA that is an authority on how to contact the top-level domains, such as those ending with .com, .edu, .net, .us, and so on. ICANN oversees the operation of 13 root servers around the world.

round trip time *See* RTT.

routable The protocols that can span more than one LAN because they carry network layer and addressing information that can be interpreted by a router.

route 1) A utility for viewing or modifying a host's routing table. 2) To intelligently direct data between networks based on addressing, patterns of usage, and availability of network segments.

router A multiport device that operates at Layer 3 of the OSI model and uses logical addressing information to direct data between networks or segments. Routers can connect dissimilar LANs and WANs running at different transmission speeds and using a variety of network layer protocols. They determine the best path between nodes based on traffic congestion, available versus unavailable routes, load balancing targets, and other factors.

Routing and Remote Access Service (RRAS) The software included with Windows 2000 Server, XP, Vista, Server 2003, and Server 2008 operating systems that enables a server to act as a router, firewall, and remote access server. Using RRAS, a server can provide network access to multiple remote clients.

Routing Information Protocol *See* RIP.

Routing Information Protocol Version 2 *See* RIPv2.

routing protocols The means by which routers communicate with each other about network status. Routing protocols determine the best path for data to take between nodes.

routing switch *See* Layer 3 switch.

RRAS *See* Routing and Remote Access Service.

RS-232 (Recommended Standard 232) A physical layer standard for serial communications, as defined by EIA/TIA.

RSA An encryption algorithm that creates a key by randomly choosing two large prime numbers and multiplying them together. RSA is named after its creators, Ronald Rivest, Adi Shamir, and Leonard Adleman. RSA was released in 1977 but remains popular today for e-commerce transactions.

RSTP (Rapid Spanning Tree Protocol) As described in IEEE's 802.1w standard, a newer version of the Spanning Tree Protocol that can detect and correct for network changes much more quickly.

RSVP (Resource Reservation Protocol) As specified in RFC 2205, a QoS technique that attempts to reserve a specific amount of network resources for a transmission before the transmission occurs.

RTCP (Real-time Transport Control Protocol) A companion protocol to RTP, defined in RFC 3550 by the IETF, RTCP provides feedback on the quality of a call or videoconference to its participants.

RTP (Real-time Transport Protocol) A transport layer protocol used with voice and video transmission. RTP operates on top of UDP and provides information about packet sequence to help receiving nodes detect delay and packet loss. It also assigns packets a timestamp that corresponds to when the data in the packet was sampled from the voice or video stream. This timestamp helps the receiving node synchronize incoming data.

RTP Control Protocol *See* RTCP.

RTS/CTS (Request to Send/Clear to Send) An exchange in which a wireless station requests the exclusive right to communicate with an access point and the access point confirms that it has granted that request.

RTT (round trip time) The length of time it takes for a packet to go from sender to receiver and then back from receiver to sender. RTT is usually measured in milliseconds.

runt A packet that is smaller than the medium's minimum packet size. For instance, any Ethernet packet that is smaller than 64 bytes is considered a runt.

sag *See* brownout.

Samba An open source software package that provides complete Windows-style file- and printer-sharing capabilities.

SAN (storage area network) A distinct network of multiple storage devices and servers that provides fast, highly available, and highly fault-tolerant access to large quantities of data for a client/server network. A SAN uses a proprietary network transmission method (such as Fibre Channel) rather than a traditional network transmission method such as Ethernet.

satellite return A type of satellite Internet access service in which a subscriber sends and receives data to and from the Internet over the satellite link. This is a symmetrical technology, in which both upstream and downstream throughputs are advertised to reach 400 to 500Kbps; in reality, throughput is often higher.

SC (subscriber connector or standard connector) A connector used with single-mode or multimode fiber-optic cable.

scalable The property of a network that allows you to add nodes or increase its size easily.

scanning The process a wireless station undergoes to find an access point. *See also* active scanning and passive scanning.

scattering The diffusion of a wireless signal that results from hitting an object that has smaller dimensions compared to the signal's wavelength. Scattering is also related to the roughness of the surface a wireless signal encounters. The rougher the surface, the more likely a signal is to scatter when it hits that surface.

schema The description of object types, or classes, and their required and optional attributes that are stored in an NOS's directory.

SCP (Secure CoPy) A method for copying files securely between hosts. SCP is part of the OpenSSH package, which comes with modern UNIX and Linux operating systems. Third-party SCP applications are available for Windows-based computers.

screening firewall *See* packet-filtering firewall.

SDH (Synchronous Digital Hierarchy) The international equivalent of SONET.

second-level support In network troubleshooting, a person or group with deeper knowledge about a subject and to whom first-level support personnel escalate problems.

Secure CoPy *See* SCP.

Secure File Transfer Protocol *See* SFTP.

Secure Shell *See* SSH.

Secure Sockets Layer *See* SSL.

security audit An assessment of an organization's security vulnerabilities. A security audit should be performed at least annually and preferably quarterly—or sooner if the network has undergone significant changes. For each risk found, it should rate the severity of a potential breach, as well as its likelihood.

security auditing The process of evaluating security measures currently in place on a network and notifying the network administrator if a security breach occurs.

security policy A document or plan that identifies an organization's security goals, risks, levels of authority, designated security coordinator and team members, responsibilities for each team member, and responsibilities for each employee. In addition, it specifies how to address security breaches.

segment 1) A part of a network. Usually, a segment is composed of a group of nodes that share the same communications channel for all their traffic. 2) A unit of data that results from subdividing a larger protocol data unit.

segmentation The process of decreasing the size of data units when moving data from a network that can handle larger data units to a network that can handle only smaller data units.

self-healing A characteristic of dual-ring topologies that allows them to automatically reroute traffic along the backup ring if the primary ring is severed.

sequencing The process of assigning a placeholder to each piece of a data block to allow the receiving node's transport layer to reassemble the data in the correct order.

serial A style of data transmission in which the pulses that represent bits follow one another along a single transmission line. In other words, they are issued sequentially, not simultaneously.

serial backbone A type of backbone that consists of two or more internetworking devices connected to each other by a single cable in a daisy chain. Hubs are often connected in this way to extend a network.

serial cable A cable, such as an RS-232 type, that permits serial data transmission.

Serial Line Internet Protocol *See* SLIP.

server A computer on the network that manages shared resources. Servers usually have more processing power, memory, and hard disk space than clients. They run network operating software that can manage not only data, but also users, groups, security, and applications on the network.

Server Manager A GUI tool provided with Windows Server 2008 that enables network administrators to manage server roles, features, resources, and users from a single interface.

Server Message Block *See* SMB.

server mirroring A fault-tolerance technique in which one server duplicates the transactions and data storage of another, identical server. Server mirroring requires a link between the servers and software running on both servers so that the servers can continually synchronize their actions and one can take over in case the other fails.

server_hello In the context of SSL encryption, a message issued from the server to the client that confirms the information the server received in the client_hello message. It also agrees to certain terms of encryption based on the options the client supplied. Depending on the Web server's preferred encryption method, the server may choose to issue your browser a public key or a digital certificate at this time.

service pack A significant patch to one of the Microsoft Windows operating systems.

service set identifier *See* SSID.

session A connection for data exchange between two parties. The term *session* may be used in the context of Web, remote access, or terminal and mainframe communications, for example.

Session Initiation Protocol *See* SIP.

session key In the context of Kerberos authentication, a key issued to both the client and the server by the authentication service that uniquely identifies their session.

session layer The fifth layer in the OSI model. The session layer establishes and maintains communication between two nodes on the network. It can be considered the "traffic cop" for network communications.

set top box In the context of IPTV, a device that decodes digital video signals and issues them to the television. Set top boxes also communicate with content servers to manage video delivery.

SFD (start-of-frame delimiter) A 1-byte field that indicates where the data field begins in an Ethernet frame.

SFTP (Secure File Transfer Protocol) A protocol available with the proprietary version of SSH that copies files between hosts securely. Like FTP, SFTP first establishes a connection with a host and then allows a remote user to browse directories, list files, and copy files. Unlike FTP, SFTP encrypts data before transmitting it.

sheath The outer cover, or jacket, of a cable.

shell Another term for the UNIX command interpreter.

shield *See* braiding.

shielded twisted pair *See* STP.

signal bounce A phenomenon, caused by improper termination on a bus-topology network, in which signals travel endlessly between the two ends of the network, preventing new signals from getting through.

signal level An ANSI standard for T-carrier technology that refers to its physical layer electrical signaling characteristics. DS0 is the equivalent of one data or voice channel. All other signal levels are multiples of DS0.

signaling The exchange of information between the components of a network or system for the purposes of establishing, monitoring, or releasing connections as well as controlling system operations.

Signaling System 7 *See* SS7.

signature scanning The comparison of a file's content with known virus signatures (unique identifying characteristics in the code) in a signature database to determine whether the file is a virus.

Simple Mail Transfer Protocol *See* SMTP.

Simple Network Management Protocol *See* SNMP.

simplex A type of transmission in which signals may travel in only one direction over a medium.

single-mode fiber *See* SMF.

SIP (Session Initiation Protocol) A protocol suite codified by the IETF (in RFC 2543) as a set of Session layer signaling and control protocols for multiservice, packet-based networks. With few exceptions, SIP performs much the same functions as the H.323 signaling protocols perform. SIP was developed as a more efficient alternative to H.323 before H.323 was revised to expedite its call setup functions. But although SIP is more efficient, because it was released later, it has never enjoyed the same widespread usage as H.323.

site license A type of software license that, for a fixed price, allows any number of users in one location to legally access a program.

site survey In the context of wireless networking, an assessment of client requirements, facility characteristics, and coverage areas to determine an access point arrangement that will ensure reliable wireless connectivity within a given area.

slash notation *See* CIDR notation.

SLIP (Serial Line Internet Protocol) A communications protocol that enables a workstation to connect to a server using a serial connection. SLIP can support only asynchronous communications and IP traffic and requires some configuration on the client workstation. SLIP has been made obsolete by PPP.

smart jack A termination for T-carrier wire pairs that is located at the customer demark and which functions as a connection protection and monitoring point.

SMB (Server Message Block) A protocol for communications and resource access between systems, such as clients and servers. SMB originated at IBM and then was adopted and further developed by Microsoft for use on its Windows operating systems. The current version of SMB is known as the CIFS (Common Internet File System) protocol.

SMF (single-mode fiber) A type of fiber-optic cable with a narrow core that carries light pulses along a single path data from one end of the cable to the other end. Data can be transmitted faster and for longer distances on single-mode fiber than on multimode fiber. However, single-mode fiber is more expensive.

SMTP (Simple Mail Transfer Protocol) The application layer TCP/IP subprotocol responsible for moving messages from one e-mail server to another.

smurf attack A threat to networked hosts in which the host is flooded with broadcast ping messages. A smurf attack is a type of denial-of-service attack.

SNAT (Static Network Address Translation) A type of address translation in which each private IP address is correlated with its own Internet-recognized IP address.

sneakernet A way of exchanging data between computers that are not connected on a network. Sneakernet requires that data be copied from a computer to a removable storage device such as a floppy disk, carried (presumably by someone wearing sneakers) to another computer, and then copied from the storage device onto the second computer.

sniffer *See* protocol analyzer.

SNMP (Simple Network Management Protocol) An application layer protocol in the TCP/IP suite used to convey data regarding the status of managed devices on a network.

social engineering The act of manipulating personal relationships to circumvent network security measures and gain access to a system.

socket A logical address assigned to a specific process running on a computer. Some sockets are reserved for operating system functions.

soft skills The skills such as customer relations, leadership ability, and dependability, which are not easily measured but are nevertheless important in a networking career.

softphone A computer configured to act like an IP telephone. Softphones present the caller with a graphical representation of a telephone dial pad and can connect to a network via a LAN, WAN, PPP dial-up connection, or leased line.

softswitch *See* MGC.

software distribution The process of automatically transferring a data file or installing a software application from the server to a client on the network.

software RAID A method of implementing RAID that uses software to implement and control RAID techniques over virtually any type of hard disk(s). RAID software may be a third-party package or utilities that come with an operating system NOS.

Solaris A proprietary implementation of the UNIX operating system by Sun Microsystems.

SONET (Synchronous Optical Network) A high-bandwidth WAN signaling technique that specifies framing and multiplexing techniques at the physical layer of the OSI model. It can integrate many other WAN technologies (for example, T-carriers, ISDN, and ATM technology) and allows for simple link additions and removals. SONET's topology includes a double ring of fiber-optic cable, which results in very high fault tolerance.

source code The computer instructions written in a programming language that is readable by humans. Source code must be translated into a form that is executable by the machine, typically called binary code (for the sequence of zeros and ones) or target code.

spam Unsolicited, unwanted e-mail.

Spanning Tree Protocol *See* STP.

SPARC The brand of computer central processing unit invented by and used in Sun Microsystems servers.

spectrum analyzer A tool that assesses the characteristics (for example, frequency, amplitude, and the effects of interference) of wireless signals.

spread spectrum A type of wireless transmission in which lower-level signals are distributed over several frequencies simultaneously. Spread-spectrum transmission is more secure than narrowband.

SS7 (Signaling System 7) A set of standards established by the ITU for handling call signaling on the PSTN (public switched telephone network).

SSH (Secure Shell) A connection utility that provides authentication and encryption. With SSH, you can securely log on to a host, execute commands on that host, and copy files to or from that host. SSH encrypts data exchanged throughout the session.

SSID (service set identifier) A unique character string used to identify an access point on an 802.11 network.

SSL (Secure Sockets Layer) A method of encrypting TCP/IP transmissions—including Web pages and data entered into Web forms—en route between the client and server using public key encryption technology.

SSL session In the context of SSL encryption, an association between the client and server that is defined by an agreement on a specific set of encryption techniques. An SSL session allows the client and server to continue to exchange data securely as long as the client is still connected to the server. SSL sessions are established by the SSL handshake protocol.

ST (straight tip) A connector used with single-mode or multimode fiber-optic cable.

stand-alone computer A computer that uses applications and data only from its local disks and that is not connected to a network.

stand-alone hub A type of hub that serves a workgroup of computers that are separate from the rest of the network, also known as a workgroup hub.

standard A documented agreement containing technical specifications or other precise criteria that are used as guidelines to ensure that materials, products, processes, and services suit their intended purpose.

standard connector *See* SC.

standby UPS A power supply that provides continuous voltage to a device by switching virtually instantaneously to the battery when it detects a loss of power from the wall outlet. Upon restoration of the power, the standby UPS switches the device to use A/C power again.

star topology A physical topology in which every node on the network is connected through a central device, such as a hub. Any single physical wire on a star network connects only two devices, so a cabling problem will affect only two nodes. Nodes transmit data to the hub, which then retransmits the data to the rest of the network segment where the destination node can pick it up.

star topology WAN A type of WAN in which a single site acts as the central connection point for several other points. This arrangement provides separate routes for data between any two sites; however, if the central connection point fails, the entire WAN fails.

start-of-frame delimiter *See* SFD.

star-wired bus topology A hybrid topology in which groups of workstations are connected in a star fashion to hubs that are networked via a single bus.

star-wired ring topology A hybrid topology that uses the physical layout of a star and the token-passing data transmission method.

stateful firewall A firewall capable of monitoring a data stream from end to end.

stateless firewall A firewall capable only of examining packets individually. Stateless firewalls perform more quickly than stateful firewalls but are not as sophisticated.

static ARP table entry A record in an ARP table that someone has manually entered using the ARP utility. Static ARP table entries remain the same until someone manually modifies them with the ARP utility.

static IP address An IP address that is manually assigned to a device and remains constant until it is manually changed.

Static Network Address Translation *See* SNAT.

static routing A technique in which a network administrator programs a router to use specific paths between nodes. Because it does not account for occasional network congestion, failed connections, or device moves, static routing is not optimal.

station An end node on a network; used most often in the context of wireless networks.

statistical multiplexing A method of multiplexing in which each node on a network is assigned a separate time slot for transmission, based on the node's priority and need.

stealth virus A type of virus that hides itself to prevent detection. Typically, stealth viruses disguise themselves as legitimate programs or replace part of a legitimate program's code with their destructive code.

storage area network *See* SAN.

store-and-forward mode A method of switching in which a switch reads the entire data frame into its memory and checks it for accuracy before transmitting it. Although this method is more time consuming than the cut-through method, it allows store-and-forward switches to transmit data more accurately.

STP (shielded twisted pair) A type of cable containing twisted-wire pairs that are not only individually insulated, but also surrounded by a shielding made of a metallic substance such as foil.

STP (Spanning Tree Protocol) A switching protocol defined in IEEE 802.1D. STP operates in the data link layer to prevent traffic loops by calculating paths that avoid potential loops and by artificially blocking links that would complete a loop. Given changes to a network's links or devices, STP recalculates its paths.

straight tip *See* ST.

straight-through cable A twisted pair patch cable in which the wire terminations in both connectors follow the same scheme.

streaming video A service in which video signals are compressed and delivered over the Internet in a continuous stream so that a user can watch and listen even before all the data has been transmitted.

structured cabling A method for uniform, enterprise-wide, multivendor cabling systems specified by the TIA/EIA 568 Commercial Building Wiring Standard. Structured cabling is based on a hierarchical design using a high-speed backbone.

subchannel One of many distinct communication paths established when a channel is multiplexed or modulated.

subnet A part of a network in which all nodes share a network addressing component and a fixed amount of bandwidth.

subnet mask In IPv4 addressing, a 32-bit number that, when combined with a device's IP address, indicates what kind of subnet the device belongs to.

subnetting The process of subdividing a single class of network into multiple, smaller networks.

subprotocols The specialized protocols that work together and belong to a protocol suite.

subscriber connector *See* SC.

supernet A type of subnet that is created using bits that normally would be reserved for network class information—by moving the subnet boundary to the left.

supernet mask A 32-bit number that, when combined with a device's IP address, indicates the kind of supernet to which the device belongs.

supernetting *See* CIDR.

supported services list A document that lists every service and software package supported within an organization, plus the names of first- and second-level support contacts for those services or software packages.

surge A momentary increase in voltage caused by distant lightning strikes or electrical problems.

surge protector A device that directs excess voltage away from equipment plugged into it and redirects it to a ground, thereby protecting the equipment from harm.

SVC (switched virtual circuit) A logical, point-to-point connection that relies on switches to determine the optimal path between sender and receiver. ATM technology uses SVCs.

swap file *See* page file.

switch 1) A connectivity device that logically subdivides a network into smaller, individual collision domains. A switch operates at the data link layer of the OSI model and can interpret MAC address information to determine whether to filter (discard) or forward packets it receives. 2) The letters or words added to a command that allow you to customize a utility's output. Switches are usually preceded by a hyphen or forward slash character.

switched virtual circuit *See* SVC.

switching A component of a network's logical topology that manages how packets are filtered and forwarded between nodes on the network.

symmetric encryption A method of encryption that requires the same key to encode the data as is used to decode the ciphertext.

symmetric multiprocessing A method of multiprocessing that splits all operations equally among two or more processors.

symmetrical A characteristic of transmission technology that provides equal throughput for data traveling both upstream and downstream and is suited to users who both upload and download significant amounts of data.

symmetrical DSL A variation of DSL that provides equal throughput both upstream and downstream between the customer and the carrier.

SYN (synchronization) The packet one node sends to request a connection with another node on the network. The SYN packet is the first of three in the three-step process of establishing a connection.

SYN-ACK (synchronization-acknowledgment) The packet a node sends to acknowledge to another node that it has received a SYN request for connection. The SYN-ACK packet is the second of three in the three-step process of establishing a connection.

synchronization *See* SYN.

synchronization-acknowledgment *See* SYN-ACK.

synchronous A transmission method in which data being transmitted and received by nodes must conform to a timing scheme.

Synchronous Digital Hierarchy *See* SDH.

Synchronous Optical Network *See* SONET.

system bus *See* bus.

system log On a computer running a UNIX or Linux operating system, the record of monitored events, which can range in priority from 0 to 7 (where "0" indicates an emergency situation and "7" simply points to information that might help in debugging a problem). You can view and modify system log locations and configurations in the file `/etc/syslog.conf` file on most systems. (On some systems this is the `/etc/rsyslog.conf` file.)

System V The proprietary version of UNIX that comes from Bell Labs.

T1 A digital carrier standard used in North America and most of Asia that provides 1.544Mbps throughput and 24 channels for voice, data, video, or audio signals. T1s rely on time division multiplexing and may use shielded or unshielded twisted pair, coaxial cable, fiber optics, or microwave links.

T3 A digital carrier standard used in North America and most of Asia that can carry the equivalent of 672 channels for voice, data, video, or audio, with a maximum data throughput of 44.736Mbps (typically rounded up to 45Mbps for purposes of discussion). T3s rely on time division multiplexing and require either fiber-optic or microwave transmission media.

TA (terminal adapter) A device used to convert digital signals into analog signals for use with ISDN phones and other analog devices. TAs are sometimes called ISDN modems.

TACACS (Terminal Access Controller Access Control System) A centralized authentication system for remote access servers that is similar to, but older than, RADIUS.

tape backup A relatively simple and economical backup method in which data is copied to magnetic tapes.

T-carrier The term for any kind of leased line that follows the standards for T1s, fractional T1s, T1Cs, T2s, T3s, or T4s.

TCP (Transmission Control Protocol) A core protocol of the TCP/IP suite. TCP belongs to the transport layer and provides reliable data delivery services.

TCP/IP (Transmission Control Protocol/Internet Protocol) A suite of networking protocols that includes TCP, IP, UDP, and many others. TCP/IP provides the foundation for data exchange across the Internet.

TCP/IP core protocols The major subprotocols of the TCP/IP suite, including IP, TCP, and UDP.

TDM (time division multiplexing) A method of multiplexing that assigns a time slot in the flow of communications to every node on the network and, in that time slot, carries data from that node.

TDR (time domain reflectometer) A high-end instrument for testing the qualities of a cable. It works by issuing a signal on a cable and measuring the way in which the signal bounces back (or reflects) to the TDR. Many performance testers rely on TDRs.

TE (terminal equipment) The end nodes (such as computers and printers) served by the same connection (such as an ISDN, DSL, or T1 link).

telecommunications closet Also known as a "telco room," the space that contains connectivity for groups of workstations in a defined area, plus cross-connections to IDFs or, in smaller organizations, an MDF. Large organizations may have several telecommunications closets per floor, but the TIA/EIA standard specifies at least one per floor.

Telecommunications Industry Association *See* TIA.

telephone test set *See* butt set.

Telnet A terminal emulation protocol used to log on to remote hosts using the TCP/IP protocol. Telnet resides in the application layer of the OSI model.

Temporal Key Integrity Protocol *See* TKIP.

terminal A device with little (if any) of its own processing or disk capacity that depends on a host to supply it with applications and data-processing services.

Terminal Access Controller Access Control System *See* TACACS.

terminal adapter *See* TA.

terminal equipment *See* TE.

terminator A resistor that is attached to each end of a bus-topology network and that causes the signal to stop rather than reflect back toward its source.

TFTP (Trivial File Transfer Protocol) A TCP/IP application layer protocol that enables file transfers between computers. Unlike FTP, TFTP relies on UDP at the transport layer and does not require a user to log on to the remote host.

TGS (Ticket Granting Service) In Kerberos terminology, an application that runs on the KDC that issues Ticket Granting Tickets to clients so that they need not request a new ticket for each new service they want to access.

TGT (Ticket Granting Ticket) In Kerberos terminology, a ticket that enables a user to be accepted as a validated principal by multiple services.

Thicknet An IEEE physical layer standard for achieving a maximum of 10Mbps throughput over coaxial copper cable. Thicknet is also known as 10Base-5. Its maximum segment length is 500 meters, and it relies on a bus topology.

thickwire Ethernet *See* Thicknet.

thin client A client that relies on another host for the majority of processing and hard disk resources necessary to run applications and share files over the network.

thin Ethernet *See* Thinnet.

Thinnet An IEEE physical layer standard for achieving 10Mbps throughput over coaxial copper cable. Thinnet is also known as 10Base-2. Its maximum segment length is 185 meters, and it relies on a bus topology.

third-level support In network troubleshooting, a person or group with deep knowledge about specific networking topics to whom second-level support personnel escalate challenging problems.

thread A well-defined, self-contained subset of a process. Using threads within a process enables a program to efficiently perform related, multiple, simultaneous activities. Threads are also used to enable processes to use multiple processors on SMP systems.

three-way handshake An authentication process that involves three steps.

throughput The amount of data that a medium can transmit during a given period of time. Throughput is usually measured in megabits (1,000,000 bits) per second, or Mbps. The physical nature of every transmission media determines its potential throughput.

TIA (Telecommunications Industry Association) A subgroup of the EIA that focuses on standards for information technology, wireless, satellite, fiber optics, and telephone equipment. Probably the best-known standards to come from the TIA/EIA alliance are its guidelines for how network cable should be installed in commercial buildings, known as the "TIA/EIA 568-B Series."

ticket In Kerberos terminology, a temporary set of credentials that a client uses to prove that its identity has been validated by the authentication service.

Ticket Granting Service *See* TGS.

Ticket Granting Ticket *See* TGT.

tiered topology WAN A type of WAN in which sites that are connected in star or ring formations are interconnected at different levels, with the interconnection points being organized into layers to form hierarchical groupings.

time division multiplexing *See* TDM.

time domain reflectometer *See* TDR.

Time to Live *See* TTL.

time-sharing *See* preemptive multitasking.

TKIP (Temporal Key Integrity Protocol) An encryption key generation and management scheme used by 802.11i.

TLD (top-level domain) The highest-level category used to distinguish domain names—for example, .org, .com, and .net. A TLD is also known as the domain suffix.

TLS (Transport Layer Security) A version of SSL being standardized by the IETF (Internet Engineering Task Force). With TLS, the IETF aims to create a version of SSL that encrypts UDP as well as TCP transmissions. TLS, which is supported by new Web browsers, uses slightly different encryption algorithms than SSL but otherwise is very similar to the most recent version of SSL.

token A special control frame that indicates to the rest of the network that a particular node has the right to transmit data.

token ring A networking technology developed by IBM in the 1980s. It relies upon direct links between nodes and a ring topology, using tokens to allow nodes to transmit data.

toll bypass A cost-savings benefit that results from organizations completing long-distance telephone calls over their packet-switched networks, thus bypassing tolls charged by common carriers on comparable PSTN calls.

tone generator A small electronic device that issues a signal on a wire pair. When used in conjunction with a tone locator, it can help locate the termination of a wire pair.

tone locator A small electronic device that emits a tone when it detects electrical activity on a wire pair. When used in conjunction with a tone generator, it can help locate the termination of a wire pair.

toner *See* tone generator.

top-level domain *See* TLD.

topology The physical layout of computers on a network.

tracepath A version of the traceroute utility found on some Linux distributions.

traceroute (tracert) A TCP/IP troubleshooting utility that uses ICMP to trace the path from one networked node to another, identifying all intermediate hops between the two nodes. Traceroute is useful for determining router or subnet connectivity problems. On Windows-based systems, the utility is known as tracert.

traffic The data transmission and processing activity taking place on a computer network at any given time.

traffic monitoring The process of determining how much data transfer activity is taking place on a network or network segment and notifying administrators when a segment becomes overloaded.

traffic policing A traffic-shaping technique in which the volume or rate of traffic traversing an interface is limited to a predefined maximum.

traffic shaping Manipulating certain characteristics of packets, data streams, or connections to manage the type and amount of traffic traversing a network or interface at any moment.

transceiver A device that transmits and receives signals.

transmission In networking, the application of data signals to a medium or the progress of data signals over a medium from one point to another.

Transmission Control Protocol *See* TCP.

Transmission Control Protocol/Internet Protocol *See* TCP/IP.

transmission media The means through which data is transmitted and received. Transmission media may be physical, such as wire or cable, or atmospheric (wireless), such as radio waves.

transmit To issue signals to the network medium.

transponder The equipment on a satellite that receives an uplinked signal from Earth, amplifies the signal, modifies its frequency, and then retransmits it (in a downlink) to an antenna on Earth.

transport layer The fourth layer of the OSI model. In the transport layer, protocols ensure that data is transferred from point A to point B reliably and without errors. Transport layer services include flow control, acknowledgment, error correction, segmentation, reassembly, and sequencing.

Transport Layer Security *See* TLS.

tree A logical representation of multiple, hierarchical levels in a directory. It is called a tree because the whole structure shares a common starting point (the root), and from that point extends branches (or containers), which may extend additional branches, and so on.

Triple DES (3DES) The modern implementation of DES, which weaves a 56-bit key through data three times, each time using a different key.

Trivial File Transfer Protocol *See* TFTP.

Trojan *See* Trojan horse.

Trojan horse A program that disguises itself as something useful but actually harms your system.

trunking The aggregation of multiple logical connections in one physical connection between connectivity devices. In the case of VLANs, trunking allows data from multiple VLANs to share a single interface on a switch.

trust relationship The relationship between two domains on a Windows Server 2003 or Server 2008 network that allows a domain controller from one domain to authenticate users from the other domain.

TTL (Time to Live) A number that indicates the maximum time that a datagram or packet can remain on the network before it is discarded. Although this field was originally meant to represent units of time, on modern networks it represents the number of router hops a datagram has endured. The TTL for datagrams is variable and configurable but is usually set at 32 or 64. Each time a datagram passes through a router, its TTL is reduced by 1. When a router receives a datagram with a TTL equal to 1, the router discards that datagram.

tunnel A secured, virtual connection between two nodes on a VPN.

tunneling The process of encapsulating one type of protocol in another. Tunneling is the way in which higher-layer data is transported over VPNs by Layer 2 protocols.

twist ratio The number of twists per meter or foot in a twisted pair cable.

twisted pair A type of cable similar to telephone wiring that consists of color-coded pairs of insulated copper wires, each with a diameter of 0.4 to 0.8mm, twisted around each other and encased in plastic coating.

two-way transitive trust The security relationship between domains in the same domain tree in which one domain grants every other domain in the tree access to its resources and, in turn, that domain can access other domains' resources. When a new domain is added to a tree, it immediately shares a two-way trust with the other domains in the tree.

UDP (User Datagram Protocol) A core protocol in the TCP/IP suite that sits in the transport layer of the OSI model. UDP is a connectionless transport service.

unicast address A type of IPv6 address that represents a single interface on a device. An IPv6 unicast address begins with either FFC0 or FF80.

unified communications The centralized management of multiple types of network-based communications, such as voice, video, fax, and messaging services.

unified messaging The centralized management of multiple types of network-based communications, such as voice, video, fax, and messaging services.

uninterruptible power supply *See* UPS.

UNIX A client or server operating system originally developed by researchers at AT&T Bell Laboratories in 1969. UNIX is a proprietary operating system, but similar operating systems, such as Linux, are freely distributable.

unpopulated segment A network segment that does not contain end nodes, such as workstations. Unpopulated segments are also called link segments.

unshielded twisted pair *See* UTP.

upgrade A major change to the existing code in a software application, which may or may not be offered free from a vendor, and may or may not be comprehensive enough to substitute for the original application.

uplink A connection from an Earth-based transmitter to an orbiting satellite.

uplink port A port on a connectivity device, such as a hub or switch, used to connect it to another connectivity device.

UPN (user principal name) The preferred Active Directory naming convention for objects when used in informal situations. This name looks like a familiar Internet address, including the positioning of the domain name after the @ sign. UPNs are typically used for e-mail and related Internet services.

UPN suffix The portion of a universal principal name (in Active Directory's naming conventions) that follows the @ sign.

UPS (uninterruptible power supply) A battery-operated power source directly attached to one or more devices and to a power supply (such as a wall outlet) that prevents undesired features of the power source from harming the device or interrupting its services.

upstream A term used to describe data traffic that flows from a customer's site to a carrier's facility. In asymmetrical communications, upstream throughput is usually much lower than downstream throughput. In symmetrical communications, upstream and downstream throughputs are equal.

USB (universal serial bus) port A standard external bus that can be used to connect multiple types of peripherals, including modems, mice, and NICs, to a computer. Two USB standards exist: USB 1.1 and USB 2.0. USB 3.0 promises to be released soon. Most modern computers support the USB 2.0 standard.

user A person who uses a computer.

user agent In SIP terminology, a user agent client or user agent server.

user agent client In SIP terminology, end-user devices such as workstations, PDAs, cell phones, or IP telephones. A user agent client initiates a SIP connection.

user agent server In SIP terminology, a server that responds to user agent clients' requests for session initiation and termination.

User Datagram Protocol *See* UDP.

user principal name *See* UPN.

UTP (unshielded twisted pair) A type of cabling that consists of one or more insulated wire pairs encased in a plastic sheath. As its name implies, UTP does not contain additional shielding for the twisted pairs. As a result, UTP is both less expensive and less resistant to noise than STP.

vault A large tape storage library.

vertical cross-connect Part of a network's backbone that supplies connectivity between a building's floors. For example, vertical cross-connects might connect an MDF and an IDF or IDFs and telecommunications closets within a building.

video bridge *See* MCU.

video over IP Any type of video service, including IPTV, videoconferencing, and streaming video, that delivers video signals over packet-switched networks using the TCP/IP protocol suite.

video phone A type of phone that includes a screen and can decode compressed video and interpret transport and signaling protocols necessary for conducting videoconference sessions.

videoconferencing The real-time reception and transmission of images and audio among two or more locations.

video-on-demand A service in which a video stored as an encoded file is delivered to a viewer upon his request.

virtual address *See* network address.

virtual circuit A connection between network nodes that, although based on potentially disparate physical links, logically appears to be a direct, dedicated link between those nodes.

virtual local area network *See* VLAN.

virtual memory The memory that is logically carved out of space on the hard drive and added to physical memory (RAM).

virtual network computing *See* VNC.

virtual private network *See* VPN.

virtualization The capability for operating multiple logical servers—or virtual servers—on a single machine.

virus A program that replicates itself to infect more computers, either through network connections or through external storage disks passed among users. Viruses might damage files or systems or simply annoy users by flashing messages or pictures on the screen or by causing the keyboard to beep.

VLAN (virtual local area network) A network within a network that is logically defined by grouping its devices' switch ports in the same broadcast domain. A VLAN can consist of any type of network node in any geographic location and can incorporate nodes connected to different switches.

VNC (virtual network computing) An open source system that enables a remote client (or viewer) workstation to manipulate and receive screen updates from a host. Examples of VNC software include RealVNC, TightVNC, and UltraVNC.

VoATM (voice over ATM) A service that uses the ATM network access method (and ATM cells) to transmit voice signals over a network.

VoDSL (voice over DSL) A service that relies on a DSL connection to transmit packetized voice signals.

voice over ATM *See* VoATM.

voice over DSL *See* VoDSL.

voice over IP *See* VoIP.

VoIP (voice over IP) The provision of telephone service over a packet-switched network running the TCP/IP protocol suite.

volt The measurement used to describe the degree of pressure an electrical current exerts on a conductor.

voltage The pressure (sometimes informally referred to as the strength) of an electrical current.

voltage event Any condition in which voltage exceeds or drops below predefined levels.

voltage event recorder A device that, when plugged into the same outlet that will be used by a network node, gathers data about the power that the outlet will provide the node.

volt-amp (VA) A measure of electrical power. A volt-amp is the product of the voltage and current (measured in amps) of the electricity on a line.

voltmeter A device used to measure voltage (or electrical pressure) on an electrical circuit.

VPN (virtual private network) A logically constructed WAN that uses existing public transmission systems. VPNs can be created through the use of software or combined software and hardware solutions. This type of network allows an organization to carve out a private WAN through the Internet, serving only its offices, while keeping the data secure and isolated from other (public) traffic.

VPN concentrator A specialized device that authenticates VPN clients and establishes tunnels for VPN connections.

WAN (wide area network) A network that spans a long distance and connects two or more LANs.

WAN link A point-to-point connection between two nodes on a WAN.

war driving The act of driving while running a laptop configured to detect and capture wireless data transmissions.

warm site A place where the computers, devices, and connectivity necessary to rebuild a network exist, though only some are appropriately configured, updated, or connected to match the network's current state.

wavelength The distance between corresponding points on a wave's cycle. Wavelength is inversely proportional to frequency.

wavelength division multiplexing *See* WDM.

WDM (wavelength division multiplexing) A multiplexing technique in which each signal on a fiber-optic cable is assigned a different wavelength, which equates to its own subchannel. Each wavelength is modulated with a data signal. In this manner, multiple signals can be simultaneously transmitted in the same direction over a length of fiber.

Web caching A technique in which Web pages are stored locally, either on a host or network, and then delivered to requestors more quickly than if they had been obtained from the original source.

Web server A computer that manages Web site services, such as supplying a Web page to multiple users on demand.

Webcast A streaming video, either on demand or live, that is delivered via the Web.

Well Known Ports The TCP/IP port numbers 0 to 1023, so named because they were long ago assigned by Internet authorities to popular services (for example, FTP and Telnet), and are, therefore, well known and frequently used.

WEP (Wired Equivalent Privacy) A key encryption technique for wireless networks that uses keys both to authenticate network clients and to encrypt data in transit.

whois The utility that allows you to query ICANN's DNS registration database and find information about a domain.

wide area network *See* WAN.

Wi-Fi *See* 802.11.

Wi-Fi Alliance An international, nonprofit organization dedicated to ensuring the interoperability of 802.11-capable devices.

Wi-Fi Protected Access *See* WPA.

WiMAX *See* 802.16.

Wired Equivalent Privacy *See* WEP.

wireless The signals made of electromagnetic energy that travel through the atmosphere.

wireless broadband The term used to describe the recently released standards for high-throughput, long-distance digital data exchange over wireless connections. WiMAX (IEEE 802.16) is one example of a wireless broadband technology.

wireless gateway An access point that provides routing functions and is used as a gateway.

wireless LAN *See* WLAN.

wireless router An access point that provides routing functions.

wireless spectrum A continuum of electromagnetic waves used for data and voice communication. The wireless spectrum (as defined by the FCC, which controls its use) spans frequencies between 9KHz and 300GHz. Each type of wireless service can be associated with one area of the wireless spectrum.

wiring schematic A graphical representation of a network's wired infrastructure.

WLAN (wireless LAN) A LAN that uses wireless connections for some or all of its transmissions.

workgroup In Microsoft terminology, a group of interconnected computers that share each others' resources without relying on a central file server.

workgroup hub *See* stand-alone hub.

workstation A computer that runs a desktop operating system and connects to a network.

Worldwide Interoperability for Microwave Access (WiMAX) *See* 802.16.

worm An unwanted program that travels between computers and across networks. Although worms do not alter other programs as viruses do, they can carry viruses.

WPA (Wi-Fi Protected Access) A wireless security method endorsed by the Wi-Fi Alliance that is considered a subset of the 802.11i standard. In WPA, authentication follows the same mechanism specified in 802.11i. The main difference between WPA and 802.11i is that WPA specifies RC4 encryption rather than AES.

WPA2 The name given to the 802.11i security standard by the Wi-Fi Alliance. The only difference between WPA2 and 802.11i is that WPA2 includes support for the older WPA security method.

X Window system The GUI environment for UNIX and Linux systems.

X.25 An analog, packet-switched WAN technology optimized for reliable, long-distance data transmission and standardized by the ITU in the mid-1970s. The X.25 standard specifies protocols at the physical, data link, and network layers of the OSI model. It provides excellent flow control and ensures data reliability over long distances by verifying the transmission at every node. X.25 can support a maximum of only 2Mbps throughput.

xDSL The term used to refer to all varieties of DSL.

Zero Configuration *See* Zeroconf.

Zeroconf (Zero Configuration) A collection of protocols designed by the IETF to simplify the setup of nodes on a TCP/IP network. Zeroconf assigns a node an IP address; resolves the node's host name and IP address without requiring a DNS server; and discovers services, such as print services, available to the node, also without requiring a DNS server.

Answers to Network+ Practice Exam Questions

1. d. Tracert
2. a. 802.11g
   b. 802.11a
   c. 802.11.b
3. e.

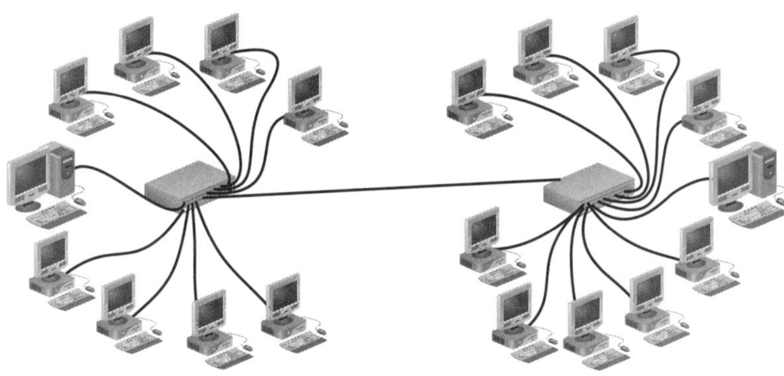

4. b. SSL
5. a. The type of server specified in his Alpha Enterprises Properties dialog box
6. d. Cat 5
7. b. It appends a node's physical address to frames before they're transmitted.
8. a. Determine the number of workstations affected, to which segment the affected workstations belong, and which area of workstations is affected.
9. c. Connecting a workstation to a router's console port
10. c. To connect the workstation to another workstation
11. a. Full mesh
12. a. C3000000FFFF
13. a. 100Base-FX
14. b. CSU/DSU
15. d. MAC addresses; the data link layer
16. c. 1,500 bytes
17. c. A DSL connection to a local telephone and Internet service provider that uses IPSec to encrypt the data before it is sent to the national office's file server over the Internet
18. b. 802.3

19. d. 80
20. b. 100 meters
21. e. SNMP
22. e. Microsoft's network is bounded by firewalls that do not accept incoming ICMP traffic.
23. e. 194.73.44.0
24. c. Hot site
25. c. Switch
26. d. It replaces each outgoing packet's Source address field with a valid IP address.
27. e. 175 feet
28. a. Determines the locations of endpoints
    d. Establishes sessions between endpoints
29. c. Network
30. d. WINS
31. b.

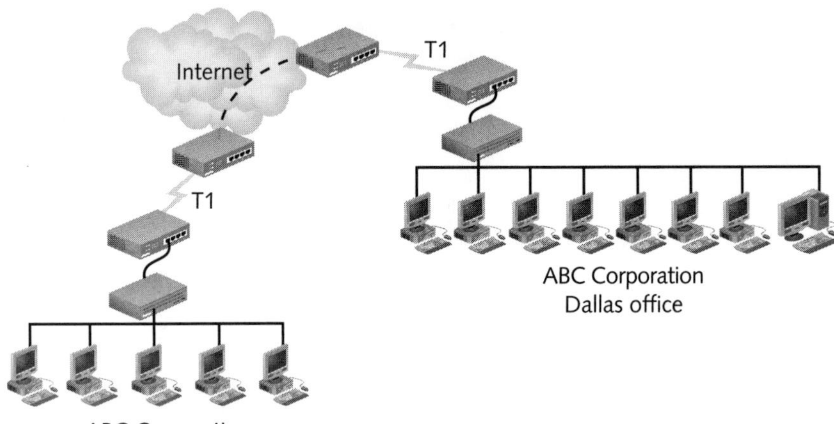

32. a. SCP
33. c. Authentication
34. b. Whether the firewall is placed in the appropriate location on the network
    c. Whether the firewall has been configured to allow access from IP addresses in the satellite office
35. a. Ipconfig; the output indicates that the machine has a MAC address of 00080DE72F0C
36. b. Its TCP/IP protocol is not installed properly.
37. b. Crimping tool
    c. Wire stripper
38. a. Cut-through switches
39. d. ::1
40. a. Hub
    e. Repeater
41. c. To make more efficient use of limited numbers of legitimate IP addresses
42. a. Circuit switching
    d. Message switching
43. a. 802.11b
44. a. Nodes 1 through 6 and nodes 8 through 14
45. c. Establish mirroring between the two servers using the T1.

46. c. SSID
47. d. TCP, port 23
48. c. Online UPS
     e. Gas-powered generator
49. a. SMTP
50. c. To associate an IP address with a given MAC address
51. e. White with orange stripe and orange
52. b. Firewall log
53. a. LDAP
54. d. To add logical addresses and properly route data
55. d. Telnet
56. b. Verify that the amount of resistance presented by terminators on coaxial cable networks
         is appropriate
     c. Check for the presence of noise on a wire (by detecting extraneous voltage)
57. a. prn *filename*
     b. lpr *filename*
58. c. 255.255.0.0
59. b.

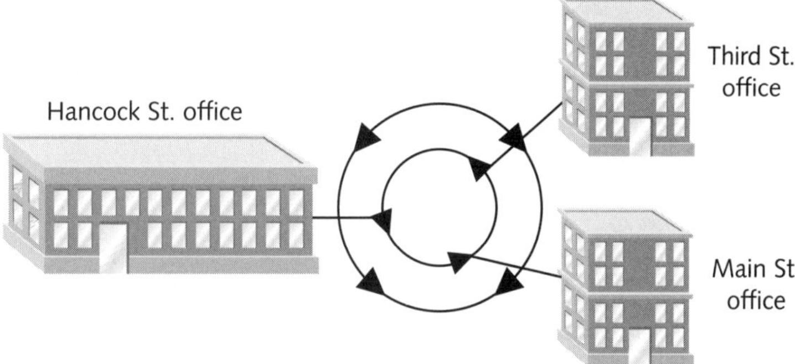

60. e. SMTP server name
61. c. ARP
62. a. PAP
63. a. Router
64. d. Network monitor
65. b. Data that changed since the previous full or incremental backup
66. e. Nothing; in Windows Vista, the DHCP option is selected by default, and the client will
         obtain IP addressing information upon connecting to the network.
67. b. RealVNC
68. e. Router
69. d. Fiber-optic cable
70. d. They will be unable to access the Internet and nodes 10 through 20.
71. b. EIGRP
72. c. 53
73. d. 255.255.255.224
74. c. L2TP
75. b. BGP
76. e. 802.11n
77. c. It enables switches to calculate paths that avoid potential loops and artificially blocks the
         links that would complete a loop.

78. a. EAPoL
79. d. 169.254.1.120
80. e. Your wireless networking client will be able to see the access point and successfully associate with it.
81. a. To identify nodes belonging to a multicast group
82. b. DNAT
83. e. (Between the Internet and the edge router)
84. a. Unicast
85. c. In a rollover cable, all wires are reversed, while in a crossover cable, only two wire pairs are reversed.
86. d. 15
87. d. Butt set
88. c. MPLS
89. b. Phishing
    c. Spoofing
90. c. It reads a tag added to each frame's header.
91. a. Traffic policing
92. d. You may set up a Web server on the company's private LAN, which is protected by a firewall.
93. b. Determine whether escalation is necessary.
94. a. Entrance facilities
95. e. Event Viewer
96. e. Geosynchronous
97. c. FF02
98. a. SONET
99. c. Stateless firewall
    d. Packet-filtering firewall
100. b. Ethernet uses variably sized packets, while ATM uses fixed-sized cells.

Special Characters

Numerics

A

Note: Page numbers referencing figures are italicized and followed by an *"f."* Page numbers referencing tables are italicized and followed by a *"t."*

Note: Page numbers referencing figures are italicized and followed by an *"f."* Page numbers referencing tables are italicized and followed by a *"t."*

Note: Page numbers referencing figures are italicized and followed by an *"f."* Page numbers referencing tables are italicized and followed by a *"t."*

Note: Page numbers referencing figures are italicized and followed by an *"f."* Page numbers referencing tables are italicized and followed by a *"t."*

Note: Page numbers referencing figures are italicized and followed by an *"f."* Page numbers referencing tables are italicized and followed by a *"t."*

Note: Page numbers referencing figures are italicized and followed by an *"f."* Page numbers referencing tables are italicized and followed by a *"t."*

Note: Page numbers referencing figures are italicized and followed by an *"f."* Page numbers referencing tables are italicized and followed by a *"t."*

Note: Page numbers referencing figures are italicized and followed by an *"f."* Page numbers referencing tables are italicized and followed by a *"t."*

Note: Page numbers referencing figures are italicized and followed by an *"f."* Page numbers referencing tables are italicized and followed by a *"t."*

Note: Page numbers referencing figures are italicized and followed by an *"f."* Page numbers referencing tables are italicized and followed by a *"t."*

Note: Page numbers referencing figures are italicized and followed by an *"f."* Page numbers referencing tables are italicized and followed by a *"t."*

Note: Page numbers referencing figures are italicized and followed by an *"f."* Page numbers referencing tables are italicized and followed by a *"t."*

Note: Page numbers referencing figures are italicized and followed by an *"f."* Page numbers referencing tables are italicized and followed by a *"t."*

Note: Page numbers referencing figures are italicized and followed by an *"f."* Page numbers referencing tables are italicized and followed by a *"t."*

Note: Page numbers referencing figures are italicized and followed by an *"f."* Page numbers referencing tables are italicized and followed by a *"t."*

Note: Page numbers referencing figures are italicized and followed by an *"f."* Page numbers referencing tables are italicized and followed by a *"t."*

Note: Page numbers referencing figures are italicized and followed by an *"f."* Page numbers referencing tables are italicized and followed by a *"t."*

Note: Page numbers referencing figures are italicized and followed by an *"f."* Page numbers referencing tables are italicized and followed by a *"t."*

Note: Page numbers referencing figures are italicized and followed by an "f." Page numbers referencing tables are italicized and followed by a "t."

Note: Page numbers referencing figures are italicized and followed by an *"f."* Page numbers referencing tables are italicized and followed by a *"t."*

the fun way to learn programming

Let's face it. C++, Java, and Perl can be a little intimidating. But now they don't have to be. The *for the absolute beginner*™ series gives you a fun, non-intimidating introduction to the world of programming. Each book in this series teaches a specific programming language using simple game programming as a teaching aid. All titles include source code on the companion CD-ROM or Web site.

**C++ Programming
for the Absolute Beginner**
By Mark Lee
1-59863-875-0 | $29.99 | 464 pages

**Microsoft WSH and VBScript
Programming for the
Absolute Beginner, Third Edition**
By Jerry Ford, Jr.
1-59863-803-3 | $34.99 | 480 pages

**C Programming for the
Absolute Beginner, Second Edition**
By Michael Vine
1-59863-480-1 | $29.99 | 336 pages

**Microsoft Excel VBA Programming for
the Absolute Beginner, Third Edition**
By Duane Birnbaum and Michael Vine
1-59863-394-5 | $29.99 | 400 pages

**Microsoft Access VBA Programming for
the Absolute Beginner, Third Edition**
By Michael Vine
1-59863-393-7 | $29.99 | 384 pages

**Microsoft Windows Powershell
Programming for the Absolute Beginner**
By Jerry Lee Ford Jr.
1-59863-354-6 | $29.99 | 376 pages

**Microsoft Visual Basic 2008 Express
Programming for the Absolute Beginner**
By Jerry Lee Ford, Jr.
1-59863-900-5 | $29.99 | 432 pages

**Ajax Programming
for the Absolute Beginner**
By Jerry Ford, Jr.
1-59863-564-6 | $29.99 | 320 pages

**Java Programming for the
Absolute Beginner, Second Edition**
By John Flynt
1-59863-275-2 | $29.99 | 480 pages

Includes CD with video tutorials!
CompTIA
A+ 2006
IN DEPTH
By best-selling author
Jean Andrews, Ph.D.
Over one million books in print!

Maps to the 2006 CompTIA A+ Certification Exams
The Ultimate CompTIA
A+ 2006 Resource Kit
Jean Andrews, Ph.D.
author of CompTIA A+ 2006 In Depth

CompTIA
Security+
2008
IN DEPTH
Mark Ciampa